Statistics Canada

Profile of Census Tracts in Abbotsford and Vancouver

Volume II

Statistique Canada

Profil des secteurs de recensement d'Abbotsford et Vancouver

Volume II

Published by authority of the Minister responsible for Statistics Canada

February 2004

Catalogue No. 95-247-XPB

ISBN 0-660-61912-1

Ottawa

Publication autorisée par le ministre responsable de Statistique Canada

Février 2004

N° 95-247-XPB au catalogue

ISBN 0-660-61912-1

Ottawa

Note of Appreciation

Canada owes the success of its statistical system to a long-standing partnership between Statistics Canada, the citizens of Canada, its businesses, governments and other institutions. Accurate and timely statistical information could not be produced without their continued co-operation and goodwill.

Note de reconnaissance

Le succès du système statistique du Canada repose sur un partenariat bien établi entre Statistique Canada et la population, les entreprises, les administrations et les autres organismes du Canada. Sans cette collaboration et cette bonne volonté, il serait impossible de produire des statistiques précises et actuelles.

National Library of Canada Cataloguing in Publication Data

Profile of census tracts in Abbotsford and Vancouver = Profil des secteurs de recensement d'Abbotsford et Vancouver

Published in 2 v.
Text in English and French.

ISBN 0-660-61912-1
CS95-247-XPB

1. Abbotsford (B.C.) - Population - Statistics.
2. Vancouver (B.C.) - Population - Statistics.
3. Census districts - British Columbia - Abbotsford - Statistics. 4. Census districts - British Columbia - Vancouver - Statistics. 5. Abbotsford (B.C.) - Census, 2001. 6. Vancouver (B.C.) - Census, 2001.
7. Canada - Census, 2001. I. Statistics Canada.
II. Title: Profil des secteurs de recensement d'Abbotsford et Vancouver.

HA741.5.2001 304.6'09711'33021
C2003-988032-XE

Données de catalogage avant publication de la Bibliothèque nationale du Canada

Profile of census tracts in Abbotsford and Vancouver = Profil des secteurs de recensement d'Abbotsford et Vancouver

Publié en 2 v.
Texte en anglais et en français.

ISBN 0-660-61912-1
CS95-247-XPB

1. Abbotsford (C.-B.) - Population - Statistiques démographiques. 2. Vancouver (C.-B.) - Population - Statistiques démographiques. 3. Secteurs de recensement - Colombie-Britannique - Abbotsford - Statistiques. 4. Secteurs de recensement - Colombie-Britannique - Vancouver - Statistiques.
5. Abbotsford (C.-B.) - Recensement, 2001.
6. Vancouver (C.-B.) - Recensement, 2001.
7. Canada - Recensement, 2001. I. Statistique Canada. II. Titre : Profil des secteurs de recensement d'Abbotsford et Vancouver.

HA741.5.2001 304.6'09711'33021
C2003-988032-XF

How to Cite this Document

Statistics Canada. Profile of Census Tracts. Ottawa: Industry Canada, 2004. 2001 Census of Canada. Catalogue number 95-247-XPB.

Pour citer ce document

Statistique Canada. Profil des secteurs de recensement. Ottawa : Industrie Canada, 2004. Recensement du Canada de 2001. Numéro 95-247-XPB au catalogue.

The paper used in this publication meets the minimum requirements of American National Standard for Information Sciences – Permanence of Paper for Printed Library Materials, ANSI Z39.48-1984.

Le papier utilisé dans la présente publication répond aux exigences minimales de l'American National Standard for Information Sciences – Permanence of Paper for Printed Library Materials, ANSI Z39.48-1984.

Table of Contents

Page

Introductory Material

Table

Reference Material

How To Get Help

Maps

Table des matières

Page

Documents d'introduction

Tableau

Documents de référence

Comment trouver de l'aide

Cartes

Introduction

The 2001 Census Area Profiles are designed to provide a statistical overview, or profile, for lower levels of geography. Each publication in this series provides a profile of census tracts (CTs) in a census metropolitan area (CMA) or a census agglomeration (CA). The Area Profiles are based on data collected by the 2001 Census of Canada from all households.

In response to client needs, variables from the 20% database are available sooner than ever before. The 2001 Census Area Profiles contain population counts for characteristics from both 100% data and 20% sample data, in each publication. New for 2001 are data on language used at work, generation status, and religion, the latter being reported every 10 years. This series also contains incidence reporting for single- or multiple-response variables. Incidence reporting will display specific categories based on the most frequently reported responses in a CMA or CA. The variables affected by incidence reporting are mother tongue, home language, knowledge of non-official languages, language used at work, and ethnic origin. On the whole, searching for 2001 Census information on your community can now be done sooner and at a greater level of detail.

Each publication in this series consists of a single table displaying the data for geographic areas in a columnar format. The data variables, also referred to as "stubs", are displayed in English on the left side of the table and in French on the right side. With the combination of variables from the 100% and 20% databases, the stubset covers 10 pages. Characteristics of the data have been grouped into blocks by theme, or universe (i.e. population, dwelling and household, family and income). Within each theme, the data are displayed showing different characteristics such as marital status, ethnic origin and census family structure and size.

The geographic headings run across the top of the page. The CTs are sequenced by numerical order within the CMAs and CAs. Reference maps showing CT boundaries are included at the back of each publication.

Definitions of the geographic areas and variables displayed in each publication can be found in the Reference Material section. Also provided at the end of each publication are data quality notes and special notes.

Introduction

Les Profils des secteurs du recensement de 2001 sont conçus de façon à fournir un aperçu statistique, ou profil, de petites régions géographiques. Chaque publication de cette série fournit un profil des secteurs de recensement (SR) d'une région métropolitaine de recensement (RMR) ou d'une agglomération de recensement (AR). Les Profils des secteurs sont fondés sur les données du Recensement du Canada de 2001 pour tous les ménages.

En réponse aux besoins des clients, les variables de la base de données-échantillon (20 %) sont disponibles plus tôt qu'elles ne l'ont jamais été. Les Profils des secteurs du recensement de 2001 contiennent les chiffres de la population selon des caractéristiques des données intégrales (100 %) et des données-échantillon (20 %), réunies dans chaque publication. Du nouveau pour 2001 : il y a des données portant sur la langue utilisée au travail, le statut des générations et la religion, cette dernière étant déclarée tous les 10 ans. Cette série comprend également des fréquences de déclaration pour les variables à réponses uniques et à réponses multiples. La fréquence de déclaration verra certaines catégories présentées selon les réponses le plus souvent déclarées dans une RMR ou une AR. Les variables touchées par la fréquence de déclaration sont la langue maternelle, la langue parlée à la maison, la connaissance des langues non officielles, la langue utilisée au travail et l'origine ethnique. En somme, vous pouvez dorénavant rechercher les informations du recensement de 2001 portant sur votre communauté plus tôt qu'auparavant, et à un niveau plus détaillé.

Chaque publication de cette série consiste en un seul tableau auquel figurent, sous forme de colonnes, les données pour les régions géographiques. Les variables de données, ou « titres », sont affichées en anglais du côté gauche du tableau et en français du côté droit. L'ensemble de titres résultant de la combinaison des variables provenant de la base de données intégrales (100 %) et de la base de données-échantillon (20 %) compte 10 pages. Les caractéristiques des données ont été regroupées en blocs, selon des thèmes ou univers (par exemple, la population, les logements et les ménages, les familles et le revenu). À partir de chacun de ces thèmes, les données sont affichées de façon à souligner les diverses caractéristiques telles l'état matrimonial, l'origine ethnique et la structure et la taille de la famille de recensement.

Les en-têtes géographiques figurent d'un côté à l'autre du haut de la page. Les SR s'enchaînent en suivant un ordre numérique à partir des RMR et des AR. Les cartes de référence démontrant les limites des SR figurent à la fin de chaque publication.

Les définitions des régions géographiques et des variables comprises dans chaque publication apparaissent dans la section sur les documents de référence. On retrouve aussi les notes sur la qualité des données et les notes spéciales à la fin de chaque publication.

Symbols

The following standard symbols are found in this publication.

...	Figures not appropriate or not applicable.
–	Nil or zero.
XXX	Figures suppressed to protect confidentiality.
A	1996 adjusted count; most of these are the result of boundary changes.
¶	Incompletely enumerated Indian reserve or Indian settlement (suppressed).
†	Excludes census data for one or more incompletely enumerated Indian reserves or Indian settlements.
◆	Data quality index showing, for the short census questionnaire (100% data), a global non-response rate higher than or equal to 5% but lower than 10%.
◆◆	Data quality index showing, for the short census questionnaire (100% data), a global non-response rate higher than or equal to 10% but lower than 25%.
◆◆◆	Data quality index showing, for the short census questionnaire (100% data), a global non-response rate higher than or equal to 25% (suppressed).
■	An error exists in the 2001 population and dwelling counts for this area. For further information, refer to the "Special Notes" section.
◇	Data quality index showing, for the long census questionnaire (20% sample data), a global non-response rate higher than or equal to 5% but lower than 10%.
◇◇	Data quality index showing, for the long census questionnaire (20% sample data), a global non-response rate higher than or equal to 10% but lower than 25%.
◇◇◇	Data quality index showing, for the long census questionnaire (20% sample data) or the short census questionnaire (100% data), a global non-response rate higher than or equal to 25% (suppressed).
•	Part of a census tract.

Signes conventionnels

Les signes conventionnels suivants sont retrouvés dans cette publication.

...	N'ayant pas lieu de figurer.
–	Néant ou zéro.
XXX	Nombres supprimés afin de protéger la confidentialité.
A	Chiffre de 1996 rajusté; la plupart de ces rajustements sont le résultat de modifications des limites.
¶	Réserve indienne ou établissement indien partiellement dénombré (supprimées).
†	Ne comprend pas les données du recensement pour une ou plusieurs réserves indiennes ou établissements indiens partiellement dénombrés.
◆	Indice de la qualité des données indiquant, pour le questionnaire de recensement abrégé (données intégrales [100 %]), un taux global de non-réponse supérieur ou égal à 5 %, mais inférieur à 10 %.
◆◆	Indice de la qualité des données indiquant, pour le questionnaire de recensement abrégé (données intégrales [100 %]), un taux global de non-réponse supérieur ou égal à 10 %, mais inférieur à 25 %.
◆◆◆	Indice de la qualité des données indiquant, pour le questionnaire de recensement abrégé (données intégrales [100 %]), un taux global de non-réponse supérieur ou égal à 25 % (supprimées).
■	Il y a une erreur dans les chiffres de population et des logements de 2001 pour cette région. Pour de plus amples renseignements, veuillez consulter la section « Notes spéciales ».
◇	Indice de la qualité des données indiquant, pour le questionnaire de recensement complet (données-échantillon [20 %]), un taux global de non-réponse supérieur ou égal à 5 %, mais inférieur à 10 %.
◇◇	Indice de la qualité des données indiquant, pour le questionnaire de recensement complet (données-échantillon [20 %]), un taux global de non-réponse supérieur ou égal à 10 %, mais inférieur à 25 %.
◇◇◇	Indice de la qualité des données indiquant, pour le questionnaire de recensement complet (données-échantillon [20 %]) ou pour le questionnaire de recensement abrégé (données intégrales [100 %]), un taux global de non-réponse supérieur ou égal à 25 % (supprimées).
•	Partie de secteur de recensement.

Abbreviations

1997 NAICS = 1997 North American Industry Classification System

2001 NOC–S = 2001 National Occupational Classification for Statistics

n.e.c. = not elsewhere classified

n.i.e. = not included elsewhere

n.o.s. = not otherwise specified

Abréviations

SCIAN de 1997 = Système de classification des industries de l'Amérique du Nord de 1997

CNP–S de 2001 = Classification nationale des professions pour statistiques de 2001

n.c.a. = non classé ailleurs

n.i.a = non inclus ailleurs

n.d.a. = non déclaré ailleurs

Census Subdivision Types – Genres de subdivisions de recensement

C	City – Cité
CC	Chartered Community
CM	County (Municipality)
COM	Community
CT	Canton (Municipalité de)
CU	Cantons unis (Municipalité de)
DM	District Municipality
HAM	Hamlet
ID	Improvement District
IGD	Indian Government District
IM	Island Municipality
LGD	Local Government District
LOT	Township and Royalty
M	Municipalité
MD	Municipal District
NH	Northern Hamlet
NL	Nisga'a Land
NV	Northern Village
NVL	Nisga'a Village
P	Paroisse (Municipalité de)
PAR	Parish
R	Indian Reserve – Réserve indienne
RC	Rural Community
RDA	Regional District Electoral Area
RG	Region
RGM	Regional Municipality
RM	Rural Municipality
RV	Resort Village
S–E	Indian Settlement – Établissement indien
SA	Special Area
SCM	Subdivision of County Municipality
SET	Settlement
SM	Specialized Municipality
SUN	Subdivision of Unorganized
SV	Summer Village
T	Town
TI	Terre inuite
TL	Teslin Land
TP	Township
TR	Terres réservées
UNO	Unorganized – Non organisé
V	Ville
VC	Village cri
VK	Village naskapi
VL	Village
VN	Village nordique

Geographic Index

Census Metropolitan Areas, Census Agglomerations and Census Tracts

Index géographique

Régions métropolitaines de recensement, agglomérations de recensement et secteurs de recensement

Abbotsford CMA/RMR - Vancouver CMA/RMR

Abbotsford CMA/RMR

Vancouver CMA/RMR

See reference material at the end of the publication. – Voir les documents de référence à la fin de la publication.

Geographic Index
Census Metropolitan Areas, Census Agglomerations and Census Tracts

Index géographique
Régions métropolitaines de recensement, agglomérations de recensement et secteurs de recensement

See reference material at the end of the publication. – Voir les documents de référence à la fin de la publication.

Geographic Index
Census Metropolitan Areas, Census Agglomerations and Census Tracts

Index géographique
Régions métropolitaines de recensement, agglomérations de recensement et secteurs de recensement

See reference material at the end of the publication. – Voir les documents de référence à la fin de la publication.

Geographic Index
Census Metropolitan Areas, Census Agglomerations and Census Tracts

Index géographique
Régions métropolitaines de recensement, agglomérations de recensement et secteurs de recensement

See reference material at the end of the publication. – Voir les documents de référence à la fin de la publication.

Geographic Index

Census Metropolitan Areas, Census Agglomerations and Census Tracts

Index géographique

Régions métropolitaines de recensement, agglomérations de recensement et secteurs de recensement

See reference material at the end of the publication. – Voir les documents de référence à la fin de la publication.

Constituent Census Tracts for Census Subdivisions

Secteurs de recensement constituant les subdivisions de recensement

Census Subdivisions Subdivisions de recensement	Census Tracts Secteurs de recensement
Abbotsford CMA/RMR	
Abbotsford, C	0001-0012, 0013•, 0014-0105, 0106.02
Fraser Valley H, RDA	0106.01
Matsqui Main 2, R	0013•
Mission, DM	0200-0207
Upper Sumas 6, R	0106.03
Vancouver CMA/RMR	
Anmore, VL	0250.02•
Barnston Island 3, R	0251•
Belcarra, VL	0250.02•
Bowen Island, IM	0250.01
Burnaby, C	0220-0243.02
Burrard Inlet 3, R	0111.01•
Capilano 5, R	0130.02•
Coquitlam, C	0270, 0280•, 0281.01-0287.07
Coquitlam 1, R	0280•
Coquitlam 2, R	0290.03•
Delta, DM	0160.01-0160.04, 0161.01•, 0161.02-0163.08
Greater Vancouver A, RDA	0069, 0250.02•, 0251•, 0260.02•
Katzie 1, R	0403.03•
Katzie 2, R	0504.02•
Langley, C	0503.01-0503.05
Langley, DM	0500•, 0501.01-0502.05, 0504.01, 0504.02•, 0504.03, 0504.04, 0505•, 0506.01, 0506.02
Langley 5, R	0400.02•
Lions Bay, VL	0250.02•
Maple Ridge, DM	0400.01, 0400.02•, 0401.01-0403.01, 0403.03•, 0403.04-0404
Matsqui 4, R	0500•
McMillan Island 6, R	0505•
Mission 1, R	0102•
Musqueam 2, R	0008•
Musqueam 4, R	0161.01•
New Westminster, C	0200-0210
North Vancouver, C	0100.01-0101.02, 0102•, 0103, 0104
North Vancouver, DM	0110.01, 0110.02, 0111.01•, 0111.02, 0111.03•, 0112-0122

See reference material at the end of the publication. – Voir les documents de référence à la fin de la publication.

Constituent Census Tracts for Census Subdivisions

Secteurs de recensement constituant les subdivisions de recensement

Census Subdivisions Subdivisions de recensement	Census Tracts Secteurs de recensement
Vancouver CMA/RMR	
Pitt Meadows, DM	0410.02-0410.04
Port Coquitlam, C	0290.02, 0290.03•, 0290.04-0292.02
Port Moody, C	0260.02•, 0260.04-0260.08
Richmond, C	0140.02-0151.04
Semiahmoo, R	0181.06•
Seymour Creek 2, R	0111.03•
Surrey, C	0180-0181.05, 0181.06•, 0181.07-0192
Tsawwassen, R	0161.01•
Vancouver, C	0001.01-0007.02, 0008•, 0009-0068
West Vancouver, DM	0130.01, 0130.02•, 0131-0135
White Rock, C	0170.03-0170.06
Whonnock 1, R	0400.02•

See reference material at the end of the publication. – Voir les documents de référence à la fin de la publication.

Conversion Table – Table de conversion

Census tract numbers in 2001 with numbers for corresponding census tracts in 1996.

Numéros des secteurs de recensement en 2001 et numéros des secteurs de recensement correspondants en 1996.

Abbotsford

2001	1996
0005.01	0005•
0005.02	0005•
0007.01	0007•
0007.02	0007•
0008.01	0008•
0008.02	0008•
0009.01	0009•
0009.02	0009•
0106.01	0106•
0106.02	0106•
0106.03	0106•

Vancouver

2001	1996
0003.01	0003•
0003.02	0003•
0004.01	0004•
0004.02	0004•
0006.01	0006•
0006.02	0006•
0007.01	0007•
0007.02	0007•
0016.03	0016.02•
0016.04	0016.02•
0037.01	0037•
0037.02	0037•
0040.01	0040•
0040.02	0040•
0041.01	0041•
0041.02	0041•
0043.01	0043•
0043.02	0043•
0047.01	0047•

See reference material at the end of the publication. – Voir les documents de référence à la fin de la publication.

Conversion Table – Table de conversion

Census tract numbers in 2001 with numbers for corresponding census tracts in 1996.

Numéros des secteurs de recensement en 2001 et numéros des secteurs de recensement correspondants en 1996.

Vancouver

2001	1996
0047.02	0047•
0050.03	0050.01•
0050.04	0050.01•
0053.01	0053•
0053.02	0053•
0054.01	0054•
0054.02	0054•
0056.01	0056•
0056.02	0056•
0057.01	0057•
0057.02	0057•
0059.03	0059.02•
0059.04	0059.02•
0059.05	0059.01•
0059.06	0059.01•
0060.01	0060•
0060.02	0060•
0110.01	0110•
0110.02	0110•
0118	0118•, 0130.02•
0130.02	0130.02•, 0118•
0133.01	0133•
0133.02	0133•
0140.03	0140.01•
0140.04	0140.01•
0144.03	0144.01•
0144.04	0144.01•
0144.05	0144.02•
0144.06	0144.02•
0147.04	0147.03•
0147.05	0147.03•
0147.06	0147.03•
0149.04	0149.01•
0149.05	0149.01•
0150	0150, 0250.02•
0151.03	0151.02•
0151.04	0151.02•
0160.01	0160.01•, 0160.04•
0160.02	0160.02•
0160.04	0160.04•
0161.01	0161.01•, 0160.01•, 0160.02•

See reference material at the end of the publication. – Voir les documents de référence à la fin de la publication.

Conversion Table – Table de conversion

Census tract numbers in 2001 with numbers for corresponding census tracts in 1996.

Numéros des secteurs de recensement en 2001 et numéros des secteurs de recensement correspondants en 1996.

Vancouver

2001	1996
0161.03	0161.03, 0161.01•
0161.05	0161.04•
0161.06	0161.04•
0163.05	0163.02•
0163.06	0163.02•
0163.07	0163.03•
0163.08	0163.03•
0170.03	0170.01•
0170.04	0170.01•
0170.05	0170.02•
0170.06	0170.02•
0181.08	0181.02•
0181.09	0181.02•
0182.01	0182•
0182.02	0182•
0182.03	0182•
0182.04	0182•
0182.05	0182•
0182.06	0182•
0183.04	0183.02•
0183.05	0183.02•
0183.06	0183.02•
0183.07	0183.02•
0184.06	0184.03•
0184.07	0184.03•
0184.08	0184.03•
0184.09	0184.04•
0184.10	0184.04•
0184.11	0184.04•
0185.06	0185.01•
0185.07	0185.01•
0185.08	0185.01•
0185.09	0185.02•
0185.10	0185.02•
0185.11	0185.02•
0185.12	0185.03•
0185.13	0185.03•
0185.14	0185.03•
0185.15	0185.04•
0185.16	0185.04•
0186.05	0186.03•

See reference material at the end of the publication. – Voir les documents de référence à la fin de la publication.

Conversion Table – Table de conversion

Census tract numbers in 2001 with numbers for corresponding census tracts in 1996.

Numéros des secteurs de recensement en 2001 et numéros des secteurs de recensement correspondants en 1996.

Vancouver

2001	1996
0186.06	0186.03•
0186.07	0186.04•
0186.08	0186.04•
0187.04	0187.01•
0187.05	0187.01•
0187.06	0187.02•
0187.07	0187.02•
0187.08	0187.02•
0187.09	0187.02•
0188.01	0188•
0188.02	0188•
0188.03	0188•
0188.04	0188•
0188.05	0188•
0188.06	0188•
0189.05	0189.01•
0189.06	0189.01•
0189.07	0189.02•
0189.08	0189.02•
0189.09	0189.04•
0189.10	0189.04•
0190.04	0190.02•
0190.05	0190.02•
0191.03	0191.01•
0191.04	0191.01•
0204.01	0204•
0204.02	0204•
0221.03	0221.02•
0221.04	0221.02•
0223.01	0223•
0223.02	0223•
0224.01	0224•
0224.02	0224•
0227.01	0227•
0227.02	0227•
0228.03	0228.01•
0228.04	0228.01•
0235.03	0235.01•
0235.04	0235.01•
0240.01	0240•
0240.02	0240•

See reference material at the end of the publication. – Voir les documents de référence à la fin de la publication.

Conversion Table – Table de conversion

Census tract numbers in 2001 with numbers for corresponding census tracts in 1996.

Numéros des secteurs de recensement en 2001 et numéros des secteurs de recensement correspondants en 1996.

Vancouver

2001	1996
0250.01	0250.01•
0250.02	0250.02•, 0250.01•
0251	0251•
0260.02	0260.02, 0250.02•
0260.04	0260.01•
0260.05	0260.01•
0260.06	0260.03•
0260.07	0260.03•
0260.08	0260.03•
0287.05	0287.03•
0287.06	0287.03•
0287.07	0287.03•
0290.02	0290.02•
0290.03	0290.03, 0290.02•
0290.04	0290.01•, 0251•
0290.05	0290.01•
0400.01	0400•
0400.02	0400•
0401.01	0401•
0401.02	0401•
0403.04	0403.02•
0403.05	0403.02•
0410.03	0410.01•, 0410.04•
0410.04	0410.01•, 0410.04•
0501.01	0501.01•
0502.01	0502.01, 0503.01•
0502.04	0502.04•
0503.01	0503.01•
0503.03	0503.03, 502.04•
0503.04	0503.02•, 0503.04•, 0501.01•
0503.05	0503.02•
0504.01	0504.01, 0503.04•

See reference material at the end of the publication. – Voir les documents de référence à la fin de la publication.

Table 1. Selected Characteristics for Census Tracts, 2001 Census – 100% Data and 20% Sample Data

No.	Characteristics	Vancouver CMA/RMR	Vancouver 0180	Vancouver 0181.01	Vancouver 0181.03	Vancouver 0181.04	Vancouver 0181.05
	POPULATION CHARACTERISTICS						
1	**Population, 1996 (1)**	**1,831,665**	**7,147**	**6,959**	**5,119**	**5,249**	**6,388**
2	**Population, 2001 (2)**	**1,986,965**	**8,199**	**7,368**	**5,419**	**6,993**	**7,148**
3	Population percentage change, 1996-2001	8.5	14.7	5.9	5.9	33.2	11.9
4	Land area in square kilometres, 2001	2,878.52	50.75	3.89	6.38	6.84	2.46
5	**Total population – 100% Data (3)**	**1,986,965**	**8,200**	**7,365**	**5,420**	**6,990**	**7,150**
	by sex and age groups						
6	Male	972,725	4,215	3,355	2,600	3,400	3,245
7	0-4 years	53,850	170	110	120	140	175
8	5-9 years	60,795	250	175	165	190	170
9	10-14 years	62,805	320	230	250	235	195
10	15-19 years	67,605	330	275	250	245	190
11	20-24 years	67,475	275	170	150	170	175
12	25-29 years	67,690	180	105	80	135	165
13	30-34 years	77,565	190	105	85	155	195
14	35-39 years	85,775	280	155	160	190	235
15	40-44 years	85,105	285	240	215	215	225
16	45-49 years	79,025	370	260	240	290	220
17	50-54 years	71,405	410	255	275	300	190
18	55-59 years	50,425	365	215	205	255	170
19	60-64 years	38,925	265	165	105	210	145
20	65-69 years	33,425	205	165	110	205	140
21	70-74 years	28,120	145	235	70	190	160
22	75-79 years	21,160	95	250	50	150	170
23	80-84 years	12,585	45	160	35	95	170
24	85 years and over	8,990	25	105	20	45	160
25	Female	1,014,240	3,985	4,010	2,825	3,600	3,905
26	0-4 years	50,960	140	115	140	155	180
27	5-9 years	57,180	250	185	190	175	195
28	10-14 years	59,805	300	225	235	215	190
29	15-19 years	63,570	245	260	225	210	160
30	20-24 years	68,320	255	160	135	160	150
31	25-29 years	72,185	175	115	90	165	160
32	30-34 years	80,890	185	150	120	155	225
33	35-39 years	88,245	250	210	195	195	225
34	40-44 years	89,480	320	300	260	270	245
35	45-49 years	81,915	415	355	290	330	255
36	50-54 years	72,430	465	280	280	345	270
37	55-59 years	50,675	335	215	165	255	205
38	60-64 years	40,375	195	200	125	240	155
39	65-69 years	35,115	170	220	130	195	170
40	70-74 years	32,745	110	315	85	205	240
41	75-79 years	29,250	90	345	70	190	290
42	80-84 years	21,365	60	220	60	95	285
43	85 years and over	19,730	35	140	35	40	295
44	**Total population 15 years and over**	**1,641,570**	**6,770**	**6,330**	**4,320**	**5,885**	**6,050**
	by legal marital status						
45	Never married (single)	556,185	1,870	1,375	1,145	1,275	1,355
46	Legally married (and not separated)	822,390	4,090	3,690	2,550	3,630	3,085
47	Separated, but still legally married	50,120	155	170	115	155	205
48	Divorced	119,970	410	470	315	475	545
49	Widowed	92,910	240	625	200	355	870
	by common-law status						
50	Not in a common-law relationship	1,540,485	6,390	6,070	4,095	5,600	5,705
51	In a common-law relationship	101,085	380	260	225	285	345
52	**Total population – 20% Sample Data (4)**	**1,967,475**	**8,150**	**7,335**	**5,405**	**6,990**	**7,015**
	by mother tongue						
53	Single responses	1,934,610	8,085	7,310	5,350	6,955	6,955
54	English	1,184,500	6,660	5,595	4,535	5,575	6,105
55	French	24,745	160	105	45	60	130
56	Non-official languages (5)	725,370	1,265	1,605	775	1,325	720
57	Chinese, n.o.s.	122,390	140	230	135	140	25
58	Cantonese	121,910	30	-	-	10	20
59	Punjabi	87,760	20	10	10	35	10
60	Mandarin	47,165	80	335	170	260	55
61	Tagalog (Pilipino)	32,560	35	30	10	20	10
62	Other languages (6)	313,575	960	995	445	865	610
63	Multiple responses	32,865	65	30	55	40	60
64	English and French	3,430	10	10	-	-	15
65	English and non-official language	27,820	45	25	45	30	40
66	French and non-official language	1,105	-	-	10	10	10
67	English, French and non-official language	510	10	-	-	-	-

See reference material at the end of the publication. – Voir les documents de référence à la fin de la publication.

Tableau 1. Certaines caractéristiques des secteurs de recensement, recensement de 2001 – Données intégrales et données-échantillon (20 %)

Vancouver 0181.06	Vancouver 0181.07	Vancouver 0181.08 A	Vancouver 0181.09 A	Vancouver 0182.01 A	Vancouver 0182.02 ◆ A	Caractéristiques	Nº
						CARACTÉRISTIQUES DE LA POPULATION	
4,850	**3,509**	**2,298**	**5,379**	**2,514**	**346**	**Population, 1996 (1)**	1
5,011	**3,597**	**2,476**	**6,253**	**2,846**	**307**	**Population, 2001 (2)**	2
3.3	2.5	7.7	16.2	13.2	-11.3	Variation en pourcentage de la population, 1996-2001	3
3.75	1.94	1.24	3.90	50.18	2.62	Superficie des terres en kilomètres carrés, 2001	4
5,015	**3,595**	**2,480**	**6,250**	**2,845**	**310**	**Population totale – Données intégrales (3)**	5
						selon le sexe et les groupes d'âge	
2,405	1,780	1,205	2,925	1,470	170	Sexe masculin	6
80	85	60	105	60	5	0-4 ans	7
120	135	75	235	85	20	5-9 ans	8
135	165	85	275	115	15	10-14 ans	9
160	185	95	295	110	20	15-19 ans	10
85	85	65	165	100	5	20-24 ans	11
65	40	45	45	55	5	25-29 ans	12
75	50	55	60	70	15	30-34 ans	13
125	90	80	120	105	20	35-39 ans	14
190	170	95	240	120	15	40-44 ans	15
180	185	105	300	145	15	45-49 ans	16
200	170	125	310	120	10	50-54 ans	17
165	135	80	185	130	5	55-59 ans	18
145	55	70	120	100	5	60-64 ans	19
155	70	55	100	55	5	65-69 ans	20
160	55	45	115	50	5	70-74 ans	21
170	60	40	130	25	-	75-79 ans	22
115	35	20	75	15	-	80-84 ans	23
90	15	20	45	10	-	85 ans et plus	24
2,600	1,810	1,270	3,325	1,375	135	Sexe féminin	25
75	90	55	95	60	5	0-4 ans	26
120	120	60	230	75	10	5-9 ans	27
135	140	95	285	110	10	10-14 ans	28
145	125	80	305	100	10	15-19 ans	29
85	85	45	170	90	10	20-24 ans	30
70	50	40	75	60	5	25-29 ans	31
85	60	65	80	65	5	30-34 ans	32
145	130	95	180	110	10	35-39 ans	33
185	195	105	330	125	20	40-44 ans	34
220	200	150	325	145	10	45-49 ans	35
200	170	110	305	125	10	50-54 ans	36
145	90	95	165	115	5	55-59 ans	37
150	80	65	130	50	-	60-64 ans	38
170	60	55	115	55	5	65-69 ans	39
175	75	55	130	35	5	70-74 ans	40
210	70	40	160	15	5	75-79 ans	41
150	35	35	120	20	-	80-84 ans	42
140	25	30	120	10	-	85 ans et plus	43
4,345	**2,865**	**2,040**	**5,030**	**2,340**	**235**	**Population totale de 15 ans et plus**	44
						selon l'état matrimonial légal	
845	675	450	1,170	640	90	Célibataire (jamais marié(e))	45
2,630	1,875	1,315	3,195	1,425	110	Légalement marié(e) (et non séparé(e))	46
95	45	45	65	70	5	Séparé(e), mais toujours légalement marié(e)	47
325	140	130	215	135	15	Divorcé(e)	48
450	130	100	390	80	10	Veuf ou veuve	49
						selon l'union libre	
4,145	2,765	1,960	4,900	2,210	225	Ne vivant pas en union libre	50
200	95	80	130	135	15	Vivant en union libre	51
4,845	**3,580**	**2,475**	**6,125**	**2,870**	**280**	**Population totale – Données-échantillon (20 %) (4)**	52
						selon la langue maternelle	
4,775	3,560	2,415	6,100	2,860	280	Réponses uniques	53
4,340	3,225	2,085	5,005	2,235	275	Anglais	54
45	20	35	35	15	-	Français	55
385	315	290	1,065	620	-	Langues non officielles (5)	56
45	-	50	150	10	-	Chinois, n.d.a.	57
-	-	-	70	35	-	Cantonais	58
-	-	-	35	145	-	Pendjabi	59
-	-	10	205	75	-	Mandarin	60
-	-	15	-	10	-	Tagalog (pilipino)	61
340	315	210	605	340	-	Autres langues (6)	62
70	20	60	25	10	-	Réponses multiples	63
40	-	20	10	-	-	Anglais et français	64
25	-	45	15	10	-	Anglais et langue non officielle	65
-	10	-	-	-	-	Français et langue non officielle	66
-	-	-	-	-	-	Anglais, français et langue non officielle	67

See reference material at the end of the publication. – Voir les documents de référence à la fin de la publication.

Table 1. Selected Characteristics for Census Tracts, 2001 Census – 100% Data and 20% Sample Data

No.	Characteristics	Vancouver CMA/RMR	Vancouver 0180	Vancouver 0181.01	Vancouver 0181.03	Vancouver 0181.04	Vancouver 0181.05
	POPULATION CHARACTERISTICS						
	by home language						
68	Single responses	1,587,675	7,655	6,415	5,070	6,480	6,630
69	English	1,285,000	7,360	5,995	4,825	6,130	6,440
70	French	3,330	45	25	-	-	50
71	Non-official languages (5)	299,340	250	395	245	350	140
72	Cantonese	73,175	-	-	-	-	10
73	Chinese, n.o.s.	55,750	110	90	100	45	10
74	Punjabi	42,970	-	-	-	-	-
75	Mandarin	26,665	50	145	80	155	20
76	Korean	14,745	15	90	20	-	15
77	Other languages (6)	86,035	65	75	45	145	95
78	Multiple responses	379,805	495	920	340	510	390
79	English and French	18,960	35	75	25	50	35
80	English and non-official language	353,615	435	835	295	450	355
81	French and non-official language	1,615	-	-	-	-	-
82	English, French and non-official language	5,615	30	-	10	10	-
	by knowledge of official languages						
83	English only	1,725,985	7,445	6,700	4,970	6,345	6,575
84	French only	1,215	-	-	-	-	10
85	English and French	147,775	635	555	355	610	415
86	Neither English nor French	92,500	70	85	85	30	20
	by knowledge of non-official languages (5) (7)						
87	Cantonese	149,445	45	10	20	15	20
88	Chinese, n.o.s.	110,065	125	170	120	115	20
89	Punjabi	104,280	30	10	10	40	10
90	Mandarin	96,095	100	430	195	295	85
91	Hindi	54,855	35	-	10	20	45
92	German	51,110	440	230	195	330	250
93	Spanish	50,945	135	120	80	135	145
	by first official language spoken						
94	English	1,839,880	7,925	7,115	5,280	6,870	6,855
95	French	24,795	145	110	40	50	125
96	English and French	12,070	10	30	-	40	15
97	Neither English nor French	90,730	65	90	85	35	20
98	Official language minority - (number) (8)	30,835	150	120	40	65	135
99	Official language minority - (percentage) (8)	1.6	1.8	1.6	0.7	0.9	1.9
	by ethnic origin (9)						
100	English	475,075	3,000	2,975	2,125	2,485	2,895
101	Canadian	378,545	2,180	1,640	1,625	1,775	2,010
102	Chinese	347,985	255	620	260	280	180
103	Scottish	311,940	1,625	1,540	1,210	1,570	1,650
104	Irish	234,675	1,230	1,160	1,050	1,065	1,315
105	German	187,410	1,440	615	770	970	1,155
106	East Indian	142,060	75	10	15	100	70
107	French	128,710	625	445	345	580	660
108	Ukrainian	76,525	505	340	460	450	370
109	Italian	69,000	345	225	140	210	260
110	Dutch (Netherlands)	67,160	500	295	185	445	365
111	Filipino	61,550	100	60	20	65	10
112	Polish	51,385	365	210	310	220	170
113	Norwegian	41,540	190	210	130	160	320
114	North American Indian	40,675	120	85	55	80	100
	by Aboriginal identity						
115	Total Aboriginal identity population (10)	36,855	135	70	45	55	155
116	Total non-Aboriginal population	1,930,620	8,015	7,270	5,360	6,935	6,860
	by Aboriginal origin						
117	Total Aboriginal origins population (11)	52,380	225	95	75	125	180
118	Total non-Aboriginal population	1,915,095	7,925	7,245	5,335	6,860	6,840
	by Registered Indian status						
119	Registered Indian (12)	17,480	30	20	10	25	55
120	Not a Registered Indian	1,950,000	8,120	7,320	5,395	6,965	6,960

Tableau 1. Certaines caractéristiques des secteurs de recensement, recensement de 2001 – Données intégrales et données-échantillon (20 %)

Vancouver 0181.06	Vancouver 0181.07	Vancouver 0181.08 A	Vancouver 0181.09 A	Vancouver 0182.01 A	Vancouver 0182.02 ◆ A	Caractéristiques	N°
						CARACTÉRISTIQUES DE LA POPULATION	
						selon la langue parlée à la maison	
4,650	3,425	2,300	5,715	2,615	275	Réponses uniques	68
4,600	3,420	2,235	5,420	2,395	275	Anglais	69
-	-	-	-	10	-	Français	70
50	10	65	295	215	-	Langues non officielles (5)	71
-	-	10	-	30	-	Cantonais	72
-	-	15	30	-	-	Chinois, n.d.a.	73
-	-	-	-	80	-	Pendjabi	74
-	-	10	125	-	-	Mandarin	75
15	-	20	55	10	-	Coréen	76
35	10	10	85	95	-	Autres langues (6)	77
195	155	180	410	260	10	Réponses multiples	78
15	35	35	25	25	-	Anglais et français	79
180	105	105	360	235	-	Anglais et langue non officielle	80
-	-	-	-	-	-	Français et langue non officielle	81
-	15	35	25	-	-	Anglais, français et langue non officielle	82
						selon la connaissance des langues officielles	
4,585	3,170	2,250	5,665	2,730	255	Anglais seulement	83
-	-	10	-	-	-	Français seulement	84
255	410	215	415	100	25	Anglais et français	85
-	-	10	45	40	-	Ni l'anglais ni le français	86
						selon la connaissance des langues non officielles (5) (7)	
-	-	35	70	40	-	Cantonais	87
45	-	35	90	-	-	Chinois, n.d.a.	88
-	-	-	40	170	-	Pendjabi	89
-	-	30	285	80	-	Mandarin	90
-	-	25	-	10	-	Hindi	91
75	140	100	225	100	-	Allemand	92
40	90	30	90	35	10	Espagnol	93
						selon la première langue officielle parlée	
4,800	3,550	2,435	6,045	2,820	280	Anglais	94
45	30	40	25	10	-	Français	95
-	-	-	10	-	-	Anglais et français	96
-	-	-	45	40	-	Ni l'anglais ni le français	97
45	30	35	35	10	-	Minorité de langue officielle - (nombre) (8)	98
0.9	0.8	1.4	0.6	0.3	-	Minorité de langue officielle - (pourcentage) (8)	99
						selon l'origine ethnique (9)	
2,095	1,480	1,050	2,515	900	85	Anglais	100
1,055	1,345	555	1,675	750	175	Canadien	101
70	10	105	435	150	10	Chinois	102
1,075	920	540	1,575	430	35	Écossais	103
1,080	750	415	915	280	15	Irlandais	104
580	420	455	775	365	20	Allemand	105
20	10	90	85	230	-	Indien de l'Inde	106
390	230	215	395	180	-	Français	107
390	250	135	290	80	-	Ukrainien	108
115	130	50	215	65	-	Italien	109
180	245	130	175	355	-	Hollandais (Néerlandais)	110
15	-	15	-	25	10	Philippin	111
165	105	80	200	45	-	Polonais	112
160	150	60	155	75	15	Norvégien	113
150	15	55	65	60	-	Indien de l'Amérique du Nord	114
						selon l'identité autochtone	
85	35	75	70	45	-	Total de la population ayant une identité autochtone (10)	115
4,755	3,550	2,405	6,055	2,825	280	Total de la population non autochtone	116
						selon l'origine autochtone	
160	45	105	80	80	-	Total de la population ayant une origine autochtone (11)	117
4,685	3,535	2,370	6,050	2,790	280	Total de la population non autochtone	118
						selon le statut d'Indien inscrit	
60	10	-	20	-	-	Oui, Indien inscrit (12)	119
4,780	3,570	2,475	6,105	2,870	280	Non, pas un Indien inscrit	120

Table 1. Selected Characteristics for Census Tracts, 2001 Census – 100% Data and 20% Sample Data

No.	Characteristics	Vancouver CMA/RMR	Vancouver 0180	Vancouver 0181.01	Vancouver 0181.03	Vancouver 0181.04	Vancouver 0181.05
	POPULATION CHARACTERISTICS						
	by visible minority groups						
121	Total visible minority population	725,660	705	1,215	520	895	415
122	Chinese	342,660	295	620	335	450	160
123	South Asian	164,365	80	30	35	135	65
124	Black	18,405	60	50	-	30	20
125	Filipino	57,025	60	60	25	65	-
126	Latin American	18,710	15	50	15	60	15
127	Southeast Asian	28,460	-	15	10	15	20
128	Arab	5,910	15	-	10	10	-
129	West Asian	21,430	-	80	10	-	10
130	Korean	28,850	90	255	65	10	65
131	Japanese	24,025	55	50	25	100	15
132	Visible minority, n.i.e. (13)	3,320	-	-	-	15	-
133	Multiple visible minorities (14)	12,490	35	-	-	10	35
	by citizenship						
134	Canadian citizenship (15)	1,734,425	7,785	6,550	5,035	6,450	6,690
135	Citizenship other than Canadian	233,050	365	785	375	540	325
	by place of birth of respondent						
136	Non-immigrant population	1,199,760	6,305	4,985	4,290	5,030	5,635
137	Born in province of residence	821,535	4,280	2,440	2,745	2,940	3,130
138	Immigrant population (16)	738,550	1,805	2,335	1,080	1,900	1,370
139	United States	23,070	125	120	95	120	95
140	Central and South America	20,585	40	90	20	85	40
141	Caribbean and Bermuda	5,960	-	15	-	15	10
142	United Kingdom	69,110	485	720	225	530	540
143	Other Europe (17)	117,535	660	420	265	515	355
144	Africa	24,700	25	65	25	95	45
145	Asia and the Middle East	455,110	405	890	410	490	235
146	Oceania and other (18)	22,490	70	25	40	45	40
147	Non-permanent residents (19)	29,165	35	25	35	55	10
148	**Total immigrant population**	**738,550**	**1,805**	**2,335**	**1,080**	**1,900**	**1,370**
	by period of immigration						
149	Before 1961	73,550	465	585	210	530	420
150	1961-1970	73,200	455	250	190	340	370
151	1971-1980	124,400	345	365	190	280	200
152	1981-1990	142,585	265	220	95	210	135
153	1991-2001 (20)	324,815	265	915	400	545	245
154	1991-1995	155,195	210	215	75	270	80
155	1996-2001 (20)	169,615	50	700	325	280	165
	by age at immigration						
156	0-4 years	58,985	165	250	115	180	135
157	5-19 years	198,510	475	580	275	585	385
158	20 years and over	481,050	1,160	1,505	685	1,140	855
159	**Total population**	**1,967,475**	**8,150**	**7,335**	**5,405**	**6,990**	**7,020**
	by religion						
160	Catholic (21)	364,785	1,505	1,180	830	1,390	1,030
161	Protestant	499,190	2,935	3,460	2,155	3,185	2,950
162	Christian Orthodox	26,520	65	80	45	90	60
163	Christian, n.i.e. (22)	101,620	630	450	290	235	355
164	Muslim	52,590	25	45	25	45	45
165	Jewish	17,275	15	30	45	25	65
166	Buddhist	74,550	105	165	105	190	45
167	Hindu	27,405	35	-	-	25	-
168	Sikh	99,005	25	15	10	45	-
169	Eastern religions (23)	5,580	-	75	-	15	10
170	Other religions (24)	6,195	15	35	20	10	50
171	No religious affiliation (25)	692,765	2,785	1,810	1,880	1,740	2,400
172	**Total population 15 years and over**	**1,620,915**	**6,730**	**6,295**	**4,305**	**5,900**	**5,920**
	by generation status						
173	1st generation (26)	721,170	1,820	2,105	1,000	1,795	1,350
174	2nd generation (27)	366,235	1,815	1,880	1,040	1,655	1,920
175	3rd generation and over (28)	533,515	3,095	2,315	2,270	2,440	2,645
176	**Total population 1 year and over (29)**	**1,946,955**	**8,095**	**7,305**	**5,385**	**6,915**	**6,950**
	by place of residence 1 year ago (mobility)						
177	Non-movers	1,628,945	6,845	6,180	4,815	5,555	5,920
178	Movers	318,015	1,255	1,125	570	1,365	1,030
179	Non-migrants	175,300	605	625	240	700	600
180	Migrants	142,720	650	500	335	665	425
181	Internal migrants	97,185	605	430	220	500	365
182	Intraprovincial migrants	77,835	540	275	165	365	305
183	Interprovincial migrants	19,350	60	155	55	135	60
184	External migrants	45,535	50	80	110	170	60

Tableau 1. Certaines caractéristiques des secteurs de recensement, recensement de 2001 – Données intégrales et données-échantillon (20 %)

Vancouver 0181.06	Vancouver 0181.07	Vancouver 0181.08 A	Vancouver 0181.09 A	Vancouver 0182.01 A	Vancouver 0182.02 ◆ A	Caractéristiques	N°
						CARACTÉRISTIQUES DE LA POPULATION	
						selon les groupes de minorités visibles	
170	45	315	845	415	20	Total de la population des minorités visibles	121
55	-	135	510	140	10	Chinois	122
10	10	90	80	225	-	Sud-Asiatique	123
30	10	-	-	-	-	Noir	124
15	-	-	10	20	10	Philippin	125
-	-	-	-	-	-	Latino-Américain	126
-	-	-	-	-	-	Asiatique du Sud-Est	127
-	-	-	50	-	-	Arabe	128
-	-	-	-	-	-	Asiatique occidental	129
25	-	20	175	15	-	Coréen	130
35	20	30	20	-	-	Japonais	131
-	-	-	-	-	-	Minorité visible, n.i.a. (13)	132
-	-	25	15	10	-	Minorités visibles multiples (14)	133
						selon la citoyenneté	
4,640	3,450	2,375	5,725	2,750	275	Citoyenneté canadienne (15)	134
200	130	105	405	125	10	Citoyenneté autre que canadienne	135
						selon le lieu de naissance du répondant	
3,865	3,055	1,915	4,520	2,125	260	Population non immigrante	136
2,110	1,920	1,110	2,785	1,515	230	Née dans la province de résidence	137
975	525	555	1,535	745	20	Population immigrante (16)	138
60	45	30	100	15	-	États-Unis	139
10	10	10	-	25	-	Amérique centrale et du Sud	140
-	-	-	10	-	-	Caraïbes et Bermudes	141
475	210	205	415	195	10	Royaume-Uni	142
230	200	160	360	255	10	Autre Europe (17)	143
85	30	10	40	20	-	Afrique	144
95	15	130	560	230	-	Asie et Moyen-Orient	145
20	15	10	40	-	-	Océanie et autre (18)	146
-	10	10	75	-	-	Résidents non permanents (19)	147
970	**520**	**555**	**1,535**	**745**	**20**	**Population immigrante totale**	148
						selon la période d'immigration	
365	160	185	440	240	10	Avant 1961	149
220	145	50	170	130	-	1961-1970	150
125	115	135	250	115	10	1971-1980	151
115	40	115	170	105	-	1981-1990	152
145	60	65	500	150	10	1991-2001 (20)	153
90	50	35	240	80	-	1991-1995	154
55	10	35	260	65	-	1996-2001 (20)	155
						selon l'âge à l'immigration	
65	35	30	145	40	-	0-4 ans	156
220	125	140	530	220	10	5-19 ans	157
685	360	385	860	485	10	20 ans et plus	158
4,845	**3,585**	**2,475**	**6,130**	**2,870**	**280**	**Population totale**	159
						selon la religion	
835	515	335	910	445	30	Catholique (21)	160
2,175	1,760	1,000	2,720	1,110	150	Protestante	161
20	65	20	20	65	-	Orthodoxe chrétienne	162
440	155	235	305	120	20	Chrétiennes, n.i.a. (22)	163
10	-	20	85	-	-	Musulmane	164
-	15	15	30	-	-	Juive	165
-	15	20	180	65	-	Bouddhiste	166
-	-	-	-	35	-	Hindoue	167
-	-	-	35	190	-	Sikh	168
15	-	-	-	-	-	Religions orientales (23)	169
10	-	10	-	-	-	Autres religions (24)	170
1,335	1,055	810	1,840	850	75	Aucune appartenance religieuse (25)	171
4,175	**2,860**	**2,035**	**4,900**	**2,355**	**215**	**Population totale de 15 ans et plus**	172
						selon le statut des générations	
980	530	555	1,525	735	20	1re génération (26)	173
1,315	835	620	1,355	665	80	2e génération (27)	174
1,875	1,490	860	2,020	950	110	3e génération et plus (28)	175
4,820	**3,565**	**2,455**	**6,100**	**2,850**	**280**	**Population totale de 1 an et plus (29)**	176
						selon le lieu de résidence 1 an auparavant (mobilité)	
4,255	2,960	2,165	5,370	2,465	240	Personnes n'ayant pas déménagé	177
565	605	290	725	385	40	Personnes ayant déménagé	178
370	405	160	525	160	40	Non-migrants	179
190	200	130	205	225	-	Migrants	180
185	175	120	160	220	-	Migrants internes	181
135	95	90	40	215	-	Migrants infraprovinciaux	182
45	80	30	120	10	-	Migrants interprovinciaux	183
10	25	15	40	-	-	Migrants externes	184

Table 1. Selected Characteristics for Census Tracts, 2001 Census – 100% Data and 20% Sample Data

No.	Characteristics	Vancouver CMA/RMR	Vancouver 0180	Vancouver 0181.01	Vancouver 0181.03	Vancouver 0181.04	Vancouver 0181.05
	POPULATION CHARACTERISTICS						
185	**Total population 5 years and over (30) by place of residence 5 years ago (mobility)**	**1,861,975**	**7,845**	**7,110**	**5,165**	**6,710**	**6,660**
186	Non-movers	970,840	4,485	3,840	3,160	3,000	3,405
187	Movers	891,135	3,360	3,270	2,005	3,710	3,255
188	Non-migrants	432,820	1,940	1,270	925	1,845	1,660
189	Migrants	458,315	1,420	2,005	1,080	1,860	1,595
190	Internal migrants	290,195	1,275	1,320	755	1,460	1,395
191	Intraprovincial migrants	223,405	1,080	1,010	610	1,140	1,150
192	Interprovincial migrants	66,785	190	315	140	320	250
193	External migrants	168,120	145	685	325	405	195
194	**Total population 15 to 24 years by school attendance**	**265,875**	**1,125**	**845**	**760**	**785**	**675**
195	Not attending school	87,675	455	235	190	225	295
196	Attending school full time	151,620	600	550	505	470	320
197	Attending school part time	26,575	80	55	65	90	60
198	**Total population 15 years and over by highest level of schooling**	**1,620,915**	**6,730**	**6,295**	**4,305**	**5,895**	**5,920**
199	Less than grade 9 (31)	100,975	170	255	85	175	350
200	Grades 9-13 without high school graduation certificate	302,050	1,505	1,200	710	1,110	1,400
201	Grades 9-13 with high school graduation certificate	197,495	820	885	465	775	705
202	Some postsecondary without degree, certificate or diploma (32)	220,990	865	965	625	795	775
203	Trades certificate or diploma (33)	157,435	905	615	450	570	805
204	College certificate or diploma (34)	250,395	1,110	985	825	1,005	975
205	University certificate below bachelor's degree	55,870	255	200	140	255	185
206	University with bachelor's degree or higher	335,710	1,090	1,185	1,005	1,220	720
	by combinations of unpaid work						
207	Males 15 years and over	787,520	3,425	2,835	2,050	2,835	2,670
208	Reported unpaid work (35)	693,120	3,075	2,555	1,840	2,505	2,340
209	Housework and child care and care or assistance to seniors	59,635	205	160	235	180	145
210	Housework and child care only	186,845	870	675	605	660	700
211	Housework and care or assistance to seniors only	54,490	255	315	185	275	235
212	Child care and care or assistance to seniors only	1,435	-	-	-	-	-
213	Housework only	377,845	1,685	1,375	785	1,345	1,235
214	Child care only	8,635	35	20	10	30	10
215	Care or assistance to seniors only	4,230	25	-	20	10	20
216	Females 15 years and over	833,400	3,300	3,455	2,255	3,065	3,245
217	Reported unpaid work (35)	770,470	3,150	3,230	2,100	2,790	2,915
218	Housework and child care and care or assistance to seniors	91,875	385	395	295	290	290
219	Housework and child care only	229,500	910	825	745	835	850
220	Housework and care or assistance to seniors only	75,405	470	405	275	335	405
221	Child care and care or assistance to seniors only	860	10	-	-	-	-
222	Housework only	364,565	1,375	1,565	775	1,305	1,355
223	Child care only	5,195	10	10	10	15	-
224	Care or assistance to seniors only	3,065	-	20	10	15	10
	by labour force activity						
225	Males 15 years and over	787,520	3,425	2,840	2,050	2,830	2,670
226	In the labour force	563,750	2,500	1,530	1,455	1,830	1,665
227	Employed	522,775	2,395	1,425	1,380	1,730	1,560
228	Unemployed	40,980	110	100	70	100	105
229	Not in the labour force	223,765	920	1,305	595	1,000	1,010
230	Participation rate	71.6	73.0	53.9	71.0	64.7	62.4
231	Employment rate	66.4	69.9	50.2	67.3	61.1	58.4
232	Unemployment rate	7.3	4.4	6.5	4.8	5.5	6.3
233	Females 15 years and over	833,400	3,300	3,455	2,255	3,065	3,245
234	In the labour force	509,255	1,955	1,590	1,335	1,705	1,570
235	Employed	472,540	1,875	1,500	1,260	1,610	1,500
236	Unemployed	36,715	80	85	75	90	70
237	Not in the labour force	324,140	1,340	1,870	920	1,360	1,675
238	Participation rate	61.1	59.2	46.0	59.2	55.6	48.4
239	Employment rate	56.7	56.8	43.4	55.9	52.5	46.2
240	Unemployment rate	7.2	4.1	5.3	5.6	5.3	4.5

Tableau 1. Certaines caractéristiques des secteurs de recensement, recensement de 2001 – Données intégrales et données-échantillon (20 %)

Vancouver 0181.06	Vancouver 0181.07	Vancouver 0181.08 A	Vancouver 0181.09 A	Vancouver 0182.01 A	Vancouver 0182.02 ◆ A	Caractéristiques	Nº
						CARACTÉRISTIQUES DE LA POPULATION	
4,660	**3,400**	**2,380**	**5,920**	**2,750**	**275**	**Population totale de 5 ans et plus (30)**	185
						selon le lieu de résidence 5 ans auparavant (mobilité)	
2,785	2,075	1,360	3,475	1,455	200	Personnes n'ayant pas déménagé	186
1,880	1,320	1,020	2,445	1,295	75	Personnes ayant déménagé	187
1,000	755	495	990	625	70	Non-migrants	188
880	565	520	1,455	675	-	Migrants	189
770	515	445	1,035	585	10	Migrants internes	190
600	280	315	655	515	10	Migrants infraprovinciaux	191
170	235	130	385	70	-	Migrants interprovinciaux	192
105	55	75	425	85	-	Migrants externes	193
410	**500**	**265**	**935**	**390**	**50**	**Population totale de 15 à 24 ans**	194
						selon la fréquentation scolaire	
165	120	50	210	160	35	Ne fréquentant pas l'école	195
210	315	210	690	205	10	Fréquentant l'école à plein temps	196
35	70	-	35	25	-	Fréquentant l'école à temps partiel	197
4,175	**2,860**	**2,035**	**4,900**	**2,350**	**215**	**Population totale de 15 ans et plus**	198
						selon le plus haut niveau de scolarité atteint	
185	20	35	110	120	10	Niveau inférieur à la 9e année (31)	199
980	405	230	900	625	40	De la 9e à la 13e année sans certificat d'études secondaires	200
480	380	175	505	335	35	De la 9e à la 13e année avec certificat d'études secondaires	201
565	355	300	725	335	25	Études postsecondaires partielles sans grade, certificat ou diplôme (32)	202
495	275	305	425	240	25	Certificat ou diplôme d'une école de métiers (33)	203
740	500	395	870	335	65	Certificat ou diplôme collégial (34)	204
80	145	60	235	80	-	Certificat universitaire inférieur au baccalauréat	205
655	780	535	1,130	280	15	Études universitaires avec baccalauréat ou diplôme supérieur	206
						selon les combinaisons de travail non rémunéré	
2,025	1,400	985	2,280	1,215	120	Hommes de 15 ans et plus	207
1,805	1,270	895	2,055	1,120	85	Travail non rémunéré déclaré (35)	208
130	130	60	195	145	20	Travaux ménagers et soins aux enfants et soins ou aide aux personnes âgées	209
430	415	285	680	280	15	Travaux ménagers et soins aux enfants seulement	210
155	95	80	175	60	10	Travaux ménagers et soins ou aide aux personnes âgées seulement	211
-	-	-	10	-	-	Soins aux enfants et soins ou aide aux personnes âgées seulement	212
1,085	615	460	960	620	50	Travaux ménagers seulement	213
-	20	10	20	-	-	Soins aux enfants seulement	214
-	-	10	15	10	-	Soins ou aide aux personnes âgées seulement	215
2,150	1,460	1,050	2,615	1,140	100	Femmes de 15 ans et plus	216
1,980	1,370	1,030	2,440	1,105	95	Travail non rémunéré déclaré (35)	217
210	185	100	355	165	15	Travaux ménagers et soins aux enfants et soins ou aide aux personnes âgées	218
495	405	300	765	385	25	Travaux ménagers et soins aux enfants seulement	219
225	155	130	275	85	-	Travaux ménagers et soins ou aide aux personnes âgées seulement	220
-	-	-	-	-	-	Soins aux enfants et soins ou aide aux personnes âgées seulement	221
1,025	615	505	1,035	460	50	Travaux ménagers seulement	222
-	-	-	-	10	-	Soins aux enfants seulement	223
20	-	-	10	15	-	Soins ou aide aux personnes âgées seulement	224
						selon l'activité	
2,025	1,395	985	2,280	1,220	115	Hommes de 15 ans et plus	225
1,200	1,030	670	1,515	960	110	Population active	226
1,145	990	645	1,460	930	100	Personnes occupées	227
45	45	30	55	30	10	Chômeurs	228
825	365	310	760	255	10	Inactifs	229
59.3	73.8	68.0	66.4	78.7	95.7	Taux d'activité	230
56.5	71.0	65.5	64.0	76.2	87.0	Taux d'emploi	231
3.8	4.4	4.5	3.6	3.1	9.1	Taux de chômage	232
2,155	1,460	1,050	2,615	1,135	95	Femmes de 15 ans et plus	233
1,045	855	650	1,365	785	65	Population active	234
1,005	835	595	1,310	745	60	Personnes occupées	235
45	20	55	55	40	10	Chômeuses	236
1,100	605	400	1,250	350	35	Inactives	237
48.5	58.6	61.9	52.2	69.2	68.4	Taux d'activité	238
46.6	57.2	56.7	50.1	65.6	63.2	Taux d'emploi	239
4.3	2.3	8.5	4.0	5.1	15.4	Taux de chômage	240

Table 1. Selected Characteristics for Census Tracts, 2001 Census – 100% Data and 20% Sample Data

No.	Characteristics	Vancouver CMA/RMR	Vancouver 0180	Vancouver 0181.01	Vancouver 0181.03	Vancouver 0181.04	Vancouver 0181.05
	POPULATION CHARACTERISTICS						
	by labour force activity – concluded						
241	Both sexes - Participation rate	66.2	66.3	49.6	64.8	60.0	54.7
242	15-24 years	59.2	62.8	55.6	57.2	59.9	64.9
243	25 years and over	67.6	67.0	48.7	66.3	60.0	53.3
244	Both sexes - Employment rate	61.4	63.5	46.5	61.3	56.7	51.7
245	15-24 years	51.0	58.4	47.9	49.3	51.9	54.8
246	25 years and over	63.4	64.5	46.3	63.9	57.3	51.3
247	Both sexes - Unemployment rate	7.2	4.3	6.1	5.4	5.5	5.4
248	15-24 years	13.8	7.0	12.9	13.6	11.8	14.9
249	25 years and over	6.1	3.6	4.9	3.6	4.6	3.8
250	**Total labour force 15 years and over**	**1,073,010**	**4,460**	**3,125**	**2,790**	**3,540**	**3,235**
	by industry based on the 1997 NAICS						
251	Industry - Not applicable (36)	23,100	70	60	45	45	50
252	All industries (37)	1,049,910	4,390	3,060	2,745	3,490	3,185
253	11 Agriculture, forestry, fishing and hunting	13,275	230	45	35	65	25
254	21 Mining and oil and gas extraction	2,250	30	10	10	10	15
255	22 Utilities	6,200	25	35	25	30	10
256	23 Construction	53,795	490	145	145	180	210
257	31-33 Manufacturing	99,055	420	200	220	200	225
258	41 Wholesale trade	56,025	295	205	170	285	175
259	44-45 Retail trade	116,520	400	330	290	365	320
260	48-49 Transportation and warehousing	65,700	305	170	135	210	215
261	51 Information and cultural industries	44,355	130	120	105	140	80
262	52 Finance and insurance	54,110	160	125	100	275	150
263	53 Real estate and rental and leasing	24,735	100	85	85	105	60
264	54 Professional, scientific and technical services	91,715	300	340	215	280	245
265	55 Management of companies and enterprises	970	10	15	15	-	-
266	56 Administrative and support, waste management and remediation services	45,530	180	105	100	80	60
267	61 Educational services	74,480	345	290	320	270	295
268	62 Health care and social assistance	99,350	315	275	330	265	425
269	71 Arts, entertainment and recreation	24,050	115	115	115	150	65
270	72 Accommodation and food services	81,555	200	155	170	215	225
271	81 Other services (except public administration)	51,610	140	145	80	190	235
272	91 Public administration	44,635	210	165	95	185	155
	by class of worker						
273	Class of worker - Not applicable (36)	23,100	70	60	45	45	50
274	All classes of worker (37)	1,049,910	4,390	3,060	2,745	3,490	3,185
275	Paid workers	956,210	3,865	2,755	2,405	3,080	2,830
276	Employees	904,735	3,425	2,540	2,105	2,735	2,715
277	Self-employed (incorporated)	51,470	445	210	305	345	120
278	Self-employed (unincorporated)	90,455	510	310	325	410	355
279	Unpaid family workers	3,245	15	-	15	-	-
	by occupation based on the 2001 NOC-S						
280	Male labour force 15 years and over	563,755	2,505	1,530	1,455	1,830	1,665
281	Occupation - Not applicable (36)	11,070	30	35	10	30	10
282	All occupations (37)	552,685	2,470	1,500	1,445	1,805	1,650
283	A Management occupations	82,510	425	305	370	435	305
284	B Business, finance and administration occupations	59,870	240	185	125	185	130
285	C Natural and applied sciences and related occupations	60,400	255	165	190	190	165
286	D Health occupations	13,415	50	20	80	45	20
287	E Occupations in social science, education, government service and religion	31,255	90	95	110	90	100
288	F Occupations in art, culture, recreation and sport	21,510	50	90	45	60	45
289	G Sales and service occupations	118,835	505	340	200	385	310
290	H Trades, transport and equipment operators and related occupations	121,700	605	230	235	295	430
291	I Occupations unique to primary industry	12,650	170	50	45	45	50
292	J Occupations unique to processing, manufacturing and utilities	30,540	80	15	40	75	85
293	Female labour force 15 years and over	509,260	1,955	1,585	1,335	1,705	1,570
294	Occupation - Not applicable (36)	12,030	40	30	30	15	35
295	All occupations (37)	497,225	1,915	1,560	1,310	1,695	1,540
296	A Management occupations	42,455	230	185	105	180	110
297	B Business, finance and administration occupations	148,020	630	460	365	620	525
298	C Natural and applied sciences and related occupations	14,750	40	50	15	30	40
299	D Health occupations	41,480	180	145	105	125	115

Tableau 1. Certaines caractéristiques des secteurs de recensement, recensement de 2001 – Données intégrales et données-échantillon (20 %)

Vancouver 0181.06	Vancouver 0181.07	Vancouver 0181.08 A	Vancouver 0181.09 A	Vancouver 0182.01 A	Vancouver 0182.02 ◆ A	Caractéristiques	N°
						CARACTÉRISTIQUES DE LA POPULATION	
						selon l'activité – fin	
53.9	66.1	64.9	59.0	74.1	81.4	Les deux sexes - Taux d'activité	241
74.4	62.0	67.9	56.1	69.2	80.0	15-24 ans	242
51.7	66.9	64.4	59.5	75.3	78.8	25 ans et plus	243
51.6	64.0	61.2	56.7	71.3	72.1	Les deux sexes - Taux d'emploi	244
67.1	53.0	49.1	48.1	64.1	70.0	15-24 ans	245
49.9	66.1	62.7	58.6	72.5	70.6	25 ans et plus	246
4.0	3.2	6.4	3.8	4.0	11.8	Les deux sexes - Taux de chômage	247
8.3	12.9	27.0	15.2	7.5	28.6	15-24 ans	248
3.4	1.3	2.6	1.3	3.4	7.4	25 ans et plus	249
2,245	**1,890**	**1,320**	**2,885**	**1,745**	**170**	**Population active totale de 15 ans et plus**	250
						selon l'industrie basée sur le SCIAN de 1997	
10	15	10	35	10	-	Industrie - Sans objet (36)	251
2,235	1,880	1,310	2,855	1,740	175	Toutes les industries (37)	252
20	25	20	25	270	-	11 Agriculture, foresterie, pêche et chasse	253
-	10	-	-	20	-	21 Extraction minière et extraction de pétrole et de gaz	254
-	35	10	10	-	-	22 Services publics	255
150	95	130	160	220	50	23 Construction	256
100	130	55	200	160	25	31-33 Fabrication	257
130	170	45	195	65	-	41 Commerce de gros	258
220	150	140	335	140	35	44-45 Commerce de détail	259
285	115	90	165	135	-	48-49 Transport et entreposage	260
50	55	35	75	50	-	51 Industrie de l'information et industrie culturelle	261
110	85	60	170	45	-	52 Finance et assurances	262
15	40	40	150	30	-	53 Services immobiliers et services de location et de location à bail	263
105	200	155	270	60	10	54 Services professionnels, scientifiques et techniques	264
-	-	-	15	-	-	55 Gestion de sociétés et d'entreprises	265
120	60	30	125	65	-	56 Services administratifs, services de soutien, services de gestion des déchets et services d'assainissement	266
195	195	155	245	95	10	61 Services d'enseignement	267
225	165	95	315	75	15	62 Soins de santé et assistance sociale	268
75	45	50	75	35	-	71 Arts, spectacles et loisirs	269
155	110	80	95	70	-	72 Hébergement et services de restauration	270
150	60	65	95	85	-	81 Autres services, sauf les administrations publiques	271
135	120	50	130	110	10	91 Administrations publiques	272
						selon la catégorie de travailleurs	
10	10	15	35	10	-	Catégorie de travailleurs - Sans objet (36)	273
2,235	1,880	1,310	2,855	1,740	170	Toutes les catégories de travailleurs (37)	274
2,035	1,690	1,190	2,595	1,450	145	Travailleurs rémunérés	275
1,910	1,535	1,020	2,275	1,300	140	Employés	276
125	150	175	320	150	-	Travailleurs autonomes (entreprise constituée en société)	277
195	190	120	250	275	25	Travailleurs autonomes (entreprise non constituée en société)	278
10	-	-	-	15	-	Travailleurs familiaux non rémunérés	279
						selon la profession basée sur la CNP-S de 2001	
1,200	1,035	675	1,520	960	105	Hommes actifs de 15 ans et plus	280
-	10	-	25	-	-	Profession - Sans objet (36)	281
1,190	1,025	670	1,500	965	105	Toutes les professions (37)	282
240	270	200	535	145	10	A Gestion	283
120	80	65	135	50	-	B Affaires, finance et administration	284
110	140	115	155	55	10	C Sciences naturelles et appliquées et professions apparentées	285
15	20	10	80	25	-	D Secteur de la santé	286
75	50	45	80	45	-	E Sciences sociales, enseignement, administration publique et religion	287
60	45	15	40	10	-	F Arts, culture, sports et loisirs	288
215	210	110	235	140	15	G Ventes et services	289
320	145	90	145	335	65	H Métiers, transport et machinerie	290
15	45	-	70	120	-	I Professions propres au secteur primaire	291
20	30	25	20	45	10	J Transformation, fabrication et services d'utilité publique	292
1,050	855	650	1,365	785	65	Femmes actives de 15 ans et plus	293
10	10	-	10	10	-	Profession - Sans objet (36)	294
1,045	850	640	1,355	775	65	Toutes les professions (37)	295
110	80	50	150	45	-	A Gestion	296
270	235	175	515	255	10	B Affaires, finance et administration	297
10	15	10	10	15	10	C Sciences naturelles et appliquées et professions apparentées	298
90	85	60	100	35	15	D Secteur de la santé	299

Table 1. Selected Characteristics for Census Tracts, 2001 Census – 100% Data and 20% Sample Data

No.	Characteristics	Vancouver CMA/RMR	Vancouver 0180	Vancouver 0181.01	Vancouver 0181.03	Vancouver 0181.04	Vancouver 0181.05
	POPULATION CHARACTERISTICS						
	by occupation based on the 2001 NOC-S – concluded						
300	E Occupations in social science, education, government service and religion	54,720	225	215	195	175	180
301	F Occupations in art, culture, recreation and sport	21,085	85	75	95	85	45
302	G Sales and service occupations	144,930	420	395	405	440	465
303	H Trades, transport and equipment operators and related occupations	8,415	15	15	-	-	10
304	I Occupations unique to primary industry	5,705	70	15	10	15	15
305	J Occupations unique to processing, manufacturing and utilities	15,670	25	10	-	15	25
306	**Total employed labour force 15 years and over**	**995,320**	**4,270**	**2,930**	**2,640**	**3,340**	**3,065**
	by place of work						
307	Males	522,780	2,395	1,430	1,380	1,735	1,560
308	Usual place of work	401,510	1,395	1,100	985	1,285	1,140
309	At home	38,490	430	125	140	285	115
310	Outside Canada	6,355	30	30	20	10	35
311	No fixed workplace address	76,425	545	170	230	160	270
312	Females	472,540	1,875	1,500	1,260	1,610	1,505
313	Usual place of work	401,895	1,350	1,195	960	1,185	1,280
314	At home	41,790	390	230	225	325	190
315	Outside Canada	2,690	10	-	30	-	-
316	No fixed workplace address	26,165	130	80	45	105	35
317	**Total employed labour force 15 years and over with usual place of work or no fixed workplace address**	**905,995**	**3,415**	**2,545**	**2,220**	**2,730**	**2,725**
	by mode of transportation						
318	Males	477,935	1,935	1,270	1,210	1,445	1,410
319	Car, truck, van, as driver	372,070	1,730	1,090	1,100	1,230	1,155
320	Car, truck, van, as passenger	22,965	110	65	50	100	45
321	Public transit	41,160	35	60	15	45	75
322	Walked	25,370	40	35	25	40	90
323	Other method	16,370	20	20	20	30	40
324	Females	428,065	1,480	1,275	1,010	1,295	1,315
325	Car, truck, van, as driver	281,985	1,300	1,035	830	1,025	935
326	Car, truck, van, as passenger	40,680	75	80	80	60	100
327	Public transit	62,855	55	70	40	65	80
328	Walked	33,335	30	85	25	95	170
329	Other method	9,200	20	10	35	40	35
330	**Total population 15 years and over who worked since January 1, 2000**	**1,148,265**	**4,890**	**3,370**	**3,105**	**3,830**	**3,440**
	by language used at work						
331	Single responses	1,027,735	4,700	3,165	3,015	3,685	3,330
332	English	991,615	4,665	3,115	2,985	3,625	3,325
333	French	830	-	-	-	10	10
334	Non-official languages (5)	35,285	40	45	35	45	-
335	Chinese, n.o.s.	11,110	25	10	20	10	10
336	Cantonese	9,925	-	-	-	-	-
337	Other languages (6)	14,245	-	45	15	40	-
338	Multiple responses	120,535	185	210	90	145	110
339	English and French	13,780	55	65	20	40	40
340	English and non-official language	103,890	110	145	70	80	65
341	French and non-official language	145	-	-	-	-	-
342	English, French and non-official language	2,720	20	-	-	20	-
	DWELLING AND HOUSEHOLD CHARACTERISTICS						
343	**Total number of occupied private dwellings**	**758,715**	**2,800**	**3,250**	**1,905**	**2,750**	**3,200**
	by tenure						
344	Owned	462,645	2,385	2,550	1,420	2,360	2,475
345	Rented	295,740	415	695	480	390	725
346	Band housing	330	-	-	-	-	-
	by structural type of dwelling						
347	Single-detached house	330,745	2,495	1,880	1,640	1,195	1,790
348	Semi-detached house	19,180	80	145	70	405	90
349	Row house	56,265	65	175	20	850	330
350	Apartment, detached duplex	65,610	45	-	30	20	15
351	Apartment, building that has five or more storeys	89,515	-	-	-	-	-
352	Apartment, building that has fewer than five storeys (38)	191,045	20	1,050	140	285	970
353	Other single-attached house	1,240	-	-	-	-	15
354	Movable dwelling (39)	5,110	100	-	-	-	-

Tableau 1. Certaines caractéristiques des secteurs de recensement, recensement de 2001 – Données intégrales et données-échantillon (20 %)

Vancouver 0181.06	Vancouver 0181.07	Vancouver 0181.08 A	Vancouver 0181.09 A	Vancouver 0182.01 A	Vancouver 0182.02 ◆ A	Caractéristiques	N°
						CARACTÉRISTIQUES DE LA POPULATION	
						selon la profession basée sur la CNP-S de 2001 – fin	
165	115	110	215	35	-	E Sciences sociales, enseignement, administration publique et religion	300
40	60	40	60	10	-	F Arts, culture, sports et loisirs	301
335	245	180	280	240	25	G Ventes et services	302
10	10	-	10	15	-	H Métiers, transport et machinerie	303
15	10	10	10	115	-	I Professions propres au secteur primaire	304
10	-	-	20	10	-	J Transformation, fabrication et services d'utilité publique	305
2,155	**1,830**	**1,240**	**2,775**	**1,675**	**155**	**Population active occupée totale de 15 ans et plus**	306
						selon le lieu de travail	
1,150	995	645	1,460	930	100	Hommes	307
785	815	450	1,195	585	60	Lieu habituel de travail	308
140	60	85	105	195	25	À domicile	309
15	10	10	15	10	-	En dehors du Canada	310
210	105	110	145	150	10	Sans adresse de travail fixe	311
1,005	835	595	1,315	750	60	Femmes	312
805	675	455	1,010	570	40	Lieu habituel de travail	313
100	95	95	225	145	10	À domicile	314
-	10	-	-	-	-	En dehors du Canada	315
100	60	45	70	35	10	Sans adresse de travail fixe	316
1,900	**1,660**	**1,050**	**2,420**	**1,340**	**120**	**Population active occupée totale de 15 ans et plus ayant un lieu habituel de travail ou sans adresse de travail fixe**	317
						selon le mode de transport	
995	920	555	1,345	735	70	Hommes	318
865	750	515	1,185	625	65	Automobile, camion ou fourgonnette, en tant que conducteur	319
65	45	20	50	45	-	Automobile, camion ou fourgonnette, en tant que passager	320
25	75	10	50	35	-	Transport en commun	321
10	30	10	50	10	-	À pied	322
25	20	10	-	15	-	Autre moyen	323
900	745	495	1,080	605	50	Femmes	324
770	565	375	855	480	45	Automobile, camion ou fourgonnette, en tant que conductrice	325
80	80	50	75	55	-	Automobile, camion ou fourgonnette, en tant que passagère	326
20	45	10	90	30	-	Transport en commun	327
30	35	45	55	10	-	À pied	328
10	20	10	15	35	-	Autre moyen	329
2,470	**2,135**	**1,450**	**3,275**	**1,895**	**170**	**Population totale de 15 ans et plus ayant travaillé depuis le 1er janvier 2000**	330
						selon la langue utilisée au travail	
2,430	2,105	1,385	3,125	1,745	175	Réponses uniques	331
2,420	2,105	1,380	3,110	1,720	175	Anglais	332
-	-	-	-	-	-	Français	333
-	-	-	20	30	-	Langues non officielles (5)	334
-	-	-	15	-	-	Chinois, n.d.a.	335
-	-	-	-	10	-	Cantonais	336
10	-	-	-	20	-	Autres langues (6)	337
40	30	60	150	145	-	Réponses multiples	338
10	10	15	20	15	-	Anglais et français	339
30	15	40	125	130	-	Anglais et langue non officielle	340
-	-	-	-	-	-	Français et langue non officielle	341
-	-	10	-	-	-	Anglais, français et langue non officielle	342
						CARACTÉRISTIQUES DES LOGEMENTS ET DES MÉNAGES	
2,075	**1,250**	**925**	**2,070**	**950**	**110**	**Nombre total de logements privés occupés**	343
						selon le mode d'occupation	
1,870	1,125	815	1,960	785	85	Possédé	344
195	130	110	110	165	20	Loué	345
-	-	-	-	-	-	Logement de bande	346
						selon le type de construction résidentielle	
1,675	1,135	875	1,655	835	100	Maison individuelle non attenante	347
60	10	20	70	-	10	Maison jumelée	348
150	35	-	135	-	-	Maison en rangée	349
65	30	25	-	10	-	Appartement, duplex non attenant	350
50	30	-	-	-	-	Appartement, immeuble de cinq étages ou plus	351
30	20	-	200	10	-	Appartement, immeuble de moins de cinq étages (38)	352
-	-	-	-	-	-	Autre maison individuelle attenante	353
50	-	-	10	100	-	Logement mobile (39)	354

Table 1. Selected Characteristics for Census Tracts, 2001 Census – 100% Data and 20% Sample Data

No.	Characteristics	Vancouver CMA/RMR	Vancouver 0180	Vancouver 0181.01	Vancouver 0181.03	Vancouver 0181.04	Vancouver 0181.05
	DWELLING AND HOUSEHOLD CHARACTERISTICS						
	by condition of dwelling						
355	Regular maintenance only	524,700	1,935	2,455	1,305	2,305	2,170
356	Minor repairs	170,685	670	625	510	380	805
357	Major repairs	63,330	195	170	85	70	225
	by period of construction						
358	Before 1946	72,360	235	10	210	25	60
359	1946-1960	91,060	275	45	200	80	230
360	1961-1970	111,400	285	50	290	125	235
361	1971-1980	152,465	730	535	485	270	820
362	1981-1990	159,145	530	1,930	315	610	1,215
363	1991-2001 (20)	172,280	745	675	405	1,635	635
364	Average number of rooms per dwelling	6.0	8.1	6.2	7.8	7.0	5.9
365	Average number of bedrooms per dwelling	2.5	3.2	2.5	3.1	2.9	2.3
366	Average value of dwelling $	294,847	428,032	266,692	459,576	325,318	191,346
367	**Total number of private households**	**758,710**	**2,800**	**3,250**	**1,900**	**2,750**	**3,195**
	by household size						
368	1 person	212,055	365	945	385	520	1,105
369	2 persons	228,230	1,070	1,335	580	1,215	1,165
370	3 persons	115,200	460	365	285	405	375
371	4-5 persons	170,360	745	565	560	535	490
372	6 or more persons	32,865	160	35	100	70	60
	by household type						
373	One-family households	483,330	2,295	2,240	1,400	2,105	1,920
374	Multiple-family households	24,755	80	-	55	70	55
375	Non-family households	250,630	425	1,010	440	575	1,220
376	Number of persons in private households	1,963,645	8,145	7,340	5,410	6,945	7,010
377	Average number of persons in private households	2.6	2.9	2.3	2.8	2.5	2.2
378	Average number of persons per room	0.4	0.4	0.4	0.4	0.4	0.4
379	Tenant households in non-farm, non-reserve private dwellings (40)	291,465	415	695	480	375	725
380	Average gross rent $ (40)	814	941	866	933	848	1,490
381	Tenant households spending 30% or more of household income on gross rent (40) (41)	125,945	185	365	215	140	350
382	Tenant households spending from 30% to 99% of household income on gross rent (40) (41)	99,260	165	345	180	100	210
383	Owner households in non-farm, non-reserve private dwellings (42)	458,780	2,295	2,540	1,410	2,350	2,475
384	Average owner's major payments $ (42)	1,057	1,192	814	1,326	1,132	833
385	Owner households spending 30% or more of household income on owner's major payments (41) (42)	109,900	495	485	325	485	515
386	Owner households spending from 30% to 99% of household income on owner's major payments (41) (42)	93,210	440	400	290	435	450
	CENSUS FAMILY CHARACTERISTICS						
387	**Total number of census families in private households**	**535,255**	**2,465**	**2,245**	**1,520**	**2,240**	**2,035**
	by census family structure and size						
388	Total couple families	453,395	2,235	1,955	1,355	1,940	1,680
389	Total families of married couples	401,385	2,030	1,825	1,255	1,790	1,505
390	Without children at home	152,540	885	1,025	455	990	865
391	With children at home	248,845	1,150	800	795	795	640
392	1 child	87,825	395	255	220	305	220
393	2 children	111,795	445	405	365	325	320
394	3 or more children	49,220	305	135	215	165	95
395	Total families of common-law couples	52,010	200	130	105	145	180
396	Without children at home	37,370	165	100	70	105	115
397	With children at home	14,635	40	30	35	40	60
398	1 child	7,945	15	20	15	30	45
399	2 children	4,755	10	10	15	15	10
400	3 or more children	1,935	15	10	10	-	10
401	Total lone-parent families	81,860	230	290	165	305	355
402	Female parent	67,055	160	245	125	255	275
403	1 child	40,440	80	160	80	170	165
404	2 children	19,310	65	50	30	75	85
405	3 or more children	7,300	15	25	15	15	25

Tableau 1. Certaines caractéristiques des secteurs de recensement, recensement de 2001 – Données intégrales et données-échantillon (20 %)

Vancouver 0181.06	Vancouver 0181.07	Vancouver 0181.08 A	Vancouver 0181.09 A	Vancouver 0182.01 A	Vancouver 0182.02 ◆ A	Caractéristiques	N°
						CARACTÉRISTIQUES DES LOGEMENTS ET DES MÉNAGES	
						selon l'état du logement	
1,535	955	650	1,705	680	80	Entretien régulier seulement	355
455	240	245	310	210	20	Réparations mineures	356
85	60	35	55	60	10	Réparations majeures	357
						selon la période de construction	
30	30	25	-	65	10	Avant 1946	358
120	95	130	25	130	20	1946-1960	359
150	170	155	30	90	20	1961-1970	360
395	315	235	190	90	20	1971-1980	361
1,070	365	240	1,220	200	20	1981-1990	362
305	275	140	605	380	20	1991-2001 (20)	363
6.5	8.0	7.8	8.3	7.8	6.9	Nombre moyen de pièces par logement	364
2.7	3.0	3.2	3.3	3.1	3.0	Nombre moyen de chambres à coucher par logement	365
214,767	360,390	366,117	392,947	367,358	323,063	Valeur moyenne du logement $	366
2,075	**1,250**	**925**	**2,065**	**950**	**105**	**Nombre total de logements privés**	367
						selon la taille du ménage	
520	165	160	295	140	30	1 personne	368
900	425	355	695	360	20	2 personnes	369
265	220	135	275	140	25	3 personnes	370
370	420	275	730	250	35	4-5 personnes	371
20	15	10	80	70	-	6 personnes ou plus	372
						selon le genre de ménage	
1,510	1,065	760	1,745	735	75	Ménages unifamiliaux	373
50	10	10	25	65	-	Ménages multifamiliaux	374
520	185	160	305	155	35	Ménages non familiaux	375
4,835	3,580	2,475	6,125	2,860	280	Nombre de personnes dans les ménages privés	376
2.3	2.9	2.7	3.0	3.0	2.7	Nombre moyen de personnes dans les ménages privés	377
0.4	0.4	0.3	0.4	0.4	0.4	Nombre moyen de personnes par pièce	378
195	125	110	110	140	10	Ménages locataires dans les logements privés non agricoles hors réserve (40)	379
909	1,389	1,434	1,412	867	-	Loyer brut moyen $ (40)	380
90	50	55	25	45	10	Ménages locataires consacrant 30 % ou plus du revenu du ménage au loyer brut (40) (41)	381
85	40	45	20	30	10	Ménages locataires consacrant de 30 % à 99 % du revenu du ménage au loyer brut (40) (41)	382
1,810	1,120	815	1,960	710	75	Ménages propriétaires dans les logements privés non agricoles hors réserve (42)	383
815	1,105	1,098	1,277	1,181	683	Principales dépenses de propriété moyennes $ (42)	384
225	130	170	320	140	10	Ménages propriétaires consacrant 30 % ou plus du revenu du ménage aux principales dépenses de propriété (41) (42)	385
205	110	145	290	100	10	Ménages propriétaires consacrant de 30 % à 99 % du revenu du ménage aux principales dépenses de propriété (41) (42)	386
						CARACTÉRISTIQUES DES FAMILLES DE RECENSEMENT	
1,605	**1,075**	**775**	**1,785**	**870**	**70**	**Total des familles de recensement dans les ménages privés**	387
						selon la structure et la taille de la famille de recensement	
1,380	985	715	1,645	785	65	Total des familles avec conjoints	388
1,275	925	660	1,585	720	60	Total des familles avec couples mariés	389
790	355	330	605	315	-	Sans enfants à la maison	390
485	565	335	975	410	50	Avec enfants à la maison	391
170	165	115	215	155	15	1 enfant	392
240	275	160	515	165	40	2 enfants	393
75	130	65	245	85	-	3 enfants ou plus	394
110	60	60	65	65	10	Total des familles en union libre	395
85	35	40	40	40	10	Sans enfants à la maison	396
20	25	15	25	20	-	Avec enfants à la maison	397
15	10	-	10	10	-	1 enfant	398
10	10	15	10	15	-	2 enfants	399
-	10	-	10	-	-	3 enfants ou plus	400
225	85	55	140	90	-	Total des familles monoparentales	401
190	70	45	125	75	10	Parent de sexe féminin	402
120	50	20	85	55	-	1 enfant	403
70	20	20	35	25	-	2 enfants	404
-	-	-	10	-	-	3 enfants ou plus	405

Table 1. Selected Characteristics for Census Tracts, 2001 Census – 100% Data and 20% Sample Data

No.	Characteristics	Vancouver CMA/RMR	Vancouver 0180	Vancouver 0181.01	Vancouver 0181.03	Vancouver 0181.04	Vancouver 0181.05
	CENSUS FAMILY CHARACTERISTICS						
	by census family structure and size – concluded						
406	Male parent	14,810	70	45	35	50	80
407	1 child	9,890	50	45	25	35	65
408	2 children	3,755	25	-	10	10	10
409	3 or more children	1,160	-	-	-	15	-
410	**Total number of children at home**	**620,755**	**2,790**	**1,940**	**1,945**	**1,990**	**1,780**
	by age groups						
411	Under 6 years	127,880	400	300	315	340	410
412	6-14 years	215,355	1,010	745	775	755	675
413	15-17 years	74,795	390	300	330	255	235
414	18-24 years	130,390	650	440	390	430	275
415	25 years and over	72,340	335	155	130	215	180
416	Average number of children at home per census family (43)	1.2	1.1	0.9	1.3	0.9	0.9
417	**Total number of persons in private households**	**1,963,645**	**8,140**	**7,340**	**5,405**	**6,940**	**7,015**
	by census family status and living arrangements						
418	Number of non-family persons	354,230	660	1,200	590	770	1,525
419	Living with relatives (44)	49,555	115	85	75	70	115
420	Living with non-relatives only	92,615	185	165	130	185	305
421	Living alone	212,055	360	945	385	520	1,110
422	Number of family persons	1,609,410	7,480	6,140	4,815	6,170	5,490
423	Average number of persons per census family	3.0	3.0	2.7	3.2	2.7	2.7
424	**Total number of persons 65 years and over**	**227,895**	**965**	**2,145**	**655**	**1,395**	**1,955**
425	Number of non-family persons 65 years and over	84,635	220	670	195	290	825
426	Living with relatives (44)	17,590	55	55	-	40	50
427	Living with non-relatives only	3,940	15	-	-	20	10
428	Living alone	63,105	150	605	185	230	765
429	Number of family persons 65 years and over	143,255	745	1,480	465	1,110	1,125
	ECONOMIC FAMILY CHARACTERISTICS						
430	**Total number of economic families in private households**	**517,625**	**2,405**	**2,255**	**1,480**	**2,195**	**2,005**
	by size of family						
431	2 persons	213,720	1,070	1,325	560	1,210	1,145
432	3 persons	108,945	455	330	280	410	340
433	4 persons	116,525	490	420	385	375	370
434	5 or more persons	78,435	385	175	255	205	155
435	Total number of persons in economic families	1,658,960	7,595	6,225	4,895	6,240	5,605
436	Average number of persons per economic family	3.2	3.2	2.8	3.3	2.8	2.8
437	Total number of unattached individuals	304,680	550	1,110	510	705	1,405
	2000 INCOME CHARACTERISTICS						
	Population 15 years and over by sex and total income groups in 2000						
438	Total - Both sexes	1,620,920	6,725	6,295	4,305	5,895	5,915
439	Without income	97,205	350	350	245	325	195
440	With income	1,523,715	6,375	5,940	4,060	5,575	5,725
441	Under $1,000 (45)	80,320	240	230	175	185	240
442	$ 1,000 - $ 2,999	68,190	240	130	175	200	150
443	$ 3,000 - $ 4,999	53,115	200	125	155	135	85
444	$ 5,000 - $ 6,999	66,555	235	200	120	195	130
445	$ 7,000 - $ 9,999	95,785	395	370	220	300	290
446	$10,000 - $11,999	66,535	245	290	180	155	305
447	$12,000 - $14,999	108,580	405	445	265	285	380
448	$15,000 - $19,999	139,105	460	700	355	385	795
449	$20,000 - $24,999	121,245	435	435	190	455	465
450	$25,000 - $29,999	102,205	405	540	280	330	330
451	$30,000 - $34,999	109,740	550	400	210	430	540
452	$35,000 - $39,999	89,535	285	360	225	390	475
453	$40,000 - $44,999	84,045	395	375	335	355	280
454	$45,000 - $49,999	63,445	235	240	125	310	230
455	$50,000 - $59,999	97,065	500	315	240	435	515
456	$60,000 and over	178,265	1,135	785	820	1,035	515
457	Average income $ (46)	31,421	38,573	31,497	41,222	44,775	29,673
458	Median income $ (46)	23,237	28,995	25,120	28,961	31,852	25,142
459	Standard error of average income $ (46)	81	1,319	723	1,631	4,308	586

Tableau 1. Certaines caractéristiques des secteurs de recensement, recensement de 2001 – Données intégrales et données-échantillon (20 %)

Vancouver 0181.06	Vancouver 0181.07	Vancouver 0181.08 A	Vancouver 0181.09 A	Vancouver 0182.01 A	Vancouver 0182.02 ◆ A	Caractéristiques	N°
						CARACTÉRISTIQUES DES FAMILLES DE RECENSEMENT	
						selon la structure et la taille de la famille de recensement – fin	
35	20	-	15	10	-	Parent de sexe masculin	406
15	10	-	10	10	-	1 enfant	407
10	10	-	10	-	-	2 enfants	408
-	10	-	-	-	-	3 enfants ou plus	409
1,220	**1,295**	**735**	**2,290**	**975**	**95**	**Nombre total d'enfants à la maison**	410
						selon les groupes d'âge	
220	220	135	265	130	-	Moins de 6 ans	411
440	505	310	960	370	60	6-14 ans	412
165	200	115	430	120	10	15-17 ans	413
205	290	125	475	245	20	18-24 ans	414
190	85	65	170	115	-	25 ans et plus	415
0.8	1.2	1.0	1.3	1.1	1.3	Nombre moyen d'enfants à la maison par famille de recensement (43)	416
4,840	**3,580**	**2,475**	**6,130**	**2,855**	**280**	**Nombre total de personnes dans les ménages privés**	417
						selon la situation des particuliers dans la famille de recensement et des particuliers dans le ménage	
630	230	245	405	230	45	Nombre de personnes hors famille de recensement	418
30	10	45	55	30	-	Vivant avec des personnes apparentées (44)	419
85	55	40	60	60	15	Vivant avec des personnes non apparentées uniquement	420
520	165	155	290	140	25	Vivant seules	421
4,205	3,355	2,230	5,725	2,625	235	Nombre de personnes membres d'une famille	422
2.6	3.1	2.9	3.2	3.0	3.4	Nombre moyen de personnes par famille de recensement	423
1,375	**490**	**400**	**995**	**300**	**20**	**Nombre total de personnes de 65 ans et plus**	424
365	70	120	260	35	15	Nombre de personnes hors famille de recensement de 65 ans et plus	425
20	-	20	50	15	-	Vivant avec des personnes apparentées (44)	426
-	15	-	-	-	-	Vivant avec des personnes non apparentées uniquement	427
340	60	100	210	15	15	Vivant seules	428
1,010	425	280	740	265	-	Nombre de personnes membres d'une famille de 65 ans et plus	429
						CARACTÉRISTIQUES DES FAMILLES ÉCONOMIQUES	
1,555	**1,065**	**765**	**1,770**	**795**	**70**	**Nombre total de familles économiques dans les ménages privés**	430
						selon la taille de la famille	
930	430	365	705	345	20	2 personnes	431
265	205	130	260	140	20	3 personnes	432
260	295	200	510	170	40	4 personnes	433
100	135	70	295	145	-	5 personnes ou plus	434
4,235	3,360	2,275	5,780	2,655	235	Nombre total de personnes dans les familles économiques	435
2.7	3.1	3.0	3.3	3.3	3.1	Nombre moyen de personnes par famille économique	436
600	220	200	350	200	45	Nombre total de personnes hors famille économique	437
						CARACTÉRISTIQUES DU REVENU DE 2000	
						Population de 15 ans et plus selon le sexe et les tranches de revenu total en 2000	
4,175	2,860	2,035	4,895	2,355	215	Total - Les deux sexes	438
110	140	80	285	120	10	Sans revenu	439
4,060	2,720	1,955	4,610	2,235	200	Avec un revenu	440
125	90	80	240	65	10	Moins de 1 000 $ (45)	441
105	105	90	210	95	20	1 000 $ - 2 999 $	442
115	80	60	145	75	-	3 000 $ - 4 999 $	443
175	125	40	145	60	-	5 000 $ - 6 999 $	444
205	135	70	305	130	15	7 000 $ - 9 999 $	445
175	110	95	145	70	-	10 000 $ - 11 999 $	446
250	80	110	180	175	15	12 000 $ - 14 999 $	447
350	185	135	300	180	10	15 000 $ - 19 999 $	448
410	155	155	365	175	30	20 000 $ - 24 999 $	449
325	155	125	235	145	20	25 000 $ - 29 999 $	450
300	195	120	205	155	10	30 000 $ - 34 999 $	451
265	90	155	295	180	35	35 000 $ - 39 999 $	452
240	215	85	220	155	20	40 000 $ - 44 999 $	453
170	150	110	145	95	10	45 000 $ - 49 999 $	454
380	140	205	335	110	15	50 000 $ - 59 999 $	455
475	715	325	1,140	375	-	60 000 $ et plus	456
32,515	49,352	37,906	46,767	37,020	26,364	Revenu moyen $ (46)	457
26,816	33,597	30,062	30,026	27,976	27,223	Revenu médian $ (46)	458
839	3,037	1,808	1,801	2,190	2,472	Erreur type de revenu moyen $ (46)	459

Table 1. Selected Characteristics for Census Tracts, 2001 Census – 100% Data and 20% Sample Data

No.	Characteristics	Vancouver CMA/RMR	Vancouver 0180	Vancouver 0181.01	Vancouver 0181.03	Vancouver 0181.04	Vancouver 0181.05
	2000 INCOME CHARACTERISTICS						
	Population 15 years and over by sex and total income groups in 2000 – concluded						
460	Total - Males	787,520	3,430	2,840	2,055	2,835	2,670
461	Without income	39,025	150	145	90	135	65
462	With income	748,500	3,285	2,695	1,965	2,700	2,605
463	Under $1,000 (45)	38,090	85	100	65	65	110
464	$ 1,000 - $ 2,999	27,250	90	50	115	90	65
465	$ 3,000 - $ 4,999	21,365	80	65	65	45	45
466	$ 5,000 - $ 6,999	27,445	80	65	30	65	45
467	$ 7,000 - $ 9,999	37,775	125	80	85	80	80
468	$10,000 - $11,999	28,620	100	80	55	70	100
469	$12,000 - $14,999	40,250	165	135	80	100	155
470	$15,000 - $19,999	59,240	205	240	180	140	260
471	$20,000 - $24,999	55,650	220	145	60	180	170
472	$25,000 - $29,999	47,460	120	230	100	130	130
473	$30,000 - $34,999	50,935	310	195	85	195	215
474	$35,000 - $39,999	43,640	125	195	50	180	210
475	$40,000 - $44,999	44,790	260	230	170	175	150
476	$45,000 - $49,999	36,150	155	140	70	160	140
477	$50,000 - $59,999	60,240	285	185	145	250	315
478	$60,000 and over	129,585	875	560	620	780	410
479	Average income $ (46)	38,151	49,517	39,647	55,787	60,584	35,237
480	Median income $ (46)	28,823	37,259	33,665	40,011	39,982	33,348
481	Standard error of average income $ (46)	150	2,305	1,274	3,060	8,499	971
482	Total - Females	833,400	3,300	3,455	2,255	3,065	3,245
483	Without income	58,175	205	210	155	190	130
484	With income	775,220	3,095	3,245	2,095	2,875	3,120
485	Under $1,000 (45)	42,230	155	130	115	120	130
486	$ 1,000 - $ 2,999	40,940	155	75	55	115	90
487	$ 3,000 - $ 4,999	31,750	120	60	90	90	40
488	$ 5,000 - $ 6,999	39,105	155	135	85	135	85
489	$ 7,000 - $ 9,999	58,010	270	295	135	215	205
490	$10,000 - $11,999	37,915	150	205	120	85	205
491	$12,000 - $14,999	68,330	240	310	180	190	225
492	$15,000 - $19,999	79,865	255	455	175	245	535
493	$20,000 - $24,999	65,595	215	290	130	275	295
494	$25,000 - $29,999	54,745	295	310	180	200	200
495	$30,000 - $34,999	58,800	240	205	130	230	330
496	$35,000 - $39,999	45,895	155	165	170	210	265
497	$40,000 - $44,999	39,250	140	145	170	180	125
498	$45,000 - $49,999	27,295	80	95	55	150	85
499	$50,000 - $59,999	36,825	215	135	95	185	200
500	$60,000 and over	48,680	260	225	205	255	110
501	Average income $ (46)	24,924	26,980	24,719	27,578	29,942	25,027
502	Median income $ (46)	19,076	21,060	18,977	22,968	24,149	20,813
503	Standard error of average income $ (46)	62	957	714	1,023	1,597	664
	by composition of total income						
504	Total - Composition of income in 2000 % (47)	100.0	100.0	100.0	100.0	100.0	100.0
505	Employment income %	78.7	74.5	60.0	76.3	69.6	65.3
506	Government transfer payments %	9.6	6.9	16.3	6.8	8.3	16.9
507	Other %	11.7	18.5	23.7	16.9	22.1	17.9
	Population 15 years and over with employment income in 2000 by sex and work activity						
508	Both sexes with employment income (48)	1,108,050	4,815	3,265	3,000	3,840	3,375
509	Average employment income $	34,007	38,106	34,399	42,570	45,220	32,821
510	Standard error of average employment income $	97	1,516	1,130	1,982	5,826	842
511	Worked full year, full time (49)	562,445	2,435	1,530	1,425	1,955	1,775
512	Average employment income $	46,806	55,338	51,221	62,747	67,294	45,503
513	Standard error of average employment income $	164	2,617	1,658	3,269	11,298	989
514	Worked part year or part time (50)	516,420	2,145	1,655	1,505	1,700	1,475
515	Average employment income $	21,244	21,488	20,127	24,566	22,271	20,060
516	Standard error of average employment income $	90	1,091	1,154	1,966	1,175	1,041
517	Males with employment income (48)	576,175	2,640	1,600	1,570	1,940	1,735
518	Average employment income $	40,665	47,176	42,503	55,548	61,876	38,212
519	Standard error of average employment income $	172	2,508	1,912	3,477	11,131	1,308
520	Worked full year, full time (49)	326,275	1,540	865	930	1,160	1,045
521	Average employment income $	53,095	64,196	58,369	72,731	84,976	50,706
522	Standard error of average employment income $	268	3,860	2,498	4,776	18,513	1,349
523	Worked part year or part time (50)	237,200	1,010	705	615	695	650
524	Average employment income $	24,976	24,449	24,327	31,046	26,733	20,601
525	Standard error of average employment income $	172	1,886	2,298	4,334	2,142	1,813

Tableau 1. Certaines caractéristiques des secteurs de recensement, recensement de 2001 – Données intégrales et données-échantillon (20 %)

Vancouver 0181.06	Vancouver 0181.07	Vancouver 0181.08 A	Vancouver 0181.09 A	Vancouver 0182.01 A	Vancouver 0182.02 ◆ A	Caractéristiques	N°
						CARACTÉRISTIQUES DU REVENU DE 2000	
						Population de 15 ans et plus selon le sexe et les tranches de revenu total en 2000 – fin	
2,025	1,400	985	2,285	1,215	115	Total - Hommes	460
25	55	35	90	35	10	Sans revenu	461
2,000	1,340	950	2,190	1,185	110	Avec un revenu	462
55	30	25	75	40	10	Moins de 1 000 $ (45)	463
45	45	65	60	20	-	1 000 $ - 2 999 $	464
25	35	-	75	25	-	3 000 $ - 4 999 $	465
60	35	10	65	30	-	5 000 $ - 6 999 $	466
40	60	10	110	40	-	7 000 $ - 9 999 $	467
35	35	35	25	30	10	10 000 $ - 11 999 $	468
35	40	45	55	70	10	12 000 $ - 14 999 $	469
170	45	35	80	95	10	15 000 $ - 19 999 $	470
200	60	55	110	95	15	20 000 $ - 24 999 $	471
175	30	55	100	75	-	25 000 $ - 29 999 $	472
155	70	45	80	60	-	30 000 $ - 34 999 $	473
140	35	85	160	115	20	35 000 $ - 39 999 $	474
170	125	35	85	80	20	40 000 $ - 44 999 $	475
65	70	45	25	50	-	45 000 $ - 49 999 $	476
285	80	155	170	60	20	50 000 $ - 59 999 $	477
340	550	240	910	285	-	60 000 $ et plus	478
40,720	68,360	49,158	68,261	46,624	30,202	Revenu moyen $ (46)	479
34,898	46,028	40,058	46,747	35,112	35,852	Revenu médian $ (46)	480
1,359	5,786	3,256	3,376	3,869	3,425	Erreur type de revenu moyen $ (46)	481
2,150	1,460	1,050	2,615	1,135	95	Total - Femmes	482
85	80	45	195	85	-	Sans revenu	483
2,065	1,380	1,005	2,425	1,055	90	Avec un revenu	484
65	55	50	165	25	-	Moins de 1 000 $ (45)	485
60	60	20	150	75	20	1 000 $ - 2 999 $	486
90	45	60	75	45	-	3 000 $ - 4 999 $	487
115	90	30	80	25	-	5 000 $ - 6 999 $	488
165	70	65	195	95	10	7 000 $ - 9 999 $	489
140	70	60	120	45	-	10 000 $ - 11 999 $	490
210	40	70	130	100	-	12 000 $ - 14 999 $	491
175	145	95	220	85	-	15 000 $ - 19 999 $	492
215	95	100	250	80	15	20 000 $ - 24 999 $	493
150	115	70	135	65	20	25 000 $ - 29 999 $	494
145	125	65	125	90	10	30 000 $ - 34 999 $	495
125	55	65	130	65	15	35 000 $ - 39 999 $	496
65	90	50	135	75	-	40 000 $ - 44 999 $	497
105	80	65	120	45	-	45 000 $ - 49 999 $	498
95	65	50	160	50	-	50 000 $ - 59 999 $	499
135	170	85	230	85	-	60 000 $ et plus	500
24,558	30,856	27,242	27,340	26,224	21,682	Revenu moyen $ (46)	501
19,984	25,454	22,188	21,520	21,402	23,863	Revenu médian $ (46)	502
853	1,516	1,456	1,026	1,396	3,263	Erreur type de revenu moyen $ (46)	503
						selon la composition du revenu total	
100.0	100.0	100.0	100.0	100.0	100.0	Total - Composition du revenu en 2000 % (47)	504
66.0	78.2	68.2	74.9	76.7	76.9	Revenu d'emploi %	505
16.5	5.2	8.4	6.6	7.3	9.0	Transferts gouvernementaux %	506
17.5	16.5	23.3	18.5	16.1	15.3	Autre %	507
						Population de 15 ans et plus ayant un revenu d'emploi en 2000 selon le sexe et le travail	
2,400	2,135	1,440	3,230	1,790	165	Les deux sexes ayant un revenu d'emploi (48)	508
36,319	49,290	35,109	50,040	35,395	24,775	Revenu moyen d'emploi $	509
1,247	3,373	1,922	2,318	1,799	2,461	Erreur type de revenu moyen d'emploi $	510
1,300	1,075	610	1,440	925	70	Ayant travaillé toute l'année à plein temps (49)	511
48,904	76,080	51,146	78,918	45,702	30,917	Revenu moyen d'emploi $	512
1,748	6,032	2,998	4,181	2,598	3,563	Erreur type de revenu moyen d'emploi $	513
1,045	1,020	780	1,695	785	95	Ayant travaillé une partie de l'année ou à temps partiel (50)	514
21,774	22,364	24,525	27,669	25,797	20,249	Revenu moyen d'emploi $	515
1,406	1,697	2,142	1,953	2,400	3,064	Erreur type de revenu moyen d'emploi $	516
1,235	1,090	735	1,690	980	100	Hommes ayant un revenu d'emploi (48)	517
43,935	67,662	43,273	70,227	43,320	25,441	Revenu moyen d'emploi $	518
1,988	6,169	3,206	4,017	2,907	3,812	Erreur type de revenu moyen d'emploi $	519
765	665	390	970	565	50	Ayant travaillé toute l'année à plein temps (49)	520
54,727	94,161	58,735	96,924	55,185	32,385	Revenu moyen d'emploi $	521
2,517	9,180	4,281	5,767	3,794	5,497	Erreur type de revenu moyen d'emploi $	522
455	410	335	675	385	50	Ayant travaillé une partie de l'année ou à temps partiel (50)	523
27,004	26,796	26,404	35,349	28,790	19,144	Revenu moyen d'emploi $	524
2,722	3,439	3,932	4,144	4,235	4,770	Erreur type de revenu moyen d'emploi $	525

Table 1. Selected Characteristics for Census Tracts, 2001 Census – 100% Data and 20% Sample Data

No.	Characteristics	Vancouver CMA/RMR	Vancouver 0180	Vancouver 0181.01	Vancouver 0181.03	Vancouver 0181.04	Vancouver 0181.05
	2000 INCOME CHARACTERISTICS						
	Population 15 years and over with employment income in 2000 by sex and work activity – concluded						
526	Females with employment income (48)	531,875	2,175	1,670	1,430	1,905	1,640
527	Average employment income $	26,793	27,104	26,635	28,331	28,268	27,118
528	Standard error of average employment income $	75	1,150	1,124	1,276	1,084	975
529	Worked full year, full time (49)	236,165	895	665	490	795	735
530	Average employment income $	38,118	40,057	41,977	43,838	41,606	38,116
531	Standard error of average employment income $	121	1,961	1,786	2,166	1,534	1,249
532	Worked part year or part time (50)	279,220	1,130	955	890	1,000	820
533	Average employment income $	18,074	18,833	17,029	20,077	19,172	19,631
534	Standard error of average employment income $	79	1,141	1,032	1,291	1,253	1,202
	Census families by structure and family income groups in 2000						
535	Total - All census families	535,255	2,460	2,245	1,520	2,245	2,035
536	Under $10,000	28,740	30	55	40	90	30
537	$ 10,000 - $19,999	38,115	95	135	15	90	120
538	$ 20,000 - $29,999	50,800	140	200	170	120	210
539	$ 30,000 - $39,999	55,435	190	255	70	165	270
540	$ 40,000 - $49,999	54,160	195	225	70	190	250
541	$ 50,000 - $59,999	49,520	215	270	145	130	225
542	$ 60,000 - $69,999	48,395	190	240	115	305	220
543	$ 70,000 - $79,999	42,105	290	210	90	210	155
544	$ 80,000 - $89,999	36,980	185	170	135	200	170
545	$ 90,000 - $99,999	28,700	140	80	85	110	140
546	$100,000 and over	102,315	785	410	580	635	240
547	Average family income $	70,196	91,256	67,733	99,797	94,989	60,886
548	Median family income $	57,926	75,596	59,139	81,161	71,401	55,950
549	Standard error of average family income $	224	3,400	1,858	4,294	11,543	1,482
550	Total - All couple census families (51)	453,395	2,235	1,955	1,360	1,935	1,680
551	Under $10,000	19,130	25	25	30	50	10
552	$ 10,000 - $19,999	23,495	40	75	-	65	65
553	$ 20,000 - $29,999	38,310	90	160	155	105	190
554	$ 30,000 - $39,999	43,530	175	195	45	100	170
555	$ 40,000 - $49,999	43,945	170	205	50	145	185
556	$ 50,000 - $59,999	42,705	195	235	130	125	195
557	$ 60,000 - $69,999	42,950	160	210	115	270	180
558	$ 70,000 - $79,999	38,835	285	205	70	195	135
559	$ 80,000 - $89,999	34,665	175	170	135	165	170
560	$ 90,000 - $99,999	27,285	135	70	85	100	125
561	$100,000 and over	98,545	780	405	545	610	245
562	Average family income $	75,585	96,436	72,249	104,439	102,273	64,954
563	Median family income $	63,146	79,319	64,228	84,955	76,640	60,252
564	Standard error of average family income $	257	3,672	2,012	4,627	13,273	1,623
	Incidence of low income in 2000						
565	Total - Economic families	515,845	2,400	2,255	1,480	2,195	2,005
566	Low income	88,045	100	210	95	185	135
567	Incidence of low income in 2000 % (52)	17.1	4.2	9.3	6.4	8.3	6.7
568	Total - Unattached individuals 15 years and over	301,305	535	1,115	510	705	1,395
569	Low income	120,030	130	280	230	135	270
570	Incidence of low income in 2000 % (52)	39.8	23.8	25.2	45.1	19.6	19.5
571	Total - Population in private households	1,955,020	8,130	7,340	5,405	6,940	7,005
572	Low income	407,135	425	960	635	735	665
573	Incidence of low income in 2000 % (52)	20.8	5.2	13.1	11.8	10.6	9.4
	Private households by household income groups in 2000						
574	Total - All private households	758,715	2,800	3,250	1,900	2,750	3,200
575	Under $10,000	54,525	70	135	70	115	35
576	$ 10,000 - $19,999	86,155	165	405	165	185	470
577	$ 20,000 - $29,999	77,280	180	390	230	170	410
578	$ 30,000 - $39,999	83,835	220	375	95	215	455
579	$ 40,000 - $49,999	77,540	200	350	125	260	340
580	$ 50,000 - $59,999	67,460	230	355	150	185	360
581	$ 60,000 - $69,999	59,960	230	275	135	320	270
582	$ 70,000 - $79,999	50,405	315	230	95	240	175
583	$ 80,000 - $89,999	43,290	210	215	140	195	225
584	$ 90,000 - $99,999	34,000	130	95	100	125	150
585	$100,000 and over	124,270	845	430	610	740	305
586	Average household income $	63,003	87,835	57,603	87,976	89,536	53,080
587	Median household income $	49,940	72,068	49,435	69,563	67,236	46,000
588	Standard error of average household income $	179	3,166	1,499	3,750	9,520	1,217

Tableau 1. Certaines caractéristiques des secteurs de recensement, recensement de 2001 – Données intégrales et données-échantillon (20 %)

Vancouver 0181.06	Vancouver 0181.07	Vancouver 0181.08 A	Vancouver 0181.09 A	Vancouver 0182.01 A	Vancouver 0182.02 ◆ A	Caractéristiques	N°
						CARACTÉRISTIQUES DU REVENU DE 2000	
						Population de 15 ans et plus ayant un revenu d'emploi en 2000 selon le sexe et le travail – fin	
1,165	1,045	710	1,540	810	70	Femmes ayant un revenu d'emploi (48)	526
28,238	30,116	26,649	27,924	25,790	23,798	Revenu moyen d'emploi $	527
1,288	1,748	1,876	1,331	1,550	2,867	Erreur type de revenu moyen d'emploi $	528
540	410	225	470	365	20	Ayant travaillé toute l'année à plein temps (49)	529
40,656	46,826	37,914	41,494	31,043	27,966	Revenu moyen d'emploi $	530
1,994	2,922	2,951	1,871	2,205	2,931	Erreur type de revenu moyen d'emploi $	531
590	610	445	1,020	400	40	Ayant travaillé une partie de l'année ou à temps partiel (50)	532
17,705	19,347	23,118	22,573	22,915	21,503	Revenu moyen d'emploi $	533
1,189	1,626	2,326	1,653	2,216	3,844	Erreur type de revenu moyen d'emploi $	534
						Familles de recensement selon la structure et les tranches de revenu de la famille en 2000	
1,605	1,075	770	1,785	870	75	Total - Toutes les familles de recensement	535
40	10	20	25	35	-	Moins de 10 000 $	536
50	25	20	40	35	-	10 000 $ - 19 999 $	537
150	25	45	65	75	-	20 000 $ - 29 999 $	538
150	60	35	80	80	10	30 000 $ - 39 999 $	539
230	45	60	165	40	30	40 000 $ - 49 999 $	540
180	55	60	180	70	10	50 000 $ - 59 999 $	541
170	65	80	85	85	20	60 000 $ - 69 999 $	542
85	115	75	105	80	-	70 000 $ - 79 999 $	543
115	100	60	100	85	-	80 000 $ - 89 999 $	544
115	100	80	135	30	-	90 000 $ - 99 999 $	545
330	480	235	810	260	10	100 000 $ et plus	546
69,650	116,987	85,843	113,058	87,236	54,861	Revenu moyen des familles $	547
60,623	94,022	78,395	93,300	74,542	46,294	Revenu médian des familles $	548
2,008	6,958	3,951	4,178	5,988	5,175	Erreur type de revenu moyen des familles $	549
1,380	985	720	1,645	780	65	Total - Toutes les familles de recensement comptant un couple (51)	550
-	-	15	10	30	-	Moins de 10 000 $	551
35	10	10	35	10	-	10 000 $ - 19 999 $	552
120	20	40	40	60	10	20 000 $ - 29 999 $	553
105	45	35	70	70	-	30 000 $ - 39 999 $	554
185	45	55	115	30	30	40 000 $ - 49 999 $	555
175	50	60	165	70	-	50 000 $ - 59 999 $	556
150	60	60	85	70	25	60 000 $ - 69 999 $	557
85	100	80	90	75	-	70 000 $ - 79 999 $	558
90	85	60	95	80	-	80 000 $ - 89 999 $	559
115	100	80	130	30	-	90 000 $ - 99 999 $	560
320	460	235	815	255	-	100 000 $ et plus	561
74,099	121,805	89,434	119,080	92,854	56,310	Revenu moyen des familles $	562
65,206	97,575	83,657	99,374	78,366	57,875	Revenu médian des familles $	563
2,116	7,447	4,051	4,386	6,493	5,403	Erreur type de revenu moyen des familles $	564
						Fréquence des unités à faible revenu en 2000	
1,520	1,070	770	1,765	795	70	Total - Familles économiques	565
60	25	45	75	40	-	Faible revenu	566
4.1	2.4	5.7	4.2	5.1	2.1	Fréquence des unités à faible revenu en 2000 % (52)	567
555	220	200	345	180	50	Total - Personnes hors famille économique de 15 ans et plus	568
100	60	55	50	50	-	Faible revenu	569
17.6	26.9	26.2	14.0	27.4	12.3	Fréquence des unités à faible revenu en 2000 % (52)	570
4,700	3,585	2,475	6,125	2,835	280	Total - Population dans les ménages privés	571
270	130	160	335	155	-	Faible revenu	572
5.8	3.6	6.6	5.5	5.6	3.3	Fréquence des unités à faible revenu en 2000 % (52)	573
						Ménages privés selon les tranches de revenu du ménage en 2000	
2,075	1,255	925	2,070	950	105	Total - Tous les ménages privés	574
40	25	25	15	40	-	Moins de 10 000 $	575
190	55	70	100	30	-	10 000 $ - 19 999 $	576
255	35	65	120	115	15	20 000 $ - 29 999 $	577
240	80	45	115	80	20	30 000 $ - 39 999 $	578
230	75	70	220	55	30	40 000 $ - 49 999 $	579
225	75	85	185	80	-	50 000 $ - 59 999 $	580
200	85	80	100	80	25	60 000 $ - 69 999 $	581
90	110	85	135	65	-	70 000 $ - 79 999 $	582
125	100	55	80	80	-	80 000 $ - 89 999 $	583
95	100	75	160	30	-	90 000 $ - 99 999 $	584
390	505	270	840	290	-	100 000 $ et plus	585
63,573	107,247	80,068	104,295	86,150	50,668	Revenu moyen des ménages $	586
55,132	88,521	72,052	81,853	66,884	42,648	Revenu médian des ménages $	587
1,786	6,188	3,569	3,831	5,826	5,024	Erreur type de revenu moyen des ménages $	588

Table 1. Selected Characteristics for Census Tracts, 2001 Census – 100% Data and 20% Sample Data

No.	Characteristics	Vancouver 0182.03 A	Vancouver 0182.04 A	Vancouver 0182.05 A	Vancouver 0182.06 ◇ A	Vancouver 0183.01	Vancouver 0183.03
	POPULATION CHARACTERISTICS						
1	**Population, 1996 (1)**	**2,435**	**1,407**	**1,468**	**1,249**	**5,105**	**5,745**
2	**Population, 2001 (2)**	**3,432**	**1,477**	**2,794**	**1,203**	**5,959**	**5,853**
3	Population percentage change, 1996-2001	40.9	5.0	90.3	-3.7	16.7	1.9
4	Land area in square kilometres, 2001	8.22	2.28	19.27	9.81	2.72	2.90
5	**Total population – 100% Data (3)**	**3,430**	**1,475**	**2,795**	**1,205**	**5,955**	**5,855**
	by sex and age groups						
6	Male	1,720	745	1,435	640	2,975	2,830
7	0-4 years	95	30	95	25	205	170
8	5-9 years	135	75	100	45	290	215
9	10-14 years	155	65	110	55	310	195
10	15-19 years	190	90	110	40	245	240
11	20-24 years	145	40	110	40	160	180
12	25-29 years	85	30	80	40	150	150
13	30-34 years	70	20	95	40	185	200
14	35-39 years	105	50	100	60	300	240
15	40-44 years	155	85	110	55	340	270
16	45-49 years	160	80	115	50	230	235
17	50-54 years	145	65	110	45	170	175
18	55-59 years	100	45	80	40	130	145
19	60-64 years	65	25	65	40	90	85
20	65-69 years	50	20	55	20	40	85
21	70-74 years	40	15	55	20	55	80
22	75-79 years	20	10	25	10	30	80
23	80-84 years	10	5	10	10	20	50
24	85 years and over	5	-	5	-	15	40
25	Female	1,710	730	1,360	565	2,985	3,030
26	0-4 years	85	35	75	30	230	160
27	5-9 years	130	45	100	45	260	195
28	10-14 years	165	85	85	55	250	215
29	15-19 years	165	70	90	35	245	205
30	20-24 years	130	50	80	30	150	175
31	25-29 years	70	20	80	25	145	165
32	30-34 years	100	25	95	35	255	200
33	35-39 years	140	55	115	40	310	235
34	40-44 years	175	100	105	65	320	270
35	45-49 years	165	85	120	40	255	235
36	50-54 years	130	60	115	50	165	170
37	55-59 years	85	30	75	30	120	150
38	60-64 years	55	20	75	20	65	95
39	65-69 years	40	20	60	25	65	110
40	70-74 years	30	15	45	10	65	115
41	75-79 years	25	5	20	10	30	115
42	80-84 years	15	5	10	5	35	110
43	85 years and over	10	-	15	5	20	115
44	**Total population 15 years and over**	**2,665**	**1,135**	**2,235**	**955**	**4,400**	**4,705**
	by legal marital status						
45	Never married (single)	790	315	610	280	1,280	1,365
46	Legally married (and not separated)	1,665	745	1,385	540	2,445	2,200
47	Separated, but still legally married	45	10	55	30	155	220
48	Divorced	90	40	90	60	355	460
49	Widowed	75	30	95	40	170	460
	by common-law status						
50	Not in a common-law relationship	2,575	1,105	2,140	905	4,115	4,335
51	In a common-law relationship	90	35	100	55	290	365
52	**Total population – 20% Sample Data (4)**	**3,430**	**1,475**	**2,795**	**1,200**	**5,950**	**5,695**
	by mother tongue						
53	Single responses	3,410	1,465	2,695	1,180	5,865	5,665
54	English	2,345	1,185	1,865	910	5,015	4,955
55	French	25	-	15	10	60	50
56	Non-official languages (5)	1,040	270	820	265	790	665
57	Chinese, n.o.s.	70	10	115	50	10	15
58	Cantonese	105	85	45	10	-	-
59	Punjabi	420	-	165	10	230	115
60	Mandarin	90	25	75	-	20	-
61	Tagalog (Pilipino)	50	10	-	-	30	10
62	Other languages (6)	310	145	420	195	510	520
63	Multiple responses	20	15	95	25	80	25
64	English and French	-	-	-	15	10	-
65	English and non-official language	10	10	95	10	75	25
66	French and non-official language	10	-	-	-	-	-
67	English, French and non-official language	-	-	-	-	-	-

See reference material at the end of the publication. – Voir les documents de référence à la fin de la publication.

Tableau 1. Certaines caractéristiques des secteurs de recensement, recensement de 2001 – Données intégrales et données-échantillon (20 %)

Vancouver 0183.04 A	Vancouver 0183.05 A	Vancouver 0183.06 A	Vancouver 0183.07 A	Vancouver 0184.01	Vancouver 0184.02 ◇	Caractéristiques	N°
						CARACTÉRISTIQUES DE LA POPULATION	
1,752	**1,865**	**2,210**	**6,403**	**3,192**	**6,439**	**Population, 1996 (1)**	1
1,776	**5,115**	**2,400**	**6,445**	**5,045**	**6,832**	**Population, 2001 (2)**	2
1.4	174.3	8.6	0.7	58.1	6.1	Variation en pourcentage de la population, 1996-2001	3
7.23	3.53	1.30	2.56	7.94	2.57	Superficie des terres en kilomètres carrés, 2001	4
1,775	**5,120**	**2,400**	**6,445**	**5,045**	**6,840**	**Population totale – Données intégrales (3)**	5
						selon le sexe et les groupes d'âge	
930	2,505	1,175	3,170	2,670	3,255	Sexe masculin	6
35	245	100	175	180	265	0-4 ans	7
50	200	100	250	155	275	5-9 ans	8
80	170	85	285	150	235	10-14 ans	9
80	175	75	280	140	200	15-19 ans	10
75	120	80	190	215	165	20-24 ans	11
50	165	90	125	235	190	25-29 ans	12
50	245	100	140	300	270	30-34 ans	13
70	235	115	210	265	315	35-39 ans	14
75	235	100	290	225	300	40-44 ans	15
65	170	85	315	155	195	45-49 ans	16
70	155	70	275	180	195	50-54 ans	17
65	110	50	170	155	145	55-59 ans	18
50	75	40	130	105	125	60-64 ans	19
40	75	30	110	75	105	65-69 ans	20
45	60	25	105	55	105	70-74 ans	21
20	35	20	75	55	90	75-79 ans	22
5	15	10	25	20	50	80-84 ans	23
5	10	5	20	10	35	85 ans et plus	24
850	2,610	1,230	3,280	2,370	3,580	Sexe féminin	25
35	215	95	160	180	260	0-4 ans	26
40	210	95	245	160	270	5-9 ans	27
60	170	80	300	140	215	10-14 ans	28
70	165	65	255	115	195	15-19 ans	29
55	135	65	200	150	195	20-24 ans	30
50	200	90	130	220	235	25-29 ans	31
50	280	90	195	220	310	30-34 ans	32
55	275	150	275	205	325	35-39 ans	33
70	215	115	330	180	285	40-44 ans	34
80	190	75	305	155	210	45-49 ans	35
65	175	80	255	185	215	50-54 ans	36
70	105	50	195	160	180	55-59 ans	37
45	90	45	130	85	140	60-64 ans	38
35	75	35	100	65	125	65-69 ans	39
30	55	45	95	60	125	70-74 ans	40
20	35	15	75	50	145	75-79 ans	41
5	15	10	25	20	90	80-84 ans	42
5	5	15	10	15	55	85 ans et plus	43
1,470	**3,910**	**1,845**	**5,035**	**4,080**	**5,320**	**Population totale de 15 ans et plus**	44
						selon l'état matrimonial légal	
495	915	485	1,275	1,200	1,505	Célibataire (jamais marié(e))	45
770	2,605	1,050	3,250	2,370	2,645	Légalement marié(e) (et non séparé(e))	46
40	110	90	95	130	250	Séparé(e), mais toujours légalement marié(e)	47
105	185	155	245	255	535	Divorcé(e)	48
60	100	70	180	125	385	Veuf ou veuve	49
						selon l'union libre	
1,360	3,675	1,705	4,830	3,845	4,885	Ne vivant pas en union libre	50
110	235	140	210	235	435	Vivant en union libre	51
1,780	**5,120**	**2,400**	**6,430**	**4,805**	**6,840**	**Population totale – Données-échantillon (20 %) (4)**	52
						selon la langue maternelle	
1,770	5,110	2,390	6,415	4,765	6,750	Réponses uniques	53
1,360	4,375	2,085	5,310	3,140	4,870	Anglais	54
10	60	20	35	60	140	Français	55
395	675	290	1,065	1,560	1,740	Langues non officielles (5)	56
-	20	75	30	30	130	Chinois, n.d.a.	57
15	10	-	10	-	30	Cantonais	58
45	35	10	290	835	320	Pendjabi	59
-	20	10	125	15	-	Mandarin	60
-	40	-	15	20	200	Tagalog (pilipino)	61
335	550	200	595	655	1,050	Autres langues (6)	62
10	10	10	15	40	85	Réponses multiples	63
-	-	-	-	15	-	Anglais et français	64
-	10	15	20	20	85	Anglais et langue non officielle	65
-	-	-	-	10	-	Français et langue non officielle	66
-	-	-	-	-	-	Anglais, français et langue non officielle	67

See reference material at the end of the publication. – Voir les documents de référence à la fin de la publication.

Table 1. Selected Characteristics for Census Tracts, 2001 Census – 100% Data and 20% Sample Data

No.	Characteristics	Vancouver 0182.03 A	Vancouver 0182.04 A	Vancouver 0182.05 A	Vancouver 0182.06 ◇ A	Vancouver 0183.01	Vancouver 0183.03
	POPULATION CHARACTERISTICS						
	by home language						
68	Single responses	2,705	1,350	2,305	1,100	5,430	5,360
69	English	2,400	1,275	1,960	1,055	5,225	5,250
70	French	10	-	-	-	-	-
71	Non-official languages (5)	285	80	340	50	200	105
72	Cantonese	45	40	25	10	-	-
73	Chinese, n.o.s.	-	-	40	30	-	-
74	Punjabi	85	-	30	-	115	45
75	Mandarin	45	15	60	-	20	-
76	Korean	50	-	40	-	-	-
77	Other languages (6)	65	25	145	10	70	55
78	Multiple responses	730	125	490	100	525	340
79	English and French	10	-	15	20	50	45
80	English and non-official language	695	130	475	70	470	290
81	French and non-official language	-	-	-	-	-	-
82	English, French and non-official language	20	-	-	10	-	-
	by knowledge of official languages						
83	English only	3,125	1,380	2,450	1,115	5,605	5,400
84	French only	10	-	-	-	-	15
85	English and French	175	90	165	65	310	240
86	Neither English nor French	130	10	170	25	35	45
	by knowledge of non-official languages (5) (7)						
87	Cantonese	125	95	40	10	-	-
88	Chinese, n.o.s.	35	10	60	45	-	15
89	Punjabi	565	15	225	20	310	165
90	Mandarin	170	60	160	10	20	-
91	Hindi	160	15	90	-	145	35
92	German	75	20	115	100	135	205
93	Spanish	25	20	40	30	65	55
	by first official language spoken						
94	English	3,235	1,455	2,585	1,160	5,845	5,600
95	French	30	15	15	-	55	55
96	English and French	35	-	20	15	15	-
97	Neither English nor French	130	10	175	20	35	40
98	Official language minority - (number) (8)	45	10	30	10	65	55
99	Official language minority - (percentage) (8)	1.3	0.7	1.1	0.8	1.1	1.0
	by ethnic origin (9)						
100	English	805	405	720	360	2,170	1,970
101	Canadian	730	430	710	305	1,710	1,775
102	Chinese	270	125	225	60	70	20
103	Scottish	490	285	495	225	1,385	1,110
104	Irish	395	165	375	195	1,025	915
105	German	475	175	520	265	1,110	1,000
106	East Indian	535	80	350	45	405	215
107	French	175	90	260	115	460	545
108	Ukrainian	235	110	75	60	300	365
109	Italian	125	45	85	75	340	120
110	Dutch (Netherlands)	170	100	230	150	555	395
111	Filipino	195	10	35	-	55	40
112	Polish	70	50	55	10	230	185
113	Norwegian	75	60	125	65	145	155
114	North American Indian	30	-	30	10	160	110
	by Aboriginal identity						
115	Total Aboriginal identity population (10)	35	10	30	-	110	155
116	Total non-Aboriginal population	3,395	1,475	2,760	1,200	5,840	5,545
	by Aboriginal origin						
117	Total Aboriginal origins population (11)	65	15	35	20	235	175
118	Total non-Aboriginal population	3,365	1,465	2,760	1,180	5,720	5,525
	by Registered Indian status						
119	Registered Indian (12)	10	-	-	-	30	35
120	Not a Registered Indian	3,425	1,480	2,785	1,200	5,925	5,660

Tableau 1. Certaines caractéristiques des secteurs de recensement, recensement de 2001 – Données intégrales et données-échantillon (20 %)

Vancouver 0183.04 A	Vancouver 0183.05 A	Vancouver 0183.06 A	Vancouver 0183.07 A	Vancouver 0184.01	Vancouver 0184.02 ◇	Caractéristiques	Nº
						CARACTÉRISTIQUES DE LA POPULATION	
						selon la langue parlée à la maison	
1,520	4,680	2,265	5,990	3,940	5,730	Réponses uniques	68
1,480	4,540	2,190	5,550	3,370	5,205	Anglais	69
-	-	-	-	15	20	Français	70
40	145	80	445	560	505	Langues non officielles (5)	71
10	-	-	-	-	40	Cantonais	72
-	15	45	25	10	45	Chinois, n.d.a.	73
10	-	-	225	415	145	Pendjabi	74
-	20	-	65	-	10	Mandarin	75
15	-	15	-	20	25	Coréen	76
15	100	15	125	120	245	Autres langues (6)	77
255	435	135	440	865	1,105	Réponses multiples	78
10	55	20	20	40	60	Anglais et français	79
240	380	115	420	820	1,015	Anglais et langue non officielle	80
-	-	-	-	-	-	Français et langue non officielle	81
-	-	10	-	-	30	Anglais, français et langue non officielle	82
						selon la connaissance des langues officielles	
1,665	4,795	2,250	6,040	4,365	6,320	Anglais seulement	83
-	-	-	-	10	-	Français seulement	84
105	290	115	235	270	365	Anglais et français	85
10	25	30	150	170	145	Ni l'anglais ni le français	86
						selon la connaissance des langues non officielles (5) (7)	
30	10	-	15	35	50	Cantonais	87
-	25	75	25	40	125	Chinois, n.d.a.	88
45	65	10	355	980	435	Pendjabi	89
10	15	-	125	30	55	Mandarin	90
-	20	-	155	170	205	Hindi	91
100	140	75	220	195	140	Allemand	92
15	120	40	80	65	155	Espagnol	93
						selon la première langue officielle parlée	
1,755	5,015	2,355	6,260	4,555	6,545	Anglais	94
10	65	20	30	55	130	Français	95
-	-	10	-	30	10	Anglais et français	96
10	25	25	145	170	145	Ni l'anglais ni le français	97
15	65	20	30	70	140	Minorité de langue officielle - (nombre) (8)	98
0.8	1.3	0.8	0.5	1.5	2.0	Minorité de langue officielle - (pourcentage) (8)	99
						selon l'origine ethnique (9)	
465	1,905	940	2,110	1,295	1,675	Anglais	100
345	1,590	615	1,805	1,015	1,800	Canadien	101
25	110	125	180	85	270	Chinois	102
340	1,090	630	1,265	875	1,165	Écossais	103
275	870	510	965	625	850	Irlandais	104
285	695	400	1,130	550	805	Allemand	105
-	95	15	425	1,005	490	Indien de l'Inde	106
90	515	185	480	370	670	Français	107
75	380	175	600	195	375	Ukrainien	108
105	220	75	185	140	205	Italien	109
350	560	195	575	225	285	Hollandais (Néerlandais)	110
-	125	-	30	40	415	Philippin	111
30	140	70	155	130	170	Polonais	112
20	220	120	320	120	155	Norvégien	113
120	110	55	110	75	205	Indien de l'Amérique du Nord	114
						selon l'identité autochtone	
115	70	30	75	30	280	Total de la population ayant une identité autochtone (10)	115
1,660	5,040	2,370	6,355	4,775	6,555	Total de la population non autochtone	116
						selon l'origine autochtone	
120	165	105	135	85	275	Total de la population ayant une origine autochtone (11)	117
1,650	4,950	2,300	6,295	4,720	6,560	Total de la population non autochtone	118
						selon le statut d'Indien inscrit	
10	35	-	15	-	170	Oui, Indien inscrit (12)	119
1,765	5,080	2,400	6,415	4,805	6,665	Non, pas un Indien inscrit	120

Table 1. Selected Characteristics for Census Tracts, 2001 Census – 100% Data and 20% Sample Data

No.	Characteristics	Vancouver 0182.03 A	Vancouver 0182.04 A	Vancouver 0182.05 A	Vancouver 0182.06 ◇ A	Vancouver 0183.01	Vancouver 0183.03
	POPULATION CHARACTERISTICS						
	by visible minority groups						
121	Total visible minority population	1,275	285	840	140	600	465
122	Chinese	345	140	230	60	35	15
123	South Asian	650	35	310	55	375	195
124	Black	-	60	10	-	45	115
125	Filipino	155	10	30	-	30	10
126	Latin American	-	10	-	10	-	20
127	Southeast Asian	-	10	65	-	65	30
128	Arab	-	10	-	-	-	-
129	West Asian	-	-	-	-	-	-
130	Korean	115	10	85	20	10	20
131	Japanese	-	-	70	-	20	50
132	Visible minority, n.i.e. (13)	10	-	10	-	10	-
133	Multiple visible minorities (14)	-	15	25	-	15	10
	by citizenship						
134	Canadian citizenship (15)	3,170	1,430	2,545	1,165	5,770	5,465
135	Citizenship other than Canadian	260	45	250	40	185	230
	by place of birth of respondent						
136	Non-immigrant population	2,475	1,165	1,965	935	5,060	4,805
137	Born in province of residence	1,875	890	1,420	745	3,720	3,285
138	Immigrant population (16)	940	310	815	255	840	850
139	United States	25	10	35	10	40	90
140	Central and South America	20	-	-	10	-	55
141	Caribbean and Bermuda	-	40	15	-	-	35
142	United Kingdom	105	30	55	20	165	175
143	Other Europe (17)	105	60	160	120	295	265
144	Africa	10	10	-	25	20	15
145	Asia and the Middle East	670	150	540	60	235	175
146	Oceania and other (18)	15	25	-	15	80	35
147	Non-permanent residents (19)	15	-	15	15	50	40
148	**Total immigrant population**	**940**	**310**	**810**	**250**	**840**	**850**
	by period of immigration						
149	Before 1961	80	60	110	90	180	215
150	1961-1970	90	45	75	40	135	155
151	1971-1980	205	95	135	30	210	220
152	1981-1990	240	10	155	65	150	130
153	1991-2001 (20)	325	95	340	25	165	125
154	1991-1995	160	35	125	15	105	60
155	1996-2001 (20)	165	60	215	15	60	65
	by age at immigration						
156	0-4 years	70	40	105	15	95	130
157	5-19 years	305	55	230	105	280	215
158	20 years and over	565	210	480	135	470	500
159	**Total population**	**3,430**	**1,475**	**2,795**	**1,205**	**5,950**	**5,700**
	by religion						
160	Catholic (21)	555	215	480	315	1,095	670
161	Protestant	1,045	605	795	355	1,945	2,415
162	Christian Orthodox	10	15	10	10	70	10
163	Christian, n.i.e. (22)	235	60	175	140	460	530
164	Muslim	35	20	20	35	65	25
165	Jewish	-	-	-	-	35	25
166	Buddhist	25	10	60	25	10	40
167	Hindu	90	10	45	-	15	-
168	Sikh	525	10	245	20	330	135
169	Eastern religions (23)	-	-	-	-	-	-
170	Other religions (24)	10	-	-	-	15	-
171	No religious affiliation (25)	915	530	975	310	1,915	1,845
172	**Total population 15 years and over**	**2,625**	**1,165**	**2,215**	**955**	**4,375**	**4,530**
	by generation status						
173	1st generation (26)	890	290	755	285	855	830
174	2nd generation (27)	725	365	585	270	1,170	1,345
175	3rd generation and over (28)	1,010	510	880	395	2,355	2,350
176	**Total population 1 year and over (29)**	**3,395**	**1,475**	**2,760**	**1,200**	**5,915**	**5,640**
	by place of residence 1 year ago (mobility)						
177	Non-movers	2,945	1,395	2,210	1,120	5,400	4,925
178	Movers	450	75	550	75	510	720
179	Non-migrants	250	45	245	40	210	455
180	Migrants	195	30	310	35	300	260
181	Internal migrants	145	30	260	40	275	205
182	Intraprovincial migrants	135	25	190	-	230	190
183	Interprovincial migrants	10	10	70	30	50	20
184	External migrants	50	-	50	-	20	55

Tableau 1. Certaines caractéristiques des secteurs de recensement, recensement de 2001 – Données intégrales et données-échantillon (20 %)

Vancouver 0183.04 A	Vancouver 0183.05 A	Vancouver 0183.06 A	Vancouver 0183.07 A	Vancouver 0184.01	Vancouver 0184.02 ◇	Caractéristiques	N°
						CARACTÉRISTIQUES DE LA POPULATION	
						selon les groupes de minorités visibles	
120	545	220	805	1,545	1,755	Total de la population des minorités visibles	121
30	80	105	185	95	225	Chinois	122
50	130	20	400	1,220	565	Sud-Asiatique	123
10	30	-	60	25	250	Noir	124
-	120	-	25	35	410	Philippin	125
-	60	10	30	25	35	Latino-Américain	126
-	85	60	20	10	35	Asiatique du Sud-Est	127
-	-	-	-	-	35	Arabe	128
-	-	-	20	30	30	Asiatique occidental	129
15	30	20	35	60	80	Coréen	130
15	20	-	25	45	85	Japonais	131
-	-	15	-	-	-	Minorité visible, n.i.a. (13)	132
-	-	-	-	-	15	Minorités visibles multiples (14)	133
						selon la citoyenneté	
1,715	4,905	2,280	6,040	4,405	6,275	Citoyenneté canadienne (15)	134
60	210	125	390	400	560	Citoyenneté autre que canadienne	135
						selon le lieu de naissance du répondant	
1,415	4,090	2,020	5,305	3,325	4,945	Population non immigrante	136
1,065	2,875	1,355	3,665	2,365	3,095	Née dans la province de résidence	137
365	1,015	380	1,055	1,475	1,820	Population immigrante (16)	138
20	60	45	70	30	60	États-Unis	139
-	40	35	25	20	65	Amérique centrale et du Sud	140
-	25	20	-	25	20	Caraïbes et Bermudes	141
45	265	105	220	205	180	Royaume-Uni	142
215	240	45	305	280	460	Autre Europe (17)	143
-	65	10	15	45	155	Afrique	144
85	315	130	390	845	820	Asie et Moyen-Orient	145
-	-	-	20	25	50	Océanie et autre (18)	146
-	10	-	70	10	70	Résidents non permanents (19)	147
365	**1,015**	**385**	**1,055**	**1,475**	**1,820**	**Population immigrante totale**	148
						selon la période d'immigration	
130	185	85	300	185	290	Avant 1961	149
80	160	40	110	250	145	1961-1970	150
75	190	105	145	335	370	1971-1980	151
40	245	40	170	290	300	1981-1990	152
45	235	110	325	420	720	1991-2001 (20)	153
25	120	50	150	225	425	1991-1995	154
20	115	60	170	200	295	1996-2001 (20)	155
						selon l'âge à l'immigration	
25	105	35	150	160	230	0-4 ans	156
85	310	115	280	405	495	5-19 ans	157
255	600	230	625	915	1,090	20 ans et plus	158
1,775	**5,115**	**2,405**	**6,430**	**4,805**	**6,835**	**Population totale**	159
						selon la religion	
365	1,075	390	1,130	750	1,500	Catholique (21)	160
600	2,105	945	2,680	1,270	2,210	Protestante	161
10	45	-	35	35	15	Orthodoxe chrétienne	162
165	275	200	430	190	340	Chrétiennes, n.i.a. (22)	163
-	70	10	25	200	245	Musulmane	164
-	40	-	-	-	10	Juive	165
-	45	20	70	15	40	Bouddhiste	166
-	-	-	-	20	115	Hindoue	167
50	55	10	380	965	390	Sikh	168
-	-	-	-	15	10	Religions orientales (23)	169
-	10	10	-	-	40	Autres religions (24)	170
590	1,395	825	1,680	1,335	1,935	Aucune appartenance religieuse (25)	171
1,445	**3,910**	**1,860**	**5,015**	**3,840**	**5,315**	**Population totale de 15 ans et plus**	172
						selon le statut des générations	
370	1,000	365	1,035	1,465	1,780	1re génération (26)	173
480	940	495	1,530	990	1,250	2e génération (27)	174
600	1,975	1,000	2,450	1,385	2,285	3e génération et plus (28)	175
1,760	**5,005**	**2,355**	**6,395**	**4,715**	**6,750**	**Population totale de 1 an et plus (29)**	176
						selon le lieu de résidence 1 an auparavant (mobilité)	
1,685	4,175	2,055	5,810	3,860	5,830	Personnes n'ayant pas déménagé	177
70	830	295	585	855	920	Personnes ayant déménagé	178
55	415	160	250	480	535	Non-migrants	179
20	415	135	335	370	385	Migrants	180
20	380	135	270	330	320	Migrants internes	181
20	345	135	220	305	280	Migrants infraprovinciaux	182
-	35	-	45	30	40	Migrants interprovinciaux	183
-	40	-	65	45	65	Migrants externes	184

Table 1. Selected Characteristics for Census Tracts, 2001 Census – 100% Data and 20% Sample Data

No.	Characteristics	Vancouver 0182.03 A	Vancouver 0182.04 A	Vancouver 0182.05 A	Vancouver 0182.06 ◇ A	Vancouver 0183.01	Vancouver 0183.03
	POPULATION CHARACTERISTICS						
185	**Total population 5 years and over (30)**	**3,235**	**1,400**	**2,615**	**1,145**	**5,515**	**5,355**
	by place of residence 5 years ago (mobility)						
186	Non-movers	1,835	870	755	805	3,220	3,490
187	Movers	1,405	530	1,855	340	2,295	1,865
188	Non-migrants	870	315	1,120	220	1,360	970
189	Migrants	530	210	735	120	940	900
190	Internal migrants	355	150	525	90	895	805
191	Intraprovincial migrants	310	125	430	80	755	665
192	Interprovincial migrants	40	25	90	10	140	140
193	External migrants	180	60	215	30	45	90
194	**Total population 15 to 24 years**	**630**	**250**	**360**	**140**	**795**	**800**
	by school attendance						
195	Not attending school	195	75	125	70	350	335
196	Attending school full time	365	155	195	55	380	400
197	Attending school part time	65	20	35	10	65	60
198	**Total population 15 years and over**	**2,625**	**1,160**	**2,215**	**955**	**4,375**	**4,530**
	by highest level of schooling						
199	Less than grade 9 (31)	85	20	120	30	265	325
200	Grades 9-13 without high school graduation certificate	520	235	465	275	1,005	1,330
201	Grades 9-13 with high school graduation certificate	370	200	315	100	635	570
202	Some postsecondary without degree, certificate or diploma (32)	315	150	280	105	650	515
203	Trades certificate or diploma (33)	305	175	275	125	705	660
204	College certificate or diploma (34)	400	170	340	180	670	745
205	University certificate below bachelor's degree	140	40	90	70	125	100
206	University with bachelor's degree or higher	475	170	325	70	325	285
	by combinations of unpaid work						
207	Males 15 years and over	1,340	600	1,120	510	2,160	2,200
208	Reported unpaid work (35)	1,160	575	1,020	460	1,975	1,950
209	Housework and child care and care or assistance to seniors	115	100	80	100	160	140
210	Housework and child care only	350	125	400	125	805	620
211	Housework and care or assistance to seniors only	90	50	45	35	165	190
212	Child care and care or assistance to seniors only	20	-	-	-	-	-
213	Housework only	575	290	465	170	825	960
214	Child care only	10	10	30	-	15	25
215	Care or assistance to seniors only	10	-	-	25	10	15
216	Females 15 years and over	1,285	560	1,100	445	2,215	2,330
217	Reported unpaid work (35)	1,175	510	1,070	415	2,140	2,190
218	Housework and child care and care or assistance to seniors	185	100	105	125	315	215
219	Housework and child care only	415	145	430	110	825	770
220	Housework and care or assistance to seniors only	95	50	70	30	160	140
221	Child care and care or assistance to seniors only	-	-	-	-	-	-
222	Housework only	460	220	445	145	815	1,040
223	Child care only	15	-	20	10	15	-
224	Care or assistance to seniors only	-	-	-	-	10	25
	by labour force activity						
225	Males 15 years and over	1,340	600	1,120	510	2,155	2,205
226	In the labour force	1,000	465	790	385	1,760	1,645
227	Employed	940	450	750	385	1,680	1,570
228	Unemployed	65	15	35	-	80	75
229	Not in the labour force	335	135	330	125	400	560
230	Participation rate	74.6	77.5	70.5	75.5	81.7	74.6
231	Employment rate	70.1	75.0	67.0	75.5	78.0	71.2
232	Unemployment rate	6.5	3.2	4.4	-	4.5	4.6
233	Females 15 years and over	1,285	565	1,095	445	2,215	2,325
234	In the labour force	860	410	640	275	1,535	1,355
235	Employed	835	385	610	260	1,470	1,270
236	Unemployed	25	25	30	10	65	85
237	Not in the labour force	425	155	455	170	680	975
238	Participation rate	66.9	72.6	58.4	61.8	69.3	58.3
239	Employment rate	65.0	68.1	55.7	58.4	66.4	54.6
240	Unemployment rate	2.9	6.1	4.7	3.6	4.2	6.3

Tableau 1. Certaines caractéristiques des secteurs de recensement, recensement de 2001 – Données intégrales et données-échantillon (20 %)

Vancouver 0183.04 A	Vancouver 0183.05 A	Vancouver 0183.06 A	Vancouver 0183.07 A	Vancouver 0184.01	Vancouver 0184.02 ◇	Caractéristiques	Nº
						CARACTÉRISTIQUES DE LA POPULATION	
1,715	**4,660**	**2,210**	**6,075**	**4,445**	**6,315**	**Population totale de 5 ans et plus (30)**	185
						selon le lieu de résidence 5 ans auparavant (mobilité)	
1,370	1,075	1,080	4,115	1,910	3,100	Personnes n'ayant pas déménagé	186
340	3,585	1,135	1,960	2,530	3,210	Personnes ayant déménagé	187
155	1,970	585	1,055	1,410	1,905	Non-migrants	188
190	1,620	545	905	1,125	1,305	Migrants	189
175	1,495	490	735	1,000	1,015	Migrants internes	190
120	1,195	455	600	825	785	Migrants infraprovinciaux	191
55	300	40	130	180	240	Migrants interprovinciaux	192
15	125	50	170	120	285	Migrants externes	193
305	**610**	**265**	**905**	**545**	**750**	**Population totale de 15 à 24 ans**	194
						selon la fréquentation scolaire	
145	255	120	350	205	315	Ne fréquentant pas l'école	195
140	270	100	495	285	365	Fréquentant l'école à plein temps	196
15	90	45	60	50	70	Fréquentant l'école à temps partiel	197
1,450	**3,915**	**1,860**	**5,015**	**3,840**	**5,315**	**Population totale de 15 ans et plus**	198
						selon le plus haut niveau de scolarité atteint	
90	120	55	220	235	350	Niveau inférieur à la 9e année (31)	199
375	665	445	1,165	635	1,410	De la 9e à la 13e année sans certificat d'études secondaires	200
195	615	280	835	500	720	De la 9e à la 13e année avec certificat d'études secondaires	201
150	515	215	725	475	735	Études postsecondaires partielles sans grade, certificat ou diplôme (32)	202
230	490	290	610	500	665	Certificat ou diplôme d'une école de métiers (33)	203
245	765	420	770	735	820	Certificat ou diplôme collégial (34)	204
25	95	35	125	135	175	Certificat universitaire inférieur au baccalauréat	205
140	650	110	570	610	445	Études universitaires avec baccalauréat ou diplôme supérieur	206
						selon les combinaisons de travail non rémunéré	
750	1,885	885	2,455	1,945	2,485	Hommes de 15 ans et plus	207
655	1,740	825	2,225	1,785	2,205	Travail non rémunéré déclaré (35)	208
55	155	15	230	210	210	Travaux ménagers et soins aux enfants et soins ou aide aux personnes âgées	209
195	630	275	715	480	625	Travaux ménagers et soins aux enfants seulement	210
75	60	40	170	135	115	Travaux ménagers et soins ou aide aux personnes âgées seulement	211
-	-	10	-	10	10	Soins aux enfants et soins ou aide aux personnes âgées seulement	212
320	875	470	1,065	925	1,200	Travaux ménagers seulement	213
-	20	10	20	15	25	Soins aux enfants seulement	214
10	-	-	25	-	30	Soins ou aide aux personnes âgées seulement	215
705	2,025	975	2,560	1,895	2,830	Femmes de 15 ans et plus	216
680	1,935	935	2,465	1,755	2,625	Travail non rémunéré déclaré (35)	217
55	280	70	375	270	380	Travaux ménagers et soins aux enfants et soins ou aide aux personnes âgées	218
230	715	345	885	580	820	Travaux ménagers et soins aux enfants seulement	219
60	115	75	235	120	205	Travaux ménagers et soins ou aide aux personnes âgées seulement	220
-	10	10	-	-	-	Soins aux enfants et soins ou aide aux personnes âgées seulement	221
325	815	435	955	780	1,185	Travaux ménagers seulement	222
-	-	-	10	10	20	Soins aux enfants seulement	223
-	-	-	10	-	10	Soins ou aide aux personnes âgées seulement	224
						selon l'activité	
745	1,885	885	2,455	1,945	2,485	Hommes de 15 ans et plus	225
535	1,490	725	1,900	1,550	1,780	Population active	226
525	1,425	685	1,830	1,475	1,620	Personnes occupées	227
10	60	35	65	75	160	Chômeurs	228
215	400	165	550	395	705	Inactifs	229
71.8	79.0	81.9	77.4	79.7	71.6	Taux d'activité	230
70.5	75.6	77.4	74.5	75.8	65.2	Taux d'emploi	231
1.9	4.0	4.8	3.4	4.8	9.0	Taux de chômage	232
705	2,030	975	2,565	1,895	2,830	Femmes de 15 ans et plus	233
435	1,365	670	1,690	1,205	1,610	Population active	234
380	1,310	640	1,630	1,130	1,450	Personnes occupées	235
50	55	40	60	80	160	Chômeuses	236
265	665	305	870	690	1,220	Inactives	237
61.7	67.2	68.7	65.9	63.6	56.9	Taux d'activité	238
53.9	64.5	65.6	63.5	59.6	51.2	Taux d'emploi	239
11.5	4.0	6.0	3.6	6.6	9.9	Taux de chômage	240

Table 1. Selected Characteristics for Census Tracts, 2001 Census – 100% Data and 20% Sample Data

No.	Characteristics	Vancouver 0182.03 A	Vancouver 0182.04 A	Vancouver 0182.05 A	Vancouver 0182.06 ◇ A	Vancouver 0183.01	Vancouver 0183.03
	POPULATION CHARACTERISTICS						
	by labour force activity – concluded						
241	Both sexes - Participation rate	70.9	75.4	64.6	69.5	75.3	66.2
242	15-24 years	64.8	66.7	59.7	78.6	71.5	60.4
243	25 years and over	73.2	77.9	65.8	66.9	76.3	67.3
244	Both sexes - Employment rate	67.7	72.0	61.4	67.5	72.0	62.8
245	15-24 years	56.3	54.9	54.2	85.2	62.0	55.3
246	25 years and over	71.4	76.4	62.5	65.2	74.3	64.3
247	Both sexes - Unemployment rate	4.6	4.0	4.9	1.5	4.4	5.2
248	15-24 years	12.5	17.6	7.0	-	14.2	9.4
249	25 years and over	2.7	1.4	4.5	1.8	2.4	4.6
250	**Total labour force 15 years and over**	**1,865**	**870**	**1,435**	**660**	**3,295**	**2,995**
	by industry based on the 1997 NAICS						
251	Industry - Not applicable (36)	35	-	20	15	30	55
252	All industries (37)	1,830	870	1,410	645	3,260	2,940
253	11 Agriculture, forestry, fishing and hunting	35	-	45	50	10	60
254	21 Mining and oil and gas extraction	-	-	-	-	20	10
255	22 Utilities	10	10	10	-	35	10
256	23 Construction	155	25	110	60	235	275
257	31-33 Manufacturing	215	95	145	130	540	420
258	41 Wholesale trade	120	30	100	25	225	190
259	44-45 Retail trade	230	105	140	65	415	365
260	48-49 Transportation and warehousing	95	60	115	30	200	180
261	51 Information and cultural industries	15	35	45	20	100	90
262	52 Finance and insurance	110	45	60	15	160	115
263	53 Real estate and rental and leasing	50	75	20	10	55	50
264	54 Professional, scientific and technical services	145	70	140	20	135	95
265	55 Management of companies and enterprises	-	-	-	-	-	-
266	56 Administrative and support, waste management and remediation services	55	20	75	10	70	105
267	61 Educational services	110	80	95	45	155	180
268	62 Health care and social assistance	135	75	80	45	310	260
269	71 Arts, entertainment and recreation	30	-	10	10	85	90
270	72 Accommodation and food services	140	85	50	30	195	150
271	81 Other services (except public administration)	80	25	85	60	150	140
272	91 Public administration	85	25	85	20	170	160
	by class of worker						
273	Class of worker - Not applicable (36)	35	10	20	10	35	55
274	All classes of worker (37)	1,830	865	1,410	645	3,260	2,945
275	Paid workers	1,615	815	1,315	540	2,985	2,565
276	Employees	1,515	755	1,190	500	2,875	2,475
277	Self-employed (incorporated)	100	65	120	40	110	90
278	Self-employed (unincorporated)	205	50	100	95	275	355
279	Unpaid family workers	10	-	-	10	-	30
	by occupation based on the 2001 NOC-S						
280	Male labour force 15 years and over	1,000	465	790	385	1,760	1,640
281	Occupation - Not applicable (36)	30	-	15	-	15	15
282	All occupations (37)	975	465	775	385	1,740	1,630
283	A Management occupations	165	145	105	95	265	180
284	B Business, finance and administration occupations	155	20	95	25	175	125
285	C Natural and applied sciences and related occupations	55	35	75	15	110	105
286	D Health occupations	40	15	20	-	20	15
287	E Occupations in social science, education, government service and religion	30	25	15	10	55	40
288	F Occupations in art, culture, recreation and sport	-	10	10	-	25	55
289	G Sales and service occupations	235	105	100	50	345	335
290	H Trades, transport and equipment operators and related occupations	230	85	270	130	510	560
291	I Occupations unique to primary industry	10	-	35	20	50	30
292	J Occupations unique to processing, manufacturing and utilities	60	30	50	40	185	180
293	Female labour force 15 years and over	855	405	640	275	1,540	1,355
294	Occupation - Not applicable (36)	10	-	10	15	20	40
295	All occupations (37)	850	405	640	260	1,520	1,315
296	A Management occupations	60	35	60	35	120	110
297	B Business, finance and administration occupations	315	110	205	40	520	355
298	C Natural and applied sciences and related occupations	10	-	40	10	-	-
299	D Health occupations	65	25	40	25	100	105

Tableau 1. Certaines caractéristiques des secteurs de recensement, recensement de 2001 – Données intégrales et données-échantillon (20 %)

Vancouver 0183.04 A	Vancouver 0183.05 A	Vancouver 0183.06 A	Vancouver 0183.07 A	Vancouver 0184.01	Vancouver 0184.02 ◇	Caractéristiques	Nº
						CARACTÉRISTIQUES DE LA POPULATION	
						selon l'activité – fin	
66.9	72.9	75.3	71.6	71.7	63.8	Les deux sexes - Taux d'activité	241
68.9	66.9	71.7	73.5	65.1	59.3	15-24 ans	242
65.9	74.0	75.9	71.3	72.8	64.4	25 ans et plus	243
62.8	69.8	71.0	69.0	67.8	57.7	Les deux sexes - Taux d'emploi	244
60.7	58.2	67.9	66.3	59.6	49.0	15-24 ans	245
63.3	72.1	71.5	69.6	69.3	59.2	25 ans et plus	246
6.2	4.2	5.4	3.6	5.5	9.3	Les deux sexes - Taux de chômage	247
14.0	12.2	5.3	9.8	9.9	17.8	15-24 ans	248
4.0	2.7	5.4	2.1	4.8	8.0	25 ans et plus	249
970	**2,850**	**1,400**	**3,595**	**2,755**	**3,385**	**Population active totale de 15 ans et plus**	250
						selon l'industrie basée sur le SCIAN de 1997	
-	20	25	30	30	120	Industrie - Sans objet (36)	251
970	2,830	1,370	3,560	2,730	3,265	Toutes les industries (37)	252
100	60	50	125	40	15	11 Agriculture, foresterie, pêche et chasse	253
-	15	10	-	-	-	21 Extraction minière et extraction de pétrole et de gaz	254
20	35	-	15	30	25	22 Services publics	255
95	125	110	245	225	260	23 Construction	256
150	315	200	270	325	475	31-33 Fabrication	257
75	280	95	270	140	240	41 Commerce de gros	258
115	335	160	525	275	345	44-45 Commerce de détail	259
45	210	80	265	200	245	48-49 Transport et entreposage	260
20	100	45	155	90	85	51 Industrie de l'information et industrie culturelle	261
-	115	45	145	110	100	52 Finance et assurances	262
10	90	60	75	70	60	53 Services immobiliers et services de location et de location à bail	263
20	220	25	240	185	170	54 Services professionnels, scientifiques et techniques	264
-	-	-	-	10	-	55 Gestion de sociétés et d'entreprises	265
55	40	45	105	135	155	56 Services administratifs, services de soutien, services de gestion des déchets et services d'assainissement	266
60	180	60	295	200	185	61 Services d'enseignement	267
60	225	145	300	160	315	62 Soins de santé et assistance sociale	268
20	35	15	70	55	100	71 Arts, spectacles et loisirs	269
60	155	100	140	170	240	72 Hébergement et services de restauration	270
50	135	55	140	130	95	81 Autres services, sauf les administrations publiques	271
20	165	70	175	175	155	91 Administrations publiques	272
						selon la catégorie de travailleurs	
-	20	25	30	30	125	Catégorie de travailleurs - Sans objet (36)	273
965	2,830	1,370	3,565	2,725	3,265	Toutes les catégories de travailleurs (37)	274
845	2,665	1,285	3,185	2,445	3,050	Travailleurs rémunérés	275
805	2,605	1,250	3,060	2,305	2,960	Employés	276
40	60	35	125	140	90	Travailleurs autonomes (entreprise constituée en société)	277
125	165	80	365	270	200	Travailleurs autonomes (entreprise non constituée en société)	278
-	10	-	10	10	15	Travailleurs familiaux non rémunérés	279
						selon la profession basée sur la CNP-S de 2001	
535	1,485	725	1,900	1,550	1,780	Hommes actifs de 15 ans et plus	280
-	20	10	15	10	50	Profession - Sans objet (36)	281
535	1,470	720	1,885	1,545	1,730	Toutes les professions (37)	282
35	315	80	360	250	210	A Gestion	283
20	135	55	130	110	95	B Affaires, finance et administration	284
25	165	65	130	155	125	C Sciences naturelles et appliquées et professions apparentées	285
-	30	20	30	20	-	D Secteur de la santé	286
10	55	-	90	55	50	E Sciences sociales, enseignement, administration publique et religion	287
-	20	-	60	30	30	F Arts, culture, sports et loisirs	288
110	310	140	425	310	360	G Ventes et services	289
210	340	235	505	450	620	H Métiers, transport et machinerie	290
85	35	30	65	75	35	I Professions propres au secteur primaire	291
40	70	95	90	90	205	J Transformation, fabrication et services d'utilité publique	292
430	1,360	675	1,695	1,205	1,605	Femmes actives de 15 ans et plus	293
-	-	15	15	20	70	Profession - Sans objet (36)	294
435	1,365	655	1,675	1,185	1,535	Toutes les professions (37)	295
20	190	65	135	140	125	A Gestion	296
120	405	230	625	420	505	B Affaires, finance et administration	297
10	15	10	15	25	35	C Sciences naturelles et appliquées et professions apparentées	298
20	75	55	100	80	145	D Secteur de la santé	299

Table 1. Selected Characteristics for Census Tracts, 2001 Census – 100% Data and 20% Sample Data

No.	Characteristics	Vancouver 0182.03 A	Vancouver 0182.04 A	Vancouver 0182.05 A	Vancouver 0182.06 ◇ A	Vancouver 0183.01	Vancouver 0183.03
	POPULATION CHARACTERISTICS						
	by occupation based on the 2001 NOC-S – concluded						
300	E Occupations in social science, education, government service and religion	95	70	75	30	150	130
301	F Occupations in art, culture, recreation and sport	20	10	20	20	55	60
302	G Sales and service occupations	240	140	160	60	500	420
303	H Trades, transport and equipment operators and related occupations	-	-	-	10	20	70
304	I Occupations unique to primary industry	20	10	20	20	-	20
305	J Occupations unique to processing, manufacturing and utilities	30	10	25	-	40	35
306	**Total employed labour force 15 years and over**	**1,775**	**835**	**1,360**	**645**	**3,150**	**2,845**
	by place of work						
307	Males	940	450	750	385	1,680	1,570
308	Usual place of work	750	400	480	255	1,390	1,185
309	At home	75	20	110	60	85	85
310	Outside Canada	-	-	-	-	-	10
311	No fixed workplace address	115	25	160	75	210	305
312	Females	835	385	605	260	1,470	1,270
313	Usual place of work	695	355	465	220	1,230	1,045
314	At home	100	30	105	20	125	115
315	Outside Canada	-	-	-	-	-	10
316	No fixed workplace address	40	10	30	15	110	105
317	**Total employed labour force 15 years and over with usual place of work or no fixed workplace address**	**1,600**	**785**	**1,135**	**565**	**2,945**	**2,630**
	by mode of transportation						
318	Males	865	425	635	330	1,595	1,485
319	Car, truck, van, as driver	815	385	560	280	1,425	1,285
320	Car, truck, van, as passenger	30	20	25	10	50	75
321	Public transit	10	20	25	10	45	30
322	Walked	-	-	20	20	55	60
323	Other method	10	-	15	10	30	35
324	Females	735	355	495	235	1,345	1,150
325	Car, truck, van, as driver	615	280	430	185	1,135	930
326	Car, truck, van, as passenger	45	35	40	35	120	75
327	Public transit	70	20	35	-	25	35
328	Walked	-	20	-	-	40	100
329	Other method	-	-	-	15	25	10
330	**Total population 15 years and over who worked since January 1, 2000**	**2,060**	**950**	**1,575**	**710**	**3,510**	**3,215**
	by language used at work						
331	Single responses	1,815	905	1,475	660	3,375	3,120
332	English	1,770	895	1,415	655	3,355	3,115
333	French	10	-	-	-	10	-
334	Non-official languages (5)	30	10	55	10	15	-
335	Chinese, n.o.s.	-	10	25	-	-	-
336	Cantonese	-	-	-	-	-	-
337	Other languages (6)	30	-	35	-	15	-
338	Multiple responses	245	45	100	50	140	95
339	English and French	15	-	15	-	20	15
340	English and non-official language	230	35	85	40	110	70
341	French and non-official language	-	-	-	-	-	-
342	English, French and non-official language	-	10	-	-	10	-
	DWELLING AND HOUSEHOLD CHARACTERISTICS						
343	**Total number of occupied private dwellings**	**980**	**420**	**890**	**385**	**1,885**	**2,215**
	by tenure						
344	Owned	845	415	725	310	1,515	1,560
345	Rented	135	-	165	80	370	660
346	Band housing	-	-	-	-	-	-
	by structural type of dwelling						
347	Single-detached house	750	415	690	375	1,590	1,170
348	Semi-detached house	20	-	140	-	50	60
349	Row house	-	-	-	10	95	120
350	Apartment, detached duplex	200	-	25	-	95	175
351	Apartment, building that has five or more storeys	-	-	-	-	-	-
352	Apartment, building that has fewer than five storeys (38)	10	-	35	-	40	665
353	Other single-attached house	10	-	-	-	-	25
354	Movable dwelling (39)	-	-	-	-	15	-

Tableau 1. Certaines caractéristiques des secteurs de recensement, recensement de 2001 – Données intégrales et données-échantillon (20 %)

Vancouver 0183.04 A	Vancouver 0183.05 A	Vancouver 0183.06 A	Vancouver 0183.07 A	Vancouver 0184.01	Vancouver 0184.02 ◇	Caractéristiques	N°
						CARACTÉRISTIQUES DE LA POPULATION	
						selon la profession basée sur la CNP-S de 2001 – fin	
40	170	70	200	100	115	E Sciences sociales, enseignement, administration publique et religion	300
10	45	-	35	35	45	F Arts, culture, sports et loisirs	301
155	410	165	435	300	485	G Ventes et services	302
10	-	10	30	40	30	H Métiers, transport et machinerie	303
30	25	20	65	10	-	I Professions propres au secteur primaire	304
30	25	25	30	40	50	J Transformation, fabrication et services d'utilité publique	305
905	**2,730**	**1,325**	**3,465**	**2,605**	**3,065**	**Population active occupée totale de 15 ans et plus**	306
						selon le lieu de travail	
525	1,425	685	1,830	1,475	1,620	Hommes	307
325	1,110	555	1,465	1,095	1,205	Lieu habituel de travail	308
50	65	15	95	105	60	À domicile	309
15	20	-	10	-	10	En dehors du Canada	310
140	230	110	270	275	345	Sans adresse de travail fixe	311
385	1,310	640	1,635	1,130	1,450	Femmes	312
305	1,165	595	1,340	980	1,245	Lieu habituel de travail	313
65	90	20	230	110	100	À domicile	314
-	-	-	-	-	-	En dehors du Canada	315
15	45	25	60	40	105	Sans adresse de travail fixe	316
775	**2,550**	**1,285**	**3,135**	**2,390**	**2,895**	**Population active occupée totale de 15 ans et plus ayant un lieu habituel de travail ou sans adresse de travail fixe**	317
						selon le mode de transport	
455	1,335	665	1,730	1,370	1,555	Hommes	318
355	1,175	585	1,510	1,245	1,195	Automobile, camion ou fourgonnette, en tant que conducteur	319
65	65	35	130	45	95	Automobile, camion ou fourgonnette, en tant que passager	320
10	35	25	30	45	120	Transport en commun	321
30	25	20	20	30	80	À pied	322
-	45	10	35	-	55	Autre moyen	323
315	1,215	615	1,405	1,015	1,345	Femmes	324
255	1,055	550	1,170	860	960	Automobile, camion ou fourgonnette, en tant que conductrice	325
35	90	25	140	85	100	Automobile, camion ou fourgonnette, en tant que passagère	326
15	55	10	50	55	210	Transport en commun	327
10	10	25	30	15	55	À pied	328
10	-	-	20	10	20	Autre moyen	329
1,075	**3,085**	**1,480**	**3,755**	**2,970**	**3,550**	**Population totale de 15 ans et plus ayant travaillé depuis le 1er janvier 2000**	330
						selon la langue utilisée au travail	
1,025	2,975	1,440	3,585	2,650	3,365	Réponses uniques	331
1,010	2,960	1,415	3,530	2,605	3,320	Anglais	332
10	-	-	-	-	-	Français	333
10	15	25	50	40	40	Langues non officielles (5)	334
-	-	25	-	-	10	Chinois, n.d.a.	335
-	-	-	-	-	-	Cantonais	336
10	15	-	50	40	35	Autres langues (6)	337
50	110	40	170	320	185	Réponses multiples	338
10	15	10	20	35	15	Anglais et français	339
40	95	25	150	280	170	Anglais et langue non officielle	340
-	-	-	-	-	-	Français et langue non officielle	341
-	-	-	-	10	-	Anglais, français et langue non officielle	342
						CARACTÉRISTIQUES DES LOGEMENTS ET DES MÉNAGES	
590	**1,675**	**905**	**2,045**	**1,640**	**2,685**	**Nombre total de logements privés occupés**	343
						selon le mode d'occupation	
455	1,590	795	1,850	1,370	2,000	Possédé	344
135	90	110	195	275	680	Loué	345
-	-	-	-	-	-	Logement de bande	346
						selon le type de construction résidentielle	
570	1,170	435	1,920	1,015	340	Maison individuelle non attenante	347
-	245	-	10	-	10	Maison jumelée	348
-	230	350	-	310	775	Maison en rangée	349
10	30	-	115	45	150	Appartement, duplex non attenant	350
-	-	-	-	-	90	Appartement, immeuble de cinq étages ou plus	351
-	-	120	-	215	665	Appartement, immeuble de moins de cinq étages (38)	352
-	-	-	-	-	-	Autre maison individuelle attenante	353
-	10	-	-	50	660	Logement mobile (39)	354

Table 1. Selected Characteristics for Census Tracts, 2001 Census – 100% Data and 20% Sample Data

No.	Characteristics	Vancouver 0182.03 A	Vancouver 0182.04 A	Vancouver 0182.05 A	Vancouver 0182.06 ◇ A	Vancouver 0183.01	Vancouver 0183.03
	DWELLING AND HOUSEHOLD CHARACTERISTICS						
	by condition of dwelling						
355	Regular maintenance only	825	360	700	245	1,300	1,445
356	Minor repairs	105	55	150	130	490	590
357	Major repairs	45	-	35	15	105	180
	by period of construction						
358	Before 1946	20	-	60	100	60	95
359	1946-1960	45	-	40	55	110	165
360	1961-1970	30	20	95	40	140	340
361	1971-1980	50	-	130	100	580	815
362	1981-1990	245	260	35	45	475	495
363	1991-2001 (20)	595	135	520	45	520	310
364	Average number of rooms per dwelling	8.8	9.9	8.1	7.7	7.5	6.1
365	Average number of bedrooms per dwelling	3.7	3.6	3.4	3.2	3.3	2.6
366	Average value of dwelling $	360,419	341,217	314,732	384,642	230,403	189,681
367	**Total number of private households**	**980**	**420**	**890**	**385**	**1,890**	**2,220**
	by household size						
368	1 person	80	25	95	55	255	650
369	2 persons	240	95	310	120	475	640
370	3 persons	130	80	140	75	370	320
371	4-5 persons	430	180	260	95	680	530
372	6 or more persons	95	45	80	45	105	80
	by household type						
373	One-family households	805	390	715	315	1,525	1,500
374	Multiple-family households	75	10	50	15	40	20
375	Non-family households	100	25	125	60	325	695
376	Number of persons in private households	3,430	1,475	2,795	1,200	5,950	5,695
377	Average number of persons in private households	3.5	3.6	3.1	3.1	3.2	2.6
378	Average number of persons per room	0.4	0.4	0.4	0.4	0.4	0.4
379	Tenant households in non-farm, non-reserve private dwellings (40)	130	-	160	80	370	650
380	Average gross rent $ (40)	706	-	992	752	799	725
381	Tenant households spending 30% or more of household income on gross rent (40) (41)	30	-	100	15	175	225
382	Tenant households spending from 30% to 99% of household income on gross rent (40) (41)	30	-	90	15	135	150
383	Owner households in non-farm, non-reserve private dwellings (42)	835	415	685	295	1,520	1,560
384	Average owner's major payments $ (42)	1,411	1,446	1,280	1,031	1,272	989
385	Owner households spending 30% or more of household income on owner's major payments (41) (42)	250	65	170	65	335	405
386	Owner households spending from 30% to 99% of household income on owner's major payments (41) (42)	195	55	150	60	280	335
	CENSUS FAMILY CHARACTERISTICS						
387	**Total number of census families in private households**	**960**	**405**	**825**	**350**	**1,615**	**1,540**
	by census family structure and size						
388	Total couple families	870	390	710	310	1,350	1,270
389	Total families of married couples	820	365	655	260	1,200	1,080
390	Without children at home	235	90	285	100	320	385
391	With children at home	580	275	370	160	880	690
392	1 child	110	70	100	35	265	230
393	2 children	335	145	170	75	420	295
394	3 or more children	135	60	100	50	200	160
395	Total families of common-law couples	50	25	55	45	145	190
396	Without children at home	35	15	25	25	60	115
397	With children at home	20	15	30	25	85	80
398	1 child	10	10	10	25	15	45
399	2 children	10	10	15	-	55	25
400	3 or more children	-	-	-	-	20	-
401	Total lone-parent families	95	10	110	40	270	270
402	Female parent	80	10	65	30	190	200
403	1 child	35	-	40	20	105	130
404	2 children	15	-	15	10	50	50
405	3 or more children	30	-	10	-	35	20

Tableau 1. Certaines caractéristiques des secteurs de recensement, recensement de 2001 – Données intégrales et données-échantillon (20 %)

Vancouver 0183.04 A	Vancouver 0183.05 A	Vancouver 0183.06 A	Vancouver 0183.07 A	Vancouver 0184.01	Vancouver 0184.02 ◇	Caractéristiques	N°
						CARACTÉRISTIQUES DES LOGEMENTS ET DES MÉNAGES	
						selon l'état du logement	
350	1,510	555	1,695	1,285	1,965	Entretien régulier seulement	355
180	150	265	325	280	580	Réparations mineures	356
60	15	80	25	75	135	Réparations majeures	357
						selon la période de construction	
45	10	-	15	55	15	Avant 1946	358
130	10	-	55	125	75	1946-1960	359
90	10	15	30	255	150	1961-1970	360
215	35	300	80	255	945	1971-1980	361
80	175	405	995	180	835	1981-1990	362
30	1,430	185	865	775	660	1991-2001 (20)	363
7.5	7.8	6.2	8.7	7.5	5.3	Nombre moyen de pièces par logement	364
3.2	3.3	2.6	3.5	3.3	2.4	Nombre moyen de chambres à coucher par logement	365
402,518	252,902	170,500	269,595	291,046	119,479	Valeur moyenne du logement $	366
590	**1,680**	**905**	**2,045**	**1,640**	**2,680**	**Nombre total de logements privés**	367
						selon la taille du ménage	
115	145	135	195	255	680	1 personne	368
170	575	360	665	580	950	2 personnes	369
95	365	175	350	300	405	3 personnes	370
170	520	210	705	395	535	4-5 personnes	371
35	75	25	120	110	110	6 personnes ou plus	372
						selon le genre de ménage	
450	1,485	730	1,745	1,230	1,825	Ménages unifamiliaux	373
25	35	15	70	85	40	Ménages multifamiliaux	374
115	160	165	225	330	815	Ménages non familiaux	375
1,780	5,115	2,400	6,430	4,805	6,800	Nombre de personnes dans les ménages privés	376
3.0	3.0	2.7	3.1	2.9	2.5	Nombre moyen de personnes dans les ménages privés	377
0.4	0.4	0.4	0.4	0.4	0.5	Nombre moyen de personnes par pièce	378
135	85	110	190	275	680	Ménages locataires dans les logements privés non agricoles hors réserve (40)	379
1,032	1,166	963	994	918	775	Loyer brut moyen $ (40)	380
65	45	40	65	130	275	Ménages locataires consacrant 30 % ou plus du revenu du ménage au loyer brut (40)	381
40	35	40	55	80	235	Ménages locataires consacrant de 30 % à 99 % du revenu du ménage au loyer brut (40) (41)	382
425	1,580	795	1,850	1,365	2,000	Ménages propriétaires dans les logements privés non agricoles hors réserve (42)	383
983	1,437	1,112	1,199	1,259	808	Principales dépenses de propriété moyennes $ (42)	384
90	345	235	325	335	475	Ménages propriétaires consacrant 30 % ou plus du revenu du ménage aux principales dépenses de propriété (41) (42)	385
80	325	230	295	305	415	Ménages propriétaires consacrant de 30 % à 99 % du revenu du ménage aux principales dépenses de propriété (41) (42)	386
						CARACTÉRISTIQUES DES FAMILLES DE RECENSEMENT	
505	**1,550**	**750**	**1,890**	**1,415**	**1,920**	**Total des familles de recensement dans les ménages privés**	387
						selon la structure et la taille de la famille de recensement	
420	1,425	610	1,730	1,280	1,515	Total des familles avec conjoints	388
380	1,295	525	1,620	1,175	1,300	Total des familles avec couples mariés	389
130	505	245	625	480	555	Sans enfants à la maison	390
250	790	275	995	690	740	Avec enfants à la maison	391
80	330	105	265	235	235	1 enfant	392
60	285	135	505	330	330	2 enfants	393
110	175	35	220	125	175	3 enfants ou plus	394
35	125	90	110	110	220	Total des familles en union libre	395
35	80	55	75	95	150	Sans enfants à la maison	396
10	45	35	30	20	70	Avec enfants à la maison	397
10	20	20	25	-	20	1 enfant	398
-	15	10	10	10	35	2 enfants	399
-	10	-	-	-	15	3 enfants ou plus	400
90	130	140	160	135	405	Total des familles monoparentales	401
60	115	100	135	105	355	Parent de sexe féminin	402
35	55	55	65	80	215	1 enfant	403
20	60	25	50	20	80	2 enfants	404
10	10	15	15	-	55	3 enfants ou plus	405

Table 1. Selected Characteristics for Census Tracts, 2001 Census – 100% Data and 20% Sample Data

No.	Characteristics	Vancouver 0182.03 A	Vancouver 0182.04 A	Vancouver 0182.05 A	Vancouver 0182.06 ◇ A	Vancouver 0183.01	Vancouver 0183.03
	CENSUS FAMILY CHARACTERISTICS						
	by census family structure and size – concluded						
406	Male parent	10	10	45	10	80	65
407	1 child	-	-	35	-	55	25
408	2 children	10	-	15	-	10	10
409	3 or more children	-	-	-	-	10	30
410	**Total number of children at home**	**1,420**	**590**	**970**	**435**	**2,370**	**1,945**
	by age groups						
411	Under 6 years	215	105	230	55	540	420
412	6-14 years	590	215	335	190	1,000	735
413	15-17 years	225	125	100	50	300	240
414	18-24 years	325	125	190	65	415	385
415	25 years and over	65	25	110	80	120	165
	Average number of children at home per						
416	census family (43)	1.5	1.5	1.2	1.3	1.5	1.3
417	**Total number of persons in private households**	**3,430**	**1,475**	**2,795**	**1,205**	**5,950**	**5,700**
	by census family status and living arrangements						
418	Number of non-family persons	180	90	280	115	620	940
419	Living with relatives (44)	45	35	80	25	195	120
420	Living with non-relatives only	60	30	105	30	170	175
421	Living alone	80	25	95	60	255	645
422	Number of family persons	3,245	1,390	2,510	1,085	5,330	4,755
423	Average number of persons per census family	3.4	3.5	3.0	3.1	3.3	3.1
424	**Total number of persons 65 years and over**	**240**	**100**	**315**	**110**	**360**	**765**
425	Number of non-family persons 65 years and over	50	25	110	35	105	365
426	Living with relatives (44)	25	15	55	15	20	45
427	Living with non-relatives only	-	-	10	-	-	15
428	Living alone	20	-	45	20	85	305
429	Number of family persons 65 years and over	190	75	210	70	255	400
	ECONOMIC FAMILY CHARACTERISTICS						
	Total number of economic families in						
430	**private households**	**885**	**395**	**765**	**330**	**1,595**	**1,530**
	by size of family						
431	2 persons	230	95	300	120	480	645
432	3 persons	125	85	130	70	340	290
433	4 persons	315	125	180	65	480	355
434	5 or more persons	215	90	160	75	295	235
435	Total number of persons in economic families	3,295	1,425	2,590	1,115	5,530	4,875
436	Average number of persons per economic family	3.7	3.6	3.4	3.4	3.5	3.2
437	Total number of unattached individuals	140	55	205	90	425	825
	2000 INCOME CHARACTERISTICS						
	Population 15 years and over by sex and total income groups in 2000						
438	Total - Both sexes	2,625	1,160	2,215	955	4,375	4,530
439	Without income	205	40	120	30	180	210
440	With income	2,425	1,120	2,095	920	4,195	4,320
441	Under $1,000 (45)	90	65	100	25	185	180
442	$ 1,000 - $ 2,999	40	80	100	30	220	235
443	$ 3,000 - $ 4,999	70	45	80	15	165	180
444	$ 5,000 - $ 6,999	165	40	85	45	150	200
445	$ 7,000 - $ 9,999	205	70	95	110	225	220
446	$10,000 - $11,999	130	15	75	55	150	170
447	$12,000 - $14,999	160	25	150	70	270	365
448	$15,000 - $19,999	195	70	180	65	315	430
449	$20,000 - $24,999	175	55	125	50	235	305
450	$25,000 - $29,999	110	70	205	95	355	230
451	$30,000 - $34,999	160	80	155	60	300	365
452	$35,000 - $39,999	155	55	85	55	265	290
453	$40,000 - $44,999	170	50	90	25	270	235
454	$45,000 - $49,999	100	35	85	35	220	260
455	$50,000 - $59,999	145	135	145	80	315	325
456	$60,000 and over	350	220	325	100	545	325
457	Average income $ (46)	34,887	38,297	33,503	31,091	31,582	27,445
458	Median income $ (46)	24,292	30,007	25,337	24,842	26,937	22,979
459	Standard error of average income $ (46)	1,727	2,550	2,171	2,662	860	710

Tableau 1. Certaines caractéristiques des secteurs de recensement, recensement de 2001 – Données intégrales et données-échantillon (20 %)

Vancouver 0183.04 A	Vancouver 0183.05 A	Vancouver 0183.06 A	Vancouver 0183.07 A	Vancouver 0184.01	Vancouver 0184.02 ◇	Caractéristiques	N°
						CARACTÉRISTIQUES DES FAMILLES DE RECENSEMENT	
						selon la structure et la taille de la famille de recensement – fin	
30	15	40	30	35	50	Parent de sexe masculin	406
30	10	25	15	25	35	1 enfant	407
-	10	10	10	10	10	2 enfants	408
-	-	-	-	10	-	3 enfants ou plus	409
695	**1,785**	**760**	**2,350**	**1,505**	**2,255**	**Nombre total d'enfants à la maison**	410
						selon les groupes d'âge	
75	555	235	420	440	635	Moins de 6 ans	411
250	620	290	985	520	885	6-14 ans	412
80	210	85	315	135	245	15-17 ans	413
170	305	100	505	265	370	18-24 ans	414
120	95	50	125	150	130	25 ans et plus	415
1.4	1.2	1.0	1.2	1.1	1.2	Nombre moyen d'enfants à la maison par famille de recensement (43)	416
1,775	**5,115**	**2,400**	**6,430**	**4,805**	**6,805**	**Nombre total de personnes dans les ménages privés**	417
						selon la situation des particuliers dans la famille de recensement et des particuliers dans le ménage	
160	355	280	460	600	1,110	Nombre de personnes hors famille de recensement	418
25	105	50	135	170	175	Vivant avec des personnes apparentées (44)	419
20	110	90	120	170	255	Vivant avec des personnes non apparentées uniquement	420
110	145	135	200	250	680	Vivant seules	421
1,620	4,760	2,125	5,970	4,205	5,685	Nombre de personnes membres d'une famille	422
3.2	3.1	2.8	3.2	3.0	3.0	Nombre moyen de personnes par famille de recensement	423
245	**390**	**185**	**610**	**425**	**915**	**Nombre total de personnes de 65 ans et plus**	424
50	85	40	135	130	345	Nombre de personnes hors famille de recensement de 65 ans et plus	425
15	20	15	85	35	45	Vivant avec des personnes apparentées (44)	426
-	20	-	-	15	25	Vivant avec des personnes non apparentées uniquement	427
30	50	25	50	85	280	Vivant seules	428
195	305	145	475	290	570	Nombre de personnes membres d'une famille de 65 ans et plus	429
						CARACTÉRISTIQUES DES FAMILLES ÉCONOMIQUES	
485	**1,530**	**755**	**1,845**	**1,360**	**1,900**	**Nombre total de familles économiques dans les ménages privés**	430
						selon la taille de la famille	
200	605	370	715	610	895	2 personnes	431
90	380	175	340	245	380	3 personnes	432
70	320	170	465	310	355	4 personnes	433
130	230	45	325	190	275	5 personnes ou plus	434
1,645	4,860	2,180	6,110	4,380	5,860	Nombre total de personnes dans les familles économiques	435
3.4	3.2	2.9	3.3	3.2	3.1	Nombre moyen de personnes par famille économique	436
130	255	225	320	425	940	Nombre total de personnes hors famille économique	437
						CARACTÉRISTIQUES DU REVENU DE 2000	
						Population de 15 ans et plus selon le sexe et les tranches de revenu total en 2000	
1,450	3,910	1,860	5,015	3,840	5,315	Total - Les deux sexes	438
70	155	60	285	210	340	Sans revenu	439
1,380	3,755	1,795	4,735	3,630	4,975	Avec un revenu	440
60	125	70	140	150	265	Moins de 1 000 $ (45)	441
70	145	60	200	135	200	1 000 $ - 2 999 $	442
45	125	25	195	145	145	3 000 $ - 4 999 $	443
90	50	40	205	135	200	5 000 $ - 6 999 $	444
70	145	95	200	210	265	7 000 $ - 9 999 $	445
45	140	75	160	120	225	10 000 $ - 11 999 $	446
95	155	100	205	230	375	12 000 $ - 14 999 $	447
230	295	230	355	250	590	15 000 $ - 19 999 $	448
105	300	130	395	245	415	20 000 $ - 24 999 $	449
90	205	95	460	235	445	25 000 $ - 29 999 $	450
90	250	140	325	290	460	30 000 $ - 34 999 $	451
85	195	135	310	250	305	35 000 $ - 39 999 $	452
75	295	180	235	255	330	40 000 $ - 44 999 $	453
60	230	115	250	180	160	45 000 $ - 49 999 $	454
60	430	170	410	305	305	50 000 $ - 59 999 $	455
100	675	130	690	495	285	60 000 $ et plus	456
25,941	38,235	30,348	33,501	33,493	25,906	Revenu moyen $ (46)	457
19,719	33,291	27,929	28,320	28,526	22,383	Revenu médian $ (46)	458
1,386	1,403	1,084	813	1,042	577	Erreur type de revenu moyen $ (46)	459

Table 1. Selected Characteristics for Census Tracts, 2001 Census – 100% Data and 20% Sample Data

No.	Characteristics	Vancouver 0182.03 A	Vancouver 0182.04 A	Vancouver 0182.05 A	Vancouver 0182.06 ◇ A	Vancouver 0183.01	Vancouver 0183.03
	2000 INCOME CHARACTERISTICS						
	Population 15 years and over by sex and total income groups in 2000 – concluded						
460	Total - Males	1,340	600	1,120	510	2,160	2,205
461	Without income	95	20	80	10	65	85
462	With income	1,245	580	1,040	500	2,095	2,120
463	Under $1,000 (45)	50	30	50	10	70	90
464	$ 1,000 - $ 2,999	10	45	15	15	90	80
465	$ 3,000 - $ 4,999	35	25	35	-	70	55
466	$ 5,000 - $ 6,999	65	25	40	-	40	70
467	$ 7,000 - $ 9,999	80	10	25	35	50	105
468	$10,000 - $11,999	60	-	-	25	65	30
469	$12,000 - $14,999	80	10	65	20	110	100
470	$15,000 - $19,999	75	30	90	40	100	135
471	$20,000 - $24,999	105	35	35	25	80	150
472	$25,000 - $29,999	35	25	110	40	115	135
473	$30,000 - $34,999	100	25	65	45	145	170
474	$35,000 - $39,999	75	20	55	25	100	150
475	$40,000 - $44,999	70	30	55	15	170	155
476	$45,000 - $49,999	50	25	30	35	155	175
477	$50,000 - $59,999	90	80	110	80	260	260
478	$60,000 and over	260	175	240	85	475	260
479	Average income $ (46)	42,569	49,333	42,956	37,248	40,595	34,264
480	Median income $ (46)	30,284	43,801	34,116	33,798	40,046	32,821
481	Standard error of average income $ (46)	2,851	4,377	3,967	2,601	1,341	1,142
482	Total - Females	1,285	560	1,095	445	2,215	2,330
483	Without income	105	20	45	25	115	130
484	With income	1,180	540	1,055	420	2,105	2,205
485	Under $1,000 (45)	45	40	45	15	120	90
486	$ 1,000 - $ 2,999	35	40	90	10	130	155
487	$ 3,000 - $ 4,999	40	20	45	10	90	120
488	$ 5,000 - $ 6,999	95	15	45	40	105	130
489	$ 7,000 - $ 9,999	125	65	65	70	180	115
490	$10,000 - $11,999	70	10	65	30	90	135
491	$12,000 - $14,999	80	20	85	50	165	260
492	$15,000 - $19,999	120	40	90	20	210	300
493	$20,000 - $24,999	70	25	95	20	160	155
494	$25,000 - $29,999	75	45	100	55	240	100
495	$30,000 - $34,999	55	60	85	15	165	195
496	$35,000 - $39,999	80	35	35	30	165	140
497	$40,000 - $44,999	95	20	40	-	100	80
498	$45,000 - $49,999	50	10	50	-	65	85
499	$50,000 - $59,999	60	60	30	10	55	70
500	$60,000 and over	85	40	80	20	70	65
501	Average income $ (46)	26,794	26,411	24,163	23,807	22,617	20,884
502	Median income $ (46)	19,437	25,117	18,106	12,716	18,992	16,691
503	Standard error of average income $ (46)	1,786	1,897	1,405	4,747	918	737
	by composition of total income						
504	Total - Composition of income in 2000 % (47)	100.0	100.0	100.0	100.0	100.0	100.0
505	Employment income %	84.1	88.9	81.2	76.4	86.6	79.3
506	Government transfer payments %	6.0	5.2	8.9	7.0	7.9	12.9
507	Other %	9.9	5.9	10.0	16.5	5.5	7.8
	Population 15 years and over with employment income in 2000 by sex and work activity						
508	Both sexes with employment income (48)	1,980	895	1,580	690	3,425	3,095
509	Average employment income $	35,887	42,664	36,079	31,795	33,522	30,376
510	Standard error of average employment income $	1,880	2,950	2,724	2,298	927	850
511	Worked full year, full time (49)	920	500	730	355	2,030	1,700
512	Average employment income $	49,430	57,174	48,259	47,375	45,047	39,659
513	Standard error of average employment income $	3,032	4,308	2,213	3,442	1,176	1,070
514	Worked part year or part time (50)	960	385	800	320	1,330	1,370
515	Average employment income $	26,303	24,092	26,729	15,785	17,191	19,307
516	Standard error of average employment income $	2,147	2,828	4,867	1,632	986	1,062
517	Males with employment income (48)	1,040	495	830	385	1,785	1,695
518	Average employment income $	43,535	52,588	45,472	39,922	43,238	36,548
519	Standard error of average employment income $	3,008	4,877	4,785	2,638	1,433	1,254
520	Worked full year, full time (49)	565	305	465	260	1,305	1,065
521	Average employment income $	55,322	67,876	52,229	49,473	51,218	43,980
522	Standard error of average employment income $	4,090	6,634	3,051	2,944	1,557	1,460
523	Worked part year or part time (50)	440	185	340	120	450	615
524	Average employment income $	31,901	28,651	39,410	19,781	22,225	24,412
525	Standard error of average employment income $	4,244	5,178	10,914	2,946	2,306	1,902

Tableau 1. Certaines caractéristiques des secteurs de recensement, recensement de 2001 – Données intégrales et données-échantillon (20 %)

Vancouver 0183.04 A	Vancouver 0183.05 A	Vancouver 0183.06 A	Vancouver 0183.07 A	Vancouver 0184.01	Vancouver 0184.02 ◇	Caractéristiques	N°
						CARACTÉRISTIQUES DU REVENU DE 2000	
						Population de 15 ans et plus selon le sexe et les tranches de revenu total en 2000 – fin	
745	1,885	885	2,455	1,940	2,485	Total - Hommes	460
25	55	15	75	80	120	Sans revenu	461
720	1,835	870	2,380	1,865	2,360	Avec un revenu	462
20	60	40	65	45	85	Moins de 1 000 $ (45)	463
25	15	-	105	40	95	1 000 $ - 2 999 $	464
20	55	15	90	65	60	3 000 $ - 4 999 $	465
35	10	10	95	40	50	5 000 $ - 6 999 $	466
35	60	70	50	100	95	7 000 $ - 9 999 $	467
-	30	25	50	40	85	10 000 $ - 11 999 $	468
25	55	10	50	90	115	12 000 $ - 14 999 $	469
125	95	105	110	105	275	15 000 $ - 19 999 $	470
80	125	75	145	85	160	20 000 $ - 24 999 $	471
35	95	20	180	110	230	25 000 $ - 29 999 $	472
65	95	60	160	150	200	30 000 $ - 34 999 $	473
65	60	65	135	135	175	35 000 $ - 39 999 $	474
40	135	100	110	165	180	40 000 $ - 44 999 $	475
30	175	60	145	120	85	45 000 $ - 49 999 $	476
45	285	110	305	195	215	50 000 $ - 59 999 $	477
70	480	105	575	385	255	60 000 $ et plus	478
30,638	47,452	35,541	41,738	40,830	31,527	Revenu moyen $ (46)	479
23,696	44,966	35,654	37,514	37,076	27,759	Revenu médian $ (46)	480
2,227	2,509	1,732	1,310	1,578	954	Erreur type de revenu moyen $ (46)	481
705	2,025	975	2,560	1,895	2,835	Total - Femmes	482
45	105	45	210	130	215	Sans revenu	483
655	1,920	930	2,355	1,770	2,615	Avec un revenu	484
40	70	30	75	110	185	Moins de 1 000 $ (45)	485
45	125	60	95	100	105	1 000 $ - 2 999 $	486
25	75	10	100	80	80	3 000 $ - 4 999 $	487
50	45	35	105	90	150	5 000 $ - 6 999 $	488
40	85	30	150	110	170	7 000 $ - 9 999 $	489
40	105	55	110	80	140	10 000 $ - 11 999 $	490
70	100	90	150	145	260	12 000 $ - 14 999 $	491
105	200	130	245	150	310	15 000 $ - 19 999 $	492
30	180	60	250	160	255	20 000 $ - 24 999 $	493
55	110	70	280	125	215	25 000 $ - 29 999 $	494
30	150	80	165	140	260	30 000 $ - 34 999 $	495
20	135	65	170	110	135	35 000 $ - 39 999 $	496
35	155	80	125	90	150	40 000 $ - 44 999 $	497
20	60	60	105	60	70	45 000 $ - 49 999 $	498
20	140	60	105	115	90	50 000 $ - 59 999 $	499
25	195	25	115	105	30	60 000 $ et plus	500
20,791	29,446	25,494	25,173	25,760	20,821	Revenu moyen $ (46)	501
16,635	24,304	21,753	23,629	20,316	17,942	Revenu médian $ (46)	502
1,504	1,151	1,225	817	1,249	606	Erreur type de revenu moyen $ (46)	503
						selon la composition du revenu total	
100.0	100.0	100.0	100.0	100.0	100.0	Total - Composition du revenu en 2000 % (47)	504
76.2	87.3	83.7	83.1	83.2	76.8	Revenu d'emploi %	505
13.8	6.0	9.0	7.7	7.5	16.9	Transferts gouvernementaux %	506
10.2	6.9	7.2	9.1	9.3	6.3	Autre %	507
						Population de 15 ans et plus ayant un revenu d'emploi en 2000 selon le sexe et le travail	
995	3,075	1,470	3,710	2,810	3,365	Les deux sexes ayant un revenu d'emploi (48)	508
27,394	40,699	31,066	35,572	35,965	29,399	Revenu moyen d'emploi $	509
1,725	1,267	1,201	942	1,207	744	Erreur type de revenu moyen d'emploi $	510
490	1,860	855	2,090	1,675	1,845	Ayant travaillé toute l'année à plein temps (49)	511
38,417	51,462	38,730	47,146	45,725	39,121	Revenu moyen d'emploi $	512
2,683	1,692	1,480	1,250	1,478	941	Erreur type de revenu moyen d'emploi $	513
480	1,165	580	1,480	1,110	1,435	Ayant travaillé une partie de l'année ou à temps partiel (50)	514
17,149	24,807	21,019	21,447	21,630	18,117	Revenu moyen d'emploi $	515
1,624	1,431	1,656	1,048	1,729	861	Erreur type de revenu moyen d'emploi $	516
570	1,575	725	1,920	1,530	1,770	Hommes ayant un revenu d'emploi (48)	517
30,202	48,672	37,038	43,969	42,033	34,644	Revenu moyen d'emploi $	518
2,663	2,037	1,906	1,466	1,748	1,137	Erreur type de revenu moyen d'emploi $	519
345	1,100	480	1,295	1,015	1,110	Ayant travaillé toute l'année à plein temps (49)	520
38,141	58,102	44,249	53,306	51,160	43,417	Revenu moyen d'emploi $	521
3,721	2,504	2,163	1,683	2,025	1,360	Erreur type de revenu moyen d'emploi $	522
215	465	220	565	495	640	Ayant travaillé une partie de l'année ou à temps partiel (50)	523
18,245	27,531	23,361	25,407	24,046	20,543	Revenu moyen d'emploi $	524
2,863	2,381	3,064	2,160	2,708	1,404	Erreur type de revenu moyen d'emploi $	525

Table 1. Selected Characteristics for Census Tracts, 2001 Census – 100% Data and 20% Sample Data

No.	Characteristics	Vancouver 0182.03 A	Vancouver 0182.04 A	Vancouver 0182.05 A	Vancouver 0182.06 ◇ A	Vancouver 0183.01	Vancouver 0183.03
	2000 INCOME CHARACTERISTICS						
	Population 15 years and over with employment income in 2000 by sex and work activity – concluded						
526	Females with employment income (48)	935	400	745	305	1,640	1,400
527	Average employment income $	27,390	30,298	25,621	21,510	22,971	22,921
528	Standard error of average employment income $	2,003	2,188	1,649	3,616	886	939
529	Worked full year, full time (49)	355	200	265	90	720	635
530	Average employment income $	40,039	40,744	41,284	41,401	33,859	32,414
531	Standard error of average employment income $	4,230	2,843	2,679	9,145	1,340	1,278
532	Worked part year or part time (50)	525	200	465	195	880	760
533	Average employment income $	21,607	19,889	17,484	13,218	14,631	15,159
534	Standard error of average employment income $	1,613	2,612	1,554	1,731	847	1,012
	Census families by structure and family income groups in 2000						
535	Total - All census families	960	400	820	345	1,615	1,540
536	Under $10,000	45	10	35	10	50	60
537	$ 10,000 - $19,999	75	-	50	30	80	55
538	$ 20,000 - $29,999	60	25	55	15	100	120
539	$ 30,000 - $39,999	80	15	100	30	140	190
540	$ 40,000 - $49,999	95	10	80	35	105	145
541	$ 50,000 - $59,999	90	25	60	30	200	245
542	$ 60,000 - $69,999	40	30	55	60	160	175
543	$ 70,000 - $79,999	60	30	50	25	145	110
544	$ 80,000 - $89,999	80	35	85	45	230	145
545	$ 90,000 - $99,999	45	35	55	-	110	135
546	$100,000 and over	290	190	205	70	300	160
547	Average family income $	82,828	99,034	77,172	72,940	71,695	61,619
548	Median family income $	67,016	98,873	62,611	64,861	69,013	57,947
549	Standard error of average family income $	5,101	6,217	5,702	6,291	2,048	1,832
550	Total - All couple census families (51)	870	395	715	305	1,350	1,265
551	Under $10,000	25	10	25	-	10	45
552	$ 10,000 - $19,999	45	10	20	20	40	25
553	$ 20,000 - $29,999	45	15	55	10	65	85
554	$ 30,000 - $39,999	70	10	90	30	100	135
555	$ 40,000 - $49,999	85	10	80	30	70	130
556	$ 50,000 - $59,999	80	25	40	25	165	195
557	$ 60,000 - $69,999	40	30	40	60	140	140
558	$ 70,000 - $79,999	55	30	40	20	140	95
559	$ 80,000 - $89,999	80	30	85	45	210	140
560	$ 90,000 - $99,999	45	40	45	-	115	130
561	$100,000 and over	285	190	195	65	300	155
562	Average family income $	88,915	100,835	81,951	72,213	78,727	65,493
563	Median family income $	75,023	99,294	70,615	67,592	76,053	60,429
564	Standard error of average family income $	5,410	6,270	6,299	4,308	2,158	2,021
	Incidence of low income in 2000						
565	Total - Economic families	880	395	765	330	1,595	1,530
566	Low income	105	35	75	10	210	175
567	Incidence of low income in 2000 % (52)	12.0	9.1	9.9	2.9	13.1	11.5
568	Total - Unattached individuals 15 years and over	135	50	200	90	385	820
569	Low income	30	15	65	10	110	395
570	Incidence of low income in 2000 % (52)	21.9	32.9	33.6	5.5	28.0	48.3
571	Total - Population in private households	3,430	1,480	2,790	1,200	5,910	5,690
572	Low income	405	135	345	40	790	915
573	Incidence of low income in 2000 % (52)	11.8	9.1	12.4	3.1	13.3	16.1
	Private households by household income groups in 2000						
574	Total - All private households	980	420	890	385	1,890	2,215
575	Under $10,000	15	10	40	10	80	150
576	$ 10,000 - $19,999	80	10	75	25	115	270
577	$ 20,000 - $29,999	65	30	60	25	140	190
578	$ 30,000 - $39,999	85	20	85	30	170	305
579	$ 40,000 - $49,999	110	10	80	50	135	210
580	$ 50,000 - $59,999	100	15	85	50	200	275
581	$ 60,000 - $69,999	50	30	60	55	200	190
582	$ 70,000 - $79,999	50	30	45	35	175	120
583	$ 80,000 - $89,999	85	25	50	50	200	145
584	$ 90,000 - $99,999	50	35	60	10	105	150
585	$100,000 and over	300	205	250	70	365	205
586	Average household income $	86,200	102,349	78,767	74,442	70,160	53,516
587	Median household income $	67,220	99,452	60,267	63,682	64,291	48,951
588	Standard error of average household income $	5,285	6,473	5,553	6,373	2,115	1,624

Tableau 1. Certaines caractéristiques des secteurs de recensement, recensement de 2001 – Données intégrales et données-échantillon (20 %)

Vancouver 0183.04 A	Vancouver 0183.05 A	Vancouver 0183.06 A	Vancouver 0183.07 A	Vancouver 0184.01	Vancouver 0184.02 ◇	Caractéristiques	N°
						CARACTÉRISTIQUES DU REVENU DE 2000	
						Population de 15 ans et plus ayant un revenu d'emploi en 2000 selon le sexe et le travail – fin	
420	1,495	750	1,790	1,285	1,595	Femmes ayant un revenu d'emploi (48)	526
23,609	32,313	25,238	26,554	28,740	23,580	Revenu moyen d'emploi $	527
1,945	1,306	1,299	982	1,538	820	Erreur type de revenu moyen d'emploi $	528
145	760	370	790	665	740	Ayant travaillé toute l'année à plein temps (49)	529
39,075	41,858	31,524	37,074	37,403	32,682	Revenu moyen d'emploi $	530
3,104	1,672	1,598	1,541	1,884	964	Erreur type de revenu moyen d'emploi $	531
260	700	360	915	615	795	Ayant travaillé une partie de l'année ou à temps partiel (50)	532
16,247	22,995	19,571	19,006	19,688	16,170	Revenu moyen d'emploi $	533
1,781	1,767	1,841	1,004	2,232	1,035	Erreur type de revenu moyen d'emploi $	534
						Familles de recensement selon la structure et les tranches de revenu de la famille en 2000	
505	1,550	750	1,890	1,415	1,920	Total - Toutes les familles de recensement	535
10	10	-	75	40	70	Moins de 10 000 $	536
35	20	45	20	55	135	10 000 $ - 19 999 $	537
50	45	40	90	120	260	20 000 $ - 29 999 $	538
85	90	110	155	140	320	30 000 $ - 39 999 $	539
55	125	125	185	65	235	40 000 $ - 49 999 $	540
50	125	100	160	165	195	50 000 $ - 59 999 $	541
45	160	105	180	160	210	60 000 $ - 69 999 $	542
65	225	65	255	180	155	70 000 $ - 79 999 $	543
25	145	70	165	125	145	80 000 $ - 89 999 $	544
30	120	35	125	75	85	90 000 $ - 99 999 $	545
70	480	60	480	290	110	100 000 $ et plus	546
61,061	85,782	60,635	75,999	74,379	52,207	Revenu moyen des familles $	547
58,072	79,321	55,645	73,304	67,333	47,951	Revenu médian des familles $	548
3,384	3,238	2,373	1,892	2,763	1,389	Erreur type de revenu moyen des familles $	549
420	1,420	610	1,730	1,285	1,515	Total - Toutes les familles de recensement comptant un couple (51)	550
15	-	-	65	30	60	Moins de 10 000 $	551
25	15	25	20	35	55	10 000 $ - 19 999 $	552
35	40	30	65	85	150	20 000 $ - 29 999 $	553
45	75	75	110	115	240	30 000 $ - 39 999 $	554
40	100	95	150	55	185	40 000 $ - 49 999 $	555
40	110	95	150	155	165	50 000 $ - 59 999 $	556
40	125	105	155	155	170	60 000 $ - 69 999 $	557
60	220	50	245	175	145	70 000 $ - 79 999 $	558
25	140	60	165	125	140	80 000 $ - 89 999 $	559
30	120	35	125	80	85	90 000 $ - 99 999 $	560
65	460	40	480	275	115	100 000 $ et plus	561
66,775	88,116	61,333	78,979	77,763	56,991	Revenu moyen des familles $	562
62,363	81,931	57,009	75,681	71,169	51,851	Revenu médian des familles $	563
3,693	3,431	2,461	1,991	2,929	1,597	Erreur type de revenu moyen des familles $	564
						Fréquence des unités à faible revenu en 2000	
485	1,530	755	1,850	1,360	1,905	Total - Familles économiques	565
60	50	70	120	125	360	Faible revenu	566
11.6	3.4	8.9	6.4	9.3	18.8	Fréquence des unités à faible revenu en 2000 % (52)	567
135	230	210	320	415	935	Total - Personnes hors famille économique de 15 ans et plus	568
60	60	60	75	160	385	Faible revenu	569
43.0	26.1	29.8	24.4	38.8	40.9	Fréquence des unités à faible revenu en 2000 % (52)	570
1,780	5,095	2,385	6,425	4,795	6,800	Total - Population dans les ménages privés	571
235	220	275	420	610	1,520	Faible revenu	572
13.3	4.3	11.5	6.5	12.8	22.3	Fréquence des unités à faible revenu en 2000 % (52)	573
						Ménages privés selon les tranches de revenu du ménage en 2000	
585	1,675	905	2,040	1,640	2,685	Total - Tous les ménages privés	574
20	20	-	40	55	120	Moins de 10 000 $	575
60	30	70	60	110	330	10 000 $ - 19 999 $	576
80	60	55	110	140	365	20 000 $ - 29 999 $	577
70	105	120	150	145	435	30 000 $ - 39 999 $	578
40	150	130	205	80	330	40 000 $ - 49 999 $	579
70	145	125	165	180	265	50 000 $ - 59 999 $	580
40	125	135	160	140	260	60 000 $ - 69 999 $	581
55	220	75	265	185	175	70 000 $ - 79 999 $	582
40	170	65	195	155	150	80 000 $ - 89 999 $	583
35	130	45	125	110	100	90 000 $ - 99 999 $	584
80	525	90	560	340	140	100 000 $ et plus	585
60,780	85,669	60,286	77,574	74,035	47,787	Revenu moyen des ménages $	586
57,307	79,702	55,020	73,499	68,435	41,893	Revenu médian des ménages $	587
3,698	3,149	2,213	1,887	2,743	1,193	Erreur type de revenu moyen des ménages $	588

Table 1. Selected Characteristics for Census Tracts, 2001 Census – 100% Data and 20% Sample Data

No.	Characteristics	Vancouver 0184.05	Vancouver 0184.06 A	Vancouver 0184.07 A	Vancouver 0184.08 A	Vancouver 0184.09 A	Vancouver 0184.10 A
	POPULATION CHARACTERISTICS						
1	**Population, 1996 (1)**	7,165	1,284	4,238	3,225	4,207	2,242
2	**Population, 2001 (2)**	7,844	1,371	4,954	3,508	4,471	3,150
3	Population percentage change, 1996-2001	9.5	6.8	16.9	8.8	6.3	40.5
4	Land area in square kilometres, 2001	2.65	2.67	1.32	1.31	1.30	1.34
5	**Total population – 100% Data (3)**	7,840	1,370	4,955	3,510	4,470	3,150
	by sex and age groups						
6	Male	3,955	705	2,270	1,705	2,240	1,575
7	0-4 years	280	30	170	150	170	115
8	5-9 years	310	55	200	185	225	140
9	10-14 years	340	55	185	170	190	140
10	15-19 years	350	50	145	110	185	135
11	20-24 years	270	40	125	105	170	135
12	25-29 years	250	40	135	100	140	110
13	30-34 years	265	40	165	115	160	110
14	35-39 years	310	60	180	190	210	125
15	40-44 years	360	65	180	160	205	105
16	45-49 years	315	50	135	125	170	110
17	50-54 years	325	40	135	80	155	125
18	55-59 years	180	30	110	75	90	65
19	60-64 years	130	35	85	35	65	50
20	65-69 years	110	45	90	40	50	30
21	70-74 years	65	25	90	30	30	35
22	75-79 years	45	30	60	10	15	20
23	80-84 years	15	5	50	5	10	10
24	85 years and over	20	10	35	5	5	10
25	Female	3,890	665	2,685	1,800	2,235	1,570
26	0-4 years	235	25	150	145	165	100
27	5-9 years	310	40	175	180	200	115
28	10-14 years	325	50	170	165	195	135
29	15-19 years	300	55	155	115	180	125
30	20-24 years	330	45	150	110	170	145
31	25-29 years	240	30	145	125	155	130
32	30-34 years	295	40	185	165	180	95
33	35-39 years	330	55	220	220	195	135
34	40-44 years	360	50	180	155	205	125
35	45-49 years	320	50	170	110	175	120
36	50-54 years	285	40	170	95	150	90
37	55-59 years	170	35	130	65	85	65
38	60-64 years	135	40	120	40	60	50
39	65-69 years	100	35	130	45	30	40
40	70-74 years	65	35	120	25	35	35
41	75-79 years	40	15	125	30	35	25
42	80-84 years	35	10	105	10	10	15
43	85 years and over	15	10	85	5	5	5
44	**Total population 15 years and over**	6,035	1,110	3,900	2,510	3,330	2,405
	by legal marital status						
45	Never married (single)	1,785	340	885	695	1,015	695
46	Legally married (and not separated)	3,620	620	2,135	1,410	1,970	1,410
47	Separated, but still legally married	145	40	150	100	75	70
48	Divorced	255	60	315	200	160	115
49	Widowed	230	50	420	95	110	110
	by common-law status						
50	Not in a common-law relationship	5,810	1,045	3,730	2,365	3,210	2,340
51	In a common-law relationship	225	65	170	150	120	65
52	**Total population – 20% Sample Data (4)**	7,825	1,370	4,830	3,510	4,470	3,145
	by mother tongue						
53	Single responses	7,600	1,345	4,785	3,465	4,320	3,085
54	English	4,130	865	2,950	2,400	2,755	1,265
55	French	70	10	40	35	10	10
56	Non-official languages (5)	3,395	475	1,795	1,030	1,555	1,810
57	Chinese, n.o.s.	255	-	60	-	90	75
58	Cantonese	140	15	40	-	70	25
59	Punjabi	1,530	350	955	485	645	1,395
60	Mandarin	155	-	15	-	25	10
61	Tagalog (Pilipino)	140	-	55	30	100	30
62	Other languages (6)	1,175	115	665	520	630	270
63	Multiple responses	230	25	45	45	145	60
64	English and French	-	-	10	-	-	-
65	English and non-official language	195	20	40	50	145	60
66	French and non-official language	10	-	-	-	-	-
67	English, French and non-official language	25	10	-	-	-	-

See reference material at the end of the publication. – Voir les documents de référence à la fin de la publication.

Tableau 1. Certaines caractéristiques des secteurs de recensement, recensement de 2001 – Données intégrales et données-échantillon (20 %)

Vancouver 0184.11 A	Vancouver 0185.05	Vancouver 0185.06 A	Vancouver 0185.07 A	Vancouver 0185.08 A	Vancouver 0185.09 A	Caractéristiques	N°
						CARACTÉRISTIQUES DE LA POPULATION	
1,444	**4,737**	**4,754**	**4,943**	**1,186**	**3,514**	**Population, 1996 (1)**	1
3,281	**4,883**	**7,052**	**5,548**	**1,209**	**3,890**	**Population, 2001 (2)**	2
127.2	3.1	48.3	12.2	1.9	10.7	Variation en pourcentage de la population, 1996-2001	3
2.58	1.34	2.66	2.62	3.75	2.69	Superficie des terres en kilomètres carrés, 2001	4
3,280	**4,880**	**7,050**	**5,550**	**1,205**	**3,895**	**Population totale – Données intégrales (3)**	5
						selon le sexe et les groupes d'âge	
1,615	2,415	3,440	2,780	610	1,885	Sexe masculin	6
110	230	205	240	20	155	0-4 ans	7
135	260	245	245	30	135	5-9 ans	8
115	205	280	240	45	100	10-14 ans	9
120	190	270	205	60	100	15-19 ans	10
135	145	245	180	45	160	20-24 ans	11
125	165	210	160	15	190	25-29 ans	12
120	200	225	215	20	215	30-34 ans	13
160	200	235	215	20	170	35-39 ans	14
125	235	240	245	60	140	40-44 ans	15
135	180	315	220	60	115	45-49 ans	16
110	115	290	185	60	85	50-54 ans	17
75	85	230	120	55	85	55-59 ans	18
60	65	175	95	40	75	60-64 ans	19
35	40	110	90	35	45	65-69 ans	20
20	40	90	45	25	45	70-74 ans	21
10	25	40	45	10	25	75-79 ans	22
5	10	35	20	5	20	80-84 ans	23
5	5	20	15	-	10	85 ans et plus	24
1,670	2,465	3,610	2,770	600	2,005	Sexe féminin	25
130	230	230	215	15	175	0-4 ans	26
110	230	225	255	30	130	5-9 ans	27
120	190	245	210	55	85	10-14 ans	28
140	175	265	175	60	95	15-19 ans	29
140	155	305	160	30	150	20-24 ans	30
125	185	235	210	10	235	25-29 ans	31
155	220	240	230	30	205	30-34 ans	32
120	245	225	250	35	155	35-39 ans	33
150	235	320	245	55	130	40-44 ans	34
145	160	305	200	55	130	45-49 ans	35
105	135	300	165	65	140	50-54 ans	36
85	95	205	115	55	75	55-59 ans	37
50	65	160	120	30	75	60-64 ans	38
35	45	115	70	25	70	65-69 ans	39
25	40	105	65	25	60	70-74 ans	40
15	30	80	45	15	45	75-79 ans	41
15	30	45	25	10	30	80-84 ans	42
5	10	20	25	5	15	85 ans et plus	43
2,565	**3,535**	**5,625**	**4,145**	**1,010**	**3,105**	**Population totale de 15 ans et plus**	44
						selon l'état matrimonial légal	
765	1,145	1,420	1,070	275	930	Célibataire (jamais marié(e))	45
1,540	1,785	3,570	2,600	610	1,655	Légalement marié(e) (et non séparé(e))	46
60	170	145	105	25	120	Séparé(e), mais toujours légalement marié(e)	47
110	295	255	190	50	230	Divorcé(e)	48
85	145	235	180	45	170	Veuf ou veuve	49
						selon l'union libre	
2,425	3,285	5,450	3,985	960	2,920	Ne vivant pas en union libre	50
130	255	180	160	50	180	Vivant en union libre	51
3,280	**4,885**	**7,050**	**5,540**	**1,210**	**3,890**	**Population totale – Données-échantillon (20 %) (4)**	52
						selon la langue maternelle	
3,205	4,735	6,790	5,405	1,200	3,760	Réponses uniques	53
2,110	2,840	3,830	2,745	955	2,225	Anglais	54
20	60	80	40	25	30	Français	55
1,075	1,830	2,870	2,620	215	1,505	Langues non officielles (5)	56
10	15	195	50	15	30	Chinois, n.d.a.	57
10	25	85	80	10	50	Cantonais	58
645	830	1,625	1,545	65	825	Pendjabi	59
10	-	100	-	20	10	Mandarin	60
40	80	35	65	10	35	Tagalog (pilipino)	61
365	890	825	880	105	565	Autres langues (6)	62
70	150	265	130	10	130	Réponses multiples	63
20	35	-	20	-	50	Anglais et français	64
30	115	260	110	10	75	Anglais et langue non officielle	65
30	-	-	-	-	-	Français et langue non officielle	66
-	10	-	-	-	-	Anglais, français et langue non officielle	67

See reference material at the end of the publication. – Voir les documents de référence à la fin de la publication.

Table 1. Selected Characteristics for Census Tracts, 2001 Census – 100% Data and 20% Sample Data

No.	Characteristics	Vancouver 0184.05	Vancouver 0184.06 A	Vancouver 0184.07 A	Vancouver 0184.08 A	Vancouver 0184.09 A	Vancouver 0184.10 A
	POPULATION CHARACTERISTICS						
	by home language						
68	Single responses	5,755	1,065	3,720	3,000	3,515	2,125
69	English	4,355	955	3,245	2,555	2,790	1,325
70	French	-	-	10	-	-	-
71	Non-official languages (5)	1,395	110	465	445	720	805
72	Cantonese	45	-	15	-	50	10
73	Chinese, n.o.s.	60	-	25	-	15	45
74	Punjabi	630	95	265	275	415	680
75	Mandarin	110	-	-	-	30	10
76	Korean	15	-	-	-	15	-
77	Other languages (6)	540	20	150	175	205	65
78	Multiple responses	2,075	305	1,110	505	955	1,020
79	English and French	30	-	30	20	10	10
80	English and non-official language	1,990	305	1,065	475	880	1,015
81	French and non-official language	-	-	-	10	-	-
82	English, French and non-official language	50	-	15	-	75	-
	by knowledge of official languages						
83	English only	7,040	1,225	4,380	3,205	4,110	2,720
84	French only	-	-	10	-	-	-
85	English and French	365	65	270	190	145	130
86	Neither English nor French	420	85	165	120	205	295
	by knowledge of non-official languages (5) (7)						
87	Cantonese	135	15	40	10	105	25
88	Chinese, n.o.s.	270	-	45	10	75	80
89	Punjabi	1,815	375	1,055	510	775	1,660
90	Mandarin	255	10	40	-	60	25
91	Hindi	985	55	310	180	355	385
92	German	90	45	95	25	75	40
93	Spanish	105	-	80	115	30	-
	by first official language spoken						
94	English	7,310	1,285	4,600	3,330	4,245	2,840
95	French	80	10	55	25	10	10
96	English and French	65	-	25	35	10	10
97	Neither English nor French	380	85	155	120	205	295
98	Official language minority - (number) (8)	105	-	65	45	15	10
99	Official language minority - (percentage) (8)	1.3	-	1.3	1.3	0.3	0.3
	by ethnic origin (9)						
100	English	1,500	415	1,090	855	955	305
101	Canadian	1,190	315	770	885	850	365
102	Chinese	735	15	185	60	275	160
103	Scottish	935	215	685	640	665	195
104	Irish	680	160	540	385	305	195
105	German	840	215	435	325	350	155
106	East Indian	2,050	255	1,030	665	725	1,650
107	French	415	85	415	430	165	100
108	Ukrainian	175	110	150	305	205	55
109	Italian	150	20	100	60	65	35
110	Dutch (Netherlands)	220	40	225	140	145	65
111	Filipino	300	-	200	105	365	100
112	Polish	60	50	75	150	190	-
113	Norwegian	150	60	85	70	110	35
114	North American Indian	75	-	125	270	115	10
	by Aboriginal identity						
115	Total Aboriginal identity population (10)	85	10	60	110	125	15
116	Total non-Aboriginal population	7,745	1,365	4,770	3,400	4,345	3,135
	by Aboriginal origin						
117	Total Aboriginal origins population (11)	110	10	165	325	155	40
118	Total non-Aboriginal population	7,720	1,360	4,670	3,185	4,315	3,110
	by Registered Indian status						
119	Registered Indian (12)	-	-	15	-	20	-
120	Not a Registered Indian	7,825	1,370	4,810	3,505	4,445	3,140

Tableau 1. Certaines caractéristiques des secteurs de recensement, recensement de 2001 – Données intégrales et données-échantillon (20 %)

Vancouver 0184.11 A	Vancouver 0185.05	Vancouver 0185.06 A	Vancouver 0185.07 A	Vancouver 0185.08 A	Vancouver 0185.09 A	Caractéristiques	N°
						CARACTÉRISTIQUES DE LA POPULATION	
						selon la langue parlée à la maison	
2,655	3,940	5,330	4,425	1,125	3,095	Réponses uniques	68
2,265	2,925	4,345	3,335	1,055	2,280	Anglais	69
-	15	15	-	-	-	Français	70
390	1,005	970	1,095	70	815	Langues non officielles (5)	71
-	10	60	65	-	40	Cantonais	72
-	15	25	35	-	20	Chinois, n.d.a.	73
320	600	630	705	10	580	Pendjabi	74
10	-	75	-	55	10	Mandarin	75
-	-	30	-	-	30	Coréen	76
60	385	150	290	10	150	Autres langues (6)	77
630	945	1,725	1,110	85	795	Réponses multiples	78
50	25	80	40	25	55	Anglais et français	79
540	920	1,640	1,055	60	720	Anglais et langue non officielle	80
-	-	-	-	-	10	Français et langue non officielle	81
35	-	-	15	-	10	Anglais, français et langue non officielle	82
						selon la connaissance des langues officielles	
3,010	4,435	6,415	4,970	1,060	3,520	Anglais seulement	83
-	10	-	20	-	-	Français seulement	84
135	185	395	265	130	170	Anglais et français	85
135	260	245	280	10	200	Ni l'anglais ni le français	86
						selon la connaissance des langues non officielles (5) (7)	
10	25	110	130	10	45	Cantonais	87
10	15	145	50	-	20	Chinois, n.d.a.	88
725	930	1,935	1,755	65	1,015	Pendjabi	89
20	10	210	10	50	50	Mandarin	90
185	490	640	720	25	705	Hindi	91
55	130	220	80	70	45	Allemand	92
85	140	55	65	15	130	Espagnol	93
						selon la première langue officielle parlée	
3,110	4,565	6,735	5,170	1,165	3,660	Anglais	94
-	50	75	55	30	25	Français	95
30	10	15	40	10	10	Anglais et français	96
140	250	230	275	15	200	Ni l'anglais ni le français	97
20	60	85	80	30	30	Minorité de langue officielle - (nombre) (8)	98
0.6	1.2	1.2	1.4	2.5	0.8	Minorité de langue officielle - (pourcentage) (8)	99
						selon l'origine ethnique (9)	
785	1,040	1,360	1,165	365	800	Anglais	100
890	935	1,170	1,085	290	835	Canadien	101
60	50	520	240	80	115	Chinois	102
445	675	980	670	315	595	Écossais	103
490	485	695	465	180	430	Irlandais	104
365	570	610	530	65	270	Allemand	105
660	1,120	2,035	2,155	130	1,165	Indien de l'Inde	106
305	400	320	270	45	170	Français	107
145	145	195	200	35	90	Ukrainien	108
275	85	120	85	80	80	Italien	109
110	115	230	100	25	95	Hollandais (Néerlandais)	110
95	210	85	90	25	90	Philippin	111
75	175	200	135	25	40	Polonais	112
80	95	165	70	60	65	Norvégien	113
50	200	80	60	15	50	Indien de l'Amérique du Nord	114
						selon l'identité autochtone	
45	210	55	60	15	75	Total de la population ayant une identité autochtone (10)	115
3,235	4,670	6,995	5,475	1,200	3,815	Total de la population non autochtone	116
						selon l'origine autochtone	
95	270	105	95	20	60	Total de la population ayant une origine autochtone (11)	117
3,185	4,615	6,950	5,445	1,190	3,830	Total de la population non autochtone	118
						selon le statut d'Indien inscrit	
10	55	20	15	10	15	Oui, Indien inscrit (12)	119
3,270	4,825	7,030	5,520	1,200	3,880	Non, pas un Indien inscrit	120

Table 1. Selected Characteristics for Census Tracts, 2001 Census – 100% Data and 20% Sample Data

No.	Characteristics	Vancouver 0184.05	Vancouver 0184.06 A	Vancouver 0184.07 A	Vancouver 0184.08 A	Vancouver 0184.09 A	Vancouver 0184.10 A
	POPULATION CHARACTERISTICS						
	by visible minority groups						
121	Total visible minority population	4,070	420	1,860	1,210	1,910	2,085
122	Chinese	615	15	180	20	275	150
123	South Asian	2,505	385	1,300	785	1,090	1,780
124	Black	30	-	85	95	15	-
125	Filipino	265	-	175	110	360	100
126	Latin American	50	-	40	75	15	-
127	Southeast Asian	350	20	10	35	75	15
128	Arab	-	-	10	15	15	-
129	West Asian	10	-	15	45	-	15
130	Korean	40	-	15	-	35	10
131	Japanese	100	-	15	-	35	-
132	Visible minority, n.i.e. (13)	-	-	-	25	-	-
133	Multiple visible minorities (14)	105	-	30	10	-	15
	by citizenship						
134	Canadian citizenship (15)	6,870	1,280	4,305	3,250	4,145	2,750
135	Citizenship other than Canadian	950	95	525	260	325	395
	by place of birth of respondent						
136	Non-immigrant population	4,755	1,025	3,215	2,540	2,945	1,745
137	Born in province of residence	3,695	635	2,290	1,900	2,365	1,420
138	Immigrant population (16)	3,005	345	1,575	960	1,520	1,365
139	United States	90	15	65	30	-	15
140	Central and South America	75	-	45	65	15	-
141	Caribbean and Bermuda	10	-	10	30	20	-
142	United Kingdom	70	35	190	160	115	120
143	Other Europe (17)	290	35	220	85	240	65
144	Africa	35	-	30	35	10	10
145	Asia and the Middle East	2,080	240	955	505	980	1,105
146	Oceania and other (18)	355	20	70	55	140	50
147	Non-permanent residents (19)	75	-	35	10	10	45
148	**Total immigrant population**	**3,000**	**340**	**1,580**	**960**	**1,520**	**1,365**
	by period of immigration						
149	Before 1961	175	90	155	85	70	55
150	1961-1970	290	10	180	65	150	80
151	1971-1980	490	70	315	120	400	385
152	1981-1990	765	70	340	305	380	360
153	1991-2001 (20)	1,280	110	585	385	520	480
154	1991-1995	760	85	225	255	285	225
155	1996-2001 (20)	520	20	355	130	235	255
	by age at immigration						
156	0-4 years	255	25	165	65	155	65
157	5-19 years	870	140	320	305	360	415
158	20 years and over	1,875	175	1,090	585	1,000	890
159	**Total population**	**7,825**	**1,375**	**4,830**	**3,510**	**4,470**	**3,150**
	by religion						
160	Catholic (21)	1,025	165	800	575	960	340
161	Protestant	1,660	450	1,365	730	1,010	500
162	Christian Orthodox	65	-	30	20	-	20
163	Christian, n.i.e. (22)	435	25	250	165	315	115
164	Muslim	200	-	50	195	85	70
165	Jewish	-	-	20	-	-	-
166	Buddhist	345	20	65	10	40	40
167	Hindu	405	10	200	90	220	75
168	Sikh	1,805	370	980	530	760	1,630
169	Eastern religions (23)	-	-	-	-	-	-
170	Other religions (24)	-	-	25	35	-	10
171	No religious affiliation (25)	1,880	320	1,035	1,160	1,075	355
172	**Total population 15 years and over**	**5,980**	**1,080**	**3,775**	**2,510**	**3,335**	**2,425**
	by generation status						
173	1st generation (26)	2,935	335	1,505	945	1,470	1,355
174	2nd generation (27)	1,295	340	865	535	745	520
175	3rd generation and over (28)	1,745	400	1,410	1,030	1,120	555
176	**Total population 1 year and over (29)**	**7,720**	**1,375**	**4,750**	**3,460**	**4,415**	**3,100**
	by place of residence 1 year ago (mobility)						
177	Non-movers	6,670	1,025	4,035	2,935	3,880	2,395
178	Movers	1,055	345	720	530	530	705
179	Non-migrants	605	285	450	455	330	520
180	Migrants	445	65	275	80	195	185
181	Internal migrants	240	55	175	65	165	120
182	Intraprovincial migrants	210	30	155	70	150	35
183	Interprovincial migrants	25	25	15	-	20	80
184	External migrants	205	15	100	10	30	70

Tableau 1. Certaines caractéristiques des secteurs de recensement, recensement de 2001 – Données intégrales et données-échantillon (20 %)

Vancouver 0184.11 A	Vancouver 0185.05	Vancouver 0185.06 A	Vancouver 0185.07 A	Vancouver 0185.08 A	Vancouver 0185.09 A	Caractéristiques	N°
						CARACTÉRISTIQUES DE LA POPULATION	
						selon les groupes de minorités visibles	
1,185	2,055	3,260	2,865	280	1,670	Total de la population des minorités visibles	121
45	50	540	215	90	100	Chinois	122
820	1,290	2,480	2,385	125	1,310	Sud-Asiatique	123
20	60	45	100	-	15	Noir	124
80	205	55	70	15	65	Philippin	125
30	105	10	20	-	105	Latino-Américain	126
115	45	45	-	-	10	Asiatique du Sud-Est	127
-	205	-	-	-	-	Arabe	128
-	40	-	10	-	-	Asiatique occidental	129
10	20	15	-	-	30	Coréen	130
25	20	15	20	35	10	Japonais	131
20	-	15	15	-	10	Minorité visible, n.i.a. (13)	132
15	10	40	35	-	20	Minorités visibles multiples (14)	133
						selon la citoyenneté	
2,890	4,300	6,315	4,900	1,165	3,300	Citoyenneté canadienne (15)	134
390	585	740	640	45	595	Citoyenneté autre que canadienne	135
						selon le lieu de naissance du répondant	
2,235	3,120	4,485	3,415	960	2,420	Population non immigrante	136
1,810	2,375	3,335	2,745	685	1,830	Née dans la province de résidence	137
1,030	1,725	2,565	2,105	235	1,445	Population immigrante (16)	138
80	35	100	25	10	35	États-Unis	139
30	95	15	60	15	60	Amérique centrale et du Sud	140
-	15	90	10	-	10	Caraïbes et Bermudes	141
95	80	260	175	15	105	Royaume-Uni	142
105	230	285	135	70	105	Autre Europe (17)	143
85	45	85	80	20	65	Afrique	144
580	1,040	1,570	1,380	105	885	Asie et Moyen-Orient	145
55	180	170	230	-	180	Océanie et autre (18)	146
10	40	10	20	15	30	Résidents non permanents (19)	147
1,030	**1,720**	**2,565**	**2,100**	**235**	**1,440**	**Population immigrante totale**	148
						selon la période d'immigration	
55	60	265	130	50	75	Avant 1961	149
130	35	265	165	75	60	1961-1970	150
265	325	585	570	50	210	1971-1980	151
100	490	540	425	35	200	1981-1990	152
490	815	910	810	25	900	1991-2001 (20)	153
260	430	430	520	10	445	1991-1995	154
235	385	485	290	20	460	1996-2001 (20)	155
						selon l'âge à l'immigration	
120	225	245	150	10	85	0-4 ans	156
320	480	815	565	65	340	5-19 ans	157
600	1,015	1,510	1,385	160	1,020	20 ans et plus	158
3,275	**4,880**	**7,055**	**5,535**	**1,210**	**3,890**	**Population totale**	159
						selon la religion	
665	775	910	665	240	530	Catholique (21)	160
805	960	1,790	1,260	295	835	Protestante	161
10	30	50	15	-	15	Orthodoxe chrétienne	162
115	350	205	205	45	255	Chrétiennes, n.i.a. (22)	163
150	325	180	455	60	50	Musulmane	164
-	-	20	10	-	50	Juive	165
35	20	80	30	20	20	Bouddhiste	166
40	280	270	340	-	285	Hindoue	167
645	860	1,905	1,675	65	945	Sikh	168
-	-	20	-	-	-	Religions orientales (23)	169
-	25	10	-	-	-	Autres religions (24)	170
815	1,255	1,615	885	470	905	Aucune appartenance religieuse (25)	171
2,595	**3,535**	**5,625**	**4,130**	**1,015**	**3,100**	**Population totale de 15 ans et plus**	172
						selon le statut des générations	
995	1,555	2,445	2,025	245	1,435	1re génération (26)	173
575	610	1,440	1,030	300	645	2e génération (27)	174
1,025	1,370	1,740	1,080	475	1,020	3e génération et plus (28)	175
3,190	**4,795**	**6,965**	**5,470**	**1,205**	**3,800**	**Population totale de 1 an et plus (29)**	176
						selon le lieu de résidence 1 an auparavant (mobilité)	
2,380	3,840	5,845	4,840	1,145	2,865	Personnes n'ayant pas déménagé	177
805	955	1,110	630	60	935	Personnes ayant déménagé	178
600	545	770	375	40	505	Non-migrants	179
210	410	350	260	20	435	Migrants	180
150	180	265	220	20	230	Migrants internes	181
120	145	235	170	25	200	Migrants infraprovinciaux	182
30	35	30	55	-	30	Migrants interprovinciaux	183
60	230	85	35	-	205	Migrants externes	184

Table 1. Selected Characteristics for Census Tracts, 2001 Census – 100% Data and 20% Sample Data

No.	Characteristics	Vancouver 0184.05	Vancouver 0184.06 A	Vancouver 0184.07 A	Vancouver 0184.08 A	Vancouver 0184.09 A	Vancouver 0184.10 A
	POPULATION CHARACTERISTICS						
185	**Total population 5 years and over (30)**	**7,250**	**1,320**	**4,505**	**3,230**	**4,135**	**2,930**
	by place of residence 5 years ago (mobility)						
186	Non-movers	4,110	790	2,295	1,845	2,555	1,315
187	Movers	3,145	530	2,215	1,385	1,585	1,610
188	Non-migrants	1,810	315	1,390	905	970	1,110
189	Migrants	1,335	210	825	480	605	500
190	Internal migrants	905	200	565	375	445	285
191	Intraprovincial migrants	755	175	505	290	390	175
192	Interprovincial migrants	155	25	60	85	60	110
193	External migrants	430	15	260	105	160	220
194	**Total population 15 to 24 years**	**1,250**	**140**	**560**	**415**	**690**	**540**
	by school attendance						
195	Not attending school	445	75	205	205	280	215
196	Attending school full time	720	35	280	155	345	265
197	Attending school part time	85	35	75	55	65	65
198	**Total population 15 years and over**	**5,980**	**1,080**	**3,775**	**2,510**	**3,330**	**2,430**
	by highest level of schooling						
199	Less than grade 9 (31)	460	120	310	185	275	235
200	Grades 9-13 without high school graduation certificate	1,535	305	1,035	490	795	525
201	Grades 9-13 with high school graduation certificate	925	145	590	385	615	425
202	Some postsecondary without degree, certificate or diploma (32)	725	130	400	385	470	330
203	Trades certificate or diploma (33)	620	105	385	425	405	235
204	College certificate or diploma (34)	770	190	540	405	435	310
205	University certificate below bachelor's degree	165	10	170	55	70	65
206	University with bachelor's degree or higher	785	80	340	185	280	310
	by combinations of unpaid work						
207	Males 15 years and over	2,985	545	1,690	1,190	1,660	1,180
208	Reported unpaid work (35)	2,705	535	1,525	1,070	1,445	1,000
209	Housework and child care and care or assistance to seniors	395	25	145	105	160	130
210	Housework and child care only	840	210	500	395	595	325
211	Housework and care or assistance to seniors only	225	25	85	65	45	50
212	Child care and care or assistance to seniors only	10	-	-	20	10	-
213	Housework only	1,205	275	790	480	635	465
214	Child care only	20	-	10	10	10	15
215	Care or assistance to seniors only	10	-	-	10	-	15
216	Females 15 years and over	2,995	530	2,085	1,320	1,675	1,245
217	Reported unpaid work (35)	2,785	525	1,905	1,265	1,455	1,190
218	Housework and child care and care or assistance to seniors	515	55	265	190	185	195
219	Housework and child care only	995	210	620	515	755	475
220	Housework and care or assistance to seniors only	210	55	170	85	60	55
221	Child care and care or assistance to seniors only	-	-	-	15	-	-
222	Housework only	1,025	180	840	435	400	430
223	Child care only	30	10	-	25	50	20
224	Care or assistance to seniors only	-	10	-	-	-	-
	by labour force activity						
225	Males 15 years and over	2,985	550	1,685	1,190	1,660	1,185
226	In the labour force	2,235	380	1,185	965	1,215	900
227	Employed	2,055	365	1,050	885	1,130	850
228	Unemployed	185	15	140	85	80	50
229	Not in the labour force	750	165	500	220	445	285
230	Participation rate	74.9	69.1	70.3	81.1	73.2	75.9
231	Employment rate	68.8	66.4	62.3	74.4	68.1	71.7
232	Unemployment rate	8.3	3.9	11.8	8.8	6.6	5.6
233	Females 15 years and over	2,990	530	2,085	1,325	1,675	1,245
234	In the labour force	1,965	260	1,185	960	1,005	765
235	Employed	1,800	245	1,095	865	955	720
236	Unemployed	165	15	90	100	55	45
237	Not in the labour force	1,030	270	905	365	665	485
238	Participation rate	65.7	49.1	56.8	72.5	60.0	61.4
239	Employment rate	60.2	46.2	52.5	65.3	57.0	57.8
240	Unemployment rate	8.4	5.8	7.6	10.4	5.5	5.9

Tableau 1. Certaines caractéristiques des secteurs de recensement, recensement de 2001 – Données intégrales et données-échantillon (20 %)

Vancouver 0184.11 A	Vancouver 0185.05	Vancouver 0185.06 A	Vancouver 0185.07 A	Vancouver 0185.08 A	Vancouver 0185.09 A	Caractéristiques	N°
						CARACTÉRISTIQUES DE LA POPULATION	
3,025	**4,415**	**6,615**	**5,080**	**1,165**	**3,555**	**Population totale de 5 ans et plus (30)**	185
						selon le lieu de résidence 5 ans auparavant (mobilité)	
1,045	2,030	3,055	2,850	845	1,335	Personnes n'ayant pas déménagé	186
1,975	2,385	3,560	2,235	325	2,215	Personnes ayant déménagé	187
1,250	1,350	2,045	1,520	135	1,220	Non-migrants	188
725	1,030	1,515	715	190	1,005	Migrants	189
500	700	1,095	535	155	605	Migrants internes	190
425	615	940	450	145	545	Migrants infraprovinciaux	191
70	80	155	85	10	60	Migrants interprovinciaux	192
225	330	420	180	35	395	Migrants externes	193
610	**655**	**1,085**	**720**	**195**	**495**	**Population totale de 15 à 24 ans**	194
						selon la fréquentation scolaire	
245	215	330	220	75	280	Ne fréquentant pas l'école	195
300	285	665	430	75	160	Fréquentant l'école à plein temps	196
65	145	90	75	50	55	Fréquentant l'école à temps partiel	197
2,595	**3,535**	**5,625**	**4,130**	**1,015**	**3,100**	**Population totale de 15 ans et plus**	198
						selon le plus haut niveau de scolarité atteint	
125	250	315	330	40	345	Niveau inférieur à la 9e année (31)	199
460	925	1,080	830	210	650	De la 9e à la 13e année sans certificat d'études secondaires	200
325	550	755	720	100	480	De la 9e à la 13e année avec certificat d'études secondaires	201
415	420	785	445	120	405	Études postsecondaires partielles sans grade, certificat ou diplôme (32)	202
285	425	605	545	150	345	Certificat ou diplôme d'une école de métiers (33)	203
440	530	890	575	140	480	Certificat ou diplôme collégial (34)	204
75	130	155	170	30	90	Certificat universitaire inférieur au baccalauréat	205
465	305	1,040	525	235	305	Études universitaires avec baccalauréat ou diplôme supérieur	206
						selon les combinaisons de travail non rémunéré	
1,270	1,720	2,715	2,055	520	1,490	Hommes de 15 ans et plus	207
1,120	1,540	2,420	1,750	475	1,355	Travail non rémunéré déclaré (35)	208
135	185	285	240	50	110	Travaux ménagers et soins aux enfants et soins ou aide aux personnes âgées	209
385	530	755	660	95	400	Travaux ménagers et soins aux enfants seulement	210
65	145	205	155	50	40	Travaux ménagers et soins ou aide aux personnes âgées seulement	211
10	-	-	10	-	-	Soins aux enfants et soins ou aide aux personnes âgées seulement	212
500	660	1,120	640	275	765	Travaux ménagers seulement	213
25	-	55	10	10	25	Soins aux enfants seulement	214
10	20	-	35	-	-	Soins ou aide aux personnes âgées seulement	215
1,325	1,820	2,910	2,075	495	1,610	Femmes de 15 ans et plus	216
1,200	1,675	2,740	1,960	485	1,570	Travail non rémunéré déclaré (35)	217
185	305	440	345	50	195	Travaux ménagers et soins aux enfants et soins ou aide aux personnes âgées	218
450	690	915	800	150	545	Travaux ménagers et soins aux enfants seulement	219
70	110	275	195	55	90	Travaux ménagers et soins ou aide aux personnes âgées seulement	220
-	-	-	-	-	-	Soins aux enfants et soins ou aide aux personnes âgées seulement	221
490	555	1,085	610	230	720	Travaux ménagers seulement	222
-	-	10	15	10	10	Soins aux enfants seulement	223
-	15	15	-	-	10	Soins ou aide aux personnes âgées seulement	224
						selon l'activité	
1,270	1,720	2,715	2,055	520	1,485	Hommes de 15 ans et plus	225
1,025	1,310	2,115	1,575	425	1,165	Population active	226
950	1,235	1,995	1,505	400	1,080	Personnes occupées	227
75	75	125	75	30	85	Chômeurs	228
245	405	600	475	95	320	Inactifs	229
80.7	76.2	77.9	76.6	81.7	78.5	Taux d'activité	230
74.8	71.8	73.5	73.2	76.9	72.7	Taux d'emploi	231
7.3	5.7	5.9	4.8	7.1	7.3	Taux de chômage	232
1,325	1,815	2,910	2,080	495	1,610	Femmes de 15 ans et plus	233
955	1,105	1,775	1,370	310	995	Population active	234
895	970	1,660	1,320	290	900	Personnes occupées	235
65	135	120	50	20	95	Chômeuses	236
375	715	1,135	710	190	615	Inactives	237
72.1	60.9	61.0	65.9	62.6	61.8	Taux d'activité	238
67.5	53.4	57.0	63.5	58.6	55.9	Taux d'emploi	239
6.8	12.2	6.8	3.6	6.5	9.5	Taux de chômage	240

Table 1. Selected Characteristics for Census Tracts, 2001 Census – 100% Data and 20% Sample Data

No.	Characteristics	Vancouver 0184.05	Vancouver 0184.06 A	Vancouver 0184.07 A	Vancouver 0184.08 A	Vancouver 0184.09 A	Vancouver 0184.10 A
	POPULATION CHARACTERISTICS						
	by labour force activity – concluded						
241	Both sexes - Participation rate	70.3	59.7	62.6	76.5	66.7	68.5
242	15-24 years	61.2	59.3	61.9	69.9	49.6	63.0
243	25 years and over	72.8	60.1	62.6	77.9	71.0	70.3
244	Both sexes - Employment rate	64.5	56.5	56.7	69.2	62.6	64.7
245	15-24 years	53.6	57.1	54.9	60.2	46.0	53.2
246	25 years and over	67.3	56.9	57.2	71.2	67.0	67.6
247	Both sexes - Unemployment rate	8.3	4.7	9.7	9.6	6.3	5.7
248	15-24 years	11.8	12.5	12.7	13.8	8.7	13.2
249	25 years and over	7.4	5.3	9.2	8.9	5.6	3.4
250	**Total labour force 15 years and over**	**4,205**	**640**	**2,370**	**1,925**	**2,225**	**1,660**
	by industry based on the 1997 NAICS						
251	Industry - Not applicable (36)	115	10	45	55	55	15
252	All industries (37)	4,090	640	2,325	1,870	2,170	1,645
253	11 Agriculture, forestry, fishing and hunting	60	10	80	60	55	40
254	21 Mining and oil and gas extraction	-	-	-	-	-	-
255	22 Utilities	40	10	10	10	10	20
256	23 Construction	280	40	100	145	115	130
257	31-33 Manufacturing	610	50	305	200	320	210
258	41 Wholesale trade	230	95	120	130	140	35
259	44-45 Retail trade	435	45	225	250	270	205
260	48-49 Transportation and warehousing	410	75	160	135	175	115
261	51 Information and cultural industries	125	10	45	60	105	35
262	52 Finance and insurance	165	20	130	65	95	100
263	53 Real estate and rental and leasing	45	25	70	10	10	30
264	54 Professional, scientific and technical services	225	20	85	55	85	95
265	55 Management of companies and enterprises	-	-	-	10	-	10
266	56 Administrative and support, waste management and remediation services	160	15	205	120	165	80
267	61 Educational services	205	30	105	60	120	45
268	62 Health care and social assistance	355	70	270	180	175	160
269	71 Arts, entertainment and recreation	60	10	50	55	20	15
270	72 Accommodation and food services	285	35	155	135	100	150
271	81 Other services (except public administration)	235	55	100	100	105	85
272	91 Public administration	160	30	110	100	100	85
	by class of worker						
273	Class of worker - Not applicable (36)	110	-	45	55	55	15
274	All classes of worker (37)	4,090	640	2,325	1,870	2,165	1,645
275	Paid workers	3,820	560	2,165	1,780	1,885	1,555
276	Employees	3,670	540	2,120	1,715	1,825	1,490
277	Self-employed (incorporated)	145	25	45	65	60	60
278	Self-employed (unincorporated)	270	80	155	80	265	80
279	Unpaid family workers	-	-	10	10	15	-
	by occupation based on the 2001 NOC-S						
280	Male labour force 15 years and over	2,240	380	1,185	965	1,210	900
281	Occupation - Not applicable (36)	45	-	30	10	35	-
282	All occupations (37)	2,195	385	1,155	955	1,180	900
283	A Management occupations	205	25	105	95	125	140
284	B Business, finance and administration occupations	225	35	155	95	50	75
285	C Natural and applied sciences and related occupations	135	25	90	80	60	35
286	D Health occupations	30	-	25	10	-	35
287	E Occupations in social science, education, government service and religion	65	10	45	25	20	10
288	F Occupations in art, culture, recreation and sport	60	-	25	25	10	10
289	G Sales and service occupations	440	100	215	225	250	195
290	H Trades, transport and equipment operators and related occupations	820	145	300	315	510	275
291	I Occupations unique to primary industry	20	-	40	20	50	25
292	J Occupations unique to processing, manufacturing and utilities	195	35	155	50	105	100
293	Female labour force 15 years and over	1,965	260	1,185	955	1,010	765
294	Occupation - Not applicable (36)	70	-	15	45	25	20
295	All occupations (37)	1,895	260	1,170	915	985	745
296	A Management occupations	120	30	70	65	55	55
297	B Business, finance and administration occupations	600	85	295	290	370	245
298	C Natural and applied sciences and related occupations	50	-	10	-	10	10
299	D Health occupations	175	20	120	60	85	90

Tableau 1. Certaines caractéristiques des secteurs de recensement, recensement de 2001 – Données intégrales et données-échantillon (20 %)

Vancouver 0184.11 A	Vancouver 0185.05	Vancouver 0185.06 A	Vancouver 0185.07 A	Vancouver 0185.08 A	Vancouver 0185.09 A	Caractéristiques	N°
						CARACTÉRISTIQUES DE LA POPULATION	
						selon l'activité – fin	
76.3	68.3	69.2	71.2	72.4	69.8	Les deux sexes - Taux d'activité	241
65.6	58.0	58.8	58.3	79.5	61.6	15-24 ans	242
79.6	70.8	71.6	74.0	70.1	71.2	25 ans et plus	243
71.1	62.2	64.9	68.3	67.5	64.0	Les deux sexes - Taux d'emploi	244
59.0	48.9	50.0	55.2	71.8	52.5	15-24 ans	245
74.6	65.5	68.4	71.0	66.5	66.2	25 ans et plus	246
6.8	8.7	6.3	4.2	6.8	8.3	Les deux sexes - Taux de chômage	247
8.8	14.5	15.7	4.8	12.5	16.4	15-24 ans	248
6.3	7.4	4.6	4.2	5.2	7.0	25 ans et plus	249
1,980	**2,415**	**3,890**	**2,945**	**730**	**2,160**	**Population active totale de 15 ans et plus**	250
						selon l'industrie basée sur le SCIAN de 1997	
45	80	45	20	20	45	Industrie - Sans objet (36)	251
1,940	2,330	3,845	2,925	715	2,115	Toutes les industries (37)	252
70	45	80	55	-	30	11 Agriculture, foresterie, pêche et chasse	253
-	-	10	-	-	-	21 Extraction minière et extraction de pétrole et de gaz	254
20	-	20	20	10	10	22 Services publics	255
110	140	165	195	95	155	23 Construction	256
135	340	460	460	30	285	31-33 Fabrication	257
75	140	245	180	15	150	41 Commerce de gros	258
185	270	410	280	95	300	44-45 Commerce de détail	259
180	215	330	310	55	260	48-49 Transport et entreposage	260
125	35	75	105	25	50	51 Industrie de l'information et industrie culturelle	261
125	80	210	135	15	80	52 Finance et assurances	262
45	25	90	75	15	20	53 Services immobiliers et services de location et de location à bail	263
110	135	350	130	60	45	54 Services professionnels, scientifiques et techniques	264
-	-	-	-	-	-	55 Gestion de sociétés et d'entreprises	265
60	180	150	155	10	140	56 Services administratifs, services de soutien, services de gestion des déchets et services d'assainissement	266
100	75	265	155	45	95	61 Services d'enseignement	267
225	215	365	255	85	200	62 Soins de santé et assistance sociale	268
45	65	65	10	20	15	71 Arts, spectacles et loisirs	269
125	180	175	145	85	100	72 Hébergement et services de restauration	270
120	105	160	145	50	110	81 Autres services, sauf les administrations publiques	271
85	95	225	125	10	85	91 Administrations publiques	272
						selon la catégorie de travailleurs	
45	75	45	20	20	45	Catégorie de travailleurs - Sans objet (36)	273
1,940	2,335	3,850	2,925	710	2,120	Toutes les catégories de travailleurs (37)	274
1,815	2,155	3,550	2,760	615	1,995	Travailleurs rémunérés	275
1,685	2,080	3,320	2,670	510	1,960	Employés	276
125	70	235	90	105	35	Travailleurs autonomes (entreprise constituée en société)	277
125	175	295	165	80	125	Travailleurs autonomes (entreprise non constituée en société)	278
-	-	-	-	15	-	Travailleurs familiaux non rémunérés	279
						selon la profession basée sur la CNP-S de 2001	
1,025	1,310	2,120	1,580	430	1,165	Hommes actifs de 15 ans et plus	280
10	45	35	10	10	20	Profession - Sans objet (36)	281
1,010	1,265	2,085	1,570	420	1,150	Toutes les professions (37)	282
155	60	355	155	95	145	A Gestion	283
105	130	295	145	40	125	B Affaires, finance et administration	284
75	110	190	150	10	60	C Sciences naturelles et appliquées et professions apparentées	285
35	20	55	10	20	20	D Secteur de la santé	286
55	-	80	35	10	25	E Sciences sociales, enseignement, administration publique et religion	287
25	20	35	20	15	10	F Arts, culture, sports et loisirs	288
240	290	425	260	105	265	G Ventes et services	289
260	460	450	545	125	435	H Métiers, transport et machinerie	290
40	35	60	20	-	10	I Professions propres au secteur primaire	291
25	130	150	230	-	65	J Transformation, fabrication et services d'utilité publique	292
955	1,105	1,780	1,365	310	995	Femmes actives de 15 ans et plus	293
30	35	15	15	15	25	Profession - Sans objet (36)	294
925	1,065	1,765	1,355	295	970	Toutes les professions (37)	295
75	45	165	65	35	55	A Gestion	296
290	260	570	430	90	300	B Affaires, finance et administration	297
10	30	15	-	-	15	C Sciences naturelles et appliquées et professions apparentées	298
120	130	165	135	20	85	D Secteur de la santé	299

Table 1. Selected Characteristics for Census Tracts, 2001 Census – 100% Data and 20% Sample Data

No.	Characteristics	Vancouver 0184.05	Vancouver 0184.06 A	Vancouver 0184.07 A	Vancouver 0184.08 A	Vancouver 0184.09 A	Vancouver 0184.10 A
	POPULATION CHARACTERISTICS						
	by occupation based on the 2001 NOC-S – concluded						
300	E Occupations in social science, education, government service and religion	145	45	70	85	80	30
301	F Occupations in art, culture, recreation and sport	45	-	20	15	30	25
302	G Sales and service occupations	550	55	450	310	215	250
303	H Trades, transport and equipment operators and related occupations	45	-	15	20	40	-
304	I Occupations unique to primary industry	55	-	65	25	50	20
305	J Occupations unique to processing, manufacturing and utilities	115	10	60	40	55	25
306	**Total employed labour force 15 years and over**	**3,860**	**610**	**2,145**	**1,740**	**2,085**	**1,570**
	by place of work						
307	Males	2,055	365	1,045	885	1,130	850
308	Usual place of work	1,670	295	755	620	840	630
309	At home	85	25	65	55	40	35
310	Outside Canada	10	-	10	-	10	-
311	No fixed workplace address	290	45	225	205	245	175
312	Females	1,800	245	1,090	860	955	720
313	Usual place of work	1,570	200	945	685	865	645
314	At home	135	30	30	70	40	55
315	Outside Canada	10	-	-	10	-	-
316	No fixed workplace address	90	10	120	90	45	25
317	**Total employed labour force 15 years and over with usual place of work or no fixed workplace address**	**3,615**	**555**	**2,035**	**1,605**	**1,990**	**1,470**
	by mode of transportation						
318	Males	1,960	340	975	820	1,080	805
319	Car, truck, van, as driver	1,600	290	820	720	960	685
320	Car, truck, van, as passenger	120	25	50	20	65	90
321	Public transit	160	10	55	55	35	20
322	Walked	45	20	25	-	10	-
323	Other method	30	-	30	25	15	-
324	Females	1,655	210	1,060	775	910	665
325	Car, truck, van, as driver	1,155	175	815	545	705	525
326	Car, truck, van, as passenger	250	15	105	115	130	75
327	Public transit	195	15	100	100	55	60
328	Walked	35	10	-	10	20	-
329	Other method	15	-	30	10	-	10
330	**Total population 15 years and over who worked since January 1, 2000**	**4,420**	**690**	**2,515**	**2,040**	**2,410**	**1,800**
	by language used at work						
331	Single responses	3,945	660	2,280	1,900	2,175	1,480
332	English	3,790	650	2,185	1,815	2,070	1,440
333	French	10	-	-	10	-	-
334	Non-official languages (5)	150	15	95	80	100	45
335	Chinese, n.o.s.	25	-	-	-	-	-
336	Cantonese	10	-	-	-	40	-
337	Other languages (6)	115	10	85	80	60	45
338	Multiple responses	475	30	235	145	240	315
339	English and French	30	-	20	10	20	10
340	English and non-official language	420	30	210	135	215	305
341	French and non-official language	-	-	-	-	-	-
342	English, French and non-official language	25	-	-	10	-	-
	DWELLING AND HOUSEHOLD CHARACTERISTICS						
343	**Total number of occupied private dwellings**	**2,170**	**480**	**1,755**	**1,100**	**1,300**	**895**
	by tenure						
344	Owned	1,750	340	1,155	830	945	580
345	Rented	425	140	605	270	355	310
346	Band housing	-	-	-	-	-	-
	by structural type of dwelling						
347	Single-detached house	1,740	265	430	420	880	330
348	Semi-detached house	45	15	40	70	-	-
349	Row house	-	-	320	345	-	-
350	Apartment, detached duplex	370	120	140	25	230	290
351	Apartment, building that has five or more storeys	-	-	-	-	-	-
352	Apartment, building that has fewer than five storeys (38)	15	75	825	235	190	270
353	Other single-attached house	-	-	-	-	-	-
354	Movable dwelling (39)	-	10	-	-	-	-

Tableau 1. Certaines caractéristiques des secteurs de recensement, recensement de 2001 – Données intégrales et données-échantillon (20 %)

Vancouver 0184.11 A	Vancouver 0185.05	Vancouver 0185.06 A	Vancouver 0185.07 A	Vancouver 0185.08 A	Vancouver 0185.09 A	Caractéristiques	N°
						CARACTÉRISTIQUES DE LA POPULATION	
						selon la profession basée sur la CNP-S de 2001 – fin	
65	75	225	115	55	90	E Sciences sociales, enseignement, administration publique et religion	300
35	25	60	15	10	10	F Arts, culture, sports et loisirs	301
295	370	435	415	75	320	G Ventes et services	302
-	20	55	40	-	25	H Métiers, transport et machinerie	303
15	40	35	40	-	20	I Professions propres au secteur primaire	304
25	70	30	100	-	55	J Transformation, fabrication et services d'utilité publique	305
1,845	**2,200**	**3,650**	**2,820**	**680**	**1,985**	**Population active occupée totale de 15 ans et plus selon le lieu de travail**	306
945	1,235	1,995	1,505	400	1,075	Hommes	307
680	935	1,575	1,130	280	840	Lieu habituel de travail	308
85	50	130	60	45	20	À domicile	309
10	10	15	-	-	-	En dehors du Canada	310
180	250	270	310	75	215	Sans adresse de travail fixe	311
895	970	1,660	1,320	285	905	Femmes	312
775	820	1,420	1,185	205	815	Lieu habituel de travail	313
55	90	115	65	60	35	À domicile	314
-	10	15	-	-	-	En dehors du Canada	315
60	55	105	70	20	50	Sans adresse de travail fixe	316
1,690	**2,060**	**3,370**	**2,685**	**580**	**1,925**	**Population active occupée totale de 15 ans et plus ayant un lieu habituel de travail ou sans adresse de travail fixe selon le mode de transport**	317
855	1,180	1,845	1,435	355	1,060	Hommes	318
740	930	1,710	1,240	315	920	Automobile, camion ou fourgonnette, en tant que conducteur	319
55	60	45	130	-	30	Automobile, camion ou fourgonnette, en tant que passager	320
40	125	20	40	20	75	Transport en commun	321
-	45	20	15	10	20	À pied	322
15	25	45	10	-	10	Autre moyen	323
835	880	1,520	1,250	230	865	Femmes	324
685	615	1,300	1,020	205	685	Automobile, camion ou fourgonnette, en tant que conductrice	325
75	135	75	120	10	45	Automobile, camion ou fourgonnette, en tant que passagère	326
75	60	100	90	-	105	Transport en commun	327
-	70	-	20	15	30	À pied	328
-	-	45	-	-	10	Autre moyen	329
2,110	**2,505**	**4,150**	**3,135**	**770**	**2,255**	**Population totale de 15 ans et plus ayant travaillé depuis le 1er janvier 2000 selon la langue utilisée au travail**	330
1,925	2,310	3,675	2,795	720	2,055	Réponses uniques	331
1,865	2,235	3,575	2,710	720	1,990	Anglais	332
-	-	-	-	-	-	Français	333
60	75	100	85	-	65	Langues non officielles (5)	334
-	-	-	10	-	-	Chinois, n.d.a.	335
-	-	10	-	-	-	Cantonais	336
60	75	95	75	-	65	Autres langues (6)	337
185	190	480	340	50	200	Réponses multiples	338
-	10	20	-	-	30	Anglais et français	339
185	180	435	330	45	170	Anglais et langue non officielle	340
-	-	-	-	-	-	Français et langue non officielle	341
-	-	20	10	-	-	Anglais, français et langue non officielle	342
						CARACTÉRISTIQUES DES LOGEMENTS ET DES MÉNAGES	
1,005	**1,580**	**2,190**	**1,575**	**400**	**1,420**	**Nombre total de logements privés occupés selon le mode d'occupation**	343
790	860	1,785	1,265	335	905	Possédé	344
215	720	405	310	65	515	Loué	345
-	-	-	-	-	-	Logement de bande	346
						selon le type de construction résidentielle	
645	565	1,335	1,115	370	405	Maison individuelle non attenante	347
20	175	75	15	-	10	Maison jumelée	348
30	100	245	-	-	380	Maison en rangée	349
160	160	345	390	10	125	Appartement, duplex non attenant	350
-	80	-	-	-	-	Appartement, immeuble de cinq étages ou plus	351
150	505	195	50	25	500	Appartement, immeuble de moins de cinq étages (38)	352
-	-	-	-	-	-	Autre maison individuelle attenante	353
-	-	-	10	-	-	Logement mobile (39)	354

Table 1. Selected Characteristics for Census Tracts, 2001 Census – 100% Data and 20% Sample Data

No.	Characteristics	Vancouver 0184.05	Vancouver 0184.06 A	Vancouver 0184.07 A	Vancouver 0184.08 A	Vancouver 0184.09 A	Vancouver 0184.10 A
	DWELLING AND HOUSEHOLD CHARACTERISTICS						
	by condition of dwelling						
355	Regular maintenance only	1,610	345	1,290	780	885	780
356	Minor repairs	465	95	320	280	365	110
357	Major repairs	100	45	145	35	45	10
	by period of construction						
358	Before 1946	10	10	-	25	-	-
359	1946-1960	110	70	35	25	45	25
360	1961-1970	75	90	80	50	110	-
361	1971-1980	570	85	205	255	265	10
362	1981-1990	720	50	645	495	690	280
363	1991-2001 (20)	690	180	795	245	185	580
364	Average number of rooms per dwelling	7.4	7.1	6.0	6.8	7.4	7.5
365	Average number of bedrooms per dwelling	3.3	3.1	2.6	3.2	3.3	3.5
366	Average value of dwelling $	251,024	257,340	203,921	202,232	223,623	330,944
367	**Total number of private households**	**2,170**	**480**	**1,755**	**1,095**	**1,300**	**895**
	by household size						
368	1 person	205	100	435	170	150	140
369	2 persons	430	155	565	260	260	185
370	3 persons	385	90	240	210	240	135
371	4-5 persons	885	100	370	360	510	310
372	6 or more persons	265	30	145	100	140	120
	by household type						
373	One-family households	1,740	340	1,205	820	1,065	605
374	Multiple-family households	200	25	80	70	60	100
375	Non-family households	225	115	470	205	175	185
376	Number of persons in private households	7,825	1,365	4,830	3,500	4,470	3,145
377	Average number of persons in private households	3.6	2.8	2.8	3.2	3.4	3.5
378	Average number of persons per room	0.5	0.4	0.5	0.5	0.5	0.5
379	Tenant households in non-farm, non-reserve private dwellings (40)	420	140	595	275	350	310
380	Average gross rent $ (40)	811	864	697	766	722	577
381	Tenant households spending 30% or more of household income on gross rent (40) (41)	175	70	245	100	135	85
382	Tenant households spending from 30% to 99% of household income on gross rent (40) (41)	135	65	235	80	120	65
383	Owner households in non-farm, non-reserve private dwellings (42)	1,745	335	1,150	830	945	585
384	Average owner's major payments $ (42)	1,244	914	984	1,182	1,229	1,578
385	Owner households spending 30% or more of household income on owner's major payments (41) (42)	570	75	280	245	335	165
386	Owner households spending from 30% to 99% of household income on owner's major payments (41) (42)	490	60	235	215	285	150
	CENSUS FAMILY CHARACTERISTICS						
387	**Total number of census families in private households**	**2,185**	**400**	**1,375**	**970**	**1,185**	**845**
	by census family structure and size						
388	Total couple families	1,895	340	1,125	765	1,010	700
389	Total families of married couples	1,765	310	1,035	650	965	670
390	Without children at home	510	150	475	170	200	205
391	With children at home	1,255	155	560	485	770	465
392	1 child	360	60	160	155	220	135
393	2 children	610	60	235	235	385	235
394	3 or more children	280	40	165	90	165	100
395	Total families of common-law couples	130	25	90	115	50	30
396	Without children at home	40	20	55	55	35	10
397	With children at home	95	-	40	55	15	15
398	1 child	40	-	10	35	-	-
399	2 children	35	10	20	10	-	15
400	3 or more children	20	-	10	10	10	-
401	Total lone-parent families	285	65	250	210	170	145
402	Female parent	220	55	215	190	140	95
403	1 child	135	20	110	95	80	40
404	2 children	55	20	75	40	35	20
405	3 or more children	30	15	30	50	25	30

Tableau 1. Certaines caractéristiques des secteurs de recensement, recensement de 2001 – Données intégrales et données-échantillon (20 %)

Vancouver 0184.11 A	Vancouver 0185.05	Vancouver 0185.06 A	Vancouver 0185.07 A	Vancouver 0185.08 A	Vancouver 0185.09 A	Caractéristiques	N°
						CARACTÉRISTIQUES DES LOGEMENTS ET DES MÉNAGES	
						selon l'état du logement	
880	1,035	1,825	1,125	315	1,040	Entretien régulier seulement	355
115	470	315	325	55	255	Réparations mineures	356
10	80	45	125	30	130	Réparations majeures	357
						selon la période de construction	
-	10	15	35	30	10	Avant 1946	358
50	105	90	80	75	100	1946-1960	359
15	115	60	155	60	60	1961-1970	360
40	650	50	200	65	155	1971-1980	361
160	550	865	695	75	390	1981-1990	362
735	160	1,105	405	90	715	1991-2001 (20)	363
8.3	5.9	7.8	7.6	9.4	5.5	Nombre moyen de pièces par logement	364
3.6	2.7	3.4	3.5	3.8	2.4	Nombre moyen de chambres à coucher par logement	365
325,403	180,265	313,117	259,076	473,774	156,144	Valeur moyenne du logement $	366
1,005	**1,580**	**2,190**	**1,575**	**400**	**1,420**	**Nombre total de logements privés**	367
						selon la taille du ménage	
75	300	275	150	60	370	1 personne	368
325	400	700	400	135	445	2 personnes	369
180	280	355	250	65	210	3 personnes	370
345	465	640	565	115	295	4-5 personnes	371
75	135	215	210	25	105	6 personnes ou plus	372
						selon le genre de ménage	
810	1,125	1,685	1,245	340	910	Ménages unifamiliaux	373
65	100	170	140	10	115	Ménages multifamiliaux	374
125	365	340	190	60	400	Ménages non familiaux	375
3,280	4,880	7,050	5,535	1,205	3,895	Nombre de personnes dans les ménages privés	376
3.3	3.1	3.2	3.5	3.1	2.7	Nombre moyen de personnes dans les ménages privés	377
0.4	0.5	0.4	0.5	0.3	0.5	Nombre moyen de personnes par pièce	378
210	715	400	315	65	515	Ménages locataires dans les logements privés non agricoles hors réserve (40)	379
778	680	772	758	891	850	Loyer brut moyen $ (40)	380
75	335	120	125	15	200	Ménages locataires consacrant 30 % ou plus du revenu du ménage au loyer brut (40) (41)	381
55	240	95	105	15	125	Ménages locataires consacrant de 30 % à 99 % du revenu du ménage au loyer brut (40) (41)	382
790	850	1,790	1,265	330	905	Ménages propriétaires dans les logements privés non agricoles hors réserve (42)	383
1,520	1,079	1,211	1,297	1,348	953	Principales dépenses de propriété moyennes $ (42)	384
255	260	400	305	90	275	Ménages propriétaires consacrant 30 % ou plus du revenu du ménage aux principales dépenses de propriété (41) (42)	385
225	225	370	270	85	265	Ménages propriétaires consacrant de 30 % à 99 % du revenu du ménage aux principales dépenses de propriété (41) (42)	386
						CARACTÉRISTIQUES DES FAMILLES DE RECENSEMENT	
945	**1,320**	**2,070**	**1,560**	**350**	**1,160**	**Total des familles de recensement dans les ménages privés**	387
						selon la structure et la taille de la famille de recensement	
815	995	1,835	1,345	305	920	Total des familles avec conjoints	388
765	865	1,740	1,260	290	820	Total des familles avec couples mariés	389
270	225	680	375	110	325	Sans enfants à la maison	390
495	640	1,065	880	180	495	Avec enfants à la maison	391
135	220	350	260	60	220	1 enfant	392
220	245	400	400	60	180	2 enfants	393
145	170	310	220	60	95	3 enfants ou plus	394
50	130	95	85	20	100	Total des familles en union libre	395
30	80	70	70	15	70	Sans enfants à la maison	396
15	55	25	15	-	25	Avec enfants à la maison	397
15	20	10	10	-	10	1 enfant	398
-	10	20	10	-	10	2 enfants	399
-	25	-	-	-	10	3 enfants ou plus	400
130	325	235	215	40	240	Total des familles monoparentales	401
100	285	185	200	35	180	Parent de sexe féminin	402
60	140	95	80	25	145	1 enfant	403
45	75	55	90	-	30	2 enfants	404
-	75	30	30	-	-	3 enfants ou plus	405

Table 1. Selected Characteristics for Census Tracts, 2001 Census – 100% Data and 20% Sample Data

No.	Characteristics	Vancouver 0184.05	Vancouver 0184.06 A	Vancouver 0184.07 A	Vancouver 0184.08 A	Vancouver 0184.09 A	Vancouver 0184.10 A
	CENSUS FAMILY CHARACTERISTICS						
	by census family structure and size – concluded						
406	Male parent	65	10	35	20	30	50
407	1 child	40	-	20	-	30	30
408	2 children	20	10	15	15	10	15
409	3 or more children	-	-	-	10	-	-
410	**Total number of children at home**	**3,125**	**445**	**1,640**	**1,415**	**1,870**	**1,220**
	by age groups						
411	Under 6 years	680	55	370	340	405	275
412	6-14 years	1,145	235	665	660	730	435
413	15-17 years	365	40	155	105	230	170
414	18-24 years	650	80	310	215	325	270
415	25 years and over	280	40	135	95	175	65
416	Average number of children at home per census family (43)	1.4	1.1	1.2	1.5	1.6	1.4
417	**Total number of persons in private households**	**7,830**	**1,365**	**4,825**	**3,505**	**4,470**	**3,150**
	by census family status and living arrangements						
418	Number of non-family persons	625	180	685	350	400	390
419	Living with relatives (44)	245	30	120	95	120	165
420	Living with non-relatives only	175	50	135	80	135	85
421	Living alone	205	100	435	175	150	140
422	Number of family persons	7,200	1,185	4,140	3,150	4,070	2,760
423	Average number of persons per census family	3.3	3.0	3.0	3.2	3.4	3.3
424	**Total number of persons 65 years and over**	**515**	**235**	**780**	**220**	**235**	**245**
425	Number of non-family persons 65 years and over	175	55	255	100	85	145
426	Living with relatives (44)	120	10	50	40	60	75
427	Living with non-relatives only	15	10	-	10	-	-
428	Living alone	45	35	205	45	30	65
429	Number of family persons 65 years and over	340	180	525	125	145	100
	ECONOMIC FAMILY CHARACTERISTICS						
430	**Total number of economic families in private households**	**1,960**	**370**	**1,290**	**905**	**1,130**	**725**
	by size of family						
431	2 persons	475	185	555	245	280	170
432	3 persons	380	65	220	210	230	125
433	4 persons	600	65	230	260	360	180
434	5 or more persons	505	60	280	185	265	245
435	Total number of persons in economic families	7,450	1,215	4,255	3,245	4,190	2,925
436	Average number of persons per economic family	3.8	3.2	3.3	3.6	3.7	4.0
437	Total number of unattached individuals	375	150	570	255	285	220
	2000 INCOME CHARACTERISTICS						
	Population 15 years and over by sex and total income groups in 2000						
438	Total - Both sexes	5,980	1,080	3,775	2,510	3,330	2,430
439	Without income	450	85	235	115	290	205
440	With income	5,530	1,000	3,540	2,395	3,040	2,225
441	Under $1,000 (45)	380	15	155	45	180	75
442	$ 1,000 - $ 2,999	415	10	85	95	165	145
443	$ 3,000 - $ 4,999	205	35	100	105	105	85
444	$ 5,000 - $ 6,999	260	30	155	135	115	120
445	$ 7,000 - $ 9,999	290	115	230	135	160	105
446	$10,000 - $11,999	285	55	160	65	105	115
447	$12,000 - $14,999	370	60	315	115	180	170
448	$15,000 - $19,999	540	110	405	225	280	205
449	$20,000 - $24,999	440	115	370	255	340	170
450	$25,000 - $29,999	275	50	275	215	170	150
451	$30,000 - $34,999	385	50	335	270	220	175
452	$35,000 - $39,999	345	50	180	215	195	145
453	$40,000 - $44,999	285	75	270	135	225	130
454	$45,000 - $49,999	220	75	70	120	175	65
455	$50,000 - $59,999	380	65	190	135	205	150
456	$60,000 and over	465	80	240	135	215	215
457	Average income $ (46)	26,062	32,549	26,177	27,648	27,443	30,992
458	Median income $ (46)	20,238	23,247	21,998	25,312	22,808	21,904
459	Standard error of average income $ (46)	652	3,176	712	928	902	1,550

Tableau 1. Certaines caractéristiques des secteurs de recensement, recensement de 2001 – Données intégrales et données-échantillon (20 %)

Vancouver 0184.11 A	Vancouver 0185.05	Vancouver 0185.06 A	Vancouver 0185.07 A	Vancouver 0185.08 A	Vancouver 0185.09 A	Caractéristiques	N°
						CARACTÉRISTIQUES DES FAMILLES DE RECENSEMENT	
						selon la structure et la taille de la famille de recensement – fin	
30	35	50	15	15	65	Parent de sexe masculin	406
25	25	35	20	10	40	1 enfant	407
-	10	15	-	-	15	2 enfants	408
-	-	-	-	-	10	3 enfants ou plus	409
1,230	**2,040**	**2,570**	**2,165**	**455**	**1,255**	**Nombre total d'enfants à la maison**	410
						selon les groupes d'âge	
290	535	575	555	45	400	Moins de 6 ans	411
390	810	850	815	145	370	6-14 ans	412
195	225	270	220	95	95	15-17 ans	413
285	275	655	425	105	255	18-24 ans	414
75	200	210	145	65	120	25 ans et plus	415
1.3	1.5	1.2	1.4	1.3	1.1	Nombre moyen d'enfants à la maison par famille de recensement (43)	416
3,280	**4,885**	**7,055**	**5,535**	**1,210**	**3,895**	**Nombre total de personnes dans les ménages privés**	417
						selon la situation des particuliers dans la famille de recensement et des particuliers dans le ménage	
285	525	580	470	100	560	Nombre de personnes hors famille de recensement	418
105	85	185	205	35	95	Vivant avec des personnes apparentées (44)	419
100	145	120	105	10	100	Vivant avec des personnes non apparentées uniquement	420
75	300	275	155	55	370	Vivant seules	421
2,995	4,355	6,475	5,070	1,105	3,330	Nombre de personnes membres d'une famille	422
3.2	3.3	3.1	3.2	3.2	2.9	Nombre moyen de personnes par famille de recensement	423
150	**265**	**630**	**440**	**165**	**375**	**Nombre total de personnes de 65 ans et plus**	424
35	80	190	150	55	165	Nombre de personnes hors famille de recensement de 65 ans et plus	425
25	10	85	95	35	45	Vivant avec des personnes apparentées (44)	426
-	-	-	-	-	10	Vivant avec des personnes non apparentées uniquement	427
10	70	105	55	20	110	Vivant seules	428
115	190	445	285	105	205	Nombre de personnes membres d'une famille de 65 ans et plus	429
						CARACTÉRISTIQUES DES FAMILLES ÉCONOMIQUES	
890	**1,230**	**1,880**	**1,395**	**340**	**1,025**	**Nombre total de familles économiques dans les ménages privés**	430
						selon la taille de la famille	
310	370	690	380	145	450	2 personnes	431
165	275	340	260	55	185	3 personnes	432
210	295	410	375	70	175	4 personnes	433
205	290	440	380	70	215	5 personnes ou plus	434
3,100	4,440	6,655	5,275	1,140	3,425	Nombre total de personnes dans les familles économiques	435
3.5	3.6	3.5	3.8	3.3	3.3	Nombre moyen de personnes par famille économique	436
175	445	400	260	65	475	Nombre total de personnes hors famille économique	437
						CARACTÉRISTIQUES DU REVENU DE 2000	
						Population de 15 ans et plus selon le sexe et les tranches de revenu total en 2000	
2,595	3,535	5,625	4,135	1,015	3,100	Total - Les deux sexes	438
200	305	450	290	50	245	Sans revenu	439
2,395	3,230	5,175	3,840	965	2,855	Avec un revenu	440
125	205	255	110	30	200	Moins de 1 000 $ (45)	441
60	175	180	120	30	140	1 000 $ - 2 999 $	442
85	175	155	200	25	120	3 000 $ - 4 999 $	443
130	190	205	230	10	110	5 000 $ - 6 999 $	444
135	270	335	225	65	170	7 000 $ - 9 999 $	445
95	135	185	150	45	125	10 000 $ - 11 999 $	446
95	290	290	265	35	210	12 000 $ - 14 999 $	447
255	265	365	350	110	285	15 000 $ - 19 999 $	448
195	230	415	290	95	220	20 000 $ - 24 999 $	449
140	185	450	195	110	245	25 000 $ - 29 999 $	450
200	255	360	315	70	200	30 000 $ - 34 999 $	451
110	215	275	210	60	170	35 000 $ - 39 999 $	452
105	185	290	285	50	175	40 000 $ - 44 999 $	453
110	90	225	215	55	125	45 000 $ - 49 999 $	454
255	155	365	255	30	165	50 000 $ - 59 999 $	455
305	210	815	425	155	200	60 000 $ et plus	456
33,333	23,266	35,140	29,208	35,361	25,252	Revenu moyen $ (46)	457
25,601	17,995	26,358	24,712	26,366	21,574	Revenu médian $ (46)	458
1,447	777	1,485	780	2,583	794	Erreur type de revenu moyen $ (46)	459

Table 1. Selected Characteristics for Census Tracts, 2001 Census – 100% Data and 20% Sample Data

No.	Characteristics	Vancouver 0184.05	Vancouver 0184.06 A	Vancouver 0184.07 A	Vancouver 0184.08 A	Vancouver 0184.09 A	Vancouver 0184.10 A
	2000 INCOME CHARACTERISTICS						
	Population 15 years and over by sex and total income groups in 2000 – concluded						
460	Total - Males	2,990	550	1,685	1,190	1,660	1,180
461	Without income	165	15	100	35	110	90
462	With income	2,815	535	1,590	1,155	1,550	1,090
463	Under $1,000 (45)	145	10	70	35	120	40
464	$ 1,000 - $ 2,999	180	10	40	50	55	60
465	$ 3,000 - $ 4,999	80	10	25	30	60	35
466	$ 5,000 - $ 6,999	135	10	35	55	40	40
467	$ 7,000 - $ 9,999	130	50	60	25	60	55
468	$10,000 - $11,999	115	40	45	30	20	60
469	$12,000 - $14,999	145	20	95	25	75	40
470	$15,000 - $19,999	280	35	150	60	145	85
471	$20,000 - $24,999	210	80	160	125	150	90
472	$25,000 - $29,999	115	25	130	105	85	70
473	$30,000 - $34,999	150	20	185	150	85	65
474	$35,000 - $39,999	205	35	75	110	75	60
475	$40,000 - $44,999	175	30	160	85	135	65
476	$45,000 - $49,999	125	50	45	85	115	35
477	$50,000 - $59,999	280	50	120	95	145	105
478	$60,000 and over	355	55	200	90	185	185
479	Average income $ (46)	30,760	35,865	31,988	32,266	32,130	39,321
480	Median income $ (46)	24,772	25,901	29,468	30,297	27,696	28,433
481	Standard error of average income $ (46)	1,028	4,637	1,187	1,551	1,486	2,727
482	Total - Females	2,995	530	2,085	1,325	1,675	1,250
483	Without income	280	65	140	80	185	115
484	With income	2,715	460	1,950	1,240	1,490	1,135
485	Under $1,000 (45)	235	10	90	10	65	40
486	$ 1,000 - $ 2,999	230	-	40	40	115	80
487	$ 3,000 - $ 4,999	125	30	75	75	50	45
488	$ 5,000 - $ 6,999	125	20	125	80	70	75
489	$ 7,000 - $ 9,999	165	65	170	105	100	55
490	$10,000 - $11,999	165	10	115	35	85	55
491	$12,000 - $14,999	225	40	215	90	105	130
492	$15,000 - $19,999	260	70	260	165	135	120
493	$20,000 - $24,999	230	40	205	125	185	80
494	$25,000 - $29,999	155	25	150	105	90	85
495	$30,000 - $34,999	230	30	150	120	140	115
496	$35,000 - $39,999	145	10	105	105	120	85
497	$40,000 - $44,999	110	45	110	55	90	65
498	$45,000 - $49,999	95	30	25	35	65	25
499	$50,000 - $59,999	100	10	70	40	60	50
500	$60,000 and over	105	25	45	45	30	30
501	Average income $ (46)	21,180	28,712	21,436	23,358	22,578	22,959
502	Median income $ (46)	16,423	18,009	17,192	20,262	20,281	18,599
503	Standard error of average income $ (46)	747	4,272	798	996	940	1,305
	by composition of total income						
504	Total - Composition of income in 2000 % (47)	100.0	100.0	100.0	100.0	100.0	100.0
505	Employment income %	84.2	64.4	70.4	84.1	84.4	86.1
506	Government transfer payments %	9.7	14.8	16.1	11.1	9.9	9.5
507	Other %	6.1	20.9	13.5	4.9	5.8	4.6
	Population 15 years and over with employment income in 2000 by sex and work activity						
508	Both sexes with employment income (48)	4,260	690	2,395	1,930	2,335	1,715
509	Average employment income $	28,526	30,293	27,279	28,788	30,172	34,595
510	Standard error of average employment income $	749	1,727	889	1,068	986	1,833
511	Worked full year, full time (49)	2,335	330	1,340	985	1,325	915
512	Average employment income $	37,501	44,354	35,477	37,126	38,898	49,378
513	Standard error of average employment income $	956	2,373	1,177	1,596	1,274	2,934
514	Worked part year or part time (50)	1,810	330	1,020	910	950	775
515	Average employment income $	18,411	18,292	17,168	20,290	19,629	17,151
516	Standard error of average employment income $	1,004	1,655	1,021	1,138	1,220	1,113
517	Males with employment income (48)	2,285	365	1,160	985	1,240	890
518	Average employment income $	33,238	35,025	32,981	33,652	35,096	43,391
519	Standard error of average employment income $	1,161	2,447	1,453	1,708	1,521	3,008
520	Worked full year, full time (49)	1,390	205	705	615	830	565
521	Average employment income $	41,254	45,566	40,565	39,594	42,350	57,440
522	Standard error of average employment income $	1,325	3,029	1,826	2,326	1,768	4,271
523	Worked part year or part time (50)	865	155	445	365	400	315
524	Average employment income $	21,272	22,431	21,281	23,938	20,962	18,441
525	Standard error of average employment income $	1,857	2,787	1,847	1,997	2,275	1,765

Tableau 1. Certaines caractéristiques des secteurs de recensement, recensement de 2001 – Données intégrales et données-échantillon (20 %)

Vancouver 0184.11 A	Vancouver 0185.05	Vancouver 0185.06 A	Vancouver 0185.07 A	Vancouver 0185.08 A	Vancouver 0185.09 A	Caractéristiques	N°
						CARACTÉRISTIQUES DU REVENU DE 2000	
						Population de 15 ans et plus selon le sexe et les tranches de revenu total en 2000 – fin	
1,265	1,715	2,715	2,060	520	1,485	Total - Hommes	460
75	160	140	135	15	85	Sans revenu	461
1,190	1,560	2,570	1,920	505	1,405	Avec un revenu	462
85	115	65	30	10	120	Moins de 1 000 $ (45)	463
20	60	90	60	10	60	1 000 $ - 2 999 $	464
25	30	80	80	-	50	3 000 $ - 4 999 $	465
65	65	40	55	-	55	5 000 $ - 6 999 $	466
40	80	150	50	40	45	7 000 $ - 9 999 $	467
25	50	100	55	40	40	10 000 $ - 11 999 $	468
40	120	90	115	15	65	12 000 $ - 14 999 $	469
95	120	160	175	20	130	15 000 $ - 19 999 $	470
90	115	185	120	55	65	20 000 $ - 24 999 $	471
65	105	220	105	55	90	25 000 $ - 29 999 $	472
95	110	145	155	30	105	30 000 $ - 34 999 $	473
50	140	75	115	20	90	35 000 $ - 39 999 $	474
35	100	155	205	45	140	40 000 $ - 44 999 $	475
60	85	165	110	35	100	45 000 $ - 49 999 $	476
180	95	220	180	10	100	50 000 $ - 59 999 $	477
225	165	635	310	120	145	60 000 $ et plus	478
40,392	28,249	44,155	35,406	42,684	29,366	Revenu moyen $ (46)	479
30,512	25,617	32,665	33,626	29,417	28,452	Revenu médian $ (46)	480
2,463	1,251	2,659	1,185	4,577	1,231	Erreur type de revenu moyen $ (46)	481
1,325	1,815	2,910	2,080	495	1,610	Total - Femmes	482
125	140	310	160	35	155	Sans revenu	483
1,200	1,675	2,605	1,925	460	1,455	Avec un revenu	484
40	80	185	80	20	75	Moins de 1 000 $ (45)	485
40	115	90	65	20	85	1 000 $ - 2 999 $	486
60	145	80	120	20	75	3 000 $ - 4 999 $	487
55	130	170	170	10	55	5 000 $ - 6 999 $	488
100	190	190	175	25	125	7 000 $ - 9 999 $	489
75	90	85	100	-	85	10 000 $ - 11 999 $	490
60	170	205	150	20	150	12 000 $ - 14 999 $	491
165	145	200	170	85	155	15 000 $ - 19 999 $	492
110	115	230	170	40	155	20 000 $ - 24 999 $	493
70	85	230	95	55	150	25 000 $ - 29 999 $	494
100	140	210	165	35	95	30 000 $ - 34 999 $	495
65	70	205	95	40	75	35 000 $ - 39 999 $	496
60	80	135	80	-	35	40 000 $ - 44 999 $	497
50	15	65	100	20	30	45 000 $ - 49 999 $	498
75	60	145	70	25	65	50 000 $ - 59 999 $	499
75	45	175	115	40	55	60 000 $ et plus	500
26,333	18,633	26,236	23,013	27,234	21,278	Revenu moyen $ (46)	501
20,080	12,880	22,424	17,445	25,025	17,074	Revenu médian $ (46)	502
1,440	888	1,262	929	1,972	951	Erreur type de revenu moyen $ (46)	503
						selon la composition du revenu total	
100.0	100.0	100.0	100.0	100.0	100.0	Total - Composition du revenu en 2000 % (47)	504
85.6	83.1	80.8	84.5	76.6	85.9	Revenu d'emploi %	505
6.2	13.8	6.6	9.4	6.9	10.1	Transferts gouvernementaux %	506
8.1	3.1	12.7	6.2	16.2	4.1	Autre %	507
						Population de 15 ans et plus ayant un revenu d'emploi en 2000 selon le sexe et le travail	
2,040	2,390	4,025	3,015	745	2,130	Les deux sexes ayant un revenu d'emploi (48)	508
33,576	26,174	36,491	31,454	35,175	29,044	Revenu moyen d'emploi $	509
1,461	956	1,399	914	2,708	935	Erreur type de revenu moyen d'emploi $	510
1,010	1,140	2,255	1,625	335	1,115	Ayant travaillé toute l'année à plein temps (49)	511
46,449	37,644	49,136	40,479	49,966	37,819	Revenu moyen d'emploi $	512
2,303	1,284	2,211	1,124	3,557	1,110	Erreur type de revenu moyen d'emploi $	513
945	1,185	1,695	1,330	395	940	Ayant travaillé une partie de l'année ou à temps partiel (50)	514
20,651	16,457	20,952	21,324	23,574	20,444	Revenu moyen d'emploi $	515
1,298	1,074	1,169	1,285	3,604	1,327	Erreur type de revenu moyen d'emploi $	516
1,030	1,295	2,120	1,585	440	1,140	Hommes ayant un revenu d'emploi (48)	517
40,116	30,509	44,883	37,923	40,508	32,644	Revenu moyen d'emploi $	518
2,351	1,384	2,430	1,306	4,348	1,352	Erreur type de revenu moyen d'emploi $	519
620	715	1,340	1,015	210	690	Ayant travaillé toute l'année à plein temps (49)	520
49,801	40,297	55,756	42,999	54,214	38,819	Revenu moyen d'emploi $	521
3,286	1,673	3,511	1,443	5,051	1,408	Erreur type de revenu moyen d'emploi $	522
385	555	755	555	230	425	Ayant travaillé une partie de l'année ou à temps partiel (50)	523
25,464	19,099	26,384	29,776	28,013	23,808	Revenu moyen d'emploi $	524
2,571	1,806	2,203	2,407	6,390	2,437	Erreur type de revenu moyen d'emploi $	525

Table 1. Selected Characteristics for Census Tracts, 2001 Census – 100% Data and 20% Sample Data

No.	Characteristics	Vancouver 0184.05	Vancouver 0184.06 A	Vancouver 0184.07 A	Vancouver 0184.08 A	Vancouver 0184.09 A	Vancouver 0184.10 A
	2000 INCOME CHARACTERISTICS						
	Population 15 years and over with employment income in 2000 by sex and work activity – concluded						
526	Females with employment income (48)	1,975	320	1,230	950	1,095	820
527	Average employment income $	23,074	24,873	21,885	23,725	24,572	25,063
528	Standard error of average employment income $	846	2,286	967	1,158	1,102	1,625
529	Worked full year, full time (49)	945	120	635	375	495	355
530	Average employment income $	31,965	42,295	29,809	33,088	33,123	36,445
531	Standard error of average employment income $	1,260	3,778	1,309	1,760	1,561	2,784
532	Worked part year or part time (50)	950	180	570	540	550	460
533	Average employment income $	15,790	14,716	13,933	17,817	18,663	16,255
534	Standard error of average employment income $	891	1,804	1,051	1,290	1,286	1,419
	Census families by structure and family income groups in 2000						
535	Total - All census families	2,180	405	1,375	975	1,185	845
536	Under $10,000	180	20	70	25	65	65
537	$ 10,000 - $19,999	130	25	85	80	40	50
538	$ 20,000 - $29,999	165	70	155	95	90	90
539	$ 30,000 - $39,999	300	50	230	110	145	110
540	$ 40,000 - $49,999	200	35	175	125	175	75
541	$ 50,000 - $59,999	255	30	115	95	130	55
542	$ 60,000 - $69,999	195	35	125	130	75	75
543	$ 70,000 - $79,999	135	10	135	90	100	35
544	$ 80,000 - $89,999	145	40	100	95	100	60
545	$ 90,000 - $99,999	160	30	50	60	85	40
546	$100,000 and over	320	50	130	75	175	190
547	Average family income $	60,096	68,839	55,227	57,809	63,834	70,499
548	Median family income $	53,302	50,229	48,946	53,565	53,160	56,455
549	Standard error of average family income $	1,772	11,700	1,928	2,242	2,461	4,242
550	Total - All couple census families (51)	1,895	335	1,125	765	1,015	700
551	Under $10,000	95	10	50	10	50	45
552	$ 10,000 - $19,999	110	15	35	15	20	40
553	$ 20,000 - $29,999	125	55	135	60	65	70
554	$ 30,000 - $39,999	250	40	165	80	125	75
555	$ 40,000 - $49,999	185	25	120	105	140	40
556	$ 50,000 - $59,999	225	35	105	95	105	50
557	$ 60,000 - $69,999	185	35	115	100	70	75
558	$ 70,000 - $79,999	130	10	125	95	85	40
559	$ 80,000 - $89,999	135	40	90	90	95	55
560	$ 90,000 - $99,999	160	30	45	50	80	25
561	$100,000 and over	305	45	130	65	170	185
562	Average family income $	64,116	74,875	59,366	63,488	67,491	77,518
563	Median family income $	58,785	54,971	53,488	61,041	59,224	63,169
564	Standard error of average family income $	1,860	13,398	2,204	2,339	2,733	4,847
	Incidence of low income in 2000						
565	Total - Economic families	1,960	370	1,285	900	1,130	730
566	Low income	350	70	200	135	145	105
567	Incidence of low income in 2000 % (52)	18.1	18.5	15.7	15.1	12.5	14.8
568	Total - Unattached individuals 15 years and over	365	150	560	260	280	220
569	Low income	200	65	255	80	175	90
570	Incidence of low income in 2000 % (52)	53.7	44.3	46.3	31.7	62.2	39.5
571	Total - Population in private households	7,820	1,365	4,815	3,505	4,470	3,145
572	Low income	1,595	300	940	555	635	485
573	Incidence of low income in 2000 % (52)	20.4	22.0	19.5	15.9	14.2	15.4
	Private households by household income groups in 2000						
574	Total - All private households	2,170	480	1,755	1,100	1,300	895
575	Under $10,000	110	15	85	35	120	30
576	$ 10,000 - $19,999	145	55	235	75	60	90
577	$ 20,000 - $29,999	160	75	180	100	90	55
578	$ 30,000 - $39,999	250	35	275	125	115	95
579	$ 40,000 - $49,999	145	60	180	130	195	65
580	$ 50,000 - $59,999	265	60	210	110	95	80
581	$ 60,000 - $69,999	175	30	155	145	125	75
582	$ 70,000 - $79,999	200	15	110	110	90	50
583	$ 80,000 - $89,999	160	35	105	90	100	85
584	$ 90,000 - $99,999	180	20	60	65	85	65
585	$100,000 and over	375	75	165	110	230	210
586	Average household income $	66,450	67,675	52,754	60,154	64,160	77,196
587	Median household income $	61,241	49,953	46,441	57,808	57,972	64,072
588	Standard error of average household income $	1,971	9,523	1,848	2,210	2,535	4,237

Tableau 1. Certaines caractéristiques des secteurs de recensement, recensement de 2001 – Données intégrales et données-échantillon (20 %)

Vancouver 0184.11 A	Vancouver 0185.05	Vancouver 0185.06 A	Vancouver 0185.07 A	Vancouver 0185.08 A	Vancouver 0185.09 A	Caractéristiques	N°
						CARACTÉRISTIQUES DU REVENU DE 2000	
						Population de 15 ans et plus ayant un revenu d'emploi en 2000 selon le sexe et le travail – fin	
1,005	1,090	1,905	1,425	310	990	Femmes ayant un revenu d'emploi (48)	526
26,863	21,042	27,177	24,248	27,552	24,920	Revenu moyen d'emploi $	527
1,622	1,208	1,038	1,141	2,395	1,206	Erreur type de revenu moyen d'emploi $	528
395	420	910	605	120	420	Ayant travaillé toute l'année à plein temps (49)	529
41,215	33,151	39,365	36,269	42,816	36,177	Revenu moyen d'emploi $	530
2,911	1,896	1,459	1,737	3,971	1,791	Erreur type de revenu moyen d'emploi $	531
560	630	945	775	165	510	Ayant travaillé une partie de l'année ou à temps partiel (50)	532
17,299	14,131	16,625	15,332	17,461	17,630	Revenu moyen d'emploi $	533
1,210	1,210	1,066	1,140	1,915	1,213	Erreur type de revenu moyen d'emploi $	534
						Familles de recensement selon la structure et les tranches de revenu de la famille en 2000	
950	1,320	2,065	1,560	345	1,160	Total - Toutes les familles de recensement	535
25	125	90	70	10	125	Moins de 10 000 $	536
60	190	110	75	15	110	10 000 $ - 19 999 $	537
75	145	165	140	10	145	20 000 $ - 29 999 $	538
80	150	145	150	45	100	30 000 $ - 39 999 $	539
95	140	180	185	60	150	40 000 $ - 49 999 $	540
70	105	190	155	10	145	50 000 $ - 59 999 $	541
80	190	205	100	25	130	60 000 $ - 69 999 $	542
85	80	225	205	40	100	70 000 $ - 79 999 $	543
40	55	120	125	15	35	80 000 $ - 89 999 $	544
65	50	95	115	15	45	90 000 $ - 99 999 $	545
270	95	545	240	115	75	100 000 $ et plus	546
77,545	47,556	79,908	65,085	87,499	48,351	Revenu moyen des familles $	547
68,368	43,091	66,557	61,003	72,903	47,757	Revenu médian des familles $	548
3,705	1,861	4,473	2,053	6,581	1,885	Erreur type de revenu moyen des familles $	549
820	995	1,835	1,345	305	920	Total - Toutes les familles de recensement comptant un couple (51)	550
15	55	75	30	-	95	Moins de 10 000 $	551
25	80	60	35	10	85	10 000 $ - 19 999 $	552
55	105	130	85	10	90	20 000 $ - 29 999 $	553
65	105	120	135	30	75	30 000 $ - 39 999 $	554
80	110	165	165	40	130	40 000 $ - 49 999 $	555
50	90	150	150	10	125	50 000 $ - 59 999 $	556
75	170	180	85	25	95	60 000 $ - 69 999 $	557
85	80	220	195	35	95	70 000 $ - 79 999 $	558
40	55	105	115	15	30	80 000 $ - 89 999 $	559
60	45	90	110	15	40	90 000 $ - 99 999 $	560
270	95	535	235	115	60	100 000 $ et plus	561
84,040	55,120	84,246	70,117	93,750	50,073	Revenu moyen des familles $	562
75,006	53,543	72,740	67,187	77,991	49,547	Revenu médian des familles $	563
4,048	2,212	5,017	2,162	6,927	2,125	Erreur type de revenu moyen des familles $	564
						Fréquence des unités à faible revenu en 2000	
895	1,235	1,880	1,395	340	1,030	Total - Familles économiques	565
110	355	195	195	10	205	Faible revenu	566
12.4	28.9	10.2	14.0	3.5	20.0	Fréquence des unités à faible revenu en 2000 % (52)	567
180	445	395	235	65	465	Total - Personnes hors famille économique de 15 ans et plus	568
85	210	145	90	-	155	Faible revenu	569
47.4	48.0	36.6	36.9	3.9	33.0	Fréquence des unités à faible revenu en 2000 % (52)	570
3,280	4,885	7,050	5,510	1,210	3,885	Total - Population dans les ménages privés	571
455	1,510	815	830	40	850	Faible revenu	572
13.8	30.9	11.6	15.1	3.3	21.9	Fréquence des unités à faible revenu en 2000 % (52)	573
						Ménages privés selon les tranches de revenu du ménage en 2000	
1,000	1,580	2,190	1,575	400	1,420	Total - Tous les ménages privés	574
25	180	40	50	10	90	Moins de 10 000 $	575
50	200	140	95	10	140	10 000 $ - 19 999 $	576
65	130	135	115	15	205	20 000 $ - 29 999 $	577
120	205	165	150	30	110	30 000 $ - 39 999 $	578
90	165	185	165	90	205	40 000 $ - 49 999 $	579
65	150	195	125	35	150	50 000 $ - 59 999 $	580
100	180	245	95	20	140	60 000 $ - 69 999 $	581
95	125	240	155	50	125	70 000 $ - 79 999 $	582
45	60	110	170	15	90	80 000 $ - 89 999 $	583
40	65	120	170	15	80	90 000 $ - 99 999 $	584
300	110	615	300	120	80	100 000 $ et plus	585
79,492	47,568	83,094	71,205	85,526	50,783	Revenu moyen des ménages $	586
68,144	43,394	69,159	69,758	69,105	48,396	Revenu médian des ménages $	587
3,608	1,694	4,282	2,201	6,199	1,663	Erreur type de revenu moyen des ménages $	588

Table 1. Selected Characteristics for Census Tracts, 2001 Census – 100% Data and 20% Sample Data

No.	Characteristics	Vancouver 0185.10 A	Vancouver 0185.11 A	Vancouver 0185.12 A	Vancouver 0185.13 ◆◇ A	Vancouver 0185.14 A	Vancouver 0185.15 A
	POPULATION CHARACTERISTICS						
1	**Population, 1996 (1)**	**4,209**	**5,844**	**5,752**	**3,537**	**5,686**	**4,470**
2	**Population, 2001 (2)**	**4,717**	**6,585**	**6,133**	**6,051**	**6,891**	**5,086**
3	Population percentage change, 1996-2001	12.1	12.7	6.6	71.1	21.2	13.8
4	Land area in square kilometres, 2001	1.29	1.32	1.37	1.33	1.34	2.67
5	**Total population – 100% Data (3)**	**4,715**	**6,585**	**6,130**	**6,050**	**6,890**	**5,085**
	by sex and age groups						
6	Male	2,360	3,265	3,115	3,010	3,360	2,585
7	0-4 years	260	350	275	270	360	260
8	5-9 years	220	290	300	270	285	225
9	10-14 years	205	215	280	225	230	150
10	15-19 years	130	190	270	215	215	175
11	20-24 years	175	240	205	250	240	205
12	25-29 years	200	290	205	275	280	210
13	30-34 years	225	320	230	290	305	240
14	35-39 years	200	320	280	265	285	220
15	40-44 years	185	210	255	215	210	190
16	45-49 years	135	210	255	150	175	150
17	50-54 years	115	185	185	150	155	110
18	55-59 years	90	140	115	140	160	120
19	60-64 years	75	95	90	100	150	115
20	65-69 years	65	85	65	90	120	75
21	70-74 years	45	65	40	55	85	65
22	75-79 years	20	40	30	25	65	35
23	80-84 years	10	15	20	15	25	20
24	85 years and over	5	10	5	10	20	20
25	Female	2,360	3,315	3,020	3,035	3,530	2,505
26	0-4 years	270	310	225	255	325	210
27	5-9 years	200	295	265	245	280	205
28	10-14 years	155	220	240	200	210	155
29	15-19 years	145	180	245	190	220	160
30	20-24 years	215	255	185	340	295	185
31	25-29 years	225	350	245	325	360	220
32	30-34 years	255	315	265	250	300	225
33	35-39 years	190	310	280	250	235	210
34	40-44 years	150	215	290	180	180	185
35	45-49 years	130	185	220	185	190	130
36	50-54 years	110	185	170	170	175	150
37	55-59 years	90	135	125	130	190	115
38	60-64 years	85	110	95	110	165	120
39	65-69 years	60	85	50	80	125	85
40	70-74 years	45	80	50	45	105	55
41	75-79 years	25	40	40	40	95	50
42	80-84 years	10	25	15	20	60	25
43	85 years and over	-	15	20	20	25	15
44	**Total population 15 years and over**	**3,410**	**4,905**	**4,550**	**4,580**	**5,205**	**3,880**
	by legal marital status						
45	Never married (single)	910	1,270	1,225	1,240	1,105	985
46	Legally married (and not separated)	2,125	2,945	2,830	2,865	3,430	2,350
47	Separated, but still legally married	110	185	120	110	150	120
48	Divorced	155	290	205	210	220	230
49	Widowed	120	220	165	155	305	200
	by common-law status						
50	Not in a common-law relationship	3,275	4,665	4,420	4,380	5,085	3,710
51	In a common-law relationship	135	235	135	195	125	170
52	**Total population – 20% Sample Data (4)**	**4,740**	**6,585**	**6,110**	**6,050**	**6,890**	**5,085**
	by mother tongue						
53	Single responses	4,615	6,440	5,965	5,775	6,670	4,980
54	English	1,310	2,400	2,985	1,910	1,285	2,020
55	French	35	40	55	25	40	65
56	Non-official languages (5)	3,275	4,000	2,925	3,845	5,340	2,895
57	Chinese, n.o.s.	-	20	-	65	10	10
58	Cantonese	10	30	30	20	65	10
59	Punjabi	2,105	2,595	1,815	2,980	4,215	2,110
60	Mandarin	-	20	-	25	25	-
61	Tagalog (Pilipino)	40	150	150	70	25	70
62	Other languages (6)	1,125	1,185	940	700	1,000	700
63	Multiple responses	120	145	140	270	220	105
64	English and French	-	-	-	10	-	15
65	English and non-official language	115	145	140	265	220	85
66	French and non-official language	-	-	-	-	-	-
67	English, French and non-official language	-	-	-	-	-	-

See reference material at the end of the publication. – Voir les documents de référence à la fin de la publication.

Tableau 1. Certaines caractéristiques des secteurs de recensement, recensement de 2001 – Données intégrales et données-échantillon (20 %)

Vancouver 0185.16 ◆◇ A	Vancouver 0186.01	Vancouver 0186.02	Vancouver 0186.05 ◇ A	Vancouver 0186.06 A	Vancouver 0186.07 A	Caractéristiques	N°
						CARACTÉRISTIQUES DE LA POPULATION	
3,665	**5,626**	**4,906**	**5,548**	**3,021**	**4,206**	**Population, 1996 (1)**	1
4,425	**6,015**	**4,977**	**5,806**	**3,469**	**4,547**	**Population, 2001 (2)**	2
20.7	6.9	1.4	4.7	14.8	8.1	Variation en pourcentage de la population, 1996-2001	3
2.65	1.98	1.90	1.25	1.28	1.33	Superficie des terres en kilomètres carrés, 2001	4
4,425	**6,015**	**4,975**	**5,810**	**3,470**	**4,545**	**Population totale – Données intégrales (3)**	5
						selon le sexe et les groupes d'âge	
2,245	3,055	2,510	2,870	1,795	2,275	Sexe masculin	6
230	235	175	265	180	225	0-4 ans	7
220	230	215	280	190	210	5-9 ans	8
170	195	175	240	115	170	10-14 ans	9
145	200	155	170	115	155	15-19 ans	10
150	220	160	215	145	160	20-24 ans	11
180	255	145	210	145	155	25-29 ans	12
205	275	190	230	145	205	30-34 ans	13
235	280	235	245	155	190	35-39 ans	14
190	275	245	230	130	180	40-44 ans	15
135	215	190	175	110	155	45-49 ans	16
100	190	160	155	100	130	50-54 ans	17
100	130	110	110	80	110	55-59 ans	18
80	115	90	120	65	85	60-64 ans	19
50	80	90	90	40	60	65-69 ans	20
40	70	90	45	30	40	70-74 ans	21
15	40	45	35	20	25	75-79 ans	22
5	20	30	20	15	5	80-84 ans	23
5	20	20	15	-	10	85 ans et plus	24
2,180	2,965	2,465	2,940	1,680	2,275	Sexe féminin	25
200	230	145	200	160	160	0-4 ans	26
200	200	180	260	135	225	5-9 ans	27
165	185	175	190	100	185	10-14 ans	28
120	195	165	165	100	155	15-19 ans	29
180	250	155	230	115	180	20-24 ans	30
195	255	155	245	175	185	25-29 ans	31
205	255	185	260	155	180	30-34 ans	32
185	240	225	235	140	195	35-39 ans	33
180	255	210	200	125	175	40-44 ans	34
125	210	145	190	100	155	45-49 ans	35
100	165	165	165	90	130	50-54 ans	36
95	140	105	160	70	95	55-59 ans	37
90	115	80	120	70	90	60-64 ans	38
50	80	115	85	55	70	65-69 ans	39
55	80	100	80	40	55	70-74 ans	40
25	45	80	65	20	20	75-79 ans	41
10	35	60	40	15	20	80-84 ans	42
5	20	30	35	10	5	85 ans et plus	43
3,235	**4,745**	**3,905**	**4,365**	**2,590**	**3,375**	**Population totale de 15 ans et plus**	44
						selon l'état matrimonial légal	
780	1,485	1,185	1,175	635	925	Célibataire (jamais marié(e))	45
2,045	2,505	2,005	2,465	1,655	2,050	Légalement marié(e) (et non séparé(e))	46
105	185	135	155	75	100	Séparé(e), mais toujours légalement marié(e)	47
160	320	315	345	110	155	Divorcé(e)	48
140	245	260	230	115	145	Veuf ou veuve	49
						selon l'union libre	
3,135	4,415	3,670	4,140	2,520	3,245	Ne vivant pas en union libre	50
95	330	240	230	70	135	Vivant en union libre	51
4,385	**5,990**	**4,950**	**5,805**	**3,460**	**4,555**	**Population totale – Données-échantillon (20 %) (4)**	52
						selon la langue maternelle	
4,285	5,855	4,870	5,555	3,390	4,460	Réponses uniques	53
1,515	3,295	3,275	2,755	1,085	1,850	Anglais	54
15	40	50	10	20	20	Français	55
2,755	2,515	1,540	2,790	2,285	2,590	Langues non officielles (5)	56
65	45	20	35	-	40	Chinois, n.d.a.	57
25	45	35	-	10	-	Cantonais	58
2,020	1,335	420	1,675	1,870	1,590	Pendjabi	59
-	30	20	30	-	-	Mandarin	60
130	85	115	75	10	140	Tagalog (pilipino)	61
520	980	925	980	400	820	Autres langues (6)	62
95	135	80	250	70	95	Réponses multiples	63
-	-	20	-	-	-	Anglais et français	64
95	135	60	240	70	95	Anglais et langue non officielle	65
-	-	-	-	-	-	Français et langue non officielle	66
-	-	-	10	-	-	Anglais, français et langue non officielle	67

See reference material at the end of the publication. – Voir les documents de référence à la fin de la publication.

Table 1. Selected Characteristics for Census Tracts, 2001 Census – 100% Data and 20% Sample Data

No.	Characteristics	Vancouver 0185.10 A	Vancouver 0185.11 A	Vancouver 0185.12 A	Vancouver 0185.13 ◆◇ A	Vancouver 0185.14 A	Vancouver 0185.15 A
	POPULATION CHARACTERISTICS						
	by home language						
68	Single responses	3,180	4,665	4,500	3,955	4,795	3,530
69	English	1,435	2,630	3,160	1,950	1,440	1,975
70	French	-	10	15	-	-	-
71	Non-official languages (5)	1,745	2,030	1,325	2,000	3,350	1,550
72	Cantonese	-	10	10	-	55	-
73	Chinese, n.o.s.	-	15	-	10	-	-
74	Punjabi	1,195	1,535	1,050	1,695	2,920	1,270
75	Mandarin	35	10	-	-	35	-
76	Korean	-	20	-	-	-	-
77	Other languages (6)	515	435	265	295	340	280
78	Multiple responses	1,560	1,915	1,605	2,100	2,095	1,555
79	English and French	35	25	60	20	20	35
80	English and non-official language	1,510	1,855	1,530	2,015	2,050	1,490
81	French and non-official language	10	15	10	-	20	-
82	English, French and non-official language	10	20	10	65	10	30
	by knowledge of official languages						
83	English only	4,085	5,760	5,360	5,195	5,465	4,320
84	French only	-	10	-	-	10	10
85	English and French	120	255	315	215	205	155
86	Neither English nor French	535	560	430	640	1,210	600
	by knowledge of non-official languages (5) (7)						
87	Cantonese	10	75	30	45	75	10
88	Chinese, n.o.s.	-	20	35	80	-	-
89	Punjabi	2,460	2,985	2,035	3,620	4,690	2,325
90	Mandarin	30	30	-	40	50	-
91	Hindi	1,020	1,305	1,075	1,050	1,345	1,210
92	German	20	60	65	50	50	50
93	Spanish	75	150	50	15	160	30
	by first official language spoken						
94	English	4,175	5,950	5,580	5,380	5,640	4,400
95	French	35	35	50	20	55	40
96	English and French	15	35	45	40	25	45
97	Neither English nor French	520	560	430	605	1,170	600
98	Official language minority - (number) (8)	40	55	75	40	70	55
99	Official language minority - (percentage) (8)	0.8	0.8	1.2	0.7	1.0	1.1
	by ethnic origin (9)						
100	English	390	665	1,165	380	450	615
101	Canadian	490	825	1,205	585	405	610
102	Chinese	125	130	145	185	105	35
103	Scottish	235	390	595	265	240	375
104	Irish	160	395	415	205	250	395
105	German	165	310	530	195	185	295
106	East Indian	2,455	3,130	1,965	3,720	4,585	2,850
107	French	130	190	255	150	95	220
108	Ukrainian	35	170	230	120	105	105
109	Italian	140	50	90	30	45	30
110	Dutch (Netherlands)	75	70	140	160	40	115
111	Filipino	55	295	290	135	50	160
112	Polish	40	95	140	50	55	30
113	Norwegian	15	60	170	45	35	65
114	North American Indian	75	185	60	70	15	130
	by Aboriginal identity						
115	Total Aboriginal identity population (10)	50	165	110	90	10	95
116	Total non-Aboriginal population	4,695	6,420	6,000	5,960	6,885	4,990
	by Aboriginal origin						
117	Total Aboriginal origins population (11)	95	200	90	95	35	160
118	Total non-Aboriginal population	4,645	6,385	6,020	5,955	6,855	4,925
	by Registered Indian status						
119	Registered Indian (12)	15	85	45	65	-	45
120	Not a Registered Indian	4,730	6,505	6,060	5,985	6,890	5,040

Tableau 1. Certaines caractéristiques des secteurs de recensement, recensement de 2001 – Données intégrales et données-échantillon (20 %)

Vancouver 0185.16 ◆◇ A	Vancouver 0186.01	Vancouver 0186.02	Vancouver 0186.05 ◇ A	Vancouver 0186.06 A	Vancouver 0186.07 A	Caractéristiques	N°
						CARACTÉRISTIQUES DE LA POPULATION	
						selon la langue parlée à la maison	
3,100	4,400	4,125	4,470	2,290	3,280	Réponses uniques	68
1,630	3,475	3,580	2,975	1,175	1,950	Anglais	69
-	-	-	-	10	-	Français	70
1,465	925	550	1,490	1,105	1,335	Langues non officielles (5)	71
-	15	35	-	10	-	Cantonais	72
30	25	10	30	-	20	Chinois, n.d.a.	73
1,195	570	290	1,160	1,000	980	Pendjabi	74
-	-	-	30	-	-	Mandarin	75
-	-	-	-	-	-	Coréen	76
245	315	210	270	95	330	Autres langues (6)	77
1,285	1,585	820	1,340	1,170	1,275	Réponses multiples	78
10	35	70	10	-	10	Anglais et français	79
1,270	1,510	715	1,315	1,150	1,245	Anglais et langue non officielle	80
-	-	-	-	20	20	Français et langue non officielle	81
-	35	35	10	-	-	Anglais, français et langue non officielle	82
						selon la connaissance des langues officielles	
3,790	5,395	4,545	5,240	2,895	3,950	Anglais seulement	83
-	-	-	-	-	40	Français seulement	84
100	225	230	165	125	125	Anglais et français	85
490	365	175	400	445	445	Ni l'anglais ni le français	86
						selon la connaissance des langues non officielles (5) (7)	
35	70	45	10	15	20	Cantonais	87
65	40	20	65	-	30	Chinois, n.d.a.	88
2,210	1,605	475	1,955	2,080	1,750	Pendjabi	89
25	45	25	30	-	15	Mandarin	90
685	870	270	815	705	640	Hindi	91
30	125	165	75	40	50	Allemand	92
50	140	55	60	95	260	Espagnol	93
						selon la première langue officielle parlée	
3,835	5,550	4,735	5,375	2,930	4,040	Anglais	94
-	35	50	10	20	50	Français	95
55	50	-	20	60	30	Anglais et français	96
490	360	160	400	445	445	Ni l'anglais ni le français	97
35	55	45	25	50	60	Minorité de langue officielle - (nombre) (8)	98
0.8	0.9	0.9	0.4	1.4	1.3	Minorité de langue officielle - (pourcentage) (8)	99
						selon l'origine ethnique (9)	
425	1,000	1,205	810	350	615	Anglais	100
495	990	1,080	815	325	325	Canadien	101
135	210	130	150	10	115	Chinois	102
395	800	930	665	290	360	Écossais	103
230	625	625	525	160	305	Irlandais	104
225	605	590	425	200	260	Allemand	105
2,050	2,080	575	2,035	2,215	1,670	Indien de l'Inde	106
155	395	475	330	100	200	Français	107
100	145	245	155	55	55	Ukrainien	108
45	65	145	160	10	80	Italien	109
95	295	145	210	45	110	Hollandais (Néerlandais)	110
235	165	170	150	40	210	Philippin	111
10	140	190	155	40	55	Polonais	112
25	85	235	95	25	110	Norvégien	113
35	185	145	155	170	40	Indien de l'Amérique du Nord	114
						selon l'identité autochtone	
20	235	155	165	50	40	Total de la population ayant une identité autochtone (10)	115
4,365	5,755	4,800	5,640	3,410	4,510	Total de la population non autochtone	116
						selon l'origine autochtone	
35	335	310	250	175	60	Total de la population ayant une origine autochtone (11)	117
4,345	5,650	4,640	5,555	3,285	4,495	Total de la population non autochtone	118
						selon le statut d'Indien inscrit	
10	105	15	65	35	15	Oui, Indien inscrit (12)	119
4,380	5,885	4,935	5,740	3,420	4,545	Non, pas un Indien inscrit	120

Table 1. Selected Characteristics for Census Tracts, 2001 Census – 100% Data and 20% Sample Data

No.	Characteristics	Vancouver 0185.10 A	Vancouver 0185.11 A	Vancouver 0185.12 A	Vancouver 0185.13 ◆◇ A	Vancouver 0185.14 A	Vancouver 0185.15 A
	POPULATION CHARACTERISTICS						
	by visible minority groups						
121	Total visible minority population	3,635	4,625	3,225	4,715	5,760	3,350
122	Chinese	75	155	60	155	105	40
123	South Asian	3,045	3,780	2,565	4,195	5,200	3,065
124	Black	190	120	115	100	185	10
125	Filipino	80	275	260	105	55	125
126	Latin American	55	80	35	-	145	15
127	Southeast Asian	145	40	20	25	25	60
128	Arab	10	-	20	15	-	-
129	West Asian	-	85	55	95	10	-
130	Korean	-	25	10	25	-	15
131	Japanese	-	20	45	-	10	-
132	Visible minority, n.i.e. (13)	-	10	-	-	-	10
133	Multiple visible minorities (14)	25	45	50	-	15	10
	by citizenship						
134	Canadian citizenship (15)	3,890	5,340	5,125	4,775	5,000	4,050
135	Citizenship other than Canadian	855	1,240	980	1,275	1,890	1,040
	by place of birth of respondent						
136	Non-immigrant population	2,420	3,310	3,525	2,775	2,790	2,705
137	Born in province of residence	2,070	2,545	2,645	2,265	2,220	2,100
138	Immigrant population (16)	2,200	3,195	2,485	3,195	4,005	2,300
139	United States	25	50	55	20	-	25
140	Central and South America	55	85	35	10	55	40
141	Caribbean and Bermuda	-	40	20	-	20	10
142	United Kingdom	70	100	165	100	55	95
143	Other Europe (17)	65	90	140	135	140	55
144	Africa	95	65	110	40	115	15
145	Asia and the Middle East	1,660	2,390	1,635	2,670	3,445	1,675
146	Oceania and other (18)	235	375	325	220	175	385
147	Non-permanent residents (19)	115	80	95	85	95	85
148	**Total immigrant population**	**2,200**	**3,200**	**2,485**	**3,195**	**4,005**	**2,300**
	by period of immigration						
149	Before 1961	65	50	85	70	100	60
150	1961-1970	130	140	125	105	195	95
151	1971-1980	475	525	485	730	525	375
152	1981-1990	485	735	585	725	1,025	630
153	1991-2001 (20)	1,040	1,745	1,215	1,570	2,160	1,140
154	1991-1995	535	850	760	735	1,020	720
155	1996-2001 (20)	505	890	450	830	1,145	425
	by age at immigration						
156	0-4 years	120	210	225	225	150	40
157	5-19 years	585	700	625	760	955	585
158	20 years and over	1,490	2,285	1,640	2,205	2,895	1,680
159	**Total population**	**4,745**	**6,585**	**6,110**	**6,050**	**6,895**	**5,085**
	by religion						
160	Catholic (21)	315	900	760	510	315	365
161	Protestant	350	800	1,035	495	570	590
162	Christian Orthodox	15	60	100	15	80	20
163	Christian, n.i.e. (22)	190	175	320	110	80	165
164	Muslim	575	615	305	350	520	215
165	Jewish	25	-	-	10	-	-
166	Buddhist	55	40	45	75	10	40
167	Hindu	280	400	355	385	305	635
168	Sikh	2,320	2,715	1,940	3,495	4,530	2,135
169	Eastern religions (23)	-	20	-	30	-	10
170	Other religions (24)	10	15	40	10	15	30
171	No religious affiliation (25)	610	850	1,205	575	465	885
172	**Total population 15 years and over**	**3,440**	**4,910**	**4,520**	**4,575**	**5,200**	**3,875**
	by generation status						
173	1st generation (26)	2,235	3,075	2,480	3,155	3,860	2,355
174	2nd generation (27)	720	735	775	905	890	610
175	3rd generation and over (28)	495	1,105	1,270	520	450	915
176	**Total population 1 year and over (29)**	**4,665**	**6,440**	**6,050**	**5,930**	**6,710**	**4,970**
	by place of residence 1 year ago (mobility)						
177	Non-movers	4,240	5,220	5,405	4,675	5,370	4,035
178	Movers	425	1,225	645	1,255	1,340	935
179	Non-migrants	260	685	420	840	860	685
180	Migrants	160	540	225	410	480	250
181	Internal migrants	95	355	120	285	200	180
182	Intraprovincial migrants	60	310	110	255	190	175
183	Interprovincial migrants	30	40	10	25	10	10
184	External migrants	70	185	100	130	280	70

Tableau 1. Certaines caractéristiques des secteurs de recensement, recensement de 2001 – Données intégrales et données-échantillon (20 %)

Vancouver 0185.16 ◆◇ A	Vancouver 0186.01	Vancouver 0186.02	Vancouver 0186.05 ◇ A	Vancouver 0186.06 A	Vancouver 0186.07 A	Caractéristiques	N°
						CARACTÉRISTIQUES DE LA POPULATION	
						selon les groupes de minorités visibles	
3,090	2,910	1,305	3,040	2,560	2,935	Total de la population des minorités visibles	121
65	155	100	140	10	110	Chinois	122
2,475	2,185	815	2,515	2,365	2,075	Sud-Asiatique	123
35	50	50	35	45	35	Noir	124
250	145	170	150	25	205	Philippin	125
45	85	40	45	70	225	Latino-Américain	126
150	95	90	50	-	240	Asiatique du Sud-Est	127
-	85	10	70	-	-	Arabe	128
-	10	-	20	-	30	Asiatique occidental	129
30	-	-	10	10	-	Coréen	130
20	55	-	-	30	-	Japonais	131
-	-	15	-	-	-	Minorité visible, n.i.a. (13)	132
10	50	10	10	10	10	Minorités visibles multiples (14)	133
						selon la citoyenneté	
3,500	5,360	4,480	4,670	2,740	3,780	Citoyenneté canadienne (15)	134
880	625	470	1,135	720	775	Citoyenneté autre que canadienne	135
						selon le lieu de naissance du répondant	
2,130	3,795	3,545	3,300	1,715	2,325	Population non immigrante	136
1,810	2,825	2,580	2,530	1,475	1,765	Née dans la province de résidence	137
2,185	2,170	1,375	2,485	1,725	2,185	Population immigrante (16)	138
25	40	30	25	15	10	États-Unis	139
40	80	20	50	55	175	Amérique centrale et du Sud	140
20	25	40	-	-	20	Caraïbes et Bermudes	141
80	125	135	145	80	85	Royaume-Uni	142
50	260	330	255	55	85	Autre Europe (17)	143
-	25	10	10	30	25	Afrique	144
1,830	1,285	660	1,665	1,350	1,605	Asie et Moyen-Orient	145
135	335	150	335	140	185	Océanie et autre (18)	146
70	25	30	25	15	45	Résidents non permanents (19)	147
2,180	**2,170**	**1,375**	**2,485**	**1,725**	**2,185**	**Population immigrante totale**	148
						selon la période d'immigration	
30	135	170	165	25	65	Avant 1961	149
130	210	200	155	55	145	1961-1970	150
410	500	215	330	290	255	1971-1980	151
420	610	290	575	495	725	1981-1990	152
1,195	715	495	1,250	865	1,000	1991-2001 (20)	153
660	345	195	500	490	555	1991-1995	154
535	365	300	750	375	450	1996-2001 (20)	155
						selon l'âge à l'immigration	
130	210	135	175	40	165	0-4 ans	156
610	605	450	750	390	535	5-19 ans	157
1,440	1,355	785	1,560	1,295	1,485	20 ans et plus	158
4,385	**5,990**	**4,945**	**5,805**	**3,460**	**4,555**	**Population totale**	159
						selon la religion	
410	710	885	635	170	740	Catholique (21)	160
530	1,150	1,375	940	415	675	Protestante	161
-	95	20	20	-	65	Orthodoxe chrétienne	162
150	240	175	110	60	245	Chrétiennes, n.i.a. (22)	163
195	155	260	345	160	60	Musulmane	164
-	-	-	-	10	-	Juive	165
100	105	55	100	-	-	Bouddhiste	166
115	435	120	270	170	200	Hindoue	167
2,185	1,535	390	1,935	2,090	1,740	Sikh	168
-	-	-	-	-	-	Religions orientales (23)	169
20	-	10	15	-	-	Autres religions (24)	170
660	1,565	1,660	1,445	385	815	Aucune appartenance religieuse (25)	171
3,175	**4,715**	**3,880**	**4,345**	**2,560**	**3,400**	**Population totale de 15 ans et plus**	172
						selon le statut des générations	
2,115	2,135	1,325	2,330	1,680	2,120	1re génération (26)	173
540	945	955	725	345	535	2e génération (27)	174
520	1,635	1,600	1,285	540	740	3e génération et plus (28)	175
4,320	**5,885**	**4,925**	**5,700**	**3,390**	**4,480**	**Population totale de 1 an et plus (29)**	176
						selon le lieu de résidence 1 an auparavant (mobilité)	
3,670	5,075	4,245	4,830	2,715	3,665	Personnes n'ayant pas déménagé	177
650	810	680	870	675	810	Personnes ayant déménagé	178
495	515	445	590	495	565	Non-migrants	179
150	290	230	280	180	250	Migrants	180
100	215	105	200	125	150	Migrants internes	181
80	155	95	145	115	50	Migrants infraprovinciaux	182
20	60	15	50	10	95	Migrants interprovinciaux	183
50	80	120	80	60	100	Migrants externes	184

Table 1. Selected Characteristics for Census Tracts, 2001 Census – 100% Data and 20% Sample Data

No.	Characteristics	Vancouver 0185.10 A	Vancouver 0185.11 A	Vancouver 0185.12 A	Vancouver 0185.13 ◆◇ A	Vancouver 0185.14 A	Vancouver 0185.15 A
	POPULATION CHARACTERISTICS						
185	**Total population 5 years and over (30)**	**4,255**	**5,930**	**5,600**	**5,525**	**6,215**	**4,610**
	by place of residence 5 years ago (mobility)						
186	Non-movers	2,200	2,440	3,010	2,095	2,895	2,460
187	Movers	2,055	3,495	2,595	3,430	3,315	2,140
188	Non-migrants	1,295	1,715	1,460	1,775	1,570	1,200
189	Migrants	760	1,780	1,130	1,655	1,750	940
190	Internal migrants	405	1,055	750	860	770	615
191	Intraprovincial migrants	320	880	535	780	520	535
192	Interprovincial migrants	85	170	210	75	250	75
193	External migrants	350	720	385	795	980	330
194	**Total population 15 to 24 years**	**715**	**860**	**895**	**1,000**	**960**	**715**
	by school attendance						
195	Not attending school	380	335	315	390	260	360
196	Attending school full time	290	430	470	525	530	285
197	Attending school part time	45	95	110	85	170	70
198	**Total population 15 years and over**	**3,440**	**4,910**	**4,525**	**4,580**	**5,205**	**3,875**
	by highest level of schooling						
199	Less than grade 9 (31)	475	595	455	605	1,000	590
200	Grades 9-13 without high school graduation certificate	905	1,250	1,075	835	1,350	1,135
201	Grades 9-13 with high school graduation certificate	560	685	575	640	680	585
202	Some postsecondary without degree, certificate or diploma (32)	450	635	505	655	610	465
203	Trades certificate or diploma (33)	320	480	590	440	285	375
204	College certificate or diploma (34)	360	550	685	470	410	375
205	University certificate below bachelor's degree	75	85	130	120	110	45
206	University with bachelor's degree or higher	285	635	505	815	750	305
	by combinations of unpaid work						
207	Males 15 years and over	1,710	2,415	2,255	2,230	2,490	1,945
208	Reported unpaid work (35)	1,500	2,125	2,065	1,940	2,140	1,710
209	Housework and child care and care or assistance to seniors	250	190	280	340	360	215
210	Housework and child care only	515	760	790	670	755	510
211	Housework and care or assistance to seniors only	80	95	140	145	225	140
212	Child care and care or assistance to seniors only	-	10	15	-	15	15
213	Housework only	625	1,030	800	730	730	725
214	Child care only	30	30	15	35	45	70
215	Care or assistance to seniors only	10	15	25	20	-	45
216	Females 15 years and over	1,735	2,500	2,265	2,350	2,715	1,930
217	Reported unpaid work (35)	1,570	2,335	2,185	2,175	2,500	1,800
218	Housework and child care and care or assistance to seniors	320	300	395	425	445	310
219	Housework and child care only	715	965	915	830	1,045	660
220	Housework and care or assistance to seniors only	115	70	100	155	250	140
221	Child care and care or assistance to seniors only	10	-	-	-	-	-
222	Housework only	380	960	735	720	685	645
223	Child care only	30	15	25	45	40	30
224	Care or assistance to seniors only	10	15	10	10	20	10
	by labour force activity						
225	Males 15 years and over	1,710	2,415	2,255	2,230	2,490	1,945
226	In the labour force	1,305	1,865	1,725	1,755	1,790	1,520
227	Employed	1,220	1,695	1,610	1,575	1,620	1,410
228	Unemployed	90	160	115	180	170	110
229	Not in the labour force	400	550	525	475	700	425
230	Participation rate	76.3	77.2	76.5	78.7	71.9	78.1
231	Employment rate	71.3	70.2	71.4	70.6	65.1	72.5
232	Unemployment rate	6.9	8.6	6.7	10.3	9.5	7.2
233	Females 15 years and over	1,735	2,500	2,265	2,350	2,715	1,930
234	In the labour force	1,005	1,655	1,600	1,455	1,400	1,215
235	Employed	895	1,480	1,420	1,280	1,245	1,080
236	Unemployed	115	175	175	185	150	135
237	Not in the labour force	730	845	670	890	1,315	715
238	Participation rate	57.9	66.2	70.6	61.9	51.6	63.0
239	Employment rate	51.6	59.2	62.7	54.5	45.9	56.0
240	Unemployment rate	11.4	10.6	10.9	12.7	10.7	11.1

Tableau 1. Certaines caractéristiques des secteurs de recensement, recensement de 2001 – Données intégrales et données-échantillon (20 %)

Vancouver 0185.16 ◆◇ A	Vancouver 0186.01	Vancouver 0186.02	Vancouver 0186.05 ◇ A	Vancouver 0186.06 A	Vancouver 0186.07 A	Caractéristiques	N°
						CARACTÉRISTIQUES DE LA POPULATION	
3,895	**5,520**	**4,625**	**5,340**	**3,135**	**4,160**	**Population totale de 5 ans et plus (30)**	185
						selon le lieu de résidence 5 ans auparavant (mobilité)	
2,010	3,180	2,800	2,740	1,855	1,830	Personnes n'ayant pas déménagé	186
1,885	2,335	1,820	2,600	1,280	2,335	Personnes ayant déménagé	187
1,085	1,160	1,280	1,370	730	1,355	Non-migrants	188
800	1,180	540	1,230	550	975	Migrants	189
385	885	325	770	255	585	Migrants internes	190
320	745	230	665	220	340	Migrants infraprovinciaux	191
70	140	100	105	35	255	Migrants interprovinciaux	192
415	295	205	460	295	390	Migrants externes	193
555	**880**	**630**	**785**	**455**	**665**	**Population totale de 15 à 24 ans**	194
						selon la fréquentation scolaire	
215	460	250	370	245	325	Ne fréquentant pas l'école	195
265	355	310	330	150	260	Fréquentant l'école à plein temps	196
70	65	70	90	60	80	Fréquentant l'école à temps partiel	197
3,175	**4,715**	**3,880**	**4,345**	**2,560**	**3,395**	**Population totale de 15 ans et plus**	198
						selon le plus haut niveau de scolarité atteint	
535	495	340	550	405	440	Niveau inférieur à la 9e année (31)	199
710	1,140	1,190	1,180	705	940	De la 9e à la 13e année sans certificat d'études secondaires	200
500	605	575	730	295	505	De la 9e à la 13e année avec certificat d'études secondaires	201
355	565	465	535	370	450	Études postsecondaires partielles sans grade, certificat ou diplôme (32)	202
350	625	475	485	290	385	Certificat ou diplôme d'une école de métiers (33)	203
270	710	590	555	185	355	Certificat ou diplôme collégial (34)	204
65	135	85	100	40	80	Certificat universitaire inférieur au baccalauréat	205
385	440	160	210	265	245	Études universitaires avec baccalauréat ou diplôme supérieur	206
						selon les combinaisons de travail non rémunéré	
1,580	2,395	1,930	2,060	1,285	1,680	Hommes de 15 ans et plus	207
1,430	2,050	1,680	1,805	1,115	1,480	Travail non rémunéré déclaré (35)	208
200	165	220	260	155	240	Travaux ménagers et soins aux enfants et soins ou aide aux personnes âgées	209
435	595	480	620	335	510	Travaux ménagers et soins aux enfants seulement	210
120	155	115	70	95	65	Travaux ménagers et soins ou aide aux personnes âgées seulement	211
15	10	15	10	-	-	Soins aux enfants et soins ou aide aux personnes âgées seulement	212
590	1,050	830	810	495	630	Travaux ménagers seulement	213
45	55	30	35	25	35	Soins aux enfants seulement	214
15	25	-	10	-	-	Soins ou aide aux personnes âgées seulement	215
1,590	2,325	1,950	2,285	1,280	1,720	Femmes de 15 ans et plus	216
1,470	2,150	1,810	2,040	1,165	1,640	Travail non rémunéré déclaré (35)	217
245	350	270	375	170	325	Travaux ménagers et soins aux enfants et soins ou aide aux personnes âgées	218
690	655	605	700	495	640	Travaux ménagers et soins aux enfants seulement	219
105	135	170	145	115	110	Travaux ménagers et soins ou aide aux personnes âgées seulement	220
-	10	10	15	-	-	Soins aux enfants et soins ou aide aux personnes âgées seulement	221
415	965	715	785	370	515	Travaux ménagers seulement	222
10	35	40	15	15	50	Soins aux enfants seulement	223
-	-	-	-	-	-	Soins ou aide aux personnes âgées seulement	224
						selon l'activité	
1,580	2,390	1,930	2,055	1,285	1,675	Hommes de 15 ans et plus	225
1,250	1,820	1,325	1,555	980	1,255	Population active	226
1,090	1,610	1,230	1,440	875	1,175	Personnes occupées	227
160	210	95	115	105	80	Chômeurs	228
335	570	605	500	300	425	Inactifs	229
79.1	76.2	68.7	75.7	76.3	74.9	Taux d'activité	230
69.0	67.4	63.7	70.1	68.1	70.1	Taux d'emploi	231
12.8	11.5	7.2	7.4	10.7	6.4	Taux de chômage	232
1,595	2,325	1,955	2,290	1,280	1,725	Femmes de 15 ans et plus	233
1,010	1,455	1,095	1,340	785	1,060	Population active	234
910	1,365	1,005	1,195	700	965	Personnes occupées	235
100	85	90	145	80	100	Chômeuses	236
580	875	850	945	495	655	Inactives	237
63.3	62.6	56.0	58.5	61.3	61.4	Taux d'activité	238
57.1	58.7	51.4	52.2	54.7	55.9	Taux d'emploi	239
9.9	5.8	8.2	10.8	10.2	9.4	Taux de chômage	240

Table 1. Selected Characteristics for Census Tracts, 2001 Census – 100% Data and 20% Sample Data

No.	Characteristics	Vancouver 0185.10 A	Vancouver 0185.11 A	Vancouver 0185.12 A	Vancouver 0185.13 ◆◇ A	Vancouver 0185.14 A	Vancouver 0185.15 A
	POPULATION CHARACTERISTICS						
	by labour force activity – concluded						
241	Both sexes - Participation rate	67.3	71.5	73.6	70.3	61.3	70.5
242	15-24 years	64.3	61.3	59.4	68.5	56.8	68.5
243	25 years and over	68.1	73.7	77.0	70.7	62.2	71.1
244	Both sexes - Employment rate	61.3	64.7	67.1	62.3	55.0	64.4
245	15-24 years	55.2	52.3	53.9	59.0	52.6	63.6
246	25 years and over	62.9	67.4	70.3	63.2	55.7	64.6
247	Both sexes - Unemployment rate	8.9	9.7	8.7	11.2	10.0	9.0
248	15-24 years	12.1	16.0	9.3	13.9	7.3	7.2
249	25 years and over	7.8	8.4	8.6	10.5	10.6	9.3
250	**Total labour force 15 years and over**	**2,310**	**3,515**	**3,325**	**3,210**	**3,185**	**2,735**
	by industry based on the 1997 NAICS						
251	Industry - Not applicable (36)	75	135	115	80	80	65
252	All industries (37)	2,240	3,385	3,210	3,135	3,105	2,670
253	11 Agriculture, forestry, fishing and hunting	85	215	135	260	225	145
254	21 Mining and oil and gas extraction	-	-	-	10	-	-
255	22 Utilities	10	15	20	10	10	-
256	23 Construction	90	210	175	135	150	135
257	31-33 Manufacturing	460	570	435	365	455	495
258	41 Wholesale trade	145	170	180	200	160	160
259	44-45 Retail trade	220	335	260	290	290	225
260	48-49 Transportation and warehousing	305	375	340	385	430	410
261	51 Information and cultural industries	35	60	70	70	60	55
262	52 Finance and insurance	95	165	115	140	125	50
263	53 Real estate and rental and leasing	40	50	50	85	35	30
264	54 Professional, scientific and technical services	105	110	105	130	110	60
265	55 Management of companies and enterprises	15	-	-	-	-	-
266	56 Administrative and support, waste management and remediation services	160	155	205	155	235	185
267	61 Educational services	40	85	180	115	85	75
268	62 Health care and social assistance	135	245	325	320	285	200
269	71 Arts, entertainment and recreation	-	30	40	35	20	10
270	72 Accommodation and food services	175	265	245	210	210	220
271	81 Other services (except public administration)	80	245	170	170	110	150
272	91 Public administration	55	85	165	45	125	65
	by class of worker						
273	Class of worker - Not applicable (36)	70	130	115	80	80	70
274	All classes of worker (37)	2,240	3,385	3,210	3,135	3,110	2,670
275	Paid workers	2,115	3,150	2,980	2,985	2,970	2,520
276	Employees	2,025	3,045	2,895	2,885	2,890	2,440
277	Self-employed (incorporated)	90	110	80	95	75	80
278	Self-employed (unincorporated)	130	230	220	145	140	145
279	Unpaid family workers	-	-	10	10	-	-
	by occupation based on the 2001 NOC-S						
280	Male labour force 15 years and over	1,310	1,860	1,730	1,750	1,790	1,520
281	Occupation - Not applicable (36)	30	45	35	40	45	25
282	All occupations (37)	1,280	1,815	1,695	1,710	1,745	1,495
283	A Management occupations	80	180	140	110	120	90
284	B Business, finance and administration occupations	110	135	140	130	165	120
285	C Natural and applied sciences and related occupations	60	80	80	105	95	50
286	D Health occupations	-	45	10	50	30	15
287	E Occupations in social science, education, government service and religion	35	10	35	60	30	15
288	F Occupations in art, culture, recreation and sport	-	35	45	-	30	20
289	G Sales and service occupations	260	295	355	370	325	235
290	H Trades, transport and equipment operators and related occupations	430	770	600	580	615	670
291	I Occupations unique to primary industry	45	65	50	125	105	75
292	J Occupations unique to processing, manufacturing and utilities	240	205	230	185	220	210
293	Female labour force 15 years and over	1,005	1,650	1,595	1,455	1,395	1,210
294	Occupation - Not applicable (36)	40	85	85	40	35	45
295	All occupations (37)	965	1,570	1,515	1,420	1,365	1,170
296	A Management occupations	25	75	25	90	60	45
297	B Business, finance and administration occupations	260	355	455	350	295	240
298	C Natural and applied sciences and related occupations	20	-	15	25	45	25
299	D Health occupations	65	115	175	155	140	60

Tableau 1. Certaines caractéristiques des secteurs de recensement, recensement de 2001 – Données intégrales et données-échantillon (20 %)

Vancouver 0185.16 ◆◇ A	Vancouver 0186.01	Vancouver 0186.02	Vancouver 0186.05 ◇ A	Vancouver 0186.06 A	Vancouver 0186.07 A	Caractéristiques	N°
						CARACTÉRISTIQUES DE LA POPULATION	
						selon l'activité – fin	
71.2	69.4	62.5	66.5	68.9	68.2	Les deux sexes - Taux d'activité	241
70.3	64.6	52.4	65.0	65.2	64.7	15-24 ans	242
71.4	70.6	64.4	66.9	69.5	69.1	25 ans et plus	243
63.0	63.2	57.5	60.8	61.5	62.9	Les deux sexes - Taux d'emploi	244
55.0	58.9	48.4	58.6	51.6	57.1	15-24 ans	245
64.6	64.3	59.4	61.2	63.7	64.4	25 ans et plus	246
11.5	9.0	7.6	9.0	10.5	7.8	Les deux sexes - Taux de chômage	247
21.8	8.9	6.1	9.8	21.3	11.5	15-24 ans	248
9.6	8.9	7.9	8.8	8.2	6.6	25 ans et plus	249
2,260	**3,270**	**2,420**	**2,895**	**1,765**	**2,320**	**Population active totale de 15 ans et plus**	250
						selon l'industrie basée sur le SCIAN de 1997	
105	60	25	75	35	35	Industrie - Sans objet (36)	251
2,155	3,205	2,395	2,820	1,730	2,290	Toutes les industries (37)	252
90	80	35	105	85	65	11 Agriculture, foresterie, pêche et chasse	253
-	-	-	-	-	-	21 Extraction minière et extraction de pétrole et de gaz	254
-	10	10	15	-	-	22 Services publics	255
125	305	210	150	130	195	23 Construction	256
475	510	400	420	370	445	31-33 Fabrication	257
85	135	110	155	70	145	41 Commerce de gros	258
150	315	325	325	130	220	44-45 Commerce de détail	259
260	290	225	345	230	330	48-49 Transport et entreposage	260
15	85	45	65	15	55	51 Industrie de l'information et industrie culturelle	261
35	160	70	70	20	50	52 Finance et assurances	262
45	50	30	55	15	10	53 Services immobiliers et services de location et de location à bail	263
60	105	95	100	60	75	54 Services professionnels, scientifiques et techniques	264
-	-	-	-	-	-	55 Gestion de sociétés et d'entreprises	265
195	125	100	165	75	110	56 Services administratifs, services de soutien, services de gestion des déchets et services d'assainissement	266
95	70	150	120	50	105	61 Services d'enseignement	267
160	275	210	210	165	140	62 Soins de santé et assistance sociale	268
55	80	30	30	10	25	71 Arts, spectacles et loisirs	269
165	295	175	200	155	135	72 Hébergement et services de restauration	270
95	160	105	165	110	115	81 Autres services, sauf les administrations publiques	271
45	170	70	120	35	75	91 Administrations publiques	272
						selon la catégorie de travailleurs	
105	65	25	75	35	30	Catégorie de travailleurs - Sans objet (36)	273
2,160	3,205	2,395	2,815	1,730	2,285	Toutes les catégories de travailleurs (37)	274
1,980	2,980	2,250	2,615	1,630	2,150	Travailleurs rémunérés	275
1,935	2,830	2,200	2,550	1,600	2,140	Employés	276
40	150	45	65	30	-	Travailleurs autonomes (entreprise constituée en société)	277
175	220	145	205	95	125	Travailleurs autonomes (entreprise non constituée en société)	278
-	10	-	-	-	-	Travailleurs familiaux non rémunérés	279
						selon la profession basée sur la CNP-S de 2001	
1,250	1,820	1,320	1,555	980	1,255	Hommes actifs de 15 ans et plus	280
60	50	15	30	20	15	Profession - Sans objet (36)	281
1,190	1,765	1,305	1,525	960	1,240	Toutes les professions (37)	282
45	130	65	90	75	95	A Gestion	283
50	150	90	120	90	100	B Affaires, finance et administration	284
30	110	100	55	15	70	C Sciences naturelles et appliquées et professions apparentées	285
-	20	10	20	10	-	D Secteur de la santé	286
40	15	40	10	10	35	E Sciences sociales, enseignement, administration publique et religion	287
10	40	15	10	-	15	F Arts, culture, sports et loisirs	288
250	295	245	295	145	165	G Ventes et services	289
450	715	580	600	355	535	H Métiers, transport et machinerie	290
45	55	25	85	55	35	I Professions propres au secteur primaire	291
250	225	140	235	200	190	J Transformation, fabrication et services d'utilité publique	292
1,015	1,455	1,100	1,340	785	1,060	Femmes actives de 15 ans et plus	293
45	10	-	45	15	20	Profession - Sans objet (36)	294
965	1,440	1,085	1,290	770	1,040	Toutes les professions (37)	295
55	60	80	35	10	55	A Gestion	296
195	490	265	295	175	235	B Affaires, finance et administration	297
15	55	25	10	-	10	C Sciences naturelles et appliquées et professions apparentées	298
70	165	90	95	65	50	D Secteur de la santé	299

Table 1. Selected Characteristics for Census Tracts, 2001 Census – 100% Data and 20% Sample Data

No.	Characteristics	Vancouver 0185.10 A	Vancouver 0185.11 A	Vancouver 0185.12 A	Vancouver 0185.13 ◆◇ A	Vancouver 0185.14 A	Vancouver 0185.15 A
	POPULATION CHARACTERISTICS						
	by occupation based on the 2001 NOC-S – concluded						
	E Occupations in social science, education,						
300	government service and religion	50	125	100	120	60	45
301	F Occupations in art, culture, recreation and sport ...	10	20	40	20	-	20
302	G Sales and service occupations	345	580	510	430	385	420
	H Trades, transport and equipment						
303	operators and related occupations	45	15	10	20	40	50
304	I Occupations unique to primary industry	55	130	90	150	135	115
	J Occupations unique to processing,						
305	manufacturing and utilities	95	145	95	65	195	150
306	**Total employed labour force 15 years and over ....**	**2,110**	**3,180**	**3,040**	**2,855**	**2,865**	**2,490**
	by place of work						
307	Males	1,220	1,700	1,610	1,575	1,615	1,410
308	Usual place of work	985	1,240	1,255	1,180	1,215	1,060
309	At home	45	50	55	95	55	75
310	Outside Canada	-	20	10	15	15	10
311	No fixed workplace address	185	385	300	285	335	265
312	Females	890	1,480	1,420	1,275	1,245	1,080
313	Usual place of work	825	1,325	1,270	1,090	1,085	955
314	At home	45	45	85	45	45	70
315	Outside Canada	-	-	-	15	-	-
316	No fixed workplace address	25	105	70	130	110	55
	Total employed labour force 15 years and over with usual place of work or no fixed						
317	**workplace address ....**	**2,020**	**3,060**	**2,890**	**2,680**	**2,750**	**2,340**
	by mode of transportation						
318	Males	1,165	1,635	1,555	1,465	1,550	1,325
319	Car, truck, van, as driver	975	1,370	1,420	1,215	1,235	1,075
320	Car, truck, van, as passenger	75	140	40	155	185	110
321	Public transit	60	80	65	75	50	55
322	Walked	40	25	10	-	45	60
323	Other method	15	20	15	25	35	25
324	Females	850	1,430	1,340	1,215	1,200	1,010
325	Car, truck, van, as driver	630	995	1,020	865	795	645
326	Car, truck, van, as passenger	100	215	125	130	280	200
327	Public transit	100	185	140	155	65	75
328	Walked	25	30	25	45	50	50
329	Other method	-	10	30	15	10	30
	Total population 15 years and over who worked						
330	**since January 1, 2000 ....**	**2,515**	**3,620**	**3,450**	**3,495**	**3,450**	**2,885**
	by language used at work						
331	Single responses	2,070	3,055	3,020	2,865	2,660	2,435
332	English	1,885	2,805	2,885	2,530	2,245	2,200
333	French	-	-	-	-	-	15
334	Non-official languages (5)	185	255	140	325	415	230
335	Chinese, n.o.s.	-	-	-	15	-	-
336	Cantonese	-	-	-	-	15	-
337	Other languages (6)	185	255	135	320	400	230
338	Multiple responses	440	565	430	635	790	450
339	English and French	15	20	10	10	10	-
340	English and non-official language	430	540	400	620	765	440
341	French and non-official language	-	-	10	-	-	-
342	English, French and non-official language	-	10	10	-	15	-
	DWELLING AND HOUSEHOLD CHARACTERISTICS						
343	**Total number of occupied private dwellings ....**	**1,230**	**1,960**	**1,585**	**1,655**	**1,895**	**1,465**
	by tenure						
344	Owned	725	1,150	1,200	1,085	1,050	895
345	Rented	510	810	385	565	845	570
346	Band housing	-	-	-	-	-	-
	by structural type of dwelling						
347	Single-detached house	620	385	1,095	425	765	720
348	Semi-detached house	25	-	10	130	145	35
349	Row house	15	360	40	210	85	95
350	Apartment, detached duplex	405	530	400	740	515	390
351	Apartment, building that has five or more storeys	-	10	-	65	55	-
	Apartment, building that has fewer than						
352	five storeys (38)	160	665	15	75	325	210
353	Other single-attached house	-	10	-	-	-	-
354	Movable dwelling (39)	-	-	30	-	-	20

Tableau 1. Certaines caractéristiques des secteurs de recensement, recensement de 2001 – Données intégrales et données-échantillon (20 %)

Vancouver 0185.16 ◆◇ A	Vancouver 0186.01	Vancouver 0186.02	Vancouver 0186.05 ◇ A	Vancouver 0186.06 A	Vancouver 0186.07 A	Caractéristiques	N°
						CARACTÉRISTIQUES DE LA POPULATION	
						selon la profession basée sur la CNP-S de 2001 – fin	
70	85	85	120	65	65	E Sciences sociales, enseignement, administration publique et religion	300
-	35	20	10	15	-	F Arts, culture, sports et loisirs	301
380	410	440	515	295	405	G Ventes et services	302
20	45	25	25	15	50	H Métiers, transport et machinerie	303
65	25	20	45	40	30	I Professions propres au secteur primaire	304
85	80	45	150	100	135	J Transformation, fabrication et services d'utilité publique	305
2,000	**2,980**	**2,235**	**2,640**	**1,580**	**2,140**	**Population active occupée totale de 15 ans et plus**	306
						selon le lieu de travail	
1,085	1,615	1,230	1,440	875	1,175	Hommes	307
785	1,190	935	1,100	615	895	Lieu habituel de travail	308
45	45	35	55	25	50	À domicile	309
10	-	-	-	-	-	En dehors du Canada	310
255	375	255	290	235	230	Sans adresse de travail fixe	311
910	1,365	1,010	1,200	700	965	Femmes	312
720	1,190	880	1,055	630	850	Lieu habituel de travail	313
60	90	65	90	20	50	À domicile	314
-	10	10	-	-	-	En dehors du Canada	315
130	90	50	55	55	60	Sans adresse de travail fixe	316
1,890	**2,840**	**2,125**	**2,490**	**1,535**	**2,035**	**Population active occupée totale de 15 ans et plus ayant un lieu habituel de travail ou sans adresse de travail fixe**	317
						selon le mode de transport	
1,040	1,565	1,195	1,385	850	1,125	Hommes	318
910	1,300	1,000	1,085	700	925	Automobile, camion ou fourgonnette, en tant que conducteur	319
40	145	85	125	85	95	Automobile, camion ou fourgonnette, en tant que passager	320
60	80	75	120	45	65	Transport en commun	321
10	-	10	20	15	15	À pied	322
30	30	20	30	10	20	Autre moyen	323
850	1,275	935	1,105	680	910	Femmes	324
595	960	665	765	505	605	Automobile, camion ou fourgonnette, en tant que conductrice	325
115	75	75	105	75	130	Automobile, camion ou fourgonnette, en tant que passagère	326
125	200	145	180	75	165	Transport en commun	327
10	35	35	50	-	15	À pied	328
-	10	20	10	25	-	Autre moyen	329
2,330	**3,530**	**2,640**	**3,110**	**1,885**	**2,550**	**Population totale de 15 ans et plus ayant travaillé depuis le 1er janvier 2000**	330
						selon la langue utilisée au travail	
1,940	3,290	2,515	2,750	1,390	2,035	Réponses uniques	331
1,760	3,170	2,470	2,595	1,265	1,880	Anglais	332
-	-	-	-	-	-	Français	333
180	115	45	155	125	160	Langues non officielles (5)	334
-	-	-	10	-	-	Chinois, n.d.a.	335
10	15	-	-	-	10	Cantonais	336
175	100	35	150	125	150	Autres langues (6)	337
390	240	125	360	490	515	Réponses multiples	338
10	-	25	-	10	10	Anglais et français	339
385	200	85	340	490	515	Anglais et langue non officielle	340
-	-	-	-	-	-	Français et langue non officielle	341
-	40	15	10	-	-	Anglais, français et langue non officielle	342
						CARACTÉRISTIQUES DES LOGEMENTS ET DES MÉNAGES	
1,130	**1,895**	**1,700**	**1,810**	**905**	**1,220**	**Nombre total de logements privés occupés**	343
						selon le mode d'occupation	
760	1,290	1,090	1,005	575	800	Possédé	344
365	610	610	805	325	420	Loué	345
-	-	-	-	-	-	Logement de bande	346
						selon le type de construction résidentielle	
695	1,230	1,100	685	580	830	Maison individuelle non attenante	347
35	30	20	105	85	15	Maison jumelée	348
-	-	15	315	90	-	Maison en rangée	349
360	505	320	325	70	355	Appartement, duplex non attenant	350
-	-	-	-	-	-	Appartement, immeuble de cinq étages ou plus	351
25	125	245	375	30	15	Appartement, immeuble de moins de cinq étages (38)	352
15	-	-	-	-	-	Autre maison individuelle attenante	353
-	-	-	-	50	-	Logement mobile (39)	354

Table 1. Selected Characteristics for Census Tracts, 2001 Census – 100% Data and 20% Sample Data

No.	Characteristics	Vancouver 0185.10 A	Vancouver 0185.11 A	Vancouver 0185.12 A	Vancouver 0185.13 ◆◇ A	Vancouver 0185.14 A	Vancouver 0185.15 A
	DWELLING AND HOUSEHOLD CHARACTERISTICS						
	by condition of dwelling						
355	Regular maintenance only	805	1,640	1,170	1,370	1,605	1,070
356	Minor repairs	285	255	340	205	145	350
357	Major repairs	140	70	80	75	150	45
	by period of construction						
358	Before 1946	60	10	10	-	-	15
359	1946-1960	45	85	40	50	10	100
360	1961-1970	55	75	120	15	25	95
361	1971-1980	140	120	440	40	35	375
362	1981-1990	435	535	805	325	605	500
363	1991-2001 (20)	495	1,130	175	1,220	1,215	375
364	Average number of rooms per dwelling	6.2	5.9	7.2	6.3	5.7	5.8
365	Average number of bedrooms per dwelling	3.1	2.9	3.4	3.3	2.6	2.8
366	Average value of dwelling $	208,518	208,483	213,883	250,805	227,143	187,929
367	**Total number of private households**	**1,230**	**1,960**	**1,590**	**1,655**	**1,900**	**1,465**
	by household size						
368	1 person	145	325	130	215	330	240
369	2 persons	245	475	270	380	410	345
370	3 persons	195	345	280	250	250	210
371	4-5 persons	375	560	665	520	550	465
372	6 or more persons	270	255	245	285	350	210
	by household type						
373	One-family households	865	1,350	1,220	1,125	1,140	1,020
374	Multiple-family households	175	230	185	260	380	180
375	Non-family households	195	380	185	270	375	265
376	Number of persons in private households	4,740	6,585	6,105	6,050	6,885	5,080
377	Average number of persons in private households	3.9	3.4	3.8	3.7	3.6	3.5
378	Average number of persons per room	0.6	0.6	0.5	0.6	0.6	0.6
379	Tenant households in non-farm, non-reserve private dwellings (40)	505	810	385	555	845	575
380	Average gross rent $ (40)	743	728	774	621	603	672
381	Tenant households spending 30% or more of household income on gross rent (40) (41)	150	285	125	200	320	200
382	Tenant households spending from 30% to 99% of household income on gross rent (40) (41)	110	215	100	170	300	155
383	Owner households in non-farm, non-reserve private dwellings (42)	725	1,150	1,200	1,085	1,045	895
384	Average owner's major payments $ (42)	1,386	1,248	1,246	1,419	1,209	1,048
385	Owner households spending 30% or more of household income on owner's major payments (41) (42)	300	375	310	480	335	280
386	Owner households spending from 30% to 99% of household income on owner's major payments (41) (42)	260	335	285	445	305	250
	CENSUS FAMILY CHARACTERISTICS						
387	**Total number of census families in private households**	**1,235**	**1,875**	**1,630**	**1,710**	**1,960**	**1,420**
	by census family structure and size						
388	Total couple families	1,085	1,530	1,440	1,455	1,725	1,215
389	Total families of married couples	1,005	1,410	1,375	1,365	1,665	1,115
390	Without children at home	275	470	310	425	680	355
391	With children at home	730	940	1,065	940	980	765
392	1 child	225	335	320	310	295	180
393	2 children	260	370	485	385	400	385
394	3 or more children	245	235	260	245	290	205
395	Total families of common-law couples	80	115	65	90	65	95
396	Without children at home	45	70	30	75	45	40
397	With children at home	40	50	30	15	20	50
398	1 child	20	10	15	10	15	35
399	2 children	10	30	10	-	-	15
400	3 or more children	10	15	-	-	-	10
401	Total lone-parent families	150	350	190	250	230	205
402	Female parent	125	295	155	200	185	170
403	1 child	65	175	85	105	105	105
404	2 children	20	90	50	40	40	50
405	3 or more children	35	30	25	50	45	20

Tableau 1. Certaines caractéristiques des secteurs de recensement, recensement de 2001 – Données intégrales et données-échantillon (20 %)

Vancouver 0185.16 ◆◇ A	Vancouver 0186.01	Vancouver 0186.02	Vancouver 0186.05 ◇ A	Vancouver 0186.06 A	Vancouver 0186.07 A	Caractéristiques	N°
						CARACTÉRISTIQUES DES LOGEMENTS ET DES MÉNAGES	
						selon l'état du logement	
820	1,225	1,035	1,195	655	920	Entretien régulier seulement	355
265	560	495	435	195	235	Réparations mineures	356
45	115	165	175	55	60	Réparations majeures	357
						selon la période de construction	
10	60	80	40	15	-	Avant 1946	358
75	515	635	160	40	80	1946-1960	359
75	445	455	265	100	80	1961-1970	360
365	300	330	680	315	515	1971-1980	361
320	325	110	505	180	255	1981-1990	362
280	250	85	160	255	280	1991-2001 (20)	363
6.2	7.0	6.5	5.9	6.3	6.7	Nombre moyen de pièces par logement	364
3.1	3.2	3.0	2.8	3.2	3.2	Nombre moyen de chambres à coucher par logement	365
210,357	216,749	215,096	182,807	207,112	223,761	Valeur moyenne du logement $	366
1,125	**1,895**	**1,700**	**1,810**	**905**	**1,215**	**Nombre total de logements privés**	367
						selon la taille du ménage	
110	310	395	350	130	110	1 personne	368
220	535	440	450	155	255	2 personnes	369
175	325	280	290	135	210	3 personnes	370
440	545	445	500	285	495	4-5 personnes	371
180	190	140	215	200	145	6 personnes ou plus	372
						selon le genre de ménage	
790	1,350	1,165	1,215	595	845	Ménages unifamiliaux	373
200	140	95	180	165	215	Ménages multifamiliaux	374
135	405	440	415	145	165	Ménages non familiaux	375
4,380	5,985	4,940	5,810	3,460	4,545	Nombre de personnes dans les ménages privés	376
3.9	3.2	2.9	3.2	3.8	3.7	Nombre moyen de personnes dans les ménages privés	377
0.6	0.5	0.5	0.5	0.6	0.6	Nombre moyen de personnes par pièce	378
365	605	605	805	320	425	Ménages locataires dans les logements privés non agricoles hors réserve (40)	379
827	842	666	723	701	693	Loyer brut moyen $ (40)	380
140	265	240	325	100	140	Ménages locataires consacrant 30 % ou plus du revenu du ménage au loyer brut (40) (41)	381
100	175	200	245	70	140	Ménages locataires consacrant de 30 % à 99 % du revenu du ménage au loyer brut (40) (41)	382
765	1,285	1,085	990	580	795	Ménages propriétaires dans les logements privés non agricoles hors réserve (42)	383
1,229	1,155	996	1,004	1,161	1,226	Principales dépenses de propriété moyennes $ (42)	384
265	330	225	290	195	280	Ménages propriétaires consacrant 30 % ou plus du revenu du ménage aux principales dépenses de propriété (41) (42)	385
240	265	205	265	185	260	Ménages propriétaires consacrant de 30 % à 99 % du revenu du ménage aux principales dépenses de propriété (41) (42)	386
						CARACTÉRISTIQUES DES FAMILLES DE RECENSEMENT	
1,205	**1,655**	**1,350**	**1,610**	**950**	**1,310**	**Total des familles de recensement dans les ménages privés**	387
						selon la structure et la taille de la famille de recensement	
1,015	1,385	1,115	1,310	820	1,070	Total des familles avec conjoints	388
980	1,215	985	1,175	800	1,015	Total des familles avec couples mariés	389
245	395	350	400	245	375	Sans enfants à la maison	390
740	825	630	785	550	640	Avec enfants à la maison	391
260	255	160	280	170	200	1 enfant	392
300	360	295	305	245	240	2 enfants	393
180	200	180	205	140	200	3 enfants ou plus	394
35	170	130	135	25	55	Total des familles en union libre	395
15	115	55	50	10	25	Sans enfants à la maison	396
20	55	70	80	15	35	Avec enfants à la maison	397
10	30	65	20	10	15	1 enfant	398
-	10	10	40	-	10	2 enfants	399
10	20	10	10	10	15	3 enfants ou plus	400
185	275	240	300	130	240	Total des familles monoparentales	401
140	195	205	220	115	170	Parent de sexe féminin	402
85	120	105	110	55	95	1 enfant	403
35	70	80	65	30	55	2 enfants	404
15	10	15	55	35	15	3 enfants ou plus	405

Table 1. Selected Characteristics for Census Tracts, 2001 Census – 100% Data and 20% Sample Data

No.	Characteristics	Vancouver 0185.10 A	Vancouver 0185.11 A	Vancouver 0185.12 A	Vancouver 0185.13 ◆◇ A	Vancouver 0185.14 A	Vancouver 0185.15 A
	CENSUS FAMILY CHARACTERISTICS						
	by census family structure and size – concluded						
406	Male parent	30	50	35	55	45	35
407	1 child	20	30	15	20	25	35
408	2 children	10	20	10	20	15	-
409	3 or more children	-	-	-	15	-	-
410	**Total number of children at home**	**1,965**	**2,480**	**2,505**	**2,375**	**2,505**	**1,980**
	by age groups						
411	Under 6 years	585	820	630	640	810	615
412	6-14 years	710	845	940	820	870	585
413	15-17 years	140	200	290	235	255	180
414	18-24 years	340	420	455	490	465	400
415	25 years and over	185	195	195	190	100	210
	Average number of children at home per						
416	census family (43)	1.6	1.3	1.5	1.4	1.3	1.4
417	**Total number of persons in private households**	**4,740**	**6,580**	**6,105**	**6,050**	**6,885**	**5,080**
	by census family status and living arrangements						
418	Number of non-family persons	455	700	530	510	690	475
419	Living with relatives (44)	145	275	245	180	250	140
420	Living with non-relatives only	165	110	150	115	115	90
421	Living alone	145	320	130	215	330	240
422	Number of family persons	4,290	5,885	5,575	5,540	6,195	4,610
423	Average number of persons per census family	3.5	3.1	3.4	3.3	3.2	3.3
424	**Total number of persons 65 years and over**	**305**	**465**	**330**	**390**	**725**	**455**
425	Number of non-family persons 65 years and over	85	200	100	90	220	145
426	Living with relatives (44)	60	115	75	45	110	60
427	Living with non-relatives only	-	-	15	-	-	-
428	Living alone	30	85	15	40	105	85
429	Number of family persons 65 years and over	220	265	225	305	510	310
	ECONOMIC FAMILY CHARACTERISTICS						
	Total number of economic families in						
430	**private households**	**1,035**	**1,605**	**1,435**	**1,425**	**1,530**	**1,220**
	by size of family						
431	2 persons	235	460	275	385	400	370
432	3 persons	170	340	265	255	230	205
433	4 persons	210	350	415	320	320	275
434	5 or more persons	420	455	480	465	580	370
435	Total number of persons in economic families	4,430	6,155	5,820	5,720	6,440	4,750
436	Average number of persons per economic family	4.3	3.8	4.1	4.0	4.2	3.9
437	Total number of unattached individuals	310	425	285	330	445	335
	2000 INCOME CHARACTERISTICS						
	Population 15 years and over by sex and total income groups in 2000						
438	Total - Both sexes	3,445	4,915	4,520	4,580	5,205	3,875
439	Without income	270	395	420	390	515	275
440	With income	3,175	4,520	4,100	4,185	4,690	3,600
441	Under $1,000 (45)	165	230	255	260	260	265
442	$ 1,000 - $ 2,999	190	220	205	340	280	245
443	$ 3,000 - $ 4,999	140	160	170	110	225	100
444	$ 5,000 - $ 6,999	175	175	135	240	275	215
445	$ 7,000 - $ 9,999	280	320	305	320	485	280
446	$10,000 - $11,999	220	310	145	265	300	215
447	$12,000 - $14,999	325	440	335	355	435	235
448	$15,000 - $19,999	305	410	315	420	510	370
449	$20,000 - $24,999	255	440	400	345	450	450
450	$25,000 - $29,999	240	270	290	285	305	245
451	$30,000 - $34,999	225	455	330	210	310	235
452	$35,000 - $39,999	180	305	215	165	210	200
453	$40,000 - $44,999	175	275	310	275	140	170
454	$45,000 - $49,999	105	140	240	115	180	95
455	$50,000 - $59,999	90	115	165	230	130	155
456	$60,000 and over	100	260	285	245	200	105
457	Average income $ (46)	21,255	23,695	25,594	22,635	22,296	21,353
458	Median income $ (46)	15,947	19,910	21,992	16,437	15,517	18,345
459	Standard error of average income $ (46)	696	593	658	636	1,332	702

Tableau 1. Certaines caractéristiques des secteurs de recensement, recensement de 2001 – Données intégrales et données-échantillon (20 %)

Vancouver 0185.16 ◆◇ A	Vancouver 0186.01	Vancouver 0186.02	Vancouver 0186.05 ◇ A	Vancouver 0186.06 A	Vancouver 0186.07 A	Caractéristiques	N°
						CARACTÉRISTIQUES DES FAMILLES DE RECENSEMENT	
						selon la structure et la taille de la famille de recensement – fin	
50	80	30	75	10	70	Parent de sexe masculin	406
40	45	25	65	10	55	1 enfant	407
-	35	10	-	-	20	2 enfants	408
-	-	-	-	-	-	3 enfants ou plus	409
1,800	**2,155**	**1,810**	**2,210**	**1,395**	**1,750**	**Nombre total d'enfants à la maison**	410
						selon les groupes d'âge	
540	525	380	560	380	495	Moins de 6 ans	411
645	710	645	900	495	630	6-14 ans	412
175	225	220	245	115	195	15-17 ans	413
280	475	315	295	280	330	18-24 ans	414
160	215	250	210	125	100	25 ans et plus	415
1.5	1.3	1.3	1.4	1.5	1.3	Nombre moyen d'enfants à la maison par famille de recensement (43)	416
4,380	**5,990**	**4,940**	**5,805**	**3,460**	**4,550**	**Nombre total de personnes dans les ménages privés**	417
						selon la situation des particuliers dans la famille de recensement et des particuliers dans le ménage	
360	795	660	670	295	420	Nombre de personnes hors famille de recensement	418
185	225	65	170	125	135	Vivant avec des personnes apparentées (44)	419
70	255	205	150	45	180	Vivant avec des personnes non apparentées uniquement	420
115	310	395	350	135	105	Vivant seules	421
4,020	5,190	4,280	5,135	3,165	4,125	Nombre de personnes membres d'une famille	422
3.3	3.1	3.2	3.2	3.3	3.2	Nombre moyen de personnes par famille de recensement	423
230	**480**	**630**	**510**	**235**	**310**	**Nombre total de personnes de 65 ans et plus**	424
35	140	220	205	75	95	Nombre de personnes hors famille de recensement de 65 ans et plus	425
25	65	35	60	50	60	Vivant avec des personnes apparentées (44)	426
-	-	30	15	-	15	Vivant avec des personnes non apparentées uniquement	427
10	65	150	120	20	15	Vivant seules	428
195	345	415	310	160	220	Nombre de personnes membres d'une famille de 65 ans et plus	429
						CARACTÉRISTIQUES DES FAMILLES ÉCONOMIQUES	
995	**1,525**	**1,260**	**1,420**	**775**	**1,095**	**Nombre total de familles économiques dans les ménages privés**	430
						selon la taille de la famille	
205	530	435	440	165	290	2 personnes	431
190	300	270	290	145	195	3 personnes	432
240	315	285	315	170	295	4 personnes	433
355	380	275	380	300	315	5 personnes ou plus	434
4,205	5,420	4,345	5,305	3,285	4,260	Nombre total de personnes dans les familles économiques	435
4.2	3.6	3.4	3.7	4.2	3.9	Nombre moyen de personnes par famille économique	436
175	570	600	505	170	290	Nombre total de personnes hors famille économique	437
						CARACTÉRISTIQUES DU REVENU DE 2000	
						Population de 15 ans et plus selon le sexe et les tranches de revenu total en 2000	
3,175	4,715	3,880	4,345	2,565	3,400	Total - Les deux sexes	438
240	275	300	320	240	265	Sans revenu	439
2,935	4,440	3,575	4,025	2,325	3,135	Avec un revenu	440
125	185	170	250	115	165	Moins de 1 000 $ (45)	441
170	200	140	245	85	165	1 000 $ - 2 999 $	442
105	200	65	155	90	150	3 000 $ - 4 999 $	443
180	285	190	195	130	145	5 000 $ - 6 999 $	444
265	310	195	305	225	260	7 000 $ - 9 999 $	445
135	220	170	205	155	195	10 000 $ - 11 999 $	446
245	310	290	400	205	245	12 000 $ - 14 999 $	447
350	430	375	415	315	365	15 000 $ - 19 999 $	448
215	420	355	355	200	315	20 000 $ - 24 999 $	449
255	345	310	270	160	245	25 000 $ - 29 999 $	450
230	330	305	250	155	145	30 000 $ - 34 999 $	451
195	215	225	220	55	140	35 000 $ - 39 999 $	452
165	235	250	180	130	105	40 000 $ - 44 999 $	453
100	200	170	165	125	200	45 000 $ - 49 999 $	454
95	255	175	215	65	160	50 000 $ - 59 999 $	455
100	310	205	205	125	145	60 000 $ et plus	456
22,301	25,100	26,057	22,899	22,483	23,062	Revenu moyen $ (46)	457
18,300	20,494	22,772	17,067	17,095	18,510	Revenu médian $ (46)	458
705	653	697	661	811	725	Erreur type de revenu moyen $ (46)	459

Table 1. Selected Characteristics for Census Tracts, 2001 Census – 100% Data and 20% Sample Data

No.	Characteristics	Vancouver 0185.10 A	Vancouver 0185.11 A	Vancouver 0185.12 A	Vancouver 0185.13 ◆◇ A	Vancouver 0185.14 A	Vancouver 0185.15 A
	2000 INCOME CHARACTERISTICS						
	Population 15 years and over by sex and total income groups in 2000 – concluded						
460	Total - Males	1,710	2,415	2,255	2,230	2,490	1,945
461	Without income	65	130	185	140	215	65
462	With income	1,650	2,280	2,070	2,090	2,275	1,880
463	Under $1,000 (45)	90	120	140	130	115	115
464	$ 1,000 - $ 2,999	65	40	95	125	120	90
465	$ 3,000 - $ 4,999	75	80	70	50	60	30
466	$ 5,000 - $ 6,999	100	65	45	70	130	105
467	$ 7,000 - $ 9,999	95	115	80	145	180	95
468	$10,000 - $11,999	95	160	40	85	150	110
469	$12,000 - $14,999	150	180	120	170	180	100
470	$15,000 - $19,999	125	190	150	210	230	185
471	$20,000 - $24,999	135	245	165	145	220	280
472	$25,000 - $29,999	105	125	120	130	145	185
473	$30,000 - $34,999	150	245	175	90	180	125
474	$35,000 - $39,999	100	150	140	85	95	115
475	$40,000 - $44,999	140	190	225	190	100	130
476	$45,000 - $49,999	80	90	175	90	100	55
477	$50,000 - $59,999	60	90	120	185	100	90
478	$60,000 and over	95	205	220	195	175	65
479	Average income $ (46)	24,981	27,591	30,753	27,726	27,647	24,255
480	Median income $ (46)	21,837	24,271	30,276	22,813	18,538	20,692
481	Standard error of average income $ (46)	1,087	930	1,013	1,016	2,657	1,067
482	Total - Females	1,735	2,500	2,265	2,350	2,715	1,930
483	Without income	210	265	235	255	300	215
484	With income	1,525	2,235	2,030	2,090	2,410	1,715
485	Under $1,000 (45)	75	105	115	135	145	155
486	$ 1,000 - $ 2,999	125	180	115	220	155	155
487	$ 3,000 - $ 4,999	65	85	105	65	160	70
488	$ 5,000 - $ 6,999	80	110	90	170	145	115
489	$ 7,000 - $ 9,999	185	205	225	175	305	185
490	$10,000 - $11,999	130	155	100	185	150	105
491	$12,000 - $14,999	170	255	225	185	250	135
492	$15,000 - $19,999	180	220	165	210	280	190
493	$20,000 - $24,999	125	195	235	200	230	165
494	$25,000 - $29,999	140	150	170	160	165	65
495	$30,000 - $34,999	75	215	155	120	125	115
496	$35,000 - $39,999	80	155	75	85	110	80
497	$40,000 - $44,999	35	85	80	85	45	40
498	$45,000 - $49,999	20	50	65	15	80	45
499	$50,000 - $59,999	30	20	50	40	35	65
500	$60,000 and over	10	55	65	45	30	40
501	Average income $ (46)	17,226	19,723	20,338	17,555	17,255	18,177
502	Median income $ (46)	13,516	15,033	15,642	13,253	13,664	13,127
503	Standard error of average income $ (46)	794	701	766	697	573	868
	by composition of total income						
504	Total - Composition of income in 2000 % (47)	100.0	100.0	100.0	100.0	100.0	100.0
505	Employment income %	83.0	85.1	86.4	83.4	74.4	76.3
506	Government transfer payments %	12.3	11.4	9.5	12.4	15.6	15.4
507	Other %	4.8	3.5	4.2	4.2	9.9	8.2
	Population 15 years and over with employment income in 2000 by sex and work activity						
508	Both sexes with employment income (48)	2,375	3,475	3,270	3,205	3,295	2,700
509	Average employment income $	23,495	26,181	27,717	24,679	23,633	21,762
510	Standard error of average employment income $	818	699	746	767	897	700
511	Worked full year, full time (49)	1,305	1,655	1,700	1,560	1,400	1,180
512	Average employment income $	29,358	36,114	36,617	36,475	34,404	31,652
513	Standard error of average employment income $	1,054	944	996	1,107	1,733	990
514	Worked part year or part time (50)	980	1,720	1,500	1,560	1,685	1,465
515	Average employment income $	17,222	17,702	18,354	13,753	16,394	14,287
516	Standard error of average employment income $	1,184	825	880	730	777	759
517	Males with employment income (48)	1,350	1,895	1,695	1,695	1,770	1,495
518	Average employment income $	27,200	29,601	33,845	29,640	27,805	24,368
519	Standard error of average employment income $	1,175	1,021	1,086	1,177	1,520	993
520	Worked full year, full time (49)	795	990	1,055	935	780	740
521	Average employment income $	31,924	39,002	40,206	40,546	39,276	32,980
522	Standard error of average employment income $	1,442	1,250	1,307	1,500	2,875	1,354
523	Worked part year or part time (50)	530	835	620	705	880	740
524	Average employment income $	21,076	19,877	23,427	16,458	19,519	15,866
525	Standard error of average employment income $	1,870	1,368	1,589	1,338	1,324	1,112

Tableau 1. Certaines caractéristiques des secteurs de recensement, recensement de 2001 – Données intégrales et données-échantillon (20 %)

Vancouver 0185.16 ◆◇ A	Vancouver 0186.01	Vancouver 0186.02	Vancouver 0186.05 ◇ A	Vancouver 0186.06 A	Vancouver 0186.07 A	Caractéristiques	N°
						CARACTÉRISTIQUES DU REVENU DE 2000	
						Population de 15 ans et plus selon le sexe et les tranches de revenu total en 2000 – fin	
1,585	2,390	1,930	2,055	1,280	1,680	Total - Hommes	460
80	95	125	90	90	100	Sans revenu	461
1,500	2,295	1,805	1,970	1,195	1,575	Avec un revenu	462
65	55	65	105	55	55	Moins de 1 000 $ (45)	463
65	120	35	145	50	70	1 000 $ - 2 999 $	464
35	75	30	25	40	40	3 000 $ - 4 999 $	465
75	110	90	55	65	60	5 000 $ - 6 999 $	466
105	130	70	85	60	80	7 000 $ - 9 999 $	467
60	130	65	95	75	65	10 000 $ - 11 999 $	468
80	130	100	135	30	85	12 000 $ - 14 999 $	469
185	200	105	180	180	170	15 000 $ - 19 999 $	470
100	180	120	185	120	165	20 000 $ - 24 999 $	471
140	190	220	115	70	145	25 000 $ - 29 999 $	472
160	145	150	105	105	95	30 000 $ - 34 999 $	473
85	115	185	145	40	75	35 000 $ - 39 999 $	474
105	125	135	130	45	95	40 000 $ - 44 999 $	475
70	145	105	110	90	145	45 000 $ - 49 999 $	476
85	175	135	165	50	125	50 000 $ - 59 999 $	477
85	280	190	175	115	115	60 000 $ et plus	478
26,376	29,796	32,008	28,357	26,514	28,755	Revenu moyen $ (46)	479
24,497	25,273	29,963	23,411	21,331	25,069	Revenu médian $ (46)	480
1,129	1,033	1,098	1,083	1,234	1,086	Erreur type de revenu moyen $ (46)	481
1,590	2,325	1,950	2,285	1,280	1,720	Total - Femmes	482
160	180	180	230	150	165	Sans revenu	483
1,435	2,140	1,770	2,055	1,130	1,555	Avec un revenu	484
60	130	105	140	65	110	Moins de 1 000 $ (45)	485
105	80	105	105	40	100	1 000 $ - 2 999 $	486
65	125	35	130	45	110	3 000 $ - 4 999 $	487
110	175	100	135	60	90	5 000 $ - 6 999 $	488
160	180	125	220	160	175	7 000 $ - 9 999 $	489
75	90	105	110	80	130	10 000 $ - 11 999 $	490
160	180	190	265	170	160	12 000 $ - 14 999 $	491
170	225	270	235	135	190	15 000 $ - 19 999 $	492
115	240	240	165	80	150	20 000 $ - 24 999 $	493
115	160	90	150	85	100	25 000 $ - 29 999 $	494
75	175	150	140	50	45	30 000 $ - 34 999 $	495
110	105	40	70	15	65	35 000 $ - 39 999 $	496
70	110	115	55	80	10	40 000 $ - 44 999 $	497
35	60	60	55	30	55	45 000 $ - 49 999 $	498
10	75	35	50	20	35	50 000 $ - 59 999 $	499
10	35	20	30	-	35	60 000 $ et plus	500
18,041	20,067	19,996	17,677	18,231	17,292	Revenu moyen $ (46)	501
14,812	16,321	18,233	13,511	13,972	12,782	Revenu médian $ (46)	502
768	705	732	693	949	845	Erreur type de revenu moyen $ (46)	503
						selon la composition du revenu total	
100.0	100.0	100.0	100.0	100.0	100.0	Total - Composition du revenu en 2000 % (47)	504
82.5	83.3	78.9	80.3	83.3	82.2	Revenu d'emploi %	505
14.0	11.2	14.8	15.0	14.0	13.0	Transferts gouvernementaux %	506
3.6	5.4	6.3	4.7	2.9	4.8	Autre %	507
						Population de 15 ans et plus ayant un revenu d'emploi en 2000 selon le sexe et le travail	
2,260	3,365	2,540	2,955	1,810	2,435	Les deux sexes ayant un revenu d'emploi (48)	508
23,918	27,643	28,950	25,010	23,989	24,397	Revenu moyen d'emploi $	509
844	784	843	824	969	858	Erreur type de revenu moyen d'emploi $	510
1,125	1,695	1,385	1,420	890	1,185	Ayant travaillé toute l'année à plein temps (49)	511
33,084	35,604	38,273	34,300	32,496	31,912	Revenu moyen d'emploi $	512
1,244	1,074	1,087	1,233	1,437	1,255	Erreur type de revenu moyen d'emploi $	513
1,065	1,590	1,085	1,445	890	1,225	Ayant travaillé une partie de l'année ou à temps partiel (50)	514
14,857	20,250	18,206	16,908	15,691	17,434	Revenu moyen d'emploi $	515
836	1,010	951	909	1,050	1,019	Erreur type de revenu moyen d'emploi $	516
1,215	1,845	1,380	1,570	980	1,300	Hommes ayant un revenu d'emploi (48)	517
28,219	31,921	34,762	30,368	28,596	30,251	Revenu moyen d'emploi $	518
1,301	1,195	1,249	1,248	1,394	1,216	Erreur type de revenu moyen d'emploi $	519
675	1,070	860	875	530	765	Ayant travaillé toute l'année à plein temps (49)	520
37,838	38,672	43,303	36,661	37,668	35,687	Revenu moyen d'emploi $	521
1,756	1,513	1,448	1,749	1,788	1,592	Erreur type de revenu moyen d'emploi $	522
505	735	500	655	440	525	Ayant travaillé une partie de l'année ou à temps partiel (50)	523
16,161	23,333	20,791	23,194	17,592	22,644	Revenu moyen d'emploi $	524
1,269	1,760	1,610	1,595	1,653	1,675	Erreur type de revenu moyen d'emploi $	525

Table 1. Selected Characteristics for Census Tracts, 2001 Census – 100% Data and 20% Sample Data

No.	Characteristics	Vancouver 0185.10 A	Vancouver 0185.11 A	Vancouver 0185.12 A	Vancouver 0185.13 ◆◇ A	Vancouver 0185.14 A	Vancouver 0185.15 A
	2000 INCOME CHARACTERISTICS						
	Population 15 years and over with employment income in 2000 by sex and work activity – concluded						
526	Females with employment income (48)	1,025	1,585	1,570	1,510	1,525	1,205
527	Average employment income $	18,633	22,082	21,107	19,128	18,784	18,528
528	Standard error of average employment income $	1,014	887	891	872	759	934
529	Worked full year, full time (49)	515	660	650	620	620	430
530	Average employment income $	25,417	31,755	30,758	30,325	28,291	29,377
531	Standard error of average employment income $	1,435	1,369	1,395	1,474	1,269	1,361
532	Worked part year or part time (50)	450	885	885	855	800	730
533	Average employment income $	12,689	15,650	14,814	11,527	12,953	12,684
534	Standard error of average employment income $	1,206	922	930	706	716	1,014
	Census families by structure and family income groups in 2000						
535	Total - All census families	1,235	1,875	1,630	1,705	1,955	1,420
536	Under $10,000	100	165	100	140	185	110
537	$ 10,000 - $19,999	140	175	90	225	285	130
538	$ 20,000 - $29,999	180	235	190	185	350	255
539	$ 30,000 - $39,999	145	275	180	230	260	230
540	$ 40,000 - $49,999	155	220	170	180	240	165
541	$ 50,000 - $59,999	170	245	205	235	160	155
542	$ 60,000 - $69,999	115	205	170	160	135	100
543	$ 70,000 - $79,999	85	105	150	105	85	85
544	$ 80,000 - $89,999	60	75	140	70	80	75
545	$ 90,000 - $99,999	25	75	90	60	95	40
546	$100,000 and over	55	100	150	105	80	85
547	Average family income $	46,972	47,372	56,703	47,883	45,773	47,285
548	Median family income $	42,776	42,580	53,368	44,089	34,707	39,258
549	Standard error of average family income $	1,886	1,464	1,669	1,623	3,270	2,056
550	Total - All couple census families (51)	1,085	1,530	1,440	1,460	1,730	1,215
551	Under $10,000	80	110	95	85	155	80
552	$ 10,000 - $19,999	100	95	60	175	205	115
553	$ 20,000 - $29,999	140	175	125	140	305	195
554	$ 30,000 - $39,999	130	230	150	200	245	190
555	$ 40,000 - $49,999	145	190	160	170	225	140
556	$ 50,000 - $59,999	170	205	185	210	150	125
557	$ 60,000 - $69,999	105	185	150	160	135	90
558	$ 70,000 - $79,999	75	105	140	95	75	80
559	$ 80,000 - $89,999	60	70	135	65	80	75
560	$ 90,000 - $99,999	25	60	90	55	85	40
561	$100,000 and over	50	90	145	110	75	85
562	Average family income $	48,881	50,821	59,166	51,472	48,222	49,949
563	Median family income $	45,976	47,580	56,091	48,920	36,950	42,212
564	Standard error of average family income $	2,050	1,589	1,796	1,784	3,654	2,339
	Incidence of low income in 2000						
565	Total - Economic families	1,035	1,605	1,430	1,425	1,535	1,225
566	Low income	230	340	225	375	490	320
567	Incidence of low income in 2000 % (52)	22.1	21.4	15.7	26.1	32.0	26.3
568	Total - Unattached individuals 15 years and over	310	425	285	325	445	335
569	Low income	145	140	110	115	185	120
570	Incidence of low income in 2000 % (52)	48.2	33.3	38.0	36.0	40.8	35.9
571	Total - Population in private households	4,740	6,580	6,105	6,045	6,885	5,085
572	Low income	1,175	1,330	985	1,445	2,010	1,215
573	Incidence of low income in 2000 % (52)	24.8	20.3	16.1	23.9	29.2	23.8
	Private households by household income groups in 2000						
574	Total - All private households	1,235	1,955	1,590	1,655	1,895	1,465
575	Under $10,000	60	145	80	120	115	85
576	$ 10,000 - $19,999	95	150	50	135	255	160
577	$ 20,000 - $29,999	115	175	90	135	275	235
578	$ 30,000 - $39,999	175	275	135	190	245	205
579	$ 40,000 - $49,999	205	230	210	180	210	145
580	$ 50,000 - $59,999	120	230	160	210	155	120
581	$ 60,000 - $69,999	110	205	160	170	155	140
582	$ 70,000 - $79,999	115	155	195	135	105	85
583	$ 80,000 - $89,999	70	100	180	105	85	80
584	$ 90,000 - $99,999	40	120	110	80	95	50
585	$100,000 and over	115	180	215	190	200	160
586	Average household income $	54,693	54,638	65,991	57,360	55,113	52,342
587	Median household income $	48,667	50,076	63,997	52,260	43,074	42,621
588	Standard error of average household income $	2,057	1,660	1,885	2,018	3,639	2,265

Tableau 1. Certaines caractéristiques des secteurs de recensement, recensement de 2001 – Données intégrales et données-échantillon (20 %)

Vancouver 0185.16 ◆◇ A	Vancouver 0186.01	Vancouver 0186.02	Vancouver 0186.05 ◇ A	Vancouver 0186.06 A	Vancouver 0186.07 A	Caractéristiques	N°
						CARACTÉRISTIQUES DU REVENU DE 2000	
						Population de 15 ans et plus ayant un revenu d'emploi en 2000 selon le sexe et le travail – fin	
1,045	1,515	1,160	1,390	830	1,135	Femmes ayant un revenu d'emploi (48)	526
18,914	22,424	22,057	18,934	18,555	17,698	Revenu moyen d'emploi $	527
930	853	929	932	1,173	1,048	Erreur type de revenu moyen d'emploi $	528
445	620	530	540	350	420	Ayant travaillé toute l'année à plein temps (49)	529
25,889	30,313	30,087	30,475	24,723	25,057	Revenu moyen d'emploi $	530
1,378	1,182	1,247	1,511	2,064	1,832	Erreur type de revenu moyen d'emploi $	531
565	855	590	790	440	700	Ayant travaillé une partie de l'année ou à temps partiel (50)	532
13,693	17,591	15,999	11,686	13,784	13,502	Revenu moyen d'emploi $	533
1,097	1,032	1,088	819	1,243	1,148	Erreur type de revenu moyen d'emploi $	534
						Familles de recensement selon la structure et les tranches de revenu de la famille en 2000	
1,200	1,655	1,350	1,615	950	1,310	Total - Toutes les familles de recensement	535
70	90	85	125	75	105	Moins de 10 000 $	536
120	115	55	165	70	200	10 000 $ - 19 999 $	537
150	170	105	220	110	170	20 000 $ - 29 999 $	538
205	215	170	225	185	110	30 000 $ - 39 999 $	539
135	145	220	175	155	155	40 000 $ - 49 999 $	540
165	170	135	210	90	120	50 000 $ - 59 999 $	541
110	165	145	180	45	155	60 000 $ - 69 999 $	542
80	170	140	110	95	70	70 000 $ - 79 999 $	543
55	165	125	70	65	90	80 000 $ - 89 999 $	544
65	70	40	30	15	40	90 000 $ - 99 999 $	545
45	170	140	105	50	105	100 000 $ et plus	546
48,207	57,634	57,448	47,076	48,525	48,668	Revenu moyen des familles $	547
43,177	54,711	54,831	43,550	43,184	45,643	Revenu médian des familles $	548
1,821	1,811	1,857	1,556	2,125	1,908	Erreur type de revenu moyen des familles $	549
1,015	1,380	1,110	1,310	820	1,070	Total - Toutes les familles de recensement comptant un couple (51)	550
45	50	55	60	45	50	Moins de 10 000 $	551
90	75	20	115	60	120	10 000 $ - 19 999 $	552
135	105	75	180	80	115	20 000 $ - 29 999 $	553
150	170	135	165	165	95	30 000 $ - 39 999 $	554
110	120	185	135	140	140	40 000 $ - 49 999 $	555
145	145	125	190	65	120	50 000 $ - 59 999 $	556
100	155	120	180	40	150	60 000 $ - 69 999 $	557
80	170	110	110	90	70	70 000 $ - 79 999 $	558
55	170	125	70	70	90	80 000 $ - 89 999 $	559
65	65	35	30	15	35	90 000 $ - 99 999 $	560
45	160	125	90	50	90	100 000 $ et plus	561
51,061	62,604	60,676	50,896	51,331	53,398	Revenu moyen des familles $	562
46,029	61,319	56,939	50,474	45,921	52,162	Revenu médian des familles $	563
2,045	1,965	2,070	1,699	2,301	2,020	Erreur type de revenu moyen des familles $	564
						Fréquence des unités à faible revenu en 2000	
1,000	1,520	1,260	1,425	775	1,095	Total - Familles économiques	565
210	260	180	385	130	260	Faible revenu	566
20.7	17.0	14.1	26.8	16.8	23.8	Fréquence des unités à faible revenu en 2000 % (52)	567
175	565	560	500	170	275	Total - Personnes hors famille économique de 15 ans et plus	568
70	265	235	220	65	125	Faible revenu	569
38.6	47.6	42.3	43.8	38.7	43.6	Fréquence des unités à faible revenu en 2000 % (52)	570
4,380	5,980	4,900	5,810	3,460	4,540	Total - Population dans les ménages privés	571
840	1,140	885	1,555	510	1,010	Faible revenu	572
19.1	19.1	18.0	26.8	14.8	22.2	Fréquence des unités à faible revenu en 2000 % (52)	573
						Ménages privés selon les tranches de revenu du ménage en 2000	
1,125	1,895	1,695	1,810	905	1,220	Total - Tous les ménages privés	574
45	135	105	145	45	40	Moins de 10 000 $	575
80	165	195	220	40	90	10 000 $ - 19 999 $	576
105	165	145	200	90	130	20 000 $ - 29 999 $	577
130	235	205	205	150	150	30 000 $ - 39 999 $	578
130	150	225	200	110	170	40 000 $ - 49 999 $	579
175	145	145	190	125	120	50 000 $ - 59 999 $	580
120	205	160	170	65	150	60 000 $ - 69 999 $	581
80	200	160	155	75	70	70 000 $ - 79 999 $	582
70	165	145	110	50	80	80 000 $ - 89 999 $	583
80	115	30	40	40	75	90 000 $ - 99 999 $	584
110	210	190	170	115	155	100 000 $ et plus	585
58,148	58,798	54,823	50,952	57,704	59,204	Revenu moyen des ménages $	586
52,617	57,916	49,443	46,004	50,294	54,702	Revenu médian des ménages $	587
2,170	1,911	1,784	1,767	2,508	2,057	Erreur type de revenu moyen des ménages $	588

Table 1. Selected Characteristics for Census Tracts, 2001 Census – 100% Data and 20% Sample Data

No.	Characteristics	Vancouver 0186.08 A	Vancouver 0187.03	Vancouver 0187.04 A	Vancouver 0187.05 A	Vancouver 0187.06 A	Vancouver 0187.07 A
	POPULATION CHARACTERISTICS						
1	**Population, 1996 (1)**	**4,777**	**6,006**	**1,728**	**5,774**	**5,067**	**722**
2	**Population, 2001 (2)**	**5,259**	**6,468**	**1,687**	**5,893**	**5,263**	**1,558**
3	Population percentage change, 1996-2001	10.1	7.7	-2.4	2.1	3.9	115.8
4	Land area in square kilometres, 2001	1.31	2.60	1.21	1.33	2.59	0.66
5	**Total population – 100% Data (3)**	**5,260**	**6,465**	**1,690**	**5,890**	**5,260**	**1,555**
	by sex and age groups						
6	Male	2,585	3,250	805	2,995	2,610	775
7	0-4 years	245	220	60	285	145	60
8	5-9 years	255	275	65	305	200	70
9	10-14 years	195	230	50	195	230	75
10	15-19 years	170	275	60	200	275	70
11	20-24 years	150	245	60	245	210	45
12	25-29 years	160	255	60	230	125	35
13	30-34 years	235	280	60	290	175	40
14	35-39 years	260	285	60	280	175	65
15	40-44 years	220	270	55	220	245	75
16	45-49 years	185	235	35	150	225	95
17	50-54 years	150	235	60	150	190	55
18	55-59 years	130	175	35	150	95	35
19	60-64 years	75	90	30	105	95	20
20	65-69 years	65	75	35	85	80	15
21	70-74 years	50	55	25	55	60	10
22	75-79 years	25	30	25	40	40	5
23	80-84 years	5	15	15	15	20	5
24	85 years and over	10	5	10	10	10	-
25	Female	2,675	3,220	885	2,900	2,650	785
26	0-4 years	230	235	65	225	160	55
27	5-9 years	230	265	55	260	195	55
28	10-14 years	215	225	45	205	230	80
29	15-19 years	170	225	60	160	220	65
30	20-24 years	170	250	50	250	190	55
31	25-29 years	225	235	65	295	160	30
32	30-34 years	235	280	40	260	175	60
33	35-39 years	240	305	65	215	220	80
34	40-44 years	230	265	55	225	260	80
35	45-49 years	195	230	45	165	235	70
36	50-54 years	160	240	50	165	170	60
37	55-59 years	130	145	45	130	100	30
38	60-64 years	90	100	35	110	90	15
39	65-69 years	60	80	40	80	90	20
40	70-74 years	45	50	30	65	70	15
41	75-79 years	35	40	35	50	65	10
42	80-84 years	10	25	35	35	25	-
43	85 years and over	10	20	70	10	20	-
44	**Total population 15 years and over**	**3,895**	**5,025**	**1,345**	**4,425**	**4,100**	**1,165**
	by legal marital status						
45	Never married (single)	1,155	1,665	350	1,175	1,285	320
46	Legally married (and not separated)	2,125	2,695	745	2,735	2,425	750
47	Separated, but still legally married	190	135	40	110	90	15
48	Divorced	305	320	70	190	130	45
49	Widowed	120	205	140	210	170	40
	by common-law status						
50	Not in a common-law relationship	3,655	4,720	1,285	4,315	3,965	1,130
51	In a common-law relationship	240	305	60	110	130	40
52	**Total population – 20% Sample Data (4)**	**5,260**	**6,470**	**1,450**	**5,885**	**5,265**	**1,555**
	by mother tongue						
53	Single responses	5,080	6,350	1,405	5,565	5,195	1,550
54	English	2,885	3,410	625	1,855	3,155	1,140
55	French	25	40	30	65	50	20
56	Non-official languages (5)	2,175	2,900	750	3,640	1,990	395
57	Chinese, n.o.s.	10	195	-	25	180	45
58	Cantonese	20	70	40	-	145	60
59	Punjabi	975	1,260	395	2,410	520	50
60	Mandarin	-	15	-	20	75	75
61	Tagalog (Pilipino)	90	140	10	195	100	35
62	Other languages (6)	1,085	1,230	305	995	965	125
63	Multiple responses	180	120	40	320	70	10
64	English and French	10	-	-	-	10	-
65	English and non-official language	170	115	40	305	45	-
66	French and non-official language	-	10	-	15	-	-
67	English, French and non-official language	-	-	-	-	10	-

See reference material at the end of the publication. – Voir les documents de référence à la fin de la publication.

Tableau 1. Certaines caractéristiques des secteurs de recensement, recensement de 2001 – Données intégrales et données-échantillon (20 %)

Vancouver 0187.08 A	Vancouver 0187.09 A	Vancouver 0188.01 A	Vancouver 0188.02 A	Vancouver 0188.03 A	Vancouver 0188.04 A	Caractéristiques	N°
						CARACTÉRISTIQUES DE LA POPULATION	
7,238	**6,709**	**1,800**	**1,605**	**4,395**	**2,534**	**Population, 1996 (1)**	1
9,534	**7,229**	**3,165**	**983**	**6,231**	**2,748**	**Population, 2001 (2)**	2
31.7	7.8	75.8	-38.8	41.8	8.4	Variation en pourcentage de la population, 1996-2001	3
3.61	2.30	3.09	0.57	3.66	3.82	Superficie des terres en kilomètres carrés, 2001	4
9,535	**7,230**	**3,165**	**985**	**6,235**	**2,745**	**Population totale – Données intégrales (3)**	5
						selon le sexe et les groupes d'âge	
4,685	3,590	1,610	485	3,125	1,375	Sexe masculin	6
340	255	120	35	190	70	0-4 ans	7
335	285	140	40	275	125	5-9 ans	8
320	275	130	35	320	115	10-14 ans	9
340	270	140	45	340	140	15-19 ans	10
315	295	120	20	195	120	20-24 ans	11
260	185	75	20	110	75	25-29 ans	12
355	275	95	40	125	85	30-34 ans	13
360	300	140	40	240	100	35-39 ans	14
385	305	170	60	345	115	40-44 ans	15
370	285	135	40	330	120	45-49 ans	16
325	250	110	45	225	85	50-54 ans	17
280	150	85	15	120	85	55-59 ans	18
185	140	60	15	95	55	60-64 ans	19
180	95	45	15	90	35	65-69 ans	20
130	95	25	15	65	25	70-74 ans	21
125	85	15	5	35	5	75-79 ans	22
50	35	10	5	15	15	80-84 ans	23
25	20	5	-	10	5	85 ans et plus	24
4,845	3,640	1,555	495	3,105	1,370	Sexe féminin	25
295	210	100	30	145	65	0-4 ans	26
285	245	120	55	235	115	5-9 ans	27
325	275	140	45	320	115	10-14 ans	28
310	300	125	25	325	120	15-19 ans	29
315	245	85	20	180	105	20-24 ans	30
315	235	90	35	120	85	25-29 ans	31
375	280	100	35	170	95	30-34 ans	32
385	305	180	55	305	110	35-39 ans	33
435	335	140	45	410	120	40-44 ans	34
375	275	155	50	290	130	45-49 ans	35
390	220	95	25	200	85	50-54 ans	36
310	160	60	20	125	70	55-59 ans	37
200	135	55	20	100	55	60-64 ans	38
155	120	40	10	70	30	65-69 ans	39
150	100	25	15	45	20	70-74 ans	40
120	110	20	5	30	15	75-79 ans	41
60	60	15	-	15	10	80-84 ans	42
45	20	10	-	15	10	85 ans et plus	43
7,640	**5,685**	**2,415**	**750**	**4,745**	**2,145**	**Population totale de 15 ans et plus**	44
						selon l'état matrimonial légal	
2,000	1,665	700	185	1,330	695	Célibataire (jamais marié(e))	45
4,450	3,265	1,480	480	3,140	1,215	Légalement marié(e) (et non séparé(e))	46
240	135	60	10	65	50	Séparé(e), mais toujours légalement marié(e)	47
545	300	100	40	110	105	Divorcé(e)	48
410	310	70	30	105	75	Veuf ou veuve	49
						selon l'union libre	
7,230	5,395	2,300	710	4,640	2,055	Ne vivant pas en union libre	50
415	285	115	30	105	90	Vivant en union libre	51
9,495	**7,220**	**3,165**	**985**	**6,225**	**2,740**	**Population totale – Données-échantillon (20 %) (4)**	52
						selon la langue maternelle	
9,350	7,075	3,075	980	6,170	2,640	Réponses uniques	53
5,985	4,440	1,935	630	3,760	1,795	Anglais	54
140	50	35	-	20	-	Français	55
3,220	2,585	1,095	345	2,395	840	Langues non officielles (5)	56
215	235	135	60	365	45	Chinois, n.d.a.	57
60	70	165	10	140	50	Cantonais	58
1,145	975	130	60	80	140	Pendjabi	59
125	75	100	35	770	-	Mandarin	60
270	110	90	-	35	30	Tagalog (pilipino)	61
1,405	1,115	475	190	1,010	575	Autres langues (6)	62
145	150	90	-	55	95	Réponses multiples	63
20	20	-	-	10	45	Anglais et français	64
125	130	85	-	45	50	Anglais et langue non officielle	65
-	-	-	10	-	-	Français et langue non officielle	66
-	-	-	-	-	-	Anglais, français et langue non officielle	67

See reference material at the end of the publication. – Voir les documents de référence à la fin de la publication.

Table 1. Selected Characteristics for Census Tracts, 2001 Census – 100% Data and 20% Sample Data

No.	Characteristics	Vancouver 0186.08 A	Vancouver 0187.03	Vancouver 0187.04 A	Vancouver 0187.05 A	Vancouver 0187.06 A	Vancouver 0187.07 A
	POPULATION CHARACTERISTICS						
	by home language						
68	Single responses	4,040	5,115	1,045	4,095	4,080	1,325
69	English	3,075	3,895	700	1,970	3,330	1,220
70	French	-	-	-	45	10	15
71	Non-official languages (5)	970	1,220	340	2,085	745	90
72	Cantonese	-	15	25	-	60	60
73	Chinese, n.o.s.	-	125	-	-	110	-
74	Punjabi	595	705	270	1,480	285	10
75	Mandarin	-	15	-	15	50	-
76	Korean	-	20	-	50	40	-
77	Other languages (6)	370	345	50	540	210	20
78	Multiple responses	1,220	1,350	405	1,785	1,185	230
79	English and French	10	30	20	10	40	-
80	English and non-official language	1,215	1,320	375	1,740	1,130	230
81	French and non-official language	-	-	-	15	-	-
82	English, French and non-official language	-	10	10	25	15	-
	by knowledge of official languages						
83	English only	4,750	5,865	1,285	5,030	4,695	1,470
84	French only	-	-	-	-	15	-
85	English and French	160	305	60	275	285	70
86	Neither English nor French	335	305	100	580	270	10
	by knowledge of non-official languages (5) (7)						
87	Cantonese	20	125	40	-	130	80
88	Chinese, n.o.s.	15	210	-	25	245	40
89	Punjabi	1,230	1,375	410	2,860	665	70
90	Mandarin	20	85	-	15	80	105
91	Hindi	640	560	145	1,030	185	20
92	German	90	65	60	100	70	20
93	Spanish	120	30	80	85	165	20
	by first official language spoken						
94	English	4,900	6,140	1,310	5,235	4,860	1,520
95	French	25	35	30	65	65	20
96	English and French	15	10	10	35	70	-
97	Neither English nor French	315	290	100	555	270	15
98	Official language minority - (number) (8)	35	40	35	85	105	20
99	Official language minority - (percentage) (8)	0.7	0.6	2.4	1.4	2.0	1.3
	by ethnic origin (9)						
100	English	810	1,065	150	345	960	445
101	Canadian	995	1,085	255	655	995	275
102	Chinese	90	435	50	80	565	300
103	Scottish	690	785	145	260	570	225
104	Irish	495	435	35	195	470	220
105	German	615	495	200	175	435	160
106	East Indian	1,540	1,610	485	3,065	605	100
107	French	245	375	80	185	295	115
108	Ukrainian	255	365	25	75	210	125
109	Italian	125	200	35	20	260	60
110	Dutch (Netherlands)	165	130	70	180	530	55
111	Filipino	225	245	55	390	260	55
112	Polish	175	210	35	115	135	25
113	Norwegian	155	115	35	30	65	30
114	North American Indian	180	110	-	50	50	15
	by Aboriginal identity						
115	Total Aboriginal identity population (10)	160	75	-	65	45	10
116	Total non-Aboriginal population	5,095	6,390	1,445	5,820	5,220	1,550
	by Aboriginal origin						
117	Total Aboriginal origins population (11)	260	145	-	90	70	20
118	Total non-Aboriginal population	5,000	6,325	1,445	5,795	5,195	1,535
	by Registered Indian status						
119	Registered Indian (12)	55	15	-	40	20	-
120	Not a Registered Indian	5,205	6,455	1,450	5,850	5,245	1,555

Tableau 1. Certaines caractéristiques des secteurs de recensement, recensement de 2001 – Données intégrales et données-échantillon (20 %)

Vancouver 0187.08 A	Vancouver 0187.09 A	Vancouver 0188.01 A	Vancouver 0188.02 A	Vancouver 0188.03 A	Vancouver 0188.04 A	Caractéristiques	Nº
						CARACTÉRISTIQUES DE LA POPULATION	
						selon la langue parlée à la maison	
7,710	5,415	2,370	805	5,190	2,150	Réponses uniques	68
6,600	4,625	2,075	710	4,050	1,985	Anglais	69
25	-	-	-	-	-	Français	70
1,085	785	295	100	1,140	165	Langues non officielles (5)	71
60	15	55	-	95	20	Cantonais	72
60	95	40	-	160	10	Chinois, n.d.a.	73
425	370	20	40	50	20	Pendjabi	74
80	35	55	-	485	-	Mandarin	75
310	10	45	55	185	95	Coréen	76
150	260	75	10	165	20	Autres langues (6)	77
1,785	1,805	790	175	1,035	585	Réponses multiples	78
60	35	30	-	30	40	Anglais et français	79
1,710	1,740	720	175	985	500	Anglais et langue non officielle	80
-	10	10	-	10	-	Français et langue non officielle	81
10	25	35	-	10	45	Anglais, français et langue non officielle	82
						selon la connaissance des langues officielles	
8,495	6,505	2,870	885	5,810	2,510	Anglais seulement	83
10	-	-	-	-	-	Français seulement	84
670	440	170	65	175	170	Anglais et français	85
315	270	125	30	240	60	Ni l'anglais ni le français	86
						selon la connaissance des langues non officielles (5) (7)	
105	125	185	10	165	65	Cantonais	87
195	235	110	55	260	35	Chinois, n.d.a.	88
1,230	1,125	210	60	205	235	Pendjabi	89
170	125	175	30	965	15	Mandarin	90
360	315	100	20	65	170	Hindi	91
245	150	60	35	170	75	Allemand	92
210	150	85	-	55	75	Espagnol	93
						selon la première langue officielle parlée	
9,020	6,900	2,975	950	5,965	2,630	Anglais	94
135	40	35	-	25	-	Français	95
40	10	25	-	-	45	Anglais et français	96
295	275	125	30	240	55	Ni l'anglais ni le français	97
155	45	50	-	20	25	Minorité de langue officielle - (nombre) (8)	98
1.6	0.6	1.6	-	0.3	0.9	Minorité de langue officielle - (pourcentage) (8)	99
						selon l'origine ethnique (9)	
2,485	1,595	700	280	1,520	715	Anglais	100
1,865	1,255	705	200	1,250	605	Canadien	101
575	570	545	135	1,220	140	Chinois	102
1,720	1,285	475	215	805	465	Écossais	103
1,410	825	205	110	700	315	Irlandais	104
1,080	765	335	115	745	205	Allemand	105
1,240	1,295	330	120	280	355	Indien de l'Inde	106
720	405	190	75	240	240	Français	107
440	315	230	15	250	265	Ukrainien	108
120	165	105	70	170	180	Italien	109
415	160	145	40	185	120	Hollandais (Néerlandais)	110
430	255	170	25	95	65	Philippin	111
365	210	110	20	230	85	Polonais	112
195	125	90	25	230	55	Norvégien	113
140	100	40	20	80	20	Indien de l'Amérique du Nord	114
						selon l'identité autochtone	
90	70	60	25	30	85	Total de la population ayant une identité autochtone (10)	115
9,405	7,150	3,110	960	6,195	2,655	Total de la population non autochtone	116
						selon l'origine autochtone	
185	150	65	25	85	70	Total de la population ayant une origine autochtone (11)	117
9,310	7,070	3,095	955	6,140	2,670	Total de la population non autochtone	118
						selon le statut d'Indien inscrit	
25	20	50	-	10	40	Oui, Indien inscrit (12)	119
9,465	7,200	3,115	985	6,215	2,695	Non, pas un Indien inscrit	120

Table 1. Selected Characteristics for Census Tracts, 2001 Census – 100% Data and 20% Sample Data

No.	Characteristics	Vancouver 0186.08 A	Vancouver 0187.03	Vancouver 0187.04 A	Vancouver 0187.05 A	Vancouver 0187.06 A	Vancouver 0187.07 A
	POPULATION CHARACTERISTICS						
	by visible minority groups						
121	Total visible minority population	2,385	2,995	790	4,305	2,050	440
122	Chinese	65	435	40	60	530	240
123	South Asian	1,650	1,755	505	3,425	735	95
124	Black	150	65	55	15	-	10
125	Filipino	200	225	55	380	230	55
126	Latin American	100	15	75	75	120	-
127	Southeast Asian	130	295	60	175	185	10
128	Arab	-	-	-	75	25	-
129	West Asian	20	45	-	-	-	-
130	Korean	-	40	-	55	140	-
131	Japanese	10	75	-	-	25	10
132	Visible minority, n.i.e. (13)	45	10	-	20	-	-
133	Multiple visible minorities (14)	15	35	-	25	65	25
	by citizenship						
134	Canadian citizenship (15)	4,505	5,695	1,285	4,875	4,805	1,435
135	Citizenship other than Canadian	750	775	165	1,010	460	120
	by place of birth of respondent						
136	Non-immigrant population	3,335	3,945	800	2,760	3,365	1,160
137	Born in province of residence	2,520	3,025	620	2,330	2,540	875
138	Immigrant population (16)	1,895	2,390	645	3,090	1,870	385
139	United States	55	70	10	-	15	30
140	Central and South America	80	40	70	70	120	-
141	Caribbean and Bermuda	25	30	10	25	10	-
142	United Kingdom	65	175	15	85	105	25
143	Other Europe (17)	290	330	90	235	330	60
144	Africa	35	10	35	60	60	-
145	Asia and the Middle East	1,075	1,600	380	2,285	1,185	270
146	Oceania and other (18)	275	145	35	310	50	-
147	Non-permanent residents (19)	30	135	-	35	30	10
148	**Total immigrant population**	**1,900**	**2,390**	**650**	**3,085**	**1,870**	**385**
	by period of immigration						
149	Before 1961	115	165	50	135	115	25
150	1961-1970	130	300	25	170	75	40
151	1971-1980	270	440	125	640	370	75
152	1981-1990	510	545	165	785	695	55
153	1991-2001 (20)	880	940	285	1,350	615	190
154	1991-1995	410	430	185	680	290	90
155	1996-2001 (20)	470	510	105	670	325	105
	by age at immigration						
156	0-4 years	90	185	30	170	140	45
157	5-19 years	550	680	200	820	560	105
158	20 years and over	1,260	1,520	415	2,095	1,175	235
159	**Total population**	**5,260**	**6,470**	**1,450**	**5,885**	**5,260**	**1,555**
	by religion						
160	Catholic (21)	870	1,095	260	735	1,365	350
161	Protestant	900	1,175	185	605	1,295	490
162	Christian Orthodox	85	100	20	10	45	35
163	Christian, n.i.e. (22)	350	150	160	385	260	105
164	Muslim	170	190	50	250	50	-
165	Jewish	30	10	-	-	-	-
166	Buddhist	50	300	15	15	110	30
167	Hindu	405	220	40	565	70	10
168	Sikh	1,130	1,415	455	2,655	580	60
169	Eastern religions (23)	-	20	-	35	10	-
170	Other religions (24)	10	-	-	-	10	-
171	No religious affiliation (25)	1,265	1,810	260	640	1,470	470
172	**Total population 15 years and over**	**3,885**	**4,995**	**1,125**	**4,415**	**4,100**	**1,155**
	by generation status						
173	1st generation (26)	1,840	2,390	630	3,005	1,805	355
174	2nd generation (27)	750	1,010	240	805	945	270
175	3rd generation and over (28)	1,290	1,595	255	600	1,350	535
176	**Total population 1 year and over (29)**	**5,200**	**6,380**	**1,435**	**5,790**	**5,200**	**1,545**
	by place of residence 1 year ago (mobility)						
177	Non-movers	4,280	5,385	1,210	5,110	4,695	1,390
178	Movers	920	1,000	220	685	505	160
179	Non-migrants	625	725	160	535	335	100
180	Migrants	300	280	60	140	175	60
181	Internal migrants	135	180	45	55	85	55
182	Intraprovincial migrants	95	160	45	50	80	45
183	Interprovincial migrants	40	20	-	10	10	10
184	External migrants	165	100	20	90	90	-

Tableau 1. Certaines caractéristiques des secteurs de recensement, recensement de 2001 – Données intégrales et données-échantillon (20 %)

Vancouver 0187.08 A	Vancouver 0187.09 A	Vancouver 0188.01 A	Vancouver 0188.02 A	Vancouver 0188.03 A	Vancouver 0188.04 A	Caractéristiques	N°
						CARACTÉRISTIQUES DE LA POPULATION	
						selon les groupes de minorités visibles	
3,350	2,960	1,420	370	2,425	895	Total de la population des minorités visibles	121
520	540	480	135	1,405	135	Chinois	122
1,505	1,435	405	120	410	380	Sud-Asiatique	123
120	50	10	-	20	20	Noir	124
370	280	170	25	95	70	Philippin	125
55	30	50	-	20	-	Latino-Américain	126
100	290	90	-	75	60	Asiatique du Sud-Est	127
20	95	20	-	25	-	Arabe	128
-	25	-	-	15	-	Asiatique occidental	129
495	100	145	90	320	195	Coréen	130
90	25	-	-	15	30	Japonais	131
-	25	25	10	20	-	Minorité visible, n.i.a. (13)	132
75	60	30	-	-	-	Minorités visibles multiples (14)	133
						selon la citoyenneté	
8,495	6,710	2,840	910	5,295	2,555	Citoyenneté canadienne (15)	134
1,000	510	320	70	930	180	Citoyenneté autre que canadienne	135
						selon le lieu de naissance du répondant	
6,455	4,765	1,970	660	3,705	1,985	Population non immigrante	136
4,405	3,710	1,485	515	2,760	1,425	Née dans la province de résidence	137
2,990	2,400	1,175	320	2,430	700	Population immigrante (16)	138
45	40	25	-	60	30	États-Unis	139
75	25	40	-	15	30	Amérique centrale et du Sud	140
30	50	10	10	-	15	Caraïbes et Bermudes	141
335	280	70	30	155	65	Royaume-Uni	142
445	315	80	45	345	65	Autre Europe (17)	143
80	30	60	-	85	-	Afrique	144
1,880	1,585	855	220	1,720	410	Asie et Moyen-Orient	145
100	85	40	20	40	80	Océanie et autre (18)	146
50	50	25	-	95	55	Résidents non permanents (19)	147
2,990	**2,400**	**1,175**	**320**	**2,430**	**700**	**Population immigrante totale**	148
						selon la période d'immigration	
375	230	70	40	240	95	Avant 1961	149
285	270	90	30	115	70	1961-1970	150
515	490	290	70	325	195	1971-1980	151
685	635	210	100	340	145	1981-1990	152
1,140	775	515	80	1,410	190	1991-2001 (20)	153
585	435	240	25	450	75	1991-1995	154
555	340	280	55	960	120	1996-2001 (20)	155
						selon l'âge à l'immigration	
200	155	90	20	250	55	0-4 ans	156
865	795	390	80	850	260	5-19 ans	157
1,925	1,455	695	220	1,330	390	20 ans et plus	158
9,495	**7,220**	**3,160**	**985**	**6,225**	**2,740**	**Population totale**	159
						selon la religion	
1,765	1,280	710	140	935	410	Catholique (21)	160
3,080	1,805	705	325	2,180	830	Protestante	161
95	105	40	10	45	20	Orthodoxe chrétienne	162
550	520	295	90	545	325	Chrétiennes, n.i.a. (22)	163
85	170	85	10	145	40	Musulmane	164
-	25	-	-	-	-	Juive	165
270	260	125	15	430	55	Bouddhiste	166
135	190	75	-	35	80	Hindoue	167
1,225	1,095	175	50	155	230	Sikh	168
-	-	25	-	15	-	Religions orientales (23)	169
-	10	-	-	-	-	Autres religions (24)	170
2,275	1,770	940	330	1,730	740	Aucune appartenance religieuse (25)	171
7,610	**5,685**	**2,395**	**755**	**4,740**	**2,055**	**Population totale de 15 ans et plus**	172
						selon le statut des générations	
2,940	2,380	1,075	310	2,220	715	1re génération (26)	173
1,905	1,340	540	150	920	605	2e génération (27)	174
2,770	1,965	780	295	1,600	740	3e génération et plus (28)	175
9,330	**7,160**	**3,130**	**970**	**6,190**	**2,715**	**Population totale de 1 an et plus (29)**	176
						selon le lieu de résidence 1 an auparavant (mobilité)	
8,025	6,285	2,675	885	5,155	2,325	Personnes n'ayant pas déménagé	177
1,305	875	455	80	1,035	395	Personnes ayant déménagé	178
780	635	210	45	595	290	Non-migrants	179
525	240	250	40	440	100	Migrants	180
400	165	190	25	225	90	Migrants internes	181
340	95	150	20	175	90	Migrants infraprovinciaux	182
60	75	35	-	55	10	Migrants interprovinciaux	183
130	70	60	15	215	10	Migrants externes	184

Table 1. Selected Characteristics for Census Tracts, 2001 Census – 100% Data and 20% Sample Data

No.	Characteristics	Vancouver 0186.08 A	Vancouver 0187.03	Vancouver 0187.04 A	Vancouver 0187.05 A	Vancouver 0187.06 A	Vancouver 0187.07 A
	POPULATION CHARACTERISTICS						
185	**Total population 5 years and over (30)**	**4,775**	**6,010**	**1,320**	**5,375**	**4,960**	**1,470**
	by place of residence 5 years ago (mobility)						
186	Non-movers	2,210	3,115	815	2,865	3,380	425
187	Movers	2,565	2,900	505	2,510	1,585	1,040
188	Non-migrants	1,640	1,710	280	1,590	865	715
189	Migrants	925	1,190	225	920	720	325
190	Internal migrants	500	810	165	445	435	240
191	Intraprovincial migrants	365	595	95	265	355	205
192	Interprovincial migrants	130	220	70	185	85	35
193	External migrants	425	380	55	470	285	90
194	**Total population 15 to 24 years**	**655**	**980**	**275**	**850**	**900**	**260**
	by school attendance						
195	Not attending school	285	460	85	365	300	75
196	Attending school full time	295	450	125	355	525	170
197	Attending school part time	75	60	70	130	80	15
198	**Total population 15 years and over**	**3,890**	**4,995**	**1,125**	**4,415**	**4,100**	**1,155**
	by highest level of schooling						
199	Less than grade 9 (31)	395	440	170	570	315	40
200	Grades 9-13 without high school graduation certificate	1,150	1,350	340	1,105	995	210
201	Grades 9-13 with high school graduation certificate	640	700	175	635	625	160
202	Some postsecondary without degree, certificate or diploma (32)	440	725	115	615	635	155
203	Trades certificate or diploma (33)	430	630	130	380	410	75
204	College certificate or diploma (34)	520	555	130	415	570	245
205	University certificate below bachelor's degree	80	230	10	90	80	60
206	University with bachelor's degree or higher	230	360	50	600	465	220
	by combinations of unpaid work						
207	Males 15 years and over	1,885	2,485	580	2,205	2,015	555
208	Reported unpaid work (35)	1,685	2,110	460	1,910	1,785	525
209	Housework and child care and care or assistance to seniors	210	140	55	240	170	55
210	Housework and child care only	575	855	135	625	530	180
211	Housework and care or assistance to seniors only	100	105	-	110	145	20
212	Child care and care or assistance to seniors only	10	10	-	-	10	-
213	Housework only	755	960	250	890	810	265
214	Child care only	25	40	15	50	85	-
215	Care or assistance to seniors only	10	-	-	-	30	10
216	Females 15 years and over	2,005	2,510	545	2,210	2,085	600
217	Reported unpaid work (35)	1,890	2,305	520	2,045	1,920	580
218	Housework and child care and care or assistance to seniors	330	250	75	335	230	85
219	Housework and child care only	780	915	205	855	740	195
220	Housework and care or assistance to seniors only	80	120	10	95	215	55
221	Child care and care or assistance to seniors only	-	10	-	-	10	-
222	Housework only	675	985	220	740	675	235
223	Child care only	25	25	10	20	35	10
224	Care or assistance to seniors only	-	-	-	10	15	-
	by labour force activity						
225	Males 15 years and over	1,880	2,485	580	2,210	2,010	560
226	In the labour force	1,505	1,985	435	1,730	1,530	410
227	Employed	1,355	1,880	425	1,615	1,430	390
228	Unemployed	150	105	15	120	105	20
229	Not in the labour force	380	505	140	475	480	145
230	Participation rate	80.1	79.9	75.0	78.3	76.1	73.2
231	Employment rate	72.1	75.7	73.3	73.1	71.1	69.6
232	Unemployment rate	10.0	5.3	3.4	6.9	6.9	4.9
233	Females 15 years and over	2,005	2,505	545	2,210	2,085	600
234	In the labour force	1,340	1,660	335	1,400	1,320	405
235	Employed	1,185	1,540	325	1,250	1,210	390
236	Unemployed	155	115	10	150	115	20
237	Not in the labour force	665	850	215	805	765	195
238	Participation rate	66.8	66.3	61.5	63.3	63.3	67.5
239	Employment rate	59.1	61.5	59.6	56.6	58.0	65.0
240	Unemployment rate	11.6	6.9	3.0	10.7	8.7	4.9

Tableau 1. Certaines caractéristiques des secteurs de recensement, recensement de 2001 – Données intégrales et données-échantillon (20 %)

Vancouver 0187.08 A	Vancouver 0187.09 A	Vancouver 0188.01 A	Vancouver 0188.02 A	Vancouver 0188.03 A	Vancouver 0188.04 A	Caractéristiques	N°
						CARACTÉRISTIQUES DE LA POPULATION	
8,880	**6,755**	**2,950**	**910**	**5,900**	**2,570**	**Population totale de 5 ans et plus (30)**	185
						selon le lieu de résidence 5 ans auparavant (mobilité)	
4,025	3,760	1,590	555	2,475	1,370	Personnes n'ayant pas déménagé	186
4,855	3,000	1,360	355	3,420	1,205	Personnes ayant déménagé	187
2,965	1,845	515	170	1,745	750	Non-migrants	188
1,890	1,150	845	190	1,675	455	Migrants	189
1,420	825	600	130	805	330	Migrants internes	190
1,250	755	430	100	730	280	Migrants infraprovinciaux	191
165	70	170	30	70	55	Migrants interprovinciaux	192
475	330	245	60	865	125	Migrants externes	193
1,310	**1,110**	**445**	**130**	**1,045**	**475**	**Population totale de 15 à 24 ans**	194
						selon la fréquentation scolaire	
450	435	135	45	300	170	Ne fréquentant pas l'école	195
690	580	270	65	660	215	Fréquentant l'école à plein temps	196
170	95	30	20	90	95	Fréquentant l'école à temps partiel	197
7,610	**5,685**	**2,400**	**750**	**4,740**	**2,060**	**Population totale de 15 ans et plus**	198
						selon le plus haut niveau de scolarité atteint	
485	395	105	45	170	90	Niveau inférieur à la 9e année (31)	199
1,570	1,295	435	150	905	615	De la 9e à la 13e année sans certificat d'études secondaires	200
1,050	970	300	90	665	250	De la 9e à la 13e année avec certificat d'études secondaires	201
1,260	795	330	135	715	310	Études postsecondaires partielles sans grade, certificat ou diplôme (32)	202
795	710	315	75	370	175	Certificat ou diplôme d'une école de métiers (33)	203
1,265	800	415	115	745	285	Certificat ou diplôme collégial (34)	204
180	80	65	35	190	80	Certificat universitaire inférieur au baccalauréat	205
1,005	645	440	105	970	255	Études universitaires avec baccalauréat ou diplôme supérieur	206
						selon les combinaisons de travail non rémunéré	
3,690	2,775	1,205	385	2,340	1,025	Hommes de 15 ans et plus	207
3,375	2,460	1,145	330	2,130	885	Travail non rémunéré déclaré (35)	208
340	255	150	10	210	95	Travaux ménagers et soins aux enfants et soins ou aide aux personnes âgées	209
985	820	405	125	815	310	Travaux ménagers et soins aux enfants seulement	210
260	150	75	55	150	50	Travaux ménagers et soins ou aide aux personnes âgées seulement	211
10	10	-	-	-	-	Soins aux enfants et soins ou aide aux personnes âgées seulement	212
1,720	1,180	505	140	950	425	Travaux ménagers seulement	213
45	35	-	-	10	-	Soins aux enfants seulement	214
15	10	10	-	-	-	Soins ou aide aux personnes âgées seulement	215
3,920	2,910	1,190	365	2,405	1,035	Femmes de 15 ans et plus	216
3,715	2,755	1,095	340	2,265	1,005	Travail non rémunéré déclaré (35)	217
515	415	230	15	280	180	Travaux ménagers et soins aux enfants et soins ou aide aux personnes âgées	218
1,215	945	425	130	920	380	Travaux ménagers et soins aux enfants seulement	219
370	270	80	50	160	55	Travaux ménagers et soins ou aide aux personnes âgées seulement	220
15	-	-	-	-	-	Soins aux enfants et soins ou aide aux personnes âgées seulement	221
1,570	1,090	355	140	895	380	Travaux ménagers seulement	222
15	25	10	-	15	10	Soins aux enfants seulement	223
20	20	10	-	-	-	Soins ou aide aux personnes âgées seulement	224
						selon l'activité	
3,690	2,775	1,205	385	2,335	1,020	Hommes de 15 ans et plus	225
2,730	2,060	920	315	1,630	740	Population active	226
2,615	1,900	885	300	1,520	680	Personnes occupées	227
120	165	40	15	115	60	Chômeurs	228
955	715	285	70	700	280	Inactifs	229
74.0	74.2	76.3	81.8	69.8	72.5	Taux d'activité	230
70.9	68.5	73.4	77.9	65.1	66.7	Taux d'emploi	231
4.4	8.0	4.3	4.8	7.1	8.1	Taux de chômage	232
3,920	2,910	1,190	370	2,405	1,035	Femmes de 15 ans et plus	233
2,535	1,935	720	275	1,445	645	Population active	234
2,325	1,755	690	260	1,365	605	Personnes occupées	235
205	180	25	10	85	40	Chômeuses	236
1,390	980	475	90	955	390	Inactives	237
64.7	66.5	60.5	74.3	60.1	62.3	Taux d'activité	238
59.3	60.3	58.0	70.3	56.8	58.5	Taux d'emploi	239
8.1	9.3	3.5	3.6	5.9	6.2	Taux de chômage	240

Table 1. Selected Characteristics for Census Tracts, 2001 Census – 100% Data and 20% Sample Data

No.	Characteristics	Vancouver 0186.08 A	Vancouver 0187.03	Vancouver 0187.04 A	Vancouver 0187.05 A	Vancouver 0187.06 A	Vancouver 0187.07 A
	POPULATION CHARACTERISTICS						
	by labour force activity – concluded						
241	Both sexes - Participation rate	73.2	72.9	68.4	70.9	69.6	70.6
242	15-24 years	64.1	70.3	67.3	68.8	65.6	58.8
243	25 years and over	74.9	73.4	68.8	71.4	70.9	73.9
244	Both sexes - Employment rate	65.5	68.5	66.7	64.8	64.5	68.0
245	15-24 years	53.0	64.6	67.3	60.0	57.2	53.8
246	25 years and over	68.0	69.4	66.5	65.9	66.5	71.7
247	Both sexes - Unemployment rate	10.7	5.9	2.6	8.6	7.5	4.3
248	15-24 years	18.8	8.7	-	12.8	11.9	6.7
249	25 years and over	9.5	5.4	2.6	7.7	6.2	3.7
250	**Total labour force 15 years and over**	**2,845**	**3,640**	**775**	**3,130**	**2,855**	**815**
	by industry based on the 1997 NAICS						
251	Industry - Not applicable (36)	80	55	10	60	55	15
252	All industries (37)	2,765	3,585	765	3,075	2,800	800
253	11 Agriculture, forestry, fishing and hunting	105	75	30	135	55	-
254	21 Mining and oil and gas extraction	10	-	-	10	-	-
255	22 Utilities	15	15	10	-	30	25
256	23 Construction	180	230	35	135	145	20
257	31-33 Manufacturing	540	590	115	540	435	70
258	41 Wholesale trade	155	300	35	145	150	40
259	44-45 Retail trade	260	475	65	375	440	125
260	48-49 Transportation and warehousing	260	255	85	335	185	65
261	51 Information and cultural industries	45	95	-	85	55	40
262	52 Finance and insurance	80	135	10	65	145	60
263	53 Real estate and rental and leasing	55	35	20	25	15	15
264	54 Professional, scientific and technical services	100	150	10	150	120	55
265	55 Management of companies and enterprises	-	10	-	-	-	-
266	56 Administrative and support, waste management and remediation services	200	205	85	155	95	25
267	61 Educational services	75	130	40	90	145	80
268	62 Health care and social assistance	300	230	60	290	275	45
269	71 Arts, entertainment and recreation	40	30	-	50	30	10
270	72 Accommodation and food services	165	310	100	255	185	40
271	81 Other services (except public administration)	145	115	45	140	130	10
272	91 Public administration	40	200	25	80	160	70
	by class of worker						
273	Class of worker - Not applicable (36)	80	55	-	60	55	20
274	All classes of worker (37)	2,765	3,585	765	3,070	2,800	800
275	Paid workers	2,555	3,385	685	2,915	2,665	750
276	Employees	2,485	3,295	675	2,850	2,620	725
277	Self-employed (incorporated)	65	90	-	65	45	20
278	Self-employed (unincorporated)	210	195	85	160	130	50
279	Unpaid family workers	-	10	-	-	-	-
	by occupation based on the 2001 NOC-S						
280	Male labour force 15 years and over	1,505	1,980	435	1,735	1,530	410
281	Occupation - Not applicable (36)	30	10	-	25	25	15
282	All occupations (37)	1,480	1,975	430	1,705	1,510	395
283	A Management occupations	125	210	30	100	170	95
284	B Business, finance and administration occupations	105	180	35	120	175	60
285	C Natural and applied sciences and related occupations	60	125	10	150	90	55
286	D Health occupations	15	25	-	20	60	-
287	E Occupations in social science, education, government service and religion	25	45	15	40	75	25
288	F Occupations in art, culture, recreation and sport	50	40	-	20	10	10
289	G Sales and service occupations	300	445	130	315	360	90
290	H Trades, transport and equipment operators and related occupations	540	620	155	665	415	45
291	I Occupations unique to primary industry	80	55	15	75	40	-
292	J Occupations unique to processing, manufacturing and utilities	180	230	35	200	125	20
293	Female labour force 15 years and over	1,340	1,655	330	1,400	1,320	405
294	Occupation - Not applicable (36)	55	50	-	30	30	10
295	All occupations (37)	1,290	1,610	335	1,370	1,290	405
296	A Management occupations	80	90	15	65	80	35
297	B Business, finance and administration occupations	320	525	75	275	420	165
298	C Natural and applied sciences and related occupations	35	60	-	15	10	10
299	D Health occupations	130	120	20	120	140	20

Tableau 1. Certaines caractéristiques des secteurs de recensement, recensement de 2001 – Données intégrales et données-échantillon (20 %)

Vancouver 0187.08 A	Vancouver 0187.09 A	Vancouver 0188.01 A	Vancouver 0188.02 A	Vancouver 0188.03 A	Vancouver 0188.04 A	Caractéristiques	N°
						CARACTÉRISTIQUES DE LA POPULATION	
						selon l'activité – fin	
69.1	70.2	68.3	78.1	65.0	67.6	Les deux sexes - Taux d'activité	241
65.6	65.0	58.0	69.2	49.8	57.3	15-24 ans	242
69.8	71.6	70.8	81.5	69.3	70.0	25 ans et plus	243
64.9	64.2	65.8	75.3	60.8	62.6	Les deux sexes - Taux d'emploi	244
55.0	55.2	53.4	61.5	41.1	50.5	15-24 ans	245
67.1	66.4	68.8	77.4	66.3	66.2	25 ans et plus	246
6.1	8.5	3.7	4.2	6.5	7.2	Les deux sexes - Taux de chômage	247
16.3	15.2	7.8	-	18.3	16.1	15-24 ans	248
4.1	7.2	3.2	4.0	4.1	5.4	25 ans et plus	249
5,265	**3,995**	**1,640**	**590**	**3,080**	**1,390**	**Population active totale de 15 ans et plus**	250
						selon l'industrie basée sur le SCIAN de 1997	
75	125	30	-	50	25	Industrie - Sans objet (36)	251
5,195	3,870	1,610	590	3,030	1,360	Toutes les industries (37)	252
35	70	10	-	15	20	11 Agriculture, foresterie, pêche et chasse	253
10	20	-	-	10	-	21 Extraction minière et extraction de pétrole et de gaz	254
50	40	40	-	50	30	22 Services publics	255
300	290	105	15	140	90	23 Construction	256
550	525	170	85	240	165	31-33 Fabrication	257
310	250	70	45	220	70	41 Commerce de gros	258
690	340	195	90	405	125	44-45 Commerce de détail	259
470	300	105	15	195	90	48-49 Transport et entreposage	260
120	105	50	10	120	20	51 Industrie de l'information et industrie culturelle	261
345	170	70	30	170	60	52 Finance et assurances	262
90	50	25	-	55	20	53 Services immobiliers et services de location et de location à bail	263
235	205	70	25	260	80	54 Services professionnels, scientifiques et techniques	264
-	-	-	-	-	-	55 Gestion de sociétés et d'entreprises	265
240	180	80	20	130	60	56 Services administratifs, services de soutien, services de gestion des déchets et services d'assainissement	266
230	160	125	35	290	45	61 Services d'enseignement	267
545	320	150	35	200	195	62 Soins de santé et assistance sociale	268
85	80	25	10	55	95	71 Arts, spectacles et loisirs	269
360	335	160	45	200	50	72 Hébergement et services de restauration	270
255	225	95	90	180	70	81 Autres services, sauf les administrations publiques	271
265	210	60	40	100	65	91 Administrations publiques	272
						selon la catégorie de travailleurs	
70	125	30	-	50	30	Catégorie de travailleurs - Sans objet (36)	273
5,190	3,875	1,615	595	3,030	1,360	Toutes les catégories de travailleurs (37)	274
4,805	3,600	1,500	555	2,745	1,225	Travailleurs rémunérés	275
4,630	3,495	1,365	545	2,515	1,185	Employés	276
175	105	140	10	230	45	Travailleurs autonomes (entreprise constituée en société)	277
320	265	95	40	280	135	Travailleurs autonomes (entreprise non constituée en société)	278
60	10	15	-	10	-	Travailleurs familiaux non rémunérés	279
						selon la profession basée sur la CNP-S de 2001	
2,735	2,060	920	320	1,630	740	Hommes actifs de 15 ans et plus	280
30	65	20	-	30	10	Profession - Sans objet (36)	281
2,700	1,995	905	320	1,600	735	Toutes les professions (37)	282
510	215	175	75	365	90	A Gestion	283
255	160	105	35	190	75	B Affaires, finance et administration	284
205	235	55	-	245	80	C Sciences naturelles et appliquées et professions apparentées	285
35	-	25	-	20	10	D Secteur de la santé	286
85	70	85	20	80	10	E Sciences sociales, enseignement, administration publique et religion	287
60	45	15	-	30	10	F Arts, culture, sports et loisirs	288
610	345	175	65	335	140	G Ventes et services	289
735	700	190	65	250	250	H Métiers, transport et machinerie	290
30	35	25	10	55	25	I Professions propres au secteur primaire	291
170	185	60	45	35	50	J Transformation, fabrication et services d'utilité publique	292
2,530	1,935	715	275	1,450	645	Femmes actives de 15 ans et plus	293
40	60	10	-	15	20	Profession - Sans objet (36)	294
2,490	1,875	705	270	1,430	630	Toutes les professions (37)	295
220	160	75	45	155	20	A Gestion	296
845	610	260	130	475	240	B Affaires, finance et administration	297
25	75	-	10	35	10	C Sciences naturelles et appliquées et professions apparentées	298
230	145	60	15	100	70	D Secteur de la santé	299

Table 1. Selected Characteristics for Census Tracts, 2001 Census – 100% Data and 20% Sample Data

No.	Characteristics	Vancouver 0186.08 A	Vancouver 0187.03	Vancouver 0187.04 A	Vancouver 0187.05 A	Vancouver 0187.06 A	Vancouver 0187.07 A
	POPULATION CHARACTERISTICS						
	by occupation based on the 2001 NOC-S – concluded						
300	E Occupations in social science, education, government service and religion	85	85	-	85	85	10
301	F Occupations in art, culture, recreation and sport	20	15	10	25	30	10
302	G Sales and service occupations	405	505	185	525	430	120
303	H Trades, transport and equipment operators and related occupations	60	30	-	50	45	10
304	I Occupations unique to primary industry	55	25	-	65	20	10
305	J Occupations unique to processing, manufacturing and utilities	100	160	20	145	35	10
306	**Total employed labour force 15 years and over**	**2,540**	**3,420**	**750**	**2,860**	**2,640**	**780**
	by place of work						
307	Males	1,355	1,880	425	1,610	1,430	390
308	Usual place of work	995	1,445	265	1,235	1,165	300
309	At home	100	30	35	45	40	35
310	Outside Canada	-	10	-	10	20	10
311	No fixed workplace address	265	390	125	330	205	45
312	Females	1,185	1,545	330	1,250	1,210	390
313	Usual place of work	1,025	1,355	255	1,095	1,110	340
314	At home	85	55	20	50	55	10
315	Outside Canada	10	-	-	-	-	-
316	No fixed workplace address	70	135	50	110	45	40
317	**Total employed labour force 15 years and over with usual place of work or no fixed workplace address**	**2,350**	**3,320**	**695**	**2,760**	**2,520**	**725**
	by mode of transportation						
318	Males	1,255	1,835	385	1,560	1,370	345
319	Car, truck, van, as driver	1,050	1,600	300	1,240	1,190	285
320	Car, truck, van, as passenger	80	135	35	110	95	35
321	Public transit	90	85	50	145	50	20
322	Walked	15	15	-	15	10	-
323	Other method	20	-	10	60	35	-
324	Females	1,095	1,480	305	1,200	1,150	380
325	Car, truck, van, as driver	775	1,105	175	930	860	310
326	Car, truck, van, as passenger	70	135	40	125	150	30
327	Public transit	175	200	70	105	95	40
328	Walked	60	30	25	15	45	-
329	Other method	20	15	-	20	-	-
330	**Total population 15 years and over who worked since January 1, 2000**	**2,975**	**3,920**	**835**	**3,290**	**3,000**	**845**
	by language used at work						
331	Single responses	2,710	3,710	765	2,875	2,760	805
332	English	2,570	3,610	720	2,670	2,665	800
333	French	-	-	-	-	-	-
334	Non-official languages (5)	145	95	45	205	100	-
335	Chinese, n.o.s.	-	40	-	-	25	-
336	Cantonese	-	-	-	-	-	-
337	Other languages (6)	145	55	45	205	70	-
338	Multiple responses	265	210	75	420	235	40
339	English and French	-	-	-	35	25	-
340	English and non-official language	265	190	65	385	210	40
341	French and non-official language	-	-	-	-	-	-
342	English, French and non-official language	-	15	-	-	-	-
	DWELLING AND HOUSEHOLD CHARACTERISTICS						
343	**Total number of occupied private dwellings**	**1,665**	**1,955**	**400**	**1,540**	**1,470**	**430**
	by tenure						
344	Owned	1,025	1,400	285	920	1,165	405
345	Rented	645	555	110	625	305	30
346	Band housing	-	-	-	-	-	-
	by structural type of dwelling						
347	Single-detached house	735	1,305	200	635	1,360	420
348	Semi-detached house	75	55	15	-	-	-
349	Row house	280	70	35	90	-	-
350	Apartment, detached duplex	165	440	65	325	30	10
351	Apartment, building that has five or more storeys	-	-	-	-	-	-
352	Apartment, building that has fewer than five storeys (38)	380	70	95	485	80	-
353	Other single-attached house	-	10	-	-	-	-
354	Movable dwelling (39)	35	-	-	-	-	-

Tableau 1. Certaines caractéristiques des secteurs de recensement, recensement de 2001 – Données intégrales et données-échantillon (20 %)

Vancouver 0187.08 A	Vancouver 0187.09 A	Vancouver 0188.01 A	Vancouver 0188.02 A	Vancouver 0188.03 A	Vancouver 0188.04 A	Caractéristiques	N°
						CARACTÉRISTIQUES DE LA POPULATION	
						selon la profession basée sur la CNP-S de 2001 – fin	
215	110	85	25	180	75	E Sciences sociales, enseignement, administration publique et religion	300
40	55	15	-	50	25	F Arts, culture, sports et loisirs	301
710	620	190	60	390	160	G Ventes et services	302
75	30	-	-	15	-	H Métiers, transport et machinerie	303
25	10	10	-	10	-	I Professions propres au secteur primaire	304
100	55	20	-	30	25	J Transformation, fabrication et services d'utilité publique	305
4,940	**3,655**	**1,580**	**565**	**2,880**	**1,285**	**Population active occupée totale de 15 ans et plus**	306
						selon le lieu de travail	
2,610	1,900	885	305	1,515	680	Hommes	307
2,030	1,505	725	270	1,145	490	Lieu habituel de travail	308
140	70	55	-	155	25	À domicile	309
20	15	-	-	-	10	En dehors du Canada	310
425	315	110	20	220	155	Sans adresse de travail fixe	311
2,325	1,755	695	260	1,360	610	Femmes	312
2,040	1,585	585	235	1,050	515	Lieu habituel de travail	313
150	65	65	25	150	35	À domicile	314
30	-	-	-	-	-	En dehors du Canada	315
105	105	40	-	160	60	Sans adresse de travail fixe	316
4,600	**3,505**	**1,455**	**525**	**2,575**	**1,220**	**Population active occupée totale de 15 ans et plus ayant un lieu habituel de travail ou sans adresse de travail fixe**	317
						selon le mode de transport	
2,455	1,820	830	290	1,360	645	Hommes	318
2,125	1,550	730	260	1,225	540	Automobile, camion ou fourgonnette, en tant que conducteur	319
155	105	35	10	55	55	Automobile, camion ou fourgonnette, en tant que passager	320
120	100	50	-	50	35	Transport en commun	321
20	30	-	10	15	-	À pied	322
35	35	15	10	20	15	Autre moyen	323
2,145	1,685	620	230	1,210	570	Femmes	324
1,660	1,295	530	170	1,010	475	Automobile, camion ou fourgonnette, en tant que conductrice	325
205	150	45	15	65	45	Automobile, camion ou fourgonnette, en tant que passagère	326
235	180	40	50	110	40	Transport en commun	327
30	40	-	-	20	10	À pied	328
20	20	-	-	10	-	Autre moyen	329
5,665	**4,110**	**1,745**	**635**	**3,370**	**1,460**	**Population totale de 15 ans et plus ayant travaillé depuis le 1er janvier 2000**	330
						selon la langue utilisée au travail	
5,260	3,755	1,545	570	3,035	1,325	Réponses uniques	331
5,130	3,665	1,520	540	2,890	1,310	Anglais	332
-	-	-	-	-	-	Français	333
130	85	20	25	145	10	Langues non officielles (5)	334
-	20	-	-	75	-	Chinois, n.d.a.	335
10	-	-	-	-	-	Cantonais	336
115	70	10	25	75	15	Autres langues (6)	337
410	355	200	65	330	135	Réponses multiples	338
85	25	10	-	-	15	Anglais et français	339
320	320	190	65	325	115	Anglais et langue non officielle	340
-	10	-	-	-	-	Français et langue non officielle	341
-	10	-	-	10	10	Anglais, français et langue non officielle	342
						CARACTÉRISTIQUES DES LOGEMENTS ET DES MÉNAGES	
3,275	**2,260**	**920**	**290**	**1,750**	**805**	**Nombre total de logements privés occupés**	343
						selon le mode d'occupation	
2,825	1,775	815	235	1,640	615	Possédé	344
450	490	105	50	105	190	Loué	345
-	-	-	-	-	-	Logement de bande	346
						selon le type de construction résidentielle	
1,060	1,495	710	270	1,675	615	Maison individuelle non attenante	347
30	30	-	-	-	10	Maison jumelée	348
1,240	365	-	-	-	-	Maison en rangée	349
410	330	125	20	75	140	Appartement, duplex non attenant	350
-	-	-	-	-	-	Appartement, immeuble de cinq étages ou plus	351
270	30	-	-	-	-	Appartement, immeuble de moins de cinq étages (38)	352
-	-	-	-	-	-	Autre maison individuelle attenante	353
270	10	75	-	-	35	Logement mobile (39)	354

Table 1. Selected Characteristics for Census Tracts, 2001 Census – 100% Data and 20% Sample Data

No.	Characteristics	Vancouver 0186.08 A	Vancouver 0187.03	Vancouver 0187.04 A	Vancouver 0187.05 A	Vancouver 0187.06 A	Vancouver 0187.07 A
	DWELLING AND HOUSEHOLD CHARACTERISTICS						
	by condition of dwelling						
355	Regular maintenance only	1,080	1,245	265	1,200	1,040	400
356	Minor repairs	495	585	110	245	340	35
357	Major repairs	85	125	20	100	90	-
	by period of construction						
358	Before 1946	20	35	-	15	10	10
359	1946-1960	90	135	15	50	25	-
360	1961-1970	375	180	25	100	55	-
361	1971-1980	695	655	170	245	120	-
362	1981-1990	280	800	70	610	735	15
363	1991-2001 (20)	200	155	110	520	540	400
364	Average number of rooms per dwelling	6.0	6.8	6.8	6.8	7.7	9.6
365	Average number of bedrooms per dwelling	2.8	3.1	3.3	3.3	3.5	4.0
366	Average value of dwelling $	181,366	220,794	213,258	241,607	252,714	321,147
367	**Total number of private households**	**1,665**	**1,955**	**395**	**1,540**	**1,470**	**435**
	by household size						
368	1 person	265	230	30	160	125	10
369	2 persons	435	495	85	305	350	100
370	3 persons	330	380	90	240	225	70
371	4-5 persons	485	675	145	550	585	220
372	6 or more persons	155	175	55	285	175	35
	by household type						
373	One-family households	1,250	1,475	295	1,040	1,190	425
374	Multiple-family households	115	165	60	280	110	-
375	Non-family households	300	315	40	215	170	10
376	Number of persons in private households	5,255	6,470	1,440	5,885	5,260	1,555
377	Average number of persons in private households	3.2	3.3	3.6	3.8	3.6	3.6
378	Average number of persons per room	0.5	0.5	0.5	0.6	0.5	0.4
379	Tenant households in non-farm, non-reserve private dwellings (40)	620	555	115	615	300	25
380	Average gross rent $ (40)	700	808	809	712	804	809
381	Tenant households spending 30% or more of household income on gross rent (40) (41)	270	275	45	210	105	10
382	Tenant households spending from 30% to 99% of household income on gross rent (40) (41)	235	220	40	185	80	10
383	Owner households in non-farm, non-reserve private dwellings (42)	1,020	1,400	285	920	1,165	405
384	Average owner's major payments $ (42)	1,183	1,165	1,124	1,267	1,134	1,393
385	Owner households spending 30% or more of household income on owner's major payments (41) (42)	330	355	80	285	265	70
386	Owner households spending from 30% to 99% of household income on owner's major payments (41) (42)	270	320	75	245	225	55
	CENSUS FAMILY CHARACTERISTICS						
387	**Total number of census families in private households**	**1,505**	**1,810**	**425**	**1,650**	**1,415**	**425**
	by census family structure and size						
388	Total couple families	1,140	1,480	350	1,370	1,275	405
389	Total families of married couples	1,020	1,310	315	1,310	1,195	390
390	Without children at home	330	390	115	380	305	105
391	With children at home	695	920	200	930	895	290
392	1 child	250	305	75	295	250	70
393	2 children	295	405	45	380	405	125
394	3 or more children	145	210	80	255	240	90
395	Total families of common-law couples	120	165	35	60	70	10
396	Without children at home	65	80	15	20	55	10
397	With children at home	55	90	25	35	20	10
398	1 child	35	10	15	10	-	-
399	2 children	15	70	10	15	-	-
400	3 or more children	-	10	-	10	10	-
401	Total lone-parent families	360	325	75	285	145	20
402	Female parent	285	265	60	180	115	15
403	1 child	150	145	20	120	60	-
404	2 children	70	85	35	55	30	10
405	3 or more children	65	30	-	-	25	10

Tableau 1. Certaines caractéristiques des secteurs de recensement, recensement de 2001 – Données intégrales et données-échantillon (20 %)

Vancouver 0187.08 A	Vancouver 0187.09 A	Vancouver 0188.01 A	Vancouver 0188.02 A	Vancouver 0188.03 A	Vancouver 0188.04 A	Caractéristiques	N°
						CARACTÉRISTIQUES DES LOGEMENTS ET DES MÉNAGES	
						selon l'état du logement	
2,595	1,585	795	235	1,500	595	Entretien régulier seulement	355
435	555	105	40	235	165	Réparations mineures	356
245	120	20	15	15	40	Réparations majeures	357
						selon la période de construction	
35	35	-	-	-	10	Avant 1946	358
70	75	20	-	10	50	1946-1960	359
100	135	30	10	35	20	1961-1970	360
255	260	20	10	50	45	1971-1980	361
515	1,105	285	60	655	320	1981-1990	362
2,310	640	565	215	995	360	1991-2001 (20)	363
6.8	7.2	8.0	8.5	8.9	7.8	Nombre moyen de pièces par logement	364
3.2	3.2	3.6	3.6	3.7	3.3	Nombre moyen de chambres à coucher par logement	365
212,440	232,727	298,787	285,129	327,699	260,628	Valeur moyenne du logement $	366
3,275	**2,255**	**920**	**290**	**1,750**	**805**	**Nombre total de logements privés**	367
						selon la taille du ménage	
570	330	120	15	70	90	1 personne	368
1,090	635	200	75	405	210	2 personnes	369
575	370	135	70	300	110	3 personnes	370
830	730	385	110	830	305	4-5 personnes	371
210	200	85	20	140	90	6 personnes ou plus	372
						selon le genre de ménage	
2,415	1,695	710	260	1,585	635	Ménages unifamiliaux	373
200	190	80	10	70	55	Ménages multifamiliaux	374
660	380	135	15	95	115	Ménages non familiaux	375
9,495	7,220	3,160	975	6,225	2,740	Nombre de personnes dans les ménages privés	376
2.9	3.2	3.4	3.4	3.6	3.4	Nombre moyen de personnes dans les ménages privés	377
0.4	0.4	0.4	0.4	0.4	0.4	Nombre moyen de personnes par pièce	378
440	480	100	50	110	185	Ménages locataires dans les logements privés non agricoles hors réserve (40)	379
907	860	915	1,035	1,129	871	Loyer brut moyen $ (40)	380
160	210	30	10	35	90	Ménages locataires consacrant 30 % ou plus du revenu du ménage au loyer brut (40) (41)	381
125	190	30	10	25	70	Ménages locataires consacrant de 30 % à 99 % du revenu du ménage au loyer brut (40) (41)	382
2,825	1,775	810	240	1,630	615	Ménages propriétaires dans les logements privés non agricoles hors réserve (42)	383
1,185	1,126	1,384	1,147	1,325	1,298	Principales dépenses de propriété moyennes $ (42)	384
730	440	280	40	470	135	Ménages propriétaires consacrant 30 % ou plus du revenu du ménage aux principales dépenses de propriété (41) (42)	385
630	425	220	35	360	105	Ménages propriétaires consacrant de 30 % à 99 % du revenu du ménage aux principales dépenses de propriété (41) (42)	386
						CARACTÉRISTIQUES DES FAMILLES DE RECENSEMENT	
2,855	**2,070**	**865**	**280**	**1,720**	**750**	**Total des familles de recensement dans les ménages privés**	387
						selon la structure et la taille de la famille de recensement	
2,455	1,775	780	265	1,605	640	Total des familles avec conjoints	388
2,200	1,620	720	250	1,550	605	Total des familles avec couples mariés	389
965	510	180	60	385	210	Sans enfants à la maison	390
1,235	1,110	540	185	1,160	395	Avec enfants à la maison	391
395	365	155	75	290	90	1 enfant	392
565	495	275	55	610	170	2 enfants	393
275	255	105	55	260	135	3 enfants ou plus	394
255	155	65	15	55	30	Total des familles en union libre	395
145	105	35	20	45	20	Sans enfants à la maison	396
110	55	30	-	10	10	Avec enfants à la maison	397
65	25	-	-	10	-	1 enfant	398
40	20	15	-	-	10	2 enfants	399
10	10	10	-	-	-	3 enfants ou plus	400
395	290	85	15	115	115	Total des familles monoparentales	401
300	225	65	10	80	95	Parent de sexe féminin	402
205	130	35	-	35	40	1 enfant	403
75	70	25	-	30	35	2 enfants	404
15	30	10	10	20	20	3 enfants ou plus	405

Table 1. Selected Characteristics for Census Tracts, 2001 Census – 100% Data and 20% Sample Data

No.	Characteristics	Vancouver 0186.08 A	Vancouver 0187.03	Vancouver 0187.04 A	Vancouver 0187.05 A	Vancouver 0187.06 A	Vancouver 0187.07 A
	CENSUS FAMILY CHARACTERISTICS						
	by census family structure and size - concluded						
406	Male parent	70	65	15	105	25	-
407	1 child	35	45	10	60	25	-
408	2 children	35	20	-	35	-	-
409	3 or more children	10	-	-	10	-	-
410	**Total number of children at home**	**2,075**	**2,495**	**550**	**2,335**	**2,170**	**670**
	by age groups						
411	Under 6 years	620	560	160	625	375	120
412	6-14 years	750	905	160	845	770	280
413	15-17 years	205	250	55	195	305	80
414	18-24 years	305	580	135	470	490	150
415	25 years and over	190	195	40	195	220	40
416	Average number of children at home per census family (43)	1.4	1.4	1.3	1.4	1.5	1.6
417	**Total number of persons in private households**	**5,260**	**6,465**	**1,440**	**5,885**	**5,260**	**1,555**
	by census family status and living arrangements						
418	Number of non-family persons	540	680	120	530	405	60
419	Living with relatives (44)	135	190	40	225	135	35
420	Living with non-relatives only	150	265	55	150	145	10
421	Living alone	260	230	30	160	125	15
422	Number of family persons	4,715	5,785	1,320	5,355	4,855	1,495
423	Average number of persons per census family	3.1	3.2	3.1	3.2	3.4	3.5
424	**Total number of persons 65 years and over**	**300**	**395**	**85**	**435**	**465**	**75**
425	Number of non-family persons 65 years and over	110	150	10	150	120	35
426	Living with relatives (44)	60	65	10	110	90	20
427	Living with non-relatives only	-	20	10	-	-	-
428	Living alone	55	70	-	40	30	10
429	Number of family persons 65 years and over	195	250	70	290	350	45
	ECONOMIC FAMILY CHARACTERISTICS						
430	**Total number of economic families in private households**	**1,370**	**1,660**	**360**	**1,330**	**1,305**	**420**
	by size of family						
431	2 persons	435	480	85	280	310	110
432	3 persons	320	375	90	220	240	70
433	4 persons	330	395	65	315	365	145
434	5 or more persons	285	410	115	515	385	100
435	Total number of persons in economic families	4,850	5,975	1,360	5,575	4,990	1,530
436	Average number of persons per economic family	3.5	3.6	3.8	4.2	3.8	3.7
437	Total number of unattached individuals	405	495	80	310	270	25
	2000 INCOME CHARACTERISTICS						
	Population 15 years and over by sex and total income groups in 2000						
438	Total - Both sexes	3,885	4,995	1,125	4,415	4,095	1,155
439	Without income	295	275	95	255	250	70
440	With income	3,595	4,720	1,030	4,160	3,850	1,090
441	Under $1,000 (45)	190	260	50	220	165	85
442	$ 1,000 - $ 2,999	175	280	55	220	245	70
443	$ 3,000 - $ 4,999	140	205	40	205	155	40
444	$ 5,000 - $ 6,999	130	240	55	200	235	65
445	$ 7,000 - $ 9,999	295	330	120	365	255	50
446	$10,000 - $11,999	205	215	30	135	225	10
447	$12,000 - $14,999	305	195	80	360	260	75
448	$15,000 - $19,999	350	370	115	505	440	80
449	$20,000 - $24,999	275	440	105	380	290	55
450	$25,000 - $29,999	200	420	70	370	195	50
451	$30,000 - $34,999	305	350	120	325	185	65
452	$35,000 - $39,999	190	375	50	195	175	45
453	$40,000 - $44,999	190	265	30	170	235	60
454	$45,000 - $49,999	180	145	10	165	140	25
455	$50,000 - $59,999	290	350	60	165	250	75
456	$60,000 and over	175	285	35	190	395	240
457	Average income $ (46)	24,831	25,845	21,713	22,272	27,830	35,652
458	Median income $ (46)	19,991	22,423	18,756	18,463	19,219	25,047
459	Standard error of average income $ (46)	687	696	1,120	583	909	2,254

Tableau 1. Certaines caractéristiques des secteurs de recensement, recensement de 2001 – Données intégrales et données-échantillon (20 %)

Vancouver 0187.08 A	Vancouver 0187.09 A	Vancouver 0188.01 A	Vancouver 0188.02 A	Vancouver 0188.03 A	Vancouver 0188.04 A	Caractéristiques	N°
						CARACTÉRISTIQUES DES FAMILLES DE RECENSEMENT	
						selon la structure et la taille de la famille de recensement – fin	
95	75	20	10	35	15	Parent de sexe masculin	406
65	35	10	10	20	-	1 enfant	407
20	20	15	-	10	15	2 enfants	408
10	20	-	-	10	-	3 enfants ou plus	409
3,145	**2,765**	**1,255**	**390**	**2,600**	**1,100**	**Nombre total d'enfants à la maison**	410
						selon les groupes d'âge	
735	590	245	80	420	220	Moins de 6 ans	411
1,145	945	520	150	1,030	455	6-14 ans	412
380	300	140	45	410	145	15-17 ans	413
675	665	220	85	555	210	18-24 ans	414
210	275	130	40	175	65	25 ans et plus	415
1.1	1.3	1.5	1.4	1.5	1.5	Nombre moyen d'enfants à la maison par famille de recensement (43)	416
9,490	**7,220**	**3,165**	**980**	**6,225**	**2,740**	**Nombre total de personnes dans les ménages privés**	417
						selon la situation des particuliers dans la famille de recensement et des particuliers dans le ménage	
1,040	605	260	45	310	255	Nombre de personnes hors famille de recensement	418
245	155	70	15	120	95	Vivant avec des personnes apparentées (44)	419
230	130	75	10	115	65	Vivant avec des personnes non apparentées uniquement	420
570	325	120	15	70	90	Vivant seules	421
8,450	6,615	2,905	940	5,920	2,485	Nombre de personnes membres d'une famille	422
3.0	3.2	3.4	3.4	3.4	3.3	Nombre moyen de personnes par famille de recensement	423
1,050	**750**	**225**	**50**	**390**	**200**	**Nombre total de personnes de 65 ans et plus**	424
390	220	45	10	85	80	Nombre de personnes hors famille de recensement de 65 ans et plus	425
105	55	30	10	60	60	Vivant avec des personnes apparentées (44)	426
15	45	-	-	10	20	Vivant avec des personnes non apparentées uniquement	427
270	125	15	10	15	10	Vivant seules	428
665	530	175	35	305	115	Nombre de personnes membres d'une famille de 65 ans et plus	429
						CARACTÉRISTIQUES DES FAMILLES ÉCONOMIQUES	
2,640	**1,900**	**795**	**270**	**1,665**	**700**	**Nombre total de familles économiques dans les ménages privés**	430
						selon la taille de la famille	
1,065	625	195	75	415	200	2 personnes	431
550	365	160	70	295	115	3 personnes	432
580	490	240	60	595	180	4 personnes	433
440	425	200	65	355	200	5 personnes ou plus	434
8,695	6,770	2,970	955	6,035	2,585	Nombre total de personnes dans les familles économiques	435
3.3	3.6	3.7	3.5	3.6	3.7	Nombre moyen de personnes par famille économique	436
800	455	195	25	190	155	Nombre total de personnes hors famille économique	437
						CARACTÉRISTIQUES DU REVENU DE 2000	
						Population de 15 ans et plus selon le sexe et les tranches de revenu total en 2000	
7,615	5,690	2,395	755	4,740	2,060	Total - Les deux sexes	438
470	345	190	30	475	145	Sans revenu	439
7,145	5,345	2,205	720	4,265	1,915	Avec un revenu	440
290	220	160	25	345	100	Moins de 1 000 $ (45)	441
325	245	100	25	245	110	1 000 $ - 2 999 $	442
150	180	110	65	165	85	3 000 $ - 4 999 $	443
250	205	105	35	215	65	5 000 $ - 6 999 $	444
480	345	170	30	275	115	7 000 $ - 9 999 $	445
370	295	150	35	115	60	10 000 $ - 11 999 $	446
425	340	170	35	225	120	12 000 $ - 14 999 $	447
585	575	120	90	270	125	15 000 $ - 19 999 $	448
560	420	120	35	285	290	20 000 $ - 24 999 $	449
520	415	90	35	185	130	25 000 $ - 29 999 $	450
650	310	150	20	250	135	30 000 $ - 34 999 $	451
335	415	145	15	185	105	35 000 $ - 39 999 $	452
425	315	80	45	305	120	40 000 $ - 44 999 $	453
390	205	165	65	215	80	45 000 $ - 49 999 $	454
510	295	105	55	350	100	50 000 $ - 59 999 $	455
880	560	270	100	635	190	60 000 $ et plus	456
30,587	28,162	29,729	29,916	32,435	29,369	Revenu moyen $ (46)	457
26,078	23,401	20,714	21,566	24,770	23,514	Revenu médian $ (46)	458
622	668	1,340	2,002	1,029	1,375	Erreur type de revenu moyen $ (46)	459

Table 1. Selected Characteristics for Census Tracts, 2001 Census – 100% Data and 20% Sample Data

No.	Characteristics	Vancouver 0186.08 A	Vancouver 0187.03	Vancouver 0187.04 A	Vancouver 0187.05 A	Vancouver 0187.06 A	Vancouver 0187.07 A
	2000 INCOME CHARACTERISTICS						
	Population 15 years and over by sex and total income groups in 2000 – concluded						
460	Total - Males	1,880	2,485	580	2,205	2,015	560
461	Without income	125	85	40	45	85	30
462	With income	1,765	2,405	540	2,155	1,930	520
463	Under $1,000 (45)	110	85	20	125	95	40
464	$ 1,000 - $ 2,999	60	115	25	90	60	20
465	$ 3,000 - $ 4,999	45	90	-	75	70	-
466	$ 5,000 - $ 6,999	70	105	10	55	120	35
467	$ 7,000 - $ 9,999	60	140	60	120	55	30
468	$10,000 - $11,999	100	115	15	45	135	-
469	$12,000 - $14,999	85	70	25	145	65	25
470	$15,000 - $19,999	180	170	65	220	190	40
471	$20,000 - $24,999	135	170	70	250	135	15
472	$25,000 - $29,999	110	215	55	215	90	15
473	$30,000 - $34,999	135	170	65	195	90	-
474	$35,000 - $39,999	120	255	30	105	105	10
475	$40,000 - $44,999	135	150	10	110	145	40
476	$45,000 - $49,999	70	115	10	110	95	10
477	$50,000 - $59,999	220	210	60	145	180	50
478	$60,000 and over	130	230	30	150	295	185
479	Average income $ (46)	29,092	29,362	27,112	26,654	33,833	47,205
480	Median income $ (46)	26,178	28,805	24,272	23,870	26,097	42,391
481	Standard error of average income $ (46)	1,053	886	1,696	901	1,488	3,834
482	Total - Females	2,005	2,510	545	2,210	2,085	600
483	Without income	170	195	55	205	165	35
484	With income	1,835	2,315	490	2,005	1,920	565
485	Under $1,000 (45)	85	180	30	95	70	45
486	$ 1,000 - $ 2,999	120	165	30	125	185	45
487	$ 3,000 - $ 4,999	95	110	40	135	85	40
488	$ 5,000 - $ 6,999	65	135	50	145	115	35
489	$ 7,000 - $ 9,999	235	195	60	245	200	20
490	$10,000 - $11,999	110	95	20	95	95	10
491	$12,000 - $14,999	215	125	60	215	190	45
492	$15,000 - $19,999	175	205	50	285	245	45
493	$20,000 - $24,999	135	275	35	125	150	45
494	$25,000 - $29,999	90	205	15	150	105	30
495	$30,000 - $34,999	170	185	50	125	100	55
496	$35,000 - $39,999	75	115	20	85	70	40
497	$40,000 - $44,999	55	110	20	60	90	25
498	$45,000 - $49,999	105	25	-	55	45	10
499	$50,000 - $59,999	70	140	-	25	75	20
500	$60,000 and over	45	55	-	35	105	55
501	Average income $ (46)	20,730	22,190	15,831	17,550	21,794	24,968
502	Median income $ (46)	14,999	18,471	12,052	13,993	15,327	19,995
503	Standard error of average income $ (46)	840	1,052	1,207	661	989	2,023
	by composition of total income						
504	Total - Composition of income in 2000 % (47)	100.0	100.0	100.0	100.0	100.0	100.0
505	Employment income %	83.6	86.4	82.5	83.2	84.9	87.7
506	Government transfer payments %	12.0	9.0	12.4	12.5	9.7	5.0
507	Other %	4.5	4.6	5.3	4.4	5.4	7.2
	Population 15 years and over with employment income in 2000 by sex and work activity						
508	Both sexes with employment income (48)	2,845	3,795	785	3,260	2,950	860
509	Average employment income $	26,204	27,763	23,447	23,635	30,769	39,817
510	Standard error of average employment income $	788	802	1,348	657	1,058	2,674
511	Worked full year, full time (49)	1,520	2,040	435	1,700	1,515	470
512	Average employment income $	35,133	37,865	31,607	31,951	43,273	58,524
513	Standard error of average employment income $	977	1,131	1,542	945	1,491	3,462
514	Worked part year or part time (50)	1,240	1,650	345	1,410	1,330	355
515	Average employment income $	16,788	16,478	13,330	14,425	17,758	18,455
516	Standard error of average employment income $	1,009	808	1,823	671	1,187	2,953
517	Males with employment income (48)	1,450	2,110	445	1,820	1,600	430
518	Average employment income $	30,476	29,934	28,422	27,156	35,913	52,473
519	Standard error of average employment income $	1,160	959	1,952	963	1,587	4,382
520	Worked full year, full time (49)	875	1,150	295	1,045	905	270
521	Average employment income $	37,876	40,090	33,687	34,721	47,911	71,245
522	Standard error of average employment income $	1,343	1,078	1,990	1,277	1,990	4,825
523	Worked part year or part time (50)	570	915	145	710	650	135
524	Average employment income $	19,491	18,123	17,614	17,094	20,417	24,100
525	Standard error of average employment income $	1,649	1,254	3,856	1,115	2,124	6,539

Tableau 1. Certaines caractéristiques des secteurs de recensement, recensement de 2001 – Données intégrales et données-échantillon (20 %)

Vancouver 0187.08 A	Vancouver 0187.09 A	Vancouver 0188.01 A	Vancouver 0188.02 A	Vancouver 0188.03 A	Vancouver 0188.04 A	Caractéristiques	N°
						CARACTÉRISTIQUES DU REVENU DE 2000	
						Population de 15 ans et plus selon le sexe et les tranches de revenu total en 2000 – fin	
3,690	2,775	1,205	385	2,335	1,025	Total - Hommes	460
170	135	60	15	200	65	Sans revenu	461
3,520	2,645	1,145	375	2,135	955	Avec un revenu	462
135	105	100	10	135	45	Moins de 1 000 $ (45)	463
130	90	55	10	70	60	1 000 $ - 2 999 $	464
50	50	50	45	40	45	3 000 $ - 4 999 $	465
80	50	65	25	80	25	5 000 $ - 6 999 $	466
155	180	80	20	95	25	7 000 $ - 9 999 $	467
160	90	65	15	55	15	10 000 $ - 11 999 $	468
125	125	30	10	105	75	12 000 $ - 14 999 $	469
270	265	55	25	130	55	15 000 $ - 19 999 $	470
230	185	30	30	170	140	20 000 $ - 24 999 $	471
270	185	15	10	80	35	25 000 $ - 29 999 $	472
270	125	50	10	90	70	30 000 $ - 34 999 $	473
175	190	70	10	115	25	35 000 $ - 39 999 $	474
210	205	45	40	135	80	40 000 $ - 44 999 $	475
260	155	105	25	95	25	45 000 $ - 49 999 $	476
320	220	85	30	185	65	50 000 $ - 59 999 $	477
690	420	245	75	550	170	60 000 $ et plus	478
37,400	33,744	37,638	34,587	41,615	35,169	Revenu moyen $ (46)	479
32,022	29,712	32,001	29,608	35,139	24,856	Revenu médian $ (46)	480
1,020	1,065	2,290	3,106	1,688	2,137	Erreur type de revenu moyen $ (46)	481
3,920	2,915	1,190	365	2,405	1,035	Total - Femmes	482
300	215	135	15	275	80	Sans revenu	483
3,620	2,700	1,055	350	2,125	960	Avec un revenu	484
160	115	65	20	200	55	Moins de 1 000 $ (45)	485
195	155	50	15	175	50	1 000 $ - 2 999 $	486
105	130	60	20	125	45	3 000 $ - 4 999 $	487
170	155	35	10	135	35	5 000 $ - 6 999 $	488
325	165	85	15	180	85	7 000 $ - 9 999 $	489
215	205	80	20	60	40	10 000 $ - 11 999 $	490
295	210	140	25	120	45	12 000 $ - 14 999 $	491
320	305	70	65	145	70	15 000 $ - 19 999 $	492
335	235	90	10	110	145	20 000 $ - 24 999 $	493
250	235	70	30	110	95	25 000 $ - 29 999 $	494
375	185	105	15	160	60	30 000 $ - 34 999 $	495
160	220	75	10	75	75	35 000 $ - 39 999 $	496
215	110	30	-	175	40	40 000 $ - 44 999 $	497
130	55	55	40	115	55	45 000 $ - 49 999 $	498
190	75	25	25	165	40	50 000 $ - 59 999 $	499
190	140	25	25	90	20	60 000 $ et plus	500
23,970	22,701	21,136	24,948	23,219	23,580	Revenu moyen $ (46)	501
20,284	18,490	16,969	18,212	17,090	21,118	Revenu médian $ (46)	502
645	752	1,051	2,337	991	1,644	Erreur type de revenu moyen $ (46)	503
						selon la composition du revenu total	
100.0	100.0	100.0	100.0	100.0	100.0	Total - Composition du revenu en 2000 % (47)	504
83.3	82.5	87.1	90.2	85.2	83.0	Revenu d'emploi %	505
9.8	11.0	7.1	6.9	6.1	9.9	Transferts gouvernementaux %	506
6.8	6.5	5.6	2.6	8.8	7.0	Autre %	507
						Population de 15 ans et plus ayant un revenu d'emploi en 2000 selon le sexe et le travail	
5,535	4,025	1,680	615	3,215	1,455	Les deux sexes ayant un revenu d'emploi (48)	508
32,913	30,847	34,085	31,823	36,604	32,072	Revenu moyen d'emploi $	509
727	824	1,612	2,192	1,224	1,697	Erreur type de revenu moyen d'emploi $	510
3,005	2,120	800	435	1,670	670	Ayant travaillé toute l'année à plein temps (49)	511
44,523	41,439	48,935	38,395	51,025	46,893	Revenu moyen d'emploi $	512
964	1,039	2,619	2,509	1,718	2,395	Erreur type de revenu moyen d'emploi $	513
2,400	1,770	810	165	1,450	735	Ayant travaillé une partie de l'année ou à temps partiel (50)	514
19,546	19,299	21,198	16,503	21,811	19,485	Revenu moyen d'emploi $	515
803	1,084	1,536	3,261	1,384	2,041	Erreur type de revenu moyen d'emploi $	516
2,880	2,060	940	340	1,710	775	Hommes ayant un revenu d'emploi (48)	517
39,624	36,789	41,325	35,064	44,971	37,580	Revenu moyen d'emploi $	518
1,155	1,257	2,597	3,253	1,932	2,482	Erreur type de revenu moyen d'emploi $	519
1,780	1,235	500	265	1,045	400	Ayant travaillé toute l'année à plein temps (49)	520
50,895	46,286	57,769	40,610	57,758	54,591	Revenu moyen d'emploi $	521
1,359	1,412	3,837	3,508	2,442	3,492	Erreur type de revenu moyen d'emploi $	522
1,045	765	405	70	635	360	Ayant travaillé une partie de l'année ou à temps partiel (50)	523
22,005	23,019	23,998	15,778	25,448	19,208	Revenu moyen d'emploi $	524
1,495	1,999	2,663	5,938	2,473	2,066	Erreur type de revenu moyen d'emploi $	525

Table 1. Selected Characteristics for Census Tracts, 2001 Census – 100% Data and 20% Sample Data

No.	Characteristics	Vancouver 0186.08 A	Vancouver 0187.03	Vancouver 0187.04 A	Vancouver 0187.05 A	Vancouver 0187.06 A	Vancouver 0187.07 A
	2000 INCOME CHARACTERISTICS						
	Population 15 years and over with employment income in 2000 by sex and work activity – concluded						
526	Females with employment income (48)	1,395	1,685	340	1,440	1,350	430
527	Average employment income $	21,762	25,045	16,926	19,169	24,661	27,191
528	Standard error of average employment income $	1,002	1,322	1,493	794	1,286	2,389
529	Worked full year, full time (49)	645	890	135	655	610	200
530	Average employment income $	31,413	34,994	27,032	27,515	36,412	41,540
531	Standard error of average employment income $	1,344	2,176	2,100	1,278	2,111	3,536
532	Worked part year or part time (50)	675	740	200	695	685	220
533	Average employment income $	14,510	14,438	10,270	11,684	15,246	14,891
534	Standard error of average employment income $	1,210	972	1,388	691	1,212	2,092
	Census families by structure and family income groups in 2000						
535	Total - All census families	1,500	1,810	425	1,650	1,420	420
536	Under $10,000	145	85	25	110	70	-
537	$ 10,000 - $19,999	180	75	25	150	130	35
538	$ 20,000 - $29,999	105	125	65	175	80	20
539	$ 30,000 - $39,999	200	270	85	260	150	10
540	$ 40,000 - $49,999	140	245	45	200	155	35
541	$ 50,000 - $59,999	200	200	35	180	65	25
542	$ 60,000 - $69,999	105	270	55	250	135	40
543	$ 70,000 - $79,999	95	170	40	50	150	40
544	$ 80,000 - $89,999	130	75	10	90	105	25
545	$ 90,000 - $99,999	50	90	35	60	105	60
546	$100,000 and over	155	205	10	120	275	145
547	Average family income $	51,088	60,007	47,671	50,070	69,369	87,934
548	Median family income $	47,687	56,315	43,806	45,977	65,709	88,999
549	Standard error of average family income $	1,798	1,765	2,734	1,620	2,576	4,961
550	Total - All couple census families (51)	1,140	1,480	350	1,370	1,270	405
551	Under $10,000	75	20	15	60	50	10
552	$ 10,000 - $19,999	90	50	15	75	100	30
553	$ 20,000 - $29,999	60	105	45	145	55	15
554	$ 30,000 - $39,999	145	205	75	225	135	-
555	$ 40,000 - $49,999	115	180	45	175	120	35
556	$ 50,000 - $59,999	185	180	25	150	60	30
557	$ 60,000 - $69,999	90	245	50	210	130	30
558	$ 70,000 - $79,999	70	150	35	45	150	30
559	$ 80,000 - $89,999	110	65	-	90	95	20
560	$ 90,000 - $99,999	50	90	30	65	95	60
561	$100,000 and over	150	195	10	120	275	145
562	Average family income $	57,294	63,519	49,723	54,027	73,219	88,920
563	Median family income $	53,613	59,966	47,238	49,654	69,277	89,820
564	Standard error of average family income $	2,044	1,820	2,652	1,730	2,731	5,145
	Incidence of low income in 2000						
565	Total - Economic families	1,375	1,660	360	1,335	1,300	425
566	Low income	345	205	70	240	230	35
567	Incidence of low income in 2000 % (52)	25.2	12.5	19.9	18.2	17.6	8.9
568	Total - Unattached individuals 15 years and over	405	490	75	310	260	25
569	Low income	185	235	40	165	130	10
570	Incidence of low income in 2000 % (52)	46.1	48.1	51.3	53.8	50.7	33.2
571	Total - Population in private households	5,255	6,465	1,440	5,885	5,250	1,555
572	Low income	1,390	945	325	1,060	950	190
573	Incidence of low income in 2000 % (52)	26.4	14.6	22.8	18.0	18.1	12.2
	Private households by household income groups in 2000						
574	Total - All private households	1,665	1,955	400	1,540	1,475	430
575	Under $10,000	125	110	10	65	60	-
576	$ 10,000 - $19,999	185	100	15	145	125	30
577	$ 20,000 - $29,999	130	175	50	120	90	20
578	$ 30,000 - $39,999	225	205	70	220	115	15
579	$ 40,000 - $49,999	180	205	35	180	150	25
580	$ 50,000 - $59,999	215	165	55	170	75	30
581	$ 60,000 - $69,999	100	270	45	185	155	25
582	$ 70,000 - $79,999	115	210	40	80	165	35
583	$ 80,000 - $89,999	125	125	25	115	100	25
584	$ 90,000 - $99,999	60	105	30	45	100	70
585	$100,000 and over	195	280	30	220	330	160
586	Average household income $	53,567	62,337	56,131	60,099	72,741	89,723
587	Median household income $	49,719	60,537	53,610	54,300	67,938	90,791
588	Standard error of average household income $	1,886	1,768	2,987	2,381	2,652	4,919

Tableau 1. Certaines caractéristiques des secteurs de recensement, recensement de 2001 – Données intégrales et données-échantillon (20 %)

Vancouver 0187.08 A	Vancouver 0187.09 A	Vancouver 0188.01 A	Vancouver 0188.02 A	Vancouver 0188.03 A	Vancouver 0188.04 A	Caractéristiques	N°
						CARACTÉRISTIQUES DU REVENU DE 2000	
						Population de 15 ans et plus ayant un revenu d'emploi en 2000 selon le sexe et le travail – fin	
2,650	1,965	735	280	1,510	680	Femmes ayant un revenu d'emploi (48)	526
25,622	24,619	24,851	27,866	27,141	25,796	Revenu moyen d'emploi $	527
759	965	1,318	2,718	1,223	2,167	Erreur type de revenu moyen d'emploi $	528
1,225	880	305	175	625	270	Ayant travaillé toute l'année à plein temps (49)	529
35,283	34,651	34,640	35,026	39,725	35,424	Revenu moyen d'emploi $	530
1,093	1,380	1,995	3,265	1,660	2,109	Erreur type de revenu moyen d'emploi $	531
1,350	1,010	405	95	815	375	Ayant travaillé une partie de l'année ou à temps partiel (50)	532
17,635	16,484	18,372	17,034	18,983	19,750	Revenu moyen d'emploi $	533
847	1,110	1,460	3,668	1,494	3,387	Erreur type de revenu moyen d'emploi $	534
						Familles de recensement selon la structure et les tranches de revenu de la famille en 2000	
2,850	2,070	865	280	1,720	750	Total - Toutes les familles de recensement	535
85	65	65	10	120	35	Moins de 10 000 $	536
230	135	65	15	95	60	10 000 $ - 19 999 $	537
255	175	65	35	125	45	20 000 $ - 29 999 $	538
205	225	110	30	110	130	30 000 $ - 39 999 $	539
285	260	50	30	125	65	40 000 $ - 49 999 $	540
295	200	60	10	105	75	50 000 $ - 59 999 $	541
335	265	70	-	140	70	60 000 $ - 69 999 $	542
235	155	70	-	140	65	70 000 $ - 79 999 $	543
175	85	110	25	140	25	80 000 $ - 89 999 $	544
200	130	40	15	140	55	90 000 $ - 99 999 $	545
555	365	160	100	480	135	100 000 $ et plus	546
66,182	63,658	67,219	72,266	76,407	65,656	Revenu moyen des familles $	547
61,978	58,924	61,403	74,562	72,198	56,878	Revenu médian des familles $	548
1,515	1,762	3,307	5,437	2,548	3,710	Erreur type de revenu moyen des familles $	549
2,455	1,775	780	265	1,605	635	Total - Toutes les familles de recensement comptant un couple (51)	550
60	55	45	-	90	25	Moins de 10 000 $	551
160	80	45	20	80	40	10 000 $ - 19 999 $	552
220	105	55	35	100	30	20 000 $ - 29 999 $	553
140	180	95	30	105	90	30 000 $ - 39 999 $	554
240	240	35	20	110	50	40 000 $ - 49 999 $	555
250	175	60	10	100	60	50 000 $ - 59 999 $	556
285	250	70	10	135	60	60 000 $ - 69 999 $	557
205	150	70	10	125	70	70 000 $ - 79 999 $	558
165	65	105	30	135	20	80 000 $ - 89 999 $	559
190	135	40	10	135	50	90 000 $ - 99 999 $	560
540	350	155	100	480	130	100 000 $ et plus	561
69,941	67,677	71,628	73,072	78,996	71,063	Revenu moyen des familles $	562
65,490	62,157	67,010	79,989	74,686	62,933	Revenu médian des familles $	563
1,623	1,892	3,502	5,653	2,636	4,065	Erreur type de revenu moyen des familles $	564
						Fréquence des unités à faible revenu en 2000	
2,635	1,900	795	270	1,665	700	Total - Familles économiques	565
295	235	135	60	345	135	Faible revenu	566
11.1	12.3	16.8	21.3	20.5	19.0	Fréquence des unités à faible revenu en 2000 % (52)	567
795	455	195	25	160	155	Total - Personnes hors famille économique de 15 ans et plus	568
275	145	80	-	75	50	Faible revenu	569
34.6	31.5	40.4	-	46.9	33.8	Fréquence des unités à faible revenu en 2000 % (52)	570
9,490	7,220	3,160	980	6,200	2,735	Total - Population dans les ménages privés	571
1,285	870	625	205	1,360	585	Faible revenu	572
13.5	12.0	19.8	21.0	22.0	21.4	Fréquence des unités à faible revenu en 2000 % (52)	573
						Ménages privés selon les tranches de revenu du ménage en 2000	
3,275	2,260	920	285	1,750	805	Total - Tous les ménages privés	574
60	60	65	10	125	40	Moins de 10 000 $	575
310	165	70	20	90	40	10 000 $ - 19 999 $	576
370	145	50	40	110	45	20 000 $ - 29 999 $	577
240	270	110	35	95	150	30 000 $ - 39 999 $	578
305	275	65	35	145	65	40 000 $ - 49 999 $	579
330	190	50	10	120	65	50 000 $ - 59 999 $	580
325	245	90	10	135	70	60 000 $ - 69 999 $	581
255	190	65	10	115	50	70 000 $ - 79 999 $	582
180	130	95	25	115	25	80 000 $ - 89 999 $	583
210	115	40	-	130	65	90 000 $ - 99 999 $	584
695	465	215	115	570	180	100 000 $ et plus	585
66,613	66,593	71,250	75,058	79,004	69,996	Revenu moyen des ménages $	586
61,089	60,038	66,608	70,004	73,331	57,049	Revenu médian des ménages $	587
1,489	1,798	3,409	5,659	2,592	3,772	Erreur type de revenu moyen des ménages $	588

Table 1. Selected Characteristics for Census Tracts, 2001 Census – 100% Data and 20% Sample Data

No.	Characteristics	Vancouver 0188.05 A	Vancouver 0188.06 A	Vancouver 0189.03	Vancouver 0189.05 A	Vancouver 0189.06 A	Vancouver 0189.07 A
	POPULATION CHARACTERISTICS						
1	**Population, 1996 (1)**	**1,988**	**712**	**3,117**	**6,674**	**2,656**	**1,841**
2	**Population, 2001 (2)**	**2,254**	**942**	**3,248**	**6,982**	**2,913**	**2,353**
3	Population percentage change, 1996-2001	13.4	32.3	4.2	4.6	9.7	27.8
4	Land area in square kilometres, 2001	6.66	3.71	1.47	1.30	2.41	0.81
5	**Total population – 100% Data (3)**	**2,255**	**945**	**3,250**	**6,985**	**2,910**	**2,355**
	by sex and age groups						
6	Male	1,125	480	1,615	3,240	1,430	1,150
7	0-4 years	55	25	110	190	105	80
8	5-9 years	90	40	120	165	120	80
9	10-14 years	125	35	130	150	110	65
10	15-19 years	130	35	105	215	120	85
11	20-24 years	75	30	95	185	95	90
12	25-29 years	40	20	115	215	95	105
13	30-34 years	50	30	130	240	100	110
14	35-39 years	75	40	180	260	140	110
15	40-44 years	120	45	175	285	135	105
16	45-49 years	120	45	110	245	125	65
17	50-54 years	80	30	80	225	90	80
18	55-59 years	65	40	65	170	50	45
19	60-64 years	45	20	70	160	35	40
20	65-69 years	30	20	50	135	35	35
21	70-74 years	10	10	35	160	30	25
22	75-79 years	5	5	35	120	15	25
23	80-84 years	5	-	10	80	10	10
24	85 years and over	5	5	5	45	5	5
25	Female	1,130	465	1,630	3,745	1,485	1,205
26	0-4 years	50	30	115	190	110	80
27	5-9 years	90	40	110	160	125	70
28	10-14 years	115	45	120	180	110	70
29	15-19 years	110	40	115	180	115	75
30	20-24 years	65	25	95	245	110	70
31	25-29 years	50	25	115	230	95	120
32	30-34 years	40	20	140	255	125	100
33	35-39 years	110	40	170	285	155	120
34	40-44 years	130	45	140	290	115	100
35	45-49 years	125	35	120	280	115	105
36	50-54 years	80	25	85	260	85	65
37	55-59 years	55	30	90	205	40	50
38	60-64 years	35	20	60	160	45	40
39	65-69 years	20	15	55	190	40	35
40	70-74 years	15	10	30	200	30	35
41	75-79 years	10	5	40	235	45	30
42	80-84 years	5	5	20	120	15	20
43	85 years and over	-	10	15	90	10	15
44	**Total population 15 years and over**	**1,725**	**730**	**2,545**	**5,950**	**2,225**	**1,900**
	by legal marital status						
45	Never married (single)	525	220	810	1,655	765	645
46	Legally married (and not separated)	1,070	435	1,345	2,935	1,100	905
47	Separated, but still legally married	35	20	80	255	95	70
48	Divorced	60	35	190	570	165	195
49	Widowed	40	15	120	540	95	85
	by common-law status						
50	Not in a common-law relationship	1,665	705	2,340	5,600	2,045	1,745
51	In a common-law relationship	60	30	205	355	185	155
52	**Total population – 20% Sample Data (4)**	**2,250**	**940**	**3,240**	**6,980**	**2,910**	**2,355**
	by mother tongue						
53	Single responses	2,210	925	3,160	6,815	2,860	2,280
54	English	1,490	760	2,510	4,155	1,610	1,485
55	French	10	10	40	35	65	15
56	Non-official languages (5)	705	155	610	2,620	1,185	785
57	Chinese, n.o.s.	155	-	15	200	45	95
58	Cantonese	30	-	65	150	15	65
59	Punjabi	20	-	-	205	350	80
60	Mandarin	100	50	-	185	-	10
61	Tagalog (Pilipino)	45	-	20	460	90	65
62	Other languages (6)	360	110	500	1,420	680	475
63	Multiple responses	45	15	80	165	50	75
64	English and French	-	15	10	25	-	-
65	English and non-official language	40	-	75	135	45	70
66	French and non-official language	-	-	-	10	-	-
67	English, French and non-official language	-	-	-	-	-	-

See reference material at the end of the publication. – Voir les documents de référence à la fin de la publication.

Tableau 1. Certaines caractéristiques des secteurs de recensement, recensement de 2001 – Données intégrales et données-échantillon (20 %)

Vancouver 0189.08 A	Vancouver 0189.09 A	Vancouver 0189.10 ◆ A	Vancouver 0190.01	Vancouver 0190.03	Vancouver 0190.04 A	Caractéristiques	Nº
						CARACTÉRISTIQUES DE LA POPULATION	
5,886	**3,555**	**4,307**	**5,062**	**4,632**	**5,901**	**Population, 1996 (1)**	1
6,119	**4,048**	**4,833**	**5,505**	**4,694**	**5,894**	**Population, 2001 (2)**	2
4.0	13.9	12.2	8.8	1.3	-0.1	Variation en pourcentage de la population, 1996-2001	3
0.68	1.30	1.33	1.48	1.93	3.07	Superficie des terres en kilomètres carrés, 2001	4
6,120	**4,050**	**4,835**	**5,505**	**4,690**	**5,895**	**Population totale – Données intégrales (3)**	5
						selon le sexe et les groupes d'âge	
2,985	1,990	2,350	2,640	2,405	3,035	Sexe masculin	6
315	115	175	175	175	215	0-4 ans	7
255	160	205	155	205	240	5-9 ans	8
200	145	200	125	195	220	10-14 ans	9
195	190	220	130	180	230	15-19 ans	10
200	170	180	165	160	165	20-24 ans	11
270	125	130	235	170	150	25-29 ans	12
300	130	135	255	195	225	30-34 ans	13
305	155	195	260	235	290	35-39 ans	14
300	175	225	250	245	290	40-44 ans	15
195	145	210	180	175	255	45-49 ans	16
145	155	170	165	155	200	50-54 ans	17
90	110	100	120	80	145	55-59 ans	18
85	60	75	105	80	115	60-64 ans	19
50	50	50	80	75	125	65-69 ans	20
35	50	30	75	25	80	70-74 ans	21
20	25	30	70	30	50	75-79 ans	22
10	10	5	50	15	35	80-84 ans	23
10	10	10	40	10	15	85 ans et plus	24
3,130	2,060	2,490	2,865	2,290	2,860	Sexe féminin	25
260	120	140	165	170	190	0-4 ans	26
255	140	205	155	170	210	5-9 ans	27
225	150	195	135	150	185	10-14 ans	28
190	180	215	130	175	180	15-19 ans	29
225	165	175	175	165	185	20-24 ans	30
300	140	170	260	165	190	25-29 ans	31
370	120	195	240	215	235	30-34 ans	32
330	185	240	255	220	265	35-39 ans	33
265	190	260	220	205	285	40-44 ans	34
190	175	225	180	175	220	45-49 ans	35
150	140	170	195	130	180	50-54 ans	36
115	90	85	145	100	140	55-59 ans	37
70	65	60	110	70	95	60-64 ans	38
55	60	60	100	55	95	65-69 ans	39
50	65	40	115	50	90	70-74 ans	40
40	30	30	100	40	70	75-79 ans	41
30	30	15	95	25	35	80-84 ans	42
10	15	10	85	15	25	85 ans et plus	43
4,610	**3,215**	**3,720**	**4,585**	**3,620**	**4,635**	**Population totale de 15 ans et plus**	44
						selon l'état matrimonial légal	
1,745	1,035	1,205	1,450	1,370	1,465	Célibataire (jamais marié(e))	45
1,805	1,840	1,990	1,930	1,535	2,470	Légalement marié(e) (et non séparé(e))	46
355	80	145	260	190	155	Séparé(e), mais toujours légalement marié(e)	47
520	115	260	545	355	330	Divorcé(e)	48
180	140	125	400	165	220	Veuf ou veuve	49
						selon l'union libre	
4,185	3,100	3,510	4,170	3,300	4,305	Ne vivant pas en union libre	50
420	110	210	420	320	335	Vivant en union libre	51
6,120	**4,045**	**4,835**	**5,505**	**4,660**	**5,875**	**Population totale – Données-échantillon (20 %) (4)**	52
						selon la langue maternelle	
5,955	3,975	4,730	5,405	4,575	5,775	Réponses uniques	53
3,485	2,110	2,560	3,705	2,875	3,885	Anglais	54
85	85	40	70	40	40	Français	55
2,385	1,780	2,130	1,630	1,660	1,850	Langues non officielles (5)	56
55	180	145	45	55	120	Chinois, n.d.a.	57
-	10	190	25	95	50	Cantonais	58
10	745	180	60	365	205	Pendjabi	59
75	145	75	115	30	75	Mandarin	60
385	75	205	145	115	115	Tagalog (pilipino)	61
1,855	635	1,335	1,240	1,005	1,285	Autres langues (6)	62
170	70	105	100	85	100	Réponses multiples	63
10	-	-	-	10	10	Anglais et français	64
145	70	100	100	65	80	Anglais et langue non officielle	65
10	-	-	-	10	10	Français et langue non officielle	66
-	-	-	-	-	-	Anglais, français et langue non officielle	67

See reference material at the end of the publication. – Voir les documents de référence à la fin de la publication.

Table 1. Selected Characteristics for Census Tracts, 2001 Census – 100% Data and 20% Sample Data

No.	Characteristics	Vancouver 0188.05 A	Vancouver 0188.06 A	Vancouver 0189.03	Vancouver 0189.05 A	Vancouver 0189.06 A	Vancouver 0189.07 A
	POPULATION CHARACTERISTICS						
	by home language						
68	Single responses	1,800	890	3,035	5,460	2,185	1,935
69	English	1,550	835	2,725	4,575	1,700	1,645
70	French	-	-	-	-	-	-
71	Non-official languages (5)	250	60	310	885	480	290
72	Cantonese	-	-	50	90	-	15
73	Chinese, n.o.s.	55	-	-	125	-	30
74	Punjabi	10	-	-	80	155	60
75	Mandarin	50	50	10	95	-	10
76	Korean	90	-	-	210	-	60
77	Other languages (6)	50	10	250	290	325	125
78	Multiple responses	455	50	205	1,520	730	420
79	English and French	10	10	10	15	50	-
80	English and non-official language	445	40	200	1,475	680	415
81	French and non-official language	-	-	-	-	-	-
82	English, French and non-official language	-	-	-	25	-	10
	by knowledge of official languages						
83	English only	2,155	900	3,010	6,425	2,635	2,130
84	French only	-	-	-	-	-	-
85	English and French	40	40	175	325	130	160
86	Neither English nor French	60	-	55	230	140	70
	by knowledge of non-official languages (5) (7)						
87	Cantonese	40	-	70	175	40	85
88	Chinese, n.o.s.	95	-	-	170	10	115
89	Punjabi	15	-	40	220	425	100
90	Mandarin	165	50	35	250	45	25
91	Hindi	-	-	130	255	220	30
92	German	45	20	70	180	35	80
93	Spanish	120	15	185	180	90	70
	by first official language spoken						
94	English	2,175	930	3,135	6,620	2,680	2,270
95	French	15	10	35	45	65	10
96	English and French	-	-	20	95	25	20
97	Neither English nor French	65	-	50	220	140	55
98	Official language minority - (number) (8)	15	10	45	95	80	20
99	Official language minority - (percentage) (8)	0.7	1.1	1.4	1.4	2.7	0.8
	by ethnic origin (9)						
100	English	605	320	960	1,485	490	525
101	Canadian	530	205	1,010	1,315	635	555
102	Chinese	335	50	95	695	55	260
103	Scottish	435	275	625	950	390	350
104	Irish	225	140	390	810	265	285
105	German	210	145	550	700	235	260
106	East Indian	30	-	230	435	450	85
107	French	110	70	235	425	225	255
108	Ukrainian	60	95	210	415	180	115
109	Italian	75	55	165	165	65	75
110	Dutch (Netherlands)	75	95	155	185	100	85
111	Filipino	70	-	45	685	145	115
112	Polish	130	30	135	420	160	105
113	Norwegian	30	70	130	140	35	70
114	North American Indian	40	40	125	195	145	20
	by Aboriginal identity						
115	Total Aboriginal identity population (10)	40	40	110	150	185	15
116	Total non-Aboriginal population	2,215	900	3,130	6,830	2,725	2,335
	by Aboriginal origin						
117	Total Aboriginal origins population (11)	45	40	135	245	190	35
118	Total non-Aboriginal population	2,215	900	3,105	6,735	2,720	2,325
	by Registered Indian status						
119	Registered Indian (12)	20	10	40	35	105	10
120	Not a Registered Indian	2,235	935	3,200	6,945	2,810	2,345

Tableau 1. Certaines caractéristiques des secteurs de recensement, recensement de 2001 – Données intégrales et données-échantillon (20 %)

Vancouver 0189.08 A	Vancouver 0189.09 A	Vancouver 0189.10 ◆ A	Vancouver 0190.01	Vancouver 0190.03	Vancouver 0190.04 A	Caractéristiques	N°
						CARACTÉRISTIQUES DE LA POPULATION	
						selon la langue parlée à la maison	
4,755	3,215	3,665	4,580	3,700	4,825	Réponses uniques	68
3,735	2,355	2,730	4,025	3,020	4,330	Anglais	69
30	50	-	-	10	-	Français	70
995	805	940	550	675	495	Langues non officielles (5)	71
-	10	135	20	25	30	Cantonais	72
35	90	45	10	15	50	Chinois, n.d.a.	73
-	240	100	20	245	55	Pendjabi	74
30	150	60	105	15	60	Mandarin	75
205	110	260	180	45	-	Coréen	76
730	210	340	220	335	310	Autres langues (6)	77
1,360	830	1,170	920	960	1,045	Réponses multiples	78
20	15	40	25	25	60	Anglais et français	79
1,320	805	1,060	875	915	965	Anglais et langue non officielle	80
15	-	20	-	-	-	Français et langue non officielle	81
10	20	55	30	20	20	Anglais, français et langue non officielle	82
						selon la connaissance des langues officielles	
5,600	3,575	4,340	5,120	4,195	5,500	Anglais seulement	83
25	-	-	-	-	-	Français seulement	84
250	255	275	230	265	270	Anglais et français	85
250	210	225	150	195	105	Ni l'anglais ni le français	86
						selon la connaissance des langues non officielles (5) (7)	
10	10	215	40	140	50	Cantonais	87
75	150	140	40	80	110	Chinois, n.d.a.	88
10	805	200	115	430	265	Pendjabi	89
75	210	140	120	80	85	Mandarin	90
65	260	125	180	165	345	Hindi	91
135	30	115	90	50	185	Allemand	92
285	45	125	90	120	165	Espagnol	93
						selon la première langue officielle parlée	
5,760	3,745	4,490	5,275	4,390	5,675	Anglais	94
85	85	30	50	50	40	Français	95
30	10	90	20	30	50	Anglais et français	96
240	210	220	155	195	105	Ni l'anglais ni le français	97
100	85	75	65	60	70	Minorité de langue officielle - (nombre) (8)	98
1.6	2.1	1.5	1.2	1.3	1.2	Minorité de langue officielle - (pourcentage) (8)	99
						selon l'origine ethnique (9)	
1,130	810	810	1,495	940	1,360	Anglais	100
1,035	760	945	1,085	920	1,605	Canadien	101
300	395	505	200	270	290	Chinois	102
795	505	575	1,100	670	935	Écossais	103
485	360	450	925	420	685	Irlandais	104
590	375	315	660	490	890	Allemand	105
120	805	255	250	500	405	Indien de l'Inde	106
445	200	290	470	415	340	Français	107
225	225	250	255	175	515	Ukrainien	108
110	70	115	90	95	175	Italien	109
150	140	200	195	140	275	Hollandais (Néerlandais)	110
740	150	435	280	170	170	Philippin	111
315	115	315	270	100	320	Polonais	112
80	135	80	250	125	185	Norvégien	113
270	95	150	225	170	205	Indien de l'Amérique du Nord	114
						selon l'identité autochtone	
230	60	135	220	180	185	Total de la population ayant une identité autochtone (10)	115
5,890	3,985	4,705	5,280	4,480	5,690	Total de la population non autochtone	116
						selon l'origine autochtone	
350	100	175	350	245	235	Total de la population ayant une origine autochtone (11)	117
5,770	3,950	4,660	5,150	4,415	5,635	Total de la population non autochtone	118
						selon le statut d'Indien inscrit	
70	55	45	60	35	90	Oui, Indien inscrit (12)	119
6,050	3,995	4,795	5,440	4,620	5,790	Non, pas un Indien inscrit	120

Table 1. Selected Characteristics for Census Tracts, 2001 Census – 100% Data and 20% Sample Data

No.	Characteristics	Vancouver 0188.05 A	Vancouver 0188.06 A	Vancouver 0189.03	Vancouver 0189.05 A	Vancouver 0189.06 A	Vancouver 0189.07 A
	POPULATION CHARACTERISTICS						
	by visible minority groups						
121	Total visible minority population	670	80	710	2,470	1,200	795
122	Chinese	340	45	80	660	160	245
123	South Asian	50	-	265	485	530	90
124	Black	-	-	65	100	55	75
125	Filipino	65	-	55	690	140	115
126	Latin American	25	-	115	50	80	35
127	Southeast Asian	25	-	25	55	140	75
128	Arab	-	-	-	15	-	10
129	West Asian	-	-	-	-	70	45
130	Korean	125	-	-	340	-	80
131	Japanese	40	-	45	25	20	30
132	Visible minority, n.i.e. (13)	-	30	30	15	-	-
133	Multiple visible minorities (14)	10	-	25	15	-	-
	by citizenship						
134	Canadian citizenship (15)	1,950	905	3,115	6,310	2,590	2,180
135	Citizenship other than Canadian	305	30	125	665	320	175
	by place of birth of respondent						
136	Non-immigrant population	1,455	775	2,485	4,210	1,875	1,550
137	Born in province of residence	1,070	565	1,825	2,480	1,410	975
138	Immigrant population (16)	775	160	750	2,700	1,025	785
139	United States	35	10	15	65	10	10
140	Central and South America	40	-	100	85	25	30
141	Caribbean and Bermuda	-	-	-	45	25	10
142	United Kingdom	50	30	115	275	45	70
143	Other Europe (17)	95	55	230	575	250	145
144	Africa	25	20	45	70	-	60
145	Asia and the Middle East	520	45	160	1,505	635	465
146	Oceania and other (18)	10	-	80	75	35	-
147	Non-permanent residents (19)	20	-	10	70	10	15
148	**Total immigrant population**	**780**	**160**	**745**	**2,695**	**1,025**	**790**
	by period of immigration						
149	Before 1961	70	35	85	355	45	70
150	1961-1970	95	30	150	205	80	70
151	1971-1980	110	-	90	520	105	140
152	1981-1990	195	45	230	545	190	175
153	1991-2001 (20)	300	45	195	1,075	615	325
154	1991-1995	65	-	120	500	360	185
155	1996-2001 (20)	240	45	75	575	255	145
	by age at immigration						
156	0-4 years	70	10	65	165	75	50
157	5-19 years	255	60	300	705	320	285
158	20 years and over	450	95	380	1,825	635	450
159	**Total population**	**2,255**	**940**	**3,235**	**6,980**	**2,910**	**2,350**
	by religion						
160	Catholic (21)	345	165	595	1,595	675	495
161	Protestant	900	410	940	2,310	705	730
162	Christian Orthodox	-	40	30	75	15	35
163	Christian, n.i.e. (22)	325	70	315	395	130	80
164	Muslim	20	-	10	55	135	45
165	Jewish	-	-	10	10	-	-
166	Buddhist	55	50	25	130	25	190
167	Hindu	-	-	105	115	15	-
168	Sikh	15	-	35	220	365	90
169	Eastern religions (23)	-	-	-	10	-	10
170	Other religions (24)	-	-	10	20	45	10
171	No religious affiliation (25)	585	210	1,160	2,070	815	660
172	**Total population 15 years and over**	**1,725**	**725**	**2,525**	**5,950**	**2,195**	**1,905**
	by generation status						
173	1st generation (26)	750	160	760	2,620	955	775
174	2nd generation (27)	350	190	640	1,330	440	345
175	3rd generation and over (28)	625	375	1,125	1,995	805	790
176	**Total population 1 year and over (29)**	**2,230**	**910**	**3,190**	**6,915**	**2,850**	**2,290**
	by place of residence 1 year ago (mobility)						
177	Non-movers	1,960	685	2,885	5,850	2,360	1,945
178	Movers	270	230	310	1,060	490	345
179	Non-migrants	130	170	185	645	310	200
180	Migrants	135	60	125	420	180	145
181	Internal migrants	100	65	120	250	100	95
182	Intraprovincial migrants	95	60	115	155	65	40
183	Interprovincial migrants	-	-	-	90	35	55
184	External migrants	35	-	-	170	75	50

Tableau 1. Certaines caractéristiques des secteurs de recensement, recensement de 2001 – Données intégrales et données-échantillon (20 %)

Vancouver 0189.08 A	Vancouver 0189.09 A	Vancouver 0189.10 ◆ A	Vancouver 0190.01	Vancouver 0190.03	Vancouver 0190.04 A	Caractéristiques	N°
						CARACTÉRISTIQUES DE LA POPULATION	
						selon les groupes de minorités visibles	
2,345	1,830	2,105	1,440	1,780	1,435	Total de la population des minorités visibles	121
165	385	440	210	225	260	Chinois	122
145	900	325	245	585	560	Sud-Asiatique	123
155	60	120	130	70	30	Noir	124
725	145	420	265	200	145	Philippin	125
225	25	90	60	40	90	Latino-Américain	126
260	150	130	95	435	225	Asiatique du Sud-Est	127
140	30	25	30	-	-	Arabe	128
95	-	40	90	10	25	Asiatique occidental	129
350	130	405	280	130	-	Coréen	130
25	-	55	20	15	60	Japonais	131
40	-	25	15	40	15	Minorité visible, n.i.a. (13)	132
25	-	30	10	20	35	Minorités visibles multiples (14)	133
						selon la citoyenneté	
4,780	3,630	4,140	4,820	4,100	5,405	Citoyenneté canadienne (15)	134
1,340	415	695	685	560	470	Citoyenneté autre que canadienne	135
						selon le lieu de naissance du répondant	
3,395	2,310	2,625	3,705	3,120	4,215	Population non immigrante	136
2,190	1,730	1,810	2,440	2,080	3,210	Née dans la province de résidence	137
2,390	1,685	2,155	1,680	1,490	1,655	Population immigrante (16)	138
70	40	35	95	30	50	États-Unis	139
210	15	80	45	40	75	Amérique centrale et du Sud	140
60	30	10	25	-	10	Caraïbes et Bermudes	141
110	155	105	205	110	115	Royaume-Uni	142
485	170	470	335	170	495	Autre Europe (17)	143
45	10	55	40	20	15	Afrique	144
1,395	1,230	1,330	870	1,100	695	Asie et Moyen-Orient	145
10	40	70	65	25	205	Océanie et autre (18)	146
335	45	55	115	50	-	Résidents non permanents (19)	147
2,395	**1,690**	**2,155**	**1,680**	**1,490**	**1,655**	**Population immigrante totale**	148
						selon la période d'immigration	
95	70	95	150	80	160	Avant 1961	149
115	160	80	195	125	210	1961-1970	150
215	340	205	135	195	320	1971-1980	151
335	375	585	410	490	420	1981-1990	152
1,625	745	1,190	785	595	540	1991-2001 (20)	153
590	465	680	340	235	275	1991-1995	154
1,035	285	505	440	360	270	1996-2001 (20)	155
						selon l'âge à l'immigration	
340	125	165	170	130	135	0-4 ans	156
745	440	625	415	390	480	5-19 ans	157
1,305	1,120	1,360	1,090	970	1,045	20 ans et plus	158
6,115	**4,045**	**4,835**	**5,505**	**4,660**	**5,875**	**Population totale**	159
						selon la religion	
1,730	835	1,190	1,095	920	1,025	Catholique (21)	160
1,415	980	1,235	1,560	1,005	1,830	Protestante	161
95	15	85	105	45	55	Orthodoxe chrétienne	162
670	285	380	355	310	255	Chrétiennes, n.i.a. (22)	163
290	45	210	130	95	200	Musulmane	164
-	-	-	15	-	10	Juive	165
120	235	220	70	380	210	Bouddhiste	166
75	55	15	185	40	90	Hindoue	167
20	810	190	55	410	220	Sikh	168
30	-	-	-	-	-	Religions orientales (23)	169
-	-	-	25	15	35	Autres religions (24)	170
1,680	780	1,295	1,910	1,440	1,935	Aucune appartenance religieuse (25)	171
4,610	**3,275**	**3,715**	**4,600**	**3,595**	**4,605**	**Population totale de 15 ans et plus**	172
						selon le statut des générations	
2,200	1,655	1,995	1,625	1,405	1,590	1re génération (26)	173
660	630	600	1,095	715	1,100	2e génération (27)	174
1,750	985	1,120	1,885	1,475	1,915	3e génération et plus (28)	175
6,015	**4,005**	**4,745**	**5,440**	**4,570**	**5,825**	**Population totale de 1 an et plus (29)**	176
						selon le lieu de résidence 1 an auparavant (mobilité)	
3,960	3,575	4,115	4,185	3,615	4,930	Personnes n'ayant pas déménagé	177
2,055	430	625	1,255	955	895	Personnes ayant déménagé	178
930	245	455	780	630	560	Non-migrants	179
1,125	185	175	475	320	335	Migrants	180
655	100	100	330	275	275	Migrants internes	181
460	95	75	285	240	240	Migrants infraprovinciaux	182
190	-	30	45	40	35	Migrants interprovinciaux	183
470	85	75	145	45	60	Migrants externes	184

Table 1. Selected Characteristics for Census Tracts, 2001 Census – 100% Data and 20% Sample Data

No.	Characteristics	Vancouver 0188.05 A	Vancouver 0188.06 A	Vancouver 0189.03	Vancouver 0189.05 A	Vancouver 0189.06 A	Vancouver 0189.07 A
	POPULATION CHARACTERISTICS						
185	**Total population 5 years and over (30)**	**2,150**	**890**	**3,005**	**6,605**	**2,675**	**2,190**
	by place of residence 5 years ago (mobility)						
186	Non-movers	1,260	310	1,830	3,350	1,395	880
187	Movers	890	580	1,175	3,250	1,280	1,310
188	Non-migrants	460	355	685	1,695	750	680
189	Migrants	430	220	490	1,555	530	630
190	Internal migrants	200	160	485	1,125	310	475
191	Intraprovincial migrants	170	100	430	840	235	330
192	Interprovincial migrants	25	65	50	285	70	145
193	External migrants	235	55	10	430	220	155
194	**Total population 15 to 24 years**	**400**	**125**	**390**	**825**	**405**	**310**
	by school attendance						
195	Not attending school	115	60	175	285	155	110
196	Attending school full time	245	55	190	435	190	160
197	Attending school part time	40	10	20	110	60	40
198	**Total population 15 years and over**	**1,725**	**725**	**2,525**	**5,950**	**2,195**	**1,905**
	by highest level of schooling						
199	Less than grade 9 (31)	75	10	110	415	215	140
200	Grades 9-13 without high school graduation certificate	360	205	695	1,400	630	470
201	Grades 9-13 with high school graduation certificate	240	130	385	660	350	200
202	Some postsecondary without degree, certificate or diploma (32)	200	115	345	745	265	290
203	Trades certificate or diploma (33)	155	90	325	780	300	200
204	College certificate or diploma (34)	300	100	475	1,010	260	380
205	University certificate below bachelor's degree	90	-	25	215	30	50
206	University with bachelor's degree or higher	300	75	170	725	150	185
	by combinations of unpaid work						
207	Males 15 years and over	865	370	1,250	2,735	1,065	925
208	Reported unpaid work (35)	760	335	1,135	2,415	955	855
209	Housework and child care and care or assistance to seniors	85	20	100	135	50	90
210	Housework and child care only	265	85	350	555	310	240
211	Housework and care or assistance to seniors only	50	35	55	160	65	30
212	Child care and care or assistance to seniors only	-	-	10	-	-	-
213	Housework only	355	190	595	1,475	505	450
214	Child care only	-	-	20	45	15	35
215	Care or assistance to seniors only	-	-	-	50	-	10
216	Females 15 years and over	860	355	1,280	3,220	1,125	985
217	Reported unpaid work (35)	805	325	1,220	2,945	1,030	910
218	Housework and child care and care or assistance to seniors	100	55	195	210	110	135
219	Housework and child care only	305	105	435	775	360	275
220	Housework and care or assistance to seniors only	75	65	75	295	85	65
221	Child care and care or assistance to seniors only	-	-	-	-	-	10
222	Housework only	305	105	485	1,660	475	395
223	Child care only	10	-	30	15	10	20
224	Care or assistance to seniors only	-	-	-	10	-	10
	by labour force activity						
225	Males 15 years and over	870	370	1,250	2,735	1,070	925
226	In the labour force	605	290	960	1,720	840	685
227	Employed	575	245	925	1,620	760	625
228	Unemployed	25	40	35	105	75	60
229	Not in the labour force	265	85	290	1,010	230	240
230	Participation rate	69.5	78.4	76.8	62.9	78.5	74.1
231	Employment rate	66.1	66.2	74.0	59.2	71.0	67.6
232	Unemployment rate	4.1	13.8	3.6	6.1	8.9	8.8
233	Females 15 years and over	860	355	1,275	3,220	1,130	985
234	In the labour force	470	225	860	1,750	695	630
235	Employed	435	210	775	1,615	605	530
236	Unemployed	35	20	80	135	85	95
237	Not in the labour force	390	130	420	1,465	435	355
238	Participation rate	54.7	63.4	67.5	54.3	61.5	64.0
239	Employment rate	50.6	59.2	60.8	50.2	53.5	53.8
240	Unemployment rate	7.4	8.9	9.3	7.7	12.2	15.1

Tableau 1. Certaines caractéristiques des secteurs de recensement, recensement de 2001 – Données intégrales et données-échantillon (20 %)

Vancouver 0189.08 A	Vancouver 0189.09 A	Vancouver 0189.10 ◆ A	Vancouver 0190.01	Vancouver 0190.03	Vancouver 0190.04 A	Caractéristiques	N°
						CARACTÉRISTIQUES DE LA POPULATION	
5,545	**3,840**	**4,500**	**5,160**	**4,280**	**5,465**	**Population totale de 5 ans et plus (30)**	185
						selon le lieu de résidence 5 ans auparavant (mobilité)	
1,300	2,305	2,010	1,945	1,915	3,150	Personnes n'ayant pas déménagé	186
4,245	1,540	2,495	3,215	2,370	2,315	Personnes ayant déménagé	187
1,965	880	1,400	1,880	1,210	1,405	Non-migrants	188
2,275	655	1,090	1,335	1,155	910	Migrants	189
1,130	470	630	865	775	640	Migrants internes	190
820	450	485	690	640	560	Migrants infraprovinciaux	191
315	20	145	175	135	80	Migrants interprovinciaux	192
1,145	180	460	470	385	275	Migrants externes	193
810	**700**	**795**	**625**	**670**	**740**	**Population totale de 15 à 24 ans**	194
						selon la fréquentation scolaire	
410	280	240	295	230	340	Ne fréquentant pas l'école	195
350	340	500	285	400	320	Fréquentant l'école à plein temps	196
50	80	55	50	40	75	Fréquentant l'école à temps partiel	197
4,610	**3,275**	**3,715**	**4,605**	**3,600**	**4,605**	**Population totale de 15 ans et plus**	198
						selon le plus haut niveau de scolarité atteint	
200	210	195	230	260	310	Niveau inférieur à la 9e année (31)	199
1,115	540	825	1,280	1,020	1,165	De la 9e à la 13e année sans certificat d'études secondaires	200
635	490	525	460	485	655	De la 9e à la 13e année avec certificat d'études secondaires	201
605	545	555	575	485	750	Études postsecondaires partielles sans grade, certificat ou diplôme (32)	202
590	365	435	635	430	570	Certificat ou diplôme d'une école de métiers (33)	203
795	490	520	685	505	720	Certificat ou diplôme collégial (34)	204
160	165	110	160	65	80	Certificat universitaire inférieur au baccalauréat	205
505	465	550	575	350	355	Études universitaires avec baccalauréat ou diplôme supérieur	206
						selon les combinaisons de travail non rémunéré	
2,215	1,600	1,770	2,155	1,810	2,345	Hommes de 15 ans et plus	207
1,835	1,420	1,575	1,910	1,545	2,080	Travail non rémunéré déclaré (35)	208
120	130	130	110	110	205	Travaux ménagers et soins aux enfants et soins ou aide aux personnes âgées	209
630	405	550	470	500	610	Travaux ménagers et soins aux enfants seulement	210
110	175	70	165	75	145	Travaux ménagers et soins ou aide aux personnes âgées seulement	211
10	-	-	-	-	15	Soins aux enfants et soins ou aide aux personnes âgées seulement	212
880	700	795	1,120	820	980	Travaux ménagers seulement	213
85	10	20	15	35	110	Soins aux enfants seulement	214
-	-	-	20	-	10	Soins ou aide aux personnes âgées seulement	215
2,395	1,675	1,945	2,450	1,790	2,260	Femmes de 15 ans et plus	216
2,210	1,610	1,875	2,335	1,620	2,090	Travail non rémunéré déclaré (35)	217
200	195	210	205	220	260	Travaux ménagers et soins aux enfants et soins ou aide aux personnes âgées	218
910	515	695	665	605	725	Travaux ménagers et soins aux enfants seulement	219
165	230	105	225	110	195	Travaux ménagers et soins ou aide aux personnes âgées seulement	220
-	-	-	-	-	-	Soins aux enfants et soins ou aide aux personnes âgées seulement	221
860	675	840	1,205	650	880	Travaux ménagers seulement	222
40	-	20	15	25	25	Soins aux enfants seulement	223
30	-	10	25	-	10	Soins ou aide aux personnes âgées seulement	224
						selon l'activité	
2,210	1,600	1,765	2,160	1,805	2,345	Hommes de 15 ans et plus	225
1,595	1,235	1,340	1,440	1,395	1,730	Population active	226
1,370	1,160	1,260	1,330	1,275	1,605	Personnes occupées	227
225	70	80	110	125	130	Chômeurs	228
615	365	425	715	405	610	Inactifs	229
72.2	77.2	75.9	66.7	77.3	73.8	Taux d'activité	230
62.0	72.5	71.4	61.6	70.6	68.4	Taux d'emploi	231
14.1	5.7	6.0	7.6	9.0	7.5	Taux de chômage	232
2,400	1,675	1,945	2,450	1,790	2,260	Femmes de 15 ans et plus	233
1,440	1,050	1,290	1,345	1,070	1,350	Population active	234
1,215	965	1,165	1,210	935	1,255	Personnes occupées	235
225	80	130	135	130	95	Chômeuses	236
955	625	650	1,100	720	915	Inactives	237
60.0	62.7	66.3	54.9	59.8	59.7	Taux d'activité	238
50.6	57.6	59.9	49.4	52.2	55.5	Taux d'emploi	239
15.6	7.6	10.1	10.0	12.1	7.0	Taux de chômage	240

Table 1. Selected Characteristics for Census Tracts, 2001 Census – 100% Data and 20% Sample Data

No.	Characteristics	Vancouver 0188.05 A	Vancouver 0188.06 A	Vancouver 0189.03	Vancouver 0189.05 A	Vancouver 0189.06 A	Vancouver 0189.07 A
	POPULATION CHARACTERISTICS						
	by labour force activity – concluded						
241	Both sexes - Participation rate	62.2	71.7	71.9	58.5	69.7	68.8
242	15-24 years	42.0	54.2	59.0	66.7	63.0	62.9
243	25 years and over	67.5	74.4	74.1	57.0	71.2	70.2
244	Both sexes - Employment rate	58.7	63.4	67.0	54.2	62.0	60.6
245	15-24 years	38.8	48.0	55.1	59.4	54.3	48.4
246	25 years and over	64.5	66.7	69.5	53.5	63.8	62.8
247	Both sexes - Unemployment rate	5.2	11.7	6.3	6.9	10.8	12.2
248	15-24 years	11.8	15.4	10.9	11.8	15.4	23.1
249	25 years and over	3.9	12.1	6.0	6.2	9.8	9.8
250	**Total labour force 15 years and over**	**1,065**	**515**	**1,820**	**3,475**	**1,530**	**1,315**
	by industry based on the 1997 NAICS						
251	Industry - Not applicable (36)	-	25	25	75	65	50
252	All industries (37)	1,070	495	1,790	3,400	1,470	1,260
253	11 Agriculture, forestry, fishing and hunting	15	-	15	40	45	30
254	21 Mining and oil and gas extraction	-	10	-	30	-	-
255	22 Utilities	10	-	20	-	10	-
256	23 Construction	55	125	80	155	105	90
257	31-33 Manufacturing	80	70	255	345	215	170
258	41 Wholesale trade	85	25	95	210	110	70
259	44-45 Retail trade	105	60	230	550	185	170
260	48-49 Transportation and warehousing	75	10	155	190	135	60
261	51 Information and cultural industries	40	10	55	95	55	65
262	52 Finance and insurance	60	10	55	150	75	90
263	53 Real estate and rental and leasing	50	-	35	30	25	25
264	54 Professional, scientific and technical services	85	-	115	210	45	45
265	55 Management of companies and enterprises	-	-	10	-	-	-
266	56 Administrative and support, waste management and remediation services	50	15	40	300	75	20
267	61 Educational services	40	50	130	120	55	75
268	62 Health care and social assistance	95	35	130	410	95	105
269	71 Arts, entertainment and recreation	15	15	45	30	15	40
270	72 Accommodation and food services	45	10	120	220	95	100
271	81 Other services (except public administration)	90	30	125	120	80	65
272	91 Public administration	75	-	80	180	55	40
	by class of worker						
273	Class of worker - Not applicable (36)	-	20	25	75	60	50
274	All classes of worker (37)	1,065	490	1,795	3,395	1,470	1,265
275	Paid workers	955	400	1,685	3,210	1,380	1,200
276	Employees	815	360	1,640	3,070	1,345	1,170
277	Self-employed (incorporated)	145	45	40	145	30	30
278	Self-employed (unincorporated)	95	90	100	175	85	65
279	Unpaid family workers	15	-	10	-	-	-
	by occupation based on the 2001 NOC-S						
280	Male labour force 15 years and over	600	290	960	1,720	835	685
281	Occupation - Not applicable (36)	-	15	-	30	15	25
282	All occupations (37)	600	280	955	1,690	825	660
283	A Management occupations	160	60	60	220	70	80
284	B Business, finance and administration occupations	25	15	95	150	75	35
285	C Natural and applied sciences and related occupations	55	30	60	270	20	75
286	D Health occupations	10	10	10	55	10	20
287	E Occupations in social science, education, government service and religion	10	10	40	45	30	20
288	F Occupations in art, culture, recreation and sport	-	10	35	30	20	30
289	G Sales and service occupations	145	10	185	410	190	170
290	H Trades, transport and equipment operators and related occupations	125	100	330	400	310	175
291	I Occupations unique to primary industry	50	20	-	15	40	10
292	J Occupations unique to processing, manufacturing and utilities	15	15	130	95	65	55
293	Female labour force 15 years and over	470	230	860	1,750	695	630
294	Occupation - Not applicable (36)	-	10	20	45	45	30
295	All occupations (37)	465	215	835	1,705	645	600
296	A Management occupations	65	40	35	125	55	60
297	B Business, finance and administration occupations	165	35	350	565	225	220
298	C Natural and applied sciences and related occupations	15	-	45	45	25	25
299	D Health occupations	40	10	65	215	45	65

Tableau 1. Certaines caractéristiques des secteurs de recensement, recensement de 2001 – Données intégrales et données-échantillon (20 %)

Vancouver 0189.08 A	Vancouver 0189.09 A	Vancouver 0189.10 ◆ A	Vancouver 0190.01	Vancouver 0190.03	Vancouver 0190.04 A	Caractéristiques	N°
						CARACTÉRISTIQUES DE LA POPULATION	
						selon l'activité – fin	
65.9	69.7	70.9	60.5	68.6	66.9	Les deux sexes - Taux d'activité	241
50.6	64.3	57.6	53.6	53.4	67.1	15-24 ans	242
69.2	71.4	74.5	61.6	72.0	66.8	25 ans et plus	243
56.1	65.0	65.4	55.2	61.6	62.0	Les deux sexes - Taux d'emploi	244
43.2	59.3	48.1	46.4	44.4	58.4	15-24 ans	245
58.9	66.7	70.0	56.4	65.4	62.7	25 ans et plus	246
14.8	6.8	8.0	9.0	10.1	7.3	Les deux sexes - Taux de chômage	247
14.6	8.9	16.5	11.9	16.7	14.0	15-24 ans	248
14.9	6.5	6.2	8.4	9.3	6.0	25 ans et plus	249
3,035	**2,280**	**2,635**	**2,780**	**2,465**	**3,085**	**Population active totale de 15 ans et plus**	250
						selon l'industrie basée sur le SCIAN de 1997	
160	65	80	85	125	60	Industrie - Sans objet (36)	251
2,875	2,220	2,550	2,705	2,340	3,015	Toutes les industries (37)	252
25	70	25	10	45	30	11 Agriculture, foresterie, pêche et chasse	253
-	-	-	-	-	-	21 Extraction minière et extraction de pétrole et de gaz	254
10	15	-	15	-	15	22 Services publics	255
225	105	130	125	185	270	23 Construction	256
410	275	300	355	380	405	31-33 Fabrication	257
180	85	135	210	85	185	41 Commerce de gros	258
340	235	360	355	270	355	44-45 Commerce de détail	259
145	150	110	230	140	280	48-49 Transport et entreposage	260
95	60	65	50	35	105	51 Industrie de l'information et industrie culturelle	261
105	155	115	80	95	50	52 Finance et assurances	262
85	35	20	60	25	30	53 Services immobiliers et services de location et de location à bail	263
200	95	165	150	125	200	54 Services professionnels, scientifiques et techniques	264
-	-	-	-	-	-	55 Gestion de sociétés et d'entreprises	265
185	90	145	135	190	195	56 Services administratifs, services de soutien, services de gestion des déchets et services d'assainissement	266
75	185	125	145	100	95	61 Services d'enseignement	267
220	260	280	345	195	315	62 Soins de santé et assistance sociale	268
45	10	35	30	45	55	71 Arts, spectacles et loisirs	269
250	140	270	175	180	135	72 Hébergement et services de restauration	270
170	120	165	115	160	190	81 Autres services, sauf les administrations publiques	271
100	135	100	135	85	105	91 Administrations publiques	272
						selon la catégorie de travailleurs	
160	60	80	80	125	65	Catégorie de travailleurs - Sans objet (36)	273
2,875	2,220	2,555	2,700	2,340	3,020	Toutes les catégories de travailleurs (37)	274
2,665	2,010	2,365	2,505	2,160	2,775	Travailleurs rémunérés	275
2,605	1,980	2,315	2,480	2,100	2,700	Employés	276
60	35	55	25	60	70	Travailleurs autonomes (entreprise constituée en société)	277
210	195	180	195	180	235	Travailleurs autonomes (entreprise non constituée en société)	278
-	10	10	-	-	10	Travailleurs familiaux non rémunérés	279
						selon la profession basée sur la CNP-S de 2001	
1,600	1,235	1,340	1,435	1,395	1,735	Hommes actifs de 15 ans et plus	280
60	25	25	20	70	20	Profession - Sans objet (36)	281
1,535	1,210	1,320	1,415	1,330	1,710	Toutes les professions (37)	282
100	125	155	140	90	80	A Gestion	283
90	95	115	165	130	170	B Affaires, finance et administration	284
140	105	160	90	60	135	C Sciences naturelles et appliquées et professions apparentées	285
10	25	-	10	25	40	D Secteur de la santé	286
30	70	35	40	55	25	E Sciences sociales, enseignement, administration publique et religion	287
15	15	30	20	25	40	F Arts, culture, sports et loisirs	288
350	270	345	325	270	300	G Ventes et services	289
510	340	340	510	445	670	H Métiers, transport et machinerie	290
65	50	40	-	45	40	I Professions propres au secteur primaire	291
225	125	105	115	190	210	J Transformation, fabrication et services d'utilité publique	292
1,440	1,050	1,295	1,345	1,070	1,350	Femmes actives de 15 ans et plus	293
105	40	55	60	55	40	Profession - Sans objet (36)	294
1,340	1,005	1,235	1,285	1,010	1,310	Toutes les professions (37)	295
85	35	85	65	80	75	A Gestion	296
465	260	365	455	290	410	B Affaires, finance et administration	297
30	10	35	15	10	25	C Sciences naturelles et appliquées et professions apparentées	298
95	135	95	145	70	120	D Secteur de la santé	299

Table 1. Selected Characteristics for Census Tracts, 2001 Census – 100% Data and 20% Sample Data

No.	Characteristics	Vancouver 0188.05 A	Vancouver 0188.06 A	Vancouver 0189.03	Vancouver 0189.05 A	Vancouver 0189.06 A	Vancouver 0189.07 A
	POPULATION CHARACTERISTICS						
	by occupation based on the 2001 NOC-S – concluded						
300	E Occupations in social science, education, government service and religion	15	15	30	75	25	40
301	F Occupations in art, culture, recreation and sport	10	15	20	30	-	-
302	G Sales and service occupations	135	85	245	535	225	150
303	H Trades, transport and equipment operators and related occupations	-	10	25	15	15	20
304	I Occupations unique to primary industry	-	-	10	10	15	15
305	J Occupations unique to processing, manufacturing and utilities	15	15	15	90	20	-
306	**Total employed labour force 15 years and over**	**1,010**	**460**	**1,700**	**3,230**	**1,365**	**1,160**
	by place of work						
307	Males	575	245	925	1,620	765	625
308	Usual place of work	365	150	735	1,240	530	515
309	At home	80	15	25	80	40	20
310	Outside Canada	10	-	10	25	-	-
311	No fixed workplace address	125	85	160	265	190	90
312	Females	435	215	775	1,610	605	535
313	Usual place of work	325	130	715	1,445	555	470
314	At home	65	45	25	105	10	40
315	Outside Canada	-	-	-	-	-	-
316	No fixed workplace address	40	40	35	65	40	25
317	**Total employed labour force 15 years and over with usual place of work or no fixed workplace address**	**850**	**405**	**1,640**	**3,015**	**1,320**	**1,095**
	by mode of transportation						
318	Males	490	235	890	1,510	720	605
319	Car, truck, van, as driver	430	190	715	1,220	590	435
320	Car, truck, van, as passenger	30	30	50	55	45	65
321	Public transit	20	15	65	140	75	60
322	Walked	10	10	25	55	10	25
323	Other method	-	-	35	35	10	20
324	Females	365	170	750	1,510	595	490
325	Car, truck, van, as driver	275	125	495	980	380	340
326	Car, truck, van, as passenger	20	40	110	140	95	55
327	Public transit	50	10	105	310	80	55
328	Walked	15	-	35	60	40	25
329	Other method	-	-	10	15	-	10
330	**Total population 15 years and over who worked since January 1, 2000**	**1,195**	**555**	**1,970**	**3,705**	**1,610**	**1,355**
	by language used at work						
331	Single responses	1,065	540	1,910	3,330	1,440	1,275
332	English	1,025	540	1,905	3,275	1,380	1,230
333	French	10	-	-	-	-	-
334	Non-official languages (5)	35	-	10	55	60	40
335	Chinese, n.o.s.	15	-	-	-	10	25
336	Cantonese	-	-	10	10	10	-
337	Other languages (6)	15	-	-	40	40	10
338	Multiple responses	125	10	50	375	165	90
339	English and French	-	-	-	25	25	-
340	English and non-official language	120	-	50	335	145	85
341	French and non-official language	-	-	-	-	-	-
342	English, French and non-official language	10	-	-	15	-	-
	DWELLING AND HOUSEHOLD CHARACTERISTICS						
343	**Total number of occupied private dwellings**	**625**	**295**	**1,090**	**3,170**	**935**	**910**
	by tenure						
344	Owned	555	230	885	1,905	625	630
345	Rented	75	65	205	1,265	305	275
346	Band housing	-	-	-	-	-	-
	by structural type of dwelling						
347	Single-detached house	595	295	740	470	530	130
348	Semi-detached house	20	-	-	-	80	-
349	Row house	-	-	85	440	115	380
350	Apartment, detached duplex	-	-	160	170	50	35
351	Apartment, building that has five or more storeys	-	-	-	670	-	-
352	Apartment, building that has fewer than five storeys (38)	-	-	100	1,415	160	355
353	Other single-attached house	-	-	-	-	-	-
354	Movable dwelling (39)	-	-	-	-	10	-

Tableau 1. Certaines caractéristiques des secteurs de recensement, recensement de 2001 – Données intégrales et données-échantillon (20 %)

Vancouver 0189.08 A	Vancouver 0189.09 A	Vancouver 0189.10 ◆ A	Vancouver 0190.01	Vancouver 0190.03	Vancouver 0190.04 A	Caractéristiques	N°
						CARACTÉRISTIQUES DE LA POPULATION	
						selon la profession basée sur la CNP-S de 2001 – fin	
55	140	90	90	65	110	E Sciences sociales, enseignement, administration publique et religion	300
30	20	30	35	25	50	F Arts, culture, sports et loisirs	301
475	305	460	405	360	405	G Ventes et services	302
35	25	15	30	35	55	H Métiers, transport et machinerie	303
-	45	-	-	25	20	I Professions propres au secteur primaire	304
70	35	50	40	50	35	J Transformation, fabrication et services d'utilité publique	305
2,585	**2,130**	**2,425**	**2,540**	**2,215**	**2,860**	**Population active occupée totale de 15 ans et plus selon le lieu de travail**	306
1,370	1,160	1,260	1,325	1,275	1,605	Hommes	307
1,005	935	1,030	1,030	895	1,120	Lieu habituel de travail	308
70	55	50	55	35	75	À domicile	309
10	25	25	-	10	35	En dehors du Canada	310
290	150	160	240	345	375	Sans adresse de travail fixe	311
1,215	965	1,165	1,210	940	1,255	Femmes	312
1,095	830	1,045	1,100	790	1,045	Lieu habituel de travail	313
55	65	35	30	75	70	À domicile	314
10	-	15	10	-	10	En dehors du Canada	315
60	70	70	75	70	125	Sans adresse de travail fixe	316
2,450	**1,985**	**2,305**	**2,445**	**2,100**	**2,670**	**Population active occupée totale de 15 ans et plus ayant un lieu habituel de travail ou sans adresse de travail fixe selon le mode de transport**	317
1,300	1,085	1,185	1,270	1,235	1,495	Hommes	318
1,000	940	935	935	970	1,160	Automobile, camion ou fourgonnette, en tant que conducteur	319
90	35	60	115	100	115	Automobile, camion ou fourgonnette, en tant que passager	320
130	85	105	195	125	150	Transport en commun	321
50	10	55	-	20	35	À pied	322
25	15	25	20	25	30	Autre moyen	323
1,155	900	1,120	1,175	860	1,170	Femmes	324
600	705	760	620	545	825	Automobile, camion ou fourgonnette, en tant que conductrice	325
100	80	120	110	125	65	Automobile, camion ou fourgonnette, en tant que passagère	326
310	75	165	305	135	245	Transport en commun	327
135	20	50	120	45	35	À pied	328
10	10	20	20	10	-	Autre moyen	329
3,090	**2,435**	**2,725**	**2,975**	**2,555**	**3,250**	**Population totale de 15 ans et plus ayant travaillé depuis le 1er janvier 2000 selon la langue utilisée au travail**	330
2,750	2,205	2,510	2,750	2,325	3,040	Réponses uniques	331
2,685	2,170	2,390	2,715	2,260	2,995	Anglais	332
-	15	-	-	-	-	Français	333
70	25	120	40	70	45	Langues non officielles (5)	334
15	-	35	-	-	20	Chinois, n.d.a.	335
-	10	15	-	25	-	Cantonais	336
55	15	70	35	40	15	Autres langues (6)	337
340	230	215	220	230	210	Réponses multiples	338
45	20	25	20	10	25	Anglais et français	339
270	205	195	200	200	170	Anglais et langue non officielle	340
-	-	-	-	-	-	Français et langue non officielle	341
15	-	-	-	20	10	Anglais, français et langue non officielle	342
						CARACTÉRISTIQUES DES LOGEMENTS ET DES MÉNAGES	
2,565	**1,210**	**1,625**	**2,535**	**1,675**	**1,935**	**Nombre total de logements privés occupés selon le mode d'occupation**	343
630	960	1,085	1,090	850	1,510	Possédé	344
1,935	245	535	1,445	820	425	Loué	345
-	-	-	-	-	-	Logement de bande	346
						selon le type de construction résidentielle	
15	1,035	435	425	710	1,665	Maison individuelle non attenante	347
-	10	40	45	55	100	Maison jumelée	348
235	15	595	395	75	-	Maison en rangée	349
225	65	40	150	95	140	Appartement, duplex non attenant	350
-	-	40	380	-	-	Appartement, immeuble de cinq étages ou plus	351
2,085	85	415	1,125	740	25	Appartement, immeuble de moins de cinq étages (38)	352
-	-	55	-	-	-	Autre maison individuelle attenante	353
-	-	-	15	-	-	Logement mobile (39)	354

Table 1. Selected Characteristics for Census Tracts, 2001 Census – 100% Data and 20% Sample Data

No.	Characteristics	Vancouver 0188.05 A	Vancouver 0188.06 A	Vancouver 0189.03	Vancouver 0189.05 A	Vancouver 0189.06 A	Vancouver 0189.07 A
	DWELLING AND HOUSEHOLD CHARACTERISTICS						
	by condition of dwelling						
355	Regular maintenance only	515	195	670	2,475	520	560
356	Minor repairs	80	85	370	445	285	220
357	Major repairs	25	10	50	250	125	120
	by period of construction						
358	Before 1946	10	-	-	20	20	10
359	1946-1960	35	30	260	60	80	25
360	1961-1970	10	35	495	260	110	90
361	1971-1980	80	80	165	460	300	280
362	1981-1990	105	40	55	1,150	200	210
363	1991-2001 (20)	395	105	115	1,215	210	290
364	Average number of rooms per dwelling	9.2	8.6	6.9	4.9	6.4	5.8
365	Average number of bedrooms per dwelling	3.8	3.3	3.2	2.0	2.8	2.4
366	Average value of dwelling $	366,056	388,804	182,382	159,532	174,722	146,343
367	**Total number of private households**	**630**	**295**	**1,095**	**3,170**	**930**	**910**
	by household size						
368	1 person	35	35	155	1,155	150	225
369	2 persons	160	90	325	1,095	260	325
370	3 persons	95	60	255	375	160	125
371	4-5 persons	280	90	305	480	270	190
372	6 or more persons	60	20	55	65	90	50
	by household type						
373	One-family households	545	240	850	1,805	680	630
374	Multiple-family households	35	15	45	60	60	20
375	Non-family households	50	45	200	1,310	195	260
376	Number of persons in private households	2,255	935	3,240	6,980	2,910	2,355
377	Average number of persons in private households	3.6	3.2	3.0	2.2	3.1	2.6
378	Average number of persons per room	0.4	0.4	0.4	0.4	0.5	0.4
379	Tenant households in non-farm, non-reserve private dwellings (40)	75	65	205	1,260	305	270
380	Average gross rent $ (40)	915	1,004	873	705	878	843
381	Tenant households spending 30% or more of household income on gross rent (40) (41)	30	20	90	695	140	85
382	Tenant households spending from 30% to 99% of household income on gross rent (40) (41)	25	20	80	595	110	65
383	Owner households in non-farm, non-reserve private dwellings (42)	550	220	885	1,905	630	635
384	Average owner's major payments $ (42)	1,281	1,291	1,074	905	1,122	964
385	Owner households spending 30% or more of household income on owner's major payments (41) (42)	135	50	200	560	205	150
386	Owner households spending from 30% to 99% of household income on owner's major payments (41) (42)	120	45	195	495	175	130
	CENSUS FAMILY CHARACTERISTICS						
387	**Total number of census families in private households**	**615**	**265**	**950**	**1,920**	**795**	**665**
	by census family structure and size						
388	Total couple families	580	235	770	1,620	655	515
389	Total families of married couples	540	210	650	1,435	545	455
390	Without children at home	135	75	200	770	200	235
391	With children at home	405	135	450	665	345	220
392	1 child	85	30	185	250	90	60
393	2 children	215	50	170	285	145	100
394	3 or more children	105	50	95	135	100	60
395	Total families of common-law couples	40	25	120	185	115	60
396	Without children at home	35	25	90	145	60	30
397	With children at home	-	-	35	40	55	35
398	1 child	10	-	25	20	20	10
399	2 children	-	-	-	10	10	20
400	3 or more children	-	-	10	10	25	-
401	Total lone-parent families	30	30	180	305	140	150
402	Female parent	15	25	140	255	130	130
403	1 child	10	20	95	145	70	85
404	2 children	10	-	25	70	30	35
405	3 or more children	-	-	15	40	25	10

Tableau 1. Certaines caractéristiques des secteurs de recensement, recensement de 2001 – Données intégrales et données-échantillon (20 %)

Vancouver 0189.08 A	Vancouver 0189.09 A	Vancouver 0189.10 ◆ A	Vancouver 0190.01	Vancouver 0190.03	Vancouver 0190.04 A	Caractéristiques	Nº
						CARACTÉRISTIQUES DES LOGEMENTS ET DES MÉNAGES	
						selon l'état du logement	
1,855	870	1,125	1,800	1,080	1,135	Entretien régulier seulement	355
505	275	345	495	445	570	Réparations mineures	356
205	60	150	240	145	225	Réparations majeures	357
						selon la période de construction	
35	-	-	45	60	100	Avant 1946	358
95	15	40	195	300	545	1946-1960	359
515	10	75	295	395	540	1961-1970	360
945	60	230	370	420	395	1971-1980	361
740	650	705	735	230	195	1981-1990	362
230	470	565	900	265	155	1991-2001 (20)	363
4.1	7.9	5.7	4.8	5.6	7.3	Nombre moyen de pièces par logement	364
1.6	3.5	2.6	1.9	2.5	3.3	Nombre moyen de chambres à coucher par logement	365
90,648	237,157	171,962	144,651	170,752	213,778	Valeur moyenne du logement $	366
2,560	**1,205**	**1,620**	**2,535**	**1,670**	**1,930**	**Nombre total de logements privés**	367
						selon la taille du ménage	
720	145	240	900	395	295	1 personne	368
865	280	450	910	475	575	2 personnes	369
475	230	350	345	295	385	3 personnes	370
445	435	500	320	410	525	4-5 personnes	371
50	125	80	60	95	150	6 personnes ou plus	372
						selon le genre de ménage	
1,610	950	1,270	1,455	1,090	1,445	Ménages unifamiliaux	373
45	80	55	45	50	95	Ménages multifamiliaux	374
905	175	295	1,035	535	400	Ménages non familiaux	375
6,120	4,045	4,835	5,500	4,650	5,875	Nombre de personnes dans les ménages privés	376
2.4	3.3	3.0	2.2	2.8	3.0	Nombre moyen de personnes dans les ménages privés	377
0.6	0.4	0.5	0.5	0.5	0.4	Nombre moyen de personnes par pièce	378
1,900	230	535	1,435	815	425	Ménages locataires dans les logements privés non agricoles hors réserve (40)	379
700	820	804	863	816	872	Loyer brut moyen $ (40)	380
1,005	90	250	735	400	160	Ménages locataires consacrant 30 % ou plus du revenu du ménage au loyer brut (40) (41)	381
710	60	185	515	290	110	Ménages locataires consacrant de 30 % à 99 % du revenu du ménage au loyer brut (40) (41)	382
620	965	1,085	1,090	850	1,505	Ménages propriétaires dans les logements privés non agricoles hors réserve (42)	383
904	1,296	1,104	773	1,045	1,106	Principales dépenses de propriété moyennes $ (42)	384
130	250	285	275	295	490	Ménages propriétaires consacrant 30 % ou plus du revenu du ménage aux principales dépenses de propriété (41) (42)	385
100	200	240	235	250	445	Ménages propriétaires consacrant de 30 % à 99 % du revenu du ménage aux principales dépenses de propriété (41) (42)	386
						CARACTÉRISTIQUES DES FAMILLES DE RECENSEMENT	
1,700	**1,125**	**1,380**	**1,540**	**1,190**	**1,640**	**Total des familles de recensement dans les ménages privés**	387
						selon la structure et la taille de la famille de recensement	
1,080	940	1,090	1,165	905	1,385	Total des familles avec conjoints	388
860	895	985	955	740	1,210	Total des familles avec couples mariés	389
320	260	275	505	240	465	Sans enfants à la maison	390
545	640	705	445	505	740	Avec enfants à la maison	391
225	200	240	220	160	255	1 enfant	392
230	330	325	165	240	315	2 enfants	393
90	105	145	60	105	175	3 enfants ou plus	394
215	50	110	215	165	175	Total des familles en union libre	395
120	30	60	130	95	85	Sans enfants à la maison	396
95	15	45	80	70	95	Avec enfants à la maison	397
65	-	20	60	25	60	1 enfant	398
25	10	10	20	25	20	2 enfants	399
10	10	15	-	20	20	3 enfants ou plus	400
625	185	290	370	285	255	Total des familles monoparentales	401
505	160	260	320	225	200	Parent de sexe féminin	402
295	75	135	245	120	125	1 enfant	403
145	60	70	50	50	60	2 enfants	404
65	25	50	20	50	15	3 enfants ou plus	405

Table 1. Selected Characteristics for Census Tracts, 2001 Census – 100% Data and 20% Sample Data

No.	Characteristics	Vancouver 0188.05 A	Vancouver 0188.06 A	Vancouver 0189.03	Vancouver 0189.05 A	Vancouver 0189.06 A	Vancouver 0189.07 A
	CENSUS FAMILY CHARACTERISTICS						
	by census family structure and size – concluded						
406	Male parent	10	-	35	45	10	20
407	1 child	-	-	30	35	10	-
408	2 children	-	-	10	10	-	10
409	3 or more children	-	-	-	-	10	10
410	**Total number of children at home**	**930**	**335**	**1,110**	**1,805**	**1,070**	**760**
	by age groups						
411	Under 6 years	150	80	285	490	285	200
412	6-14 years	360	135	420	540	425	245
413	15-17 years	155	55	120	210	100	120
414	18-24 years	210	40	190	360	205	135
415	25 years and over	55	20	105	200	55	60
416	Average number of children at home per census family (43)	1.5	1.3	1.2	0.9	1.3	1.1
417	**Total number of persons in private households**	**2,255**	**940**	**3,235**	**6,980**	**2,910**	**2,350**
	by census family status and living arrangements						
418	Number of non-family persons	130	100	405	1,635	385	415
419	Living with relatives (44)	40	40	80	210	80	80
420	Living with non-relatives only	55	30	165	275	155	110
421	Living alone	35	35	155	1,150	150	225
422	Number of family persons	2,125	840	2,835	5,345	2,525	1,940
423	Average number of persons per census family	3.5	3.2	3.0	2.8	3.2	2.9
424	**Total number of persons 65 years and over**	**125**	**65**	**255**	**1,360**	**225**	**255**
425	Number of non-family persons 65 years and over	30	25	75	640	105	120
426	Living with relatives (44)	10	15	25	55	45	40
427	Living with non-relatives only	-	-	-	15	-	10
428	Living alone	10	-	40	565	55	75
429	Number of family persons 65 years and over	100	40	180	720	120	135
	ECONOMIC FAMILY CHARACTERISTICS						
430	**Total number of economic families in private households**	**595**	**255**	**895**	**1,915**	**735**	**660**
	by size of family						
431	2 persons	165	95	330	1,030	250	335
432	3 persons	100	50	225	340	145	110
433	4 persons	190	45	195	350	175	125
434	5 or more persons	140	70	145	195	170	95
435	Total number of persons in economic families	2,165	880	2,920	5,555	2,610	2,025
436	Average number of persons per economic family	3.7	3.5	3.3	2.9	3.5	3.0
437	Total number of unattached individuals	85	60	320	1,425	305	330
	2000 INCOME CHARACTERISTICS						
	Population 15 years and over by sex and total income groups in 2000						
438	Total - Both sexes	1,725	730	2,530	5,950	2,200	1,905
439	Without income	215	55	115	320	120	105
440	With income	1,510	670	2,415	5,625	2,075	1,800
441	Under $1,000 (45)	115	10	125	230	90	70
442	$ 1,000 - $ 2,999	75	40	80	255	155	75
443	$ 3,000 - $ 4,999	40	20	75	165	65	35
444	$ 5,000 - $ 6,999	75	-	110	280	70	140
445	$ 7,000 - $ 9,999	125	55	135	370	70	110
446	$10,000 - $11,999	65	60	120	280	95	60
447	$12,000 - $14,999	40	45	140	520	175	75
448	$15,000 - $19,999	105	45	155	630	200	175
449	$20,000 - $24,999	115	55	190	485	140	175
450	$25,000 - $29,999	85	55	230	370	225	115
451	$30,000 - $34,999	50	55	195	505	200	150
452	$35,000 - $39,999	105	25	140	315	185	130
453	$40,000 - $44,999	125	30	195	395	105	115
454	$45,000 - $49,999	85	25	100	220	85	110
455	$50,000 - $59,999	115	25	225	220	100	150
456	$60,000 and over	200	125	205	380	115	120
457	Average income $ (46)	32,832	43,850	28,685	25,313	25,850	28,157
458	Median income $ (46)	25,300	26,098	26,024	20,507	24,348	24,620
459	Standard error of average income $ (46)	1,788	5,981	897	554	950	1,023

Tableau 1. Certaines caractéristiques des secteurs de recensement, recensement de 2001 – Données intégrales et données-échantillon (20 %)

Vancouver 0189.08 A	Vancouver 0189.09 A	Vancouver 0189.10 ◆ A	Vancouver 0190.01	Vancouver 0190.03	Vancouver 0190.04 A	Caractéristiques	N°
						CARACTÉRISTIQUES DES FAMILLES DE RECENSEMENT	
						selon la structure et la taille de la famille de recensement – fin	
115	25	30	55	60	55	Parent de sexe masculin	406
115	-	15	40	30	30	1 enfant	407
-	25	15	10	30	25	2 enfants	408
10	-	-	10	-	-	3 enfants ou plus	409
2,045	**1,610**	**1,945**	**1,350**	**1,615**	**2,015**	**Nombre total d'enfants à la maison**	410
						selon les groupes d'âge	
655	225	400	425	440	510	Moins de 6 ans	411
855	535	720	460	595	725	6-14 ans	412
215	175	255	140	200	230	15-17 ans	413
220	435	430	155	280	350	18-24 ans	414
105	240	135	175	90	205	25 ans et plus	415
1.2	1.4	1.4	0.9	1.4	1.2	Nombre moyen d'enfants à la maison par famille de recensement (43)	416
6,120	**4,045**	**4,835**	**5,505**	**4,650**	**5,875**	**Nombre total de personnes dans les ménages privés**	417
						selon la situation des particuliers dans la famille de recensement et des particuliers dans le ménage	
1,295	365	430	1,450	940	830	Nombre de personnes hors famille de recensement	418
185	120	110	185	190	235	Vivant avec des personnes apparentées (44)	419
390	100	75	365	350	300	Vivant avec des personnes non apparentées uniquement	420
720	145	240	900	395	295	Vivant seules	421
4,820	3,680	4,410	4,055	3,710	5,045	Nombre de personnes membres d'une famille	422
2.8	3.3	3.2	2.6	3.1	3.1	Nombre moyen de personnes par famille de recensement	423
300	**325**	**265**	**815**	**305**	**615**	**Nombre total de personnes de 65 ans et plus**	424
135	125	80	390	175	190	Nombre de personnes hors famille de recensement de 65 ans et plus	425
30	90	30	45	70	75	Vivant avec des personnes apparentées (44)	426
-	-	-	20	25	20	Vivant avec des personnes non apparentées uniquement	427
105	35	50	330	75	100	Vivant seules	428
165	200	185	420	135	420	Nombre de personnes membres d'une famille de 65 ans et plus	429
						CARACTÉRISTIQUES DES FAMILLES ÉCONOMIQUES	
1,690	**1,045**	**1,355**	**1,540**	**1,170**	**1,580**	**Nombre total de familles économiques dans les ménages privés**	430
						selon la taille de la famille	
760	275	445	860	405	570	2 personnes	431
465	225	340	325	290	400	3 personnes	432
315	320	350	235	270	320	4 personnes	433
160	225	225	110	200	290	5 personnes ou plus	434
5,010	3,805	4,520	4,245	3,900	5,280	Nombre total de personnes dans les familles économiques	435
3.0	3.7	3.3	2.8	3.3	3.3	Nombre moyen de personnes par famille économique	436
1,115	240	315	1,265	750	595	Nombre total de personnes hors famille économique	437
						CARACTÉRISTIQUES DU REVENU DE 2000	
						Population de 15 ans et plus selon le sexe et les tranches de revenu total en 2000	
4,605	3,275	3,715	4,605	3,600	4,605	Total - Les deux sexes	438
330	250	290	320	260	240	Sans revenu	439
4,275	3,025	3,420	4,285	3,335	4,365	Avec un revenu	440
290	160	180	320	200	265	Moins de 1 000 $ (45)	441
290	185	155	110	255	230	1 000 $ - 2 999 $	442
150	110	145	150	170	145	3 000 $ - 4 999 $	443
240	135	160	155	240	170	5 000 $ - 6 999 $	444
365	225	230	265	185	290	7 000 $ - 9 999 $	445
190	180	190	205	95	120	10 000 $ - 11 999 $	446
355	230	240	350	275	375	12 000 $ - 14 999 $	447
520	240	310	460	375	510	15 000 $ - 19 999 $	448
365	240	235	435	270	285	20 000 $ - 24 999 $	449
275	150	220	390	235	355	25 000 $ - 29 999 $	450
350	130	255	365	210	435	30 000 $ - 34 999 $	451
225	190	235	305	210	215	35 000 $ - 39 999 $	452
275	155	230	220	165	265	40 000 $ - 44 999 $	453
125	165	170	125	120	130	45 000 $ - 49 999 $	454
165	170	235	200	155	290	50 000 $ - 59 999 $	455
95	345	230	220	185	275	60 000 $ et plus	456
20,846	27,485	26,833	24,473	22,838	25,649	Revenu moyen $ (46)	457
17,463	20,269	21,612	21,035	18,041	21,371	Revenu médian $ (46)	458
537	932	809	657	715	672	Erreur type de revenu moyen $ (46)	459

Table 1. Selected Characteristics for Census Tracts, 2001 Census – 100% Data and 20% Sample Data

No.	Characteristics	Vancouver 0188.05 A	Vancouver 0188.06 A	Vancouver 0189.03	Vancouver 0189.05 A	Vancouver 0189.06 A	Vancouver 0189.07 A
	2000 INCOME CHARACTERISTICS						
	Population 15 years and over by sex and total income groups in 2000 – concluded						
460	Total - Males	870	370	1,250	2,730	1,065	920
461	Without income	100	20	30	130	45	40
462	With income	770	355	1,220	2,605	1,020	880
463	Under $1,000 (45)	50	-	35	105	40	40
464	$ 1,000 - $ 2,999	20	10	25	105	40	10
465	$ 3,000 - $ 4,999	15	15	25	60	15	10
466	$ 5,000 - $ 6,999	30	-	20	85	30	50
467	$ 7,000 - $ 9,999	50	20	50	140	25	50
468	$10,000 - $11,999	35	25	75	120	50	25
469	$12,000 - $14,999	20	-	65	150	55	30
470	$15,000 - $19,999	30	25	70	205	105	50
471	$20,000 - $24,999	50	25	95	265	60	60
472	$25,000 - $29,999	50	35	125	195	115	90
473	$30,000 - $34,999	-	20	45	250	90	105
474	$35,000 - $39,999	40	10	95	140	110	60
475	$40,000 - $44,999	65	20	115	225	70	65
476	$45,000 - $49,999	65	30	50	140	50	70
477	$50,000 - $59,999	75	20	190	140	90	115
478	$60,000 and over	165	105	150	290	85	70
479	Average income $ (46)	42,062	61,432	34,441	30,195	31,463	31,882
480	Median income $ (46)	37,800	35,196	31,822	26,096	28,478	31,278
481	Standard error of average income $ (46)	3,022	10,697	1,380	913	1,542	1,420
482	Total - Females	855	355	1,275	3,215	1,130	985
483	Without income	115	40	85	200	70	65
484	With income	745	320	1,190	3,020	1,055	920
485	Under $1,000 (45)	65	10	90	130	55	30
486	$ 1,000 - $ 2,999	55	25	60	150	120	60
487	$ 3,000 - $ 4,999	30	-	55	110	55	25
488	$ 5,000 - $ 6,999	40	-	85	190	35	90
489	$ 7,000 - $ 9,999	70	35	90	235	45	60
490	$10,000 - $11,999	35	35	50	160	45	35
491	$12,000 - $14,999	25	40	75	370	120	50
492	$15,000 - $19,999	70	20	85	425	100	130
493	$20,000 - $24,999	65	30	95	220	80	120
494	$25,000 - $29,999	35	15	100	180	110	30
495	$30,000 - $34,999	45	45	145	255	105	45
496	$35,000 - $39,999	70	15	45	175	80	75
497	$40,000 - $44,999	60	10	80	170	40	50
498	$45,000 - $49,999	20	-	45	75	35	40
499	$50,000 - $59,999	35	10	35	80	10	40
500	$60,000 and over	30	20	55	85	30	55
501	Average income $ (46)	23,321	24,319	22,796	21,098	20,411	24,589
502	Median income $ (46)	18,087	17,991	20,849	16,707	16,056	19,303
503	Standard error of average income $ (46)	1,562	2,864	1,049	624	1,027	1,431
	by composition of total income						
504	Total - Composition of income in 2000 % (47)	100.0	100.0	100.0	100.0	100.0	100.0
505	Employment income %	81.4	77.7	85.0	70.7	80.9	79.5
506	Government transfer payments %	7.2	5.7	9.2	17.6	12.6	12.2
507	Other %	11.3	16.6	6.0	11.7	6.4	8.0
	Population 15 years and over with employment income in 2000 by sex and work activity						
508	Both sexes with employment income (48)	1,165	570	1,865	3,530	1,575	1,335
509	Average employment income $	34,642	40,209	31,461	28,524	27,569	30,283
510	Standard error of average employment income $	2,115	6,550	1,050	731	1,181	1,175
511	Worked full year, full time (49)	585	255	1,155	1,820	870	705
512	Average employment income $	49,737	64,304	39,585	37,617	35,130	40,500
513	Standard error of average employment income $	2,890	12,816	1,239	970	1,579	1,437
514	Worked part year or part time (50)	540	285	690	1,635	635	615
515	Average employment income $	20,102	21,954	18,537	19,093	19,999	19,088
516	Standard error of average employment income $	2,712	2,928	1,415	895	1,587	1,434
517	Males with employment income (48)	620	300	990	1,770	835	670
518	Average employment income $	43,026	55,915	37,166	33,669	32,617	33,765
519	Standard error of average employment income $	3,508	11,744	1,552	1,126	1,818	1,547
520	Worked full year, full time (49)	345	175	690	1,020	495	405
521	Average employment income $	59,004	77,010	42,546	41,919	40,239	39,715
522	Standard error of average employment income $	4,157	18,280	1,770	1,447	2,356	1,712
523	Worked part year or part time (50)	265	115	295	715	305	255
524	Average employment income $	24,100	27,293	25,332	22,698	22,387	24,577
525	Standard error of average employment income $	5,182	5,776	2,578	1,456	2,422	2,567

Tableau 1. Certaines caractéristiques des secteurs de recensement, recensement de 2001 – Données intégrales et données-échantillon (20 %)

Vancouver 0189.08 A	Vancouver 0189.09 A	Vancouver 0189.10 ◆ A	Vancouver 0190.01	Vancouver 0190.03	Vancouver 0190.04 A	Caractéristiques	N°
						CARACTÉRISTIQUES DU REVENU DE 2000	
						Population de 15 ans et plus selon le sexe et les tranches de revenu total en 2000 – fin	
2,210	1,600	1,770	2,155	1,805	2,345	Total - Hommes	460
170	105	135	115	105	125	Sans revenu	461
2,045	1,490	1,635	2,040	1,700	2,215	Avec un revenu	462
135	65	80	175	95	110	Moins de 1 000 $ (45)	463
125	65	45	40	130	70	1 000 $ - 2 999 $	464
30	70	65	35	105	45	3 000 $ - 4 999 $	465
110	60	70	55	60	35	5 000 $ - 6 999 $	466
150	115	95	135	60	145	7 000 $ - 9 999 $	467
55	45	70	80	20	60	10 000 $ - 11 999 $	468
145	95	65	85	120	145	12 000 $ - 14 999 $	469
200	75	135	175	160	180	15 000 $ - 19 999 $	470
190	80	110	225	125	155	20 000 $ - 24 999 $	471
110	60	100	215	135	175	25 000 $ - 29 999 $	472
190	40	130	165	130	235	30 000 $ - 34 999 $	473
140	100	120	175	100	105	35 000 $ - 39 999 $	474
185	100	125	105	115	175	40 000 $ - 44 999 $	475
70	110	105	100	75	110	45 000 $ - 49 999 $	476
135	85	150	130	120	240	50 000 $ - 59 999 $	477
70	330	160	145	155	235	60 000 $ et plus	478
24,315	34,861	31,609	27,494	27,003	31,782	Revenu moyen $ (46)	479
21,305	31,608	28,795	25,049	24,151	29,340	Revenu médian $ (46)	480
863	1,549	1,359	1,021	1,138	1,056	Erreur type de revenu moyen $ (46)	481
2,395	1,675	1,945	2,450	1,790	2,260	Total - Femmes	482
165	140	160	205	155	110	Sans revenu	483
2,235	1,530	1,790	2,235	1,635	2,145	Avec un revenu	484
155	100	100	145	100	160	Moins de 1 000 $ (45)	485
165	125	105	75	125	155	1 000 $ - 2 999 $	486
120	45	75	120	65	100	3 000 $ - 4 999 $	487
130	80	95	95	175	135	5 000 $ - 6 999 $	488
215	110	140	130	130	140	7 000 $ - 9 999 $	489
135	135	120	130	70	60	10 000 $ - 11 999 $	490
220	135	170	270	150	235	12 000 $ - 14 999 $	491
320	160	175	280	210	330	15 000 $ - 19 999 $	492
170	155	120	205	150	135	20 000 $ - 24 999 $	493
165	90	120	175	100	180	25 000 $ - 29 999 $	494
165	90	120	205	75	205	30 000 $ - 34 999 $	495
85	90	110	130	110	110	35 000 $ - 39 999 $	496
85	55	105	120	45	90	40 000 $ - 44 999 $	497
55	60	70	25	50	25	45 000 $ - 49 999 $	498
25	85	85	65	40	55	50 000 $ - 59 999 $	499
25	20	75	75	35	40	60 000 $ et plus	500
17,674	20,289	22,469	21,716	18,512	19,322	Revenu moyen $ (46)	501
14,641	16,312	18,148	17,632	14,887	16,400	Revenu médian $ (46)	502
631	880	870	822	806	706	Erreur type de revenu moyen $ (46)	503
						selon la composition du revenu total	
100.0	100.0	100.0	100.0	100.0	100.0	Total - Composition du revenu en 2000 % (47)	504
78.8	84.4	84.1	73.5	79.9	78.1	Revenu d'emploi %	505
17.7	9.8	9.7	16.1	14.6	12.8	Transferts gouvernementaux %	506
3.4	5.9	6.2	10.3	5.4	9.0	Autre %	507
						Population de 15 ans et plus ayant un revenu d'emploi en 2000 selon le sexe et le travail	
2,880	2,400	2,665	2,810	2,360	3,095	Les deux sexes ayant un revenu d'emploi (48)	508
24,423	29,199	28,985	27,448	25,807	28,257	Revenu moyen d'emploi $	509
652	1,040	935	851	874	808	Erreur type de revenu moyen d'emploi $	510
1,440	1,180	1,390	1,520	1,270	1,700	Ayant travaillé toute l'année à plein temps (49)	511
31,568	40,810	39,622	35,977	33,134	36,787	Revenu moyen d'emploi $	512
842	1,475	1,141	1,063	1,147	1,092	Erreur type de revenu moyen d'emploi $	513
1,380	1,135	1,220	1,245	1,090	1,335	Ayant travaillé une partie de l'année ou à temps partiel (50)	514
17,456	18,821	17,464	17,420	17,301	18,175	Revenu moyen d'emploi $	515
835	1,114	1,220	1,101	1,125	928	Erreur type de revenu moyen d'emploi $	516
1,550	1,280	1,370	1,465	1,350	1,740	Hommes ayant un revenu d'emploi (48)	517
26,909	35,659	33,086	30,811	29,546	33,709	Revenu moyen d'emploi $	518
961	1,628	1,458	1,272	1,276	1,198	Erreur type de revenu moyen d'emploi $	519
815	725	790	890	755	1,060	Ayant travaillé toute l'année à plein temps (49)	520
34,355	48,674	42,031	37,479	36,494	41,352	Revenu moyen d'emploi $	521
1,209	2,017	1,681	1,497	1,563	1,510	Erreur type de revenu moyen d'emploi $	522
710	540	560	530	590	655	Ayant travaillé une partie de l'année ou à temps partiel (50)	523
19,070	19,385	21,175	20,567	20,734	21,943	Revenu moyen d'emploi $	524
1,253	1,719	2,222	1,999	1,844	1,557	Erreur type de revenu moyen d'emploi $	525

Table 1. Selected Characteristics for Census Tracts, 2001 Census – 100% Data and 20% Sample Data

No.	Characteristics	Vancouver 0188.05 A	Vancouver 0188.06 A	Vancouver 0189.03	Vancouver 0189.05 A	Vancouver 0189.06 A	Vancouver 0189.07 A
	2000 INCOME CHARACTERISTICS						
	Population 15 years and over with employment income in 2000 by sex and work activity – concluded						
526	Females with employment income (48)	540	270	875	1,760	745	665
527	Average employment income $	24,974	22,705	24,984	23,347	21,932	26,787
528	Standard error of average employment income $	1,839	3,088	1,256	860	1,338	1,727
529	Worked full year, full time (49)	240	80	465	805	370	300
530	Average employment income $	36,436	35,908	35,186	32,167	28,228	41,564
531	Standard error of average employment income $	2,863	6,828	1,506	1,115	1,583	2,445
532	Worked part year or part time (50)	270	170	395	920	330	355
533	Average employment income $	16,146	18,335	13,458	16,298	17,784	15,102
534	Standard error of average employment income $	1,982	2,819	1,365	1,076	2,063	1,473
	Census families by structure and family income groups in 2000						
535	Total - All census families	610	265	950	1,925	795	665
536	Under $10,000	15	10	55	85	60	45
537	$ 10,000 - $19,999	25	25	80	155	80	45
538	$ 20,000 - $29,999	40	20	65	265	65	45
539	$ 30,000 - $39,999	45	15	65	235	65	85
540	$ 40,000 - $49,999	85	30	80	235	100	120
541	$ 50,000 - $59,999	55	15	135	205	95	55
542	$ 60,000 - $69,999	60	45	95	185	65	55
543	$ 70,000 - $79,999	70	15	115	185	100	55
544	$ 80,000 - $89,999	30	15	90	110	60	60
545	$ 90,000 - $99,999	45	15	60	45	20	25
546	$100,000 and over	145	65	110	210	85	75
547	Average family income $	76,601	96,656	60,526	53,653	55,260	57,592
548	Median family income $	67,588	66,794	58,322	49,125	51,046	48,097
549	Standard error of average family income $	4,376	14,557	2,206	1,474	2,431	2,713
550	Total - All couple census families (51)	585	235	775	1,615	655	515
551	Under $10,000	20	10	-	70	40	15
552	$ 10,000 - $19,999	20	15	45	90	20	15
553	$ 20,000 - $29,999	40	15	40	220	50	20
554	$ 30,000 - $39,999	35	15	55	195	50	75
555	$ 40,000 - $49,999	80	25	65	170	85	100
556	$ 50,000 - $59,999	55	10	140	185	95	40
557	$ 60,000 - $69,999	55	50	85	175	60	40
558	$ 70,000 - $79,999	65	15	100	180	90	55
559	$ 80,000 - $89,999	30	10	75	105	60	60
560	$ 90,000 - $99,999	45	20	50	40	20	25
561	$100,000 and over	145	60	110	185	80	75
562	Average family income $	78,587	103,728	67,041	56,252	61,252	64,842
563	Median family income $	68,895	68,963	65,234	53,272	57,175	59,683
564	Standard error of average family income $	4,516	16,021	2,294	1,623	2,644	3,109
	Incidence of low income in 2000						
565	Total - Economic families	590	260	895	1,920	735	665
566	Low income	80	15	150	375	130	100
567	Incidence of low income in 2000 % (52)	13.3	5.0	16.7	19.5	17.9	15.3
568	Total - Unattached individuals 15 years and over	70	65	315	1,425	305	335
569	Low income	35	10	75	680	110	100
570	Incidence of low income in 2000 % (52)	55.2	5.5	23.5	47.7	37.1	31.7
571	Total - Population in private households	2,235	940	3,235	6,980	2,910	2,350
572	Low income	330	55	585	1,840	610	445
573	Incidence of low income in 2000 % (52)	14.8	6.0	18.0	26.3	20.9	18.9
	Private households by household income groups in 2000						
574	Total - All private households	625	295	1,095	3,170	930	910
575	Under $10,000	10	-	15	250	45	30
576	$ 10,000 - $19,999	25	10	85	560	100	70
577	$ 20,000 - $29,999	45	25	110	400	85	85
578	$ 30,000 - $39,999	40	10	95	400	100	105
579	$ 40,000 - $49,999	75	20	70	390	120	170
580	$ 50,000 - $59,999	65	40	155	255	95	90
581	$ 60,000 - $69,999	40	35	110	290	105	85
582	$ 70,000 - $79,999	70	10	125	200	80	80
583	$ 80,000 - $89,999	35	40	110	130	60	65
584	$ 90,000 - $99,999	55	20	60	65	30	30
585	$100,000 and over	155	85	155	230	120	85
586	Average household income $	78,907	99,605	63,297	44,946	57,645	55,916
587	Median household income $	70,903	70,102	61,078	39,010	51,355	49,415
588	Standard error of average household income $	4,355	12,727	2,059	1,145	2,562	2,155

Tableau 1. Certaines caractéristiques des secteurs de recensement, recensement de 2001 – Données intégrales et données-échantillon (20 %)

Vancouver 0189.08 A	Vancouver 0189.09 A	Vancouver 0189.10 ◆ A	Vancouver 0190.01	Vancouver 0190.03	Vancouver 0190.04 A	Caractéristiques	N°
						CARACTÉRISTIQUES DU REVENU DE 2000	
						Population de 15 ans et plus ayant un revenu d'emploi en 2000 selon le sexe et le travail – fin	
1,330	1,115	1,295	1,350	1,005	1,355	Femmes ayant un revenu d'emploi (48)	526
21,523	21,765	24,655	23,805	20,782	21,280	Revenu moyen d'emploi $	527
835	1,044	1,090	1,076	1,075	867	Erreur type de revenu moyen d'emploi $	528
630	450	600	630	510	645	Ayant travaillé toute l'année à plein temps (49)	529
27,985	28,216	36,444	33,861	28,152	29,298	Revenu moyen d'emploi $	530
1,065	1,445	1,353	1,444	1,561	1,225	Erreur type de revenu moyen d'emploi $	531
665	600	660	710	495	680	Ayant travaillé une partie de l'année ou à temps partiel (50)	532
15,732	18,316	14,337	15,073	13,208	14,533	Revenu moyen d'emploi $	533
1,082	1,439	1,210	1,162	1,144	935	Erreur type de revenu moyen d'emploi $	534
						Familles de recensement selon la structure et les tranches de revenu de la famille en 2000	
1,700	1,130	1,380	1,540	1,190	1,645	Total - Toutes les familles de recensement	535
290	55	95	155	130	55	Moins de 10 000 $	536
250	85	125	235	155	140	10 000 $ - 19 999 $	537
300	110	135	150	100	165	20 000 $ - 29 999 $	538
215	70	150	205	190	180	30 000 $ - 39 999 $	539
235	95	135	140	150	190	40 000 $ - 49 999 $	540
155	100	105	220	125	200	50 000 $ - 59 999 $	541
115	90	205	160	70	195	60 000 $ - 69 999 $	542
65	120	130	120	85	185	70 000 $ - 79 999 $	543
35	95	120	50	70	130	80 000 $ - 89 999 $	544
15	65	35	25	55	95	90 000 $ - 99 999 $	545
30	235	155	75	55	110	100 000 $ et plus	546
35,004	66,129	57,734	44,662	45,436	55,908	Revenu moyen des familles $	547
30,696	65,876	56,469	41,869	40,117	53,782	Revenu médian des familles $	548
1,273	2,469	2,046	1,675	1,834	1,600	Erreur type de revenu moyen des familles $	549
1,075	940	1,090	1,165	905	1,390	Total - Toutes les familles de recensement comptant un couple (51)	550
130	50	70	90	80	35	Moins de 10 000 $	551
115	50	40	100	65	95	10 000 $ - 19 999 $	552
175	70	85	125	70	130	20 000 $ - 29 999 $	553
145	50	120	165	135	140	30 000 $ - 39 999 $	554
170	70	95	110	130	165	40 000 $ - 49 999 $	555
125	80	85	165	110	155	50 000 $ - 59 999 $	556
75	90	170	150	70	175	60 000 $ - 69 999 $	557
60	115	115	105	85	175	70 000 $ - 79 999 $	558
35	100	110	50	70	115	80 000 $ - 89 999 $	559
10	65	40	25	50	85	90 000 $ - 99 999 $	560
30	210	155	75	40	115	100 000 $ et plus	561
40,370	71,052	64,025	50,032	50,269	58,907	Revenu moyen des familles $	562
37,297	72,792	62,078	49,793	47,510	58,141	Revenu médian des familles $	563
1,705	2,636	2,345	1,911	1,991	1,749	Erreur type de revenu moyen des familles $	564
						Fréquence des unités à faible revenu en 2000	
1,690	1,045	1,360	1,535	1,170	1,580	Total - Familles économiques	565
725	170	365	430	350	220	Faible revenu	566
43.0	16.3	26.9	28.0	29.7	13.7	Fréquence des unités à faible revenu en 2000 % (52)	567
1,105	230	310	1,245	725	560	Total - Personnes hors famille économique de 15 ans et plus	568
445	80	100	490	330	195	Faible revenu	569
40.2	35.2	32.5	39.4	45.6	35.1	Fréquence des unités à faible revenu en 2000 % (52)	570
6,115	4,035	4,830	5,485	4,625	5,840	Total - Population dans les ménages privés	571
2,790	775	1,385	1,690	1,570	905	Faible revenu	572
45.7	19.3	28.6	30.8	34.0	15.6	Fréquence des unités à faible revenu en 2000 % (52)	573
						Ménages privés selon les tranches de revenu du ménage en 2000	
2,560	1,210	1,620	2,535	1,670	1,935	Total - Tous les ménages privés	574
395	55	110	240	195	55	Moins de 10 000 $	575
415	60	190	450	225	170	10 000 $ - 19 999 $	576
395	100	160	330	110	185	20 000 $ - 29 999 $	577
345	125	180	345	300	210	30 000 $ - 39 999 $	578
390	125	145	270	230	225	40 000 $ - 49 999 $	579
235	100	120	305	165	225	50 000 $ - 59 999 $	580
170	95	205	195	115	240	60 000 $ - 69 999 $	581
115	105	130	185	65	220	70 000 $ - 79 999 $	582
35	110	135	75	115	120	80 000 $ - 89 999 $	583
15	70	55	45	55	90	90 000 $ - 99 999 $	584
50	255	190	100	100	190	100 000 $ et plus	585
34,804	68,816	56,598	41,352	45,408	57,903	Revenu moyen des ménages $	586
31,295	64,347	52,714	37,262	40,028	54,089	Revenu médian des ménages $	587
1,043	2,575	2,013	1,268	1,667	1,599	Erreur type de revenu moyen des ménages $	588

Table 1. Selected Characteristics for Census Tracts, 2001 Census – 100% Data and 20% Sample Data

No.	Characteristics	Vancouver 0190.05 A	Vancouver 0191.02 ◇	Vancouver 0191.03 A	Vancouver 0191.04 ◆ A	Vancouver 0192	Vancouver 0200
	POPULATION CHARACTERISTICS						
1	**Population, 1996 (1)**	**1,638**	**7,020**	**4,327**	**4,363**	**4,206**	**3,020**
2	**Population, 2001 (2)**	**1,682**	**7,477**	**4,484**	**4,603**	**4,096**	**4,553**
3	Population percentage change, 1996-2001	2.7	6.5	3.6	5.5	-2.6	50.8
4	Land area in square kilometres, 2001	0.60	2.62	1.30	1.31	9.70	3.34
5	**Total population – 100% Data (3)**	**1,680**	**7,480**	**4,485**	**4,605**	**4,095**	**4,555**
	by sex and age groups						
6	Male	860	3,720	2,310	2,280	2,240	2,310
7	0-4 years	70	240	180	105	140	170
8	5-9 years	70	230	205	120	175	175
9	10-14 years	55	190	170	95	155	135
10	15-19 years	85	215	140	110	105	145
11	20-24 years	45	285	155	120	130	160
12	25-29 years	55	310	165	170	155	210
13	30-34 years	80	360	170	210	230	260
14	35-39 years	90	380	225	220	225	255
15	40-44 years	85	345	210	190	230	180
16	45-49 years	55	280	175	190	200	150
17	50-54 years	40	200	145	195	150	125
18	55-59 years	25	180	80	130	100	100
19	60-64 years	30	135	85	130	70	95
20	65-69 years	25	135	70	85	70	70
21	70-74 years	20	85	70	80	55	35
22	75-79 years	15	80	40	60	30	25
23	80-84 years	10	50	25	30	10	10
24	85 years and over	5	35	10	35	5	10
25	Female	820	3,760	2,175	2,325	1,850	2,245
26	0-4 years	65	245	140	130	130	180
27	5-9 years	70	215	180	120	160	180
28	10-14 years	60	215	170	90	140	155
29	15-19 years	60	205	165	105	105	125
30	20-24 years	50	305	145	135	140	190
31	25-29 years	65	295	165	155	120	185
32	30-34 years	80	310	155	180	175	250
33	35-39 years	85	345	220	215	195	205
34	40-44 years	60	300	170	150	155	180
35	45-49 years	60	245	150	165	135	125
36	50-54 years	35	210	105	155	115	140
37	55-59 years	30	155	95	135	85	100
38	60-64 years	35	140	85	120	55	80
39	65-69 years	20	105	80	110	45	55
40	70-74 years	25	125	70	90	45	45
41	75-79 years	10	120	50	85	20	30
42	80-84 years	15	110	25	75	20	15
43	85 years and over	5	115	15	110	5	5
44	**Total population 15 years and over**	**1,300**	**6,140**	**3,445**	**3,940**	**3,190**	**3,555**
	by legal marital status						
45	Never married (single)	510	2,250	1,095	1,175	1,195	1,200
46	Legally married (and not separated)	560	2,405	1,805	1,610	1,425	1,885
47	Separated, but still legally married	50	345	145	210	160	110
48	Divorced	110	705	240	545	285	215
49	Widowed	75	440	155	400	125	145
	by common-law status						
50	Not in a common-law relationship	1,205	5,600	3,235	3,715	2,905	3,290
51	In a common-law relationship	95	545	210	220	280	260
52	**Total population – 20% Sample Data (4)**	**1,675**	**7,255**	**4,460**	**4,425**	**4,070**	**4,550**
	by mother tongue						
53	Single responses	1,585	7,080	4,330	4,395	4,000	4,380
54	English	1,025	4,870	2,565	2,695	2,590	2,025
55	French	20	140	20	60	15	55
56	Non-official languages (5)	540	2,065	1,745	1,640	1,390	2,295
57	Chinese, n.o.s.	20	140	60	10	70	60
58	Cantonese	-	15	80	10	95	110
59	Punjabi	35	500	570	485	320	1,125
60	Mandarin	25	75	35	-	15	10
61	Tagalog (Pilipino)	20	140	115	130	60	55
62	Other languages (6)	440	1,200	885	1,010	830	945
63	Multiple responses	95	180	130	25	75	170
64	English and French	-	-	-	15	10	10
65	English and non-official language	90	145	115	15	65	165
66	French and non-official language	-	35	-	-	-	-
67	English, French and non-official language	-	-	15	-	-	-

See reference material at the end of the publication. – Voir les documents de référence à la fin de la publication.

Tableau 1. Certaines caractéristiques des secteurs de recensement, recensement de 2001 – Données intégrales et données-échantillon (20 %)

Vancouver 0201	Vancouver 0202	Vancouver 0203	Vancouver 0204.01 A	Vancouver 0204.02 ◆ A	Vancouver 0205	Caractéristiques	N°
						CARACTÉRISTIQUES DE LA POPULATION	
1,481	**5,605**	**4,068**	**3,866**	**4,439**	**7,388**	**Population, 1996 (1)**	1
1,687	**6,047**	**4,313**	**4,304**	**5,081**	**8,327**	**Population, 2001 (2)**	2
13.9	7.9	6.0	11.3	14.5	12.7	Variation en pourcentage de la population, 1996-2001	3
0.75	1.30	1.11	0.39	0.71	1.12	Superficie des terres en kilomètres carrés, 2001	4
1,685	**6,045**	**4,315**	**4,300**	**5,080**	**8,325**	**Population totale – Données intégrales (3)**	5
						selon le sexe et les groupes d'âge	
855	2,920	2,175	2,140	2,550	3,975	Sexe masculin	6
60	135	150	125	150	135	0-4 ans	7
65	80	155	80	130	140	5-9 ans	8
35	70	145	60	100	105	10-14 ans	9
55	120	130	70	105	170	15-19 ans	10
50	170	155	160	185	240	20-24 ans	11
80	265	105	215	240	320	25-29 ans	12
85	350	170	280	295	400	30-34 ans	13
80	280	210	265	310	395	35-39 ans	14
70	265	230	255	235	380	40-44 ans	15
60	225	190	160	225	375	45-49 ans	16
60	230	190	145	185	280	50-54 ans	17
45	200	90	90	115	215	55-59 ans	18
25	155	70	80	75	150	60-64 ans	19
30	120	70	60	65	150	65-69 ans	20
20	115	50	30	55	175	70-74 ans	21
10	65	30	35	30	155	75-79 ans	22
5	50	25	10	30	100	80-84 ans	23
10	25	20	10	15	100	85 ans et plus	24
830	3,120	2,145	2,165	2,525	4,355	Sexe féminin	25
55	125	115	95	140	140	0-4 ans	26
60	90	165	75	110	125	5-9 ans	27
40	55	140	50	90	95	10-14 ans	28
40	100	115	85	120	135	15-19 ans	29
65	195	130	195	210	290	20-24 ans	30
65	280	115	245	230	310	25-29 ans	31
75	270	205	235	255	315	30-34 ans	32
65	280	205	265	250	335	35-39 ans	33
70	285	205	225	220	325	40-44 ans	34
55	270	180	175	195	290	45-49 ans	35
60	290	150	155	160	270	50-54 ans	36
35	225	95	110	110	220	55-59 ans	37
25	140	70	50	80	195	60-64 ans	38
35	145	70	60	70	205	65-69 ans	39
15	140	60	50	75	255	70-74 ans	40
20	100	55	45	90	315	75-79 ans	41
15	70	50	35	60	290	80-84 ans	42
15	45	25	20	60	235	85 ans et plus	43
1,365	**5,490**	**3,450**	**3,815**	**4,365**	**7,590**	**Population totale de 15 ans et plus**	44
						selon l'état matrimonial légal	
480	1,990	1,095	1,730	1,810	2,830	Célibataire (jamais marié(e))	45
690	2,230	1,775	1,200	1,540	2,465	Légalement marié(e) (et non séparé(e))	46
30	230	140	180	220	405	Séparé(e), mais toujours légalement marié(e)	47
95	745	260	550	525	1,000	Divorcé(e)	48
65	295	180	150	275	905	Veuf ou veuve	49
						selon l'union libre	
1,275	4,850	3,225	3,285	3,945	6,910	Ne vivant pas en union libre	50
90	640	220	525	415	685	Vivant en union libre	51
1,685	**6,040**	**4,310**	**4,300**	**5,075**	**8,245**	**Population totale – Données-échantillon (20 %) (4)**	52
						selon la langue maternelle	
1,645	6,005	4,275	4,180	4,920	8,130	Réponses uniques	53
1,030	4,440	2,960	3,145	3,380	5,735	Anglais	54
15	100	25	80	75	140	Français	55
600	1,460	1,290	955	1,465	2,250	Langues non officielles (5)	56
10	165	25	50	55	165	Chinois, n.d.a.	57
15	150	50	-	65	25	Cantonais	58
290	15	385	35	205	15	Pendjabi	59
10	15	-	80	15	170	Mandarin	60
80	215	45	60	180	205	Tagalog (pilipino)	61
195	900	790	735	950	1,670	Autres langues (6)	62
40	35	35	125	155	110	Réponses multiples	63
-	10	-	-	15	40	Anglais et français	64
40	30	35	125	115	70	Anglais et langue non officielle	65
-	-	-	-	30	-	Français et langue non officielle	66
-	-	-	-	-	-	Anglais, français et langue non officielle	67

See reference material at the end of the publication. – Voir les documents de référence à la fin de la publication.

Table 1. Selected Characteristics for Census Tracts, 2001 Census – 100% Data and 20% Sample Data

No.	Characteristics	Vancouver 0190.05 A	Vancouver 0191.02 ◇	Vancouver 0191.03 A	Vancouver 0191.04 ◆ A	Vancouver 0192	Vancouver 0200
	POPULATION CHARACTERISTICS						
	by home language						
68	Single responses	1,410	6,085	3,515	3,550	3,210	3,175
69	English	1,090	5,310	2,815	2,965	2,740	2,130
70	French	-	10	-	-	-	10
71	Non-official languages (5)	315	760	700	580	475	1,045
72	Cantonese	25	10	50	-	75	75
73	Chinese, n.o.s.	-	75	30	10	-	10
74	Punjabi	20	270	365	335	175	620
75	Mandarin	25	60	10	-	15	-
76	Korean	10	95	20	25	-	-
77	Other languages (6)	240	250	220	220	210	335
78	Multiple responses	270	1,170	945	870	860	1,365
79	English and French	10	50	35	85	15	35
80	English and non-official language	260	1,065	915	760	845	1,330
81	French and non-official language	-	-	-	-	-	-
82	English, French and non-official language	-	60	-	20	10	-
	by knowledge of official languages						
83	English only	1,560	6,765	3,895	4,045	3,930	3,900
84	French only	-	10	-	-	-	-
85	English and French	40	310	255	300	75	295
86	Neither English nor French	80	175	310	75	65	345
	by knowledge of non-official languages (5) (7)						
87	Cantonese	10	20	95	-	170	190
88	Chinese, n.o.s.	10	175	85	10	75	45
89	Punjabi	40	610	650	570	425	1,295
90	Mandarin	30	85	40	-	30	50
91	Hindi	65	415	385	200	320	730
92	German	45	120	85	195	65	80
93	Spanish	110	110	125	90	50	50
	by first official language spoken						
94	English	1,585	6,935	4,110	4,230	3,985	4,120
95	French	20	100	10	35	20	55
96	English and French	-	45	35	85	-	20
97	Neither English nor French	75	170	305	80	65	345
98	Official language minority - (number) (8)	15	125	30	75	20	65
99	Official language minority - (percentage) (8)	0.9	1.7	0.7	1.7	0.5	1.4
	by ethnic origin (9)						
100	English	315	1,865	825	830	785	540
101	Canadian	360	1,595	715	895	1,025	585
102	Chinese	65	285	245	95	265	270
103	Scottish	195	1,100	580	650	555	405
104	Irish	235	765	460	550	275	310
105	German	145	845	305	660	320	220
106	East Indian	95	895	720	605	720	1,520
107	French	130	730	320	380	195	310
108	Ukrainian	70	425	145	205	145	205
109	Italian	65	330	75	35	90	180
110	Dutch (Netherlands)	90	315	115	125	150	145
111	Filipino	25	270	185	185	95	160
112	Polish	20	215	50	115	135	115
113	Norwegian	35	235	95	225	140	45
114	North American Indian	50	385	160	115	145	60
	by Aboriginal identity						
115	Total Aboriginal identity population (10)	65	395	175	130	160	60
116	Total non-Aboriginal population	1,610	6,855	4,290	4,295	3,910	4,485
	by Aboriginal origin						
117	Total Aboriginal origins population (11)	80	560	200	150	165	155
118	Total non-Aboriginal population	1,595	6,690	4,260	4,275	3,905	4,390
	by Registered Indian status						
119	Registered Indian (12)	10	170	85	40	40	20
120	Not a Registered Indian	1,670	7,080	4,370	4,385	4,025	4,525

Tableau 1. Certaines caractéristiques des secteurs de recensement, recensement de 2001 – Données intégrales et données-échantillon (20 %)

Vancouver 0201	Vancouver 0202	Vancouver 0203	Vancouver 0204.01 A	Vancouver 0204.02 ◆ A	Vancouver 0205	Caractéristiques	N°
						CARACTÉRISTIQUES DE LA POPULATION	
						selon la langue parlée à la maison	
1,370	5,050	3,540	3,730	4,160	6,990	Réponses uniques	68
1,105	4,680	3,185	3,390	3,630	6,340	Anglais	69
-	20	-	10	10	25	Français	70
265	355	355	330	535	625	Langues non officielles (5)	71
-	30	20	25	45	-	Cantonais	72
10	80	-	10	20	75	Chinois, n.d.a.	73
150	-	175	15	50	-	Pendjabi	74
20	-	-	65	10	75	Mandarin	75
15	50	10	10	95	55	Coréen	76
75	200	145	195	320	425	Autres langues (6)	77
315	990	770	575	915	1,255	Réponses multiples	78
10	45	20	50	70	65	Anglais et français	79
305	935	745	515	810	1,165	Anglais et langue non officielle	80
-	-	-	-	-	-	Français et langue non officielle	81
-	-	-	10	30	20	Anglais, français et langue non officielle	82
						selon la connaissance des langues officielles	
1,540	5,595	3,995	3,940	4,580	7,510	Anglais seulement	83
-	10	-	-	10	10	Français seulement	84
60	355	185	295	340	560	Anglais et français	85
90	85	130	75	150	160	Ni l'anglais ni le français	86
						selon la connaissance des langues non officielles (5) (7)	
-	215	65	30	70	45	Cantonais	87
10	145	25	30	60	125	Chinois, n.d.a.	88
300	15	480	30	255	25	Pendjabi	89
30	85	15	75	20	215	Mandarin	90
60	55	115	45	55	20	Hindi	91
35	120	85	120	120	245	Allemand	92
20	225	85	125	170	245	Espagnol	93
						selon la première langue officielle parlée	
1,590	5,850	4,150	4,160	4,810	7,875	Anglais	94
15	95	25	70	95	135	Français	95
-	25	-	20	15	75	Anglais et français	96
80	65	135	55	155	165	Ni l'anglais ni le français	97
15	110	30	85	100	175	Minorité de langue officielle - (nombre) (8)	98
0.9	1.8	0.7	2.0	2.0	2.1	Minorité de langue officielle - (pourcentage) (8)	99
						selon l'origine ethnique (9)	
425	1,720	1,105	1,195	1,145	2,260	Anglais	100
380	1,095	780	1,055	905	1,815	Canadien	101
40	470	210	160	275	495	Chinois	102
205	1,125	815	835	870	1,560	Écossais	103
210	880	660	635	810	1,255	Irlandais	104
195	560	490	600	395	990	Allemand	105
290	150	535	95	305	60	Indien de l'Inde	106
110	450	200	405	405	750	Français	107
50	370	225	180	285	290	Ukrainien	108
30	145	210	115	105	230	Italien	109
50	205	155	225	125	355	Hollandais (Néerlandais)	110
150	315	125	185	350	335	Philippin	111
35	205	160	115	115	235	Polonais	112
105	220	190	105	85	235	Norvégien	113
10	205	30	150	275	265	Indien de l'Amérique du Nord	114
						selon l'identité autochtone	
20	200	55	160	220	210	Total de la population ayant une identité autochtone (10)	115
1,665	5,845	4,260	4,145	4,860	8,035	Total de la population non autochtone	116
						selon l'origine autochtone	
15	255	105	175	320	315	Total de la population ayant une origine autochtone (11)	117
1,670	5,785	4,205	4,125	4,755	7,930	Total de la population non autochtone	118
						selon le statut d'Indien inscrit	
15	140	25	70	100	135	Oui, Indien inscrit (12)	119
1,670	5,900	4,285	4,230	4,975	8,105	Non, pas un Indien inscrit	120

Table 1. Selected Characteristics for Census Tracts, 2001 Census – 100% Data and 20% Sample Data

No.	Characteristics	Vancouver 0190.05 A	Vancouver 0191.02 ◇	Vancouver 0191.03 A	Vancouver 0191.04 ◆ A	Vancouver 0192	Vancouver 0200
	POPULATION CHARACTERISTICS						
	by visible minority groups						
121	Total visible minority population	435	2,150	2,005	1,495	1,500	2,835
122	Chinese	60	280	240	85	285	235
123	South Asian	110	1,060	995	865	755	1,940
124	Black	20	90	25	55	-	170
125	Filipino	25	255	175	165	85	165
126	Latin American	80	60	55	70	35	15
127	Southeast Asian	105	180	365	120	255	20
128	Arab	-	-	30	-	-	25
129	West Asian	-	25	35	15	-	130
130	Korean	10	135	60	45	-	-
131	Japanese	10	20	15	55	45	70
132	Visible minority, n.i.e. (13)	-	20	-	-	-	10
133	Multiple visible minorities (14)	-	30	20	25	30	65
	by citizenship						
134	Canadian citizenship (15)	1,455	6,440	3,830	4,040	3,765	3,940
135	Citizenship other than Canadian	225	815	630	390	310	605
	by place of birth of respondent						
136	Non-immigrant population	1,135	5,160	2,790	3,090	2,685	2,445
137	Born in province of residence	695	3,425	2,120	1,835	2,005	1,950
138	Immigrant population (16)	485	2,005	1,675	1,320	1,385	2,020
139	United States	20	45	10	35	60	15
140	Central and South America	15	40	50	60	25	35
141	Caribbean and Bermuda	50	10	15	25	10	40
142	United Kingdom	20	205	55	70	140	70
143	Other Europe (17)	185	370	220	265	245	115
144	Africa	10	45	15	20	30	105
145	Asia and the Middle East	155	1,085	1,095	775	680	1,340
146	Oceania and other (18)	35	200	215	65	190	290
147	Non-permanent residents (19)	50	95	-	20	10	80
148	**Total immigrant population**	**485**	**2,000**	**1,675**	**1,320**	**1,380**	**2,015**
	by period of immigration						
149	Before 1961	65	220	145	105	80	110
150	1961-1970	35	155	110	80	145	150
151	1971-1980	70	320	240	370	205	360
152	1981-1990	90	390	500	285	535	480
153	1991-2001 (20)	225	910	675	470	415	915
154	1991-1995	80	465	270	265	240	510
155	1996-2001 (20)	145	445	405	205	170	410
	by age at immigration						
156	0-4 years	30	190	165	60	90	125
157	5-19 years	180	590	440	290	400	525
158	20 years and over	270	1,220	1,070	970	895	1,375
159	**Total population**	**1,675**	**7,255**	**4,465**	**4,425**	**4,070**	**4,545**
	by religion						
160	Catholic (21)	390	1,265	705	780	780	665
161	Protestant	275	1,730	960	1,150	595	530
162	Christian Orthodox	15	55	20	60	50	10
163	Christian, n.i.e. (22)	70	590	280	165	165	75
164	Muslim	115	215	185	270	115	465
165	Jewish	-	10	25	10	-	-
166	Buddhist	30	220	170	35	220	110
167	Hindu	50	155	155	155	275	240
168	Sikh	50	575	595	495	315	1,415
169	Eastern religions (23)	-	25	-	-	-	15
170	Other religions (24)	-	65	10	-	15	15
171	No religious affiliation (25)	680	2,355	1,355	1,300	1,535	1,005
172	**Total population 15 years and over**	**1,275**	**5,910**	**3,390**	**3,760**	**3,175**	**3,570**
	by generation status						
173	1st generation (26)	470	1,945	1,590	1,300	1,345	2,055
174	2nd generation (27)	275	1,315	640	960	595	780
175	3rd generation and over (28)	530	2,650	1,170	1,505	1,235	735
176	**Total population 1 year and over (29)**	**1,635**	**7,105**	**4,410**	**4,355**	**4,020**	**4,480**
	by place of residence 1 year ago (mobility)						
177	Non-movers	1,190	5,120	3,590	3,750	3,345	3,570
178	Movers	445	1,980	810	615	670	910
179	Non-migrants	205	1,325	550	415	440	350
180	Migrants	240	655	265	195	235	560
181	Internal migrants	185	570	195	150	185	410
182	Intraprovincial migrants	140	515	185	155	150	350
183	Interprovincial migrants	40	55	10	-	35	60
184	External migrants	60	90	65	45	50	155

Tableau 1. Certaines caractéristiques des secteurs de recensement, recensement de 2001 – Données intégrales et données-échantillon (20 %)

Vancouver 0201	Vancouver 0202	Vancouver 0203	Vancouver 0204.01 A	Vancouver 0204.02 ◆ A	Vancouver 0205	Caractéristiques	N°
						CARACTÉRISTIQUES DE LA POPULATION	
						selon les groupes de minorités visibles	
620	1,445	1,165	785	1,485	1,515	Total de la population des minorités visibles	121
45	465	140	145	195	425	Chinois	122
345	125	620	105	345	70	Sud-Asiatique	123
10	145	60	90	165	165	Noir	124
150	310	110	235	340	325	Philippin	125
10	45	35	25	95	55	Latino-Américain	126
15	20	70	40	30	60	Asiatique du Sud-Est	127
-	25	-	90	35	10	Arabe	128
-	70	70	-	55	100	Asiatique occidental	129
20	120	25	35	135	145	Coréen	130
10	105	-	10	40	85	Japonais	131
-	-	-	-	15	-	Minorité visible, n.i.a. (13)	132
10	15	25	10	40	75	Minorités visibles multiples (14)	133
						selon la citoyenneté	
1,460	5,475	4,045	3,855	4,360	7,360	Citoyenneté canadienne (15)	134
225	570	265	445	715	885	Citoyenneté autre que canadienne	135
						selon le lieu de naissance du répondant	
1,055	4,205	3,050	3,030	3,340	5,705	Population non immigrante	136
725	2,475	2,275	1,815	2,245	3,215	Née dans la province de résidence	137
610	1,785	1,230	1,225	1,625	2,395	Population immigrante (16)	138
25	60	10	45	70	95	États-Unis	139
10	80	30	60	55	55	Amérique centrale et du Sud	140
-	70	-	25	35	15	Caraïbes et Bermudes	141
40	345	165	185	120	300	Royaume-Uni	142
125	320	315	395	470	940	Autre Europe (17)	143
-	80	40	55	125	80	Afrique	144
410	770	650	435	730	865	Asie et Moyen-Orient	145
10	65	15	30	15	40	Océanie et autre (18)	146
25	55	30	40	115	145	Résidents non permanents (19)	147
605	**1,785**	**1,230**	**1,225**	**1,625**	**2,390**	**Population immigrante totale**	148
						selon la période d'immigration	
40	220	165	165	205	555	Avant 1961	149
65	275	120	90	140	235	1961-1970	150
85	350	295	175	210	245	1971-1980	151
90	325	315	180	205	255	1981-1990	152
330	615	345	625	860	1,105	1991-2001 (20)	153
120	315	145	235	360	370	1991-1995	154
210	300	200	385	500	740	1996-2001 (20)	155
						selon l'âge à l'immigration	
50	180	135	95	125	205	0-4 ans	156
100	440	435	380	430	550	5-19 ans	157
455	1,165	660	750	1,075	1,645	20 ans et plus	158
1,690	**6,045**	**4,310**	**4,305**	**5,080**	**8,245**	**Population totale**	159
						selon la religion	
275	1,280	835	845	1,075	1,655	Catholique (21)	160
495	1,960	1,145	1,165	1,285	2,735	Protestante	161
60	75	70	155	220	305	Orthodoxe chrétienne	162
140	295	150	290	210	380	Chrétiennes, n.i.a. (22)	163
10	155	145	115	110	100	Musulmane	164
-	25	-	20	10	25	Juive	165
15	175	25	80	85	120	Bouddhiste	166
10	35	10	30	-	30	Hindoue	167
315	15	415	25	285	30	Sikh	168
-	-	105	15	25	45	Religions orientales (23)	169
10	30	-	20	20	90	Autres religions (24)	170
365	2,005	1,410	1,530	1,760	2,725	Aucune appartenance religieuse (25)	171
1,355	**5,480**	**3,440**	**3,820**	**4,350**	**7,490**	**Population totale de 15 ans et plus**	172
						selon le statut des générations	
595	1,760	1,170	1,205	1,625	2,405	1re génération (26)	173
245	1,270	900	790	950	1,945	2e génération (27)	174
515	2,445	1,370	1,830	1,780	3,145	3e génération et plus (28)	175
1,675	**5,980**	**4,250**	**4,220**	**4,985**	**8,185**	**Population totale de 1 an et plus (29)**	176
						selon le lieu de résidence 1 an auparavant (mobilité)	
1,435	4,625	3,700	3,260	3,835	6,180	Personnes n'ayant pas déménagé	177
240	1,360	550	960	1,150	2,005	Personnes ayant déménagé	178
50	445	265	475	530	760	Non-migrants	179
190	910	285	480	620	1,240	Migrants	180
135	800	205	380	445	970	Migrants internes	181
135	715	185	330	385	850	Migrants infraprovinciaux	182
-	85	15	55	55	125	Migrants interprovinciaux	183
55	110	75	100	180	265	Migrants externes	184

Table 1. Selected Characteristics for Census Tracts, 2001 Census – 100% Data and 20% Sample Data

No.	Characteristics	Vancouver 0190.05 A	Vancouver 0191.02 ◇	Vancouver 0191.03 A	Vancouver 0191.04 ◆ A	Vancouver 0192	Vancouver 0200
	POPULATION CHARACTERISTICS						
185	**Total population 5 years and over (30)**	**1,570**	**6,760**	**4,135**	**4,190**	**3,800**	**4,220**
	by place of residence 5 years ago (mobility)						
186	Non-movers	655	2,750	2,310	2,195	2,195	1,925
187	Movers	920	4,015	1,825	1,990	1,605	2,295
188	Non-migrants	280	2,180	890	1,155	825	930
189	Migrants	635	1,835	935	835	780	1,365
190	Internal migrants	455	1,435	665	690	600	1,000
191	Intraprovincial migrants	270	1,135	555	580	540	905
192	Interprovincial migrants	185	295	110	105	60	95
193	External migrants	180	395	270	155	180	365
194	**Total population 15 to 24 years**	**255**	**1,010**	**600**	**445**	**575**	**655**
	by school attendance						
195	Not attending school	105	435	210	135	235	245
196	Attending school full time	135	430	315	255	270	305
197	Attending school part time	20	145	70	65	70	100
198	**Total population 15 years and over**	**1,270**	**5,910**	**3,395**	**3,765**	**3,170**	**3,570**
	by highest level of schooling						
199	Less than grade 9 (31)	160	520	385	375	205	480
200	Grades 9-13 without high school graduation certificate	395	1,680	875	1,085	895	825
201	Grades 9-13 with high school graduation certificate	175	745	565	485	480	500
202	Some postsecondary without degree, certificate or diploma (32)	160	740	370	320	280	475
203	Trades certificate or diploma (33)	155	730	410	600	505	390
204	College certificate or diploma (34)	160	895	540	530	460	480
205	University certificate below bachelor's degree	-	125	50	105	45	80
206	University with bachelor's degree or higher	75	470	195	260	305	340
	by combinations of unpaid work						
207	Males 15 years and over	665	2,980	1,725	1,885	1,745	1,845
208	Reported unpaid work (35)	540	2,560	1,550	1,655	1,465	1,675
209	Housework and child care and care or assistance to seniors	45	120	140	110	125	275
210	Housework and child care only	170	755	480	350	415	535
211	Housework and care or assistance to seniors only	30	160	100	95	85	100
212	Child care and care or assistance to seniors only	-	10	25	-	-	-
213	Housework only	275	1,475	765	1,050	815	730
214	Child care only	25	25	30	45	35	15
215	Care or assistance to seniors only	-	25	15	-	-	10
216	Females 15 years and over	610	2,930	1,665	1,880	1,430	1,720
217	Reported unpaid work (35)	575	2,715	1,605	1,745	1,295	1,620
218	Housework and child care and care or assistance to seniors	55	235	235	155	175	275
219	Housework and child care only	245	865	550	520	460	655
220	Housework and care or assistance to seniors only	50	220	120	160	60	120
221	Child care and care or assistance to seniors only	-	-	10	-	-	10
222	Housework only	215	1,370	655	900	585	530
223	Child care only	-	20	20	-	15	30
224	Care or assistance to seniors only	-	-	20	15	-	10
	by labour force activity						
225	Males 15 years and over	665	2,980	1,730	1,880	1,745	1,850
226	In the labour force	440	2,025	1,260	1,295	1,365	1,340
227	Employed	385	1,790	1,190	1,210	1,245	1,205
228	Unemployed	50	230	70	90	120	135
229	Not in the labour force	225	955	465	580	380	505
230	Participation rate	66.2	68.0	72.8	68.9	78.2	72.4
231	Employment rate	57.9	60.1	68.8	64.4	71.3	65.1
232	Unemployment rate	11.4	11.4	5.6	6.9	8.8	10.1
233	Females 15 years and over	610	2,930	1,665	1,885	1,425	1,720
234	In the labour force	305	1,710	1,010	965	905	1,100
235	Employed	260	1,480	935	925	725	1,005
236	Unemployed	40	230	75	40	180	95
237	Not in the labour force	300	1,220	655	920	520	620
238	Participation rate	50.0	58.4	60.7	51.2	63.5	64.0
239	Employment rate	42.6	50.5	56.2	49.1	50.9	58.4
240	Unemployment rate	13.1	13.5	7.4	4.1	19.9	8.6

Tableau 1. Certaines caractéristiques des secteurs de recensement, recensement de 2001 – Données intégrales et données-échantillon (20 %)

Vancouver 0201	Vancouver 0202	Vancouver 0203	Vancouver 0204.01 A	Vancouver 0204.02 ◆ A	Vancouver 0205	Caractéristiques	N°
						CARACTÉRISTIQUES DE LA POPULATION	
1,555	**5,785**	**4,045**	**4,085**	**4,760**	**7,980**	**Population totale de 5 ans et plus (30)**	185
						selon le lieu de résidence 5 ans auparavant (mobilité)	
820	2,440	2,295	1,225	1,935	3,190	Personnes n'ayant pas déménagé	186
735	3,340	1,750	2,860	2,825	4,790	Personnes ayant déménagé	187
270	1,155	765	1,160	1,115	1,675	Non-migrants	188
470	2,190	985	1,700	1,710	3,115	Migrants	189
345	1,870	825	1,285	1,190	2,420	Migrants internes	190
320	1,660	775	1,115	995	2,085	Migrants infraprovinciaux	191
25	215	50	165	200	335	Migrants interprovinciaux	192
125	320	160	415	515	690	Migrants externes	193
170	**595**	**545**	**525**	**590**	**795**	**Population totale de 15 à 24 ans**	194
						selon la fréquentation scolaire	
80	290	220	210	265	340	Ne fréquentant pas l'école	195
75	210	260	195	245	365	Fréquentant l'école à plein temps	196
15	100	65	110	85	90	Fréquentant l'école à temps partiel	197
1,350	**5,480**	**3,440**	**3,820**	**4,355**	**7,490**	**Population totale de 15 ans et plus**	198
						selon le plus haut niveau de scolarité atteint	
150	125	200	115	215	520	Niveau inférieur à la 9e année (31)	199
265	1,045	670	665	850	1,705	De la 9e à la 13e année sans certificat d'études secondaires	200
180	575	445	435	535	800	De la 9e à la 13e année avec certificat d'études secondaires	201
210	715	375	480	680	935	Études postsecondaires partielles sans grade, certificat ou diplôme (32)	202
200	585	345	495	530	945	Certificat ou diplôme d'une école de métiers (33)	203
180	1,145	730	840	760	1,130	Certificat ou diplôme collégial (34)	204
50	200	65	200	170	260	Certificat universitaire inférieur au baccalauréat	205
135	1,090	615	595	615	1,190	Études universitaires avec baccalauréat ou diplôme supérieur	206
						selon les combinaisons de travail non rémunéré	
665	2,640	1,720	1,860	2,180	3,505	Hommes de 15 ans et plus	207
595	2,340	1,545	1,655	1,875	2,920	Travail non rémunéré déclaré (35)	208
60	110	110	45	85	105	Travaux ménagers et soins aux enfants et soins ou aide aux personnes âgées	209
190	360	470	340	365	550	Travaux ménagers et soins aux enfants seulement	210
35	230	90	105	75	230	Travaux ménagers et soins ou aide aux personnes âgées seulement	211
-	10	10	-	-	-	Soins aux enfants et soins ou aide aux personnes âgées seulement	212
295	1,605	845	1,125	1,320	1,980	Travaux ménagers seulement	213
25	15	15	25	15	30	Soins aux enfants seulement	214
-	15	20	10	15	25	Soins ou aide aux personnes âgées seulement	215
690	2,840	1,725	1,965	2,170	3,980	Femmes de 15 ans et plus	216
615	2,695	1,565	1,840	2,050	3,495	Travail non rémunéré déclaré (35)	217
85	240	165	155	170	180	Travaux ménagers et soins aux enfants et soins ou aide aux personnes âgées	218
200	455	480	435	475	625	Travaux ménagers et soins aux enfants seulement	219
55	355	110	215	185	470	Travaux ménagers et soins ou aide aux personnes âgées seulement	220
-	-	-	-	-	-	Soins aux enfants et soins ou aide aux personnes âgées seulement	221
245	1,630	785	1,030	1,205	2,180	Travaux ménagers seulement	222
30	10	15	-	-	15	Soins aux enfants seulement	223
-	-	-	-	10	25	Soins ou aide aux personnes âgées seulement	224
						selon l'activité	
670	2,640	1,720	1,860	2,185	3,505	Hommes de 15 ans et plus	225
505	1,930	1,390	1,420	1,570	2,210	Population active	226
470	1,785	1,365	1,240	1,430	1,985	Personnes occupées	227
30	145	30	175	145	225	Chômeurs	228
165	715	320	440	610	1,300	Inactifs	229
75.4	73.1	80.8	76.3	71.9	63.1	Taux d'activité	230
70.1	67.6	79.4	66.7	65.4	56.6	Taux d'emploi	231
5.9	7.5	2.2	12.3	9.2	10.2	Taux de chômage	232
685	2,835	1,720	1,965	2,170	3,980	Femmes de 15 ans et plus	233
450	1,880	1,135	1,345	1,270	2,055	Population active	234
405	1,720	1,075	1,245	1,150	1,845	Personnes occupées	235
45	155	65	105	120	205	Chômeuses	236
235	960	585	620	905	1,925	Inactives	237
65.7	66.3	66.0	68.4	58.5	51.6	Taux d'activité	238
59.1	60.7	62.5	63.4	53.0	46.4	Taux d'emploi	239
10.0	8.2	5.7	7.8	9.4	10.0	Taux de chômage	240

Table 1. Selected Characteristics for Census Tracts, 2001 Census – 100% Data and 20% Sample Data

No.	Characteristics	Vancouver 0190.05 A	Vancouver 0191.02 ◇	Vancouver 0191.03 A	Vancouver 0191.04 ◆ A	Vancouver 0192	Vancouver 0200
	POPULATION CHARACTERISTICS						
	by labour force activity – concluded						
241	Both sexes - Participation rate	58.7	63.2	67.0	60.0	71.3	68.5
242	15-24 years	41.2	59.4	68.3	66.7	60.9	61.4
243	25 years and over	63.1	64.0	66.7	59.1	73.8	69.8
244	Both sexes - Employment rate	51.0	55.3	62.6	56.7	62.0	61.9
245	15-24 years	31.4	48.0	56.7	62.9	47.4	59.1
246	25 years and over	56.2	56.9	63.8	56.0	65.3	62.7
247	Both sexes - Unemployment rate	12.1	12.3	6.6	5.5	13.2	9.4
248	15-24 years	23.8	19.2	16.0	5.0	22.9	3.7
249	25 years and over	10.9	10.8	4.6	5.4	11.4	10.6
250	**Total labour force 15 years and over**	**740**	**3,735**	**2,270**	**2,260**	**2,270**	**2,440**
	by industry based on the 1997 NAICS						
251	Industry - Not applicable (36)	30	190	40	35	110	70
252	All industries (37)	715	3,545	2,230	2,230	2,160	2,375
253	11 Agriculture, forestry, fishing and hunting	10	55	55	30	15	40
254	21 Mining and oil and gas extraction	10	10	-	-	-	10
255	22 Utilities	-	25	10	-	35	10
256	23 Construction	75	300	110	105	170	95
257	31-33 Manufacturing	95	520	400	315	250	385
258	41 Wholesale trade	50	120	115	160	120	100
259	44-45 Retail trade	45	410	265	175	265	365
260	48-49 Transportation and warehousing	35	315	245	285	175	280
261	51 Information and cultural industries	10	135	40	40	40	70
262	52 Finance and insurance	35	70	45	110	110	70
263	53 Real estate and rental and leasing	10	60	20	45	25	25
264	54 Professional, scientific and technical services	20	190	45	120	95	65
265	55 Management of companies and enterprises	-	-	-	-	-	-
266	56 Administrative and support, waste management and remediation services	90	330	150	135	110	165
267	61 Educational services	25	130	70	20	120	55
268	62 Health care and social assistance	70	280	240	265	205	200
269	71 Arts, entertainment and recreation	20	70	40	50	30	45
270	72 Accommodation and food services	70	240	160	215	150	185
271	81 Other services (except public administration)	45	165	135	90	150	115
272	91 Public administration	20	125	100	65	80	90
	by class of worker						
273	Class of worker - Not applicable (36)	30	190	40	30	110	70
274	All classes of worker (37)	710	3,545	2,230	2,225	2,160	2,375
275	Paid workers	630	3,300	2,095	2,075	1,910	2,275
276	Employees	625	3,225	2,025	2,025	1,870	2,210
277	Self-employed (incorporated)	10	70	70	50	40	70
278	Self-employed (unincorporated)	80	240	135	150	245	100
279	Unpaid family workers	-	10	-	10	-	-
	by occupation based on the 2001 NOC-S						
280	Male labour force 15 years and over	440	2,025	1,265	1,295	1,370	1,345
281	Occupation - Not applicable (36)	25	95	15	25	40	25
282	All occupations (37)	420	1,935	1,250	1,270	1,330	1,315
283	A Management occupations	25	130	45	120	100	140
284	B Business, finance and administration occupations	15	210	100	140	145	135
285	C Natural and applied sciences and related occupations	25	140	55	85	95	90
286	D Health occupations	-	20	35	10	25	35
287	E Occupations in social science, education, government service and religion	25	55	50	-	40	25
288	F Occupations in art, culture, recreation and sport	-	60	10	35	25	30
289	G Sales and service occupations	90	385	250	250	300	315
290	H Trades, transport and equipment operators and related occupations	160	735	465	470	425	360
291	I Occupations unique to primary industry	10	55	55	35	65	60
292	J Occupations unique to processing, manufacturing and utilities	55	150	180	130	115	130
293	Female labour force 15 years and over	305	1,710	1,010	960	905	1,105
294	Occupation - Not applicable (36)	-	95	25	10	70	40
295	All occupations (37)	300	1,615	985	955	830	1,055
296	A Management occupations	-	70	30	55	60	60
297	B Business, finance and administration occupations	110	590	270	315	235	315
298	C Natural and applied sciences and related occupations	10	10	10	10	-	35
299	D Health occupations	30	115	115	80	55	80

Tableau 1. Certaines caractéristiques des secteurs de recensement, recensement de 2001 – Données intégrales et données-échantillon (20 %)

Vancouver 0201	Vancouver 0202	Vancouver 0203	Vancouver 0204.01 A	Vancouver 0204.02 ◆ A	Vancouver 0205	Caractéristiques	N°
						CARACTÉRISTIQUES DE LA POPULATION	
						selon l'activité – fin	
70.5	69.6	73.4	72.4	65.3	56.9	Les deux sexes - Taux d'activité	241
62.9	70.6	67.9	70.5	68.1	64.2	15-24 ans	242
71.2	69.3	74.8	72.7	64.8	56.0	25 ans et plus	243
64.6	64.0	70.7	65.2	59.2	51.1	Les deux sexes - Taux d'emploi	244
57.1	62.7	63.9	57.1	58.5	53.5	15-24 ans	245
65.7	64.2	72.1	66.5	59.3	50.9	25 ans et plus	246
7.9	8.0	3.7	9.9	9.3	10.1	Les deux sexes - Taux de chômage	247
9.1	11.8	5.4	18.7	16.0	16.7	15-24 ans	248
7.7	7.5	3.5	8.8	8.2	9.2	25 ans et plus	249
950	**3,810**	**2,530**	**2,765**	**2,840**	**4,265**	**Population active totale de 15 ans et plus**	250
						selon l'industrie basée sur le SCIAN de 1997	
10	95	25	35	95	105	Industrie - Sans objet (36)	251
940	3,715	2,510	2,725	2,745	4,165	Toutes les industries (37)	252
15	10	30	10	-	40	11 Agriculture, foresterie, pêche et chasse	253
-	-	10	-	-	10	21 Extraction minière et extraction de pétrole et de gaz	254
15	-	50	30	10	20	22 Services publics	255
75	235	110	230	255	205	23 Construction	256
80	340	260	320	280	390	31-33 Fabrication	257
45	205	120	130	145	290	41 Commerce de gros	258
115	395	315	285	355	460	44-45 Commerce de détail	259
85	275	140	225	175	190	48-49 Transport et entreposage	260
20	160	105	145	125	190	51 Industrie de l'information et industrie culturelle	261
55	215	90	125	80	160	52 Finance et assurances	262
-	110	60	45	35	110	53 Services immobiliers et services de location et de location à bail	263
30	365	230	180	225	210	54 Services professionnels, scientifiques et techniques	264
-	-	-	10	10	-	55 Gestion de sociétés et d'entreprises	265
75	175	80	100	155	275	56 Services administratifs, services de soutien, services de gestion des déchets et services d'assainissement	266
90	225	175	140	180	280	61 Services d'enseignement	267
95	340	270	285	290	420	62 Soins de santé et assistance sociale	268
10	70	15	50	65	110	71 Arts, spectacles et loisirs	269
40	230	145	145	120	290	72 Hébergement et services de restauration	270
80	170	160	120	115	270	81 Autres services, sauf les administrations publiques	271
15	180	150	165	135	245	91 Administrations publiques	272
						selon la catégorie de travailleurs	
15	95	25	35	100	100	Catégorie de travailleurs - Sans objet (36)	273
940	3,710	2,510	2,730	2,745	4,165	Toutes les catégories de travailleurs (37)	274
855	3,415	2,295	2,600	2,595	3,850	Travailleurs rémunérés	275
835	3,240	2,190	2,555	2,555	3,795	Employés	276
25	180	100	40	40	50	Travailleurs autonomes (entreprise constituée en société)	277
80	300	215	115	135	295	Travailleurs autonomes (entreprise non constituée en société)	278
10	-	-	15	10	15	Travailleurs familiaux non rémunérés	279
						selon la profession basée sur la CNP-S de 2001	
500	1,930	1,395	1,420	1,570	2,205	Hommes actifs de 15 ans et plus	280
-	45	-	15	45	70	Profession - Sans objet (36)	281
500	1,885	1,385	1,405	1,525	2,140	Toutes les professions (37)	282
40	240	185	115	165	185	A Gestion	283
30	270	170	200	130	220	B Affaires, finance et administration	284
40	270	145	115	150	240	C Sciences naturelles et appliquées et professions apparentées	285
10	60	30	35	15	55	D Secteur de la santé	286
20	80	55	25	75	155	E Sciences sociales, enseignement, administration publique et religion	287
25	45	50	50	40	65	F Arts, culture, sports et loisirs	288
90	340	245	285	310	485	G Ventes et services	289
195	475	330	505	520	560	H Métiers, transport et machinerie	290
10	15	15	10	10	55	I Professions propres au secteur primaire	291
30	85	160	70	115	120	J Transformation, fabrication et services d'utilité publique	292
455	1,880	1,140	1,345	1,270	2,055	Femmes actives de 15 ans et plus	293
15	50	15	25	50	30	Profession - Sans objet (36)	294
440	1,830	1,125	1,320	1,220	2,025	Toutes les professions (37)	295
15	190	75	125	95	155	A Gestion	296
170	600	375	470	335	660	B Affaires, finance et administration	297
25	40	20	105	20	30	C Sciences naturelles et appliquées et professions apparentées	298
50	140	160	130	130	155	D Secteur de la santé	299

Table 1. Selected Characteristics for Census Tracts, 2001 Census – 100% Data and 20% Sample Data

No.	Characteristics	Vancouver 0190.05 A	Vancouver 0191.02 ◇	Vancouver 0191.03 A	Vancouver 0191.04 ◆ A	Vancouver 0192	Vancouver 0200
	POPULATION CHARACTERISTICS						
	by occupation based on the 2001 NOC-S – concluded						
300	E Occupations in social science, education, government service and religion	10	95	65	65	55	30
301	F Occupations in art, culture, recreation and sport	-	20	10	15	25	25
302	G Sales and service occupations	110	495	335	345	315	395
303	H Trades, transport and equipment operators and related occupations	15	80	80	30	35	25
304	I Occupations unique to primary industry	-	30	50	-	-	-
305	J Occupations unique to processing, manufacturing and utilities	15	100	35	45	40	100
306	**Total employed labour force 15 years and over**	**650**	**3,275**	**2,125**	**2,135**	**1,970**	**2,210**
	by place of work						
307	Males	385	1,790	1,190	1,210	1,245	1,200
308	Usual place of work	275	1,310	935	930	900	995
309	At home	25	70	30	10	85	50
310	Outside Canada	-	25	15	-	-	-
311	No fixed workplace address	85	395	205	270	260	160
312	Females	260	1,480	935	925	725	1,010
313	Usual place of work	195	1,295	860	805	615	910
314	At home	15	60	15	55	55	40
315	Outside Canada	-	-	-	-	10	-
316	No fixed workplace address	50	125	60	65	40	50
317	**Total employed labour force 15 years and over with usual place of work or no fixed workplace address**	**610**	**3,125**	**2,060**	**2,070**	**1,805**	**2,120**
	by mode of transportation						
318	Males	365	1,700	1,140	1,200	1,155	1,155
319	Car, truck, van, as driver	255	1,150	925	870	800	835
320	Car, truck, van, as passenger	45	130	90	55	70	60
321	Public transit	45	355	100	175	195	175
322	Walked	15	30	25	100	25	50
323	Other method	-	35	10	10	60	35
324	Females	245	1,425	915	870	650	960
325	Car, truck, van, as driver	150	775	580	445	475	595
326	Car, truck, van, as passenger	60	140	105	55	25	85
327	Public transit	15	395	145	270	135	225
328	Walked	-	90	90	95	10	35
329	Other method	20	20	10	-	-	25
330	**Total population 15 years and over who worked since January 1, 2000**	**740**	**3,950**	**2,385**	**2,310**	**2,335**	**2,615**
	by language used at work						
331	Single responses	680	3,630	2,055	2,165	2,205	2,340
332	English	680	3,530	1,940	2,135	2,190	2,270
333	French	-	-	-	-	-	-
334	Non-official languages (5)	-	100	115	25	10	60
335	Chinese, n.o.s.	-	45	10	-	-	-
336	Cantonese	-	-	10	-	10	15
337	Other languages (6)	-	60	100	25	10	50
338	Multiple responses	60	325	330	150	135	270
339	English and French	-	-	10	15	10	35
340	English and non-official language	60	320	300	135	130	235
341	French and non-official language	-	-	-	-	-	-
342	English, French and non-official language	-	-	25	10	-	-
	DWELLING AND HOUSEHOLD CHARACTERISTICS						
343	**Total number of occupied private dwellings**	**560**	**3,040**	**1,360**	**2,130**	**1,470**	**1,445**
	by tenure						
344	Owned	275	1,120	890	965	1,035	915
345	Rented	290	1,925	470	1,170	435	535
346	Band housing	-	-	-	-	-	-
	by structural type of dwelling						
347	Single-detached house	370	1,055	890	575	940	680
348	Semi-detached house	35	50	35	65	20	-
349	Row house	-	95	-	85	10	10
350	Apartment, detached duplex	30	380	350	-	350	420
351	Apartment, building that has five or more storeys	-	605	-	715	-	-
352	Apartment, building that has fewer than five storeys (38)	140	855	90	690	10	205
353	Other single-attached house	-	-	-	-	-	80
354	Movable dwelling (39)	-	-	-	-	135	45

Tableau 1. Certaines caractéristiques des secteurs de recensement, recensement de 2001 – Données intégrales et données-échantillon (20 %)

Vancouver 0201	Vancouver 0202	Vancouver 0203	Vancouver 0204.01 A	Vancouver 0204.02 ◆ A	Vancouver 0205	Caractéristiques	N°
						CARACTÉRISTIQUES DE LA POPULATION	
						selon la profession basée sur la CNP-S de 2001 – fin	
40	235	140	135	120	235	E Sciences sociales, enseignement, administration publique et religion	300
10	110	55	40	65	85	F Arts, culture, sports et loisirs	301
125	460	245	260	370	570	G Ventes et services	302
-	25	10	30	30	45	H Métiers, transport et machinerie	303
-	15	10	-	10	10	I Professions propres au secteur primaire	304
15	25	35	30	45	75	J Transformation, fabrication et services d'utilité publique	305
880	**3,505**	**2,435**	**2,485**	**2,580**	**3,835**	**Population active occupée totale de 15 ans et plus**	306
						selon le lieu de travail	
470	1,780	1,360	1,240	1,430	1,990	Hommes	307
345	1,355	1,110	950	1,090	1,575	Lieu habituel de travail	308
15	100	35	40	115	75	À domicile	309
-	10	-	10	10	-	En dehors du Canada	310
115	315	220	240	220	330	Sans adresse de travail fixe	311
410	1,720	1,075	1,240	1,150	1,845	Femmes	312
355	1,490	920	1,185	1,035	1,610	Lieu habituel de travail	313
20	150	75	35	45	130	À domicile	314
-	-	20	-	10	10	En dehors du Canada	315
30	75	60	25	55	95	Sans adresse de travail fixe	316
845	**3,240**	**2,310**	**2,400**	**2,405**	**3,610**	**Population active occupée totale de 15 ans et plus ayant un lieu habituel de travail ou sans adresse de travail fixe**	317
						selon le mode de transport	
460	1,675	1,330	1,195	1,310	1,910	Hommes	318
375	1,200	965	890	945	1,220	Automobile, camion ou fourgonnette, en tant que conducteur	319
10	55	60	65	65	80	Automobile, camion ou fourgonnette, en tant que passager	320
70	300	165	145	205	345	Transport en commun	321
-	75	80	50	80	200	À pied	322
10	40	55	50	15	65	Autre moyen	323
385	1,570	980	1,210	1,095	1,700	Femmes	324
190	950	575	675	585	820	Automobile, camion ou fourgonnette, en tant que conductrice	325
20	130	110	45	95	95	Automobile, camion ou fourgonnette, en tant que passagère	326
145	425	235	395	285	505	Transport en commun	327
15	65	60	85	120	265	À pied	328
10	-	15	-	10	10	Autre moyen	329
1,035	**4,005**	**2,700**	**3,025**	**3,045**	**4,610**	**Population totale de 15 ans et plus ayant travaillé depuis le 1er janvier 2000**	330
						selon la langue utilisée au travail	
895	3,785	2,550	2,910	2,780	4,340	Réponses uniques	331
885	3,740	2,535	2,885	2,740	4,270	Anglais	332
-	-	-	10	-	10	Français	333
10	30	15	20	35	70	Langues non officielles (5)	334
-	25	-	-	-	15	Chinois, n.d.a.	335
-	-	-	-	-	-	Cantonais	336
10	-	10	20	30	50	Autres langues (6)	337
145	220	155	110	265	265	Réponses multiples	338
-	50	10	20	65	80	Anglais et français	339
135	170	150	90	200	180	Anglais et langue non officielle	340
-	-	-	-	-	-	Français et langue non officielle	341
-	10	-	-	-	15	Anglais, français et langue non officielle	342
						CARACTÉRISTIQUES DES LOGEMENTS ET DES MÉNAGES	
605	**3,215**	**1,570**	**2,385**	**2,645**	**4,970**	**Nombre total de logements privés occupés**	343
						selon le mode d'occupation	
365	1,845	1,110	915	720	1,750	Possédé	344
240	1,365	465	1,470	1,925	3,225	Loué	345
-	-	-	-	-	-	Logement de bande	346
						selon le type de construction résidentielle	
360	130	1,025	190	370	410	Maison individuelle non attenante	347
10	10	30	10	-	20	Maison jumelée	348
-	200	30	135	-	85	Maison en rangée	349
145	125	310	80	165	135	Appartement, duplex non attenant	350
-	1,640	-	395	370	2,070	Appartement, immeuble de cinq étages ou plus	351
90	1,115	155	1,575	1,735	2,250	Appartement, immeuble de moins de cinq étages (38)	352
-	-	25	-	10	-	Autre maison individuelle attenante	353
-	-	-	-	-	10	Logement mobile (39)	354

Table 1. Selected Characteristics for Census Tracts, 2001 Census – 100% Data and 20% Sample Data

No.	Characteristics	Vancouver 0190.05 A	Vancouver 0191.02 ◇	Vancouver 0191.03 A	Vancouver 0191.04 ◆ A	Vancouver 0192	Vancouver 0200
	DWELLING AND HOUSEHOLD CHARACTERISTICS						
	by condition of dwelling						
355	Regular maintenance only	330	1,935	815	1,650	865	1,035
356	Minor repairs	165	740	485	300	395	275
357	Major repairs	65	365	60	185	210	135
	by period of construction						
358	Before 1946	35	205	50	30	195	155
359	1946-1960	200	680	370	175	375	155
360	1961-1970	200	660	425	275	175	95
361	1971-1980	115	425	210	730	325	65
362	1981-1990	10	265	240	640	225	155
363	1991-2001 (20)	-	810	60	275	165	815
364	Average number of rooms per dwelling	6.2	5.3	6.7	4.6	6.2	6.2
365	Average number of bedrooms per dwelling	2.7	2.2	3.1	1.9	2.8	3.0
366	Average value of dwelling $	201,160	186,300	200,225	144,847	184,135	238,087
367	**Total number of private households**	**565**	**3,040**	**1,360**	**2,130**	**1,465**	**1,450**
	by household size						
368	1 person	95	970	200	1,045	400	275
369	2 persons	165	1,000	355	535	370	375
370	3 persons	110	495	255	205	225	235
371	4-5 persons	150	455	400	270	380	405
372	6 or more persons	45	125	145	80	85	155
	by household type						
373	One-family households	430	1,780	950	915	915	940
374	Multiple-family households	-	75	135	70	50	140
375	Non-family households	130	1,180	275	1,150	505	375
376	Number of persons in private households	1,675	7,215	4,460	4,415	4,055	4,535
377	Average number of persons in private households	3.0	2.4	3.3	2.1	2.8	3.1
378	Average number of persons per room	0.5	0.5	0.5	0.5	0.4	0.5
379	Tenant households in non-farm, non-reserve private dwellings (40)	285	1,925	470	1,150	430	530
380	Average gross rent $ (40)	785	712	822	600	739	705
381	Tenant households spending 30% or more of household income on gross rent (40) (41)	165	940	295	655	225	155
382	Tenant households spending from 30% to 99% of household income on gross rent (40) (41)	140	740	270	545	175	130
383	Owner households in non-farm, non-reserve private dwellings (42)	275	1,115	890	960	1,035	910
384	Average owner's major payments $ (42)	833	932	1,079	907	1,098	1,233
385	Owner households spending 30% or more of household income on owner's major payments (41) (42)	70	360	245	275	405	370
386	Owner households spending from 30% to 99% of household income on owner's major payments (41) (42)	60	310	210	230	345	340
	CENSUS FAMILY CHARACTERISTICS						
387	**Total number of census families in private households**	**445**	**1,940**	**1,240**	**1,055**	**1,015**	**1,245**
	by census family structure and size						
388	Total couple families	325	1,430	915	865	840	1,035
389	Total families of married couples	280	1,150	860	750	700	925
390	Without children at home	90	540	285	330	200	310
391	With children at home	185	610	575	420	490	615
392	1 child	40	210	210	110	185	195
393	2 children	100	225	215	210	180	255
394	3 or more children	40	170	150	100	125	165
395	Total families of common-law couples	50	275	55	115	140	105
396	Without children at home	25	160	25	75	75	65
397	With children at home	25	120	25	40	70	45
398	1 child	15	60	15	35	15	10
399	2 children	-	55	-	10	30	20
400	3 or more children	10	-	-	-	20	15
401	Total lone-parent families	115	505	330	190	175	210
402	Female parent	100	420	255	135	130	150
403	1 child	50	275	115	95	85	85
404	2 children	30	110	90	25	30	40
405	3 or more children	15	35	50	10	15	30

Tableau 1. Certaines caractéristiques des secteurs de recensement, recensement de 2001 – Données intégrales et données-échantillon (20 %)

Vancouver 0201	Vancouver 0202	Vancouver 0203	Vancouver 0204.01 A	Vancouver 0204.02 ◆ A	Vancouver 0205	Caractéristiques	N°
						CARACTÉRISTIQUES DES LOGEMENTS ET DES MÉNAGES	
						selon l'état du logement	
370	1,680	1,025	1,505	1,865	3,470	Entretien régulier seulement	355
210	680	425	485	550	1,000	Réparations mineures	356
25	850	115	395	230	505	Réparations majeures	357
						selon la période de construction	
155	175	625	230	440	645	Avant 1946	358
155	180	410	155	270	480	1946-1960	359
70	125	135	575	655	1,295	1961-1970	360
50	130	125	500	615	1,300	1971-1980	361
55	1,215	160	470	345	635	1981-1990	362
120	1,380	115	455	315	610	1991-2001 (20)	363
5.9	4.6	6.7	4.3	4.3	4.1	Nombre moyen de pièces par logement	364
2.6	1.8	2.8	1.6	1.6	1.4	Nombre moyen de chambres à coucher par logement	365
249,388	162,976	271,620	131,324	202,957	177,440	Valeur moyenne du logement $	366
605	**3,210**	**1,570**	**2,385**	**2,640**	**4,970**	**Nombre total de logements privés**	367
						selon la taille du ménage	
130	1,270	355	1,110	1,245	2,835	1 personne	368
200	1,370	470	865	805	1,430	2 personnes	369
95	350	295	250	290	415	3 personnes	370
145	205	390	150	250	260	4-5 personnes	371
35	15	65	15	50	30	6 personnes ou plus	372
						selon le genre de ménage	
415	1,700	1,100	1,060	1,105	1,755	Ménages unifamiliaux	373
30	15	45	15	40	35	Ménages multifamiliaux	374
160	1,495	425	1,315	1,495	3,180	Ménages non familiaux	375
1,685	6,040	4,315	4,300	5,075	8,240	Nombre de personnes dans les ménages privés	376
2.8	1.9	2.7	1.8	1.9	1.7	Nombre moyen de personnes dans les ménages privés	377
0.5	0.4	0.4	0.4	0.5	0.4	Nombre moyen de personnes par pièce	378
240	1,350	465	1,455	1,910	3,170	Ménages locataires dans les logements privés non agricoles hors réserve (40)	379
669	741	753	670	669	616	Loyer brut moyen $ (40)	380
75	490	195	535	870	1,455	Ménages locataires consacrant 30 % ou plus du revenu du ménage au loyer brut (40) (41)	381
75	335	180	430	720	1,220	Ménages locataires consacrant de 30 % à 99 % du revenu du ménage au loyer brut (40) (41)	382
365	1,845	1,110	920	720	1,745	Ménages propriétaires dans les logements privés non agricoles hors réserve (42)	383
1,157	955	1,063	937	1,050	744	Principales dépenses de propriété moyennes $ (42)	384
85	485	195	225	245	315	Ménages propriétaires consacrant 30 % ou plus du revenu du ménage aux principales dépenses de propriété (41) (42)	385
80	450	165	190	225	265	Ménages propriétaires consacrant de 30 % à 99 % du revenu du ménage aux principales dépenses de propriété (41) (42)	386
						CARACTÉRISTIQUES DES FAMILLES DE RECENSEMENT	
480	**1,735**	**1,210**	**1,090**	**1,185**	**1,830**	**Total des familles de recensement dans les ménages privés**	387
						selon la structure et la taille de la famille de recensement	
410	1,405	985	860	955	1,550	Total des familles avec conjoints	388
345	1,080	875	595	740	1,210	Total des familles avec couples mariés	389
125	715	325	295	320	740	Sans enfants à la maison	390
220	365	555	300	430	470	Avec enfants à la maison	391
75	205	180	185	215	265	1 enfant	392
85	135	270	95	155	150	2 enfants	393
60	30	105	20	65	55	3 enfants ou plus	394
70	320	115	265	210	340	Total des familles en union libre	395
55	270	75	225	160	255	Sans enfants à la maison	396
15	50	40	40	50	85	Avec enfants à la maison	397
10	25	20	40	40	55	1 enfant	398
-	20	-	-	-	30	2 enfants	399
-	10	15	-	-	10	3 enfants ou plus	400
65	330	220	225	235	280	Total des familles monoparentales	401
55	255	180	190	195	225	Parent de sexe féminin	402
30	185	100	135	145	175	1 enfant	403
15	50	55	60	35	35	2 enfants	404
10	15	20	-	15	15	3 enfants ou plus	405

Table 1. Selected Characteristics for Census Tracts, 2001 Census – 100% Data and 20% Sample Data

No.	Characteristics	Vancouver 0190.05 A	Vancouver 0191.02 ◇	Vancouver 0191.03 A	Vancouver 0191.04 ◆ A	Vancouver 0192	Vancouver 0200
	CENSUS FAMILY CHARACTERISTICS						
	by census family structure and size – concluded						
406	Male parent	15	85	75	55	45	65
407	1 child	-	55	55	40	15	55
408	2 children	-	30	20	15	15	10
409	3 or more children	10	-	-	-	10	-
410	**Total number of children at home**	**660**	**2,125**	**1,745**	**1,140**	**1,410**	**1,685**
	by age groups						
411	Under 6 years	110	600	395	310	340	390
412	6-14 years	295	735	650	355	535	585
413	15-17 years	110	260	170	115	190	150
414	18-24 years	100	355	325	215	225	380
415	25 years and over	50	175	210	150	120	180
416	Average number of children at home per census family (43)	1.5	1.1	1.4	1.1	1.4	1.3
417	**Total number of persons in private households**	**1,680**	**7,215**	**4,460**	**4,410**	**4,055**	**4,535**
	by census family status and living arrangements						
418	Number of non-family persons	245	1,725	565	1,355	800	575
419	Living with relatives (44)	55	240	105	195	125	160
420	Living with non-relatives only	100	525	265	120	270	140
421	Living alone	95	965	195	1,045	405	275
422	Number of family persons	1,430	5,490	3,900	3,055	3,260	3,960
423	Average number of persons per census family	3.2	2.8	3.1	2.9	3.2	3.2
424	**Total number of persons 65 years and over**	**170**	**740**	**440**	**685**	**260**	**315**
425	Number of non-family persons 65 years and over	75	380	80	355	110	120
426	Living with relatives (44)	25	45	45	10	45	60
427	Living with non-relatives only	-	50	-	15	10	-
428	Living alone	45	275	35	335	60	60
429	Number of family persons 65 years and over	90	365	365	335	150	195
	ECONOMIC FAMILY CHARACTERISTICS						
430	**Total number of economic families in private households**	**440**	**1,905**	**1,090**	**1,030**	**970**	**1,125**
	by size of family						
431	2 persons	155	945	310	485	325	335
432	3 persons	95	420	270	195	205	245
433	4 persons	110	290	260	190	190	265
434	5 or more persons	80	250	250	155	255	280
435	Total number of persons in economic families	1,480	5,725	4,000	3,250	3,385	4,120
436	Average number of persons per economic family	3.4	3.0	3.7	3.2	3.5	3.7
437	Total number of unattached individuals	195	1,490	460	1,165	670	415
	2000 INCOME CHARACTERISTICS						
	Population 15 years and over by sex and total income groups in 2000						
438	Total - Both sexes	1,275	5,910	3,395	3,765	3,175	3,570
439	Without income	170	315	180	180	230	295
440	With income	1,105	5,595	3,215	3,585	2,940	3,275
441	Under $1,000 (45)	30	305	130	150	115	250
442	$ 1,000 - $ 2,999	50	250	135	125	125	120
443	$ 3,000 - $ 4,999	75	225	160	105	115	95
444	$ 5,000 - $ 6,999	70	315	145	170	180	185
445	$ 7,000 - $ 9,999	75	480	270	375	150	200
446	$10,000 - $11,999	55	340	205	195	80	175
447	$12,000 - $14,999	140	550	255	295	275	315
448	$15,000 - $19,999	125	620	310	330	330	350
449	$20,000 - $24,999	130	475	325	365	295	305
450	$25,000 - $29,999	80	510	345	410	240	315
451	$30,000 - $34,999	65	395	215	260	265	195
452	$35,000 - $39,999	70	220	160	305	135	190
453	$40,000 - $44,999	40	285	190	135	140	150
454	$45,000 - $49,999	20	175	95	175	95	95
455	$50,000 - $59,999	50	260	165	80	235	155
456	$60,000 and over	35	205	100	105	155	175
457	Average income $ (46)	22,070	22,236	22,777	23,098	24,963	23,301
458	Median income $ (46)	16,318	17,342	19,801	20,434	20,732	18,654
459	Standard error of average income $ (46)	1,312	537	674	706	781	718

Tableau 1. Certaines caractéristiques des secteurs de recensement, recensement de 2001 – Données intégrales et données-échantillon (20 %)

Vancouver 0201	Vancouver 0202	Vancouver 0203	Vancouver 0204.01 A	Vancouver 0204.02 ◆ A	Vancouver 0205	Caractéristiques	N°
						CARACTÉRISTIQUES DES FAMILLES DE RECENSEMENT	
						selon la structure et la taille de la famille de recensement – fin	
15	80	40	35	35	55	Parent de sexe masculin	406
10	75	25	30	25	35	1 enfant	407
-	-	15	-	10	10	2 enfants	408
-	-	-	10	10	-	3 enfants ou plus	409
565	**1,075**	**1,470**	**770**	**1,100**	**1,225**	**Nombre total d'enfants à la maison**	410
						selon les groupes d'âge	
165	300	310	255	375	310	Moins de 6 ans	411
165	265	560	220	345	445	6-14 ans	412
55	65	150	65	85	140	15-17 ans	413
70	250	295	155	185	190	18-24 ans	414
105	195	155	65	115	150	25 ans et plus	415
1.2	0.6	1.2	0.7	0.9	0.7	Nombre moyen d'enfants à la maison par famille de recensement (43)	416
1,690	**6,040**	**4,310**	**4,300**	**5,075**	**8,240**	**Nombre total de personnes dans les ménages privés**	417
						selon la situation des particuliers dans la famille de recensement et des particuliers dans le ménage	
230	1,830	645	1,585	1,830	3,635	Nombre de personnes hors famille de recensement	418
25	105	110	120	120	200	Vivant avec des personnes apparentées (44)	419
75	460	175	355	460	595	Vivant avec des personnes non apparentées uniquement	420
130	1,265	355	1,105	1,250	2,835	Vivant seules	421
1,455	4,210	3,665	2,720	3,250	4,610	Nombre de personnes membres d'une famille	422
3.1	2.4	3.0	2.5	2.7	2.5	Nombre moyen de personnes par famille de recensement	423
165	**880**	**440**	**365**	**550**	**1,980**	**Nombre total de personnes de 65 ans et plus**	424
70	320	125	195	345	1,110	Nombre de personnes hors famille de recensement de 65 ans et plus	425
10	20	30	10	20	35	Vivant avec des personnes apparentées (44)	426
-	-	10	10	25	15	Vivant avec des personnes non apparentées uniquement	427
60	300	80	170	305	1,055	Vivant seules	428
95	555	315	165	205	865	Nombre de personnes membres d'une famille de 65 ans et plus	429
						CARACTÉRISTIQUES DES FAMILLES ÉCONOMIQUES	
450	**1,760**	**1,160**	**1,115**	**1,185**	**1,875**	**Nombre total de familles économiques dans les ménages privés**	430
						selon la taille de la famille	
195	1,260	450	700	595	1,230	2 personnes	431
100	290	280	285	315	360	3 personnes	432
65	150	250	85	180	185	4 personnes	433
95	60	180	45	100	100	5 personnes ou plus	434
1,480	4,320	3,775	2,845	3,365	4,815	Nombre total de personnes dans les familles économiques	435
3.3	2.5	3.2	2.5	2.8	2.6	Nombre moyen de personnes par famille économique	436
205	1,725	535	1,460	1,710	3,430	Nombre total de personnes hors famille économique	437
						CARACTÉRISTIQUES DU REVENU DE 2000	
						Population de 15 ans et plus selon le sexe et les tranches de revenu total en 2000	
1,355	5,475	3,440	3,820	4,350	7,490	Total - Les deux sexes	438
115	175	165	130	215	295	Sans revenu	439
1,240	5,300	3,275	3,695	4,140	7,195	Avec un revenu	440
60	235	95	160	240	270	Moins de 1 000 $ (45)	441
35	175	135	155	115	275	1 000 $ - 2 999 $	442
30	130	95	105	115	200	3 000 $ - 4 999 $	443
40	190	120	185	170	265	5 000 $ - 6 999 $	444
55	270	225	120	255	440	7 000 $ - 9 999 $	445
45	150	110	125	230	290	10 000 $ - 11 999 $	446
125	370	165	265	370	880	12 000 $ - 14 999 $	447
110	355	325	360	395	960	15 000 $ - 19 999 $	448
120	445	285	285	430	600	20 000 $ - 24 999 $	449
110	470	165	310	235	470	25 000 $ - 29 999 $	450
110	365	220	320	365	630	30 000 $ - 34 999 $	451
70	360	240	360	230	490	35 000 $ - 39 999 $	452
85	400	215	260	265	330	40 000 $ - 44 999 $	453
70	230	165	190	185	335	45 000 $ - 49 999 $	454
115	430	330	225	245	325	50 000 $ - 59 999 $	455
70	725	385	260	300	440	60 000 $ et plus	456
27,822	34,962	34,338	28,422	28,107	26,476	Revenu moyen $ (46)	457
24,997	28,358	28,099	25,901	21,947	20,058	Revenu médian $ (46)	458
1,102	1,316	1,563	805	1,041	862	Erreur type de revenu moyen $ (46)	459

Table 1. Selected Characteristics for Census Tracts, 2001 Census – 100% Data and 20% Sample Data

No.	Characteristics	Vancouver 0190.05 A	Vancouver 0191.02 ◇	Vancouver 0191.03 A	Vancouver 0191.04 ◆ A	Vancouver 0192	Vancouver 0200
	2000 INCOME CHARACTERISTICS						
	Population 15 years and over by sex and total income groups in 2000 – concluded						
460	Total - Males	665	2,980	1,730	1,880	1,745	1,845
461	Without income	60	165	60	95	85	110
462	With income	605	2,810	1,670	1,790	1,660	1,735
463	Under $1,000 (45)	15	140	65	30	50	170
464	$ 1,000 - $ 2,999	15	110	65	75	65	40
465	$ 3,000 - $ 4,999	40	100	65	40	50	45
466	$ 5,000 - $ 6,999	60	190	70	85	80	65
467	$ 7,000 - $ 9,999	30	195	100	130	55	110
468	$10,000 - $11,999	25	175	85	85	45	85
469	$12,000 - $14,999	75	170	145	90	165	150
470	$15,000 - $19,999	55	275	140	145	165	185
471	$20,000 - $24,999	65	280	160	200	170	170
472	$25,000 - $29,999	35	215	170	235	150	150
473	$30,000 - $34,999	25	180	140	170	145	95
474	$35,000 - $39,999	45	105	75	185	105	90
475	$40,000 - $44,999	25	185	125	70	70	55
476	$45,000 - $49,999	15	120	50	115	50	75
477	$50,000 - $59,999	45	190	135	70	165	120
478	$60,000 and over	35	180	80	65	120	130
479	Average income $ (46)	25,555	25,668	25,619	26,552	27,356	25,138
480	Median income $ (46)	19,001	20,905	22,954	25,356	23,737	20,236
481	Standard error of average income $ (46)	2,184	867	1,030	1,037	1,114	1,084
482	Total - Females	605	2,930	1,665	1,880	1,430	1,725
483	Without income	105	145	125	90	145	185
484	With income	505	2,785	1,545	1,795	1,280	1,540
485	Under $1,000 (45)	15	170	65	120	65	75
486	$ 1,000 - $ 2,999	40	140	65	55	65	75
487	$ 3,000 - $ 4,999	30	125	95	65	70	50
488	$ 5,000 - $ 6,999	10	125	70	85	100	115
489	$ 7,000 - $ 9,999	40	285	170	245	90	90
490	$10,000 - $11,999	35	165	120	110	30	95
491	$12,000 - $14,999	65	375	115	205	115	160
492	$15,000 - $19,999	65	350	180	190	160	165
493	$20,000 - $24,999	65	190	160	165	125	135
494	$25,000 - $29,999	50	295	180	175	90	170
495	$30,000 - $34,999	35	210	75	85	120	105
496	$35,000 - $39,999	25	110	85	120	25	100
497	$40,000 - $44,999	15	95	60	70	70	90
498	$45,000 - $49,999	-	50	50	60	45	20
499	$50,000 - $59,999	10	65	30	10	70	40
500	$60,000 and over	-	25	25	40	35	50
501	Average income $ (46)	17,916	18,770	19,704	19,655	21,864	21,231
502	Median income $ (46)	16,006	15,080	16,283	15,347	18,329	18,044
503	Standard error of average income $ (46)	1,129	590	826	911	1,054	903
	by composition of total income						
504	Total - Composition of income in 2000 % (47)	100.0	100.0	100.0	100.0	100.0	100.0
505	Employment income %	64.4	75.3	78.9	75.0	80.7	84.5
506	Government transfer payments %	23.2	18.1	15.9	18.6	11.6	11.8
507	Other %	12.5	6.7	5.2	6.4	7.7	3.7
	Population 15 years and over with employment income in 2000 by sex and work activity						
508	Both sexes with employment income (48)	660	3,835	2,340	2,215	2,290	2,490
509	Average employment income $	23,892	24,423	24,655	28,087	25,871	25,838
510	Standard error of average employment income $	1,622	684	800	971	852	835
511	Worked full year, full time (49)	320	1,780	1,140	1,290	1,190	1,340
512	Average employment income $	30,688	34,666	34,526	35,958	34,072	33,875
513	Standard error of average employment income $	1,647	1,006	1,140	1,250	1,143	1,156
514	Worked part year or part time (50)	320	1,915	1,120	880	1,060	1,065
515	Average employment income $	18,112	15,940	15,666	17,095	17,162	17,136
516	Standard error of average employment income $	2,783	722	776	1,024	968	965
517	Males with employment income (48)	370	2,075	1,280	1,235	1,380	1,330
518	Average employment income $	27,619	28,054	27,379	30,410	28,042	28,527
519	Standard error of average employment income $	2,563	1,034	1,128	1,338	1,214	1,257
520	Worked full year, full time (49)	180	1,055	715	765	795	755
521	Average employment income $	34,036	37,973	35,547	36,781	35,309	37,533
522	Standard error of average employment income $	2,310	1,443	1,507	1,756	1,584	1,620
523	Worked part year or part time (50)	175	945	535	460	555	525
524	Average employment income $	22,643	18,127	16,858	20,265	18,415	17,390
525	Standard error of average employment income $	4,883	1,160	1,175	1,475	1,423	1,503

Tableau 1. Certaines caractéristiques des secteurs de recensement, recensement de 2001 – Données intégrales et données-échantillon (20 %)

Vancouver 0201	Vancouver 0202	Vancouver 0203	Vancouver 0204.01 A	Vancouver 0204.02 ◆ A	Vancouver 0205	Caractéristiques	N°
						CARACTÉRISTIQUES DU REVENU DE 2000	
						Population de 15 ans et plus selon le sexe et les tranches de revenu total en 2000 – fin	
670	2,640	1,720	1,855	2,180	3,510	Total - Hommes	460
30	65	40	30	95	125	Sans revenu	461
635	2,570	1,680	1,825	2,090	3,385	Avec un revenu	462
40	145	60	105	135	125	Moins de 1 000 $ (45)	463
10	85	65	110	60	105	1 000 $ - 2 999 $	464
20	70	45	35	35	80	3 000 $ - 4 999 $	465
10	95	30	95	70	125	5 000 $ - 6 999 $	466
10	90	50	40	150	150	7 000 $ - 9 999 $	467
-	60	70	35	65	160	10 000 $ - 11 999 $	468
55	160	55	125	130	305	12 000 $ - 14 999 $	469
50	105	150	135	170	360	15 000 $ - 19 999 $	470
60	155	105	135	170	330	20 000 $ - 24 999 $	471
45	190	90	170	110	265	25 000 $ - 29 999 $	472
55	190	125	135	220	360	30 000 $ - 34 999 $	473
55	195	130	165	140	200	35 000 $ - 39 999 $	474
30	225	135	105	145	190	40 000 $ - 44 999 $	475
50	115	100	85	105	185	45 000 $ - 49 999 $	476
100	210	175	155	145	175	50 000 $ - 59 999 $	477
40	485	290	190	230	275	60 000 $ et plus	478
31,335	39,506	41,513	30,556	32,503	30,134	Revenu moyen $ (46)	479
30,230	33,495	34,638	27,426	28,327	24,056	Revenu médian $ (46)	480
1,600	1,621	2,777	1,314	1,698	1,643	Erreur type de revenu moyen $ (46)	481
690	2,835	1,720	1,965	2,170	3,980	Total - Femmes	482
85	110	125	95	120	165	Sans revenu	483
605	2,730	1,595	1,865	2,050	3,815	Avec un revenu	484
15	90	35	55	110	150	Moins de 1 000 $ (45)	485
30	90	65	40	55	170	1 000 $ - 2 999 $	486
15	65	55	70	80	115	3 000 $ - 4 999 $	487
30	100	85	90	100	145	5 000 $ - 6 999 $	488
45	180	175	80	105	290	7 000 $ - 9 999 $	489
35	90	40	90	160	130	10 000 $ - 11 999 $	490
65	210	110	140	245	580	12 000 $ - 14 999 $	491
50	250	180	225	225	600	15 000 $ - 19 999 $	492
60	285	175	155	260	270	20 000 $ - 24 999 $	493
65	285	75	140	125	200	25 000 $ - 29 999 $	494
50	175	95	185	140	275	30 000 $ - 34 999 $	495
20	165	115	195	90	290	35 000 $ - 39 999 $	496
55	180	80	150	120	140	40 000 $ - 44 999 $	497
20	120	65	110	75	150	45 000 $ - 49 999 $	498
15	220	155	75	100	150	50 000 $ - 59 999 $	499
30	240	100	70	70	165	60 000 $ et plus	500
24,118	30,675	26,777	26,336	23,638	23,229	Revenu moyen $ (46)	501
20,914	25,035	20,332	24,278	17,823	16,943	Revenu médian $ (46)	502
1,452	2,028	1,149	911	1,160	677	Erreur type de revenu moyen $ (46)	503
						selon la composition du revenu total	
100.0	100.0	100.0	100.0	100.0	100.0	Total - Composition du revenu en 2000 % (47)	504
80.7	78.8	81.4	85.4	80.4	68.3	Revenu d'emploi %	505
10.4	8.9	9.2	10.1	13.3	18.0	Transferts gouvernementaux %	506
8.9	12.3	9.3	4.5	6.3	13.7	Autre %	507
						Population de 15 ans et plus ayant un revenu d'emploi en 2000 selon le sexe et le travail	
995	3,940	2,595	2,905	2,870	4,355	Les deux sexes ayant un revenu d'emploi (48)	508
27,982	37,064	35,380	30,899	32,637	29,916	Revenu moyen d'emploi $	509
1,277	1,582	1,852	929	1,418	1,329	Erreur type de revenu moyen d'emploi $	510
545	2,180	1,360	1,680	1,495	2,110	Ayant travaillé toute l'année à plein temps (49)	511
35,636	48,485	51,239	40,237	42,824	39,976	Revenu moyen d'emploi $	512
1,673	2,504	3,054	1,138	2,196	1,337	Erreur type de revenu moyen d'emploi $	513
440	1,665	1,195	1,175	1,325	2,045	Ayant travaillé une partie de l'année ou à temps partiel (50)	514
19,004	22,227	17,800	18,456	21,935	21,561	Revenu moyen d'emploi $	515
1,568	1,225	1,078	1,150	1,530	2,367	Erreur type de revenu moyen d'emploi $	516
530	1,955	1,460	1,440	1,565	2,240	Hommes ayant un revenu d'emploi (48)	517
30,929	41,800	41,317	34,032	37,369	33,964	Revenu moyen d'emploi $	518
1,807	1,843	3,105	1,513	2,132	2,358	Erreur type de revenu moyen d'emploi $	519
310	1,145	810	835	915	1,130	Ayant travaillé toute l'année à plein temps (49)	520
38,003	51,984	59,263	44,234	47,555	43,019	Revenu moyen d'emploi $	521
2,091	2,318	4,951	1,941	3,320	2,060	Erreur type de revenu moyen d'emploi $	522
210	780	620	595	645	1,015	Ayant travaillé une partie de l'année ou à temps partiel (50)	523
21,120	25,284	18,766	20,175	23,226	26,164	Revenu moyen d'emploi $	524
2,616	2,227	1,613	1,712	1,604	4,561	Erreur type de revenu moyen d'emploi $	525

Table 1. Selected Characteristics for Census Tracts, 2001 Census – 100% Data and 20% Sample Data

No.	Characteristics	Vancouver 0190.05 A	Vancouver 0191.02 ◇	Vancouver 0191.03 A	Vancouver 0191.04 ◆ A	Vancouver 0192	Vancouver 0200
	2000 INCOME CHARACTERISTICS						
	Population 15 years and over with employment income in 2000 by sex and work activity – concluded						
526	Females with employment income (48)	285	1,760	1,065	975	915	1,160
527	Average employment income $	19,060	20,145	21,392	25,140	22,584	22,759
528	Standard error of average employment income $	1,511	790	1,088	1,364	1,092	1,031
529	Worked full year, full time (49)	135	725	425	525	395	585
530	Average employment income $	26,233	29,858	32,800	34,769	31,587	29,142
531	Standard error of average employment income $	2,069	1,159	1,701	1,675	1,380	1,513
532	Worked part year or part time (50)	140	975	585	425	500	540
533	Average employment income $	12,545	13,820	14,574	13,641	15,787	16,889
534	Standard error of average employment income $	1,575	838	1,015	1,286	1,297	1,221
	Census families by structure and family income groups in 2000						
535	Total - All census families	445	1,940	1,240	1,050	1,010	1,245
536	Under $10,000	45	140	55	60	50	85
537	$ 10,000 - $19,999	90	260	140	110	75	160
538	$ 20,000 - $29,999	55	300	195	70	90	150
539	$ 30,000 - $39,999	60	310	130	170	140	160
540	$ 40,000 - $49,999	35	175	190	185	190	140
541	$ 50,000 - $59,999	40	190	115	150	90	130
542	$ 60,000 - $69,999	35	175	115	90	135	135
543	$ 70,000 - $79,999	50	95	125	110	70	100
544	$ 80,000 - $89,999	15	100	60	20	70	35
545	$ 90,000 - $99,999	10	80	35	35	30	40
546	$100,000 and over	10	115	80	55	60	115
547	Average family income $	40,933	46,033	49,415	50,637	52,989	50,213
548	Median family income $	34,401	38,800	43,998	48,125	46,054	46,702
549	Standard error of average family income $	2,998	1,525	1,781	2,521	2,207	1,967
550	Total - All couple census families (51)	330	1,425	910	865	835	1,035
551	Under $10,000	35	55	30	30	35	80
552	$ 10,000 - $19,999	30	125	50	65	35	105
553	$ 20,000 - $29,999	40	175	120	60	55	100
554	$ 30,000 - $39,999	50	240	100	150	125	110
555	$ 40,000 - $49,999	40	125	140	140	160	125
556	$ 50,000 - $59,999	30	170	95	140	70	115
557	$ 60,000 - $69,999	30	165	110	90	130	105
558	$ 70,000 - $79,999	45	90	110	100	70	100
559	$ 80,000 - $89,999	15	90	60	20	75	40
560	$ 90,000 - $99,999	10	80	35	25	30	40
561	$100,000 and over	10	115	60	35	55	115
562	Average family income $	47,791	53,108	54,328	52,261	57,303	53,242
563	Median family income $	44,857	48,009	51,111	49,251	50,734	49,479
564	Standard error of average family income $	3,539	1,853	1,977	2,746	2,497	2,213
	Incidence of low income in 2000						
565	Total - Economic families	440	1,905	1,090	1,030	970	1,125
566	Low income	185	555	260	215	200	220
567	Incidence of low income in 2000 % (52)	41.2	29.2	24.3	20.9	20.5	19.6
568	Total - Unattached individuals 15 years and over	190	1,490	445	1,160	670	410
569	Low income	120	900	195	640	270	175
570	Incidence of low income in 2000 % (52)	61.6	60.7	44.7	54.8	40.2	43.2
571	Total - Population in private households	1,680	7,210	4,445	4,415	4,055	4,530
572	Low income	755	2,585	1,105	1,295	980	930
573	Incidence of low income in 2000 % (52)	44.8	35.8	24.8	29.3	24.2	20.5
	Private households by household income groups in 2000						
574	Total - All private households	560	3,040	1,360	2,130	1,465	1,445
575	Under $10,000	35	375	80	325	135	85
576	$ 10,000 - $19,999	125	580	140	425	150	185
577	$ 20,000 - $29,999	70	410	185	310	140	145
578	$ 30,000 - $39,999	80	410	140	250	185	180
579	$ 40,000 - $49,999	45	290	175	225	225	155
580	$ 50,000 - $59,999	50	275	135	155	120	140
581	$ 60,000 - $69,999	45	195	130	105	170	180
582	$ 70,000 - $79,999	50	120	85	130	120	110
583	$ 80,000 - $89,999	15	115	85	40	65	65
584	$ 90,000 - $99,999	20	115	55	30	30	50
585	$100,000 and over	25	160	135	125	125	150
586	Average household income $	43,323	40,693	53,848	38,679	49,820	52,432
587	Median household income $	34,829	32,573	46,185	30,722	45,002	48,207
588	Standard error of average household income $	2,806	1,196	2,193	1,739	1,950	1,954

Tableau 1. Certaines caractéristiques des secteurs de recensement, recensement de 2001 – Données intégrales et données-échantillon (20 %)

Vancouver 0201	Vancouver 0202	Vancouver 0203	Vancouver 0204.01 A	Vancouver 0204.02 ◆ A	Vancouver 0205	Caractéristiques	N°
						CARACTÉRISTIQUES DU REVENU DE 2000	
						Population de 15 ans et plus ayant un revenu d'emploi en 2000 selon le sexe et le travail – fin	
465	1,980	1,135	1,455	1,305	2,115	Femmes ayant un revenu d'emploi (48)	526
24,635	32,380	27,727	27,799	26,956	25,625	Revenu moyen d'emploi $	527
1,743	2,533	1,327	1,026	1,721	1,029	Erreur type de revenu moyen d'emploi $	528
235	1,040	550	840	585	985	Ayant travaillé toute l'année à plein temps (49)	529
32,469	44,635	39,468	36,267	35,402	36,481	Revenu moyen d'emploi $	530
2,654	4,576	1,771	1,010	2,130	1,572	Erreur type de revenu moyen d'emploi $	531
225	880	575	580	685	1,035	Ayant travaillé une partie de l'année ou à temps partiel (50)	532
17,030	19,513	16,751	16,680	20,721	17,019	Revenu moyen d'emploi $	533
1,737	1,221	1,406	1,513	2,586	1,097	Erreur type de revenu moyen d'emploi $	534
						Familles de recensement selon la structure et les tranches de revenu de la famille en 2000	
480	1,735	1,210	1,090	1,185	1,825	Total - Toutes les familles de recensement	535
-	45	20	45	85	170	Moins de 10 000 $	536
55	100	95	85	125	210	10 000 $ - 19 999 $	537
40	180	125	155	175	230	20 000 $ - 29 999 $	538
45	140	80	150	95	290	30 000 $ - 39 999 $	539
70	190	80	170	145	215	40 000 $ - 49 999 $	540
45	205	110	100	120	125	50 000 $ - 59 999 $	541
55	185	95	55	105	170	60 000 $ - 69 999 $	542
40	140	125	90	80	135	70 000 $ - 79 999 $	543
45	85	155	105	60	70	80 000 $ - 89 999 $	544
20	100	55	20	65	55	90 000 $ - 99 999 $	545
60	355	270	120	130	165	100 000 $ et plus	546
60,884	73,931	75,843	54,452	57,675	52,743	Revenu moyen des familles $	547
54,754	60,976	70,003	44,977	48,126	41,102	Revenu médian des familles $	548
3,421	3,920	4,109	2,377	3,739	3,224	Erreur type de revenu moyen des familles $	549
410	1,400	985	860	955	1,550	Total - Toutes les familles de recensement comptant un couple (51)	550
-	35	10	45	45	130	Moins de 10 000 $	551
25	65	55	60	70	135	10 000 $ - 19 999 $	552
40	100	85	110	120	215	20 000 $ - 29 999 $	553
35	105	50	125	70	240	30 000 $ - 39 999 $	554
60	160	60	110	120	170	40 000 $ - 49 999 $	555
30	155	95	75	115	120	50 000 $ - 59 999 $	556
50	145	90	30	85	135	60 000 $ - 69 999 $	557
45	130	95	70	80	130	70 000 $ - 79 999 $	558
40	80	135	95	60	70	80 000 $ - 89 999 $	559
15	100	55	15	65	50	90 000 $ - 99 999 $	560
60	330	270	125	130	160	100 000 $ et plus	561
65,438	79,601	83,399	57,462	65,075	56,020	Revenu moyen des familles $	562
63,050	66,746	74,697	47,877	55,543	42,397	Revenu médian des familles $	563
3,666	4,555	4,662	2,801	4,594	3,754	Erreur type de revenu moyen des familles $	564
						Fréquence des unités à faible revenu en 2000	
450	1,760	1,160	1,115	1,185	1,875	Total - Familles économiques	565
60	220	160	200	290	485	Faible revenu	566
13.9	12.8	13.8	17.9	24.6	25.7	Fréquence des unités à faible revenu en 2000 % (52)	567
205	1,725	535	1,460	1,710	3,425	Total - Personnes hors famille économique de 15 ans et plus	568
105	535	180	550	720	1,555	Faible revenu	569
49.1	31.0	33.4	37.6	42.2	45.4	Fréquence des unités à faible revenu en 2000 % (52)	570
1,690	6,040	4,310	4,300	5,075	8,235	Total - Population dans les ménages privés	571
260	1,140	735	1,070	1,500	2,815	Faible revenu	572
15.6	18.9	17.0	24.8	29.5	34.2	Fréquence des unités à faible revenu en 2000 % (52)	573
						Ménages privés selon les tranches de revenu du ménage en 2000	
600	3,210	1,570	2,385	2,645	4,975	Total - Tous les ménages privés	574
20	260	45	235	240	540	Moins de 10 000 $	575
90	295	170	340	515	1,175	10 000 $ - 19 999 $	576
60	415	160	285	380	685	20 000 $ - 29 999 $	577
50	350	140	385	395	865	30 000 $ - 39 999 $	578
65	380	125	305	285	570	40 000 $ - 49 999 $	579
60	350	120	220	225	265	50 000 $ - 59 999 $	580
75	290	95	170	155	300	60 000 $ - 69 999 $	581
55	225	115	125	135	195	70 000 $ - 79 999 $	582
40	130	190	150	80	80	80 000 $ - 89 999 $	583
15	120	65	30	70	50	90 000 $ - 99 999 $	584
75	400	335	135	155	235	100 000 $ et plus	585
57,079	57,725	71,653	43,998	43,997	38,297	Revenu moyen des ménages $	586
51,677	46,696	60,651	38,161	34,244	30,657	Revenu médian des ménages $	587
3,197	2,397	3,566	1,401	1,939	1,378	Erreur type de revenu moyen des ménages $	588

Table 1. Selected Characteristics for Census Tracts, 2001 Census – 100% Data and 20% Sample Data

No.	Characteristics	Vancouver 0206 ◆◇◇	Vancouver 0207	Vancouver 0208	Vancouver 0209	Vancouver 0210	Vancouver 0220
	POPULATION CHARACTERISTICS						
1	**Population, 1996 (1)**	**1,587**	**2,111**	**5,015**	**6,505**	**4,265**	**1,023**
2	**Population, 2001 (2)**	**1,793**	**2,145**	**5,193**	**6,610**	**4,603**	**1,016**
3	Population percentage change, 1996-2001	13.0	1.6	3.5	1.6	7.9	-0.7
4	Land area in square kilometres, 2001	0.31	0.34	1.68	2.01	2.34	9.12
5	**Total population – 100% Data (3)**	**1,795**	**2,140**	**5,190**	**6,610**	**4,605**	**1,015**
	by sex and age groups						
6	Male	975	1,115	2,445	3,060	2,240	505
7	0-4 years	25	35	150	155	150	25
8	5-9 years	5	20	155	180	130	25
9	10-14 years	15	20	165	175	100	30
10	15-19 years	25	40	145	170	90	35
11	20-24 years	90	110	140	170	150	40
12	25-29 years	135	125	125	145	135	35
13	30-34 years	130	140	170	180	220	35
14	35-39 years	120	135	215	225	265	55
15	40-44 years	110	130	240	265	230	55
16	45-49 years	95	105	240	275	215	45
17	50-54 years	90	90	190	235	180	40
18	55-59 years	45	45	115	220	110	25
19	60-64 years	35	30	100	160	65	15
20	65-69 years	20	40	85	135	50	15
21	70-74 years	20	35	85	120	60	15
22	75-79 years	15	20	60	105	40	5
23	80-84 years	5	10	30	95	30	5
24	85 years and over	5	5	40	55	20	-
25	Female	820	1,030	2,745	3,545	2,365	510
26	0-4 years	30	30	140	165	140	20
27	5-9 years	10	20	140	170	145	20
28	10-14 years	10	20	175	155	120	45
29	15-19 years	25	40	155	160	115	45
30	20-24 years	95	125	155	170	125	25
31	25-29 years	125	140	145	150	165	50
32	30-34 years	105	110	200	215	200	35
33	35-39 years	85	105	230	270	245	40
34	40-44 years	60	85	225	305	220	50
35	45-49 years	70	75	235	275	175	45
36	50-54 years	75	80	180	305	160	45
37	55-59 years	40	60	130	220	110	20
38	60-64 years	40	40	70	195	75	20
39	65-69 years	10	30	85	150	70	20
40	70-74 years	20	25	100	175	80	10
41	75-79 years	10	20	125	145	80	5
42	80-84 years	5	20	100	140	55	5
43	85 years and over	5	10	145	195	85	5
44	**Total population 15 years and over**	**1,700**	**2,005**	**4,265**	**5,610**	**3,825**	**845**
	by legal marital status						
45	Never married (single)	845	950	1,330	1,525	1,355	340
46	Legally married (and not separated)	495	560	1,965	2,800	1,600	385
47	Separated, but still legally married	90	115	135	190	170	30
48	Divorced	230	300	460	515	415	45
49	Widowed	45	75	380	575	280	45
	by common-law status						
50	Not in a common-law relationship	1,505	1,750	3,950	5,260	3,455	780
51	In a common-law relationship	195	250	315	350	365	65
52	**Total population – 20% Sample Data (4)**	**1,755**	**2,130**	**5,100**	**6,155**	**4,455**	**980**
	by mother tongue						
53	Single responses	1,750	2,095	5,070	5,980	4,360	970
54	English	1,205	1,610	4,225	4,865	3,530	650
55	French	50	70	50	35	20	-
56	Non-official languages (5)	495	415	795	1,070	810	320
57	Chinese, n.o.s.	175	10	75	45	35	55
58	Cantonese	15	65	15	25	45	50
59	Punjabi	-	10	120	55	35	10
60	Mandarin	-	10	65	-	15	10
61	Tagalog (Pilipino)	85	15	85	90	160	25
62	Other languages (6)	215	315	430	850	525	180
63	Multiple responses	-	30	35	175	95	10
64	English and French	-	-	10	-	10	-
65	English and non-official language	10	25	35	170	80	10
66	French and non-official language	-	-	-	10	-	-
67	English, French and non-official language	-	-	-	-	-	-

See reference material at the end of the publication. – Voir les documents de référence à la fin de la publication.

Tableau 1. Certaines caractéristiques des secteurs de recensement, recensement de 2001 – Données intégrales et données-échantillon (20 %)

Vancouver 0221.01	Vancouver 0221.03 A	Vancouver 0221.04 A	Vancouver 0222	Vancouver 0223.01 A	Vancouver 0223.02 ◇ A	Caractéristiques	N°
						CARACTÉRISTIQUES DE LA POPULATION	
1,648	**3,099**	**4,482**	**7,389**	**4,551**	**3,936**	**Population, 1996 (1)**	1
1,656	**3,003**	**4,992**	**8,689**	**5,201**	**4,580**	**Population, 2001 (2)**	2
0.5	-3.1	11.4	17.6	14.3	16.4	Variation en pourcentage de la population, 1996-2001	3
1.21	1.28	1.31	2.91	1.43	0.76	Superficie des terres en kilomètres carrés, 2001	4
1,655	**3,000**	**4,985**	**8,685**	**5,205**	**4,580**	**Population totale – Données intégrales (3)**	5
						selon le sexe et les groupes d'âge	
850	1,495	2,450	4,125	2,515	2,305	Sexe masculin	6
40	80	105	215	195	165	0-4 ans	7
55	80	140	225	225	175	5-9 ans	8
85	85	150	250	185	160	10-14 ans	9
65	105	185	300	190	170	15-19 ans	10
45	105	250	255	190	210	20-24 ans	11
30	75	190	260	185	190	25-29 ans	12
50	60	175	345	255	225	30-34 ans	13
60	135	170	390	250	210	35-39 ans	14
85	125	185	390	235	210	40-44 ans	15
75	115	180	370	175	155	45-49 ans	16
65	140	170	355	125	135	50-54 ans	17
50	100	145	205	85	75	55-59 ans	18
30	70	95	140	75	75	60-64 ans	19
30	60	80	135	60	50	65-69 ans	20
25	65	75	130	45	45	70-74 ans	21
20	45	65	85	25	20	75-79 ans	22
15	30	50	40	10	10	80-84 ans	23
15	25	35	25	5	5	85 ans et plus	24
805	1,505	2,535	4,565	2,690	2,275	Sexe féminin	25
35	65	115	190	165	185	0-4 ans	26
35	95	110	230	210	170	5-9 ans	27
60	105	130	250	190	155	10-14 ans	28
45	95	175	320	175	155	15-19 ans	29
55	110	205	325	180	190	20-24 ans	30
35	80	165	290	230	185	25-29 ans	31
55	95	155	385	300	230	30-34 ans	32
55	95	165	420	285	205	35-39 ans	33
75	125	190	445	240	205	40-44 ans	34
85	145	225	430	200	150	45-49 ans	35
55	110	185	345	140	125	50-54 ans	36
50	100	120	220	105	100	55-59 ans	37
30	65	85	175	80	60	60-64 ans	38
25	65	90	155	55	50	65-69 ans	39
40	70	90	160	45	50	70-74 ans	40
40	55	95	115	45	35	75-79 ans	41
25	35	85	75	25	15	80-84 ans	42
10	15	160	40	20	15	85 ans et plus	43
1,340	**2,505**	**4,235**	**7,325**	**4,030**	**3,565**	**Population totale de 15 ans et plus**	44
						selon l'état matrimonial légal	
385	730	1,500	2,410	1,465	1,405	Célibataire (jamais marié(e))	45
785	1,505	2,115	3,880	1,985	1,625	Légalement marié(e) (et non séparé(e))	46
25	45	80	165	160	165	Séparé(e), mais toujours légalement marié(e)	47
75	110	180	520	265	240	Divorcé(e)	48
75	120	360	350	155	135	Veuf ou veuve	49
						selon l'union libre	
1,280	2,410	4,090	6,930	3,790	3,305	Ne vivant pas en union libre	50
55	95	145	390	240	260	Vivant en union libre	51
1,660	**2,990**	**4,695**	**8,660**	**5,185**	**4,575**	**Population totale – Données-échantillon (20 %) (4)**	52
						selon la langue maternelle	
1,640	2,955	4,540	8,530	4,995	4,400	Réponses uniques	53
1,135	1,595	1,820	4,150	2,015	1,830	Anglais	54
20	25	40	110	50	30	Français	55
485	1,335	2,685	4,275	2,935	2,545	Langues non officielles (5)	56
55	285	665	755	560	365	Chinois, n.d.a.	57
85	230	180	620	235	140	Cantonais	58
75	150	380	335	435	235	Pendjabi	59
25	75	415	630	50	145	Mandarin	60
20	15	65	120	275	130	Tagalog (pilipino)	61
225	575	975	1,810	1,380	1,530	Autres langues (6)	62
15	35	155	130	185	175	Réponses multiples	63
10	-	-	20	-	35	Anglais et français	64
10	20	150	95	185	140	Anglais et langue non officielle	65
-	15	10	10	-	-	Français et langue non officielle	66
-	-	-	10	-	-	Anglais, français et langue non officielle	67

See reference material at the end of the publication. – Voir les documents de référence à la fin de la publication.

Table 1. Selected Characteristics for Census Tracts, 2001 Census – 100% Data and 20% Sample Data

No.	Characteristics	Vancouver 0206 ◆◇◇	Vancouver 0207	Vancouver 0208	Vancouver 0209	Vancouver 0210	Vancouver 0220
	POPULATION CHARACTERISTICS						
	by home language						
68	Single responses	1,500	1,830	4,635	5,350	3,980	880
69	English	1,310	1,715	4,500	5,115	3,860	730
70	French	-	-	-	-	10	-
71	Non-official languages (5)	190	110	135	235	120	145
72	Cantonese	10	35	-	-	20	40
73	Chinese, n.o.s.	145	-	-	-	-	55
74	Punjabi	-	-	30	15	-	-
75	Mandarin	-	-	10	-	10	-
76	Korean	-	45	-	40	-	20
77	Other languages (6)	40	15	90	180	75	15
78	Multiple responses	255	305	465	805	475	105
79	English and French	25	35	30	45	20	-
80	English and non-official language	220	250	435	735	430	105
81	French and non-official language	-	-	-	-	-	-
82	English, French and non-official language	10	20	-	25	20	-
	by knowledge of official languages						
83	English only	1,525	1,910	4,670	5,735	4,150	895
84	French only	-	-	-	-	10	-
85	English and French	170	195	400	400	260	15
86	Neither English nor French	60	25	30	20	45	75
	by knowledge of non-official languages (5) (7)						
87	Cantonese	15	75	20	40	60	65
88	Chinese, n.o.s.	160	10	60	75	30	85
89	Punjabi	10	10	120	105	30	10
90	Mandarin	15	45	80	-	30	30
91	Hindi	10	35	80	60	10	30
92	German	40	50	175	145	60	10
93	Spanish	80	70	115	60	30	20
	by first official language spoken						
94	English	1,635	2,015	5,010	6,065	4,380	905
95	French	50	75	50	45	20	-
96	English and French	15	10	15	35	10	-
97	Neither English nor French	55	25	30	15	45	75
98	Official language minority - (number) (8)	60	80	55	65	25	-
99	Official language minority - (percentage) (8)	3.4	3.8	1.1	1.1	0.6	-
	by ethnic origin (9)						
100	English	400	570	2,015	1,775	1,525	165
101	Canadian	350	515	1,300	1,535	1,140	145
102	Chinese	210	110	210	285	190	225
103	Scottish	285	390	1,200	1,435	915	205
104	Irish	280	365	980	985	690	165
105	German	235	230	635	775	435	55
106	East Indian	20	75	200	170	90	25
107	French	190	200	455	530	405	80
108	Ukrainian	85	95	265	290	195	95
109	Italian	30	55	240	215	185	55
110	Dutch (Netherlands)	135	100	145	320	180	65
111	Filipino	130	75	100	220	375	25
112	Polish	65	55	170	235	145	10
113	Norwegian	25	50	180	325	120	-
114	North American Indian	50	155	155	105	100	60
	by Aboriginal identity						
115	Total Aboriginal identity population (10)	55	170	190	125	130	55
116	Total non-Aboriginal population	1,700	1,955	4,915	6,030	4,325	930
	by Aboriginal origin						
117	Total Aboriginal origins population (11)	60	195	250	175	145	80
118	Total non-Aboriginal population	1,695	1,935	4,850	5,985	4,315	900
	by Registered Indian status						
119	Registered Indian (12)	20	55	35	10	55	25
120	Not a Registered Indian	1,735	2,070	5,065	6,140	4,400	955

Tableau 1. Certaines caractéristiques des secteurs de recensement, recensement de 2001 – Données intégrales et données-échantillon (20 %)

Vancouver 0221.01	Vancouver 0221.03 A	Vancouver 0221.04 A	Vancouver 0222	Vancouver 0223.01 A	Vancouver 0223.02 ◇ A	Caractéristiques	N°
						CARACTÉRISTIQUES DE LA POPULATION	
						selon la langue parlée à la maison	
1,365	2,305	3,365	6,460	3,240	2,945	Réponses uniques	68
1,250	1,865	1,985	4,560	1,980	2,025	Anglais	69
-	-	-	35	35	10	Français	70
110	440	1,385	1,870	1,220	915	Langues non officielles (5)	71
60	110	155	415	145	75	Cantonais	72
25	85	300	380	210	110	Chinois, n.d.a.	73
-	25	120	100	240	50	Pendjabi	74
-	70	325	380	40	110	Mandarin	75
-	25	135	180	80	-	Coréen	76
25	120	350	410	505	575	Autres langues (6)	77
290	680	1,325	2,195	1,945	1,635	Réponses multiples	78
20	25	20	40	65	20	Anglais et français	79
255	640	1,300	2,135	1,885	1,550	Anglais et langue non officielle	80
20	-	-	-	-	45	Français et langue non officielle	81
-	15	10	20	-	25	Anglais, français et langue non officielle	82
						selon la connaissance des langues officielles	
1,540	2,735	4,080	7,745	4,515	4,070	Anglais seulement	83
-	-	-	10	25	15	Français seulement	84
110	140	195	420	345	250	Anglais et français	85
10	120	425	485	290	245	Ni l'anglais ni le français	86
						selon la connaissance des langues non officielles (5) (7)	
120	270	325	895	340	205	Cantonais	87
45	240	480	680	575	305	Chinois, n.d.a.	88
90	145	435	405	505	295	Pendjabi	89
65	305	740	1,065	145	220	Mandarin	90
15	80	150	215	300	360	Hindi	91
55	110	70	245	100	45	Allemand	92
15	45	90	245	260	260	Espagnol	93
						selon la première langue officielle parlée	
1,630	2,840	4,255	8,000	4,760	4,230	Anglais	94
15	25	30	110	65	30	Français	95
-	-	30	75	65	75	Anglais et français	96
10	120	380	475	295	235	Ni l'anglais ni le français	97
20	30	45	150	100	70	Minorité de langue officielle - (nombre) (8)	98
1.2	1.0	1.0	1.7	1.9	1.5	Minorité de langue officielle - (pourcentage) (8)	99
						selon l'origine ethnique (9)	
335	650	585	1,750	535	470	Anglais	100
295	410	485	1,150	520	680	Canadien	101
255	705	1,320	2,510	1,165	735	Chinois	102
280	365	420	1,125	250	410	Écossais	103
140	305	410	690	320	275	Irlandais	104
195	290	240	680	210	175	Allemand	105
160	260	620	655	700	550	Indien de l'Inde	106
85	180	165	480	215	195	Français	107
60	80	165	180	55	150	Ukrainien	108
90	125	150	175	145	95	Italien	109
50	145	70	225	90	95	Hollandais (Néerlandais)	110
30	55	105	295	450	235	Philippin	111
40	15	85	230	215	85	Polonais	112
55	15	70	60	65	40	Norvégien	113
-	10	70	55	220	210	Indien de l'Amérique du Nord	114
						selon l'identité autochtone	
-	20	90	40	185	185	Total de la population ayant une identité autochtone (10)	115
1,660	2,970	4,605	8,615	5,000	4,395	Total de la population non autochtone	116
						selon l'origine autochtone	
-	25	110	80	240	230	Total de la population ayant une origine autochtone (11)	117
1,655	2,960	4,585	8,580	4,945	4,350	Total de la population non autochtone	118
						selon le statut d'Indien inscrit	
-	-	10	10	145	155	Oui, Indien inscrit (12)	119
1,655	2,990	4,685	8,645	5,040	4,425	Non, pas un Indien inscrit	120

Table 1. Selected Characteristics for Census Tracts, 2001 Census – 100% Data and 20% Sample Data

No.	Characteristics	Vancouver 0206 ◆◇◇	Vancouver 0207	Vancouver 0208	Vancouver 0209	Vancouver 0210	Vancouver 0220
	POPULATION CHARACTERISTICS						
	by visible minority groups						
121	Total visible minority population	455	450	670	1,120	870	365
122	Chinese	195	100	225	290	145	205
123	South Asian	30	80	240	225	95	35
124	Black	10	90	10	130	85	-
125	Filipino	130	60	90	210	380	15
126	Latin American	15	15	25	-	15	-
127	Southeast Asian	10	-	-	-	25	55
128	Arab	-	10	10	-	-	-
129	West Asian	-	-	25	15	25	-
130	Korean	10	75	15	90	75	25
131	Japanese	30	-	25	90	15	35
132	Visible minority, n.i.e. (13)	10	10	-	70	-	-
133	Multiple visible minorities (14)	10	-	15	-	10	-
	by citizenship						
134	Canadian citizenship (15)	1,540	1,870	4,840	5,905	4,155	895
135	Citizenship other than Canadian	215	255	260	245	300	90
	by place of birth of respondent						
136	Non-immigrant population	1,130	1,490	4,080	4,850	3,365	645
137	Born in province of residence	710	790	2,765	3,325	2,310	460
138	Immigrant population (16)	565	575	965	1,265	1,025	320
139	United States	15	25	60	55	15	-
140	Central and South America	25	20	30	15	15	35
141	Caribbean and Bermuda	20	20	10	40	20	-
142	United Kingdom	95	85	205	160	155	20
143	Other Europe (17)	95	140	250	515	260	70
144	Africa	40	45	25	100	40	-
145	Asia and the Middle East	265	230	320	350	485	160
146	Oceania and other (18)	-	10	65	35	35	25
147	Non-permanent residents (19)	55	60	55	40	75	20
148	**Total immigrant population**	**565**	**580**	**965**	**1,270**	**1,025**	**320**
	by period of immigration						
149	Before 1961	30	75	260	245	205	60
150	1961-1970	50	90	110	220	125	25
151	1971-1980	120	60	195	210	245	40
152	1981-1990	120	135	160	260	150	50
153	1991-2001 (20)	245	220	245	335	290	145
154	1991-1995	155	65	120	165	100	140
155	1996-2001 (20)	85	150	125	175	190	10
	by age at immigration						
156	0-4 years	25	45	90	115	110	25
157	5-19 years	115	160	270	275	305	90
158	20 years and over	420	365	600	885	605	200
159	**Total population**	**1,755**	**2,125**	**5,105**	**6,155**	**4,455**	**980**
	by religion						
160	Catholic (21)	340	360	900	1,450	1,070	35
161	Protestant	405	635	1,860	2,285	1,330	240
162	Christian Orthodox	25	10	25	125	30	-
163	Christian, n.i.e. (22)	145	135	295	295	345	75
164	Muslim	20	20	55	125	40	-
165	Jewish	10	40	30	10	-	-
166	Buddhist	20	20	20	25	35	25
167	Hindu	10	30	75	30	10	20
168	Sikh	-	-	85	95	35	-
169	Eastern religions (23)	-	10	10	-	10	-
170	Other religions (24)	10	30	40	10	25	-
171	No religious affiliation (25)	780	845	1,710	1,720	1,530	595
172	**Total population 15 years and over**	**1,655**	**1,975**	**4,170**	**5,145**	**3,670**	**775**
	by generation status						
173	1st generation (26)	610	605	1,005	1,260	1,055	335
174	2nd generation (27)	320	335	1,255	1,530	735	150
175	3rd generation and over (28)	725	1,035	1,905	2,350	1,880	295
176	**Total population 1 year and over (29)**	**1,740**	**2,115**	**5,050**	**6,115**	**4,405**	**970**
	by place of residence 1 year ago (mobility)						
177	Non-movers	1,155	1,475	4,230	5,380	3,675	825
178	Movers	580	640	820	730	730	145
179	Non-migrants	220	265	380	365	255	25
180	Migrants	360	370	435	360	475	115
181	Internal migrants	315	295	320	300	400	120
182	Intraprovincial migrants	300	250	280	285	355	100
183	Interprovincial migrants	15	45	40	20	50	20
184	External migrants	50	75	115	65	75	-

Tableau 1. Certaines caractéristiques des secteurs de recensement, recensement de 2001 – Données intégrales et données-échantillon (20 %)

Vancouver 0221.01	Vancouver 0221.03 A	Vancouver 0221.04 A	Vancouver 0222	Vancouver 0223.01 A	Vancouver 0223.02 ◇ A	Caractéristiques	N°
						CARACTÉRISTIQUES DE LA POPULATION	
						selon les groupes de minorités visibles	
595	1,315	2,805	4,305	2,995	2,445	Total de la population des minorités visibles	121
255	785	1,445	2,440	995	710	Chinois	122
160	280	670	695	825	665	Sud-Asiatique	123
-	-	30	105	110	130	Noir	124
30	50	95	255	420	220	Philippin	125
-	25	55	130	240	205	Latino-Américain	126
15	-	75	95	65	120	Asiatique du Sud-Est	127
-	10	15	30	35	-	Arabe	128
25	-	25	100	115	250	Asiatique occidental	129
25	45	210	215	95	115	Coréen	130
80	110	95	130	25	-	Japonais	131
20	-	10	20	-	10	Minorité visible, n.i.a. (13)	132
-	10	80	90	60	20	Minorités visibles multiples (14)	133
						selon la citoyenneté	
1,540	2,770	3,675	7,245	4,160	3,565	Citoyenneté canadienne (15)	134
115	215	1,020	1,415	1,025	1,010	Citoyenneté autre que canadienne	135
						selon le lieu de naissance du répondant	
1,200	1,760	2,070	4,205	2,315	2,020	Population non immigrante	136
930	1,390	1,540	3,115	1,715	1,415	Née dans la province de résidence	137
435	1,210	2,495	4,320	2,820	2,450	Population immigrante (16)	138
30	15	15	120	40	25	États-Unis	139
10	15	45	130	160	145	Amérique centrale et du Sud	140
-	-	15	25	15	15	Caraïbes et Bermudes	141
75	85	70	185	90	40	Royaume-Uni	142
90	190	235	705	555	485	Autre Europe (17)	143
-	55	80	85	60	160	Afrique	144
230	825	1,995	2,945	1,845	1,510	Asie et Moyen-Orient	145
10	25	35	135	50	70	Océanie et autre (18)	146
15	20	130	135	45	110	Résidents non permanents (19)	147
435	**1,210**	**2,500**	**4,320**	**2,820**	**2,445**	**Population immigrante totale**	148
						selon la période d'immigration	
80	145	125	280	125	115	Avant 1961	149
60	255	260	415	160	50	1961-1970	150
125	135	360	520	300	260	1971-1980	151
110	185	320	605	530	465	1981-1990	152
65	485	1,430	2,500	1,700	1,555	1991-2001 (20)	153
25	320	440	1,120	865	575	1991-1995	154
40	165	990	1,380	840	980	1996-2001 (20)	155
						selon l'âge à l'immigration	
30	70	165	330	255	205	0-4 ans	156
120	405	720	1,295	650	730	5-19 ans	157
290	735	1,610	2,695	1,920	1,510	20 ans et plus	158
1,655	**2,990**	**4,695**	**8,660**	**5,185**	**4,580**	**Population totale**	159
						selon la religion	
215	465	735	1,475	1,320	780	Catholique (21)	160
530	825	910	1,710	705	710	Protestante	161
40	20	55	220	200	225	Orthodoxe chrétienne	162
90	150	235	670	330	255	Chrétiennes, n.i.a. (22)	163
-	15	75	315	275	570	Musulmane	164
10	-	10	15	10	10	Juive	165
60	120	390	365	190	355	Bouddhiste	166
10	70	160	150	135	130	Hindoue	167
145	170	500	360	500	305	Sikh	168
25	-	30	-	30	-	Religions orientales (23)	169
-	10	-	-	20	35	Autres religions (24)	170
535	1,140	1,575	3,380	1,485	1,205	Aucune appartenance religieuse (25)	171
1,370	**2,480**	**3,930**	**7,300**	**4,030**	**3,555**	**Population totale de 15 ans et plus**	172
						selon le statut des générations	
425	1,180	2,340	4,085	2,655	2,225	1re génération (26)	173
510	700	810	1,675	590	635	2e génération (27)	174
435	605	785	1,540	780	690	3e génération et plus (28)	175
1,650	**2,950**	**4,675**	**8,590**	**5,155**	**4,500**	**Population totale de 1 an et plus (29)**	176
						selon le lieu de résidence 1 an auparavant (mobilité)	
1,520	2,755	3,825	7,465	4,460	3,510	Personnes n'ayant pas déménagé	177
130	190	850	1,125	695	990	Personnes ayant déménagé	178
30	75	425	635	265	410	Non-migrants	179
100	110	425	490	430	580	Migrants	180
70	90	285	320	305	380	Migrants internes	181
70	65	230	290	285	305	Migrants infraprovinciaux	182
-	25	50	30	25	75	Migrants interprovinciaux	183
30	25	140	165	125	200	Migrants externes	184

Table 1. Selected Characteristics for Census Tracts, 2001 Census – 100% Data and 20% Sample Data

No.	Characteristics	Vancouver 0206 ◆◇◇	Vancouver 0207	Vancouver 0208	Vancouver 0209	Vancouver 0210	Vancouver 0220
	POPULATION CHARACTERISTICS						
185	**Total population 5 years and over (30)**	**1,710**	**2,045**	**4,800**	**5,820**	**4,175**	**920**
	by place of residence 5 years ago (mobility)						
186	Non-movers	485	745	2,520	3,545	2,370	600
187	Movers	1,220	1,305	2,280	2,275	1,800	320
188	Non-migrants	380	395	1,200	895	675	115
189	Migrants	840	905	1,080	1,375	1,125	205
190	Internal migrants	705	725	920	1,210	920	180
191	Intraprovincial migrants	620	600	790	1,015	820	130
192	Interprovincial migrants	80	125	130	195	100	45
193	External migrants	135	180	160	170	210	30
194	**Total population 15 to 24 years**	**205**	**325**	**595**	**660**	**480**	**130**
	by school attendance						
195	Not attending school	95	145	240	205	195	55
196	Attending school full time	75	125	290	370	255	65
197	Attending school part time	30	60	65	85	30	15
198	**Total population 15 years and over**	**1,655**	**1,975**	**4,170**	**5,145**	**3,670**	**775**
	by highest level of schooling						
199	Less than grade 9 (31)	65	100	190	160	165	75
200	Grades 9-13 without high school graduation certificate	275	430	795	1,000	775	150
201	Grades 9-13 with high school graduation certificate	110	215	440	710	465	115
202	Some postsecondary without degree, certificate or diploma (32)	300	280	595	670	485	105
203	Trades certificate or diploma (33)	250	230	395	605	475	65
204	College certificate or diploma (34)	330	375	765	925	700	145
205	University certificate below bachelor's degree	30	75	70	150	105	25
206	University with bachelor's degree or higher	295	275	920	930	505	105
	by combinations of unpaid work						
207	Males 15 years and over	880	1,005	1,955	2,380	1,820	400
208	Reported unpaid work (35)	790	955	1,800	2,115	1,640	380
209	Housework and child care and care or assistance to seniors	15	20	150	120	85	35
210	Housework and child care only	120	160	455	665	450	90
211	Housework and care or assistance to seniors only	30	100	125	255	130	-
212	Child care and care or assistance to seniors only	20	-	10	-	10	-
213	Housework only	565	670	1,015	1,040	965	225
214	Child care only	25	-	30	20	-	25
215	Care or assistance to seniors only	10	10	15	15	-	-
216	Females 15 years and over	775	970	2,215	2,770	1,845	380
217	Reported unpaid work (35)	700	940	2,010	2,575	1,735	350
218	Housework and child care and care or assistance to seniors	55	50	220	230	205	30
219	Housework and child care only	110	140	545	730	540	140
220	Housework and care or assistance to seniors only	50	95	235	355	160	15
221	Child care and care or assistance to seniors only	20	-	-	-	-	-
222	Housework only	435	640	1,000	1,210	815	155
223	Child care only	20	10	10	35	10	-
224	Care or assistance to seniors only	-	10	15	15	10	-
	by labour force activity						
225	Males 15 years and over	880	1,010	1,955	2,375	1,820	400
226	In the labour force	690	785	1,355	1,680	1,380	310
227	Employed	635	690	1,280	1,590	1,290	290
228	Unemployed	50	100	80	95	90	15
229	Not in the labour force	195	225	600	695	445	95
230	Participation rate	78.4	77.7	69.3	70.7	75.8	77.5
231	Employment rate	72.2	68.3	65.5	66.9	70.9	72.5
232	Unemployment rate	7.2	12.7	5.9	5.7	6.5	4.8
233	Females 15 years and over	775	970	2,215	2,770	1,850	380
234	In the labour force	555	690	1,345	1,640	1,145	260
235	Employed	525	625	1,295	1,525	1,120	260
236	Unemployed	35	65	50	115	20	10
237	Not in the labour force	220	280	870	1,125	705	115
238	Participation rate	71.6	71.1	60.7	59.2	61.9	68.4
239	Employment rate	67.7	64.4	58.5	55.1	60.5	68.4
240	Unemployment rate	6.3	9.4	3.7	7.0	1.7	3.8

Tableau 1. Certaines caractéristiques des secteurs de recensement, recensement de 2001 – Données intégrales et données-échantillon (20 %)

Vancouver 0221.01	Vancouver 0221.03 A	Vancouver 0221.04 A	Vancouver 0222	Vancouver 0223.01 A	Vancouver 0223.02 ◇ A	Caractéristiques	Nº
						CARACTÉRISTIQUES DE LA POPULATION	
1,580	**2,860**	**4,470**	**8,255**	**4,830**	**4,235**	**Population totale de 5 ans et plus (30)**	185
						selon le lieu de résidence 5 ans auparavant (mobilité)	
1,260	2,080	2,355	4,505	1,870	1,745	Personnes n'ayant pas déménagé	186
325	775	2,115	3,750	2,955	2,490	Personnes ayant déménagé	187
160	365	870	1,615	1,250	845	Non-migrants	188
165	410	1,240	2,135	1,710	1,640	Migrants	189
135	235	505	1,065	965	820	Migrants internes	190
115	230	440	915	830	610	Migrants infraprovinciaux	191
20	10	65	155	135	210	Migrants interprovinciaux	192
30	175	735	1,065	740	820	Migrants externes	193
235	**375**	**790**	**1,195**	**735**	**725**	**Population totale de 15 à 24 ans**	194
						selon la fréquentation scolaire	
65	75	200	330	195	315	Ne fréquentant pas l'école	195
145	270	450	730	470	345	Fréquentant l'école à plein temps	196
25	25	145	140	70	65	Fréquentant l'école à temps partiel	197
1,370	**2,480**	**3,930**	**7,300**	**4,030**	**3,550**	**Population totale de 15 ans et plus**	198
						selon le plus haut niveau de scolarité atteint	
65	160	255	345	320	290	Niveau inférieur à la 9e année (31)	199
185	360	625	1,360	780	725	De la 9e à la 13e année sans certificat d'études secondaires	200
190	315	575	860	615	370	De la 9e à la 13e année avec certificat d'études secondaires	201
190	295	485	1,000	470	580	Études postsecondaires partielles sans grade, certificat ou diplôme (32)	202
220	305	430	505	445	395	Certificat ou diplôme d'une école de métiers (33)	203
235	495	615	1,185	530	495	Certificat ou diplôme collégial (34)	204
35	50	190	305	185	140	Certificat universitaire inférieur au baccalauréat	205
255	500	760	1,740	690	555	Études universitaires avec baccalauréat ou diplôme supérieur	206
						selon les combinaisons de travail non rémunéré	
705	1,225	1,970	3,410	1,900	1,790	Hommes de 15 ans et plus	207
650	1,110	1,730	3,045	1,760	1,510	Travail non rémunéré déclaré (35)	208
60	110	160	255	205	130	Travaux ménagers et soins aux enfants et soins ou aide aux personnes âgées	209
210	265	410	870	525	470	Travaux ménagers et soins aux enfants seulement	210
55	95	165	290	145	95	Travaux ménagers et soins ou aide aux personnes âgées seulement	211
-	-	10	-	-	-	Soins aux enfants et soins ou aide aux personnes âgées seulement	212
320	630	925	1,545	870	795	Travaux ménagers seulement	213
-	10	30	50	15	10	Soins aux enfants seulement	214
-	10	35	25	-	-	Soins ou aide aux personnes âgées seulement	215
670	1,260	1,955	3,885	2,130	1,765	Femmes de 15 ans et plus	216
615	1,160	1,840	3,655	2,015	1,625	Travail non rémunéré déclaré (35)	217
85	150	220	430	350	135	Travaux ménagers et soins aux enfants et soins ou aide aux personnes âgées	218
195	315	490	1,055	685	700	Travaux ménagers et soins aux enfants seulement	219
55	190	180	395	155	130	Travaux ménagers et soins ou aide aux personnes âgées seulement	220
-	-	10	-	-	10	Soins aux enfants et soins ou aide aux personnes âgées seulement	221
270	495	890	1,720	805	645	Travaux ménagers seulement	222
-	10	20	25	10	10	Soins aux enfants seulement	223
-	10	25	25	20	-	Soins ou aide aux personnes âgées seulement	224
						selon l'activité	
700	1,225	1,975	3,410	1,900	1,785	Hommes de 15 ans et plus	225
490	840	1,210	2,325	1,455	1,265	Population active	226
440	800	1,080	2,130	1,300	1,090	Personnes occupées	227
55	40	125	200	155	175	Chômeurs	228
210	385	765	1,085	445	525	Inactifs	229
70.0	68.6	61.3	68.2	76.6	70.9	Taux d'activité	230
62.9	65.3	54.7	62.5	68.4	61.1	Taux d'emploi	231
11.2	4.8	10.3	8.6	10.7	13.8	Taux de chômage	232
670	1,255	1,960	3,890	2,130	1,765	Femmes de 15 ans et plus	233
420	750	1,000	2,300	1,420	1,120	Population active	234
375	720	920	2,160	1,265	925	Personnes occupées	235
45	30	80	145	155	190	Chômeuses	236
255	505	955	1,585	705	645	Inactives	237
62.7	59.8	51.0	59.1	66.7	63.5	Taux d'activité	238
56.0	57.4	46.9	55.5	59.4	52.4	Taux d'emploi	239
10.7	4.0	8.0	6.3	10.9	17.0	Taux de chômage	240

Table 1. Selected Characteristics for Census Tracts, 2001 Census – 100% Data and 20% Sample Data

No.	Characteristics	Vancouver 0206 ◆◇◇	Vancouver 0207	Vancouver 0208	Vancouver 0209	Vancouver 0210	Vancouver 0220
	POPULATION CHARACTERISTICS						
	by labour force activity – concluded						
241	Both sexes - Participation rate	75.2	74.7	64.7	64.5	68.8	73.5
242	15-24 years	65.9	80.0	67.2	59.1	60.4	55.6
243	25 years and over	76.3	73.4	64.3	65.5	69.9	77.5
244	Both sexes - Employment rate	70.1	66.6	61.9	60.5	65.7	71.6
245	15-24 years	53.7	61.5	61.3	47.0	46.9	55.6
246	25 years and over	71.8	67.4	61.8	62.7	68.5	74.4
247	Both sexes - Unemployment rate	6.8	10.5	4.6	6.2	4.6	3.5
248	15-24 years	14.8	23.1	7.5	20.5	22.4	-
249	25 years and over	5.8	8.2	4.1	4.4	2.0	4.0
250	**Total labour force 15 years and over**	**1,245**	**1,475**	**2,700**	**3,325**	**2,520**	**570**
	by industry based on the 1997 NAICS						
251	Industry - Not applicable (36)	10	30	40	65	20	10
252	All industries (37)	1,235	1,450	2,665	3,255	2,505	565
253	11 Agriculture, forestry, fishing and hunting	-	-	10	20	15	50
254	21 Mining and oil and gas extraction	-	-	10	-	-	25
255	22 Utilities	-	10	55	40	20	10
256	23 Construction	80	90	160	160	180	-
257	31-33 Manufacturing	135	115	250	345	320	35
258	41 Wholesale trade	90	75	135	160	95	40
259	44-45 Retail trade	125	240	240	340	275	60
260	48-49 Transportation and warehousing	80	105	100	210	210	55
261	51 Information and cultural industries	75	25	200	180	105	25
262	52 Finance and insurance	80	45	110	155	100	15
263	53 Real estate and rental and leasing	50	20	60	70	25	-
264	54 Professional, scientific and technical services	115	105	170	210	170	50
265	55 Management of companies and enterprises	-	-	-	-	-	-
266	56 Administrative and support, waste management and remediation services	65	115	85	120	125	25
267	61 Educational services	70	85	285	280	145	25
268	62 Health care and social assistance	110	115	255	445	350	50
269	71 Arts, entertainment and recreation	20	50	70	45	35	-
270	72 Accommodation and food services	65	95	135	160	135	50
271	81 Other services (except public administration)	35	100	95	170	60	20
272	91 Public administration	35	65	230	150	130	30
	by class of worker						
273	Class of worker - Not applicable (36)	10	25	40	70	15	10
274	All classes of worker (37)	1,235	1,450	2,660	3,255	2,505	565
275	Paid workers	1,145	1,380	2,445	2,965	2,290	465
276	Employees	1,115	1,360	2,340	2,870	2,220	450
277	Self-employed (incorporated)	25	20	100	95	75	20
278	Self-employed (unincorporated)	95	65	220	275	215	85
279	Unpaid family workers	-	-	-	15	-	15
	by occupation based on the 2001 NOC-S						
280	Male labour force 15 years and over	690	785	1,355	1,680	1,380	310
281	Occupation - Not applicable (36)	10	15	10	25	10	-
282	All occupations (37)	680	765	1,345	1,660	1,375	305
283	A Management occupations	55	40	190	260	140	20
284	B Business, finance and administration occupations	145	90	160	160	135	15
285	C Natural and applied sciences and related occupations	90	65	135	165	110	30
286	D Health occupations	-	30	30	40	40	-
287	E Occupations in social science, education, government service and religion	35	45	145	100	70	25
288	F Occupations in art, culture, recreation and sport	15	15	45	30	35	10
289	G Sales and service occupations	150	230	230	325	220	90
290	H Trades, transport and equipment operators and related occupations	145	165	305	410	500	65
291	I Occupations unique to primary industry	-	35	25	25	20	30
292	J Occupations unique to processing, manufacturing and utilities	45	60	80	145	100	20
293	Female labour force 15 years and over	555	690	1,340	1,645	1,140	260
294	Occupation - Not applicable (36)	-	-	30	50	10	10
295	All occupations (37)	555	685	1,315	1,595	1,130	255
296	A Management occupations	40	50	90	115	100	15
297	B Business, finance and administration occupations	230	230	390	580	320	45
298	C Natural and applied sciences and related occupations	15	-	35	40	15	25
299	D Health occupations	55	60	90	150	140	15

Tableau 1. Certaines caractéristiques des secteurs de recensement, recensement de 2001 – Données intégrales et données-échantillon (20 %)

Vancouver 0221.01	Vancouver 0221.03 A	Vancouver 0221.04 A	Vancouver 0222	Vancouver 0223.01 A	Vancouver 0223.02 ◇ A	Caractéristiques	N°
						CARACTÉRISTIQUES DE LA POPULATION	
						selon l'activité – fin	
66.1	64.3	56.2	63.4	71.3	67.0	Les deux sexes - Taux d'activité	241
75.0	68.9	54.7	54.8	60.5	60.0	15-24 ans	242
64.3	63.7	56.5	65.0	73.7	69.1	25 ans et plus	243
59.1	61.5	51.0	58.6	63.6	56.7	Les deux sexes - Taux d'emploi	244
57.4	58.1	44.7	44.4	55.8	49.3	15-24 ans	245
59.9	62.0	52.4	61.4	65.4	58.5	25 ans et plus	246
11.0	4.4	9.3	7.4	10.9	15.3	Les deux sexes - Taux de chômage	247
27.8	15.7	17.2	19.1	7.9	16.3	15-24 ans	248
6.9	2.6	7.3	5.4	11.3	15.1	25 ans et plus	249
905	**1,595**	**2,210**	**4,625**	**2,875**	**2,385**	**Population active totale de 15 ans et plus**	250
						selon l'industrie basée sur le SCIAN de 1997	
20	20	65	110	55	230	Industrie - Sans objet (36)	251
885	1,575	2,140	4,515	2,820	2,155	Toutes les industries (37)	252
10	15	20	20	25	10	11 Agriculture, foresterie, pêche et chasse	253
-	-	-	35	-	15	21 Extraction minière et extraction de pétrole et de gaz	254
10	10	10	35	30	25	22 Services publics	255
60	80	100	205	125	155	23 Construction	256
105	165	220	370	320	245	31-33 Fabrication	257
20	55	125	270	145	75	41 Commerce de gros	258
75	205	275	540	340	385	44-45 Commerce de détail	259
45	35	120	285	175	130	48-49 Transport et entreposage	260
50	120	90	230	160	60	51 Industrie de l'information et industrie culturelle	261
45	55	55	175	105	75	52 Finance et assurances	262
15	55	30	105	50	30	53 Services immobiliers et services de location et de location à bail	263
90	125	220	510	230	135	54 Services professionnels, scientifiques et techniques	264
-	-	-	-	-	-	55 Gestion de sociétés et d'entreprises	265
55	30	155	250	135	170	56 Services administratifs, services de soutien, services de gestion des déchets et services d'assainissement	266
60	120	105	315	140	65	61 Services d'enseignement	267
85	210	135	450	275	180	62 Soins de santé et assistance sociale	268
45	-	25	95	30	20	71 Arts, spectacles et loisirs	269
55	70	235	300	340	180	72 Hébergement et services de restauration	270
40	150	125	180	115	130	81 Autres services, sauf les administrations publiques	271
45	75	95	150	75	70	91 Administrations publiques	272
						selon la catégorie de travailleurs	
20	15	60	115	55	225	Catégorie de travailleurs - Sans objet (36)	273
890	1,580	2,145	4,510	2,820	2,155	Toutes les catégories de travailleurs (37)	274
805	1,415	1,930	4,125	2,655	1,980	Travailleurs rémunérés	275
730	1,340	1,830	3,875	2,585	1,945	Employés	276
75	80	100	255	70	35	Travailleurs autonomes (entreprise constituée en société)	277
85	135	200	375	145	165	Travailleurs autonomes (entreprise non constituée en société)	278
-	25	15	10	20	10	Travailleurs familiaux non rémunérés	279
						selon la profession basée sur la CNP-S de 2001	
490	840	1,210	2,325	1,450	1,265	Hommes actifs de 15 ans et plus	280
-	10	20	80	30	90	Profession - Sans objet (36)	281
490	830	1,185	2,250	1,425	1,175	Toutes les professions (37)	282
140	135	175	345	150	80	A Gestion	283
45	55	160	365	145	115	B Affaires, finance et administration	284
50	120	190	385	205	155	C Sciences naturelles et appliquées et professions apparentées	285
15	35	20	85	25	15	D Secteur de la santé	286
15	25	65	130	45	30	E Sciences sociales, enseignement, administration publique et religion	287
15	40	30	50	30	-	F Arts, culture, sports et loisirs	288
95	190	260	345	300	290	G Ventes et services	289
80	175	225	410	360	390	H Métiers, transport et machinerie	290
-	15	20	45	20	35	I Professions propres au secteur primaire	291
20	45	45	100	155	65	J Transformation, fabrication et services d'utilité publique	292
415	755	1,000	2,295	1,420	1,120	Femmes actives de 15 ans et plus	293
15	-	45	40	30	135	Profession - Sans objet (36)	294
400	745	960	2,265	1,395	980	Toutes les professions (37)	295
35	105	60	170	75	70	A Gestion	296
145	190	255	810	420	260	B Affaires, finance et administration	297
10	15	35	70	20	80	C Sciences naturelles et appliquées et professions apparentées	298
50	80	75	200	95	55	D Secteur de la santé	299

Table 1. Selected Characteristics for Census Tracts, 2001 Census – 100% Data and 20% Sample Data

No.	Characteristics	Vancouver 0206 ◆◇◇	Vancouver 0207	Vancouver 0208	Vancouver 0209	Vancouver 0210	Vancouver 0220
	POPULATION CHARACTERISTICS						
	by occupation based on the 2001 NOC-S – concluded						
300	E Occupations in social science, education, government service and religion	35	60	210	255	120	30
301	F Occupations in art, culture, recreation and sport	10	25	80	55	65	25
302	G Sales and service occupations	110	230	405	330	335	45
303	H Trades, transport and equipment operators and related occupations	15	-	10	30	30	20
304	I Occupations unique to primary industry	-	-	-	10	-	20
305	J Occupations unique to processing, manufacturing and utilities	40	15	-	30	10	15
306	**Total employed labour force 15 years and over**	**1,160**	**1,320**	**2,580**	**3,115**	**2,410**	**550**
	by place of work						
307	Males	635	690	1,280	1,590	1,290	290
308	Usual place of work	485	540	1,040	1,220	965	215
309	At home	45	20	75	120	45	40
310	Outside Canada	10	-	15	10	15	-
311	No fixed workplace address	100	135	160	240	265	35
312	Females	525	630	1,300	1,525	1,120	260
313	Usual place of work	475	535	1,105	1,350	965	170
314	At home	35	15	145	100	80	55
315	Outside Canada	-	-	-	-	10	-
316	No fixed workplace address	10	80	40	75	65	35
317	**Total employed labour force 15 years and over with usual place of work or no fixed workplace address**	**1,070**	**1,280**	**2,335**	**2,880**	**2,255**	**455**
	by mode of transportation						
318	Males	580	670	1,195	1,460	1,230	250
319	Car, truck, van, as driver	310	375	900	1,200	955	170
320	Car, truck, van, as passenger	10	60	40	50	25	-
321	Public transit	170	170	145	110	140	40
322	Walked	65	45	65	65	75	30
323	Other method	35	20	45	40	30	10
324	Females	495	615	1,140	1,420	1,025	205
325	Car, truck, van, as driver	195	250	700	960	605	125
326	Car, truck, van, as passenger	10	25	95	115	120	30
327	Public transit	230	265	160	195	200	30
328	Walked	50	75	160	125	95	10
329	Other method	10	-	25	25	10	20
330	**Total population 15 years and over who worked since January 1, 2000**	**1,345**	**1,540**	**2,845**	**3,600**	**2,720**	**620**
	by language used at work						
331	Single responses	1,230	1,450	2,745	3,470	2,675	570
332	English	1,185	1,440	2,730	3,450	2,665	515
333	French	-	-	-	-	-	-
334	Non-official languages (5)	50	10	15	15	10	55
335	Chinese, n.o.s.	45	-	10	-	-	30
336	Cantonese	-	10	-	-	-	15
337	Other languages (6)	-	-	-	15	10	10
338	Multiple responses	115	90	100	130	45	50
339	English and French	20	20	15	45	10	-
340	English and non-official language	95	50	90	80	35	50
341	French and non-official language	-	-	-	-	-	-
342	English, French and non-official language	-	20	-	10	-	-
	DWELLING AND HOUSEHOLD CHARACTERISTICS						
343	**Total number of occupied private dwellings**	**1,010**	**1,310**	**2,265**	**2,615**	**1,995**	**330**
	by tenure						
344	Owned	340	355	1,160	1,855	1,080	210
345	Rented	670	955	1,105	760	920	120
346	Band housing	-	-	-	-	-	-
	by structural type of dwelling						
347	Single-detached house	-	15	1,065	1,070	895	245
348	Semi-detached house	-	10	-	15	30	15
349	Row house	15	-	30	170	25	10
350	Apartment, detached duplex	10	20	180	170	190	50
351	Apartment, building that has five or more storeys	610	465	465	385	50	-
352	Apartment, building that has fewer than five storeys (38)	380	805	515	805	805	15
353	Other single-attached house	-	-	-	-	-	-
354	Movable dwelling (39)	-	-	-	-	-	-

Tableau 1. Certaines caractéristiques des secteurs de recensement, recensement de 2001 – Données intégrales et données-échantillon (20 %)

Vancouver 0221.01	Vancouver 0221.03 A	Vancouver 0221.04 A	Vancouver 0222	Vancouver 0223.01 A	Vancouver 0223.02 ◇ A	Caractéristiques	Nº
						CARACTÉRISTIQUES DE LA POPULATION	
						selon la profession basée sur la CNP-S de 2001 – fin	
40	80	45	240	140	60	E Sciences sociales, enseignement, administration publique et religion	300
20	40	35	55	30	10	F Arts, culture, sports et loisirs	301
100	190	395	645	520	390	G Ventes et services	302
-	20	10	30	15	15	H Métiers, transport et machinerie	303
-	10	10	10	10	-	I Professions propres au secteur primaire	304
-	10	45	40	65	50	J Transformation, fabrication et services d'utilité publique	305
815	**1,520**	**2,000**	**4,285**	**2,565**	**2,015**	**Population active occupée totale de 15 ans et plus**	306
						selon le lieu de travail	
435	800	1,080	2,130	1,295	1,085	Hommes	307
370	660	795	1,740	1,095	840	Lieu habituel de travail	308
35	40	105	115	55	55	À domicile	309
-	15	15	35	-	-	En dehors du Canada	310
40	90	165	240	150	185	Sans adresse de travail fixe	311
375	720	925	2,160	1,265	930	Femmes	312
335	615	790	1,870	1,145	835	Lieu habituel de travail	313
20	70	85	175	55	35	À domicile	314
-	-	-	10	10	10	En dehors du Canada	315
25	35	45	110	60	40	Sans adresse de travail fixe	316
760	**1,395**	**1,795**	**3,955**	**2,450**	**1,905**	**Population active occupée totale de 15 ans et plus ayant un lieu habituel de travail ou sans adresse de travail fixe**	317
						selon le mode de transport	
405	745	960	1,980	1,245	1,025	Hommes	318
365	625	745	1,480	885	805	Automobile, camion ou fourgonnette, en tant que conducteur	319
20	25	30	70	40	45	Automobile, camion ou fourgonnette, en tant que passager	320
20	80	100	315	285	130	Transport en commun	321
-	10	70	90	15	40	À pied	322
-	10	15	30	20	10	Autre moyen	323
355	650	840	1,980	1,205	875	Femmes	324
260	460	450	1,135	585	470	Automobile, camion ou fourgonnette, en tant que conductrice	325
30	65	55	170	65	110	Automobile, camion ou fourgonnette, en tant que passagère	326
60	80	260	625	490	245	Transport en commun	327
-	30	45	35	65	45	À pied	328
-	10	25	20	-	10	Autre moyen	329
985	**1,680**	**2,435**	**5,075**	**3,070**	**2,315**	**Population totale de 15 ans et plus ayant travaillé depuis le 1er janvier 2000**	330
						selon la langue utilisée au travail	
910	1,470	2,070	4,420	2,700	2,070	Réponses uniques	331
910	1,445	1,950	4,310	2,565	2,000	Anglais	332
-	10	-	-	10	-	Français	333
-	20	120	110	125	65	Langues non officielles (5)	334
-	10	55	35	60	40	Chinois, n.d.a.	335
-	10	10	30	35	10	Cantonais	336
-	-	65	40	30	15	Autres langues (6)	337
80	215	365	655	375	240	Réponses multiples	338
10	-	10	30	25	15	Anglais et français	339
65	205	330	600	345	230	Anglais et langue non officielle	340
-	-	-	-	-	-	Français et langue non officielle	341
-	-	30	20	-	-	Anglais, français et langue non officielle	342
						CARACTÉRISTIQUES DES LOGEMENTS ET DES MÉNAGES	
570	**1,020**	**1,490**	**3,290**	**1,685**	**1,525**	**Nombre total de logements privés occupés**	343
						selon le mode d'occupation	
500	815	985	2,450	750	630	Possédé	344
70	210	505	835	940	895	Loué	345
-	-	-	-	-	-	Logement de bande	346
						selon le type de construction résidentielle	
510	910	1,010	1,385	305	545	Maison individuelle non attenante	347
10	10	160	130	190	145	Maison jumelée	348
-	-	-	210	375	200	Maison en rangée	349
50	80	150	45	310	75	Appartement, duplex non attenant	350
-	-	-	435	45	50	Appartement, immeuble de cinq étages ou plus	351
10	25	160	1,085	465	515	Appartement, immeuble de moins de cinq étages (38)	352
-	-	-	-	-	-	Autre maison individuelle attenante	353
-	-	-	-	-	-	Logement mobile (39)	354

Table 1. Selected Characteristics for Census Tracts, 2001 Census – 100% Data and 20% Sample Data

No.	Characteristics	Vancouver 0206 ◆◇◇	Vancouver 0207	Vancouver 0208	Vancouver 0209	Vancouver 0210	Vancouver 0220
	DWELLING AND HOUSEHOLD CHARACTERISTICS						
	by condition of dwelling						
355	Regular maintenance only	690	755	1,535	1,725	1,230	165
356	Minor repairs	185	330	505	570	625	130
357	Major repairs	135	225	220	320	145	35
	by period of construction						
358	Before 1946	65	135	855	160	530	25
359	1946-1960	70	240	420	595	450	105
360	1961-1970	235	215	265	355	400	45
361	1971-1980	140	365	420	160	375	40
362	1981-1990	170	220	65	695	145	70
363	1991-2001 (20)	340	130	240	650	100	40
364	Average number of rooms per dwelling	3.8	3.7	5.7	6.2	5.7	6.8
365	Average number of bedrooms per dwelling	1.4	1.3	2.3	2.5	2.2	3.1
366	Average value of dwelling $	104,807	122,016	315,037	246,209	207,472	327,301
367	**Total number of private households**	**1,010**	**1,305**	**2,265**	**2,615**	**1,995**	**330**
	by household size						
368	1 person	520	710	920	725	750	55
369	2 persons	350	460	585	990	600	100
370	3 persons	110	70	270	410	295	65
371	4-5 persons	30	70	435	420	305	85
372	6 or more persons	-	-	55	70	50	25
	by household type						
373	One-family households	350	475	1,230	1,765	1,095	225
374	Multiple-family households	20	-	50	20	25	25
375	Non-family households	635	835	980	830	880	80
376	Number of persons in private households	1,695	2,130	5,100	6,155	4,455	980
377	Average number of persons in private households	1.7	1.6	2.3	2.4	2.2	3.0
378	Average number of persons per room	0.4	0.4	0.4	0.4	0.4	0.4
379	Tenant households in non-farm, non-reserve private dwellings (40)	670	960	1,095	760	920	120
380	Average gross rent $ (40)	718	652	544	779	647	819
381	Tenant households spending 30% or more of household income on gross rent (40) (41)	260	340	395	245	320	45
382	Tenant households spending from 30% to 99% of household income on gross rent (40) (41)	205	250	380	200	235	35
383	Owner households in non-farm, non-reserve private dwellings (42)	345	355	1,155	1,850	1,070	205
384	Average owner's major payments $ (42)	853	743	1,268	965	1,090	919
385	Owner households spending 30% or more of household income on owner's major payments (41) (42)	70	75	230	385	270	20
386	Owner households spending from 30% to 99% of household income on owner's major payments (41) (42)	65	50	200	360	240	20
	CENSUS FAMILY CHARACTERISTICS						
387	**Total number of census families in private households**	**395**	**475**	**1,330**	**1,810**	**1,150**	**275**
	by census family structure and size						
388	Total couple families	345	390	1,140	1,525	970	230
389	Total families of married couples	245	265	980	1,350	780	185
390	Without children at home	140	200	410	680	290	80
391	With children at home	100	65	570	670	495	100
392	1 child	95	30	185	275	250	35
393	2 children	10	20	260	265	140	55
394	3 or more children	-	15	125	130	105	10
395	Total families of common-law couples	105	125	165	175	190	45
396	Without children at home	95	100	120	100	155	-
397	With children at home	-	25	35	80	35	40
398	1 child	-	-	30	60	25	15
399	2 children	-	20	10	10	10	10
400	3 or more children	-	-	-	15	-	10
401	Total lone-parent families	45	80	190	285	180	50
402	Female parent	35	70	155	245	160	30
403	1 child	35	60	105	140	115	20
404	2 children	-	10	35	70	35	-
405	3 or more children	-	-	10	30	10	10

Tableau 1. Certaines caractéristiques des secteurs de recensement, recensement de 2001 – Données intégrales et données-échantillon (20 %)

Vancouver 0221.01	Vancouver 0221.03 A	Vancouver 0221.04 A	Vancouver 0222	Vancouver 0223.01 A	Vancouver 0223.02 ◇ A	Caractéristiques	N°
						CARACTÉRISTIQUES DES LOGEMENTS ET DES MÉNAGES	
						selon l'état du logement	
375	680	1,075	2,360	1,105	980	Entretien régulier seulement	355
160	295	365	700	405	405	Réparations mineures	356
30	50	50	230	180	140	Réparations majeures	357
						selon la période de construction	
25	105	220	150	65	100	Avant 1946	358
370	460	310	550	200	305	1946-1960	359
55	175	150	240	155	360	1961-1970	360
50	75	225	230	140	235	1971-1980	361
10	65	180	590	460	310	1981-1990	362
60	140	390	1,525	675	210	1991-2001 (20)	363
8.0	7.8	7.0	5.8	5.5	5.2	Nombre moyen de pièces par logement	364
3.5	3.3	3.2	2.5	2.6	2.4	Nombre moyen de chambres à coucher par logement	365
345,503	355,923	369,749	257,821	218,763	228,984	Valeur moyenne du logement $	366
565	**1,020**	**1,490**	**3,290**	**1,685**	**1,530**	**Nombre total de logements privés**	367
						selon la taille du ménage	
95	180	245	800	290	295	1 personne	368
170	335	360	1,040	440	395	2 personnes	369
100	155	280	565	325	305	3 personnes	370
165	310	475	735	505	405	4-5 personnes	371
35	50	130	145	130	120	6 personnes ou plus	372
						selon le genre de ménage	
440	715	1,055	2,275	1,190	1,030	Ménages unifamiliaux	373
25	75	100	80	95	75	Ménages multifamiliaux	374
110	230	330	930	400	425	Ménages non familiaux	375
1,655	2,990	4,685	8,665	5,185	4,565	Nombre de personnes dans les ménages privés	376
2.9	2.9	3.2	2.6	3.1	3.0	Nombre moyen de personnes dans les ménages privés	377
0.4	0.4	0.4	0.5	0.6	0.6	Nombre moyen de personnes par pièce	378
70	210	490	835	930	885	Ménages locataires dans les logements privés non agricoles hors réserve (40)	379
941	953	889	833	810	767	Loyer brut moyen $ (40)	380
40	90	215	260	345	405	Ménages locataires consacrant 30 % ou plus du revenu du ménage au loyer brut (40) (41)	381
35	90	185	205	275	255	Ménages locataires consacrant de 30 % à 99 % du revenu du ménage au loyer brut (40) (41)	382
495	815	980	2,435	745	625	Ménages propriétaires dans les logements privés non agricoles hors réserve (42)	383
1,054	896	837	937	1,137	990	Principales dépenses de propriété moyennes $ (42)	384
90	125	180	520	220	190	Ménages propriétaires consacrant 30 % ou plus du revenu du ménage aux principales dépenses de propriété (41) (42)	385
85	115	140	365	195	165	Ménages propriétaires consacrant de 30 % à 99 % du revenu du ménage aux principales dépenses de propriété (41) (42)	386
						CARACTÉRISTIQUES DES FAMILLES DE RECENSEMENT	
485	**880**	**1,265**	**2,445**	**1,400**	**1,175**	**Total des familles de recensement dans les ménages privés**	387
						selon la structure et la taille de la famille de recensement	
435	785	1,075	2,115	1,085	935	Total des familles avec conjoints	388
390	750	1,000	1,905	965	805	Total des familles avec couples mariés	389
160	305	310	760	275	215	Sans enfants à la maison	390
230	445	695	1,135	700	585	Avec enfants à la maison	391
70	130	200	405	225	205	1 enfant	392
95	230	375	520	335	255	2 enfants	393
60	85	120	205	140	130	3 enfants ou plus	394
45	35	75	215	115	135	Total des familles en union libre	395
25	20	40	185	90	55	Sans enfants à la maison	396
20	10	35	30	25	80	Avec enfants à la maison	397
20	10	30	10	20	30	1 enfant	398
-	-	-	15	10	20	2 enfants	399
-	10	-	10	-	30	3 enfants ou plus	400
55	95	190	330	315	235	Total des familles monoparentales	401
35	65	155	270	255	195	Parent de sexe féminin	402
20	50	105	165	135	115	1 enfant	403
20	20	40	90	80	60	2 enfants	404
-	-	10	10	40	20	3 enfants ou plus	405

Table 1. Selected Characteristics for Census Tracts, 2001 Census – 100% Data and 20% Sample Data

No.	Characteristics	Vancouver 0206 ◆◇◇	Vancouver 0207	Vancouver 0208	Vancouver 0209	Vancouver 0210	Vancouver 0220
	CENSUS FAMILY CHARACTERISTICS						
	by census family structure and size – concluded						
406	Male parent	15	20	40	40	15	20
407	1 child	-	15	20	25	15	15
408	2 children	15	-	20	10	10	-
409	3 or more children	-	-	-	-	-	-
410	**Total number of children at home**	**185**	**250**	**1,440**	**1,770**	**1,145**	**310**
	by age groups						
411	Under 6 years	55	90	345	385	320	75
412	6-14 years	45	55	575	620	450	125
413	15-17 years	20	60	190	150	100	40
414	18-24 years	20	40	225	385	150	65
415	25 years and over	45	10	110	220	135	10
	Average number of children at home per						
416	census family (43)	0.5	0.5	1.1	1.0	1.0	1.1
417	**Total number of persons in private households**	**1,695**	**2,130**	**5,100**	**6,150**	**4,455**	**980**
	by census family status and living arrangements						
418	Number of non-family persons	770	1,010	1,195	1,050	1,190	170
419	Living with relatives (44)	15	105	50	130	150	30
420	Living with non-relatives only	230	195	220	200	285	85
421	Living alone	520	710	920	725	750	55
422	Number of family persons	925	1,115	3,910	5,100	3,265	810
423	Average number of persons per census family	2.3	2.4	2.9	2.8	2.8	3.0
424	**Total number of persons 65 years and over**	**125**	**185**	**780**	**930**	**465**	**55**
425	Number of non-family persons 65 years and over	40	115	420	330	235	25
426	Living with relatives (44)	-	-	10	40	45	10
427	Living with non-relatives only	-	-	15	10	30	15
428	Living alone	40	110	390	280	160	10
429	Number of family persons 65 years and over	85	70	360	605	225	30
	ECONOMIC FAMILY CHARACTERISTICS						
	Total number of economic families in						
430	**private households**	**380**	**505**	**1,295**	**1,815**	**1,180**	**270**
	by size of family						
431	2 persons	260	375	585	935	585	110
432	3 persons	95	80	265	395	285	60
433	4 persons	10	40	285	315	180	45
434	5 or more persons	20	15	165	165	130	45
435	Total number of persons in economic families	940	1,220	3,960	5,225	3,415	845
436	Average number of persons per economic family	2.4	2.4	3.1	2.9	2.9	3.2
437	Total number of unattached individuals	750	910	1,140	925	1,040	135
	2000 INCOME CHARACTERISTICS						
	Population 15 years and over by sex and total income groups in 2000						
438	Total - Both sexes	1,655	1,975	4,170	5,140	3,670	775
439	Without income	40	25	135	270	155	35
440	With income	1,610	1,945	4,035	4,875	3,520	745
441	Under $1,000 (45)	75	90	155	165	145	50
442	$ 1,000 - $ 2,999	40	45	165	140	115	30
443	$ 3,000 - $ 4,999	30	60	90	110	155	10
444	$ 5,000 - $ 6,999	15	105	215	150	105	35
445	$ 7,000 - $ 9,999	120	145	190	220	250	45
446	$10,000 - $11,999	45	110	165	215	80	55
447	$12,000 - $14,999	65	140	335	325	145	55
448	$15,000 - $19,999	165	185	365	390	385	25
449	$20,000 - $24,999	160	160	310	310	275	60
450	$25,000 - $29,999	150	160	300	395	255	70
451	$30,000 - $34,999	185	110	335	375	255	55
452	$35,000 - $39,999	145	150	200	380	310	45
453	$40,000 - $44,999	150	115	195	355	245	50
454	$45,000 - $49,999	85	115	165	180	155	35
455	$50,000 - $59,999	75	100	245	425	240	35
456	$60,000 and over	95	160	605	740	380	75
457	Average income $ (46)	28,959	27,773	32,812	34,170	30,152	29,366
458	Median income $ (46)	28,311	23,393	25,026	29,996	26,618	23,503
459	Standard error of average income $ (46)	996	1,177	1,081	820	874	2,162

Tableau 1. Certaines caractéristiques des secteurs de recensement, recensement de 2001 – Données intégrales et données-échantillon (20 %)

Vancouver 0221.01	Vancouver 0221.03 A	Vancouver 0221.04 A	Vancouver 0222	Vancouver 0223.01 A	Vancouver 0223.02 ◇ A	Caractéristiques	N°
						CARACTÉRISTIQUES DES FAMILLES DE RECENSEMENT	
						selon la structure et la taille de la famille de recensement – fin	
15	30	35	60	65	40	Parent de sexe masculin	406
-	15	15	20	45	20	1 enfant	407
15	15	20	30	10	15	2 enfants	408
-	-	-	10	15	10	3 enfants ou plus	409
570	**1,000**	**1,620**	**2,695**	**1,915**	**1,680**	**Nombre total d'enfants à la maison**	410
						selon les groupes d'âge	
85	170	265	495	430	395	Moins de 6 ans	411
195	345	465	860	725	615	6-14 ans	412
95	80	195	320	205	160	15-17 ans	413
115	245	440	605	380	385	18-24 ans	414
75	160	250	415	170	135	25 ans et plus	415
1.2	1.1	1.3	1.1	1.4	1.4	Nombre moyen d'enfants à la maison par famille de recensement (43)	416
1,655	**2,990**	**4,680**	**8,660**	**5,180**	**4,560**	**Nombre total de personnes dans les ménages privés**	417
						selon la situation des particuliers dans la famille de recensement et des particuliers dans le ménage	
165	330	725	1,405	785	770	Nombre de personnes hors famille de recensement	418
20	50	195	265	270	260	Vivant avec des personnes apparentées (44)	419
50	95	285	335	220	210	Vivant avec des personnes non apparentées uniquement	420
95	180	245	800	290	300	Vivant seules	421
1,490	2,660	3,965	7,260	4,395	3,790	Nombre de personnes membres d'une famille	422
3.0	3.0	3.1	3.0	3.1	3.2	Nombre moyen de personnes par famille de recensement	423
260	**475**	**600**	**965**	**370**	**300**	**Nombre total de personnes de 65 ans et plus**	424
70	100	215	340	140	115	Nombre de personnes hors famille de recensement de 65 ans et plus	425
10	10	80	90	75	55	Vivant avec des personnes apparentées (44)	426
10	25	25	40	-	-	Vivant avec des personnes non apparentées uniquement	427
60	65	110	210	65	55	Vivant seules	428
185	375	390	625	230	185	Nombre de personnes membres d'une famille de 65 ans et plus	429
						CARACTÉRISTIQUES DES FAMILLES ÉCONOMIQUES	
465	**810**	**1,200**	**2,395**	**1,330**	**1,160**	**Nombre total de familles économiques dans les ménages privés**	430
						selon la taille de la famille	
170	305	365	995	420	345	2 personnes	431
115	150	280	550	290	300	3 personnes	432
115	220	305	540	345	260	4 personnes	433
75	135	250	315	275	250	5 personnes ou plus	434
1,510	2,715	4,160	7,525	4,670	4,055	Nombre total de personnes dans les familles économiques	435
3.2	3.3	3.5	3.1	3.5	3.5	Nombre moyen de personnes par famille économique	436
145	275	525	1,140	515	510	Nombre total de personnes hors famille économique	437
						CARACTÉRISTIQUES DU REVENU DE 2000	
						Population de 15 ans et plus selon le sexe et les tranches de revenu total en 2000	
1,375	2,480	3,930	7,300	4,025	3,550	Total - Les deux sexes	438
65	145	320	465	270	300	Sans revenu	439
1,310	2,335	3,610	6,835	3,755	3,255	Avec un revenu	440
50	60	250	455	255	250	Moins de 1 000 $ (45)	441
45	80	220	300	215	200	1 000 $ - 2 999 $	442
50	115	150	400	175	235	3 000 $ - 4 999 $	443
35	115	215	300	225	140	5 000 $ - 6 999 $	444
60	140	200	290	285	330	7 000 $ - 9 999 $	445
30	90	175	275	220	160	10 000 $ - 11 999 $	446
100	160	260	500	220	245	12 000 $ - 14 999 $	447
70	210	395	605	320	355	15 000 $ - 19 999 $	448
80	240	300	405	320	265	20 000 $ - 24 999 $	449
115	190	295	410	320	160	25 000 $ - 29 999 $	450
70	90	255	530	335	300	30 000 $ - 34 999 $	451
110	155	135	345	190	150	35 000 $ - 39 999 $	452
135	95	180	480	110	135	40 000 $ - 44 999 $	453
60	125	165	295	130	90	45 000 $ - 49 999 $	454
115	210	110	480	210	130	50 000 $ - 59 999 $	455
190	255	300	770	240	115	60 000 $ et plus	456
35,876	30,517	25,520	28,645	23,496	20,614	Revenu moyen $ (46)	457
30,553	24,326	18,923	23,479	19,736	15,339	Revenu médian $ (46)	458
1,804	1,119	916	674	690	699	Erreur type de revenu moyen $ (46)	459

Table 1. Selected Characteristics for Census Tracts, 2001 Census – 100% Data and 20% Sample Data

No.	Characteristics	Vancouver 0206 ◆◇◇	Vancouver 0207	Vancouver 0208	Vancouver 0209	Vancouver 0210	Vancouver 0220
	2000 INCOME CHARACTERISTICS						
	Population 15 years and over by sex and total income groups in 2000 – concluded						
460	Total - Males	880	1,005	1,955	2,380	1,820	400
461	Without income	10	10	90	85	55	15
462	With income	875	1,000	1,865	2,290	1,765	390
463	Under $1,000 (45)	45	50	70	75	110	20
464	$ 1,000 - $ 2,999	20	20	40	85	55	10
465	$ 3,000 - $ 4,999	10	35	15	60	85	-
466	$ 5,000 - $ 6,999	10	25	85	50	35	-
467	$ 7,000 - $ 9,999	55	55	50	50	70	20
468	$10,000 - $11,999	30	50	60	85	45	10
469	$12,000 - $14,999	10	75	120	105	25	25
470	$15,000 - $19,999	100	100	100	120	155	15
471	$20,000 - $24,999	80	65	165	110	140	45
472	$25,000 - $29,999	80	75	130	180	100	50
473	$30,000 - $34,999	125	65	145	190	135	30
474	$35,000 - $39,999	100	105	90	130	130	25
475	$40,000 - $44,999	70	60	140	170	170	40
476	$45,000 - $49,999	35	40	50	100	80	25
477	$50,000 - $59,999	55	55	170	270	155	40
478	$60,000 and over	60	115	425	505	280	45
479	Average income $ (46)	30,774	30,753	42,135	40,213	34,573	37,158
480	Median income $ (46)	30,263	25,321	30,990	36,058	32,006	30,007
481	Standard error of average income $ (46)	1,319	1,809	1,937	1,419	1,457	3,297
482	Total - Females	770	965	2,215	2,765	1,850	375
483	Without income	35	15	45	180	100	20
484	With income	740	950	2,170	2,585	1,750	355
485	Under $1,000 (45)	30	40	85	85	35	30
486	$ 1,000 - $ 2,999	20	25	125	55	65	20
487	$ 3,000 - $ 4,999	20	25	70	55	70	15
488	$ 5,000 - $ 6,999	15	75	125	100	70	30
489	$ 7,000 - $ 9,999	60	90	140	170	175	20
490	$10,000 - $11,999	20	60	110	125	30	45
491	$12,000 - $14,999	60	65	215	225	125	35
492	$15,000 - $19,999	65	85	260	270	230	15
493	$20,000 - $24,999	80	95	145	200	140	15
494	$25,000 - $29,999	75	80	170	205	155	20
495	$30,000 - $34,999	60	50	195	180	125	25
496	$35,000 - $39,999	50	45	105	250	180	20
497	$40,000 - $44,999	80	55	60	190	75	10
498	$45,000 - $49,999	55	70	115	75	75	10
499	$50,000 - $59,999	20	50	70	155	90	10
500	$60,000 and over	35	45	175	235	100	25
501	Average income $ (46)	26,822	24,643	24,804	28,816	25,682	20,877
502	Median income $ (46)	24,975	21,131	18,212	24,995	21,937	13,135
503	Standard error of average income $ (46)	1,503	1,437	964	862	921	2,324
	by composition of total income						
504	Total - Composition of income in 2000 % (47)	100.0	100.0	100.0	100.0	100.0	100.0
505	Employment income %	86.1	81.6	80.8	75.8	83.2	85.1
506	Government transfer payments %	8.4	10.2	10.3	10.2	10.4	8.4
507	Other %	5.4	8.0	8.9	13.9	6.4	6.6
	Population 15 years and over with employment income in 2000 by sex and work activity						
508	Both sexes with employment income (48)	1,355	1,485	2,780	3,510	2,645	565
509	Average employment income $	29,685	29,747	38,525	36,026	33,367	32,618
510	Standard error of average employment income $	1,046	1,226	1,337	950	942	2,631
511	Worked full year, full time (49)	885	795	1,565	1,990	1,495	265
512	Average employment income $	34,733	39,286	49,772	46,340	41,563	46,564
513	Standard error of average employment income $	1,307	1,658	1,802	1,131	1,142	3,963
514	Worked part year or part time (50)	430	660	1,175	1,450	1,105	290
515	Average employment income $	21,629	19,338	23,947	22,957	21,922	20,446
516	Standard error of average employment income $	1,386	1,309	1,673	1,345	1,259	2,966
517	Males with employment income (48)	735	780	1,380	1,745	1,430	305
518	Average employment income $	31,990	32,464	48,053	41,352	37,161	40,488
519	Standard error of average employment income $	1,321	1,722	2,213	1,576	1,421	4,034
520	Worked full year, full time (49)	500	465	920	1,085	855	160
521	Average employment income $	35,009	40,557	57,188	50,377	46,176	48,270
522	Standard error of average employment income $	1,767	2,264	2,671	1,770	1,637	5,897
523	Worked part year or part time (50)	225	310	465	640	550	130
524	Average employment income $	26,452	21,270	29,833	26,908	21,987	32,125
525	Standard error of average employment income $	1,604	1,975	3,370	2,620	1,898	5,611

Tableau 1. Certaines caractéristiques des secteurs de recensement, recensement de 2001 – Données intégrales et données-échantillon (20 %)

Vancouver 0221.01	Vancouver 0221.03 A	Vancouver 0221.04 A	Vancouver 0222	Vancouver 0223.01 A	Vancouver 0223.02 ◇ A	Caractéristiques	N°
						CARACTÉRISTIQUES DU REVENU DE 2000	
						Population de 15 ans et plus selon le sexe et les tranches de revenu total en 2000 – fin	
700	1,225	1,975	3,415	1,900	1,785	Total - Hommes	460
25	45	155	200	115	120	Sans revenu	461
675	1,180	1,820	3,215	1,785	1,670	Avec un revenu	462
20	20	140	175	80	190	Moins de 1 000 $ (45)	463
25	25	65	95	95	45	1 000 $ - 2 999 $	464
20	40	80	125	75	115	3 000 $ - 4 999 $	465
25	45	75	85	80	50	5 000 $ - 6 999 $	466
35	45	125	105	115	120	7 000 $ - 9 999 $	467
-	30	80	110	90	75	10 000 $ - 11 999 $	468
45	65	75	190	80	95	12 000 $ - 14 999 $	469
15	125	195	250	125	195	15 000 $ - 19 999 $	470
30	145	120	220	175	135	20 000 $ - 24 999 $	471
80	85	175	160	150	105	25 000 $ - 29 999 $	472
35	30	140	230	145	135	30 000 $ - 34 999 $	473
25	105	70	140	125	80	35 000 $ - 39 999 $	474
50	65	90	275	55	90	40 000 $ - 44 999 $	475
35	55	95	160	50	80	45 000 $ - 49 999 $	476
85	140	75	280	125	85	50 000 $ - 59 999 $	477
140	160	225	600	215	80	60 000 $ et plus	478
42,704	34,634	30,334	35,352	28,212	23,080	Revenu moyen $ (46)	479
33,969	27,087	22,479	30,787	24,451	17,230	Revenu médian $ (46)	480
3,099	1,648	1,561	1,165	1,119	1,080	Erreur type de revenu moyen $ (46)	481
670	1,255	1,960	3,890	2,130	1,765	Total - Femmes	482
35	95	170	260	155	180	Sans revenu	483
635	1,155	1,785	3,625	1,970	1,585	Avec un revenu	484
30	40	105	275	175	60	Moins de 1 000 $ (45)	485
25	50	150	205	115	160	1 000 $ - 2 999 $	486
30	75	75	270	95	120	3 000 $ - 4 999 $	487
10	65	145	215	140	85	5 000 $ - 6 999 $	488
30	95	80	180	170	205	7 000 $ - 9 999 $	489
15	60	95	160	130	85	10 000 $ - 11 999 $	490
55	100	185	310	135	145	12 000 $ - 14 999 $	491
50	85	195	355	190	160	15 000 $ - 19 999 $	492
55	95	180	185	150	130	20 000 $ - 24 999 $	493
35	110	115	245	165	50	25 000 $ - 29 999 $	494
30	60	110	305	200	165	30 000 $ - 34 999 $	495
85	50	70	205	60	70	35 000 $ - 39 999 $	496
85	35	95	205	55	50	40 000 $ - 44 999 $	497
25	65	70	135	80	10	45 000 $ - 49 999 $	498
30	70	40	195	80	45	50 000 $ - 59 999 $	499
55	100	75	175	30	35	60 000 $ et plus	500
28,652	26,335	20,608	22,707	19,229	18,011	Revenu moyen $ (46)	501
26,251	20,324	16,374	17,014	15,394	13,508	Revenu médian $ (46)	502
1,566	1,465	873	687	771	848	Erreur type de revenu moyen $ (46)	503
						selon la composition du revenu total	
100.0	100.0	100.0	100.0	100.0	100.0	Total - Composition du revenu en 2000 % (47)	504
75.1	72.3	73.0	79.3	82.6	78.5	Revenu d'emploi %	505
10.8	13.0	13.7	9.3	12.9	15.2	Transferts gouvernementaux %	506
14.0	14.7	13.2	11.3	4.4	6.3	Autre %	507
						Population de 15 ans et plus ayant un revenu d'emploi en 2000 selon le sexe et le travail	
960	1,640	2,310	4,870	2,795	2,225	Les deux sexes ayant un revenu d'emploi (48)	508
36,629	31,468	29,146	31,930	26,153	23,662	Revenu moyen d'emploi $	509
2,142	1,412	1,182	852	816	888	Erreur type de revenu moyen d'emploi $	510
535	840	1,050	2,595	1,375	1,020	Ayant travaillé toute l'année à plein temps (49)	511
48,716	46,067	43,416	44,520	36,535	30,791	Revenu moyen d'emploi $	512
2,903	2,038	1,807	1,220	1,117	1,142	Erreur type de revenu moyen d'emploi $	513
390	760	1,150	2,125	1,350	1,160	Ayant travaillé une partie de l'année ou à temps partiel (50)	514
21,401	16,660	17,029	18,177	16,480	17,934	Revenu moyen d'emploi $	515
1,961	1,125	932	809	903	1,255	Erreur type de revenu moyen d'emploi $	516
520	870	1,240	2,460	1,425	1,195	Hommes ayant un revenu d'emploi (48)	517
43,261	34,595	33,787	37,881	31,129	26,417	Revenu moyen d'emploi $	518
3,487	2,059	1,943	1,420	1,254	1,323	Erreur type de revenu moyen d'emploi $	519
320	490	605	1,510	790	615	Ayant travaillé toute l'année à plein temps (49)	520
54,945	47,944	48,906	48,496	39,904	32,746	Revenu moyen d'emploi $	521
4,286	2,757	2,826	1,923	1,699	1,542	Erreur type de revenu moyen d'emploi $	522
180	365	595	900	595	550	Ayant travaillé une partie de l'année ou à temps partiel (50)	523
22,159	18,107	18,379	21,811	21,172	20,128	Revenu moyen d'emploi $	524
3,440	1,818	1,489	1,439	1,525	2,146	Erreur type de revenu moyen d'emploi $	525

Table 1. Selected Characteristics for Census Tracts, 2001 Census – 100% Data and 20% Sample Data

No.	Characteristics	Vancouver 0206 ◆◇◇	Vancouver 0207	Vancouver 0208	Vancouver 0209	Vancouver 0210	Vancouver 0220
	2000 INCOME CHARACTERISTICS						
	Population 15 years and over with employment income in 2000 by sex and work activity – concluded						
526	Females with employment income (48)	620	700	1,395	1,760	1,215	265
527	Average employment income $	26,963	26,713	29,115	30,746	28,893	23,515
528	Standard error of average employment income $	1,678	1,703	1,275	1,025	1,138	2,759
529	Worked full year, full time (49)	385	330	645	905	640	100
530	Average employment income $	34,372	37,521	39,212	41,502	35,412	43,782
531	Standard error of average employment income $	1,901	2,400	1,829	1,239	1,389	3,927
532	Worked part year or part time (50)	210	350	715	815	555	160
533	Average employment income $	16,512	17,604	20,151	19,849	21,857	11,188
534	Standard error of average employment income $	2,197	1,691	1,500	1,262	1,664	1,542
	Census families by structure and family income groups in 2000						
535	Total - All census families	395	475	1,330	1,810	1,150	270
536	Under $10,000	10	30	35	40	80	15
537	$ 10,000 - $19,999	35	35	70	90	40	15
538	$ 20,000 - $29,999	60	50	50	160	60	15
539	$ 30,000 - $39,999	30	60	175	135	85	40
540	$ 40,000 - $49,999	55	55	110	180	115	20
541	$ 50,000 - $59,999	70	85	120	165	175	25
542	$ 60,000 - $69,999	30	35	155	180	150	40
543	$ 70,000 - $79,999	40	40	85	205	115	15
544	$ 80,000 - $89,999	35	30	100	155	100	30
545	$ 90,000 - $99,999	20	10	105	105	45	10
546	$100,000 and over	10	50	320	390	185	45
547	Average family income $	51,920	55,856	78,066	72,208	65,400	64,723
548	Median family income $	51,281	50,747	63,070	67,288	60,965	59,129
549	Standard error of average family income $	3,202	3,556	3,260	2,193	2,391	6,008
550	Total - All couple census families (51)	345	390	1,140	1,520	975	230
551	Under $10,000	10	10	25	25	50	10
552	$ 10,000 - $19,999	30	15	25	30	20	10
553	$ 20,000 - $29,999	55	40	45	120	20	15
554	$ 30,000 - $39,999	15	55	155	105	75	30
555	$ 40,000 - $49,999	35	40	55	135	85	15
556	$ 50,000 - $59,999	70	75	110	140	150	20
557	$ 60,000 - $69,999	25	25	140	150	125	40
558	$ 70,000 - $79,999	35	45	75	200	115	15
559	$ 80,000 - $89,999	30	30	100	135	95	35
560	$ 90,000 - $99,999	20	10	95	95	45	10
561	$100,000 and over	-	50	325	380	185	45
562	Average family income $	53,005	60,196	84,501	77,088	71,054	72,061
563	Median family income $	51,444	51,154	71,818	72,390	66,984	66,505
564	Standard error of average family income $	3,442	3,966	3,567	2,308	2,589	6,551
	Incidence of low income in 2000						
565	Total - Economic families	385	510	1,295	1,810	1,175	265
566	Low income	65	85	95	210	155	40
567	Incidence of low income in 2000 % (52)	16.9	16.4	7.5	11.6	13.3	15.4
568	Total - Unattached individuals 15 years and over	750	905	1,125	920	1,020	135
569	Low income	195	370	595	205	440	50
570	Incidence of low income in 2000 % (52)	26.0	41.0	53.1	22.3	43.3	33.8
571	Total - Population in private households	1,695	2,130	5,085	6,150	4,445	980
572	Low income	360	585	890	785	845	165
573	Incidence of low income in 2000 % (52)	21.1	27.6	17.5	12.8	19.0	17.0
	Private households by household income groups in 2000						
574	Total - All private households	1,010	1,310	2,260	2,615	1,995	330
575	Under $10,000	75	175	155	100	165	15
576	$ 10,000 - $19,999	115	180	450	220	240	10
577	$ 20,000 - $29,999	140	225	175	285	185	50
578	$ 30,000 - $39,999	170	185	285	195	235	35
579	$ 40,000 - $49,999	115	155	165	315	225	15
580	$ 50,000 - $59,999	110	120	200	285	235	35
581	$ 60,000 - $69,999	75	65	170	225	190	50
582	$ 70,000 - $79,999	85	70	70	245	140	30
583	$ 80,000 - $89,999	50	35	110	170	105	20
584	$ 90,000 - $99,999	60	-	100	135	55	10
585	$100,000 and over	10	95	385	445	230	65
586	Average household income $	44,841	41,339	58,562	63,661	53,089	66,519
587	Median household income $	40,973	32,946	44,357	57,388	47,103	61,063
588	Standard error of average household income $	1,856	2,018	2,378	1,768	1,798	5,530

Tableau 1. Certaines caractéristiques des secteurs de recensement, recensement de 2001 – Données intégrales et données-échantillon (20 %)

Vancouver 0221.01	Vancouver 0221.03 A	Vancouver 0221.04 A	Vancouver 0222	Vancouver 0223.01 A	Vancouver 0223.02 ◇ A	Caractéristiques	N°
						CARACTÉRISTIQUES DU REVENU DE 2000	
						Population de 15 ans et plus ayant un revenu d'emploi en 2000 selon le sexe et le travail – fin	
440	770	1,065	2,405	1,360	1,030	Femmes ayant un revenu d'emploi (48)	526
28,745	27,946	23,712	25,850	20,941	20,462	Revenu moyen d'emploi $	527
1,945	1,868	1,126	875	932	1,103	Erreur type de revenu moyen d'emploi $	528
215	355	445	1,085	590	400	Ayant travaillé toute l'année à plein temps (49)	529
39,226	43,477	35,998	39,004	32,030	27,797	Revenu moyen d'emploi $	530
2,712	2,966	1,694	1,178	1,194	1,604	Erreur type de revenu moyen d'emploi $	531
210	395	555	1,225	755	610	Ayant travaillé une partie de l'année ou à temps partiel (50)	532
20,744	15,328	15,574	15,513	12,782	15,977	Revenu moyen d'emploi $	533
2,176	1,368	1,080	893	957	1,366	Erreur type de revenu moyen d'emploi $	534
						Familles de recensement selon la structure et les tranches de revenu de la famille en 2000	
485	880	1,265	2,445	1,400	1,175	Total - Toutes les familles de recensement	535
10	10	105	130	105	155	Moins de 10 000 $	536
15	60	105	190	180	130	10 000 $ - 19 999 $	537
25	75	170	250	135	155	20 000 $ - 29 999 $	538
30	80	165	255	175	210	30 000 $ - 39 999 $	539
30	60	130	255	130	135	40 000 $ - 49 999 $	540
20	120	90	215	175	130	50 000 $ - 59 999 $	541
30	125	115	230	145	65	60 000 $ - 69 999 $	542
100	50	60	200	125	60	70 000 $ - 79 999 $	543
45	95	45	215	90	50	80 000 $ - 89 999 $	544
50	45	85	115	50	25	90 000 $ - 99 999 $	545
135	160	200	390	95	65	100 000 $ et plus	546
85,210	69,399	59,287	62,537	49,956	42,741	Revenu moyen des familles $	547
79,676	63,389	45,881	56,644	47,946	36,626	Revenu médian des familles $	548
4,308	2,921	2,820	1,800	1,754	1,904	Erreur type de revenu moyen des familles $	549
430	785	1,075	2,110	1,085	935	Total - Toutes les familles de recensement comptant un couple (51)	550
10	-	90	85	45	105	Moins de 10 000 $	551
10	55	75	135	85	65	10 000 $ - 19 999 $	552
15	55	115	205	95	140	20 000 $ - 29 999 $	553
30	70	135	190	100	175	30 000 $ - 39 999 $	554
20	60	105	185	120	105	40 000 $ - 49 999 $	555
15	105	80	195	160	120	50 000 $ - 59 999 $	556
20	105	110	225	130	45	60 000 $ - 69 999 $	557
95	45	60	195	115	55	70 000 $ - 79 999 $	558
40	80	35	220	80	50	80 000 $ - 89 999 $	559
45	45	80	110	50	20	90 000 $ - 99 999 $	560
130	160	195	375	95	60	100 000 $ et plus	561
89,124	71,778	63,373	66,572	56,826	45,755	Revenu moyen des familles $	562
81,501	63,972	53,944	62,576	55,017	39,480	Revenu médian des familles $	563
4,523	3,129	3,181	1,950	1,874	2,216	Erreur type de revenu moyen des familles $	564
						Fréquence des unités à faible revenu en 2000	
470	810	1,200	2,400	1,330	1,160	Total - Familles économiques	565
35	80	305	440	385	390	Faible revenu	566
7.6	9.6	25.6	18.3	29.2	33.8	Fréquence des unités à faible revenu en 2000 % (52)	567
145	270	495	1,130	515	495	Total - Personnes hors famille économique de 15 ans et plus	568
55	95	210	410	175	230	Faible revenu	569
40.2	35.5	42.6	36.2	33.6	46.3	Fréquence des unités à faible revenu en 2000 % (52)	570
1,655	2,990	4,650	8,655	5,180	4,550	Total - Population dans les ménages privés	571
215	395	1,350	1,995	1,400	1,685	Faible revenu	572
12.9	13.3	29.0	23.0	27.0	37.0	Fréquence des unités à faible revenu en 2000 % (52)	573
						Ménages privés selon les tranches de revenu du ménage en 2000	
570	1,025	1,485	3,285	1,685	1,525	Total - Tous les ménages privés	574
15	30	105	170	125	200	Moins de 10 000 $	575
40	100	165	370	210	180	10 000 $ - 19 999 $	576
25	85	145	295	175	185	20 000 $ - 29 999 $	577
45	85	205	340	205	245	30 000 $ - 39 999 $	578
30	65	135	385	160	200	40 000 $ - 49 999 $	579
25	135	120	315	155	155	50 000 $ - 59 999 $	580
35	115	140	275	175	85	60 000 $ - 69 999 $	581
115	70	50	240	130	85	70 000 $ - 79 999 $	582
35	95	60	270	145	65	80 000 $ - 89 999 $	583
65	35	75	120	50	30	90 000 $ - 99 999 $	584
150	215	285	500	165	90	100 000 $ et plus	585
82,574	69,795	61,901	59,592	52,338	43,710	Revenu moyen des ménages $	586
79,128	61,641	46,301	51,547	47,938	36,658	Revenu médian des ménages $	587
4,234	3,053	2,791	1,539	1,740	1,817	Erreur type de revenu moyen des ménages $	588

Table 1. Selected Characteristics for Census Tracts, 2001 Census – 100% Data and 20% Sample Data

No.	Characteristics	Vancouver 0224.01 A	Vancouver 0224.02 A	Vancouver 0225	Vancouver 0226.01	Vancouver 0226.02	Vancouver 0227.01 A
	POPULATION CHARACTERISTICS						
1	**Population, 1996 (1)**	**3,796**	**3,724**	**7,088**	**6,639**	**3,463**	**3,476**
2	**Population, 2001 (2)**	**3,907**	**4,058**	**9,163**	**8,162**	**3,732**	**4,074**
3	Population percentage change, 1996-2001	2.9	9.0	29.3	22.9	7.8	17.2
4	Land area in square kilometres, 2001	0.48	0.69	2.89	1.00	1.31	0.27
5	**Total population - 100% Data (3)**	**3,910**	**4,055**	**9,160**	**8,165**	**3,730**	**4,075**
	by sex and age groups						
6	Male	1,910	1,850	4,525	3,845	1,900	1,980
7	0-4 years	105	100	250	180	90	135
8	5-9 years	80	135	255	170	100	110
9	10-14 years	65	85	250	160	120	85
10	15-19 years	75	110	305	195	150	95
11	20-24 years	130	120	365	325	170	175
12	25-29 years	180	110	395	365	145	230
13	30-34 years	210	145	475	395	155	290
14	35-39 years	215	170	440	430	185	275
15	40-44 years	185	120	340	300	120	170
16	45-49 years	150	125	340	270	125	140
17	50-54 years	120	95	300	210	120	90
18	55-59 years	95	75	205	130	100	45
19	60-64 years	90	100	170	135	90	40
20	65-69 years	80	85	145	145	95	35
21	70-74 years	55	95	135	160	70	20
22	75-79 years	45	70	90	135	45	15
23	80-84 years	20	60	50	95	15	15
24	85 years and over	20	60	35	55	15	5
25	Female	2,000	2,205	4,635	4,315	1,830	2,095
26	0-4 years	95	100	255	185	75	130
27	5-9 years	70	90	200	145	75	125
28	10-14 years	65	85	255	140	105	90
29	15-19 years	75	90	275	195	115	100
30	20-24 years	120	115	385	310	150	175
31	25-29 years	200	140	420	385	120	275
32	30-34 years	205	145	470	500	155	285
33	35-39 years	200	125	435	400	140	265
34	40-44 years	140	135	375	320	140	165
35	45-49 years	125	125	340	260	165	135
36	50-54 years	135	105	310	245	125	80
37	55-59 years	105	85	210	180	115	55
38	60-64 years	65	120	170	185	85	50
39	65-69 years	90	100	135	185	85	35
40	70-74 years	90	95	170	190	50	40
41	75-79 years	90	135	125	210	60	40
42	80-84 years	60	145	65	165	30	35
43	85 years and over	70	270	45	125	20	25
44	**Total population 15 years and over**	**3,425**	**3,460**	**7,705**	**7,190**	**3,165**	**3,390**
	by legal marital status						
45	Never married (single)	1,190	940	2,775	2,400	1,125	1,365
46	Legally married (and not separated)	1,405	1,455	3,925	3,550	1,660	1,505
47	Separated, but still legally married	160	130	215	185	65	150
48	Divorced	385	335	415	500	160	250
49	Widowed	285	600	375	550	145	125
	by common-law status						
50	Not in a common-law relationship	3,225	3,330	7,280	6,860	3,050	3,195
51	In a common-law relationship	200	125	425	325	115	200
52	**Total population - 20% Sample Data (4)**	**3,875**	**3,570**	**9,150**	**8,160**	**3,700**	**4,075**
	by mother tongue						
53	Single responses	3,730	3,540	8,895	7,985	3,645	3,980
54	English	1,920	1,455	3,985	2,270	1,815	1,210
55	French	60	50	65	50	50	15
56	Non-official languages (5)	1,750	2,035	4,835	5,655	1,780	2,755
57	Chinese, n.o.s.	280	325	985	1,265	330	555
58	Cantonese	190	165	840	660	215	50
59	Punjabi	30	105	415	20	50	-
60	Mandarin	145	240	575	1,085	395	300
61	Tagalog (Pilipino)	60	60	250	130	35	345
62	Other languages (6)	1,050	1,135	1,775	2,490	750	1,510
63	Multiple responses	145	35	260	180	55	95
64	English and French	10	10	-	15	-	25
65	English and non-official language	120	20	250	150	50	70
66	French and non-official language	-	-	-	10	10	-
67	English, French and non-official language	20	-	-	10	-	-

See reference material at the end of the publication. – Voir les documents de référence à la fin de la publication.

Tableau 1. Certaines caractéristiques des secteurs de recensement, recensement de 2001 – Données intégrales et données-échantillon (20 %)

Vancouver 0227.02 A	Vancouver 0228.02	Vancouver 0228.03 A	Vancouver 0228.04 A	Vancouver 0229	Vancouver 0230.01	Caractéristiques	N°
						CARACTÉRISTIQUES DE LA POPULATION	
4,599	**3,283**	**3,522**	**4,285**	**6,442**	**5,054**	**Population, 1996 (1)**	1
4,923	**3,461**	**4,190**	**4,803**	**6,678**	**5,358**	**Population, 2001 (2)**	2
7.0	5.4	19.0	12.1	3.7	6.0	Variation en pourcentage de la population, 1996-2001	3
1.11	0.99	0.34	0.71	3.09	4.22	Superficie des terres en kilomètres carrés, 2001	4
4,925	**3,465**	**4,190**	**4,805**	**6,680**	**5,355**	**Population totale – Données intégrales (3)**	5
						selon le sexe et les groupes d'âge	
2,250	1,750	2,025	2,170	3,155	2,580	Sexe masculin	6
100	85	100	110	160	105	0-4 ans	7
55	105	80	85	160	135	5-9 ans	8
55	130	55	100	150	180	10-14 ans	9
70	120	95	110	235	210	15-19 ans	10
125	150	190	140	230	240	20-24 ans	11
180	110	235	180	225	135	25-29 ans	12
275	110	285	205	225	130	30-34 ans	13
220	140	210	220	245	170	35-39 ans	14
205	150	150	175	255	230	40-44 ans	15
140	145	145	155	230	230	45-49 ans	16
175	100	105	125	210	230	50-54 ans	17
105	115	75	100	160	185	55-59 ans	18
105	70	60	85	140	135	60-64 ans	19
110	55	70	85	150	100	65-69 ans	20
115	70	55	90	125	85	70-74 ans	21
110	55	60	70	130	45	75-79 ans	22
75	25	35	65	70	20	80-84 ans	23
40	15	20	60	55	10	85 ans et plus	24
2,670	1,715	2,165	2,630	3,530	2,775	Sexe féminin	25
85	95	95	105	135	105	0-4 ans	26
70	110	65	95	165	135	5-9 ans	27
50	100	55	90	160	185	10-14 ans	28
70	95	95	110	220	230	15-19 ans	29
150	110	230	170	190	170	20-24 ans	30
215	125	220	175	230	150	25-29 ans	31
255	115	270	170	225	145	30-34 ans	32
215	135	210	240	260	220	35-39 ans	33
220	160	155	190	290	270	40-44 ans	34
195	145	140	180	245	270	45-49 ans	35
150	130	120	150	225	275	50-54 ans	36
140	85	75	150	175	180	55-59 ans	37
135	70	90	110	165	155	60-64 ans	38
170	65	70	115	170	100	65-69 ans	39
150	75	85	120	170	75	70-74 ans	40
170	60	75	160	160	70	75-79 ans	41
135	25	75	140	125	25	80-84 ans	42
90	10	30	170	220	15	85 ans et plus	43
4,510	**2,840**	**3,740**	**4,215**	**5,750**	**4,510**	**Population totale de 15 ans et plus**	44
						selon l'état matrimonial légal	
1,445	880	1,435	1,425	1,955	1,445	Célibataire (jamais marié(e))	45
1,970	1,620	1,710	1,740	2,660	2,525	Légalement marié(e) (et non séparé(e))	46
155	60	105	125	175	95	Séparé(e), mais toujours légalement marié(e)	47
475	145	265	400	375	285	Divorcé(e)	48
460	130	225	530	590	160	Veuf ou veuve	49
						selon l'union libre	
4,190	2,730	3,500	3,960	5,470	4,305	Ne vivant pas en union libre	50
320	110	240	255	280	205	Vivant en union libre	51
4,920	**3,455**	**4,190**	**4,590**	**6,215**	**5,350**	**Population totale – Données-échantillon (20 %) (4)**	52
						selon la langue maternelle	
4,850	3,380	4,125	4,485	6,080	5,280	Réponses uniques	53
2,075	1,630	1,475	2,340	3,145	3,230	Anglais	54
45	20	70	20	20	40	Français	55
2,735	1,735	2,575	2,125	2,915	2,005	Langues non officielles (5)	56
585	465	470	375	455	345	Chinois, n.d.a.	57
180	290	315	290	355	370	Cantonais	58
-	75	10	30	120	50	Pendjabi	59
185	90	325	85	115	160	Mandarin	60
75	100	90	65	80	50	Tagalog (pilipino)	61
1,705	720	1,370	1,275	1,790	1,035	Autres langues (6)	62
70	75	70	105	135	70	Réponses multiples	63
-	-	-	15	10	-	Anglais et français	64
60	75	60	85	110	60	Anglais et langue non officielle	65
10	-	-	10	10	15	Français et langue non officielle	66
-	-	-	-	20	-	Anglais, français et langue non officielle	67

See reference material at the end of the publication. – Voir les documents de référence à la fin de la publication.

Table 1. Selected Characteristics for Census Tracts, 2001 Census – 100% Data and 20% Sample Data

No.	Characteristics	Vancouver 0224.01 A	Vancouver 0224.02 A	Vancouver 0225	Vancouver 0226.01	Vancouver 0226.02	Vancouver 0227.01 A
	POPULATION CHARACTERISTICS						
	by home language						
68	Single responses	2,960	2,630	6,700	5,965	2,825	2,555
69	English	2,110	1,555	4,525	2,810	2,115	1,445
70	French	-	-	-	-	10	10
71	Non-official languages (5)	850	1,075	2,175	3,150	705	1,110
72	Cantonese	150	120	425	495	160	25
73	Chinese, n.o.s.	180	145	405	845	115	320
74	Punjabi	10	40	130	-	-	-
75	Mandarin	105	155	455	640	170	185
76	Korean	50	115	175	265	45	85
77	Other languages (6)	360	490	585	900	210	495
78	Multiple responses	910	940	2,450	2,195	875	1,520
79	English and French	25	55	35	60	50	20
80	English and non-official language	800	885	2,400	2,105	825	1,495
81	French and non-official language	60	-	10	-	-	-
82	English, French and non-official language	25	-	10	35	-	-
	by knowledge of official languages						
83	English only	3,355	3,000	8,290	6,840	3,220	3,690
84	French only	-	-	-	-	10	-
85	English and French	250	125	320	445	255	175
86	Neither English nor French	270	445	530	885	215	210
	by knowledge of non-official languages (5) (7)						
87	Cantonese	235	285	1,000	935	445	70
88	Chinese, n.o.s.	315	320	900	1,140	195	515
89	Punjabi	45	115	475	25	115	-
90	Mandarin	260	315	985	1,440	465	380
91	Hindi	195	100	280	55	85	50
92	German	60	80	165	290	110	95
93	Spanish	190	160	325	165	65	130
	by first official language spoken						
94	English	3,505	3,065	8,505	7,100	3,435	3,825
95	French	40	50	80	60	40	15
96	English and French	70	15	60	120	10	35
97	Neither English nor French	265	450	505	880	215	200
98	Official language minority - (number) (8)	75	55	110	125	45	35
99	Official language minority - (percentage) (8)	1.9	1.5	1.2	1.5	1.2	0.9
	by ethnic origin (9)						
100	English	540	580	1,330	830	700	360
101	Canadian	600	390	1,270	685	635	425
102	Chinese	740	925	2,675	3,055	975	995
103	Scottish	450	345	890	480	285	295
104	Irish	340	270	695	420	325	195
105	German	245	185	495	395	320	240
106	East Indian	245	215	630	105	190	55
107	French	165	155	365	230	110	135
108	Ukrainian	155	95	260	135	185	110
109	Italian	50	110	300	115	85	40
110	Dutch (Netherlands)	85	35	235	55	75	55
111	Filipino	175	80	420	350	85	530
112	Polish	45	65	240	85	35	55
113	Norwegian	75	45	130	40	25	30
114	North American Indian	130	95	170	65	65	40
	by Aboriginal identity						
115	Total Aboriginal identity population (10)	120	55	205	60	55	40
116	Total non-Aboriginal population	3,760	3,520	8,945	8,105	3,640	4,035
	by Aboriginal origin						
117	Total Aboriginal origins population (11)	160	100	205	75	65	50
118	Total non-Aboriginal population	3,715	3,470	8,945	8,085	3,635	4,025
	by Registered Indian status						
119	Registered Indian (12)	60	25	115	10	45	20
120	Not a Registered Indian	3,820	3,545	9,040	8,155	3,650	4,055

Tableau 1. Certaines caractéristiques des secteurs de recensement, recensement de 2001 – Données intégrales et données-échantillon (20 %)

Vancouver 0227.02 A	Vancouver 0228.02	Vancouver 0228.03 A	Vancouver 0228.04 A	Vancouver 0229	Vancouver 0230.01	Caractéristiques	N°
						CARACTÉRISTIQUES DE LA POPULATION	
						selon la langue parlée à la maison	
3,700	2,710	3,060	3,515	4,395	4,260	Réponses uniques	68
2,460	1,965	1,670	2,650	3,285	3,560	Anglais	69
15	10	10	10	10	-	Français	70
1,225	740	1,380	860	1,100	700	Langues non officielles (5)	71
145	155	225	125	195	115	Cantonais	72
290	185	330	185	140	95	Chinois, n.d.a.	73
-	10	-	10	45	10	Pendjabi	74
110	90	210	95	50	100	Mandarin	75
110	10	295	90	40	100	Coréen	76
570	285	325	355	625	280	Autres langues (6)	77
1,225	745	1,130	1,075	1,820	1,090	Réponses multiples	78
15	10	60	10	15	35	Anglais et français	79
1,205	740	1,060	1,050	1,795	1,030	Anglais et langue non officielle	80
-	-	10	-	-	-	Français et langue non officielle	81
10	-	-	20	10	20	Anglais, français et langue non officielle	82
						selon la connaissance des langues officielles	
4,355	3,015	3,600	4,165	5,525	4,770	Anglais seulement	83
-	10	-	-	-	-	Français seulement	84
270	195	290	205	410	350	Anglais et français	85
295	245	305	215	280	230	Ni l'anglais ni le français	86
						selon la connaissance des langues non officielles (5) (7)	
315	350	495	350	525	435	Cantonais	87
455	410	405	360	465	310	Chinois, n.d.a.	88
10	125	45	50	200	80	Pendjabi	89
425	190	550	230	280	345	Mandarin	90
20	135	65	250	430	65	Hindi	91
205	65	135	170	95	190	Allemand	92
220	80	110	105	200	90	Espagnol	93
						selon la première langue officielle parlée	
4,505	3,165	3,730	4,320	5,855	5,050	Anglais	94
50	25	85	45	20	40	Français	95
80	20	80	10	55	40	Anglais et français	96
295	245	290	215	280	225	Ni l'anglais ni le français	97
85	35	125	50	50	60	Minorité de langue officielle - (nombre) (8)	98
1.7	1.0	3.0	1.1	0.8	1.1	Minorité de langue officielle - (pourcentage) (8)	99
						selon l'origine ethnique (9)	
925	515	455	820	865	1,300	Anglais	100
645	490	535	730	805	960	Canadien	101
1,030	1,075	1,285	975	1,355	1,150	Chinois	102
485	370	360	480	700	780	Écossais	103
395	215	200	490	395	565	Irlandais	104
335	215	250	465	455	615	Allemand	105
60	230	125	260	1,065	195	Indien de l'Inde	106
145	135	200	185	290	215	Français	107
160	130	80	175	140	245	Ukrainien	108
50	105	85	115	280	280	Italien	109
130	35	40	110	100	170	Hollandais (Néerlandais)	110
135	190	145	155	155	150	Philippin	111
165	85	90	190	35	270	Polonais	112
65	65	35	45	85	120	Norvégien	113
30	55	90	60	155	25	Indien de l'Amérique du Nord	114
						selon l'identité autochtone	
30	55	85	35	150	15	Total de la population ayant une identité autochtone (10)	115
4,895	3,405	4,110	4,555	6,065	5,335	Total de la population non autochtone	116
						selon l'origine autochtone	
35	50	95	55	190	40	Total de la population ayant une origine autochtone (11)	117
4,890	3,405	4,095	4,535	6,020	5,315	Total de la population non autochtone	118
						selon le statut d'Indien inscrit	
20	25	60	30	45	10	Oui, Indien inscrit (12)	119
4,905	3,430	4,125	4,560	6,165	5,340	Non, pas un Indien inscrit	120

Table 1. Selected Characteristics for Census Tracts, 2001 Census – 100% Data and 20% Sample Data

No.	Characteristics	Vancouver 0224.01 A	Vancouver 0224.02 A	Vancouver 0225	Vancouver 0226.01	Vancouver 0226.02	Vancouver 0227.01 A
	POPULATION CHARACTERISTICS						
	by visible minority groups						
121	Total visible minority population	1,675	1,715	4,990	4,875	1,875	2,440
122	Chinese	735	820	2,685	3,145	1,085	955
123	South Asian	255	300	830	135	190	120
124	Black	95	30	110	45	130	145
125	Filipino	160	80	375	315	55	535
126	Latin American	150	45	160	100	55	115
127	Southeast Asian	55	45	150	130	65	75
128	Arab	-	80	60	45	10	25
129	West Asian	55	110	45	240	35	150
130	Korean	95	160	305	445	110	180
131	Japanese	50	15	135	155	65	85
132	Visible minority, n.i.e. (13)	-	30	20	45	-	10
133	Multiple visible minorities (14)	15	-	110	70	75	50
	by citizenship						
134	Canadian citizenship (15)	3,170	2,495	7,480	5,040	2,925	2,305
135	Citizenship other than Canadian	705	1,075	1,675	3,120	775	1,765
	by place of birth of respondent						
136	Non-immigrant population	2,005	1,555	4,505	2,405	1,850	1,250
137	Born in province of residence	1,270	1,005	3,195	1,455	1,335	780
138	Immigrant population (16)	1,785	1,980	4,505	5,260	1,690	2,555
139	United States	20	50	85	40	35	20
140	Central and South America	135	55	130	70	50	70
141	Caribbean and Bermuda	10	-	65	10	10	-
142	United Kingdom	110	45	185	170	130	30
143	Other Europe (17)	315	465	535	1,095	215	505
144	Africa	85	50	115	95	125	80
145	Asia and the Middle East	1,015	1,225	3,310	3,775	1,135	1,835
146	Oceania and other (18)	100	90	85	15	10	15
147	Non-permanent residents (19)	85	35	145	495	160	275
148	**Total immigrant population**	**1,790**	**1,985**	**4,510**	**5,260**	**1,690**	**2,555**
	by period of immigration						
149	Before 1961	115	110	245	310	115	25
150	1961-1970	130	85	340	180	135	20
151	1971-1980	175	315	705	305	280	95
152	1981-1990	260	155	665	600	235	165
153	1991-2001 (20)	1,115	1,310	2,550	3,860	930	2,240
154	1991-1995	355	375	1,070	1,160	385	450
155	1996-2001 (20)	760	935	1,485	2,705	540	1,790
	by age at immigration						
156	0-4 years	120	100	365	360	125	200
157	5-19 years	420	585	1,235	1,175	500	510
158	20 years and over	1,250	1,295	2,910	3,725	1,070	1,845
159	**Total population**	**3,875**	**3,570**	**9,150**	**8,160**	**3,700**	**4,075**
	by religion						
160	Catholic (21)	765	595	2,100	1,190	550	880
161	Protestant	845	520	1,770	1,390	830	745
162	Christian Orthodox	130	175	160	550	25	230
163	Christian, n.i.e. (22)	150	210	540	620	360	235
164	Muslim	255	225	230	410	70	260
165	Jewish	25	10	30	-	30	15
166	Buddhist	80	135	535	630	200	120
167	Hindu	85	80	195	60	50	45
168	Sikh	35	95	450	15	95	-
169	Eastern religions (23)	-	-	45	40	10	-
170	Other religions (24)	30	-	15	-	-	30
171	No religious affiliation (25)	1,470	1,530	3,080	3,260	1,465	1,520
172	**Total population 15 years and over**	**3,390**	**2,975**	**7,690**	**7,135**	**3,140**	**3,395**
	by generation status						
173	1st generation (26)	1,700	1,740	4,275	5,155	1,690	2,445
174	2nd generation (27)	665	545	1,570	1,055	765	435
175	3rd generation and over (28)	1,015	685	1,855	915	690	515
176	**Total population 1 year and over (29)**	**3,830**	**3,530**	**9,045**	**8,065**	**3,660**	**4,025**
	by place of residence 1 year ago (mobility)						
177	Non-movers	2,960	2,700	7,045	5,815	2,865	2,620
178	Movers	875	830	2,000	2,250	795	1,405
179	Non-migrants	355	295	930	860	385	515
180	Migrants	520	535	1,075	1,385	410	890
181	Internal migrants	315	250	685	530	140	380
182	Intraprovincial migrants	255	210	640	450	115	320
183	Interprovincial migrants	65	40	40	85	25	60
184	External migrants	205	285	390	860	265	510

Tableau 1. Certaines caractéristiques des secteurs de recensement, recensement de 2001 – Données intégrales et données-échantillon (20 %)

Vancouver 0227.02 A	Vancouver 0228.02	Vancouver 0228.03 A	Vancouver 0228.04 A	Vancouver 0229	Vancouver 0230.01	Caractéristiques	N°
						CARACTÉRISTIQUES DE LA POPULATION	
						selon les groupes de minorités visibles	
2,095	1,925	2,375	2,050	3,380	2,025	Total de la population des minorités visibles	121
1,050	1,070	1,300	950	1,245	1,155	Chinois	122
90	300	125	350	1,270	270	Sud-Asiatique	123
75	30	80	55	130	45	Noir	124
110	115	130	150	110	150	Philippin	125
150	30	45	10	130	35	Latino-Américain	126
75	85	60	60	210	45	Asiatique du Sud-Est	127
20	15	10	75	10	-	Arabe	128
185	110	80	105	55	-	Asiatique occidental	129
195	35	485	150	65	150	Coréen	130
105	30	40	85	40	145	Japonais	131
-	-	-	10	10	-	Minorité visible, n.i.a. (13)	132
35	100	25	55	125	25	Minorités visibles multiples (14)	133
						selon la citoyenneté	
3,700	2,980	3,015	3,850	5,720	4,790	Citoyenneté canadienne (15)	134
1,225	475	1,180	745	495	565	Citoyenneté autre que canadienne	135
						selon le lieu de naissance du répondant	
2,085	1,850	1,520	2,420	3,215	3,235	Population non immigrante	136
1,105	1,410	970	1,590	2,350	2,360	Née dans la province de résidence	137
2,690	1,570	2,445	2,050	2,945	2,090	Population immigrante (16)	138
10	20	60	35	35	85	États-Unis	139
170	20	65	25	115	35	Amérique centrale et du Sud	140
50	-	30	30	-	10	Caraïbes et Bermudes	141
150	95	65	65	145	230	Royaume-Uni	142
750	235	365	440	450	420	Autre Europe (17)	143
35	55	40	120	680	115	Afrique	144
1,515	1,085	1,795	1,240	1,395	1,135	Asie et Moyen-Orient	145
15	55	25	85	120	65	Océanie et autre (18)	146
150	45	220	120	60	30	Résidents non permanents (19)	147
2,685	**1,570**	**2,445**	**2,050**	**2,945**	**2,090**	**Population immigrante totale**	148
						selon la période d'immigration	
255	205	215	220	240	210	Avant 1961	149
190	145	110	160	230	190	1961-1970	150
200	280	165	335	975	510	1971-1980	151
340	260	340	380	675	280	1981-1990	152
1,705	675	1,615	960	820	905	1991-2001 (20)	153
620	260	570	345	455	485	1991-1995	154
1,085	415	1,040	610	360	425	1996-2001 (20)	155
						selon l'âge à l'immigration	
145	85	115	140	255	215	0-4 ans	156
605	505	580	490	755	485	5-19 ans	157
1,940	975	1,750	1,420	1,935	1,390	20 ans et plus	158
4,925	**3,460**	**4,190**	**4,590**	**6,210**	**5,350**	**Population totale**	159
						selon la religion	
1,035	580	840	865	1,115	1,040	Catholique (21)	160
1,320	910	640	1,225	1,195	1,565	Protestante	161
235	20	110	105	85	60	Orthodoxe chrétienne	162
240	180	475	360	385	260	Chrétiennes, n.i.a. (22)	163
215	95	155	280	875	175	Musulmane	164
-	-	10	30	-	20	Juive	165
240	220	150	250	235	170	Bouddhiste	166
15	90	60	195	275	15	Hindoue	167
-	140	10	40	120	80	Sikh	168
20	60	20	-	55	-	Religions orientales (23)	169
20	10	20	10	10	-	Autres religions (24)	170
1,575	1,140	1,710	1,230	1,865	1,950	Aucune appartenance religieuse (25)	171
4,505	**2,830**	**3,740**	**3,995**	**5,280**	**4,505**	**Population totale de 15 ans et plus**	172
						selon le statut des générations	
2,595	1,510	2,475	2,080	2,880	1,940	1re génération (26)	173
935	590	465	1,015	1,275	1,125	2e génération (27)	174
975	735	805	900	1,120	1,440	3e génération et plus (28)	175
4,890	**3,435**	**4,145**	**4,565**	**6,175**	**5,320**	**Population totale de 1 an et plus (29)**	176
						selon le lieu de résidence 1 an auparavant (mobilité)	
3,810	2,925	3,000	3,770	5,060	4,670	Personnes n'ayant pas déménagé	177
1,075	510	1,140	790	1,120	645	Personnes ayant déménagé	178
490	220	505	405	525	210	Non-migrants	179
585	285	630	385	595	440	Migrants	180
295	120	405	220	450	325	Migrants internes	181
265	100	325	195	420	295	Migrants infraprovinciaux	182
30	20	80	30	30	30	Migrants interprovinciaux	183
285	170	230	165	145	110	Migrants externes	184

Table 1. Selected Characteristics for Census Tracts, 2001 Census – 100% Data and 20% Sample Data

No.	Characteristics	Vancouver 0224.01 A	Vancouver 0224.02 A	Vancouver 0225	Vancouver 0226.01	Vancouver 0226.02	Vancouver 0227.01 A
	POPULATION CHARACTERISTICS						
185	**Total population 5 years and over (30)**	**3,675**	**3,365**	**8,645**	**7,800**	**3,535**	**3,805**
	by place of residence 5 years ago (mobility)						
186	Non-movers	1,505	1,560	3,710	2,245	1,950	845
187	Movers	2,170	1,805	4,930	5,555	1,580	2,960
188	Non-migrants	815	590	1,835	1,450	520	655
189	Migrants	1,360	1,210	3,095	4,105	1,060	2,305
190	Internal migrants	655	440	1,750	1,200	515	595
191	Intraprovincial migrants	440	320	1,565	910	480	395
192	Interprovincial migrants	210	115	185	290	30	205
193	External migrants	710	780	1,345	2,905	550	1,705
194	**Total population 15 to 24 years**	**395**	**425**	**1,315**	**990**	**640**	**530**
	by school attendance						
195	Not attending school	130	135	345	185	170	180
196	Attending school full time	230	235	845	740	415	285
197	Attending school part time	40	65	125	65	55	70
198	**Total population 15 years and over**	**3,385**	**2,975**	**7,690**	**7,135**	**3,140**	**3,390**
	by highest level of schooling						
199	Less than grade 9 (31)	400	385	620	480	155	140
200	Grades 9-13 without high school graduation certificate	560	800	1,300	1,050	565	460
201	Grades 9-13 with high school graduation certificate	300	395	880	920	325	420
202	Some postsecondary without degree, certificate or diploma (32)	445	340	1,315	905	545	450
203	Trades certificate or diploma (33)	400	270	665	555	285	190
204	College certificate or diploma (34)	535	355	1,145	955	475	390
205	University certificate below bachelor's degree	170	120	375	485	130	150
206	University with bachelor's degree or higher	580	315	1,400	1,775	665	1,190
	by combinations of unpaid work						
207	Males 15 years and over	1,645	1,420	3,795	3,315	1,545	1,655
208	Reported unpaid work (35)	1,345	1,245	3,240	2,815	1,415	1,505
209	Housework and child care and care or assistance to seniors	105	65	240	185	115	95
210	Housework and child care only	355	360	880	710	375	370
211	Housework and care or assistance to seniors only	90	135	240	215	65	70
212	Child care and care or assistance to seniors only	-	-	-	-	-	-
213	Housework only	755	655	1,835	1,620	800	945
214	Child care only	20	25	40	65	10	25
215	Care or assistance to seniors only	15	10	-	25	40	-
216	Females 15 years and over	1,740	1,555	3,895	3,820	1,595	1,740
217	Reported unpaid work (35)	1,470	1,370	3,540	3,475	1,405	1,635
218	Housework and child care and care or assistance to seniors	110	135	445	265	140	120
219	Housework and child care only	380	405	1,140	865	425	505
220	Housework and care or assistance to seniors only	160	160	255	345	125	65
221	Child care and care or assistance to seniors only	-	10	-	-	-	-
222	Housework only	795	645	1,660	1,955	685	930
223	Child care only	10	10	30	40	-	10
224	Care or assistance to seniors only	10	15	10	10	30	-
	by labour force activity						
225	Males 15 years and over	1,645	1,420	3,795	3,315	1,550	1,655
226	In the labour force	1,065	720	2,445	1,775	1,020	1,200
227	Employed	960	555	2,320	1,605	930	1,050
228	Unemployed	105	165	125	170	95	155
229	Not in the labour force	580	695	1,350	1,535	530	455
230	Participation rate	64.7	50.7	64.4	53.5	65.8	72.5
231	Employment rate	58.4	39.1	61.1	48.4	60.0	63.4
232	Unemployment rate	9.9	22.9	5.1	9.6	9.3	12.9
233	Females 15 years and over	1,740	1,555	3,900	3,820	1,595	1,740
234	In the labour force	885	635	2,165	1,665	835	1,040
235	Employed	775	535	2,035	1,470	795	910
236	Unemployed	105	95	130	195	40	125
237	Not in the labour force	860	920	1,735	2,155	755	705
238	Participation rate	50.9	40.8	55.5	43.6	52.4	59.8
239	Employment rate	44.5	34.4	52.2	38.5	49.8	52.3
240	Unemployment rate	11.9	15.0	6.0	11.7	4.8	12.0

Tableau 1. Certaines caractéristiques des secteurs de recensement, recensement de 2001 – Données intégrales et données-échantillon (20 %)

Vancouver 0227.02 A	Vancouver 0228.02	Vancouver 0228.03 A	Vancouver 0228.04 A	Vancouver 0229	Vancouver 0230.01	Caractéristiques	Nº
						CARACTÉRISTIQUES DE LA POPULATION	
4,745	**3,275**	**4,010**	**4,375**	**5,910**	**5,145**	**Population totale de 5 ans et plus (30)**	185
						selon le lieu de résidence 5 ans auparavant (mobilité)	
1,950	2,170	1,130	2,245	3,285	3,345	Personnes n'ayant pas déménagé	186
2,800	1,110	2,875	2,140	2,630	1,795	Personnes ayant déménagé	187
905	395	900	860	970	780	Non-migrants	188
1,895	715	1,975	1,280	1,660	1,020	Migrants	189
805	370	905	655	1,235	640	Migrants internes	190
645	330	655	510	1,055	535	Migrants infraprovinciaux	191
165	45	250	145	180	110	Migrants interprovinciaux	192
1,090	345	1,070	620	420	380	Migrants externes	193
435	**410**	**610**	**525**	**815**	**845**	**Population totale de 15 à 24 ans**	194
						selon la fréquentation scolaire	
170	120	155	140	195	225	Ne fréquentant pas l'école	195
235	230	415	295	550	580	Fréquentant l'école à plein temps	196
30	60	40	85	75	45	Fréquentant l'école à temps partiel	197
4,505	**2,830**	**3,745**	**3,995**	**5,280**	**4,510**	**Population totale de 15 ans et plus**	198
						selon le plus haut niveau de scolarité atteint	
255	205	220	330	440	160	Niveau inférieur à la 9ᵉ année (31)	199
730	445	370	730	1,075	565	De la 9ᵉ à la 13ᵉ année sans certificat d'études secondaires	200
530	375	430	485	735	450	De la 9ᵉ à la 13ᵉ année avec certificat d'études secondaires	201
495	340	685	505	720	765	Études postsecondaires partielles sans grade, certificat ou diplôme (32)	202
470	325	250	315	630	385	Certificat ou diplôme d'une école de métiers (33)	203
800	515	460	580	830	630	Certificat ou diplôme collégial (34)	204
230	110	205	180	150	245	Certificat universitaire inférieur au baccalauréat	205
990	515	1,120	870	695	1,300	Études universitaires avec baccalauréat ou diplôme supérieur	206
						selon les combinaisons de travail non rémunéré	
2,035	1,440	1,785	1,810	2,530	2,150	Hommes de 15 ans et plus	207
1,815	1,235	1,520	1,615	2,150	1,880	Travail non rémunéré déclaré (35)	208
145	135	60	95	235	165	Travaux ménagers et soins aux enfants et soins ou aide aux personnes âgées	209
290	345	310	280	455	580	Travaux ménagers et soins aux enfants seulement	210
175	75	120	155	225	125	Travaux ménagers et soins ou aide aux personnes âgées seulement	211
-	-	-	-	10	-	Soins aux enfants et soins ou aide aux personnes âgées seulement	212
1,175	670	990	1,060	1,190	985	Travaux ménagers seulement	213
25	10	15	15	25	10	Soins aux enfants seulement	214
-	-	25	15	10	15	Soins ou aide aux personnes âgées seulement	215
2,465	1,385	1,960	2,190	2,750	2,355	Femmes de 15 ans et plus	216
2,250	1,325	1,750	2,000	2,485	2,150	Travail non rémunéré déclaré (35)	217
205	200	85	125	400	235	Travaux ménagers et soins aux enfants et soins ou aide aux personnes âgées	218
395	385	385	445	570	660	Travaux ménagers et soins aux enfants seulement	219
280	155	145	270	370	250	Travaux ménagers et soins ou aide aux personnes âgées seulement	220
-	-	-	10	-	-	Soins aux enfants et soins ou aide aux personnes âgées seulement	221
1,345	575	1,120	1,155	1,110	975	Travaux ménagers seulement	222
15	-	10	-	30	10	Soins aux enfants seulement	223
-	-	10	10	-	10	Soins ou aide aux personnes âgées seulement	224
						selon l'activité	
2,035	1,445	1,785	1,805	2,530	2,155	Hommes de 15 ans et plus	225
1,340	970	1,120	1,170	1,660	1,620	Population active	226
1,175	900	985	1,060	1,530	1,500	Personnes occupées	227
165	70	135	115	135	120	Chômeurs	228
695	475	660	635	870	530	Inactifs	229
65.8	67.1	62.7	64.8	65.6	75.2	Taux d'activité	230
57.7	62.3	55.2	58.7	60.5	69.6	Taux d'emploi	231
12.3	7.2	12.1	9.8	8.1	7.4	Taux de chômage	232
2,465	1,385	1,960	2,190	2,750	2,355	Femmes de 15 ans et plus	233
1,265	795	1,000	1,120	1,655	1,555	Population active	234
1,145	735	880	1,065	1,550	1,475	Personnes occupées	235
120	65	120	55	105	80	Chômeuses	236
1,200	590	955	1,065	1,090	800	Inactives	237
51.3	57.4	51.0	51.1	60.2	66.0	Taux d'activité	238
46.5	53.1	44.9	48.6	56.4	62.6	Taux d'emploi	239
9.5	8.2	12.0	4.9	6.3	5.1	Taux de chômage	240

Table 1. Selected Characteristics for Census Tracts, 2001 Census – 100% Data and 20% Sample Data

No.	Characteristics	Vancouver 0224.01 A	Vancouver 0224.02 A	Vancouver 0225	Vancouver 0226.01	Vancouver 0226.02	Vancouver 0227.01 A
	POPULATION CHARACTERISTICS						
	by labour force activity – concluded						
241	Both sexes - Participation rate	57.6	45.6	59.9	48.3	59.2	66.2
242	15-24 years	53.2	43.0	44.3	32.3	46.9	54.7
243	25 years and over	58.1	46.0	63.0	50.9	62.1	68.4
244	Both sexes - Employment rate	51.3	36.8	56.6	43.2	54.8	57.7
245	15-24 years	39.7	34.9	39.3	26.1	40.2	47.2
246	25 years and over	53.0	37.1	60.1	45.9	58.5	59.8
247	Both sexes - Unemployment rate	10.8	19.2	5.4	10.6	7.3	12.5
248	15-24 years	26.2	18.9	12.1	18.8	13.3	15.8
249	25 years and over	9.2	19.2	4.6	9.8	5.8	12.1
250	**Total labour force 15 years and over by industry based on the 1997 NAICS**	**1,950**	**1,355**	**4,610**	**3,440**	**1,855**	**2,240**
251	Industry - Not applicable (36)	90	135	120	160	35	60
252	All industries (37)	1,860	1,220	4,490	3,285	1,825	2,180
253	11 Agriculture, forestry, fishing and hunting	15	-	25	15	25	20
254	21 Mining and oil and gas extraction	-	-	-	-	-	30
255	22 Utilities	10	10	35	10	-	20
256	23 Construction	90	70	270	105	80	60
257	31-33 Manufacturing	295	110	480	320	195	305
258	41 Wholesale trade	100	70	300	155	115	120
259	44-45 Retail trade	235	165	515	395	235	250
260	48-49 Transportation and warehousing	90	65	205	160	50	90
261	51 Information and cultural industries	70	25	200	215	110	145
262	52 Finance and insurance	65	50	305	225	110	80
263	53 Real estate and rental and leasing	45	50	70	90	10	15
264	54 Professional, scientific and technical services	140	100	435	485	165	260
265	55 Management of companies and enterprises	-	-	-	-	-	10
266	56 Administrative and support, waste management and remediation services	110	70	195	135	90	120
267	61 Educational services	85	80	295	215	85	75
268	62 Health care and social assistance	160	85	395	265	115	175
269	71 Arts, entertainment and recreation	25	20	65	25	45	20
270	72 Accommodation and food services	210	160	230	225	180	220
271	81 Other services (except public administration)	70	70	210	155	110	105
272	91 Public administration	45	25	260	85	95	70
	by class of worker						
273	Class of worker - Not applicable (36)	90	135	120	160	35	60
274	All classes of worker (37)	1,860	1,220	4,490	3,280	1,825	2,185
275	Paid workers	1,750	1,120	4,160	3,025	1,730	2,085
276	Employees	1,715	1,110	3,920	2,875	1,595	2,085
277	Self-employed (incorporated)	35	15	250	140	130	-
278	Self-employed (unincorporated)	105	80	320	250	85	95
279	Unpaid family workers	10	20	10	10	10	-
	by occupation based on the 2001 NOC-S						
280	Male labour force 15 years and over	1,070	720	2,445	1,775	1,020	1,205
281	Occupation - Not applicable (36)	35	75	40	45	20	15
282	All occupations (37)	1,030	645	2,405	1,735	1,005	1,185
283	A Management occupations	110	65	365	250	135	70
284	B Business, finance and administration occupations	95	75	295	195	60	145
285	C Natural and applied sciences and related occupations	140	55	330	455	180	310
286	D Health occupations	10	25	60	30	-	10
287	E Occupations in social science, education, government service and religion	25	10	90	70	50	30
288	F Occupations in art, culture, recreation and sport	35	15	80	55	60	30
289	G Sales and service occupations	265	205	430	335	300	270
290	H Trades, transport and equipment operators and related occupations	260	165	550	275	145	195
291	I Occupations unique to primary industry	15	-	40	-	30	25
292	J Occupations unique to processing, manufacturing and utilities	75	35	170	65	45	110
293	Female labour force 15 years and over	885	630	2,165	1,665	835	1,040
294	Occupation - Not applicable (36)	50	60	80	115	15	40
295	All occupations (37)	830	575	2,085	1,545	820	995
296	A Management occupations	40	50	195	145	60	55
297	B Business, finance and administration occupations	265	150	675	550	240	260
298	C Natural and applied sciences and related occupations	15	15	120	110	30	130
299	D Health occupations	45	25	165	105	50	70

Tableau 1. Certaines caractéristiques des secteurs de recensement, recensement de 2001 – Données intégrales et données-échantillon (20 %)

Vancouver 0227.02 A	Vancouver 0228.02	Vancouver 0228.03 A	Vancouver 0228.04 A	Vancouver 0229	Vancouver 0230.01	Caractéristiques	N°
						CARACTÉRISTIQUES DE LA POPULATION	
						selon l'activité – fin	
57.8	62.4	56.6	57.4	62.8	70.5	Les deux sexes - Taux d'activité	241
58.1	58.5	53.7	61.9	59.5	53.8	15-24 ans	242
57.7	63.2	57.5	56.9	63.5	74.2	25 ans et plus	243
51.5	57.7	49.9	53.2	58.2	65.9	Les deux sexes - Taux d'emploi	244
48.3	53.7	44.3	54.8	53.0	42.4	15-24 ans	245
51.8	58.7	51.0	53.0	59.2	71.3	25 ans et plus	246
10.9	7.6	12.2	7.4	7.4	6.5	Les deux sexes - Taux de chômage	247
16.0	10.4	18.5	12.5	11.2	19.8	15-24 ans	248
10.4	7.2	11.1	6.6	6.5	4.0	25 ans et plus	249
2,610	**1,765**	**2,120**	**2,290**	**3,320**	**3,175**	**Population active totale de 15 ans et plus**	250
						selon l'industrie basée sur le SCIAN de 1997	
90	30	105	25	55	50	Industrie - Sans objet (36)	251
2,515	1,740	2,015	2,275	3,260	3,125	Toutes les industries (37)	252
10	25	10	10	15	25	11 Agriculture, foresterie, pêche et chasse	253
15	10	10	10	-	-	21 Extraction minière et extraction de pétrole et de gaz	254
40	-	25	35	15	25	22 Services publics	255
70	90	100	60	120	65	23 Construction	256
235	190	155	175	310	210	31-33 Fabrication	257
150	85	70	155	170	145	41 Commerce de gros	258
255	200	160	330	385	300	44-45 Commerce de détail	259
160	100	100	125	200	120	48-49 Transport et entreposage	260
180	105	120	175	180	225	51 Industrie de l'information et industrie culturelle	261
135	80	160	170	240	230	52 Finance et assurances	262
120	25	45	35	65	30	53 Services immobiliers et services de location et de location à bail	263
245	140	220	200	245	375	54 Services professionnels, scientifiques et techniques	264
-	-	-	-	-	10	55 Gestion de sociétés et d'entreprises	265
115	75	60	85	150	115	56 Services administratifs, services de soutien, services de gestion des déchets et services d'assainissement	266
115	90	155	105	195	300	61 Services d'enseignement	267
240	125	230	200	305	360	62 Soins de santé et assistance sociale	268
30	30	55	25	65	40	71 Arts, spectacles et loisirs	269
180	130	220	190	235	165	72 Hébergement et services de restauration	270
85	130	65	105	190	160	81 Autres services, sauf les administrations publiques	271
135	110	70	90	165	225	91 Administrations publiques	272
						selon la catégorie de travailleurs	
90	30	105	20	55	50	Catégorie de travailleurs - Sans objet (36)	273
2,515	1,735	2,020	2,270	3,265	3,125	Toutes les catégories de travailleurs (37)	274
2,365	1,585	1,870	2,150	3,020	2,850	Travailleurs rémunérés	275
2,310	1,475	1,820	2,070	2,920	2,715	Employés	276
55	105	55	80	95	135	Travailleurs autonomes (entreprise constituée en société)	277
110	140	140	125	220	235	Travailleurs autonomes (entreprise non constituée en société)	278
45	15	10	-	30	40	Travailleurs familiaux non rémunérés	279
						selon la profession basée sur la CNP-S de 2001	
1,335	970	1,120	1,170	1,660	1,620	Hommes actifs de 15 ans et plus	280
45	15	40	10	30	15	Profession - Sans objet (36)	281
1,290	955	1,085	1,165	1,635	1,600	Toutes les professions (37)	282
115	155	110	135	235	205	A Gestion	283
150	95	115	140	215	195	B Affaires, finance et administration	284
225	115	205	215	190	235	C Sciences naturelles et appliquées et professions apparentées	285
25	15	55	20	25	90	D Secteur de la santé	286
30	25	120	60	90	155	E Sciences sociales, enseignement, administration publique et religion	287
55	30	40	45	40	55	F Arts, culture, sports et loisirs	288
335	220	220	320	380	265	G Ventes et services	289
220	225	180	185	345	305	H Métiers, transport et machinerie	290
15	25	10	-	45	35	I Professions propres au secteur primaire	291
110	50	25	50	65	60	J Transformation, fabrication et services d'utilité publique	292
1,270	800	1,000	1,120	1,655	1,555	Femmes actives de 15 ans et plus	293
40	15	65	15	25	30	Profession - Sans objet (36)	294
1,220	780	935	1,110	1,630	1,525	Toutes les professions (37)	295
60	35	60	110	130	105	A Gestion	296
380	290	305	355	615	525	B Affaires, finance et administration	297
90	25	35	50	20	80	C Sciences naturelles et appliquées et professions apparentées	298
125	35	95	110	110	180	D Secteur de la santé	299

Table 1. Selected Characteristics for Census Tracts, 2001 Census – 100% Data and 20% Sample Data

No.	Characteristics	Vancouver 0224.01 A	Vancouver 0224.02 A	Vancouver 0225	Vancouver 0226.01	Vancouver 0226.02	Vancouver 0227.01 A
	POPULATION CHARACTERISTICS						
	by occupation based on the 2001 NOC-S – concluded						
300	E Occupations in social science, education, government service and religion	70	55	210	175	75	65
301	F Occupations in art, culture, recreation and sport	20	20	90	50	55	20
302	G Sales and service occupations	300	225	505	360	225	355
303	H Trades, transport and equipment operators and related occupations	35	25	45	20	30	10
304	I Occupations unique to primary industry	-	-	10	-	10	10
305	J Occupations unique to processing, manufacturing and utilities	30	10	70	50	45	30
306	**Total employed labour force 15 years and over**	**1,740**	**1,090**	**4,360**	**3,080**	**1,720**	**1,960**
	by place of work						
307	Males	960	555	2,320	1,610	925	1,050
308	Usual place of work	785	430	1,830	1,240	735	915
309	At home	20	45	145	160	70	45
310	Outside Canada	15	10	30	55	-	-
311	No fixed workplace address	140	75	320	155	115	80
312	Females	775	535	2,035	1,470	795	910
313	Usual place of work	650	475	1,755	1,330	695	840
314	At home	10	50	135	85	60	40
315	Outside Canada	-	-	25	20	-	-
316	No fixed workplace address	115	15	120	35	35	30
317	**Total employed labour force 15 years and over with usual place of work or no fixed workplace address**	**1,695**	**995**	**4,020**	**2,755**	**1,585**	**1,870**
	by mode of transportation						
318	Males	925	505	2,150	1,390	855	1,000
319	Car, truck, van, as driver	600	365	1,680	880	580	555
320	Car, truck, van, as passenger	55	40	120	30	30	20
321	Public transit	225	65	280	305	155	350
322	Walked	15	25	35	130	75	55
323	Other method	30	10	35	50	20	20
324	Females	765	490	1,870	1,365	735	870
325	Car, truck, van, as driver	370	255	1,160	560	355	190
326	Car, truck, van, as passenger	45	85	200	95	70	90
327	Public transit	275	125	400	500	240	445
328	Walked	60	20	110	185	60	135
329	Other method	20	-	10	25	10	15
330	**Total population 15 years and over who worked since January 1, 2000**	**2,085**	**1,365**	**5,035**	**3,705**	**2,075**	**2,485**
	by language used at work						
331	Single responses	1,800	1,150	4,370	2,935	1,725	2,135
332	English	1,715	1,075	4,130	2,675	1,640	1,995
333	French	-	-	-	-	-	-
334	Non-official languages (5)	85	75	240	260	85	140
335	Chinese, n.o.s.	35	45	40	95	35	80
336	Cantonese	25	10	65	50	30	-
337	Other languages (6)	30	20	130	110	20	55
338	Multiple responses	280	215	660	770	345	350
339	English and French	25	-	15	40	20	-
340	English and non-official language	235	195	655	715	325	335
341	French and non-official language	-	-	-	-	-	-
342	English, French and non-official language	20	10	-	15	-	-
	DWELLING AND HOUSEHOLD CHARACTERISTICS						
343	**Total number of occupied private dwellings**	**2,045**	**1,560**	**3,390**	**3,985**	**1,300**	**1,875**
	by tenure						
344	Owned	820	450	2,110	1,620	800	155
345	Rented	1,220	1,115	1,280	2,365	500	1,725
346	Band housing	-	-	-	-	-	-
	by structural type of dwelling						
347	Single-detached house	165	530	1,540	60	740	20
348	Semi-detached house	20	60	120	20	80	-
349	Row house	60	-	445	20	-	40
350	Apartment, detached duplex	20	15	240	-	205	-
351	Apartment, building that has five or more storeys	800	390	190	2,520	-	-
352	Apartment, building that has fewer than five storeys (38)	980	570	840	1,365	270	1,815
353	Other single-attached house	-	-	10	-	-	-
354	Movable dwelling (39)	-	-	-	-	-	-

Tableau 1. Certaines caractéristiques des secteurs de recensement, recensement de 2001 – Données intégrales et données-échantillon (20 %)

Vancouver 0227.02 A	Vancouver 0228.02	Vancouver 0228.03 A	Vancouver 0228.04 A	Vancouver 0229	Vancouver 0230.01	Caractéristiques	N°
						CARACTÉRISTIQUES DE LA POPULATION	
						selon la profession basée sur la CNP-S de 2001 – fin	
115	70	75	125	165	200	E Sciences sociales, enseignement, administration publique et religion	300
60	-	15	40	10	75	F Arts, culture, sports et loisirs	301
330	265	295	285	500	330	G Ventes et services	302
15	-	30	15	20	10	H Métiers, transport et machinerie	303
-	20	-	-	-	-	I Professions propres au secteur primaire	304
60	45	30	25	50	20	J Transformation, fabrication et services d'utilité publique	305
2,320	**1,635**	**1,865**	**2,125**	**3,080**	**2,975**	**Population active occupée totale de 15 ans et plus**	306
						selon le lieu de travail	
1,175	900	985	1,060	1,530	1,500	Hommes	307
955	675	770	875	1,210	1,225	Lieu habituel de travail	308
65	65	80	65	90	115	À domicile	309
15	10	20	-	10	15	En dehors du Canada	310
135	150	110	125	220	145	Sans adresse de travail fixe	311
1,150	730	880	1,065	1,545	1,475	Femmes	312
1,015	650	805	950	1,385	1,300	Lieu habituel de travail	313
95	65	20	65	85	110	À domicile	314
-	-	-	15	-	25	En dehors du Canada	315
35	20	40	35	75	35	Sans adresse de travail fixe	316
2,140	**1,495**	**1,735**	**1,980**	**2,890**	**2,715**	**Population active occupée totale de 15 ans et plus ayant un lieu habituel de travail ou sans adresse de travail fixe**	317
						selon le mode de transport	
1,085	825	880	995	1,430	1,370	Hommes	318
645	610	590	680	1,110	1,100	Automobile, camion ou fourgonnette, en tant que conducteur	319
30	60	20	50	35	60	Automobile, camion ou fourgonnette, en tant que passager	320
315	95	220	240	140	95	Transport en commun	321
85	25	25	20	85	75	À pied	322
15	35	20	10	55	40	Autre moyen	323
1,050	670	855	990	1,460	1,335	Femmes	324
510	345	275	475	870	1,015	Automobile, camion ou fourgonnette, en tant que conductrice	325
50	90	65	70	145	100	Automobile, camion ou fourgonnette, en tant que passagère	326
385	190	385	350	315	165	Transport en commun	327
85	30	115	80	120	65	À pied	328
20	10	10	10	15	-	Autre moyen	329
2,725	**1,905**	**2,220**	**2,500**	**3,620**	**3,405**	**Population totale de 15 ans et plus ayant travaillé depuis le 1er janvier 2000**	330
						selon la langue utilisée au travail	
2,335	1,545	1,895	2,195	3,145	3,095	Réponses uniques	331
2,285	1,470	1,810	2,105	3,100	3,005	Anglais	332
-	-	-	-	-	10	Français	333
50	70	85	90	50	80	Langues non officielles (5)	334
10	10	20	25	30	15	Chinois, n.d.a.	335
10	-	20	-	10	15	Cantonais	336
25	55	45	60	10	50	Autres langues (6)	337
390	365	325	310	470	310	Réponses multiples	338
30	-	50	45	15	25	Anglais et français	339
355	345	270	250	445	280	Anglais et langue non officielle	340
-	-	-	10	-	-	Français et langue non officielle	341
-	15	-	10	15	10	Anglais, français et langue non officielle	342
						CARACTÉRISTIQUES DES LOGEMENTS ET DES MÉNAGES	
2,765	**1,180**	**2,075**	**2,210**	**2,495**	**1,850**	**Nombre total de logements privés occupés**	343
						selon le mode d'occupation	
1,280	760	595	1,280	1,305	1,560	Possédé	344
1,480	420	1,480	930	1,185	285	Loué	345
-	-	-	-	-	-	Logement de bande	346
						selon le type de construction résidentielle	
-	620	15	265	845	780	Maison individuelle non attenante	347
10	80	-	165	85	30	Maison jumelée	348
10	75	-	100	100	805	Maison en rangée	349
-	275	-	85	385	55	Appartement, duplex non attenant	350
1,735	-	1,275	515	-	95	Appartement, immeuble de cinq étages ou plus	351
995	125	775	1,090	1,075	80	Appartement, immeuble de moins de cinq étages (38)	352
-	10	-	-	-	-	Autre maison individuelle attenante	353
-	-	-	-	-	-	Logement mobile (39)	354

Table 1. Selected Characteristics for Census Tracts, 2001 Census – 100% Data and 20% Sample Data

No.	Characteristics	Vancouver 0224.01 A	Vancouver 0224.02 A	Vancouver 0225	Vancouver 0226.01	Vancouver 0226.02	Vancouver 0227.01 A
	DWELLING AND HOUSEHOLD CHARACTERISTICS						
	by condition of dwelling						
355	Regular maintenance only	1,495	1,030	2,415	3,145	880	1,145
356	Minor repairs	290	455	805	590	345	540
357	Major repairs	255	80	170	250	75	195
	by period of construction						
358	Before 1946	30	70	240	120	65	50
359	1946-1960	210	260	660	260	310	220
360	1961-1970	400	530	485	675	370	915
361	1971-1980	680	300	515	795	230	445
362	1981-1990	390	230	345	1,015	180	200
363	1991-2001 (20)	340	170	1,145	1,125	145	50
364	Average number of rooms per dwelling	3.9	4.2	5.9	3.9	6.6	3.4
365	Average number of bedrooms per dwelling	1.5	1.7	2.6	1.4	3.1	1.1
366	Average value of dwelling $	167,471	293,646	292,513	205,620	335,601	115,109
367	**Total number of private households**	**2,040**	**1,560**	**3,390**	**3,990**	**1,295**	**1,880**
	by household size						
368	1 person	1,010	660	820	1,555	255	635
369	2 persons	560	365	1,030	1,310	390	615
370	3 persons	260	225	565	635	240	395
371	4-5 persons	180	260	810	455	335	210
372	6 or more persons	25	60	155	40	85	25
	by household type						
373	One-family households	880	800	2,270	2,140	855	1,020
374	Multiple-family households	20	35	120	30	85	25
375	Non-family households	1,140	725	1,005	1,820	360	825
376	Number of persons in private households	3,875	3,565	9,145	8,160	3,700	4,070
377	Average number of persons in private households	1.9	2.3	2.7	2.0	2.8	2.2
378	Average number of persons per room	0.5	0.5	0.5	0.5	0.4	0.6
379	Tenant households in non-farm, non-reserve private dwellings (40)	1,205	1,080	1,235	2,270	495	1,655
380	Average gross rent $ (40)	611	576	765	796	877	678
381	Tenant households spending 30% or more of household income on gross rent (40) (41)	630	595	610	1,265	230	720
382	Tenant households spending from 30% to 99% of household income on gross rent (40) (41)	475	440	400	970	165	535
383	Owner households in non-farm, non-reserve private dwellings (42)	820	450	2,105	1,610	795	155
384	Average owner's major payments $ (42)	872	812	952	650	867	665
385	Owner households spending 30% or more of household income on owner's major payments (41) (42)	270	105	595	450	215	35
386	Owner households spending from 30% to 99% of household income on owner's major payments (41) (42)	210	60	480	320	175	25
	CENSUS FAMILY CHARACTERISTICS						
387	**Total number of census families in private households**	**925**	**880**	**2,535**	**2,195**	**1,020**	**1,080**
	by census family structure and size						
388	Total couple families	770	720	2,160	1,890	860	835
389	Total families of married couples	680	660	1,930	1,725	810	735
390	Without children at home	270	225	725	815	300	285
391	With children at home	410	440	1,205	910	510	450
392	1 child	240	185	445	505	210	295
393	2 children	120	145	555	355	215	120
394	3 or more children	45	110	200	45	85	35
395	Total families of common-law couples	95	60	225	165	50	100
396	Without children at home	90	55	150	130	40	90
397	With children at home	10	-	80	40	15	15
398	1 child	-	-	35	20	15	10
399	2 children	-	-	25	20	-	-
400	3 or more children	-	-	20	-	-	-
401	Total lone-parent families	155	155	380	305	165	240
402	Female parent	120	135	325	260	160	225
403	1 child	85	80	200	185	95	105
404	2 children	25	45	100	80	45	95
405	3 or more children	10	10	20	-	20	25

Tableau 1. Certaines caractéristiques des secteurs de recensement, recensement de 2001 – Données intégrales et données-échantillon (20 %)

Vancouver 0227.02 A	Vancouver 0228.02	Vancouver 0228.03 A	Vancouver 0228.04 A	Vancouver 0229	Vancouver 0230.01	Caractéristiques	N°
						CARACTÉRISTIQUES DES LOGEMENTS ET DES MÉNAGES	
						selon l'état du logement	
1,940	720	1,640	1,640	1,680	1,375	Entretien régulier seulement	355
520	380	310	420	605	400	Réparations mineures	356
305	85	125	160	205	75	Réparations majeures	357
						selon la période de construction	
-	110	-	75	165	20	Avant 1946	358
95	495	130	200	630	215	1946-1960	359
590	190	480	420	365	300	1961-1970	360
665	160	670	685	350	600	1971-1980	361
1,095	140	325	435	605	125	1981-1990	362
315	85	470	395	380	585	1991-2001 (20)	363
3.8	6.7	3.7	4.5	5.4	7.1	Nombre moyen de pièces par logement	364
1.4	3.1	1.3	1.8	2.4	3.1	Nombre moyen de chambres à coucher par logement	365
160,169	331,062	227,742	193,821	293,301	325,391	Valeur moyenne du logement $	366
2,760	**1,185**	**2,075**	**2,215**	**2,495**	**1,845**	**Nombre total de logements privés**	367
						selon la taille du ménage	
1,315	210	785	935	780	290	1 personne	368
945	345	750	695	780	585	2 personnes	369
315	230	335	265	320	375	3 personnes	370
180	330	190	295	510	525	4-5 personnes	371
-	65	10	25	100	70	6 personnes ou plus	372
						selon le genre de ménage	
1,280	895	1,090	1,120	1,545	1,420	Ménages unifamiliaux	373
-	50	25	50	70	75	Ménages multifamiliaux	374
1,480	235	960	1,040	875	350	Ménages non familiaux	375
4,925	3,455	4,190	4,590	6,215	5,265	Nombre de personnes dans les ménages privés	376
1.8	2.9	2.0	2.1	2.5	2.8	Nombre moyen de personnes dans les ménages privés	377
0.5	0.4	0.6	0.5	0.5	0.4	Nombre moyen de personnes par pièce	378
1,410	415	1,425	935	1,190	270	Ménages locataires dans les logements privés non agricoles hors réserve (40)	379
708	920	796	668	744	1,054	Loyer brut moyen $ (40)	380
680	155	655	360	425	85	Ménages locataires consacrant 30 % ou plus du revenu du ménage au loyer brut (40) (41)	381
505	120	430	235	300	85	Ménages locataires consacrant de 30 % à 99 % du revenu du ménage au loyer brut (40) (41)	382
1,275	760	595	1,280	1,305	1,555	Ménages propriétaires dans les logements privés non agricoles hors réserve (42)	383
607	847	603	720	916	964	Principales dépenses de propriété moyennes $ (42)	384
275	180	165	265	270	255	Ménages propriétaires consacrant 30 % ou plus du revenu du ménage aux principales dépenses de propriété (41) (42)	385
205	150	100	225	205	235	Ménages propriétaires consacrant de 30 % à 99 % du revenu du ménage aux principales dépenses de propriété (41) (42)	386
						CARACTÉRISTIQUES DES FAMILLES DE RECENSEMENT	
1,285	**1,000**	**1,140**	**1,230**	**1,690**	**1,580**	**Total des familles de recensement dans les ménages privés**	387
						selon la structure et la taille de la famille de recensement	
1,120	860	935	965	1,390	1,350	Total des familles avec conjoints	388
970	795	825	830	1,245	1,245	Total des familles avec couples mariés	389
555	310	450	410	530	465	Sans enfants à la maison	390
420	490	375	420	715	770	Avec enfants à la maison	391
270	155	240	185	255	290	1 enfant	392
120	215	115	175	325	355	2 enfants	393
25	110	20	65	145	125	3 enfants ou plus	394
150	65	110	130	145	105	Total des familles en union libre	395
145	30	95	95	110	75	Sans enfants à la maison	396
-	35	15	35	40	30	Avec enfants à la maison	397
-	20	10	30	25	15	1 enfant	398
-	-	10	-	15	15	2 enfants	399
-	-	10	-	-	-	3 enfants ou plus	400
165	145	210	270	300	225	Total des familles monoparentales	401
145	105	160	230	265	165	Parent de sexe féminin	402
105	55	110	175	205	115	1 enfant	403
40	40	30	55	35	40	2 enfants	404
-	-	20	-	25	10	3 enfants ou plus	405

Table 1. Selected Characteristics for Census Tracts, 2001 Census – 100% Data and 20% Sample Data

No.	Characteristics	Vancouver 0224.01 A	Vancouver 0224.02 A	Vancouver 0225	Vancouver 0226.01	Vancouver 0226.02	Vancouver 0227.01 A
	CENSUS FAMILY CHARACTERISTICS						
	by census family structure and size – concluded						
406	Male parent	35	20	60	45	-	20
407	1 child	25	10	30	30	-	-
408	2 children	-	15	20	-	-	15
409	3 or more children	-	-	10	15	-	-
410	**Total number of children at home**	**850**	**1,085**	**2,925**	**1,820**	**1,170**	**1,060**
	by age groups						
411	Under 6 years	245	245	595	440	195	325
412	6-14 years	245	355	855	590	350	355
413	15-17 years	75	110	330	190	165	80
414	18-24 years	145	210	715	325	260	200
415	25 years and over	140	160	430	280	200	100
416	Average number of children at home per census family (43)	0.9	1.2	1.2	0.8	1.1	1.0
417	**Total number of persons in private households**	**3,870**	**3,565**	**9,145**	**8,160**	**3,700**	**4,075**
	by census family status and living arrangements						
418	Number of non-family persons	1,330	880	1,530	2,260	650	1,100
419	Living with relatives (44)	100	70	250	190	60	100
420	Living with non-relatives only	220	155	455	515	335	355
421	Living alone	1,015	660	820	1,550	255	640
422	Number of family persons	2,540	2,675	7,615	5,905	3,050	2,980
423	Average number of persons per census family	2.7	3.1	3.0	2.7	3.0	2.8
424	**Total number of persons 65 years and over**	**580**	**660**	**1,010**	**1,460**	**440**	**265**
425	Number of non-family persons 65 years and over	390	380	330	625	120	110
426	Living with relatives (44)	30	10	85	35	40	-
427	Living with non-relatives only	15	10	10	10	-	10
428	Living alone	350	360	235	590	75	95
429	Number of family persons 65 years and over	185	285	680	835	325	160
	ECONOMIC FAMILY CHARACTERISTICS						
430	**Total number of economic families in private households**	**930**	**855**	**2,425**	**2,230**	**965**	**1,090**
	by size of family						
431	2 persons	475	330	970	1,145	370	500
432	3 persons	260	225	535	610	225	370
433	4 persons	120	155	555	400	225	160
434	5 or more persons	75	145	370	70	150	60
435	Total number of persons in economic families	2,640	2,750	7,865	6,095	3,110	3,075
436	Average number of persons per economic family	2.8	3.2	3.2	2.7	3.2	2.8
437	Total number of unattached individuals	1,235	815	1,280	2,065	590	1,000
	2000 INCOME CHARACTERISTICS						
	Population 15 years and over by sex and total income groups in 2000						
438	Total - Both sexes	3,385	2,975	7,695	7,130	3,145	3,395
439	Without income	235	360	620	595	240	400
440	With income	3,150	2,615	7,070	6,535	2,900	3,000
441	Under $1,000 (45)	205	220	655	575	310	210
442	$ 1,000 - $ 2,999	135	195	305	405	125	155
443	$ 3,000 - $ 4,999	100	70	295	355	110	145
444	$ 5,000 - $ 6,999	160	105	280	345	180	165
445	$ 7,000 - $ 9,999	200	220	455	455	210	235
446	$10,000 - $11,999	170	125	350	300	170	170
447	$12,000 - $14,999	335	405	535	630	180	300
448	$15,000 - $19,999	315	345	590	660	280	305
449	$20,000 - $24,999	290	240	505	590	230	280
450	$25,000 - $29,999	245	145	450	420	160	225
451	$30,000 - $34,999	230	140	520	390	160	240
452	$35,000 - $39,999	215	90	415	285	120	205
453	$40,000 - $44,999	100	65	400	255	170	100
454	$45,000 - $49,999	110	55	280	210	110	45
455	$50,000 - $59,999	200	80	435	235	120	125
456	$60,000 and over	125	120	600	425	255	90
457	Average income $ (46)	23,327	20,922	27,577	22,755	26,156	21,048
458	Median income $ (46)	18,407	14,596	20,606	16,204	17,463	16,265
459	Standard error of average income $ (46)	731	1,352	978	665	1,364	688

Tableau 1. Certaines caractéristiques des secteurs de recensement, recensement de 2001 – Données intégrales et données-échantillon (20 %)

Vancouver 0227.02 A	Vancouver 0228.02	Vancouver 0228.03 A	Vancouver 0228.04 A	Vancouver 0229	Vancouver 0230.01	Caractéristiques	N°
						CARACTÉRISTIQUES DES FAMILLES DE RECENSEMENT	
						selon la structure et la taille de la famille de recensement – fin	
20	40	50	35	30	60	Parent de sexe masculin	406
20	30	30	30	20	45	1 enfant	407
-	10	15	10	10	10	2 enfants	408
-	-	-	-	-	-	3 enfants ou plus	409
800	**1,215**	**855**	**1,135**	**1,845**	**1,780**	**Nombre total d'enfants à la maison**	410
						selon les groupes d'âge	
205	250	210	230	345	225	Moins de 6 ans	411
215	380	235	345	560	615	6-14 ans	412
70	75	60	115	230	255	15-17 ans	413
140	295	200	275	415	450	18-24 ans	414
170	220	155	170	295	240	25 ans et plus	415
0.6	1.2	0.7	0.9	1.1	1.1	Nombre moyen d'enfants à la maison par famille de recensement (43)	416
4,925	**3,455**	**4,190**	**4,590**	**6,210**	**5,265**	**Nombre total de personnes dans les ménages privés**	417
						selon la situation des particuliers dans la famille de recensement et des particuliers dans le ménage	
1,720	385	1,255	1,260	1,285	555	Nombre de personnes hors famille de recensement	418
110	60	135	135	205	130	Vivant avec des personnes apparentées (44)	419
295	110	335	195	300	145	Vivant avec des personnes non apparentées uniquement	420
1,310	210	785	930	780	285	Vivant seules	421
3,205	3,075	2,935	3,325	4,925	4,705	Nombre de personnes membres d'une famille	422
2.5	3.1	2.6	2.7	2.9	3.0	Nombre moyen de personnes par famille de recensement	423
1,120	**495**	**570**	**895**	**995**	**545**	**Nombre total de personnes de 65 ans et plus**	424
565	105	205	445	365	105	Nombre de personnes hors famille de recensement de 65 ans et plus	425
30	20	25	30	95	30	Vivant avec des personnes apparentées (44)	426
35	-	-	10	15	10	Vivant avec des personnes non apparentées uniquement	427
500	80	175	410	250	75	Vivant seules	428
550	395	365	445	635	435	Nombre de personnes membres d'une famille de 65 ans et plus	429
						CARACTÉRISTIQUES DES FAMILLES ÉCONOMIQUES	
1,315	**955**	**1,150**	**1,190**	**1,650**	**1,535**	**Nombre total de familles économiques dans les ménages privés**	430
						selon la taille de la famille	
825	355	660	625	760	580	2 personnes	431
305	225	290	250	310	380	3 personnes	432
155	210	155	195	350	400	4 personnes	433
30	165	45	125	230	170	5 personnes ou plus	434
3,315	3,135	3,070	3,460	5,135	4,835	Nombre total de personnes dans les familles économiques	435
2.5	3.3	2.7	2.9	3.1	3.2	Nombre moyen de personnes par famille économique	436
1,610	320	1,120	1,125	1,080	430	Nombre total de personnes hors famille économique	437
						CARACTÉRISTIQUES DU REVENU DE 2000	
						Population de 15 ans et plus selon le sexe et les tranches de revenu total en 2000	
4,505	2,830	3,740	3,995	5,280	4,505	Total - Les deux sexes	438
385	190	330	185	265	315	Sans revenu	439
4,120	2,640	3,415	3,810	5,020	4,190	Avec un revenu	440
175	190	380	165	245	130	Moins de 1 000 $ (45)	441
275	120	165	180	275	115	1 000 $ - 2 999 $	442
110	90	145	160	150	150	3 000 $ - 4 999 $	443
160	130	145	190	235	215	5 000 $ - 6 999 $	444
215	165	210	245	300	250	7 000 $ - 9 999 $	445
165	100	160	170	235	150	10 000 $ - 11 999 $	446
440	220	260	320	385	260	12 000 $ - 14 999 $	447
480	230	230	405	500	220	15 000 $ - 19 999 $	448
305	245	355	285	385	240	20 000 $ - 24 999 $	449
350	215	250	320	480	265	25 000 $ - 29 999 $	450
305	140	245	275	410	390	30 000 $ - 34 999 $	451
215	190	165	260	260	225	35 000 $ - 39 999 $	452
210	135	175	175	270	205	40 000 $ - 44 999 $	453
240	100	95	150	305	230	45 000 $ - 49 999 $	454
195	165	195	245	245	415	50 000 $ - 59 999 $	455
280	205	230	275	340	740	60 000 $ et plus	456
26,251	26,412	23,998	26,654	26,522	38,125	Revenu moyen $ (46)	457
20,310	21,063	20,047	20,851	21,291	30,665	Revenu médian $ (46)	458
777	1,045	777	781	803	1,296	Erreur type de revenu moyen $ (46)	459

Table 1. Selected Characteristics for Census Tracts, 2001 Census – 100% Data and 20% Sample Data

No.	Characteristics	Vancouver 0224.01 A	Vancouver 0224.02 A	Vancouver 0225	Vancouver 0226.01	Vancouver 0226.02	Vancouver 0227.01 A
	2000 INCOME CHARACTERISTICS						
	Population 15 years and over by sex and total income groups in 2000 – concluded						
460	Total - Males	1,645	1,420	3,795	3,315	1,550	1,655
461	Without income	55	145	270	230	115	160
462	With income	1,590	1,275	3,530	3,085	1,430	1,495
463	Under $1,000 (45)	125	105	370	325	145	125
464	$ 1,000 - $ 2,999	95	115	95	160	45	65
465	$ 3,000 - $ 4,999	30	10	120	140	50	45
466	$ 5,000 - $ 6,999	65	40	115	155	100	70
467	$ 7,000 - $ 9,999	85	110	190	175	65	90
468	$10,000 - $11,999	80	75	170	130	55	55
469	$12,000 - $14,999	130	155	175	210	55	120
470	$15,000 - $19,999	145	150	295	285	105	130
471	$20,000 - $24,999	125	125	220	260	110	145
472	$25,000 - $29,999	140	100	215	225	95	145
473	$30,000 - $34,999	65	75	255	205	65	155
474	$35,000 - $39,999	140	35	220	185	55	115
475	$40,000 - $44,999	50	35	205	150	85	60
476	$45,000 - $49,999	95	20	175	90	75	25
477	$50,000 - $59,999	135	55	250	145	95	90
478	$60,000 and over	85	80	460	240	225	40
479	Average income $ (46)	25,886	24,122	33,160	25,300	33,082	23,098
480	Median income $ (46)	21,223	15,395	25,037	19,435	24,228	21,029
481	Standard error of average income $ (46)	1,162	2,620	1,833	1,133	2,191	986
482	Total - Females	1,740	1,555	3,900	3,820	1,595	1,735
483	Without income	175	210	350	370	125	235
484	With income	1,565	1,340	3,545	3,450	1,470	1,500
485	Under $1,000 (45)	85	120	290	255	165	90
486	$ 1,000 - $ 2,999	45	80	210	245	80	85
487	$ 3,000 - $ 4,999	75	60	180	215	60	95
488	$ 5,000 - $ 6,999	90	65	165	190	80	95
489	$ 7,000 - $ 9,999	120	105	260	275	145	140
490	$10,000 - $11,999	95	50	185	170	110	110
491	$12,000 - $14,999	200	250	360	415	130	180
492	$15,000 - $19,999	165	195	295	375	175	175
493	$20,000 - $24,999	165	115	285	330	130	135
494	$25,000 - $29,999	105	45	230	190	65	80
495	$30,000 - $34,999	170	60	265	185	95	85
496	$35,000 - $39,999	75	55	195	100	70	90
497	$40,000 - $44,999	50	35	195	105	80	40
498	$45,000 - $49,999	20	40	105	120	30	15
499	$50,000 - $59,999	65	25	185	95	25	35
500	$60,000 and over	35	40	145	185	30	50
501	Average income $ (46)	20,728	17,878	22,021	20,481	19,407	19,008
502	Median income $ (46)	17,167	13,370	15,962	14,393	13,965	13,747
503	Standard error of average income $ (46)	869	874	664	736	1,568	948
	by composition of total income						
504	Total - Composition of income in 2000 % (47)	100.0	100.0	100.0	100.0	100.0	100.0
505	Employment income %	74.1	64.3	80.0	66.0	76.2	82.5
506	Government transfer payments %	15.8	23.8	10.8	15.9	10.1	14.3
507	Other %	10.1	12.0	9.3	18.1	13.6	3.3
	Population 15 years and over with employment income in 2000 by sex and work activity						
508	Both sexes with employment income (48)	1,970	1,275	4,825	3,470	1,950	2,215
509	Average employment income $	27,598	27,615	32,330	28,270	29,630	23,466
510	Standard error of average employment income $	960	2,551	1,337	1,038	1,777	831
511	Worked full year, full time (49)	920	530	2,430	1,620	995	855
512	Average employment income $	36,755	41,899	45,701	40,297	43,508	36,199
513	Standard error of average employment income $	1,186	5,434	2,340	1,804	2,993	1,320
514	Worked part year or part time (50)	1,000	675	2,190	1,725	880	1,245
515	Average employment income $	20,337	17,912	19,440	17,405	16,253	15,853
516	Standard error of average employment income $	1,290	1,471	914	873	1,154	796
517	Males with employment income (48)	1,035	650	2,510	1,770	1,070	1,155
518	Average employment income $	31,913	32,770	38,575	31,564	35,268	26,059
519	Standard error of average employment income $	1,418	4,771	2,434	1,720	2,468	1,137
520	Worked full year, full time (49)	540	295	1,355	905	610	490
521	Average employment income $	39,005	49,975	51,834	43,436	48,991	37,608
522	Standard error of average employment income $	1,506	9,566	4,115	2,974	3,561	1,702
523	Worked part year or part time (50)	485	335	1,100	825	420	645
524	Average employment income $	24,473	19,091	23,161	19,496	17,939	17,581
525	Standard error of average employment income $	2,302	2,536	1,515	1,278	2,000	1,094

Tableau 1. Certaines caractéristiques des secteurs de recensement, recensement de 2001 – Données intégrales et données-échantillon (20 %)

Vancouver 0227.02 A	Vancouver 0228.02	Vancouver 0228.03 A	Vancouver 0228.04 A	Vancouver 0229	Vancouver 0230.01	Caractéristiques	N°
						CARACTÉRISTIQUES DU REVENU DE 2000	
						Population de 15 ans et plus selon le sexe et les tranches de revenu total en 2000 – fin	
2,035	1,445	1,785	1,805	2,535	2,150	Total - Hommes	460
145	70	85	70	130	120	Sans revenu	461
1,895	1,375	1,695	1,735	2,400	2,035	Avec un revenu	462
105	90	210	70	150	85	Moins de 1 000 $ (45)	463
110	95	80	90	115	35	1 000 $ - 2 999 $	464
30	40	65	70	65	50	3 000 $ - 4 999 $	465
85	40	90	75	100	90	5 000 $ - 6 999 $	466
90	45	45	115	100	115	7 000 $ - 9 999 $	467
75	55	90	55	90	55	10 000 $ - 11 999 $	468
120	65	90	105	150	75	12 000 $ - 14 999 $	469
135	115	100	125	280	85	15 000 $ - 19 999 $	470
215	110	180	145	155	75	20 000 $ - 24 999 $	471
160	95	150	145	205	125	25 000 $ - 29 999 $	472
160	70	80	135	165	180	30 000 $ - 34 999 $	473
65	125	95	125	135	125	35 000 $ - 39 999 $	474
140	90	100	85	145	90	40 000 $ - 44 999 $	475
130	50	35	65	175	115	45 000 $ - 49 999 $	476
105	145	130	155	130	240	50 000 $ - 59 999 $	477
175	145	165	185	235	495	60 000 $ et plus	478
29,673	31,335	26,640	30,205	28,464	43,738	Revenu moyen $ (46)	479
24,367	25,967	22,092	25,516	24,970	36,301	Revenu médian $ (46)	480
1,355	1,721	1,253	1,313	924	1,703	Erreur type de revenu moyen $ (46)	481
2,465	1,385	1,960	2,190	2,745	2,355	Total - Femmes	482
240	110	240	115	130	195	Sans revenu	483
2,225	1,275	1,720	2,075	2,615	2,160	Avec un revenu	484
70	105	175	90	100	45	Moins de 1 000 $ (45)	485
160	25	85	90	160	75	1 000 $ - 2 999 $	486
80	50	80	85	80	105	3 000 $ - 4 999 $	487
85	95	55	115	140	125	5 000 $ - 6 999 $	488
120	125	165	130	195	140	7 000 $ - 9 999 $	489
90	50	70	110	145	95	10 000 $ - 11 999 $	490
320	155	175	215	240	185	12 000 $ - 14 999 $	491
350	110	130	275	220	135	15 000 $ - 19 999 $	492
90	130	175	145	230	160	20 000 $ - 24 999 $	493
195	120	100	170	275	140	25 000 $ - 29 999 $	494
145	65	165	140	240	215	30 000 $ - 34 999 $	495
150	70	70	140	120	100	35 000 $ - 39 999 $	496
65	45	80	90	120	115	40 000 $ - 44 999 $	497
115	50	60	85	135	115	45 000 $ - 49 999 $	498
85	20	70	85	115	175	50 000 $ - 59 999 $	499
110	65	70	90	100	240	60 000 $ et plus	500
23,335	21,112	21,388	23,676	24,742	32,842	Revenu moyen $ (46)	501
17,398	16,926	16,282	18,026	20,211	25,265	Revenu médian $ (46)	502
838	1,046	923	898	1,289	1,927	Erreur type de revenu moyen $ (46)	503
						selon la composition du revenu total	
100.0	100.0	100.0	100.0	100.0	100.0	Total - Composition du revenu en 2000 % (47)	504
70.0	72.9	70.4	70.5	76.6	81.2	Revenu d'emploi %	505
15.7	12.7	12.9	14.4	14.5	6.4	Transferts gouvernementaux %	506
14.2	14.3	16.8	15.2	8.9	12.3	Autre %	507
						Population de 15 ans et plus ayant un revenu d'emploi en 2000 selon le sexe et le travail	
2,505	1,780	2,110	2,420	3,480	3,310	Les deux sexes ayant un revenu d'emploi (48)	508
30,214	28,628	27,303	29,562	29,248	39,254	Revenu moyen d'emploi $	509
1,097	1,190	998	1,043	998	1,479	Erreur type de revenu moyen d'emploi $	510
1,310	900	1,020	1,255	1,810	1,720	Ayant travaillé toute l'année à plein temps (49)	511
38,178	38,956	38,459	38,166	39,919	56,657	Revenu moyen d'emploi $	512
1,324	1,816	1,296	1,468	1,570	2,585	Erreur type de revenu moyen d'emploi $	513
1,150	840	1,025	1,105	1,600	1,525	Ayant travaillé une partie de l'année ou à temps partiel (50)	514
22,316	18,242	17,258	20,749	18,158	20,955	Revenu moyen d'emploi $	515
1,674	1,197	1,209	1,293	936	907	Erreur type de revenu moyen d'emploi $	516
1,295	995	1,150	1,225	1,695	1,655	Hommes ayant un revenu d'emploi (48)	517
32,757	32,327	30,197	31,773	31,044	44,338	Revenu moyen d'emploi $	518
1,765	1,833	1,503	1,634	1,117	1,778	Erreur type de revenu moyen d'emploi $	519
715	545	585	665	1,010	995	Ayant travaillé toute l'année à plein temps (49)	520
39,168	43,182	40,279	40,326	38,863	59,135	Revenu moyen d'emploi $	521
1,874	2,700	1,914	2,287	1,318	2,575	Erreur type de revenu moyen d'emploi $	522
545	430	540	540	650	650	Ayant travaillé une partie de l'année ou à temps partiel (50)	523
26,430	19,394	20,444	21,915	20,349	22,471	Revenu moyen d'emploi $	524
3,228	1,817	2,038	2,005	1,671	1,477	Erreur type de revenu moyen d'emploi $	525

Table 1. Selected Characteristics for Census Tracts, 2001 Census – 100% Data and 20% Sample Data

No.	Characteristics	Vancouver 0224.01 A	Vancouver 0224.02 A	Vancouver 0225	Vancouver 0226.01	Vancouver 0226.02	Vancouver 0227.01 A
	2000 INCOME CHARACTERISTICS						
	Population 15 years and over with employment income in 2000 by sex and work activity – concluded						
526	Females with employment income (48)	940	620	2,315	1,700	885	1,060
527	Average employment income $	22,843	22,243	25,556	24,830	22,828	20,623
528	Standard error of average employment income $	1,194	1,377	847	1,100	2,465	1,189
529	Worked full year, full time (49)	385	240	1,080	715	380	365
530	Average employment income $	33,584	32,078	37,999	36,330	34,676	34,322
531	Standard error of average employment income $	1,862	2,291	1,013	1,649	5,161	2,059
532	Worked part year or part time (50)	510	345	1,090	895	460	605
533	Average employment income $	16,381	16,754	15,670	15,478	14,708	14,005
534	Standard error of average employment income $	1,156	1,505	979	1,177	1,257	1,136
	Census families by structure and family income groups in 2000						
535	Total - All census families	920	875	2,535	2,195	1,025	1,080
536	Under $10,000	110	150	255	360	120	185
537	$ 10,000 - $19,999	115	145	225	325	105	125
538	$ 20,000 - $29,999	115	120	200	325	105	240
539	$ 30,000 - $39,999	100	130	355	305	90	185
540	$ 40,000 - $49,999	100	65	180	255	80	80
541	$ 50,000 - $59,999	115	80	195	175	130	100
542	$ 60,000 - $69,999	60	25	200	60	90	45
543	$ 70,000 - $79,999	70	15	260	145	55	35
544	$ 80,000 - $89,999	40	40	205	60	50	45
545	$ 90,000 - $99,999	45	35	90	35	40	15
546	$100,000 and over	50	75	370	145	155	35
547	Average family income $	45,574	41,454	62,256	41,352	57,598	35,737
548	Median family income $	40,897	30,845	51,456	32,647	51,037	29,957
549	Standard error of average family income $	2,235	2,468	2,944	1,864	3,393	1,795
550	Total - All couple census families (51)	770	725	2,160	1,890	860	835
551	Under $10,000	85	120	185	300	75	135
552	$ 10,000 - $19,999	60	100	145	205	80	65
553	$ 20,000 - $29,999	105	85	170	280	80	190
554	$ 30,000 - $39,999	80	115	290	295	75	145
555	$ 40,000 - $49,999	90	55	145	225	65	55
556	$ 50,000 - $59,999	95	75	160	145	120	90
557	$ 60,000 - $69,999	55	20	180	60	95	45
558	$ 70,000 - $79,999	70	15	235	140	35	30
559	$ 80,000 - $89,999	40	40	205	55	30	40
560	$ 90,000 - $99,999	45	35	85	40	40	15
561	$100,000 and over	50	65	355	145	150	30
562	Average family income $	49,537	43,212	67,218	44,337	61,714	38,075
563	Median family income $	48,684	33,103	57,125	34,734	53,136	32,135
564	Standard error of average family income $	2,509	2,651	3,366	2,111	3,857	2,090
	Incidence of low income in 2000						
565	Total - Economic families	935	855	2,430	2,230	965	1,090
566	Low income	310	415	620	980	240	435
567	Incidence of low income in 2000 % (52)	33.3	48.4	25.5	44.1	24.9	40.2
568	Total - Unattached individuals 15 years and over	1,235	810	1,275	2,065	575	1,000
569	Low income	665	565	540	870	260	470
570	Incidence of low income in 2000 % (52)	53.8	70.0	41.9	42.0	45.2	47.1
571	Total - Population in private households	3,875	3,560	9,145	8,160	3,685	4,075
572	Low income	1,565	1,970	2,650	3,725	1,070	1,780
573	Incidence of low income in 2000 % (52)	40.4	55.2	29.0	45.7	29.0	43.7
	Private households by household income groups in 2000						
574	Total - All private households	2,040	1,560	3,390	3,985	1,295	1,880
575	Under $10,000	340	280	400	565	140	310
576	$ 10,000 - $19,999	455	500	430	770	155	285
577	$ 20,000 - $29,999	260	195	260	625	125	345
578	$ 30,000 - $39,999	225	180	415	610	110	360
579	$ 40,000 - $49,999	195	75	320	450	120	165
580	$ 50,000 - $59,999	180	85	300	310	145	170
581	$ 60,000 - $69,999	105	40	210	150	105	90
582	$ 70,000 - $79,999	110	35	250	170	85	30
583	$ 80,000 - $89,999	45	45	260	80	40	50
584	$ 90,000 - $99,999	40	35	115	80	75	25
585	$100,000 and over	90	100	440	170	200	45
586	Average household income $	35,963	34,873	57,490	37,305	58,483	33,556
587	Median household income $	28,251	20,037	45,073	30,379	48,726	29,995
588	Standard error of average household income $	1,398	2,570	2,362	1,180	3,093	1,221

Tableau 1. Certaines caractéristiques des secteurs de recensement, recensement de 2001 – Données intégrales et données-échantillon (20 %)

Vancouver 0227.02 A	Vancouver 0228.02	Vancouver 0228.03 A	Vancouver 0228.04 A	Vancouver 0229	Vancouver 0230.01	Caractéristiques	N°
						CARACTÉRISTIQUES DU REVENU DE 2000	
						Population de 15 ans et plus ayant un revenu d'emploi en 2000 selon le sexe et le travail – fin	
1,210	785	960	1,195	1,785	1,645	Femmes ayant un revenu d'emploi (48)	526
27,495	23,936	23,849	27,297	27,544	34,144	Revenu moyen d'emploi $	527
1,245	1,283	1,240	1,275	1,637	2,371	Erreur type de revenu moyen d'emploi $	528
595	355	435	590	805	730	Ayant travaillé toute l'année à plein temps (49)	529
36,980	32,503	36,039	35,736	41,246	53,275	Revenu moyen d'emploi $	530
1,842	1,820	1,646	1,756	3,141	5,035	Erreur type de revenu moyen d'emploi $	531
610	410	490	565	950	870	Ayant travaillé une partie de l'année ou à temps partiel (50)	532
18,661	17,023	13,764	19,631	16,649	19,821	Revenu moyen d'emploi $	533
1,313	1,519	1,158	1,643	1,060	1,111	Erreur type de revenu moyen d'emploi $	534
						Familles de recensement selon la structure et les tranches de revenu de la famille en 2000	
1,280	1,000	1,145	1,225	1,690	1,575	Total - Toutes les familles de recensement	535
170	60	160	85	95	35	Moins de 10 000 $	536
120	35	160	90	85	55	10 000 $ - 19 999 $	537
150	125	160	160	220	100	20 000 $ - 29 999 $	538
210	85	115	140	190	90	30 000 $ - 39 999 $	539
140	145	140	155	225	145	40 000 $ - 49 999 $	540
140	115	95	145	170	105	50 000 $ - 59 999 $	541
120	145	60	85	220	135	60 000 $ - 69 999 $	542
40	70	100	100	90	125	70 000 $ - 79 999 $	543
55	55	55	80	105	130	80 000 $ - 89 999 $	544
50	40	15	40	100	175	90 000 $ - 99 999 $	545
95	130	85	140	185	470	100 000 $ et plus	546
47,382	60,431	43,358	56,589	57,168	83,890	Revenu moyen des familles $	547
39,205	53,603	38,262	47,378	50,888	79,216	Revenu médian des familles $	548
2,245	2,870	2,087	2,293	1,731	2,661	Erreur type de revenu moyen des familles $	549
1,120	860	935	960	1,390	1,350	Total - Toutes les familles de recensement comptant un couple (51)	550
165	45	135	50	50	35	Moins de 10 000 $	551
95	20	110	35	55	20	10 000 $ - 19 999 $	552
130	95	140	100	185	80	20 000 $ - 29 999 $	553
185	75	75	115	135	85	30 000 $ - 39 999 $	554
115	110	130	140	170	90	40 000 $ - 49 999 $	555
105	100	70	130	150	85	50 000 $ - 59 999 $	556
105	125	55	80	200	125	60 000 $ - 69 999 $	557
35	70	90	75	95	90	70 000 $ - 79 999 $	558
50	50	50	65	85	120	80 000 $ - 89 999 $	559
50	40	15	40	100	150	90 000 $ - 99 999 $	560
90	120	75	135	180	460	100 000 $ et plus	561
48,023	62,541	45,400	61,949	61,089	87,249	Revenu moyen des familles $	562
39,176	57,542	40,345	51,903	55,895	86,054	Revenu médian des familles $	563
2,546	2,945	2,446	2,619	1,940	2,774	Erreur type de revenu moyen des familles $	564
						Fréquence des unités à faible revenu en 2000	
1,315	955	1,150	1,195	1,650	1,535	Total - Familles économiques	565
355	170	385	265	280	145	Faible revenu	566
27.3	17.8	33.3	22.1	17.0	9.3	Fréquence des unités à faible revenu en 2000 % (52)	567
1,610	320	1,125	1,125	1,050	430	Total - Personnes hors famille économique de 15 ans et plus	568
710	160	470	500	385	110	Faible revenu	569
43.9	49.5	41.9	44.4	36.9	25.6	Fréquence des unités à faible revenu en 2000 % (52)	570
4,920	3,460	4,190	4,585	6,180	5,270	Total - Population dans les ménages privés	571
1,710	810	1,570	1,305	1,270	575	Faible revenu	572
34.7	23.4	37.5	28.5	20.6	10.9	Fréquence des unités à faible revenu en 2000 % (52)	573
						Ménages privés selon les tranches de revenu du ménage en 2000	
2,760	1,185	2,075	2,210	2,495	1,845	Total - Tous les ménages privés	574
350	50	365	215	190	40	Moins de 10 000 $	575
535	115	285	395	265	80	10 000 $ - 19 999 $	576
355	120	290	285	355	135	20 000 $ - 29 999 $	577
420	145	230	335	300	95	30 000 $ - 39 999 $	578
335	165	250	215	325	150	40 000 $ - 49 999 $	579
265	110	165	205	205	165	50 000 $ - 59 999 $	580
200	140	135	125	250	155	60 000 $ - 69 999 $	581
40	65	125	95	105	190	70 000 $ - 79 999 $	582
60	50	80	115	85	135	80 000 $ - 89 999 $	583
70	55	40	45	130	180	90 000 $ - 99 999 $	584
130	165	105	180	280	520	100 000 $ et plus	585
39,130	59,021	39,499	45,843	53,320	85,870	Revenu moyen des ménages $	586
33,439	48,700	32,490	36,618	44,961	75,828	Revenu médian des ménages $	587
1,289	2,614	1,414	1,651	1,869	3,118	Erreur type de revenu moyen des ménages $	588

Table 1. Selected Characteristics for Census Tracts, 2001 Census – 100% Data and 20% Sample Data

No.	Characteristics	Vancouver 0230.02	Vancouver 0231	Vancouver 0232	Vancouver 0233	Vancouver 0234	Vancouver 0235.02
	POPULATION CHARACTERISTICS						
1	**Population, 1996 (1)**	**3,882**	**3,732**	**2,987**	**6,094**	**5,474**	**4,206**
2	**Population, 2001 (2)**	**3,874**	**4,008**	**3,280**	**6,755**	**6,582**	**4,235**
3	Population percentage change, 1996-2001	-0.2	7.4	9.8	10.8	20.2	0.7
4	Land area in square kilometres, 2001	3.95	1.98	2.89	1.52	4.53	1.44
5	**Total population – 100% Data (3)**	**3,875**	**4,010**	**3,280**	**6,760**	**6,580**	**4,235**
	by sex and age groups						
6	Male	1,930	2,015	1,660	3,330	3,330	2,065
7	0-4 years	95	80	75	255	210	145
8	5-9 years	75	105	100	225	230	160
9	10-14 years	100	145	120	235	240	150
10	15-19 years	140	195	135	240	260	145
11	20-24 years	180	195	155	255	210	145
12	25-29 years	175	125	125	265	175	105
13	30-34 years	140	125	125	270	210	155
14	35-39 years	125	135	125	290	265	215
15	40-44 years	130	155	115	240	265	210
16	45-49 years	140	175	125	260	270	195
17	50-54 years	135	160	125	215	230	135
18	55-59 years	120	110	95	140	130	85
19	60-64 years	115	85	80	105	95	65
20	65-69 years	95	100	55	125	90	55
21	70-74 years	70	70	40	80	100	50
22	75-79 years	40	30	30	80	135	25
23	80-84 years	30	25	15	30	120	10
24	85 years and over	20	10	10	30	95	10
25	Female	1,945	1,990	1,620	3,430	3,250	2,170
26	0-4 years	60	85	85	210	210	125
27	5-9 years	110	100	75	210	230	135
28	10-14 years	105	140	95	200	225	165
29	15-19 years	135	165	115	230	270	155
30	20-24 years	165	155	145	260	210	125
31	25-29 years	145	110	125	295	185	120
32	30-34 years	140	125	140	300	270	185
33	35-39 years	125	160	115	290	285	220
34	40-44 years	165	175	110	270	315	230
35	45-49 years	145	170	145	250	275	215
36	50-54 years	140	170	135	205	230	155
37	55-59 years	105	115	85	145	125	105
38	60-64 years	80	95	95	130	90	70
39	65-69 years	65	70	50	130	105	55
40	70-74 years	70	60	40	95	90	55
41	75-79 years	45	45	25	85	65	25
42	80-84 years	65	30	20	50	40	25
43	85 years and over	75	15	15	85	35	10
44	**Total population 15 years and over**	**3,330**	**3,350**	**2,730**	**5,430**	**5,235**	**3,350**
	by legal marital status						
45	Never married (single)	1,270	1,155	950	1,780	1,615	1,135
46	Legally married (and not separated)	1,405	1,870	1,460	2,845	2,940	1,680
47	Separated, but still legally married	110	65	70	165	115	130
48	Divorced	255	135	125	310	265	290
49	Widowed	290	125	120	325	295	125
	by common-law status						
50	Not in a common-law relationship	3,200	3,255	2,590	5,190	5,035	3,115
51	In a common-law relationship	135	100	145	240	200	240
52	**Total population – 20% Sample Data (4)**	**3,790**	**3,970**	**3,300**	**6,635**	**6,290**	**4,235**
	by mother tongue						
53	Single responses	3,725	3,945	3,215	6,530	6,120	4,205
54	English	1,810	2,085	1,515	3,055	3,170	2,825
55	French	35	15	40	75	50	75
56	Non-official languages (5)	1,880	1,840	1,660	3,400	2,905	1,305
57	Chinese, n.o.s.	345	520	240	455	485	115
58	Cantonese	310	135	185	525	570	115
59	Punjabi	160	90	255	775	235	40
60	Mandarin	25	335	190	140	295	115
61	Tagalog (Pilipino)	140	40	130	195	60	130
62	Other languages (6)	900	720	665	1,315	1,255	790
63	Multiple responses	65	35	90	110	170	35
64	English and French	30	-	-	10	15	10
65	English and non-official language	35	35	85	85	150	20
66	French and non-official language	-	-	-	10	-	-
67	English, French and non-official language	-	-	10	-	-	-

See reference material at the end of the publication. – Voir les documents de référence à la fin de la publication.

Tableau 1. Certaines caractéristiques des secteurs de recensement, recensement de 2001 – Données intégrales et données-échantillon (20 %)

Vancouver 0235.03 A	Vancouver 0235.04 A	Vancouver 0236	Vancouver 0237	Vancouver 0238.01	Vancouver 0238.02	Caractéristiques	N[o]
						CARACTÉRISTIQUES DE LA POPULATION	
2,741	**5,619**	**3,803**	**7,418**	**2,736**	**6,943**	**Population, 1996 (1)**	1
2,807	**5,965**	**3,703**	**7,600**	**2,896**	**6,986**	**Population, 2001 (2)**	2
2.4	6.2	-2.6	2.5	5.8	0.6	Variation en pourcentage de la population, 1996-2001	3
0.41	1.04	4.00	2.58	1.25	2.34	Superficie des terres en kilomètres carrés, 2001	4
2,805	**5,965**	**3,705**	**7,600**	**2,895**	**6,990**	**Population totale – Données intégrales (3)**	5
						selon le sexe et les groupes d'âge	
1,395	2,895	1,820	3,775	1,450	3,500	Sexe masculin	6
40	155	80	160	60	125	0-4 ans	7
25	140	90	225	80	190	5-9 ans	8
20	110	125	250	120	235	10-14 ans	9
30	150	190	305	120	340	15-19 ans	10
100	300	155	295	125	325	20-24 ans	11
130	310	100	250	75	270	25-29 ans	12
140	345	90	265	105	200	30-34 ans	13
155	305	100	275	90	215	35-39 ans	14
120	225	130	335	120	255	40-44 ans	15
120	235	160	350	105	290	45-49 ans	16
90	155	190	295	110	290	50-54 ans	17
85	110	95	185	75	190	55-59 ans	18
80	110	115	165	70	145	60-64 ans	19
80	85	80	165	75	150	65-69 ans	20
60	65	50	100	65	120	70-74 ans	21
45	55	30	80	35	85	75-79 ans	22
40	25	15	45	20	45	80-84 ans	23
25	15	10	35	5	25	85 ans et plus	24
1,415	3,070	1,885	3,825	1,445	3,490	Sexe féminin	25
25	145	75	155	60	110	0-4 ans	26
30	150	95	190	65	150	5-9 ans	27
20	110	145	245	90	210	10-14 ans	28
25	150	170	280	120	290	15-19 ans	29
110	290	140	275	105	330	20-24 ans	30
125	305	100	225	75	245	25-29 ans	31
115	305	90	260	95	185	30-34 ans	32
100	310	115	335	100	245	35-39 ans	33
90	240	170	380	140	325	40-44 ans	34
80	205	200	345	115	330	45-49 ans	35
120	200	175	275	115	260	50-54 ans	36
80	160	110	185	75	135	55-59 ans	37
90	120	90	165	85	140	60-64 ans	38
65	100	85	130	65	165	65-69 ans	39
115	105	50	145	55	130	70-74 ans	40
90	80	35	120	40	110	75-79 ans	41
65	55	25	70	25	70	80-84 ans	42
60	35	20	50	15	80	85 ans et plus	43
2,640	**5,150**	**3,090**	**6,385**	**2,420**	**5,970**	**Population totale de 15 ans et plus**	44
						selon l'état matrimonial légal	
965	1,955	1,005	2,145	785	2,180	Célibataire (jamais marié(e))	45
825	2,205	1,810	3,335	1,405	3,115	Légalement marié(e) (et non séparé(e))	46
135	180	50	160	40	95	Séparé(e), mais toujours légalement marié(e)	47
425	540	95	425	90	250	Divorcé(e)	48
280	270	130	315	100	330	Veuf ou veuve	49
						selon l'union libre	
2,345	4,720	3,000	6,020	2,345	5,740	Ne vivant pas en union libre	50
300	430	90	365	75	230	Vivant en union libre	51
2,805	**5,965**	**3,700**	**7,600**	**2,890**	**6,875**	**Population totale – Données-échantillon (20 %) (4)**	52
						selon la langue maternelle	
2,785	5,765	3,665	7,415	2,820	6,835	Réponses uniques	53
1,840	3,120	1,890	3,400	1,180	3,205	Anglais	54
55	60	15	70	35	45	Français	55
895	2,590	1,765	3,950	1,605	3,580	Langues non officielles (5)	56
55	380	555	695	285	670	Chinois, n.d.a.	57
65	340	550	1,010	370	685	Cantonais	58
10	-	-	55	-	75	Pendjabi	59
30	175	115	370	145	470	Mandarin	60
25	90	10	30	45	120	Tagalog (pilipino)	61
720	1,600	525	1,775	755	1,565	Autres langues (6)	62
20	195	35	185	75	40	Réponses multiples	63
-	10	-	20	-	-	Anglais et français	64
25	190	30	160	75	45	Anglais et langue non officielle	65
-	-	-	-	-	-	Français et langue non officielle	66
-	-	-	-	-	-	Anglais, français et langue non officielle	67

See reference material at the end of the publication. – Voir les documents de référence à la fin de la publication.

Table 1. Selected Characteristics for Census Tracts, 2001 Census – 100% Data and 20% Sample Data

No.	Characteristics	Vancouver 0230.02	Vancouver 0231	Vancouver 0232	Vancouver 0233	Vancouver 0234	Vancouver 0235.02
	POPULATION CHARACTERISTICS						
	by home language						
68	Single responses	2,585	3,005	2,360	4,600	4,580	3,385
69	English	1,985	2,205	1,695	3,245	3,390	3,100
70	French	-	-	-	10	-	10
71	Non-official languages (5)	595	800	665	1,350	1,190	285
72	Cantonese	140	135	40	350	275	55
73	Chinese, n.o.s.	135	210	50	150	225	15
74	Punjabi	15	35	135	310	60	10
75	Mandarin	25	185	75	50	145	50
76	Korean	-	30	20	100	205	20
77	Other languages (6)	285	205	340	390	280	125
78	Multiple responses	1,205	970	945	2,035	1,710	850
79	English and French	25	20	20	95	55	60
80	English and non-official language	1,140	940	915	1,920	1,625	770
81	French and non-official language	25	10	10	10	-	20
82	English, French and non-official language	20	-	-	15	20	-
	by knowledge of official languages						
83	English only	3,410	3,555	2,900	5,915	5,675	3,865
84	French only	-	-	-	10	-	-
85	English and French	255	220	185	335	335	330
86	Neither English nor French	125	195	220	380	275	40
	by knowledge of non-official languages (5) (7)						
87	Cantonese	300	220	245	620	615	150
88	Chinese, n.o.s.	295	385	210	495	500	100
89	Punjabi	185	135	365	945	260	50
90	Mandarin	190	575	230	330	540	150
91	Hindi	260	115	175	490	215	125
92	German	70	45	65	110	65	55
93	Spanish	160	140	140	85	150	145
	by first official language spoken						
94	English	3,630	3,765	3,045	6,125	5,930	4,075
95	French	35	10	35	110	50	70
96	English and French	15	10	-	30	35	45
97	Neither English nor French	115	190	220	370	275	45
98	Official language minority - (number) (8)	40	15	35	120	70	95
99	Official language minority - (percentage) (8)	1.1	0.4	1.1	1.8	1.1	2.2
	by ethnic origin (9)						
100	English	595	805	495	995	1,070	1,140
101	Canadian	540	585	510	690	970	750
102	Chinese	780	1,180	715	1,520	1,555	445
103	Scottish	280	420	250	630	685	790
104	Irish	295	405	295	520	530	675
105	German	215	180	275	640	535	375
106	East Indian	565	350	625	1,165	445	245
107	French	185	225	155	440	285	360
108	Ukrainian	135	135	75	195	250	125
109	Italian	245	315	250	270	310	390
110	Dutch (Netherlands)	55	145	20	185	220	145
111	Filipino	180	105	195	320	120	190
112	Polish	70	130	60	340	125	105
113	Norwegian	20	90	75	75	175	130
114	North American Indian	75	40	95	155	100	60
	by Aboriginal identity						
115	Total Aboriginal identity population (10)	125	35	90	170	75	50
116	Total non-Aboriginal population	3,665	3,935	3,210	6,465	6,215	4,190
	by Aboriginal origin						
117	Total Aboriginal origins population (11)	150	45	105	200	185	60
118	Total non-Aboriginal population	3,635	3,925	3,195	6,435	6,100	4,180
	by Registered Indian status						
119	Registered Indian (12)	40	10	15	90	30	10
120	Not a Registered Indian	3,750	3,965	3,290	6,550	6,260	4,225

Tableau 1. Certaines caractéristiques des secteurs de recensement, recensement de 2001 – Données intégrales et données-échantillon (20 %)

Vancouver 0235.03 A	Vancouver 0235.04 A	Vancouver 0236	Vancouver 0237	Vancouver 0238.01	Vancouver 0238.02	Caractéristiques	N°
						CARACTÉRISTIQUES DE LA POPULATION	
						selon la langue parlée à la maison	
2,395	4,725	2,775	5,590	1,975	5,020	Réponses uniques	68
2,120	3,535	2,130	4,010	1,395	3,500	Anglais	69
-	-	-	-	-	20	Français	70
275	1,195	645	1,585	585	1,505	Langues non officielles (5)	71
35	230	385	560	155	355	Cantonais	72
10	175	95	285	85	225	Chinois, n.d.a.	73
-	-	-	10	-	45	Pendjabi	74
30	105	60	125	85	325	Mandarin	75
85	260	30	215	20	145	Coréen	76
115	420	75	395	245	410	Autres langues (6)	77
410	1,240	925	2,010	915	1,855	Réponses multiples	78
20	35	45	50	15	10	Anglais et français	79
360	1,190	860	1,940	895	1,820	Anglais et langue non officielle	80
25	10	-	10	-	-	Français et langue non officielle	81
-	10	20	10	-	20	Anglais, français et langue non officielle	82
						selon la connaissance des langues officielles	
2,530	5,230	3,275	6,655	2,645	6,145	Anglais seulement	83
-	-	-	10	-	10	Français seulement	84
205	520	185	540	125	360	Anglais et français	85
70	215	240	400	125	370	Ni l'anglais ni le français	86
						selon la connaissance des langues non officielles (5) (7)	
80	425	660	1,160	475	845	Cantonais	87
25	360	470	605	250	475	Chinois, n.d.a.	88
10	15	45	85	-	140	Pendjabi	89
55	285	320	815	285	885	Mandarin	90
50	190	65	130	15	125	Hindi	91
105	120	60	155	40	75	Allemand	92
70	225	45	140	20	200	Espagnol	93
						selon la première langue officielle parlée	
2,650	5,650	3,430	7,045	2,720	6,420	Anglais	94
75	50	15	75	35	55	Français	95
15	60	20	85	15	40	Anglais et français	96
70	200	230	395	125	365	Ni l'anglais ni le français	97
80	85	25	115	40	75	Minorité de langue officielle - (nombre) (8)	98
2.9	1.4	0.7	1.5	1.4	1.1	Minorité de langue officielle - (pourcentage) (8)	99
						selon l'origine ethnique (9)	
745	1,305	575	1,135	315	915	Anglais	100
540	925	360	830	345	1,165	Canadien	101
150	1,110	1,600	2,470	990	1,995	Chinois	102
545	795	375	735	270	615	Écossais	103
385	615	215	680	120	450	Irlandais	104
315	475	325	460	135	305	Allemand	105
90	340	130	275	100	255	Indien de l'Inde	106
205	320	100	290	125	210	Français	107
90	235	90	225	65	160	Ukrainien	108
60	130	430	500	375	890	Italien	109
105	130	40	75	60	210	Hollandais (Néerlandais)	110
35	230	20	65	75	155	Philippin	111
130	205	130	190	10	140	Polonais	112
70	110	75	100	10	130	Norvégien	113
15	125	10	125	35	65	Indien de l'Amérique du Nord	114
						selon l'identité autochtone	
15	150	-	130	35	135	Total de la population ayant une identité autochtone (10)	115
2,790	5,810	3,700	7,470	2,860	6,740	Total de la population non autochtone	116
						selon l'origine autochtone	
25	175	10	140	35	120	Total de la population ayant une origine autochtone (11)	117
2,785	5,785	3,695	7,460	2,855	6,755	Total de la population non autochtone	118
						selon le statut d'Indien inscrit	
10	85	-	95	-	40	Oui, Indien inscrit (12)	119
2,800	5,875	3,700	7,505	2,890	6,840	Non, pas un Indien inscrit	120

Table 1. Selected Characteristics for Census Tracts, 2001 Census – 100% Data and 20% Sample Data

No.	Characteristics	Vancouver 0230.02	Vancouver 0231	Vancouver 0232	Vancouver 0233	Vancouver 0234	Vancouver 0235.02
	POPULATION CHARACTERISTICS						
	by visible minority groups						
121	Total visible minority population	1,965	2,145	1,900	3,550	2,965	1,300
122	Chinese	780	1,230	725	1,375	1,570	455
123	South Asian	590	375	725	1,265	660	290
124	Black	90	65	50	130	25	30
125	Filipino	175	105	195	245	125	150
126	Latin American	75	85	60	50	65	45
127	Southeast Asian	-	15	-	100	45	65
128	Arab	-	-	-	10	10	65
129	West Asian	90	55	-	105	40	35
130	Korean	40	85	35	155	335	65
131	Japanese	35	65	90	40	70	85
132	Visible minority, n.i.e. (13)	-	25	-	-	-	-
133	Multiple visible minorities (14)	75	45	25	75	25	15
	by citizenship						
134	Canadian citizenship (15)	3,395	3,450	2,905	5,900	5,345	3,850
135	Citizenship other than Canadian	390	525	400	740	945	385
	by place of birth of respondent						
136	Non-immigrant population	1,930	2,050	1,695	3,580	3,360	2,840
137	Born in province of residence	1,370	1,535	1,345	2,770	2,635	1,985
138	Immigrant population (16)	1,825	1,840	1,595	3,005	2,870	1,380
139	United States	25	20	55	65	65	25
140	Central and South America	100	80	90	40	40	60
141	Caribbean and Bermuda	10	55	-	15	10	10
142	United Kingdom	95	65	25	95	160	65
143	Other Europe (17)	240	215	165	430	320	255
144	Africa	235	115	245	220	215	175
145	Asia and the Middle East	1,055	1,275	960	2,030	2,005	745
146	Oceania and other (18)	60	15	45	110	50	50
147	Non-permanent residents (19)	35	85	-	50	60	15
148	**Total immigrant population**	**1,825**	**1,835**	**1,595**	**3,005**	**2,870**	**1,385**
	by period of immigration						
149	Before 1961	165	130	85	155	175	95
150	1961-1970	155	185	145	300	185	75
151	1971-1980	365	270	460	780	395	370
152	1981-1990	510	200	305	680	505	385
153	1991-2001 (20)	630	1,050	600	1,095	1,605	460
154	1991-1995	280	565	330	570	835	190
155	1996-2001 (20)	350	485	275	525	770	275
	by age at immigration						
156	0-4 years	135	155	130	210	240	125
157	5-19 years	560	515	465	840	990	375
158	20 years and over	1,130	1,160	995	1,960	1,640	880
159	**Total population**	**3,790**	**3,975**	**3,300**	**6,635**	**6,290**	**4,235**
	by religion						
160	Catholic (21)	880	740	720	1,280	1,360	1,135
161	Protestant	650	875	695	1,170	1,540	980
162	Christian Orthodox	20	55	20	190	100	45
163	Christian, n.i.e. (22)	220	145	125	190	570	225
164	Muslim	415	245	345	290	335	315
165	Jewish	-	-	10	20	15	25
166	Buddhist	155	390	190	375	195	90
167	Hindu	145	85	30	140	70	25
168	Sikh	175	115	340	910	260	15
169	Eastern religions (23)	10	10	-	10	15	-
170	Other religions (24)	25	40	25	50	35	15
171	No religious affiliation (25)	1,100	1,285	800	2,030	1,795	1,365
172	**Total population 15 years and over**	**3,265**	**3,335**	**2,715**	**5,290**	**4,950**	**3,330**
	by generation status						
173	1st generation (26)	1,770	1,755	1,525	2,935	2,645	1,305
174	2nd generation (27)	760	845	605	1,230	910	800
175	3rd generation and over (28)	740	735	585	1,120	1,395	1,230
176	**Total population 1 year and over (29)**	**3,765**	**3,950**	**3,275**	**6,540**	**6,235**	**4,185**
	by place of residence 1 year ago (mobility)						
177	Non-movers	3,050	3,420	2,850	5,375	5,240	3,660
178	Movers	715	535	420	1,165	985	525
179	Non-migrants	305	240	220	605	525	245
180	Migrants	405	295	200	555	460	280
181	Internal migrants	350	195	155	435	360	225
182	Intraprovincial migrants	340	170	150	365	295	175
183	Interprovincial migrants	15	25	10	75	65	55
184	External migrants	55	100	40	120	100	55

Tableau 1. Certaines caractéristiques des secteurs de recensement, recensement de 2001 – Données intégrales et données-échantillon (20 %)

Vancouver 0235.03 A	Vancouver 0235.04 A	Vancouver 0236	Vancouver 0237	Vancouver 0238.01	Vancouver 0238.02	Caractéristiques	N°
						CARACTÉRISTIQUES DE LA POPULATION	
						selon les groupes de minorités visibles	
665	2,665	1,985	3,900	1,610	3,405	Total de la population des minorités visibles	121
150	1,060	1,515	2,480	995	2,105	Chinois	122
115	395	175	315	175	325	Sud-Asiatique	123
50	150	-	65	45	50	Noir	124
40	215	-	35	60	155	Philippin	125
10	145	10	40	10	135	Latino-Américain	126
-	95	30	70	40	100	Asiatique du Sud-Est	127
50	30	15	10	-	-	Arabe	128
35	95	-	205	75	95	Asiatique occidental	129
195	400	95	345	30	215	Coréen	130
10	30	90	180	125	215	Japonais	131
-	-	-	105	10	-	Minorité visible, n.i.a. (13)	132
-	40	45	45	45	25	Minorités visibles multiples (14)	133
						selon la citoyenneté	
2,450	4,980	3,345	6,420	2,515	5,985	Citoyenneté canadienne (15)	134
360	985	350	1,180	380	895	Citoyenneté autre que canadienne	135
						selon le lieu de naissance du répondant	
1,825	3,175	1,925	3,760	1,400	3,555	Population non immigrante	136
1,010	1,975	1,585	2,660	1,040	2,815	Née dans la province de résidence	137
920	2,520	1,750	3,705	1,430	3,220	Population immigrante (16)	138
40	50	20	65	15	45	États-Unis	139
35	85	10	45	-	95	Amérique centrale et du Sud	140
10	30	10	15	-	10	Caraïbes et Bermudes	141
110	160	110	200	45	90	Royaume-Uni	142
275	335	265	585	250	560	Autre Europe (17)	143
65	255	40	275	120	150	Afrique	144
385	1,580	1,260	2,490	995	2,255	Asie et Moyen-Orient	145
-	25	40	30	-	30	Océanie et autre (18)	146
65	270	30	135	60	100	Résidents non permanents (19)	147
915	**2,525**	**1,750**	**3,705**	**1,430**	**3,220**	**Population immigrante totale**	148
						selon la période d'immigration	
230	165	185	255	135	380	Avant 1961	149
60	205	260	230	150	270	1961-1970	150
115	455	390	710	225	495	1971-1980	151
95	350	240	505	380	465	1981-1990	152
415	1,355	675	2,015	530	1,610	1991-2001 (20)	153
145	710	355	885	300	860	1991-1995	154
275	645	320	1,130	235	750	1996-2001 (20)	155
						selon l'âge à l'immigration	
60	230	165	280	130	290	0-4 ans	156
225	660	500	1,040	400	1,065	5-19 ans	157
635	1,635	1,085	2,390	900	1,860	20 ans et plus	158
2,805	**5,965**	**3,700**	**7,605**	**2,890**	**6,880**	**Population totale**	159
						selon la religion	
540	1,160	915	1,645	795	1,815	Catholique (21)	160
800	1,450	735	1,470	525	1,215	Protestante	161
95	165	40	210	45	80	Orthodoxe chrétienne	162
195	315	230	455	240	515	Chrétiennes, n.i.a. (22)	163
160	485	65	545	205	190	Musulmane	164
10	25	10	-	-	40	Juive	165
15	165	135	415	145	425	Bouddhiste	166
30	20	40	25	-	105	Hindoue	167
10	-	50	75	-	85	Sikh	168
30	30	10	10	-	10	Religions orientales (23)	169
10	10	-	15	20	-	Autres religions (24)	170
920	2,140	1,470	2,735	925	2,390	Aucune appartenance religieuse (25)	171
2,645	**5,145**	**3,125**	**6,385**	**2,385**	**5,840**	**Population totale de 15 ans et plus**	172
						selon le statut des générations	
930	2,575	1,730	3,470	1,440	3,025	1re génération (26)	173
710	970	745	1,440	485	1,470	2e génération (27)	174
995	1,595	655	1,475	460	1,340	3e génération et plus (28)	175
2,795	**5,920**	**3,670**	**7,515**	**2,875**	**6,840**	**Population totale de 1 an et plus (29)**	176
						selon le lieu de résidence 1 an auparavant (mobilité)	
2,125	4,490	3,385	6,445	2,655	5,805	Personnes n'ayant pas déménagé	177
670	1,435	285	1,070	215	1,035	Personnes ayant déménagé	178
285	695	90	420	85	600	Non-migrants	179
390	740	195	655	130	440	Migrants	180
335	395	155	495	90	225	Migrants internes	181
315	335	120	405	85	165	Migrants infraprovinciaux	182
25	70	30	90	10	60	Migrants interprovinciaux	183
50	335	40	160	45	210	Migrants externes	184

Table 1. Selected Characteristics for Census Tracts, 2001 Census – 100% Data and 20% Sample Data

No.	Characteristics	Vancouver 0230.02	Vancouver 0231	Vancouver 0232	Vancouver 0233	Vancouver 0234	Vancouver 0235.02
	POPULATION CHARACTERISTICS						
185	**Total population 5 years and over (30)**	**3,645**	**3,825**	**3,120**	**6,170**	**5,870**	**3,965**
	by place of residence 5 years ago (mobility)						
186	Non-movers	1,875	2,580	1,920	3,440	3,055	2,300
187	Movers	1,775	1,245	1,205	2,735	2,815	1,670
188	Non-migrants	620	585	720	1,500	1,055	675
189	Migrants	1,155	660	485	1,235	1,760	995
190	Internal migrants	825	195	305	820	1,070	715
191	Intraprovincial migrants	765	165	250	635	865	635
192	Interprovincial migrants	60	30	55	185	200	85
193	External migrants	320	465	180	410	690	280
194	**Total population 15 to 24 years**	**630**	**755**	**490**	**955**	**965**	**545**
	by school attendance						
195	Not attending school	245	145	145	350	245	135
196	Attending school full time	310	540	280	480	575	370
197	Attending school part time	75	65	60	130	140	40
198	**Total population 15 years and over**	**3,265**	**3,340**	**2,720**	**5,285**	**4,950**	**3,330**
	by highest level of schooling						
199	Less than grade 9 (31)	305	100	190	505	260	95
200	Grades 9-13 without high school graduation certificate	650	630	440	1,200	805	485
201	Grades 9-13 with high school graduation certificate	395	405	395	660	675	450
202	Some postsecondary without degree, certificate or diploma (32)	520	465	275	660	730	455
203	Trades certificate or diploma (33)	440	195	320	605	485	425
204	College certificate or diploma (34)	385	440	475	680	890	665
205	University certificate below bachelor's degree	105	240	135	185	170	80
206	University with bachelor's degree or higher	460	870	495	785	930	680
	by combinations of unpaid work						
207	Males 15 years and over	1,675	1,645	1,400	2,575	2,375	1,605
208	Reported unpaid work (35)	1,475	1,440	1,240	2,335	2,080	1,460
209	Housework and child care and care or assistance to seniors	90	150	160	260	175	95
210	Housework and child care only	330	375	350	750	615	485
211	Housework and care or assistance to seniors only	115	110	115	215	170	115
212	Child care and care or assistance to seniors only	10	-	-	10	-	-
213	Housework only	900	755	595	1,065	1,020	755
214	Child care only	20	40	15	40	40	-
215	Care or assistance to seniors only	10	-	-	-	50	10
216	Females 15 years and over	1,595	1,695	1,320	2,710	2,570	1,725
217	Reported unpaid work (35)	1,480	1,560	1,245	2,525	2,400	1,660
218	Housework and child care and care or assistance to seniors	120	225	280	425	350	145
219	Housework and child care only	380	385	380	905	775	585
220	Housework and care or assistance to seniors only	145	180	105	135	220	185
221	Child care and care or assistance to seniors only	-	-	-	-	-	10
222	Housework only	805	745	465	1,040	1,015	730
223	Child care only	25	20	10	15	-	-
224	Care or assistance to seniors only	10	-	-	10	25	-
	by labour force activity						
225	Males 15 years and over	1,675	1,645	1,395	2,575	2,380	1,600
226	In the labour force	1,155	1,065	960	1,880	1,625	1,250
227	Employed	1,095	1,020	910	1,720	1,500	1,150
228	Unemployed	60	50	50	165	130	95
229	Not in the labour force	520	575	440	695	745	355
230	Participation rate	69.0	64.7	68.8	73.0	68.3	78.1
231	Employment rate	65.4	62.0	65.2	66.8	63.0	71.9
232	Unemployment rate	5.2	4.7	5.2	8.8	8.0	7.6
233	Females 15 years and over	1,590	1,695	1,320	2,710	2,575	1,725
234	In the labour force	885	870	845	1,695	1,495	1,205
235	Employed	785	850	750	1,555	1,315	1,100
236	Unemployed	100	25	95	140	175	105
237	Not in the labour force	710	820	475	1,015	1,080	520
238	Participation rate	55.7	51.3	64.0	62.5	58.1	69.9
239	Employment rate	49.4	50.1	56.8	57.4	51.1	63.8
240	Unemployment rate	11.3	2.9	11.2	8.3	11.7	8.7

Tableau 1. Certaines caractéristiques des secteurs de recensement, recensement de 2001 – Données intégrales et données-échantillon (20 %)

Vancouver 0235.03 A	Vancouver 0235.04 A	Vancouver 0236	Vancouver 0237	Vancouver 0238.01	Vancouver 0238.02	Caractéristiques	N°
						CARACTÉRISTIQUES DE LA POPULATION	
2,745	**5,655**	**3,540**	**7,285**	**2,775**	**6,650**	**Population totale de 5 ans et plus (30)**	185
						selon le lieu de résidence 5 ans auparavant (mobilité)	
1,300	2,240	2,620	4,025	2,040	3,955	Personnes n'ayant pas déménagé	186
1,450	3,420	925	3,260	735	2,700	Personnes ayant déménagé	187
545	1,250	360	1,315	285	1,100	Non-migrants	188
905	2,170	565	1,940	455	1,595	Migrants	189
640	1,390	305	810	255	805	Migrants internes	190
475	1,045	235	620	155	635	Migrants infraprovinciaux	191
160	340	70	185	100	170	Migrants interprovinciaux	192
260	780	260	1,130	195	790	Migrants externes	193
265	**880**	**580**	**1,165**	**545**	**1,275**	**Population totale de 15 à 24 ans**	194
						selon la fréquentation scolaire	
130	300	95	280	125	345	Ne fréquentant pas l'école	195
75	510	430	800	375	780	Fréquentant l'école à plein temps	196
60	70	60	85	50	145	Fréquentant l'école à temps partiel	197
2,640	**5,145**	**3,125**	**6,385**	**2,385**	**5,835**	**Population totale de 15 ans et plus**	198
						selon le plus haut niveau de scolarité atteint	
145	220	215	360	230	405	Niveau inférieur à la 9e année (31)	199
470	840	515	1,050	475	925	De la 9e à la 13e année sans certificat d'études secondaires	200
260	485	380	830	290	965	De la 9e à la 13e année avec certificat d'études secondaires	201
310	690	545	795	310	820	Études postsecondaires partielles sans grade, certificat ou diplôme (32)	202
350	470	185	550	255	695	Certificat ou diplôme d'une école de métiers (33)	203
540	1,115	450	935	260	725	Certificat ou diplôme collégial (34)	204
125	230	60	210	85	240	Certificat universitaire inférieur au baccalauréat	205
445	1,100	770	1,650	475	1,065	Études universitaires avec baccalauréat ou diplôme supérieur	206
						selon les combinaisons de travail non rémunéré	
1,310	2,500	1,550	3,145	1,150	2,915	Hommes de 15 ans et plus	207
1,115	2,125	1,325	2,715	1,040	2,605	Travail non rémunéré déclaré (35)	208
65	95	90	220	110	310	Travaux ménagers et soins aux enfants et soins ou aide aux personnes âgées	209
130	360	395	665	240	605	Travaux ménagers et soins aux enfants seulement	210
85	130	145	220	150	315	Travaux ménagers et soins ou aide aux personnes âgées seulement	211
-	10	-	-	10	10	Soins aux enfants et soins ou aide aux personnes âgées seulement	212
805	1,455	675	1,525	515	1,310	Travaux ménagers seulement	213
10	65	10	35	10	25	Soins aux enfants seulement	214
15	-	10	50	10	30	Soins ou aide aux personnes âgées seulement	215
1,335	2,650	1,580	3,240	1,230	2,920	Femmes de 15 ans et plus	216
1,230	2,385	1,445	3,025	1,140	2,740	Travail non rémunéré déclaré (35)	217
90	190	210	300	185	380	Travaux ménagers et soins aux enfants et soins ou aide aux personnes âgées	218
215	610	390	830	290	685	Travaux ménagers et soins aux enfants seulement	219
110	295	145	325	125	445	Travaux ménagers et soins ou aide aux personnes âgées seulement	220
-	-	-	10	-	-	Soins aux enfants et soins ou aide aux personnes âgées seulement	221
785	1,265	685	1,540	530	1,195	Travaux ménagers seulement	222
30	15	15	-	10	-	Soins aux enfants seulement	223
10	-	-	15	-	30	Soins ou aide aux personnes âgées seulement	224
						selon l'activité	
1,305	2,495	1,550	3,145	1,150	2,915	Hommes de 15 ans et plus	225
950	1,785	1,005	2,160	660	2,075	Population active	226
875	1,665	950	2,015	605	1,865	Personnes occupées	227
75	115	60	145	55	210	Chômeurs	228
355	715	545	980	490	835	Inactifs	229
72.8	71.5	64.8	68.7	57.4	71.2	Taux d'activité	230
67.0	66.7	61.3	64.1	52.6	64.0	Taux d'emploi	231
7.9	6.4	6.0	6.7	8.3	10.1	Taux de chômage	232
1,335	2,650	1,575	3,240	1,235	2,925	Femmes de 15 ans et plus	233
740	1,635	900	1,820	650	1,655	Population active	234
650	1,490	855	1,645	585	1,490	Personnes occupées	235
85	145	50	180	65	165	Chômeuses	236
595	1,015	675	1,420	580	1,270	Inactives	237
55.4	61.7	57.1	56.2	52.6	56.6	Taux d'activité	238
48.7	56.2	54.3	50.8	47.4	50.9	Taux d'emploi	239
11.5	8.9	5.6	9.9	10.0	10.0	Taux de chômage	240

Table 1. Selected Characteristics for Census Tracts, 2001 Census – 100% Data and 20% Sample Data

No.	Characteristics	Vancouver 0230.02	Vancouver 0231	Vancouver 0232	Vancouver 0233	Vancouver 0234	Vancouver 0235.02
	POPULATION CHARACTERISTICS						
	by labour force activity – concluded						
241	Both sexes - Participation rate	62.2	58.2	66.3	67.8	63.0	73.7
242	15-24 years	61.9	48.0	63.6	63.4	54.6	59.3
243	25 years and over	62.4	61.2	66.8	68.7	65.0	76.7
244	Both sexes - Employment rate	57.4	56.0	60.8	62.0	56.9	67.9
245	15-24 years	52.8	42.1	51.0	56.0	46.4	43.1
246	25 years and over	58.6	59.9	63.4	63.2	59.4	72.5
247	Both sexes - Unemployment rate	7.9	3.6	8.3	8.7	9.9	8.1
248	15-24 years	16.7	11.0	20.6	10.7	15.1	25.0
249	25 years and over	5.8	1.9	5.4	8.1	8.7	5.4
250	**Total labour force 15 years and over**	**2,035**	**1,940**	**1,805**	**3,585**	**3,120**	**2,455**
	by industry based on the 1997 NAICS						
251	Industry - Not applicable (36)	50	40	60	95	130	55
252	All industries (37)	1,980	1,905	1,740	3,490	2,990	2,400
253	11 Agriculture, forestry, fishing and hunting	-	10	15	25	-	10
254	21 Mining and oil and gas extraction	10	-	-	-	-	10
255	22 Utilities	25	10	10	20	20	10
256	23 Construction	190	170	95	220	120	130
257	31-33 Manufacturing	105	140	220	455	235	165
258	41 Wholesale trade	115	110	125	165	145	130
259	44-45 Retail trade	275	125	215	420	355	230
260	48-49 Transportation and warehousing	140	90	110	270	195	150
261	51 Information and cultural industries	100	50	55	145	215	160
262	52 Finance and insurance	90	135	60	105	145	120
263	53 Real estate and rental and leasing	20	45	15	50	30	45
264	54 Professional, scientific and technical services	160	220	105	185	300	230
265	55 Management of companies and enterprises	-	-	-	-	-	-
266	56 Administrative and support, waste management and remediation services	75	85	70	155	130	130
267	61 Educational services	75	130	85	175	190	260
268	62 Health care and social assistance	160	160	175	390	355	190
269	71 Arts, entertainment and recreation	40	40	15	75	20	55
270	72 Accommodation and food services	170	195	140	280	225	140
271	81 Other services (except public administration)	185	85	145	225	205	145
272	91 Public administration	45	105	90	125	110	95
	by class of worker						
273	Class of worker - Not applicable (36)	50	40	60	95	130	60
274	All classes of worker (37)	1,980	1,905	1,745	3,485	2,990	2,395
275	Paid workers	1,765	1,675	1,620	3,215	2,780	2,220
276	Employees	1,685	1,515	1,515	3,130	2,675	2,105
277	Self-employed (incorporated)	80	155	110	80	110	120
278	Self-employed (unincorporated)	200	220	120	250	190	170
279	Unpaid family workers	15	10	-	25	20	-
	by occupation based on the 2001 NOC-S						
280	Male labour force 15 years and over	1,150	1,070	960	1,885	1,630	1,250
281	Occupation - Not applicable (36)	15	30	25	55	45	25
282	All occupations (37)	1,135	1,040	940	1,830	1,590	1,225
283	A Management occupations	175	210	185	205	265	160
284	B Business, finance and administration occupations	125	115	95	170	200	125
285	C Natural and applied sciences and related occupations	145	80	90	190	160	160
286	D Health occupations	-	45	45	15	45	20
287	E Occupations in social science, education, government service and religion	20	95	25	75	60	45
288	F Occupations in art, culture, recreation and sport	40	30	10	35	20	65
289	G Sales and service occupations	275	180	200	380	330	310
290	H Trades, transport and equipment operators and related occupations	310	235	225	580	380	270
291	I Occupations unique to primary industry	10	35	15	35	40	25
292	J Occupations unique to processing, manufacturing and utilities	20	-	50	150	80	40
293	Female labour force 15 years and over	885	870	845	1,700	1,495	1,205
294	Occupation - Not applicable (36)	40	10	35	40	85	30
295	All occupations (37)	845	865	805	1,655	1,405	1,175
296	A Management occupations	65	95	55	95	95	115
297	B Business, finance and administration occupations	265	285	345	480	475	410
298	C Natural and applied sciences and related occupations	35	45	25	20	65	15
299	D Health occupations	65	60	35	190	95	65

Tableau 1. Certaines caractéristiques des secteurs de recensement, recensement de 2001 – Données intégrales et données-échantillon (20 %)

Vancouver 0235.03 A	Vancouver 0235.04 A	Vancouver 0236	Vancouver 0237	Vancouver 0238.01	Vancouver 0238.02	Caractéristiques	N°
						CARACTÉRISTIQUES DE LA POPULATION	
						selon l'activité – fin	
64.0	66.5	61.1	62.3	54.9	64.0	Les deux sexes - Taux d'activité	241
76.9	60.2	45.7	51.9	50.9	63.1	15-24 ans	242
62.6	67.8	64.6	64.7	56.1	64.2	25 ans et plus	243
57.7	61.3	57.7	57.3	49.9	57.4	Les deux sexes - Taux d'emploi	244
65.4	54.0	41.4	42.1	40.0	53.5	15-24 ans	245
57.3	63.0	61.3	60.8	52.9	58.6	25 ans et plus	246
9.8	7.7	5.5	8.0	9.2	10.2	Les deux sexes - Taux de chômage	247
12.8	12.3	9.4	19.0	20.0	15.5	15-24 ans	248
9.4	7.1	5.2	6.1	5.8	8.7	25 ans et plus	249
1,690	**3,420**	**1,910**	**3,980**	**1,310**	**3,735**	**Population active totale de 15 ans et plus**	250
						selon l'industrie basée sur le SCIAN de 1997	
70	75	40	80	30	105	Industrie - Sans objet (36)	251
1,615	3,350	1,870	3,900	1,285	3,625	Toutes les industries (37)	252
-	-	10	15	-	-	11 Agriculture, foresterie, pêche et chasse	253
10	-	-	10	-	10	21 Extraction minière et extraction de pétrole et de gaz	254
-	35	20	20	10	50	22 Services publics	255
135	165	55	225	50	295	23 Construction	256
215	285	160	275	125	320	31-33 Fabrication	257
90	210	140	330	100	185	41 Commerce de gros	258
235	365	210	360	150	520	44-45 Commerce de détail	259
85	195	50	170	40	215	48-49 Transport et entreposage	260
75	210	90	240	25	165	51 Industrie de l'information et industrie culturelle	261
70	160	160	290	55	165	52 Finance et assurances	262
60	130	65	90	40	75	53 Services immobiliers et services de location et de location à bail	263
120	400	190	385	115	325	54 Services professionnels, scientifiques et techniques	264
-	-	-	-	-	-	55 Gestion de sociétés et d'entreprises	265
50	145	75	150	30	150	56 Services administratifs, services de soutien, services de gestion des déchets et services d'assainissement	266
115	215	190	300	65	215	61 Services d'enseignement	267
100	250	145	185	150	255	62 Soins de santé et assistance sociale	268
10	75	15	85	65	75	71 Arts, spectacles et loisirs	269
85	220	70	315	145	320	72 Hébergement et services de restauration	270
100	175	100	210	80	175	81 Autres services, sauf les administrations publiques	271
50	115	115	250	35	115	91 Administrations publiques	272
						selon la catégorie de travailleurs	
70	75	40	85	25	110	Catégorie de travailleurs - Sans objet (36)	273
1,615	3,345	1,870	3,895	1,285	3,625	Toutes les catégories de travailleurs (37)	274
1,505	3,165	1,705	3,565	1,175	3,260	Travailleurs rémunérés	275
1,465	3,065	1,590	3,365	1,115	3,060	Employés	276
40	110	115	195	60	200	Travailleurs autonomes (entreprise constituée en société)	277
110	175	145	320	100	350	Travailleurs autonomes (entreprise non constituée en société)	278
-	10	15	15	10	15	Travailleurs familiaux non rémunérés	279
						selon la profession basée sur la CNP-S de 2001	
950	1,785	1,005	2,160	665	2,080	Hommes actifs de 15 ans et plus	280
35	30	10	45	10	50	Profession - Sans objet (36)	281
910	1,760	990	2,115	655	2,030	Toutes les professions (37)	282
135	240	215	325	95	325	A Gestion	283
110	205	155	245	90	295	B Affaires, finance et administration	284
110	335	130	370	60	195	C Sciences naturelles et appliquées et professions apparentées	285
10	15	40	50	15	50	D Secteur de la santé	286
70	80	85	130	55	75	E Sciences sociales, enseignement, administration publique et religion	287
-	50	30	75	-	55	F Arts, culture, sports et loisirs	288
170	355	145	435	115	405	G Ventes et services	289
230	435	140	370	175	520	H Métiers, transport et machinerie	290
10	-	25	15	-	20	I Professions propres au secteur primaire	291
65	35	35	75	55	85	J Transformation, fabrication et services d'utilité publique	292
735	1,640	905	1,820	650	1,655	Femmes actives de 15 ans et plus	293
30	40	25	30	20	55	Profession - Sans objet (36)	294
705	1,595	875	1,785	630	1,600	Toutes les professions (37)	295
50	95	105	145	45	160	A Gestion	296
235	605	310	640	160	525	B Affaires, finance et administration	297
20	110	20	90	30	35	C Sciences naturelles et appliquées et professions apparentées	298
55	80	45	95	35	105	D Secteur de la santé	299

Table 1. Selected Characteristics for Census Tracts, 2001 Census – 100% Data and 20% Sample Data

No.	Characteristics	Vancouver 0230.02	Vancouver 0231	Vancouver 0232	Vancouver 0233	Vancouver 0234	Vancouver 0235.02
	POPULATION CHARACTERISTICS						
	by occupation based on the 2001 NOC-S – concluded						
300	E Occupations in social science, education, government service and religion	105	80	55	125	175	130
301	F Occupations in art, culture, recreation and sport	30	50	25	50	40	90
302	G Sales and service occupations	260	210	220	570	410	335
303	H Trades, transport and equipment operators and related occupations	15	10	20	50	15	10
304	I Occupations unique to primary industry	-	10	-	20	10	-
305	J Occupations unique to processing, manufacturing and utilities	10	20	25	60	25	10
306	**Total employed labour force 15 years and over**	**1,870**	**1,870**	**1,655**	**3,275**	**2,815**	**2,260**
	by place of work						
307	Males	1,095	1,020	910	1,720	1,495	1,155
308	Usual place of work	805	695	725	1,420	1,185	905
309	At home	70	90	30	60	75	95
310	Outside Canada	15	45	10	15	40	10
311	No fixed workplace address	200	190	145	225	195	145
312	Females	785	850	745	1,555	1,315	1,100
313	Usual place of work	690	665	655	1,360	1,125	985
314	At home	70	125	40	85	120	75
315	Outside Canada	-	10	-	35	20	-
316	No fixed workplace address	20	50	50	80	50	45
317	**Total employed labour force 15 years and over with usual place of work or no fixed workplace address**	**1,715**	**1,595**	**1,580**	**3,085**	**2,555**	**2,080**
	by mode of transportation						
318	Males	1,005	885	870	1,645	1,380	1,055
319	Car, truck, van, as driver	805	735	720	1,260	1,180	950
320	Car, truck, van, as passenger	55	80	50	90	90	20
321	Public transit	70	60	75	200	90	45
322	Walked	35	-	10	50	10	-
323	Other method	25	10	30	50	20	30
324	Females	710	715	705	1,435	1,175	1,025
325	Car, truck, van, as driver	490	550	465	1,025	840	770
326	Car, truck, van, as passenger	80	80	105	95	180	90
327	Public transit	85	75	110	235	110	125
328	Walked	40	-	15	75	35	40
329	Other method	10	10	10	10	15	-
330	**Total population 15 years and over who worked since January 1, 2000**	**2,190**	**2,155**	**1,925**	**3,795**	**3,220**	**2,605**
	by language used at work						
331	Single responses	1,960	1,905	1,670	3,410	2,830	2,380
332	English	1,895	1,805	1,605	3,335	2,740	2,370
333	French	-	-	-	-	-	-
334	Non-official languages (5)	70	100	65	75	85	10
335	Chinese, n.o.s.	-	35	20	35	20	-
336	Cantonese	30	10	15	20	10	-
337	Other languages (6)	35	65	25	20	65	15
338	Multiple responses	230	250	255	390	390	220
339	English and French	10	20	10	20	45	40
340	English and non-official language	225	230	235	365	335	165
341	French and non-official language	-	-	-	-	-	-
342	English, French and non-official language	-	-	10	-	15	15
	DWELLING AND HOUSEHOLD CHARACTERISTICS						
343	**Total number of occupied private dwellings**	**1,535**	**1,260**	**1,025**	**2,075**	**2,015**	**1,545**
	by tenure						
344	Owned	620	980	745	1,260	1,450	1,185
345	Rented	915	275	280	815	570	355
346	Band housing	-	-	-	-	-	-
	by structural type of dwelling						
347	Single-detached house	530	835	430	1,270	1,070	400
348	Semi-detached house	295	190	135	110	265	-
349	Row house	-	-	10	115	445	710
350	Apartment, detached duplex	135	135	465	435	170	65
351	Apartment, building that has five or more storeys	-	-	-	-	-	-
352	Apartment, building that has fewer than five storeys (38)	570	100	-	130	60	375
353	Other single-attached house	-	-	-	15	10	-
354	Movable dwelling (39)	-	-	-	-	-	-

Tableau 1. Certaines caractéristiques des secteurs de recensement, recensement de 2001 – Données intégrales et données-échantillon (20 %)

Vancouver 0235.03 A	Vancouver 0235.04 A	Vancouver 0236	Vancouver 0237	Vancouver 0238.01	Vancouver 0238.02	Caractéristiques	N°
						CARACTÉRISTIQUES DE LA POPULATION	
						selon la profession basée sur la CNP-S de 2001 – fin	
70	165	95	210	60	155	E Sciences sociales, enseignement, administration publique et religion	300
20	65	70	45	45	35	F Arts, culture, sports et loisirs	301
190	410	210	500	235	535	G Ventes et services	302
10	-	10	35	-	15	H Métiers, transport et machinerie	303
-	-	-	-	-	10	I Professions propres au secteur primaire	304
50	55	10	30	15	15	J Transformation, fabrication et services d'utilité publique	305
1,525	**3,155**	**1,805**	**3,655**	**1,195**	**3,350**	**Population active occupée totale de 15 ans et plus**	306
						selon le lieu de travail	
875	1,665	950	2,020	605	1,865	Hommes	307
695	1,270	820	1,575	490	1,310	Lieu habituel de travail	308
25	135	55	160	15	90	À domicile	309
-	25	10	40	20	40	En dehors du Canada	310
155	235	65	240	80	420	Sans adresse de travail fixe	311
655	1,490	855	1,640	585	1,485	Femmes	312
620	1,330	675	1,460	510	1,305	Lieu habituel de travail	313
15	70	110	125	50	85	À domicile	314
-	20	-	20	10	15	En dehors du Canada	315
15	65	70	40	20	75	Sans adresse de travail fixe	316
1,485	**2,900**	**1,630**	**3,310**	**1,100**	**3,115**	**Population active occupée totale de 15 ans et plus ayant un lieu habituel de travail ou sans adresse de travail fixe**	317
						selon le mode de transport	
850	1,510	885	1,815	570	1,730	Hommes	318
670	1,095	800	1,545	500	1,460	Automobile, camion ou fourgonnette, en tant que conducteur	319
35	105	50	80	50	120	Automobile, camion ou fourgonnette, en tant que passager	320
80	195	35	115	15	100	Transport en commun	321
40	30	-	45	-	25	À pied	322
20	80	-	35	15	35	Autre moyen	323
640	1,390	745	1,500	525	1,385	Femmes	324
375	905	650	1,110	320	880	Automobile, camion ou fourgonnette, en tant que conductrice	325
25	140	40	205	80	190	Automobile, camion ou fourgonnette, en tant que passagère	326
160	265	50	125	100	235	Transport en commun	327
65	55	-	45	35	55	À pied	328
15	15	-	10	-	25	Autre moyen	329
1,745	**3,600**	**2,025**	**4,280**	**1,475**	**3,935**	**Population totale de 15 ans et plus ayant travaillé depuis le 1er janvier 2000**	330
						selon la langue utilisée au travail	
1,565	3,260	1,710	3,530	1,215	3,375	Réponses uniques	331
1,545	3,105	1,665	3,395	1,155	3,230	Anglais	332
-	-	-	15	10	-	Français	333
20	155	45	125	50	145	Langues non officielles (5)	334
10	10	10	55	20	25	Chinois, n.d.a.	335
-	60	20	40	15	30	Cantonais	336
10	95	15	30	15	90	Autres langues (6)	337
185	340	315	745	265	560	Réponses multiples	338
35	50	20	35	25	35	Anglais et français	339
145	290	275	710	235	520	Anglais et langue non officielle	340
-	-	-	-	-	-	Français et langue non officielle	341
-	-	15	-	-	-	Anglais, français et langue non officielle	342
						CARACTÉRISTIQUES DES LOGEMENTS ET DES MÉNAGES	
1,765	**2,785**	**1,095**	**2,865**	**945**	**2,245**	**Nombre total de logements privés occupés**	343
						selon le mode d'occupation	
580	1,360	980	1,695	750	1,480	Possédé	344
1,180	1,430	115	1,170	200	765	Loué	345
-	-	-	-	-	-	Logement de bande	346
						selon le type de construction résidentielle	
-	-	1,035	1,045	615	1,400	Maison individuelle non attenante	347
10	-	-	15	-	125	Maison jumelée	348
-	335	-	505	60	35	Maison en rangée	349
-	10	60	100	185	215	Appartement, duplex non attenant	350
1,425	1,145	-	535	-	-	Appartement, immeuble de cinq étages ou plus	351
335	1,290	-	645	90	475	Appartement, immeuble de moins de cinq étages (38)	352
-	-	-	15	-	-	Autre maison individuelle attenante	353
-	15	-	-	-	-	Logement mobile (39)	354

Table 1. Selected Characteristics for Census Tracts, 2001 Census – 100% Data and 20% Sample Data

No.	Characteristics	Vancouver 0230.02	Vancouver 0231	Vancouver 0232	Vancouver 0233	Vancouver 0234	Vancouver 0235.02
	DWELLING AND HOUSEHOLD CHARACTERISTICS						
	by condition of dwelling						
355	Regular maintenance only	1,140	925	665	1,310	1,410	1,005
356	Minor repairs	300	255	285	585	505	430
357	Major repairs	90	80	85	175	110	110
	by period of construction						
358	Before 1946	95	70	85	360	110	-
359	1946-1960	95	215	165	520	485	235
360	1961-1970	285	265	160	240	195	360
361	1971-1980	515	315	250	220	110	725
362	1981-1990	250	240	180	255	125	175
363	1991-2001 (20)	295	150	190	480	995	50
364	Average number of rooms per dwelling	5.4	7.6	7.5	6.6	7.1	6.4
365	Average number of bedrooms per dwelling	2.5	3.4	3.4	3.1	3.1	2.8
366	Average value of dwelling $	319,054	466,256	341,740	292,855	320,280	193,097
367	**Total number of private households**	**1,530**	**1,260**	**1,030**	**2,075**	**2,015**	**1,545**
	by household size						
368	1 person	585	155	130	305	250	315
369	2 persons	330	360	300	565	555	450
370	3 persons	210	220	190	385	435	315
371	4-5 persons	325	445	320	605	680	405
372	6 or more persons	80	80	90	210	105	55
	by household type						
373	One-family households	790	970	775	1,495	1,610	1,130
374	Multiple-family households	45	65	75	185	85	15
375	Non-family households	695	225	185	395	320	395
376	Number of persons in private households	3,790	3,975	3,295	6,630	6,290	4,235
377	Average number of persons in private households	2.5	3.2	3.2	3.2	3.1	2.8
378	Average number of persons per room	0.5	0.4	0.4	0.5	0.4	0.4
379	Tenant households in non-farm, non-reserve private dwellings (40)	910	280	285	815	565	355
380	Average gross rent $ (40)	699	955	903	816	855	864
381	Tenant households spending 30% or more of household income on gross rent (40) (41)	405	130	90	265	245	100
382	Tenant households spending from 30% to 99% of household income on gross rent (40) (41)	305	85	65	175	205	80
383	Owner households in non-farm, non-reserve private dwellings (42)	615	970	745	1,260	1,440	1,185
384	Average owner's major payments $ (42)	1,215	1,319	1,260	1,001	1,100	924
385	Owner households spending 30% or more of household income on owner's major payments (41) (42)	200	235	215	325	330	200
386	Owner households spending from 30% to 99% of household income on owner's major payments (41) (42)	180	165	180	265	240	160
	CENSUS FAMILY CHARACTERISTICS						
387	**Total number of census families in private households**	**880**	**1,095**	**935**	**1,880**	**1,785**	**1,160**
	by census family structure and size						
388	Total couple families	750	940	845	1,520	1,480	950
389	Total families of married couples	685	885	760	1,400	1,380	830
390	Without children at home	225	290	275	445	380	250
391	With children at home	460	600	490	950	995	580
392	1 child	175	170	180	345	335	195
393	2 children	155	275	195	395	455	265
394	3 or more children	125	155	110	210	205	120
395	Total families of common-law couples	65	55	85	125	100	120
396	Without children at home	50	35	40	45	55	70
397	With children at home	20	20	45	75	50	45
398	1 child	15	10	30	60	25	30
399	2 children	-	-	10	15	10	20
400	3 or more children	-	-	-	-	20	-
401	Total lone-parent families	125	155	95	365	305	210
402	Female parent	85	125	80	305	280	145
403	1 child	60	85	40	210	165	105
404	2 children	20	30	20	60	65	40
405	3 or more children	10	15	20	30	45	10

Tableau 1. Certaines caractéristiques des secteurs de recensement, recensement de 2001 – Données intégrales et données-échantillon (20 %)

Vancouver 0235.03 A	Vancouver 0235.04 A	Vancouver 0236	Vancouver 0237	Vancouver 0238.01	Vancouver 0238.02	Caractéristiques	N°
						CARACTÉRISTIQUES DES LOGEMENTS ET DES MÉNAGES	
						selon l'état du logement	
1,460	1,690	710	2,010	610	1,410	Entretien régulier seulement	355
210	540	285	655	255	685	Réparations mineures	356
95	560	95	200	80	155	Réparations majeures	357
						selon la période de construction	
20	-	55	35	10	90	Avant 1946	358
75	30	105	245	290	465	1946-1960	359
255	120	350	415	235	780	1961-1970	360
1,190	1,065	415	995	340	450	1971-1980	361
220	1,225	95	880	35	235	1981-1990	362
10	355	75	285	35	235	1991-2001 (20)	363
3.7	4.4	8.4	6.1	7.1	7.2	Nombre moyen de pièces par logement	364
1.3	1.8	3.6	2.6	3.2	3.2	Nombre moyen de chambres à coucher par logement	365
107,376	121,324	387,892	301,731	313,600	383,040	Valeur moyenne du logement $	366
1,765	**2,785**	**1,095**	**2,865**	**945**	**2,250**	**Nombre total de logements privés**	367
						selon la taille du ménage	
1,015	960	70	735	145	330	1 personne	368
545	1,030	270	780	285	665	2 personnes	369
125	410	230	480	140	375	3 personnes	370
80	350	445	785	315	765	4-5 personnes	371
-	30	80	80	60	120	6 personnes ou plus	372
						selon le genre de ménage	
645	1,455	890	1,960	740	1,675	Ménages unifamiliaux	373
10	45	100	60	30	105	Ménages multifamiliaux	374
1,115	1,285	95	845	180	465	Ménages non familiaux	375
2,810	5,960	3,700	7,605	2,895	6,865	Nombre de personnes dans les ménages privés	376
1.6	2.1	3.4	2.7	3.1	3.1	Nombre moyen de personnes dans les ménages privés	377
0.4	0.5	0.4	0.4	0.4	0.4	Nombre moyen de personnes par pièce	378
1,185	1,410	115	1,160	195	765	Ménages locataires dans les logements privés non agricoles hors réserve (40)	379
733	762	1,291	933	854	942	Loyer brut moyen $ (40)	380
525	605	25	505	65	340	Ménages locataires consacrant 30 % ou plus du revenu du ménage au loyer brut (40) (41)	381
455	460	20	390	65	260	Ménages locataires consacrant de 30 % à 99 % du revenu du ménage au loyer brut (40) (41)	382
580	1,360	980	1,685	740	1,470	Ménages propriétaires dans les logements privés non agricoles hors réserve (42)	383
676	880	908	881	907	832	Principales dépenses de propriété moyennes $ (42)	384
140	380	145	415	175	375	Ménages propriétaires consacrant 30 % ou plus du revenu du ménage aux principales dépenses de propriété (41) (42)	385
115	325	120	310	145	330	Ménages propriétaires consacrant de 30 % à 99 % du revenu du ménage aux principales dépenses de propriété (41) (42)	386
						CARACTÉRISTIQUES DES FAMILLES DE RECENSEMENT	
650	**1,545**	**1,100**	**2,075**	**795**	**1,905**	**Total des familles de recensement dans les ménages privés**	387
						selon la structure et la taille de la famille de recensement	
560	1,290	970	1,850	720	1,630	Total des familles avec conjoints	388
410	1,060	900	1,650	675	1,510	Total des familles avec couples mariés	389
270	495	300	535	250	465	Sans enfants à la maison	390
145	570	600	1,120	430	1,045	Avec enfants à la maison	391
70	265	190	385	125	340	1 enfant	392
70	245	300	555	195	505	2 enfants	393
-	60	110	180	110	195	3 enfants ou plus	394
150	225	75	190	35	120	Total des familles en union libre	395
135	165	45	135	25	90	Sans enfants à la maison	396
15	60	30	55	10	30	Avec enfants à la maison	397
15	40	25	30	10	30	1 enfant	398
-	15	-	25	-	-	2 enfants	399
-	-	-	10	10	-	3 enfants ou plus	400
90	255	130	225	80	270	Total des familles monoparentales	401
65	220	115	200	50	175	Parent de sexe féminin	402
50	155	55	85	30	105	1 enfant	403
-	65	60	90	-	45	2 enfants	404
10	-	-	20	15	25	3 enfants ou plus	405

Table 1. Selected Characteristics for Census Tracts, 2001 Census – 100% Data and 20% Sample Data

No.	Characteristics	Vancouver 0230.02	Vancouver 0231	Vancouver 0232	Vancouver 0233	Vancouver 0234	Vancouver 0235.02
	CENSUS FAMILY CHARACTERISTICS						
	by census family structure and size – concluded						
406	Male parent	40	30	10	60	30	65
407	1 child	35	30	10	50	30	30
408	2 children	10	-	-	10	-	35
409	3 or more children	-	-	-	-	-	-
410	**Total number of children at home**	**1,105**	**1,480**	**1,150**	**2,430**	**2,510**	**1,490**
	by age groups						
411	Under 6 years	155	200	210	585	495	305
412	6-14 years	350	420	375	745	835	595
413	15-17 years	140	225	105	250	290	210
414	18-24 years	245	410	285	495	560	245
415	25 years and over	220	220	175	350	330	135
416	Average number of children at home per census family (43)	1.3	1.4	1.2	1.3	1.4	1.3
417	**Total number of persons in private households**	**3,790**	**3,975**	**3,295**	**6,630**	**6,285**	**4,235**
	by census family status and living arrangements						
418	Number of non-family persons	1,050	460	365	795	515	635
419	Living with relatives (44)	130	185	105	195	110	150
420	Living with non-relatives only	335	115	125	300	160	170
421	Living alone	590	155	130	300	250	315
422	Number of family persons	2,735	3,515	2,930	5,830	5,775	3,600
423	Average number of persons per census family	3.1	3.2	3.1	3.1	3.2	3.1
424	**Total number of persons 65 years and over**	**510**	**425**	**335**	**680**	**565**	**320**
425	Number of non-family persons 65 years and over	290	120	85	210	170	90
426	Living with relatives (44)	55	65	35	80	50	35
427	Living with non-relatives only	10	-	30	20	25	-
428	Living alone	225	55	20	115	85	55
429	Number of family persons 65 years and over	225	310	250	470	395	230
	ECONOMIC FAMILY CHARACTERISTICS						
430	**Total number of economic families in private households**	**860**	**1,080**	**865**	**1,710**	**1,725**	**1,170**
	by size of family						
431	2 persons	335	375	305	560	540	430
432	3 persons	160	200	175	380	400	275
433	4 persons	195	280	200	385	485	310
434	5 or more persons	175	225	185	390	295	150
435	Total number of persons in economic families	2,870	3,700	3,035	6,025	5,885	3,755
436	Average number of persons per economic family	3.3	3.4	3.5	3.5	3.4	3.2
437	Total number of unattached individuals	925	275	260	600	400	480
	2000 INCOME CHARACTERISTICS						
	Population 15 years and over by sex and total income groups in 2000						
438	Total - Both sexes	3,265	3,340	2,720	5,285	4,950	3,330
439	Without income	215	250	145	320	360	175
440	With income	3,055	3,090	2,575	4,965	4,585	3,150
441	Under $1,000 (45)	120	270	155	260	425	140
442	$ 1,000 - $ 2,999	165	220	125	200	255	130
443	$ 3,000 - $ 4,999	145	115	145	195	135	75
444	$ 5,000 - $ 6,999	180	140	75	220	210	145
445	$ 7,000 - $ 9,999	220	135	165	425	295	140
446	$10,000 - $11,999	130	170	100	215	170	170
447	$12,000 - $14,999	280	185	115	425	300	155
448	$15,000 - $19,999	225	255	220	425	385	210
449	$20,000 - $24,999	295	225	105	425	300	220
450	$25,000 - $29,999	270	130	175	265	345	230
451	$30,000 - $34,999	200	165	170	465	280	250
452	$35,000 - $39,999	210	120	215	300	315	275
453	$40,000 - $44,999	145	130	145	310	195	295
454	$45,000 - $49,999	90	160	85	165	140	160
455	$50,000 - $59,999	125	210	180	295	300	255
456	$60,000 and over	240	475	395	375	525	315
457	Average income $ (46)	26,049	34,096	33,571	26,721	28,310	30,975
458	Median income $ (46)	20,309	21,485	26,099	20,570	21,336	29,408
459	Standard error of average income $ (46)	1,069	1,826	1,571	906	836	880

Tableau 1. Certaines caractéristiques des secteurs de recensement, recensement de 2001 – Données intégrales et données-échantillon (20 %)

Vancouver 0235.03 A	Vancouver 0235.04 A	Vancouver 0236	Vancouver 0237	Vancouver 0238.01	Vancouver 0238.02	Caractéristiques	N°
						CARACTÉRISTIQUES DES FAMILLES DE RECENSEMENT	
						selon la structure et la taille de la famille de recensement – fin	
35	35	10	30	30	100	Parent de sexe masculin	406
25	20	10	10	15	70	1 enfant	407
10	15	10	20	15	-	2 enfants	408
-	-	-	-	-	30	3 enfants ou plus	409
340	**1,385**	**1,375**	**2,545**	**1,050**	**2,485**	**Nombre total d'enfants à la maison**	410
						selon les groupes d'âge	
65	385	195	385	160	310	Moins de 6 ans	411
100	435	375	830	340	720	6-14 ans	412
25	130	205	360	160	350	15-17 ans	413
70	265	320	620	260	755	18-24 ans	414
80	180	280	355	125	355	25 ans et plus	415
0.5	0.9	1.2	1.2	1.3	1.3	Nombre moyen d'enfants à la maison par famille de recensement (43)	416
2,810	**5,960**	**3,700**	**7,605**	**2,895**	**6,865**	**Nombre total de personnes dans les ménages privés**	417
						selon la situation des particuliers dans la famille de recensement et des particuliers dans le ménage	
1,250	1,745	250	1,140	330	845	Nombre de personnes hors famille de recensement	418
20	210	95	130	110	200	Vivant avec des personnes apparentées (44)	419
220	575	80	270	75	315	Vivant avec des personnes non apparentées uniquement	420
1,015	960	75	735	145	330	Vivant seules	421
1,555	4,220	3,450	6,465	2,560	6,020	Nombre de personnes membres d'une famille	422
2.4	2.7	3.1	3.1	3.2	3.2	Nombre moyen de personnes par famille de recensement	423
645	**625**	**420**	**935**	**385**	**870**	**Nombre total de personnes de 65 ans et plus**	424
390	295	100	360	95	170	Nombre de personnes hors famille de recensement de 65 ans et plus	425
-	40	60	60	40	45	Vivant avec des personnes apparentées (44)	426
-	10	15	20	-	15	Vivant avec des personnes non apparentées uniquement	427
390	245	25	280	60	115	Vivant seules	428
255	330	320	575	285	700	Nombre de personnes membres d'une famille de 65 ans et plus	429
						CARACTÉRISTIQUES DES FAMILLES ÉCONOMIQUES	
655	**1,580**	**1,015**	**2,035**	**785**	**1,815**	**Nombre total de familles économiques dans les ménages privés**	430
						selon la taille de la famille	
480	835	280	720	280	595	2 personnes	431
95	365	235	470	150	385	3 personnes	432
80	290	305	570	205	515	4 personnes	433
-	90	200	275	150	320	5 personnes ou plus	434
1,575	4,430	3,545	6,595	2,675	6,225	Nombre total de personnes dans les familles économiques	435
2.4	2.8	3.5	3.2	3.4	3.4	Nombre moyen de personnes par famille économique	436
1,235	1,530	150	1,005	220	645	Nombre total de personnes hors famille économique	437
						CARACTÉRISTIQUES DU REVENU DE 2000	
						Population de 15 ans et plus selon le sexe et les tranches de revenu total en 2000	
2,640	5,145	3,130	6,380	2,385	5,840	Total - Les deux sexes	438
85	355	245	430	165	360	Sans revenu	439
2,560	4,790	2,885	5,950	2,220	5,480	Avec un revenu	440
100	215	185	275	205	400	Moins de 1 000 $ (45)	441
80	230	175	295	135	350	1 000 $ - 2 999 $	442
75	240	60	290	75	235	3 000 $ - 4 999 $	443
75	180	110	350	85	255	5 000 $ - 6 999 $	444
135	250	150	375	220	370	7 000 $ - 9 999 $	445
70	240	110	265	125	380	10 000 $ - 11 999 $	446
285	315	180	425	155	405	12 000 $ - 14 999 $	447
280	580	210	585	210	470	15 000 $ - 19 999 $	448
165	440	245	485	200	425	20 000 $ - 24 999 $	449
200	355	100	355	120	320	25 000 $ - 29 999 $	450
210	445	220	375	135	415	30 000 $ - 34 999 $	451
210	240	155	380	145	285	35 000 $ - 39 999 $	452
150	285	165	335	75	250	40 000 $ - 44 999 $	453
130	215	115	175	75	210	45 000 $ - 49 999 $	454
175	245	225	350	125	245	50 000 $ - 59 999 $	455
210	320	490	645	140	465	60 000 $ et plus	456
29,155	25,900	33,881	27,880	23,610	25,705	Revenu moyen $ (46)	457
25,272	21,072	25,321	20,702	17,658	17,988	Revenu médian $ (46)	458
1,047	686	1,269	712	972	801	Erreur type de revenu moyen $ (46)	459

Table 1. Selected Characteristics for Census Tracts, 2001 Census – 100% Data and 20% Sample Data

No.	Characteristics	Vancouver 0230.02	Vancouver 0231	Vancouver 0232	Vancouver 0233	Vancouver 0234	Vancouver 0235.02
	2000 INCOME CHARACTERISTICS						
	Population 15 years and over by sex and total income groups in 2000 – concluded						
460	Total - Males	1,675	1,640	1,400	2,580	2,375	1,605
461	Without income	70	90	45	105	155	85
462	With income	1,600	1,550	1,350	2,470	2,220	1,520
463	Under $1,000 (45)	55	150	90	110	215	60
464	$ 1,000 - $ 2,999	45	80	55	60	145	40
465	$ 3,000 - $ 4,999	50	65	80	70	60	40
466	$ 5,000 - $ 6,999	80	80	40	50	85	45
467	$ 7,000 - $ 9,999	90	55	75	190	110	60
468	$10,000 - $11,999	80	40	40	125	40	75
469	$12,000 - $14,999	105	80	40	145	110	40
470	$15,000 - $19,999	165	85	110	195	145	60
471	$20,000 - $24,999	125	115	55	230	140	110
472	$25,000 - $29,999	160	75	95	130	125	95
473	$30,000 - $34,999	125	55	70	205	105	95
474	$35,000 - $39,999	135	55	70	185	140	165
475	$40,000 - $44,999	90	65	75	195	100	175
476	$45,000 - $49,999	65	85	50	100	110	70
477	$50,000 - $59,999	60	120	135	190	175	130
478	$60,000 and over	170	335	280	295	420	250
479	Average income $ (46)	30,885	42,821	39,324	32,555	33,952	36,472
480	Median income $ (46)	25,040	25,131	29,994	27,004	26,756	36,149
481	Standard error of average income $ (46)	1,766	3,381	2,671	1,632	1,366	1,428
482	Total - Females	1,595	1,695	1,320	2,710	2,575	1,725
483	Without income	140	155	95	215	210	90
484	With income	1,450	1,540	1,225	2,500	2,365	1,635
485	Under $1,000 (45)	70	115	70	150	215	80
486	$ 1,000 - $ 2,999	125	135	70	140	110	90
487	$ 3,000 - $ 4,999	100	50	65	130	80	35
488	$ 5,000 - $ 6,999	95	60	35	170	125	100
489	$ 7,000 - $ 9,999	130	75	90	235	190	75
490	$10,000 - $11,999	50	130	65	90	125	95
491	$12,000 - $14,999	170	100	75	285	190	115
492	$15,000 - $19,999	60	165	105	230	240	145
493	$20,000 - $24,999	170	100	50	195	160	105
494	$25,000 - $29,999	110	50	80	135	215	130
495	$30,000 - $34,999	80	110	105	265	170	150
496	$35,000 - $39,999	75	60	145	115	180	110
497	$40,000 - $44,999	50	65	65	115	90	125
498	$45,000 - $49,999	25	75	35	65	35	85
499	$50,000 - $59,999	70	95	55	100	125	125
500	$60,000 and over	70	135	115	75	105	60
501	Average income $ (46)	20,722	25,310	27,210	20,949	23,001	25,866
502	Median income $ (46)	14,067	17,491	24,232	15,782	17,798	23,823
503	Standard error of average income $ (46)	1,030	1,253	1,452	739	935	993
	by composition of total income						
504	Total - Composition of income in 2000 % (47)	100.0	100.0	100.0	100.0	100.0	100.0
505	Employment income %	78.7	77.2	76.0	80.7	79.3	82.7
506	Government transfer payments %	12.8	7.0	7.5	10.6	10.2	7.9
507	Other %	8.4	15.9	16.6	8.8	10.5	9.4
	Population 15 years and over with employment income in 2000 by sex and work activity						
508	Both sexes with employment income (48)	2,135	2,100	1,900	3,710	3,155	2,555
509	Average employment income $	29,366	38,639	34,488	28,828	32,584	31,652
510	Standard error of average employment income $	1,426	2,401	1,783	1,138	1,037	981
511	Worked full year, full time (49)	1,115	955	910	1,820	1,490	1,460
512	Average employment income $	38,743	58,721	51,663	40,303	45,487	42,500
513	Standard error of average employment income $	2,158	4,420	2,925	2,010	1,425	1,219
514	Worked part year or part time (50)	945	1,070	900	1,775	1,570	1,065
515	Average employment income $	19,777	22,275	19,664	18,345	21,442	17,146
516	Standard error of average employment income $	1,702	1,963	1,417	901	1,305	1,082
517	Males with employment income (48)	1,210	1,110	1,050	1,925	1,640	1,250
518	Average employment income $	33,113	49,430	39,459	35,339	38,142	37,221
519	Standard error of average employment income $	2,260	4,290	2,853	2,005	1,572	1,569
520	Worked full year, full time (49)	670	575	535	1,105	860	815
521	Average employment income $	41,167	71,261	57,988	44,904	50,257	47,166
522	Standard error of average employment income $	3,407	7,076	4,480	3,175	1,969	1,788
523	Worked part year or part time (50)	490	500	460	760	745	425
524	Average employment income $	23,750	26,567	21,270	23,042	24,953	18,606
525	Standard error of average employment income $	2,823	3,790	2,352	1,621	2,178	1,942

Tableau 1. Certaines caractéristiques des secteurs de recensement, recensement de 2001 – Données intégrales et données-échantillon (20 %)

Vancouver 0235.03 A	Vancouver 0235.04 A	Vancouver 0236	Vancouver 0237	Vancouver 0238.01	Vancouver 0238.02	Caractéristiques	N°
						CARACTÉRISTIQUES DU REVENU DE 2000	
						Population de 15 ans et plus selon le sexe et les tranches de revenu total en 2000 – fin	
1,305	2,495	1,550	3,145	1,150	2,915	Total - Hommes	460
15	135	135	210	75	155	Sans revenu	461
1,285	2,360	1,415	2,935	1,075	2,755	Avec un revenu	462
75	100	95	145	85	175	Moins de 1 000 $ (45)	463
15	95	70	105	40	145	1 000 $ - 2 999 $	464
45	100	25	130	45	70	3 000 $ - 4 999 $	465
25	60	20	135	40	105	5 000 $ - 6 999 $	466
40	95	50	125	55	155	7 000 $ - 9 999 $	467
35	90	45	135	60	135	10 000 $ - 11 999 $	468
130	125	70	150	80	150	12 000 $ - 14 999 $	469
85	260	125	215	105	260	15 000 $ - 19 999 $	470
70	220	85	240	100	220	20 000 $ - 24 999 $	471
85	200	40	155	60	145	25 000 $ - 29 999 $	472
145	175	90	195	75	205	30 000 $ - 34 999 $	473
100	115	60	185	85	170	35 000 $ - 39 999 $	474
70	160	55	185	50	145	40 000 $ - 44 999 $	475
100	140	70	90	45	160	45 000 $ - 49 999 $	476
100	170	135	240	85	175	50 000 $ - 59 999 $	477
170	245	380	495	85	325	60 000 $ et plus	478
33,883	30,290	42,334	33,690	27,315	30,960	Revenu moyen $ (46)	479
30,380	25,206	34,016	27,158	20,873	23,604	Revenu médian $ (46)	480
1,792	1,196	2,215	1,156	1,477	1,298	Erreur type de revenu moyen $ (46)	481
1,335	2,645	1,575	3,240	1,230	2,920	Total - Femmes	482
65	220	110	225	90	205	Sans revenu	483
1,270	2,430	1,465	3,015	1,145	2,725	Avec un revenu	484
20	115	90	125	125	225	Moins de 1 000 $ (45)	485
70	135	105	190	100	205	1 000 $ - 2 999 $	486
30	140	30	160	30	165	3 000 $ - 4 999 $	487
50	115	90	215	45	150	5 000 $ - 6 999 $	488
100	150	95	250	170	215	7 000 $ - 9 999 $	489
40	150	70	135	65	245	10 000 $ - 11 999 $	490
150	190	115	280	70	250	12 000 $ - 14 999 $	491
195	315	85	365	110	210	15 000 $ - 19 999 $	492
95	220	165	245	95	205	20 000 $ - 24 999 $	493
115	150	60	205	60	170	25 000 $ - 29 999 $	494
70	265	130	180	65	205	30 000 $ - 34 999 $	495
115	125	100	190	55	115	35 000 $ - 39 999 $	496
80	125	110	150	25	100	40 000 $ - 44 999 $	497
30	70	40	80	35	50	45 000 $ - 49 999 $	498
70	80	85	105	40	75	50 000 $ - 59 999 $	499
40	80	105	145	60	135	60 000 $ et plus	500
24,357	21,636	25,728	22,226	20,122	20,385	Revenu moyen $ (46)	501
18,693	18,278	21,910	16,970	13,207	13,092	Revenu médian $ (46)	502
1,048	686	1,147	779	1,235	884	Erreur type de revenu moyen $ (46)	503
						selon la composition du revenu total	
100.0	100.0	100.0	100.0	100.0	100.0	Total - Composition du revenu en 2000 % (47)	504
73.3	81.6	76.8	77.8	73.1	74.9	Revenu d'emploi %	505
15.4	11.1	7.8	11.0	13.8	11.8	Transferts gouvernementaux %	506
11.4	7.2	15.5	11.2	13.3	13.4	Autre %	507
						Population de 15 ans et plus ayant un revenu d'emploi en 2000 selon le sexe et le travail	
1,700	3,520	1,965	4,105	1,445	3,750	Les deux sexes ayant un revenu d'emploi (48)	508
32,106	28,771	38,157	31,453	26,435	28,121	Revenu moyen d'emploi $	509
1,174	868	1,427	905	1,270	1,009	Erreur type de revenu moyen d'emploi $	510
920	1,925	1,030	2,035	655	1,805	Ayant travaillé toute l'année à plein temps (49)	511
39,890	37,470	54,066	45,637	39,858	40,339	Revenu moyen d'emploi $	512
1,284	1,260	2,031	1,224	1,813	1,467	Erreur type de revenu moyen d'emploi $	513
750	1,535	905	1,970	760	1,835	Ayant travaillé une partie de l'année ou à temps partiel (50)	514
23,421	18,862	20,753	17,785	15,200	17,215	Revenu moyen d'emploi $	515
1,868	887	1,313	997	1,303	1,198	Erreur type de revenu moyen d'emploi $	516
920	1,870	1,045	2,180	725	2,025	Hommes ayant un revenu d'emploi (48)	517
37,041	32,672	46,103	36,956	30,520	32,340	Revenu moyen d'emploi $	518
1,810	1,447	2,255	1,375	1,856	1,493	Erreur type de revenu moyen d'emploi $	519
520	1,020	690	1,190	400	1,130	Ayant travaillé toute l'année à plein temps (49)	520
43,164	42,119	58,491	50,174	41,507	42,343	Revenu moyen d'emploi $	521
1,935	2,129	2,798	1,739	2,468	1,992	Erreur type de revenu moyen d'emploi $	522
400	815	350	945	310	830	Ayant travaillé une partie de l'année ou à temps partiel (50)	523
29,322	22,151	22,514	21,550	16,939	19,688	Revenu moyen d'emploi $	524
3,093	1,454	2,439	1,753	2,000	2,054	Erreur type de revenu moyen d'emploi $	525

Table 1. Selected Characteristics for Census Tracts, 2001 Census – 100% Data and 20% Sample Data

No.	Characteristics	Vancouver 0230.02	Vancouver 0231	Vancouver 0232	Vancouver 0233	Vancouver 0234	Vancouver 0235.02
	2000 INCOME CHARACTERISTICS						
	Population 15 years and over with employment income in 2000 by sex and work activity – concluded						
526	Females with employment income (48)	925	990	850	1,790	1,520	1,300
527	Average employment income $	24,444	26,533	28,355	21,831	26,584	26,301
528	Standard error of average employment income $	1,390	1,408	1,809	880	1,265	1,124
529	Worked full year, full time (49)	440	385	380	710	630	650
530	Average employment income $	35,079	39,949	42,687	33,149	38,971	36,610
531	Standard error of average employment income $	1,765	2,191	2,957	1,282	1,924	1,469
532	Worked part year or part time (50)	450	565	435	1,020	825	645
533	Average employment income $	15,467	18,476	17,976	14,840	18,275	16,184
534	Standard error of average employment income $	1,670	1,536	1,510	956	1,493	1,262
	Census families by structure and family income groups in 2000						
535	Total - All census families	880	1,100	935	1,885	1,785	1,160
536	Under $10,000	50	55	30	130	95	10
537	$ 10,000 - $19,999	90	80	50	180	125	55
538	$ 20,000 - $29,999	60	90	85	145	195	115
539	$ 30,000 - $39,999	75	110	70	240	215	75
540	$ 40,000 - $49,999	115	110	50	185	175	150
541	$ 50,000 - $59,999	45	85	85	225	135	125
542	$ 60,000 - $69,999	120	50	65	145	135	150
543	$ 70,000 - $79,999	50	70	80	160	115	135
544	$ 80,000 - $89,999	70	45	75	110	140	85
545	$ 90,000 - $99,999	65	50	85	155	105	70
546	$100,000 and over	140	355	260	210	340	195
547	Average family income $	66,792	85,950	81,687	60,128	65,310	67,069
548	Median family income $	60,027	66,032	73,376	51,675	55,923	62,588
549	Standard error of average family income $	3,866	5,168	4,674	2,624	2,225	2,114
550	Total - All couple census families (51)	750	940	845	1,520	1,475	950
551	Under $10,000	30	35	15	65	75	-
552	$ 10,000 - $19,999	65	20	40	135	55	20
553	$ 20,000 - $29,999	40	80	80	85	95	90
554	$ 30,000 - $39,999	60	85	60	175	165	55
555	$ 40,000 - $49,999	85	95	45	155	145	95
556	$ 50,000 - $59,999	45	70	70	185	110	115
557	$ 60,000 - $69,999	105	45	45	120	130	115
558	$ 70,000 - $79,999	55	65	65	145	115	115
559	$ 80,000 - $89,999	65	45	75	110	140	85
560	$ 90,000 - $99,999	65	45	85	145	100	60
561	$100,000 and over	135	355	255	190	340	190
562	Average family income $	71,848	95,124	85,352	63,389	72,918	72,121
563	Median family income $	61,895	74,885	79,637	57,940	66,545	68,151
564	Standard error of average family income $	4,299	5,683	5,015	2,111	2,447	2,310
	Incidence of low income in 2000						
565	Total - Economic families	865	1,085	865	1,710	1,720	1,170
566	Low income	190	195	115	315	350	140
567	Incidence of low income in 2000 % (52)	22.0	17.9	13.3	18.5	20.5	11.6
568	Total - Unattached individuals 15 years and over	905	270	260	590	400	475
569	Low income	495	140	140	265	190	135
570	Incidence of low income in 2000 % (52)	55.0	53.5	53.5	45.1	48.0	28.5
571	Total - Population in private households	3,770	3,970	3,295	6,615	6,285	4,230
572	Low income	1,170	800	570	1,210	1,485	545
573	Incidence of low income in 2000 % (52)	31.0	20.1	17.3	18.3	23.6	12.9
	Private households by household income groups in 2000						
574	Total - All private households	1,535	1,260	1,030	2,075	2,020	1,545
575	Under $10,000	195	115	35	150	110	55
576	$ 10,000 - $19,999	315	80	75	215	175	100
577	$ 20,000 - $29,999	195	100	80	155	255	130
578	$ 30,000 - $39,999	95	70	110	240	235	130
579	$ 40,000 - $49,999	135	110	70	165	195	215
580	$ 50,000 - $59,999	85	100	75	225	150	155
581	$ 60,000 - $69,999	100	90	85	145	115	165
582	$ 70,000 - $79,999	70	60	45	170	130	160
583	$ 80,000 - $89,999	75	75	80	120	150	95
584	$ 90,000 - $99,999	65	55	80	150	120	65
585	$100,000 and over	205	395	290	345	390	265
586	Average household income $	51,856	83,733	83,866	63,957	64,397	63,272
587	Median household income $	37,993	66,810	69,357	53,937	52,014	59,168
588	Standard error of average household income $	2,819	4,832	4,913	2,643	2,199	1,957

Tableau 1. Certaines caractéristiques des secteurs de recensement, recensement de 2001 – Données intégrales et données-échantillon (20 %)

Vancouver 0235.03 A	Vancouver 0235.04 A	Vancouver 0236	Vancouver 0237	Vancouver 0238.01	Vancouver 0238.02	Caractéristiques	N°
						CARACTÉRISTIQUES DU REVENU DE 2000	
						Population de 15 ans et plus ayant un revenu d'emploi en 2000 selon le sexe et le travail – fin	
780	1,655	915	1,920	715	1,730	Femmes ayant un revenu d'emploi (48)	526
26,235	24,366	29,116	25,195	22,270	23,175	Revenu moyen d'emploi $	527
1,311	864	1,445	1,050	1,660	1,274	Erreur type de revenu moyen d'emploi $	528
395	905	340	845	255	675	Ayant travaillé toute l'année à plein temps (49)	529
35,564	32,237	45,174	39,267	37,237	36,961	Revenu moyen d'emploi $	530
1,493	1,139	2,112	1,540	2,548	2,032	Erreur type de revenu moyen d'emploi $	531
355	720	560	1,030	450	1,010	Ayant travaillé une partie de l'année ou à temps partiel (50)	532
16,811	15,133	19,654	14,321	13,987	15,187	Revenu moyen d'emploi $	533
1,619	921	1,479	938	1,705	1,369	Erreur type de revenu moyen d'emploi $	534
						Familles de recensement selon la structure et les tranches de revenu de la famille en 2000	
650	1,545	1,100	2,075	795	1,900	Total - Toutes les familles de recensement	535
25	150	55	115	25	130	Moins de 10 000 $	536
70	165	80	145	85	225	10 000 $ - 19 999 $	537
80	215	80	250	110	200	20 000 $ - 29 999 $	538
85	200	95	170	130	190	30 000 $ - 39 999 $	539
65	125	50	220	40	250	40 000 $ - 49 999 $	540
65	150	60	185	65	105	50 000 $ - 59 999 $	541
85	165	75	210	110	160	60 000 $ - 69 999 $	542
80	95	80	185	50	140	70 000 $ - 79 999 $	543
40	80	60	115	40	110	80 000 $ - 89 999 $	544
15	65	95	85	35	90	90 000 $ - 99 999 $	545
50	125	365	395	100	310	100 000 $ et plus	546
54,807	49,570	82,818	63,327	56,762	62,469	Revenu moyen des familles $	547
50,110	42,776	72,702	56,813	50,133	48,005	Revenu médian des familles $	548
3,204	1,879	3,651	1,961	2,816	2,579	Erreur type de revenu moyen des familles $	549
560	1,290	970	1,850	715	1,635	Total - Toutes les familles de recensement comptant un couple (51)	550
15	100	30	85	25	95	Moins de 10 000 $	551
60	105	75	100	55	125	10 000 $ - 19 999 $	552
75	200	70	205	100	190	20 000 $ - 29 999 $	553
75	160	90	160	110	170	30 000 $ - 39 999 $	554
55	90	35	195	45	220	40 000 $ - 49 999 $	555
55	140	50	170	60	95	50 000 $ - 59 999 $	556
65	160	75	200	110	120	60 000 $ - 69 999 $	557
80	75	75	175	50	135	70 000 $ - 79 999 $	558
40	75	50	110	45	110	80 000 $ - 89 999 $	559
15	70	75	75	30	85	90 000 $ - 99 999 $	560
45	125	350	380	90	300	100 000 $ et plus	561
53,633	53,219	86,344	66,208	59,131	67,169	Revenu moyen des familles $	562
52,095	49,646	79,366	60,104	55,797	51,813	Revenu médian des familles $	563
2,738	2,112	3,939	2,111	2,919	2,826	Erreur type de revenu moyen des familles $	564
						Fréquence des unités à faible revenu en 2000	
660	1,580	1,020	2,035	780	1,815	Total - Familles économiques	565
135	450	150	460	165	395	Faible revenu	566
20.0	28.5	14.6	22.5	21.0	21.8	Fréquence des unités à faible revenu en 2000 % (52)	567
1,235	1,530	150	1,000	220	635	Total - Personnes hors famille économique de 15 ans et plus	568
490	545	50	425	95	235	Faible revenu	569
39.7	35.9	32.6	42.3	43.4	36.7	Fréquence des unités à faible revenu en 2000 % (52)	570
2,805	5,960	3,695	7,600	2,890	6,860	Total - Population dans les ménages privés	571
850	1,950	585	2,085	685	1,610	Faible revenu	572
30.4	32.7	15.9	27.5	23.8	23.5	Fréquence des unités à faible revenu en 2000 % (52)	573
						Ménages privés selon les tranches de revenu du ménage en 2000	
1,765	2,790	1,095	2,860	945	2,250	Total - Tous les ménages privés	574
115	230	25	225	35	115	Moins de 10 000 $	575
390	445	50	345	95	245	10 000 $ - 19 999 $	576
220	335	60	315	135	240	20 000 $ - 29 999 $	577
235	425	105	295	180	285	30 000 $ - 39 999 $	578
225	325	50	295	60	260	40 000 $ - 49 999 $	579
150	250	120	190	80	135	50 000 $ - 59 999 $	580
140	305	50	275	95	165	60 000 $ - 69 999 $	581
110	130	65	225	70	210	70 000 $ - 79 999 $	582
70	105	95	155	40	120	80 000 $ - 89 999 $	583
35	90	95	95	40	110	90 000 $ - 99 999 $	584
75	150	380	460	110	355	100 000 $ et plus	585
42,282	44,401	89,087	57,933	55,257	62,606	Revenu moyen des ménages $	586
35,579	38,454	81,924	48,459	43,180	49,136	Revenu médian des ménages $	587
1,586	1,268	3,682	1,689	2,654	2,365	Erreur type de revenu moyen des ménages $	588

Table 1. Selected Characteristics for Census Tracts, 2001 Census – 100% Data and 20% Sample Data

No.	Characteristics	Vancouver 0239	Vancouver 0240.01 A	Vancouver 0240.02 A	Vancouver 0241	Vancouver 0242	Vancouver 0243.01
	POPULATION CHARACTERISTICS						
1	**Population, 1996 (1)**	**7,454**	**3,123**	**5,198**	**6,997**	**7,009**	**5,883**
2	**Population, 2001 (2)**	**7,810**	**3,793**	**5,082**	**7,483**	**6,870**	**6,129**
3	Population percentage change, 1996-2001	4.8	21.5	-2.2	6.9	-2.0	4.2
4	Land area in square kilometres, 2001	2.37	2.20	0.90	1.88	4.45	1.71
5	**Total population - 100% Data (3)**	**7,815**	**3,790**	**5,080**	**7,480**	**6,870**	**6,130**
	by sex and age groups						
6	Male	3,875	1,815	2,550	3,610	3,445	3,050
7	0-4 years	180	90	135	190	120	120
8	5-9 years	200	90	165	160	150	170
9	10-14 years	200	75	125	195	195	215
10	15-19 years	275	115	145	225	215	270
11	20-24 years	310	150	185	275	265	325
12	25-29 years	340	165	195	270	290	240
13	30-34 years	340	175	235	285	235	185
14	35-39 years	370	170	230	330	275	215
15	40-44 years	315	145	220	315	320	225
16	45-49 years	300	135	180	310	295	260
17	50-54 years	240	120	175	290	280	230
18	55-59 years	165	85	120	190	215	135
19	60-64 years	150	85	115	125	180	135
20	65-69 years	160	50	135	125	145	115
21	70-74 years	140	55	85	130	120	90
22	75-79 years	100	50	75	85	90	60
23	80-84 years	60	25	25	55	40	30
24	85 years and over	35	30	15	50	15	20
25	Female	3,940	1,980	2,525	3,875	3,425	3,080
26	0-4 years	195	100	115	195	135	95
27	5-9 years	210	80	115	170	160	140
28	10-14 years	185	75	120	200	195	210
29	15-19 years	215	100	135	205	190	260
30	20-24 years	300	145	175	280	240	325
31	25-29 years	315	205	200	305	250	195
32	30-34 years	315	195	215	330	215	185
33	35-39 years	340	160	210	335	290	240
34	40-44 years	345	140	210	300	325	300
35	45-49 years	300	135	165	310	270	260
36	50-54 years	255	145	195	310	275	245
37	55-59 years	180	85	135	155	210	150
38	60-64 years	170	60	150	145	190	130
39	65-69 years	210	65	115	120	140	120
40	70-74 years	160	60	85	125	135	85
41	75-79 years	130	85	80	150	90	65
42	80-84 years	65	75	55	115	65	40
43	85 years and over	45	70	45	145	45	35
44	**Total population 15 years and over**	**6,645**	**3,280**	**4,300**	**6,370**	**5,920**	**5,175**
	by legal marital status						
45	Never married (single)	2,405	1,235	1,480	2,310	2,115	1,985
46	Legally married (and not separated)	3,290	1,455	2,185	2,950	2,870	2,555
47	Separated, but still legally married	175	90	110	180	170	160
48	Divorced	415	240	265	435	465	245
49	Widowed	360	260	260	505	295	235
	by common-law status						
50	Not in a common-law relationship	6,255	3,060	4,115	5,990	5,525	4,980
51	In a common-law relationship	390	220	185	385	390	200
52	**Total population - 20% Sample Data (4)**	**7,810**	**3,790**	**5,075**	**7,230**	**6,845**	**6,100**
	by mother tongue						
53	Single responses	7,620	3,745	4,950	7,120	6,760	5,990
54	English	3,355	1,905	1,840	4,125	3,675	2,750
55	French	45	65	70	35	40	10
56	Non-official languages (5)	4,220	1,780	3,035	2,950	3,050	3,230
57	Chinese, n.o.s.	1,060	175	575	785	625	1,015
58	Cantonese	1,005	450	970	585	725	590
59	Punjabi	80	80	55	60	95	75
60	Mandarin	220	90	90	195	290	280
61	Tagalog (Pilipino)	50	55	25	50	40	20
62	Other languages (6)	1,805	935	1,320	1,275	1,275	1,245
63	Multiple responses	190	45	120	110	85	115
64	English and French	10	-	10	10	-	-
65	English and non-official language	175	45	115	100	90	95
66	French and non-official language	-	-	-	10	-	-
67	English, French and non-official language	-	-	-	-	-	15

See reference material at the end of the publication. – Voir les documents de référence à la fin de la publication.

Tableau 1. Certaines caractéristiques des secteurs de recensement, recensement de 2001 – Données intégrales et données-échantillon (20 %)

Vancouver 0243.02 ◆	Vancouver 0250.01 A	Vancouver 0250.02 A	Vancouver 0251	Vancouver 0260.02 A	Vancouver 0260.04 A	Caractéristiques	N°
						CARACTÉRISTIQUES DE LA POPULATION	
6,411	**2,738**	**3,170**	**168**	**3,807**	**3,622**	**Population, 1996 (1)**	1
6,450	**2,957**	**3,514**	**155**	**4,308**	**3,758**	**Population, 2001 (2)**	2
0.6	8.0	10.9	-7.7	13.2	3.8	Variation en pourcentage de la population, 1996-2001	3
13.51	49.94	834.19	6.19	14.46	1.15	Superficie des terres en kilomètres carrés, 2001	4
6,450	**2,955**	**3,510**	**155**	**4,305**	**3,760**	**Population totale – Données intégrales (3)**	5
						selon le sexe et les groupes d'âge	
3,115	1,445	1,740	85	2,150	1,870	Sexe masculin	6
200	80	90	5	120	135	0-4 ans	7
245	115	120	10	125	145	5-9 ans	8
285	135	130	10	130	155	10-14 ans	9
290	110	120	5	145	155	15-19 ans	10
290	35	65	10	150	110	20-24 ans	11
200	25	70	5	165	105	25-29 ans	12
230	55	85	-	170	135	30-34 ans	13
265	120	150	10	225	180	35-39 ans	14
295	165	165	10	200	175	40-44 ans	15
260	155	185	5	200	155	45-49 ans	16
220	150	165	5	145	150	50-54 ans	17
140	105	140	5	125	95	55-59 ans	18
80	50	105	-	75	65	60-64 ans	19
55	45	70	5	60	40	65-69 ans	20
40	45	40	5	40	25	70-74 ans	21
20	30	30	-	35	25	75-79 ans	22
10	15	5	-	15	5	80-84 ans	23
5	5	5	-	15	5	85 ans et plus	24
3,335	1,510	1,775	70	2,160	1,885	Sexe féminin	25
175	75	105	5	125	110	0-4 ans	26
240	120	125	5	125	150	5-9 ans	27
260	140	135	5	135	145	10-14 ans	28
270	90	110	5	135	155	15-19 ans	29
290	40	75	5	150	125	20-24 ans	30
220	30	60	5	195	90	25-29 ans	31
275	85	125	5	215	150	30-34 ans	32
340	130	175	5	215	190	35-39 ans	33
360	195	180	5	200	200	40-44 ans	34
310	160	170	5	185	160	45-49 ans	35
240	130	170	5	130	130	50-54 ans	36
125	100	130	5	100	110	55-59 ans	37
80	60	85	-	90	65	60-64 ans	38
45	40	55	5	50	45	65-69 ans	39
45	55	35	5	40	20	70-74 ans	40
30	35	20	5	40	25	75-79 ans	41
10	10	15	-	20	10	80-84 ans	42
15	20	5	-	10	10	85 ans et plus	43
5,050	**2,295**	**2,800**	**120**	**3,545**	**2,915**	**Population totale de 15 ans et plus**	44
						selon l'état matrimonial légal	
1,770	550	665	40	1,265	915	Célibataire (jamais marié(e))	45
2,655	1,335	1,795	50	1,575	1,635	Légalement marié(e) (et non séparé(e))	46
165	90	65	5	190	100	Séparé(e), mais toujours légalement marié(e)	47
350	240	205	15	375	185	Divorcé(e)	48
115	80	70	-	145	75	Veuf ou veuve	49
						selon l'union libre	
4,830	2,030	2,580	95	3,215	2,715	Ne vivant pas en union libre	50
220	265	220	25	330	200	Vivant en union libre	51
6,450	**2,960**	**3,510**	**140**	**4,310**	**3,760**	**Population totale – Données-échantillon (20 %) (4)**	52
						selon la langue maternelle	
6,360	2,930	3,505	145	4,280	3,725	Réponses uniques	53
3,710	2,735	3,020	140	3,300	2,690	Anglais	54
35	30	30	-	45	15	Français	55
2,615	165	460	-	940	1,015	Langues non officielles (5)	56
490	-	-	-	25	35	Chinois, n.d.a.	57
415	10	10	-	65	55	Cantonais	58
10	-	-	-	10	-	Pendjabi	59
230	-	35	-	10	75	Mandarin	60
20	10	10	-	115	55	Tagalog (pilipino)	61
1,465	150	410	10	710	790	Autres langues (6)	62
90	25	10	-	35	40	Réponses multiples	63
10	-	-	-	10	-	Anglais et français	64
50	25	10	-	25	40	Anglais et langue non officielle	65
20	-	-	-	-	-	Français et langue non officielle	66
10	-	-	-	-	-	Anglais, français et langue non officielle	67

See reference material at the end of the publication. – Voir les documents de référence à la fin de la publication.

Table 1. Selected Characteristics for Census Tracts, 2001 Census – 100% Data and 20% Sample Data

No.	Characteristics	Vancouver 0239	Vancouver 0240.01 A	Vancouver 0240.02 A	Vancouver 0241	Vancouver 0242	Vancouver 0243.01
	POPULATION CHARACTERISTICS						
	by home language						
68	Single responses	5,525	2,680	3,775	5,640	5,350	4,350
69	English	3,955	2,180	2,230	4,525	4,170	3,205
70	French	-	-	40	10	-	-
71	Non-official languages (5)	1,575	485	1,505	1,105	1,180	1,140
72	Cantonese	515	290	600	360	485	240
73	Chinese, n.o.s.	465	55	340	380	205	370
74	Punjabi	-	-	-	20	35	-
75	Mandarin	125	35	45	140	210	135
76	Korean	-	10	40	15	10	55
77	Other languages (6)	460	105	480	200	235	350
78	Multiple responses	2,285	1,110	1,300	1,585	1,490	1,755
79	English and French	40	10	15	40	45	15
80	English and non-official language	2,215	1,020	1,280	1,525	1,435	1,670
81	French and non-official language	10	20	-	-	-	75
82	English, French and non-official language	25	60	-	25	15	-
	by knowledge of official languages						
83	English only	7,055	3,415	4,450	6,365	6,100	5,450
84	French only	10	-	-	-	-	-
85	English and French	310	270	240	465	400	290
86	Neither English nor French	440	95	375	405	345	360
	by knowledge of non-official languages (5) (7)						
87	Cantonese	1,110	520	1,050	875	910	775
88	Chinese, n.o.s.	1,025	150	610	705	570	730
89	Punjabi	85	100	55	60	135	75
90	Mandarin	510	135	280	425	450	730
91	Hindi	170	45	100	60	240	80
92	German	110	70	20	130	220	60
93	Spanish	335	120	185	130	140	195
	by first official language spoken						
94	English	7,315	3,610	4,565	6,760	6,450	5,685
95	French	65	50	80	35	40	10
96	English and French	30	30	55	25	20	50
97	Neither English nor French	405	100	380	400	340	360
98	Official language minority - (number) (8)	75	65	105	50	45	30
99	Official language minority - (percentage) (8)	1.0	1.7	2.1	0.7	0.7	0.5
	by ethnic origin (9)						
100	English	940	590	525	1,260	1,200	795
101	Canadian	850	520	485	1,225	1,165	750
102	Chinese	2,520	875	1,800	1,920	2,040	1,990
103	Scottish	740	365	420	790	895	680
104	Irish	560	195	350	770	745	460
105	German	490	240	200	510	535	500
106	East Indian	275	260	130	210	360	210
107	French	210	155	220	320	350	285
108	Ukrainian	185	120	95	250	125	150
109	Italian	1,065	645	585	1,120	570	865
110	Dutch (Netherlands)	75	100	55	145	120	90
111	Filipino	115	90	55	55	75	35
112	Polish	160	30	85	135	165	130
113	Norwegian	140	65	30	65	105	115
114	North American Indian	80	40	50	220	100	45
	by Aboriginal identity						
115	Total Aboriginal identity population (10)	65	50	30	220	80	65
116	Total non-Aboriginal population	7,745	3,745	5,045	7,010	6,765	6,030
	by Aboriginal origin						
117	Total Aboriginal origins population (11)	90	85	60	265	115	75
118	Total non-Aboriginal population	7,715	3,710	5,010	6,965	6,730	6,030
	by Registered Indian status						
119	Registered Indian (12)	35	25	20	95	45	-
120	Not a Registered Indian	7,780	3,765	5,055	7,140	6,800	6,100

Tableau 1. Certaines caractéristiques des secteurs de recensement, recensement de 2001 – Données intégrales et données-échantillon (20 %)

Vancouver 0243.02 ◆	Vancouver 0250.01 A	Vancouver 0250.02 A	Vancouver 0251	Vancouver 0260.02 A	Vancouver 0260.04 A	Caractéristiques	N°
						CARACTÉRISTIQUES DE LA POPULATION	
						selon la langue parlée à la maison	
4,900	2,830	3,180	140	3,675	3,460	Réponses uniques	68
3,915	2,800	3,130	135	3,450	2,960	Anglais	69
10	-	-	-	-	-	Français	70
985	30	45	-	220	500	Langues non officielles (5)	71
190	-	-	-	25	25	Cantonais	72
250	-	-	-	20	10	Chinois, n.d.a.	73
-	-	-	-	-	-	Pendjabi	74
145	-	25	-	10	75	Mandarin	75
145	25	-	-	30	160	Coréen	76
260	-	20	-	135	235	Autres langues (6)	77
1,545	130	330	-	645	295	Réponses multiples	78
65	10	25	-	65	15	Anglais et français	79
1,440	120	275	-	555	270	Anglais et langue non officielle	80
-	-	-	-	15	-	Français et langue non officielle	81
35	-	30	-	10	10	Anglais, français et langue non officielle	82
						selon la connaissance des langues officielles	
5,695	2,665	3,260	140	3,975	3,330	Anglais seulement	83
-	-	-	-	-	-	Français seulement	84
615	290	250	-	325	355	Anglais et français	85
145	-	-	-	15	75	Ni l'anglais ni le français	86
						selon la connaissance des langues non officielles (5) (7)	
480	-	20	-	95	70	Cantonais	87
450	-	-	-	45	25	Chinois, n.d.a.	88
55	-	-	-	10	-	Pendjabi	89
460	10	45	-	40	95	Mandarin	90
75	10	25	-	50	25	Hindi	91
125	115	180	-	95	110	Allemand	92
190	110	40	-	95	85	Espagnol	93
						selon la première langue officielle parlée	
6,200	2,915	3,450	145	4,245	3,605	Anglais	94
55	35	30	-	40	15	Français	95
60	-	30	-	15	75	Anglais et français	96
135	-	-	-	10	65	Ni l'anglais ni le français	97
85	45	45	-	45	55	Minorité de langue officielle - (nombre) (8)	98
1.3	1.5	1.3	-	1.0	1.5	Minorité de langue officielle - (pourcentage) (8)	99
						selon l'origine ethnique (9)	
1,600	1,640	1,555	-	1,485	1,200	Anglais	100
1,185	655	855	25	990	945	Canadien	101
1,345	10	85	-	205	310	Chinois	102
1,145	925	800	40	900	885	Écossais	103
690	490	690	25	640	610	Irlandais	104
545	385	720	25	480	600	Allemand	105
345	-	30	-	125	95	Indien de l'Inde	106
405	220	295	-	255	310	Français	107
220	90	160	20	120	220	Ukrainien	108
275	75	160	-	205	120	Italien	109
285	245	165	-	155	225	Hollandais (Néerlandais)	110
50	30	10	-	185	105	Philippin	111
325	80	55	-	145	155	Polonais	112
140	75	285	-	105	140	Norvégien	113
145	45	25	60	105	170	Indien de l'Amérique du Nord	114
						selon l'identité autochtone	
135	15	30	45	95	140	Total de la population ayant une identité autochtone (10)	115
6,315	2,945	3,485	100	4,215	3,625	Total de la population non autochtone	116
						selon l'origine autochtone	
165	55	40	55	150	200	Total de la population ayant une origine autochtone (11)	117
6,285	2,905	3,470	85	4,165	3,560	Total de la population non autochtone	118
						selon le statut d'Indien inscrit	
65	-	25	45	10	50	Oui, Indien inscrit (12)	119
6,385	2,955	3,485	105	4,305	3,705	Non, pas un Indien inscrit	120

Table 1. Selected Characteristics for Census Tracts, 2001 Census – 100% Data and 20% Sample Data

No.	Characteristics	Vancouver 0239	Vancouver 0240.01 A	Vancouver 0240.02 A	Vancouver 0241	Vancouver 0242	Vancouver 0243.01
	POPULATION CHARACTERISTICS						
	by visible minority groups						
121	Total visible minority population	3,675	1,530	2,650	2,530	2,870	3,010
122	Chinese	2,645	840	1,795	1,910	2,030	2,175
123	South Asian	340	290	130	215	390	230
124	Black	90	35	65	40	45	-
125	Filipino	100	90	45	60	80	35
126	Latin American	260	15	140	30	30	95
127	Southeast Asian	60	65	210	85	60	110
128	Arab	-	10	25	-	10	10
129	West Asian	20	-	15	20	35	135
130	Korean	30	80	60	65	20	120
131	Japanese	95	80	135	100	120	45
132	Visible minority, n.i.e. (13)	10	-	-	10	10	-
133	Multiple visible minorities (14)	25	30	20	-	50	55
	by citizenship						
134	Canadian citizenship (15)	6,710	3,305	4,420	6,585	6,110	5,400
135	Citizenship other than Canadian	1,100	485	655	645	735	700
	by place of birth of respondent						
136	Non-immigrant population	4,035	2,125	2,440	4,505	3,890	2,965
137	Born in province of residence	3,140	1,590	1,925	3,385	2,765	2,230
138	Immigrant population (16)	3,550	1,575	2,585	2,650	2,940	3,090
139	United States	40	10	25	55	70	45
140	Central and South America	110	35	125	55	45	70
141	Caribbean and Bermuda	25	15	-	-	20	-
142	United Kingdom	110	85	55	140	150	90
143	Other Europe (17)	730	415	575	655	735	645
144	Africa	80	20	60	65	65	125
145	Asia and the Middle East	2,375	900	1,700	1,610	1,735	2,075
146	Oceania and other (18)	75	95	45	75	125	45
147	Non-permanent residents (19)	230	90	50	75	10	50
148	**Total immigrant population**	**3,545**	**1,575**	**2,590**	**2,650**	**2,945**	**3,090**
	by period of immigration						
149	Before 1961	425	155	215	300	425	300
150	1961-1970	355	305	300	285	305	285
151	1971-1980	530	320	580	685	595	550
152	1981-1990	635	290	555	600	435	595
153	1991-2001 (20)	1,595	500	935	790	1,190	1,355
154	1991-1995	970	330	545	460	580	820
155	1996-2001 (20)	620	175	390	330	610	530
	by age at immigration						
156	0-4 years	265	90	165	245	260	310
157	5-19 years	1,000	500	745	645	835	845
158	20 years and over	2,285	980	1,680	1,760	1,850	1,935
159	**Total population**	**7,810**	**3,790**	**5,075**	**7,230**	**6,850**	**6,100**
	by religion						
160	Catholic (21)	2,080	1,155	1,600	2,205	1,695	1,500
161	Protestant	1,365	745	630	1,320	1,125	1,045
162	Christian Orthodox	215	10	55	60	80	80
163	Christian, n.i.e. (22)	410	175	335	220	355	280
164	Muslim	150	50	25	75	305	210
165	Jewish	10	-	10	40	10	10
166	Buddhist	515	95	245	420	300	345
167	Hindu	90	45	60	95	15	40
168	Sikh	100	130	10	80	145	70
169	Eastern religions (23)	25	-	70	30	-	30
170	Other religions (24)	15	10	-	-	40	20
171	No religious affiliation (25)	2,845	1,360	2,040	2,675	2,770	2,480
172	**Total population 15 years and over**	**6,640**	**3,285**	**4,295**	**6,120**	**5,895**	**5,150**
	by generation status						
173	1st generation (26)	3,480	1,595	2,520	2,630	2,740	2,865
174	2nd generation (27)	1,655	975	1,020	1,825	1,670	1,235
175	3rd generation and over (28)	1,500	710	760	1,665	1,490	1,055
176	**Total population 1 year and over (29)**	**7,745**	**3,760**	**5,000**	**7,160**	**6,775**	**6,060**
	by place of residence 1 year ago (mobility)						
177	Non-movers	6,495	3,060	4,340	6,095	5,990	4,955
178	Movers	1,245	695	660	1,060	790	1,105
179	Non-migrants	570	420	320	540	445	560
180	Migrants	680	280	340	525	345	545
181	Internal migrants	560	220	255	410	280	390
182	Intraprovincial migrants	440	200	185	310	250	300
183	Interprovincial migrants	115	15	65	100	35	90
184	External migrants	120	65	85	115	65	155

Tableau 1. Certaines caractéristiques des secteurs de recensement, recensement de 2001 – Données intégrales et données-échantillon (20 %)

Vancouver 0243.02 ◆	Vancouver 0250.01 A	Vancouver 0250.02 A	Vancouver 0251	Vancouver 0260.02 A	Vancouver 0260.04 A	Caractéristiques	N°
						CARACTÉRISTIQUES DE LA POPULATION	
						selon les groupes de minorités visibles	
2,515	145	190	-	935	800	Total de la population des minorités visibles	121
1,295	10	85	-	200	260	Chinois	122
395	-	10	-	140	90	Sud-Asiatique	123
105	10	10	-	115	45	Noir	124
35	30	-	-	170	45	Philippin	125
30	25	-	-	40	25	Latino-Américain	126
15	-	-	-	30	-	Asiatique du Sud-Est	127
45	-	-	-	70	25	Arabe	128
125	-	20	-	95	-	Asiatique occidental	129
265	30	-	-	40	235	Coréen	130
145	35	25	-	-	10	Japonais	131
-	10	-	-	-	-	Minorité visible, n.i.a. (13)	132
65	-	25	-	40	55	Minorités visibles multiples (14)	133
						selon la citoyenneté	
5,440	2,760	3,165	...	3,950	3,285	Citoyenneté canadienne (15)	134
1,010	195	345	...	360	470	Citoyenneté autre que canadienne	135
						selon le lieu de naissance du répondant	
3,570	2,265	2,700	...	3,165	2,625	Population non immigrante	136
2,535	1,530	1,885	...	2,270	1,855	Née dans la province de résidence	137
2,615	660	795	...	1,115	1,090	Population immigrante (16)	138
75	90	120	...	65	100	États-Unis	139
70	35	20	...	55	25	Amérique centrale et du Sud	140
-	-	-	...	40	-	Caraïbes et Bermudes	141
190	310	205	...	150	125	Royaume-Uni	142
510	115	250	...	250	280	Autre Europe (17)	143
230	35	70	...	30	60	Afrique	144
1,485	55	110	...	520	490	Asie et Moyen-Orient	145
55	20	25	...	15	-	Océanie et autre (18)	146
260	30	15	...	30	45	Résidents non permanents (19)	147
2,615	**660**	**795**	**...**	**1,120**	**1,090**	**Population immigrante totale**	148
						selon la période d'immigration	
180	140	125	...	130	120	Avant 1961	149
175	180	180	...	120	70	1961-1970	150
380	120	130	...	205	145	1971-1980	151
455	95	145	...	210	80	1981-1990	152
1,430	130	215	...	450	685	1991-2001 (20)	153
555	35	60	...	250	220	1991-1995	154
875	95	160	...	195	460	1996-2001 (20)	155
						selon l'âge à l'immigration	
285	80	90	...	125	140	0-4 ans	156
780	165	160	...	310	325	5-19 ans	157
1,550	420	540	...	690	620	20 ans et plus	158
6,450	**2,955**	**3,510**	**140**	**4,315**	**3,760**	**Population totale**	159
						selon la religion	
925	310	620	30	860	390	Catholique (21)	160
1,095	915	1,240	35	1,290	1,425	Protestante	161
130	-	15	-	55	105	Orthodoxe chrétienne	162
605	95	120	-	180	225	Chrétiennes, n.i.a. (22)	163
370	-	25	-	170	85	Musulmane	164
30	25	30	-	20	-	Juive	165
285	50	25	-	35	45	Bouddhiste	166
80	35	-	-	40	35	Hindoue	167
15	-	-	-	10	-	Sikh	168
45	-	15	-	20	10	Religions orientales (23)	169
55	10	15	-	35	-	Autres religions (24)	170
2,810	1,515	1,410	70	1,610	1,440	Aucune appartenance religieuse (25)	171
5,050	**2,300**	**2,770**	**110**	**3,560**	**2,910**	**Population totale de 15 ans et plus**	172
						selon le statut des générations	
2,600	665	770	10	1,095	910	1re génération (26)	173
870	535	680	20	825	700	2e génération (27)	174
1,580	1,095	1,325	80	1,635	1,300	3e génération et plus (28)	175
6,385	**2,900**	**3,480**	**145**	**4,260**	**3,730**	**Population totale de 1 an et plus (29)**	176
						selon le lieu de résidence 1 an auparavant (mobilité)	
5,365	2,265	3,145	135	3,450	2,880	Personnes n'ayant pas déménagé	177
1,020	640	340	10	810	850	Personnes ayant déménagé	178
495	230	120	-	315	300	Non-migrants	179
525	405	220	10	495	550	Migrants	180
360	365	215	-	420	345	Migrants internes	181
295	315	205	10	400	335	Migrants infraprovinciaux	182
70	45	-	-	20	15	Migrants interprovinciaux	183
160	40	10	-	75	200	Migrants externes	184

Table 1. Selected Characteristics for Census Tracts, 2001 Census – 100% Data and 20% Sample Data

No.	Characteristics	Vancouver 0239	Vancouver 0240.01 A	Vancouver 0240.02 A	Vancouver 0241	Vancouver 0242	Vancouver 0243.01
	POPULATION CHARACTERISTICS						
185	**Total population 5 years and over (30)**	**7,470**	**3,640**	**4,825**	**6,865**	**6,535**	**5,885**
	by place of residence 5 years ago (mobility)						
186	Non-movers	4,155	1,860	3,010	3,895	4,075	3,380
187	Movers	3,315	1,780	1,815	2,960	2,460	2,505
188	Non-migrants	1,500	900	695	1,460	1,135	1,150
189	Migrants	1,820	885	1,125	1,505	1,325	1,350
190	Internal migrants	1,175	685	755	1,110	825	765
191	Intraprovincial migrants	1,015	525	480	875	615	555
192	Interprovincial migrants	160	160	275	240	210	205
193	External migrants	640	200	365	390	500	585
194	**Total population 15 to 24 years**	**1,090**	**520**	**645**	**990**	**930**	**1,170**
	by school attendance						
195	Not attending school	260	185	240	325	320	235
196	Attending school full time	645	260	325	570	500	785
197	Attending school part time	190	75	80	95	110	145
198	**Total population 15 years and over**	**6,640**	**3,285**	**4,295**	**6,120**	**5,895**	**5,150**
	by highest level of schooling						
199	Less than grade 9 (31)	535	220	595	545	375	395
200	Grades 9-13 without high school graduation certificate	1,155	580	960	1,050	1,105	815
201	Grades 9-13 with high school graduation certificate	865	570	595	745	860	655
202	Some postsecondary without degree, certificate or diploma (32)	915	480	555	840	805	810
203	Trades certificate or diploma (33)	795	255	340	590	535	645
204	College certificate or diploma (34)	1,100	590	600	945	870	780
205	University certificate below bachelor's degree	190	105	95	195	125	175
206	University with bachelor's degree or higher	1,075	485	570	1,210	1,225	875
	by combinations of unpaid work						
207	Males 15 years and over	3,285	1,550	2,120	2,980	2,980	2,545
208	Reported unpaid work (35)	2,880	1,310	1,775	2,615	2,610	2,215
209	Housework and child care and care or assistance to seniors	235	145	210	285	185	185
210	Housework and child care only	765	310	515	625	640	545
211	Housework and care or assistance to seniors only	235	130	160	185	270	200
212	Child care and care or assistance to seniors only	10	10	-	10	-	-
213	Housework only	1,580	690	865	1,465	1,360	1,245
214	Child care only	40	15	20	35	120	35
215	Care or assistance to seniors only	20	15	-	15	40	-
216	Females 15 years and over	3,350	1,735	2,175	3,145	2,910	2,605
217	Reported unpaid work (35)	3,140	1,500	1,955	2,895	2,690	2,385
218	Housework and child care and care or assistance to seniors	330	210	210	435	280	305
219	Housework and child care only	940	365	630	740	810	685
220	Housework and care or assistance to seniors only	280	175	230	310	300	210
221	Child care and care or assistance to seniors only	-	-	10	-	-	-
222	Housework only	1,580	735	860	1,395	1,245	1,165
223	Child care only	10	10	20	10	30	15
224	Care or assistance to seniors only	10	10	-	10	25	10
	by labour force activity						
225	Males 15 years and over	3,285	1,545	2,120	2,980	2,985	2,540
226	In the labour force	2,255	1,065	1,420	2,230	2,075	1,645
227	Employed	2,115	955	1,295	2,080	1,930	1,535
228	Unemployed	140	110	125	150	145	110
229	Not in the labour force	1,030	480	700	745	910	905
230	Participation rate	68.6	68.9	67.0	74.8	69.5	64.8
231	Employment rate	64.4	61.8	61.1	69.8	64.7	60.4
232	Unemployment rate	6.2	10.3	8.8	6.7	7.0	6.7
233	Females 15 years and over	3,350	1,735	2,175	3,145	2,915	2,610
234	In the labour force	2,065	990	1,250	1,955	1,720	1,545
235	Employed	1,975	930	1,135	1,840	1,655	1,410
236	Unemployed	95	55	115	115	70	135
237	Not in the labour force	1,285	750	925	1,190	1,190	1,060
238	Participation rate	61.6	57.1	57.5	62.2	59.0	59.2
239	Employment rate	59.0	53.6	52.2	58.5	56.8	54.0
240	Unemployment rate	4.6	5.6	9.2	5.9	4.1	8.7

Tableau 1. Certaines caractéristiques des secteurs de recensement, recensement de 2001 – Données intégrales et données-échantillon (20 %)

Vancouver 0243.02 ◆	Vancouver 0250.01 A	Vancouver 0250.02 A	Vancouver 0251	Vancouver 0260.02 A	Vancouver 0260.04 A	Caractéristiques	Nº
						CARACTÉRISTIQUES DE LA POPULATION	
6,070	**2,805**	**3,315**	**135**	**4,065**	**3,530**	**Population totale de 5 ans et plus (30)**	185
						selon le lieu de résidence 5 ans auparavant (mobilité)	
3,055	1,460	1,870	85	1,785	1,735	Personnes n'ayant pas déménagé	186
3,020	1,345	1,440	45	2,280	1,790	Personnes ayant déménagé	187
1,085	345	430	15	740	380	Non-migrants	188
1,940	1,000	1,010	30	1,540	1,410	Migrants	189
1,010	895	870	30	1,335	995	Migrants internes	190
820	695	825	30	1,160	935	Migrants infraprovinciaux	191
185	200	40	-	170	60	Migrants interprovinciaux	192
925	105	145	-	210	420	Migrants externes	193
1,075	**270**	**325**	**15**	**610**	**605**	**Population totale de 15 à 24 ans**	194
						selon la fréquentation scolaire	
190	105	150	-	240	250	Ne fréquentant pas l'école	195
815	145	150	-	325	290	Fréquentant l'école à plein temps	196
70	15	30	-	40	65	Fréquentant l'école à temps partiel	197
5,050	**2,305**	**2,770**	**110**	**3,560**	**2,910**	**Population totale de 15 ans et plus**	198
						selon le plus haut niveau de scolarité atteint	
145	15	25	-	105	45	Niveau inférieur à la 9e année (31)	199
795	305	375	45	690	480	De la 9e à la 13e année sans certificat d'études secondaires	200
430	205	300	-	480	400	De la 9e à la 13e année avec certificat d'études secondaires	201
685	270	365	15	605	435	Études postsecondaires partielles sans grade, certificat ou diplôme (32)	202
365	170	325	10	390	240	Certificat ou diplôme d'une école de métiers (33)	203
705	490	520	25	640	500	Certificat ou diplôme collégial (34)	204
250	65	75	-	65	75	Certificat universitaire inférieur au baccalauréat	205
1,675	785	795	-	580	730	Études universitaires avec baccalauréat ou diplôme supérieur	206
						selon les combinaisons de travail non rémunéré	
2,430	1,090	1,420	55	1,770	1,430	Hommes de 15 ans et plus	207
2,145	1,030	1,325	50	1,595	1,275	Travail non rémunéré déclaré (35)	208
170	65	50	-	125	110	Travaux ménagers et soins aux enfants et soins ou aide aux personnes âgées	209
685	420	410	10	445	425	Travaux ménagers et soins aux enfants seulement	210
110	70	145	15	100	100	Travaux ménagers et soins ou aide aux personnes âgées seulement	211
-	-	-	-	10	10	Soins aux enfants et soins ou aide aux personnes âgées seulement	212
1,130	480	690	25	885	625	Travaux ménagers seulement	213
30	-	10	-	25	-	Soins aux enfants seulement	214
15	-	20	-	10	-	Soins ou aide aux personnes âgées seulement	215
2,620	1,210	1,350	50	1,790	1,480	Femmes de 15 ans et plus	216
2,470	1,160	1,315	50	1,655	1,345	Travail non rémunéré déclaré (35)	217
330	95	100	10	165	210	Travaux ménagers et soins aux enfants et soins ou aide aux personnes âgées	218
950	455	415	15	545	475	Travaux ménagers et soins aux enfants seulement	219
170	100	175	-	165	145	Travaux ménagers et soins ou aide aux personnes âgées seulement	220
-	-	-	-	10	10	Soins aux enfants et soins ou aide aux personnes âgées seulement	221
1,010	495	600	25	720	515	Travaux ménagers seulement	222
-	15	-	-	10	-	Soins aux enfants seulement	223
-	-	20	-	30	-	Soins ou aide aux personnes âgées seulement	224
						selon l'activité	
2,425	1,090	1,420	55	1,765	1,430	Hommes de 15 ans et plus	225
1,745	895	1,150	45	1,360	1,095	Population active	226
1,615	895	1,085	45	1,280	1,010	Personnes occupées	227
130	10	60	-	80	90	Chômeurs	228
680	195	280	-	410	330	Inactifs	229
72.0	82.1	81.0	81.8	77.1	76.6	Taux d'activité	230
66.6	82.1	76.4	81.8	72.5	70.6	Taux d'emploi	231
7.4	1.1	5.2	-	5.9	8.2	Taux de chômage	232
2,625	1,215	1,345	55	1,790	1,480	Femmes de 15 ans et plus	233
1,685	835	940	35	1,345	1,035	Population active	234
1,570	765	890	30	1,270	945	Personnes occupées	235
110	75	50	-	75	95	Chômeuses	236
935	375	410	25	450	445	Inactives	237
64.2	68.7	69.9	63.6	75.1	69.9	Taux d'activité	238
59.8	63.0	66.2	54.5	70.9	63.9	Taux d'emploi	239
6.5	9.0	5.3	-	5.6	9.2	Taux de chômage	240

Table 1. Selected Characteristics for Census Tracts, 2001 Census – 100% Data and 20% Sample Data

No.	Characteristics	Vancouver 0239	Vancouver 0240.01 A	Vancouver 0240.02 A	Vancouver 0241	Vancouver 0242	Vancouver 0243.01
	POPULATION CHARACTERISTICS						
	by labour force activity – concluded						
241	Both sexes - Participation rate	65.1	62.5	62.2	68.4	64.4	61.9
242	15-24 years	56.4	65.4	60.5	68.2	56.8	51.1
243	25 years and over	66.8	62.0	62.6	68.5	65.8	65.0
244	Both sexes - Employment rate	61.6	57.5	56.6	64.1	60.8	57.2
245	15-24 years	50.9	53.8	43.8	56.6	51.9	44.6
246	25 years and over	63.8	57.9	58.9	65.5	62.5	61.0
247	Both sexes - Unemployment rate	5.3	8.0	8.8	6.5	5.7	7.7
248	15-24 years	10.6	16.4	26.0	17.0	9.5	13.3
249	25 years and over	4.6	6.1	5.9	4.3	5.0	6.4
250	**Total labour force 15 years and over**	**4,320**	**2,050**	**2,670**	**4,185**	**3,800**	**3,190**
	by industry based on the 1997 NAICS						
251	Industry - Not applicable (36)	45	50	55	45	80	85
252	All industries (37)	4,275	2,000	2,610	4,140	3,720	3,105
253	11 Agriculture, forestry, fishing and hunting	-	-	10	30	-	10
254	21 Mining and oil and gas extraction	10	-	-	10	20	-
255	22 Utilities	50	-	25	-	10	50
256	23 Construction	195	160	200	265	245	165
257	31-33 Manufacturing	480	150	270	395	370	270
258	41 Wholesale trade	220	80	200	220	250	215
259	44-45 Retail trade	535	205	255	365	400	300
260	48-49 Transportation and warehousing	185	120	155	210	180	155
261	51 Information and cultural industries	215	95	100	240	255	100
262	52 Finance and insurance	240	120	170	255	150	190
263	53 Real estate and rental and leasing	135	20	25	115	65	40
264	54 Professional, scientific and technical services	310	165	190	325	360	265
265	55 Management of companies and enterprises	-	-	-	20	-	-
266	56 Administrative and support, waste management and remediation services	150	90	115	130	215	150
267	61 Educational services	260	105	115	370	305	260
268	62 Health care and social assistance	425	220	200	310	230	275
269	71 Arts, entertainment and recreation	105	130	75	55	120	85
270	72 Accommodation and food services	410	140	270	425	255	200
271	81 Other services (except public administration)	180	130	175	260	150	195
272	91 Public administration	185	60	65	145	140	180
	by class of worker						
273	Class of worker - Not applicable (36)	45	50	60	45	75	85
274	All classes of worker (37)	4,275	2,000	2,610	4,140	3,720	3,105
275	Paid workers	3,920	1,835	2,395	3,810	3,330	2,845
276	Employees	3,790	1,795	2,335	3,660	3,155	2,705
277	Self-employed (incorporated)	130	45	65	150	180	135
278	Self-employed (unincorporated)	340	165	210	320	385	250
279	Unpaid family workers	15	-	10	-	10	-
	by occupation based on the 2001 NOC-S						
280	Male labour force 15 years and over	2,255	1,065	1,420	2,230	2,075	1,640
281	Occupation - Not applicable (36)	20	15	25	15	40	40
282	All occupations (37)	2,230	1,050	1,395	2,215	2,035	1,605
283	A Management occupations	315	120	115	320	270	195
284	B Business, finance and administration occupations	330	135	155	205	220	275
285	C Natural and applied sciences and related occupations	250	115	140	220	245	165
286	D Health occupations	50	25	15	60	30	25
287	E Occupations in social science, education, government service and religion	75	45	35	110	155	80
288	F Occupations in art, culture, recreation and sport	60	30	55	95	125	80
289	G Sales and service occupations	475	260	330	475	405	300
290	H Trades, transport and equipment operators and related occupations	550	250	450	570	485	380
291	I Occupations unique to primary industry	15	20	35	30	15	20
292	J Occupations unique to processing, manufacturing and utilities	105	55	65	115	85	75
293	Female labour force 15 years and over	2,065	985	1,250	1,955	1,720	1,545
294	Occupation - Not applicable (36)	25	30	35	30	35	45
295	All occupations (37)	2,045	955	1,215	1,925	1,690	1,495
296	A Management occupations	160	100	50	120	130	115
297	B Business, finance and administration occupations	700	355	370	565	495	530
298	C Natural and applied sciences and related occupations	55	35	70	75	85	55
299	D Health occupations	145	80	50	85	85	100

Tableau 1. Certaines caractéristiques des secteurs de recensement, recensement de 2001 – Données intégrales et données-échantillon (20 %)

Vancouver 0243.02 ◆	Vancouver 0250.01 A	Vancouver 0250.02 A	Vancouver 0251	Vancouver 0260.02 A	Vancouver 0260.04 A	Caractéristiques	N°
						CARACTÉRISTIQUES DE LA POPULATION	
						selon l'activité – fin	
67.9	75.3	75.3	76.2	76.0	73.2	Les deux sexes - Taux d'activité	241
48.8	64.8	80.3	100.0	70.2	66.1	15-24 ans	242
73.1	76.7	74.6	73.7	77.5	75.1	25 ans et plus	243
63.2	71.8	71.3	71.4	71.5	67.0	Les deux sexes - Taux d'emploi	244
40.0	53.7	63.1	-	65.6	59.2	15-24 ans	245
69.4	74.1	72.4	68.4	72.7	69.3	25 ans et plus	246
7.0	4.9	5.3	-	5.9	8.5	Les deux sexes - Taux de chômage	247
19.0	16.7	20.8	-	4.7	11.2	15-24 ans	248
4.8	3.5	3.0	-	5.9	7.8	25 ans et plus	249
3,435	**1,735**	**2,085**	**80**	**2,705**	**2,130**	**Population active totale de 15 ans et plus**	250
						selon l'industrie basée sur le SCIAN de 1997	
70	10	-	-	30	60	Industrie - Sans objet (36)	251
3,360	1,720	2,080	80	2,675	2,065	Toutes les industries (37)	252
-	15	25	10	-	-	11 Agriculture, foresterie, pêche et chasse	253
15	10	10	-	10	-	21 Extraction minière et extraction de pétrole et de gaz	254
10	-	30	-	10	20	22 Services publics	255
200	115	175	10	145	140	23 Construction	256
185	140	65	-	230	90	31-33 Fabrication	257
135	35	120	-	175	105	41 Commerce de gros	258
295	130	150	10	400	280	44-45 Commerce de détail	259
130	35	85	10	130	100	48-49 Transport et entreposage	260
160	125	140	-	90	125	51 Industrie de l'information et industrie culturelle	261
180	70	120	-	115	80	52 Finance et assurances	262
100	35	40	-	60	25	53 Services immobiliers et services de location et de location à bail	263
325	300	220	-	215	200	54 Services professionnels, scientifiques et techniques	264
10	15	-	-	-	-	55 Gestion de sociétés et d'entreprises	265
170	60	65	-	85	110	56 Services administratifs, services de soutien, services de gestion des déchets et services d'assainissement	266
560	135	215	10	210	190	61 Services d'enseignement	267
355	130	210	15	280	215	62 Soins de santé et assistance sociale	268
60	100	90	-	60	45	71 Arts, spectacles et loisirs	269
225	90	70	-	200	135	72 Hébergement et services de restauration	270
110	80	160	10	95	110	81 Autres services, sauf les administrations publiques	271
150	95	100	10	175	85	91 Administrations publiques	272
						selon la catégorie de travailleurs	
70	10	10	-	30	65	Catégorie de travailleurs - Sans objet (36)	273
3,360	1,725	2,080	75	2,675	2,065	Toutes les catégories de travailleurs (37)	274
3,105	1,305	1,820	70	2,470	1,860	Travailleurs rémunérés	275
2,890	1,050	1,570	70	2,400	1,770	Employés	276
215	255	250	-	70	95	Travailleurs autonomes (entreprise constituée en société)	277
250	410	245	10	200	175	Travailleurs autonomes (entreprise non constituée en société)	278
-	10	15	-	-	25	Travailleurs familiaux non rémunérés	279
						selon la profession basée sur la CNP-S de 2001	
1,745	900	1,150	45	1,360	1,100	Hommes actifs de 15 ans et plus	280
50	-	-	-	10	30	Profession - Sans objet (36)	281
1,700	900	1,145	45	1,350	1,070	Toutes les professions (37)	282
285	125	240	-	190	175	A Gestion	283
205	85	120	10	100	85	B Affaires, finance et administration	284
245	165	135	-	120	145	C Sciences naturelles et appliquées et professions apparentées	285
45	20	55	-	20	25	D Secteur de la santé	286
250	95	95	-	75	70	E Sciences sociales, enseignement, administration publique et religion	287
65	110	75	-	45	15	F Arts, culture, sports et loisirs	288
285	100	190	-	335	265	G Ventes et services	289
265	160	205	30	340	270	H Métiers, transport et machinerie	290
15	15	30	10	45	-	I Professions propres au secteur primaire	291
30	30	10	-	70	25	J Transformation, fabrication et services d'utilité publique	292
1,685	835	935	30	1,340	1,035	Femmes actives de 15 ans et plus	293
20	15	10	-	15	35	Profession - Sans objet (36)	294
1,665	825	935	30	1,325	995	Toutes les professions (37)	295
175	75	90	-	105	115	A Gestion	296
530	230	310	15	410	305	B Affaires, finance et administration	297
70	25	10	-	70	30	C Sciences naturelles et appliquées et professions apparentées	298
160	45	60	-	160	85	D Secteur de la santé	299

Table 1. Selected Characteristics for Census Tracts, 2001 Census – 100% Data and 20% Sample Data

No.	Characteristics	Vancouver 0239	Vancouver 0240.01 A	Vancouver 0240.02 A	Vancouver 0241	Vancouver 0242	Vancouver 0243.01
	POPULATION CHARACTERISTICS						
	by occupation based on the 2001 NOC-S – concluded						
300	E Occupations in social science, education, government service and religion	220	75	130	290	180	230
301	F Occupations in art, culture, recreation and sport	60	35	35	85	65	20
302	G Sales and service occupations	525	230	405	585	565	335
303	H Trades, transport and equipment operators and related occupations	35	40	25	50	55	25
304	I Occupations unique to primary industry	-	-	15	10	10	-
305	J Occupations unique to processing, manufacturing and utilities	125	-	65	65	30	85
306	**Total employed labour force 15 years and over**	**4,090**	**1,885**	**2,435**	**3,920**	**3,585**	**2,945**
	by place of work						
307	Males	2,115	955	1,300	2,075	1,935	1,535
308	Usual place of work	1,715	775	965	1,630	1,475	1,115
309	At home	150	40	55	60	120	95
310	Outside Canada	15	-	-	25	15	50
311	No fixed workplace address	240	140	280	360	320	275
312	Females	1,975	930	1,135	1,840	1,650	1,410
313	Usual place of work	1,790	830	965	1,595	1,395	1,175
314	At home	110	55	75	120	155	135
315	Outside Canada	10	-	-	-	-	10
316	No fixed workplace address	70	45	90	125	100	90
317	**Total employed labour force 15 years and over with usual place of work or no fixed workplace address**	**3,810**	**1,790**	**2,300**	**3,710**	**3,290**	**2,655**
	by mode of transportation						
318	Males	1,950	920	1,240	1,990	1,795	1,395
319	Car, truck, van, as driver	1,605	815	980	1,650	1,515	1,140
320	Car, truck, van, as passenger	100	20	65	45	85	120
321	Public transit	150	35	120	160	125	80
322	Walked	55	40	30	70	40	30
323	Other method	40	-	45	65	25	20
324	Females	1,860	880	1,055	1,715	1,495	1,260
325	Car, truck, van, as driver	1,215	565	630	1,120	995	850
326	Car, truck, van, as passenger	200	40	105	185	225	150
327	Public transit	340	180	245	285	210	230
328	Walked	90	75	60	105	35	30
329	Other method	20	15	15	20	20	10
330	**Total population 15 years and over who worked since January 1, 2000**	**4,630**	**2,180**	**2,850**	**4,420**	**4,110**	**3,400**
	by language used at work						
331	Single responses	3,940	1,880	2,215	3,955	3,550	3,015
332	English	3,745	1,800	2,055	3,865	3,445	2,830
333	French	10	-	-	-	-	10
334	Non-official languages (5)	185	80	165	90	100	180
335	Chinese, n.o.s.	55	30	50	20	45	60
336	Cantonese	60	30	50	50	45	20
337	Other languages (6)	70	20	65	15	20	95
338	Multiple responses	695	300	635	460	555	390
339	English and French	50	35	30	35	100	25
340	English and non-official language	635	265	600	415	445	360
341	French and non-official language	-	-	-	-	-	-
342	English, French and non-official language	10	-	-	15	10	-
	DWELLING AND HOUSEHOLD CHARACTERISTICS						
343	**Total number of occupied private dwellings**	**3,020**	**1,625**	**1,855**	**2,825**	**2,735**	**2,080**
	by tenure						
344	Owned	1,790	860	1,075	1,745	1,655	1,265
345	Rented	1,235	760	780	1,080	1,075	815
346	Band housing	-	-	-	-	-	-
	by structural type of dwelling						
347	Single-detached house	1,395	555	1,055	1,330	1,700	1,015
348	Semi-detached house	10	20	15	25	10	130
349	Row house	60	30	-	30	35	115
350	Apartment, detached duplex	455	250	295	480	335	215
351	Apartment, building that has five or more storeys	510	465	100	285	35	-
352	Apartment, building that has fewer than five storeys (38)	585	305	390	665	610	600
353	Other single-attached house	-	-	-	10	-	-
354	Movable dwelling (39)	-	-	-	-	-	-

Tableau 1. Certaines caractéristiques des secteurs de recensement, recensement de 2001 – Données intégrales et données-échantillon (20 %)

Vancouver 0243.02 ◆	Vancouver 0250.01 A	Vancouver 0250.02 A	Vancouver 0251	Vancouver 0260.02 A	Vancouver 0260.04 A	Caractéristiques	N°
						CARACTÉRISTIQUES DE LA POPULATION	
						selon la profession basée sur la CNP-S de 2001 – fin	
						E Sciences sociales, enseignement,	
320	130	175	-	135	115	administration publique et religion	300
55	115	50	-	40	65	F Arts, culture, sports et loisirs	301
320	145	200	-	380	260	G Ventes et services	302
10	35	25	-	15	-	H Métiers, transport et machinerie	303
10	15	10	-	-	10	I Professions propres au secteur primaire	304
						J Transformation, fabrication et	
20	15	10	-	10	-	services d'utilité publique	305
3,190	**1,655**	**1,975**	**75**	**2,545**	**1,950**	**Population active occupée totale de 15 ans et plus**	306
						selon le lieu de travail	
1,615	890	1,085	45	1,275	1,010	Hommes	307
1,270	505	785	15	1,070	720	Lieu habituel de travail	308
160	195	135	10	65	60	À domicile	309
40	10	15	-	-	10	En dehors du Canada	310
150	185	155	15	145	215	Sans adresse de travail fixe	311
1,570	765	890	35	1,270	940	Femmes	312
1,305	520	700	20	1,120	795	Lieu habituel de travail	313
180	205	145	10	70	95	À domicile	314
10	-	-	-	-	10	En dehors du Canada	315
85	35	45	-	80	30	Sans adresse de travail fixe	316
2,805	**1,245**	**1,680**	**55**	**2,405**	**1,770**	**Population active occupée totale de 15 ans et plus ayant un lieu habituel de travail ou sans adresse de travail fixe**	317
						selon le mode de transport	
1,420	690	935	35	1,210	940	Hommes	318
1,150	545	860	30	930	775	Automobile, camion ou fourgonnette, en tant que conducteur	319
65	35	40	-	60	45	Automobile, camion ou fourgonnette, en tant que passager	320
75	80	15	-	155	90	Transport en commun	321
90	15	15	-	45	10	À pied	322
35	25	10	-	25	20	Autre moyen	323
1,385	550	745	20	1,195	830	Femmes	324
980	355	595	15	850	670	Automobile, camion ou fourgonnette, en tant que conductrice	325
155	50	60	-	135	65	Automobile, camion ou fourgonnette, en tant que passagère	326
145	105	55	-	155	75	Transport en commun	327
90	35	20	-	45	15	À pied	328
15	10	15	-	10	15	Autre moyen	329
3,860	**1,845**	**2,180**	**90**	**2,880**	**2,220**	**Population totale de 15 ans et plus ayant travaillé depuis le 1er janvier 2000**	330
						selon la langue utilisée au travail	
3,450	1,785	2,075	90	2,790	2,135	Réponses uniques	331
3,345	1,790	2,075	90	2,775	2,105	Anglais	332
-	-	-	-	-	10	Français	333
95	-	-	-	15	25	Langues non officielles (5)	334
20	-	-	-	-	-	Chinois, n.d.a.	335
25	-	-	-	10	-	Cantonais	336
50	-	-	-	-	25	Autres langues (6)	337
415	60	105	-	90	85	Réponses multiples	338
40	40	30	-	30	10	Anglais et français	339
370	20	65	-	60	80	Anglais et langue non officielle	340
-	-	-	-	-	-	Français et langue non officielle	341
-	-	-	-	-	-	Anglais, français et langue non officielle	342
						CARACTÉRISTIQUES DES LOGEMENTS ET DES MÉNAGES	
2,075	**1,150**	**1,240**	**50**	**1,825**	**1,225**	**Nombre total de logements privés occupés**	343
						selon le mode d'occupation	
1,165	885	1,030	25	1,120	780	Possédé	344
905	260	205	25	710	445	Loué	345
-	-	-		-	-	Logement de bande	346
						selon le type de construction résidentielle	
475	1,070	1,055	50	600	550	Maison individuelle non attenante	347
85	10	20	-	10	40	Maison jumelée	348
1,240	20	15	-	250	345	Maison en rangée	349
55	10	55	-	190	70	Appartement, duplex non attenant	350
195	-	-	-	90	-	Appartement, immeuble de cinq étages ou plus	351
35	15	-	-	630	215	Appartement, immeuble de moins de cinq étages (38)	352
-	15	-	-	10	-	Autre maison individuelle attenante	353
-	-	95	10	45	-	Logement mobile (39)	354

Table 1. Selected Characteristics for Census Tracts, 2001 Census – 100% Data and 20% Sample Data

No.	Characteristics	Vancouver 0239	Vancouver 0240.01 A	Vancouver 0240.02 A	Vancouver 0241	Vancouver 0242	Vancouver 0243.01
	DWELLING AND HOUSEHOLD CHARACTERISTICS						
	by condition of dwelling						
355	Regular maintenance only	1,960	1,200	1,250	1,830	1,620	1,460
356	Minor repairs	765	330	445	660	935	460
357	Major repairs	295	90	160	325	185	155
	by period of construction						
358	Before 1946	130	65	250	590	185	90
359	1946-1960	765	355	220	520	835	190
360	1961-1970	495	155	245	350	470	620
361	1971-1980	925	260	320	420	620	580
362	1981-1990	425	360	430	425	335	435
363	1991-2001 (20)	285	425	395	525	300	160
364	Average number of rooms per dwelling	6.0	5.6	6.3	6.2	6.4	6.7
365	Average number of bedrooms per dwelling	2.7	2.5	2.8	2.6	2.7	3.1
366	Average value of dwelling $	311,547	281,449	313,978	320,764	345,624	367,727
367	**Total number of private households**	**3,020**	**1,625**	**1,855**	**2,825**	**2,735**	**2,080**
	by household size						
368	1 person	785	565	465	830	790	350
369	2 persons	960	515	505	830	840	590
370	3 persons	500	205	325	420	405	400
371	4-5 persons	665	275	445	620	625	630
372	6 or more persons	115	60	110	115	75	110
	by household type						
373	One-family households	1,960	895	1,175	1,710	1,670	1,480
374	Multiple-family households	120	45	115	105	95	90
375	Non-family households	940	680	560	1,005	975	505
376	Number of persons in private households	7,810	3,790	5,075	7,205	6,850	6,105
377	Average number of persons in private households	2.6	2.3	2.7	2.6	2.5	2.9
378	Average number of persons per room	0.4	0.4	0.4	0.4	0.4	0.4
379	Tenant households in non-farm, non-reserve private dwellings (40)	1,215	750	775	1,065	1,060	805
380	Average gross rent $ (40)	817	1,019	822	771	791	914
381	Tenant households spending 30% or more of household income on gross rent (40) (41)	445	380	340	410	445	325
382	Tenant households spending from 30% to 99% of household income on gross rent (40) (41)	360	290	240	355	380	255
383	Owner households in non-farm, non-reserve private dwellings (42)	1,790	860	1,075	1,745	1,650	1,260
384	Average owner's major payments $ (42)	833	1,022	778	1,008	918	850
385	Owner households spending 30% or more of household income on owner's major payments (41) (42)	420	215	240	365	315	300
386	Owner households spending from 30% to 99% of household income on owner's major payments (41) (42)	330	195	185	305	260	265
	CENSUS FAMILY CHARACTERISTICS						
387	**Total number of census families in private households**	**2,205**	**990**	**1,415**	**1,925**	**1,875**	**1,665**
	by census family structure and size						
388	Total couple families	1,845	830	1,175	1,610	1,610	1,360
389	Total families of married couples	1,615	715	1,080	1,415	1,415	1,250
390	Without children at home	610	295	375	475	555	420
391	With children at home	1,005	420	710	940	855	830
392	1 child	430	125	315	395	305	290
393	2 children	410	190	280	425	425	375
394	3 or more children	165	100	105	120	125	160
395	Total families of common-law couples	230	115	90	195	195	105
396	Without children at home	170	85	55	135	150	50
397	With children at home	55	35	35	60	45	60
398	1 child	15	30	35	20	20	30
399	2 children	35	-	10	25	15	20
400	3 or more children	10	-	-	15	10	-
401	Total lone-parent families	360	160	240	320	265	310
402	Female parent	285	135	205	255	240	260
403	1 child	160	80	165	165	140	135
404	2 children	90	60	30	55	70	70
405	3 or more children	35	-	10	35	30	55

Tableau 1. Certaines caractéristiques des secteurs de recensement, recensement de 2001 – Données intégrales et données-échantillon (20 %)

Vancouver 0243.02 ◆	Vancouver 0250.01 A	Vancouver 0250.02 A	Vancouver 0251	Vancouver 0260.02 A	Vancouver 0260.04 A	Caractéristiques	N°
						CARACTÉRISTIQUES DES LOGEMENTS ET DES MÉNAGES	
						selon l'état du logement	
1,455	630	815	25	1,105	795	Entretien régulier seulement	355
440	335	315	20	405	360	Réparations mineures	356
180	180	105	10	315	65	Réparations majeures	357
						selon la période de construction	
15	75	15	15	205	10	Avant 1946	358
35	110	60	10	155	100	1946-1960	359
160	100	200	10	335	540	1961-1970	360
460	265	380	-	470	335	1971-1980	361
1,305	265	290	-	180	100	1981-1990	362
100	340	295	10	485	140	1991-2001 (20)	363
6.6	6.8	8.3	6.6	5.9	7.1	Nombre moyen de pièces par logement	364
2.9	2.7	3.2	2.8	2.4	3.1	Nombre moyen de chambres à coucher par logement	365
308,158	357,914	475,183	-	197,384	243,260	Valeur moyenne du logement $	366
2,070	**1,150**	**1,235**	**50**	**1,825**	**1,225**	**Nombre total de logements privés**	367
						selon la taille du ménage	
270	225	185	10	580	145	1 personne	368
575	435	475	20	550	330	2 personnes	369
495	185	175	10	340	250	3 personnes	370
670	290	365	20	300	460	4-5 personnes	371
55	15	40	-	50	30	6 personnes ou plus	372
						selon le genre de ménage	
1,720	890	1,000	40	1,125	975	Ménages unifamiliaux	373
35	10	25	-	30	60	Ménages multifamiliaux	374
320	250	215	-	670	185	Ménages non familiaux	375
6,115	2,950	3,500	145	4,285	3,755	Nombre de personnes dans les ménages privés	376
2.9	2.6	2.8	2.9	2.3	3.1	Nombre moyen de personnes dans les ménages privés	377
0.4	0.4	0.3	0.4	0.4	0.4	Nombre moyen de personnes par pièce	378
905	260	205	-	710	415	Ménages locataires dans les logements privés non agricoles hors réserve (40)	379
819	932	1,224	-	693	1,006	Loyer brut moyen $ (40)	380
370	95	45	-	170	160	Ménages locataires consacrant 30 % ou plus du revenu du ménage au loyer brut (40) (41)	381
305	85	40	-	140	140	Ménages locataires consacrant de 30 % à 99 % du revenu du ménage au loyer brut (40) (41)	382
1,165	880	1,030	-	1,115	780	Ménages propriétaires dans les logements privés non agricoles hors réserve (42)	383
1,220	1,235	1,184	-	1,082	1,104	Principales dépenses de propriété moyennes $ (42)	384
320	215	175	-	240	205	Ménages propriétaires consacrant 30 % ou plus du revenu du ménage aux principales dépenses de propriété (41) (42)	385
275	185	145	-	215	165	Ménages propriétaires consacrant de 30 % à 99 % du revenu du ménage aux principales dépenses de propriété (41) (42)	386
						CARACTÉRISTIQUES DES FAMILLES DE RECENSEMENT	
1,790	**905**	**1,045**	**45**	**1,185**	**1,100**	**Total des familles de recensement dans les ménages privés**	387
						selon la structure et la taille de la famille de recensement	
1,435	830	970	40	935	915	Total des familles avec conjoints	388
1,315	670	880	20	775	810	Total des familles avec couples mariés	389
365	285	430	10	310	260	Sans enfants à la maison	390
950	385	450	15	460	550	Avec enfants à la maison	391
330	120	115	-	225	175	1 enfant	392
475	195	210	-	165	235	2 enfants	393
145	70	125	-	75	140	3 enfants ou plus	394
125	160	85	20	160	105	Total des familles en union libre	395
55	100	60	10	75	75	Sans enfants à la maison	396
65	60	30	-	85	30	Avec enfants à la maison	397
35	30	25	-	45	20	1 enfant	398
20	10	-	-	40	-	2 enfants	399
10	15	-	-	-	-	3 enfants ou plus	400
355	70	75	-	255	185	Total des familles monoparentales	401
320	50	50	-	200	165	Parent de sexe féminin	402
175	40	15	-	125	85	1 enfant	403
115	10	30	-	60	50	2 enfants	404
30	-	10	-	15	35	3 enfants ou plus	405

Table 1. Selected Characteristics for Census Tracts, 2001 Census – 100% Data and 20% Sample Data

No.	Characteristics	Vancouver 0239	Vancouver 0240.01 A	Vancouver 0240.02 A	Vancouver 0241	Vancouver 0242	Vancouver 0243.01
	CENSUS FAMILY CHARACTERISTICS						
	by census family structure and size - concluded						
406	Male parent	75	20	30	65	20	50
407	1 child	50	25	15	55	20	35
408	2 children	25	-	10	-	10	10
409	3 or more children	-	-	-	10	-	-
410	**Total number of children at home**	**2,410**	**1,095**	**1,580**	**2,245**	**2,020**	**2,155**
	by age groups						
411	Under 6 years	430	215	300	445	345	285
412	6-14 years	730	290	485	655	605	665
413	15-17 years	265	110	145	230	205	300
414	18-24 years	495	280	325	485	510	570
415	25 years and over	495	190	330	425	355	325
416	Average number of children at home per census family (43)	1.1	1.1	1.1	1.2	1.1	1.3
417	**Total number of persons in private households**	**7,810**	**3,785**	**5,075**	**7,205**	**6,845**	**6,100**
	by census family status and living arrangements						
418	Number of non-family persons	1,350	875	905	1,425	1,350	920
419	Living with relatives (44)	220	135	190	195	200	175
420	Living with non-relatives only	350	170	255	395	360	400
421	Living alone	785	570	465	835	790	350
422	Number of family persons	6,460	2,915	4,165	5,780	5,500	5,180
423	Average number of persons per census family	2.9	2.9	3.0	3.0	2.9	3.1
424	**Total number of persons 65 years and over**	**1,105**	**560**	**710**	**870**	**905**	**655**
425	Number of non-family persons 65 years and over	300	305	215	360	300	155
426	Living with relatives (44)	85	60	75	70	80	65
427	Living with non-relatives only	10	15	25	15	10	-
428	Living alone	205	225	110	275	200	95
429	Number of family persons 65 years and over	800	255	495	505	605	500
	ECONOMIC FAMILY CHARACTERISTICS						
430	**Total number of economic families in private households**	**2,125**	**985**	**1,310**	**1,845**	**1,815**	**1,595**
	by size of family						
431	2 persons	900	460	470	745	760	530
432	3 persons	470	190	295	380	370	360
433	4 persons	450	185	305	435	465	415
434	5 or more persons	300	150	240	290	215	290
435	Total number of persons in economic families	6,680	3,050	4,355	5,980	5,695	5,350
436	Average number of persons per economic family	3.1	3.1	3.3	3.2	3.1	3.4
437	Total number of unattached individuals	1,130	740	720	1,225	1,150	755
	2000 INCOME CHARACTERISTICS						
	Population 15 years and over by sex and total income groups in 2000						
438	Total - Both sexes	6,635	3,285	4,300	6,120	5,895	5,150
439	Without income	395	155	195	315	270	460
440	With income	6,245	3,130	4,105	5,805	5,620	4,690
441	Under $1,000 (45)	265	155	320	360	305	360
442	$ 1,000 - $ 2,999	365	110	225	235	310	185
443	$ 3,000 - $ 4,999	290	70	150	150	160	210
444	$ 5,000 - $ 6,999	245	135	140	235	160	250
445	$ 7,000 - $ 9,999	340	165	295	390	395	335
446	$10,000 - $11,999	275	210	135	240	220	255
447	$12,000 - $14,999	415	255	360	400	315	355
448	$15,000 - $19,999	605	260	475	450	520	435
449	$20,000 - $24,999	550	245	365	505	530	395
450	$25,000 - $29,999	475	185	315	405	390	350
451	$30,000 - $34,999	430	270	285	400	370	255
452	$35,000 - $39,999	400	290	270	380	290	225
453	$40,000 - $44,999	370	205	275	420	335	260
454	$45,000 - $49,999	245	125	130	300	255	170
455	$50,000 - $59,999	420	195	205	340	395	280
456	$60,000 and over	550	265	145	595	670	365
457	Average income $ (46)	27,263	28,788	23,083	30,491	32,771	25,662
458	Median income $ (46)	22,393	24,322	18,863	24,177	24,020	19,428
459	Standard error of average income $ (46)	577	1,190	606	956	1,810	801

Tableau 1. Certaines caractéristiques des secteurs de recensement, recensement de 2001 – Données intégrales et données-échantillon (20 %)

Vancouver 0243.02 ◆	Vancouver 0250.01 A	Vancouver 0250.02 A	Vancouver 0251	Vancouver 0260.02 A	Vancouver 0260.04 A	Caractéristiques	Nº
						CARACTÉRISTIQUES DES FAMILLES DE RECENSEMENT	
						selon la structure et la taille de la famille de recensement – fin	
35	25	25	-	55	25	Parent de sexe masculin	406
15	15	25	-	35	-	1 enfant	407
20	-	-	-	20	15	2 enfants	408
-	-	-	-	-	10	3 enfants ou plus	409
2,380	**925**	**1,110**	**45**	**1,290**	**1,435**	**Nombre total d'enfants à la maison**	410
						selon les groupes d'âge	
455	195	270	10	285	290	Moins de 6 ans	411
945	455	460	25	470	550	6-14 ans	412
320	105	105	10	150	170	15-17 ans	413
440	150	200	-	275	360	18-24 ans	414
225	10	70	-	110	75	25 ans et plus	415
1.3	1.0	1.1	1.0	1.1	1.3	Nombre moyen d'enfants à la maison par famille de recensement (43)	416
6,115	**2,950**	**3,495**	**140**	**4,285**	**3,760**	**Nombre total de personnes dans les ménages privés**	417
						selon la situation des particuliers dans la famille de recensement et des particuliers dans le ménage	
510	290	375	15	870	310	Nombre de personnes hors famille de recensement	418
95	-	60	10	65	80	Vivant avec des personnes apparentées (44)	419
140	60	125	-	225	80	Vivant avec des personnes non apparentées uniquement	420
270	230	185	-	580	150	Vivant seules	421
5,605	2,660	3,120	130	3,410	3,445	Nombre de personnes membres d'une famille	422
3.1	2.9	3.0	2.8	2.9	3.1	Nombre moyen de personnes par famille de recensement	423
280	**305**	**290**	**20**	**300**	**205**	**Nombre total de personnes de 65 ans et plus**	424
85	100	70	-	155	45	Nombre de personnes hors famille de recensement de 65 ans et plus	425
30	-	15	-	30	25	Vivant avec des personnes apparentées (44)	426
-	-	10	-	-	-	Vivant avec des personnes non apparentées uniquement	427
55	100	45	10	125	10	Vivant seules	428
190	205	215	15	145	165	Nombre de personnes membres d'une famille de 65 ans et plus	429
						CARACTÉRISTIQUES DES FAMILLES ÉCONOMIQUES	
1,760	**900**	**1,035**	**45**	**1,165**	**1,065**	**Nombre total de familles économiques dans les ménages privés**	430
						selon la taille de la famille	
560	425	495	20	510	365	2 personnes	431
490	175	165	-	305	240	3 personnes	432
510	215	230	20	250	275	4 personnes	433
200	85	145	-	95	190	5 personnes ou plus	434
5,705	2,660	3,185	130	3,475	3,530	Nombre total de personnes dans les familles économiques	435
3.2	3.0	3.1	3.4	3.0	3.3	Nombre moyen de personnes par famille économique	436
405	290	315	10	810	230	Nombre total de personnes hors famille économique	437
						CARACTÉRISTIQUES DU REVENU DE 2000	
						Population de 15 ans et plus selon le sexe et les tranches de revenu total en 2000	
5,050	2,305	2,770	XXX	3,560	2,910	Total - Les deux sexes	438
330	65	115		195	280	Sans revenu	439
4,720	2,240	2,655		3,365	2,630	Avec un revenu	440
320	50	70		140	135	Moins de 1 000 $ (45)	441
310	65	145		100	140	1 000 $ - 2 999 $	442
195	75	110		130	110	3 000 $ - 4 999 $	443
295	60	40		135	95	5 000 $ - 6 999 $	444
250	105	65		105	95	7 000 $ - 9 999 $	445
225	60	65		70	110	10 000 $ - 11 999 $	446
250	115	120		225	135	12 000 $ - 14 999 $	447
445	180	180		270	200	15 000 $ - 19 999 $	448
300	215	170		285	225	20 000 $ - 24 999 $	449
245	145	160		290	185	25 000 $ - 29 999 $	450
310	185	180		275	140	30 000 $ - 34 999 $	451
250	145	160		255	150	35 000 $ - 39 999 $	452
220	105	115		230	220	40 000 $ - 44 999 $	453
210	115	115		175	170	45 000 $ - 49 999 $	454
315	165	260		250	220	50 000 $ - 59 999 $	455
585	450	705		435	305	60 000 $ et plus	456
31,680	42,542	53,527		32,528	31,013	Revenu moyen $ (46)	457
21,053	30,213	35,893		28,513	26,884	Revenu médian $ (46)	458
1,128	2,424	2,950		903	1,091	Erreur type de revenu moyen $ (46)	459

Table 1. Selected Characteristics for Census Tracts, 2001 Census – 100% Data and 20% Sample Data

No.	Characteristics	Vancouver 0239	Vancouver 0240.01 A	Vancouver 0240.02 A	Vancouver 0241	Vancouver 0242	Vancouver 0243.01
	2000 INCOME CHARACTERISTICS						
	Population 15 years and over by sex and total income groups in 2000 – concluded						
460	Total - Males	3,285	1,550	2,120	2,975	2,985	2,545
461	Without income	175	60	95	120	145	190
462	With income	3,105	1,490	2,030	2,860	2,840	2,355
463	Under $1,000 (45)	155	95	145	165	120	170
464	$ 1,000 - $ 2,999	165	35	95	100	130	70
465	$ 3,000 - $ 4,999	100	10	45	85	85	85
466	$ 5,000 - $ 6,999	100	65	55	95	85	110
467	$ 7,000 - $ 9,999	90	110	95	140	150	180
468	$10,000 - $11,999	130	85	70	85	80	110
469	$12,000 - $14,999	180	55	155	105	120	150
470	$15,000 - $19,999	245	95	245	175	270	210
471	$20,000 - $24,999	245	95	170	250	250	185
472	$25,000 - $29,999	245	65	120	235	145	120
473	$30,000 - $34,999	215	150	150	145	205	130
474	$35,000 - $39,999	215	185	160	170	160	125
475	$40,000 - $44,999	200	105	185	215	170	160
476	$45,000 - $49,999	175	60	95	180	140	90
477	$50,000 - $59,999	290	120	135	245	220	185
478	$60,000 and over	365	170	105	470	520	275
479	Average income $ (46)	31,239	32,897	26,661	37,222	40,155	29,314
480	Median income $ (46)	26,919	31,115	23,961	29,372	29,103	22,019
481	Standard error of average income $ (46)	898	2,248	945	1,683	3,499	1,247
482	Total - Females	3,350	1,740	2,175	3,140	2,915	2,610
483	Without income	220	90	100	195	130	270
484	With income	3,135	1,640	2,075	2,945	2,785	2,335
485	Under $1,000 (45)	110	55	180	195	180	195
486	$ 1,000 - $ 2,999	200	75	130	130	185	115
487	$ 3,000 - $ 4,999	185	60	105	70	70	125
488	$ 5,000 - $ 6,999	145	75	80	145	75	145
489	$ 7,000 - $ 9,999	250	55	205	250	245	155
490	$10,000 - $11,999	145	125	65	155	140	140
491	$12,000 - $14,999	235	200	210	290	200	205
492	$15,000 - $19,999	360	165	235	280	245	225
493	$20,000 - $24,999	305	150	195	255	280	210
494	$25,000 - $29,999	230	125	200	170	245	225
495	$30,000 - $34,999	215	125	130	260	170	130
496	$35,000 - $39,999	185	110	110	215	135	100
497	$40,000 - $44,999	170	100	90	200	170	100
498	$45,000 - $49,999	70	65	35	115	115	85
499	$50,000 - $59,999	130	75	65	95	180	90
500	$60,000 and over	190	95	40	130	155	90
501	Average income $ (46)	23,317	25,065	19,578	23,955	25,239	21,982
502	Median income $ (46)	18,962	20,039	16,346	18,551	20,277	16,309
503	Standard error of average income $ (46)	697	991	736	882	890	983
	by composition of total income						
504	Total - Composition of income in 2000 % (47)	100.0	100.0	100.0	100.0	100.0	100.0
505	Employment income %	75.7	74.2	76.0	79.5	78.3	75.3
506	Government transfer payments %	11.1	12.9	15.1	10.0	9.4	11.4
507	Other %	13.2	12.9	8.9	10.5	12.2	13.3
	Population 15 years and over with employment income in 2000 by sex and work activity						
508	Both sexes with employment income (48)	4,485	2,180	2,790	4,225	3,995	3,155
509	Average employment income $	28,755	30,639	25,758	33,280	36,111	28,749
510	Standard error of average employment income $	674	1,564	724	951	2,457	1,051
511	Worked full year, full time (49)	2,330	1,105	1,285	2,180	1,970	1,370
512	Average employment income $	38,763	41,838	35,256	43,701	51,205	42,342
513	Standard error of average employment income $	857	2,601	1,082	1,470	4,780	1,597
514	Worked part year or part time (50)	2,055	975	1,400	2,000	1,890	1,690
515	Average employment income $	17,903	18,501	17,936	22,283	22,188	18,675
516	Standard error of average employment income $	849	1,118	776	989	1,147	1,176
517	Males with employment income (48)	2,310	1,180	1,445	2,210	2,125	1,580
518	Average employment income $	32,755	32,879	29,254	39,442	43,626	33,108
519	Standard error of average employment income $	999	2,687	1,055	1,528	4,511	1,611
520	Worked full year, full time (49)	1,350	565	770	1,205	1,175	740
521	Average employment income $	41,671	45,249	37,353	50,708	59,581	47,605
522	Standard error of average employment income $	1,194	4,878	1,405	2,264	7,979	2,610
523	Worked part year or part time (50)	925	525	625	980	880	775
524	Average employment income $	20,477	20,090	20,134	26,185	24,456	20,734
525	Standard error of average employment income $	1,367	1,680	1,272	1,632	1,509	1,394

Tableau 1. Certaines caractéristiques des secteurs de recensement, recensement de 2001 – Données intégrales et données-échantillon (20 %)

Vancouver 0243.02 ◆	Vancouver 0250.01 A	Vancouver 0250.02 A	Vancouver 0251	Vancouver 0260.02 A	Vancouver 0260.04 A	Caractéristiques	N°
						CARACTÉRISTIQUES DU REVENU DE 2000	
						Population de 15 ans et plus selon le sexe et les tranches de revenu total en 2000 – fin	
2,425	1,090	1,420	xxx	1,765	1,430	Total - Hommes	460
120	15	35		80	140	Sans revenu	461
2,305	1,075	1,385		1,690	1,290	Avec un revenu	462
165	15	20		55	50	Moins de 1 000 $ (45)	463
130	10	50		30	40	1 000 $ - 2 999 $	464
85	-	50		45	55	3 000 $ - 4 999 $	465
135	30	15		70	40	5 000 $ - 6 999 $	466
95	35	25		45	35	7 000 $ - 9 999 $	467
65	30	25		25	60	10 000 $ - 11 999 $	468
105	75	65		110	30	12 000 $ - 14 999 $	469
215	50	35		105	80	15 000 $ - 19 999 $	470
165	105	85		155	70	20 000 $ - 24 999 $	471
120	50	75		155	70	25 000 $ - 29 999 $	472
125	80	55		125	65	30 000 $ - 34 999 $	473
90	90	70		140	95	35 000 $ - 39 999 $	474
105	60	60		105	135	40 000 $ - 44 999 $	475
130	50	55		105	95	45 000 $ - 49 999 $	476
155	90	185		135	140	50 000 $ - 59 999 $	477
415	310	515		300	230	60 000 $ et plus	478
37,617	55,462	64,952		36,752	37,626	Revenu moyen $ (46)	479
24,490	36,881	49,961		32,100	36,419	Revenu médian $ (46)	480
1,831	4,509	4,559		1,385	1,831	Erreur type de revenu moyen $ (46)	481
2,625	1,210	1,345		1,795	1,480	Total - Femmes	482
210	45	80		115	140	Sans revenu	483
2,415	1,165	1,270		1,675	1,340	Avec un revenu	484
155	35	50		80	80	Moins de 1 000 $ (45)	485
180	60	95		70	100	1 000 $ - 2 999 $	486
110	75	60		85	65	3 000 $ - 4 999 $	487
160	30	20		65	50	5 000 $ - 6 999 $	488
155	70	35		60	60	7 000 $ - 9 999 $	489
160	30	35		45	45	10 000 $ - 11 999 $	490
140	45	55		115	100	12 000 $ - 14 999 $	491
220	135	145		165	125	15 000 $ - 19 999 $	492
140	115	85		130	155	20 000 $ - 24 999 $	493
125	90	85		135	115	25 000 $ - 29 999 $	494
185	105	120		150	75	30 000 $ - 34 999 $	495
160	55	90		115	50	35 000 $ - 39 999 $	496
115	45	60		125	80	40 000 $ - 44 999 $	497
80	60	65		70	75	45 000 $ - 49 999 $	498
160	70	75		115	85	50 000 $ - 59 999 $	499
170	145	195		140	70	60 000 $ et plus	500
26,011	30,606	41,063		28,276	24,667	Revenu moyen $ (46)	501
18,448	24,495	27,403		25,148	21,161	Revenu médian $ (46)	502
1,258	1,750	3,564		1,114	1,121	Erreur type de revenu moyen $ (46)	503
						selon la composition du revenu total	
100.0	100.0	100.0		100.0	100.0	Total - Composition du revenu en 2000 % (47)	504
86.1	72.8	85.8		86.8	86.3	Revenu d'emploi %	505
6.2	6.3	4.2		7.4	7.5	Transferts gouvernementaux %	506
7.7	20.8	10.0		5.7	6.2	Autre %	507
						Population de 15 ans et plus ayant un revenu d'emploi en 2000 selon le sexe et le travail	
3,765	1,740	2,140		2,750	2,195	Les deux sexes ayant un revenu d'emploi (48)	508
34,232	39,888	56,966		34,551	32,115	Revenu moyen d'emploi $	509
1,335	2,277	3,390		1,003	1,228	Erreur type de revenu moyen d'emploi $	510
1,685	840	1,175		1,535	1,050	Ayant travaillé toute l'année à plein temps (49)	511
54,319	51,081	72,696		44,570	44,972	Revenu moyen d'emploi $	512
2,743	2,904	4,835		1,262	1,949	Erreur type de revenu moyen d'emploi $	513
1,955	875	900		1,135	1,055	Ayant travaillé une partie de l'année ou à temps partiel (50)	514
18,547	29,734	28,789		22,337	19,954	Revenu moyen d'emploi $	515
953	3,373	2,484		1,309	1,171	Erreur type de revenu moyen d'emploi $	516
1,890	880	1,145		1,410	1,115	Hommes ayant un revenu d'emploi (48)	517
40,631	50,694	67,562		38,425	38,806	Revenu moyen d'emploi $	518
2,160	3,911	4,964		1,535	2,054	Erreur type de revenu moyen d'emploi $	519
890	525	775		815	615	Ayant travaillé toute l'année à plein temps (49)	520
64,905	56,633	83,260		48,284	51,762	Revenu moyen d'emploi $	521
4,398	4,098	6,697		1,896	2,906	Erreur type de revenu moyen d'emploi $	522
935	350	360		565	435	Ayant travaillé une partie de l'année ou à temps partiel (50)	523
19,441	42,135	33,949		25,969	21,507	Revenu moyen d'emploi $	524
1,112	7,362	4,732		2,133	2,032	Erreur type de revenu moyen d'emploi $	525

Table 1. Selected Characteristics for Census Tracts, 2001 Census – 100% Data and 20% Sample Data

No.	Characteristics	Vancouver 0239	Vancouver 0240.01 A	Vancouver 0240.02 A	Vancouver 0241	Vancouver 0242	Vancouver 0243.01
	2000 INCOME CHARACTERISTICS						
	Population 15 years and over with employment income in 2000 by sex and work activity – concluded						
526	Females with employment income (48)	2,175	1,005	1,350	2,015	1,875	1,575
527	Average employment income $	24,508	28,002	22,004	26,530	27,604	24,380
528	Standard error of average employment income $	861	1,335	950	1,010	1,163	1,308
529	Worked full year, full time (49)	980	540	510	975	795	630
530	Average employment income $	34,760	38,257	32,091	35,033	38,768	36,136
531	Standard error of average employment income $	1,155	1,703	1,661	1,563	1,297	1,473
532	Worked part year or part time (50)	1,130	445	775	1,020	1,010	910
533	Average employment income $	15,790	16,633	16,156	18,532	20,207	16,918
534	Standard error of average employment income $	1,051	1,382	941	1,102	1,687	1,818
	Census families by structure and family income groups in 2000						
535	Total - All census families	2,210	990	1,415	1,930	1,875	1,670
536	Under $10,000	170	15	135	105	70	115
537	$ 10,000 - $19,999	200	65	125	125	115	100
538	$ 20,000 - $29,999	145	60	145	120	230	220
539	$ 30,000 - $39,999	210	125	175	190	170	145
540	$ 40,000 - $49,999	285	100	185	220	185	205
541	$ 50,000 - $59,999	285	95	110	220	125	185
542	$ 60,000 - $69,999	210	135	155	115	210	105
543	$ 70,000 - $79,999	170	80	100	155	105	175
544	$ 80,000 - $89,999	115	90	120	165	140	110
545	$ 90,000 - $99,999	105	85	60	145	105	75
546	$100,000 and over	310	125	100	375	420	235
547	Average family income $	59,628	62,956	51,470	70,382	78,664	60,043
548	Median family income $	51,660	61,779	45,510	59,679	62,414	52,447
549	Standard error of average family income $	1,756	2,249	1,871	2,944	5,894	2,263
550	Total - All couple census families (51)	1,850	830	1,175	1,610	1,605	1,360
551	Under $10,000	115	15	70	55	60	85
552	$ 10,000 - $19,999	125	30	95	90	60	65
553	$ 20,000 - $29,999	115	65	105	75	180	140
554	$ 30,000 - $39,999	185	75	140	140	140	105
555	$ 40,000 - $49,999	225	75	145	175	145	140
556	$ 50,000 - $59,999	250	95	90	190	95	155
557	$ 60,000 - $69,999	180	115	140	90	195	100
558	$ 70,000 - $79,999	155	65	95	140	100	165
559	$ 80,000 - $89,999	110	90	120	155	145	105
560	$ 90,000 - $99,999	100	80	60	145	95	80
561	$100,000 and over	290	115	105	355	395	220
562	Average family income $	63,049	66,564	56,462	74,265	84,377	65,401
563	Median family income $	56,070	63,566	54,060	68,520	66,252	57,600
564	Standard error of average family income $	1,915	2,482	2,089	2,967	6,790	2,595
	Incidence of low income in 2000						
565	Total - Economic families	2,125	985	1,310	1,845	1,815	1,595
566	Low income	410	145	305	260	315	310
567	Incidence of low income in 2000 % (52)	19.4	14.7	23.2	14.2	17.4	19.4
568	Total - Unattached individuals 15 years and over	1,125	740	720	1,220	1,145	755
569	Low income	355	265	310	440	460	400
570	Incidence of low income in 2000 % (52)	31.8	35.5	42.8	35.9	40.1	52.5
571	Total - Population in private households	7,805	3,785	5,075	7,200	6,840	6,105
572	Low income	1,710	745	1,265	1,300	1,495	1,570
573	Incidence of low income in 2000 % (52)	21.9	19.7	24.9	18.0	21.9	25.8
	Private households by household income groups in 2000						
574	Total - All private households	3,020	1,620	1,855	2,825	2,735	2,080
575	Under $10,000	180	75	160	125	205	170
576	$ 10,000 - $19,999	370	220	240	325	290	200
577	$ 20,000 - $29,999	255	165	205	255	300	215
578	$ 30,000 - $39,999	375	195	210	360	300	235
579	$ 40,000 - $49,999	335	190	250	340	280	250
580	$ 50,000 - $59,999	365	180	175	300	210	165
581	$ 60,000 - $69,999	280	155	135	180	245	120
582	$ 70,000 - $79,999	190	100	75	165	150	200
583	$ 80,000 - $89,999	150	95	135	175	145	150
584	$ 90,000 - $99,999	110	80	95	140	115	105
585	$100,000 and over	395	170	175	455	495	275
586	Average household income $	56,299	55,444	51,042	62,654	67,376	57,885
587	Median household income $	49,474	47,561	43,390	49,981	49,534	48,201
588	Standard error of average household income $	1,500	2,508	1,761	2,279	4,240	2,062

Tableau 1. Certaines caractéristiques des secteurs de recensement, recensement de 2001 – Données intégrales et données-échantillon (20 %)

Vancouver 0243.02 ◆	Vancouver 0250.01 A	Vancouver 0250.02 A	Vancouver 0251	Vancouver 0260.02 A	Vancouver 0260.04 A	Caractéristiques	N°
						CARACTÉRISTIQUES DU REVENU DE 2000	
						Population de 15 ans et plus ayant un revenu d'emploi en 2000 selon le sexe et le travail – fin	
1,875	860	995	XXX	1,345	1,080	Femmes ayant un revenu d'emploi (48)	526
27,796	28,826	44,809		30,475	25,217	Revenu moyen d'emploi $	527
1,483	1,982	4,431		1,228	1,207	Erreur type de revenu moyen d'emploi $	528
790	320	395		720	430	Ayant travaillé toute l'année à plein temps (49)	529
42,395	41,923	52,196		40,404	35,341	Revenu moyen d'emploi $	530
2,750	3,492	5,107		1,546	1,840	Erreur type de revenu moyen d'emploi $	531
1,025	525	545		570	620	Ayant travaillé une partie de l'année ou à temps partiel (50)	532
17,731	21,362	25,386		18,754	18,860	Revenu moyen d'emploi $	533
1,534	2,146	2,716		1,475	1,396	Erreur type de revenu moyen d'emploi $	534
						Familles de recensement selon la structure et les tranches de revenu de la famille en 2000	
1,790	905	1,050		1,190	1,095	Total - Toutes les familles de recensement	535
110	10	25		45	75	Moins de 10 000 $	536
175	15	30		60	50	10 000 $ - 19 999 $	537
165	50	30		50	75	20 000 $ - 29 999 $	538
180	75	65		140	75	30 000 $ - 39 999 $	539
130	110	60		135	115	40 000 $ - 49 999 $	540
155	100	90		110	150	50 000 $ - 59 999 $	541
150	55	80		150	120	60 000 $ - 69 999 $	542
120	65	55		110	95	70 000 $ - 79 999 $	543
125	100	70		95	90	80 000 $ - 89 999 $	544
120	75	60		75	45	90 000 $ - 99 999 $	545
360	250	480		225	210	100 000 $ et plus	546
73,383	92,952	120,246		68,354	66,521	Revenu moyen des familles $	547
57,387	73,932	91,982		64,182	60,757	Revenu médian des familles $	548
3,750	5,836	8,138		2,375	2,665	Erreur type de revenu moyen des familles $	549
1,435	835	970		935	910	Total - Toutes les familles de recensement comptant un couple (51)	550
75	10	15		10	60	Moins de 10 000 $	551
85	15	30		40	25	10 000 $ - 19 999 $	552
140	30	25		15	45	20 000 $ - 29 999 $	553
115	60	55		95	50	30 000 $ - 39 999 $	554
115	95	35		90	90	40 000 $ - 49 999 $	555
105	80	75		95	120	50 000 $ - 59 999 $	556
140	55	80		130	115	60 000 $ - 69 999 $	557
105	60	55		110	80	70 000 $ - 79 999 $	558
120	105	70		75	75	80 000 $ - 89 999 $	559
100	75	60		65	50	90 000 $ - 99 999 $	560
340	240	465		210	210	100 000 $ et plus	561
81,220	97,457	125,707		74,664	71,983	Revenu moyen des familles $	562
63,776	81,588	95,268		68,783	64,721	Revenu médian des familles $	563
4,521	6,234	8,642		2,547	2,997	Erreur type de revenu moyen des familles $	564
						Fréquence des unités à faible revenu en 2000	
1,760	895	1,040		1,165	1,070	Total - Familles économiques	565
385	40	50		150	175	Faible revenu	566
22.0	4.1	4.9		12.8	16.4	Fréquence des unités à faible revenu en 2000 % (52)	567
410	290	305		810	215	Total - Personnes hors famille économique de 15 ans et plus	568
140	65	50		295	50	Faible revenu	569
34.6	23.9	15.4		37.1	23.5	Fréquence des unités à faible revenu en 2000 % (52)	570
6,110	2,950	3,490		4,285	3,740	Total - Population dans les ménages privés	571
1,410	170	175		740	620	Faible revenu	572
23.1	5.7	5.0		17.3	16.5	Fréquence des unités à faible revenu en 2000 % (52)	573
						Ménages privés selon les tranches de revenu du ménage en 2000	
2,070	1,150	1,235		1,825	1,220	Total - Tous les ménages privés	574
130	30	40		95	75	Moins de 10 000 $	575
225	75	60		215	60	10 000 $ - 19 999 $	576
160	65	50		135	115	20 000 $ - 29 999 $	577
240	105	90		210	95	30 000 $ - 39 999 $	578
170	140	70		195	115	40 000 $ - 49 999 $	579
205	115	130		155	190	50 000 $ - 59 999 $	580
165	80	85		220	105	60 000 $ - 69 999 $	581
130	75	50		140	105	70 000 $ - 79 999 $	582
130	100	70		120	75	80 000 $ - 89 999 $	583
125	90	60		85	60	90 000 $ - 99 999 $	584
385	275	535		250	235	100 000 $ et plus	585
69,989	82,837	114,662		59,530	66,717	Revenu moyen des ménages $	586
53,736	64,979	85,862		54,099	56,535	Revenu médian des ménages $	587
3,313	5,019	7,336		2,170	2,775	Erreur type de revenu moyen des ménages $	588

Table 1. Selected Characteristics for Census Tracts, 2001 Census – 100% Data and 20% Sample Data

No.	Characteristics	Vancouver 0260.05 A	Vancouver 0260.06 A	Vancouver 0260.07 A	Vancouver 0260.08 A	Vancouver 0280	Vancouver 0281.01
	POPULATION CHARACTERISTICS						
1	**Population, 1996 (1)**	**3,924**	**3,168**	**3,194**	**3,132**	**3,975**	**6,127**
2	**Population, 2001 (2)**	**3,966**	**3,882**	**3,913**	**3,989**	**4,021**	**6,417**
3	Population percentage change, 1996-2001	1.1	22.5	22.5	27.4	1.2	4.7
4	Land area in square kilometres, 2001	3.06	2.42	1.08	3.47	4.33	2.11
5	**Total population – 100% Data (3)**	**3,970**	**3,880**	**3,915**	**3,990**	**4,025**	**6,415**
	by sex and age groups						
6	Male	1,990	1,900	1,875	1,950	2,070	3,215
7	0-4 years	145	110	160	130	70	160
8	5-9 years	180	150	155	185	90	210
9	10-14 years	160	120	170	165	140	245
10	15-19 years	115	140	140	140	145	255
11	20-24 years	95	90	90	95	150	275
12	25-29 years	75	90	110	105	130	205
13	30-34 years	165	95	205	120	100	200
14	35-39 years	215	170	215	170	120	220
15	40-44 years	205	195	180	215	220	260
16	45-49 years	195	175	130	195	235	345
17	50-54 years	110	190	115	165	190	260
18	55-59 years	75	140	65	100	170	225
19	60-64 years	80	95	40	75	90	145
20	65-69 years	70	65	35	30	90	90
21	70-74 years	45	40	20	20	50	65
22	75-79 years	30	30	15	15	45	30
23	80-84 years	10	10	10	10	25	10
24	85 years and over	5	10	10	5	10	10
25	Female	1,975	1,980	2,040	2,040	1,955	3,200
26	0-4 years	140	100	140	130	60	150
27	5-9 years	175	130	150	145	110	180
28	10-14 years	130	110	140	155	130	235
29	15-19 years	115	140	130	170	165	280
30	20-24 years	80	115	90	120	135	255
31	25-29 years	75	95	150	110	85	200
32	30-34 years	165	130	235	170	90	210
33	35-39 years	235	195	205	210	140	225
34	40-44 years	220	195	230	255	205	340
35	45-49 years	165	205	180	185	230	305
36	50-54 years	120	195	130	140	195	300
37	55-59 years	105	130	75	100	130	170
38	60-64 years	75	90	35	65	95	125
39	65-69 years	60	50	30	35	55	85
40	70-74 years	55	40	30	20	50	55
41	75-79 years	35	30	25	20	45	40
42	80-84 years	15	15	30	5	30	25
43	85 years and over	10	15	40	-	20	20
44	**Total population 15 years and over**	**3,030**	**3,160**	**2,995**	**3,075**	**3,425**	**5,230**
	by legal marital status						
45	Never married (single)	800	785	910	825	1,260	1,665
46	Legally married (and not separated)	1,800	2,040	1,575	2,025	1,750	3,030
47	Separated, but still legally married	85	70	110	50	70	130
48	Divorced	235	185	275	115	190	245
49	Widowed	110	90	125	60	155	155
	by common-law status						
50	Not in a common-law relationship	2,845	2,985	2,750	2,965	3,315	4,975
51	In a common-law relationship	185	175	250	120	110	255
52	**Total population – 20% Sample Data (4)**	**3,965**	**3,875**	**3,835**	**3,990**	**3,310**	**6,415**
	by mother tongue						
53	Single responses	3,915	3,860	3,745	3,915	3,280	6,345
54	English	3,250	3,145	2,990	2,630	2,005	4,330
55	French	15	60	65	30	30	75
56	Non-official languages (5)	655	655	690	1,255	1,245	1,930
57	Chinese, n.o.s.	20	135	25	305	230	245
58	Cantonese	15	30	30	60	225	310
59	Punjabi	-	-	10	-	25	100
60	Mandarin	-	10	30	225	130	130
61	Tagalog (Pilipino)	40	20	80	30	-	45
62	Other languages (6)	570	465	520	635	630	1,105
63	Multiple responses	45	25	90	70	35	75
64	English and French	15	10	15	-	20	-
65	English and non-official language	30	10	75	75	15	65
66	French and non-official language	-	-	-	-	-	10
67	English, French and non-official language	-	-	-	-	-	-

See reference material at the end of the publication. – Voir les documents de référence à la fin de la publication.

Tableau 1. Certaines caractéristiques des secteurs de recensement, recensement de 2001 – Données intégrales et données-échantillon (20 %)

Vancouver 0281.02	Vancouver 0282	Vancouver 0283	Vancouver 0284.01	Vancouver 0284.02	Vancouver 0285.01	Caractéristiques	N°
						CARACTÉRISTIQUES DE LA POPULATION	
5,931	**6,942**	**6,022**	**6,489**	**6,005**	**3,067**	**Population, 1996 (1)**	1
6,000	**7,822**	**6,166**	**6,744**	**5,938**	**3,202**	**Population, 2001 (2)**	2
1.2	12.7	2.4	3.9	-1.1	4.4	Variation en pourcentage de la population, 1996-2001	3
2.60	2.76	2.20	2.13	2.10	0.64	Superficie des terres en kilomètres carrés, 2001	4
6,000	**7,820**	**6,165**	**6,745**	**5,935**	**3,200**	**Population totale – Données intégrales (3)**	5
						selon le sexe et les groupes d'âge	
3,025	3,820	2,995	3,370	2,980	1,595	Sexe masculin	6
155	255	195	190	160	70	0-4 ans	7
185	265	180	230	175	90	5-9 ans	8
210	255	140	230	190	75	10-14 ans	9
220	240	190	270	200	100	15-19 ans	10
210	220	235	320	255	100	20-24 ans	11
210	305	240	235	185	140	25-29 ans	12
215	340	305	210	235	170	30-34 ans	13
305	395	305	290	260	190	35-39 ans	14
225	370	250	295	270	175	40-44 ans	15
260	320	210	270	260	145	45-49 ans	16
220	225	210	220	220	100	50-54 ans	17
140	135	130	170	160	75	55-59 ans	18
145	150	110	110	110	55	60-64 ans	19
120	115	95	110	110	35	65-69 ans	20
90	100	80	100	85	30	70-74 ans	21
60	45	50	70	50	25	75-79 ans	22
25	50	40	35	35	15	80-84 ans	23
15	40	40	15	15	10	85 ans et plus	24
2,975	4,005	3,165	3,375	2,960	1,605	Sexe féminin	25
150	230	160	165	140	75	0-4 ans	26
175	250	150	195	160	75	5-9 ans	27
200	240	155	165	165	70	10-14 ans	28
190	220	185	245	200	80	15-19 ans	29
195	235	255	280	215	120	20-24 ans	30
195	310	265	270	190	145	25-29 ans	31
245	395	305	250	230	170	30-34 ans	32
275	380	275	275	250	155	35-39 ans	33
280	385	230	290	290	145	40-44 ans	34
245	290	220	275	250	115	45-49 ans	35
200	225	190	230	230	100	50-54 ans	36
150	170	140	165	160	80	55-59 ans	37
155	150	130	125	135	60	60-64 ans	38
105	115	90	135	110	60	65-69 ans	39
95	105	105	125	100	50	70-74 ans	40
75	85	105	85	75	45	75-79 ans	41
30	110	105	55	40	35	80-84 ans	42
20	110	110	40	25	15	85 ans et plus	43
4,925	**6,330**	**5,180**	**5,575**	**4,950**	**2,735**	**Population totale de 15 ans et plus**	44
						selon l'état matrimonial légal	
1,635	2,250	1,850	2,030	1,685	1,090	Célibataire (jamais marié(e))	45
2,450	2,855	2,345	2,715	2,490	915	Légalement marié(e) (et non séparé(e))	46
195	285	200	180	155	175	Séparé(e), mais toujours légalement marié(e)	47
405	580	420	385	400	385	Divorcé(e)	48
235	365	365	270	220	170	Veuf ou veuve	49
						selon l'union libre	
4,500	5,840	4,800	5,285	4,585	2,485	Ne vivant pas en union libre	50
425	495	380	295	365	255	Vivant en union libre	51
5,975	**7,650**	**5,910**	**6,735**	**5,930**	**3,190**	**Population totale – Données-échantillon (20 %) (4)**	52
						selon la langue maternelle	
5,925	7,570	5,830	6,595	5,865	3,110	Réponses uniques	53
4,600	5,150	3,570	3,390	3,825	1,975	Anglais	54
160	315	105	105	85	65	Français	55
1,170	2,100	2,150	3,100	1,955	1,075	Langues non officielles (5)	56
250	265	295	420	325	80	Chinois, n.d.a.	57
80	310	85	300	285	10	Cantonais	58
-	145	75	15	50	-	Pendjabi	59
85	115	95	315	65	95	Mandarin	60
50	175	75	50	60	95	Tagalog (pilipino)	61
700	1,100	1,525	2,000	1,170	785	Autres langues (6)	62
50	85	85	140	70	80	Réponses multiples	63
-	35	15	20	10	-	Anglais et français	64
40	35	70	125	55	80	Anglais et langue non officielle	65
-	10	-	-	-	-	Français et langue non officielle	66
-	-	-	-	10	-	Anglais, français et langue non officielle	67

See reference material at the end of the publication. – Voir les documents de référence à la fin de la publication.

Table 1. Selected Characteristics for Census Tracts, 2001 Census – 100% Data and 20% Sample Data

No.	Characteristics	Vancouver 0260.05 A	Vancouver 0260.06 A	Vancouver 0260.07 A	Vancouver 0260.08 A	Vancouver 0280	Vancouver 0281.01
	POPULATION CHARACTERISTICS						
	by home language						
68	Single responses	3,630	3,545	3,400	3,265	2,785	5,385
69	English	3,475	3,350	3,190	2,800	2,260	4,765
70	French	-	-	25	-	-	10
71	Non-official languages (5)	150	190	180	465	525	605
72	Cantonese	10	20	10	20	150	140
73	Chinese, n.o.s.	-	60	-	180	15	120
74	Punjabi	-	-	-	-	-	-
75	Mandarin	-	-	35	85	65	90
76	Korean	20	70	15	110	180	150
77	Other languages (6)	115	30	120	70	115	95
78	Multiple responses	335	335	440	725	525	1,030
79	English and French	40	45	-	25	10	30
80	English and non-official language	295	275	435	685	510	945
81	French and non-official language	-	-	-	15	-	-
82	English, French and non-official language	-	15	-	-	10	55
	by knowledge of official languages						
83	English only	3,640	3,560	3,550	3,580	2,995	5,850
84	French only	-	-	-	10	-	-
85	English and French	275	285	255	295	230	465
86	Neither English nor French	35	35	25	105	80	105
	by knowledge of non-official languages (5) (7)						
87	Cantonese	15	80	50	125	290	395
88	Chinese, n.o.s.	20	110	15	260	150	210
89	Punjabi	-	-	-	-	35	130
90	Mandarin	-	65	55	335	255	180
91	Hindi	10	15	35	85	10	225
92	German	60	85	65	60	50	230
93	Spanish	60	75	75	90	25	95
	by first official language spoken						
94	English	3,890	3,790	3,745	3,825	3,200	6,195
95	French	20	55	65	45	25	90
96	English and French	15	-	-	15	15	30
97	Neither English nor French	40	35	25	105	70	105
98	Official language minority - (number) (8)	30	60	65	50	30	105
99	Official language minority - (percentage) (8)	0.8	1.5	1.7	1.3	0.9	1.6
	by ethnic origin (9)						
100	English	1,420	1,405	1,350	1,110	750	1,855
101	Canadian	870	1,090	1,080	725	735	1,395
102	Chinese	75	295	210	810	830	785
103	Scottish	935	925	865	740	540	1,245
104	Irish	615	845	645	545	325	865
105	German	565	445	620	425	280	745
106	East Indian	85	65	60	105	85	455
107	French	400	355	385	215	180	500
108	Ukrainian	280	245	250	240	180	225
109	Italian	250	220	265	285	155	290
110	Dutch (Netherlands)	120	240	140	120	65	280
111	Filipino	75	25	170	50	10	115
112	Polish	125	215	125	155	105	195
113	Norwegian	205	135	160	85	60	225
114	North American Indian	35	30	115	35	20	100
	by Aboriginal identity						
115	Total Aboriginal identity population (10)	45	50	140	20	20	95
116	Total non-Aboriginal population	3,915	3,835	3,700	3,965	3,290	6,320
	by Aboriginal origin						
117	Total Aboriginal origins population (11)	70	75	175	35	25	140
118	Total non-Aboriginal population	3,890	3,800	3,655	3,955	3,285	6,275
	by Registered Indian status						
119	Registered Indian (12)	10	10	35	20	20	20
120	Not a Registered Indian	3,950	3,870	3,795	3,970	3,290	6,395

Tableau 1. Certaines caractéristiques des secteurs de recensement, recensement de 2001 – Données intégrales et données-échantillon (20 %)

Vancouver 0281.02	Vancouver 0282	Vancouver 0283	Vancouver 0284.01	Vancouver 0284.02	Vancouver 0285.01	Caractéristiques	N°
						CARACTÉRISTIQUES DE LA POPULATION	
						selon la langue parlée à la maison	
5,320	6,335	4,640	5,115	4,840	2,565	Réponses uniques	68
4,955	5,545	3,725	3,520	4,180	2,205	Anglais	69
20	45	10	10	25	15	Français	70
350	745	900	1,590	645	340	Langues non officielles (5)	71
45	155	65	200	245	10	Cantonais	72
65	85	120	145	105	45	Chinois, n.d.a.	73
-	15	10	-	30	-	Pendjabi	74
35	50	65	235	30	50	Mandarin	75
45	165	65	440	-	10	Coréen	76
160	270	580	565	235	230	Autres langues (6)	77
655	1,315	1,275	1,620	1,090	630	Réponses multiples	78
65	210	55	85	85	30	Anglais et français	79
540	1,080	1,170	1,525	985	595	Anglais et langue non officielle	80
40	-	15	-	10	-	Français et langue non officielle	81
15	25	40	10	10	-	Anglais, français et langue non officielle	82
						selon la connaissance des langues officielles	
5,425	6,575	5,200	5,790	5,285	2,945	Anglais seulement	83
35	10	-	-	15	-	Français seulement	84
415	905	515	455	455	170	Anglais et français	85
105	160	190	480	185	70	Ni l'anglais ni le français	86
						selon la connaissance des langues non officielles (5) (7)	
85	400	190	290	460	15	Cantonais	87
210	205	280	420	295	80	Chinois, n.d.a.	88
-	150	100	20	40	10	Pendjabi	89
165	210	140	540	215	100	Mandarin	90
70	70	105	15	65	10	Hindi	91
55	110	140	255	135	70	Allemand	92
65	190	145	175	225	60	Espagnol	93
						selon la première langue officielle parlée	
5,715	7,130	5,550	6,085	5,625	3,080	Anglais	94
145	290	115	100	75	55	Français	95
20	75	55	90	60	10	Anglais et français	96
95	160	190	465	175	50	Ni l'anglais ni le français	97
155	325	140	145	105	60	Minorité de langue officielle - (nombre) (8)	98
2.6	4.2	2.4	2.2	1.8	1.9	Minorité de langue officielle - (pourcentage) (8)	99
						selon l'origine ethnique (9)	
1,865	1,870	1,650	1,210	1,705	830	Anglais	100
1,590	1,870	1,265	1,010	1,420	835	Canadien	101
515	810	685	1,205	1,080	215	Chinois	102
1,375	1,310	865	895	900	405	Écossais	103
830	950	620	730	740	410	Irlandais	104
850	705	585	600	505	310	Allemand	105
120	335	265	25	235	10	Indien de l'Inde	106
625	1,045	695	465	460	275	Français	107
400	355	280	315	180	135	Ukrainien	108
295	400	290	555	505	35	Italien	109
255	205	225	185	195	90	Hollandais (Néerlandais)	110
105	370	150	135	65	185	Philippin	111
185	215	315	185	110	225	Polonais	112
185	125	190	150	90	60	Norvégien	113
125	175	140	150	90	95	Indien de l'Amérique du Nord	114
						selon l'identité autochtone	
90	135	90	130	45	45	Total de la population ayant une identité autochtone (10)	115
5,885	7,515	5,820	6,610	5,890	3,145	Total de la population non autochtone	116
						selon l'origine autochtone	
210	275	200	195	110	110	Total de la population ayant une origine autochtone (11)	117
5,770	7,375	5,710	6,535	5,825	3,085	Total de la population non autochtone	118
						selon le statut d'Indien inscrit	
35	45	40	70	30	25	Oui, Indien inscrit (12)	119
5,940	7,610	5,870	6,670	5,910	3,165	Non, pas un Indien inscrit	120

Table 1. Selected Characteristics for Census Tracts, 2001 Census – 100% Data and 20% Sample Data

No.	Characteristics	Vancouver 0260.05 A	Vancouver 0260.06 A	Vancouver 0260.07 A	Vancouver 0260.08 A	Vancouver 0280	Vancouver 0281.01
	POPULATION CHARACTERISTICS						
	by visible minority groups						
121	Total visible minority population	445	625	670	1,425	1,445	1,870
122	Chinese	70	240	195	770	810	760
123	South Asian	90	40	75	120	120	465
124	Black	20	45	20	30	35	40
125	Filipino	65	20	160	55	10	105
126	Latin American	30	10	30	35	-	15
127	Southeast Asian	20	-	10	10	35	75
128	Arab	10	40	10	65	10	35
129	West Asian	55	-	65	-	115	35
130	Korean	40	110	60	235	300	320
131	Japanese	25	40	40	70	10	10
132	Visible minority, n.i.e. (13)	10	25	-	-	-	-
133	Multiple visible minorities (14)	15	50	10	45	15	15
	by citizenship						
134	Canadian citizenship (15)	3,665	3,595	3,535	3,545	2,880	5,785
135	Citizenship other than Canadian	300	280	300	445	430	635
	by place of birth of respondent						
136	Non-immigrant population	3,090	2,905	2,910	2,420	1,985	4,420
137	Born in province of residence	2,205	2,015	2,135	1,850	1,450	3,360
138	Immigrant population (16)	825	935	885	1,550	1,310	1,905
139	United States	50	40	55	70	15	55
140	Central and South America	30	20	30	30	-	30
141	Caribbean and Bermuda	-	25	10	25	30	30
142	United Kingdom	130	150	120	160	45	160
143	Other Europe (17)	320	210	250	180	165	360
144	Africa	140	55	70	125	45	55
145	Asia and the Middle East	145	415	315	925	995	1,110
146	Oceania and other (18)	-	15	30	35	-	105
147	Non-permanent residents (19)	50	35	35	20	15	95
148	**Total immigrant population**	**820**	**930**	**890**	**1,545**	**1,310**	**1,900**
	by period of immigration						
149	Before 1961	110	165	55	55	90	210
150	1961-1970	115	140	85	100	70	265
151	1971-1980	105	180	135	325	210	365
152	1981-1990	115	205	215	330	175	335
153	1991-2001 (20)	380	245	395	735	770	730
154	1991-1995	160	85	205	290	320	415
155	1996-2001 (20)	220	165	185	445	445	310
	by age at immigration						
156	0-4 years	140	95	75	165	90	140
157	5-19 years	265	280	280	425	420	570
158	20 years and over	425	555	535	960	800	1,195
159	**Total population**	**3,960**	**3,875**	**3,835**	**3,985**	**3,310**	**6,415**
	by religion						
160	Catholic (21)	695	930	830	930	625	1,470
161	Protestant	1,285	1,270	1,135	1,050	935	1,790
162	Christian Orthodox	130	10	75	40	40	50
163	Christian, n.i.e. (22)	295	195	230	145	170	325
164	Muslim	140	55	55	80	155	80
165	Jewish	10	-	15	-	-	35
166	Buddhist	10	10	20	255	170	115
167	Hindu	-	-	35	75	30	125
168	Sikh	-	-	-	-	30	120
169	Eastern religions (23)	10	-	-	115	-	30
170	Other religions (24)	10	10	45	20	-	-
171	No religious affiliation (25)	1,395	1,400	1,385	1,260	1,155	2,275
172	**Total population 15 years and over**	**3,020**	**3,155**	**2,915**	**3,075**	**2,710**	**5,240**
	by generation status						
173	1st generation (26)	760	945	880	1,395	1,245	1,905
174	2nd generation (27)	830	810	635	680	615	1,270
175	3rd generation and over (28)	1,425	1,400	1,400	1,000	850	2,065
176	**Total population 1 year and over (29)**	**3,910**	**3,830**	**3,770**	**3,950**	**3,285**	**6,355**
	by place of residence 1 year ago (mobility)						
177	Non-movers	3,545	3,325	3,275	3,440	3,040	5,685
178	Movers	365	510	500	510	250	670
179	Non-migrants	105	245	150	175	110	250
180	Migrants	255	260	350	345	135	420
181	Internal migrants	225	250	345	310	95	340
182	Intraprovincial migrants	190	240	325	270	85	310
183	Interprovincial migrants	35	10	20	40	10	40
184	External migrants	35	10	-	30	40	75

Tableau 1. Certaines caractéristiques des secteurs de recensement, recensement de 2001 – Données intégrales et données-échantillon (20 %)

Vancouver 0281.02	Vancouver 0282	Vancouver 0283	Vancouver 0284.01	Vancouver 0284.02	Vancouver 0285.01	Caractéristiques	N°
						CARACTÉRISTIQUES DE LA POPULATION	
						selon les groupes de minorités visibles	
1,090	2,210	1,745	2,710	1,690	850	Total de la population des minorités visibles	121
550	760	665	1,150	955	200	Chinois	122
115	335	315	30	165	45	Sud-Asiatique	123
70	105	30	65	55	40	Noir	124
95	355	140	85	65	135	Philippin	125
10	100	45	70	110	45	Latino-Américain	126
65	85	55	85	110	80	Asiatique du Sud-Est	127
-	-	15	75	10	45	Arabe	128
70	190	350	355	40	145	Asiatique occidental	129
60	215	85	635	40	80	Coréen	130
55	10	40	120	90	30	Japonais	131
-	-	-	-	-	-	Minorité visible, n.i.a. (13)	132
-	55	10	35	50	10	Minorités visibles multiples (14)	133
						selon la citoyenneté	
5,520	6,980	4,875	5,020	5,340	2,775	Citoyenneté canadienne (15)	134
455	670	1,035	1,720	595	415	Citoyenneté autre que canadienne	135
						selon le lieu de naissance du répondant	
4,745	5,360	3,665	3,520	3,885	2,005	Population non immigrante	136
3,530	3,810	2,580	2,425	2,775	1,280	Née dans la province de résidence	137
1,205	2,215	2,105	2,980	2,010	1,145	Population immigrante (16)	138
35	70	35	55	45	35	États-Unis	139
15	85	50	75	125	40	Amérique centrale et du Sud	140
-	20	15	15	10	25	Caraïbes et Bermudes	141
170	195	155	115	160	125	Royaume-Uni	142
330	415	640	660	420	350	Autre Europe (17)	143
10	105	75	25	125	10	Afrique	144
625	1,290	1,120	2,005	1,070	555	Asie et Moyen-Orient	145
25	30	20	30	55	10	Océanie et autre (18)	146
20	75	140	235	40	40	Résidents non permanents (19)	147
1,210	**2,215**	**2,105**	**2,985**	**2,015**	**1,145**	**Population immigrante totale**	148
						selon la période d'immigration	
205	230	220	250	165	115	Avant 1961	149
100	140	120	145	200	100	1961-1970	150
230	390	240	175	365	100	1971-1980	151
200	420	405	335	515	270	1981-1990	152
470	1,035	1,125	2,080	760	565	1991-2001 (20)	153
125	540	280	580	370	190	1991-1995	154
340	490	845	1,505	395	375	1996-2001 (20)	155
						selon l'âge à l'immigration	
95	220	180	180	225	105	0-4 ans	156
365	695	520	945	505	325	5-19 ans	157
740	1,300	1,405	1,855	1,285	710	20 ans et plus	158
5,980	**7,650**	**5,910**	**6,735**	**5,930**	**3,190**	**Population totale**	159
						selon la religion	
1,240	2,175	1,370	1,705	1,420	740	Catholique (21)	160
1,765	1,620	1,300	1,440	1,450	775	Protestante	161
135	165	280	260	95	85	Orthodoxe chrétienne	162
235	320	300	475	560	215	Chrétiennes, n.i.a. (22)	163
110	230	420	275	120	215	Musulmane	164
10	-	30	25	-	-	Juive	165
120	220	65	220	160	60	Bouddhiste	166
95	60	40	-	25	10	Hindoue	167
-	105	105	10	40	-	Sikh	168
-	25	50	180	-	10	Religions orientales (23)	169
-	10	15	25	20	15	Autres religions (24)	170
2,270	2,735	1,935	2,120	2,040	1,080	Aucune appartenance religieuse (25)	171
4,895	**6,150**	**4,925**	**5,565**	**4,940**	**2,725**	**Population totale de 15 ans et plus**	172
						selon le statut des générations	
1,160	2,120	2,055	2,840	1,900	1,065	1re génération (26)	173
1,210	1,185	1,050	1,055	1,250	500	2e génération (27)	174
2,525	2,850	1,815	1,675	1,790	1,160	3e génération et plus (28)	175
5,915	**7,560**	**5,855**	**6,670**	**5,880**	**3,160**	**Population totale de 1 an et plus (29)**	176
						selon le lieu de résidence 1 an auparavant (mobilité)	
5,190	6,300	4,665	5,135	5,010	2,365	Personnes n'ayant pas déménagé	177
725	1,255	1,190	1,535	870	800	Personnes ayant déménagé	178
295	600	390	605	315	310	Non-migrants	179
430	660	800	930	550	485	Migrants	180
385	585	530	475	420	360	Migrants internes	181
325	555	490	410	400	310	Migrants infraprovinciaux	182
65	25	40	65	20	50	Migrants interprovinciaux	183
40	75	270	455	135	125	Migrants externes	184

Table 1. Selected Characteristics for Census Tracts, 2001 Census – 100% Data and 20% Sample Data

No.	Characteristics	Vancouver 0260.05 A	Vancouver 0260.06 A	Vancouver 0260.07 A	Vancouver 0260.08 A	Vancouver 0280	Vancouver 0281.01
	POPULATION CHARACTERISTICS						
185	**Total population 5 years and over (30)**	**3,670**	**3,670**	**3,535**	**3,725**	**3,210**	**6,105**
	by place of residence 5 years ago (mobility)						
186	Non-movers	2,190	1,910	1,765	2,125	2,125	4,045
187	Movers	1,480	1,755	1,765	1,595	1,085	2,060
188	Non-migrants	470	570	510	410	435	780
189	Migrants	1,005	1,180	1,255	1,190	655	1,275
190	Internal migrants	775	995	1,070	835	245	920
191	Intraprovincial migrants	675	850	910	735	220	745
192	Interprovincial migrants	100	145	160	100	30	175
193	External migrants	235	190	190	355	405	360
194	**Total population 15 to 24 years**	**395**	**490**	**450**	**525**	**530**	**1,080**
	by school attendance						
195	Not attending school	140	190	160	105	120	430
196	Attending school full time	220	260	250	375	375	575
197	Attending school part time	25	35	45	40	35	75
198	**Total population 15 years and over**	**3,020**	**3,160**	**2,910**	**3,075**	**2,710**	**5,240**
	by highest level of schooling						
199	Less than grade 9 (31)	85	55	40	70	25	170
200	Grades 9-13 without high school graduation certificate	595	460	390	475	460	995
201	Grades 9-13 with high school graduation certificate	365	385	370	260	355	595
202	Some postsecondary without degree, certificate or diploma (32)	370	495	455	440	365	860
203	Trades certificate or diploma (33)	420	245	320	255	185	625
204	College certificate or diploma (34)	540	560	650	490	425	945
205	University certificate below bachelor's degree	120	110	45	160	165	155
206	University with bachelor's degree or higher	530	845	635	925	730	890
	by combinations of unpaid work						
207	Males 15 years and over	1,490	1,525	1,355	1,465	1,290	2,585
208	Reported unpaid work (35)	1,360	1,455	1,225	1,350	1,145	2,295
209	Housework and child care and care or assistance to seniors	85	155	80	105	105	255
210	Housework and child care only	460	415	470	520	335	605
211	Housework and care or assistance to seniors only	95	130	80	85	95	100
212	Child care and care or assistance to seniors only	-	-	-	20	-	20
213	Housework only	690	725	590	585	590	1,285
214	Child care only	20	30	-	25	-	20
215	Care or assistance to seniors only	10	-	15	10	15	10
216	Females 15 years and over	1,530	1,635	1,555	1,610	1,415	2,650
217	Reported unpaid work (35)	1,470	1,520	1,480	1,530	1,290	2,430
218	Housework and child care and care or assistance to seniors	165	250	145	165	135	400
219	Housework and child care only	570	450	600	560	415	680
220	Housework and care or assistance to seniors only	155	195	130	130	115	215
221	Child care and care or assistance to seniors only	-	-	-	15	-	-
222	Housework only	565	615	595	640	615	1,105
223	Child care only	10	10	10	15	-	15
224	Care or assistance to seniors only	10	-	-	-	-	15
	by labour force activity						
225	Males 15 years and over	1,495	1,520	1,355	1,460	1,290	2,585
226	In the labour force	1,140	1,205	1,115	1,095	955	2,055
227	Employed	1,040	1,170	1,045	1,070	895	1,965
228	Unemployed	105	30	70	30	60	90
229	Not in the labour force	350	320	240	365	340	530
230	Participation rate	76.3	79.3	82.3	75.0	74.0	79.5
231	Employment rate	69.6	77.0	77.1	73.3	69.4	76.0
232	Unemployment rate	9.2	2.5	6.3	2.7	6.3	4.4
233	Females 15 years and over	1,530	1,635	1,560	1,610	1,420	2,650
234	In the labour force	980	1,145	1,180	985	925	1,745
235	Employed	925	1,090	1,125	935	845	1,650
236	Unemployed	50	55	55	55	80	90
237	Not in the labour force	550	485	375	625	490	910
238	Participation rate	64.1	70.0	75.6	61.2	65.1	65.8
239	Employment rate	60.5	66.7	72.1	58.1	59.5	62.3
240	Unemployment rate	5.1	4.8	4.7	5.6	8.6	5.2

Tableau 1. Certaines caractéristiques des secteurs de recensement, recensement de 2001 – Données intégrales et données-échantillon (20 %)

Vancouver 0281.02	Vancouver 0282	Vancouver 0283	Vancouver 0284.01	Vancouver 0284.02	Vancouver 0285.01	Caractéristiques	Nº
						CARACTÉRISTIQUES DE LA POPULATION	
5,670	**7,160**	**5,555**	**6,380**	**5,635**	**3,045**	**Population totale de 5 ans et plus (30) selon le lieu de résidence 5 ans auparavant (mobilité)**	185
3,340	3,495	2,355	2,540	3,115	1,120	Personnes n'ayant pas déménagé	186
2,325	3,660	3,200	3,840	2,520	1,925	Personnes ayant déménagé	187
960	1,620	1,035	1,190	825	535	Non-migrants	188
1,370	2,035	2,165	2,645	1,700	1,385	Migrants	189
1,070	1,665	1,370	1,135	1,280	955	Migrants internes	190
850	1,455	1,095	910	985	720	Migrants infraprovinciaux	191
215	210	270	220	290	230	Migrants interprovinciaux	192
300	375	795	1,510	420	435	Migrants externes	193
805	**895**	**865**	**1,120**	**870**	**405**	**Population totale de 15 à 24 ans selon la fréquentation scolaire**	194
275	350	355	295	280	130	Ne fréquentant pas l'école	195
425	455	395	755	495	230	Fréquentant l'école à plein temps	196
110	90	110	65	95	45	Fréquentant l'école à temps partiel	197
4,895	**6,150**	**4,925**	**5,565**	**4,940**	**2,725**	**Population totale de 15 ans et plus selon le plus haut niveau de scolarité atteint**	198
200	305	240	245	255	130	Niveau inférieur à la 9e année (31)	199
1,100	1,305	895	1,190	1,015	600	De la 9e à la 13e année sans certificat d'études secondaires	200
760	795	640	620	650	240	De la 9e à la 13e année avec certificat d'études secondaires	201
670	770	710	910	790	430	Études postsecondaires partielles sans grade, certificat ou diplôme (32)	202
655	665	675	550	575	385	Certificat ou diplôme d'une école de métiers (33)	203
760	1,285	695	800	830	525	Certificat ou diplôme collégial (34)	204
100	145	130	240	110	85	Certificat universitaire inférieur au baccalauréat	205
645	880	945	995	720	335	Études universitaires avec baccalauréat ou diplôme supérieur	206
						selon les combinaisons de travail non rémunéré	
2,455	2,985	2,425	2,730	2,450	1,355	Hommes de 15 ans et plus	207
2,170	2,660	2,100	2,520	2,200	1,215	Travail non rémunéré déclaré (35)	208
210	225	185	265	175	45	Travaux ménagers et soins aux enfants et soins ou aide aux personnes âgées	209
575	810	505	630	540	300	Travaux ménagers et soins aux enfants seulement	210
155	225	125	175	130	35	Travaux ménagers et soins ou aide aux personnes âgées seulement	211
10	10	-	-	-	10	Soins aux enfants et soins ou aide aux personnes âgées seulement	212
1,175	1,345	1,240	1,425	1,335	810	Travaux ménagers seulement	213
30	30	30	10	10	10	Soins aux enfants seulement	214
15	25	15	20	10	10	Soins ou aide aux personnes âgées seulement	215
2,440	3,160	2,505	2,840	2,490	1,365	Femmes de 15 ans et plus	216
2,320	2,965	2,320	2,695	2,300	1,245	Travail non rémunéré déclaré (35)	217
310	420	230	345	230	95	Travaux ménagers et soins aux enfants et soins ou aide aux personnes âgées	218
695	945	715	825	715	415	Travaux ménagers et soins aux enfants seulement	219
185	295	130	240	215	95	Travaux ménagers et soins ou aide aux personnes âgées seulement	220
-	10	-	-	10	10	Soins aux enfants et soins ou aide aux personnes âgées seulement	221
1,105	1,290	1,190	1,260	1,115	630	Travaux ménagers seulement	222
-	10	40	10	-	-	Soins aux enfants seulement	223
10	-	-	10	15	-	Soins ou aide aux personnes âgées seulement	224
						selon l'activité	
2,455	2,990	2,425	2,730	2,455	1,355	Hommes de 15 ans et plus	225
1,845	2,180	1,850	1,855	1,790	1,025	Population active	226
1,685	1,955	1,690	1,630	1,665	915	Personnes occupées	227
155	220	160	225	120	110	Chômeurs	228
610	805	575	875	665	335	Inactifs	229
75.2	72.9	76.3	67.9	72.9	75.6	Taux d'activité	230
68.6	65.4	69.7	59.7	67.8	67.5	Taux d'emploi	231
8.4	10.1	8.6	12.1	6.7	10.7	Taux de chômage	232
2,440	3,160	2,505	2,835	2,490	1,365	Femmes de 15 ans et plus	233
1,610	2,060	1,540	1,490	1,640	845	Population active	234
1,485	1,965	1,440	1,295	1,560	745	Personnes occupées	235
125	95	95	190	75	105	Chômeuses	236
830	1,100	970	1,350	850	520	Inactives	237
66.0	65.2	61.5	52.6	65.9	61.9	Taux d'activité	238
60.9	62.2	57.5	45.7	62.7	54.6	Taux d'emploi	239
7.8	4.6	6.2	12.8	4.6	12.4	Taux de chômage	240

Table 1. Selected Characteristics for Census Tracts, 2001 Census – 100% Data and 20% Sample Data

No.	Characteristics	Vancouver 0260.05 A	Vancouver 0260.06 A	Vancouver 0260.07 A	Vancouver 0260.08 A	Vancouver 0280	Vancouver 0281.01
	POPULATION CHARACTERISTICS						
	by labour force activity – concluded						
241	Both sexes - Participation rate	70.2	74.4	78.9	67.8	69.5	72.4
242	15-24 years	51.3	70.1	65.6	43.8	54.7	65.4
243	25 years and over	72.8	75.3	81.1	72.5	72.9	74.3
244	Both sexes - Employment rate	65.1	71.6	74.4	65.1	64.3	69.1
245	15-24 years	39.2	62.9	57.8	39.0	40.6	59.3
246	25 years and over	68.8	73.2	77.5	70.4	70.1	71.6
247	Both sexes - Unemployment rate	7.3	3.6	5.4	3.8	7.7	4.7
248	15-24 years	22.0	8.8	11.9	10.6	27.1	10.6
249	25 years and over	5.7	2.7	4.5	3.0	3.8	3.6
250	**Total labour force 15 years and over**	**2,120**	**2,350**	**2,295**	**2,085**	**1,880**	**3,800**
	by industry based on the 1997 NAICS						
251	Industry - Not applicable (36)	60	35	55	35	40	45
252	All industries (37)	2,065	2,315	2,245	2,045	1,845	3,750
253	11 Agriculture, forestry, fishing and hunting	10	-	-	-	10	30
254	21 Mining and oil and gas extraction	-	15	-	10	-	-
255	22 Utilities	40	25	45	25	20	40
256	23 Construction	150	85	135	95	50	245
257	31-33 Manufacturing	175	235	130	160	155	315
258	41 Wholesale trade	165	155	95	105	90	215
259	44-45 Retail trade	210	220	245	210	250	405
260	48-49 Transportation and warehousing	105	100	60	65	95	285
261	51 Information and cultural industries	165	90	185	110	125	130
262	52 Finance and insurance	80	115	140	220	140	225
263	53 Real estate and rental and leasing	40	100	-	50	25	90
264	54 Professional, scientific and technical services	160	195	180	195	160	270
265	55 Management of companies and enterprises	-	-	-	-	-	-
266	56 Administrative and support, waste management and remediation services	75	55	110	30	30	110
267	61 Educational services	120	290	210	240	250	270
268	62 Health care and social assistance	200	225	245	230	175	430
269	71 Arts, entertainment and recreation	40	50	35	85	35	110
270	72 Accommodation and food services	70	115	130	65	65	225
271	81 Other services (except public administration)	125	85	115	50	70	195
272	91 Public administration	135	140	165	115	100	140
	by class of worker						
273	Class of worker - Not applicable (36)	60	35	50	35	35	50
274	All classes of worker (37)	2,065	2,315	2,240	2,050	1,840	3,750
275	Paid workers	1,910	2,120	2,050	1,925	1,720	3,525
276	Employees	1,865	1,970	1,980	1,785	1,590	3,315
277	Self-employed (incorporated)	40	150	70	135	130	215
278	Self-employed (unincorporated)	145	155	180	120	115	215
279	Unpaid family workers	10	40	10	-	10	15
	by occupation based on the 2001 NOC-S						
280	Male labour force 15 years and over	1,140	1,200	1,115	1,100	955	2,055
281	Occupation - Not applicable (36)	40	10	25	10	10	15
282	All occupations (37)	1,100	1,195	1,090	1,085	945	2,040
283	A Management occupations	120	285	140	235	230	385
284	B Business, finance and administration occupations	145	110	115	215	180	265
285	C Natural and applied sciences and related occupations	165	150	135	120	105	175
286	D Health occupations	15	10	30	65	25	95
287	E Occupations in social science, education, government service and religion	45	105	80	85	50	65
288	F Occupations in art, culture, recreation and sport	25	50	55	20	55	30
289	G Sales and service occupations	235	265	250	175	160	405
290	H Trades, transport and equipment operators and related occupations	300	175	210	130	80	470
291	I Occupations unique to primary industry	10	15	10	10	-	40
292	J Occupations unique to processing, manufacturing and utilities	45	30	50	25	60	115
293	Female labour force 15 years and over	980	1,150	1,180	985	925	1,745
294	Occupation - Not applicable (36)	20	30	25	25	25	30
295	All occupations (37)	965	1,125	1,155	965	900	1,710
296	A Management occupations	110	135	125	80	60	140
297	B Business, finance and administration occupations	360	310	425	405	285	585
298	C Natural and applied sciences and related occupations	35	50	20	10	40	45
299	D Health occupations	80	105	105	80	95	230

Tableau 1. Certaines caractéristiques des secteurs de recensement, recensement de 2001 – Données intégrales et données-échantillon (20 %)

Vancouver 0281.02	Vancouver 0282	Vancouver 0283	Vancouver 0284.01	Vancouver 0284.02	Vancouver 0285.01	Caractéristiques	Nº
						CARACTÉRISTIQUES DE LA POPULATION	
						selon l'activité – fin	
70.5	68.9	68.8	60.0	69.3	68.6	Les deux sexes - Taux d'activité	241
64.0	59.2	62.4	49.3	62.1	56.8	15-24 ans	242
71.8	70.7	70.2	62.8	70.9	70.5	25 ans et plus	243
64.8	63.8	63.5	52.5	65.3	60.7	Les deux sexes - Taux d'emploi	244
57.1	50.8	54.9	38.8	51.4	51.9	15-24 ans	245
66.1	66.0	65.3	56.0	68.2	62.3	25 ans et plus	246
8.1	7.5	7.7	12.6	5.7	11.2	Les deux sexes - Taux de chômage	247
10.7	14.2	11.2	20.7	15.9	8.7	15-24 ans	248
7.7	6.6	6.8	10.6	3.8	11.9	25 ans et plus	249
3,450	**4,240**	**3,385**	**3,340**	**3,425**	**1,865**	**Population active totale de 15 ans et plus**	250
						selon l'industrie basée sur le SCIAN de 1997	
85	95	85	125	50	70	Industrie - Sans objet (36)	251
3,365	4,145	3,305	3,215	3,380	1,800	Toutes les industries (37)	252
-	35	10	15	15	-	11 Agriculture, foresterie, pêche et chasse	253
-	-	-	-	10	-	21 Extraction minière et extraction de pétrole et de gaz	254
30	65	25	10	10	10	22 Services publics	255
300	265	250	270	240	170	23 Construction	256
350	400	350	415	275	160	31-33 Fabrication	257
315	330	190	205	280	80	41 Commerce de gros	258
370	620	395	375	385	235	44-45 Commerce de détail	259
245	300	225	140	185	105	48-49 Transport et entreposage	260
185	165	110	130	195	100	51 Industrie de l'information et industrie culturelle	261
95	160	95	115	170	70	52 Finance et assurances	262
80	100	80	90	35	75	53 Services immobiliers et services de location et de location à bail	263
165	185	280	215	220	95	54 Services professionnels, scientifiques et techniques	264
-	15	-	-	-	-	55 Gestion de sociétés et d'entreprises	265
135	170	180	145	90	60	56 Services administratifs, services de soutien, services de gestion des déchets et services d'assainissement	266
260	260	180	145	310	110	61 Services d'enseignement	267
365	465	340	335	280	140	62 Soins de santé et assistance sociale	268
45	60	70	65	70	50	71 Arts, spectacles et loisirs	269
155	190	195	325	230	125	72 Hébergement et services de restauration	270
90	195	185	135	185	130	81 Autres services, sauf les administrations publiques	271
175	160	135	80	180	80	91 Administrations publiques	272
						selon la catégorie de travailleurs	
80	95	80	125	45	70	Catégorie de travailleurs - Sans objet (36)	273
3,370	4,145	3,305	3,215	3,375	1,800	Toutes les catégories de travailleurs (37)	274
3,120	3,870	3,065	2,970	3,150	1,680	Travailleurs rémunérés	275
2,990	3,755	2,995	2,805	3,085	1,670	Employés	276
130	115	70	170	70	15	Travailleurs autonomes (entreprise constituée en société)	277
240	275	235	220	230	115	Travailleurs autonomes (entreprise non constituée en société)	278
10	-	-	25	-	-	Travailleurs familiaux non rémunérés	279
						selon la profession basée sur la CNP-S de 2001	
1,840	2,180	1,850	1,850	1,790	1,020	Hommes actifs de 15 ans et plus	280
25	45	30	55	20	25	Profession - Sans objet (36)	281
1,820	2,135	1,820	1,795	1,765	1,000	Toutes les professions (37)	282
220	250	175	220	245	35	A Gestion	283
150	210	185	205	150	85	B Affaires, finance et administration	284
160	240	175	165	205	85	C Sciences naturelles et appliquées et professions apparentées	285
20	50	35	45	20	20	D Secteur de la santé	286
75	70	125	85	140	75	E Sciences sociales, enseignement, administration publique et religion	287
20	30	65	95	85	35	F Arts, culture, sports et loisirs	288
410	445	340	355	350	210	G Ventes et services	289
650	680	540	450	405	370	H Métiers, transport et machinerie	290
20	40	50	40	55	15	I Professions propres au secteur primaire	291
90	120	130	120	110	65	J Transformation, fabrication et services d'utilité publique	292
1,610	2,060	1,540	1,485	1,640	845	Femmes actives de 15 ans et plus	293
55	50	50	65	30	45	Profession - Sans objet (36)	294
1,550	2,015	1,485	1,420	1,610	800	Toutes les professions (37)	295
110	115	130	75	115	45	A Gestion	296
465	640	545	430	495	305	B Affaires, finance et administration	297
65	65	25	60	25	20	C Sciences naturelles et appliquées et professions apparentées	298
120	185	90	80	100	45	D Secteur de la santé	299

Table 1. Selected Characteristics for Census Tracts, 2001 Census – 100% Data and 20% Sample Data

No.	Characteristics	Vancouver 0260.05 A	Vancouver 0260.06 A	Vancouver 0260.07 A	Vancouver 0260.08 A	Vancouver 0280	Vancouver 0281.01
	POPULATION CHARACTERISTICS						
	by occupation based on the 2001 NOC-S – concluded						
300	E Occupations in social science, education, government service and religion	135	170	95	170	135	195
301	F Occupations in art, culture, recreation and sport	35	50	35	30	30	45
302	G Sales and service occupations	195	265	325	175	225	395
303	H Trades, transport and equipment operators and related occupations	15	25	-	10	-	25
304	I Occupations unique to primary industry	-	-	-	-	-	10
305	J Occupations unique to processing, manufacturing and utilities	-	15	15	-	10	45
306	**Total employed labour force 15 years and over**	**1,965**	**2,265**	**2,175**	**2,005**	**1,735**	**3,620**
	by place of work						
307	Males	1,045	1,170	1,050	1,070	890	1,960
308	Usual place of work	800	915	785	865	755	1,560
309	At home	45	130	80	85	30	110
310	Outside Canada	15	-	-	15	10	25
311	No fixed workplace address	185	130	175	105	90	265
312	Females	925	1,090	1,125	930	840	1,650
313	Usual place of work	800	955	990	835	730	1,460
314	At home	60	100	75	90	45	140
315	Outside Canada	-	10	-	-	20	-
316	No fixed workplace address	60	35	55	-	50	45
317	**Total employed labour force 15 years and over with usual place of work or no fixed workplace address**	**1,850**	**2,030**	**2,010**	**1,815**	**1,625**	**3,330**
	by mode of transportation						
318	Males	985	1,045	965	970	850	1,825
319	Car, truck, van, as driver	890	970	785	885	740	1,585
320	Car, truck, van, as passenger	30	30	55	30	35	85
321	Public transit	35	40	80	45	40	105
322	Walked	10	-	40	-	15	10
323	Other method	25	10	-	10	15	40
324	Females	860	990	1,045	840	775	1,510
325	Car, truck, van, as driver	670	830	725	685	630	1,180
326	Car, truck, van, as passenger	70	60	110	50	80	160
327	Public transit	95	75	155	100	50	150
328	Walked	20	15	45	10	20	15
329	Other method	10	-	15	-	-	-
330	**Total population 15 years and over who worked since January 1, 2000**	**2,250**	**2,540**	**2,410**	**2,255**	**2,020**	**4,050**
	by language used at work						
331	Single responses	2,190	2,350	2,290	2,025	1,860	3,765
332	English	2,175	2,330	2,265	1,970	1,825	3,745
333	French	-	-	-	-	10	-
334	Non-official languages (5)	15	25	20	60	30	25
335	Chinese, n.o.s.	-	20	-	20	-	-
336	Cantonese	-	-	10	-	10	10
337	Other languages (6)	15	10	10	35	20	20
338	Multiple responses	60	185	120	230	155	280
339	English and French	30	20	40	30	-	10
340	English and non-official language	30	160	80	200	155	250
341	French and non-official language	-	-	-	-	-	-
342	English, French and non-official language	-	-	-	-	-	25
	DWELLING AND HOUSEHOLD CHARACTERISTICS						
343	**Total number of occupied private dwellings**	**1,445**	**1,360**	**1,445**	**1,240**	**1,050**	**2,065**
	by tenure						
344	Owned	1,065	1,235	1,180	1,125	970	1,730
345	Rented	380	125	265	120	75	335
346	Band housing	-	-	-	-	-	-
	by structural type of dwelling						
347	Single-detached house	700	870	305	775	755	1,410
348	Semi-detached house	10	185	-	35	40	105
349	Row house	300	125	510	195	85	100
350	Apartment, detached duplex	50	175	30	200	135	370
351	Apartment, building that has five or more storeys	-	-	115	-	-	-
352	Apartment, building that has fewer than five storeys (38)	385	-	490	25	30	80
353	Other single-attached house	-	-	-	-	-	-
354	Movable dwelling (39)	-	-	-	-	10	-

Tableau 1. Certaines caractéristiques des secteurs de recensement, recensement de 2001 – Données intégrales et données-échantillon (20 %)

Vancouver 0281.02	Vancouver 0282	Vancouver 0283	Vancouver 0284.01	Vancouver 0284.02	Vancouver 0285.01	Caractéristiques	N°
						CARACTÉRISTIQUES DE LA POPULATION	
						selon la profession basée sur la CNP-S de 2001 – fin	
270	295	170	115	240	55	E Sciences sociales, enseignement, administration publique et religion	300
70	65	35	45	55	20	F Arts, culture, sports et loisirs	301
400	515	410	520	465	235	G Ventes et services	302
15	85	45	30	45	25	H Métiers, transport et machinerie	303
-	10	-	-	10	20	I Professions propres au secteur primaire	304
35	40	40	70	60	25	J Transformation, fabrication et services d'utilité publique	305
3,170	**3,925**	**3,130**	**2,920**	**3,225**	**1,655**	**Population active occupée totale de 15 ans et plus**	306
						selon le lieu de travail	
1,685	1,955	1,690	1,630	1,670	910	Hommes	307
1,315	1,615	1,290	1,290	1,200	680	Lieu habituel de travail	308
45	80	75	95	110	40	À domicile	309
-	-	35	25	25	10	En dehors du Canada	310
325	260	295	225	335	195	Sans adresse de travail fixe	311
1,485	1,965	1,440	1,295	1,560	745	Femmes	312
1,270	1,755	1,240	1,155	1,395	695	Lieu habituel de travail	313
120	100	105	55	100	15	À domicile	314
-	10	20	20	20	-	En dehors du Canada	315
85	110	75	65	45	35	Sans adresse de travail fixe	316
2,995	**3,740**	**2,900**	**2,730**	**2,970**	**1,595**	**Population active occupée totale de 15 ans et plus ayant un lieu habituel de travail ou sans adresse de travail fixe**	317
						selon le mode de transport	
1,635	1,875	1,585	1,515	1,535	870	Hommes	318
1,420	1,625	1,220	1,180	1,245	670	Automobile, camion ou fourgonnette, en tant que conducteur	319
70	80	95	80	105	15	Automobile, camion ou fourgonnette, en tant que passager	320
50	60	155	160	110	85	Transport en commun	321
50	70	60	75	30	85	À pied	322
45	45	45	15	40	15	Autre moyen	323
1,360	1,865	1,310	1,220	1,445	730	Femmes	324
985	1,390	870	715	1,045	420	Automobile, camion ou fourgonnette, en tant que conductrice	325
190	210	140	180	120	125	Automobile, camion ou fourgonnette, en tant que passagère	326
120	170	195	195	205	100	Transport en commun	327
45	80	100	100	75	70	À pied	328
20	-	10	30	-	15	Autre moyen	329
3,615	**4,500**	**3,600**	**3,655**	**3,660**	**1,925**	**Population totale de 15 ans et plus ayant travaillé depuis le 1er janvier 2000**	330
						selon la langue utilisée au travail	
3,455	4,110	3,340	3,080	3,295	1,795	Réponses uniques	331
3,410	4,050	3,240	2,905	3,205	1,735	Anglais	332
-	-	10	-	-	15	Français	333
50	65	95	175	85	50	Langues non officielles (5)	334
10	20	25	30	30	30	Chinois, n.d.a.	335
-	-	10	20	25	15	Cantonais	336
50	35	70	125	30	-	Autres langues (6)	337
160	390	260	580	365	130	Réponses multiples	338
25	110	30	60	40	50	Anglais et français	339
135	255	230	515	315	75	Anglais et langue non officielle	340
-	-	-	-	-	-	Français et langue non officielle	341
-	20	-	10	10	10	Anglais, français et langue non officielle	342
						CARACTÉRISTIQUES DES LOGEMENTS ET DES MÉNAGES	
2,315	**3,030**	**2,490**	**2,685**	**2,335**	**1,705**	**Nombre total de logements privés occupés**	343
						selon le mode d'occupation	
1,660	1,840	1,170	1,280	1,485	490	Possédé	344
650	1,190	1,315	1,410	850	1,215	Loué	345
-	-	-	-	-	-	Logement de bande	346
						selon le type de construction résidentielle	
1,555	1,040	980	725	1,195	155	Maison individuelle non attenante	347
40	260	150	25	230	10	Maison jumelée	348
170	405	15	20	50	70	Maison en rangée	349
285	245	165	140	195	15	Appartement, duplex non attenant	350
-	10	335	260	135	10	Appartement, immeuble de cinq étages ou plus	351
260	870	820	1,525	520	1,440	Appartement, immeuble de moins de cinq étages (38)	352
-	-	-	-	10	-	Autre maison individuelle attenante	353
10	205	15	-	-	-	Logement mobile (39)	354

Table 1. Selected Characteristics for Census Tracts, 2001 Census – 100% Data and 20% Sample Data

No.	Characteristics	Vancouver 0260.05 A	Vancouver 0260.06 A	Vancouver 0260.07 A	Vancouver 0260.08 A	Vancouver 0280	Vancouver 0281.01
	DWELLING AND HOUSEHOLD CHARACTERISTICS						
	by condition of dwelling						
355	Regular maintenance only	975	1,075	935	1,045	690	1,340
356	Minor repairs	390	210	260	165	310	595
357	Major repairs	75	70	245	30	45	130
	by period of construction						
358	Before 1946	35	35	10	10	-	-
359	1946-1960	315	75	-	-	-	75
360	1961-1970	550	90	10	10	-	365
361	1971-1980	435	375	465	35	10	485
362	1981-1990	50	155	495	395	865	750
363	1991-2001 (20)	60	630	460	805	170	380
364	Average number of rooms per dwelling	6.7	8.2	6.1	8.3	8.2	8.0
365	Average number of bedrooms per dwelling	2.9	3.4	2.6	3.5	3.5	3.4
366	Average value of dwelling $	222,688	344,310	183,104	331,835	320,056	303,267
367	**Total number of private households**	**1,445**	**1,360**	**1,440**	**1,240**	**1,050**	**2,065**
	by household size						
368	1 person	270	155	295	120	100	250
369	2 persons	480	505	460	315	310	580
370	3 persons	245	270	280	255	175	395
371	4-5 persons	420	390	380	495	425	735
372	6 or more persons	25	35	20	55	40	105
	by household type						
373	One-family households	1,125	1,155	1,090	1,030	910	1,690
374	Multiple-family households	10	20	15	60	30	65
375	Non-family households	310	185	340	150	110	315
376	Number of persons in private households	3,940	3,875	3,835	3,985	3,305	6,415
377	Average number of persons in private households	2.7	2.8	2.7	3.2	3.2	3.1
378	Average number of persons per room	0.4	0.3	0.4	0.4	0.4	0.4
379	Tenant households in non-farm, non-reserve private dwellings (40)	385	125	260	105	75	340
380	Average gross rent $ (40)	784	963	919	958	1,112	941
381	Tenant households spending 30% or more of household income on gross rent (40) (41)	100	60	100	30	35	125
382	Tenant households spending from 30% to 99% of household income on gross rent (40) (41)	95	45	75	15	30	110
383	Owner households in non-farm, non-reserve private dwellings (42)	1,060	1,230	1,180	1,125	965	1,725
384	Average owner's major payments $ (42)	1,005	1,395	1,086	1,266	1,090	1,166
385	Owner households spending 30% or more of household income on owner's major payments (41) (42)	150	285	225	260	175	400
386	Owner households spending from 30% to 99% of household income on owner's major payments (41) (42)	140	235	180	235	150	345
	CENSUS FAMILY CHARACTERISTICS						
387	**Total number of census families in private households**	**1,150**	**1,195**	**1,115**	**1,160**	**965**	**1,825**
	by census family structure and size						
388	Total couple families	990	1,100	895	1,060	875	1,640
389	Total families of married couples	895	1,015	765	1,010	820	1,505
390	Without children at home	325	395	255	300	250	505
391	With children at home	575	615	510	705	565	1,000
392	1 child	190	210	190	220	145	335
393	2 children	290	300	240	345	315	450
394	3 or more children	100	105	70	140	110	215
395	Total families of common-law couples	95	90	130	55	55	135
396	Without children at home	70	55	90	30	40	80
397	With children at home	25	40	45	20	15	60
398	1 child	15	35	25	10	15	30
399	2 children	10	-	10	10	-	20
400	3 or more children	-	-	15	10	-	10
401	Total lone-parent families	165	90	215	95	95	190
402	Female parent	150	70	170	75	55	150
403	1 child	90	40	80	50	45	70
404	2 children	40	35	55	30	10	50
405	3 or more children	20	-	40	-	-	35

Tableau 1. Certaines caractéristiques des secteurs de recensement, recensement de 2001 – Données intégrales et données-échantillon (20 %)

Vancouver 0281.02	Vancouver 0282	Vancouver 0283	Vancouver 0284.01	Vancouver 0284.02	Vancouver 0285.01	Caractéristiques	N°
						CARACTÉRISTIQUES DES LOGEMENTS ET DES MÉNAGES	
						selon l'état du logement	
1,380	1,960	1,670	1,725	1,555	1,200	Entretien régulier seulement	355
715	735	610	590	620	435	Réparations mineures	356
215	340	205	375	155	75	Réparations majeures	357
						selon la période de construction	
60	310	145	25	95	40	Avant 1946	358
420	505	510	290	335	130	1946-1960	359
770	515	530	650	825	545	1961-1970	360
500	325	685	815	520	665	1971-1980	361
160	635	370	580	290	275	1981-1990	362
400	730	245	325	270	45	1991-2001 (20)	363
6.7	5.7	5.5	5.4	6.3	4.1	Nombre moyen de pièces par logement	364
2.8	2.5	2.3	2.2	2.7	1.5	Nombre moyen de chambres à coucher par logement	365
210,105	190,797	244,682	237,938	239,130	158,029	Valeur moyenne du logement $	366
2,315	**3,030**	**2,490**	**2,690**	**2,335**	**1,705**	**Nombre total de logements privés**	367
						selon la taille du ménage	
540	780	775	750	605	845	1 personne	368
755	995	790	825	780	485	2 personnes	369
420	565	400	465	365	185	3 personnes	370
545	580	460	565	505	170	4-5 personnes	371
55	105	65	80	75	10	6 personnes ou plus	372
						selon le genre de ménage	
1,625	1,960	1,460	1,750	1,555	765	Ménages unifamiliaux	373
50	85	55	20	60	10	Ménages multifamiliaux	374
640	990	970	910	715	935	Ménages non familiaux	375
5,980	7,650	5,905	6,735	5,925	3,190	Nombre de personnes dans les ménages privés	376
2.6	2.5	2.4	2.5	2.5	1.9	Nombre moyen de personnes dans les ménages privés	377
0.4	0.4	0.4	0.5	0.4	0.5	Nombre moyen de personnes par pièce	378
655	1,185	1,290	1,385	825	1,200	Ménages locataires dans les logements privés non agricoles hors réserve (40)	379
835	759	741	752	834	638	Loyer brut moyen $ (40)	380
245	460	560	695	265	555	Ménages locataires consacrant 30 % ou plus du revenu du ménage au loyer brut (40) (41)	381
175	395	450	495	235	375	Ménages locataires consacrant de 30 % à 99 % du revenu du ménage au loyer brut (40) (41)	382
1,665	1,840	1,175	1,285	1,475	480	Ménages propriétaires dans les logements privés non agricoles hors réserve (42)	383
898	1,006	917	841	834	793	Principales dépenses de propriété moyennes $ (42)	384
310	410	265	260	235	85	Ménages propriétaires consacrant 30 % ou plus du revenu du ménage aux principales dépenses de propriété (41) (42)	385
280	365	235	205	200	55	Ménages propriétaires consacrant de 30 % à 99 % du revenu du ménage aux principales dépenses de propriété (41) (42)	386
						CARACTÉRISTIQUES DES FAMILLES DE RECENSEMENT	
1,725	**2,135**	**1,595**	**1,800**	**1,680**	**775**	**Total des familles de recensement dans les ménages privés**	387
						selon la structure et la taille de la famille de recensement	
1,440	1,655	1,320	1,485	1,415	565	Total des familles avec conjoints	388
1,215	1,410	1,135	1,335	1,230	445	Total des familles avec couples mariés	389
500	545	445	465	505	195	Sans enfants à la maison	390
720	865	690	875	725	250	Avec enfants à la maison	391
245	360	285	340	270	115	1 enfant	392
340	380	295	380	360	100	2 enfants	393
130	135	115	150	90	35	3 enfants ou plus	394
225	245	180	150	180	120	Total des familles en union libre	395
135	150	135	105	120	105	Sans enfants à la maison	396
90	95	50	45	60	20	Avec enfants à la maison	397
60	40	35	10	15	15	1 enfant	398
30	40	15	30	50	-	2 enfants	399
-	10	-	-	-	-	3 enfants ou plus	400
285	480	280	315	270	210	Total des familles monoparentales	401
185	405	260	255	215	195	Parent de sexe féminin	402
95	250	170	160	125	155	1 enfant	403
55	130	70	65	90	25	2 enfants	404
30	25	15	25	10	15	3 enfants ou plus	405

Table 1. Selected Characteristics for Census Tracts, 2001 Census – 100% Data and 20% Sample Data

No.	Characteristics	Vancouver 0260.05 A	Vancouver 0260.06 A	Vancouver 0260.07 A	Vancouver 0260.08 A	Vancouver 0280	Vancouver 0281.01
	CENSUS FAMILY CHARACTERISTICS						
	by census family structure and size - concluded						
406	Male parent	15	20	45	15	40	45
407	1 child	15	15	20	10	40	30
408	2 children	-	-	20	-	-	10
409	3 or more children	-	-	-	10	-	-
410	**Total number of children at home**	**1,340**	**1,310**	**1,370**	**1,525**	**1,240**	**2,330**
	by age groups						
411	Under 6 years	365	260	355	330	135	400
412	6-14 years	570	465	570	585	465	765
413	15-17 years	165	140	130	200	175	320
414	18-24 years	145	305	270	270	320	650
415	25 years and over	100	140	50	140	145	190
416	Average number of children at home per census family (43)	1.2	1.1	1.2	1.3	1.3	1.3
417	**Total number of persons in private households**	**3,940**	**3,880**	**3,830**	**3,985**	**3,310**	**6,415**
	by census family status and living arrangements						
418	Number of non-family persons	455	270	455	240	225	615
419	Living with relatives (44)	80	40	50	30	75	150
420	Living with non-relatives only	110	80	110	85	60	220
421	Living alone	270	155	295	120	100	250
422	Number of family persons	3,485	3,610	3,385	3,745	3,080	5,795
423	Average number of persons per census family	3.0	3.0	3.0	3.2	3.2	3.2
424	**Total number of persons 65 years and over**	**350**	**300**	**160**	**170**	**210**	**430**
425	Number of non-family persons 65 years and over	105	60	40	25	50	90
426	Living with relatives (44)	10	20	10	10	30	50
427	Living with non-relatives only	-	-	-	-	-	10
428	Living alone	95	40	30	15	15	40
429	Number of family persons 65 years and over	245	240	120	150	160	330
	ECONOMIC FAMILY CHARACTERISTICS						
430	**Total number of economic families in private households**	**1,155**	**1,180**	**1,120**	**1,100**	**945**	**1,780**
	by size of family						
431	2 persons	470	490	440	310	330	605
432	3 persons	265	265	295	245	155	365
433	4 persons	300	285	280	350	300	500
434	5 or more persons	120	135	110	190	155	300
435	Total number of persons in economic families	3,555	3,645	3,430	3,785	3,150	5,945
436	Average number of persons per economic family	3.1	3.1	3.1	3.4	3.3	3.3
437	Total number of unattached individuals	385	230	405	205	160	470
	2000 INCOME CHARACTERISTICS						
	Population 15 years and over by sex and total income groups in 2000						
438	Total - Both sexes	3,020	3,155	2,910	3,075	2,710	5,240
439	Without income	210	120	145	295	180	385
440	With income	2,815	3,035	2,765	2,785	2,525	4,860
441	Under $1,000 (45)	105	90	145	140	230	190
442	$ 1,000 - $ 2,999	100	130	105	110	115	225
443	$ 3,000 - $ 4,999	45	130	70	80	105	110
444	$ 5,000 - $ 6,999	80	105	60	100	105	190
445	$ 7,000 - $ 9,999	125	145	160	145	115	275
446	$10,000 - $11,999	75	65	40	115	30	200
447	$12,000 - $14,999	85	155	130	110	140	265
448	$15,000 - $19,999	255	160	200	150	165	350
449	$20,000 - $24,999	160	170	180	205	140	295
450	$25,000 - $29,999	215	195	155	95	130	375
451	$30,000 - $34,999	245	220	215	220	185	450
452	$35,000 - $39,999	250	220	205	150	130	305
453	$40,000 - $44,999	195	135	230	155	135	255
454	$45,000 - $49,999	120	140	200	175	145	250
455	$50,000 - $59,999	290	230	190	195	185	445
456	$60,000 and over	470	735	470	650	480	685
457	Average income $ (46)	36,833	41,829	35,054	40,062	35,454	34,405
458	Median income $ (46)	32,640	32,272	32,379	33,034	29,566	29,699
459	Standard error of average income $ (46)	1,121	1,462	1,014	1,629	1,444	1,004

Tableau 1. Certaines caractéristiques des secteurs de recensement, recensement de 2001 – Données intégrales et données-échantillon (20 %)

Vancouver 0281.02	Vancouver 0282	Vancouver 0283	Vancouver 0284.01	Vancouver 0284.02	Vancouver 0285.01	Caractéristiques	N°
						CARACTÉRISTIQUES DES FAMILLES DE RECENSEMENT	
						selon la structure et la taille de la famille de recensement – fin	
100	75	15	60	55	15	Parent de sexe masculin	406
70	45	15	45	35	10	1 enfant	407
15	25	-	20	10	-	2 enfants	408
15	-	-	-	15	-	3 enfants ou plus	409
1,905	**2,420**	**1,700**	**2,140**	**1,830**	**745**	**Nombre total d'enfants à la maison**	410
						selon les groupes d'âge	
395	570	425	435	375	185	Moins de 6 ans	411
685	910	560	720	620	280	6-14 ans	412
225	285	195	315	225	90	15-17 ans	413
385	380	365	450	445	135	18-24 ans	414
225	275	160	220	170	55	25 ans et plus	415
1.1	1.1	1.1	1.2	1.1	1.0	Nombre moyen d'enfants à la maison par famille de recensement (43)	416
5,980	**7,655**	**5,905**	**6,735**	**5,925**	**3,190**	**Nombre total de personnes dans les ménages privés**	417
						selon la situation des particuliers dans la famille de recensement et des particuliers dans le ménage	
905	1,445	1,295	1,305	1,005	1,105	Nombre de personnes hors famille de recensement	418
135	195	105	220	115	135	Vivant avec des personnes apparentées (44)	419
235	465	410	345	290	125	Vivant avec des personnes non apparentées uniquement	420
540	780	780	750	605	850	Vivant seules	421
5,070	6,210	4,615	5,425	4,925	2,085	Nombre de personnes membres d'une famille	422
2.9	2.9	2.9	3.0	2.9	2.7	Nombre moyen de personnes par famille de recensement	423
630	**720**	**570**	**770**	**635**	**315**	**Nombre total de personnes de 65 ans et plus**	424
195	275	230	265	195	210	Nombre de personnes hors famille de recensement de 65 ans et plus	425
50	35	10	70	40	30	Vivant avec des personnes apparentées (44)	426
-	20	10	-	20	10	Vivant avec des personnes non apparentées uniquement	427
145	220	210	190	135	165	Vivant seules	428
440	440	340	510	435	105	Nombre de personnes membres d'une famille de 65 ans et plus	429
						CARACTÉRISTIQUES DES FAMILLES ÉCONOMIQUES	
1,700	**2,080**	**1,560**	**1,815**	**1,630**	**795**	**Nombre total de familles économiques dans les ménages privés**	430
						selon la taille de la famille	
735	905	680	750	720	430	2 personnes	431
380	520	390	445	345	190	3 personnes	432
400	415	310	380	360	130	4 personnes	433
190	245	175	240	200	50	5 personnes ou plus	434
5,205	6,400	4,720	5,640	5,040	2,220	Nombre total de personnes dans les familles économiques	435
3.1	3.1	3.0	3.1	3.1	2.8	Nombre moyen de personnes par famille économique	436
775	1,250	1,185	1,095	890	970	Nombre total de personnes hors famille économique	437
						CARACTÉRISTIQUES DU REVENU DE 2000	
						Population de 15 ans et plus selon le sexe et les tranches de revenu total en 2000	
4,895	6,145	4,930	5,565	4,940	2,725	Total - Les deux sexes	438
195	340	325	420	295	160	Sans revenu	439
4,700	5,810	4,605	5,140	4,645	2,570	Avec un revenu	440
225	275	225	295	180	175	Moins de 1 000 $ (45)	441
230	235	210	295	200	165	1 000 $ - 2 999 $	442
170	190	160	265	90	130	3 000 $ - 4 999 $	443
200	205	250	230	220	120	5 000 $ - 6 999 $	444
220	340	225	420	315	155	7 000 $ - 9 999 $	445
145	205	190	230	180	70	10 000 $ - 11 999 $	446
325	380	425	460	320	150	12 000 $ - 14 999 $	447
365	510	400	550	395	275	15 000 $ - 19 999 $	448
345	510	425	325	370	195	20 000 $ - 24 999 $	449
385	395	420	385	310	190	25 000 $ - 29 999 $	450
410	520	360	315	425	225	30 000 $ - 34 999 $	451
290	405	325	310	380	190	35 000 $ - 39 999 $	452
285	545	215	235	345	140	40 000 $ - 44 999 $	453
245	220	195	170	180	110	45 000 $ - 49 999 $	454
345	460	220	225	330	145	50 000 $ - 59 999 $	455
520	410	365	425	425	145	60 000 $ et plus	456
29,745	28,374	32,066	25,243	29,897	24,317	Revenu moyen $ (46)	457
26,315	25,291	22,487	18,052	25,422	21,675	Revenu médian $ (46)	458
734	587	2,323	705	854	822	Erreur type de revenu moyen $ (46)	459

Table 1. Selected Characteristics for Census Tracts, 2001 Census – 100% Data and 20% Sample Data

No.	Characteristics	Vancouver 0260.05 A	Vancouver 0260.06 A	Vancouver 0260.07 A	Vancouver 0260.08 A	Vancouver 0280	Vancouver 0281.01
	2000 INCOME CHARACTERISTICS						
	Population 15 years and over by sex and total income groups in 2000 – concluded						
460	Total - Males	1,490	1,525	1,355	1,465	1,290	2,585
461	Without income	100	30	60	90	55	130
462	With income	1,395	1,490	1,295	1,370	1,235	2,455
463	Under $1,000 (45)	50	45	65	55	75	70
464	$ 1,000 - $ 2,999	35	50	30	20	40	85
465	$ 3,000 - $ 4,999	-	25	20	25	50	40
466	$ 5,000 - $ 6,999	40	40	35	40	35	65
467	$ 7,000 - $ 9,999	20	65	75	65	35	120
468	$10,000 - $11,999	25	10	-	45	20	65
469	$12,000 - $14,999	45	65	35	40	45	165
470	$15,000 - $19,999	110	55	90	50	90	95
471	$20,000 - $24,999	55	60	50	110	35	135
472	$25,000 - $29,999	100	80	50	25	65	185
473	$30,000 - $34,999	105	80	90	60	95	180
474	$35,000 - $39,999	140	90	105	70	30	160
475	$40,000 - $44,999	95	75	100	80	70	110
476	$45,000 - $49,999	65	70	80	65	100	165
477	$50,000 - $59,999	155	145	100	115	105	240
478	$60,000 and over	360	530	370	505	335	570
479	Average income $ (46)	44,460	53,030	42,330	51,632	44,831	42,764
480	Median income $ (46)	38,689	44,874	40,026	43,983	39,734	34,935
481	Standard error of average income $ (46)	1,795	2,469	1,630	2,824	2,430	1,731
482	Total - Females	1,530	1,635	1,560	1,615	1,415	2,650
483	Without income	105	85	90	205	125	250
484	With income	1,420	1,545	1,470	1,410	1,295	2,405
485	Under $1,000 (45)	50	45	80	85	160	120
486	$ 1,000 - $ 2,999	70	85	75	90	70	140
487	$ 3,000 - $ 4,999	45	100	50	50	55	65
488	$ 5,000 - $ 6,999	40	70	30	65	70	125
489	$ 7,000 - $ 9,999	105	80	85	85	85	155
490	$10,000 - $11,999	50	55	40	70	10	140
491	$12,000 - $14,999	40	90	95	65	95	105
492	$15,000 - $19,999	150	105	115	100	65	250
493	$20,000 - $24,999	105	110	130	90	100	160
494	$25,000 - $29,999	115	120	110	65	60	185
495	$30,000 - $34,999	140	145	125	160	90	275
496	$35,000 - $39,999	110	125	100	80	100	145
497	$40,000 - $44,999	100	60	135	75	65	140
498	$45,000 - $49,999	55	70	120	105	45	80
499	$50,000 - $59,999	135	85	90	80	80	205
500	$60,000 and over	110	205	100	145	145	115
501	Average income $ (46)	29,377	31,032	28,650	28,766	26,508	25,862
502	Median income $ (46)	26,023	25,839	27,773	25,318	22,540	22,953
503	Standard error of average income $ (46)	1,201	1,432	1,141	1,354	1,377	851
	by composition of total income						
504	Total - Composition of income in 2000 % (47)	100.0	100.0	100.0	100.0	100.0	100.0
505	Employment income %	80.6	83.4	89.8	89.2	85.0	83.3
506	Government transfer payments %	8.0	4.7	5.5	3.9	4.8	6.2
507	Other %	11.4	11.9	4.7	6.8	10.1	10.4
	Population 15 years and over with employment income in 2000 by sex and work activity						
508	Both sexes with employment income (48)	2,200	2,450	2,335	2,210	1,930	3,930
509	Average employment income $	37,930	43,233	37,288	45,024	39,400	35,465
510	Standard error of average employment income $	1,290	1,555	1,088	1,905	1,678	1,126
511	Worked full year, full time (49)	1,235	1,285	1,450	1,235	1,070	2,035
512	Average employment income $	50,565	60,216	45,928	58,340	54,943	48,507
513	Standard error of average employment income $	1,710	2,120	1,236	2,252	2,388	1,451
514	Worked part year or part time (50)	915	1,125	845	930	815	1,815
515	Average employment income $	22,109	24,224	23,493	29,167	20,097	21,415
516	Standard error of average employment income $	1,423	1,720	1,680	3,004	1,557	1,505
517	Males with employment income (48)	1,150	1,215	1,135	1,145	990	2,100
518	Average employment income $	44,925	53,983	44,464	57,807	47,811	42,871
519	Standard error of average employment income $	1,999	2,495	1,698	3,190	2,794	1,894
520	Worked full year, full time (49)	705	775	800	775	645	1,255
521	Average employment income $	57,486	67,528	50,454	66,600	62,412	55,656
522	Standard error of average employment income $	2,465	3,008	1,738	3,129	3,568	2,107
523	Worked part year or part time (50)	425	425	310	365	320	820
524	Average employment income $	26,129	29,940	31,400	40,730	20,729	23,873
525	Standard error of average employment income $	2,328	3,353	3,564	7,191	2,779	3,112

Tableau 1. Certaines caractéristiques des secteurs de recensement, recensement de 2001 – Données intégrales et données-échantillon (20 %)

Vancouver 0281.02	Vancouver 0282	Vancouver 0283	Vancouver 0284.01	Vancouver 0284.02	Vancouver 0285.01	Caractéristiques	Nº
						CARACTÉRISTIQUES DU REVENU DE 2000	
						Population de 15 ans et plus selon le sexe et les tranches de revenu total en 2000 – fin	
2,455	2,990	2,425	2,730	2,455	1,355	Total - Hommes	460
90	120	130	190	115	95	Sans revenu	461
2,370	2,865	2,295	2,535	2,335	1,265	Avec un revenu	462
80	160	115	140	80	100	Moins de 1 000 $ (45)	463
85	120	70	145	60	50	1 000 $ - 2 999 $	464
40	115	75	140	20	50	3 000 $ - 4 999 $	465
80	65	105	80	90	45	5 000 $ - 6 999 $	466
80	190	75	135	125	60	7 000 $ - 9 999 $	467
75	70	75	90	70	25	10 000 $ - 11 999 $	468
115	120	140	220	125	45	12 000 $ - 14 999 $	469
130	210	205	245	240	115	15 000 $ - 19 999 $	470
175	270	230	180	160	110	20 000 $ - 24 999 $	471
180	150	225	170	145	85	25 000 $ - 29 999 $	472
215	245	170	165	185	95	30 000 $ - 34 999 $	473
170	215	155	145	160	125	35 000 $ - 39 999 $	474
150	310	130	120	145	75	40 000 $ - 44 999 $	475
180	95	95	95	130	55	45 000 $ - 49 999 $	476
220	240	140	125	225	125	50 000 $ - 59 999 $	477
385	290	285	325	380	110	60 000 $ et plus	478
35,827	30,785	40,633	28,667	36,046	28,567	Revenu moyen $ (46)	479
32,931	27,331	25,336	21,583	30,972	25,978	Revenu médian $ (46)	480
1,109	942	4,485	1,036	1,420	1,375	Erreur type de revenu moyen $ (46)	481
2,440	3,160	2,505	2,840	2,485	1,365	Total - Femmes	482
105	210	200	230	175	65	Sans revenu	483
2,335	2,950	2,310	2,605	2,310	1,300	Avec un revenu	484
145	120	105	155	100	75	Moins de 1 000 $ (45)	485
145	120	140	150	140	115	1 000 $ - 2 999 $	486
135	75	90	120	70	75	3 000 $ - 4 999 $	487
125	145	140	150	130	75	5 000 $ - 6 999 $	488
135	145	155	285	190	95	7 000 $ - 9 999 $	489
70	135	115	140	115	40	10 000 $ - 11 999 $	490
205	255	285	240	190	105	12 000 $ - 14 999 $	491
225	305	200	310	155	160	15 000 $ - 19 999 $	492
165	245	195	145	200	85	20 000 $ - 24 999 $	493
200	245	190	215	170	100	25 000 $ - 29 999 $	494
200	270	190	145	240	130	30 000 $ - 34 999 $	495
120	185	170	160	220	60	35 000 $ - 39 999 $	496
130	235	85	115	200	70	40 000 $ - 44 999 $	497
70	130	100	75	50	55	45 000 $ - 49 999 $	498
120	220	80	100	105	20	50 000 $ - 59 999 $	499
130	125	80	100	40	35	60 000 $ et plus	500
23,578	26,029	23,556	21,910	23,677	20,184	Revenu moyen $ (46)	501
19,218	22,502	17,391	15,811	22,214	16,739	Revenu médian $ (46)	502
873	700	1,190	935	846	905	Erreur type de revenu moyen $ (46)	503
						selon la composition du revenu total	
100.0	100.0	100.0	100.0	100.0	100.0	Total - Composition du revenu en 2000 % (47)	504
82.1	82.4	80.9	75.6	82.0	78.4	Revenu d'emploi %	505
9.6	10.5	8.9	13.6	9.8	14.0	Transferts gouvernementaux %	506
8.2	7.1	10.3	10.8	8.2	7.5	Autre %	507
						Population de 15 ans et plus ayant un revenu d'emploi en 2000 selon le sexe et le travail	
3,530	4,355	3,475	3,555	3,555	1,820	Les deux sexes ayant un revenu d'emploi (48)	508
32,547	31,205	34,314	27,624	32,032	26,916	Revenu moyen d'emploi $	509
866	666	2,818	910	1,003	1,017	Erreur type de revenu moyen d'emploi $	510
1,925	2,515	1,810	1,580	1,855	1,045	Ayant travaillé toute l'année à plein temps (49)	511
43,004	40,418	49,462	42,218	43,085	35,234	Revenu moyen d'emploi $	512
1,157	823	5,331	1,358	1,461	1,359	Erreur type de revenu moyen d'emploi $	513
1,555	1,770	1,565	1,880	1,670	760	Ayant travaillé une partie de l'année ou à temps partiel (50)	514
20,105	18,952	18,231	16,433	20,021	16,002	Revenu moyen d'emploi $	515
972	786	964	928	1,077	1,131	Erreur type de revenu moyen d'emploi $	516
1,860	2,215	1,865	1,880	1,835	1,015	Hommes ayant un revenu d'emploi (48)	517
38,009	33,477	42,406	31,196	38,488	30,274	Revenu moyen d'emploi $	518
1,267	1,047	5,148	1,302	1,619	1,571	Erreur type de revenu moyen d'emploi $	519
1,145	1,315	985	925	1,050	615	Ayant travaillé toute l'année à plein temps (49)	520
46,026	42,505	62,364	44,978	49,232	37,909	Revenu moyen d'emploi $	521
1,608	1,276	9,596	1,729	2,225	2,093	Erreur type de revenu moyen d'emploi $	522
705	870	830	930	785	390	Ayant travaillé une partie de l'année ou à temps partiel (50)	523
25,110	20,031	20,428	18,318	24,203	18,945	Revenu moyen d'emploi $	524
1,632	1,358	1,391	1,467	1,872	1,804	Erreur type de revenu moyen d'emploi $	525

Table 1. Selected Characteristics for Census Tracts, 2001 Census – 100% Data and 20% Sample Data

No.	Characteristics	Vancouver 0260.05 A	Vancouver 0260.06 A	Vancouver 0260.07 A	Vancouver 0260.08 A	Vancouver 0280	Vancouver 0281.01
	2000 INCOME CHARACTERISTICS						
	Population 15 years and over with employment income in 2000 by sex and work activity – concluded						
526	Females with employment income (48)	1,055	1,230	1,205	1,065	945	1,825
527	Average employment income $	30,290	32,586	30,533	31,253	30,580	26,955
528	Standard error of average employment income $	1,404	1,675	1,245	1,504	1,522	905
529	Worked full year, full time (49)	525	505	650	460	425	775
530	Average employment income $	41,322	49,008	40,307	44,544	43,629	36,919
531	Standard error of average employment income $	1,837	2,532	1,607	2,372	1,929	1,233
532	Worked part year or part time (50)	495	705	535	565	490	990
533	Average employment income $	18,628	20,806	18,869	21,731	19,678	19,366
534	Standard error of average employment income $	1,664	1,830	1,461	1,495	1,809	1,035
	Census families by structure and family income groups in 2000						
535	Total - All census families	1,150	1,195	1,115	1,155	970	1,825
536	Under $10,000	25	10	45	60	15	60
537	$ 10,000 - $19,999	25	25	25	65	55	55
538	$ 20,000 - $29,999	55	60	50	70	45	120
539	$ 30,000 - $39,999	95	40	115	80	100	115
540	$ 40,000 - $49,999	130	85	100	50	100	135
541	$ 50,000 - $59,999	170	60	140	40	25	175
542	$ 60,000 - $69,999	110	120	125	105	70	230
543	$ 70,000 - $79,999	90	110	65	85	75	160
544	$ 80,000 - $89,999	85	110	115	75	95	195
545	$ 90,000 - $99,999	100	105	105	95	90	125
546	$100,000 and over	265	465	240	435	290	465
547	Average family income $	75,623	97,789	73,760	85,693	85,619	80,676
548	Median family income $	66,798	88,714	67,540	84,324	78,838	74,011
549	Standard error of average family income $	2,638	3,408	2,615	3,355	4,139	2,558
550	Total - All couple census families (51)	990	1,105	895	1,060	875	1,640
551	Under $10,000	-	10	25	50	15	20
552	$ 10,000 - $19,999	25	15	15	55	45	20
553	$ 20,000 - $29,999	35	50	20	55	45	110
554	$ 30,000 - $39,999	80	45	85	70	95	90
555	$ 40,000 - $49,999	115	85	50	40	65	115
556	$ 50,000 - $59,999	120	45	125	35	20	145
557	$ 60,000 - $69,999	115	100	105	90	50	205
558	$ 70,000 - $79,999	80	90	60	80	75	160
559	$ 80,000 - $89,999	75	100	90	70	90	185
560	$ 90,000 - $99,999	90	105	100	90	90	125
561	$100,000 and over	260	455	230	430	275	465
562	Average family income $	80,812	100,826	79,859	89,308	89,098	85,992
563	Median family income $	72,134	92,149	75,487	87,868	83,454	77,971
564	Standard error of average family income $	2,872	3,570	2,924	3,484	4,421	2,675
	Incidence of low income in 2000						
565	Total - Economic families	1,150	1,180	1,120	1,095	940	1,780
566	Low income	80	80	105	145	140	190
567	Incidence of low income in 2000 % (52)	7.1	6.7	9.1	13.1	14.6	10.6
568	Total - Unattached individuals 15 years and over	380	230	400	205	145	465
569	Low income	80	55	130	50	25	125
570	Incidence of low income in 2000 % (52)	21.2	23.5	31.6	24.5	17.1	26.9
571	Total - Population in private households	3,940	3,880	3,830	3,985	3,290	6,410
572	Low income	325	320	460	585	560	800
573	Incidence of low income in 2000 % (52)	8.2	8.3	12.1	14.6	17.0	12.4
	Private households by household income groups in 2000						
574	Total - All private households	1,445	1,360	1,440	1,245	1,050	2,065
575	Under $10,000	15	20	95	55	15	75
576	$ 10,000 - $19,999	70	75	45	60	55	60
577	$ 20,000 - $29,999	105	90	95	45	60	150
578	$ 30,000 - $39,999	160	60	150	80	100	150
579	$ 40,000 - $49,999	155	75	185	110	105	140
580	$ 50,000 - $59,999	185	70	165	60	60	190
581	$ 60,000 - $69,999	140	120	140	105	90	205
582	$ 70,000 - $79,999	135	115	85	95	85	180
583	$ 80,000 - $89,999	100	100	125	70	85	240
584	$ 90,000 - $99,999	90	125	115	105	90	125
585	$100,000 and over	305	510	250	470	310	545
586	Average household income $	71,123	93,466	67,169	89,695	85,393	80,926
587	Median household income $	62,974	84,781	59,012	84,124	74,868	74,265
588	Standard error of average household income $	2,361	3,336	2,324	3,630	3,945	2,532

Tableau 1. Certaines caractéristiques des secteurs de recensement, recensement de 2001 – Données intégrales et données-échantillon (20 %)

Vancouver 0281.02	Vancouver 0282	Vancouver 0283	Vancouver 0284.01	Vancouver 0284.02	Vancouver 0285.01	Caractéristiques	N°
						CARACTÉRISTIQUES DU REVENU DE 2000	
						Population de 15 ans et plus ayant un revenu d'emploi en 2000 selon le sexe et le travail – fin	
1,670	2,140	1,615	1,670	1,720	805	Femmes ayant un revenu d'emploi (48)	526
26,465	28,854	24,955	23,597	25,152	22,690	Revenu moyen d'emploi $	527
1,078	803	1,042	1,227	1,024	1,193	Erreur type de revenu moyen d'emploi $	528
780	1,190	825	650	805	435	Ayant travaillé toute l'année à plein temps (49)	529
38,565	38,114	34,053	38,287	35,100	31,418	Revenu moyen d'emploi $	530
1,533	988	1,399	2,148	1,487	1,525	Erreur type de revenu moyen d'emploi $	531
850	900	735	955	885	365	Ayant travaillé une partie de l'année ou à temps partiel (50)	532
15,971	17,909	15,738	14,601	16,316	12,851	Revenu moyen d'emploi $	533
1,053	829	1,300	1,140	1,095	1,316	Erreur type de revenu moyen d'emploi $	534
						Familles de recensement selon la structure et les tranches de revenu de la famille en 2000	
1,725	2,135	1,600	1,800	1,680	775	Total - Toutes les familles de recensement	535
50	95	90	170	55	135	Moins de 10 000 $	536
120	190	145	225	75	75	10 000 $ - 19 999 $	537
125	180	170	190	170	70	20 000 $ - 29 999 $	538
180	270	245	305	240	95	30 000 $ - 39 999 $	539
210	255	170	130	190	95	40 000 $ - 49 999 $	540
135	250	145	135	190	95	50 000 $ - 59 999 $	541
210	220	145	165	140	45	60 000 $ - 69 999 $	542
175	170	105	90	105	75	70 000 $ - 79 999 $	543
115	165	110	50	150	20	80 000 $ - 89 999 $	544
80	90	75	60	60	20	90 000 $ - 99 999 $	545
315	250	195	275	300	40	100 000 $ et plus	546
66,182	57,480	73,036	53,858	65,338	43,629	Revenu moyen des familles $	547
60,986	52,602	48,975	40,429	55,851	40,350	Revenu médian des familles $	548
1,999	1,560	7,362	2,114	2,372	2,579	Erreur type de revenu moyen des familles $	549
1,445	1,650	1,315	1,485	1,415	565	Total - Toutes les familles de recensement comptant un couple (51)	550
25	70	85	130	35	95	Moins de 10 000 $	551
80	95	85	130	30	30	10 000 $ - 19 999 $	552
95	120	135	150	135	50	20 000 $ - 29 999 $	553
140	165	140	255	185	65	30 000 $ - 39 999 $	554
170	175	145	110	145	50	40 000 $ - 49 999 $	555
105	190	125	110	175	85	50 000 $ - 59 999 $	556
180	205	115	160	100	45	60 000 $ - 69 999 $	557
170	130	110	85	105	70	70 000 $ - 79 999 $	558
110	160	105	45	145	20	80 000 $ - 89 999 $	559
75	90	75	60	55	20	90 000 $ - 99 999 $	560
295	250	200	240	295	40	100 000 $ et plus	561
70,708	63,617	81,034	56,988	70,026	49,320	Revenu moyen des familles $	562
65,516	60,499	54,638	46,053	58,163	48,193	Revenu médian des familles $	563
2,205	1,833	8,544	2,412	2,668	3,328	Erreur type de revenu moyen des familles $	564
						Fréquence des unités à faible revenu en 2000	
1,700	2,080	1,560	1,810	1,625	795	Total - Familles économiques	565
245	365	415	565	205	285	Faible revenu	566
14.4	17.5	26.6	31.1	12.5	35.6	Fréquence des unités à faible revenu en 2000 % (52)	567
765	1,245	1,190	1,080	890	970	Total - Personnes hors famille économique de 15 ans et plus	568
255	440	495	460	315	340	Faible revenu	569
32.8	35.4	41.6	42.3	35.3	35.5	Fréquence des unités à faible revenu en 2000 % (52)	570
5,970	7,650	5,910	6,725	5,925	3,190	Total - Population dans les ménages privés	571
1,000	1,675	1,790	2,360	1,040	1,125	Faible revenu	572
16.8	21.9	30.3	35.1	17.5	35.4	Fréquence des unités à faible revenu en 2000 % (52)	573
						Ménages privés selon les tranches de revenu du ménage en 2000	
2,315	3,035	2,490	2,690	2,330	1,705	Total - Tous les ménages privés	574
100	145	200	300	160	260	Moins de 10 000 $	575
235	355	355	385	150	255	10 000 $ - 19 999 $	576
245	285	375	300	205	250	20 000 $ - 29 999 $	577
260	395	360	465	355	275	30 000 $ - 39 999 $	578
280	395	255	280	320	210	40 000 $ - 49 999 $	579
185	370	195	205	205	170	50 000 $ - 59 999 $	580
215	200	145	180	195	105	60 000 $ - 69 999 $	581
190	200	140	135	135	65	70 000 $ - 79 999 $	582
135	225	130	70	170	45	80 000 $ - 89 999 $	583
100	115	95	65	80	20	90 000 $ - 99 999 $	584
365	350	245	305	355	40	100 000 $ et plus	585
60,422	54,397	59,262	48,273	59,426	36,624	Revenu moyen des ménages $	586
51,656	49,014	38,113	36,618	49,531	33,666	Revenu médian des ménages $	587
1,815	1,307	4,947	1,678	1,943	1,452	Erreur type de revenu moyen des ménages $	588

Table 1. Selected Characteristics for Census Tracts, 2001 Census – 100% Data and 20% Sample Data

No.	Characteristics	Vancouver 0285.02	Vancouver 0286.01	Vancouver 0286.02	Vancouver 0286.03	Vancouver 0287.01	Vancouver 0287.02
	POPULATION CHARACTERISTICS						
1	**Population, 1996 (1)**	**5,489**	**5,755**	**6,866**	**4,243**	**6,708**	**3,666**
2	**Population, 2001 (2)**	**5,522**	**5,815**	**6,978**	**4,125**	**7,197**	**3,914**
3	Population percentage change, 1996-2001	0.6	1.0	1.6	-2.8	7.3	6.8
4	Land area in square kilometres, 2001	2.22	4.05	2.79	2.96	1.89	55.60
5	**Total population – 100% Data (3)**	**5,525**	**5,815**	**6,975**	**4,125**	**7,195**	**3,915**
	by sex and age groups						
6	Male	2,785	2,895	3,490	2,070	3,555	1,975
7	0-4 years	155	150	235	95	250	150
8	5-9 years	170	190	285	130	315	180
9	10-14 years	235	225	265	160	380	190
10	15-19 years	235	250	280	170	360	160
11	20-24 years	210	215	235	150	200	105
12	25-29 years	160	160	180	105	150	70
13	30-34 years	155	165	245	110	260	115
14	35-39 years	220	205	295	160	315	190
15	40-44 years	230	255	330	170	405	225
16	45-49 years	225	265	305	180	345	185
17	50-54 years	210	235	275	175	220	130
18	55-59 years	170	165	195	150	100	95
19	60-64 years	125	150	155	105	75	65
20	65-69 years	110	110	95	85	55	50
21	70-74 years	80	75	65	60	55	30
22	75-79 years	55	45	40	35	35	25
23	80-84 years	25	30	15	15	20	10
24	85 years and over	15	10	5	5	10	5
25	Female	2,745	2,925	3,480	2,055	3,640	1,935
26	0-4 years	130	145	195	115	215	140
27	5-9 years	170	175	235	130	285	165
28	10-14 years	195	205	260	155	340	170
29	15-19 years	215	255	280	160	300	165
30	20-24 years	170	210	215	110	210	105
31	25-29 years	135	155	185	95	200	75
32	30-34 years	165	165	255	110	275	135
33	35-39 years	205	225	320	185	410	220
34	40-44 years	270	265	355	170	415	210
35	45-49 years	235	270	320	195	340	165
36	50-54 years	200	225	260	180	190	115
37	55-59 years	155	170	200	150	125	80
38	60-64 years	130	155	130	100	85	65
39	65-69 years	100	100	95	90	70	50
40	70-74 years	105	95	75	40	70	35
41	75-79 years	65	55	55	40	60	30
42	80-84 years	55	45	15	20	35	10
43	85 years and over	50	10	25	15	15	5
44	**Total population 15 years and over**	**4,465**	**4,730**	**5,495**	**3,335**	**5,415**	**2,920**
	by legal marital status						
45	Never married (single)	1,385	1,470	1,705	940	1,735	805
46	Legally married (and not separated)	2,510	2,755	3,155	2,005	2,965	1,795
47	Separated, but still legally married	90	115	150	80	170	75
48	Divorced	240	200	310	190	330	155
49	Widowed	235	185	175	130	215	80
	by common-law status						
50	Not in a common-law relationship	4,275	4,500	5,185	3,205	5,090	2,745
51	In a common-law relationship	190	230	310	135	325	180
52	**Total population – 20% Sample Data (4)**	**5,425**	**5,810**	**6,965**	**4,115**	**7,190**	**3,910**
	by mother tongue						
53	Single responses	5,390	5,740	6,865	4,085	7,110	3,850
54	English	3,800	3,920	4,980	3,215	4,525	3,095
55	French	60	65	105	25	90	85
56	Non-official languages (5)	1,520	1,750	1,775	845	2,490	665
57	Chinese, n.o.s.	220	275	220	110	580	10
58	Cantonese	170	155	190	135	530	30
59	Punjabi	-	10	15	40	-	40
60	Mandarin	335	265	160	50	45	10
61	Tagalog (Pilipino)	25	45	135	45	235	15
62	Other languages (6)	775	1,000	1,055	465	1,105	560
63	Multiple responses	35	70	100	35	80	65
64	English and French	-	10	10	-	10	25
65	English and non-official language	25	50	85	35	75	45
66	French and non-official language	-	10	-	-	-	-
67	English, French and non-official language	-	10	-	-	-	-

See reference material at the end of the publication. – Voir les documents de référence à la fin de la publication.

Tableau 1. Certaines caractéristiques des secteurs de recensement, recensement de 2001 – Données intégrales et données-échantillon (20 %)

Vancouver 0287.04	Vancouver 0287.05 A	Vancouver 0287.06 A	Vancouver 0287.07 A	Vancouver 0290.02	Vancouver 0290.03	Caractéristiques	Nº
						CARACTÉRISTIQUES DE LA POPULATION	
7,368	**6,837**	**3,895**	**6,433**	**5,193**	**5,930**	**Population, 1996 (1)**	1
8,217	**8,711**	**4,202**	**11,914**	**6,072**	**6,248**	**Population, 2001 (2)**	2
11.5	27.4	7.9	85.2	16.9	5.4	Variation en pourcentage de la population, 1996-2001	3
3.16	2.82	1.19	21.85	4.53	3.26	Superficie des terres en kilomètres carrés, 2001	4
8,220	**8,710**	**4,200**	**11,915**	**6,070**	**6,250**	**Population totale – Données intégrales (3)**	5
						selon le sexe et les groupes d'âge	
4,085	3,990	1,890	5,910	2,840	3,130	Sexe masculin	6
270	200	105	335	200	245	0-4 ans	7
295	215	120	430	170	265	5-9 ans	8
425	235	140	550	155	285	10-14 ans	9
435	250	195	575	145	240	15-19 ans	10
245	250	120	445	160	175	20-24 ans	11
155	280	80	315	235	200	25-29 ans	12
245	370	90	340	370	255	30-34 ans	13
305	410	130	420	350	300	35-39 ans	14
380	345	150	595	270	335	40-44 ans	15
445	335	180	625	195	275	45-49 ans	16
355	280	145	530	150	165	50-54 ans	17
210	180	85	290	80	130	55-59 ans	18
105	130	70	170	80	90	60-64 ans	19
80	150	70	140	70	75	65-69 ans	20
50	125	65	95	50	45	70-74 ans	21
45	125	60	35	60	30	75-79 ans	22
15	65	40	10	40	15	80-84 ans	23
10	45	50	5	55	-	85 ans et plus	24
4,135	4,720	2,310	6,005	3,225	3,120	Sexe féminin	25
235	190	75	275	175	250	0-4 ans	26
280	150	135	425	160	235	5-9 ans	27
325	220	165	520	130	230	10-14 ans	28
375	235	145	550	140	255	15-19 ans	29
260	265	100	410	180	185	20-24 ans	30
205	350	85	340	290	180	25-29 ans	31
305	410	130	430	335	270	30-34 ans	32
395	440	160	595	310	355	35-39 ans	33
495	425	200	685	240	345	40-44 ans	34
455	375	165	645	225	230	45-49 ans	35
315	345	160	455	195	170	50-54 ans	36
165	200	80	210	110	140	55-59 ans	37
100	250	95	165	80	95	60-64 ans	38
80	210	110	120	95	70	65-69 ans	39
55	250	80	90	110	40	70-74 ans	40
55	200	120	55	140	30	75-79 ans	41
30	125	125	25	140	15	80-84 ans	42
15	75	170	15	185	10	85 ans et plus	43
6,395	**7,500**	**3,475**	**9,375**	**5,085**	**4,745**	**Population totale de 15 ans et plus**	44
						selon l'état matrimonial légal	
1,840	2,185	870	2,805	1,790	1,440	Célibataire (jamais marié(e))	45
3,930	3,770	1,855	5,860	1,840	2,670	Légalement marié(e) (et non séparé(e))	46
145	255	85	145	300	160	Séparé(e), mais toujours légalement marié(e)	47
315	700	205	335	605	345	Divorcé(e)	48
165	585	460	230	545	125	Veuf ou veuve	49
						selon l'union libre	
6,105	6,970	3,385	9,015	4,530	4,355	Ne vivant pas en union libre	50
285	535	90	360	560	385	Vivant en union libre	51
8,215	**8,710**	**4,060**	**11,915**	**5,700**	**6,235**	**Population totale – Données-échantillon (20 %) (4)**	52
						selon la langue maternelle	
8,140	8,590	3,995	11,770	5,520	6,155	Réponses uniques	53
5,075	5,085	2,300	4,435	4,295	4,925	Anglais	54
65	80	25	70	70	40	Français	55
3,005	3,425	1,670	7,265	1,155	1,190	Langues non officielles (5)	56
520	425	255	1,395	110	135	Chinois, n.d.a.	57
830	805	390	2,080	90	115	Cantonais	58
15	30	20	205	-	95	Pendjabi	59
275	250	50	775	75	20	Mandarin	60
35	80	135	120	105	65	Tagalog (pilipino)	61
1,325	1,830	820	2,685	775	760	Autres langues (6)	62
75	120	70	150	180	85	Réponses multiples	63
20	15	-	10	20	20	Anglais et français	64
55	100	65	145	135	65	Anglais et langue non officielle	65
-	-	-	-	25	-	Français et langue non officielle	66
-	-	-	-	-	-	Anglais, français et langue non officielle	67

See reference material at the end of the publication. – Voir les documents de référence à la fin de la publication.

Table 1. Selected Characteristics for Census Tracts, 2001 Census – 100% Data and 20% Sample Data

No.	Characteristics	Vancouver 0285.02	Vancouver 0286.01	Vancouver 0286.02	Vancouver 0286.03	Vancouver 0287.01	Vancouver 0287.02
	POPULATION CHARACTERISTICS						
	by home language						
68	Single responses	4,685	4,905	5,920	3,745	5,870	3,415
69	English	4,210	4,265	5,325	3,525	4,680	3,290
70	French	-	10	25	-	-	10
71	Non-official languages (5)	475	640	565	220	1,190	115
72	Cantonese	100	95	110	20	365	15
73	Chinese, n.o.s.	45	150	100	45	255	-
74	Punjabi	-	10	10	-	-	10
75	Mandarin	185	160	70	15	50	-
76	Korean	40	50	35	35	165	-
77	Other languages (6)	110	175	235	100	355	95
78	Multiple responses	735	900	1,040	370	1,315	495
79	English and French	45	55	30	15	55	75
80	English and non-official language	690	840	1,005	355	1,245	405
81	French and non-official language	-	-	-	-	-	-
82	English, French and non-official language	-	15	10	-	15	20
	by knowledge of official languages						
83	English only	4,965	5,150	6,410	3,680	6,625	3,595
84	French only	-	-	-	-	-	-
85	English and French	345	540	455	375	300	305
86	Neither English nor French	115	120	95	55	260	15
	by knowledge of non-official languages (5) (7)						
87	Cantonese	250	215	365	110	745	45
88	Chinese, n.o.s.	165	335	185	100	515	25
89	Punjabi	40	45	30	40	10	65
90	Mandarin	430	345	200	90	295	65
91	Hindi	10	10	75	20	55	15
92	German	95	125	170	155	130	65
93	Spanish	140	195	220	35	135	135
	by first official language spoken						
94	English	5,240	5,600	6,740	4,025	6,825	3,815
95	French	60	65	100	25	90	80
96	English and French	-	40	35	15	15	-
97	Neither English nor French	115	100	95	60	260	10
98	Official language minority - (number) (8)	60	85	120	30	95	85
99	Official language minority - (percentage) (8)	1.1	1.5	1.7	0.7	1.3	2.2
	by ethnic origin (9)						
100	English	1,285	1,505	2,150	1,180	1,740	1,485
101	Canadian	1,375	1,315	1,650	1,300	1,935	1,225
102	Chinese	915	970	860	425	1,530	230
103	Scottish	920	1,100	1,465	885	1,010	840
104	Irish	615	775	810	630	925	700
105	German	525	550	740	530	765	340
106	East Indian	90	85	165	90	120	50
107	French	515	420	560	215	710	300
108	Ukrainian	175	310	350	215	345	210
109	Italian	520	565	445	280	130	180
110	Dutch (Netherlands)	265	175	335	160	175	195
111	Filipino	45	55	355	85	305	75
112	Polish	165	160	345	105	205	75
113	Norwegian	90	230	190	90	70	145
114	North American Indian	65	60	210	120	140	95
	by Aboriginal identity						
115	Total Aboriginal identity population (10)	100	120	150	10	80	75
116	Total non-Aboriginal population	5,325	5,690	6,815	4,105	7,110	3,835
	by Aboriginal origin						
117	Total Aboriginal origins population (11)	195	100	235	120	185	105
118	Total non-Aboriginal population	5,230	5,710	6,725	3,995	7,005	3,810
	by Registered Indian status						
119	Registered Indian (12)	40	70	65	10	-	20
120	Not a Registered Indian	5,380	5,740	6,905	4,110	7,185	3,895

Tableau 1. Certaines caractéristiques des secteurs de recensement, recensement de 2001 – Données intégrales et données-échantillon (20 %)

Vancouver 0287.04	Vancouver 0287.05 A	Vancouver 0287.06 A	Vancouver 0287.07 A	Vancouver 0290.02	Vancouver 0290.03	Caractéristiques	N°
						CARACTÉRISTIQUES DE LA POPULATION	
						selon la langue parlée à la maison	
6,880	7,145	3,150	8,490	4,845	5,510	Réponses uniques	68
5,455	5,630	2,495	4,805	4,585	5,135	Anglais	69
-	10	-	10	-	30	Français	70
1,425	1,510	655	3,675	260	350	Langues non officielles (5)	71
490	510	255	1,360	55	30	Cantonais	72
195	140	85	590	35	15	Chinois, n.d.a.	73
-	-	10	35	-	70	Pendjabi	74
215	150	40	420	-	-	Mandarin	75
285	285	125	655	35	70	Coréen	76
235	425	140	625	140	160	Autres langues (6)	77
1,340	1,565	910	3,430	850	725	Réponses multiples	78
45	45	25	130	90	25	Anglais et français	79
1,280	1,515	890	3,265	745	680	Anglais et langue non officielle	80
10	-	-	-	-	-	Français et langue non officielle	81
-	10	-	35	15	20	Anglais, français et langue non officielle	82
						selon la connaissance des langues officielles	
7,455	7,815	3,695	10,490	5,290	5,670	Anglais seulement	83
-	-	-	-	-	-	Français seulement	84
465	455	215	590	370	450	Anglais et français	85
300	445	150	830	40	115	Ni l'anglais ni le français	86
						selon la connaissance des langues non officielles (5) (7)	
1,000	910	460	2,325	205	125	Cantonais	87
385	315	235	1,155	105	145	Chinois, n.d.a.	88
15	65	65	205	-	140	Pendjabi	89
665	665	140	1,720	105	55	Mandarin	90
10	60	75	95	40	75	Hindi	91
230	220	75	205	140	115	Allemand	92
190	230	55	290	100	110	Espagnol	93
						selon la première langue officielle parlée	
7,850	8,130	3,835	10,955	5,580	6,070	Anglais	94
50	90	20	75	60	35	Français	95
20	50	65	65	15	15	Anglais et français	96
285	445	145	820	35	115	Ni l'anglais ni le français	97
65	115	50	105	70	50	Minorité de langue officielle - (nombre) (8)	98
0.8	1.3	1.2	0.9	1.2	0.8	Minorité de langue officielle - (pourcentage) (8)	99
						selon l'origine ethnique (9)	
2,255	2,135	970	1,815	1,550	2,255	Anglais	100
1,765	1,520	525	1,370	1,445	1,730	Canadien	101
1,890	1,805	920	4,835	485	390	Chinois	102
1,090	1,350	495	1,160	1,215	1,520	Écossais	103
935	1,075	340	740	790	920	Irlandais	104
845	825	230	710	725	735	Allemand	105
140	120	95	525	45	260	Indien de l'Inde	106
665	520	205	355	525	570	Français	107
270	405	145	335	260	300	Ukrainien	108
515	355	165	400	180	300	Italien	109
200	240	90	160	250	360	Hollandais (Néerlandais)	110
145	140	260	225	235	85	Philippin	111
315	350	85	210	215	230	Polonais	112
170	135	75	120	190	100	Norvégien	113
75	120	50	45	230	140	Indien de l'Amérique du Nord	114
						selon l'identité autochtone	
155	75	45	40	215	150	Total de la population ayant une identité autochtone (10)	115
8,060	8,640	4,015	11,875	5,485	6,085	Total de la population non autochtone	116
						selon l'origine autochtone	
175	140	55	55	280	275	Total de la population ayant une origine autochtone (11)	117
8,040	8,570	4,005	11,860	5,420	5,960	Total de la population non autochtone	118
						selon le statut d'Indien inscrit	
10	25	25	15	50	25	Oui, Indien inscrit (12)	119
8,205	8,685	4,040	11,905	5,645	6,215	Non, pas un Indien inscrit	120

Table 1. Selected Characteristics for Census Tracts, 2001 Census – 100% Data and 20% Sample Data

No.	Characteristics	Vancouver 0285.02	Vancouver 0286.01	Vancouver 0286.02	Vancouver 0286.03	Vancouver 0287.01	Vancouver 0287.02
	POPULATION CHARACTERISTICS						
	by visible minority groups						
121	Total visible minority population	1,465	1,535	1,980	770	2,735	515
122	Chinese	940	895	840	390	1,505	200
123	South Asian	100	80	245	95	120	85
124	Black	110	50	75	10	90	20
125	Filipino	25	55	335	70	300	75
126	Latin American	45	120	135	20	80	35
127	Southeast Asian	-	90	75	10	25	-
128	Arab	-	-	15	-	20	15
129	West Asian	55	35	105	65	180	15
130	Korean	65	85	85	45	210	-
131	Japanese	60	40	15	45	70	20
132	Visible minority, n.i.e. (13)	-	-	10	10	40	20
133	Multiple visible minorities (14)	60	65	35	25	100	30
	by citizenship						
134	Canadian citizenship (15)	5,005	5,240	6,455	3,735	6,275	3,775
135	Citizenship other than Canadian	420	575	505	385	915	135
	by place of birth of respondent						
136	Non-immigrant population	3,825	3,925	4,730	3,120	4,465	3,080
137	Born in province of residence	2,920	2,840	3,475	2,315	3,260	2,270
138	Immigrant population (16)	1,560	1,850	2,190	970	2,675	830
139	United States	25	45	75	55	45	20
140	Central and South America	65	90	135	20	95	35
141	Caribbean and Bermuda	20	25	30	-	15	10
142	United Kingdom	165	120	250	130	175	150
143	Other Europe (17)	325	525	480	220	360	305
144	Africa	30	80	90	60	55	50
145	Asia and the Middle East	905	930	1,100	470	1,870	240
146	Oceania and other (18)	20	30	35	20	55	20
147	Non-permanent residents (19)	35	40	45	25	50	-
148	**Total immigrant population**	**1,560**	**1,845**	**2,185**	**970**	**2,680**	**830**
	by period of immigration						
149	Before 1961	185	235	240	165	145	140
150	1961-1970	250	205	280	160	260	135
151	1971-1980	170	320	415	185	310	190
152	1981-1990	285	280	520	195	495	150
153	1991-2001 (20)	670	805	740	265	1,470	220
154	1991-1995	320	335	375	25	645	145
155	1996-2001 (20)	350	470	365	240	825	75
	by age at immigration						
156	0-4 years	160	155	140	115	195	125
157	5-19 years	470	600	675	270	790	240
158	20 years and over	935	1,095	1,375	585	1,695	465
159	**Total population**	**5,420**	**5,810**	**6,965**	**4,120**	**7,190**	**3,910**
	by religion						
160	Catholic (21)	1,065	1,455	1,760	810	1,615	800
161	Protestant	1,645	1,830	1,950	1,475	1,685	1,245
162	Christian Orthodox	30	205	25	25	100	70
163	Christian, n.i.e. (22)	205	320	450	300	510	175
164	Muslim	60	30	220	65	190	35
165	Jewish	95	35	100	-	10	20
166	Buddhist	160	125	70	40	115	50
167	Hindu	30	10	50	10	90	10
168	Sikh	40	40	25	30	-	60
169	Eastern religions (23)	25	15	45	30	10	35
170	Other religions (24)	15	10	65	20	30	10
171	No religious affiliation (25)	2,050	1,735	2,190	1,315	2,840	1,385
172	**Total population 15 years and over**	**4,375**	**4,735**	**5,480**	**3,330**	**5,400**	**2,920**
	by generation status						
173	1st generation (26)	1,515	1,765	2,120	935	2,515	770
174	2nd generation (27)	1,180	1,220	1,240	935	910	675
175	3rd generation and over (28)	1,680	1,750	2,115	1,460	1,975	1,470
176	**Total population 1 year and over (29)**	**5,385**	**5,735**	**6,870**	**4,070**	**7,060**	**3,855**
	by place of residence 1 year ago (mobility)						
177	Non-movers	4,600	5,205	6,035	3,750	6,145	3,545
178	Movers	790	530	830	320	920	315
179	Non-migrants	290	220	395	145	460	130
180	Migrants	500	305	435	175	460	185
181	Internal migrants	395	260	370	135	325	180
182	Intraprovincial migrants	325	215	315	120	295	140
183	Interprovincial migrants	70	45	60	15	25	40
184	External migrants	105	50	65	40	140	10

Tableau 1. Certaines caractéristiques des secteurs de recensement, recensement de 2001 – Données intégrales et données-échantillon (20 %)

Vancouver 0287.04	Vancouver 0287.05 A	Vancouver 0287.06 A	Vancouver 0287.07 A	Vancouver 0290.02	Vancouver 0290.03	Caractéristiques	N°
						CARACTÉRISTIQUES DE LA POPULATION	
						selon les groupes de minorités visibles	
2,950	3,310	1,770	7,550	1,135	1,215	Total de la population des minorités visibles	121
1,925	1,760	860	4,770	380	330	Chinois	122
130	200	135	500	45	255	Sud-Asiatique	123
95	110	80	50	170	125	Noir	124
135	160	255	180	230	90	Philippin	125
85	55	30	110	10	65	Latino-Américain	126
20	50	10	275	25	15	Asiatique du Sud-Est	127
-	40	30	85	85	35	Arabe	128
40	380	200	220	75	65	Asiatique occidental	129
420	390	165	1,035	50	100	Coréen	130
40	105	-	100	15	105	Japonais	131
-	-	-	40	10	-	Minorité visible, n.i.a. (13)	132
75	55	10	180	50	30	Minorités visibles multiples (14)	133
						selon la citoyenneté	
6,895	7,480	3,500	9,170	5,300	5,845	Citoyenneté canadienne (15)	134
1,320	1,230	555	2,745	395	395	Citoyenneté autre que canadienne	135
						selon le lieu de naissance du répondant	
4,680	4,805	2,115	4,535	4,125	4,720	Population non immigrante	136
3,395	3,095	1,350	3,125	2,700	3,505	Née dans la province de résidence	137
3,470	3,795	1,925	7,155	1,535	1,490	Population immigrante (16)	138
75	75	35	130	105	40	États-Unis	139
100	95	30	165	10	55	Amérique centrale et du Sud	140
70	25	40	25	40	35	Caraïbes et Bermudes	141
295	410	200	180	230	220	Royaume-Uni	142
570	620	280	485	390	355	Autre Europe (17)	143
170	180	40	250	65	135	Afrique	144
2,160	2,365	1,300	5,865	650	610	Asie et Moyen-Orient	145
20	25	10	55	55	35	Océanie et autre (18)	146
65	105	25	230	40	25	Résidents non permanents (19)	147
3,465	**3,800**	**1,925**	**7,150**	**1,535**	**1,490**	**Population immigrante totale**	148
						selon la période d'immigration	
190	385	140	105	185	125	Avant 1961	149
230	270	135	230	160	180	1961-1970	150
540	405	305	550	210	345	1971-1980	151
495	690	415	1,050	355	330	1981-1990	152
2,015	2,050	940	5,220	620	510	1991-2001 (20)	153
860	865	390	2,365	280	315	1991-1995	154
1,155	1,180	550	2,855	340	190	1996-2001 (20)	155
						selon l'âge à l'immigration	
350	300	175	555	220	145	0-4 ans	156
1,050	975	480	2,200	450	455	5-19 ans	157
2,065	2,520	1,270	4,400	865	890	20 ans et plus	158
8,215	**8,710**	**4,060**	**11,915**	**5,695**	**6,240**	**Population totale**	159
						selon la religion	
2,105	1,810	760	2,240	1,295	1,280	Catholique (21)	160
2,270	2,490	1,295	2,225	1,760	2,000	Protestante	161
45	75	125	115	100	65	Orthodoxe chrétienne	162
490	530	230	945	290	430	Chrétiennes, n.i.a. (22)	163
145	390	220	520	130	120	Musulmane	164
20	50	-	-	-	20	Juive	165
195	190	125	775	45	65	Bouddhiste	166
20	85	30	80	20	35	Hindoue	167
15	60	70	220	-	145	Sikh	168
-	90	-	30	-	-	Religions orientales (23)	169
65	-	20	10	55	10	Autres religions (24)	170
2,830	2,955	1,180	4,750	2,005	2,080	Aucune appartenance religieuse (25)	171
6,395	**7,500**	**3,320**	**9,375**	**4,665**	**4,720**	**Population totale de 15 ans et plus**	172
						selon le statut des générations	
3,090	3,595	1,750	6,390	1,405	1,450	1re génération (26)	173
1,185	1,755	765	1,145	1,080	1,045	2e génération (27)	174
2,125	2,145	810	1,845	2,175	2,225	3e génération et plus (28)	175
8,140	**8,650**	**4,000**	**11,790**	**5,610**	**6,115**	**Population totale de 1 an et plus (29)**	176
						selon le lieu de résidence 1 an auparavant (mobilité)	
7,185	7,165	3,380	9,645	4,310	5,285	Personnes n'ayant pas déménagé	177
950	1,480	630	2,145	1,300	825	Personnes ayant déménagé	178
360	705	400	1,005	590	445	Non-migrants	179
590	775	225	1,145	710	380	Migrants	180
370	525	85	730	625	315	Migrants internes	181
350	475	85	575	545	275	Migrants infraprovinciaux	182
30	45	-	160	80	35	Migrants interprovinciaux	183
220	255	140	410	85	70	Migrants externes	184

Table 1. Selected Characteristics for Census Tracts, 2001 Census – 100% Data and 20% Sample Data

No.	Characteristics	Vancouver 0285.02	Vancouver 0286.01	Vancouver 0286.02	Vancouver 0286.03	Vancouver 0287.01	Vancouver 0287.02
	POPULATION CHARACTERISTICS						
185	**Total population 5 years and over (30)**	**5,130**	**5,495**	**6,550**	**3,910**	**6,725**	**3,620**
	by place of residence 5 years ago (mobility)						
186	Non-movers	3,535	3,630	4,285	2,690	3,005	2,480
187	Movers	1,600	1,865	2,265	1,220	3,725	1,145
188	Non-migrants	635	635	940	370	1,505	370
189	Migrants	960	1,235	1,325	845	2,225	780
190	Internal migrants	665	730	1,010	585	1,555	660
191	Intraprovincial migrants	600	555	865	485	1,365	520
192	Interprovincial migrants	65	175	150	95	195	140
193	External migrants	300	505	315	265	670	125
194	**Total population 15 to 24 years**	**835**	**970**	**985**	**590**	**1,075**	**530**
	by school attendance						
195	Not attending school	205	280	250	185	380	155
196	Attending school full time	525	615	585	350	580	325
197	Attending school part time	105	75	150	50	115	50
198	**Total population 15 years and over**	**4,370**	**4,740**	**5,480**	**3,330**	**5,400**	**2,920**
	by highest level of schooling						
199	Less than grade 9 (31)	135	175	135	80	205	50
200	Grades 9-13 without high school graduation certificate	815	875	1,045	425	1,185	520
201	Grades 9-13 with high school graduation certificate	645	730	755	480	830	445
202	Some postsecondary without degree, certificate or diploma (32)	590	760	855	495	710	390
203	Trades certificate or diploma (33)	525	480	555	435	640	425
204	College certificate or diploma (34)	785	860	1,015	575	975	600
205	University certificate below bachelor's degree	110	115	180	95	125	60
206	University with bachelor's degree or higher	765	745	940	740	735	420
	by combinations of unpaid work						
207	Males 15 years and over	2,195	2,335	2,705	1,680	2,615	1,460
208	Reported unpaid work (35)	2,015	2,150	2,415	1,495	2,385	1,320
209	Housework and child care and care or assistance to seniors	225	225	310	150	260	165
210	Housework and child care only	600	650	715	395	1,010	510
211	Housework and care or assistance to seniors only	140	200	135	140	80	100
212	Child care and care or assistance to seniors only	-	-	-	-	10	-
213	Housework only	1,025	1,050	1,210	790	975	540
214	Child care only	10	15	35	-	30	10
215	Care or assistance to seniors only	10	20	10	15	20	-
216	Females 15 years and over	2,180	2,400	2,775	1,655	2,785	1,460
217	Reported unpaid work (35)	2,070	2,215	2,585	1,525	2,605	1,390
218	Housework and child care and care or assistance to seniors	340	315	415	205	310	200
219	Housework and child care only	670	715	930	505	1,110	600
220	Housework and care or assistance to seniors only	195	290	125	115	135	110
221	Child care and care or assistance to seniors only	-	-	-	15	-	-
222	Housework only	870	875	1,095	680	1,020	470
223	Child care only	-	25	10	-	35	10
224	Care or assistance to seniors only	-	-	-	-	-	-
	by labour force activity						
225	Males 15 years and over	2,195	2,335	2,705	1,675	2,615	1,460
226	In the labour force	1,605	1,760	2,085	1,305	1,980	1,135
227	Employed	1,465	1,660	1,995	1,200	1,845	1,100
228	Unemployed	140	105	95	100	135	35
229	Not in the labour force	590	570	620	375	635	325
230	Participation rate	73.1	75.4	77.1	77.9	75.7	77.7
231	Employment rate	66.7	71.1	73.8	71.6	70.6	75.3
232	Unemployment rate	8.7	6.0	4.6	7.7	6.8	3.1
233	Females 15 years and over	2,180	2,405	2,775	1,650	2,785	1,460
234	In the labour force	1,215	1,530	1,895	1,045	1,810	1,140
235	Employed	1,130	1,420	1,795	995	1,710	1,105
236	Unemployed	80	110	105	55	105	35
237	Not in the labour force	970	875	875	605	975	320
238	Participation rate	55.7	63.6	68.3	63.3	65.0	78.1
239	Employment rate	51.8	59.0	64.7	60.3	61.4	75.7
240	Unemployment rate	6.6	7.2	5.5	5.3	5.8	3.1

Tableau 1. Certaines caractéristiques des secteurs de recensement, recensement de 2001 – Données intégrales et données-échantillon (20 %)

Vancouver 0287.04	Vancouver 0287.05 A	Vancouver 0287.06 A	Vancouver 0287.07 A	Vancouver 0290.02	Vancouver 0290.03	Caractéristiques	N°
						CARACTÉRISTIQUES DE LA POPULATION	
7,710	**8,325**	**3,865**	**11,310**	**5,330**	**5,740**	**Population totale de 5 ans et plus (30)**	185
						selon le lieu de résidence 5 ans auparavant (mobilité)	
4,155	3,365	2,130	3,810	2,220	3,105	Personnes n'ayant pas déménagé	186
3,560	4,955	1,740	7,505	3,110	2,635	Personnes ayant déménagé	187
1,030	1,860	650	2,315	1,315	1,270	Non-migrants	188
2,535	3,100	1,085	5,195	1,795	1,365	Migrants	189
1,400	1,890	585	2,555	1,455	1,145	Migrants internes	190
1,105	1,660	550	1,940	1,280	930	Migrants infraprovinciaux	191
290	230	40	615	175	220	Migrants interprovinciaux	192
1,135	1,210	495	2,635	345	220	Migrants externes	193
1,335	**1,000**	**560**	**1,965**	**620**	**850**	**Population totale de 15 à 24 ans**	194
						selon la fréquentation scolaire	
325	310	130	410	260	380	Ne fréquentant pas l'école	195
950	550	355	1,425	315	400	Fréquentant l'école à plein temps	196
65	140	70	140	50	70	Fréquentant l'école à temps partiel	197
6,400	**7,495**	**3,320**	**9,380**	**4,665**	**4,720**	**Population totale de 15 ans et plus**	198
						selon le plus haut niveau de scolarité atteint	
170	430	245	300	225	150	Niveau inférieur à la 9e année (31)	199
1,230	1,460	660	1,555	1,020	885	De la 9e à la 13e année sans certificat d'études secondaires	200
740	790	360	1,100	640	835	De la 9e à la 13e année avec certificat d'études secondaires	201
770	1,070	460	1,420	600	645	Études postsecondaires partielles sans grade, certificat ou diplôme (32)	202
630	690	295	505	635	645	Certificat ou diplôme d'une école de métiers (33)	203
1,175	1,290	580	1,540	955	935	Certificat ou diplôme collégial (34)	204
305	285	115	490	115	105	Certificat universitaire inférieur au baccalauréat	205
1,380	1,480	615	2,450	470	530	Études universitaires avec baccalauréat ou diplôme supérieur	206
						selon les combinaisons de travail non rémunéré	
3,095	3,330	1,490	4,580	2,120	2,315	Hommes de 15 ans et plus	207
2,745	2,925	1,325	4,090	1,890	2,085	Travail non rémunéré déclaré (35)	208
275	220	95	455	120	190	Travaux ménagers et soins aux enfants et soins ou aide aux personnes âgées	209
1,125	790	445	1,395	615	865	Travaux ménagers et soins aux enfants seulement	210
115	200	135	220	75	75	Travaux ménagers et soins ou aide aux personnes âgées seulement	211
10	-	-	15	-	20	Soins aux enfants et soins ou aide aux personnes âgées seulement	212
1,185	1,625	620	1,920	1,050	905	Travaux ménagers seulement	213
15	45	15	55	20	30	Soins aux enfants seulement	214
15	40	20	35	10	10	Soins ou aide aux personnes âgées seulement	215
3,305	4,170	1,830	4,795	2,540	2,410	Femmes de 15 ans et plus	216
3,105	3,900	1,610	4,500	2,290	2,280	Travail non rémunéré déclaré (35)	217
355	360	210	550	175	290	Travaux ménagers et soins aux enfants et soins ou aide aux personnes âgées	218
1,205	1,055	485	1,645	815	990	Travaux ménagers et soins aux enfants seulement	219
150	405	235	230	150	115	Travaux ménagers et soins ou aide aux personnes âgées seulement	220
-	-	-	10	-	-	Soins aux enfants et soins ou aide aux personnes âgées seulement	221
1,370	2,030	665	2,015	1,140	845	Travaux ménagers seulement	222
20	45	-	45	-	30	Soins aux enfants seulement	223
10	-	10	10	-	10	Soins ou aide aux personnes âgées seulement	224
						selon l'activité	
3,095	3,335	1,490	4,585	2,120	2,315	Hommes de 15 ans et plus	225
2,285	2,200	960	3,075	1,710	1,845	Population active	226
2,195	2,050	905	2,875	1,570	1,710	Personnes occupées	227
95	155	55	200	140	135	Chômeurs	228
805	1,130	530	1,510	410	470	Inactifs	229
73.8	66.0	64.4	67.1	80.7	79.7	Taux d'activité	230
70.9	61.5	60.7	62.7	74.1	73.9	Taux d'emploi	231
4.2	7.0	5.7	6.5	8.2	7.3	Taux de chômage	232
3,305	4,170	1,830	4,790	2,540	2,405	Femmes de 15 ans et plus	233
2,175	2,300	950	2,565	1,580	1,545	Population active	234
2,070	2,105	870	2,335	1,485	1,455	Personnes occupées	235
105	195	75	235	95	95	Chômeuses	236
1,125	1,865	880	2,230	955	860	Inactives	237
65.8	55.2	51.9	53.5	62.2	64.2	Taux d'activité	238
62.6	50.5	47.5	48.7	58.5	60.5	Taux d'emploi	239
4.8	8.5	7.9	9.2	6.0	6.1	Taux de chômage	240

Table 1. Selected Characteristics for Census Tracts, 2001 Census – 100% Data and 20% Sample Data

No.	Characteristics	Vancouver 0285.02	Vancouver 0286.01	Vancouver 0286.02	Vancouver 0286.03	Vancouver 0287.01	Vancouver 0287.02
	POPULATION CHARACTERISTICS						
	by labour force activity – concluded						
241	Both sexes - Participation rate	64.4	69.6	72.7	70.6	70.3	78.1
242	15-24 years	55.1	66.5	59.9	59.3	47.9	71.7
243	25 years and over	66.7	70.3	75.5	73.0	75.6	79.3
244	Both sexes - Employment rate	59.4	65.0	69.1	65.9	65.7	75.7
245	15-24 years	43.7	58.2	53.8	46.6	45.1	67.9
246	25 years and over	62.9	66.7	72.4	70.1	70.8	77.2
247	Both sexes - Unemployment rate	8.0	6.4	5.0	6.4	6.3	3.1
248	15-24 years	19.6	13.1	10.2	20.3	6.8	5.3
249	25 years and over	5.5	4.9	4.1	4.0	6.4	2.6
250	**Total labour force 15 years and over**	**2,820**	**3,300**	**3,985**	**2,350**	**3,790**	**2,280**
	by industry based on the 1997 NAICS						
251	Industry - Not applicable (36)	70	85	70	25	70	10
252	All industries (37)	2,750	3,210	3,920	2,330	3,725	2,265
253	11 Agriculture, forestry, fishing and hunting	15	-	15	-	-	10
254	21 Mining and oil and gas extraction	10	-	-	-	-	-
255	22 Utilities	55	15	55	30	20	40
256	23 Construction	200	255	235	160	225	200
257	31-33 Manufacturing	200	315	320	200	380	145
258	41 Wholesale trade	160	275	245	180	245	140
259	44-45 Retail trade	375	480	370	215	550	250
260	48-49 Transportation and warehousing	165	170	220	85	250	95
261	51 Information and cultural industries	130	125	160	140	140	85
262	52 Finance and insurance	125	190	205	80	150	135
263	53 Real estate and rental and leasing	90	25	55	40	55	55
264	54 Professional, scientific and technical services	180	195	360	190	265	210
265	55 Management of companies and enterprises	-	-	-	-	-	-
266	56 Administrative and support, waste management and remediation services	95	70	150	75	165	60
267	61 Educational services	280	245	360	285	190	260
268	62 Health care and social assistance	255	215	430	215	380	245
269	71 Arts, entertainment and recreation	60	75	50	75	75	60
270	72 Accommodation and food services	95	215	285	115	295	135
271	81 Other services (except public administration)	140	175	225	110	180	60
272	91 Public administration	145	165	170	110	150	80
	by class of worker						
273	Class of worker - Not applicable (36)	70	85	70	20	65	10
274	All classes of worker (37)	2,750	3,210	3,920	2,330	3,725	2,265
275	Paid workers	2,570	2,900	3,615	2,135	3,470	2,115
276	Employees	2,380	2,750	3,435	1,990	3,260	1,980
277	Self-employed (incorporated)	190	155	185	145	205	135
278	Self-employed (unincorporated)	180	285	300	195	245	145
279	Unpaid family workers	-	25	-	-	15	-
	by occupation based on the 2001 NOC-S						
280	Male labour force 15 years and over	1,605	1,760	2,085	1,300	1,980	1,135
281	Occupation - Not applicable (36)	40	45	25	20	35	-
282	All occupations (37)	1,565	1,720	2,060	1,280	1,940	1,140
283	A Management occupations	255	240	300	205	240	200
284	B Business, finance and administration occupations	150	160	185	90	155	105
285	C Natural and applied sciences and related occupations	190	190	265	170	220	130
286	D Health occupations	15	15	25	20	25	15
287	E Occupations in social science, education, government service and religion	105	100	130	95	70	65
288	F Occupations in art, culture, recreation and sport	85	40	15	25	50	20
289	G Sales and service occupations	290	330	475	260	485	210
290	H Trades, transport and equipment operators and related occupations	390	545	535	330	555	340
291	I Occupations unique to primary industry	40	-	15	30	15	15
292	J Occupations unique to processing, manufacturing and utilities	50	90	100	50	125	40
293	Female labour force 15 years and over	1,215	1,535	1,895	1,050	1,815	1,140
294	Occupation - Not applicable (36)	25	40	40	-	30	10
295	All occupations (37)	1,185	1,490	1,860	1,045	1,780	1,130
296	A Management occupations	95	100	160	75	115	85
297	B Business, finance and administration occupations	345	500	595	385	510	350
298	C Natural and applied sciences and related occupations	25	85	45	15	40	35
299	D Health occupations	125	90	160	85	190	110

Tableau 1. Certaines caractéristiques des secteurs de recensement, recensement de 2001 – Données intégrales et données-échantillon (20 %)

Vancouver 0287.04	Vancouver 0287.05 A	Vancouver 0287.06 A	Vancouver 0287.07 A	Vancouver 0290.02	Vancouver 0290.03	Caractéristiques	N°
						CARACTÉRISTIQUES DE LA POPULATION	
						selon l'activité – fin	
69.8	60.1	57.5	60.1	70.5	71.7	Les deux sexes - Taux d'activité	241
51.3	53.8	64.9	39.7	60.0	59.4	15-24 ans	242
74.6	61.0	56.1	65.6	72.2	74.5	25 ans et plus	243
66.6	55.4	53.5	55.6	65.5	67.0	Les deux sexes - Taux d'emploi	244
45.7	47.0	57.7	32.8	48.4	53.5	15-24 ans	245
72.1	56.7	52.8	61.5	68.2	70.0	25 ans et plus	246
4.5	7.7	6.8	7.7	7.1	6.8	Les deux sexes - Taux de chômage	247
10.2	12.0	11.1	16.8	18.7	9.9	15-24 ans	248
3.4	7.2	6.1	6.2	5.5	6.1	25 ans et plus	249
4,465	**4,505**	**1,910**	**5,640**	**3,295**	**3,390**	**Population active totale de 15 ans et plus**	250
						selon l'industrie basée sur le SCIAN de 1997	
95	125	25	170	65	80	Industrie - Sans objet (36)	251
4,370	4,375	1,875	5,475	3,230	3,310	Toutes les industries (37)	252
10	20	-	20	15	45	11 Agriculture, foresterie, pêche et chasse	253
10	-	-	10	-	-	21 Extraction minière et extraction de pétrole et de gaz	254
35	50	10	25	30	35	22 Services publics	255
250	160	60	220	250	235	23 Construction	256
350	430	185	415	370	355	31-33 Fabrication	257
265	305	105	365	215	225	41 Commerce de gros	258
495	585	270	795	355	400	44-45 Commerce de détail	259
220	205	45	330	230	255	48-49 Transport et entreposage	260
265	185	105	235	115	150	51 Industrie de l'information et industrie culturelle	261
315	270	95	390	135	160	52 Finance et assurances	262
140	70	65	170	70	85	53 Services immobiliers et services de location et de location à bail	263
380	325	130	500	165	170	54 Services professionnels, scientifiques et techniques	264
-	-	-	-	-	-	55 Gestion de sociétés et d'entreprises	265
175	140	55	165	160	85	56 Services administratifs, services de soutien, services de gestion des déchets et services d'assainissement	266
300	325	140	445	85	200	61 Services d'enseignement	267
335	440	185	490	375	370	62 Soins de santé et assistance sociale	268
135	85	35	80	70	65	71 Arts, spectacles et loisirs	269
300	340	190	370	230	175	72 Hébergement et services de restauration	270
195	175	105	215	200	130	81 Autres services, sauf les administrations publiques	271
195	255	100	240	155	175	91 Administrations publiques	272
						selon la catégorie de travailleurs	
90	130	30	170	65	80	Catégorie de travailleurs - Sans objet (36)	273
4,375	4,375	1,880	5,475	3,230	3,310	Toutes les catégories de travailleurs (37)	274
3,895	4,070	1,695	4,955	3,105	3,110	Travailleurs rémunérés	275
3,610	3,910	1,650	4,455	3,050	3,035	Employés	276
290	160	45	495	55	75	Travailleurs autonomes (entreprise constituée en société)	277
465	295	160	485	115	195	Travailleurs autonomes (entreprise non constituée en société)	278
10	10	25	30	10	-	Travailleurs familiaux non rémunérés	279
						selon la profession basée sur la CNP-S de 2001	
2,285	2,205	960	3,075	1,710	1,845	Hommes actifs de 15 ans et plus	280
50	40	10	60	30	45	Profession - Sans objet (36)	281
2,235	2,165	950	3,015	1,680	1,795	Toutes les professions (37)	282
440	465	160	950	165	225	A Gestion	283
270	245	90	295	195	220	B Affaires, finance et administration	284
275	325	125	340	150	205	C Sciences naturelles et appliquées et professions apparentées	285
50	40	35	80	10	25	D Secteur de la santé	286
80	90	55	140	35	55	E Sciences sociales, enseignement, administration publique et religion	287
90	35	40	115	35	40	F Arts, culture, sports et loisirs	288
540	470	250	600	325	360	G Ventes et services	289
390	385	130	405	605	575	H Métiers, transport et machinerie	290
40	25	-	10	35	15	I Professions propres au secteur primaire	291
50	80	50	80	125	85	J Transformation, fabrication et services d'utilité publique	292
2,180	2,300	945	2,570	1,585	1,550	Femmes actives de 15 ans et plus	293
40	90	20	110	35	35	Profession - Sans objet (36)	294
2,140	2,215	930	2,455	1,550	1,515	Toutes les professions (37)	295
205	155	45	355	110	105	A Gestion	296
730	805	315	755	575	515	B Affaires, finance et administration	297
65	70	25	90	10	30	C Sciences naturelles et appliquées et professions apparentées	298
145	155	75	170	135	145	D Secteur de la santé	299

Table 1. Selected Characteristics for Census Tracts, 2001 Census – 100% Data and 20% Sample Data

No.	Characteristics	Vancouver 0285.02	Vancouver 0286.01	Vancouver 0286.02	Vancouver 0286.03	Vancouver 0287.01	Vancouver 0287.02
	POPULATION CHARACTERISTICS						
	by occupation based on the 2001 NOC-S – concluded						
	E Occupations in social science, education,						
300	government service and religion	130	175	245	165	170	210
301	F Occupations in art, culture, recreation and sport	50	40	45	50	60	15
302	G Sales and service occupations	375	475	550	250	595	315
	H Trades, transport and equipment						
303	operators and related occupations	25	15	30	10	40	15
304	I Occupations unique to primary industry	-	10	15	-	-	-
	J Occupations unique to processing,						
305	manufacturing and utilities	15	10	15	10	50	10
306	**Total employed labour force 15 years and over**	**2,595**	**3,080**	**3,785**	**2,200**	**3,550**	**2,205**
	by place of work						
307	Males	1,465	1,655	1,995	1,200	1,840	1,105
308	Usual place of work	1,020	1,180	1,615	880	1,430	775
309	At home	120	135	65	85	80	95
310	Outside Canada	50	20	10	15	20	-
311	No fixed workplace address	270	320	305	220	310	230
312	Females	1,130	1,420	1,790	995	1,710	1,105
313	Usual place of work	925	1,240	1,550	825	1,440	925
314	At home	105	115	160	120	135	130
315	Outside Canada	10	10	-	-	10	-
316	No fixed workplace address	95	50	80	50	130	55
	Total employed labour force 15 years and over with usual place of work or no fixed						
317	**workplace address**	**2,315**	**2,800**	**3,550**	**1,975**	**3,310**	**1,975**
	by mode of transportation						
318	Males	1,300	1,500	1,920	1,100	1,740	1,000
319	Car, truck, van, as driver	1,140	1,350	1,645	990	1,530	835
320	Car, truck, van, as passenger	50	55	105	15	85	85
321	Public transit	75	70	115	60	80	55
322	Walked	20	10	35	15	15	10
323	Other method	10	30	15	10	35	15
324	Females	1,020	1,295	1,635	875	1,570	975
325	Car, truck, van, as driver	765	1,030	1,205	680	1,095	825
326	Car, truck, van, as passenger	90	110	135	65	230	75
327	Public transit	125	120	180	115	165	50
328	Walked	25	30	100	10	65	-
329	Other method	10	10	10	10	10	20
	Total population 15 years and over who worked						
330	**since January 1, 2000**	**3,030**	**3,435**	**4,235**	**2,505**	**4,030**	**2,405**
	by language used at work						
331	Single responses	2,780	3,155	3,995	2,330	3,600	2,290
332	English	2,715	3,120	3,945	2,320	3,445	2,275
333	French	-	-	10	-	-	-
334	Non-official languages (5)	60	25	40	-	155	15
335	Chinese, n.o.s.	-	10	10	-	60	10
336	Cantonese	10	-	20	-	40	-
337	Other languages (6)	45	20	-	10	55	-
338	Multiple responses	255	280	240	180	425	115
339	English and French	20	30	15	25	-	40
340	English and non-official language	220	245	220	155	425	75
341	French and non-official language	-	-	-	-	-	-
342	English, French and non-official language	10	10	-	10	-	-
	DWELLING AND HOUSEHOLD CHARACTERISTICS						
343	**Total number of occupied private dwellings**	**1,760**	**1,930**	**2,235**	**1,415**	**2,305**	**1,215**
	by tenure						
344	Owned	1,400	1,565	1,800	1,220	1,540	1,065
345	Rented	360	360	430	190	765	150
346	Band housing	-	-	-	-	-	-
	by structural type of dwelling						
347	Single-detached house	1,540	1,550	1,610	1,200	1,355	1,095
348	Semi-detached house	10	10	140	-	15	-
349	Row house	10	-	175	-	325	-
350	Apartment, detached duplex	125	340	295	200	135	115
351	Apartment, building that has five or more storeys	-	-	-	-	-	-
	Apartment, building that has fewer than						
352	five storeys (38)	75	35	10	10	320	10
353	Other single-attached house	-	-	10	-	10	-
354	Movable dwelling (39)	-	-	-	-	155	-

Tableau 1. Certaines caractéristiques des secteurs de recensement, recensement de 2001 – Données intégrales et données-échantillon (20 %)

Vancouver 0287.04	Vancouver 0287.05 A	Vancouver 0287.06 A	Vancouver 0287.07 A	Vancouver 0290.02	Vancouver 0290.03	Caractéristiques	N°
						CARACTÉRISTIQUES DE LA POPULATION	
						selon la profession basée sur la CNP-S de 2001 – fin	
220	270	75	270	125	170	E Sciences sociales, enseignement, administration publique et religion	300
85	35	30	75	20	55	F Arts, culture, sports et loisirs	301
575	610	320	635	490	420	G Ventes et services	302
35	30	15	20	55	45	H Métiers, transport et machinerie	303
10	10	-	-	-	15	I Professions propres au secteur primaire	304
75	75	35	80	30	20	J Transformation, fabrication et services d'utilité publique	305
4,260	**4,150**	**1,775**	**5,210**	**3,055**	**3,170**	**Population active occupée totale de 15 ans et plus**	306
						selon le lieu de travail	
2,190	2,050	905	2,875	1,570	1,710	Hommes	307
1,675	1,670	725	2,130	1,205	1,350	Lieu habituel de travail	308
160	130	80	320	90	90	À domicile	309
45	25	15	90	-	10	En dehors du Canada	310
310	225	85	335	265	265	Sans adresse de travail fixe	311
2,070	2,105	875	2,335	1,485	1,460	Femmes	312
1,765	1,820	765	1,925	1,345	1,255	Lieu habituel de travail	313
190	140	55	300	85	115	À domicile	314
-	10	-	15	10	-	En dehors du Canada	315
115	135	50	90	55	85	Sans adresse de travail fixe	316
3,865	**3,845**	**1,625**	**4,485**	**2,865**	**2,950**	**Population active occupée totale de 15 ans et plus ayant un lieu habituel de travail ou sans adresse de travail fixe**	317
						selon le mode de transport	
1,985	1,890	810	2,460	1,470	1,615	Hommes	318
1,755	1,635	645	2,190	1,225	1,410	Automobile, camion ou fourgonnette, en tant que conducteur	319
75	75	80	135	40	80	Automobile, camion ou fourgonnette, en tant que passager	320
110	110	55	110	130	60	Transport en commun	321
10	65	30	10	40	30	À pied	322
40	-	-	20	35	30	Autre moyen	323
1,880	1,955	820	2,020	1,395	1,340	Femmes	324
1,340	1,435	535	1,570	895	1,030	Automobile, camion ou fourgonnette, en tant que conductrice	325
280	155	95	255	130	130	Automobile, camion ou fourgonnette, en tant que passagère	326
150	200	125	150	240	95	Transport en commun	327
95	155	60	35	100	60	À pied	328
10	-	-	10	35	30	Autre moyen	329
4,725	**4,805**	**2,100**	**6,100**	**3,460**	**3,610**	**Population totale de 15 ans et plus ayant travaillé depuis le 1er janvier 2000**	330
						selon la langue utilisée au travail	
4,200	4,290	1,875	4,935	3,185	3,490	Réponses uniques	331
4,115	4,115	1,795	4,635	3,170	3,430	Anglais	332
-	-	-	10	-	-	Français	333
75	175	75	295	10	55	Langues non officielles (5)	334
15	30	10	80	-	-	Chinois, n.d.a.	335
20	105	35	100	10	35	Cantonais	336
35	35	35	115	-	20	Autres langues (6)	337
525	520	230	1,170	275	125	Réponses multiples	338
35	50	15	50	60	30	Anglais et français	339
490	465	210	1,105	215	90	Anglais et langue non officielle	340
-	-	-	-	-	-	Français et langue non officielle	341
-	-	10	20	10	-	Anglais, français et langue non officielle	342
						CARACTÉRISTIQUES DES LOGEMENTS ET DES MÉNAGES	
2,525	**4,095**	**1,605**	**3,475**	**2,775**	**2,055**	**Nombre total de logements privés occupés**	343
						selon le mode d'occupation	
2,120	3,020	950	3,070	1,615	1,595	Possédé	344
410	1,070	660	405	1,160	460	Loué	345
-	-	-	-	-	-	Logement de bande	346
						selon le type de construction résidentielle	
1,490	505	670	2,120	270	1,140	Maison individuelle non attenante	347
150	-	65	130	25	65	Maison jumelée	348
640	210	180	670	270	475	Maison en rangée	349
135	45	80	300	120	300	Appartement, duplex non attenant	350
-	880	-	-	-	-	Appartement, immeuble de cinq étages ou plus	351
105	2,460	605	250	2,080	65	Appartement, immeuble de moins de cinq étages (38)	352
-	-	-	-	15	-	Autre maison individuelle attenante	353
-	-	-	-	-	-	Logement mobile (39)	354

Table 1. Selected Characteristics for Census Tracts, 2001 Census – 100% Data and 20% Sample Data

No.	Characteristics	Vancouver 0285.02	Vancouver 0286.01	Vancouver 0286.02	Vancouver 0286.03	Vancouver 0287.01	Vancouver 0287.02
	DWELLING AND HOUSEHOLD CHARACTERISTICS						
	by condition of dwelling						
355	Regular maintenance only	1,210	1,275	1,460	960	1,525	880
356	Minor repairs	485	575	650	380	650	285
357	Major repairs	60	80	125	70	130	55
	by period of construction						
358	Before 1946	60	30	20	-	10	20
359	1946-1960	350	400	125	180	15	45
360	1961-1970	705	915	490	700	130	100
361	1971-1980	375	330	890	370	710	315
362	1981-1990	175	170	500	110	985	410
363	1991-2001 (20)	85	80	210	45	460	330
364	Average number of rooms per dwelling	8.0	7.7	7.6	8.1	6.5	8.2
365	Average number of bedrooms per dwelling	3.4	3.3	3.3	3.3	2.9	3.3
366	Average value of dwelling $	317,566	289,454	253,200	282,231	215,147	306,735
367	**Total number of private households**	**1,760**	**1,930**	**2,235**	**1,415**	**2,305**	**1,215**
	by household size						
368	1 person	225	250	265	210	335	140
369	2 persons	500	535	595	435	515	290
370	3 persons	335	415	460	250	465	235
371	4-5 persons	595	655	805	510	875	485
372	6 or more persons	110	75	110	15	115	60
	by household type						
373	One-family households	1,415	1,495	1,805	1,130	1,755	990
374	Multiple-family households	50	125	80	35	130	65
375	Non-family households	295	315	345	250	415	160
376	Number of persons in private households	5,420	5,810	6,960	4,115	7,190	3,910
377	Average number of persons in private households	3.1	3.0	3.1	2.9	3.1	3.2
378	Average number of persons per room	0.4	0.4	0.4	0.4	0.5	0.4
379	Tenant households in non-farm, non-reserve private dwellings (40)	360	365	430	185	760	150
380	Average gross rent $ (40)	917	1,000	908	964	989	875
381	Tenant households spending 30% or more of household income on gross rent (40) (41)	130	120	170	75	280	50
382	Tenant households spending from 30% to 99% of household income on gross rent (40) (41)	105	120	145	40	230	40
383	Owner households in non-farm, non-reserve private dwellings (42)	1,400	1,570	1,800	1,220	1,535	1,060
384	Average owner's major payments $ (42)	946	940	1,115	1,043	1,076	1,194
385	Owner households spending 30% or more of household income on owner's major payments (41) (42)	285	335	365	230	505	200
386	Owner households spending from 30% to 99% of household income on owner's major payments (41) (42)	250	295	325	175	430	190
	CENSUS FAMILY CHARACTERISTICS						
387	**Total number of census families in private households**	**1,520**	**1,740**	**1,975**	**1,195**	**2,025**	**1,120**
	by census family structure and size						
388	Total couple families	1,330	1,475	1,725	1,035	1,625	980
389	Total families of married couples	1,235	1,345	1,560	985	1,460	890
390	Without children at home	415	410	480	365	345	240
391	With children at home	815	940	1,085	615	1,115	650
392	1 child	235	350	330	200	345	185
393	2 children	410	510	565	275	580	315
394	3 or more children	175	75	190	145	190	145
395	Total families of common-law couples	95	120	165	45	165	90
396	Without children at home	50	60	125	20	70	55
397	With children at home	45	60	45	30	95	35
398	1 child	30	45	20	20	50	20
399	2 children	10	10	20	-	35	20
400	3 or more children	-	10	10	10	15	-
401	Total lone-parent families	190	265	245	160	400	135
402	Female parent	145	180	205	130	330	85
403	1 child	65	115	90	70	200	70
404	2 children	60	40	90	55	110	15
405	3 or more children	20	15	30	10	25	10

Tableau 1. Certaines caractéristiques des secteurs de recensement, recensement de 2001 – Données intégrales et données-échantillon (20 %)

Vancouver 0287.04	Vancouver 0287.05 A	Vancouver 0287.06 A	Vancouver 0287.07 A	Vancouver 0290.02	Vancouver 0290.03	Caractéristiques	N°
						CARACTÉRISTIQUES DES LOGEMENTS ET DES MÉNAGES	
						selon l'état du logement	
1,840	2,575	1,175	3,115	1,680	1,405	Entretien régulier seulement	355
550	520	345	280	465	530	Réparations mineures	356
135	1,005	85	75	630	120	Réparations majeures	357
						selon la période de construction	
-	-	-	-	55	30	Avant 1946	358
10	10	-	-	125	175	1946-1960	359
15	15	35	10	220	800	1961-1970	360
375	95	65	10	425	400	1971-1980	361
1,215	1,035	1,210	195	405	195	1981-1990	362
910	2,945	290	3,255	1,545	460	1991-2001 (20)	363
7.9	4.9	6.0	8.0	4.6	7.3	Nombre moyen de pièces par logement	364
3.4	2.0	2.5	3.8	1.9	3.2	Nombre moyen de chambres à coucher par logement	365
282,564	156,967	240,342	355,028	119,504	222,594	Valeur moyenne du logement $	366
2,525	**4,095**	**1,605**	**3,475**	**2,780**	**2,050**	**Nombre total de logements privés**	367
						selon la taille du ménage	
210	1,455	530	245	1,155	265	1 personne	368
635	1,470	405	810	890	555	2 personnes	369
540	570	220	685	355	445	3 personnes	370
1,010	565	395	1,465	345	710	4-5 personnes	371
130	30	55	275	40	80	6 personnes ou plus	372
						selon le genre de ménage	
2,210	2,450	1,030	2,975	1,480	1,655	Ménages unifamiliaux	373
75	20	25	190	15	45	Ménages multifamiliaux	374
240	1,625	550	315	1,290	355	Ménages non familiaux	375
8,215	8,710	4,060	11,915	5,670	6,240	Nombre de personnes dans les ménages privés	376
3.3	2.1	2.5	3.4	2.0	3.0	Nombre moyen de personnes dans les ménages privés	377
0.4	0.4	0.4	0.4	0.4	0.4	Nombre moyen de personnes par pièce	378
400	1,065	655	400	1,150	460	Ménages locataires dans les logements privés non agricoles hors réserve (40)	379
1,028	797	980	1,311	745	760	Loyer brut moyen $ (40)	380
140	485	355	175	605	165	Ménages locataires consacrant 30 % ou plus du revenu du ménage au loyer brut (40) (41)	381
100	375	295	120	505	115	Ménages locataires consacrant de 30 % à 99 % du revenu du ménage au loyer brut (40) (41)	382
2,115	3,020	950	3,060	1,615	1,590	Ménages propriétaires dans les logements privés non agricoles hors réserve (42)	383
1,231	873	987	1,439	900	1,111	Principales dépenses de propriété moyennes $ (42)	384
585	860	260	1,125	335	355	Ménages propriétaires consacrant 30 % ou plus du revenu du ménage aux principales dépenses de propriété (41) (42)	385
460	700	200	825	290	305	Ménages propriétaires consacrant de 30 % à 99 % du revenu du ménage aux principales dépenses de propriété (41) (42)	386
						CARACTÉRISTIQUES DES FAMILLES DE RECENSEMENT	
2,365	**2,495**	**1,085**	**3,370**	**1,505**	**1,750**	**Total des familles de recensement dans les ménages privés**	387
						selon la structure et la taille de la famille de recensement	
2,110	2,100	950	3,080	1,145	1,515	Total des familles avec conjoints	388
1,960	1,835	905	2,890	865	1,320	Total des familles avec couples mariés	389
565	890	310	760	400	330	Sans enfants à la maison	390
1,390	945	595	2,130	460	985	Avec enfants à la maison	391
415	425	190	640	190	350	1 enfant	392
700	405	305	1,120	215	490	2 enfants	393
275	115	100	370	55	145	3 enfants ou plus	394
145	265	45	185	280	195	Total des familles en union libre	395
75	245	25	125	185	85	Sans enfants à la maison	396
70	15	20	60	95	110	Avec enfants à la maison	397
55	10	10	35	70	70	1 enfant	398
10	-	10	20	25	10	2 enfants	399
10	-	-	10	-	25	3 enfants ou plus	400
260	390	130	295	355	235	Total des familles monoparentales	401
215	325	105	235	325	180	Parent de sexe féminin	402
85	230	70	120	190	110	1 enfant	403
100	85	15	80	70	50	2 enfants	404
30	15	15	35	55	20	3 enfants ou plus	405

Table 1. Selected Characteristics for Census Tracts, 2001 Census – 100% Data and 20% Sample Data

No.	Characteristics	Vancouver 0285.02	Vancouver 0286.01	Vancouver 0286.02	Vancouver 0286.03	Vancouver 0287.01	Vancouver 0287.02
	CENSUS FAMILY CHARACTERISTICS						
	by census family structure and size – concluded						
406	Male parent	40	95	40	30	70	45
407	1 child	20	55	25	10	40	40
408	2 children	20	25	15	10	20	10
409	3 or more children	-	10	-	10	10	-
410	**Total number of children at home**	**2,015**	**2,090**	**2,550**	**1,500**	**2,880**	**1,525**
	by age groups						
411	Under 6 years	380	365	505	275	565	350
412	6-14 years	670	705	955	515	1,220	630
413	15-17 years	270	240	335	185	430	180
414	18-24 years	475	550	570	355	485	285
415	25 years and over	230	235	190	175	180	85
416	Average number of children at home per census family (43)	1.3	1.2	1.3	1.3	1.4	1.4
417	**Total number of persons in private households**	**5,420**	**5,810**	**6,965**	**4,120**	**7,190**	**3,910**
	by census family status and living arrangements						
418	Number of non-family persons	560	510	705	390	660	290
419	Living with relatives (44)	80	125	210	105	110	55
420	Living with non-relatives only	255	135	235	75	215	100
421	Living alone	225	255	270	210	335	135
422	Number of family persons	4,860	5,300	6,255	3,730	6,530	3,625
423	Average number of persons per census family	3.2	3.0	3.2	3.1	3.2	3.2
424	**Total number of persons 65 years and over**	**570**	**585**	**495**	**415**	**425**	**265**
425	Number of non-family persons 65 years and over	110	130	200	100	170	55
426	Living with relatives (44)	40	20	110	30	45	25
427	Living with non-relatives only	10	15	30	10	-	-
428	Living alone	65	95	55	70	120	30
429	Number of family persons 65 years and over	460	455	295	310	260	210
	ECONOMIC FAMILY CHARACTERISTICS						
430	**Total number of economic families in private households**	**1,470**	**1,645**	**1,925**	**1,190**	**1,905**	**1,060**
	by size of family						
431	2 persons	470	515	610	430	505	305
432	3 persons	355	410	445	255	435	210
433	4 persons	420	525	580	325	635	345
434	5 or more persons	230	195	290	185	325	195
435	Total number of persons in economic families	4,945	5,425	6,460	3,830	6,640	3,680
436	Average number of persons per economic family	3.3	3.3	3.4	3.2	3.5	3.5
437	Total number of unattached individuals	480	380	505	285	555	235
	2000 INCOME CHARACTERISTICS						
	Population 15 years and over by sex and total income groups in 2000						
438	Total - Both sexes	4,375	4,735	5,480	3,330	5,400	2,920
439	Without income	290	300	345	195	590	95
440	With income	4,080	4,435	5,135	3,130	4,810	2,825
441	Under $1,000 (45)	185	260	275	135	200	105
442	$ 1,000 - $ 2,999	225	195	260	165	315	105
443	$ 3,000 - $ 4,999	130	155	145	100	195	85
444	$ 5,000 - $ 6,999	210	215	175	125	240	155
445	$ 7,000 - $ 9,999	245	355	210	155	245	175
446	$10,000 - $11,999	170	200	215	115	210	60
447	$12,000 - $14,999	235	235	280	130	285	180
448	$15,000 - $19,999	360	335	290	235	345	165
449	$20,000 - $24,999	280	345	330	135	400	130
450	$25,000 - $29,999	195	295	380	200	395	210
451	$30,000 - $34,999	280	330	350	265	375	190
452	$35,000 - $39,999	245	350	310	165	260	210
453	$40,000 - $44,999	195	305	385	185	265	235
454	$45,000 - $49,999	205	140	415	175	210	145
455	$50,000 - $59,999	275	235	430	280	400	210
456	$60,000 and over	650	480	685	565	475	465
457	Average income $ (46)	33,637	28,866	34,332	36,184	30,222	35,328
458	Median income $ (46)	24,975	24,023	29,977	30,295	24,840	30,049
459	Standard error of average income $ (46)	1,620	835	1,082	1,308	1,271	1,691

Tableau 1. Certaines caractéristiques des secteurs de recensement, recensement de 2001 – Données intégrales et données-échantillon (20 %)

Vancouver 0287.04	Vancouver 0287.05 A	Vancouver 0287.06 A	Vancouver 0287.07 A	Vancouver 0290.02	Vancouver 0290.03	Caractéristiques	N°
						CARACTÉRISTIQUES DES FAMILLES DE RECENSEMENT	
						selon la structure et la taille de la famille de recensement – fin	
45	60	30	60	35	55	Parent de sexe masculin	406
20	40	15	45	30	35	1 enfant	407
20	20	15	10	10	20	2 enfants	408
10	-	-	-	-	10	3 enfants ou plus	409
3,250	**2,150**	**1,375**	**4,630**	**1,495**	**2,335**	**Nombre total d'enfants à la maison**	410
						selon les groupes d'âge	
625	440	235	780	480	585	Moins de 6 ans	411
1,180	765	505	1,755	550	920	6-14 ans	412
555	300	205	685	180	305	15-17 ans	413
665	425	310	1,035	200	400	18-24 ans	414
215	220	120	380	85	125	25 ans et plus	415
1.4	0.9	1.3	1.4	1.0	1.3	Nombre moyen d'enfants à la maison par famille de recensement (43)	416
8,215	**8,710**	**4,065**	**11,915**	**5,670**	**6,235**	**Nombre total de personnes dans les ménages privés**	417
						selon la situation des particuliers dans la famille de recensement et des particuliers dans le ménage	
490	1,960	650	840	1,530	640	Nombre de personnes hors famille de recensement	418
120	220	70	335	60	145	Vivant avec des personnes apparentées (44)	419
160	290	55	265	310	235	Vivant avec des personnes non apparentées uniquement	420
210	1,455	525	245	1,155	265	Vivant seules	421
7,725	6,745	3,410	11,075	4,145	5,600	Nombre de personnes membres d'une famille	422
3.3	2.7	3.1	3.3	2.8	3.2	Nombre moyen de personnes par famille de recensement	423
465	**1,370**	**760**	**605**	**680**	**315**	**Nombre total de personnes de 65 ans et plus**	424
155	590	410	135	465	140	Nombre de personnes hors famille de recensement de 65 ans et plus	425
75	65	50	100	15	85	Vivant avec des personnes apparentées (44)	426
25	20	20	-	-	-	Vivant avec des personnes non apparentées uniquement	427
55	510	340	35	450	50	Vivant seules	428
315	780	350	470	215	175	Nombre de personnes membres d'une famille de 65 ans et plus	429
						CARACTÉRISTIQUES DES FAMILLES ÉCONOMIQUES	
2,295	**2,520**	**1,060**	**3,185**	**1,505**	**1,725**	**Nombre total de familles économiques dans les ménages privés**	430
						selon la taille de la famille	
650	1,380	390	815	810	530	2 personnes	431
560	565	215	680	320	430	3 personnes	432
725	410	295	1,035	290	530	4 personnes	433
365	170	160	655	90	230	5 personnes ou plus	434
7,845	6,965	3,480	11,410	4,205	5,740	Nombre total de personnes dans les familles économiques	435
3.4	2.8	3.3	3.6	2.8	3.3	Nombre moyen de personnes par famille économique	436
370	1,740	580	505	1,460	495	Nombre total de personnes hors famille économique	437
						CARACTÉRISTIQUES DU REVENU DE 2000	
						Population de 15 ans et plus selon le sexe et les tranches de revenu total en 2000	
6,400	7,495	3,320	9,375	4,665	4,725	Total - Les deux sexes	438
665	540	195	1,035	220	355	Sans revenu	439
5,730	6,960	3,130	8,340	4,440	4,365	Avec un revenu	440
350	325	125	695	125	215	Moins de 1 000 $ (45)	441
305	295	160	535	165	195	1 000 $ - 2 999 $	442
220	250	105	380	90	190	3 000 $ - 4 999 $	443
295	285	145	440	135	130	5 000 $ - 6 999 $	444
350	485	215	625	300	205	7 000 $ - 9 999 $	445
235	255	205	320	165	175	10 000 $ - 11 999 $	446
300	495	255	610	410	270	12 000 $ - 14 999 $	447
440	550	375	615	435	280	15 000 $ - 19 999 $	448
280	605	180	460	275	285	20 000 $ - 24 999 $	449
295	430	170	390	360	250	25 000 $ - 29 999 $	450
445	675	230	450	410	410	30 000 $ - 34 999 $	451
300	400	185	370	405	305	35 000 $ - 39 999 $	452
340	465	145	370	300	345	40 000 $ - 44 999 $	453
195	305	150	250	210	210	45 000 $ - 49 999 $	454
470	520	210	470	350	380	50 000 $ - 59 999 $	455
905	610	265	1,355	300	520	60 000 $ et plus	456
34,867	28,429	26,934	33,230	28,918	31,791	Revenu moyen $ (46)	457
25,323	24,177	19,144	19,315	26,304	29,751	Revenu médian $ (46)	458
1,649	565	893	1,402	781	783	Erreur type de revenu moyen $ (46)	459

Table 1. Selected Characteristics for Census Tracts, 2001 Census – 100% Data and 20% Sample Data

No.	Characteristics	Vancouver 0285.02	Vancouver 0286.01	Vancouver 0286.02	Vancouver 0286.03	Vancouver 0287.01	Vancouver 0287.02
	2000 INCOME CHARACTERISTICS						
	Population 15 years and over by sex and total income groups in 2000 – concluded						
460	Total - Males	2,190	2,330	2,705	1,675	2,615	1,460
461	Without income	100	105	140	80	270	35
462	With income	2,095	2,225	2,565	1,595	2,350	1,425
463	Under $1,000 (45)	65	125	100	45	105	55
464	$ 1,000 - $ 2,999	70	75	140	70	120	25
465	$ 3,000 - $ 4,999	40	65	55	70	70	25
466	$ 5,000 - $ 6,999	90	85	95	65	60	70
467	$ 7,000 - $ 9,999	90	120	50	25	65	50
468	$10,000 - $11,999	45	95	60	70	80	10
469	$12,000 - $14,999	115	120	100	35	145	70
470	$15,000 - $19,999	200	155	110	50	125	100
471	$20,000 - $24,999	100	135	130	45	145	30
472	$25,000 - $29,999	110	110	170	90	190	145
473	$30,000 - $34,999	150	145	155	95	140	85
474	$35,000 - $39,999	110	185	155	75	165	60
475	$40,000 - $44,999	85	175	175	135	130	130
476	$45,000 - $49,999	120	105	265	100	125	60
477	$50,000 - $59,999	190	145	265	165	310	130
478	$60,000 and over	515	390	540	455	380	370
479	Average income $ (46)	42,694	34,807	42,165	45,356	38,676	44,080
480	Median income $ (46)	33,790	30,476	38,055	41,092	32,303	36,252
481	Standard error of average income $ (46)	2,913	1,392	1,915	2,289	2,437	3,093
482	Total - Females	2,180	2,405	2,775	1,655	2,785	1,460
483	Without income	195	195	205	115	325	60
484	With income	1,985	2,210	2,565	1,540	2,460	1,400
485	Under $1,000 (45)	120	140	180	90	95	55
486	$ 1,000 - $ 2,999	150	120	120	90	195	80
487	$ 3,000 - $ 4,999	85	85	85	30	120	60
488	$ 5,000 - $ 6,999	120	130	80	60	185	80
489	$ 7,000 - $ 9,999	155	240	160	125	180	125
490	$10,000 - $11,999	125	105	155	40	130	45
491	$12,000 - $14,999	120	120	180	90	135	115
492	$15,000 - $19,999	160	175	180	190	225	65
493	$20,000 - $24,999	185	205	200	90	255	105
494	$25,000 - $29,999	85	185	215	110	205	65
495	$30,000 - $34,999	130	190	195	175	235	110
496	$35,000 - $39,999	135	170	145	95	90	145
497	$40,000 - $44,999	110	130	215	60	135	105
498	$45,000 - $49,999	80	35	155	80	85	85
499	$50,000 - $59,999	85	90	170	110	90	75
500	$60,000 and over	135	95	145	110	95	95
501	Average income $ (46)	24,092	22,874	26,510	26,672	22,148	26,429
502	Median income $ (46)	17,472	19,848	22,519	23,106	19,035	24,235
503	Standard error of average income $ (46)	1,014	842	872	1,106	775	1,102
	by composition of total income						
504	Total - Composition of income in 2000 % (47)	100.0	100.0	100.0	100.0	100.0	100.0
505	Employment income %	77.2	77.4	85.8	82.8	87.2	85.8
506	Government transfer payments %	8.9	9.4	6.6	6.7	7.8	5.7
507	Other %	13.9	13.2	7.6	10.5	5.0	8.5
	Population 15 years and over with employment income in 2000 by sex and work activity						
508	Both sexes with employment income (48)	2,950	3,260	4,180	2,455	3,795	2,325
509	Average employment income $	35,878	30,413	36,192	38,185	33,403	36,849
510	Standard error of average employment income $	1,806	940	1,184	1,554	1,526	1,916
511	Worked full year, full time (49)	1,460	1,750	2,280	1,240	2,100	1,265
512	Average employment income $	53,350	42,889	48,875	52,175	43,877	51,846
513	Standard error of average employment income $	3,243	1,224	1,827	1,891	2,521	3,017
514	Worked part year or part time (50)	1,410	1,425	1,760	1,165	1,575	1,005
515	Average employment income $	19,430	16,386	20,926	24,500	21,228	19,243
516	Standard error of average employment income $	989	984	1,037	2,251	1,234	1,462
517	Males with employment income (48)	1,630	1,685	2,210	1,290	2,010	1,175
518	Average employment income $	43,415	36,675	43,108	47,487	40,982	45,597
519	Standard error of average employment income $	3,028	1,473	2,028	2,682	2,738	3,480
520	Worked full year, full time (49)	985	1,030	1,385	815	1,220	760
521	Average employment income $	58,726	47,086	55,538	57,366	51,024	58,621
522	Standard error of average employment income $	4,664	1,771	2,837	2,650	4,177	4,827
523	Worked part year or part time (50)	640	620	760	450	735	395
524	Average employment income $	20,526	20,712	22,149	31,465	26,934	22,681
525	Standard error of average employment income $	1,559	1,932	1,846	5,526	2,347	3,094

Tableau 1. Certaines caractéristiques des secteurs de recensement, recensement de 2001 – Données intégrales et données-échantillon (20 %)

Vancouver 0287.04	Vancouver 0287.05 A	Vancouver 0287.06 A	Vancouver 0287.07 A	Vancouver 0290.02	Vancouver 0290.03	Caractéristiques	N°
						CARACTÉRISTIQUES DU REVENU DE 2000	
						Population de 15 ans et plus selon le sexe et les tranches de revenu total en 2000 – fin	
3,095	3,330	1,490	4,580	2,125	2,315	Total - Hommes	460
330	185	100	370	135	100	Sans revenu	461
2,765	3,145	1,385	4,210	1,985	2,215	Avec un revenu	462
180	165	65	355	40	65	Moins de 1 000 $ (45)	463
95	140	65	185	35	75	1 000 $ - 2 999 $	464
65	105	40	140	40	90	3 000 $ - 4 999 $	465
150	105	70	150	35	45	5 000 $ - 6 999 $	466
130	165	80	280	90	80	7 000 $ - 9 999 $	467
80	85	55	155	20	70	10 000 $ - 11 999 $	468
95	135	65	255	60	95	12 000 $ - 14 999 $	469
210	205	165	280	220	105	15 000 $ - 19 999 $	470
130	215	95	225	105	130	20 000 $ - 24 999 $	471
150	245	65	205	155	105	25 000 $ - 29 999 $	472
175	285	70	165	195	140	30 000 $ - 34 999 $	473
130	185	55	150	210	150	35 000 $ - 39 999 $	474
140	200	65	185	180	200	40 000 $ - 44 999 $	475
120	175	80	130	145	165	45 000 $ - 49 999 $	476
280	290	125	280	235	235	50 000 $ - 59 999 $	477
635	455	225	1,065	230	480	60 000 $ et plus	478
43,763	33,431	32,534	43,823	35,696	40,074	Revenu moyen $ (46)	479
32,020	30,022	24,506	25,695	34,963	38,815	Revenu médian $ (46)	480
3,205	986	1,612	2,639	1,195	1,244	Erreur type de revenu moyen $ (46)	481
3,300	4,165	1,830	4,795	2,540	2,410	Total - Femmes	482
340	355	95	660	90	255	Sans revenu	483
2,965	3,815	1,740	4,135	2,455	2,150	Avec un revenu	484
175	165	60	335	95	150	Moins de 1 000 $ (45)	485
215	160	95	355	130	125	1 000 $ - 2 999 $	486
150	145	70	245	55	100	3 000 $ - 4 999 $	487
145	180	80	295	95	80	5 000 $ - 6 999 $	488
225	320	135	350	210	130	7 000 $ - 9 999 $	489
150	170	155	160	140	105	10 000 $ - 11 999 $	490
200	360	190	360	345	175	12 000 $ - 14 999 $	491
225	350	210	340	215	175	15 000 $ - 19 999 $	492
155	390	85	235	170	155	20 000 $ - 24 999 $	493
140	190	105	180	205	145	25 000 $ - 29 999 $	494
275	390	160	285	215	270	30 000 $ - 34 999 $	495
170	215	130	220	200	160	35 000 $ - 39 999 $	496
200	270	80	185	120	145	40 000 $ - 44 999 $	497
80	130	70	120	65	45	45 000 $ - 49 999 $	498
185	230	85	190	115	145	50 000 $ - 59 999 $	499
270	150	40	285	75	40	60 000 $ et plus	500
26,571	24,301	22,471	22,440	23,421	23,268	Revenu moyen $ (46)	501
19,870	20,317	17,178	14,875	18,556	20,456	Revenu médian $ (46)	502
1,071	610	907	728	968	789	Erreur type de revenu moyen $ (46)	503
						selon la composition du revenu total	
100.0	100.0	100.0	100.0	100.0	100.0	Total - Composition du revenu en 2000 % (47)	504
84.5	75.0	71.8	82.0	79.4	87.5	Revenu d'emploi %	505
5.4	12.7	15.3	5.1	12.7	7.2	Transferts gouvernementaux %	506
10.1	12.3	13.0	12.9	7.9	5.2	Autre %	507
						Population de 15 ans et plus ayant un revenu d'emploi en 2000 selon le sexe et le travail	
4,455	4,620	2,000	5,870	3,320	3,515	Les deux sexes ayant un revenu d'emploi (48)	508
37,903	32,110	30,218	38,718	30,754	34,577	Revenu moyen d'emploi $	509
1,280	716	1,220	1,834	768	867	Erreur type de revenu moyen d'emploi $	510
2,460	2,825	1,000	2,780	1,945	2,045	Ayant travaillé toute l'année à plein temps (49)	511
51,368	41,092	43,476	57,683	38,832	44,878	Revenu moyen d'emploi $	512
1,858	851	1,735	3,564	904	1,046	Erreur type de revenu moyen d'emploi $	513
1,960	1,680	970	2,860	1,335	1,400	Ayant travaillé une partie de l'année ou à temps partiel (50)	514
21,429	18,300	16,363	21,575	19,565	20,667	Revenu moyen d'emploi $	515
1,384	957	1,224	1,015	1,051	1,112	Erreur type de revenu moyen d'emploi $	516
2,260	2,275	995	3,180	1,710	1,860	Hommes ayant un revenu d'emploi (48)	517
45,187	36,678	36,268	48,731	35,600	43,112	Revenu moyen d'emploi $	518
2,128	1,192	2,036	3,248	1,084	1,290	Erreur type de revenu moyen d'emploi $	519
1,420	1,560	545	1,705	1,105	1,205	Ayant travaillé toute l'année à plein temps (49)	520
58,709	44,531	50,658	68,174	41,466	52,899	Revenu moyen d'emploi $	521
2,959	1,322	2,687	5,630	1,238	1,346	Erreur type de revenu moyen d'emploi $	522
820	670	430	1,380	565	625	Ayant travaillé une partie de l'année ou à temps partiel (50)	523
22,296	20,642	17,991	26,152	25,621	25,746	Revenu moyen d'emploi $	524
1,611	1,948	2,137	1,820	1,775	2,090	Erreur type de revenu moyen d'emploi $	525

Table 1. Selected Characteristics for Census Tracts, 2001 Census – 100% Data and 20% Sample Data

No.	Characteristics	Vancouver 0285.02	Vancouver 0286.01	Vancouver 0286.02	Vancouver 0286.03	Vancouver 0287.01	Vancouver 0287.02
	2000 INCOME CHARACTERISTICS						
	Population 15 years and over with employment income in 2000 by sex and work activity – concluded						
526	Females with employment income (48)	1,320	1,575	1,970	1,170	1,785	1,150
527	Average employment income $	26,583	23,698	28,429	27,889	24,860	27,887
528	Standard error of average employment income $	1,273	1,027	933	1,246	932	1,219
529	Worked full year, full time (49)	480	715	895	420	885	510
530	Average employment income $	42,362	36,862	38,543	42,112	34,041	41,748
531	Standard error of average employment income $	2,103	1,450	1,144	1,999	1,331	1,425
532	Worked part year or part time (50)	780	810	995	715	840	610
533	Average employment income $	18,529	13,086	19,991	20,137	16,230	17,031
534	Standard error of average employment income $	1,259	826	1,162	1,252	1,030	1,297
	Census families by structure and family income groups in 2000						
535	Total - All census families	1,520	1,740	1,975	1,195	2,030	1,120
536	Under $10,000	35	80	55	40	165	10
537	$ 10,000 - $19,999	60	80	90	25	140	45
538	$ 20,000 - $29,999	115	215	125	70	200	65
539	$ 30,000 - $39,999	140	140	155	65	150	65
540	$ 40,000 - $49,999	165	200	160	90	235	135
541	$ 50,000 - $59,999	85	190	200	110	210	95
542	$ 60,000 - $69,999	165	160	200	95	275	90
543	$ 70,000 - $79,999	125	145	125	70	185	125
544	$ 80,000 - $89,999	125	160	180	100	135	105
545	$ 90,000 - $99,999	130	70	155	120	90	85
546	$100,000 and over	360	305	535	410	245	300
547	Average family income $	76,789	65,199	79,206	86,556	62,169	81,757
548	Median family income $	68,821	58,783	70,266	81,753	55,504	74,407
549	Standard error of average family income $	3,470	2,150	2,839	3,352	2,965	4,239
550	Total - All couple census families (51)	1,330	1,470	1,725	1,030	1,625	985
551	Under $10,000	25	50	40	15	110	10
552	$ 10,000 - $19,999	35	55	55	10	85	20
553	$ 20,000 - $29,999	95	155	70	55	140	45
554	$ 30,000 - $39,999	90	110	120	40	115	45
555	$ 40,000 - $49,999	150	145	120	65	175	115
556	$ 50,000 - $59,999	80	165	180	100	175	80
557	$ 60,000 - $69,999	145	140	175	85	235	80
558	$ 70,000 - $79,999	110	130	125	60	170	105
559	$ 80,000 - $89,999	125	150	170	100	130	105
560	$ 90,000 - $99,999	120	65	150	120	75	85
561	$100,000 and over	350	295	525	385	225	295
562	Average family income $	81,418	69,698	84,267	92,275	66,407	86,885
563	Median family income $	76,160	64,217	77,416	89,564	60,608	79,302
564	Standard error of average family income $	3,848	2,362	3,124	3,554	3,498	4,727
	Incidence of low income in 2000						
565	Total - Economic families	1,475	1,645	1,925	1,185	1,905	1,060
566	Low income	185	230	240	95	365	65
567	Incidence of low income in 2000 % (52)	12.5	13.8	12.4	8.3	19.3	6.2
568	Total - Unattached individuals 15 years and over	480	375	485	285	550	215
569	Low income	225	135	170	120	145	50
570	Incidence of low income in 2000 % (52)	47.0	35.4	34.7	42.3	26.3	23.7
571	Total - Population in private households	5,425	5,800	6,945	4,115	7,190	3,895
572	Low income	870	895	1,035	400	1,445	265
573	Incidence of low income in 2000 % (52)	16.0	15.4	14.9	9.7	20.1	6.9
	Private households by household income groups in 2000						
574	Total - All private households	1,755	1,930	2,235	1,410	2,305	1,215
575	Under $10,000	45	40	70	65	120	10
576	$ 10,000 - $19,999	110	110	135	95	175	55
577	$ 20,000 - $29,999	150	235	120	85	245	85
578	$ 30,000 - $39,999	165	160	170	85	210	80
579	$ 40,000 - $49,999	175	210	225	105	280	120
580	$ 50,000 - $59,999	115	245	210	110	215	110
581	$ 60,000 - $69,999	155	175	185	120	275	95
582	$ 70,000 - $79,999	155	175	125	60	215	120
583	$ 80,000 - $89,999	125	145	195	110	160	125
584	$ 90,000 - $99,999	150	85	140	135	105	100
585	$100,000 and over	420	350	650	430	300	330
586	Average household income $	78,029	66,326	78,848	80,302	63,118	82,133
587	Median household income $	67,253	59,044	68,956	74,401	54,650	74,662
588	Standard error of average household income $	3,724	2,001	2,701	3,063	2,720	3,951

Tableau 1. Certaines caractéristiques des secteurs de recensement, recensement de 2001 – Données intégrales et données-échantillon (20 %)

Vancouver 0287.04	Vancouver 0287.05 A	Vancouver 0287.06 A	Vancouver 0287.07 A	Vancouver 0290.02	Vancouver 0290.03	Caractéristiques	N°
						CARACTÉRISTIQUES DU REVENU DE 2000	
						Population de 15 ans et plus ayant un revenu d'emploi en 2000 selon le sexe et le travail – fin	
2,195	2,340	1,005	2,690	1,615	1,655	Femmes ayant un revenu d'emploi (48)	526
30,421	27,670	24,255	26,883	25,614	24,983	Revenu moyen d'emploi $	527
1,331	780	1,239	910	1,017	921	Erreur type de revenu moyen d'emploi $	528
1,040	1,265	455	1,075	835	845	Ayant travaillé toute l'année à plein temps (49)	529
41,334	36,863	34,812	41,069	35,359	33,392	Revenu moyen d'emploi $	530
1,366	942	1,595	1,348	1,275	1,281	Erreur type de revenu moyen d'emploi $	531
1,140	1,005	535	1,485	765	775	Ayant travaillé une partie de l'année ou à temps partiel (50)	532
20,805	16,740	15,050	17,317	15,089	16,579	Revenu moyen d'emploi $	533
2,046	941	1,395	952	1,135	1,016	Erreur type de revenu moyen d'emploi $	534
						Familles de recensement selon la structure et les tranches de revenu de la famille en 2000	
2,370	2,490	1,085	3,370	1,505	1,745	Total - Toutes les familles de recensement	535
100	215	60	290	90	90	Moins de 10 000 $	536
215	200	110	295	100	90	10 000 $ - 19 999 $	537
165	280	100	380	180	65	20 000 $ - 29 999 $	538
175	275	95	270	200	135	30 000 $ - 39 999 $	539
155	340	70	250	155	180	40 000 $ - 49 999 $	540
175	205	95	245	125	180	50 000 $ - 59 999 $	541
205	200	105	220	145	225	60 000 $ - 69 999 $	542
270	215	100	195	220	175	70 000 $ - 79 999 $	543
170	155	85	170	130	150	80 000 $ - 89 999 $	544
175	160	75	160	60	105	90 000 $ - 99 999 $	545
565	245	190	885	85	365	100 000 $ et plus	546
78,680	54,158	62,812	74,536	52,939	69,312	Revenu moyen des familles $	547
68,727	46,316	60,771	56,971	50,480	65,963	Revenu médian des familles $	548
3,988	1,476	2,478	3,399	1,647	1,837	Erreur type de revenu moyen des familles $	549
2,110	2,100	950	3,075	1,150	1,510	Total - Toutes les familles de recensement comptant un couple (51)	550
80	160	45	220	30	50	Moins de 10 000 $	551
180	115	85	240	30	40	10 000 $ - 19 999 $	552
120	245	85	340	115	45	20 000 $ - 29 999 $	553
135	210	95	240	155	100	30 000 $ - 39 999 $	554
135	290	65	230	110	165	40 000 $ - 49 999 $	555
150	180	65	245	105	150	50 000 $ - 59 999 $	556
175	170	90	210	130	210	60 000 $ - 69 999 $	557
255	205	100	195	210	160	70 000 $ - 79 999 $	558
160	140	75	160	125	145	80 000 $ - 89 999 $	559
165	160	55	155	60	105	90 000 $ - 99 999 $	560
550	240	195	850	75	335	100 000 $ et plus	561
82,681	57,439	65,568	78,034	59,836	73,546	Revenu moyen des familles $	562
73,787	50,883	64,049	60,877	62,420	69,214	Revenu médian des familles $	563
4,381	1,643	2,702	3,663	1,804	1,892	Erreur type de revenu moyen des familles $	564
						Fréquence des unités à faible revenu en 2000	
2,300	2,520	1,060	3,190	1,505	1,720	Total - Familles économiques	565
420	615	230	835	315	220	Faible revenu	566
18.3	24.3	22.0	26.2	21.0	13.0	Fréquence des unités à faible revenu en 2000 % (52)	567
365	1,740	585	505	1,455	490	Total - Personnes hors famille économique de 15 ans et plus	568
135	480	265	225	585	165	Faible revenu	569
36.8	27.6	45.8	44.8	39.9	33.2	Fréquence des unités à faible revenu en 2000 % (52)	570
8,215	8,705	4,060	11,910	5,665	6,230	Total - Population dans les ménages privés	571
1,580	2,375	1,055	3,540	1,530	835	Faible revenu	572
19.3	27.3	26.1	29.7	27.0	13.5	Fréquence des unités à faible revenu en 2000 % (52)	573
						Ménages privés selon les tranches de revenu du ménage en 2000	
2,525	4,095	1,610	3,475	2,780	2,055	Total - Tous les ménages privés	574
120	345	100	225	175	100	Moins de 10 000 $	575
190	490	340	275	475	155	10 000 $ - 19 999 $	576
170	510	175	375	340	120	20 000 $ - 29 999 $	577
185	520	195	280	390	150	30 000 $ - 39 999 $	578
190	570	95	240	345	200	40 000 $ - 49 999 $	579
230	435	130	265	240	200	50 000 $ - 59 999 $	580
210	290	90	210	195	235	60 000 $ - 69 999 $	581
255	265	90	235	250	160	70 000 $ - 79 999 $	582
155	180	90	185	150	155	80 000 $ - 89 999 $	583
225	195	65	150	75	155	90 000 $ - 99 999 $	584
610	290	235	1,025	145	425	100 000 $ et plus	585
79,127	48,268	52,413	79,783	46,038	67,589	Revenu moyen des ménages $	586
67,901	42,461	40,065	62,206	40,058	64,799	Revenu médian des ménages $	587
3,748	1,079	2,055	3,360	1,362	1,799	Erreur type de revenu moyen des ménages $	588

Table 1. Selected Characteristics for Census Tracts, 2001 Census – 100% Data and 20% Sample Data

No.	Characteristics	Vancouver 0290.04 A	Vancouver 0290.05 A	Vancouver 0291.01	Vancouver 0291.02	Vancouver 0292.01	Vancouver 0292.02
	POPULATION CHARACTERISTICS						
1	**Population, 1996 (1)**	**5,866**	**3,485**	**6,287**	**7,388**	**5,762**	**6,771**
2	**Population, 2001 (2)**	**6,724**	**3,522**	**6,509**	**7,772**	**5,762**	**8,653**
3	Population percentage change, 1996-2001	14.6	1.1	3.5	5.2	-	27.8
4	Land area in square kilometres, 2001	4.90	1.55	2.28	3.11	2.08	7.86
5	**Total population - 100% Data (3)**	**6,720**	**3,520**	**6,510**	**7,775**	**5,760**	**8,655**
	by sex and age groups						
6	Male	3,325	1,830	3,225	3,890	2,930	4,320
7	0-4 years	185	145	210	265	205	285
8	5-9 years	250	155	225	315	250	400
9	10-14 years	270	175	230	305	300	375
10	15-19 years	260	150	245	330	270	385
11	20-24 years	220	105	200	255	180	245
12	25-29 years	140	100	235	255	140	220
13	30-34 years	190	145	295	310	190	310
14	35-39 years	280	180	325	345	245	405
15	40-44 years	330	200	300	390	305	445
16	45-49 years	315	150	255	315	230	395
17	50-54 years	300	115	185	280	225	290
18	55-59 years	205	85	145	175	150	200
19	60-64 years	145	50	105	120	85	130
20	65-69 years	100	30	95	85	65	100
21	70-74 years	65	20	75	65	35	70
22	75-79 years	40	15	50	35	25	35
23	80-84 years	20	5	30	30	5	15
24	85 years and over	15	5	15	15	10	10
25	Female	3,400	1,695	3,285	3,880	2,840	4,330
26	0-4 years	210	110	210	260	170	265
27	5-9 years	240	155	200	280	235	385
28	10-14 years	260	140	205	275	265	330
29	15-19 years	245	120	245	295	245	370
30	20-24 years	210	95	210	270	145	230
31	25-29 years	135	110	240	245	130	210
32	30-34 years	200	145	300	315	215	355
33	35-39 years	350	195	340	360	290	500
34	40-44 years	385	170	295	380	320	460
35	45-49 years	350	140	250	355	270	355
36	50-54 years	255	105	185	260	210	275
37	55-59 years	190	80	155	190	120	200
38	60-64 years	130	40	135	110	80	125
39	65-69 years	105	35	100	105	55	100
40	70-74 years	85	20	85	70	40	70
41	75-79 years	30	25	65	55	30	50
42	80-84 years	20	10	40	40	10	35
43	85 years and over	5	5	20	20	10	15
44	**Total population 15 years and over**	**5,315**	**2,645**	**5,230**	**6,075**	**4,335**	**6,605**
	by legal marital status						
45	Never married (single)	1,315	780	1,840	2,005	1,220	1,890
46	Legally married (and not separated)	3,505	1,545	2,415	3,160	2,650	3,940
47	Separated, but still legally married	105	75	250	220	125	195
48	Divorced	245	165	475	475	225	390
49	Widowed	145	80	255	230	115	190
	by common-law status						
50	Not in a common-law relationship	5,105	2,490	4,820	5,575	4,095	6,215
51	In a common-law relationship	210	155	410	500	245	390
52	**Total population - 20% Sample Data (4)**	**6,720**	**3,505**	**6,475**	**7,755**	**5,765**	**8,640**
	by mother tongue						
53	Single responses	6,635	3,380	6,410	7,650	5,715	8,555
54	English	4,780	2,490	4,670	5,925	4,615	5,910
55	French	10	65	170	75	125	70
56	Non-official languages (5)	1,850	825	1,570	1,650	970	2,570
57	Chinese, n.o.s.	290	90	60	90	75	455
58	Cantonese	525	185	255	210	75	555
59	Punjabi	20	50	60	220	55	90
60	Mandarin	30	15	55	45	30	130
61	Tagalog (Pilipino)	60	80	120	100	50	55
62	Other languages (6)	915	395	1,020	985	680	1,285
63	Multiple responses	85	130	65	110	50	90
64	English and French	-	20	10	20	-	-
65	English and non-official language	80	105	65	90	45	65
66	French and non-official language	10	-	-	-	-	20
67	English, French and non-official language	-	-	-	-	-	-

See reference material at the end of the publication. – Voir les documents de référence à la fin de la publication.

Tableau 1. Certaines caractéristiques des secteurs de recensement, recensement de 2001 – Données intégrales et données-échantillon (20 %)

Vancouver 0400.01 A	Vancouver 0400.02 A	Vancouver 0401.01 A	Vancouver 0401.02 A	Vancouver 0402.01	Vancouver 0402.02	Caractéristiques	N°
						CARACTÉRISTIQUES DE LA POPULATION	
5,883	**3,476**	**2,255**	**6,205**	**7,312**	**4,785**	**Population, 1996 (1)**	1
9,186	**3,436**	**2,676**	**6,898**	**7,865**	**4,968**	**Population, 2001 (2)**	2
56.1	-1.2	18.7	11.2	7.6	3.8	Variation en pourcentage de la population, 1996-2001	3
18.97	37.64	1.11	3.14	3.06	2.99	Superficie des terres en kilomètres carrés, 2001	4
9,180	**3,435**	**2,680**	**6,895**	**7,865**	**4,965**	**Population totale – Données intégrales (3)**	5
						selon le sexe et les groupes d'âge	
4,580	1,760	1,325	3,270	3,760	2,420	Sexe masculin	6
350	65	90	190	245	150	0-4 ans	7
445	120	85	190	310	185	5-9 ans	8
425	130	80	155	330	225	10-14 ans	9
380	125	105	175	240	220	15-19 ans	10
210	115	85	170	225	145	20-24 ans	11
225	60	85	200	170	115	25-29 ans	12
370	80	90	295	270	145	30-34 ans	13
445	140	120	285	330	190	35-39 ans	14
480	175	125	280	385	240	40-44 ans	15
345	155	90	230	285	200	45-49 ans	16
265	175	85	195	230	175	50-54 ans	17
175	135	75	170	160	110	55-59 ans	18
155	100	65	160	140	85	60-64 ans	19
110	80	45	145	115	70	65-69 ans	20
90	50	40	145	115	65	70-74 ans	21
55	25	30	145	110	55	75-79 ans	22
30	15	20	90	60	25	80-84 ans	23
20	10	15	50	50	10	85 ans et plus	24
4,605	1,675	1,355	3,630	4,110	2,540	Sexe féminin	25
325	80	85	200	245	160	0-4 ans	26
395	120	75	180	290	205	5-9 ans	27
445	125	85	140	305	205	10-14 ans	28
310	110	85	155	300	185	15-19 ans	29
205	105	70	170	195	125	20-24 ans	30
280	55	75	210	215	100	25-29 ans	31
435	80	120	230	295	170	30-34 ans	32
475	150	125	295	360	230	35-39 ans	33
470	160	105	255	395	250	40-44 ans	34
325	160	85	225	290	240	45-49 ans	35
265	190	90	230	210	160	50-54 ans	36
185	120	85	195	160	115	55-59 ans	37
140	70	65	205	145	85	60-64 ans	38
125	50	60	200	150	80	65-69 ans	39
90	40	60	220	170	80	70-74 ans	40
65	25	45	205	160	60	75-79 ans	41
40	15	35	135	125	55	80-84 ans	42
35	10	20	160	100	20	85 ans et plus	43
6,795	**2,790**	**2,175**	**5,830**	**6,145**	**3,835**	**Population totale de 15 ans et plus**	44
						selon l'état matrimonial légal	
1,750	830	685	1,585	1,685	1,125	Célibataire (jamais marié(e))	45
4,110	1,555	965	2,545	3,175	2,105	Légalement marié(e) (et non séparé(e))	46
230	110	135	365	275	150	Séparé(e), mais toujours légalement marié(e)	47
470	195	235	705	495	265	Divorcé(e)	48
235	100	165	625	510	190	Veuf ou veuve	49
						selon l'union libre	
6,315	2,560	1,975	5,310	5,725	3,600	Ne vivant pas en union libre	50
485	230	205	520	415	235	Vivant en union libre	51
9,165	**3,425**	**2,620**	**6,690**	**7,815**	**4,935**	**Population totale – Données-échantillon (20 %) (4)**	52
						selon la langue maternelle	
9,125	3,415	2,620	6,655	7,730	4,880	Réponses uniques	53
8,025	3,035	2,190	5,645	6,770	4,340	Anglais	54
100	70	30	155	85	75	Français	55
1,000	305	395	850	875	470	Langues non officielles (5)	56
30	-	10	50	40	20	Chinois, n.d.a.	57
65	-	-	10	-	-	Cantonais	58
20	-	-	35	45	30	Pendjabi	59
20	-	-	-	45	10	Mandarin	60
45	-	-	40	20	15	Tagalog (pilipino)	61
825	305	380	715	720	390	Autres langues (6)	62
40	15	-	40	80	50	Réponses multiples	63
10	15	-	10	15	-	Anglais et français	64
35	-	-	35	60	50	Anglais et langue non officielle	65
-	-	-	-	-	-	Français et langue non officielle	66
-	-	-	-	10	-	Anglais, français et langue non officielle	67

See reference material at the end of the publication. – Voir les documents de référence à la fin de la publication.

Table 1. Selected Characteristics for Census Tracts, 2001 Census – 100% Data and 20% Sample Data

No.	Characteristics	Vancouver 0290.04 A	Vancouver 0290.05 A	Vancouver 0291.01	Vancouver 0291.02	Vancouver 0292.01	Vancouver 0292.02
	POPULATION CHARACTERISTICS						
	by home language						
68	Single responses	5,715	2,915	5,530	6,880	5,135	7,145
69	English	5,195	2,645	4,930	6,255	4,865	6,360
70	French	-	35	-	15	45	10
71	Non-official languages (5)	525	240	595	605	225	780
72	Cantonese	205	150	175	185	50	310
73	Chinese, n.o.s.	115	20	20	30	20	120
74	Punjabi	10	25	15	115	15	45
75	Mandarin	20	-	15	10	25	40
76	Korean	85	-	10	-	20	95
77	Other languages (6)	95	50	365	270	90	170
78	Multiple responses	1,005	595	945	880	630	1,500
79	English and French	10	80	140	25	30	75
80	English and non-official language	990	495	800	830	600	1,400
81	French and non-official language	10	10	-	-	-	-
82	English, French and non-official language	-	15	-	25	-	25
	by knowledge of official languages						
83	English only	6,235	3,075	5,910	7,105	5,295	8,025
84	French only	-	-	-	-	10	-
85	English and French	380	335	425	455	405	465
86	Neither English nor French	110	95	140	195	55	150
	by knowledge of non-official languages (5) (7)						
87	Cantonese	555	235	275	205	90	655
88	Chinese, n.o.s.	300	90	75	85	105	415
89	Punjabi	85	115	65	245	65	100
90	Mandarin	275	50	140	95	60	345
91	Hindi	135	100	75	250	215	185
92	German	165	40	135	165	125	175
93	Spanish	140	35	175	110	85	130
	by first official language spoken						
94	English	6,570	3,320	6,140	7,480	5,600	8,405
95	French	10	65	155	65	95	70
96	English and French	45	25	40	10	10	20
97	Neither English nor French	100	90	140	195	60	145
98	Official language minority - (number) (8)	35	80	175	70	95	80
99	Official language minority - (percentage) (8)	0.5	2.3	2.7	0.9	1.6	0.9
	by ethnic origin (9)						
100	English	1,980	1,145	1,785	2,415	1,975	2,335
101	Canadian	1,590	730	1,630	2,420	1,690	2,250
102	Chinese	1,150	430	425	405	365	1,490
103	Scottish	1,295	685	1,270	1,715	1,450	1,425
104	Irish	790	400	990	1,130	965	1,245
105	German	795	405	770	975	745	1,030
106	East Indian	275	325	150	395	265	305
107	French	525	435	675	805	680	715
108	Ukrainian	345	130	365	370	345	320
109	Italian	240	250	330	285	340	515
110	Dutch (Netherlands)	365	150	230	380	235	420
111	Filipino	105	110	220	165	120	80
112	Polish	265	65	275	320	195	360
113	Norwegian	185	165	275	315	225	300
114	North American Indian	75	20	130	225	130	130
	by Aboriginal identity						
115	Total Aboriginal identity population (10)	50	55	125	200	65	165
116	Total non-Aboriginal population	6,670	3,455	6,350	7,560	5,700	8,480
	by Aboriginal origin						
117	Total Aboriginal origins population (11)	105	75	155	280	135	215
118	Total non-Aboriginal population	6,620	3,430	6,320	7,475	5,625	8,420
	by Registered Indian status						
119	Registered Indian (12)	-	-	55	70	10	55
120	Not a Registered Indian	6,715	3,510	6,420	7,685	5,755	8,585

Tableau 1. Certaines caractéristiques des secteurs de recensement, recensement de 2001 – Données intégrales et données-échantillon (20 %)

Vancouver 0400.01 A	Vancouver 0400.02 A	Vancouver 0401.01 A	Vancouver 0401.02 A	Vancouver 0402.01	Vancouver 0402.02	Caractéristiques	N°
						CARACTÉRISTIQUES DE LA POPULATION	
						selon la langue parlée à la maison	
8,635	3,255	2,370	6,215	7,275	4,740	Réponses uniques	68
8,470	3,245	2,325	5,995	7,100	4,685	Anglais	69
-	-	-	50	10	-	Français	70
160	10	50	170	170	55	Langues non officielles (5)	71
30	-	-	10	-	-	Cantonais	72
-	-	-	20	15	20	Chinois, n.d.a.	73
-	-	-	35	30	-	Pendjabi	74
25	-	-	-	25	-	Mandarin	75
15	-	-	20	20	-	Coréen	76
95	15	50	90	85	30	Autres langues (6)	77
530	170	250	480	535	195	Réponses multiples	78
60	30	15	30	85	15	Anglais et français	79
445	145	235	445	430	180	Anglais et langue non officielle	80
-	-	-	-	-	-	Français et langue non officielle	81
25	-	10	10	20	-	Anglais, français et langue non officielle	82
						selon la connaissance des langues officielles	
8,460	3,170	2,475	6,275	7,280	4,500	Anglais seulement	83
-	-	-	10	-	-	Français seulement	84
675	260	130	345	510	400	Anglais et français	85
35	-	15	60	25	30	Ni l'anglais ni le français	86
						selon la connaissance des langues non officielles (5) (7)	
85	-	-	30	10	-	Cantonais	87
35	-	-	15	35	20	Chinois, n.d.a.	88
40	-	10	40	65	30	Pendjabi	89
30	-	-	30	55	20	Mandarin	90
20	-	80	45	50	50	Hindi	91
250	195	70	195	225	100	Allemand	92
105	30	20	100	110	70	Espagnol	93
						selon la première langue officielle parlée	
9,035	3,360	2,575	6,450	7,695	4,835	Anglais	94
90	65	30	135	85	70	Français	95
15	-	-	40	-	-	Anglais et français	96
35	-	15	60	30	30	Ni l'anglais ni le français	97
95	65	30	155	85	70	Minorité de langue officielle - (nombre) (8)	98
1.0	1.9	1.1	2.3	1.1	1.4	Minorité de langue officielle - (pourcentage) (8)	99
						selon l'origine ethnique (9)	
3,035	1,430	765	2,340	2,840	1,900	Anglais	100
3,125	1,090	770	2,130	2,215	1,615	Canadien	101
345	20	10	110	145	75	Chinois	102
1,990	735	580	1,390	1,705	1,310	Écossais	103
1,330	670	495	865	1,300	740	Irlandais	104
1,445	570	465	860	1,100	800	Allemand	105
130	10	70	45	160	65	Indien de l'Inde	106
935	505	280	725	930	570	Français	107
610	235	160	330	515	380	Ukrainien	108
460	100	45	190	290	190	Italien	109
590	285	160	255	525	415	Hollandais (Néerlandais)	110
90	-	10	55	80	45	Philippin	111
360	65	135	205	240	280	Polonais	112
285	70	130	160	255	220	Norvégien	113
250	125	75	250	195	105	Indien de l'Amérique du Nord	114
						selon l'identité autochtone	
245	125	50	170	155	135	Total de la population ayant une identité autochtone (10)	115
8,915	3,300	2,570	6,520	7,655	4,795	Total de la population non autochtone	116
						selon l'origine autochtone	
430	185	100	295	300	155	Total de la population ayant une origine autochtone (11)	117
8,740	3,235	2,520	6,390	7,515	4,780	Total de la population non autochtone	118
						selon le statut d'Indien inscrit	
65	30	-	35	30	35	Oui, Indien inscrit (12)	119
9,100	3,395	2,615	6,660	7,785	4,900	Non, pas un Indien inscrit	120

Table 1. Selected Characteristics for Census Tracts, 2001 Census – 100% Data and 20% Sample Data

No.	Characteristics	Vancouver 0290.04 A	Vancouver 0290.05 A	Vancouver 0291.01	Vancouver 0291.02	Vancouver 0292.01	Vancouver 0292.02
	POPULATION CHARACTERISTICS						
	by visible minority groups						
121	Total visible minority population	1,920	980	1,210	1,415	1,045	2,400
122	Chinese	1,135	385	430	380	340	1,430
123	South Asian	275	340	170	500	360	350
124	Black	15	35	120	35	45	160
125	Filipino	105	90	200	175	85	75
126	Latin American	35	15	75	55	25	15
127	Southeast Asian	15	-	45	25	30	40
128	Arab	50	10	20	-	-	25
129	West Asian	60	25	95	135	85	65
130	Korean	170	-	35	10	35	125
131	Japanese	30	25	20	80	20	10
132	Visible minority, n.i.e. (13)	15	10	-	-	-	90
133	Multiple visible minorities (14)	10	50	15	25	20	15
	by citizenship						
134	Canadian citizenship (15)	6,300	3,305	5,905	7,225	5,460	7,900
135	Citizenship other than Canadian	420	205	575	530	305	740
	by place of birth of respondent						
136	Non-immigrant population	4,630	2,570	4,805	5,980	4,510	5,835
137	Born in province of residence	3,250	2,140	3,410	4,630	3,335	4,330
138	Immigrant population (16)	2,055	925	1,665	1,745	1,225	2,760
139	United States	35	20	70	50	45	40
140	Central and South America	45	25	55	40	35	30
141	Caribbean and Bermuda	35	20	25	10	40	55
142	United Kingdom	235	90	185	245	215	280
143	Other Europe (17)	340	165	500	480	230	600
144	Africa	90	80	45	25	115	225
145	Asia and the Middle East	1,165	465	730	735	395	1,450
146	Oceania and other (18)	110	60	55	170	155	80
147	Non-permanent residents (19)	45	-	10	25	25	50
148	**Total immigrant population**	**2,050**	**925**	**1,665**	**1,745**	**1,230**	**2,760**
	by period of immigration						
149	Before 1961	190	90	165	200	100	180
150	1961-1970	215	85	115	185	155	280
151	1971-1980	455	205	305	310	360	425
152	1981-1990	390	275	270	335	235	490
153	1991-2001 (20)	795	275	810	725	375	1,390
154	1991-1995	480	105	440	440	210	700
155	1996-2001 (20)	315	165	365	280	165	685
	by age at immigration						
156	0-4 years	175	95	190	175	140	280
157	5-19 years	675	250	455	490	345	840
158	20 years and over	1,210	585	1,025	1,080	740	1,640
159	**Total population**	**6,720**	**3,505**	**6,480**	**7,755**	**5,765**	**8,640**
	by religion						
160	Catholic (21)	1,255	790	1,570	1,290	1,325	1,855
161	Protestant	2,215	935	1,780	2,145	1,530	2,335
162	Christian Orthodox	115	25	90	50	60	60
163	Christian, n.i.e. (22)	345	230	290	410	280	730
164	Muslim	105	120	160	115	50	200
165	Jewish	30	15	-	25	40	-
166	Buddhist	245	60	60	50	30	110
167	Hindu	155	60	55	165	185	40
168	Sikh	10	135	35	240	130	110
169	Eastern religions (23)	20	30	-	85	45	-
170	Other religions (24)	30	10	15	-	-	15
171	No religious affiliation (25)	2,190	1,100	2,420	3,185	2,095	3,170
172	**Total population 15 years and over**	**5,310**	**2,645**	**5,205**	**6,075**	**4,335**	**6,590**
	by generation status						
173	1st generation (26)	1,920	870	1,530	1,705	1,205	2,535
174	2nd generation (27)	1,290	560	1,125	1,320	1,030	1,380
175	3rd generation and over (28)	2,095	1,220	2,550	3,045	2,100	2,680
176	**Total population 1 year and over (29)**	**6,650**	**3,420**	**6,390**	**7,675**	**5,715**	**8,545**
	by place of residence 1 year ago (mobility)						
177	Non-movers	6,045	3,135	5,430	6,680	5,005	7,345
178	Movers	605	285	960	995	705	1,205
179	Non-migrants	160	135	440	565	300	545
180	Migrants	450	155	520	430	410	660
181	Internal migrants	410	145	395	380	370	540
182	Intraprovincial migrants	355	145	370	330	345	470
183	Interprovincial migrants	60	-	25	50	25	70
184	External migrants	35	10	125	45	40	120

Tableau 1. Certaines caractéristiques des secteurs de recensement, recensement de 2001 – Données intégrales et données-échantillon (20 %)

Vancouver 0400.01 A	Vancouver 0400.02 A	Vancouver 0401.01 A	Vancouver 0401.02 A	Vancouver 0402.01	Vancouver 0402.02	Caractéristiques	N°
						CARACTÉRISTIQUES DE LA POPULATION	
						selon les groupes de minorités visibles	
850	40	190	485	605	330	Total de la population des minorités visibles	121
215	10	10	95	110	75	Chinois	122
135	-	105	115	170	30	Sud-Asiatique	123
135	10	-	30	75	85	Noir	124
75	-	-	55	60	40	Philippin	125
-	-	-	25	50	40	Latino-Américain	126
30	-	-	20	30	-	Asiatique du Sud-Est	127
-	-	-	-	30	-	Arabe	128
30	-	30	-	25	-	Asiatique occidental	129
20	-	20	90	20	-	Coréen	130
150	-	-	10	30	-	Japonais	131
15	20	10	40	-	10	Minorité visible, n.i.a. (13)	132
45	-	-	-	10	45	Minorités visibles multiples (14)	133
						selon la citoyenneté	
8,845	3,305	2,545	6,405	7,450	4,690	Citoyenneté canadienne (15)	134
320	120	75	285	360	245	Citoyenneté autre que canadienne	135
						selon le lieu de naissance du répondant	
7,745	2,875	2,140	5,380	6,310	4,185	Population non immigrante	136
5,520	2,140	1,475	3,620	4,125	3,130	Née dans la province de résidence	137
1,370	545	480	1,305	1,475	710	Population immigrante (16)	138
60	45	40	105	190	55	États-Unis	139
20	20	20	55	35	65	Amérique centrale et du Sud	140
55	-	-	20	10	35	Caraïbes et Bermudes	141
345	200	125	350	395	165	Royaume-Uni	142
450	280	165	445	475	215	Autre Europe (17)	143
145	10	10	30	135	50	Afrique	144
265	-	80	250	225	95	Asie et Moyen-Orient	145
35	-	50	45	10	30	Océanie et autre (18)	146
50	-	-	10	25	40	Résidents non permanents (19)	147
1,370	**545**	**485**	**1,305**	**1,475**	**705**	**Population immigrante totale**	148
						selon la période d'immigration	
355	130	105	405	370	175	Avant 1961	149
210	185	115	255	255	100	1961-1970	150
170	130	90	185	270	100	1971-1980	151
225	65	115	170	170	90	1981-1990	152
405	35	55	295	415	245	1991-2001 (20)	153
210	25	10	120	265	205	1991-1995	154
200	-	45	175	150	45	1996-2001 (20)	155
						selon l'âge à l'immigration	
160	85	45	245	170	85	0-4 ans	156
445	130	120	260	465	220	5-19 ans	157
765	330	315	805	840	405	20 ans et plus	158
9,165	**3,425**	**2,625**	**6,690**	**7,815**	**4,930**	**Population totale**	159
						selon la religion	
1,590	545	490	1,185	1,445	820	Catholique (21)	160
3,030	1,245	720	2,575	3,105	1,925	Protestante	161
55	25	35	70	70	10	Orthodoxe chrétienne	162
555	220	140	270	485	200	Chrétiennes, n.i.a. (22)	163
55	10	-	-	90	20	Musulmane	164
-	10	-	30	-	-	Juive	165
50	-	-	10	25	-	Bouddhiste	166
25	-	25	60	30	-	Hindoue	167
40	-	10	35	65	30	Sikh	168
60	-	30	10	10	40	Religions orientales (23)	169
25	10	-	50	-	-	Autres religions (24)	170
3,675	1,370	1,175	2,405	2,500	1,885	Aucune appartenance religieuse (25)	171
6,745	**2,780**	**2,165**	**5,615**	**6,060**	**3,760**	**Population totale de 15 ans et plus**	172
						selon le statut des générations	
1,300	545	485	1,250	1,465	670	1re génération (26)	173
1,560	745	590	1,495	1,720	1,085	2e génération (27)	174
3,890	1,485	1,090	2,870	2,875	2,005	3e génération et plus (28)	175
9,015	**3,395**	**2,580**	**6,610**	**7,715**	**4,895**	**Population totale de 1 an et plus (29)**	176
						selon le lieu de résidence 1 an auparavant (mobilité)	
7,540	3,220	1,990	5,335	6,745	4,380	Personnes n'ayant pas déménagé	177
1,480	180	595	1,270	965	515	Personnes ayant déménagé	178
685	105	285	600	485	340	Non-migrants	179
790	75	310	670	480	170	Migrants	180
760	65	295	610	465	165	Migrants internes	181
655	70	250	575	365	145	Migrants infraprovinciaux	182
110	-	45	40	95	20	Migrants interprovinciaux	183
30	10	10	60	15	10	Migrants externes	184

Table 1. Selected Characteristics for Census Tracts, 2001 Census – 100% Data and 20% Sample Data

No.	Characteristics	Vancouver 0290.04 A	Vancouver 0290.05 A	Vancouver 0291.01	Vancouver 0291.02	Vancouver 0292.01	Vancouver 0292.02
	POPULATION CHARACTERISTICS						
185	**Total population 5 years and over (30)**	**6,320**	**3,225**	**6,055**	**7,235**	**5,380**	**8,085**
	by place of residence 5 years ago (mobility)						
186	Non-movers	3,870	2,105	3,250	4,085	3,680	3,815
187	Movers	2,445	1,120	2,805	3,145	1,700	4,275
188	Non-migrants	1,010	430	1,125	1,600	750	1,585
189	Migrants	1,435	690	1,680	1,550	950	2,685
190	Internal migrants	1,125	580	1,370	1,370	815	2,060
191	Intraprovincial migrants	990	535	1,190	1,205	700	1,720
192	Interprovincial migrants	135	45	185	165	120	345
193	External migrants	315	110	310	180	130	625
194	**Total population 15 to 24 years**	**935**	**505**	**910**	**1,155**	**825**	**1,220**
	by school attendance						
195	Not attending school	280	180	415	480	340	385
196	Attending school full time	510	270	420	590	400	725
197	Attending school part time	150	45	75	85	85	110
198	**Total population 15 years and over**	**5,310**	**2,645**	**5,205**	**6,070**	**4,340**	**6,590**
	by highest level of schooling						
199	Less than grade 9 (31)	120	100	255	325	115	245
200	Grades 9-13 without high school graduation certificate	860	585	1,405	1,380	915	1,420
201	Grades 9-13 with high school graduation certificate	710	380	845	1,185	560	915
202	Some postsecondary without degree, certificate or diploma (32)	780	320	705	790	500	960
203	Trades certificate or diploma (33)	540	350	600	900	660	880
204	College certificate or diploma (34)	1,190	570	870	1,020	880	1,105
205	University certificate below bachelor's degree	180	75	125	100	135	160
206	University with bachelor's degree or higher	930	265	400	375	575	900
	by combinations of unpaid work						
207	Males 15 years and over	2,605	1,335	2,535	2,995	2,150	3,250
208	Reported unpaid work (35)	2,315	1,200	2,305	2,690	1,960	2,940
209	Housework and child care and care or assistance to seniors	250	105	165	230	220	360
210	Housework and child care only	765	410	740	925	770	1,040
211	Housework and care or assistance to seniors only	150	110	125	165	155	195
212	Child care and care or assistance to seniors only	-	-	-	10	10	10
213	Housework only	1,105	535	1,240	1,325	780	1,300
214	Child care only	45	30	20	30	20	30
215	Care or assistance to seniors only	10	10	-	-	10	20
216	Females 15 years and over	2,705	1,310	2,670	3,075	2,185	3,335
217	Reported unpaid work (35)	2,560	1,240	2,520	2,905	2,125	3,110
218	Housework and child care and care or assistance to seniors	330	190	305	355	310	460
219	Housework and child care only	910	495	875	1,140	850	1,295
220	Housework and care or assistance to seniors only	255	60	225	225	165	155
221	Child care and care or assistance to seniors only	-	-	-	-	-	-
222	Housework only	1,045	465	1,095	1,170	780	1,175
223	Child care only	20	10	20	15	10	25
224	Care or assistance to seniors only	-	15	10	-	10	-
	by labour force activity						
225	Males 15 years and over	2,610	1,335	2,540	3,000	2,150	3,255
226	In the labour force	2,020	1,115	1,880	2,340	1,710	2,505
227	Employed	1,945	1,040	1,750	2,220	1,625	2,315
228	Unemployed	75	75	130	120	80	185
229	Not in the labour force	585	220	655	655	445	755
230	Participation rate	77.4	83.5	74.0	78.0	79.5	77.0
231	Employment rate	74.5	77.9	68.9	74.0	75.6	71.1
232	Unemployment rate	3.7	6.7	6.9	5.1	4.7	7.4
233	Females 15 years and over	2,705	1,315	2,670	3,075	2,190	3,335
234	In the labour force	1,875	985	1,710	2,150	1,625	2,130
235	Employed	1,805	920	1,540	1,960	1,555	1,995
236	Unemployed	75	65	170	190	70	130
237	Not in the labour force	830	330	965	925	565	1,205
238	Participation rate	69.3	74.9	64.0	69.9	74.2	63.9
239	Employment rate	66.7	70.0	57.7	63.7	71.0	59.8
240	Unemployment rate	4.0	6.6	9.9	8.8	4.3	6.1

Tableau 1. Certaines caractéristiques des secteurs de recensement, recensement de 2001 – Données intégrales et données-échantillon (20 %)

Vancouver 0400.01 A	Vancouver 0400.02 A	Vancouver 0401.01 A	Vancouver 0401.02 A	Vancouver 0402.01	Vancouver 0402.02	Caractéristiques	N°
						CARACTÉRISTIQUES DE LA POPULATION	
8,465	**3,275**	**2,450**	**6,275**	**7,300**	**4,620**	**Population totale de 5 ans et plus (30)**	185
						selon le lieu de résidence 5 ans auparavant (mobilité)	
3,350	2,555	1,110	2,745	3,820	2,725	Personnes n'ayant pas déménagé	186
5,120	720	1,340	3,530	3,480	1,895	Personnes ayant déménagé	187
2,345	400	510	1,925	1,750	1,045	Non-migrants	188
2,770	320	830	1,610	1,735	845	Migrants	189
2,580	320	800	1,450	1,640	770	Migrants internes	190
2,255	300	690	1,320	1,340	700	Migrants infraprovinciaux	191
325	15	115	130	295	70	Migrants interprovinciaux	192
190	-	25	155	95	75	Migrants externes	193
1,095	**455**	**330**	**645**	**925**	**660**	**Population totale de 15 à 24 ans**	194
						selon la fréquentation scolaire	
400	240	160	330	335	250	Ne fréquentant pas l'école	195
590	180	145	235	490	345	Fréquentant l'école à plein temps	196
100	30	35	75	90	65	Fréquentant l'école à temps partiel	197
6,745	**2,780**	**2,165**	**5,615**	**6,055**	**3,765**	**Population totale de 15 ans et plus**	198
						selon le plus haut niveau de scolarité atteint	
225	100	140	275	400	140	Niveau inférieur à la 9e année (31)	199
1,505	600	555	1,785	1,505	875	De la 9e à la 13e année sans certificat d'études secondaires	200
785	420	325	685	830	530	De la 9e à la 13e année avec certificat d'études secondaires	201
940	290	275	710	830	530	Études postsecondaires partielles sans grade, certificat ou diplôme (32)	202
960	435	295	680	900	570	Certificat ou diplôme d'une école de métiers (33)	203
1,240	540	360	930	960	730	Certificat ou diplôme collégial (34)	204
180	55	30	130	135	65	Certificat universitaire inférieur au baccalauréat	205
915	335	175	425	505	320	Études universitaires avec baccalauréat ou diplôme supérieur	206
						selon les combinaisons de travail non rémunéré	
3,335	1,430	1,045	2,665	2,855	1,825	Hommes de 15 ans et plus	207
3,065	1,280	965	2,375	2,545	1,670	Travail non rémunéré déclaré (35)	208
205	90	80	95	175	165	Travaux ménagers et soins aux enfants et soins ou aide aux personnes âgées	209
1,390	350	225	630	945	575	Travaux ménagers et soins aux enfants seulement	210
135	110	65	180	150	130	Travaux ménagers et soins ou aide aux personnes âgées seulement	211
-	-	10	10	-	-	Soins aux enfants et soins ou aide aux personnes âgées seulement	212
1,295	725	565	1,430	1,230	770	Travaux ménagers seulement	213
25	10	20	20	40	15	Soins aux enfants seulement	214
10	10	-	15	10	-	Soins ou aide aux personnes âgées seulement	215
3,405	1,350	1,125	2,950	3,200	1,935	Femmes de 15 ans et plus	216
3,265	1,250	1,045	2,705	3,025	1,840	Travail non rémunéré déclaré (35)	217
435	170	165	215	345	300	Travaux ménagers et soins aux enfants et soins ou aide aux personnes âgées	218
1,365	345	285	755	1,120	725	Travaux ménagers et soins aux enfants seulement	219
235	150	145	320	265	170	Travaux ménagers et soins ou aide aux personnes âgées seulement	220
-	-	-	-	-	10	Soins aux enfants et soins ou aide aux personnes âgées seulement	221
1,215	580	430	1,390	1,275	620	Travaux ménagers seulement	222
-	-	-	10	10	10	Soins aux enfants seulement	223
-	-	20	25	10	20	Soins ou aide aux personnes âgées seulement	224
						selon l'activité	
3,340	1,435	1,040	2,660	2,860	1,825	Hommes de 15 ans et plus	225
2,605	1,070	770	1,735	2,110	1,375	Population active	226
2,435	1,010	700	1,620	1,945	1,330	Personnes occupées	227
165	55	65	110	160	50	Chômeurs	228
730	365	275	930	750	445	Inactifs	229
78.0	74.6	74.0	65.2	73.8	75.3	Taux d'activité	230
72.9	70.4	67.3	60.9	68.0	72.9	Taux d'emploi	231
6.3	5.1	8.4	6.3	7.6	3.6	Taux de chômage	232
3,405	1,345	1,120	2,950	3,200	1,940	Femmes de 15 ans et plus	233
2,265	895	635	1,535	1,850	1,220	Population active	234
2,130	825	595	1,450	1,690	1,135	Personnes occupées	235
135	70	40	85	160	85	Chômeuses	236
1,140	450	490	1,415	1,350	720	Inactives	237
66.5	66.5	56.7	52.0	57.8	62.9	Taux d'activité	238
62.6	61.3	53.1	49.2	52.8	58.5	Taux d'emploi	239
6.0	7.8	6.3	5.5	8.6	7.0	Taux de chômage	240

Table 1. Selected Characteristics for Census Tracts, 2001 Census – 100% Data and 20% Sample Data

No.	Characteristics	Vancouver 0290.04 A	Vancouver 0290.05 A	Vancouver 0291.01	Vancouver 0291.02	Vancouver 0292.01	Vancouver 0292.02
	POPULATION CHARACTERISTICS						
	by labour force activity – concluded						
241	Both sexes - Participation rate	73.4	79.2	68.9	73.9	76.6	70.3
242	15-24 years	65.2	68.3	68.3	64.9	64.8	54.9
243	25 years and over	75.1	81.8	68.9	76.1	79.6	73.8
244	Both sexes - Employment rate	70.5	74.1	63.1	68.8	73.4	65.4
245	15-24 years	56.1	58.0	53.3	55.0	53.9	44.7
246	25 years and over	73.5	77.9	65.4	72.1	77.8	70.1
247	Both sexes - Unemployment rate	3.9	6.7	8.4	6.9	4.5	6.9
248	15-24 years	13.1	15.9	22.4	15.3	15.9	18.7
249	25 years and over	2.1	4.6	5.4	5.2	2.3	4.9
250	**Total labour force 15 years and over**	**3,895**	**2,095**	**3,585**	**4,485**	**3,330**	**4,630**
	by industry based on the 1997 NAICS						
251	Industry - Not applicable (36)	45	20	100	85	30	90
252	All industries (37)	3,850	2,075	3,485	4,400	3,300	4,540
253	11 Agriculture, forestry, fishing and hunting	-	15	-	15	45	35
254	21 Mining and oil and gas extraction	15	-	10	-	15	10
255	22 Utilities	55	10	15	10	10	30
256	23 Construction	170	190	370	405	210	345
257	31-33 Manufacturing	325	220	360	620	265	430
258	41 Wholesale trade	270	95	220	265	160	355
259	44-45 Retail trade	485	215	495	585	415	555
260	48-49 Transportation and warehousing	225	95	235	310	175	280
261	51 Information and cultural industries	140	120	190	105	125	145
262	52 Finance and insurance	345	105	130	190	165	190
263	53 Real estate and rental and leasing	110	40	40	105	65	100
264	54 Professional, scientific and technical services	320	155	160	205	270	380
265	55 Management of companies and enterprises	10	-	-	-	-	-
266	56 Administrative and support, waste management and remediation services	70	75	160	230	125	195
267	61 Educational services	300	110	95	195	260	255
268	62 Health care and social assistance	305	245	275	370	415	525
269	71 Arts, entertainment and recreation	40	30	45	100	30	110
270	72 Accommodation and food services	195	180	280	340	190	270
271	81 Other services (except public administration)	270	85	155	150	145	125
272	91 Public administration	195	90	240	195	215	210
	by class of worker						
273	Class of worker - Not applicable (36)	45	25	100	90	30	90
274	All classes of worker (37)	3,850	2,075	3,485	4,400	3,300	4,540
275	Paid workers	3,600	1,970	3,230	4,120	3,125	4,125
276	Employees	3,370	1,920	3,120	4,020	3,000	4,005
277	Self-employed (incorporated)	230	45	105	100	125	120
278	Self-employed (unincorporated)	250	110	260	275	170	420
279	Unpaid family workers	-	-	-	-	-	-
	by occupation based on the 2001 NOC-S						
280	Male labour force 15 years and over	2,020	1,115	1,880	2,340	1,710	2,500
281	Occupation - Not applicable (36)	20	-	35	25	15	30
282	All occupations (37)	2,000	1,115	1,840	2,315	1,690	2,475
283	A Management occupations	495	165	210	295	260	350
284	B Business, finance and administration occupations	245	95	145	105	110	240
285	C Natural and applied sciences and related occupations	230	65	145	185	235	195
286	D Health occupations	20	45	15	10	30	35
287	E Occupations in social science, education, government service and religion	75	30	45	60	75	140
288	F Occupations in art, culture, recreation and sport	35	35	30	20	35	85
289	G Sales and service occupations	455	220	350	480	410	525
290	H Trades, transport and equipment operators and related occupations	340	365	775	995	475	690
291	I Occupations unique to primary industry	35	10	10	20	15	50
292	J Occupations unique to processing, manufacturing and utilities	75	80	110	145	40	160
293	Female labour force 15 years and over	1,875	985	1,705	2,150	1,625	2,130
294	Occupation - Not applicable (36)	25	20	65	65	10	65
295	All occupations (37)	1,850	960	1,645	2,085	1,610	2,070
296	A Management occupations	270	95	125	155	95	230
297	B Business, finance and administration occupations	645	305	645	675	640	645
298	C Natural and applied sciences and related occupations	35	25	45	40	15	55
299	D Health occupations	180	90	105	195	190	210

Tableau 1. Certaines caractéristiques des secteurs de recensement, recensement de 2001 – Données intégrales et données-échantillon (20 %)

Vancouver 0400.01 A	Vancouver 0400.02 A	Vancouver 0401.01 A	Vancouver 0401.02 A	Vancouver 0402.01	Vancouver 0402.02	Caractéristiques	N°
						CARACTÉRISTIQUES DE LA POPULATION	
						selon l'activité – fin	
72.3	70.6	64.7	58.2	65.3	68.9	Les deux sexes - Taux d'activité	241
62.6	72.2	59.7	63.1	67.9	69.7	15-24 ans	242
74.0	70.5	65.7	57.6	64.9	68.9	25 ans et plus	243
67.8	66.0	60.0	54.8	60.1	65.3	Les deux sexes - Taux d'emploi	244
50.7	54.4	49.3	53.1	55.4	59.1	15-24 ans	245
71.0	68.4	61.7	54.8	60.9	66.9	25 ans et plus	246
6.3	6.1	7.8	5.8	8.1	5.2	Les deux sexes - Taux de chômage	247
18.8	24.6	17.5	14.8	18.4	15.2	15-24 ans	248
4.2	2.8	6.2	4.5	6.3	3.0	25 ans et plus	249
4,875	**1,960**	**1,405**	**3,265**	**3,960**	**2,595**	**Population active totale de 15 ans et plus**	250
						selon l'industrie basée sur le SCIAN de 1997	
75	25	35	50	70	40	Industrie - Sans objet (36)	251
4,795	1,935	1,365	3,220	3,890	2,560	Toutes les industries (37)	252
100	95	30	115	45	40	11 Agriculture, foresterie, pêche et chasse	253
20	-	-	-	20	10	21 Extraction minière et extraction de pétrole et de gaz	254
10	-	10	10	15	20	22 Services publics	255
345	250	115	205	260	145	23 Construction	256
480	200	185	415	480	275	31-33 Fabrication	257
275	135	55	160	245	90	41 Commerce de gros	258
495	170	190	440	505	295	44-45 Commerce de détail	259
330	120	100	195	245	185	48-49 Transport et entreposage	260
170	35	65	95	130	130	51 Industrie de l'information et industrie culturelle	261
200	25	15	165	175	70	52 Finance et assurances	262
100	25	25	25	50	70	53 Services immobiliers et services de location et de location à bail	263
325	95	35	110	225	140	54 Services professionnels, scientifiques et techniques	264
-	-	-	10	10	-	55 Gestion de sociétés et d'entreprises	265
155	75	65	180	145	75	56 Services administratifs, services de soutien, services de gestion des déchets et services d'assainissement	266
510	175	125	130	260	190	61 Services d'enseignement	267
485	250	110	335	365	270	62 Soins de santé et assistance sociale	268
105	30	10	35	85	75	71 Arts, spectacles et loisirs	269
195	60	60	225	280	185	72 Hébergement et services de restauration	270
225	115	70	210	210	155	81 Autres services, sauf les administrations publiques	271
260	85	110	155	145	135	91 Administrations publiques	272
						selon la catégorie de travailleurs	
80	30	35	50	70	40	Catégorie de travailleurs - Sans objet (36)	273
4,795	1,930	1,365	3,220	3,890	2,560	Toutes les catégories de travailleurs (37)	274
4,360	1,680	1,275	2,935	3,545	2,320	Travailleurs rémunérés	275
4,180	1,535	1,215	2,845	3,455	2,265	Employés	276
180	145	55	85	90	50	Travailleurs autonomes (entreprise constituée en société)	277
430	240	85	290	345	225	Travailleurs autonomes (entreprise non constituée en société)	278
-	15	-	-	-	15	Travailleurs familiaux non rémunérés	279
						selon la profession basée sur la CNP-S de 2001	
2,605	1,065	770	1,735	2,110	1,375	Hommes actifs de 15 ans et plus	280
30	10	10	25	30	-	Profession - Sans objet (36)	281
2,575	1,055	760	1,710	2,075	1,375	Toutes les professions (37)	282
375	135	115	145	270	115	A Gestion	283
165	40	50	150	165	105	B Affaires, finance et administration	284
175	55	30	155	145	125	C Sciences naturelles et appliquées et professions apparentées	285
35	30	15	50	45	30	D Secteur de la santé	286
190	45	35	50	65	90	E Sciences sociales, enseignement, administration publique et religion	287
60	25	10	30	40	35	F Arts, culture, sports et loisirs	288
505	145	105	330	485	290	G Ventes et services	289
785	420	340	530	600	415	H Métiers, transport et machinerie	290
100	40	10	95	60	55	I Professions propres au secteur primaire	291
195	120	50	165	205	115	J Transformation, fabrication et services d'utilité publique	292
2,265	895	635	1,535	1,850	1,220	Femmes actives de 15 ans et plus	293
45	20	30	25	35	35	Profession - Sans objet (36)	294
2,225	875	605	1,510	1,815	1,185	Toutes les professions (37)	295
175	45	45	115	170	80	A Gestion	296
700	220	135	455	520	375	B Affaires, finance et administration	297
40	30	20	50	20	10	C Sciences naturelles et appliquées et professions apparentées	298
220	110	55	150	135	145	D Secteur de la santé	299

Table 1. Selected Characteristics for Census Tracts, 2001 Census – 100% Data and 20% Sample Data

No.	Characteristics	Vancouver 0290.04 A	Vancouver 0290.05 A	Vancouver 0291.01	Vancouver 0291.02	Vancouver 0292.01	Vancouver 0292.02
	POPULATION CHARACTERISTICS						
	by occupation based on the 2001 NOC-S – concluded						
300	E Occupations in social science, education, government service and religion	160	100	80	180	210	165
301	F Occupations in art, culture, recreation and sport	40	20	25	40	45	80
302	G Sales and service occupations	455	280	535	685	385	615
303	H Trades, transport and equipment operators and related occupations	20	15	55	40	25	25
304	I Occupations unique to primary industry	-	10	-	-	-	25
305	J Occupations unique to processing, manufacturing and utilities	40	20	30	70	15	30
306	**Total employed labour force 15 years and over**	**3,745**	**1,960**	**3,285**	**4,180**	**3,180**	**4,310**
	by place of work						
307	Males	1,940	1,040	1,745	2,220	1,625	2,315
308	Usual place of work	1,500	795	1,260	1,700	1,295	1,790
309	At home	190	35	50	90	85	140
310	Outside Canada	55	10	-	20	20	30
311	No fixed workplace address	200	200	440	415	230	355
312	Females	1,800	920	1,540	1,955	1,555	1,995
313	Usual place of work	1,520	800	1,300	1,780	1,350	1,750
314	At home	175	55	130	60	120	140
315	Outside Canada	-	-	-	-	10	-
316	No fixed workplace address	110	65	110	115	75	105
317	**Total employed labour force 15 years and over with usual place of work or no fixed workplace address**	**3,325**	**1,855**	**3,105**	**4,005**	**2,950**	**4,000**
	by mode of transportation						
318	Males	1,700	995	1,700	2,110	1,525	2,145
319	Car, truck, van, as driver	1,485	935	1,375	1,870	1,360	1,855
320	Car, truck, van, as passenger	105	25	120	115	55	90
321	Public transit	70	20	115	65	80	105
322	Walked	30	-	80	45	-	45
323	Other method	10	15	10	25	15	45
324	Females	1,625	865	1,410	1,895	1,425	1,855
325	Car, truck, van, as driver	1,275	650	1,020	1,425	1,110	1,330
326	Car, truck, van, as passenger	190	60	115	175	105	195
327	Public transit	140	130	120	170	135	220
328	Walked	10	15	130	110	50	90
329	Other method	15	10	20	15	25	15
330	**Total population 15 years and over who worked since January 1, 2000**	**4,195**	**2,190**	**3,735**	**4,705**	**3,570**	**4,950**
	by language used at work						
331	Single responses	3,840	2,070	3,545	4,490	3,435	4,620
332	English	3,785	2,045	3,505	4,440	3,420	4,555
333	French	-	-	-	-	-	-
334	Non-official languages (5)	55	25	40	50	20	65
335	Chinese, n.o.s.	15	-	-	15	10	15
336	Cantonese	40	25	25	15	-	10
337	Other languages (6)	-	-	20	20	-	35
338	Multiple responses	355	120	190	215	130	330
339	English and French	35	45	20	40	-	30
340	English and non-official language	315	75	165	165	120	285
341	French and non-official language	-	-	-	-	-	-
342	English, French and non-official language	-	-	-	10	10	15
	DWELLING AND HOUSEHOLD CHARACTERISTICS						
343	**Total number of occupied private dwellings**	**2,190**	**1,105**	**2,495**	**2,640**	**1,750**	**2,750**
	by tenure						
344	Owned	2,020	890	1,515	1,925	1,490	2,175
345	Rented	170	215	980	710	265	570
346	Band housing	-	-	-	-	-	-
	by structural type of dwelling						
347	Single-detached house	1,230	910	1,135	1,570	1,385	1,720
348	Semi-detached house	105	15	60	215	40	220
349	Row house	660	65	315	110	160	465
350	Apartment, detached duplex	195	100	260	375	160	255
351	Apartment, building that has five or more storeys	-	-	-	-	-	-
352	Apartment, building that has fewer than five storeys (38)	-	10	680	380	10	75
353	Other single-attached house	-	-	-	-	-	10
354	Movable dwelling (39)	-	-	50	-	-	-

Tableau 1. Certaines caractéristiques des secteurs de recensement, recensement de 2001 – Données intégrales et données-échantillon (20 %)

Vancouver 0400.01 A	Vancouver 0400.02 A	Vancouver 0401.01 A	Vancouver 0401.02 A	Vancouver 0402.01	Vancouver 0402.02	Caractéristiques	N°
						CARACTÉRISTIQUES DE LA POPULATION	
						selon la profession basée sur la CNP-S de 2001 – fin	
						E Sciences sociales, enseignement,	
290	155	70	130	145	140	administration publique et religion	300
85	15	10	25	45	30	F Arts, culture, sports et loisirs	301
645	245	230	495	685	335	G Ventes et services	302
50	15	20	30	30	35	H Métiers, transport et machinerie	303
15	40	20	35	20	-	I Professions propres au secteur primaire	304
						J Transformation, fabrication et	
10	-	-	25	45	35	services d'utilité publique	305
4,570	**1,840**	**1,295**	**3,075**	**3,640**	**2,465**	**Population active occupée totale de 15 ans et plus**	306
						selon le lieu de travail	
2,440	1,015	700	1,625	1,950	1,330	Hommes	307
1,860	675	475	1,250	1,440	1,025	Lieu habituel de travail	308
115	95	40	80	100	90	À domicile	309
15	-	10	-	15	10	En dehors du Canada	310
445	245	180	295	400	205	Sans adresse de travail fixe	311
2,135	825	595	1,450	1,690	1,135	Femmes	312
1,855	665	520	1,275	1,480	980	Lieu habituel de travail	313
175	110	35	95	155	115	À domicile	314
10	-	-	-	-	-	En dehors du Canada	315
95	45	40	80	55	40	Sans adresse de travail fixe	316
						Population active occupée totale de 15 ans et plus ayant un lieu habituel de travail ou	
4,260	**1,635**	**1,210**	**2,900**	**3,365**	**2,250**	**sans adresse de travail fixe**	317
						selon le mode de transport	
2,305	920	655	1,540	1,835	1,235	Hommes	318
						Automobile, camion ou fourgonnette, en tant	
1,995	815	485	1,275	1,595	1,095	que conducteur	319
						Automobile, camion ou fourgonnette, en tant	
100	55	65	130	40	50	que passager	320
105	15	60	45	70	35	Transport en commun	321
30	15	25	55	80	10	À pied	322
75	15	25	45	55	40	Autre moyen	323
1,955	715	565	1,360	1,530	1,015	Femmes	324
						Automobile, camion ou fourgonnette, en tant	
1,655	595	390	1,075	1,180	840	que conductrice	325
						Automobile, camion ou fourgonnette, en tant	
135	75	55	90	155	85	que passagère	326
105	20	50	60	65	50	Transport en commun	327
50	20	60	120	115	40	À pied	328
-	-	10	15	25	-	Autre moyen	329
						Population totale de 15 ans et plus ayant travaillé	
5,220	**2,140**	**1,515**	**3,535**	**4,160**	**2,760**	**depuis le 1er janvier 2000**	330
						selon la langue utilisée au travail	
5,080	2,080	1,495	3,400	4,045	2,725	Réponses uniques	331
5,055	2,080	1,495	3,395	4,025	2,715	Anglais	332
15	-	-	-	10	-	Français	333
10	-	-	-	15	-	Langues non officielles (5)	334
-	-	-	-	-	-	Chinois, n.d.a.	335
-	-	-	-	-	-	Cantonais	336
10	-	-	10	10	10	Autres langues (6)	337
150	60	20	135	120	35	Réponses multiples	338
45	15	10	45	50	20	Anglais et français	339
95	45	10	90	70	15	Anglais et langue non officielle	340
-	-	-	-	-	-	Français et langue non officielle	341
10	-	-	-	-	-	Anglais, français et langue non officielle	342
						CARACTÉRISTIQUES DES LOGEMENTS ET DES MÉNAGES	
2,950	**1,240**	**1,115**	**3,215**	**3,000**	**1,715**	**Nombre total de logements privés occupés**	343
						selon le mode d'occupation	
2,535	1,105	595	1,975	2,140	1,395	Possédé	344
420	135	515	1,245	860	325	Loué	345
-	-	-	-	-	-	Logement de bande	346
						selon le type de construction résidentielle	
2,160	1,195	550	745	1,790	1,170	Maison individuelle non attenante	347
65	10	20	120	-	50	Maison jumelée	348
580	10	80	640	95	265	Maison en rangée	349
60	15	95	50	165	110	Appartement, duplex non attenant	350
-	-	205	280	155	-	Appartement, immeuble de cinq étages ou plus	351
85	-	115	1,375	795	120	Appartement, immeuble de moins de cinq étages (38)	352
-	-	-	10	-	-	Autre maison individuelle attenante	353
-	25	40	-	-	-	Logement mobile (39)	354

Table 1. Selected Characteristics for Census Tracts, 2001 Census – 100% Data and 20% Sample Data

No.	Characteristics	Vancouver 0290.04 A	Vancouver 0290.05 A	Vancouver 0291.01	Vancouver 0291.02	Vancouver 0292.01	Vancouver 0292.02
	DWELLING AND HOUSEHOLD CHARACTERISTICS						
	by condition of dwelling						
355	Regular maintenance only	1,920	710	1,585	1,730	1,250	2,075
356	Minor repairs	235	355	715	700	380	555
357	Major repairs	30	40	195	210	120	115
	by period of construction						
358	Before 1946	-	30	85	60	15	70
359	1946-1960	-	30	295	275	50	75
360	1961-1970	10	200	410	630	150	470
361	1971-1980	10	285	670	840	630	685
362	1981-1990	995	345	480	345	665	250
363	1991-2001 (20)	1,180	220	555	490	235	1,205
364	Average number of rooms per dwelling	8.2	7.6	6.1	6.9	7.9	7.2
365	Average number of bedrooms per dwelling	3.4	3.3	2.6	3.0	3.4	3.2
366	Average value of dwelling $	284,555	221,935	198,936	208,934	229,712	231,489
367	**Total number of private households**	**2,190**	**1,105**	**2,495**	**2,640**	**1,750**	**2,750**
	by household size						
368	1 person	195	110	655	425	140	285
369	2 persons	725	260	770	775	405	745
370	3 persons	410	270	410	525	370	590
371	4-5 persons	770	410	585	795	755	1,005
372	6 or more persons	90	45	85	120	80	130
	by household type						
373	One-family households	1,935	910	1,625	2,000	1,510	2,345
374	Multiple-family households	25	30	70	135	75	70
375	Non-family households	220	165	805	500	165	325
376	Number of persons in private households	6,720	3,510	6,475	7,755	5,765	8,635
377	Average number of persons in private households	3.1	3.2	2.6	2.9	3.3	3.1
378	Average number of persons per room	0.4	0.4	0.4	0.4	0.4	0.4
	Tenant households in non-farm, non-reserve						
379	private dwellings (40)	170	215	975	705	255	575
380	Average gross rent $ (40)	1,025	885	743	872	900	893
	Tenant households spending 30% or more of						
381	household income on gross rent (40) (41)	40	70	520	290	85	240
	Tenant households spending from 30% to 99% of						
382	household income on gross rent (40) (41)	30	60	365	240	65	200
	Owner households in non-farm, non-reserve						
383	private dwellings (42)	2,015	885	1,515	1,925	1,485	2,160
384	Average owner's major payments $ (42)	1,195	1,202	1,053	1,067	1,215	1,180
	Owner households spending 30% or more of household income on owner's major						
385	payments (41) (42)	385	230	290	465	300	625
	Owner households spending from 30% to 99% of household income on						
386	owner's major payments (41) (42)	340	205	255	385	280	525
	CENSUS FAMILY CHARACTERISTICS						
	Total number of census families in						
387	**private households**	**1,995**	**970**	**1,765**	**2,280**	**1,660**	**2,500**
	by census family structure and size						
388	Total couple families	1,855	850	1,410	1,830	1,460	2,155
389	Total families of married couples	1,740	770	1,195	1,555	1,335	1,960
390	Without children at home	590	195	450	545	335	510
391	With children at home	1,150	580	745	1,015	1,000	1,455
392	1 child	355	180	270	345	310	440
393	2 children	565	310	315	470	510	760
394	3 or more children	230	85	160	200	180	250
395	Total families of common-law couples	110	80	215	270	130	195
396	Without children at home	70	50	95	95	80	155
397	With children at home	40	30	115	175	45	35
398	1 child	20	20	80	110	25	10
399	2 children	10	10	30	50	20	10
400	3 or more children	15	-	10	20	-	10
401	Total lone-parent families	145	120	355	450	200	350
402	Female parent	115	85	300	355	160	290
403	1 child	80	20	170	210	75	140
404	2 children	30	55	80	105	60	130
405	3 or more children	10	15	50	40	25	20

Tableau 1. Certaines caractéristiques des secteurs de recensement, recensement de 2001 – Données intégrales et données-échantillon (20 %)

Vancouver 0400.01 A	Vancouver 0400.02 A	Vancouver 0401.01 A	Vancouver 0401.02 A	Vancouver 0402.01	Vancouver 0402.02	Caractéristiques	N°
						CARACTÉRISTIQUES DES LOGEMENTS ET DES MÉNAGES	
						selon l'état du logement	
2,275	670	715	2,445	2,150	1,205	Entretien régulier seulement	355
530	445	265	540	715	395	Réparations mineures	356
140	125	135	230	135	115	Réparations majeures	357
						selon la période de construction	
115	185	55	75	75	65	Avant 1946	358
170	170	190	250	140	200	1946-1960	359
195	170	320	365	325	295	1961-1970	360
185	390	210	480	755	280	1971-1980	361
475	165	215	940	935	535	1981-1990	362
1,810	155	130	1,110	765	340	1991-2001 (20)	363
7.9	7.6	5.8	5.3	6.5	7.4	Nombre moyen de pièces par logement	364
3.3	3.1	2.4	2.1	2.8	3.2	Nombre moyen de chambres à coucher par logement	365
239,158	302,482	187,190	146,241	192,720	192,430	Valeur moyenne du logement $	366
2,950	**1,240**	**1,115**	**3,220**	**3,000**	**1,720**	**Nombre total de logements privés**	367
						selon la taille du ménage	
365	240	355	1,260	765	300	1 personne	368
825	430	340	1,130	935	530	2 personnes	369
585	190	185	360	475	300	3 personnes	370
1,025	330	220	440	725	520	4-5 personnes	371
155	55	15	25	105	70	6 personnes ou plus	372
						selon le genre de ménage	
2,445	920	710	1,815	2,100	1,370	Ménages unifamiliaux	373
105	35	20	25	35	20	Ménages multifamiliaux	374
400	280	385	1,375	865	335	Ménages non familiaux	375
9,145	3,425	2,625	6,665	7,810	4,935	Nombre de personnes dans les ménages privés	376
3.1	2.8	2.4	2.1	2.6	2.9	Nombre moyen de personnes dans les ménages privés	377
0.4	0.4	0.4	0.4	0.4	0.4	Nombre moyen de personnes par pièce	378
410	120	515	1,245	860	320	Ménages locataires dans les logements privés non agricoles hors réserve (40)	379
878	860	698	678	701	806	Loyer brut moyen $ (40)	380
170	35	255	640	365	140	Ménages locataires consacrant 30 % ou plus du revenu du ménage au loyer brut (40) (41)	381
140	25	215	535	280	125	Ménages locataires consacrant de 30 % à 99 % du revenu du ménage au loyer brut (40) (41)	382
2,515	1,060	600	1,975	2,140	1,395	Ménages propriétaires dans les logements privés non agricoles hors réserve (42)	383
1,264	1,002	1,063	874	1,000	1,012	Principales dépenses de propriété moyennes $ (42)	384
635	245	145	565	475	310	Ménages propriétaires consacrant 30 % ou plus du revenu du ménage aux principales dépenses de propriété (41) (42)	385
605	210	130	480	380	285	Ménages propriétaires consacrant de 30 % à 99 % du revenu du ménage aux principales dépenses de propriété (41) (42)	386
						CARACTÉRISTIQUES DES FAMILLES DE RECENSEMENT	
2,655	**995**	**745**	**1,875**	**2,170**	**1,405**	**Total des familles de recensement dans les ménages privés**	387
						selon la structure et la taille de la famille de recensement	
2,340	905	620	1,505	1,770	1,120	Total des familles avec conjoints	388
2,050	780	475	1,240	1,560	1,035	Total des familles avec couples mariés	389
700	335	215	685	610	350	Sans enfants à la maison	390
1,350	445	265	555	950	685	Avec enfants à la maison	391
420	125	80	195	255	225	1 enfant	392
675	200	125	265	490	295	2 enfants	393
255	120	55	95	200	165	3 enfants ou plus	394
295	125	145	265	210	85	Total des familles en union libre	395
140	80	85	205	145	55	Sans enfants à la maison	396
160	45	60	65	60	30	Avec enfants à la maison	397
75	10	45	35	50	10	1 enfant	398
50	25	15	25	10	15	2 enfants	399
35	15	-	-	-	10	3 enfants ou plus	400
315	90	125	365	400	285	Total des familles monoparentales	401
260	65	105	295	315	225	Parent de sexe féminin	402
130	65	75	190	165	120	1 enfant	403
95	-	20	85	125	55	2 enfants	404
35	-	15	25	25	50	3 enfants ou plus	405

Table 1. Selected Characteristics for Census Tracts, 2001 Census – 100% Data and 20% Sample Data

No.	Characteristics	Vancouver 0290.04 A	Vancouver 0290.05 A	Vancouver 0291.01	Vancouver 0291.02	Vancouver 0292.01	Vancouver 0292.02
	CENSUS FAMILY CHARACTERISTICS						
	by census family structure and size – concluded						
406	Male parent	30	35	55	95	40	60
407	1 child	20	25	35	75	15	40
408	2 children	10	-	10	25	15	10
409	3 or more children	-	-	10	-	-	10
410	**Total number of children at home**	**2,490**	**1,325**	**2,150**	**2,830**	**2,310**	**3,395**
	by age groups						
411	Under 6 years	490	355	505	640	440	755
412	6-14 years	925	495	765	1,040	990	1,290
413	15-17 years	290	160	325	380	320	520
414	18-24 years	600	260	410	580	415	595
415	25 years and over	185	55	155	190	155	250
416	Average number of children at home per census family (43)	1.2	1.4	1.2	1.2	1.4	1.4
417	**Total number of persons in private households**	**6,720**	**3,510**	**6,475**	**7,760**	**5,765**	**8,635**
	by census family status and living arrangements						
418	Number of non-family persons	385	360	1,145	820	330	590
419	Living with relatives (44)	100	110	190	165	80	140
420	Living with non-relatives only	90	140	305	225	110	170
421	Living alone	200	110	655	425	140	280
422	Number of family persons	6,335	3,145	5,330	6,940	5,430	8,045
423	Average number of persons per census family	3.2	3.2	3.0	3.0	3.3	3.2
424	**Total number of persons 65 years and over**	**485**	**150**	**565**	**560**	**290**	**490**
425	Number of non-family persons 65 years and over	110	65	265	150	90	140
426	Living with relatives (44)	70	45	40	60	40	45
427	Living with non-relatives only	-	10	40	20	-	-
428	Living alone	40	15	190	70	45	95
429	Number of family persons 65 years and over	375	90	295	410	205	345
	ECONOMIC FAMILY CHARACTERISTICS						
430	**Total number of economic families in private households**	**1,965**	**950**	**1,740**	**2,175**	**1,590**	**2,440**
	by size of family						
431	2 persons	705	255	705	755	410	750
432	3 persons	420	250	395	555	380	580
433	4 persons	550	280	405	530	545	745
434	5 or more persons	295	160	235	335	265	360
435	Total number of persons in economic families	6,430	3,255	5,525	7,105	5,510	8,185
436	Average number of persons per economic family	3.3	3.4	3.2	3.3	3.5	3.4
437	Total number of unattached individuals	290	250	955	650	250	450
	2000 INCOME CHARACTERISTICS						
	Population 15 years and over by sex and total income groups in 2000						
438	Total - Both sexes	5,310	2,645	5,205	6,070	4,335	6,585
439	Without income	245	135	310	355	260	530
440	With income	5,070	2,515	4,890	5,715	4,075	6,060
441	Under $1,000 (45)	205	115	285	255	180	395
442	$ 1,000 - $ 2,999	210	70	215	235	210	345
443	$ 3,000 - $ 4,999	140	135	205	210	140	205
444	$ 5,000 - $ 6,999	215	175	225	240	155	255
445	$ 7,000 - $ 9,999	225	105	285	420	205	330
446	$10,000 - $11,999	170	90	195	235	125	260
447	$12,000 - $14,999	230	105	415	375	210	295
448	$15,000 - $19,999	405	95	380	460	265	525
449	$20,000 - $24,999	270	115	355	415	275	545
450	$25,000 - $29,999	340	215	345	395	350	385
451	$30,000 - $34,999	270	175	405	400	350	365
452	$35,000 - $39,999	235	210	320	325	195	385
453	$40,000 - $44,999	320	220	395	400	275	295
454	$45,000 - $49,999	290	150	285	320	200	235
455	$50,000 - $59,999	465	220	235	525	350	540
456	$60,000 and over	1,065	310	340	495	580	705
457	Average income $ (46)	38,557	32,065	27,087	28,759	32,893	30,265
458	Median income $ (46)	31,598	30,035	23,864	25,048	27,987	23,937
459	Standard error of average income $ (46)	1,012	1,020	666	626	889	843

Tableau 1. Certaines caractéristiques des secteurs de recensement, recensement de 2001 – Données intégrales et données-échantillon (20 %)

Vancouver 0400.01 A	Vancouver 0400.02 A	Vancouver 0401.01 A	Vancouver 0401.02 A	Vancouver 0402.01	Vancouver 0402.02	Caractéristiques	N°
						CARACTÉRISTIQUES DES FAMILLES DE RECENSEMENT	
						selon la structure et la taille de la famille de recensement – fin	
55	20	20	70	85	60	Parent de sexe masculin	406
30	20	15	65	65	55	1 enfant	407
15	10	-	-	15	-	2 enfants	408
-	-	-	-	10	-	3 enfants ou plus	409
3,400	**1,100**	**760**	**1,615**	**2,620**	**1,855**	**Nombre total d'enfants à la maison**	410
						selon les groupes d'âge	
880	190	205	455	615	345	Moins de 6 ans	411
1,480	450	250	600	1,120	810	6-14 ans	412
435	125	105	200	345	225	15-17 ans	413
415	255	155	200	360	365	18-24 ans	414
195	80	45	150	175	115	25 ans et plus	415
1.3	1.1	1.0	0.9	1.2	1.3	Nombre moyen d'enfants à la maison par famille de recensement (43)	416
9,145	**3,425**	**2,620**	**6,665**	**7,810**	**4,935**	**Nombre total de personnes dans les ménages privés**	417
						selon la situation des particuliers dans la famille de recensement et des particuliers dans le ménage	
745	425	490	1,675	1,255	560	Nombre de personnes hors famille de recensement	418
125	45	60	85	200	130	Vivant avec des personnes apparentées (44)	419
255	145	80	325	295	135	Vivant avec des personnes non apparentées uniquement	420
360	240	350	1,260	765	300	Vivant seules	421
8,400	3,000	2,135	4,985	6,555	4,375	Nombre de personnes membres d'une famille	422
3.2	3.0	2.9	2.7	3.0	3.1	Nombre moyen de personnes par famille de recensement	423
640	**325**	**350**	**1,285**	**1,105**	**545**	**Nombre total de personnes de 65 ans et plus**	424
205	125	155	625	445	175	Nombre de personnes hors famille de recensement de 65 ans et plus	425
90	15	10	30	55	25	Vivant avec des personnes apparentées (44)	426
-	10	15	35	15	-	Vivant avec des personnes non apparentées uniquement	427
115	100	135	560	380	145	Vivant seules	428
435	200	195	665	655	370	Nombre de personnes membres d'une famille de 65 ans et plus	429
						CARACTÉRISTIQUES DES FAMILLES ÉCONOMIQUES	
2,570	**975**	**740**	**1,865**	**2,165**	**1,400**	**Nombre total de familles économiques dans les ménages privés**	430
						selon la taille de la famille	
840	455	345	1,115	925	525	2 personnes	431
590	145	170	315	465	315	3 personnes	432
765	230	155	310	530	355	4 personnes	433
380	150	70	130	245	210	5 personnes ou plus	434
8,520	3,045	2,190	5,075	6,755	4,500	Nombre total de personnes dans les familles économiques	435
3.3	3.1	2.9	2.7	3.1	3.2	Nombre moyen de personnes par famille économique	436
615	385	435	1,590	1,055	430	Nombre total de personnes hors famille économique	437
						CARACTÉRISTIQUES DU REVENU DE 2000	
						Population de 15 ans et plus selon le sexe et les tranches de revenu total en 2000	
6,745	2,775	2,165	5,615	6,060	3,765	Total - Les deux sexes	438
405	125	80	195	255	255	Sans revenu	439
6,345	2,655	2,085	5,420	5,805	3,510	Avec un revenu	440
190	95	75	195	250	140	Moins de 1 000 $ (45)	441
295	165	105	200	295	125	1 000 $ - 2 999 $	442
260	80	60	200	225	105	3 000 $ - 4 999 $	443
240	80	130	280	220	125	5 000 $ - 6 999 $	444
345	155	155	355	365	190	7 000 $ - 9 999 $	445
225	80	110	220	240	115	10 000 $ - 11 999 $	446
375	155	175	420	570	205	12 000 $ - 14 999 $	447
450	250	170	545	505	380	15 000 $ - 19 999 $	448
465	215	135	465	525	180	20 000 $ - 24 999 $	449
385	165	150	350	420	285	25 000 $ - 29 999 $	450
500	160	120	525	395	290	30 000 $ - 34 999 $	451
325	275	165	440	400	250	35 000 $ - 39 999 $	452
445	160	125	385	305	240	40 000 $ - 44 999 $	453
350	115	145	220	235	150	45 000 $ - 49 999 $	454
605	215	180	385	345	305	50 000 $ - 59 999 $	455
885	295	105	225	525	435	60 000 $ et plus	456
33,215	30,623	25,984	26,048	27,781	31,419	Revenu moyen $ (46)	457
29,265	26,340	23,050	22,468	21,965	28,125	Revenu médian $ (46)	458
737	1,008	929	540	700	878	Erreur type de revenu moyen $ (46)	459

Table 1. Selected Characteristics for Census Tracts, 2001 Census – 100% Data and 20% Sample Data

No.	Characteristics	Vancouver 0290.04 A	Vancouver 0290.05 A	Vancouver 0291.01	Vancouver 0291.02	Vancouver 0292.01	Vancouver 0292.02
	2000 INCOME CHARACTERISTICS						
	Population 15 years and over by sex and total income groups in 2000 – concluded						
460	Total - Males	2,605	1,335	2,535	2,995	2,150	3,250
461	Without income	115	25	130	155	135	205
462	With income	2,490	1,305	2,410	2,840	2,020	3,050
463	Under $1,000 (45)	85	90	105	110	45	175
464	$ 1,000 - $ 2,999	85	15	90	85	65	110
465	$ 3,000 - $ 4,999	25	45	80	85	65	60
466	$ 5,000 - $ 6,999	60	95	115	65	70	100
467	$ 7,000 - $ 9,999	75	25	130	145	120	90
468	$10,000 - $11,999	80	20	75	120	55	95
469	$12,000 - $14,999	80	40	100	125	95	105
470	$15,000 - $19,999	165	45	165	155	120	250
471	$20,000 - $24,999	135	60	160	175	90	235
472	$25,000 - $29,999	120	105	170	175	145	215
473	$30,000 - $34,999	95	65	195	195	140	140
474	$35,000 - $39,999	70	110	165	175	85	185
475	$40,000 - $44,999	160	120	170	220	135	170
476	$45,000 - $49,999	145	65	190	205	130	170
477	$50,000 - $59,999	300	145	195	385	175	400
478	$60,000 and over	805	255	290	420	490	545
479	Average income $ (46)	47,971	37,591	32,689	35,335	40,645	37,097
480	Median income $ (46)	44,839	37,046	30,001	33,911	35,330	33,083
481	Standard error of average income $ (46)	1,592	1,577	1,082	988	1,487	1,287
482	Total - Females	2,700	1,310	2,670	3,080	2,190	3,335
483	Without income	130	105	185	200	130	325
484	With income	2,575	1,210	2,480	2,875	2,060	3,010
485	Under $1,000 (45)	120	30	180	140	140	225
486	$ 1,000 - $ 2,999	130	50	130	145	145	235
487	$ 3,000 - $ 4,999	120	90	120	125	75	145
488	$ 5,000 - $ 6,999	155	80	110	175	85	155
489	$ 7,000 - $ 9,999	150	80	160	275	90	240
490	$10,000 - $11,999	90	75	120	115	70	170
491	$12,000 - $14,999	145	60	310	255	115	190
492	$15,000 - $19,999	245	50	220	305	150	275
493	$20,000 - $24,999	130	50	195	235	190	305
494	$25,000 - $29,999	215	110	170	225	200	165
495	$30,000 - $34,999	175	110	210	200	210	225
496	$35,000 - $39,999	165	100	155	150	110	195
497	$40,000 - $44,999	160	100	220	180	140	120
498	$45,000 - $49,999	150	80	95	120	70	70
499	$50,000 - $59,999	170	75	40	145	175	140
500	$60,000 and over	260	55	50	75	90	155
501	Average income $ (46)	29,457	26,085	21,661	22,260	25,297	23,342
502	Median income $ (46)	25,021	27,197	17,611	18,453	23,988	17,230
503	Standard error of average income $ (46)	1,145	1,158	722	681	858	1,030
	by composition of total income						
504	Total - Composition of income in 2000 % (47)	100.0	100.0	100.0	100.0	100.0	100.0
505	Employment income %	85.7	87.4	80.9	83.3	87.4	87.2
506	Government transfer payments %	4.8	6.4	11.2	9.7	6.3	7.7
507	Other %	9.5	6.2	7.9	7.0	6.3	5.1
	Population 15 years and over with employment income in 2000 by sex and work activity						
508	Both sexes with employment income (48)	4,075	2,150	3,530	4,510	3,520	4,760
509	Average employment income $	41,110	32,747	30,334	30,330	33,322	33,617
510	Standard error of average employment income $	1,103	1,078	813	717	982	1,004
511	Worked full year, full time (49)	2,395	1,240	1,905	2,515	1,865	2,585
512	Average employment income $	56,028	43,192	40,136	40,932	45,688	45,292
513	Standard error of average employment income $	1,458	1,265	1,066	896	1,334	1,368
514	Worked part year or part time (50)	1,605	875	1,545	1,905	1,590	2,050
515	Average employment income $	19,570	19,016	19,408	17,600	19,367	20,206
516	Standard error of average employment income $	1,018	1,337	1,013	814	1,077	1,282
517	Males with employment income (48)	2,100	1,130	1,845	2,395	1,760	2,565
518	Average employment income $	49,356	38,670	35,952	36,270	41,491	39,899
519	Standard error of average employment income $	1,642	1,639	1,276	1,082	1,630	1,450
520	Worked full year, full time (49)	1,400	785	1,075	1,515	1,105	1,650
521	Average employment income $	62,921	46,066	44,967	45,361	52,054	48,114
522	Standard error of average employment income $	1,951	1,827	1,564	1,228	1,992	1,600
523	Worked part year or part time (50)	680	335	715	845	650	850
524	Average employment income $	22,009	22,577	24,234	21,466	23,540	25,558
525	Standard error of average employment income $	1,776	2,513	1,853	1,508	2,123	2,708

Tableau 1. Certaines caractéristiques des secteurs de recensement, recensement de 2001 – Données intégrales et données-échantillon (20 %)

Vancouver 0400.01 A	Vancouver 0400.02 A	Vancouver 0401.01 A	Vancouver 0401.02 A	Vancouver 0402.01	Vancouver 0402.02	Caractéristiques	N°
						CARACTÉRISTIQUES DU REVENU DE 2000	
						Population de 15 ans et plus selon le sexe et les tranches de revenu total en 2000 – fin	
3,340	1,435	1,040	2,665	2,855	1,825	Total - Hommes	460
200	55	30	85	125	85	Sans revenu	461
3,140	1,375	1,015	2,575	2,730	1,740	Avec un revenu	462
60	35	35	125	95	40	Moins de 1 000 $ (45)	463
130	45	30	65	120	45	1 000 $ - 2 999 $	464
85	-	30	75	60	25	3 000 $ - 4 999 $	465
85	30	45	120	45	45	5 000 $ - 6 999 $	466
85	40	80	80	120	65	7 000 $ - 9 999 $	467
95	35	40	95	90	30	10 000 $ - 11 999 $	468
75	55	55	110	135	65	12 000 $ - 14 999 $	469
150	115	30	200	200	160	15 000 $ - 19 999 $	470
210	120	50	240	225	75	20 000 $ - 24 999 $	471
180	85	80	175	190	145	25 000 $ - 29 999 $	472
250	110	55	230	205	185	30 000 $ - 34 999 $	473
125	155	90	220	240	95	35 000 $ - 39 999 $	474
255	105	85	210	190	115	40 000 $ - 44 999 $	475
220	60	85	155	165	105	45 000 $ - 49 999 $	476
445	145	135	310	215	205	50 000 $ - 59 999 $	477
695	260	95	175	430	355	60 000 $ et plus	478
41,981	38,807	31,724	30,736	35,748	39,065	Revenu moyen $ (46)	479
40,087	36,125	31,086	29,955	31,298	35,112	Revenu médian $ (46)	480
1,163	1,537	1,457	862	1,214	1,374	Erreur type de revenu moyen $ (46)	481
3,410	1,345	1,125	2,955	3,200	1,940	Total - Femmes	482
200	70	50	110	130	170	Sans revenu	483
3,205	1,275	1,070	2,845	3,070	1,770	Avec un revenu	484
125	60	30	70	150	100	Moins de 1 000 $ (45)	485
165	120	75	135	170	80	1 000 $ - 2 999 $	486
180	75	30	125	160	80	3 000 $ - 4 999 $	487
165	50	85	160	170	80	5 000 $ - 6 999 $	488
260	115	80	280	245	130	7 000 $ - 9 999 $	489
125	50	70	130	145	85	10 000 $ - 11 999 $	490
300	100	115	310	435	140	12 000 $ - 14 999 $	491
295	140	135	345	315	225	15 000 $ - 19 999 $	492
255	100	85	230	300	100	20 000 $ - 24 999 $	493
200	85	75	170	230	140	25 000 $ - 29 999 $	494
250	50	65	295	190	100	30 000 $ - 34 999 $	495
200	120	75	220	160	155	35 000 $ - 39 999 $	496
190	55	40	175	115	120	40 000 $ - 44 999 $	497
125	55	60	70	65	50	45 000 $ - 49 999 $	498
165	75	40	80	125	100	50 000 $ - 59 999 $	499
190	30	15	55	100	80	60 000 $ et plus	500
24,633	21,796	20,559	21,803	20,698	23,910	Revenu moyen $ (46)	501
19,616	17,620	16,735	18,004	16,292	19,130	Revenu médian $ (46)	502
776	1,063	1,039	622	658	966	Erreur type de revenu moyen $ (46)	503
						selon la composition du revenu total	
100.0	100.0	100.0	100.0	100.0	100.0	Total - Composition du revenu en 2000 % (47)	504
86.3	79.6	79.9	69.6	78.7	79.8	Revenu d'emploi %	505
7.8	9.7	13.4	16.7	14.0	11.2	Transferts gouvernementaux %	506
5.8	10.8	6.6	13.8	7.4	9.0	Autre %	507
						Population de 15 ans et plus ayant un revenu d'emploi en 2000 selon le sexe et le travail	
5,070	2,115	1,460	3,435	4,025	2,710	Les deux sexes ayant un revenu d'emploi (48)	508
35,887	30,561	29,608	28,576	31,525	32,494	Revenu moyen d'emploi $	509
851	1,162	1,133	715	956	1,015	Erreur type de revenu moyen d'emploi $	510
2,850	1,030	815	1,990	2,035	1,430	Ayant travaillé toute l'année à plein temps (49)	511
46,296	42,821	39,498	37,639	43,921	42,899	Revenu moyen d'emploi $	512
1,059	1,719	1,145	860	1,434	1,302	Erreur type de revenu moyen d'emploi $	513
2,110	1,020	610	1,325	1,880	1,195	Ayant travaillé une partie de l'année ou à temps partiel (50)	514
23,275	19,425	17,959	16,810	19,546	21,396	Revenu moyen d'emploi $	515
1,176	1,215	1,597	881	897	1,325	Erreur type de revenu moyen d'emploi $	516
2,665	1,125	805	1,785	2,085	1,460	Hommes ayant un revenu d'emploi (48)	517
44,402	38,232	33,875	32,983	39,354	39,866	Revenu moyen d'emploi $	518
1,290	1,795	1,613	1,101	1,519	1,515	Erreur type de revenu moyen d'emploi $	519
1,760	670	490	1,140	1,210	895	Ayant travaillé toute l'année à plein temps (49)	520
51,594	49,017	42,910	41,379	50,514	48,608	Revenu moyen d'emploi $	521
1,494	2,260	1,540	1,225	2,098	1,735	Erreur type de revenu moyen d'emploi $	522
875	400	295	605	850	525	Ayant travaillé une partie de l'année ou à temps partiel (50)	523
30,862	24,454	20,734	18,518	24,625	26,167	Revenu moyen d'emploi $	524
2,195	2,265	2,666	1,561	1,534	2,414	Erreur type de revenu moyen d'emploi $	525

Table 1. Selected Characteristics for Census Tracts, 2001 Census – 100% Data and 20% Sample Data

No.	Characteristics	Vancouver 0290.04 A	Vancouver 0290.05 A	Vancouver 0291.01	Vancouver 0291.02	Vancouver 0292.01	Vancouver 0292.02
	2000 INCOME CHARACTERISTICS						
	Population 15 years and over with employment income in 2000 by sex and work activity – concluded						
526	Females with employment income (48)	1,970	1,015	1,690	2,125	1,760	2,195
527	Average employment income $	32,326	26,170	24,209	23,639	25,142	26,304
528	Standard error of average employment income $	1,345	1,218	879	814	927	1,306
529	Worked full year, full time (49)	995	460	825	1,000	760	935
530	Average employment income $	46,354	38,292	33,848	34,255	36,433	40,301
531	Standard error of average employment income $	2,032	1,261	1,238	1,127	1,188	2,465
532	Worked part year or part time (50)	930	535	830	1,060	940	1,195
533	Average employment income $	17,785	16,784	15,214	14,530	16,476	16,391
534	Standard error of average employment income $	1,151	1,451	873	795	1,035	1,028
	Census families by structure and family income groups in 2000						
535	Total - All census families	1,990	970	1,765	2,280	1,660	2,500
536	Under $10,000	20	20	100	120	75	90
537	$ 10,000 - $19,999	85	45	175	180	45	145
538	$ 20,000 - $29,999	110	60	160	155	65	180
539	$ 30,000 - $39,999	95	85	205	280	120	270
540	$ 40,000 - $49,999	120	80	150	205	160	290
541	$ 50,000 - $59,999	190	100	175	220	175	275
542	$ 60,000 - $69,999	180	80	215	245	210	240
543	$ 70,000 - $79,999	100	115	190	155	175	245
544	$ 80,000 - $89,999	190	65	115	235	150	180
545	$ 90,000 - $99,999	165	110	110	165	105	145
546	$100,000 and over	730	210	165	325	385	425
547	Average family income $	91,215	72,218	56,878	61,211	74,561	67,297
548	Median family income $	85,026	71,285	55,169	59,435	69,289	59,822
549	Standard error of average family income $	2,690	2,504	1,715	1,543	2,094	2,028
550	Total - All couple census families (51)	1,855	855	1,415	1,830	1,460	2,150
551	Under $10,000	15	10	65	60	55	70
552	$ 10,000 - $19,999	55	40	60	85	25	75
553	$ 20,000 - $29,999	90	25	105	105	50	125
554	$ 30,000 - $39,999	95	60	135	205	70	220
555	$ 40,000 - $49,999	95	75	95	145	120	235
556	$ 50,000 - $59,999	175	85	165	155	150	235
557	$ 60,000 - $69,999	175	80	205	220	205	220
558	$ 70,000 - $79,999	90	100	180	145	165	230
559	$ 80,000 - $89,999	185	65	120	220	145	185
560	$ 90,000 - $99,999	160	115	115	165	95	145
561	$100,000 and over	705	210	165	320	385	415
562	Average family income $	94,238	77,320	64,240	67,494	79,523	70,646
563	Median family income $	87,075	76,161	61,939	67,306	74,789	64,732
564	Standard error of average family income $	2,825	2,596	1,893	1,696	2,223	2,032
	Incidence of low income in 2000						
565	Total - Economic families	1,970	950	1,745	2,175	1,595	2,440
566	Low income	175	95	375	330	140	390
567	Incidence of low income in 2000 % (52)	8.8	9.8	21.4	15.3	9.0	15.9
568	Total - Unattached individuals 15 years and over	290	250	955	645	250	435
569	Low income	65	70	460	240	70	185
570	Incidence of low income in 2000 % (52)	23.4	26.9	48.1	37.3	27.9	42.1
571	Total - Population in private households	6,720	3,505	6,475	7,750	5,765	8,620
572	Low income	590	410	1,620	1,350	575	1,490
573	Incidence of low income in 2000 % (52)	8.8	11.7	25.0	17.4	10.0	17.3
	Private households by household income groups in 2000						
574	Total - All private households	2,185	1,105	2,495	2,640	1,750	2,750
575	Under $10,000	30	25	220	125	50	125
576	$ 10,000 - $19,999	95	45	345	225	60	165
577	$ 20,000 - $29,999	115	70	235	160	80	225
578	$ 30,000 - $39,999	125	80	265	270	110	270
579	$ 40,000 - $49,999	130	130	225	275	180	285
580	$ 50,000 - $59,999	210	105	180	275	180	290
581	$ 60,000 - $69,999	235	95	245	280	195	260
582	$ 70,000 - $79,999	120	110	210	215	200	320
583	$ 80,000 - $89,999	210	65	155	240	160	185
584	$ 90,000 - $99,999	165	115	145	150	115	165
585	$100,000 and over	760	265	265	425	420	470
586	Average household income $	89,194	73,058	53,071	62,235	76,624	66,711
587	Median household income $	80,875	70,282	47,973	59,536	71,773	60,287
588	Standard error of average household income $	2,563	2,425	1,570	1,498	2,105	1,953

Tableau 1. Certaines caractéristiques des secteurs de recensement, recensement de 2001 – Données intégrales et données-échantillon (20 %)

Vancouver 0400.01 A	Vancouver 0400.02 A	Vancouver 0401.01 A	Vancouver 0401.02 A	Vancouver 0402.01	Vancouver 0402.02	Caractéristiques	N°
						CARACTÉRISTIQUES DU REVENU DE 2000	
						Population de 15 ans et plus ayant un revenu d'emploi en 2000 selon le sexe et le travail – fin	
2,410	990	655	1,650	1,935	1,250	Femmes ayant un revenu d'emploi (48)	526
26,474	21,845	24,330	23,820	23,074	23,852	Revenu moyen d'emploi $	527
910	1,183	1,421	827	945	1,095	Erreur type de revenu moyen d'emploi $	528
1,095	360	320	850	825	535	Ayant travaillé toute l'année à plein temps (49)	529
37,773	31,233	34,217	32,605	34,252	33,309	Revenu moyen d'emploi $	530
1,146	1,942	1,428	1,054	1,443	1,545	Erreur type de revenu moyen d'emploi $	531
1,230	620	320	715	1,035	665	Ayant travaillé une partie de l'année ou à temps partiel (50)	532
17,868	16,172	15,419	15,369	15,351	17,624	Revenu moyen d'emploi $	533
1,131	1,307	1,787	938	943	1,318	Erreur type de revenu moyen d'emploi $	534
						Familles de recensement selon la structure et les tranches de revenu de la famille en 2000	
2,660	990	745	1,870	2,170	1,405	Total - Toutes les familles de recensement	535
80	35	35	135	110	25	Moins de 10 000 $	536
120	45	60	115	110	90	10 000 $ - 19 999 $	537
150	65	75	220	280	140	20 000 $ - 29 999 $	538
260	65	70	185	245	130	30 000 $ - 39 999 $	539
220	75	75	275	245	140	40 000 $ - 49 999 $	540
255	95	80	230	225	165	50 000 $ - 59 999 $	541
250	140	55	235	235	110	60 000 $ - 69 999 $	542
340	120	120	195	190	90	70 000 $ - 79 999 $	543
225	75	70	90	130	145	80 000 $ - 89 999 $	544
185	90	40	85	110	110	90 000 $ - 99 999 $	545
575	190	70	90	305	265	100 000 $ et plus	546
71,815	69,679	57,572	51,317	60,760	67,574	Revenu moyen des familles $	547
68,490	68,254	57,650	50,188	53,619	61,034	Revenu médian des familles $	548
1,690	2,427	2,557	1,387	1,843	2,284	Erreur type de revenu moyen des familles $	549
2,340	905	625	1,505	1,770	1,120	Total - Toutes les familles de recensement comptant un couple (51)	550
55	10	15	75	50	20	Moins de 10 000 $	551
65	35	10	40	50	40	10 000 $ - 19 999 $	552
95	45	60	180	205	80	20 000 $ - 29 999 $	553
215	60	60	115	155	65	30 000 $ - 39 999 $	554
200	70	65	205	200	105	40 000 $ - 49 999 $	555
205	95	75	205	195	155	50 000 $ - 59 999 $	556
225	130	55	225	220	90	60 000 $ - 69 999 $	557
320	120	110	195	165	80	70 000 $ - 79 999 $	558
210	70	70	85	125	135	80 000 $ - 89 999 $	559
185	90	40	85	105	115	90 000 $ - 99 999 $	560
565	185	70	90	305	245	100 000 $ et plus	561
76,262	73,743	63,488	56,356	67,093	74,227	Revenu moyen des familles $	562
72,726	70,388	64,476	56,172	61,531	72,714	Revenu médian des familles $	563
1,781	2,434	2,591	1,496	2,078	2,543	Erreur type de revenu moyen des familles $	564
						Fréquence des unités à faible revenu en 2000	
2,570	975	740	1,865	2,165	1,400	Total - Familles économiques	565
215	50	165	350	370	170	Faible revenu	566
8.3	5.2	22.1	18.8	17.0	12.2	Fréquence des unités à faible revenu en 2000 % (52)	567
560	375	435	1,570	1,045	425	Total - Personnes hors famille économique de 15 ans et plus	568
205	90	225	655	505	130	Faible revenu	569
37.2	23.7	52.0	41.8	49.0	30.6	Fréquence des unités à faible revenu en 2000 % (52)	570
9,085	3,415	2,625	6,645	7,795	4,930	Total - Population dans les ménages privés	571
895	225	675	1,570	1,600	675	Faible revenu	572
9.8	6.6	25.6	23.7	20.6	13.8	Fréquence des unités à faible revenu en 2000 % (52)	573
						Ménages privés selon les tranches de revenu du ménage en 2000	
2,950	1,235	1,115	3,220	3,000	1,720	Total - Tous les ménages privés	574
80	35	100	290	170	55	Moins de 10 000 $	575
200	120	210	490	380	150	10 000 $ - 19 999 $	576
160	85	110	445	395	175	20 000 $ - 29 999 $	577
300	130	120	415	380	155	30 000 $ - 39 999 $	578
260	110	80	400	285	170	40 000 $ - 49 999 $	579
280	95	105	330	310	195	50 000 $ - 59 999 $	580
250	130	50	260	235	130	60 000 $ - 69 999 $	581
335	135	105	235	200	100	70 000 $ - 79 999 $	582
230	85	90	105	165	155	80 000 $ - 89 999 $	583
200	100	60	105	145	130	90 000 $ - 99 999 $	584
660	215	90	140	335	285	100 000 $ et plus	585
71,206	65,668	48,573	43,729	53,752	64,200	Revenu moyen des ménages $	586
66,693	62,276	41,390	39,036	46,031	57,813	Revenu médian des ménages $	587
1,637	2,483	2,237	1,096	1,560	2,106	Erreur type de revenu moyen des ménages $	588

Table 1. Selected Characteristics for Census Tracts, 2001 Census – 100% Data and 20% Sample Data

No.	Characteristics	Vancouver 0403.01	Vancouver 0403.03	Vancouver 0403.04 A	Vancouver 0403.05 A	Vancouver 0404	Vancouver 0410.02
	POPULATION CHARACTERISTICS						
1	**Population, 1996 (1)**	**5,405**	**5,305**	**4,751**	**3,588**	**7,395**	**5,461**
2	**Population, 2001 (2)**	**5,500**	**5,617**	**4,730**	**4,247**	**8,275**	**6,001**
3	Population percentage change, 1996-2001	1.8	5.9	-0.4	18.4	11.9	9.9
4	Land area in square kilometres, 2001	2.32	3.81	4.97	1.82	188.12	22.25
5	**Total population – 100% Data (3)**	**5,500**	**5,610**	**4,730**	**4,245**	**8,275**	**6,000**
	by sex and age groups						
6	Male	2,790	2,775	2,395	2,105	4,320	2,875
7	0-4 years	155	235	160	135	230	180
8	5-9 years	275	280	195	170	340	215
9	10-14 years	270	260	235	200	370	230
10	15-19 years	245	220	225	190	355	210
11	20-24 years	165	130	130	130	280	150
12	25-29 years	135	125	95	90	200	155
13	30-34 years	170	245	155	120	290	225
14	35-39 years	270	320	215	200	405	260
15	40-44 years	260	260	245	220	450	290
16	45-49 years	195	210	215	180	395	205
17	50-54 years	205	170	195	165	325	185
18	55-59 years	135	85	95	90	210	155
19	60-64 years	95	70	70	60	185	100
20	65-69 years	75	70	55	65	130	95
21	70-74 years	55	35	50	40	85	100
22	75-79 years	45	30	45	35	45	60
23	80-84 years	35	15	20	20	20	40
24	85 years and over	15	15	10	10	10	20
25	Female	2,710	2,835	2,335	2,140	3,955	3,125
26	0-4 years	140	220	145	135	190	155
27	5-9 years	205	250	205	175	330	235
28	10-14 years	210	240	170	165	355	215
29	15-19 years	190	195	205	190	300	205
30	20-24 years	130	155	110	120	205	155
31	25-29 years	135	185	115	75	190	170
32	30-34 years	205	250	170	140	280	285
33	35-39 years	275	320	235	205	405	275
34	40-44 years	270	315	235	250	425	270
35	45-49 years	220	200	235	185	365	230
36	50-54 years	185	145	150	145	285	205
37	55-59 years	125	90	80	90	185	165
38	60-64 years	95	70	70	65	145	130
39	65-69 years	65	70	60	60	130	105
40	70-74 years	65	45	60	55	80	120
41	75-79 years	70	30	45	45	50	110
42	80-84 years	50	30	25	25	25	60
43	85 years and over	70	25	15	15	15	25
44	**Total population 15 years and over**	**4,250**	**4,120**	**3,620**	**3,270**	**6,450**	**4,765**
	by legal marital status						
45	Never married (single)	1,280	1,225	1,060	915	1,925	1,305
46	Legally married (and not separated)	2,185	2,225	2,015	1,955	3,710	2,570
47	Separated, but still legally married	170	165	130	80	215	200
48	Divorced	370	335	275	205	425	385
49	Widowed	245	170	135	115	185	300
	by common-law status						
50	Not in a common-law relationship	3,960	3,755	3,330	3,085	6,030	4,445
51	In a common-law relationship	295	365	290	180	420	320
52	**Total population – 20% Sample Data (4)**	**5,345**	**5,610**	**4,725**	**4,230**	**8,050**	**5,970**
	by mother tongue						
53	Single responses	5,335	5,570	4,680	4,220	8,005	5,955
54	English	4,805	5,015	4,075	3,480	7,000	4,665
55	French	70	125	35	50	105	120
56	Non-official languages (5)	460	440	575	690	905	1,160
57	Chinese, n.o.s.	25	30	40	25	20	25
58	Cantonese	-	-	-	15	60	45
59	Punjabi	30	25	105	245	85	305
60	Mandarin	10	35	70	10	115	10
61	Tagalog (Pilipino)	10	40	10	-	-	25
62	Other languages (6)	390	310	355	390	620	755
63	Multiple responses	10	35	45	10	40	15
64	English and French	10	-	-	-	20	10
65	English and non-official language	-	30	45	15	20	10
66	French and non-official language	-	-	-	-	-	-
67	English, French and non-official language	-	-	-	-	-	-

See reference material at the end of the publication. – Voir les documents de référence à la fin de la publication.

Tableau 1. Certaines caractéristiques des secteurs de recensement, recensement de 2001 – Données intégrales et données-échantillon (20 %)

Vancouver 0410.03 A	Vancouver 0410.04 ◆ A	Vancouver 0500	Vancouver 0501.01 ◇ A	Vancouver 0501.02	Vancouver 0501.03	Caractéristiques	N°
						CARACTÉRISTIQUES DE LA POPULATION	
7,121	**854**	**6,292**	**2,526**	**5,611**	**3,403**	**Population, 1996 (1)**	1
7,752	**917**	**6,290**	**2,980**	**5,425**	**3,228**	**Population, 2001 (2)**	2
8.9	7.4	-	18.0	-3.3	-5.1	Variation en pourcentage de la population, 1996-2001	3
3.97	59.16	72.51	19.57	18.93	23.21	Superficie des terres en kilomètres carrés, 2001	4
7,750	**920**	**6,285**	**2,980**	**5,425**	**3,230**	**Population totale – Données intégrales (3)**	5
						selon le sexe et les groupes d'âge	
3,780	480	3,135	1,395	2,755	1,695	Sexe masculin	6
270	20	150	70	110	90	0-4 ans	7
265	25	205	80	160	130	5-9 ans	8
330	35	200	85	215	150	10-14 ans	9
335	45	230	100	255	185	15-19 ans	10
210	40	135	80	170	115	20-24 ans	11
190	30	130	70	100	65	25-29 ans	12
270	30	175	85	95	110	30-34 ans	13
355	30	240	110	185	145	35-39 ans	14
385	35	255	95	255	160	40-44 ans	15
330	40	240	90	255	140	45-49 ans	16
255	30	230	80	265	120	50-54 ans	17
195	20	235	85	240	95	55-59 ans	18
120	25	170	70	160	60	60-64 ans	19
90	35	160	70	105	40	65-69 ans	20
90	20	135	70	90	40	70-74 ans	21
55	10	145	60	55	25	75-79 ans	22
25	5	75	45	30	15	80-84 ans	23
15	-	30	50	15	10	85 ans et plus	24
3,975	440	3,155	1,580	2,665	1,530	Sexe féminin	25
230	20	160	80	90	75	0-4 ans	26
330	25	175	70	185	115	5-9 ans	27
325	30	230	85	220	135	10-14 ans	28
325	35	210	85	240	140	15-19 ans	29
195	35	135	90	160	85	20-24 ans	30
210	15	145	60	95	75	25-29 ans	31
320	20	170	85	120	100	30-34 ans	32
400	25	240	85	175	135	35-39 ans	33
405	40	255	95	265	170	40-44 ans	34
320	35	240	95	255	135	45-49 ans	35
270	30	255	105	275	120	50-54 ans	36
180	20	215	95	205	55	55-59 ans	37
125	35	150	65	125	55	60-64 ans	38
105	25	155	70	90	40	65-69 ans	39
85	20	140	90	55	35	70-74 ans	40
70	10	145	100	60	25	75-79 ans	41
65	5	100	90	40	20	80-84 ans	42
15	5	35	130	20	10	85 ans et plus	43
6,010	**760**	**5,170**	**2,520**	**4,450**	**2,520**	**Population totale de 15 ans et plus**	44
						selon l'état matrimonial légal	
1,670	245	1,315	595	1,265	770	Célibataire (jamais marié(e))	45
3,405	430	2,945	1,365	2,675	1,445	Légalement marié(e) (et non séparé(e))	46
280	15	170	55	115	70	Séparé(e), mais toujours légalement marié(e)	47
415	40	425	175	235	160	Divorcé(e)	48
240	35	310	320	160	85	Veuf ou veuve	49
						selon l'union libre	
5,655	710	4,770	2,385	4,230	2,365	Ne vivant pas en union libre	50
355	60	400	130	220	160	Vivant en union libre	51
7,745	**940**	**6,285**	**2,720**	**5,385**	**3,190**	**Population totale – Données-échantillon (20 %) (4)**	52
						selon la langue maternelle	
7,685	935	6,245	2,675	5,375	3,190	Réponses uniques	53
6,940	630	5,445	2,225	4,695	2,865	Anglais	54
95	55	55	60	60	15	Français	55
645	250	740	385	620	305	Langues non officielles (5)	56
-	10	-	-	15	25	Chinois, n.d.a.	57
10	-	-	-	-	10	Cantonais	58
70	175	15	20	10	40	Pendjabi	59
75	-	15	60	25	-	Mandarin	60
20	-	10	-	-	-	Tagalog (pilipino)	61
465	65	700	300	575	235	Autres langues (6)	62
60	10	45	45	10	-	Réponses multiples	63
10	10	-	20	10	-	Anglais et français	64
55	-	45	30	10	-	Anglais et langue non officielle	65
-	-	-	-	-	-	Français et langue non officielle	66
-	-	-	-	-	-	Anglais, français et langue non officielle	67

See reference material at the end of the publication. – Voir les documents de référence à la fin de la publication.

Table 1. Selected Characteristics for Census Tracts, 2001 Census – 100% Data and 20% Sample Data

No.	Characteristics	Vancouver 0403.01	Vancouver 0403.03	Vancouver 0403.04 A	Vancouver 0403.05 A	Vancouver 0404	Vancouver 0410.02
	POPULATION CHARACTERISTICS						
	by home language						
68	Single responses	4,975	5,335	4,265	3,820	7,630	5,310
69	English	4,885	5,305	4,205	3,680	7,290	5,035
70	French	15	-	-	-	10	10
71	Non-official languages (5)	75	35	65	140	330	265
72	Cantonese	-	-	-	10	35	-
73	Chinese, n.o.s.	-	10	15	10	-	25
74	Punjabi	25	10	20	50	95	60
75	Mandarin	-	15	-	-	95	-
76	Korean	-	-	-	25	50	15
77	Other languages (6)	50	10	30	35	50	165
78	Multiple responses	370	270	460	415	420	665
79	English and French	135	65	70	15	75	60
80	English and non-official language	230	195	375	400	345	590
81	French and non-official language	-	-	-	-	-	-
82	English, French and non-official language	-	15	15	-	-	15
	by knowledge of official languages						
83	English only	4,900	5,240	4,330	3,920	7,470	5,430
84	French only	-	-	-	-	-	-
85	English and French	410	360	395	280	515	470
86	Neither English nor French	40	10	-	35	65	70
	by knowledge of non-official languages (5) (7)						
87	Cantonese	-	-	-	35	60	60
88	Chinese, n.o.s.	25	10	35	40	15	30
89	Punjabi	30	35	105	285	115	395
90	Mandarin	15	90	75	20	125	25
91	Hindi	-	35	35	30	20	130
92	German	90	105	95	65	165	160
93	Spanish	125	40	80	35	65	90
	by first official language spoken						
94	English	5,195	5,495	4,695	4,150	7,875	5,800
95	French	75	105	20	45	90	100
96	English and French	35	-	10	10	20	10
97	Neither English nor French	40	10	-	30	60	70
98	Official language minority - (number) (8)	90	110	25	50	100	100
99	Official language minority - (percentage) (8)	1.7	2.0	0.5	1.2	1.2	1.7
	by ethnic origin (9)						
100	English	1,985	1,985	2,010	1,630	3,105	1,685
101	Canadian	1,560	1,650	1,465	1,220	2,305	1,275
102	Chinese	60	105	145	120	215	170
103	Scottish	1,385	1,500	1,030	1,130	1,925	1,170
104	Irish	1,105	975	875	900	1,460	1,045
105	German	785	815	545	610	1,170	790
106	East Indian	10	150	110	330	105	365
107	French	480	640	540	315	825	600
108	Ukrainian	165	435	255	220	605	290
109	Italian	215	190	130	195	375	190
110	Dutch (Netherlands)	450	295	290	405	460	430
111	Filipino	25	60	15	20	15	85
112	Polish	185	190	175	80	215	230
113	Norwegian	155	200	235	150	345	280
114	North American Indian	220	330	210	85	190	170
	by Aboriginal identity						
115	Total Aboriginal identity population (10)	205	275	110	80	205	125
116	Total non-Aboriginal population	5,140	5,335	4,615	4,155	7,840	5,850
	by Aboriginal origin						
117	Total Aboriginal origins population (11)	295	365	270	130	305	220
118	Total non-Aboriginal population	5,050	5,245	4,455	4,105	7,740	5,755
	by Registered Indian status						
119	Registered Indian (12)	140	200	10	30	65	65
120	Not a Registered Indian	5,210	5,410	4,710	4,205	7,980	5,905

Tableau 1. Certaines caractéristiques des secteurs de recensement, recensement de 2001 – Données intégrales et données-échantillon (20 %)

Vancouver 0410.03 A	Vancouver 0410.04 ◆ A	Vancouver 0500	Vancouver 0501.01 ◇ A	Vancouver 0501.02	Vancouver 0501.03	Caractéristiques	N°
						CARACTÉRISTIQUES DE LA POPULATION	
						selon la langue parlée à la maison	
7,385	740	5,910	2,520	5,135	3,070	Réponses uniques	68
7,275	660	5,880	2,500	5,085	3,030	Anglais	69
-	10	15	-	-	10	Français	70
110	75	25	20	55	35	Langues non officielles (5)	71
-	-	-	-	-	-	Cantonais	72
-	10	-	-	-	10	Chinois, n.d.a.	73
10	60	-	-	-	10	Pendjabi	74
55	-	-	20	-	-	Mandarin	75
-	-	-	-	25	-	Coréen	76
45	10	20	-	30	10	Autres langues (6)	77
360	195	375	205	245	125	Réponses multiples	78
80	30	-	40	20	-	Anglais et français	79
270	170	370	165	210	120	Anglais et langue non officielle	80
-	-	-	-	10	-	Français et langue non officielle	81
10	-	-	-	10	-	Anglais, français et langue non officielle	82
						selon la connaissance des langues officielles	
7,180	810	6,035	2,560	5,170	3,030	Anglais seulement	83
10	-	-	-	-	-	Français seulement	84
520	95	250	150	200	155	Anglais et français	85
40	35	10	10	10	10	Ni l'anglais ni le français	86
						selon la connaissance des langues non officielles (5) (7)	
10	-	10	-	-	10	Cantonais	87
10	15	-	-	-	50	Chinois, n.d.a.	88
85	190	10	20	10	50	Pendjabi	89
75	-	20	60	45	15	Mandarin	90
70	-	20	10	-	-	Hindi	91
110	10	375	155	250	115	Allemand	92
75	25	45	35	40	35	Espagnol	93
						selon la première langue officielle parlée	
7,590	855	6,230	2,655	5,310	3,175	Anglais	94
85	45	50	45	40	15	Français	95
30	-	-	-	15	-	Anglais et français	96
40	35	10	10	10	-	Ni l'anglais ni le français	97
100	45	50	50	45	20	Minorité de langue officielle - (nombre) (8)	98
1.3	4.8	0.8	1.8	0.8	0.6	Minorité de langue officielle - (pourcentage) (8)	99
						selon l'origine ethnique (9)	
3,160	270	2,290	1,015	2,095	1,235	Anglais	100
2,685	275	1,720	750	1,675	855	Canadien	101
150	25	80	75	45	65	Chinois	102
2,120	170	1,235	415	1,035	680	Écossais	103
1,335	120	1,125	460	835	685	Irlandais	104
940	60	1,150	450	1,095	510	Allemand	105
115	195	30	20	20	50	Indien de l'Inde	106
880	105	425	280	480	255	Français	107
435	75	245	95	395	195	Ukrainien	108
390	20	180	65	210	195	Italien	109
335	85	555	350	465	260	Hollandais (Néerlandais)	110
35	-	40	10	-	-	Philippin	111
135	25	155	65	260	110	Polonais	112
300	15	205	70	265	90	Norvégien	113
160	-	245	10	145	35	Indien de l'Amérique du Nord	114
						selon l'identité autochtone	
180	-	205	15	145	80	Total de la population ayant une identité autochtone (10)	115
7,560	940	6,085	2,700	5,235	3,115	Total de la population non autochtone	116
						selon l'origine autochtone	
225	-	330	15	240	90	Total de la population ayant une origine autochtone (11)	117
7,520	930	5,960	2,705	5,145	3,105	Total de la population non autochtone	118
						selon le statut d'Indien inscrit	
85	-	85	-	-	-	Oui, Indien inscrit (12)	119
7,655	940	6,200	2,715	5,375	3,195	Non, pas un Indien inscrit	120

Table 1. Selected Characteristics for Census Tracts, 2001 Census – 100% Data and 20% Sample Data

No.	Characteristics	Vancouver 0403.01	Vancouver 0403.03	Vancouver 0403.04 A	Vancouver 0403.05 A	Vancouver 0404	Vancouver 0410.02
	POPULATION CHARACTERISTICS						
	by visible minority groups						
121	Total visible minority population	335	450	505	560	675	905
122	Chinese	65	120	150	105	230	165
123	South Asian	65	155	105	325	160	450
124	Black	40	65	120	10	75	60
125	Filipino	10	75	15	20	10	60
126	Latin American	45	-	15	-	10	35
127	Southeast Asian	-	-	75	-	10	45
128	Arab	35	-	-	-	-	-
129	West Asian	45	-	15	15	15	10
130	Korean	10	-	-	45	100	15
131	Japanese	15	-	-	10	55	35
132	Visible minority, n.i.e. (13)	-	-	-	30	10	15
133	Multiple visible minorities (14)	10	20	-	-	-	15
	by citizenship						
134	Canadian citizenship (15)	5,105	5,420	4,540	4,085	7,505	5,505
135	Citizenship other than Canadian	240	190	185	145	540	465
	by place of birth of respondent						
136	Non-immigrant population	4,570	4,820	3,975	3,385	6,655	4,390
137	Born in province of residence	3,295	3,615	2,960	2,575	5,010	3,075
138	Immigrant population (16)	755	790	740	820	1,350	1,555
139	United States	60	45	30	65	75	35
140	Central and South America	45	10	20	-	15	15
141	Caribbean and Bermuda	10	55	30	35	10	50
142	United Kingdom	230	285	220	185	395	345
143	Other Europe (17)	210	185	150	235	355	545
144	Africa	10	20	20	25	35	75
145	Asia and the Middle East	170	155	235	250	450	450
146	Oceania and other (18)	20	35	30	10	20	35
147	Non-permanent residents (19)	20	-	10	30	40	20
148	**Total immigrant population**	**755**	**790**	**740**	**820**	**1,350**	**1,560**
	by period of immigration						
149	Before 1961	145	85	110	150	280	320
150	1961-1970	135	105	205	185	265	165
151	1971-1980	150	240	195	180	235	375
152	1981-1990	140	185	90	150	205	310
153	1991-2001 (20)	185	170	130	150	370	400
154	1991-1995	115	140	75	85	120	165
155	1996-2001 (20)	75	30	55	65	250	235
	by age at immigration						
156	0-4 years	135	105	110	115	135	170
157	5-19 years	275	190	190	280	410	490
158	20 years and over	345	490	435	430	810	900
159	**Total population**	**5,350**	**5,610**	**4,725**	**4,235**	**8,050**	**5,975**
	by religion						
160	Catholic (21)	1,120	1,090	950	960	1,480	1,205
161	Protestant	1,885	1,630	1,870	1,590	2,580	2,175
162	Christian Orthodox	15	80	30	50	35	140
163	Christian, n.i.e. (22)	250	270	70	100	500	235
164	Muslim	120	20	-	15	15	10
165	Jewish	-	10	-	10	-	-
166	Buddhist	-	-	-	20	50	25
167	Hindu	-	15	10	-	-	50
168	Sikh	-	30	105	265	110	365
169	Eastern religions (23)	50	-	25	10	30	10
170	Other religions (24)	25	65	20	-	20	-
171	No religious affiliation (25)	1,895	2,395	1,655	1,215	3,220	1,755
172	**Total population 15 years and over**	**4,095**	**4,115**	**3,605**	**3,245**	**6,235**	**4,760**
	by generation status						
173	1st generation (26)	710	760	750	795	1,340	1,490
174	2nd generation (27)	955	990	985	840	1,420	1,195
175	3rd generation and over (28)	2,425	2,365	1,870	1,605	3,475	2,075
176	**Total population 1 year and over (29)**	**5,300**	**5,550**	**4,665**	**4,205**	**7,975**	**5,935**
	by place of residence 1 year ago (mobility)						
177	Non-movers	4,660	4,755	4,180	3,710	7,335	4,955
178	Movers	635	795	485	505	635	975
179	Non-migrants	415	380	290	190	275	320
180	Migrants	215	415	195	310	365	660
181	Internal migrants	190	410	180	245	320	600
182	Intraprovincial migrants	180	325	180	245	245	595
183	Interprovincial migrants	-	90	-	-	65	-
184	External migrants	30	-	15	65	50	55

Tableau 1. Certaines caractéristiques des secteurs de recensement, recensement de 2001 – Données intégrales et données-échantillon (20 %)

Vancouver 0410.03 A	Vancouver 0410.04 ◆ A	Vancouver 0500	Vancouver 0501.01 ◇ A	Vancouver 0501.02	Vancouver 0501.03	Caractéristiques	N°
						CARACTÉRISTIQUES DE LA POPULATION	
						selon les groupes de minorités visibles	
415	260	295	135	235	150	Total de la population des minorités visibles	121
115	25	35	75	45	65	Chinois	122
130	215	35	20	20	50	Sud-Asiatique	123
55	-	10	-	75	10	Noir	124
25	-	35	-	10	-	Philippin	125
15	20	10	10	10	20	Latino-Américain	126
25	-	25	-	25	-	Asiatique du Sud-Est	127
-	-	-	-	-	-	Arabe	128
-	-	-	-	-	-	Asiatique occidental	129
10	-	15	-	25	-	Coréen	130
30	-	105	25	25	15	Japonais	131
20	-	-	-	-	-	Minorité visible, n.i.a. (13)	132
10	-	25	-	-	-	Minorités visibles multiples (14)	133
						selon la citoyenneté	
7,445	865	6,010	2,610	5,170	3,055	Citoyenneté canadienne (15)	134
305	70	280	110	215	135	Citoyenneté autre que canadienne	135
						selon le lieu de naissance du répondant	
6,625	695	5,220	2,150	4,555	2,800	Population non immigrante	136
4,775	525	3,800	1,290	3,555	2,105	Née dans la province de résidence	137
1,080	240	1,070	540	815	365	Population immigrante (16)	138
65	-	115	40	60	40	États-Unis	139
20	15	20	15	-	25	Amérique centrale et du Sud	140
30	-	-	-	20	-	Caraïbes et Bermudes	141
430	45	290	165	210	70	Royaume-Uni	142
275	55	495	230	380	145	Autre Europe (17)	143
30	-	25	10	10	10	Afrique	144
195	120	110	85	105	70	Asie et Moyen-Orient	145
40	-	10	-	20	-	Océanie et autre (18)	146
35	-	-	25	-	25	Résidents non permanents (19)	147
1,085	**240**	**1,070**	**540**	**820**	**360**	**Population immigrante totale**	148
						selon la période d'immigration	
260	35	320	175	315	105	Avant 1961	149
250	50	280	110	145	65	1961-1970	150
160	10	245	100	120	95	1971-1980	151
150	65	95	40	75	50	1981-1990	152
270	85	130	110	160	50	1991-2001 (20)	153
135	45	30	25	110	10	1991-1995	154
130	40	95	90	50	45	1996-2001 (20)	155
						selon l'âge à l'immigration	
120	-	165	55	100	45	0-4 ans	156
320	55	340	160	320	95	5-19 ans	157
645	185	565	325	395	220	20 ans et plus	158
7,745	**940**	**6,290**	**2,720**	**5,380**	**3,190**	**Population totale**	159
						selon la religion	
1,370	110	785	375	685	485	Catholique (21)	160
2,745	300	2,820	1,245	2,185	1,090	Protestante	161
15	-	55	70	15	-	Orthodoxe chrétienne	162
350	45	400	310	265	280	Chrétiennes, n.i.a. (22)	163
10	-	10	-	-	-	Musulmane	164
10	-	-	-	-	15	Juive	165
45	-	40	70	50	10	Bouddhiste	166
20	-	-	-	-	10	Hindoue	167
110	195	15	20	20	50	Sikh	168
-	-	15	-	-	-	Religions orientales (23)	169
10	-	25	-	25	-	Autres religions (24)	170
3,065	285	2,125	625	2,130	1,255	Aucune appartenance religieuse (25)	171
5,995	**755**	**5,120**	**2,265**	**4,385**	**2,455**	**Population totale de 15 ans et plus**	172
						selon le statut des générations	
1,085	240	1,015	575	795	390	1re génération (26)	173
1,565	145	1,710	635	1,305	645	2e génération (27)	174
3,345	375	2,395	1,060	2,290	1,420	3e génération et plus (28)	175
7,680	**915**	**6,230**	**2,670**	**5,360**	**3,160**	**Population totale de 1 an et plus (29)**	176
						selon le lieu de résidence 1 an auparavant (mobilité)	
6,865	800	5,495	2,310	5,010	2,770	Personnes n'ayant pas déménagé	177
815	110	735	360	345	385	Personnes ayant déménagé	178
370	45	340	165	170	110	Non-migrants	179
440	65	395	190	175	270	Migrants	180
370	70	400	135	165	245	Migrants internes	181
355	65	365	115	160	190	Migrants infraprovinciaux	182
15	10	30	20	-	55	Migrants interprovinciaux	183
70	-	-	60	-	30	Migrants externes	184

Table 1. Selected Characteristics for Census Tracts, 2001 Census – 100% Data and 20% Sample Data

No.	Characteristics	Vancouver 0403.01	Vancouver 0403.03	Vancouver 0403.04 A	Vancouver 0403.05 A	Vancouver 0404	Vancouver 0410.02
	POPULATION CHARACTERISTICS						
185	**Total population 5 years and over (30)**	**5,050**	**5,150**	**4,420**	**3,965**	**7,635**	**5,635**
	by place of residence 5 years ago (mobility)						
186	Non-movers	2,780	2,850	2,635	2,090	4,445	3,055
187	Movers	2,270	2,300	1,785	1,875	3,190	2,575
188	Non-migrants	1,355	780	765	860	1,715	750
189	Migrants	920	1,520	1,020	1,015	1,475	1,830
190	Internal migrants	835	1,505	900	905	1,225	1,595
191	Intraprovincial migrants	810	1,255	850	820	1,040	1,450
192	Interprovincial migrants	25	245	55	85	185	145
193	External migrants	85	20	115	110	250	235
194	**Total population 15 to 24 years**	**725**	**710**	**665**	**635**	**1,070**	**760**
	by school attendance						
195	Not attending school	360	390	270	240	350	265
196	Attending school full time	305	295	355	355	625	410
197	Attending school part time	60	25	40	40	100	85
198	**Total population 15 years and over**	**4,090**	**4,120**	**3,610**	**3,240**	**6,235**	**4,760**
	by highest level of schooling						
199	Less than grade 9 (31)	160	120	75	115	190	180
200	Grades 9-13 without high school graduation certificate	1,080	1,090	805	795	1,420	1,130
201	Grades 9-13 with high school graduation certificate	590	725	595	435	755	660
202	Some postsecondary without degree, certificate or diploma (32)	515	515	475	445	765	615
203	Trades certificate or diploma (33)	610	570	475	475	855	755
204	College certificate or diploma (34)	795	790	710	590	1,250	890
205	University certificate below bachelor's degree	90	65	95	80	205	70
206	University with bachelor's degree or higher	250	250	380	310	790	445
	by combinations of unpaid work						
207	Males 15 years and over	2,055	1,995	1,810	1,580	3,150	2,210
208	Reported unpaid work (35)	1,850	1,805	1,600	1,430	2,835	1,950
209	Housework and child care and care or assistance to seniors	100	195	80	125	250	110
210	Housework and child care only	625	680	645	555	1,025	645
211	Housework and care or assistance to seniors only	155	100	135	90	185	115
212	Child care and care or assistance to seniors only	-	-	-	10	-	-
213	Housework only	920	785	720	610	1,340	1,050
214	Child care only	35	35	20	25	25	25
215	Care or assistance to seniors only	15	10	-	15	-	-
216	Females 15 years and over	2,035	2,125	1,800	1,660	3,090	2,545
217	Reported unpaid work (35)	1,925	2,060	1,700	1,580	2,940	2,355
218	Housework and child care and care or assistance to seniors	270	330	220	235	460	225
219	Housework and child care only	680	860	670	645	1,085	755
220	Housework and care or assistance to seniors only	195	165	155	130	230	235
221	Child care and care or assistance to seniors only	-	-	-	-	10	-
222	Housework only	760	695	650	565	1,135	1,085
223	Child care only	20	10	-	-	15	30
224	Care or assistance to seniors only	-	-	-	10	-	15
	by labour force activity						
225	Males 15 years and over	2,060	1,995	1,805	1,585	3,145	2,215
226	In the labour force	1,590	1,575	1,370	1,220	2,520	1,645
227	Employed	1,475	1,445	1,275	1,160	2,405	1,525
228	Unemployed	120	135	95	60	115	120
229	Not in the labour force	470	420	440	365	625	570
230	Participation rate	77.2	78.9	75.9	77.0	80.1	74.3
231	Employment rate	71.6	72.4	70.6	73.2	76.5	68.8
232	Unemployment rate	7.5	8.6	6.9	4.9	4.6	7.3
233	Females 15 years and over	2,030	2,125	1,805	1,660	3,090	2,545
234	In the labour force	1,300	1,515	1,240	1,120	1,965	1,655
235	Employed	1,210	1,420	1,165	1,040	1,895	1,510
236	Unemployed	95	95	75	80	75	145
237	Not in the labour force	730	610	565	535	1,125	895
238	Participation rate	64.0	71.3	68.7	67.5	63.6	65.0
239	Employment rate	59.6	66.8	64.5	62.7	61.3	59.3
240	Unemployment rate	7.3	6.3	6.0	7.1	3.8	8.8

Tableau 1. Certaines caractéristiques des secteurs de recensement, recensement de 2001 – Données intégrales et données-échantillon (20 %)

Vancouver 0410.03 A	Vancouver 0410.04 ◆ A	Vancouver 0500	Vancouver 0501.01 ◇ A	Vancouver 0501.02	Vancouver 0501.03	Caractéristiques	N°
						CARACTÉRISTIQUES DE LA POPULATION	
7,250	**880**	**5,960**	**2,580**	**5,180**	**3,045**	**Population totale de 5 ans et plus (30)**	185
						selon le lieu de résidence 5 ans auparavant (mobilité)	
3,910	575	3,940	1,260	3,905	1,935	Personnes n'ayant pas déménagé	186
3,340	305	2,020	1,315	1,275	1,110	Personnes ayant déménagé	187
1,350	95	880	535	555	565	Non-migrants	188
1,990	215	1,140	785	720	545	Migrants	189
1,865	165	1,070	695	665	480	Migrants internes	190
1,740	155	985	585	650	405	Migrants infraprovinciaux	191
125	10	85	110	15	75	Migrants interprovinciaux	192
125	50	65	95	55	65	Migrants externes	193
1,055	**125**	**680**	**385**	**810**	**520**	**Population totale de 15 à 24 ans**	194
						selon la fréquentation scolaire	
440	55	295	165	295	185	Ne fréquentant pas l'école	195
555	70	335	190	425	290	Fréquentant l'école à plein temps	196
65	-	45	35	90	45	Fréquentant l'école à temps partiel	197
5,995	**755**	**5,125**	**2,270**	**4,385**	**2,455**	**Population totale de 15 ans et plus**	198
						selon le plus haut niveau de scolarité atteint	
115	55	230	160	135	85	Niveau inférieur à la 9e année (31)	199
1,625	220	1,445	540	1,100	565	De la 9e à la 13e année sans certificat d'études secondaires	200
870	85	690	370	575	390	De la 9e à la 13e année avec certificat d'études secondaires	201
840	100	585	260	545	395	Études postsecondaires partielles sans grade, certificat ou diplôme (32)	202
870	90	750	320	630	395	Certificat ou diplôme d'une école de métiers (33)	203
1,045	125	770	325	895	345	Certificat ou diplôme collégial (34)	204
135	15	140	45	130	70	Certificat universitaire inférieur au baccalauréat	205
490	70	515	250	385	220	Études universitaires avec baccalauréat ou diplôme supérieur	206
						selon les combinaisons de travail non rémunéré	
2,915	415	2,545	1,100	2,225	1,290	Hommes de 15 ans et plus	207
2,565	340	2,350	950	1,985	1,220	Travail non rémunéré déclaré (35)	208
220	35	170	60	150	60	Travaux ménagers et soins aux enfants et soins ou aide aux personnes âgées	209
975	75	560	305	560	470	Travaux ménagers et soins aux enfants seulement	210
195	15	165	105	165	75	Travaux ménagers et soins ou aide aux personnes âgées seulement	211
-	-	-	10	-	-	Soins aux enfants et soins ou aide aux personnes âgées seulement	212
1,130	210	1,435	465	1,100	595	Travaux ménagers seulement	213
40	-	-	10	10	15	Soins aux enfants seulement	214
-	10	15	10	-	-	Soins ou aide aux personnes âgées seulement	215
3,080	340	2,570	1,170	2,170	1,165	Femmes de 15 ans et plus	216
2,910	335	2,440	1,090	2,065	1,105	Travail non rémunéré déclaré (35)	217
400	40	290	115	235	130	Travaux ménagers et soins aux enfants et soins ou aide aux personnes âgées	218
1,090	105	715	335	630	470	Travaux ménagers et soins aux enfants seulement	219
320	30	245	125	230	120	Travaux ménagers et soins ou aide aux personnes âgées seulement	220
-	-	-	-	10	-	Soins aux enfants et soins ou aide aux personnes âgées seulement	221
1,060	145	1,160	510	955	390	Travaux ménagers seulement	222
25	-	20	-	-	-	Soins aux enfants seulement	223
10	15	-	-	10	10	Soins ou aide aux personnes âgées seulement	224
						selon l'activité	
2,915	415	2,545	1,100	2,220	1,290	Hommes de 15 ans et plus	225
2,320	335	1,845	730	1,665	1,100	Population active	226
2,170	315	1,780	695	1,575	1,050	Personnes occupées	227
145	15	60	30	90	50	Chômeurs	228
595	80	705	370	555	195	Inactifs	229
79.6	80.7	72.5	66.4	75.0	85.3	Taux d'activité	230
74.4	75.9	69.9	63.2	70.9	81.4	Taux d'emploi	231
6.2	4.5	3.3	4.1	5.4	4.5	Taux de chômage	232
3,080	340	2,575	1,165	2,165	1,160	Femmes de 15 ans et plus	233
2,090	195	1,725	610	1,550	885	Population active	234
1,990	185	1,605	570	1,495	820	Personnes occupées	235
95	15	115	45	55	65	Chômeuses	236
995	145	855	555	620	275	Inactives	237
67.9	57.4	67.0	52.4	71.6	76.3	Taux d'activité	238
64.6	54.4	62.3	48.9	69.1	70.7	Taux d'emploi	239
4.5	7.7	6.7	7.4	3.5	7.3	Taux de chômage	240

Table 1. Selected Characteristics for Census Tracts, 2001 Census – 100% Data and 20% Sample Data

No.	Characteristics	Vancouver 0403.01	Vancouver 0403.03	Vancouver 0403.04 A	Vancouver 0403.05 A	Vancouver 0404	Vancouver 0410.02
	POPULATION CHARACTERISTICS						
	by labour force activity – concluded						
241	Both sexes - Participation rate	70.8	75.1	72.3	72.3	71.9	69.2
242	15-24 years	61.6	66.9	60.6	68.5	60.0	66.2
243	25 years and over	72.5	76.7	75.0	73.2	74.3	69.9
244	Both sexes - Employment rate	65.4	69.5	67.6	68.0	69.0	63.8
245	15-24 years	50.3	58.5	49.2	59.8	51.2	50.7
246	25 years and over	68.8	71.8	71.8	69.7	72.6	66.2
247	Both sexes - Unemployment rate	7.3	7.3	6.5	5.8	4.1	7.9
248	15-24 years	17.8	11.6	18.8	12.6	14.7	23.2
249	25 years and over	5.1	6.5	4.1	4.5	2.3	5.2
250	**Total labour force 15 years and over**	**2,895**	**3,090**	**2,610**	**2,345**	**4,485**	**3,290**
	by industry based on the 1997 NAICS						
251	Industry - Not applicable (36)	35	75	40	20	55	55
252	All industries (37)	2,860	3,015	2,565	2,320	4,425	3,240
253	11 Agriculture, forestry, fishing and hunting	40	30	30	25	135	200
254	21 Mining and oil and gas extraction	10	-	20	10	-	20
255	22 Utilities	10	15	10	35	10	25
256	23 Construction	260	260	170	175	395	170
257	31-33 Manufacturing	355	360	230	335	550	390
258	41 Wholesale trade	135	195	160	80	220	150
259	44-45 Retail trade	340	310	315	290	385	400
260	48-49 Transportation and warehousing	270	210	135	120	245	215
261	51 Information and cultural industries	65	100	120	70	95	90
262	52 Finance and insurance	105	145	95	100	165	100
263	53 Real estate and rental and leasing	45	30	70	45	55	50
264	54 Professional, scientific and technical services	70	165	135	110	300	190
265	55 Management of companies and enterprises	-	-	-	-	-	-
266	56 Administrative and support, waste management and remediation services	130	145	90	90	135	135
267	61 Educational services	80	130	240	170	305	165
268	62 Health care and social assistance	380	335	315	225	535	350
269	71 Arts, entertainment and recreation	65	45	40	30	90	70
270	72 Accommodation and food services	220	180	160	180	315	260
271	81 Other services (except public administration)	150	155	80	95	270	155
272	91 Public administration	125	195	135	125	220	105
	by class of worker						
273	Class of worker - Not applicable (36)	35	75	45	20	55	55
274	All classes of worker (37)	2,855	3,015	2,565	2,320	4,425	3,235
275	Paid workers	2,570	2,770	2,375	2,165	3,990	2,940
276	Employees	2,495	2,695	2,300	2,095	3,695	2,810
277	Self-employed (incorporated)	75	75	75	70	295	130
278	Self-employed (unincorporated)	275	240	175	150	425	290
279	Unpaid family workers	10	10	10	10	15	10
	by occupation based on the 2001 NOC-S						
280	Male labour force 15 years and over	1,590	1,575	1,370	1,220	2,515	1,640
281	Occupation - Not applicable (36)	25	30	10	10	25	15
282	All occupations (37)	1,565	1,545	1,360	1,220	2,490	1,630
283	A Management occupations	245	155	175	215	325	220
284	B Business, finance and administration occupations	120	115	155	85	140	115
285	C Natural and applied sciences and related occupations	120	95	105	70	195	125
286	D Health occupations	50	35	35	30	35	40
287	E Occupations in social science, education, government service and religion	10	55	45	65	150	30
288	F Occupations in art, culture, recreation and sport	30	20	50	20	60	60
289	G Sales and service occupations	235	315	290	275	515	270
290	H Trades, transport and equipment operators and related occupations	605	575	365	315	850	525
291	I Occupations unique to primary industry	35	55	25	25	75	110
292	J Occupations unique to processing, manufacturing and utilities	120	125	115	115	145	130
293	Female labour force 15 years and over	1,305	1,515	1,240	1,120	1,965	1,650
294	Occupation - Not applicable (36)	15	40	30	15	25	40
295	All occupations (37)	1,290	1,470	1,205	1,105	1,935	1,610
296	A Management occupations	85	85	80	120	165	145
297	B Business, finance and administration occupations	345	455	355	355	560	445
298	C Natural and applied sciences and related occupations	30	40	30	15	40	15
299	D Health occupations	155	110	135	85	245	120

Tableau 1. Certaines caractéristiques des secteurs de recensement, recensement de 2001 – Données intégrales et données-échantillon (20 %)

Vancouver 0410.03 A	Vancouver 0410.04 ◆ A	Vancouver 0500	Vancouver 0501.01 ◇ A	Vancouver 0501.02	Vancouver 0501.03	Caractéristiques	N°
						CARACTÉRISTIQUES DE LA POPULATION	
						selon l'activité – fin	
73.6	70.9	69.6	59.4	73.2	80.7	Les deux sexes - Taux d'activité	241
68.7	40.0	75.0	71.4	68.3	81.7	15-24 ans	242
74.5	76.2	68.7	56.8	74.4	80.4	25 ans et plus	243
69.4	66.2	66.0	55.7	69.9	76.0	Les deux sexes - Taux d'emploi	244
61.1	40.0	66.2	61.0	57.4	75.0	15-24 ans	245
71.3	71.2	66.2	54.4	72.6	76.2	25 ans et plus	246
5.4	5.7	4.9	5.9	4.7	5.8	Les deux sexes - Taux de chômage	247
11.0	-	11.9	13.0	16.2	8.2	15-24 ans	248
4.3	7.3	3.9	4.2	2.3	5.4	25 ans et plus	249
4,405	**530**	**3,565**	**1,340**	**3,215**	**1,985**	**Population active totale de 15 ans et plus**	250
						selon l'industrie basée sur le SCIAN de 1997	
45	10	45	10	20	15	Industrie - Sans objet (36)	251
4,360	525	3,520	1,330	3,200	1,965	Toutes les industries (37)	252
65	125	605	150	140	195	11 Agriculture, foresterie, pêche et chasse	253
-	-	15	10	-	-	21 Extraction minière et extraction de pétrole et de gaz	254
25	-	30	-	20	30	22 Services publics	255
345	60	260	140	335	145	23 Construction	256
485	25	355	120	310	165	31-33 Fabrication	257
310	20	180	90	225	130	41 Commerce de gros	258
370	45	320	120	325	215	44-45 Commerce de détail	259
255	30	255	100	210	120	48-49 Transport et entreposage	260
155	-	75	25	95	35	51 Industrie de l'information et industrie culturelle	261
145	10	90	35	135	45	52 Finance et assurances	262
55	35	50	55	50	20	53 Services immobiliers et services de location et de location à bail	263
175	40	195	35	160	155	54 Services professionnels, scientifiques et techniques	264
-	-	-	-	10	-	55 Gestion de sociétés et d'entreprises	265
125	30	135	60	70	95	56 Services administratifs, services de soutien, services de gestion des déchets et services d'assainissement	266
295	15	170	65	255	145	61 Services d'enseignement	267
570	15	220	150	290	130	62 Soins de santé et assistance sociale	268
110	15	115	50	50	15	71 Arts, spectacles et loisirs	269
360	35	165	-	200	115	72 Hébergement et services de restauration	270
200	20	160	90	150	115	81 Autres services, sauf les administrations publiques	271
315	-	120	35	185	110	91 Administrations publiques	272
						selon la catégorie de travailleurs	
45	-	45	10	20	15	Catégorie de travailleurs - Sans objet (36)	273
4,355	525	3,520	1,330	3,200	1,970	Toutes les catégories de travailleurs (37)	274
4,055	455	2,765	1,100	2,910	1,770	Travailleurs rémunérés	275
3,965	365	2,385	1,000	2,765	1,665	Employés	276
95	85	380	100	150	110	Travailleurs autonomes (entreprise constituée en société)	277
300	55	660	195	285	180	Travailleurs autonomes (entreprise non constituée en société)	278
-	15	95	40	10	20	Travailleurs familiaux non rémunérés	279
						selon la profession basée sur la CNP-S de 2001	
2,320	335	1,845	730	1,670	1,095	Hommes actifs de 15 ans et plus	280
30	10	-	10	10	10	Profession - Sans objet (36)	281
2,290	325	1,840	725	1,655	1,090	Toutes les professions (37)	282
330	40	245	165	205	115	A Gestion	283
200	20	105	20	115	80	B Affaires, finance et administration	284
120	20	105	25	110	65	C Sciences naturelles et appliquées et professions apparentées	285
25	-	25	10	25	45	D Secteur de la santé	286
70	15	95	40	80	60	E Sciences sociales, enseignement, administration publique et religion	287
65	10	35	-	30	-	F Arts, culture, sports et loisirs	288
440	35	315	95	315	230	G Ventes et services	289
790	85	480	245	625	335	H Métiers, transport et machinerie	290
75	100	330	90	75	130	I Professions propres au secteur primaire	291
185	-	115	35	85	40	J Transformation, fabrication et services d'utilité publique	292
2,090	195	1,720	615	1,545	885	Femmes actives de 15 ans et plus	293
15	-	45	-	10	10	Profession - Sans objet (36)	294
2,070	195	1,675	610	1,535	880	Toutes les professions (37)	295
125	30	175	45	95	50	A Gestion	296
605	50	450	150	515	300	B Affaires, finance et administration	297
20	10	10	15	35	10	C Sciences naturelles et appliquées et professions apparentées	298
250	10	150	70	120	50	D Secteur de la santé	299

Table 1. Selected Characteristics for Census Tracts, 2001 Census – 100% Data and 20% Sample Data

No.	Characteristics	Vancouver 0403.01	Vancouver 0403.03	Vancouver 0403.04 A	Vancouver 0403.05 A	Vancouver 0404	Vancouver 0410.02
	POPULATION CHARACTERISTICS						
	by occupation based on the 2001 NOC-S – concluded						
300	E Occupations in social science, education, government service and religion	145	140	140	85	240	125
301	F Occupations in art, culture, recreation and sport	15	50	35	35	35	45
302	G Sales and service occupations	435	450	375	345	535	565
303	H Trades, transport and equipment operators and related occupations	20	50	20	20	20	30
304	I Occupations unique to primary industry	10	10	10	25	70	85
305	J Occupations unique to processing, manufacturing and utilities	40	80	25	25	25	40
306	**Total employed labour force 15 years and over**	**2,680**	**2,865**	**2,440**	**2,205**	**4,300**	**3,035**
	by place of work						
307	Males	1,475	1,445	1,275	1,160	2,405	1,525
308	Usual place of work	1,000	1,105	970	905	1,720	1,125
309	At home	85	50	70	25	140	110
310	Outside Canada	-	-	-	10	-	20
311	No fixed workplace address	390	290	235	225	550	275
312	Females	1,210	1,425	1,170	1,040	1,890	1,510
313	Usual place of work	1,065	1,225	1,000	845	1,510	1,335
314	At home	75	125	85	140	255	130
315	Outside Canada	10	-	-	15	10	-
316	No fixed workplace address	60	70	80	40	120	40
317	**Total employed labour force 15 years and over with usual place of work or no fixed workplace address**	**2,520**	**2,690**	**2,290**	**2,020**	**3,900**	**2,775**
	by mode of transportation						
318	Males	1,390	1,390	1,210	1,135	2,265	1,400
319	Car, truck, van, as driver	1,175	1,150	1,015	945	1,945	1,250
320	Car, truck, van, as passenger	45	95	65	70	95	55
321	Public transit	85	55	65	45	125	55
322	Walked	30	55	30	45	55	10
323	Other method	50	30	35	20	45	30
324	Females	1,125	1,300	1,080	890	1,630	1,375
325	Car, truck, van, as driver	860	1,025	835	750	1,385	1,100
326	Car, truck, van, as passenger	90	105	95	45	185	95
327	Public transit	70	80	80	30	30	115
328	Walked	100	70	65	50	10	55
329	Other method	10	25	-	10	20	10
330	**Total population 15 years and over who worked since January 1, 2000**	**3,070**	**3,255**	**2,765**	**2,445**	**4,870**	**3,565**
	by language used at work						
331	Single responses	2,980	3,195	2,670	2,365	4,685	3,415
332	English	2,965	3,180	2,665	2,355	4,665	3,410
333	French	-	-	10	-	-	-
334	Non-official languages (5)	15	20	-	-	20	-
335	Chinese, n.o.s.	-	-	-	-	-	10
336	Cantonese	-	-	-	-	10	-
337	Other languages (6)	10	10	-	10	10	-
338	Multiple responses	85	55	90	75	185	145
339	English and French	25	40	10	25	50	30
340	English and non-official language	55	15	70	50	135	105
341	French and non-official language	-	-	-	-	-	-
342	English, French and non-official language	10	-	15	-	-	-
	DWELLING AND HOUSEHOLD CHARACTERISTICS						
343	**Total number of occupied private dwellings**	**1,875**	**1,920**	**1,590**	**1,370**	**2,660**	**2,300**
	by tenure						
344	Owned	1,415	1,515	1,340	1,180	2,355	1,685
345	Rented	460	380	250	195	310	615
346	Band housing	-	25	-	-	-	-
	by structural type of dwelling						
347	Single-detached house	1,180	1,370	1,310	1,055	2,385	900
348	Semi-detached house	125	45	25	-	30	115
349	Row house	335	195	145	160	115	625
350	Apartment, detached duplex	90	165	60	110	55	115
351	Apartment, building that has five or more storeys	-	-	-	-	-	35
352	Apartment, building that has fewer than five storeys (38)	75	135	60	40	40	510
353	Other single-attached house	10	10	-	-	-	-
354	Movable dwelling (39)	55	-	-	-	30	10

Tableau 1. Certaines caractéristiques des secteurs de recensement, recensement de 2001 – Données intégrales et données-échantillon (20 %)

Vancouver 0410.03 A	Vancouver 0410.04 ◆ A	Vancouver 0500	Vancouver 0501.01 ◇ A	Vancouver 0501.02	Vancouver 0501.03	Caractéristiques	N°
						CARACTÉRISTIQUES DE LA POPULATION	
						selon la profession basée sur la CNP-S de 2001 – fin	
190	-	80	50	175	70	E Sciences sociales, enseignement, administration publique et religion	300
60	-	75	30	25	10	F Arts, culture, sports et loisirs	301
700	45	435	145	440	280	G Ventes et services	302
45	10	35	10	50	-	H Métiers, transport et machinerie	303
20	35	235	90	85	95	I Professions propres au secteur primaire	304
45	10	40	10	10	15	J Transformation, fabrication et services d'utilité publique	305
4,160	**500**	**3,385**	**1,265**	**3,065**	**1,870**	**Population active occupée totale de 15 ans et plus selon le lieu de travail**	306
2,170	315	1,780	695	1,580	1,045	Hommes	307
1,700	115	960	390	1,015	690	Lieu habituel de travail	308
95	135	440	100	170	200	À domicile	309
25	-	-	10	25	10	En dehors du Canada	310
355	65	370	200	355	150	Sans adresse de travail fixe	311
1,990	180	1,605	570	1,490	815	Femmes	312
1,740	130	990	385	1,230	550	Lieu habituel de travail	313
130	50	505	165	210	195	À domicile	314
-	-	-	-	15	-	En dehors du Canada	315
125	-	105	20	45	65	Sans adresse de travail fixe	316
3,915	**310**	**2,435**	**995**	**2,645**	**1,465**	**Population active occupée totale de 15 ans et plus ayant un lieu habituel de travail ou sans adresse de travail fixe selon le mode de transport**	317
2,060	175	1,340	590	1,375	840	Hommes	318
1,745	160	1,165	535	1,270	750	Automobile, camion ou fourgonnette, en tant que conducteur	319
125	10	70	15	50	55	Automobile, camion ou fourgonnette, en tant que passager	320
85	10	10	10	30	-	Transport en commun	321
45	10	70	10	15	10	À pied	322
50	-	30	20	10	25	Autre moyen	323
1,865	130	1,095	405	1,270	620	Femmes	324
1,475	115	980	360	1,160	540	Automobile, camion ou fourgonnette, en tant que conductrice	325
180	10	50	30	60	60	Automobile, camion ou fourgonnette, en tant que passagère	326
150	-	-	-	15	-	Transport en commun	327
50	-	45	-	20	10	À pied	328
10	-	30	10	15	-	Autre moyen	329
4,675	**605**	**3,770**	**1,495**	**3,405**	**2,025**	**Population totale de 15 ans et plus ayant travaillé depuis le 1er janvier 2000 selon la langue utilisée au travail**	330
4,555	525	3,690	1,390	3,315	1,975	Réponses uniques	331
4,540	510	3,690	1,370	3,315	1,945	Anglais	332
10	-	-	-	-	10	Français	333
10	20	-	15	-	20	Langues non officielles (5)	334
-	-	-	-	-	10	Chinois, n.d.a.	335
-	-	-	-	-	-	Cantonais	336
-	10	-	15	-	15	Autres langues (6)	337
130	75	75	100	100	50	Réponses multiples	338
50	15	10	10	15	-	Anglais et français	339
80	60	70	90	80	55	Anglais et langue non officielle	340
-	-	-	-	-	-	Français et langue non officielle	341
-	-	-	-	10	-	Anglais, français et langue non officielle	342
						CARACTÉRISTIQUES DES LOGEMENTS ET DES MÉNAGES	
2,715	**290**	**2,385**	**1,015**	**1,815**	**1,015**	**Nombre total de logements privés occupés selon le mode d'occupation**	343
2,190	205	1,920	820	1,615	800	Possédé	344
525	85	465	195	200	215	Loué	345
-	-	-	-	-	-	Logement de bande	346
						selon le type de construction résidentielle	
1,965	290	1,610	760	1,805	950	Maison individuelle non attenante	347
50	-	25	-	-	15	Maison jumelée	348
280	-	-	235	10	-	Maison en rangée	349
80	-	75	-	10	-	Appartement, duplex non attenant	350
-	-	-	-	-	-	Appartement, immeuble de cinq étages ou plus	351
335	-	-	-	-	-	Appartement, immeuble de moins de cinq étages (38)	352
-	-	20	-	-	25	Autre maison individuelle attenante	353
-	-	650	15	10	30	Logement mobile (39)	354

Table 1. Selected Characteristics for Census Tracts, 2001 Census – 100% Data and 20% Sample Data

No.	Characteristics	Vancouver 0403.01	Vancouver 0403.03	Vancouver 0403.04 A	Vancouver 0403.05 A	Vancouver 0404	Vancouver 0410.02
	DWELLING AND HOUSEHOLD CHARACTERISTICS						
	by condition of dwelling						
355	Regular maintenance only	1,185	1,255	1,005	1,005	1,845	1,595
356	Minor repairs	500	510	485	235	615	450
357	Major repairs	190	155	105	140	200	260
	by period of construction						
358	Before 1946	75	225	100	10	140	85
359	1946-1960	200	150	185	55	260	80
360	1961-1970	335	80	245	175	295	75
361	1971-1980	680	100	605	85	420	255
362	1981-1990	370	1,010	340	520	590	810
363	1991-2001 (20)	215	355	110	525	960	995
364	Average number of rooms per dwelling	7.0	6.7	7.6	7.8	7.9	6.5
365	Average number of bedrooms per dwelling	3.0	3.0	3.1	3.2	3.3	2.7
366	Average value of dwelling $	202,453	186,352	217,563	232,406	273,582	202,385
367	**Total number of private households**	**1,870**	**1,925**	**1,590**	**1,370**	**2,665**	**2,295**
	by household size						
368	1 person	330	305	240	170	365	540
369	2 persons	560	550	450	400	815	770
370	3 persons	350	395	310	255	480	375
371	4-5 persons	560	600	540	480	845	525
372	6 or more persons	70	70	55	75	155	85
	by household type						
373	One-family households	1,465	1,525	1,305	1,100	2,135	1,660
374	Multiple-family households	25	25	20	70	90	20
375	Non-family households	375	370	260	200	440	615
376	Number of persons in private households	5,345	5,595	4,725	4,230	8,045	5,975
377	Average number of persons in private households	2.9	2.9	3.0	3.1	3.0	2.6
378	Average number of persons per room	0.4	0.4	0.4	0.4	0.4	0.4
379	Tenant households in non-farm, non-reserve private dwellings (40)	460	370	250	190	295	605
380	Average gross rent $ (40)	900	886	905	943	902	701
381	Tenant households spending 30% or more of household income on gross rent (40) (41)	200	160	125	95	100	245
382	Tenant households spending from 30% to 99% of household income on gross rent (40) (41)	185	135	115	75	70	205
383	Owner households in non-farm, non-reserve private dwellings (42)	1,420	1,485	1,340	1,180	2,315	1,645
384	Average owner's major payments $ (42)	994	1,030	1,054	1,162	1,199	951
385	Owner households spending 30% or more of household income on owner's major payments (41) (42)	285	365	310	280	545	315
386	Owner households spending from 30% to 99% of household income on owner's major payments (41) (42)	245	330	285	230	500	270
	CENSUS FAMILY CHARACTERISTICS						
387	**Total number of census families in private households**	**1,525**	**1,575**	**1,350**	**1,250**	**2,310**	**1,705**
	by census family structure and size						
388	Total couple families	1,210	1,290	1,155	1,075	2,060	1,435
389	Total families of married couples	1,065	1,105	1,015	975	1,850	1,275
390	Without children at home	440	325	325	305	695	485
391	With children at home	625	775	690	670	1,155	785
392	1 child	200	235	205	230	325	245
393	2 children	305	385	330	310	575	375
394	3 or more children	115	155	155	130	250	170
395	Total families of common-law couples	145	190	140	100	210	165
396	Without children at home	30	95	60	65	115	145
397	With children at home	115	90	80	40	95	15
398	1 child	40	55	20	15	55	-
399	2 children	70	20	50	20	35	-
400	3 or more children	10	15	10	-	-	10
401	Total lone-parent families	320	285	195	180	255	270
402	Female parent	260	240	170	145	195	230
403	1 child	120	135	90	90	95	110
404	2 children	70	65	50	50	75	95
405	3 or more children	70	40	30	10	25	30

Tableau 1. Certaines caractéristiques des secteurs de recensement, recensement de 2001 – Données intégrales et données-échantillon (20 %)

Vancouver 0410.03 A	Vancouver 0410.04 ◆ A	Vancouver 0500	Vancouver 0501.01 ◇ A	Vancouver 0501.02	Vancouver 0501.03	Caractéristiques	N°
						CARACTÉRISTIQUES DES LOGEMENTS ET DES MÉNAGES	
						selon l'état du logement	
1,970	215	1,640	785	1,180	605	Entretien régulier seulement	355
605	30	570	195	515	370	Réparations mineures	356
140	45	180	40	130	35	Réparations majeures	357
						selon la période de construction	
15	35	225	85	115	50	Avant 1946	358
40	25	240	70	170	80	1946-1960	359
170	30	295	85	235	120	1961-1970	360
970	90	855	145	740	360	1971-1980	361
885	50	520	340	400	325	1981-1990	362
630	65	250	290	160	80	1991-2001 (20)	363
7.1	7.9	7.0	7.0	8.2	7.3	Nombre moyen de pièces par logement	364
3.1	3.3	2.9	2.9	3.3	3.1	Nombre moyen de chambres à coucher par logement	365
196,693	401,524	339,651	272,385	326,123	313,061	Valeur moyenne du logement $	366
2,715	**290**	**2,385**	**1,015**	**1,820**	**1,015**	**Nombre total de logements privés**	367
						selon la taille du ménage	
445	40	495	260	245	145	1 personne	368
835	95	955	390	600	305	2 personnes	369
525	55	320	85	320	130	3 personnes	370
835	75	525	215	555	355	4-5 personnes	371
75	25	100	70	90	80	6 personnes ou plus	372
						selon le genre de ménage	
2,190	225	1,755	710	1,485	815	Ménages unifamiliaux	373
20	20	45	25	65	35	Ménages multifamiliaux	374
510	50	590	280	270	165	Ménages non familiaux	375
7,745	935	6,285	2,660	5,380	3,185	Nombre de personnes dans les ménages privés	376
2.9	3.2	2.6	2.6	3.0	3.1	Nombre moyen de personnes dans les ménages privés	377
0.4	0.4	0.4	0.4	0.4	0.4	Nombre moyen de personnes par pièce	378
525	90	430	190	195	210	Ménages locataires dans les logements privés non agricoles hors réserve (40)	379
796	610	930	824	711	790	Loyer brut moyen $ (40)	380
185	20	135	70	90	70	Ménages locataires consacrant 30 % ou plus du revenu du ménage au loyer brut (40) (41)	381
160	10	95	70	70	60	Ménages locataires consacrant de 30 % à 99 % du revenu du ménage au loyer brut (40) (41)	382
2,185	150	1,360	740	1,575	730	Ménages propriétaires dans les logements privés non agricoles hors réserve (42)	383
1,079	1,173	975	913	1,087	1,137	Principales dépenses de propriété moyennes $ (42)	384
460	25	345	145	325	195	Ménages propriétaires consacrant 30 % ou plus du revenu du ménage aux principales dépenses de propriété (41) (42)	385
390	25	295	130	270	160	Ménages propriétaires consacrant de 30 % à 99 % du revenu du ménage aux principales dépenses de propriété (41) (42)	386
						CARACTÉRISTIQUES DES FAMILLES DE RECENSEMENT	
2,220	**270**	**1,840**	**755**	**1,610**	**885**	**Total des familles de recensement dans les ménages privés**	387
						selon la structure et la taille de la famille de recensement	
1,905	255	1,665	720	1,430	765	Total des familles avec conjoints	388
1,690	215	1,465	630	1,330	700	Total des familles avec couples mariés	389
575	95	760	340	545	225	Sans enfants à la maison	390
1,120	125	710	285	785	480	Avec enfants à la maison	391
390	30	235	85	250	110	1 enfant	392
530	40	300	115	360	230	2 enfants	393
200	55	175	95	175	135	3 enfants ou plus	394
215	40	200	95	100	60	Total des familles en union libre	395
115	15	125	55	50	45	Sans enfants à la maison	396
100	25	80	35	45	20	Avec enfants à la maison	397
40	20	35	10	10	-	1 enfant	398
45	-	25	15	15	10	2 enfants	399
15	-	15	10	25	10	3 enfants ou plus	400
315	10	170	40	180	125	Total des familles monoparentales	401
240	10	110	35	110	85	Parent de sexe féminin	402
130	10	35	10	75	55	1 enfant	403
65	-	40	20	20	30	2 enfants	404
50	10	35	-	15	-	3 enfants ou plus	405

Table 1. Selected Characteristics for Census Tracts, 2001 Census – 100% Data and 20% Sample Data

No.	Characteristics	Vancouver 0403.01	Vancouver 0403.03	Vancouver 0403.04 A	Vancouver 0403.05 A	Vancouver 0404	Vancouver 0410.02
	CENSUS FAMILY CHARACTERISTICS						
	by census family structure and size – concluded						
406	Male parent	65	50	25	30	60	45
407	1 child	40	30	10	20	30	35
408	2 children	10	20	10	10	20	10
409	3 or more children	15	-	10	-	15	-
410	**Total number of children at home**	**2,025**	**2,140**	**1,865**	**1,600**	**2,885**	**2,050**
	by age groups						
411	Under 6 years	350	560	405	350	545	440
412	6-14 years	890	925	715	635	1,250	775
413	15-17 years	270	255	265	210	420	280
414	18-24 years	385	275	345	305	515	365
415	25 years and over	130	125	140	105	150	185
416	Average number of children at home per census family (43)	1.3	1.4	1.4	1.3	1.2	1.2
417	**Total number of persons in private households**	**5,345**	**5,595**	**4,725**	**4,230**	**8,045**	**5,975**
	by census family status and living arrangements						
418	Number of non-family persons	585	595	355	315	785	785
419	Living with relatives (44)	90	90	55	40	240	90
420	Living with non-relatives only	170	200	55	105	180	155
421	Living alone	330	305	240	170	365	540
422	Number of family persons	4,755	5,000	4,365	3,915	7,255	5,190
423	Average number of persons per census family	3.1	3.2	3.2	3.1	3.1	3.0
424	**Total number of persons 65 years and over**	**430**	**365**	**380**	**345**	**540**	**715**
425	Number of non-family persons 65 years and over	155	150	100	100	165	255
426	Living with relatives (44)	40	20	25	20	70	20
427	Living with non-relatives only	-	25	-	15	-	10
428	Living alone	115	105	75	65	85	225
429	Number of family persons 65 years and over	270	210	270	245	375	460
	ECONOMIC FAMILY CHARACTERISTICS						
430	**Total number of economic families in private households**	**1,525**	**1,570**	**1,330**	**1,195**	**2,260**	**1,685**
	by size of family						
431	2 persons	580	540	445	420	805	710
432	3 persons	350	380	295	265	455	365
433	4 persons	435	440	395	335	645	390
434	5 or more persons	155	205	195	185	355	220
435	Total number of persons in economic families	4,845	5,090	4,425	3,960	7,500	5,280
436	Average number of persons per economic family	3.2	3.2	3.3	3.3	3.3	3.1
437	Total number of unattached individuals	500	505	300	275	540	695
	2000 INCOME CHARACTERISTICS						
	Population 15 years and over by sex and total income groups in 2000						
438	Total - Both sexes	4,090	4,120	3,605	3,240	6,235	4,760
439	Without income	300	210	270	175	340	190
440	With income	3,795	3,905	3,335	3,070	5,895	4,565
441	Under $1,000 (45)	175	195	150	195	295	140
442	$ 1,000 - $ 2,999	165	200	145	150	265	195
443	$ 3,000 - $ 4,999	130	125	150	190	315	145
444	$ 5,000 - $ 6,999	115	195	90	120	215	100
445	$ 7,000 - $ 9,999	225	205	160	150	350	370
446	$10,000 - $11,999	90	155	160	105	130	185
447	$12,000 - $14,999	180	270	135	195	355	300
448	$15,000 - $19,999	390	315	245	235	395	415
449	$20,000 - $24,999	270	205	270	140	400	450
450	$25,000 - $29,999	235	315	180	215	210	345
451	$30,000 - $34,999	370	310	330	255	485	300
452	$35,000 - $39,999	360	195	205	145	395	320
453	$40,000 - $44,999	315	325	210	200	360	255
454	$45,000 - $49,999	235	235	190	130	310	160
455	$50,000 - $59,999	280	305	280	285	450	370
456	$60,000 and over	265	355	435	360	960	530
457	Average income $ (46)	29,535	29,002	31,856	30,910	34,218	30,128
458	Median income $ (46)	27,492	26,037	29,011	26,396	29,996	24,923
459	Standard error of average income $ (46)	790	681	927	1,191	895	761

Tableau 1. Certaines caractéristiques des secteurs de recensement, recensement de 2001 – Données intégrales et données-échantillon (20 %)

Vancouver 0410.03 A	Vancouver 0410.04 ◆ A	Vancouver 0500	Vancouver 0501.01 ◇ A	Vancouver 0501.02	Vancouver 0501.03	Caractéristiques	N°
						CARACTÉRISTIQUES DES FAMILLES DE RECENSEMENT	
						selon la structure et la taille de la famille de recensement – fin	
75	-	65	-	70	35	Parent de sexe masculin	406
35	-	50	-	60	30	1 enfant	407
20	-	15	-	-	-	2 enfants	408
25	-	-	-	-	-	3 enfants ou plus	409
2,800	**330**	**1,920**	**775**	**1,915**	**1,270**	**Nombre total d'enfants à la maison**	410
						selon les groupes d'âge	
580	60	375	160	260	235	Moins de 6 ans	411
1,145	125	770	270	725	500	6-14 ans	412
400	60	280	130	255	195	15-17 ans	413
550	55	310	150	490	285	18-24 ans	414
125	40	180	65	180	45	25 ans et plus	415
1.3	1.3	1.0	1.0	1.2	1.4	Nombre moyen d'enfants à la maison par famille de recensement (43)	416
7,745	**935**	**6,285**	**2,660**	**5,380**	**3,180**	**Nombre total de personnes dans les ménages privés**	417
						selon la situation des particuliers dans la famille de recensement et des particuliers dans le ménage	
815	80	860	415	435	265	Nombre de personnes hors famille de recensement	418
150	30	145	50	70	10	Vivant avec des personnes apparentées (44)	419
215	10	220	100	115	110	Vivant avec des personnes non apparentées uniquement	420
445	45	495	260	240	140	Vivant seules	421
6,930	855	5,420	2,250	4,950	2,920	Nombre de personnes membres d'une famille	422
3.1	3.2	2.9	3.0	3.1	3.3	Nombre moyen de personnes par famille de recensement	423
615	**150**	**1,120**	**550**	**520**	**280**	**Nombre total de personnes de 65 ans et plus**	424
205	25	315	210	130	60	Nombre de personnes hors famille de recensement de 65 ans et plus	425
55	10	55	15	35	10	Vivant avec des personnes apparentées (44)	426
20	-	45	-	-	10	Vivant avec des personnes non apparentées uniquement	427
130	15	220	190	95	40	Vivant seules	428
410	125	805	335	395	220	Nombre de personnes membres d'une famille de 65 ans et plus	429
						CARACTÉRISTIQUES DES FAMILLES ÉCONOMIQUES	
2,215	**250**	**1,820**	**740**	**1,555**	**865**	**Nombre total de familles économiques dans les ménages privés**	430
						selon la taille de la famille	
820	90	895	385	620	325	2 personnes	431
505	55	335	85	300	140	3 personnes	432
610	40	325	140	380	230	4 personnes	433
280	60	260	125	260	170	5 personnes ou plus	434
7,080	885	5,565	2,300	5,020	2,935	Nombre total de personnes dans les familles économiques	435
3.2	3.6	3.1	3.1	3.2	3.4	Nombre moyen de personnes par famille économique	436
660	50	720	360	360	250	Nombre total de personnes hors famille économique	437
						CARACTÉRISTIQUES DU REVENU DE 2000	
						Population de 15 ans et plus selon le sexe et les tranches de revenu total en 2000	
5,995	755	5,120	2,265	4,390	2,460	Total - Les deux sexes	438
315	70	205	100	225	90	Sans revenu	439
5,685	680	4,920	2,170	4,160	2,365	Avec un revenu	440
240	15	200	45	195	75	Moins de 1 000 $ (45)	441
260	30	175	85	135	85	1 000 $ - 2 999 $	442
230	30	195	80	140	125	3 000 $ - 4 999 $	443
255	20	140	75	135	100	5 000 $ - 6 999 $	444
340	40	320	155	240	125	7 000 $ - 9 999 $	445
170	-	225	115	150	110	10 000 $ - 11 999 $	446
335	50	475	220	240	95	12 000 $ - 14 999 $	447
390	50	520	245	350	220	15 000 $ - 19 999 $	448
360	75	480	170	400	235	20 000 $ - 24 999 $	449
380	85	375	175	235	140	25 000 $ - 29 999 $	450
435	75	370	145	360	180	30 000 $ - 34 999 $	451
430	30	250	150	245	105	35 000 $ - 39 999 $	452
415	25	195	110	220	215	40 000 $ - 44 999 $	453
240	20	195	60	165	120	45 000 $ - 49 999 $	454
570	30	275	115	315	190	50 000 $ - 59 999 $	455
610	95	525	215	630	240	60 000 $ et plus	456
30,631	32,902	28,922	33,540	33,008	30,302	Revenu moyen $ (46)	457
28,391	26,930	21,953	21,903	26,343	25,284	Revenu médian $ (46)	458
654	2,356	805	3,227	973	1,074	Erreur type de revenu moyen $ (46)	459

Table 1. Selected Characteristics for Census Tracts, 2001 Census – 100% Data and 20% Sample Data

No.	Characteristics	Vancouver 0403.01	Vancouver 0403.03	Vancouver 0403.04 A	Vancouver 0403.05 A	Vancouver 0404	Vancouver 0410.02
	2000 INCOME CHARACTERISTICS						
	Population 15 years and over by sex and total income groups in 2000 – concluded						
460	Total - Males	2,060	1,990	1,810	1,580	3,150	2,215
461	Without income	155	60	115	45	100	75
462	With income	1,900	1,930	1,695	1,540	3,050	2,135
463	Under $1,000 (45)	55	100	65	85	125	40
464	$ 1,000 - $ 2,999	45	80	55	35	70	30
465	$ 3,000 - $ 4,999	50	55	60	125	185	50
466	$ 5,000 - $ 6,999	40	60	30	40	50	25
467	$ 7,000 - $ 9,999	80	60	50	55	115	100
468	$10,000 - $11,999	25	60	45	30	60	80
469	$12,000 - $14,999	65	105	45	65	115	125
470	$15,000 - $19,999	180	135	95	90	145	145
471	$20,000 - $24,999	115	65	130	55	155	180
472	$25,000 - $29,999	110	125	70	95	80	165
473	$30,000 - $34,999	180	110	130	105	225	105
474	$35,000 - $39,999	170	90	100	90	215	140
475	$40,000 - $44,999	190	215	145	110	195	120
476	$45,000 - $49,999	150	150	115	75	195	100
477	$50,000 - $59,999	230	215	195	215	295	275
478	$60,000 and over	220	300	375	275	820	450
479	Average income $ (46)	36,198	35,090	40,038	38,797	43,625	39,142
480	Median income $ (46)	34,892	34,415	39,097	34,431	39,685	35,366
481	Standard error of average income $ (46)	1,243	1,075	1,481	2,069	1,447	1,273
482	Total - Females	2,035	2,125	1,800	1,655	3,085	2,545
483	Without income	140	145	160	130	245	110
484	With income	1,890	1,980	1,645	1,530	2,845	2,430
485	Under $1,000 (45)	120	90	90	110	175	105
486	$ 1,000 - $ 2,999	120	120	95	120	200	160
487	$ 3,000 - $ 4,999	80	70	95	65	135	95
488	$ 5,000 - $ 6,999	75	135	60	70	165	70
489	$ 7,000 - $ 9,999	145	140	105	95	230	265
490	$10,000 - $11,999	60	90	115	75	70	105
491	$12,000 - $14,999	115	165	90	135	235	175
492	$15,000 - $19,999	210	185	155	140	245	265
493	$20,000 - $24,999	150	140	140	90	245	270
494	$25,000 - $29,999	130	190	110	120	135	180
495	$30,000 - $34,999	185	200	200	155	265	190
496	$35,000 - $39,999	195	105	105	55	180	185
497	$40,000 - $44,999	120	105	70	90	165	135
498	$45,000 - $49,999	85	90	70	60	115	65
499	$50,000 - $59,999	55	90	85	70	150	90
500	$60,000 and over	50	60	60	85	140	80
501	Average income $ (46)	22,820	23,062	23,414	22,977	24,135	22,207
502	Median income $ (46)	20,332	18,778	20,449	17,408	19,417	19,288
503	Standard error of average income $ (46)	847	765	926	1,031	876	719
	by composition of total income						
504	Total - Composition of income in 2000 % (47)	100.0	100.0	100.0	100.0	100.0	100.0
505	Employment income %	80.4	84.2	83.5	84.5	84.7	80.0
506	Government transfer payments %	12.0	9.5	7.9	8.8	6.8	11.9
507	Other %	7.5	6.3	8.7	6.5	8.4	8.0
	Population 15 years and over with employment income in 2000 by sex and work activity						
508	Both sexes with employment income (48)	2,900	3,095	2,645	2,320	4,740	3,370
509	Average employment income $	31,113	30,775	33,490	34,586	36,046	32,712
510	Standard error of average employment income $	974	772	1,057	1,472	973	914
511	Worked full year, full time (49)	1,545	1,610	1,490	1,225	2,580	1,850
512	Average employment income $	41,657	41,764	44,304	44,899	48,953	42,054
513	Standard error of average employment income $	1,281	982	1,241	1,720	1,309	1,032
514	Worked part year or part time (50)	1,300	1,465	1,125	1,060	2,085	1,510
515	Average employment income $	18,888	19,146	19,818	23,113	21,018	21,423
516	Standard error of average employment income $	1,145	912	1,448	2,272	1,128	1,379
517	Males with employment income (48)	1,575	1,595	1,415	1,225	2,600	1,725
518	Average employment income $	37,640	37,313	41,353	42,637	45,052	40,861
519	Standard error of average employment income $	1,477	1,163	1,640	2,460	1,478	1,443
520	Worked full year, full time (49)	905	940	955	705	1,685	1,075
521	Average employment income $	47,883	46,551	49,447	51,010	56,165	48,252
522	Standard error of average employment income $	1,834	1,363	1,632	2,539	1,720	1,441
523	Worked part year or part time (50)	630	640	440	490	880	650
524	Average employment income $	23,994	24,214	24,351	31,008	24,873	28,640
525	Standard error of average employment income $	1,961	1,620	3,246	4,621	2,150	2,755

Tableau 1. Certaines caractéristiques des secteurs de recensement, recensement de 2001 – Données intégrales et données-échantillon (20 %)

Vancouver 0410.03 A	Vancouver 0410.04 ◆ A	Vancouver 0500	Vancouver 0501.01 ◇ A	Vancouver 0501.02	Vancouver 0501.03	Caractéristiques	N°
						CARACTÉRISTIQUES DU REVENU DE 2000	
						Population de 15 ans et plus selon le sexe et les tranches de revenu total en 2000 – fin	
2,915	415	2,550	1,100	2,220	1,295	Total - Hommes	460
120	35	70	50	75	25	Sans revenu	461
2,795	385	2,475	1,050	2,145	1,265	Avec un revenu	462
125	10	100	35	100	40	Moins de 1 000 $ (45)	463
120	10	90	30	30	35	1 000 $ - 2 999 $	464
75	15	65	20	50	50	3 000 $ - 4 999 $	465
90	20	50	10	60	30	5 000 $ - 6 999 $	466
145	15	130	45	75	65	7 000 $ - 9 999 $	467
65	-	85	40	80	65	10 000 $ - 11 999 $	468
65	25	165	90	100	15	12 000 $ - 14 999 $	469
160	25	210	95	140	120	15 000 $ - 19 999 $	470
150	40	235	80	215	100	20 000 $ - 24 999 $	471
145	40	190	105	120	50	25 000 $ - 29 999 $	472
160	35	180	70	130	105	30 000 $ - 34 999 $	473
165	20	135	65	110	60	35 000 $ - 39 999 $	474
185	25	105	75	105	130	40 000 $ - 44 999 $	475
165	15	145	20	140	75	45 000 $ - 49 999 $	476
450	20	205	95	205	125	50 000 $ - 59 999 $	477
535	60	390	170	490	215	60 000 $ et plus	478
37,897	34,436	35,421	45,897	40,117	36,378	Revenu moyen $ (46)	479
38,204	28,973	27,087	29,323	32,414	33,831	Revenu médian $ (46)	480
1,047	2,899	1,375	6,216	1,609	1,690	Erreur type de revenu moyen $ (46)	481
3,080	340	2,575	1,165	2,170	1,160	Total - Femmes	482
190	45	135	45	150	65	Sans revenu	483
2,885	295	2,440	1,120	2,015	1,100	Avec un revenu	484
115	10	105	10	100	35	Moins de 1 000 $ (45)	485
140	30	85	50	105	50	1 000 $ - 2 999 $	486
160	15	130	65	85	80	3 000 $ - 4 999 $	487
165	-	90	65	70	65	5 000 $ - 6 999 $	488
195	20	190	115	170	70	7 000 $ - 9 999 $	489
105	10	140	75	65	50	10 000 $ - 11 999 $	490
270	20	310	135	140	85	12 000 $ - 14 999 $	491
235	25	310	150	210	100	15 000 $ - 19 999 $	492
210	35	250	90	185	135	20 000 $ - 24 999 $	493
230	40	195	70	110	90	25 000 $ - 29 999 $	494
280	45	190	75	235	80	30 000 $ - 34 999 $	495
265	-	115	85	140	50	35 000 $ - 39 999 $	496
235	-	90	30	120	85	40 000 $ - 44 999 $	497
80	10	50	35	30	45	45 000 $ - 49 999 $	498
120	10	70	20	110	65	50 000 $ - 59 999 $	499
80	30	135	45	140	25	60 000 $ et plus	500
23,597	30,921	22,337	21,993	25,441	23,300	Revenu moyen $ (46)	501
20,962	23,112	17,729	17,194	21,331	20,088	Revenu médian $ (46)	502
682	3,862	743	1,271	964	1,136	Erreur type de revenu moyen $ (46)	503
						selon la composition du revenu total	
100.0	100.0	100.0	100.0	100.0	100.0	Total - Composition du revenu en 2000 % (47)	504
84.7	75.9	70.0	71.0	80.2	81.7	Revenu d'emploi %	505
8.6	9.9	13.9	12.9	8.7	8.3	Transferts gouvernementaux %	506
6.7	14.3	16.1	16.2	11.1	10.0	Autre %	507
						Population de 15 ans et plus ayant un revenu d'emploi en 2000 selon le sexe et le travail	
4,530	550	3,450	1,490	3,330	1,945	Les deux sexes ayant un revenu d'emploi (48)	508
32,570	30,683	28,813	34,708	33,061	30,080	Revenu moyen d'emploi $	509
748	2,306	1,079	3,743	1,111	1,202	Erreur type de revenu moyen d'emploi $	510
2,560	275	1,715	635	1,745	1,010	Ayant travaillé toute l'année à plein temps (49)	511
44,519	42,127	37,683	46,292	44,673	40,700	Revenu moyen d'emploi $	512
880	3,289	1,546	3,711	1,598	1,695	Erreur type de revenu moyen d'emploi $	513
1,860	255	1,690	805	1,475	905	Ayant travaillé une partie de l'année ou à temps partiel (50)	514
17,697	20,553	20,387	26,354	21,094	19,092	Revenu moyen d'emploi $	515
909	2,661	1,399	6,139	1,321	1,389	Erreur type de revenu moyen d'emploi $	516
2,350	315	1,835	790	1,790	1,095	Hommes ayant un revenu d'emploi (48)	517
40,145	32,403	35,155	46,305	38,985	34,833	Revenu moyen d'emploi $	518
1,116	3,054	1,740	6,598	1,792	1,856	Erreur type de revenu moyen d'emploi $	519
1,585	175	1,090	410	1,015	650	Ayant travaillé toute l'année à plein temps (49)	520
49,677	44,246	41,639	53,963	51,893	45,374	Revenu moyen d'emploi $	521
1,152	3,495	2,060	5,428	2,448	2,483	Erreur type de revenu moyen d'emploi $	522
725	130	725	360	690	425	Ayant travaillé une partie de l'année ou à temps partiel (50)	523
21,260	20,231	26,316	38,660	23,644	20,411	Revenu moyen d'emploi $	524
1,808	4,062	2,952	12,493	2,189	2,145	Erreur type de revenu moyen d'emploi $	525

Table 1. Selected Characteristics for Census Tracts, 2001 Census – 100% Data and 20% Sample Data

No.	Characteristics	Vancouver 0403.01	Vancouver 0403.03	Vancouver 0403.04 A	Vancouver 0403.05 A	Vancouver 0404	Vancouver 0410.02
	2000 INCOME CHARACTERISTICS						
	Population 15 years and over with employment income in 2000 by sex and work activity – concluded						
526	Females with employment income (48)	1,325	1,500	1,235	1,100	2,145	1,645
527	Average employment income $	23,358	23,820	24,466	25,672	25,101	24,154
528	Standard error of average employment income $	1,041	882	1,059	1,270	1,014	906
529	Worked full year, full time (49)	635	665	530	520	895	775
530	Average employment income $	32,786	34,978	34,989	36,549	35,376	33,443
531	Standard error of average employment income $	1,327	1,215	1,577	1,826	1,576	1,172
532	Worked part year or part time (50)	670	820	685	570	1,200	860
533	Average employment income $	14,125	15,177	16,902	16,341	18,203	15,947
534	Standard error of average employment income $	1,140	910	1,076	1,316	1,167	1,056
	Census families by structure and family income groups in 2000						
535	Total - All census families	1,525	1,575	1,350	1,245	2,310	1,705
536	Under $10,000	30	45	35	65	35	55
537	$ 10,000 - $19,999	100	105	80	80	110	75
538	$ 20,000 - $29,999	105	90	85	95	120	150
539	$ 30,000 - $39,999	180	140	100	95	175	145
540	$ 40,000 - $49,999	175	175	135	105	130	200
541	$ 50,000 - $59,999	210	215	125	125	280	155
542	$ 60,000 - $69,999	170	170	150	130	335	155
543	$ 70,000 - $79,999	155	195	175	120	200	150
544	$ 80,000 - $89,999	130	180	145	120	145	185
545	$ 90,000 - $99,999	90	60	80	60	235	145
546	$100,000 and over	190	200	260	250	560	275
547	Average family income $	63,185	62,799	70,046	69,537	76,966	67,084
548	Median family income $	57,303	61,005	68,081	63,360	68,876	64,514
549	Standard error of average family income $	1,878	1,480	2,277	2,832	1,900	1,942
550	Total - All couple census families (51)	1,210	1,285	1,155	1,070	2,055	1,430
551	Under $10,000	15	25	10	35	25	-
552	$ 10,000 - $19,999	25	45	35	55	55	65
553	$ 20,000 - $29,999	70	50	70	50	65	95
554	$ 30,000 - $39,999	110	100	65	80	130	90
555	$ 40,000 - $49,999	120	135	90	100	100	165
556	$ 50,000 - $59,999	180	175	115	110	260	135
557	$ 60,000 - $69,999	155	150	120	115	305	150
558	$ 70,000 - $79,999	140	175	165	115	195	145
559	$ 80,000 - $89,999	115	180	140	115	140	160
560	$ 90,000 - $99,999	90	60	80	60	235	145
561	$100,000 and over	190	195	260	245	535	280
562	Average family income $	70,024	68,176	75,912	75,485	80,556	73,337
563	Median family income $	66,471	66,270	74,403	68,981	72,454	71,218
564	Standard error of average family income $	2,091	1,616	2,390	3,032	1,931	2,032
	Incidence of low income in 2000						
565	Total - Economic families	1,520	1,510	1,330	1,195	2,260	1,685
566	Low income	245	175	130	170	145	215
567	Incidence of low income in 2000 % (52)	16.4	11.5	10.0	13.8	6.4	12.7
568	Total - Unattached individuals 15 years and over	500	485	300	275	525	700
569	Low income	175	220	85	85	120	275
570	Incidence of low income in 2000 % (52)	35.2	45.5	28.5	30.7	23.4	39.9
571	Total - Population in private households	5,345	5,360	4,720	4,230	8,025	5,970
572	Low income	1,060	850	565	640	645	900
573	Incidence of low income in 2000 % (52)	19.8	15.9	12.0	15.1	8.0	15.0
	Private households by household income groups in 2000						
574	Total - All private households	1,875	1,920	1,590	1,375	2,660	2,295
575	Under $10,000	50	65	25	40	45	85
576	$ 10,000 - $19,999	160	185	105	100	150	295
577	$ 20,000 - $29,999	180	140	125	105	135	245
578	$ 30,000 - $39,999	195	190	155	135	225	180
579	$ 40,000 - $49,999	240	210	170	105	170	245
580	$ 50,000 - $59,999	260	250	165	175	325	200
581	$ 60,000 - $69,999	195	200	155	145	370	175
582	$ 70,000 - $79,999	160	215	180	115	205	190
583	$ 80,000 - $89,999	125	190	125	120	160	200
584	$ 90,000 - $99,999	90	55	85	70	275	155
585	$100,000 and over	225	220	290	260	610	320
586	Average household income $	59,827	58,763	66,832	69,192	75,691	59,890
587	Median household income $	53,349	56,007	63,317	61,129	66,942	55,484
588	Standard error of average household income $	1,757	1,433	2,061	2,620	1,848	1,741

Tableau 1. Certaines caractéristiques des secteurs de recensement, recensement de 2001 – Données intégrales et données-échantillon (20 %)

Vancouver 0410.03 A	Vancouver 0410.04 ◆ A	Vancouver 0500	Vancouver 0501.01 ◇ A	Vancouver 0501.02	Vancouver 0501.03	Caractéristiques	Nº
						CARACTÉRISTIQUES DU REVENU DE 2000	
						Population de 15 ans et plus ayant un revenu d'emploi en 2000 selon le sexe et le travail – fin	
2,175	240	1,620	695	1,535	850	Femmes ayant un revenu d'emploi (48)	526
24,370	28,440	21,643	21,531	26,162	23,942	Revenu moyen d'emploi $	527
834	3,497	1,088	1,364	1,133	1,293	Erreur type de revenu moyen d'emploi $	528
975	95	630	220	730	365	Ayant travaillé toute l'année à plein temps (49)	529
36,124	38,384	30,818	32,218	34,599	32,316	Revenu moyen d'emploi $	530
1,134	6,697	2,180	2,053	1,442	1,463	Erreur type de revenu moyen d'emploi $	531
1,145	130	965	445	780	480	Ayant travaillé une partie de l'année ou à temps partiel (50)	532
15,440	20,881	15,930	16,296	18,838	17,922	Revenu moyen d'emploi $	533
875	3,416	901	1,597	1,573	1,799	Erreur type de revenu moyen d'emploi $	534
						Familles de recensement selon la structure et les tranches de revenu de la famille en 2000	
2,220	270	1,840	760	1,610	890	Total - Toutes les familles de recensement	535
40	-	75	10	45	20	Moins de 10 000 $	536
115	10	75	10	65	30	10 000 $ - 19 999 $	537
115	10	245	95	80	50	20 000 $ - 29 999 $	538
220	55	180	60	100	105	30 000 $ - 39 999 $	539
240	40	195	130	165	90	40 000 $ - 49 999 $	540
245	30	185	65	120	110	50 000 $ - 59 999 $	541
275	30	170	60	195	95	60 000 $ - 69 999 $	542
225	25	170	115	155	75	70 000 $ - 79 999 $	543
200	-	145	25	140	75	80 000 $ - 89 999 $	544
145	20	95	20	125	55	90 000 $ - 99 999 $	545
400	40	305	165	415	180	100 000 $ et plus	546
68,102	67,130	64,957	81,666	77,795	71,924	Revenu moyen des familles $	547
65,254	57,907	56,515	60,388	72,364	64,142	Revenu médian des familles $	548
1,549	5,177	2,092	10,255	2,255	3,079	Erreur type de revenu moyen des familles $	549
1,910	255	1,665	720	1,430	765	Total - Toutes les familles de recensement comptant un couple (51)	550
25	-	60	10	20	-	Moins de 10 000 $	551
55	10	40	10	45	20	10 000 $ - 19 999 $	552
65	-	200	85	65	35	20 000 $ - 29 999 $	553
180	55	160	50	80	80	30 000 $ - 39 999 $	554
190	35	180	120	150	70	40 000 $ - 49 999 $	555
195	30	175	50	90	95	50 000 $ - 59 999 $	556
245	30	170	50	195	95	60 000 $ - 69 999 $	557
220	25	145	115	150	75	70 000 $ - 79 999 $	558
200	10	140	25	125	60	80 000 $ - 89 999 $	559
145	20	95	20	115	55	90 000 $ - 99 999 $	560
385	40	295	170	395	170	100 000 $ et plus	561
72,835	68,910	67,414	83,706	81,214	77,007	Revenu moyen des familles $	562
69,885	58,250	60,036	63,823	75,188	67,758	Revenu médian des familles $	563
1,637	5,285	2,240	10,813	2,354	3,301	Erreur type de revenu moyen des familles $	564
						Fréquence des unités à faible revenu en 2000	
2,215	250	1,660	735	1,555	865	Total - Familles économiques	565
230	10	95	30	105	45	Faible revenu	566
10.4	4.7	5.8	3.5	6.9	5.1	Fréquence des unités à faible revenu en 2000 % (52)	567
640	50	625	345	355	250	Total - Personnes hors famille économique de 15 ans et plus	568
225	15	185	90	135	70	Faible revenu	569
35.1	31.3	29.7	26.2	39.6	28.7	Fréquence des unités à faible revenu en 2000 % (52)	570
7,720	930	5,860	2,645	5,375	3,180	Total - Population dans les ménages privés	571
915	50	455	175	465	210	Faible revenu	572
11.8	5.2	7.8	6.5	8.7	6.5	Fréquence des unités à faible revenu en 2000 % (52)	573
						Ménages privés selon les tranches de revenu du ménage en 2000	
2,715	290	2,385	1,015	1,820	1,015	Total - Tous les ménages privés	574
70	15	150	15	70	30	Moins de 10 000 $	575
215	10	185	165	150	50	10 000 $ - 19 999 $	576
180	10	295	125	120	70	20 000 $ - 29 999 $	577
320	55	250	85	110	120	30 000 $ - 39 999 $	578
295	45	280	135	145	120	40 000 $ - 49 999 $	579
290	30	220	65	135	115	50 000 $ - 59 999 $	580
255	20	215	75	190	90	60 000 $ - 69 999 $	581
255	15	175	95	160	80	70 000 $ - 79 999 $	582
225	10	155	40	140	65	80 000 $ - 89 999 $	583
155	15	110	15	100	60	90 000 $ - 99 999 $	584
450	75	350	195	490	220	100 000 $ et plus	585
64,077	76,440	59,553	70,559	75,558	70,434	Revenu moyen des ménages $	586
59,213	56,542	51,849	48,076	68,643	59,997	Revenu médian des ménages $	587
1,450	6,620	1,847	7,999	2,393	3,038	Erreur type de revenu moyen des ménages $	588

Table 1. Selected Characteristics for Census Tracts, 2001 Census – 100% Data and 20% Sample Data

No.	Characteristics	Vancouver 0502.01 A	Vancouver 0502.02	Vancouver 0502.03	Vancouver 0502.04 A	Vancouver 0502.05 ◇	Vancouver 0503.01 A
	POPULATION CHARACTERISTICS						
1	**Population, 1996 (1)**	**2,529**	**4,065**	**5,265**	**6,754**	**2,580**	**2,665**
2	**Population, 2001 (2)**	**2,496**	**3,984**	**5,203**	**8,455**	**2,495**	**2,589**
3	Population percentage change, 1996-2001	-1.3	-2.0	-1.2	25.2	-3.3	-2.9
4	Land area in square kilometres, 2001	1.47	9.42	2.62	6.46	33.52	1.08
5	**Total population – 100% Data (3)**	**2,495**	**3,985**	**5,200**	**8,460**	**2,495**	**2,585**
	by sex and age groups						
6	Male	1,230	1,950	2,635	4,070	1,215	1,340
7	0-4 years	55	80	145	240	40	90
8	5-9 years	110	90	225	310	85	115
9	10-14 years	115	135	250	340	100	115
10	15-19 years	90	140	260	385	105	125
11	20-24 years	80	110	160	290	55	85
12	25-29 years	60	75	125	220	55	60
13	30-34 years	80	100	165	190	60	75
14	35-39 years	100	120	235	275	85	125
15	40-44 years	100	130	255	385	115	130
16	45-49 years	120	195	220	355	100	105
17	50-54 years	130	155	200	295	110	105
18	55-59 years	75	135	160	245	115	65
19	60-64 years	35	120	80	140	70	50
20	65-69 years	25	105	55	135	45	30
21	70-74 years	15	90	35	105	40	20
22	75-79 years	20	90	35	95	25	15
23	80-84 years	10	50	20	45	10	10
24	85 years and over	10	35	10	20	5	10
25	Female	1,265	2,035	2,565	4,385	1,275	1,250
26	0-4 years	75	80	175	220	55	70
27	5-9 years	90	95	220	305	85	95
28	10-14 years	110	120	210	375	95	105
29	15-19 years	115	145	210	390	105	100
30	20-24 years	85	105	135	265	75	70
31	25-29 years	55	95	110	200	50	70
32	30-34 years	70	80	195	230	85	90
33	35-39 years	110	125	250	390	90	120
34	40-44 years	105	135	280	415	110	115
35	45-49 years	120	165	220	365	125	120
36	50-54 years	125	185	200	320	120	115
37	55-59 years	50	150	145	235	90	55
38	60-64 years	35	120	75	175	60	45
39	65-69 years	25	125	30	160	45	20
40	70-74 years	30	105	35	130	35	20
41	75-79 years	40	115	35	130	25	25
42	80-84 years	15	65	30	60	20	10
43	85 years and over	10	30	20	25	10	5
44	**Total population 15 years and over**	**1,945**	**3,380**	**3,980**	**6,675**	**2,035**	**2,000**
	by legal marital status						
45	Never married (single)	555	815	1,240	1,860	610	560
46	Legally married (and not separated)	1,100	1,945	2,240	3,940	1,135	1,200
47	Separated, but still legally married	65	115	115	195	55	55
48	Divorced	120	260	270	395	145	125
49	Widowed	100	245	120	285	85	55
	by common-law status						
50	Not in a common-law relationship	1,840	3,160	3,700	6,400	1,865	1,900
51	In a common-law relationship	105	220	285	275	170	105
52	**Total population – 20% Sample Data (4)**	**2,510**	**3,960**	**5,180**	**8,400**	**2,495**	**2,590**
	by mother tongue						
53	Single responses	2,505	3,945	5,165	8,360	2,470	2,575
54	English	2,335	3,525	4,730	7,280	2,220	2,150
55	French	20	70	55	85	20	30
56	Non-official languages (5)	150	355	375	995	235	395
57	Chinese, n.o.s.	15	-	-	120	-	45
58	Cantonese	10	-	-	10	-	-
59	Punjabi	-	80	10	40	10	-
60	Mandarin	-	-	-	65	-	-
61	Tagalog (Pilipino)	10	10	-	10	-	10
62	Other languages (6)	125	260	355	760	225	340
63	Multiple responses	-	15	20	40	20	20
64	English and French	10	-	-	10	-	-
65	English and non-official language	-	15	15	35	15	10
66	French and non-official language	-	-	-	-	-	15
67	English, French and non-official language	-	-	-	-	-	-

See reference material at the end of the publication. – Voir les documents de référence à la fin de la publication.

Tableau 1. Certaines caractéristiques des secteurs de recensement, recensement de 2001 – Données intégrales et données-échantillon (20 %)

Vancouver 0503.03 A	Vancouver 0503.04 A	Vancouver 0503.05 A	Vancouver 0504.01 A	Vancouver 0504.02	Vancouver 0504.03	Caractéristiques	N°
						CARACTÉRISTIQUES DE LA POPULATION	
7,257	**4,862**	**7,739**	**7,436**	**5,684**	**6,041**	**Population, 1996 (1)**	1
7,198	**5,330**	**8,526**	**7,567**	**8,052**	**6,501**	**Population, 2001 (2)**	2
-0.8	9.6	10.2	1.8	41.7	7.6	Variation en pourcentage de la population, 1996-2001	3
3.64	4.08	1.42	21.60	8.15	13.74	Superficie des terres en kilomètres carrés, 2001	4
7,200	**5,330**	**8,525**	**7,565**	**8,055**	**6,505**	**Population totale – Données intégrales (3)**	5
						selon le sexe et les groupes d'âge	
3,580	2,490	3,815	3,755	3,950	3,215	Sexe masculin	6
255	155	245	250	285	275	0-4 ans	7
275	165	200	280	330	320	5-9 ans	8
280	125	170	285	340	290	10-14 ans	9
340	130	220	320	325	270	15-19 ans	10
240	215	280	260	170	170	20-24 ans	11
185	260	385	230	115	150	25-29 ans	12
265	215	320	265	245	260	30-34 ans	13
320	210	295	285	345	315	35-39 ans	14
300	190	245	310	370	345	40-44 ans	15
290	170	225	305	350	275	45-49 ans	16
260	140	220	280	250	195	50-54 ans	17
200	85	185	195	210	135	55-59 ans	18
120	95	140	170	155	65	60-64 ans	19
60	80	135	115	155	45	65-69 ans	20
65	100	160	85	110	50	70-74 ans	21
70	70	150	55	95	30	75-79 ans	22
40	60	135	45	60	10	80-84 ans	23
25	25	100	25	40	10	85 ans et plus	24
3,625	2,840	4,710	3,810	4,105	3,285	Sexe féminin	25
210	165	235	200	220	245	0-4 ans	26
295	150	235	265	310	305	5-9 ans	27
295	155	165	300	335	295	10-14 ans	28
330	160	190	290	300	285	15-19 ans	29
240	215	375	230	165	170	20-24 ans	30
190	270	380	235	150	190	25-29 ans	31
255	190	350	275	280	290	30-34 ans	32
340	210	295	320	375	355	35-39 ans	33
330	205	280	340	440	345	40-44 ans	34
290	170	260	330	335	265	45-49 ans	35
285	160	260	260	240	195	50-54 ans	36
175	125	230	175	205	115	55-59 ans	37
95	120	180	160	175	60	60-64 ans	38
65	110	190	110	140	60	65-69 ans	39
65	145	245	115	145	55	70-74 ans	40
85	135	315	95	115	40	75-79 ans	41
50	85	265	75	95	20	80-84 ans	42
20	85	260	30	75	5	85 ans et plus	43
5,585	**4,420**	**7,275**	**5,985**	**6,235**	**4,775**	**Population totale de 15 ans et plus**	44
						selon l'état matrimonial légal	
1,730	1,525	2,305	1,820	1,370	1,265	Célibataire (jamais marié(e))	45
3,085	1,725	2,545	3,245	4,005	2,990	Légalement marié(e) (et non séparé(e))	46
170	250	435	205	165	125	Séparé(e), mais toujours légalement marié(e)	47
390	560	1,055	440	365	270	Divorcé(e)	48
215	355	935	280	325	125	Veuf ou veuve	49
						selon l'union libre	
5,195	3,980	6,585	5,620	5,980	4,490	Ne vivant pas en union libre	50
390	435	690	365	255	280	Vivant en union libre	51
7,180	**5,275**	**8,360**	**7,555**	**7,965**	**6,505**	**Population totale – Données-échantillon (20 %) (4)**	52
						selon la langue maternelle	
7,080	5,215	8,290	7,480	7,845	6,460	Réponses uniques	53
6,305	4,545	6,935	5,965	6,785	5,840	Anglais	54
70	120	135	85	110	80	Français	55
705	550	1,220	1,435	950	530	Langues non officielles (5)	56
45	15	115	110	40	50	Chinois, n.d.a.	57
-	10	10	35	20	55	Cantonais	58
10	-	-	225	40	10	Pendjabi	59
25	25	15	70	130	10	Mandarin	60
10	15	25	45	40	-	Tagalog (pilipino)	61
615	485	1,060	955	675	415	Autres langues (6)	62
95	55	75	65	125	45	Réponses multiples	63
30	-	-	10	20	30	Anglais et français	64
65	45	70	55	105	20	Anglais et langue non officielle	65
-	-	-	-	-	-	Français et langue non officielle	66
-	-	-	-	-	-	Anglais, français et langue non officielle	67

See reference material at the end of the publication. – Voir les documents de référence à la fin de la publication.

Table 1. Selected Characteristics for Census Tracts, 2001 Census – 100% Data and 20% Sample Data

No.	Characteristics	Vancouver 0502.01 A	Vancouver 0502.02	Vancouver 0502.03	Vancouver 0502.04 A	Vancouver 0502.05 ◇	Vancouver 0503.01 A
	POPULATION CHARACTERISTICS						
	by home language						
68	Single responses	2,440	3,780	4,995	7,905	2,375	2,270
69	English	2,435	3,775	4,920	7,605	2,370	2,240
70	French	-	-	-	-	-	-
71	Non-official languages (5)	-	10	70	305	10	35
72	Cantonese	-	-	-	-	-	-
73	Chinese, n.o.s.	-	-	-	75	-	-
74	Punjabi	-	-	-	-	10	-
75	Mandarin	-	-	-	80	-	-
76	Korean	-	-	10	105	-	25
77	Other languages (6)	-	-	60	45	-	10
78	Multiple responses	75	180	190	490	115	320
79	English and French	15	20	40	45	10	35
80	English and non-official language	55	165	145	440	95	270
81	French and non-official language	-	-	-	-	-	-
82	English, French and non-official language	-	-	10	-	-	15
	by knowledge of official languages						
83	English only	2,345	3,705	4,795	7,900	2,275	2,465
84	French only	-	-	-	20	-	-
85	English and French	160	255	360	400	210	120
86	Neither English nor French	-	-	25	75	10	15
	by knowledge of non-official languages (5) (7)						
87	Cantonese	-	-	-	15	-	-
88	Chinese, n.o.s.	15	-	-	70	-	45
89	Punjabi	-	85	15	75	15	-
90	Mandarin	-	-	10	120	-	-
91	Hindi	-	15	-	40	10	-
92	German	55	80	115	240	135	50
93	Spanish	10	65	30	90	30	150
	by first official language spoken						
94	English	2,490	3,895	5,110	8,215	2,465	2,540
95	French	20	70	45	95	20	40
96	English and French	-	-	-	10	-	-
97	Neither English nor French	-	-	25	75	10	15
98	Official language minority - (number) (8)	20	70	45	100	20	45
99	Official language minority - (percentage) (8)	0.8	1.8	0.9	1.2	0.8	1.7
	by ethnic origin (9)						
100	English	1,285	1,445	2,210	3,150	875	885
101	Canadian	810	1,175	1,535	2,500	750	760
102	Chinese	45	-	10	120	25	45
103	Scottish	580	850	1,535	1,910	690	500
104	Irish	370	685	840	1,620	490	335
105	German	390	600	695	1,170	485	355
106	East Indian	-	95	10	85	15	40
107	French	210	450	635	680	230	285
108	Ukrainian	115	230	350	545	110	125
109	Italian	45	130	185	265	135	140
110	Dutch (Netherlands)	240	375	470	825	180	175
111	Filipino	10	20	-	20	-	40
112	Polish	95	95	140	230	115	110
113	Norwegian	15	130	195	330	55	75
114	North American Indian	110	45	130	120	50	85
	by Aboriginal identity						
115	Total Aboriginal identity population (10)	110	60	80	155	55	90
116	Total non-Aboriginal population	2,395	3,900	5,100	8,245	2,440	2,505
	by Aboriginal origin						
117	Total Aboriginal origins population (11)	130	70	245	185	60	110
118	Total non-Aboriginal population	2,385	3,895	4,935	8,210	2,440	2,480
	by Registered Indian status						
119	Registered Indian (12)	55	-	-	80	-	35
120	Not a Registered Indian	2,455	3,955	5,180	8,315	2,495	2,555

Tableau 1. Certaines caractéristiques des secteurs de recensement, recensement de 2001 – Données intégrales et données-échantillon (20 %)

Vancouver 0503.03 A	Vancouver 0503.04 A	Vancouver 0503.05 A	Vancouver 0504.01 A	Vancouver 0504.02	Vancouver 0504.03	Caractéristiques	N°
						CARACTÉRISTIQUES DE LA POPULATION	
						selon la langue parlée à la maison	
6,755	5,035	7,615	6,745	7,495	6,185	Réponses uniques	68
6,665	4,905	7,325	6,320	7,235	6,075	Anglais	69
-	-	-	25	25	10	Français	70
95	135	285	400	235	95	Langues non officielles (5)	71
-	-	10	20	-	25	Cantonais	72
-	-	25	50	35	25	Chinois, n.d.a.	73
-	-	-	105	20	-	Pendjabi	74
10	10	-	30	75	-	Mandarin	75
-	25	135	70	55	-	Coréen	76
90	100	125	125	45	45	Autres langues (6)	77
420	235	745	805	470	315	Réponses multiples	78
40	55	65	25	25	95	Anglais et français	79
360	170	670	780	435	220	Anglais et langue non officielle	80
-	10	-	-	-	-	Français et langue non officielle	81
20	-	10	-	10	-	Anglais, français et langue non officielle	82
						selon la connaissance des langues officielles	
6,750	4,910	7,805	7,040	7,400	6,070	Anglais seulement	83
-	-	-	30	-	10	Français seulement	84
420	335	420	385	465	410	Anglais et français	85
10	30	140	110	100	20	Ni l'anglais ni le français	86
						selon la connaissance des langues non officielles (5) (7)	
-	10	15	35	45	55	Cantonais	87
60	15	105	110	60	80	Chinois, n.d.a.	88
10	10	10	225	165	10	Pendjabi	89
50	50	90	90	145	25	Mandarin	90
20	25	10	60	55	25	Hindi	91
235	160	200	275	185	185	Allemand	92
105	100	190	80	15	65	Espagnol	93
						selon la première langue officielle parlée	
7,095	5,145	8,080	7,330	7,765	6,410	Anglais	94
65	95	135	85	95	80	Français	95
-	-	10	30	15	-	Anglais et français	96
10	30	140	105	85	10	Ni l'anglais ni le français	97
70	95	140	100	105	80	Minorité de langue officielle - (nombre) (8)	98
1.0	1.8	1.7	1.3	1.3	1.2	Minorité de langue officielle - (pourcentage) (8)	99
						selon l'origine ethnique (9)	
2,645	2,090	2,540	2,340	3,035	2,680	Anglais	100
2,330	1,445	2,440	2,005	2,360	2,290	Canadien	101
175	85	225	225	265	170	Chinois	102
1,795	1,420	1,810	1,385	1,810	1,845	Écossais	103
1,290	930	1,380	1,220	1,210	1,575	Irlandais	104
1,425	885	1,030	1,235	1,255	1,280	Allemand	105
50	35	40	335	245	55	Indien de l'Inde	106
745	530	1,110	770	775	825	Français	107
485	325	360	380	565	505	Ukrainien	108
405	185	165	210	170	150	Italien	109
615	445	495	585	550	580	Hollandais (Néerlandais)	110
35	50	65	75	65	-	Philippin	111
245	175	235	270	195	200	Polonais	112
415	165	270	205	240	175	Norvégien	113
190	140	375	215	170	125	Indien de l'Amérique du Nord	114
						selon l'identité autochtone	
175	105	375	155	170	50	Total de la population ayant une identité autochtone (10)	115
7,000	5,170	7,990	7,400	7,795	6,450	Total de la population non autochtone	116
						selon l'origine autochtone	
240	235	550	295	230	195	Total de la population ayant une origine autochtone (11)	117
6,935	5,040	7,815	7,260	7,740	6,305	Total de la population non autochtone	118
						selon le statut d'Indien inscrit	
35	35	110	80	90	15	Oui, Indien inscrit (12)	119
7,140	5,240	8,250	7,475	7,880	6,485	Non, pas un Indien inscrit	120

Table 1. Selected Characteristics for Census Tracts, 2001 Census – 100% Data and 20% Sample Data

No.	Characteristics	Vancouver 0502.01 A	Vancouver 0502.02	Vancouver 0502.03	Vancouver 0502.04 A	Vancouver 0502.05 ◇	Vancouver 0503.01 A
	POPULATION CHARACTERISTICS						
	by visible minority groups						
121	Total visible minority population	95	115	105	585	125	335
122	Chinese	45	-	15	200	30	45
123	South Asian	-	95	15	75	25	30
124	Black	25	-	-	30	-	10
125	Filipino	10	10	10	25	-	20
126	Latin American	-	-	-	15	-	130
127	Southeast Asian	15	10	15	100	20	-
128	Arab	-	-	-	-	-	-
129	West Asian	-	-	10	-	-	-
130	Korean	-	-	10	105	30	30
131	Japanese	-	-	10	35	15	45
132	Visible minority, n.i.e. (13)	-	-	10	-	-	-
133	Multiple visible minorities (14)	-	-	10	10	-	25
	by citizenship						
134	Canadian citizenship (15)	2,455	3,835	4,960	7,930	2,380	2,475
135	Citizenship other than Canadian	50	125	220	470	115	120
	by place of birth of respondent						
136	Non-immigrant population	2,215	3,515	4,555	6,850	2,080	2,065
137	Born in province of residence	1,625	2,435	3,330	4,895	1,540	1,545
138	Immigrant population (16)	280	410	600	1,425	410	525
139	United States	55	50	30	120	35	20
140	Central and South America	15	10	10	25	10	135
141	Caribbean and Bermuda	10	-	-	-	-	-
142	United Kingdom	85	110	220	505	120	110
143	Other Europe (17)	80	200	255	395	160	155
144	Africa	-	-	15	15	-	10
145	Asia and the Middle East	40	40	45	345	55	85
146	Oceania and other (18)	-	10	25	30	20	15
147	Non-permanent residents (19)	10	35	25	120	10	-
148	**Total immigrant population**	**285**	**410**	**600**	**1,425**	**405**	**525**
	by period of immigration						
149	Before 1961	50	165	120	415	175	65
150	1961-1970	85	100	170	285	95	55
151	1971-1980	40	135	170	155	80	60
152	1981-1990	75	10	40	185	50	245
153	1991-2001 (20)	35	-	95	390	15	100
154	1991-1995	30	-	45	185	10	65
155	1996-2001 (20)	-	-	50	205	10	40
	by age at immigration						
156	0-4 years	60	30	80	190	50	115
157	5-19 years	50	120	190	485	110	145
158	20 years and over	170	255	335	755	250	265
159	**Total population**	**2,505**	**3,960**	**5,180**	**8,395**	**2,490**	**2,595**
	by religion						
160	Catholic (21)	235	525	930	1,145	380	435
161	Protestant	1,190	1,815	1,755	3,685	935	830
162	Christian Orthodox	20	30	90	10	-	60
163	Christian, n.i.e. (22)	175	200	195	910	135	315
164	Muslim	-	-	10	-	-	-
165	Jewish	-	100	60	-	-	10
166	Buddhist	-	-	25	85	-	10
167	Hindu	-	-	-	30	-	-
168	Sikh	-	80	15	35	15	-
169	Eastern religions (23)	-	-	10	-	-	-
170	Other religions (24)	-	-	15	-	15	-
171	No religious affiliation (25)	880	1,210	2,075	2,485	1,015	945
172	**Total population 15 years and over**	**1,920**	**3,385**	**3,995**	**6,610**	**1,980**	**1,970**
	by generation status						
173	1st generation (26)	285	450	605	1,480	410	495
174	2nd generation (27)	590	1,185	950	1,750	535	445
175	3rd generation and over (28)	1,040	1,755	2,445	3,375	1,035	1,030
176	**Total population 1 year and over (29)**	**2,495**	**3,940**	**5,130**	**8,300**	**2,475**	**2,570**
	by place of residence 1 year ago (mobility)						
177	Non-movers	2,215	3,455	4,520	7,020	2,105	2,420
178	Movers	285	480	605	1,285	365	150
179	Non-migrants	145	275	365	715	95	60
180	Migrants	135	210	245	570	270	90
181	Internal migrants	125	195	210	485	250	55
182	Intraprovincial migrants	105	190	210	440	240	35
183	Interprovincial migrants	20	-	-	45	-	20
184	External migrants	10	10	30	85	20	30

Tableau 1. Certaines caractéristiques des secteurs de recensement, recensement de 2001 – Données intégrales et données-échantillon (20 %)

Vancouver 0503.03 A	Vancouver 0503.04 A	Vancouver 0503.05 A	Vancouver 0504.01 A	Vancouver 0504.02	Vancouver 0504.03	Caractéristiques	N°
						CARACTÉRISTIQUES DE LA POPULATION	
						selon les groupes de minorités visibles	
450	410	850	1,135	1,045	385	Total de la population des minorités visibles	121
130	60	155	270	280	170	Chinois	122
55	40	15	315	280	65	Sud-Asiatique	123
30	50	55	40	20	25	Noir	124
35	50	50	80	65	-	Philippin	125
10	60	110	40	-	15	Latino-Américain	126
20	50	125	55	30	30	Asiatique du Sud-Est	127
20	-	-	-	10	10	Arabe	128
10	15	45	-	25	15	Asiatique occidental	129
55	50	190	220	200	20	Coréen	130
60	10	20	105	100	45	Japonais	131
-	10	10	-	30	-	Minorité visible, n.i.a. (13)	132
25	10	75	10	10	-	Minorités visibles multiples (14)	133
						selon la citoyenneté	
6,825	5,050	7,810	7,090	7,550	6,260	Citoyenneté canadienne (15)	134
355	220	545	460	420	240	Citoyenneté autre que canadienne	135
						selon le lieu de naissance du répondant	
6,160	4,625	6,715	5,945	6,500	5,635	Population non immigrante	136
4,310	2,905	3,995	4,250	4,340	4,235	Née dans la province de résidence	137
1,005	585	1,515	1,465	1,385	855	Population immigrante (16)	138
170	35	90	60	65	75	États-Unis	139
15	55	95	20	35	25	Amérique centrale et du Sud	140
10	-	20	-	15	10	Caraïbes et Bermudes	141
260	125	340	335	280	270	Royaume-Uni	142
245	115	465	420	285	260	Autre Europe (17)	143
30	15	15	30	80	55	Afrique	144
250	210	460	580	580	135	Asie et Moyen-Orient	145
25	25	25	20	45	25	Océanie et autre (18)	146
15	60	130	140	80	15	Résidents non permanents (19)	147
1,005	**585**	**1,515**	**1,470**	**1,390**	**855**	**Population immigrante totale**	148
						selon la période d'immigration	
195	160	435	250	260	180	Avant 1961	149
155	60	180	340	160	135	1961-1970	150
245	100	270	275	205	205	1971-1980	151
205	120	155	265	260	130	1981-1990	152
210	145	480	350	500	200	1991-2001 (20)	153
85	55	95	230	275	55	1991-1995	154
120	90	385	120	225	145	1996-2001 (20)	155
						selon l'âge à l'immigration	
150	50	175	155	160	90	0-4 ans	156
335	175	420	385	430	315	5-19 ans	157
520	355	925	925	805	450	20 ans et plus	158
7,175	**5,275**	**8,360**	**7,550**	**7,965**	**6,500**	**Population totale**	159
						selon la religion	
1,195	865	1,415	1,130	1,360	990	Catholique (21)	160
2,375	1,820	3,115	2,570	3,265	2,735	Protestante	161
30	35	30	100	40	15	Orthodoxe chrétienne	162
590	380	660	640	505	425	Chrétiennes, n.i.a. (22)	163
25	35	100	-	40	35	Musulmane	164
-	10	25	20	-	-	Juive	165
15	65	190	145	130	25	Bouddhiste	166
25	10	-	-	20	20	Hindoue	167
40	10	-	230	200	15	Sikh	168
30	25	-	-	15	-	Religions orientales (23)	169
25	10	30	15	10	20	Autres religions (24)	170
2,825	2,005	2,790	2,695	2,385	2,220	Aucune appartenance religieuse (25)	171
5,605	**4,355**	**7,130**	**5,975**	**6,150**	**4,745**	**Population totale de 15 ans et plus**	172
						selon le statut des générations	
965	640	1,560	1,540	1,380	835	1re génération (26)	173
1,415	1,355	1,910	1,595	1,730	1,080	2e génération (27)	174
3,215	2,365	3,660	2,835	3,040	2,840	3e génération et plus (28)	175
7,120	**5,220**	**8,275**	**7,475**	**7,850**	**6,390**	**Population totale de 1 an et plus (29)**	176
						selon le lieu de résidence 1 an auparavant (mobilité)	
6,445	4,005	5,990	6,505	6,720	5,685	Personnes n'ayant pas déménagé	177
675	1,215	2,285	965	1,125	705	Personnes ayant déménagé	178
295	650	1,085	485	545	195	Non-migrants	179
390	565	1,195	485	585	515	Migrants	180
360	515	1,045	380	535	475	Migrants internes	181
320	440	925	330	460	455	Migrants infraprovinciaux	182
40	75	120	45	70	20	Migrants interprovinciaux	183
20	50	155	105	55	40	Migrants externes	184

Table 1. Selected Characteristics for Census Tracts, 2001 Census – 100% Data and 20% Sample Data

No.	Characteristics	Vancouver 0502.01 A	Vancouver 0502.02	Vancouver 0502.03	Vancouver 0502.04 A	Vancouver 0502.05 ◇	Vancouver 0503.01 A
	POPULATION CHARACTERISTICS						
185	**Total population 5 years and over (30)**	**2,340**	**3,840**	**4,880**	**7,940**	**2,370**	**2,400**
	by place of residence 5 years ago (mobility)						
186	Non-movers	1,530	2,595	3,205	3,690	1,485	1,555
187	Movers	810	1,250	1,675	4,250	885	845
188	Non-migrants	385	550	915	2,035	280	375
189	Migrants	425	700	755	2,215	610	475
190	Internal migrants	405	675	660	1,895	585	430
191	Intraprovincial migrants	380	605	605	1,605	565	425
192	Interprovincial migrants	20	75	60	285	20	10
193	External migrants	20	25	95	315	20	45
194	**Total population 15 to 24 years**	**350**	**515**	**790**	**1,310**	**285**	**365**
	by school attendance						
195	Not attending school	195	190	270	505	130	185
196	Attending school full time	140	245	395	655	150	165
197	Attending school part time	15	80	125	150	10	20
198	**Total population 15 years and over**	**1,920**	**3,385**	**3,995**	**6,610**	**1,980**	**1,970**
	by highest level of schooling						
199	Less than grade 9 (31)	35	205	130	235	65	110
200	Grades 9-13 without high school graduation certificate	585	920	895	1,545	415	470
201	Grades 9-13 with high school graduation certificate	290	595	665	925	375	310
202	Some postsecondary without degree, certificate or diploma (32)	245	380	565	940	310	235
203	Trades certificate or diploma (33)	310	455	610	865	295	335
204	College certificate or diploma (34)	210	535	775	1,050	230	270
205	University certificate below bachelor's degree	40	60	50	310	15	40
206	University with bachelor's degree or higher	200	235	305	735	275	215
	by combinations of unpaid work						
207	Males 15 years and over	920	1,670	2,010	3,160	990	1,005
208	Reported unpaid work (35)	885	1,475	1,820	2,815	890	875
209	Housework and child care and care or assistance to seniors	85	160	170	285	100	60
210	Housework and child care only	270	375	590	880	200	300
211	Housework and care or assistance to seniors only	80	115	135	285	105	50
212	Child care and care or assistance to seniors only	-	-	-	-	-	-
213	Housework only	425	810	900	1,355	475	460
214	Child care only	20	-	10	10	10	-
215	Care or assistance to seniors only	-	10	-	10	10	-
216	Females 15 years and over	1,000	1,720	1,985	3,445	990	965
217	Reported unpaid work (35)	930	1,575	1,880	3,235	960	910
218	Housework and child care and care or assistance to seniors	170	250	220	585	145	95
219	Housework and child care only	275	385	700	965	300	330
220	Housework and care or assistance to seniors only	85	155	220	315	110	100
221	Child care and care or assistance to seniors only	-	-	-	-	-	-
222	Housework only	380	770	735	1,335	410	380
223	Child care only	20	10	-	20	-	10
224	Care or assistance to seniors only	-	10	10	20	-	-
	by labour force activity						
225	Males 15 years and over	920	1,670	2,005	3,155	990	1,000
226	In the labour force	735	1,110	1,675	2,450	815	765
227	Employed	705	1,080	1,565	2,325	765	685
228	Unemployed	20	35	105	125	45	75
229	Not in the labour force	190	560	340	705	175	240
230	Participation rate	79.9	66.5	83.5	77.7	82.3	76.5
231	Employment rate	76.6	64.7	78.1	73.7	77.3	68.5
232	Unemployment rate	2.7	3.2	6.3	5.1	5.5	9.8
233	Females 15 years and over	1,000	1,715	1,985	3,450	990	970
234	In the labour force	645	950	1,545	2,270	670	650
235	Employed	640	875	1,470	2,150	650	630
236	Unemployed	10	75	75	115	20	25
237	Not in the labour force	355	765	440	1,180	320	310
238	Participation rate	64.5	55.4	77.8	65.8	67.7	67.0
239	Employment rate	64.0	51.0	74.1	62.3	65.7	64.9
240	Unemployment rate	1.6	7.9	4.9	5.1	3.0	3.8

Tableau 1. Certaines caractéristiques des secteurs de recensement, recensement de 2001 – Données intégrales et données-échantillon (20 %)

Vancouver 0503.03 A	Vancouver 0503.04 A	Vancouver 0503.05 A	Vancouver 0504.01 A	Vancouver 0504.02	Vancouver 0504.03	Caractéristiques	N°
						CARACTÉRISTIQUES DE LA POPULATION	
6,735	**4,950**	**7,895**	**7,105**	**7,460**	**5,995**	**Population totale de 5 ans et plus (30)**	185
						selon le lieu de résidence 5 ans auparavant (mobilité)	
4,390	1,945	2,600	4,410	3,420	3,275	Personnes n'ayant pas déménagé	186
2,345	3,000	5,300	2,695	4,040	2,720	Personnes ayant déménagé	187
1,100	1,440	2,010	1,100	1,515	1,040	Non-migrants	188
1,245	1,565	3,290	1,590	2,525	1,685	Migrants	189
1,120	1,400	2,755	1,440	2,220	1,565	Migrants internes	190
1,000	1,205	2,380	1,220	1,905	1,330	Migrants infraprovinciaux	191
125	190	375	220	310	235	Migrants interprovinciaux	192
120	165	535	150	310	120	Migrants externes	193
1,155	**720**	**1,005**	**1,105**	**945**	**905**	**Population totale de 15 à 24 ans**	194
						selon la fréquentation scolaire	
435	355	510	315	320	365	Ne fréquentant pas l'école	195
540	295	375	610	580	470	Fréquentant l'école à plein temps	196
180	70	115	175	45	75	Fréquentant l'école à temps partiel	197
5,600	**4,355**	**7,125**	**5,975**	**6,150**	**4,750**	**Population totale de 15 ans et plus**	198
						selon le plus haut niveau de scolarité atteint	
105	320	615	315	170	75	Niveau inférieur à la 9e année (31)	199
1,300	1,260	2,050	1,430	1,330	950	De la 9e à la 13e année sans certificat d'études secondaires	200
850	595	800	765	860	810	De la 9e à la 13e année avec certificat d'études secondaires	201
810	575	940	880	825	750	Études postsecondaires partielles sans grade, certificat ou diplôme (32)	202
790	640	920	895	725	500	Certificat ou diplôme d'une école de métiers (33)	203
980	580	1,120	860	1,205	940	Certificat ou diplôme collégial (34)	204
155	85	135	200	150	140	Certificat universitaire inférieur au baccalauréat	205
610	285	550	625	880	590	Études universitaires avec baccalauréat ou diplôme supérieur	206
						selon les combinaisons de travail non rémunéré	
2,775	2,030	3,160	2,935	2,970	2,335	Hommes de 15 ans et plus	207
2,545	1,800	2,645	2,715	2,665	2,100	Travail non rémunéré déclaré (35)	208
215	70	95	290	180	230	Travaux ménagers et soins aux enfants et soins ou aide aux personnes âgées	209
835	470	705	815	960	755	Travaux ménagers et soins aux enfants seulement	210
205	130	250	270	190	105	Travaux ménagers et soins ou aide aux personnes âgées seulement	211
-	-	-	-	10	-	Soins aux enfants et soins ou aide aux personnes âgées seulement	212
1,280	1,120	1,570	1,310	1,270	990	Travaux ménagers seulement	213
20	-	20	30	35	10	Soins aux enfants seulement	214
-	-	-	10	20	-	Soins ou aide aux personnes âgées seulement	215
2,830	2,325	3,970	3,040	3,180	2,410	Femmes de 15 ans et plus	216
2,695	2,205	3,520	2,820	3,015	2,285	Travail non rémunéré déclaré (35)	217
305	115	215	410	370	375	Travaux ménagers et soins aux enfants et soins ou aide aux personnes âgées	218
1,075	690	1,085	900	1,125	895	Travaux ménagers et soins aux enfants seulement	219
195	210	365	305	285	165	Travaux ménagers et soins ou aide aux personnes âgées seulement	220
-	-	-	-	-	-	Soins aux enfants et soins ou aide aux personnes âgées seulement	221
1,090	1,190	1,835	1,185	1,215	850	Travaux ménagers seulement	222
30	10	10	-	15	-	Soins aux enfants seulement	223
-	-	20	10	10	-	Soins ou aide aux personnes âgées seulement	224
						selon l'activité	
2,775	2,030	3,160	2,930	2,970	2,335	Hommes de 15 ans et plus	225
2,305	1,345	2,130	2,200	2,175	1,940	Population active	226
2,200	1,220	1,960	2,110	2,075	1,895	Personnes occupées	227
105	125	165	85	100	45	Chômeurs	228
465	685	1,025	735	800	395	Inactifs	229
83.1	66.3	67.4	75.1	73.2	83.1	Taux d'activité	230
79.3	60.1	62.0	72.0	69.9	81.2	Taux d'emploi	231
4.6	9.3	7.7	3.9	4.6	2.3	Taux de chômage	232
2,830	2,325	3,965	3,040	3,175	2,410	Femmes de 15 ans et plus	233
2,005	1,380	1,970	1,985	2,070	1,770	Population active	234
1,885	1,265	1,785	1,885	1,955	1,685	Personnes occupées	235
120	110	180	105	120	85	Chômeuses	236
825	950	1,995	1,055	1,105	640	Inactives	237
70.8	59.4	49.7	65.3	65.2	73.4	Taux d'activité	238
66.6	54.4	45.0	62.0	61.6	69.9	Taux d'emploi	239
6.0	8.0	9.1	5.3	5.8	4.8	Taux de chômage	240

Table 1. Selected Characteristics for Census Tracts, 2001 Census – 100% Data and 20% Sample Data

No.	Characteristics	Vancouver 0502.01 A	Vancouver 0502.02	Vancouver 0502.03	Vancouver 0502.04 A	Vancouver 0502.05 ◇	Vancouver 0503.01 A
	POPULATION CHARACTERISTICS						
	by labour force activity – concluded						
241	Both sexes - Participation rate	71.6	60.9	80.6	71.3	75.0	72.1
242	15-24 years	62.9	69.9	74.1	69.1	65.5	57.5
243	25 years and over	73.2	59.1	82.2	72.0	76.6	75.4
244	Both sexes - Employment rate	70.3	57.6	76.0	67.8	71.2	67.0
245	15-24 years	61.4	62.1	65.2	63.2	55.2	41.1
246	25 years and over	72.0	57.0	78.6	68.9	74.0	72.9
247	Both sexes - Unemployment rate	1.8	5.3	5.8	5.2	4.7	7.0
248	15-24 years	4.5	11.1	12.1	8.3	18.9	31.0
249	25 years and over	1.7	3.8	4.2	4.3	3.1	3.3
250	**Total labour force 15 years and over**	**1,375**	**2,060**	**3,215**	**4,720**	**1,485**	**1,420**
	by industry based on the 1997 NAICS						
251	Industry - Not applicable (36)	15	50	65	40	30	45
252	All industries (37)	1,360	2,015	3,155	4,675	1,450	1,375
253	11 Agriculture, forestry, fishing and hunting	30	75	60	100	220	10
254	21 Mining and oil and gas extraction	-	-	-	25	-	-
255	22 Utilities	15	10	15	30	15	10
256	23 Construction	90	205	355	395	160	75
257	31-33 Manufacturing	155	185	345	450	105	205
258	41 Wholesale trade	75	155	200	230	60	100
259	44-45 Retail trade	190	295	450	565	180	125
260	48-49 Transportation and warehousing	130	165	255	225	90	150
261	51 Information and cultural industries	70	50	100	115	30	20
262	52 Finance and insurance	65	75	120	230	10	85
263	53 Real estate and rental and leasing	10	20	35	85	30	15
264	54 Professional, scientific and technical services	65	60	200	260	95	60
265	55 Management of companies and enterprises	-	-	-	10	-	-
266	56 Administrative and support, waste management and remediation services	30	90	100	150	50	40
267	61 Educational services	105	115	185	460	90	120
268	62 Health care and social assistance	90	175	195	375	75	110
269	71 Arts, entertainment and recreation	15	35	60	95	70	45
270	72 Accommodation and food services	65	85	165	380	50	75
271	81 Other services (except public administration)	75	95	195	245	90	50
272	91 Public administration	75	125	125	260	40	80
	by class of worker						
273	Class of worker - Not applicable (36)	15	45	65	40	30	45
274	All classes of worker (37)	1,355	2,015	3,155	4,680	1,450	1,375
275	Paid workers	1,245	1,805	2,810	4,215	1,190	1,270
276	Employees	1,195	1,690	2,645	3,885	1,015	1,250
277	Self-employed (incorporated)	55	115	165	335	175	25
278	Self-employed (unincorporated)	105	195	330	445	255	105
279	Unpaid family workers	10	15	10	20	10	-
	by occupation based on the 2001 NOC-S						
280	Male labour force 15 years and over	730	1,110	1,670	2,455	810	770
281	Occupation - Not applicable (36)	10	15	30	25	20	30
282	All occupations (37)	720	1,095	1,645	2,430	795	735
283	A Management occupations	95	225	250	400	130	80
284	B Business, finance and administration occupations	70	85	85	155	20	80
285	C Natural and applied sciences and related occupations	40	40	100	225	100	40
286	D Health occupations	10	10	-	25	35	-
287	E Occupations in social science, education, government service and religion	45	25	65	115	35	30
288	F Occupations in art, culture, recreation and sport	15	30	45	20	15	15
289	G Sales and service occupations	90	215	300	595	100	120
290	H Trades, transport and equipment operators and related occupations	300	355	600	740	250	265
291	I Occupations unique to primary industry	15	75	100	65	95	-
292	J Occupations unique to processing, manufacturing and utilities	50	45	105	90	15	90
293	Female labour force 15 years and over	640	950	1,545	2,265	675	650
294	Occupation - Not applicable (36)	-	35	40	15	10	15
295	All occupations (37)	635	915	1,510	2,250	660	640
296	A Management occupations	35	80	160	170	80	55
297	B Business, finance and administration occupations	225	290	550	745	215	270
298	C Natural and applied sciences and related occupations	20	-	45	10	20	10
299	D Health occupations	55	90	90	195	30	60

Tableau 1. Certaines caractéristiques des secteurs de recensement, recensement de 2001 – Données intégrales et données-échantillon (20 %)

Vancouver 0503.03 A	Vancouver 0503.04 A	Vancouver 0503.05 A	Vancouver 0504.01 A	Vancouver 0504.02	Vancouver 0504.03	Caractéristiques	N°
						CARACTÉRISTIQUES DE LA POPULATION	
						selon l'activité – fin	
77.0	62.6	57.5	70.0	69.0	78.2	Les deux sexes - Taux d'activité	241
71.3	63.9	65.3	68.8	69.3	70.2	15-24 ans	242
78.3	62.3	56.3	70.4	68.9	80.1	25 ans et plus	243
72.9	57.1	52.7	66.9	65.4	75.4	Les deux sexes - Taux d'emploi	244
65.2	54.2	57.4	60.8	60.3	65.7	15-24 ans	245
74.9	57.7	51.9	68.2	66.4	77.5	25 ans et plus	246
5.1	9.0	8.5	4.5	5.2	3.5	Les deux sexes - Taux de chômage	247
8.5	14.0	12.1	11.2	12.9	6.3	15-24 ans	248
4.3	7.7	7.7	2.9	3.6	3.1	25 ans et plus	249
4,310	**2,730**	**4,100**	**4,185**	**4,240**	**3,710**	**Population active totale de 15 ans et plus**	250
						selon l'industrie basée sur le SCIAN de 1997	
45	65	100	40	45	25	Industrie - Sans objet (36)	251
4,270	2,660	4,005	4,140	4,200	3,690	Toutes les industries (37)	252
70	70	70	165	55	55	11 Agriculture, foresterie, pêche et chasse	253
10	-	10	-	-	-	21 Extraction minière et extraction de pétrole et de gaz	254
15	-	-	20	55	30	22 Services publics	255
320	170	290	340	245	215	23 Construction	256
540	365	530	420	435	425	31-33 Fabrication	257
300	280	285	280	280	275	41 Commerce de gros	258
585	360	550	545	635	530	44-45 Commerce de détail	259
250	165	240	315	255	200	48-49 Transport et entreposage	260
150	45	125	155	175	105	51 Industrie de l'information et industrie culturelle	261
170	45	95	145	225	210	52 Finance et assurances	262
65	35	90	50	70	45	53 Services immobiliers et services de location et de location à bail	263
215	135	175	210	280	200	54 Services professionnels, scientifiques et techniques	264
-	-	-	-	15	-	55 Gestion de sociétés et d'entreprises	265
155	110	205	125	95	155	56 Services administratifs, services de soutien, services de gestion des déchets et services d'assainissement	266
295	130	155	205	275	250	61 Services d'enseignement	267
375	215	380	315	330	320	62 Soins de santé et assistance sociale	268
75	60	55	90	95	100	71 Arts, spectacles et loisirs	269
295	215	345	255	200	280	72 Hébergement et services de restauration	270
240	155	285	255	175	125	81 Autres services, sauf les administrations publiques	271
155	90	125	240	305	170	91 Administrations publiques	272
						selon la catégorie de travailleurs	
45	65	95	45	45	25	Catégorie de travailleurs - Sans objet (36)	273
4,270	2,655	4,005	4,140	4,200	3,685	Toutes les catégories de travailleurs (37)	274
3,815	2,500	3,650	3,725	3,805	3,360	Travailleurs rémunérés	275
3,680	2,440	3,585	3,445	3,585	3,155	Employés	276
140	60	65	280	220	200	Travailleurs autonomes (entreprise constituée en société)	277
445	155	315	400	370	320	Travailleurs autonomes (entreprise non constituée en société)	278
10	-	45	15	20	10	Travailleurs familiaux non rémunérés	279
						selon la profession basée sur la CNP-S de 2001	
2,305	1,345	2,130	2,195	2,175	1,940	Hommes actifs de 15 ans et plus	280
25	15	55	20	10	10	Profession - Sans objet (36)	281
2,275	1,330	2,080	2,180	2,165	1,930	Toutes les professions (37)	282
330	150	305	330	420	305	A Gestion	283
195	140	160	215	250	200	B Affaires, finance et administration	284
120	100	225	200	195	160	C Sciences naturelles et appliquées et professions apparentées	285
30	-	40	30	50	20	D Secteur de la santé	286
95	45	65	35	80	85	E Sciences sociales, enseignement, administration publique et religion	287
35	20	55	30	70	20	F Arts, culture, sports et loisirs	288
520	285	395	405	530	485	G Ventes et services	289
735	445	650	675	380	495	H Métiers, transport et machinerie	290
55	20	65	130	40	40	I Professions propres au secteur primaire	291
160	120	125	140	150	120	J Transformation, fabrication et services d'utilité publique	292
2,000	1,380	1,970	1,985	2,070	1,770	Femmes actives de 15 ans et plus	293
15	55	45	25	35	15	Profession - Sans objet (36)	294
1,990	1,325	1,925	1,960	2,035	1,755	Toutes les professions (37)	295
140	85	155	150	225	145	A Gestion	296
545	425	530	675	680	635	B Affaires, finance et administration	297
35	-	25	25	15	55	C Sciences naturelles et appliquées et professions apparentées	298
130	55	200	140	130	100	D Secteur de la santé	299

Table 1. Selected Characteristics for Census Tracts, 2001 Census – 100% Data and 20% Sample Data

No.	Characteristics	Vancouver 0502.01 A	Vancouver 0502.02	Vancouver 0502.03	Vancouver 0502.04 A	Vancouver 0502.05 ◇	Vancouver 0503.01 A
	POPULATION CHARACTERISTICS						
	by occupation based on the 2001 NOC-S – concluded						
300	E Occupations in social science, education, government service and religion	35	85	135	255	45	80
301	F Occupations in art, culture, recreation and sport	40	25	35	75	25	10
302	G Sales and service occupations	185	270	450	670	140	140
303	H Trades, transport and equipment operators and related occupations	10	10	10	35	10	10
304	I Occupations unique to primary industry	30	40	20	50	105	10
305	J Occupations unique to processing, manufacturing and utilities	10	20	10	30	-	10
306	**Total employed labour force 15 years and over**	**1,350**	**1,950**	**3,035**	**4,480**	**1,415**	**1,315**
	by place of work						
307	Males	710	1,080	1,560	2,325	765	685
308	Usual place of work	510	750	1,155	1,685	420	535
309	At home	45	75	75	120	165	60
310	Outside Canada	-	-	20	10	-	-
311	No fixed workplace address	160	250	315	510	170	95
312	Females	640	875	1,475	2,150	650	630
313	Usual place of work	540	665	1,140	1,775	395	555
314	At home	55	120	200	230	220	55
315	Outside Canada	-	-	10	15	-	-
316	No fixed workplace address	45	90	130	135	30	25
317	**Total employed labour force 15 years and over with usual place of work or no fixed workplace address**	**1,250**	**1,750**	**2,735**	**4,105**	**1,020**	**1,205**
	by mode of transportation						
318	Males	670	1,000	1,465	2,195	590	630
319	Car, truck, van, as driver	600	935	1,345	1,970	550	565
320	Car, truck, van, as passenger	30	30	75	105	15	45
321	Public transit	15	10	10	35	10	10
322	Walked	25	-	10	40	10	10
323	Other method	-	20	30	40	10	10
324	Females	580	755	1,270	1,905	430	575
325	Car, truck, van, as driver	540	660	1,130	1,640	370	500
326	Car, truck, van, as passenger	30	65	95	165	40	70
327	Public transit	10	10	15	15	-	-
328	Walked	-	-	15	70	20	10
329	Other method	10	10	10	15	-	-
330	**Total population 15 years and over who worked since January 1, 2000**	**1,460**	**2,180**	**3,275**	**5,020**	**1,580**	**1,490**
	by language used at work						
331	Single responses	1,450	2,105	3,205	4,905	1,545	1,410
332	English	1,445	2,105	3,205	4,850	1,550	1,400
333	French	-	-	-	25	-	-
334	Non-official languages (5)	-	-	-	30	-	10
335	Chinese, n.o.s.	-	-	-	-	-	-
336	Cantonese	-	-	-	-	-	-
337	Other languages (6)	-	-	-	30	-	-
338	Multiple responses	10	75	75	115	35	80
339	English and French	10	20	35	40	10	15
340	English and non-official language	-	50	30	75	25	60
341	French and non-official language	-	-	-	-	-	-
342	English, French and non-official language	10	10	-	-	-	10
	DWELLING AND HOUSEHOLD CHARACTERISTICS						
343	**Total number of occupied private dwellings**	**835**	**1,565**	**1,620**	**2,870**	**890**	**835**
	by tenure						
344	Owned	775	1,315	1,475	2,475	670	740
345	Rented	65	250	150	390	220	95
346	Band housing	-	-	-	-	-	-
	by structural type of dwelling						
347	Single-detached house	770	945	1,510	1,715	700	750
348	Semi-detached house	10	-	10	25	10	-
349	Row house	-	-	-	355	-	-
350	Apartment, detached duplex	65	50	85	295	55	85
351	Apartment, building that has five or more storeys	-	-	-	-	-	-
352	Apartment, building that has fewer than five storeys (38)	10	10	-	485	-	-
353	Other single-attached house	-	10	15	-	-	-
354	Movable dwelling (39)	-	555	-	-	125	-

Tableau 1. Certaines caractéristiques des secteurs de recensement, recensement de 2001 – Données intégrales et données-échantillon (20 %)

Vancouver 0503.03 A	Vancouver 0503.04 A	Vancouver 0503.05 A	Vancouver 0504.01 A	Vancouver 0504.02	Vancouver 0504.03	Caractéristiques	N°
						CARACTÉRISTIQUES DE LA POPULATION	
						selon la profession basée sur la CNP-S de 2001 – fin	
290	115	155	180	260	235	E Sciences sociales, enseignement, administration publique et religion	300
65	45	35	65	60	35	F Arts, culture, sports et loisirs	301
700	485	700	610	580	500	G Ventes et services	302
15	30	25	35	40	10	H Métiers, transport et machinerie	303
40	45	45	45	15	45	I Professions propres au secteur primaire	304
30	45	55	25	30	-	J Transformation, fabrication et services d'utilité publique	305
4,085	**2,485**	**3,750**	**4,000**	**4,025**	**3,580**	**Population active occupée totale de 15 ans et plus**	306
						selon le lieu de travail	
2,200	1,220	1,965	2,115	2,075	1,890	Hommes	307
1,640	995	1,500	1,465	1,585	1,555	Lieu habituel de travail	308
175	55	90	140	125	95	À domicile	309
15	10	10	-	35	10	En dehors du Canada	310
370	150	360	505	325	235	Sans adresse de travail fixe	311
1,885	1,270	1,790	1,880	1,950	1,685	Femmes	312
1,675	1,155	1,595	1,500	1,635	1,380	Lieu habituel de travail	313
145	60	105	270	250	210	À domicile	314
15	-	20	-	10	-	En dehors du Canada	315
55	55	70	115	60	85	Sans adresse de travail fixe	316
3,735	**2,355**	**3,525**	**3,580**	**3,605**	**3,265**	**Population active occupée totale de 15 ans et plus ayant un lieu habituel de travail ou sans adresse de travail fixe**	317
						selon le mode de transport	
2,010	1,150	1,855	1,970	1,910	1,795	Hommes	318
1,755	950	1,505	1,685	1,745	1,575	Automobile, camion ou fourgonnette, en tant que conducteur	319
150	45	125	155	45	110	Automobile, camion ou fourgonnette, en tant que passager	320
30	10	60	25	70	40	Transport en commun	321
40	85	70	60	25	35	À pied	322
30	60	95	45	30	40	Autre moyen	323
1,725	1,210	1,665	1,615	1,690	1,470	Femmes	324
1,515	960	1,270	1,335	1,420	1,275	Automobile, camion ou fourgonnette, en tant que conductrice	325
105	100	140	125	165	105	Automobile, camion ou fourgonnette, en tant que passagère	326
50	45	65	75	45	50	Transport en commun	327
45	100	155	50	60	25	À pied	328
10	-	35	30	-	25	Autre moyen	329
4,555	**2,915**	**4,355**	**4,420**	**4,525**	**3,990**	**Population totale de 15 ans et plus ayant travaillé depuis le 1er janvier 2000**	330
						selon la langue utilisée au travail	
4,470	2,845	4,165	4,245	4,430	3,930	Réponses uniques	331
4,470	2,850	4,100	4,235	4,395	3,925	Anglais	332
-	-	-	-	-	-	Français	333
10	-	60	15	35	10	Langues non officielles (5)	334
-	-	20	-	15	-	Chinois, n.d.a.	335
-	-	-	-	-	-	Cantonais	336
-	-	35	15	15	-	Autres langues (6)	337
90	70	195	175	100	55	Réponses multiples	338
35	-	55	35	50	20	Anglais et français	339
50	50	140	140	50	35	Anglais et langue non officielle	340
-	-	-	-	-	-	Français et langue non officielle	341
-	-	-	-	-	-	Anglais, français et langue non officielle	342
						CARACTÉRISTIQUES DES LOGEMENTS ET DES MÉNAGES	
2,350	**2,440**	**4,460**	**2,630**	**2,750**	**2,010**	**Nombre total de logements privés occupés**	343
						selon le mode d'occupation	
2,095	1,270	1,760	2,080	2,485	1,800	Possédé	344
255	1,175	2,700	550	260	215	Loué	345
-	-	-	-	-	-	Logement de bande	346
						selon le type de construction résidentielle	
1,930	240	170	1,930	1,655	1,625	Maison individuelle non attenante	347
40	205	55	10	35	75	Maison jumelée	348
155	360	435	130	390	155	Maison en rangée	349
190	25	100	75	230	90	Appartement, duplex non attenant	350
-	-	-	-	-	-	Appartement, immeuble de cinq étages ou plus	351
35	1,610	3,675	405	375	10	Appartement, immeuble de moins de cinq étages (38)	352
-	-	25	10	-	10	Autre maison individuelle attenante	353
-	-	-	70	70	55	Logement mobile (39)	354

Table 1. Selected Characteristics for Census Tracts, 2001 Census – 100% Data and 20% Sample Data

No.	Characteristics	Vancouver 0502.01 A	Vancouver 0502.02	Vancouver 0502.03	Vancouver 0502.04 A	Vancouver 0502.05 ◇	Vancouver 0503.01 A
	DWELLING AND HOUSEHOLD CHARACTERISTICS						
	by condition of dwelling						
355	Regular maintenance only	575	985	1,080	2,520	550	555
356	Minor repairs	220	465	400	250	255	210
357	Major repairs	40	115	135	100	85	70
	by period of construction						
358	Before 1946	25	50	10	45	70	10
359	1946-1960	50	145	50	85	85	10
360	1961-1970	115	175	230	55	140	115
361	1971-1980	570	530	1,140	215	315	440
362	1981-1990	60	580	145	320	150	220
363	1991-2001 (20)	20	85	45	2,160	130	35
364	Average number of rooms per dwelling	8.0	6.8	8.0	7.5	7.3	7.8
365	Average number of bedrooms per dwelling	3.3	2.8	3.4	3.1	3.0	3.4
366	Average value of dwelling $	220,650	240,534	234,680	263,703	430,026	227,280
367	**Total number of private households**	**835**	**1,565**	**1,625**	**2,875**	**890**	**835**
	by household size						
368	1 person	155	330	170	470	170	105
369	2 persons	215	660	440	965	320	230
370	3 persons	150	190	345	475	135	160
371	4-5 persons	255	365	560	800	225	305
372	6 or more persons	60	25	110	165	45	35
	by household type						
373	One-family households	620	1,135	1,405	2,230	670	675
374	Multiple-family households	40	35	20	75	15	10
375	Non-family households	180	395	195	570	210	145
376	Number of persons in private households	2,510	3,960	5,180	8,400	2,465	2,590
377	Average number of persons in private households	3.0	2.5	3.2	2.9	2.8	3.1
378	Average number of persons per room	0.4	0.4	0.4	0.4	0.4	0.4
379	Tenant households in non-farm, non-reserve private dwellings (40)	60	250	145	390	200	90
380	Average gross rent $ (40)	845	1,105	966	898	914	952
381	Tenant households spending 30% or more of household income on gross rent (40) (41)	20	85	70	145	80	40
382	Tenant households spending from 30% to 99% of household income on gross rent (40) (41)	15	60	50	135	80	20
383	Owner households in non-farm, non-reserve private dwellings (42)	770	1,300	1,480	2,480	520	740
384	Average owner's major payments $ (42)	1,093	771	1,191	1,161	1,144	1,223
385	Owner households spending 30% or more of household income on owner's major payments (41) (42)	135	185	380	545	115	135
386	Owner households spending from 30% to 99% of household income on owner's major payments (41) (42)	115	170	355	510	95	125
	CENSUS FAMILY CHARACTERISTICS						
387	**Total number of census families in private households**	**695**	**1,205**	**1,450**	**2,385**	**695**	**700**
	by census family structure and size						
388	Total couple families	605	1,090	1,270	2,090	640	635
389	Total families of married couples	530	985	1,105	1,945	570	595
390	Without children at home	165	540	315	790	250	175
391	With children at home	355	445	790	1,150	325	425
392	1 child	100	125	210	355	130	120
393	2 children	165	185	355	430	110	195
394	3 or more children	95	135	220	365	90	105
395	Total families of common-law couples	75	105	170	145	65	40
396	Without children at home	30	50	80	105	55	15
397	With children at home	45	55	85	40	15	25
398	1 child	30	20	35	30	10	25
399	2 children	15	25	30	10	-	10
400	3 or more children	-	10	25	10	-	-
401	Total lone-parent families	95	120	180	295	55	60
402	Female parent	70	70	145	220	45	55
403	1 child	60	35	85	115	20	35
404	2 children	10	35	55	65	10	20
405	3 or more children	10	-	10	45	20	-

Tableau 1. Certaines caractéristiques des secteurs de recensement, recensement de 2001 – Données intégrales et données-échantillon (20 %)

Vancouver 0503.03 A	Vancouver 0503.04 A	Vancouver 0503.05 A	Vancouver 0504.01 A	Vancouver 0504.02	Vancouver 0504.03	Caractéristiques	N°
						CARACTÉRISTIQUES DES LOGEMENTS ET DES MÉNAGES	
						selon l'état du logement	
1,545	1,760	3,180	1,795	2,365	1,435	Entretien régulier seulement	355
670	445	815	675	270	490	Réparations mineures	356
135	235	465	160	110	85	Réparations majeures	357
						selon la période de construction	
10	15	85	175	15	10	Avant 1946	358
105	100	110	60	-	40	1946-1960	359
215	230	435	200	50	30	1961-1970	360
1,390	420	1,350	535	225	105	1971-1980	361
545	665	895	1,080	390	1,210	1981-1990	362
85	1,010	1,590	585	2,065	610	1991-2001 (20)	363
7.7	5.1	4.3	7.1	7.6	7.8	Nombre moyen de pièces par logement	364
3.3	2.0	1.7	3.0	3.0	3.2	Nombre moyen de chambres à coucher par logement	365
227,210	149,375	123,230	288,099	240,552	240,086	Valeur moyenne du logement $	366
2,350	**2,440**	**4,465**	**2,625**	**2,750**	**2,010**	**Nombre total de logements privés**	367
						selon la taille du ménage	
300	805	2,080	505	395	205	1 personne	368
690	960	1,485	800	940	515	2 personnes	369
435	335	460	430	435	390	3 personnes	370
830	310	415	750	855	800	4-5 personnes	371
100	40	25	145	120	105	6 personnes ou plus	372
						selon le genre de ménage	
1,885	1,420	2,105	1,950	2,245	1,720	Ménages unifamiliaux	373
55	15	25	70	50	30	Ménages multifamiliaux	374
405	1,005	2,330	605	455	260	Ménages non familiaux	375
7,180	5,255	8,340	7,550	7,960	6,500	Nombre de personnes dans les ménages privés	376
3.1	2.1	1.9	2.9	2.9	3.2	Nombre moyen de personnes dans les ménages privés	377
0.4	0.4	0.4	0.4	0.4	0.4	Nombre moyen de personnes par pièce	378
255	1,170	2,685	535	265	215	Ménages locataires dans les logements privés non agricoles hors réserve (40)	379
950	756	674	998	1,288	915	Loyer brut moyen $ (40)	380
85	520	1,335	225	145	65	Ménages locataires consacrant 30 % ou plus du revenu du ménage au loyer brut (40) (41)	381
65	395	1,080	175	100	50	Ménages locataires consacrant de 30 % à 99 % du revenu du ménage au loyer brut (40) (41)	382
2,090	1,265	1,760	2,015	2,475	1,785	Ménages propriétaires dans les logements privés non agricoles hors réserve (42)	383
1,118	865	792	1,062	1,205	1,287	Principales dépenses de propriété moyennes $ (42)	384
465	315	565	480	425	380	Ménages propriétaires consacrant 30 % ou plus du revenu du ménage aux principales dépenses de propriété (41) (42)	385
430	275	500	405	380	345	Ménages propriétaires consacrant de 30 % à 99 % du revenu du ménage aux principales dépenses de propriété (41) (42)	386
						CARACTÉRISTIQUES DES FAMILLES DE RECENSEMENT	
2,005	**1,460**	**2,160**	**2,100**	**2,345**	**1,785**	**Total des familles de recensement dans les ménages privés**	387
						selon la structure et la taille de la famille de recensement	
1,720	1,070	1,555	1,800	2,120	1,610	Total des familles avec conjoints	388
1,540	850	1,210	1,605	1,985	1,470	Total des familles avec couples mariés	389
480	505	780	635	795	420	Sans enfants à la maison	390
1,055	345	430	970	1,190	1,050	Avec enfants à la maison	391
315	105	165	275	345	285	1 enfant	392
510	160	185	455	585	525	2 enfants	393
230	70	75	240	260	240	3 enfants ou plus	394
180	225	350	190	135	145	Total des familles en union libre	395
105	140	230	115	65	65	Sans enfants à la maison	396
80	85	115	80	70	75	Avec enfants à la maison	397
40	70	60	25	25	35	1 enfant	398
25	10	50	50	45	25	2 enfants	399
15	-	15	-	10	15	3 enfants ou plus	400
285	385	600	305	225	170	Total des familles monoparentales	401
210	330	540	235	180	140	Parent de sexe féminin	402
95	170	320	130	95	50	1 enfant	403
55	105	140	70	60	80	2 enfants	404
60	55	80	35	25	10	3 enfants ou plus	405

Table 1. Selected Characteristics for Census Tracts, 2001 Census – 100% Data and 20% Sample Data

No.	Characteristics	Vancouver 0502.01 A	Vancouver 0502.02	Vancouver 0502.03	Vancouver 0502.04 A	Vancouver 0502.05 ◇	Vancouver 0503.01 A
	CENSUS FAMILY CHARACTERISTICS						
	by census family structure and size – concluded						
406	Male parent	20	50	30	70	15	-
407	1 child	25	40	30	60	-	-
408	2 children	-	10	-	-	-	-
409	3 or more children	-	-	-	10	10	-
410	**Total number of children at home**	**920**	**1,160**	**2,100**	**3,015**	**810**	**980**
	by age groups						
411	Under 6 years	230	150	350	550	175	215
412	6-14 years	360	420	820	1,235	335	370
413	15-17 years	110	150	275	420	105	100
414	18-24 years	165	320	475	680	150	225
415	25 years and over	55	115	185	130	40	60
416	Average number of children at home per census family (43)	1.3	1.0	1.5	1.3	1.2	1.4
417	**Total number of persons in private households**	**2,510**	**3,960**	**5,180**	**8,395**	**2,470**	**2,595**
	by census family status and living arrangements						
418	Number of non-family persons	295	510	360	905	325	280
419	Living with relatives (44)	85	25	30	170	50	70
420	Living with non-relatives only	65	165	160	270	105	105
421	Living alone	155	325	170	465	170	105
422	Number of family persons	2,215	3,450	4,820	7,490	2,140	2,315
423	Average number of persons per census family	3.2	2.9	3.3	3.1	3.1	3.3
424	**Total number of persons 65 years and over**	**245**	**760**	**260**	**890**	**275**	**175**
425	Number of non-family persons 65 years and over	115	220	70	260	95	45
426	Living with relatives (44)	35	10	15	65	30	20
427	Living with non-relatives only	10	-	10	10	-	-
428	Living alone	70	210	50	185	60	25
429	Number of family persons 65 years and over	130	540	190	630	185	130
	ECONOMIC FAMILY CHARACTERISTICS						
430	**Total number of economic families in private households**	**675**	**1,175**	**1,435**	**2,345**	**680**	**715**
	by size of family						
431	2 persons	240	620	480	975	290	225
432	3 persons	130	170	295	445	135	155
433	4 persons	190	235	380	495	155	220
434	5 or more persons	125	150	280	435	105	105
435	Total number of persons in economic families	2,295	3,470	4,850	7,655	2,195	2,380
436	Average number of persons per economic family	3.4	2.9	3.4	3.3	3.2	3.3
437	Total number of unattached individuals	215	490	330	735	270	210
	2000 INCOME CHARACTERISTICS						
	Population 15 years and over by sex and total income groups in 2000						
438	Total - Both sexes	1,920	3,385	3,995	6,605	1,980	1,970
439	Without income	105	220	270	370	100	105
440	With income	1,820	3,165	3,725	6,240	1,885	1,865
441	Under $1,000 (45)	105	70	100	200	75	125
442	$ 1,000 - $ 2,999	35	75	160	290	75	115
443	$ 3,000 - $ 4,999	70	90	110	160	55	55
444	$ 5,000 - $ 6,999	85	170	105	310	65	55
445	$ 7,000 - $ 9,999	90	230	235	310	80	75
446	$10,000 - $11,999	45	210	145	240	75	60
447	$12,000 - $14,999	75	295	200	365	130	120
448	$15,000 - $19,999	165	355	445	510	160	105
449	$20,000 - $24,999	90	205	255	485	135	80
450	$25,000 - $29,999	110	220	235	445	140	120
451	$30,000 - $34,999	185	230	250	505	145	185
452	$35,000 - $39,999	125	205	320	310	130	115
453	$40,000 - $44,999	120	165	215	340	115	125
454	$45,000 - $49,999	115	60	95	310	70	115
455	$50,000 - $59,999	210	220	400	580	115	90
456	$60,000 and over	190	355	460	895	335	325
457	Average income $ (46)	32,168	29,221	32,102	34,131	36,582	32,751
458	Median income $ (46)	30,304	22,037	27,330	27,622	28,290	30,068
459	Standard error of average income $ (46)	1,158	974	884	914	1,873	1,334

Tableau 1. Certaines caractéristiques des secteurs de recensement, recensement de 2001 – Données intégrales et données-échantillon (20 %)

Vancouver 0503.03 A	Vancouver 0503.04 A	Vancouver 0503.05 A	Vancouver 0504.01 A	Vancouver 0504.02	Vancouver 0504.03	Caractéristiques	N°
						CARACTÉRISTIQUES DES FAMILLES DE RECENSEMENT	
						selon la structure et la taille de la famille de recensement – fin	
75	60	55	65	50	30	Parent de sexe masculin	406
45	45	55	55	40	20	1 enfant	407
20	15	-	15	10	-	2 enfants	408
10	-	-	-	-	10	3 enfants ou plus	409
2,745	**1,380**	**1,870**	**2,640**	**2,825**	**2,585**	**Nombre total d'enfants à la maison**	410
						selon les groupes d'âge	
530	375	585	540	635	615	Moins de 6 ans	411
1,025	530	650	1,010	1,170	1,110	6-14 ans	412
385	175	245	330	380	345	15-17 ans	413
620	210	255	530	495	425	18-24 ans	414
185	90	135	225	140	90	25 ans et plus	415
1.4	0.9	0.9	1.3	1.2	1.4	Nombre moyen d'enfants à la maison par famille de recensement (43)	416
7,175	**5,255**	**8,345**	**7,555**	**7,960**	**6,500**	**Nombre total de personnes dans les ménages privés**	417
						selon la situation des particuliers dans la famille de recensement et des particuliers dans le ménage	
710	1,350	2,755	1,015	670	525	Nombre de personnes hors famille de recensement	418
120	130	145	105	130	130	Vivant avec des personnes apparentées (44)	419
295	415	535	400	145	190	Vivant avec des personnes non apparentées uniquement	420
295	805	2,075	505	395	205	Vivant seules	421
6,465	3,910	5,590	6,540	7,290	5,980	Nombre de personnes membres d'une famille	422
3.2	2.7	2.6	3.1	3.1	3.3	Nombre moyen de personnes par famille de recensement	423
535	**835**	**1,805**	**750**	**960**	**335**	**Nombre total de personnes de 65 ans et plus**	424
160	325	1,055	205	300	110	Nombre de personnes hors famille de recensement de 65 ans et plus	425
-	20	30	30	45	50	Vivant avec des personnes apparentées (44)	426
25	20	45	-	20	-	Vivant avec des personnes non apparentées uniquement	427
130	285	980	175	230	65	Vivant seules	428
375	510	755	545	655	220	Nombre de personnes membres d'une famille de 65 ans et plus	429
						CARACTÉRISTIQUES DES FAMILLES ÉCONOMIQUES	
1,970	**1,475**	**2,170**	**2,055**	**2,310**	**1,765**	**Nombre total de familles économiques dans les ménages privés**	430
						selon la taille de la famille	
640	855	1,360	850	915	500	2 personnes	431
435	290	370	375	425	400	3 personnes	432
590	220	320	530	650	560	4 personnes	433
305	105	120	305	320	305	5 personnes ou plus	434
6,580	4,040	5,735	6,645	7,420	6,110	Nombre total de personnes dans les familles économiques	435
3.3	2.7	2.6	3.2	3.2	3.5	Nombre moyen de personnes par famille économique	436
595	1,220	2,610	910	540	390	Nombre total de personnes hors famille économique	437
						CARACTÉRISTIQUES DU REVENU DE 2000	
						Population de 15 ans et plus selon le sexe et les tranches de revenu total en 2000	
5,600	4,355	7,125	5,975	6,150	4,745	Total - Les deux sexes	438
285	205	305	255	375	230	Sans revenu	439
5,320	4,150	6,820	5,720	5,775	4,520	Avec un revenu	440
180	180	285	325	135	165	Moins de 1 000 $ (45)	441
345	165	275	215	220	185	1 000 $ - 2 999 $	442
140	110	135	255	190	125	3 000 $ - 4 999 $	443
225	150	325	250	245	150	5 000 $ - 6 999 $	444
340	285	470	305	225	270	7 000 $ - 9 999 $	445
195	175	310	190	190	90	10 000 $ - 11 999 $	446
250	375	815	360	330	215	12 000 $ - 14 999 $	447
415	405	820	460	450	325	15 000 $ - 19 999 $	448
385	375	685	515	375	425	20 000 $ - 24 999 $	449
335	345	605	425	435	240	25 000 $ - 29 999 $	450
325	385	530	480	500	320	30 000 $ - 34 999 $	451
385	270	440	355	370	320	35 000 $ - 39 999 $	452
330	215	335	370	355	375	40 000 $ - 44 999 $	453
305	260	255	240	200	235	45 000 $ - 49 999 $	454
435	190	260	420	565	405	50 000 $ - 59 999 $	455
720	275	285	555	985	665	60 000 $ et plus	456
34,256	26,457	23,852	31,889	37,382	34,085	Revenu moyen $ (46)	457
26,875	23,192	19,908	24,573	30,563	30,223	Revenu médian $ (46)	458
1,226	640	468	1,296	998	848	Erreur type de revenu moyen $ (46)	459

Table 1. Selected Characteristics for Census Tracts, 2001 Census – 100% Data and 20% Sample Data

No.	Characteristics	Vancouver 0502.01 A	Vancouver 0502.02	Vancouver 0502.03	Vancouver 0502.04 A	Vancouver 0502.05 ◇	Vancouver 0503.01 A
	2000 INCOME CHARACTERISTICS						
	Population 15 years and over by sex and total income groups in 2000 – concluded						
460	Total - Males	920	1,670	2,010	3,155	990	1,005
461	Without income	35	70	70	135	30	50
462	With income	890	1,600	1,940	3,025	960	960
463	Under $1,000 (45)	25	30	50	40	15	60
464	$ 1,000 - $ 2,999	10	35	70	130	45	50
465	$ 3,000 - $ 4,999	30	45	55	40	20	10
466	$ 5,000 - $ 6,999	30	70	60	135	15	45
467	$ 7,000 - $ 9,999	25	80	100	110	55	15
468	$10,000 - $11,999	10	35	60	90	35	15
469	$12,000 - $14,999	20	115	75	130	45	15
470	$15,000 - $19,999	70	125	140	155	65	45
471	$20,000 - $24,999	25	110	140	210	45	20
472	$25,000 - $29,999	30	130	75	185	55	65
473	$30,000 - $34,999	75	135	125	200	95	85
474	$35,000 - $39,999	45	110	145	180	60	60
475	$40,000 - $44,999	90	95	100	170	65	55
476	$45,000 - $49,999	60	50	70	195	25	80
477	$50,000 - $59,999	175	160	305	325	80	60
478	$60,000 and over	165	285	375	730	235	265
479	Average income $ (46)	41,278	37,152	38,968	42,850	43,358	40,883
480	Median income $ (46)	40,325	30,305	35,829	37,686	34,194	36,468
481	Standard error of average income $ (46)	1,724	1,646	1,431	1,566	3,059	2,105
482	Total - Females	1,000	1,715	1,985	3,450	995	970
483	Without income	75	150	195	230	65	55
484	With income	925	1,565	1,790	3,215	925	905
485	Under $1,000 (45)	80	40	55	155	55	65
486	$ 1,000 - $ 2,999	25	40	90	165	30	60
487	$ 3,000 - $ 4,999	40	50	55	120	35	45
488	$ 5,000 - $ 6,999	50	100	45	175	45	10
489	$ 7,000 - $ 9,999	60	155	135	200	25	55
490	$10,000 - $11,999	40	175	85	145	50	45
491	$12,000 - $14,999	55	175	130	240	85	105
492	$15,000 - $19,999	90	235	305	350	95	65
493	$20,000 - $24,999	65	100	115	275	85	55
494	$25,000 - $29,999	80	95	160	260	85	50
495	$30,000 - $34,999	105	90	125	305	50	100
496	$35,000 - $39,999	80	90	175	125	70	55
497	$40,000 - $44,999	30	75	110	170	45	70
498	$45,000 - $49,999	50	15	25	110	40	40
499	$50,000 - $59,999	40	60	95	260	30	30
500	$60,000 and over	25	65	85	160	105	65
501	Average income $ (46)	23,419	21,136	24,664	25,929	29,582	24,189
502	Median income $ (46)	20,906	15,644	19,385	20,873	22,097	20,293
503	Standard error of average income $ (46)	1,279	862	870	893	2,043	1,376
	by composition of total income						
504	Total - Composition of income in 2000 % (47)	100.0	100.0	100.0	100.0	100.0	100.0
505	Employment income %	86.3	70.8	86.6	79.2	79.8	87.4
506	Government transfer payments %	8.9	14.0	7.1	8.3	8.3	6.3
507	Other %	4.8	15.1	6.4	12.5	12.0	6.3
	Population 15 years and over with employment income in 2000 by sex and work activity						
508	Both sexes with employment income (48)	1,455	2,105	3,145	4,830	1,500	1,480
509	Average employment income $	34,607	31,151	32,943	34,910	36,603	36,168
510	Standard error of average employment income $	1,238	1,370	970	916	2,195	1,484
511	Worked full year, full time (49)	925	1,015	1,805	2,515	805	970
512	Average employment income $	43,676	47,072	43,818	47,262	46,491	45,311
513	Standard error of average employment income $	1,346	2,180	1,253	1,140	2,548	1,836
514	Worked part year or part time (50)	505	1,040	1,305	2,235	670	480
515	Average employment income $	18,743	16,832	18,521	22,021	26,118	18,805
516	Standard error of average employment income $	1,753	998	1,079	1,261	3,634	1,647
517	Males with employment income (48)	750	1,130	1,660	2,490	820	815
518	Average employment income $	42,547	39,460	40,329	43,115	42,997	43,488
519	Standard error of average employment income $	1,779	2,229	1,549	1,457	3,373	2,261
520	Worked full year, full time (49)	590	640	1,095	1,520	500	575
521	Average employment income $	48,042	54,921	49,468	53,180	47,093	53,852
522	Standard error of average employment income $	1,779	3,113	1,787	1,516	2,817	2,452
523	Worked part year or part time (50)	160	470	545	910	315	230
524	Average employment income $	22,186	19,580	23,132	28,505	37,034	18,512
525	Standard error of average employment income $	3,650	1,747	2,269	2,720	7,453	2,840

Tableau 1. Certaines caractéristiques des secteurs de recensement, recensement de 2001 – Données intégrales et données-échantillon (20 %)

Vancouver 0503.03 A	Vancouver 0503.04 A	Vancouver 0503.05 A	Vancouver 0504.01 A	Vancouver 0504.02	Vancouver 0504.03	Caractéristiques	Nº
						CARACTÉRISTIQUES DU REVENU DE 2000	
						Population de 15 ans et plus selon le sexe et les tranches de revenu total en 2000 – fin	
2,770	2,030	3,160	2,935	2,975	2,340	Total - Hommes	460
95	90	135	120	125	100	Sans revenu	461
2,680	1,935	3,025	2,815	2,845	2,235	Avec un revenu	462
110	85	160	85	65	85	Moins de 1 000 $ (45)	463
140	40	100	105	65	90	1 000 $ - 2 999 $	464
40	30	40	40	70	65	3 000 $ - 4 999 $	465
75	25	95	100	80	40	5 000 $ - 6 999 $	466
95	50	165	85	40	65	7 000 $ - 9 999 $	467
65	60	130	95	90	20	10 000 $ - 11 999 $	468
85	125	195	150	125	100	12 000 $ - 14 999 $	469
160	210	290	215	180	90	15 000 $ - 19 999 $	470
155	185	295	195	160	140	20 000 $ - 24 999 $	471
140	210	250	145	115	90	25 000 $ - 29 999 $	472
145	190	245	255	170	130	30 000 $ - 34 999 $	473
165	130	215	215	180	130	35 000 $ - 39 999 $	474
240	115	220	235	170	180	40 000 $ - 44 999 $	475
190	195	155	135	145	140	45 000 $ - 49 999 $	476
300	105	205	310	415	310	50 000 $ - 59 999 $	477
575	190	255	460	785	555	60 000 $ et plus	478
44,598	31,432	29,313	39,636	47,398	42,432	Revenu moyen $ (46)	479
38,347	28,391	25,326	33,138	41,745	40,358	Revenu médian $ (46)	480
2,240	988	858	1,963	1,646	1,433	Erreur type de revenu moyen $ (46)	481
2,830	2,325	3,965	3,040	3,175	2,410	Total - Femmes	482
190	110	175	140	250	130	Sans revenu	483
2,640	2,215	3,790	2,900	2,925	2,280	Avec un revenu	484
80	100	125	240	70	75	Moins de 1 000 $ (45)	485
210	125	175	115	160	90	1 000 $ - 2 999 $	486
100	80	95	215	130	60	3 000 $ - 4 999 $	487
145	120	225	150	160	110	5 000 $ - 6 999 $	488
250	235	300	220	185	215	7 000 $ - 9 999 $	489
130	120	180	100	105	75	10 000 $ - 11 999 $	490
160	250	620	215	200	110	12 000 $ - 14 999 $	491
265	195	535	245	270	230	15 000 $ - 19 999 $	492
230	185	385	320	220	285	20 000 $ - 24 999 $	493
200	135	355	285	315	145	25 000 $ - 29 999 $	494
180	195	285	225	330	190	30 000 $ - 34 999 $	495
215	140	225	145	190	195	35 000 $ - 39 999 $	496
90	100	110	130	180	195	40 000 $ - 44 999 $	497
115	65	95	105	55	95	45 000 $ - 49 999 $	498
140	85	55	115	155	95	50 000 $ - 59 999 $	499
145	90	30	95	205	110	60 000 $ et plus	500
23,761	22,108	19,494	24,383	27,644	25,899	Revenu moyen $ (46)	501
18,755	16,364	16,847	18,373	24,107	23,311	Revenu médian $ (46)	502
765	783	444	1,655	1,043	811	Erreur type de revenu moyen $ (46)	503
						selon la composition du revenu total	
100.0	100.0	100.0	100.0	100.0	100.0	Total - Composition du revenu en 2000 % (47)	504
85.3	74.3	69.9	82.7	80.9	87.9	Revenu d'emploi %	505
6.8	16.4	20.8	9.1	9.0	6.0	Transferts gouvernementaux %	506
7.8	9.3	9.2	8.1	10.1	6.0	Autre %	507
						Population de 15 ans et plus ayant un revenu d'emploi en 2000 selon le sexe et le travail	
4,410	2,815	4,110	4,250	4,380	3,875	Les deux sexes ayant un revenu d'emploi (48)	508
35,279	28,965	27,659	35,555	39,915	34,945	Revenu moyen d'emploi $	509
1,252	839	643	1,659	1,248	941	Erreur type de revenu moyen d'emploi $	510
2,455	1,635	2,210	2,110	2,425	2,245	Ayant travaillé toute l'année à plein temps (49)	511
48,865	36,972	36,993	51,244	54,862	46,575	Revenu moyen d'emploi $	512
1,758	1,044	837	2,935	1,791	1,250	Erreur type de revenu moyen d'emploi $	513
1,885	1,130	1,790	2,040	1,855	1,600	Ayant travaillé une partie de l'année ou à temps partiel (50)	514
18,540	18,219	17,318	20,178	21,952	19,082	Revenu moyen d'emploi $	515
1,448	1,097	723	1,166	1,314	928	Erreur type de revenu moyen d'emploi $	516
2,315	1,420	2,100	2,245	2,215	2,000	Hommes ayant un revenu d'emploi (48)	517
45,482	33,745	32,868	42,299	50,785	43,019	Revenu moyen d'emploi $	518
2,154	1,229	1,040	2,354	2,002	1,537	Erreur type de revenu moyen d'emploi $	519
1,570	885	1,265	1,360	1,520	1,325	Ayant travaillé toute l'année à plein temps (49)	520
56,626	40,190	42,123	52,853	62,564	54,200	Revenu moyen d'emploi $	521
2,570	1,544	1,252	3,403	2,395	1,787	Erreur type de revenu moyen d'emploi $	522
720	505	805	835	670	670	Ayant travaillé une partie de l'année ou à temps partiel (50)	523
22,910	23,947	19,239	26,177	25,783	21,340	Revenu moyen d'emploi $	524
3,426	1,700	1,256	2,571	2,806	1,816	Erreur type de revenu moyen d'emploi $	525

Table 1. Selected Characteristics for Census Tracts, 2001 Census – 100% Data and 20% Sample Data

No.	Characteristics	Vancouver 0502.01 A	Vancouver 0502.02	Vancouver 0502.03	Vancouver 0502.04 A	Vancouver 0502.05 ◇	Vancouver 0503.01 A
	2000 INCOME CHARACTERISTICS						
	Population 15 years and over with employment income in 2000 by sex and work activity – concluded						
526	Females with employment income (48)	705	975	1,480	2,340	680	660
527	Average employment income $	26,116	21,528	24,688	26,188	28,905	27,125
528	Standard error of average employment income $	1,442	1,200	930	957	2,557	1,494
529	Worked full year, full time (49)	335	370	705	990	305	395
530	Average employment income $	35,966	33,569	35,080	38,193	45,513	32,913
531	Standard error of average employment income $	1,649	2,022	1,304	1,545	4,866	1,998
532	Worked part year or part time (50)	345	575	755	1,325	350	250
533	Average employment income $	17,175	14,593	15,195	17,564	16,243	19,076
534	Standard error of average employment income $	1,892	1,097	859	961	1,501	1,869
	Census families by structure and family income groups in 2000						
535	Total - All census families	695	1,205	1,445	2,385	695	695
536	Under $10,000	10	-	15	30	20	25
537	$ 10,000 - $19,999	20	90	60	90	30	15
538	$ 20,000 - $29,999	25	120	75	205	65	40
539	$ 30,000 - $39,999	50	115	125	195	80	25
540	$ 40,000 - $49,999	60	160	120	205	55	55
541	$ 50,000 - $59,999	85	145	165	180	65	30
542	$ 60,000 - $69,999	75	100	120	260	80	105
543	$ 70,000 - $79,999	90	55	125	285	55	100
544	$ 80,000 - $89,999	95	90	165	190	55	80
545	$ 90,000 - $99,999	70	80	145	200	35	80
546	$100,000 and over	120	235	330	550	165	145
547	Average family income $	72,236	66,992	76,754	77,584	81,795	76,618
548	Median family income $	70,570	56,462	72,717	70,432	66,719	76,071
549	Standard error of average family income $	2,456	2,353	2,147	2,326	5,204	2,852
550	Total - All couple census families (51)	600	1,085	1,270	2,090	640	635
551	Under $10,000	10	-	15	10	20	10
552	$ 10,000 - $19,999	10	55	25	40	10	-
553	$ 20,000 - $29,999	20	105	40	150	40	30
554	$ 30,000 - $39,999	25	115	100	175	65	20
555	$ 40,000 - $49,999	50	130	95	150	55	45
556	$ 50,000 - $59,999	70	130	145	155	65	35
557	$ 60,000 - $69,999	65	90	100	245	75	95
558	$ 70,000 - $79,999	85	50	110	265	55	90
559	$ 80,000 - $89,999	90	95	165	175	60	85
560	$ 90,000 - $99,999	60	75	145	200	35	80
561	$100,000 and over	110	235	330	530	165	145
562	Average family income $	75,804	70,051	81,969	81,439	86,710	80,569
563	Median family income $	73,899	60,024	80,009	73,464	68,131	78,754
564	Standard error of average family income $	2,541	2,495	2,227	2,451	5,456	2,858
	Incidence of low income in 2000						
565	Total - Economic families	675	1,180	1,435	2,350	685	710
566	Low income	30	125	130	220	45	55
567	Incidence of low income in 2000 % (52)	4.2	10.6	9.1	9.4	6.9	7.5
568	Total - Unattached individuals 15 years and over	215	485	320	740	270	180
569	Low income	90	230	160	205	40	55
570	Incidence of low income in 2000 % (52)	41.6	47.8	49.9	28.3	14.3	30.8
571	Total - Population in private households	2,510	3,955	5,170	8,400	2,470	2,560
572	Low income	200	610	555	985	160	260
573	Incidence of low income in 2000 % (52)	7.9	15.4	10.7	11.7	6.5	10.0
	Private households by household income groups in 2000						
574	Total - All private households	835	1,565	1,620	2,870	890	835
575	Under $10,000	15	35	30	35	40	35
576	$ 10,000 - $19,999	55	250	95	155	65	25
577	$ 20,000 - $29,999	40	150	105	305	105	55
578	$ 30,000 - $39,999	50	155	135	275	70	20
579	$ 40,000 - $49,999	65	175	135	245	70	85
580	$ 50,000 - $59,999	130	155	180	220	70	35
581	$ 60,000 - $69,999	80	140	135	280	105	130
582	$ 70,000 - $79,999	85	75	145	300	70	110
583	$ 80,000 - $89,999	110	100	165	195	70	115
584	$ 90,000 - $99,999	55	85	140	230	45	70
585	$100,000 and over	145	245	355	615	185	160
586	Average household income $	69,860	59,143	73,703	74,158	76,833	73,276
587	Median household income $	68,178	50,806	69,249	66,678	62,461	73,135
588	Standard error of average household income $	2,590	2,097	2,129	2,119	4,690	2,705

Tableau 1. Certaines caractéristiques des secteurs de recensement, recensement de 2001 – Données intégrales et données-échantillon (20 %)

Vancouver 0503.03 A	Vancouver 0503.04 A	Vancouver 0503.05 A	Vancouver 0504.01 A	Vancouver 0504.02	Vancouver 0504.03	Caractéristiques	N°
						CARACTÉRISTIQUES DU REVENU DE 2000	
						Population de 15 ans et plus ayant un revenu d'emploi en 2000 selon le sexe et le travail – fin	
2,090	1,390	2,015	2,005	2,160	1,880	Femmes ayant un revenu d'emploi (48)	526
23,985	24,093	22,228	28,012	28,771	26,361	Revenu moyen d'emploi $	527
852	1,071	676	2,287	1,327	918	Erreur type de revenu moyen d'emploi $	528
890	750	945	750	910	925	Ayant travaillé toute l'année à plein temps (49)	529
35,177	33,145	30,129	48,335	41,933	35,667	Revenu moyen d'emploi $	530
1,237	1,316	868	5,387	2,407	1,340	Erreur type de revenu moyen d'emploi $	531
1,165	625	990	1,205	1,185	930	Ayant travaillé une partie de l'année ou à temps partiel (50)	532
15,832	13,629	15,765	15,999	19,785	17,460	Revenu moyen d'emploi $	533
894	1,294	811	739	1,278	959	Erreur type de revenu moyen d'emploi $	534
						Familles de recensement selon la structure et les tranches de revenu de la famille en 2000	
2,000	1,455	2,155	2,105	2,350	1,785	Total - Toutes les familles de recensement	535
35	75	175	60	40	45	Moins de 10 000 $	536
55	105	230	135	60	50	10 000 $ - 19 999 $	537
105	210	375	200	145	80	20 000 $ - 29 999 $	538
185	245	265	200	265	100	30 000 $ - 39 999 $	539
210	170	330	165	120	130	40 000 $ - 49 999 $	540
210	160	205	215	200	195	50 000 $ - 59 999 $	541
225	125	215	280	240	230	60 000 $ - 69 999 $	542
210	110	130	180	220	210	70 000 $ - 79 999 $	543
170	70	85	175	245	190	80 000 $ - 89 999 $	544
155	100	90	140	185	140	90 000 $ - 99 999 $	545
440	90	70	350	610	405	100 000 $ et plus	546
78,502	50,864	44,228	73,659	83,260	77,134	Revenu moyen des familles $	547
68,964	45,266	41,242	62,134	74,388	72,353	Revenu médian des familles $	548
2,839	1,649	1,258	3,913	2,462	2,034	Erreur type de revenu moyen des familles $	549
1,720	1,065	1,560	1,795	2,120	1,610	Total - Toutes les familles de recensement comptant un couple (51)	550
10	35	45	35	25	25	Moins de 10 000 $	551
25	65	75	90	40	25	10 000 $ - 19 999 $	552
70	95	225	160	115	60	20 000 $ - 29 999 $	553
140	190	220	140	220	65	30 000 $ - 39 999 $	554
170	110	280	140	105	110	40 000 $ - 49 999 $	555
180	140	180	185	170	175	50 000 $ - 59 999 $	556
205	110	195	235	225	210	60 000 $ - 69 999 $	557
185	90	115	175	215	205	70 000 $ - 79 999 $	558
155	60	80	165	230	185	80 000 $ - 89 999 $	559
145	90	80	125	180	140	90 000 $ - 99 999 $	560
435	85	55	340	595	400	100 000 $ et plus	561
84,178	56,569	50,910	79,153	86,601	80,964	Revenu moyen des familles $	562
73,507	51,172	47,916	66,039	76,783	76,213	Revenu médian des familles $	563
3,194	1,977	1,384	4,458	2,602	2,163	Erreur type de revenu moyen des familles $	564
						Fréquence des unités à faible revenu en 2000	
1,970	1,475	2,170	2,055	2,300	1,765	Total - Familles économiques	565
150	285	600	210	75	100	Faible revenu	566
7.6	19.3	27.6	10.1	3.3	5.5	Fréquence des unités à faible revenu en 2000 % (52)	567
575	1,215	2,615	885	530	360	Total - Personnes hors famille économique de 15 ans et plus	568
165	500	1,265	320	100	85	Faible revenu	569
28.6	41.0	48.5	36.2	18.7	23.7	Fréquence des unités à faible revenu en 2000 % (52)	570
7,155	5,260	8,345	7,530	7,925	6,470	Total - Population dans les ménages privés	571
630	1,290	2,935	950	325	450	Faible revenu	572
8.8	24.6	35.2	12.6	4.1	7.0	Fréquence des unités à faible revenu en 2000 % (52)	573
						Ménages privés selon les tranches de revenu du ménage en 2000	
2,350	2,440	4,460	2,630	2,750	2,010	Total - Tous les ménages privés	574
65	210	470	90	35	40	Moins de 10 000 $	575
90	300	1,080	245	130	75	10 000 $ - 19 999 $	576
165	365	765	305	215	90	20 000 $ - 29 999 $	577
200	460	515	240	345	110	30 000 $ - 39 999 $	578
220	275	485	235	165	165	40 000 $ - 49 999 $	579
240	215	320	240	265	225	50 000 $ - 59 999 $	580
250	160	295	290	265	245	60 000 $ - 69 999 $	581
215	130	180	185	200	215	70 000 $ - 79 999 $	582
205	70	125	205	265	205	80 000 $ - 89 999 $	583
185	100	110	160	195	165	90 000 $ - 99 999 $	584
520	160	115	440	665	465	100 000 $ et plus	585
77,507	44,828	36,320	69,396	78,475	76,558	Revenu moyen des ménages $	586
67,308	38,037	29,271	58,104	68,241	71,681	Revenu médian des ménages $	587
2,809	1,349	858	3,313	2,239	1,939	Erreur type de revenu moyen des ménages $	588

Table 1. Selected Characteristics for Census Tracts, 2001 Census – 100% Data and 20% Sample Data

No.	Characteristics	Vancouver 0504.04	Vancouver 0505	Vancouver 0506.01	Vancouver 0506.02		
	POPULATION CHARACTERISTICS						
1	**Population, 1996 (1)**	**5,947**	**6,346**	**3,723**	**6,511**		
2	**Population, 2001 (2)**	**7,524**	**6,530**	**3,759**	**6,914**		
3	Population percentage change, 1996-2001	26.5	2.9	1.0	6.2		
4	Land area in square kilometres, 2001	2.11	66.62	3.05	6.26		
5	**Total population – 100% Data (3)**	**7,525**	**6,530**	**3,760**	**6,915**		
	by sex and age groups						
6	Male	3,670	3,240	1,865	3,425		
7	0-4 years	260	165	175	260		
8	5-9 years	280	235	210	315		
9	10-14 years	310	280	190	310		
10	15-19 years	295	265	135	295		
11	20-24 years	160	175	120	190		
12	25-29 years	155	150	120	185		
13	30-34 years	260	160	150	235		
14	35-39 years	325	240	175	335		
15	40-44 years	305	300	180	295		
16	45-49 years	275	290	110	240		
17	50-54 years	265	275	90	220		
18	55-59 years	140	240	75	145		
19	60-64 years	125	160	35	105		
20	65-69 years	165	100	30	85		
21	70-74 years	150	80	20	90		
22	75-79 years	130	55	25	60		
23	80-84 years	40	35	15	30		
24	85 years and over	15	40	5	30		
25	Female	3,850	3,290	1,895	3,495		
26	0-4 years	235	175	165	210		
27	5-9 years	255	215	175	285		
28	10-14 years	280	285	155	325		
29	15-19 years	230	295	130	275		
30	20-24 years	155	180	115	195		
31	25-29 years	160	155	140	200		
32	30-34 years	305	180	170	275		
33	35-39 years	355	245	220	340		
34	40-44 years	365	310	190	290		
35	45-49 years	335	300	135	255		
36	50-54 years	240	270	85	195		
37	55-59 years	175	205	70	140		
38	60-64 years	160	140	30	95		
39	65-69 years	200	80	35	100		
40	70-74 years	160	85	30	105		
41	75-79 years	135	70	30	90		
42	80-84 years	65	50	25	60		
43	85 years and over	35	35	5	60		
44	**Total population 15 years and over**	**5,900**	**5,175**	**2,695**	**5,210**		
	by legal marital status						
45	Never married (single)	1,225	1,525	830	1,470		
46	Legally married (and not separated)	3,865	2,830	1,365	2,695		
47	Separated, but still legally married	160	185	140	255		
48	Divorced	365	430	260	470		
49	Widowed	285	205	100	315		
	by common-law status						
50	Not in a common-law relationship	5,610	4,815	2,465	4,805		
51	In a common-law relationship	290	360	225	405		
52	**Total population – 20% Sample Data (4)**	**7,525**	**6,450**	**3,795**	**6,825**		
	by mother tongue						
53	Single responses	7,510	6,415	3,790	6,750		
54	English	6,585	5,750	3,385	5,710		
55	French	195	25	25	150		
56	Non-official languages (5)	725	645	375	885		
57	Chinese, n.o.s.	35	25	-	15		
58	Cantonese	-	-	15	20		
59	Punjabi	10	35	50	230		
60	Mandarin	25	-	-	40		
61	Tagalog (Pilipino)	10	10	-	25		
62	Other languages (6)	650	570	305	565		
63	Multiple responses	20	35	10	70		
64	English and French	-	-	10	15		
65	English and non-official language	20	30	-	60		
66	French and non-official language	-	-	-	-		
67	English, French and non-official language	-	-	-	-		

See reference material at the end of the publication. – Voir les documents de référence à la fin de la publication.

Tableau 1. Certaines caractéristiques des secteurs de recensement, recensement de 2001 – Données intégrales et données-échantillon (20 %)

Caractéristiques	N°
CARACTÉRISTIQUES DE LA POPULATION	
Population, 1996 (1)	1
Population, 2001 (2)	2
Variation en pourcentage de la population, 1996-2001	3
Superficie des terres en kilomètres carrés, 2001	4
Population totale – Données intégrales (3)	5
selon le sexe et les groupes d'âge	
Sexe masculin	6
0-4 ans	7
5-9 ans	8
10-14 ans	9
15-19 ans	10
20-24 ans	11
25-29 ans	12
30-34 ans	13
35-39 ans	14
40-44 ans	15
45-49 ans	16
50-54 ans	17
55-59 ans	18
60-64 ans	19
65-69 ans	20
70-74 ans	21
75-79 ans	22
80-84 ans	23
85 ans et plus	24
Sexe féminin	25
0-4 ans	26
5-9 ans	27
10-14 ans	28
15-19 ans	29
20-24 ans	30
25-29 ans	31
30-34 ans	32
35-39 ans	33
40-44 ans	34
45-49 ans	35
50-54 ans	36
55-59 ans	37
60-64 ans	38
65-69 ans	39
70-74 ans	40
75-79 ans	41
80-84 ans	42
85 ans et plus	43
Population totale de 15 ans et plus	44
selon l'état matrimonial légal	
Célibataire (jamais marié(e))	45
Légalement marié(e) (et non séparé(e))	46
Séparé(e), mais toujours légalement marié(e)	47
Divorcé(e)	48
Veuf ou veuve	49
selon l'union libre	
Ne vivant pas en union libre	50
Vivant en union libre	51
Population totale – Données-échantillon (20 %) (4)	52
selon la langue maternelle	
Réponses uniques	53
Anglais	54
Français	55
Langues non officielles (5)	56
Chinois, n.d.a.	57
Cantonais	58
Pendjabi	59
Mandarin	60
Tagalog (pilipino)	61
Autres langues (6)	62
Réponses multiples	63
Anglais et français	64
Anglais et langue non officielle	65
Français et langue non officielle	66
Anglais, français et langue non officielle	67

See reference material at the end of the publication. – Voir les documents de référence à la fin de la publication.

Table 1. Selected Characteristics for Census Tracts, 2001 Census – 100% Data and 20% Sample Data

No.	Characteristics	Vancouver 0504.04	Vancouver 0505	Vancouver 0506.01	Vancouver 0506.02		
	POPULATION CHARACTERISTICS						
	by home language						
68	Single responses	7,085	6,145	3,690	6,335		
69	English	6,930	6,095	3,490	6,035		
70	French	10	-	-	65		
71	Non-official languages (5)	145	50	205	235		
72	Cantonese	-	-	10	20		
73	Chinese, n.o.s.	30	20	-	-		
74	Punjabi	-	-	50	135		
75	Mandarin	-	-	-	15		
76	Korean	95	-	-	40		
77	Other languages (6)	15	30	145	35		
78	Multiple responses	445	310	100	495		
79	English and French	160	30	20	90		
80	English and non-official language	275	235	85	400		
81	French and non-official language	-	10	-	-		
82	English, French and non-official language	-	35	-	-		
	by knowledge of official languages						
83	English only	6,895	6,105	3,540	6,225		
84	French only	-	-	-	-		
85	English and French	550	315	185	470		
86	Neither English nor French	80	30	65	125		
	by knowledge of non-official languages (5) (7)						
87	Cantonese	-	10	15	10		
88	Chinese, n.o.s.	40	25	-	10		
89	Punjabi	10	40	50	245		
90	Mandarin	25	10	10	45		
91	Hindi	20	-	-	30		
92	German	205	245	65	175		
93	Spanish	35	100	15	95		
	by first official language spoken						
94	English	7,245	6,385	3,690	6,575		
95	French	190	35	30	120		
96	English and French	10	10	10	-		
97	Neither English nor French	80	25	65	125		
98	Official language minority - (number) (8)	200	35	30	120		
99	Official language minority - (percentage) (8)	2.7	0.5	0.8	1.8		
	by ethnic origin (9)						
100	English	2,650	2,510	1,250	2,500		
101	Canadian	2,160	1,845	1,455	1,705		
102	Chinese	150	60	40	60		
103	Scottish	1,660	1,680	810	1,485		
104	Irish	1,670	1,030	545	1,095		
105	German	1,165	1,300	665	1,205		
106	East Indian	145	45	30	270		
107	French	730	425	475	855		
108	Ukrainian	505	255	115	670		
109	Italian	375	215	95	270		
110	Dutch (Netherlands)	355	765	345	560		
111	Filipino	30	-	-	35		
112	Polish	305	210	85	205		
113	Norwegian	440	195	220	255		
114	North American Indian	85	180	80	245		
	by Aboriginal identity						
115	Total Aboriginal identity population (10)	135	190	155	295		
116	Total non-Aboriginal population	7,390	6,260	3,635	6,530		
	by Aboriginal origin						
117	Total Aboriginal origins population (11)	165	260	165	400		
118	Total non-Aboriginal population	7,360	6,190	3,630	6,420		
	by Registered Indian status						
119	Registered Indian (12)	50	80	20	20		
120	Not a Registered Indian	7,475	6,375	3,770	6,805		

Tableau 1. Certaines caractéristiques des secteurs de recensement, recensement de 2001 – Données intégrales et données-échantillon (20 %)

					Caractéristiques	Nº
					CARACTÉRISTIQUES DE LA POPULATION	
					selon la langue parlée à la maison	
					Réponses uniques	68
					Anglais	69
					Français	70
					Langues non officielles (5)	71
					Cantonais	72
					Chinois, n.d.a.	73
					Pendjabi	74
					Mandarin	75
					Coréen	76
					Autres langues (6)	77
					Réponses multiples	78
					Anglais et français	79
					Anglais et langue non officielle	80
					Français et langue non officielle	81
					Anglais, français et langue non officielle	82
					selon la connaissance des langues officielles	
					Anglais seulement	83
					Français seulement	84
					Anglais et français	85
					Ni l'anglais ni le français	86
					selon la connaissance des langues non officielles (5) (7)	
					Cantonais	87
					Chinois, n.d.a.	88
					Pendjabi	89
					Mandarin	90
					Hindi	91
					Allemand	92
					Espagnol	93
					selon la première langue officielle parlée	
					Anglais	94
					Français	95
					Anglais et français	96
					Ni l'anglais ni le français	97
					Minorité de langue officielle - (nombre) (8)	98
					Minorité de langue officielle - (pourcentage) (8)	99
					selon l'origine ethnique (9)	
					Anglais	100
					Canadien	101
					Chinois	102
					Écossais	103
					Irlandais	104
					Allemand	105
					Indien de l'Inde	106
					Français	107
					Ukrainien	108
					Italien	109
					Hollandais (Néerlandais)	110
					Philippin	111
					Polonais	112
					Norvégien	113
					Indien de l'Amérique du Nord	114
					selon l'identité autochtone	
					Total de la population ayant une identité autochtone (10)	115
					Total de la population non autochtone	116
					selon l'origine autochtone	
					Total de la population ayant une origine autochtone (11)	117
					Total de la population non autochtone	118
					selon le statut d'Indien inscrit	
					Oui, Indien inscrit (12)	119
					Non, pas un Indien inscrit	120

Table 1. Selected Characteristics for Census Tracts, 2001 Census – 100% Data and 20% Sample Data

No.	Characteristics	Vancouver 0504.04	Vancouver 0505	Vancouver 0506.01	Vancouver 0506.02		
	POPULATION CHARACTERISTICS						
	by visible minority groups						
121	Total visible minority population	510	260	265	635		
122	Chinese	115	60	20	70		
123	South Asian	115	50	55	280		
124	Black	10	20	10	-		
125	Filipino	25	10	-	40		
126	Latin American	10	25	-	40		
127	Southeast Asian	15	55	155	55		
128	Arab	-	-	-	-		
129	West Asian	-	-	-	-		
130	Korean	185	-	-	65		
131	Japanese	40	30	15	75		
132	Visible minority, n.i.e. (13)	-	-	10	-		
133	Multiple visible minorities (14)	15	10	-	15		
	by citizenship						
134	Canadian citizenship (15)	7,020	6,145	3,590	6,470		
135	Citizenship other than Canadian	510	305	205	355		
	by place of birth of respondent						
136	Non-immigrant population	6,250	5,415	3,255	5,710		
137	Born in province of residence	3,900	3,930	2,570	4,085		
138	Immigrant population (16)	1,160	1,010	535	1,085		
139	United States	140	100	20	95		
140	Central and South America	10	40	10	45		
141	Caribbean and Bermuda	25	-	-	-		
142	United Kingdom	335	295	175	235		
143	Other Europe (17)	290	335	90	245		
144	Africa	45	35	40	70		
145	Asia and the Middle East	295	140	180	340		
146	Oceania and other (18)	20	65	15	45		
147	Non-permanent residents (19)	115	30	-	30		
148	**Total immigrant population**	**1,160**	**1,005**	**530**	**1,085**		
	by period of immigration						
149	Before 1961	335	295	75	160		
150	1961-1970	150	205	65	190		
151	1971-1980	265	240	135	160		
152	1981-1990	30	160	70	245		
153	1991-2001 (20)	370	115	185	340		
154	1991-1995	105	35	45	140		
155	1996-2001 (20)	265	80	140	195		
	by age at immigration						
156	0-4 years	110	110	60	50		
157	5-19 years	395	305	155	365		
158	20 years and over	655	590	315	670		
159	**Total population**	**7,525**	**6,450**	**3,790**	**6,825**		
	by religion						
160	Catholic (21)	1,515	675	315	1,065		
161	Protestant	3,170	2,675	1,370	2,365		
162	Christian Orthodox	75	15	25	20		
163	Christian, n.i.e. (22)	550	515	200	450		
164	Muslim	25	-	-	15		
165	Jewish	10	10	-	10		
166	Buddhist	55	70	30	85		
167	Hindu	15	-	-	20		
168	Sikh	15	40	50	260		
169	Eastern religions (23)	15	-	-	-		
170	Other religions (24)	20	15	10	15		
171	No religious affiliation (25)	2,060	2,445	1,800	2,520		
172	**Total population 15 years and over**	**5,890**	**5,085**	**2,750**	**5,105**		
	by generation status						
173	1st generation (26)	1,170	1,045	520	1,100		
174	2nd generation (27)	1,560	1,270	625	1,260		
175	3rd generation and over (28)	3,150	2,770	1,605	2,750		
176	**Total population 1 year and over (29)**	**7,440**	**6,365**	**3,710**	**6,755**		
	by place of residence 1 year ago (mobility)						
177	Non-movers	6,475	5,695	3,030	5,720		
178	Movers	970	670	685	1,030		
179	Non-migrants	520	400	395	620		
180	Migrants	445	270	285	415		
181	Internal migrants	330	240	255	355		
182	Intraprovincial migrants	290	175	205	300		
183	Interprovincial migrants	40	65	50	55		
184	External migrants	115	35	35	55		

Tableau 1. Certaines caractéristiques des secteurs de recensement, recensement de 2001 – Données intégrales et données-échantillon (20 %)

					Caractéristiques	N°
					CARACTÉRISTIQUES DE LA POPULATION	
					selon les groupes de minorités visibles	
					Total de la population des minorités visibles	121
					Chinois	122
					Sud-Asiatique	123
					Noir	124
					Philippin	125
					Latino-Américain	126
					Asiatique du Sud-Est	127
					Arabe	128
					Asiatique occidental	129
					Coréen	130
					Japonais	131
					Minorité visible, n.i.a. (13)	132
					Minorités visibles multiples (14)	133
					selon la citoyenneté	
					Citoyenneté canadienne (15)	134
					Citoyenneté autre que canadienne	135
					selon le lieu de naissance du répondant	
					Population non immigrante	136
					Née dans la province de résidence	137
					Population immigrante (16)	138
					États-Unis	139
					Amérique centrale et du Sud	140
					Caraïbes et Bermudes	141
					Royaume-Uni	142
					Autre Europe (17)	143
					Afrique	144
					Asie et Moyen-Orient	145
					Océanie et autre (18)	146
					Résidents non permanents (19)	147
					Population immigrante totale	148
					selon la période d'immigration	
					Avant 1961	149
					1961-1970	150
					1971-1980	151
					1981-1990	152
					1991-2001 (20)	153
					1991-1995	154
					1996-2001 (20)	155
					selon l'âge à l'immigration	
					0-4 ans	156
					5-19 ans	157
					20 ans et plus	158
					Population totale	159
					selon la religion	
					Catholique (21)	160
					Protestante	161
					Orthodoxe chrétienne	162
					Chrétiennes, n.i.a. (22)	163
					Musulmane	164
					Juive	165
					Bouddhiste	166
					Hindoue	167
					Sikh	168
					Religions orientales (23)	169
					Autres religions (24)	170
					Aucune appartenance religieuse (25)	171
					Population totale de 15 ans et plus	172
					selon le statut des générations	
					1re génération (26)	173
					2e génération (27)	174
					3e génération et plus (28)	175
					Population totale de 1 an et plus (29)	176
					selon le lieu de résidence 1 an auparavant (mobilité)	
					Personnes n'ayant pas déménagé	177
					Personnes ayant déménagé	178
					Non-migrants	179
					Migrants	180
					Migrants internes	181
					Migrants infraprovinciaux	182
					Migrants interprovinciaux	183
					Migrants externes	184

Table 1. Selected Characteristics for Census Tracts, 2001 Census – 100% Data and 20% Sample Data

No.	Characteristics	Vancouver 0504.04	Vancouver 0505	Vancouver 0506.01	Vancouver 0506.02		
	POPULATION CHARACTERISTICS						
185	**Total population 5 years and over (30)**	**7,030**	**6,115**	**3,425**	**6,355**		
	by place of residence 5 years ago (mobility)						
186	Non-movers	3,295	3,740	1,590	3,735		
187	Movers	3,735	2,370	1,840	2,620		
188	Non-migrants	1,395	1,195	885	1,430		
189	Migrants	2,335	1,180	955	1,190		
190	Internal migrants	1,970	1,055	820	975		
191	Intraprovincial migrants	1,480	930	755	845		
192	Interprovincial migrants	490	125	70	130		
193	External migrants	370	125	130	220		
194	**Total population 15 to 24 years**	**840**	**900**	**515**	**955**		
	by school attendance						
195	Not attending school	295	260	330	445		
196	Attending school full time	460	550	170	420		
197	Attending school part time	75	100	15	95		
198	**Total population 15 years and over**	**5,885**	**5,085**	**2,750**	**5,105**		
	by highest level of schooling						
199	Less than grade 9 (31)	185	145	135	360		
200	Grades 9-13 without high school graduation certificate	1,125	1,170	715	1,525		
201	Grades 9-13 with high school graduation certificate	790	725	495	745		
202	Some postsecondary without degree, certificate or diploma (32)	950	640	335	590		
203	Trades certificate or diploma (33)	635	615	425	775		
204	College certificate or diploma (34)	1,045	775	395	680		
205	University certificate below bachelor's degree	245	135	115	125		
206	University with bachelor's degree or higher	920	875	140	305		
	by combinations of unpaid work						
207	Males 15 years and over	2,810	2,515	1,310	2,505		
208	Reported unpaid work (35)	2,560	2,240	1,140	2,220		
209	Housework and child care and care or assistance to seniors	210	220	50	160		
210	Housework and child care only	825	685	500	795		
211	Housework and care or assistance to seniors only	165	155	55	155		
212	Child care and care or assistance to seniors only	10	-	-	-		
213	Housework only	1,315	1,155	525	1,055		
214	Child care only	20	10	-	40		
215	Care or assistance to seniors only	20	-	10	10		
216	Females 15 years and over	3,080	2,565	1,440	2,605		
217	Reported unpaid work (35)	2,920	2,375	1,345	2,460		
218	Housework and child care and care or assistance to seniors	375	300	90	320		
219	Housework and child care only	1,000	830	630	970		
220	Housework and care or assistance to seniors only	265	215	105	220		
221	Child care and care or assistance to seniors only	10	-	10	-		
222	Housework only	1,255	1,015	500	915		
223	Child care only	20	15	-	30		
224	Care or assistance to seniors only	10	10	-	10		
	by labour force activity						
225	Males 15 years and over	2,810	2,515	1,310	2,505		
226	In the labour force	1,990	2,040	1,010	1,920		
227	Employed	1,870	1,945	945	1,775		
228	Unemployed	125	95	70	150		
229	Not in the labour force	820	475	300	585		
230	Participation rate	70.8	81.1	77.1	76.6		
231	Employment rate	66.5	77.3	72.1	70.9		
232	Unemployment rate	6.3	4.7	6.9	7.8		
233	Females 15 years and over	3,080	2,565	1,440	2,605		
234	In the labour force	1,895	1,795	985	1,670		
235	Employed	1,825	1,710	920	1,545		
236	Unemployed	70	85	65	120		
237	Not in the labour force	1,180	775	455	930		
238	Participation rate	61.5	70.0	68.4	64.1		
239	Employment rate	59.3	66.7	63.9	59.3		
240	Unemployment rate	3.7	4.7	6.6	7.2		

Tableau 1. Certaines caractéristiques des secteurs de recensement, recensement de 2001 – Données intégrales et données-échantillon (20 %)

						Caractéristiques	N°
						CARACTÉRISTIQUES DE LA POPULATION	
						Population totale de 5 ans et plus (30)	185
						selon le lieu de résidence 5 ans auparavant (mobilité)	
						Personnes n'ayant pas déménagé	186
						Personnes ayant déménagé	187
						Non-migrants	188
						Migrants	189
						Migrants internes	190
						Migrants infraprovinciaux	191
						Migrants interprovinciaux	192
						Migrants externes	193
						Population totale de 15 à 24 ans	194
						selon la fréquentation scolaire	
						Ne fréquentant pas l'école	195
						Fréquentant l'école à plein temps	196
						Fréquentant l'école à temps partiel	197
						Population totale de 15 ans et plus	198
						selon le plus haut niveau de scolarité atteint	
						Niveau inférieur à la 9e année (31)	199
						De la 9e à la 13e année sans certificat d'études secondaires	200
						De la 9e à la 13e année avec certificat d'études secondaires	201
						Études postsecondaires partielles sans grade, certificat ou diplôme (32)	202
						Certificat ou diplôme d'une école de métiers (33)	203
						Certificat ou diplôme collégial (34)	204
						Certificat universitaire inférieur au baccalauréat	205
						Études universitaires avec baccalauréat ou diplôme supérieur	206
						selon les combinaisons de travail non rémunéré	
						Hommes de 15 ans et plus	207
						Travail non rémunéré déclaré (35)	208
						Travaux ménagers et soins aux enfants et soins ou aide aux personnes âgées	209
						Travaux ménagers et soins aux enfants seulement	210
						Travaux ménagers et soins ou aide aux personnes âgées seulement	211
						Soins aux enfants et soins ou aide aux personnes âgées seulement	212
						Travaux ménagers seulement	213
						Soins aux enfants seulement	214
						Soins ou aide aux personnes âgées seulement	215
						Femmes de 15 ans et plus	216
						Travail non rémunéré déclaré (35)	217
						Travaux ménagers et soins aux enfants et soins ou aide aux personnes âgées	218
						Travaux ménagers et soins aux enfants seulement	219
						Travaux ménagers et soins ou aide aux personnes âgées seulement	220
						Soins aux enfants et soins ou aide aux personnes âgées seulement	221
						Travaux ménagers seulement	222
						Soins aux enfants seulement	223
						Soins ou aide aux personnes âgées seulement	224
						selon l'activité	
						Hommes de 15 ans et plus	225
						Population active	226
						Personnes occupées	227
						Chômeurs	228
						Inactifs	229
						Taux d'activité	230
						Taux d'emploi	231
						Taux de chômage	232
						Femmes de 15 ans et plus	233
						Population active	234
						Personnes occupées	235
						Chômeuses	236
						Inactives	237
						Taux d'activité	238
						Taux d'emploi	239
						Taux de chômage	240

Table 1. Selected Characteristics for Census Tracts, 2001 Census – 100% Data and 20% Sample Data

No.	Characteristics	Vancouver 0504.04	Vancouver 0505	Vancouver 0506.01	Vancouver 0506.02
	POPULATION CHARACTERISTICS				
	by labour force activity – concluded				
241	Both sexes - Participation rate	66.0	75.4	72.5	70.3
242	15-24 years	66.5	68.9	66.7	67.0
243	25 years and over	65.8	76.9	73.9	71.0
244	Both sexes - Employment rate	62.7	71.8	67.5	64.9
245	15-24 years	56.9	62.8	60.2	58.6
246	25 years and over	63.7	73.9	69.4	66.4
247	Both sexes - Unemployment rate	4.9	4.8	7.0	7.7
248	15-24 years	15.2	8.9	8.8	12.5
249	25 years and over	3.3	4.0	6.3	6.6
250	**Total labour force 15 years and over**	**3,885**	**3,840**	**1,995**	**3,590**
	by industry based on the 1997 NAICS				
251	Industry - Not applicable (36)	10	40	35	60
252	All industries (37)	3,880	3,800	1,960	3,530
253	11 Agriculture, forestry, fishing and hunting	10	350	80	180
254	21 Mining and oil and gas extraction	-	-	-	-
255	22 Utilities	20	35	-	-
256	23 Construction	230	390	95	320
257	31-33 Manufacturing	355	295	305	560
258	41 Wholesale trade	250	225	95	215
259	44-45 Retail trade	515	390	310	430
260	48-49 Transportation and warehousing	180	270	130	185
261	51 Information and cultural industries	110	95	25	55
262	52 Finance and insurance	265	105	50	95
263	53 Real estate and rental and leasing	140	25	35	25
264	54 Professional, scientific and technical services	185	210	75	130
265	55 Management of companies and enterprises	-	-	-	-
266	56 Administrative and support, waste management and remediation services	130	105	75	105
267	61 Educational services	335	350	95	165
268	62 Health care and social assistance	375	350	215	305
269	71 Arts, entertainment and recreation	85	90	20	55
270	72 Accommodation and food services	140	165	175	255
271	81 Other services (except public administration)	230	175	140	250
272	91 Public administration	325	160	50	190
	by class of worker				
273	Class of worker - Not applicable (36)	10	45	35	55
274	All classes of worker (37)	3,880	3,800	1,965	3,530
275	Paid workers	3,535	3,175	1,795	3,215
276	Employees	3,425	2,915	1,700	3,115
277	Self-employed (incorporated)	110	265	95	100
278	Self-employed (unincorporated)	345	605	165	305
279	Unpaid family workers	-	15	-	10
	by occupation based on the 2001 NOC-S				
280	Male labour force 15 years and over	1,990	2,040	1,010	1,920
281	Occupation - Not applicable (36)	-	25	20	35
282	All occupations (37)	1,990	2,020	990	1,885
283	A Management occupations	400	285	180	275
284	B Business, finance and administration occupations	190	110	50	100
285	C Natural and applied sciences and related occupations	200	140	40	80
286	D Health occupations	15	70	10	10
287	E Occupations in social science, education, government service and religion	145	135	25	80
288	F Occupations in art, culture, recreation and sport	30	50	10	15
289	G Sales and service occupations	560	290	175	340
290	H Trades, transport and equipment operators and related occupations	325	595	390	630
291	I Occupations unique to primary industry	45	250	20	90
292	J Occupations unique to processing, manufacturing and utilities	90	105	85	270
293	Female labour force 15 years and over	1,895	1,795	985	1,670
294	Occupation - Not applicable (36)	-	20	20	20
295	All occupations (37)	1,890	1,780	965	1,645
296	A Management occupations	210	130	60	145
297	B Business, finance and administration occupations	635	460	265	400
298	C Natural and applied sciences and related occupations	25	25	15	-
299	D Health occupations	185	150	50	155

Tableau 1. Certaines caractéristiques des secteurs de recensement, recensement de 2001 – Données intégrales et données-échantillon (20 %)

						Caractéristiques	N°
						CARACTÉRISTIQUES DE LA POPULATION	
						selon l'activité – fin	
						Les deux sexes - Taux d'activité	241
						15-24 ans	242
						25 ans et plus	243
						Les deux sexes - Taux d'emploi	244
						15-24 ans	245
						25 ans et plus	246
						Les deux sexes - Taux de chômage	247
						15-24 ans	248
						25 ans et plus	249
						Population active totale de 15 ans et plus	250
						selon l'industrie basée sur le SCIAN de 1997	
						Industrie - Sans objet (36)	251
						Toutes les industries (37)	252
						11 Agriculture, foresterie, pêche et chasse	253
						21 Extraction minière et extraction de pétrole et de gaz	254
						22 Services publics	255
						23 Construction	256
						31-33 Fabrication	257
						41 Commerce de gros	258
						44-45 Commerce de détail	259
						48-49 Transport et entreposage	260
						51 Industrie de l'information et industrie culturelle	261
						52 Finance et assurances	262
						53 Services immobiliers et services de location et de location à bail	263
						54 Services professionnels, scientifiques et techniques	264
						55 Gestion de sociétés et d'entreprises	265
						56 Services administratifs, services de soutien, services de gestion des déchets et services d'assainissement	266
						61 Services d'enseignement	267
						62 Soins de santé et assistance sociale	268
						71 Arts, spectacles et loisirs	269
						72 Hébergement et services de restauration	270
						81 Autres services, sauf les administrations publiques	271
						91 Administrations publiques	272
						selon la catégorie de travailleurs	
						Catégorie de travailleurs - Sans objet (36)	273
						Toutes les catégories de travailleurs (37)	274
						Travailleurs rémunérés	275
						Employés	276
						Travailleurs autonomes (entreprise constituée en société)	277
						Travailleurs autonomes (entreprise non constituée en société)	278
						Travailleurs familiaux non rémunérés	279
						selon la profession basée sur la CNP-S de 2001	
						Hommes actifs de 15 ans et plus	280
						Profession - Sans objet (36)	281
						Toutes les professions (37)	282
						A Gestion	283
						B Affaires, finance et administration	284
						C Sciences naturelles et appliquées et professions apparentées	285
						D Secteur de la santé	286
						E Sciences sociales, enseignement, administration publique et religion	287
						F Arts, culture, sports et loisirs	288
						G Ventes et services	289
						H Métiers, transport et machinerie	290
						I Professions propres au secteur primaire	291
						J Transformation, fabrication et services d'utilité publique	292
						Femmes actives de 15 ans et plus	293
						Profession - Sans objet (36)	294
						Toutes les professions (37)	295
						A Gestion	296
						B Affaires, finance et administration	297
						C Sciences naturelles et appliquées et professions apparentées	298
						D Secteur de la santé	299

Table 1. Selected Characteristics for Census Tracts, 2001 Census – 100% Data and 20% Sample Data

No.	Characteristics	Vancouver 0504.04	Vancouver 0505	Vancouver 0506.01	Vancouver 0506.02		
	POPULATION CHARACTERISTICS						
	by occupation based on the 2001 NOC-S – concluded						
300	E Occupations in social science, education, government service and religion	250	260	100	140		
301	F Occupations in art, culture, recreation and sport	85	95	20	55		
302	G Sales and service occupations	470	450	370	610		
303	H Trades, transport and equipment operators and related occupations	25	55	35	25		
304	I Occupations unique to primary industry	-	135	40	85		
305	J Occupations unique to processing, manufacturing and utilities	10	20	25	30		
306	**Total employed labour force 15 years and over**	**3,695**	**3,655**	**1,860**	**3,320**		
	by place of work						
307	Males	1,865	1,945	940	1,775		
308	Usual place of work	1,445	1,225	755	1,355		
309	At home	135	305	30	65		
310	Outside Canada	15	-	-	-		
311	No fixed workplace address	270	415	160	360		
312	Females	1,825	1,710	915	1,545		
313	Usual place of work	1,585	1,285	795	1,335		
314	At home	145	270	85	110		
315	Outside Canada	-	-	-	-		
316	No fixed workplace address	100	150	35	105		
317	**Total employed labour force 15 years and over with usual place of work or no fixed workplace address**	**3,400**	**3,070**	**1,745**	**3,145**		
	by mode of transportation						
318	Males	1,720	1,635	910	1,705		
319	Car, truck, van, as driver	1,465	1,415	825	1,540		
320	Car, truck, van, as passenger	60	105	40	95		
321	Public transit	85	25	10	25		
322	Walked	65	60	30	25		
323	Other method	40	30	10	20		
324	Females	1,680	1,435	830	1,440		
325	Car, truck, van, as driver	1,425	1,185	715	1,195		
326	Car, truck, van, as passenger	145	105	50	85		
327	Public transit	60	30	-	15		
328	Walked	45	95	45	110		
329	Other method	10	15	15	35		
330	**Total population 15 years and over who worked since January 1, 2000**	**4,310**	**4,170**	**2,220**	**3,800**		
	by language used at work						
331	Single responses	4,190	4,100	2,165	3,630		
332	English	4,160	4,065	2,115	3,585		
333	French	10	10	-	-		
334	Non-official languages (5)	25	25	45	50		
335	Chinese, n.o.s.	10	-	-	-		
336	Cantonese	-	-	-	-		
337	Other languages (6)	25	25	45	45		
338	Multiple responses	120	65	55	170		
339	English and French	60	20	-	10		
340	English and non-official language	60	45	50	150		
341	French and non-official language	-	-	-	-		
342	English, French and non-official language	-	-	-	-		
	DWELLING AND HOUSEHOLD CHARACTERISTICS						
343	**Total number of occupied private dwellings**	**2,735**	**2,210**	**1,285**	**2,320**		
	by tenure						
344	Owned	2,540	1,765	975	1,715		
345	Rented	190	440	310	595		
346	Band housing	-	10	-	-		
	by structural type of dwelling						
347	Single-detached house	1,085	1,920	645	1,555		
348	Semi-detached house	690	20	10	50		
349	Row house	575	10	435	245		
350	Apartment, detached duplex	10	20	35	170		
351	Apartment, building that has five or more storeys	-	-	-	-		
352	Apartment, building that has fewer than five storeys (38)	375	50	160	200		
353	Other single-attached house	-	-	-	10		
354	Movable dwelling (39)	-	185	-	90		

Tableau 1. Certaines caractéristiques des secteurs de recensement, recensement de 2001 – Données intégrales et données-échantillon (20 %)

Caractéristiques	N°
CARACTÉRISTIQUES DE LA POPULATION	
selon la profession basée sur la CNP-S de 2001 – fin	
E Sciences sociales, enseignement, administration publique et religion	300
F Arts, culture, sports et loisirs	301
G Ventes et services	302
H Métiers, transport et machinerie	303
I Professions propres au secteur primaire	304
J Transformation, fabrication et services d'utilité publique	305
Population active occupée totale de 15 ans et plus	306
selon le lieu de travail	
Hommes	307
Lieu habituel de travail	308
À domicile	309
En dehors du Canada	310
Sans adresse de travail fixe	311
Femmes	312
Lieu habituel de travail	313
À domicile	314
En dehors du Canada	315
Sans adresse de travail fixe	316
Population active occupée totale de 15 ans et plus ayant un lieu habituel de travail ou sans adresse de travail fixe	317
selon le mode de transport	
Hommes	318
Automobile, camion ou fourgonnette, en tant que conducteur	319
Automobile, camion ou fourgonnette, en tant que passager	320
Transport en commun	321
À pied	322
Autre moyen	323
Femmes	324
Automobile, camion ou fourgonnette, en tant que conductrice	325
Automobile, camion ou fourgonnette, en tant que passagère	326
Transport en commun	327
À pied	328
Autre moyen	329
Population totale de 15 ans et plus ayant travaillé depuis le 1er janvier 2000	330
selon la langue utilisée au travail	
Réponses uniques	331
Anglais	332
Français	333
Langues non officielles (5)	334
Chinois, n.d.a.	335
Cantonais	336
Autres langues (6)	337
Réponses multiples	338
Anglais et français	339
Anglais et langue non officielle	340
Français et langue non officielle	341
Anglais, français et langue non officielle	342
CARACTÉRISTIQUES DES LOGEMENTS ET DES MÉNAGES	
Nombre total de logements privés occupés	343
selon le mode d'occupation	
Possédé	344
Loué	345
Logement de bande	346
selon le type de construction résidentielle	
Maison individuelle non attenante	347
Maison jumelée	348
Maison en rangée	349
Appartement, duplex non attenant	350
Appartement, immeuble de cinq étages ou plus	351
Appartement, immeuble de moins de cinq étages (38)	352
Autre maison individuelle attenante	353
Logement mobile (39)	354

Table 1. Selected Characteristics for Census Tracts, 2001 Census – 100% Data and 20% Sample Data

No.	Characteristics	Vancouver 0504.04	Vancouver 0505	Vancouver 0506.01	Vancouver 0506.02		
	DWELLING AND HOUSEHOLD CHARACTERISTICS						
	by condition of dwelling						
355	Regular maintenance only	2,355	1,460	930	1,455		
356	Minor repairs	350	545	280	680		
357	Major repairs	25	200	75	185		
	by period of construction						
358	Before 1946	-	210	10	20		
359	1946-1960	-	195	25	130		
360	1961-1970	10	300	45	245		
361	1971-1980	15	845	375	865		
362	1981-1990	890	355	565	580		
363	1991-2001 (20)	1,825	305	265	475		
364	Average number of rooms per dwelling	7.1	7.7	6.5	6.7		
365	Average number of bedrooms per dwelling	3.0	3.1	3.0	3.0		
366	Average value of dwelling $	210,778	315,181	160,518	210,787		
367	**Total number of private households**	**2,730**	**2,210**	**1,285**	**2,315**		
	by household size						
368	1 person	390	375	200	430		
369	2 persons	1,030	730	335	650		
370	3 persons	475	370	280	410		
371	4-5 persons	780	610	435	710		
372	6 or more persons	55	125	35	110		
	by household type						
373	One-family households	2,235	1,750	1,030	1,765		
374	Multiple-family households	40	30	30	60		
375	Non-family households	450	430	225	490		
376	Number of persons in private households	7,525	6,410	3,795	6,825		
377	Average number of persons in private households	2.8	2.9	2.9	2.9		
378	Average number of persons per room	0.4	0.4	0.5	0.4		
379	Tenant households in non-farm, non-reserve private dwellings (40)	185	435	310	590		
380	Average gross rent $ (40)	1,172	861	787	709		
381	Tenant households spending 30% or more of household income on gross rent (40) (41)	50	165	90	335		
382	Tenant households spending from 30% to 99% of household income on gross rent (40) (41)	35	130	80	265		
383	Owner households in non-farm, non-reserve private dwellings (42)	2,530	1,560	980	1,700		
384	Average owner's major payments $ (42)	1,145	1,070	1,032	1,065		
385	Owner households spending 30% or more of household income on owner's major payments (41) (42)	455	325	310	425		
386	Owner households spending from 30% to 99% of household income on owner's major payments (41) (42)	425	290	270	400		
	CENSUS FAMILY CHARACTERISTICS						
387	**Total number of census families in private households**	**2,320**	**1,815**	**1,090**	**1,890**		
	by census family structure and size						
388	Total couple families	2,045	1,570	825	1,535		
389	Total families of married couples	1,925	1,390	680	1,325		
390	Without children at home	855	565	190	470		
391	With children at home	1,065	820	490	855		
392	1 child	365	215	150	240		
393	2 children	560	385	270	420		
394	3 or more children	145	225	75	195		
395	Total families of common-law couples	120	180	140	205		
396	Without children at home	70	105	85	85		
397	With children at home	45	75	55	125		
398	1 child	20	25	35	35		
399	2 children	20	30	15	80		
400	3 or more children	10	15	-	-		
401	Total lone-parent families	280	245	270	360		
402	Female parent	260	185	235	280		
403	1 child	120	80	105	105		
404	2 children	115	75	90	95		
405	3 or more children	20	25	35	75		

Tableau 1. Certaines caractéristiques des secteurs de recensement, recensement de 2001 – Données intégrales et données-échantillon (20 %)

						Caractéristiques	N°
						CARACTÉRISTIQUES DES LOGEMENTS ET DES MÉNAGES	
						selon l'état du logement	
						Entretien régulier seulement	355
						Réparations mineures	356
						Réparations majeures	357
						selon la période de construction	
						Avant 1946	358
						1946-1960	359
						1961-1970	360
						1971-1980	361
						1981-1990	362
						1991-2001 (20)	363
						Nombre moyen de pièces par logement	364
						Nombre moyen de chambres à coucher par logement	365
						Valeur moyenne du logement $	366
						Nombre total de logements privés	367
						selon la taille du ménage	
						1 personne	368
						2 personnes	369
						3 personnes	370
						4-5 personnes	371
						6 personnes ou plus	372
						selon le genre de ménage	
						Ménages unifamiliaux	373
						Ménages multifamiliaux	374
						Ménages non familiaux	375
						Nombre de personnes dans les ménages privés	376
						Nombre moyen de personnes dans les ménages privés	377
						Nombre moyen de personnes par pièce	378
						Ménages locataires dans les logements privés non agricoles hors réserve (40)	379
						Loyer brut moyen $ (40)	380
						Ménages locataires consacrant 30 % ou plus du revenu du ménage au loyer brut (40) (41)	381
						Ménages locataires consacrant de 30 % à 99 % du revenu du ménage au loyer brut (40) (41)	382
						Ménages propriétaires dans les logements privés non agricoles hors réserve (42)	383
						Principales dépenses de propriété moyennes $ (42)	384
						Ménages propriétaires consacrant 30 % ou plus du revenu du ménage aux principales dépenses de propriété (41) (42)	385
						Ménages propriétaires consacrant de 30 % à 99 % du revenu du ménage aux principales dépenses de propriété (41) (42)	386
						CARACTÉRISTIQUES DES FAMILLES DE RECENSEMENT	
						Total des familles de recensement dans les ménages privés	387
						selon la structure et la taille de la famille de recensement	
						Total des familles avec conjoints	388
						Total des familles avec couples mariés	389
						Sans enfants à la maison	390
						Avec enfants à la maison	391
						1 enfant	392
						2 enfants	393
						3 enfants ou plus	394
						Total des familles en union libre	395
						Sans enfants à la maison	396
						Avec enfants à la maison	397
						1 enfant	398
						2 enfants	399
						3 enfants ou plus	400
						Total des familles monoparentales	401
						Parent de sexe féminin	402
						1 enfant	403
						2 enfants	404
						3 enfants ou plus	405

Table 1. Selected Characteristics for Census Tracts, 2001 Census – 100% Data and 20% Sample Data

No.	Characteristics	Vancouver 0504.04	Vancouver 0505	Vancouver 0506.01	Vancouver 0506.02		
	CENSUS FAMILY CHARACTERISTICS						
	by census family structure and size – concluded						
406	Male parent	15	60	35	80		
407	1 child	-	50	25	50		
408	2 children	15	-	15	25		
409	3 or more children	-	-	-	-		
410	**Total number of children at home**	**2,500**	**2,350**	**1,450**	**2,640**		
	by age groups						
411	Under 6 years	625	405	430	545		
412	6-14 years	995	950	600	1,175		
413	15-17 years	350	320	160	325		
414	18-24 years	430	470	180	450		
415	25 years and over	100	205	80	155		
416	Average number of children at home per census family (43)	1.1	1.3	1.3	1.4		
417	**Total number of persons in private households**	**7,520**	**6,415**	**3,795**	**6,825**		
	by census family status and living arrangements						
418	Number of non-family persons	660	680	430	765		
419	Living with relatives (44)	110	100	50	95		
420	Living with non-relatives only	155	210	175	230		
421	Living alone	390	370	200	435		
422	Number of family persons	6,865	5,735	3,365	6,060		
423	Average number of persons per census family	3.0	3.2	3.1	3.2		
424	**Total number of persons 65 years and over**	**1,090**	**565**	**190**	**620**		
425	Number of non-family persons 65 years and over	250	125	50	260		
426	Living with relatives (44)	35	45	10	30		
427	Living with non-relatives only	-	-	10	15		
428	Living alone	215	80	25	220		
429	Number of family persons 65 years and over	840	440	140	360		
	ECONOMIC FAMILY CHARACTERISTICS						
430	**Total number of economic families in private households**	**2,310**	**1,800**	**1,060**	**1,835**		
	by size of family						
431	2 persons	1,010	760	375	650		
432	3 persons	475	335	255	385		
433	4 persons	615	420	305	500		
434	5 or more persons	205	290	130	305		
435	Total number of persons in economic families	6,980	5,835	3,410	6,155		
436	Average number of persons per economic family	3.0	3.2	3.2	3.4		
437	Total number of unattached individuals	545	575	380	665		
	2000 INCOME CHARACTERISTICS						
	Population 15 years and over by sex and total income groups in 2000						
438	Total - Both sexes	5,890	5,080	2,750	5,110		
439	Without income	275	230	150	255		
440	With income	5,615	4,855	2,595	4,850		
441	Under $1,000 (45)	165	210	55	265		
442	$ 1,000 - $ 2,999	260	170	120	295		
443	$ 3,000 - $ 4,999	110	160	115	155		
444	$ 5,000 - $ 6,999	200	205	125	145		
445	$ 7,000 - $ 9,999	320	295	180	270		
446	$10,000 - $11,999	170	220	155	225		
447	$12,000 - $14,999	245	260	155	330		
448	$15,000 - $19,999	440	400	175	525		
449	$20,000 - $24,999	360	360	305	400		
450	$25,000 - $29,999	420	400	195	325		
451	$30,000 - $34,999	410	360	190	405		
452	$35,000 - $39,999	370	250	140	335		
453	$40,000 - $44,999	370	295	225	245		
454	$45,000 - $49,999	270	170	150	220		
455	$50,000 - $59,999	515	390	170	310		
456	$60,000 and over	990	695	150	395		
457	Average income $ (46)	35,630	36,096	26,529	27,107		
458	Median income $ (46)	30,326	26,086	23,291	22,450		
459	Standard error of average income $ (46)	752	1,879	785	685		

Tableau 1. Certaines caractéristiques des secteurs de recensement, recensement de 2001 – Données intégrales et données-échantillon (20 %)

Caractéristiques	N°
CARACTÉRISTIQUES DES FAMILLES DE RECENSEMENT	
selon la structure et la taille de la famille de recensement – fin	
Parent de sexe masculin	406
1 enfant	407
2 enfants	408
3 enfants ou plus	409
Nombre total d'enfants à la maison	410
selon les groupes d'âge	
Moins de 6 ans	411
6-14 ans	412
15-17 ans	413
18-24 ans	414
25 ans et plus	415
Nombre moyen d'enfants à la maison par famille de recensement (43)	416
Nombre total de personnes dans les ménages privés	417
selon la situation des particuliers dans la famille de recensement et des particuliers dans le ménage	
Nombre de personnes hors famille de recensement	418
Vivant avec des personnes apparentées (44)	419
Vivant avec des personnes non apparentées uniquement	420
Vivant seules	421
Nombre de personnes membres d'une famille	422
Nombre moyen de personnes par famille de recensement	423
Nombre total de personnes de 65 ans et plus	424
Nombre de personnes hors famille de recensement de 65 ans et plus	425
Vivant avec des personnes apparentées (44)	426
Vivant avec des personnes non apparentées uniquement	427
Vivant seules	428
Nombre de personnes membres d'une famille de 65 ans et plus	429
CARACTÉRISTIQUES DES FAMILLES ÉCONOMIQUES	
Nombre total de familles économiques dans les ménages privés	430
selon la taille de la famille	
2 personnes	431
3 personnes	432
4 personnes	433
5 personnes ou plus	434
Nombre total de personnes dans les familles économiques	435
Nombre moyen de personnes par famille économique	436
Nombre total de personnes hors famille économique	437
CARACTÉRISTIQUES DU REVENU DE 2000	
Population de 15 ans et plus selon le sexe et les tranches de revenu total en 2000	
Total - Les deux sexes	438
Sans revenu	439
Avec un revenu	440
Moins de 1 000 $ (45)	441
1 000 $ - 2 999 $	442
3 000 $ - 4 999 $	443
5 000 $ - 6 999 $	444
7 000 $ - 9 999 $	445
10 000 $ - 11 999 $	446
12 000 $ - 14 999 $	447
15 000 $ - 19 999 $	448
20 000 $ - 24 999 $	449
25 000 $ - 29 999 $	450
30 000 $ - 34 999 $	451
35 000 $ - 39 999 $	452
40 000 $ - 44 999 $	453
45 000 $ - 49 999 $	454
50 000 $ - 59 999 $	455
60 000 $ et plus	456
Revenu moyen $ (46)	457
Revenu médian $ (46)	458
Erreur type de revenu moyen $ (46)	459

Table 1. Selected Characteristics for Census Tracts, 2001 Census – 100% Data and 20% Sample Data

No.	Characteristics	Vancouver 0504.04	Vancouver 0505	Vancouver 0506.01	Vancouver 0506.02		
	2000 INCOME CHARACTERISTICS						
	Population 15 years and over by sex and total income groups in 2000 – concluded						
460	Total - Males	2,810	2,520	1,310	2,500		
461	Without income	140	85	60	100		
462	With income	2,670	2,430	1,250	2,405		
463	Under $1,000 (45)	55	100	25	100		
464	$ 1,000 - $ 2,999	70	70	35	140		
465	$ 3,000 - $ 4,999	40	65	45	55		
466	$ 5,000 - $ 6,999	80	90	25	60		
467	$ 7,000 - $ 9,999	65	130	55	85		
468	$10,000 - $11,999	60	95	55	70		
469	$12,000 - $14,999	70	70	40	95		
470	$15,000 - $19,999	165	185	70	245		
471	$20,000 - $24,999	145	140	135	185		
472	$25,000 - $29,999	180	180	105	140		
473	$30,000 - $34,999	165	150	85	190		
474	$35,000 - $39,999	180	110	50	165		
475	$40,000 - $44,999	165	175	150	160		
476	$45,000 - $49,999	150	95	110	170		
477	$50,000 - $59,999	305	240	140	220		
478	$60,000 and over	775	540	115	320		
479	Average income $ (46)	45,173	44,734	32,774	33,201		
480	Median income $ (46)	41,002	32,536	32,334	30,431		
481	Standard error of average income $ (46)	1,218	3,490	1,239	1,135		
482	Total - Females	3,080	2,565	1,435	2,600		
483	Without income	135	145	90	155		
484	With income	2,945	2,420	1,350	2,445		
485	Under $1,000 (45)	110	115	25	165		
486	$ 1,000 - $ 2,999	185	100	90	150		
487	$ 3,000 - $ 4,999	75	95	70	100		
488	$ 5,000 - $ 6,999	120	115	100	85		
489	$ 7,000 - $ 9,999	255	165	120	185		
490	$10,000 - $11,999	115	130	95	160		
491	$12,000 - $14,999	170	190	115	240		
492	$15,000 - $19,999	275	220	110	280		
493	$20,000 - $24,999	215	225	170	215		
494	$25,000 - $29,999	240	225	85	185		
495	$30,000 - $34,999	245	210	105	220		
496	$35,000 - $39,999	195	140	90	170		
497	$40,000 - $44,999	205	125	70	85		
498	$45,000 - $49,999	125	75	40	50		
499	$50,000 - $59,999	215	150	30	90		
500	$60,000 and over	215	155	35	70		
501	Average income $ (46)	26,967	27,407	20,747	21,117		
502	Median income $ (46)	24,191	21,592	18,004	16,944		
503	Standard error of average income $ (46)	780	1,250	878	698		
	by composition of total income						
504	Total - Composition of income in 2000 % (47)	100.0	100.0	100.0	100.0		
505	Employment income %	80.1	81.9	84.6	82.4		
506	Government transfer payments %	8.8	7.8	11.2	10.8		
507	Other %	11.0	10.4	4.2	6.8		
	Population 15 years and over with employment income in 2000 by sex and work activity						
508	Both sexes with employment income (48)	4,200	4,015	2,140	3,685		
509	Average employment income $	38,144	35,666	27,250	29,418		
510	Standard error of average employment income $	898	2,220	875	802		
511	Worked full year, full time (49)	2,430	1,990	1,155	2,045		
512	Average employment income $	50,803	48,245	36,191	39,023		
513	Standard error of average employment income $	999	4,204	1,063	1,115		
514	Worked part year or part time (50)	1,695	1,950	980	1,560		
515	Average employment income $	21,241	23,129	16,780	17,671		
516	Standard error of average employment income $	1,249	1,319	1,062	844		
517	Males with employment income (48)	2,115	2,085	1,090	1,930		
518	Average employment income $	47,587	44,891	33,713	35,335		
519	Standard error of average employment income $	1,413	4,028	1,276	1,253		
520	Worked full year, full time (49)	1,395	1,225	720	1,270		
521	Average employment income $	58,390	56,200	39,190	42,573		
522	Standard error of average employment income $	1,386	6,671	1,389	1,566		
523	Worked part year or part time (50)	700	840	370	640		
524	Average employment income $	27,326	29,764	22,931	21,939		
525	Standard error of average employment income $	2,566	2,396	2,125	1,591		

Tableau 1. Certaines caractéristiques des secteurs de recensement, recensement de 2001 – Données intégrales et données-échantillon (20 %)

					Caractéristiques	N°
					CARACTÉRISTIQUES DU REVENU DE 2000	
					Population de 15 ans et plus selon le sexe et les tranches de revenu total en 2000 – fin	
					Total - Hommes	460
					Sans revenu	461
					Avec un revenu	462
					Moins de 1 000 $ (45)	463
					1 000 $ - 2 999 $	464
					3 000 $ - 4 999 $	465
					5 000 $ - 6 999 $	466
					7 000 $ - 9 999 $	467
					10 000 $ - 11 999 $	468
					12 000 $ - 14 999 $	469
					15 000 $ - 19 999 $	470
					20 000 $ - 24 999 $	471
					25 000 $ - 29 999 $	472
					30 000 $ - 34 999 $	473
					35 000 $ - 39 999 $	474
					40 000 $ - 44 999 $	475
					45 000 $ - 49 999 $	476
					50 000 $ - 59 999 $	477
					60 000 $ et plus	478
					Revenu moyen $ (46)	479
					Revenu médian $ (46)	480
					Erreur type de revenu moyen $ (46)	481
					Total - Femmes	482
					Sans revenu	483
					Avec un revenu	484
					Moins de 1 000 $ (45)	485
					1 000 $ - 2 999 $	486
					3 000 $ - 4 999 $	487
					5 000 $ - 6 999 $	488
					7 000 $ - 9 999 $	489
					10 000 $ - 11 999 $	490
					12 000 $ - 14 999 $	491
					15 000 $ - 19 999 $	492
					20 000 $ - 24 999 $	493
					25 000 $ - 29 999 $	494
					30 000 $ - 34 999 $	495
					35 000 $ - 39 999 $	496
					40 000 $ - 44 999 $	497
					45 000 $ - 49 999 $	498
					50 000 $ - 59 999 $	499
					60 000 $ et plus	500
					Revenu moyen $ (46)	501
					Revenu médian $ (46)	502
					Erreur type de revenu moyen $ (46)	503
					selon la composition du revenu total	
					Total - Composition du revenu en 2000 % (47)	504
					Revenu d'emploi %	505
					Transferts gouvernementaux %	506
					Autre %	507
					Population de 15 ans et plus ayant un revenu d'emploi en 2000 selon le sexe et le travail	
					Les deux sexes ayant un revenu d'emploi (48)	508
					Revenu moyen d'emploi $	509
					Erreur type de revenu moyen d'emploi $	510
					Ayant travaillé toute l'année à plein temps (49)	511
					Revenu moyen d'emploi $	512
					Erreur type de revenu moyen d'emploi $	513
					Ayant travaillé une partie de l'année ou à temps partiel (50)	514
					Revenu moyen d'emploi $	515
					Erreur type de revenu moyen d'emploi $	516
					Hommes ayant un revenu d'emploi (48)	517
					Revenu moyen d'emploi $	518
					Erreur type de revenu moyen d'emploi $	519
					Ayant travaillé toute l'année à plein temps (49)	520
					Revenu moyen d'emploi $	521
					Erreur type de revenu moyen d'emploi $	522
					Ayant travaillé une partie de l'année ou à temps partiel (50)	523
					Revenu moyen d'emploi $	524
					Erreur type de revenu moyen d'emploi $	525

Table 1. Selected Characteristics for Census Tracts, 2001 Census – 100% Data and 20% Sample Data

No.	Characteristics	Vancouver 0504.04	Vancouver 0505	Vancouver 0506.01	Vancouver 0506.02		
	2000 INCOME CHARACTERISTICS						
	Population 15 years and over with employment income in 2000 by sex and work activity – concluded						
526	Females with employment income (48)	2,085	1,930	1,060	1,755		
527	Average employment income $	28,565	25,710	20,607	22,923		
528	Standard error of average employment income $	920	1,387	1,046	866		
529	Worked full year, full time (49)	1,035	770	440	780		
530	Average employment income $	40,586	35,656	31,249	33,254		
531	Standard error of average employment income $	1,126	2,485	1,533	1,316		
532	Worked part year or part time (50)	995	1,115	610	920		
533	Average employment income $	16,971	18,113	13,095	14,714		
534	Standard error of average employment income $	1,038	1,347	1,040	865		
	Census families by structure and family income groups in 2000						
535	Total - All census families	2,325	1,815	1,090	1,890		
536	Under $10,000	50	55	50	60		
537	$ 10,000 - $19,999	70	20	100	125		
538	$ 20,000 - $29,999	145	150	110	195		
539	$ 30,000 - $39,999	160	140	125	210		
540	$ 40,000 - $49,999	250	185	140	235		
541	$ 50,000 - $59,999	215	190	150	195		
542	$ 60,000 - $69,999	250	140	110	170		
543	$ 70,000 - $79,999	175	180	110	235		
544	$ 80,000 - $89,999	235	150	50	140		
545	$ 90,000 - $99,999	185	140	60	80		
546	$100,000 and over	585	445	75	245		
547	Average family income $	76,470	84,416	52,877	61,096		
548	Median family income $	72,271	70,357	50,487	56,102		
549	Standard error of average family income $	1,730	5,224	1,843	1,695		
550	Total - All couple census families (51)	2,040	1,570	825	1,535		
551	Under $10,000	30	35	25	50		
552	$ 10,000 - $19,999	40	10	20	35		
553	$ 20,000 - $29,999	95	110	55	145		
554	$ 30,000 - $39,999	135	110	95	145		
555	$ 40,000 - $49,999	205	140	95	185		
556	$ 50,000 - $59,999	190	155	135	145		
557	$ 60,000 - $69,999	215	130	105	160		
558	$ 70,000 - $79,999	170	170	110	220		
559	$ 80,000 - $89,999	230	155	55	130		
560	$ 90,000 - $99,999	160	135	55	80		
561	$100,000 and over	565	420	75	240		
562	Average family income $	80,342	89,640	60,674	66,485		
563	Median family income $	78,148	75,465	59,277	64,013		
564	Standard error of average family income $	1,813	6,034	2,019	1,925		
	Incidence of low income in 2000						
565	Total - Economic families	2,310	1,785	1,060	1,835		
566	Low income	110	60	160	195		
567	Incidence of low income in 2000 % (52)	4.9	3.5	15.1	10.7		
568	Total - Unattached individuals 15 years and over	525	570	360	665		
569	Low income	50	145	110	280		
570	Incidence of low income in 2000 % (52)	10.1	25.7	30.1	42.3		
571	Total - Population in private households	7,505	6,345	3,780	6,825		
572	Low income	440	335	585	1,050		
573	Incidence of low income in 2000 % (52)	5.8	5.2	15.4	15.3		
	Private households by household income groups in 2000						
574	Total - All private households	2,735	2,205	1,290	2,315		
575	Under $10,000	45	85	70	145		
576	$ 10,000 - $19,999	150	115	100	305		
577	$ 20,000 - $29,999	220	215	130	200		
578	$ 30,000 - $39,999	225	180	140	220		
579	$ 40,000 - $49,999	295	235	165	255		
580	$ 50,000 - $59,999	250	215	175	240		
581	$ 60,000 - $69,999	270	175	150	180		
582	$ 70,000 - $79,999	180	175	110	215		
583	$ 80,000 - $89,999	240	155	105	130		
584	$ 90,000 - $99,999	215	160	40	125		
585	$100,000 and over	640	500	105	290		
586	Average household income $	73,240	78,677	53,587	56,767		
587	Median household income $	67,239	61,059	51,694	51,535		
588	Standard error of average household income $	1,675	4,503	1,725	1,640		

Tableau 1. Certaines caractéristiques des secteurs de recensement, recensement de 2001 – Données intégrales et données-échantillon (20 %)

					Caractéristiques	N°
					CARACTÉRISTIQUES DU REVENU DE 2000	
					Population de 15 ans et plus ayant un revenu d'emploi en 2000 selon le sexe et le travail – fin	
					Femmes ayant un revenu d'emploi (48)	526
					Revenu moyen d'emploi $	527
					Erreur type de revenu moyen d'emploi $	528
					Ayant travaillé toute l'année à plein temps (49)	529
					Revenu moyen d'emploi $	530
					Erreur type de revenu moyen d'emploi $	531
					Ayant travaillé une partie de l'année ou à temps partiel (50)	532
					Revenu moyen d'emploi $	533
					Erreur type de revenu moyen d'emploi $	534
					Familles de recensement selon la structure et les tranches de revenu de la famille en 2000	
					Total - Toutes les familles de recensement	535
					Moins de 10 000 $	536
					10 000 $ - 19 999 $	537
					20 000 $ - 29 999 $	538
					30 000 $ - 39 999 $	539
					40 000 $ - 49 999 $	540
					50 000 $ - 59 999 $	541
					60 000 $ - 69 999 $	542
					70 000 $ - 79 999 $	543
					80 000 $ - 89 999 $	544
					90 000 $ - 99 999 $	545
					100 000 $ et plus	546
					Revenu moyen des familles $	547
					Revenu médian des familles $	548
					Erreur type de revenu moyen des familles $	549
					Total - Toutes les familles de recensement comptant un couple (51)	550
					Moins de 10 000 $	551
					10 000 $ - 19 999 $	552
					20 000 $ - 29 999 $	553
					30 000 $ - 39 999 $	554
					40 000 $ - 49 999 $	555
					50 000 $ - 59 999 $	556
					60 000 $ - 69 999 $	557
					70 000 $ - 79 999 $	558
					80 000 $ - 89 999 $	559
					90 000 $ - 99 999 $	560
					100 000 $ et plus	561
					Revenu moyen des familles $	562
					Revenu médian des familles $	563
					Erreur type de revenu moyen des familles $	564
					Fréquence des unités à faible revenu en 2000	
					Total - Familles économiques	565
					Faible revenu	566
					Fréquence des unités à faible revenu en 2000 % (52)	567
					Total - Personnes hors famille économique de 15 ans et plus	568
					Faible revenu	569
					Fréquence des unités à faible revenu en 2000 % (52)	570
					Total - Population dans les ménages privés	571
					Faible revenu	572
					Fréquence des unités à faible revenu en 2000 % (52)	573
					Ménages privés selon les tranches de revenu du ménage en 2000	
					Total - Tous les ménages privés	574
					Moins de 10 000 $	575
					10 000 $ - 19 999 $	576
					20 000 $ - 29 999 $	577
					30 000 $ - 39 999 $	578
					40 000 $ - 49 999 $	579
					50 000 $ - 59 999 $	580
					60 000 $ - 69 999 $	581
					70 000 $ - 79 999 $	582
					80 000 $ - 89 999 $	583
					90 000 $ - 99 999 $	584
					100 000 $ et plus	585
					Revenu moyen des ménages $	586
					Revenu médian des ménages $	587
					Erreur type de revenu moyen des ménages $	588

Footnotes

(1) Based on 2001 area. These figures have not been subjected to random rounding.

(2) These figures have not been subjected to random rounding.

(3) Includes institutional residents.

(4) Excludes institutional residents. These data are based on weighted sample data (20%). In some instances, due to weighting factors, it is possible for small areas to have an "estimated population excluding institutional residents" higher than the "population including institutional residents".

(5) Non-official language categories are based on the most frequently reported responses in the census metropolitan area or census agglomeration. When zero values are obtained for most of the non-official languages in some geographic areas, the number of non-official languages shown is less.

(6) This is a subtotal of all non-official languages collected by the census that are not displayed separately here.

(7) Indicates the number of respondents reporting knowledge of each of these non-official languages.

(8) The official language minority is English in Quebec and French in all other provinces and territories.

(9) This table shows total response counts for the 15 most frequently reported ethnic origins in the census metropolitan area or census agglomeration. Total responses indicate the number of respondents who reported each ethnic origin, either as their only response or in addition to one or more other ethnic origins. Total responses represent the sum of single ethnic origin responses and multiple ethnic origin responses received in the census.

(10) Refers to those persons identifying with at least one Aboriginal group, i.e. North American Indian, Métis or Inuit (Eskimo), and/or those who reported being a Treaty Indian or a Registered Indian as defined by the *Indian Act* of Canada and/or who were members of an Indian Band or First Nation.

Renvois

(1) Selon la superficie de 2001. Ces chiffres n'ont pas fait l'objet d'un arrondissement aléatoire.

(2) Ces chiffres n'ont pas fait l'objet d'un arrondissement aléatoire.

(3) Comprend les pensionnaires d'un établissement institutionnel.

(4) Ne comprend pas les pensionnaires d'un établissement institutionnel. Ces données sont basées sur les données-échantillon pondérées (20 %). Dans certains cas, en raison des coefficients de pondération, il est possible que, dans les petites régions, « l'estimation de la population ne comprenant pas les pensionnaires d'un établissement institutionnel » soit plus élevée que « la population comprenant les pensionnaires d'un établissement institutionnel ».

(5) Les catégories de langues non officielles sont basées sur les réponses le plus souvent déclarées dans la région métropolitaine de recensement ou l'agglomération de recensement. Le nombre de langues non officielles présentées est moindre lorsque des valeurs égales à zéro sont obtenues pour la plupart des langues non officielles dans certaines régions géographiques.

(6) Ceci est un sous-total de toutes les langues non officielles recueillies par le recensement qui ne sont pas affichées séparément ici.

(7) Indique le nombre de répondants qui ont indiqué avoir une connaissance de chacune de ces langues non officielles.

(8) Au Québec, la langue officielle minoritaire est l'anglais, et dans les autres provinces et territoires, la langue officielle minoritaire est le français.

(9) Ce tableau présente les chiffres des réponses totales des 15 origines ethniques le plus souvent déclarées dans la région métropolitaine de recensement ou l'agglomération de recensement. Le total des réponses correspond au nombre de recensés ayant indiqué chaque origine ethnique, soit comme étant leur seule réponse ou comme étant associée à une autre origine ethnique ou plus. Le total des réponses représente la somme des réponses uniques portant sur l'origine ethnique et des réponses multiples portant sur l'origine ethnique déclarées dans le cadre du recensement.

(10) S'entend des personnes ayant déclaré appartenir à au moins un groupe autochtone, c'est-à-dire Indien de l'Amérique du Nord, Métis, ou Inuit (Esquimau) et/ou ayant déclaré être un Indien des traités ou un Indien inscrit aux termes de la *Loi sur les Indiens* du Canada et/ou ayant déclaré être membre d'une bande indienne ou d'une première nation.

(11) Refers to those persons who reported at least one Aboriginal origin (North American Indian, Métis or Inuit) to the ethnic origin question. Ethnic origin refers to the ethnic or cultural group(s) to which the respondent's ancestors belong. Additional information on ethnic origin can be obtained from the 2001 Census Dictionary.

(12) Registered or Treaty Indian: The expression "Registered Indian" refers to those persons who reported they were registered under the *Indian Act* of Canada. Treaty Indians are persons who are registered under the *Indian Act* and can prove descent from a Band that signed a treaty.

The Registered Indian counts in this table may differ from the administrative counts maintained by the Department of Indian Affairs and Northern Development, with the most important causes of these differences being the incompletely enumerated Indian reserves and Indian settlements as well as methodological and conceptual differences between the two sources.

(13) Includes respondents who reported a write-in response classified as a visible minority such as "Polynesian", "Guyanese", "Mauritian", etc.

(14) Includes respondents who reported more than one visible minority group by checking two or more mark-in circles, e.g. "Black" and "South Asian".

(15) Includes those who reported dual citizenship including Canadian.

(16) Refers to people who are, or have been, landed immigrants in Canada. A landed immigrant is a person who has been granted the right to live in Canada permanently by immigration authorities. Some immigrants have resided in Canada for a number of years, while others are recent arrivals. Most immigrants are born outside Canada, but a small number were born in Canada.

(17) "Other Europe" includes Southern Europe, Eastern Europe, Northern and Western Europe, excluding the United Kingdom. Data not directly comparable to censuses prior to 1996, where Europe included Cyprus and the U.S.S.R. In 1996 and 2001, Cyprus and the former Soviet republics of Armenia, Azerbaijan, Georgia, Kazakhstan, Kyrgyzstan, Tajikistan, Turkmenistan and Uzbekistan are included in Asia.

(11) Personne ayant indiqué appartenir à au moins un groupe autochtone à la question sur l'origine ethnique, c'est-à-dire Indien de l'Amérique du Nord, Métis ou Inuit. L'origine ethnique se rapporte au(x) groupe(s) ethnique(s) ou culturel(s) auquel (auxquels) appartenaient les ancêtres du recensé. Pour de plus amples renseignements au sujet de l'origine ethnique, veuillez consulter le Dictionnaire du recensement de 2001.

(12) Indien inscrit ou Indien des traités : Les Indiens inscrits sont des personnes ayant déclaré être inscrites en vertu de la *Loi sur les Indiens* du Canada. Les Indiens des traités sont des personnes qui sont inscrites en vertu de la *Loi sur les Indiens* et qui peuvent démontrer qu'elles descendent d'une bande qui a signé un traité.

Il est possible que les nombres d'Indiens inscrits qui figurent dans le présent tableau ne concordent pas avec les chiffres du ministère des Affaires indiennes et du Nord canadien, les divergences étant surtout attribuables au dénombrement partiel des réserves indiennes et des établissements indiens et à la diversité des méthodes et concepts adoptés.

(13) Comprend les répondants ayant fourni une réponse écrite classifiée comme faisant partie des minorités visibles, p. ex. « Polynésien », « Guyanais », « Mauricien », etc.

(14) Comprend les répondants ayant déclaré plus d'un groupe de minorités visibles en cochant au moins deux cercles, p. ex. « Noir » et « Sud-Asiatique ».

(15) Comprend les personnes qui ont indiqué une double citoyenneté, y compris « Canadien ».

(16) Personnes ayant le statut d'immigrant reçu au Canada, ou l'ayant déjà eu. Un immigrant reçu est une personne à qui les autorités de l'immigration ont accordé le droit de résider au Canada en permanence. Certains immigrants résident au Canada depuis un certain nombre d'années, alors que d'autres sont arrivés récemment. La plupart des immigrants sont nés à l'extérieur du Canada, mais un petit nombre d'entre eux sont nés ici.

(17) « Autre Europe » comprend l'Europe méridionale, l'Europe orientale, l'Europe septentrionale et l'Europe occidentale excluant le Royaume-Uni. Les données ne sont pas directement comparables avec celles des recensements antérieurs à celui de 1996, alors que l'Europe comprenait Chypre et l'URSS. En 1996 et en 2001, Chypre et les anciennes républiques soviétiques d'Arménie, d'Azerbaïdjan, de Géorgie, du Kazakhstan, du Kirghizistan, d'Ouzbékistan, du Tadjikistan et du Turkménistan sont comprises dans l'Asie.

(18) "Other" includes Greenland, Saint Pierre and Miquelon, the category "Other country", as well as immigrants born in Canada.

(19) Refers to persons who, at the time of the census, held a student or employment authorization, Minister's permit or who were refugee claimants, as well as family members living with them.

(20) Includes data up to May 15, 2001.

(21) Includes Roman Catholic, Eastern Catholic, Polish National Catholic Church, Old Catholic.

(22) Includes mostly answers of "Christian", not otherwise stated.

(23) Includes Baha'i, Eckankar, Jains, Shinto, Taoist, Zoroastrian and Eastern religions, not identified elsewhere.

(24) Includes Aboriginal spirituality, Pagan, Wicca, Unity - New Thought - Pantheist, Scientology, Rastafarian, New Age, Gnostic, Satanist, etc.

(25) Includes Agnostic, Atheist, Humanist, and No religion, and other responses, such as Darwinism, etc.

(26) Refers to persons born outside Canada.

(27) Refers to persons born inside Canada with at least one parent born outside Canada.

(28) Refers to persons born inside Canada with both parents born inside Canada.

(29) Population 1 year of age and over residing in Canada, excluding institutional residents and Canadians (military and government personnel) in households outside Canada.

The concept of "migrants" is defined at the Census Subdivision (CSD) level. For geographic levels below the CSD, such as census tracts (CTs), the distinction between the migrant and non-migrant population refers to the corresponding CSD of the CT. For example, migrants within a CT are those persons who moved from a different CSD, while non-migrants are those who moved within the same CSD, although they moved in from a different CT in the same CSD or moved within the same CT.

(18) « Autre » comprend le Groenland, Saint-Pierre-et-Miquelon, la catégorie « Autre pays » ainsi que les immigrants nés au Canada.

(19) Personnes qui, au moment du recensement, étaient titulaires d'un permis de séjour pour étudiants, d'un permis de travail ou d'un permis ministériel, ou qui revendiquaient le statut de réfugié, ainsi que les membres de leur famille vivant avec elles.

(20) Comprend les données jusqu'au 15 mai 2001.

(21) Comprend Catholique romaine, Catholique orientale, Église catholique nationale polonaise, Vieille-catholique.

(22) Comprend la plupart des réponses « Chrétienne » non déterminées autrement.

(23) Comprend Baha'i, Eckankar, Djaïn, Shintoïste, Taoïste, Zoroastrienne et les religions orientales, non incluses ailleurs.

(24) Comprend Spiritualité autochtone, Païenne, Wicca, Unité - Nouvelle Pensée - Panthéiste, Scientologie, Rasta, Nouvel Âge, Gnostique, Satanique, etc.

(25) Comprend Agnostique, Athée, Humaniste et Aucune religion, et autres réponses, telles que darwiniste, etc.

(26) Comprend les personnes nées à l'extérieur du Canada.

(27) Comprend les personnes nées au Canada avec au moins un parent né à l'extérieur du Canada.

(28) Comprend les personnes nées au Canada de parents qui sont nés au Canada.

(29) Population de 1 an et plus résidant au Canada, à l'exclusion des pensionnaires d'un établissement institutionnel et des Canadiens (militaires et fonctionnaires) appartenant à un ménage à l'extérieur du Canada.

Le concept de « migrants » est défini au niveau des subdivisions de recensement (SDR). Pour les niveaux géographiques inférieurs aux SDR, comme les secteurs de recensement (SR), la distinction entre la population des migrants et des non-migrants est faite au niveau de la SDR correspondant au SR. Par exemple, les migrants au sein d'un SR sont les personnes qui sont originaires d'une SDR différente, alors que les non-migrants sont celles qui ont déménagé à l'intérieur de la même SDR, même s'ils sont passés d'un SR à un autre à l'intérieur de la même SDR ou ont déménagé à l'intérieur du même SR.

(30) Population 5 years of age and over residing in Canada, excluding institutional residents and Canadians (military and government personnel) in households outside Canada.

The concept of "migrants" is defined at the Census Subdivision (CSD) level. For geographic levels below the CSD, such as census tracts (CTs), the distinction between the migrant and non-migrant population refers to the corresponding CSD of the CT. For example, migrants within a CT are those persons who moved from a different CSD, while non-migrants are those who moved within the same CSD, although they moved in from a different CT in the same CSD or moved within the same CT.

(31) Includes "Never attended school or attended kindergarten only".

(32) Excludes persons with a postsecondary certificate, diploma or degree. Refers to courses completed at postsecondary institutions (university or college) which normally require a high school graduation certificate or equivalent for entrance, as well as to other courses in related or similar institutions which may not require a high school graduation certificate for entrance.

(33) Includes persons who may or may not have, in addition to a Trades certificate or diploma, some postsecondary courses without any degree, certificate or diploma.

(34) Referred to as "Other **non-university** certificate or diploma" in previous censuses, this sector includes non-degree-granting institutions such as community colleges, CEGEPs, private business colleges and technical institutes.

(35) Refers to persons who reported time spent doing one or more of the following unpaid work activities: (a) unpaid housework; (b) unpaid child care; (c) unpaid care or assistance to seniors. For example, a respondent who reported 5 to 14 hours of housework, 30 to 59 hours of child care and no hours of care or assistance to seniors would fall into the category "Housework and child care only".

(36) Unemployed persons 15 years and over who have never worked for pay or in self-employment or who had last worked prior to January 1, 2000.

(30) Population de 5 ans et plus résidant au Canada, à l'exclusion des pensionnaires d'un établissement institutionnel et des Canadiens (militaires et fonctionnaires) appartenant à un ménage à l'extérieur du Canada.

Le concept de « migrants » est défini au niveau des subdivisions de recensement (SDR). Pour les niveaux géographiques inférieurs aux SDR, comme les secteurs de recensement (SR), la distinction entre la population des migrants et des non-migrants est faite au niveau de la SDR correspondant au SR. Par exemple, les migrants au sein d'un SR sont les personnes qui sont originaires d'une SDR différente, alors que les non-migrants sont celles qui ont déménagé à l'intérieur de la même SDR, même s'ils sont passés d'un SR à un autre à l'intérieur de la même SDR ou ont déménagé à l'intérieur du même SR.

(31) Comprend la catégorie « Aucune scolarité ou uniquement l'école maternelle ».

(32) Ne comprend pas les personnes ayant un certificat, un diplôme ou un grade postsecondaire. Désigne les cours terminés dans un établissement postsecondaire (université ou collège) qui exige habituellement comme condition d'admission un certificat d'études secondaires ou l'équivalent; il peut aussi s'agir d'autres cours dans des établissements similaires ou connexes qui ne demandent pas nécessairement comme condition d'admission un certificat d'études secondaires.

(33) Comprend les personnes pouvant avoir ou ne pas avoir des études postsecondaires partielles sans aucun grade, certificat ou diplôme, en plus d'un certificat ou un diplôme d'une école de métiers.

(34) Désigné par l'expression « Certificat ou diplôme d'autres études **non universitaires** » dans les recensements précédents, ce secteur comprend tous les autres établissements ne décernant pas de grade, tels que les collèges communautaires, les cégeps, les collèges commerciaux privés et les instituts techniques.

(35) Personnes qui ont déclaré du temps consacré à une ou plusieurs des activités de travail non rémunéré suivantes : a) travaux ménagers, sans paye ou sans salaire; b) soins aux enfants, sans paye ou sans salaire; c) soins ou aide aux personnes âgées, sans paye ou sans salaire. Par exemple, un répondant qui a déclaré 5 à 14 heures de travaux ménagers, 30 à 59 heures de soins aux enfants et aucune heure de soins ou d'aide aux personnes âgées serait classé dans la catégorie « Travaux ménagers et soins aux enfants seulement ».

(36) Chômeurs de 15 ans et plus qui n'ont jamais travaillé à un emploi salarié ou à leur compte ou qui ont travaillé la dernière fois avant le 1er janvier 2000.

(37) Refers to the experienced labour force: persons who, during the week prior to Census Day, were employed or unemployed who worked for pay or in self-employment since January 1, 2000.

(38) Includes apartments without direct ground access in buildings that have fewer than five storeys and apartments with direct ground access in buildings that have fewer than five storeys.

(39) Includes mobile homes and other movable dwellings such as houseboats and railroad cars.

(40) Includes households in tenant-occupied, non-farm, non-reserve dwellings with household income greater than $0 in 2000 (i.e. excludes negative or zero household income).

(41) It should be noted that not all households spending 30% or more of incomes on shelter costs are necessarily experiencing housing affordability problems. This is particularly true of households with high incomes. There are also other households who choose to spend more on shelter than on other goods. Nevertheless, the allocation of 30% or more of a household's income to housing expenses provides a useful benchmark for assessing trends in housing affordability.

The relatively high shelter cost to household income ratios for some households may have resulted from the difference in the reference period for shelter cost and household income data. The reference period for shelter cost data (gross rent for tenants, and owner's major payments for owners) is 2001, while household income is reported for the year 2000. As well, for some households the 2000 household income may represent income for only part of a year.

(42) Includes households in owner-occupied, non-farm, non-reserve dwellings with household income greater than $0 in 2000 (i.e. excludes negative or zero household income).

(43) The average number of children at home per family is calculated using the total number of children at home and the total number of families.

(44) Non-relatives may be present.

(45) Including loss.

(37) S'entend de la population active expérimentée : les personnes qui, pendant la semaine ayant précédé le jour du recensement, étaient occupées ou en chômage et qui avaient travaillé à un emploi salarié ou à leur compte depuis le 1er janvier 2000.

(38) Comprend les appartements sans accès direct au niveau du sol dans les immeubles de moins de cinq étages et les appartements avec accès direct au niveau du sol dans les immeubles de moins de cinq étages.

(39) Comprend les maisons mobiles et les autres logements mobiles tels que les bateaux-maisons et les wagons de chemin de fer.

(40) Comprend les ménages ayant un revenu supérieur à 0 $ en 2000 dans les logements non agricoles hors réserve occupés par un locataire (sont exclus les ménages ayant un revenu négatif ou nul).

(41) Il convient de souligner que les ménages qui consacrent 30 % ou plus de leur revenu aux coûts d'habitation n'éprouvent pas nécessairement des problèmes d'abordabilité du logement. C'est notamment le cas des ménages ayant un revenu élevé. D'autres ménages choisissent de consacrer une plus grande part de leur revenu aux coûts d'habitation qu'à d'autres biens. Néanmoins, ce seuil (30 % ou plus du revenu du ménage consacré aux coûts d'habitation) constitue un repère utile pour l'évaluation des tendances en matière d'abordabilité du logement.

Les rapports entre les coûts d'habitation et le revenu du ménage relativement élevés pour certains ménages s'expliquent du fait que les périodes de référence utilisées pour les données sur les coûts d'habitation et pour les données sur le revenu du ménage ne sont pas les mêmes. En effet, la période de référence est l'année 2001 dans le cas des données sur les coûts d'habitation (loyer brut pour les locataires et principales dépenses de propriété pour les propriétaires), et l'année 2000 dans le cas des données sur le revenu du ménage. En outre, pour certains ménages, le revenu du ménage déclaré ne correspond qu'à une partie de l'année 2000.

(42) Comprend les ménages ayant un revenu supérieur à 0 $ en 2000 dans les logements non agricoles hors réserve occupés par le propriétaire (sont exclus les ménages ayant un revenu négatif ou nul).

(43) Le nombre moyen d'enfants à la maison par famille est calculé à partir du nombre total d'enfants à la maison et du nombre total de familles.

(44) Il peut y avoir des personnes non apparentées.

(45) Comprend les pertes.

(46) For persons with income.

(47) Percentages may not add to 100% due to rounding of the data.

(48) Includes persons who did not work in 2000 but reported employment income.

(49) Worked 49-52 weeks in 2000, mostly full time.

(50) Worked less than 49 weeks or worked mostly part time in 2000.

(51) Refers to married, opposite-sex and same-sex common-law couple families.

(52) Incidence of low income rates are calculated from rounded counts of low-income persons or families and the total number of persons or families. These counts have been rounded independently of the rounded counts shown in the table; thus, there may be a small difference between the rate shown and the one derived from the counts shown. Users are advised to interpret incidence of low income rates based upon small counts with caution.

(46) S'applique aux personnes ayant un revenu.

(47) Il est possible que la somme des pourcentages ne soit pas de 100 % en raison de l'arrondissement des données.

(48) Comprend les personnes qui n'ont pas travaillé en 2000 mais qui ont déclaré un revenu d'emploi.

(49) A travaillé 49-52 semaines en 2000, surtout à plein temps.

(50) A travaillé moins de 49 semaines ou a travaillé surtout à temps partiel en 2000.

(51) Comprend les familles comptant un couple marié et les familles comptant un couple en union libre formé de partenaires de sexe opposé ou de même sexe.

(52) Les taux de fréquence des unités à faible revenu sont calculés à partir des chiffres arrondis des personnes ou des familles à faible revenu et du nombre total de personnes ou de familles. Ces chiffres ont été arrondis séparément des chiffres arrondis figurant dans le tableau; par conséquent, il peut y avoir une légère différence entre la fréquence indiquée et une fréquence calculée à partir des chiffres figurant dans le tableau. Les utilisateurs doivent faire preuve de circonspection lorsqu'ils interprètent les fréquences des unités à faible revenu fondées sur des chiffres peu élevés.

Definitions

For further information on definitions and special notes, refer to the 2001 Census Dictionary, Catalogue No. 92-378-XIE or 92-378-XPE.

Aboriginal Identity

Refers to those persons who reported identifying with at least one Aboriginal group, i.e. North American Indian, Métis or Inuit (Eskimo), and/or those who reported being a Treaty Indian or a Registered Indian as defined by the *Indian Act* of Canada and/or who were members of an Indian Band or First Nation. In 1991 and previous censuses, Aboriginal persons were determined using the ethnic origin question (ancestry). The 1996 Census included a question on the individual's own perception of his/her Aboriginal identity. The 2001 Census question is the same as the one used in 1996.

Aboriginal Origin

Refers to those persons who reported at least one Aboriginal origin to the ethnic origin question (North American Indian, Métis or Inuit). Ethnic origin refers to the ethnic or cultural group(s) to which the respondent's ancestors belong. See Ethnic Origin.

Age

Refers to the age at last birthday (as of the census reference date, May 15, 2001). This variable is derived from date of birth.

Age at Immigration

Refers to the age at which the respondent first obtained landed immigrant status. A landed immigrant is a person who has been granted the right to live in Canada permanently by immigration authorities.

Bedrooms

Refers to all rooms designed and furnished as bedrooms and used mainly for sleeping purposes, even though the use may be occasional (e.g. spare bedroom).

Census Agglomeration (CA)

See the definition of Census Metropolitan Area (CMA) and Census Agglomeration (CA).

Census Division (CD)

Census division (CD) is the general term for provincially legislated areas (such as county, municipalité régionale de comté and regional district) or their equivalents. Census divisions are intermediate geographic areas between the province level and the municipality (census subdivision).

Census Family

Refers to a married couple (with or without children of either or both spouses), a couple living common-law (with or without children of either or both partners) or a lone parent of any marital status, with at least one child living in the same dwelling. A couple living common-law may be of opposite or same sex. "Children" in a census family include grandchildren living with their grandparent(s) but with no parents present.

Census Family Status

Refers to the classification of the population according to whether or not the persons are members of a census family.

Family persons refer to household members who belong to a census family. They, in turn, are further classified as follows:

Spouses refer to persons of opposite sex who are legally married to each other and living in the same dwelling.

Common-law partners are two persons of opposite sex or of the same sex who are not legally married to each other, but live together as a couple in the same dwelling.

Lone parent refers to a mother or a father, with no spouse or common-law partner present, living in a dwelling with one or more children.

Children refer to blood, step- or adopted sons and daughters (regardless of age or marital status) who are living in the same dwelling as their parent(s), as well as grandchildren in households where there are no parents present. Sons and daughters who are living with their spouse or common-law partner, or with one or more of their own children, are not considered to be members of the census family of their parent(s), even if they are living in the same dwelling. In addition, those sons and daughters who do not live in the same dwelling as their parent(s) are not considered members of the census family of their parent(s). The category of children can be further distinguished as follows:

Never-married sons and/or daughters in a census family, as used in censuses prior to 2001.

Other sons and/or daughters in a census family who would not have been included in the census family of their parents according to the previous concept.

Grandchildren living in the same household as their grandparent(s), with no parents present.

Non-family persons refer to household members who do not belong to a census family. They may be related to Person 1 (e.g. Person 1's sister, brother-in-law, cousin, grandparent), or unrelated to Person 1 (e.g. lodger, room-mate, employee). A person living alone is always a non-family person.

Census Family Structure

Refers to the classification of census families into married couples (with or without children of either or both spouses), common-law couples (with or without children of either or both partners), and lone-parent families by sex of parent. A couple living common-law may be of opposite or same sex. "Children" in a census family include grandchildren living with their grandparent(s) but with no parents present.

Census Metropolitan Area (CMA) and Census Agglomeration (CA)

A census metropolitan area (CMA) or a census agglomeration (CA) is formed by one or more adjacent municipalities centred on a large urban area (known as the urban core). The census population count of the urban core is at least 10,000 to form a census agglomeration and at least 100,000 to form a census metropolitan area. To be included in the CMA or CA, other adjacent municipalities must have a high degree of integration with the central urban area, as measured by commuting flows derived from census place of work data.

If the population of the urban core of a CA declines below 10,000, the CA is retired. However, once an area becomes a CMA, it is retained as a CMA even if the population of its urban core declines below 100,000. The urban areas in the CMA or CA that are not contiguous to the urban core are called the urban fringe. Rural areas in the CMA or CA are called the rural fringe.

When a CA has an urban core of at least 50,000 based on census counts, it is subdivided into census tracts. Census tracts are maintained for the CA even if the population of the urban core subsequently falls below 50,000. All CMAs are subdivided into census tracts.

Census Subdivision (CSD)

Census subdivision (CSD) is the general term for municipalities (as determined by provincial legislation) or areas treated as municipal equivalents for statistical purposes (for example, Indian reserves, Indian settlements and unorganized territories).

Census Subdivision Type

Census subdivisions (CSDs) are classified into 46 types according to official designations adopted by provincial or federal authorities. Two exceptions are "Subdivision of Unorganized" in Newfoundland and Labrador, and "Subdivision of County Municipality" in Nova Scotia, which are geographic areas created as equivalents for municipalities by Statistics Canada, in cooperation with those provinces, for the purpose of disseminating statistical data.

The **census subdivision type** accompanies the census subdivision name in order to distinguish CSDs from each other, for example, Granby, V (for the *ville* of Granby) and Granby, CT (for the *municipalité de canton* of Granby).

Census Tract (CT)

Census tracts (CTs) are small, relatively stable geographic areas that usually have a population of 2,500 to 8,000. They are located in census metropolitan areas and in census agglomerations with an urban core population of 50,000 or more in the previous census.

A committee of local specialists (for example, planners, health and social workers and educators) initially delineates CTs in conjunction with Statistics Canada. Once a census metropolitan area (CMA) or census agglomeration (CA) has been subdivided into census tracts, the census tracts are maintained even if the urban core population subsequently declines below 50,000.

Citizenship

Refers to the legal citizenship status of the respondent. Persons who are citizens of more than one country were instructed to provide the name of the other country(ies).

Class of Worker

This variable classifies persons who reported a job into the following categories:

(a) persons who worked mainly for wages, salaries, commissions, tips, piece-rates, or payments "in kind" (payments in goods or services rather than money);

(b) persons who worked mainly for themselves, with or without paid help, operating a business, farm or professional practice, alone or in partnership;

(c) persons who worked without pay in a family business, farm or professional practice owned or operated by a related household member; unpaid family work does not include unpaid housework, unpaid childcare, unpaid care to seniors and volunteer work.

The job reported was the one held in the week (Sunday to Saturday) prior to enumeration (May 15, 2001) if the person was employed, or the job of longest duration since January 1, 2000, if the person was not employed during the reference week. Persons with two or more jobs in the reference week were asked to provide information for the job at which they worked the most hours.

Incorporation Status

Refers to the legal status of a business, farm or professional practice. It is directed at persons who were mainly self-employed, either with or without paid help in the job reported (i.e. their job in the week [Sunday to Saturday] prior to enumeration [May 15, 2001] or the one of longest duration since January 1, 2000). An **incorporated business** is a business, farm or professional practice that has been formed into a legal corporation, thus constituting a legal entity under either federal or provincial laws. An **unincorporated business**, farm or professional practice is not a separate legal entity, but may be a partnership, family business or owner-operated business.

Common-law Status

Refers to two people of the opposite sex or of the same sex who live together as a couple, but who are not legally married to each other.

Condition of Dwelling

Refers to whether, in the judgement of the respondent, the dwelling requires any repairs (excluding desirable remodelling or additions).

Dwelling, Occupied Private

Refers to a private dwelling in which a person or a group of persons is permanently residing. Also included are private dwellings whose usual residents are temporarily absent on Census Day. Unless otherwise specified, all data in housing products are for occupied private dwellings, rather than for unoccupied private dwellings or dwellings occupied solely by foreign and/or temporary residents.

Dwelling, Private

Refers to a separate set of living quarters with a private entrance either from outside or from a common hall, lobby, vestibule or stairway inside the building. The entrance to the dwelling must be one that can be used without passing through the living quarters of someone else. The dwelling must meet the two conditions necessary for year-round occupancy:

(a) a source of heat or power (as evidenced by chimneys, power lines, oil or gas pipes or meters, generators, woodpiles, electric lights, heating pumps, solar heating panels, etc.);

(b) an enclosed space that provides shelter from the elements (as evidenced by complete and enclosed walls and roof, and by doors and windows that provide protection from wind, rain and snow).

The census classifies private dwellings into **regular private dwellings** and **occupied marginal dwellings**. Regular private dwellings are further classified into three major groups: **occupied dwellings** (occupied by usual residents), **dwellings occupied by foreign and/or temporary residents** and **unoccupied dwellings**. Marginal dwellings are classified as occupied by usual residents or by foreign and/or temporary residents. Marginal dwellings that were unoccupied on Census Day are not counted in the housing stock.

Earner or Employment Income Recipient

Refers to a person 15 years of age and over who received wages and salaries, net income from a non-farm unincorporated business and/or professional practice, and/or net farm self-employment income during calendar year 2000.

Economic Family

Refers to a group of two or more persons who live in the same dwelling and are related to each other by blood, marriage, common-law or adoption.

Ethnic Origin

Refers to the ethnic or cultural group(s) to which the respondent's ancestors belong.

First Official Language Spoken

Refers to a variable specified within the framework of the *Official Languages Act*.

Generation Status

Generation status of the respondent, i.e. "1st", "2nd" or "3rd +" generation, refers to whether the respondent or the respondent's parents were born in or outside Canada.

Highest Level of Schooling

Refers to the highest grade or year of elementary or secondary (high) school attended, or to the highest year of university or college education completed. University education is considered to be a higher level of schooling than college education. Also, the attainment of a degree, certificate or diploma is considered to be at a higher level than years completed or attended without an educational qualification.

Home Language

Refers to the language spoken most often or on a regular basis at home by the individual at the time of the census.

Hours Spent Doing Unpaid Housework

Refers to the number of hours persons spent doing unpaid housework, yard work or home maintenance in the week (Sunday to Saturday) prior to Census Day (May 15, 2001). It includes hours spent doing unpaid housework for members of one's own household, for other family members outside the household, and for friends or neighbours.

Unpaid housework does not include volunteer work for a non-profit organization, a religious organization, a charity or community group, or work without pay in the operation of a family farm, business or professional practice.

Hours Spent Looking After Children, Without Pay

Refers to the number of hours persons spent looking after children without pay. It includes hours spent providing unpaid child care for members of one's own household, for other family members outside the household, for friends or neighbours or for other family members outside the household in the week (Sunday to Saturday) prior to Census Day (May 15, 2001).

Unpaid child care does not include volunteer work for a non-profit organization, a religious organization, a charity or community group, or work without pay in the operation of a family farm, business or professional practice.

Hours Spent Providing Unpaid Care or Assistance to Seniors

Refers to the number of hours persons spent providing unpaid care or assistance to seniors of one's own household, to other senior family members outside the household, and to friends or neighbours in the week (Sunday to Saturday) prior to Census Day (May 15, 2001).

Unpaid care or assistance to seniors does not include volunteer work for a non-profit organization, religious organization, charity or community group, or work without pay in the operation of a family farm, business or professional practice.

Household Living Arrangements

Refers to the classification of persons in terms of whether they are members of a family household or of a non-family household, and whether they are family or non-family persons.

Household, Private

Refers to a person or a group of persons (other than foreign residents) who occupy a private dwelling and do not have a usual place of residence elsewhere in Canada.

Household Size

Refers to the number of persons in a private household.

Household Type

Refers to the basic division of private households into family and non-family households. Family household refers to a household that contains at least one census family, that is, a married couple with or without children, or a couple living common-law with or without children, or a lone parent living with one or more children (lone-parent family). One-family household refers to a single census family (with or without other non-family persons) that occupies a private dwelling. Multiple-family household refers to a household in which two or more census families (with or without additional non-family persons) occupy the same private dwelling.

Non-family household refers to either one person living alone in a private dwelling or to a group of two or more people who share a private dwelling, but who do not constitute a census family.

Immigrant Population

Refers to people who are, or have been, landed immigrants in Canada. A landed immigrant is a person who has been granted the right to live in Canada permanently by immigration authorities. Some immigrants have resided in Canada for a number of years, while others have arrived recently. Most immigrants are born outside Canada, but a small number were born in Canada.

Incidence of Low Income

The incidence of low income is the proportion or percentage of economic families or unattached individuals in a given classification below the low income cut-offs. These incidence rates are calculated from unrounded estimates of economic families and unattached individuals 15 years of age and over.

Income Status

Refers to the position of an economic family or an unattached individual 15 years of age and over in relation to Statistics Canada's low income cut-offs (LICOs).

Industry (Based on the 1997 North American Industry Classification System [NAICS])

Refers to the general nature of the business carried out in the establishment where the person worked. If the person did not have a job during the week (Sunday to Saturday) prior to enumeration (May 15, 2001), the data relate to the job of longest duration since January 1, 2000. Persons with two or more jobs were required to report the information for the job at which they worked the most hours.

The 2001 industry data are produced according to the 1997 NAICS. The NAICS provides enhanced industry comparability among the three North American Free Trade Agreement (NAFTA) trading partners (Canada, United States and Mexico). This classification consists of a systematic and comprehensive arrangement of industries structured into 20 sectors, 99 subsectors and 300 industry groups. The criteria used to create these categories are similarity of input structures, labour skills or production processes used by the establishment. For further information on the classification, see *North American Industry Classification System, Canada, 1997*, Catalogue No. 12-501-XPE.

The variable "Industry (based on the 1997 NAICS)" does not permit direct comparison to any previous census industry data. The 1980 Standard Industrial Classification should be used for comparisons between the 1986, 1991, 1996 and 2001 Censuses.

Knowledge of Non-official Languages

Refers to languages, other than English or French, in which the respondent can conduct a conversation.

Knowledge of Official Languages

Refers to the ability to conduct a conversation in English only, in French only, in both English and French, or in neither of the official languages of Canada.

Labour Force Activity (in Reference Week)

Refers to the labour market activity of the population 15 years of age and over in the week (Sunday to Saturday) prior to Census Day (May 15, 2001). Respondents were classified as either employed, or unemployed, or as not in the labour force. The labour force includes the employed and the unemployed.

Employed (in Reference Week)
Refers to persons 15 years of age and over, excluding institutional residents, who, during the week (Sunday to Saturday) prior to Census Day (May 15, 2001):

(a) did any work at all for pay or in self-employment or without pay in a family farm, business or professional practice;

(b) were absent from their job or business, with or without pay, for the entire week because of a vacation, an illness, a labour dispute at their place of work, or any other reasons.

Unemployed (in Reference Week)
Refers to persons 15 years of age and over, excluding institutional residents, who, during the week (Sunday to Saturday) prior to Census Day (May 15, 2001), were without paid work or without self-employment work and were available for work and either:

(a) had actively looked for paid work in the past four weeks; or

(b) were on temporary lay-off and expected to return to their job; or

(c) had definite arrangements to start a new job in four weeks or less.

Not in the Labour Force (in Reference Week)
Refers to persons 15 years of age and over, excluding institutional residents, who, in the week (Sunday to Saturday) prior to Census Day (May 15, 2001), were neither employed nor unemployed. It includes students, homemakers, retired workers, seasonal workers in an "off" season who were not looking for work, and persons who could not work because of a long-term illness or disability.

Labour Force (in Reference Week)
Refers to persons who were either employed or unemployed during the week (Sunday to Saturday) prior to Census Day (May 15, 2001).

In past censuses, this was called "Total Labour Force".

Participation Rate (in Reference Week)
Refers to the labour force in the week (Sunday to Saturday) prior to Census Day (May 15, 2001), expressed as a percentage of the population 15 years of age and over excluding institutional residents.

The participation rate for a particular group (age, sex, marital status, geographic area, etc.) is the total labour force in that group, expressed as a percentage of the population 15 years of age and over, in that group.

Employment Rate (in Reference Week)
Refers to the number of persons employed in the week (Sunday to Saturday) prior to Census Day (May 15, 2001), expressed as a percentage of the total population 15 years of age and over excluding institutional residents.

The employment rate for a particular group (age, sex, marital status, geographic area, etc.) is the number of employed in that group, expressed as a percentage of the population 15 years of age and over in that group.

In past censuses, this was called the Employment-population Ratio.

Unemployment Rate (in Reference Week)
Refers to the unemployed expressed as a percentage of the labour force in the week (Sunday to Saturday) prior to Census Day (May 15, 2001).

The unemployment rate for a particular group (age, sex, marital status, geographic area, etc.) is the unemployed in that group, expressed as a percentage of the labour force in that group, in the week prior to enumeration.

Land Area

Land area is the area in square kilometres of the land-based portions of standard geographic areas.

The land area measurements are unofficial, and are provided for the sole purpose of calculating population density.

Landed Immigrant Status

Refers to people who have been granted the right to live in Canada permanently by immigration authorities.

Language Used at Work

Refers to the language used most often at work by the individual at the time of the census. Other languages used at work on a regular basis are also collected.

Legal Marital Status

Refers to the legal conjugal status of a person.

The various responses are defined as follows:

Never legally married (single) – Persons who have never married (including all persons less than 15 years of age) and persons whose marriage has been annulled and who have not remarried.

Legally married (and not separated) – Persons whose husband or wife is living, unless the couple is separated or a divorce has been obtained.

Separated, but still legally married – Persons currently married, but who are no longer living with their spouse (for any reason other than illness or work) and have not obtained a divorce.

Divorced – Persons who have obtained a legal divorce and who have not remarried.

Widowed – Persons who have lost their spouse through death and who have not remarried.

Low Income Cut-offs (LICOs)

Measures of low income known as low income cut-offs (LICOs) were first introduced in Canada in 1968 based on 1961 Census income data and 1959 family expenditure patterns. At that time, expenditure patterns indicated that Canadian families spent about 50% of their total income on food, shelter and clothing. It was arbitrarily estimated that families spending 70% or more of their income (20 percentage points more than the average) on these basic necessities would be in "straitened" circumstances. With this assumption, low income cut-off points were set for five different sizes of families.

Subsequent to these initial cut-offs, revised low income cut-offs were established based on national family expenditure data from 1969, 1978, 1986 and 1992. These data indicated that Canadian families spent, on average, 42% in 1969, 38.5% in 1978, 36.2% in 1986 and 34.7% in 1992 of their total income on basic necessities. Since 1992, data from the expenditure survey have indicated that this proportion has remained fairly stable. By adding the original difference of 20 percentage points to the basic level of expenditure on necessities, new low income cut-offs were set at income levels differentiated by family size and degree of urbanization. Since 1992, these cut-offs have been updated yearly by changes in the consumer price index.

Mode of Transportation

Refers to the mode of transportation to work of non-institutional residents 15 years of age and over who worked at some time since January 1, 2000. Persons who indicate in the place of work question that they either had no fixed workplace address, or specified a usual workplace address, are asked to identify the mode of transportation they most frequently use to commute from home to work. The variable usually relates to the individual's job in the week prior to enumeration. However, if the person did not work during that week but had worked at some time since January 1, 2000, the information relates to the job held longest during that period.

Persons who use more than one mode of transportation are asked to identify the single mode they use for most of the travel distance. As a result, the question provides data on the primary mode of transportation to work. The question does not measure multiple modes of transportation, nor does it measure the seasonal variation in mode of transportation or trips made for purposes other than the commute from home to work.

Mother Tongue

Refers to the first language learned at home in childhood and still understood by the individual at the time of the census.

Non-immigrant Population

Refers to people who are Canadian citizens by birth. Although most were born in Canada, a small number of them were born outside Canada to Canadian parents.

Occupation (Based on the 2001 National Occupational Classification for Statistics [2001 NOC–S])

Refers to the kind of work persons were doing during the reference week, as determined by their kind of work and the description of the main activities in their job. If the person did not have a job during the week (Sunday to Saturday) prior to enumeration (May 15, 2001), the data relate to the job of longest duration since January 1, 2000. Persons with two or more jobs were to report the information for the job at which they worked the most hours.

The 2001 occupation data are classified according to the 2001 National Occupational Classification for Statistics (2001 NOC–S). This classification is composed of four levels of aggregation. There are 10 broad occupational categories containing 47 major groups that are further subdivided into 140 minor groups. At the most detailed level, there are 520 occupation unit groups. Occupation unit groups are formed on the basis of the education, training, or skill level required to enter the job, as well as the kind of work performed, as determined by the tasks, duties and responsibilities of the occupation.

For information on the 2001 NOC–S, see the *National Occupational Classification for Statistics, 2001*, Catalogue No. 12-583-XPE.

Owner's Major Payments or Gross Rent as a Percentage of Household Income

Refers to the proportion of average monthly 2000 total household income which is spent on owner's major payments (in the case of owner-occupied dwellings) or on gross rent (in the case of tenant-occupied dwellings). This concept is illustrated below:

(a) **Owner-occupied non-farm dwellings:**

$$\frac{\text{Owner's major payments}}{\text{(2000 total annual household income) /12}} \times 100 = \_\_\_\%$$

(b) **Tenant-occupied non-farm dwellings:**

$$\frac{\text{Gross rent}}{\text{(2000 total annual household income) /12}} \times 100 = \_\_\_\%$$

Period of Construction

Refers to the period in time during which the building or dwelling was originally constructed.

Period of Immigration

Refers to ranges of years based on the year of immigration question. Year of immigration refers to the year in which landed immigrant status was first obtained.

Place of Birth of Respondent

Refers to specific provinces or territories for respondents who were born in Canada, or to specific countries if born outside Canada.

Place of Residence 1 Year Ago (Mobility)

Refers to the relationship between a person's usual place of residence on Census Day and his or her usual place of residence one year earlier. A person is classified as a non-mover if no difference exists. Otherwise, a person is classified as a mover and this categorization is called Mobility Status (1 Year Ago). Within the category of movers, a further distinction is made between non-migrants and migrants; this difference is called migration status.

Non-movers are persons who, on Census Day, were living at the same address as the one at which they resided one year earlier.

Movers are persons who, on Census Day, were living at a different address than the one at which they resided one year earlier.

Non-migrants are movers who, on Census Day, were living at a different address, but in the same census subdivision (CSD) as the one they lived in one year earlier.

Migrants are movers who, on Census Day, were residing in a different CSD one year earlier (internal migrants) or who were living outside Canada one year earlier (external migrants).

Intraprovincial migrants are movers who, on Census Day, were living in a different census subdivision than the one at which they resided one year earlier, in the same province.

Interprovincial migrants are movers who, on Census Day, were living in a different census subdivision than the one at which they resided one year earlier, in a different province.

Place of Residence 5 Years Ago (Mobility)

Refers to the relationship between a person's usual place of residence on Census Day and his or her usual place of residence five years earlier. A person is classified as a non-mover if no difference exists. Otherwise, a person is classified as a mover and this categorization is called Mobility Status (5 Years Ago). Within the movers category, a further distinction is made between non-migrants and migrants; this difference is called migration status.

Non-movers are persons who, on Census Day, were living at the same address as the one at which they resided five years earlier.

Movers are persons who, on Census Day, were living at a different address than the one at which they resided five years earlier.

Non-migrants are movers who, on Census Day, were living at a different address, but in the same census subdivision (CSD) as the one they lived in five years earlier.

Migrants are movers who, on Census Day, were residing in a different CSD five years earlier (internal migrants) or who were living outside Canada five years earlier (external migrants).

Intraprovincial migrants are movers who, on Census Day, were living in a different census subdivision than the one in which they resided five years earlier, in the same province.

Interprovincial migrants are movers who, on Census Day, were living in a different census subdivision than the one in which they resided five years earlier, in a different province.

Place of Work Status

Refers to the place of work of non-institutional residents 15 years of age and over who worked at some time since January 1, 2000. The variable usually relates to the individual's job held in the week prior to enumeration. However, if the person did not work during that week but had worked at some time since January 1, 2000, the information relates to the job held longest during that period.

Worked at home – Persons whose job is located in the same building as their place of residence, persons who live and work on the same farm, building superintendents and teleworkers who spend most of their work week working at home.

Worked outside Canada – Persons who work at a location outside Canada. This can include diplomats, Armed Forces personnel and other persons enumerated abroad. This category also includes recent immigrants who may not currently be employed, but whose job of longest duration since January 1, 2000 was held outside Canada.

No fixed workplace address – Persons who do not go from home to the same workplace location at the beginning of each shift. Such persons include building and landscape contractors, travelling salespersons, independent truck drivers, etc.

Worked at the address specified below – Persons who are not included in the categories described above and who report to the same (usual) workplace location at the beginning of each shift are included here. Respondents are asked to provide the street address, city, town, village, township, municipality or Indian reserve, province/territory and postal code of their workplace. If the full street address was not known, the name of the building or nearest street intersection could be substituted.

Teleworkers who spend less than one-half of their workweek working at their home office are asked to report the full address of their employer. Persons whose workplace location varied, but who reported regularly to an employer's address at the beginning of each shift, are asked to report the full address of the employer.

Population Universe

The Population Universe of the 2001 Census includes the following groups:

- Canadian citizens (by birth or by naturalization) and landed immigrants with a usual place of residence in Canada;
- Canadian citizens (by birth or by naturalization) and landed immigrants who are abroad, either on a military base or attached to a diplomatic mission;
- Canadian citizens (by birth or by naturalization) and landed immigrants at sea or in port aboard merchant vessels under Canadian registry;
- persons with a usual place of residence in Canada who are claiming refugee status and members of their families living with them;
- persons with a usual place of residence in Canada who hold student authorizations (student visas or student permits) and members of their families living with them;
- persons with a usual place of residence in Canada who hold employment authorizations (or work permits) and members of their families living with them;
- persons with a usual place of residence in Canada who hold Minister's permits (including extensions) and members of their families living with them.

For census purposes, the last four groups in this list are referred to as "non-permanent residents".

Presence of Children

Refers to the number of children in private households by age groups.

Province or Territory

Province and territory refer to the major political units of Canada. From a statistical point of view, province and territory are basic areas for which data are tabulated. Canada is divided into ten provinces and three territories.

Registered or Treaty Indian

Refers to those persons who reported they were registered under the *Indian Act* of Canada. Treaty Indians are persons who are registered under the *Indian Act* and can prove descent from a Band that signed a treaty. Although there was a question in the 1991 Census on registration status, the layout of the 1996 question was somewhat different. In 1991, registration status was a subcomponent of Question 16 on Registered Indians. In the first part of the question, respondents were asked about their registration status, while the second part of the question dealt with Band membership. In 1996, one direct question was developed to collect data on registration or treaty status.

The wording of the 1996 question differed slightly from the one in previous years. Prior to 1996, the term "treaty" was excluded from the question. It was added in 1996 at the request of individuals from the Western provinces, where the term is more widely used.

Religion

Refers to specific religious denominations, groups or bodies, as well as to sects, cults, or other religiously defined communities or systems of belief.

Rent, Gross

Refers to the total average monthly payments paid by tenant households to secure shelter.

Rooms

Refers to the number of rooms in a dwelling. A room is an enclosed area within a dwelling which is finished and suitable for year-round living.

School Attendance

Refers to either full-time or part-time (day or evening) attendance at school, college or university during the nine-month period between September 2000 and May 15, 2001. Attendance is counted only for courses which could be used as credits towards a certificate, diploma or degree.

Sex

Refers to the gender of the respondent.

Structural Type of Dwelling

Refers to the structural characteristics and/or dwelling configuration, that is, whether the dwelling is a single-detached house, an apartment in a high-rise building, a row house, a mobile home, etc.

Tenure

Refers to whether some member of the household owns or rents the dwelling, or whether the dwelling is Band housing (on an Indian reserve or settlement).

Total Income

Refers to the total money income received from the following sources during calendar year 2000 by persons 15 years of age and over:

- wages and salaries (total);
- net farm income;
- net non-farm income from unincorporated business and/or professional practice;
- Canada Child Tax Benefits;
- Old Age Security pension and Guaranteed Income Supplement;
- benefits from Canada or Quebec Pension Plan;
- benefits from Employment Insurance;
- other income from government sources;
- dividends, interest on bonds, deposits and savings certificates, and other investment income;
- retirement pensions, superannuation and annuities, including those from RRSPs and RRIFs;
- other money income.

Receipts Not Counted as Income – The income concept excluded gambling gains and losses, lottery prizes, money inherited during the year in a lump sum, capital gains or losses, receipts from the sale of property, income tax refunds, loan payments received, lump-sum settlements of insurance policies, rebates received on property taxes, refunds of pension contributions, as well as all income "in kind", such as free meals, living accommodations, or agricultural products produced and consumed on the farm.

Average Income of Individuals – Average income of individuals refers to the weighted mean total income of individuals 15 years of age and over who reported income for 2000. Average income is calculated from unrounded data by dividing the aggregate income of a specified group of individuals (e.g. males 45 to 54 years of age) by the number of individuals with income in that group.

Average and median incomes and standard errors for average income of individuals will be calculated for those individuals who are at least 15 years of age and who have an income (positive or negative). For all other universes (e.g. census families or private households), these statistics will be calculated over all units, whether or not they reported any income.

Median Income of Individuals – The median income of a specified group of income recipients is that amount which divides their income size distribution into two halves, i.e. the incomes of the first half of individuals are below the median, while those of the second half are above the median. Median income is calculated from the unrounded number of individuals (e.g. males 45 to 54 years of age) with income in that group.

Average and median incomes and standard errors for average income of individuals will be calculated for those individuals who are at least 15 years of age and who have an income (positive or negative). For all other universes (e.g. census families or private households), these statistics will be calculated over all units, whether or not they reported any income.

Standard Error of Average Income – Refers to the estimated standard error of average income for an income size distribution. If interpreted as shown below, it serves as a rough indicator of the precision of the corresponding estimate of average income. For about 68% of the samples which could be selected from the sample frame, the difference between the sample estimate of average income and the corresponding figure based on complete enumeration would be less than one standard error. For about 95% of the possible samples, the difference would be less than two standard errors and, in about 99% of the samples, the difference would be approximately two and one half standard errors.

Unattached Individuals

Refers to household members who are not members of an economic family. Persons living alone are included in this category.

Value of Dwelling

Refers to the dollar amount expected by the owner if the dwelling were to be sold.

Visible Minorities

Refers to the visible minority group to which the respondent belongs. The *Employment Equity Act* defines visible minorities as "persons, other than Aboriginal peoples, who are non-Caucasian in race or non-white in colour".

The visible minority population includes the following groups: Chinese, South Asian, Black, Filipino, Latin American, Southeast Asian, Arab, West Asian, Korean, Japanese, Visible Minority, n.i.e. and Multiple Visible Minorities.

Data Quality

General

The 2001 Census was a large and complex undertaking and, while considerable effort was taken to ensure high standards throughout all collection and processing operations, the resulting estimates are inevitably subject to a certain degree of error. Users of census data should be aware that such error exists, and should have some appreciation of its main components, so that they can assess the usefulness of census data for their purposes and the risks involved in basing conclusions or decisions on these data.

Errors can arise at virtually every stage of the census process, from the preparation of materials through data processing, including the listing of dwellings and the collection of data. Some errors occur at random, and when the individual responses are aggregated for a sufficiently large group, such errors tend to cancel out. For errors of this nature, the larger the group, the more accurate the corresponding estimate. It is for this reason that users are advised to be cautious when using small estimates. There are some errors, however, which might occur more systematically, and which result in "biased" estimates. Because the bias from such errors is persistent no matter how large the group for which responses are aggregated, and because bias is particularly difficult to measure, systematic errors are a more serious problem for most data users than the random errors referred to previously.

For census data in general, the principal types of error are as follows:

- **coverage errors**, which occur when dwellings or individuals are missed, incorrectly enumerated or counted more than once;
- **non-response errors**, which result when responses cannot be obtained from a certain number of households and/or individuals, because of extended absence or some other reason;
- **response errors**, which occur when the respondent, or sometimes the Census Representative, misunderstands a census question, and records an incorrect response or simply uses the wrong response box;
- **processing errors**, which can occur at various steps including **coding**, when "write-in" responses are transformed into numerical codes; **data capture**, when responses are transferred from the census questionnaire in an electronic format, by key-entry operators; and **imputation**, when a "valid", but not necessarily correct, response is inserted into a record by the computer to replace missing or "invalid" data ("valid" and "invalid" referring to whether or not the response is consistent with other information on the record);
- **sampling errors**, which apply only to the supplementary questions on the "long form" asked of a one-fifth sample of households, and which arise from the fact that the responses to these questions, when weighted up to represent the whole population, inevitably differ somewhat from the responses which would have been obtained if these questions had been asked of all households.

The above types of error each have both random and systematic components. Usually, however, the systematic component of sampling error is very small in relation to its random component. For the other non sampling errors, both random and systematic components may be significant.

Coverage Errors

Coverage errors affect the accuracy of the census counts, that is, the sizes of the various census universes: population, families, households and dwellings. While steps have been taken to correct certain identifiable errors, the final counts are still subject to some degree of error because persons or dwellings have been missed, incorrectly enumerated in the census or counted more than once.

Missed dwellings or persons result in **undercoverage**. Dwellings can be missed because of the misunderstanding of enumeration area (EA) boundaries, or because either they do not look like dwellings or they appear uninhabitable. Persons can be missed when their dwelling is missed or is classified as vacant, or because the respondent misinterprets the instructions on whom to include on the questionnaire. Some individuals may be missed because they have no usual residence and did not spend census night in a dwelling.

Dwellings or persons incorrectly enumerated or double counted result in **overcoverage**. Overcoverage of dwellings can occur when structures unfit for habitation are listed as dwellings (incorrectly enumerated), when there is a certain ambiguity regarding the EA boundaries or when units (for example, rooms) are listed separately instead of being treated as part of one dwelling (double counted). Persons can be counted more than once because their dwelling is double counted or because the guidelines on whom to include on the questionnaire have been misunderstood. Occasionally, someone who is not in the census population universe, such as a foreign resident or a fictitious person, may, incorrectly, be enumerated in the census. On average, overcoverage is less likely to occur than undercoverage and, as a result, counts of dwellings and persons are likely to be slightly underestimated.

For the 2001 Census, three studies are used to measure coverage error. In the Dwelling Classification Study, dwellings listed as vacant were revisited to verify that they were vacant on Census Day, and dwellings whose households were listed as non-respondent were revisited to determine the number of usual residents and their characteristics. Adjustments have been made to the final census counts for households and persons missed because their dwelling was incorrectly classified as vacant. The census counts may also have been adjusted for dwellings whose households were classified as non-respondent. Despite these adjustments, the final counts are still subject to some undercoverage. Undercoverage tends to be higher for certain segments of the population, such as young adults (especially young adult males) and recent immigrants. The Reverse Record Check Study is used to measure the residual undercoverage for Canada, and each province and territory. The Overcoverage Study is designed to investigate overcoverage errors. The results of the Reverse Record Check and the Overcoverage Study, when taken together, furnish an estimate of net undercoverage.

Other Non-sampling Errors

While coverage errors affect the number of units in the various census universes, other errors affect the characteristics of those units.

Sometimes it is not possible to obtain a complete response from a household, even though the dwelling was identified as occupied and a questionnaire was dropped off. The household members may have been away throughout the census period or, in rare instances, the householder may have refused to complete the form. More frequently, the questionnaire is returned but no response is provided to certain questions. Effort is devoted to ensure as complete a questionnaire as possible. Census representatives edit the questionnaires and follow up on missing information. Their work is then checked by a supervisor and a quality control technician. Despite this, at the end of the collection stage, a small number of responses are still missing, i.e. **non-response errors**. Although missing responses are eliminated during processing by replacing each one of them by the corresponding response for a "similar" record, there remain some potential imputation errors. This is particularly serious if the non-respondents differ in some respects from the respondents; this procedure will then introduce a **non-response bias**.

Even when a response is obtained, it may not be entirely accurate. The respondent may have misinterpreted the question or may have guessed the answer, especially when answering on behalf of another, possibly absent, household member. The respondent may also have entered the answer in the wrong place on the questionnaire. Such errors are referred to as **response errors**. While response errors usually arise from inaccurate information provided by respondents, they can also result from mistakes by the Census Representative who completed certain parts of the questionnaire, such as the structural type of dwelling, or who followed up to obtain a missing response.

Some of the census questions require a written response. During processing, these "write-in" entries are given a numeric code. **Coding errors** can occur when the written response is ambiguous, incomplete, difficult to read or when the code list is extensive (e.g. major field of study, place of work). A formal Quality Control (QC) operation is used to detect, rectify and reduce coding errors. Within each work unit, a sample of responses is independently coded a second time. The resolution of discrepancies between the first and second codings determines whether recoding of the work unit is necessary. Except for the Industry and Occupation variables, much of the census coding is now automated, resulting in a reduction of coding errors.

The information on the questionnaires is typed into a computer file. Two procedures are used to control the number of **data capture errors**. First, certain edits (such as range checks) are performed as the data are keyed in. Second, a sample from each batch of documents is retyped and compared with the original entries. Unsatisfactory work is identified and corrected, and the remainder of the batch is captured as needed.

Once captured, the data are edited where they undergo a series of computer checks to identify missing or inconsistent responses. These are replaced during the imputation stage of processing where either a response consistent with the other respondents' data is inferred or a response from a similar donor is substituted. Imputation ensures a complete database where the data correspond to the census counts and facilitate multivariate analyses. Although errors may have been introduced during **imputation**, the methods used have been rigorously tested to minimize systematic errors.

Various studies are being carried out to evaluate the quality of the responses obtained in the 2001 Census. For each question, non-response rates and edit failure rates have been calculated. These can be useful in identifying the potential for non-response errors and other types of errors. Also, tabulations from the 2001 Census have been or will be compared with corresponding estimates from previous censuses, from sample surveys (such as the Labour Force Survey) and from various administrative records (such as birth registrations and municipal assessment records). Such comparisons can indicate potential quality problems or at least discrepancies between the sources.

In addition to these aggregate-level comparisons, there are some micro-match studies in progress, in which census responses are compared with another source of information at the individual record level. For certain "stable" characteristics (such as age, sex, mother tongue and place of birth), the responses obtained in the 2001 Census, for a sample of individuals, are being compared with those for the same individuals in the 1996 Census.

Sampling Errors

Estimates obtained by weighting up responses collected on a sample basis are subject to error due to the fact that the distribution of characteristics within the sample will not usually be identical to the distribution of characteristics within the population from which the sample has been selected.

The potential error introduced by sampling will vary according to the relative scarcity of the characteristics in the population. For large cell values, the potential error due to sampling, as a proportion of the cell value, will be relatively small. For small cell values, this potential error, as a proportion of the cell value, will be relatively large.

The potential error due to sampling is usually expressed in terms of the so-called "standard error". This is the square root of the average, taken over all possible samples of the same size and design, of the squared deviation of the sample estimate from the value for the total population.

The following table provides approximate measures of the standard error due to sampling. These measures are intended as a general guide only.

Approximate Standard Error Due to Sampling for 2001 Census Sample Data

Cell Value	Approximate Standard Error
50 or less	15
100	20
200	30
500	45
1,000	65
2,000	90
5,000	140
10,000	200
20,000	280
50,000	450
100,000	630
500,000	1,400

Users wishing to determine the approximate error due to sampling for any given cell of data, based upon the 20% sample, should choose the standard error value corresponding to the cell value that is closest to the value of the given cell in the census tabulation. When using the obtained standard error value, the user, in general, can be reasonably certain that, for the enumerated population, the true value (discounting all forms of error other than sampling) lies within plus or minus three times the standard error (e.g. for a cell value of 1,000, the range would be 1,000 ± [3 x 65] or 1,000 ± 195).

The standard errors given in the table above will not apply to population, household, dwelling or family counts for the geographic area under consideration (see Sampling and Weighting below). The effect of sampling for these cells can be determined by a comparison with a corresponding 100% data product.

The effect of the particular sample design and weighting procedure used in the 2001 Census will vary, however, from one characteristic to another and from one geographic area to another. The standard error values in the table may, therefore, understate or overstate the error due to sampling.

Sampling and Weighting

The 2001 Census data were collected either from 100% of the households or on a sample basis (i.e. from a random sample of one in five households) with the data weighted up to provide estimates for the entire population. The information was collected on a 20% sample basis and weighted up to compensate for sampling. All table headings are noted accordingly. Note that, on Indian reserves and in remote areas, all data were collected on a 100% basis.

For any given geographic area, the weighted population, household, dwelling or family total or subtotal may differ from that shown in reports containing data collected on a 100% basis. Such variations are due to sampling and to the fact that, unlike sample data, 100% data do not exclude institutional residents.

Confidentiality and Random Rounding

The figures shown in the tables have been subjected to a confidentiality procedure known as **random rounding** to prevent the possibility of associating statistical data with any identifiable individual. Under this method, all figures, including totals and margins, are randomly rounded either up or down to a multiple of "5", and in some cases "10". While providing strong protection against disclosure, this technique does not add significant error to the census data. The user should be aware that totals and margins are rounded independently of the cell data so that some differences between these and the sum of rounded cell data may exist. Also, minor differences can be expected in corresponding totals and cell values among various census tabulations. Similarly, percentages, which are calculated on rounded figures, do not necessarily add up to 100%. Order statistics (median, quartiles, percentiles, etc.) and measures of dispersion such as the standard error are computed in the usual manner. When a statistic is defined as the quotient of two numbers (which is the case for averages, percentages, and proportions), the two numbers are rounded before the division is performed. For income, owner's payments, value of dwelling, hours worked, weeks worked and age, the sum is defined as the product of the average and the rounded weighted frequency. Otherwise, it is the weighted sum that is rounded. It should also be noted that small cell counts may suffer a significant distortion as a result of random rounding. Individual data cells containing small numbers may lose their precision as a result. Also, a statistic is suppressed if the number of actual records used in the calculation is less than 4 or if the sum of the weight of these records is less than 10. In addition, for values expressed in dollar units, other rules are applied. For standard products, if all the values are the same, the statistic is suppressed. For all other products, the statistic is suppressed if the range of the values is too narrow or if all values are less than, in absolute value, to a specified threshold.

Users should be aware of possible data distortions when they are aggregating these rounded data. Imprecisions as a result of rounding tend to cancel each other out when data cells are re-aggregated. However, users can minimize these distortions by using, whenever possible, the appropriate subtotals when aggregating.

For those requiring maximum precision, the option exists to use custom tabulations. With custom products, aggregation is done using individual census database records. Random rounding occurs only after the data cells have been aggregated, thus minimizing any distortion.

In addition to random rounding, **area suppression** has been adopted to further protect the confidentiality of individual responses.

Area suppression is the deletion of all characteristic data for geographic areas with populations below a specified size. The extent to which data are suppressed depends upon the following factors:

- If the data are tabulated from the 100% database, they are suppressed if the total population in the area is less than 40.
- If the data are tabulated from the 20% sample database, they are suppressed if the total non-institutional population in the area from either the 100% or 20% database is less than 40.

There are some exceptions to these rules:

- Income distributions and related statistics are suppressed if the population in the area, excluding institutional residents, is less than 250 from either the 100% or the 20% database, or if the number of private households is less than 40 from the 20% database.
- Place-of-work distributions and related statistics are suppressed if the total number of employed persons in the area is less than 40, according to the sample database. If the data also include an income distribution, the threshold is raised to 250, again according to the sample database.
- Tabulations covering both place of work and place of residence along with related statistics are suppressed, if the total number of employed persons in the area is less than 40 according to the sample database, or if the area's total population, excluding institutional residents, according to either the 100% or the sample database, is less than 40. If the tabulations also include an income distribution, the threshold is raised to 250 in all cases and the tabulations are suppressed if the number of private dwellings in the place of residence area is less than 40.
- Same-sex couples distributions and related statistics are suppressed if the population in private households in the area is less than 5,000, according to the 20% sample database.
- If the data are tabulated from the 100% database and refer to six-character postal codes or to groups of either blocks or block-faces, they are suppressed if the total population in the area is less than 100.
- If the data are tabulated from the 20% sample database and refer to six-character postal codes or to groups of either blocks or block-faces, they are suppressed if the total non-institutional population in the area from either the 100% or 20% database is less than 100.
- If the data refer to groups of either blocks or block-faces, and cover place of work, they are suppressed if the total number of employed persons in the area is less than 100, according to the sample database.
- If the data refer to groups of either blocks or block-faces, and cover both place of work and place of residence, they are suppressed if the total number of employed persons in the area is less than 100, according to the sample database, or if the area's total population, excluding institutional residents, according to either 100% or the sample database, is less than 100.

In all cases, suppressed data are included in the appropriate higher aggregate subtotals and totals.

The suppression technique is being implemented for all products involving subprovincial data (i.e. Profile series, basic cross-tabulations, semi-custom and custom data products) collected on a 100% or 20% sample basis.

For further information on the quality of census data, contact the Social Survey Methods Division at Statistics Canada, Ottawa, Ontario, Canada K1A 0T6, or by calling (613) 951-4783.

Special Notes

Aboriginal Identity

Users should be aware that the population counts associated with this variable are more affected than most by the incomplete enumeration of certain Indian reserves and Indian settlements. The extent of the impact will depend on the geographical area under study. In 2001, a total of 30 Indian reserves and Indian settlements were incompletely enumerated by the census. The population of these 30 communities are not included in the census counts.

Changes to Family Concepts for the 2001 Census

For the 1996 Census, the definition of census family was as follows:

Refers to a now-married couple (with or without never-married sons and/or daughters of either or both spouses), a couple living common-law (with or without never-married sons and/or daughters of either or both partners) or a lone-parent of any marital status, with at least one never-married son or daughter living in the same dwelling.

This reflected a concept that had not changed since 1976. However, during the planning for the 2001 Census, it was decided that some changes were required, due to the following factors: (1) changes to federal and provincial legislation putting same-sex couples on an equal footing with opposite-sex common-law couples (most notably Bill C-23, the *Modernization of Benefits and Obligations Act*, which was passed by the Government of Canada in 2000); (2) recommendations by the United Nations as part of a process of standardization of concepts for the 2000-2001 round of censuses in member countries; and (3) a significant number of persons less than 15 years of age classified as "non-family persons" in previous censuses.

As a result, the census family concept for the 2001 Census reflects the following changes:

- Two persons living in a same-sex common-law relationship, along with any of their children residing in the household, are considered a census family.
- Children in a census family can have been previously married (as long as they are not currently living with a spouse or common-law partner). Previously, they had to be "never-married".
- A grandchild living in a three-generation household where the parent (middle generation) is never-married is, contrary to previous censuses, now considered as a child in the census family of his or her parent, provided the grandchild is not living with his or her own spouse, common-law partner, or child. Traditionally, the census family usually consisted of the two older generations.
- A grandchild of another household member, where a middle-generation parent is not present, is now considered as a child in the census family of his or her grandparent, provided the grandchild is not living with his or her own spouse, common-law partner, or child. Traditionally, such a grandchild would not be considered as a member of a census family.

The last three changes listed (definition of "child"), together, result in a 1.5% increase in the total number of census families, and in a 10.1% increase in the number of lone-parent families. The inclusion of same-sex couples results in a 0.4% increase in the number of census families at the national level.

The term economic family refers to a group of two or more persons who live in the same dwelling and are related to each other by blood, marriage, common-law or adoption. This definition has not changed for 2001. The only effect of conceptual changes on economic families is that same-sex partners are now considered to be common-law partners. Thus they are considered related and members of the same economic family.

Outside of the "family universe", there are two related concepts that are affected by the change in the census family definition: common-law status and household type. Prior to 2001, two people living together as husband and wife without being legally married to each other were considered to be living common-law. For 2001, this has been expanded to include persons living in a same-sex partnership. The concept of household type refers to the basic division of private households into family and non-family households. Since it is based on the census family concept, the household type (whether a household is "family" or "non-family") is affected by the change. Also, the detailed classification of this variable is affected, since married couples and common-law couples were broken down into those "without never-married sons or daughters" and "with never-married sons or daughters". For 2001 this reads "without children" and "with children", with the attendant change in meaning.

Comparability of 2001 Place of Work Data

Working at home can be measured in different ways. In the census, the "Worked at home" category includes persons who live and work at the same physical location, such as farmers, teleworkers and work camp workers. In addition, the 2001 Census Guide instructed persons who worked part of the time at home and part of the time at an employer's address to indicate that they "Worked at home" if most of their time was spent working at home (e.g. three days out of five).

Other Statistics Canada surveys such as the General Social Survey, the Survey of Labour and Income Dynamics, and the Workplace and Employee Survey also collect information on working at home. However, the survey data are not directly comparable to the census data since the surveys ask respondents whether they did some or all of their paid work at home, whereas the census asks them where they usually worked most of the time. Consequently, census estimates on work at home are lower than survey estimates.

The place-of-work question has remained in virtually the same format in each census since 1971. However, in 1996, the category "No fixed workplace address" replaced "No usual place of work". In 1996, the census questionnaire was modified by adding a check box for the "No fixed workplace" response category. In previous censuses, respondents were asked to write "No usual place of work" in the address fields. It is believed that previous censuses have undercounted the number of persons with "No fixed workplace address".

Annexations, incorporations and amalgamations of municipalities could create some difficulties when comparing spatial units and structures which change over time.

Data Quality for School Attendance

The overall quality of the education variables from the 2001 Census is acceptable. However, users of the 2001 Census data on school attendance are cautioned that the counts for the 15 to 19 year olds not attending school category may be too high. The proportion of persons aged 15 to 19 who indicated they had not attended school in the school year prior to the census increased from 18% in 1996 to 23% in 2001. This variable requires further research.

Data Quality – Relationship of Census Income Estimates to the National Accounts and Survey of Labour and Income Dynamics

Census income estimates of aggregate income in 2000 were compared to similar personal income estimates from the national accounts. After adjustments to the personal income estimates for differences in concepts and coverage, the census estimate of aggregate income in 2000 from comparable sources was 4.1% lower than the national accounts estimate. As in the past, census estimates for some income components and for some provinces compared more favourably than for others.

Census estimates of aggregate wages and salaries, the largest component of income, were almost identical to the national accounts estimates. Although there was a large difference between the two estimates of net income from farm self-employment (the smallest component of individual earnings), census estimates of aggregate income from both farm and non-farm self-employment were lower by 1%. Overall, estimates of total income from employment were nearly identical.

Census estimates of Old Age Security pensions and the Guaranteed Income Supplement were about 5% higher, while those for Canada/Quebec Pension Plan benefits were about 9% lower, than adjusted national accounts estimates. Employment Insurance benefits reported in the census were smaller by about 6%. Estimates of aggregate Canada Child Tax benefits were nearly identical in both estimates. Census estimates of other government transfer payments, which include such items as social welfare benefits, provincial income supplements to seniors, veterans' pensions and GST/HST/QST refunds, were significantly below the estimates from the national accounts. Overall, census estimates of aggregate income from all government transfer payments were lower by about 13%. As in previous census-year comparisons, the census estimate of investment income was significantly lower, by 32% in 2000, than the national accounts estimate.

Census income statistics were also compared with similar statistics from the annual Survey of Labour and Income Dynamics (SLID). SLID estimates reflect adjustments made for population undercoverage, while census estimates do not include such an adjustment. This adjustment contributes to census estimates showing fewer income recipients (by 3.4%) and earners (by 7.2%) than SLID estimates. Consequently, census estimates of aggregate earnings are 4% lower than the SLID estimate, while the census estimate of aggregate total income of individuals is lower by 3%. Most of the observed provincial differences were considered acceptable in the light of sampling errors in the Survey.

Immigration and Citizenship Data

Persons living on Indian reserves and Indian settlements, who were enumerated with the 2001 Census Form 2D questionnaire, were not asked the citizenship and immigration questions. Consequently, data are not shown for Indian reserves and Indian settlements at the lower geographic levels. These data, however, are included in the totals for larger geographic areas, such as census divisions and provinces.

Impact of Municipal Restructuring

The boundaries and names of municipalities (census subdivisions) can change from one census to the next because of annexations, dissolutions and incorporations. However, since the 1996 Census, the changes are more numerous and more dramatic, especially in the provinces of Quebec, Ontario and British Columbia. In general, data from the 2001 Census are available for fewer and larger census subdivisions, and historical analyses are more complex. To bridge the impact of these municipal changes on data dissemination, the 2001 Census is producing a profile for dissolved census subdivisions.

Income Reference Period

Canadian censuses were conducted in 1996 and 2001. Income data from these censuses relate to the calendar year prior to the census year, i.e. 1995 and 2000 respectively.

Income Suppression

Area suppression is the deletion of all characteristic data for geographic areas with populations below a specified size. Income distributions and related statistics are suppressed if the population in the area, excluding institutional residents, is less than 250 from either the 100% or the 20% database, or if the number of private households is less than 40 from the 20% database.

Migration Data for Small Geographic Areas

Estimates of internal migration may be less accurate for small geographic areas, areas with a place name which is duplicated elsewhere, and for some Census Subdivisions (CSD) where previous residents may have provided the name of the Census Metropolitan Area or Census Agglomeration instead of the specific name of the component CSD from which they migrated.

Non-permanent Residents

In 1991, 1996 and 2001, the Census of Population enumerated both permanent and non-permanent residents of Canada. Non-permanent residents are persons who held a student or employment authorization, Minister's permit, or who were refugee claimants, at the time of the census. Family members living with these persons are also classified as non-permanent residents.

Prior to 1991, only permanent residents of Canada were included in the census. (The only exception to this occurred in 1941.) Non-permanent residents were considered foreign residents and were not enumerated.

Today in Canada, non-permanent residents make up a significant segment of the population, especially in several census metropolitan areas. Their presence can affect the demand for such government services as health care, schooling, employment programs and language training. The inclusion of non-permanent residents in the census facilitates comparisons with provincial and territorial statistics (marriages, divorces, births and deaths) which include this population. In addition, this inclusion of non-permanent residents brings Canadian practice closer to the UN recommendation that long-term residents (persons living in a country for one year or longer) be enumerated in the census.

According to the 1996 Census, there were 166,715 non-permanent residents in Canada, representing 0.6% of the total population. There were slightly more non-permanent residents in Canada at the time of the 2001 Census: 198,645 non-permanent residents, or 0.7% of the total population.

Total population counts, as well as counts for all variables, are affected by this change in the census universe. Users should be especially careful when comparing data from 1991, 1996 or 2001 with data from previous censuses in geographic areas where there is a concentration of non-permanent residents. Such areas include the major metropolitan areas in Ontario, Quebec and British Columbia.

Although every attempt has been made to enumerate non-permanent residents, factors such as language difficulties, the reluctance to complete a government form or to understand the need to participate may have affected the enumeration of this population.

Nunavut

Data from the 2001 Census are available for Nunavut, the new territory that came into effect on April 1, 1999.

Standard data products released only at the Canada/Province/Territory geographic levels will not contain data for Nunavut for the census years prior to 2001.

Standard data products released at the Census Metropolitan Area (CMA) and Census Agglomeration (CA) geographic levels will contain data for Nunavut for the 2001, 1996 and/or 1991 Censuses.

The 1996 and 1991 CMA/CA data have been adjusted to reflect as closely as possible the 2001 CMA/CA geographic boundaries. This has been done to facilitate data comparisons using the 2001 geographic boundaries.

Ontario Census Tracts

A database error affected the presentation of the 1996 population counts for two census tracts (CTs), namely CTs 0520.05 and 0520.06, in the Census Metropolitan Area (CMA) of Toronto. The data for these CTs are correct but inverted: 0520.05 contains the data for 0520.06, and 0520.06 contains the data for 0520.05. Because of operational constraints, it was not possible to make adjustments to the 1996 database (adjusted counts) for these two CTs. Care should therefore be exercised when using these data.

Population 15 Years and Over Who Worked Since 2000

Refers to those who have worked since January 1, 2000, regardless of whether or not they were in the labour force in the reference week.

Population and Dwelling Count Amendments

After the release of the population and dwelling counts, errors are occasionally uncovered in the data. It is not possible to make changes to the 2001 Census data presented in these tables. Users can, however, obtain the population and dwelling count amendments listed by census subdivisions and other levels of geography by visiting the 2001 Census portion of the Statistics Canada Web site at www.statcan.ca. In addition, users can contact the nearest Statistics Canada regional reference centre by telephone at 1 800 263-1136 or by e-mail at infostats@statcan.ca.

Population Counts

The 2001 Census population counts for a particular area represent the number of Canadians whose usual place of residence is in that area, regardless of where they happened to be on Census Day. Also included are any Canadians who were staying in that area on Census Day and who had no usual place of residence elsewhere in Canada, as well as those considered to be "non-permanent residents" (see the Special Notes). For most areas, there is little difference between the number of usual residents and the number of people staying in the area on Census Day. For certain places, however, such as tourist or vacation areas, or those including large work camps, the number of people staying in that area at any particular time could significantly exceed the number of usual residents shown here. The population counts include Canadians living in other countries, but do not include foreign residents living in Canada (the "foreign residents" category does not include "non-permanent residents" - see the Special Notes). Given these differences, users are advised not to interpret population counts as being the number of people living in the reported dwellings.

Structural Type of Dwelling

The 2001 Census collected data for two new categories for structural type of dwelling:

Apartment with direct ground access in a building that has fewer than five storeys; and Apartment without direct ground access in a building that has fewer than five storeys.

Postcensal data evaluation has revealed a serious misclassification problem with these dwellings. As a result, the data will not be released.

Data for "Apartment in a building that has fewer than five storeys" have been released in 2001 products. This category is an aggregate of the two new previously mentioned categories, and is directly comparable with the same category from previous censuses. It presents no data problems.

Appendix 1. Incompletely Enumerated Indian Reserves and Indian Settlements, 1996 and 1991 Population Counts

Province	Incompletely enumerated Indian reserves and Indian settlements, 2001	Population	
		1996	1991
Quebec	Akwesasne (Partie)	¶	¶
	Doncaster 17	0	4
	Kahnawake 14	¶	¶
	Kanesatake	¶	¶
	Lac-Rapide	228	¶
Ontario	Akwesasne (Part) 59 (formerly Akwesasne [Part])	¶	¶
	Bear Island 1	153	¶
	Chippewas of the Thames First Nation 42 (formerly Chippewa of the Thames First Nation)	¶	¶
	Goulais Bay 15A	¶	¶
	Marten Falls 65	204	187
	Moose Factory 68	0	0
	Munsee-Delaware Nation 1	¶	¶
	Ojibway Nation of Saugeen (Savant Lake) (formerly Savant Lake)	¶	171
	Oneida 41	¶	¶
	Pikangikum 14	1,170	1,303
	Rankin Location 15D	¶	¶
	Six Nations (Part) 40 (Brant County)	¶	¶
	Six Nations (Part) 40 (Haldimand-Norfolk Regional Municipality)	¶	¶
	Tyendinaga Mohawk Territory (formerly Tyendinaga 38)	¶	¶
	Wahta Mohawk Territory (formerly Gibson 31)	¶	130
	Whitefish Bay 32A	¶	¶
	Whitesand	115	0
Manitoba	Dakota Tipi 1	¶	72
Saskatchewan	Big Head 124	¶	¶
Alberta	Ermineskin 138	¶	¶
	Little Buffalo	¶	186
	Saddle Lake 125	¶	1,893
British Columbia	Esquimalt	¶	¶
	Marble Canyon 3	67	¶
	Pavilion 1	76	73

Appendix 2. Suppressed Census Tracts Showing Population Counts by Census Metropolitan Area and Census Agglomeration, 2001 Census

Suppressed Census Tracts	Population Counts (100% Data)	Population Counts (20% Sample Data)
Belleville CA		
0010	35	34
0013 **A**	10	4
0014 **A**	33	33
0405	-	-
0407	-	-
Edmonton CMA		
0015.01	5	4
0016.01	-	-
0019.01	-	-
0052.01	-	-
0064.02	-	-
0065.03	-	-
0090.07	-	-
Granby CA		
0003 **A**	38	38
Greater Sudbury CMA		
0013	-	-
Halifax CMA		
0155 ◆◆◆◇◇◇ **A**	15	14
Kitchener CMA		
0106.03 ◆◆◆◇◇◇	5	2
Lethbridge CA		
0010	25	15
London CMA		
0035	-	-
Montréal CMA		
0014.02	23	23
0040	-	-
0071	-	-
0091	-	-
0094.02	-	-
0127.02	17	17
0145	-	-
0189	-	-
0229	-	-
0268.03	-	-
0440	-	-
0832 ¶		-
Ottawa - Hull CMA		
0140.01	20	16
Saint John CMA		
0005	15	6
Saint-Jean-sur-Richelieu CA		
0006	5	-
0010	-	-
0303	-	-
Toronto CMA		
0003	-	-
0376.06 ◇	35	20
0401.05	5	5
Trois-Rivières CMA		
0301	39	38
Vancouver CMA		
0270	-	-
Winnipeg CMA		
0052	-	-

Note:

For more information on the 2001 suppression rules, please see the Data Quality section in the Reference Material of this publication.

Regional Reference Centres

The Advisory Services Division of Statistics Canada provides an information dissemination network across the country through eight regional reference centres. Each reference centre has a collection of current publications and reference documents that can be consulted or purchased, along with diskettes, CD-ROMs, maps, and other products. Copying facilities for printed materials are available on site.

Each reference centre provides a wide range of additional services. Advisory Services can provide assistance in helping you identify your informational needs, establish sources of available data, consolidate and integrate data from different sources, develop profiles, provide analysis of highlights or tendencies and, finally, provide training on products, services, Statistics Canada concepts and the use of statistical data.

For more information, call the National Toll-free Enquiries Line listed below or send an e-mail to infostats@statcan.ca.

Contact Us

National Toll-free **Enquiries** Line (Canada and United States):
1 800 263-1136

TTY: 1 800 363-7629

Toll-free **Order Only** Line (Canada and United States): 1 800 267-6677

National Toll-free **Fax Order** Line (Canada and United States):
1 877 287-4369

E-mail: infostats@statcan.ca

Atlantic Region

Serving the provinces of Newfoundland and Labrador, Nova Scotia, Prince Edward Island and New Brunswick.

Advisory Services
Statistics Canada
2nd Floor, Box 11
1741 Brunswick Street
Halifax, Nova Scotia
B3J 3X8

Toll-free number: 1 800 263-1136
Local calls: (902) 426-5331
Fax number: (902) 426-9538
E-mail: infostats@statcan.ca

Quebec Region

Serving the province of Quebec and the territory of Nunavut except the National Capital Region.

Advisory Services
Statistics Canada
4th Floor, East Tower
Guy Favreau Complex
200 René Lévesque Blvd. W
Montréal, Quebec
H2Z 1X4

Toll-free number: 1 800 263-1136
Local calls: (514) 283-5725
Fax number: (514) 283-9350
E-mail: infostats@statcan.ca

National Capital Region

Serving the National Capital Region.

Statistical Reference Centre
(National Capital Region)
Statistics Canada
Main Building, Room 1500
120 Parkdale Avenue
Ottawa, Ontario
K1A 0T6

Toll-free number: 1 800 263-1136
Local calls: (613) 951-8116
Fax number: (613) 951-0581
E-mail: infostats@statcan.ca

Ontario Region

Serving the province of Ontario except the National Capital Region.

Advisory Services
Statistics Canada
Arthur Meighen Building, 10th Floor
25 St. Clair Avenue E
Toronto, Ontario
M4T 1M4

Toll-free number: 1 800 263-1136
Local calls: (416) 973-6586
Fax number: (416) 973-7475
E-mail: infostats@statcan.ca

Prairie Region

This region has three reference centres serving the provinces of Manitoba, Saskatchewan, Alberta and the Northwest Territories.

Serving the province of Manitoba:

Advisory Services
Statistics Canada
Via Rail Building, Suite 200
123 Main Street
Winnipeg, Manitoba
R3C 4V9

Toll-free number: 1 800 263-1136
Local calls: (204) 983-4020
Fax number: (204) 983-7543
E-mail: infostats@statcan.ca

Prairie Region – concluded

Serving the province of Saskatchewan:

Advisory Services
Statistics Canada
Park Plaza, Suite 440
2365 Albert Street
Regina, Saskatchewan
S4P 4K1

Toll-free number: 1 800 263-1136
Local calls: (306) 780-5405
Fax number: (306) 780-5403
E-mail: infostats@statcan.ca

Serving Alberta and the Northwest Territories:

Advisory Services
Statistics Canada
Pacific Plaza, Suite 900
10909 Jasper Avenue NW
Edmonton, Alberta
T5J 4J3

Toll-free number: 1 800 263-1136
Local calls: (780) 495-3027
Fax number: (780) 495-5318
E-mail: infostats@statcan.ca

Pacific Region

Serving the province of British Columbia and the Yukon Territory.

Advisory Services
Statistics Canada
Library Square Tower
600-300 West Georgia Street
Vancouver, British Columbia
V6B 6C7

Toll-free number: 1 800 263-1136
Local calls: (604) 666-3691
Fax number: (604) 666-4863
E-mail: infostats@statcan.ca

Définitions

Pour de plus amples renseignements sur les définitions et les notes spéciales, veuillez consultez le Dictionnaire du recensement de 2001, n° 92-378-XIF ou 92-378-XPF au catalogue.

Activité (pendant la semaine de référence)

Activité sur le marché du travail des personnes âgées de 15 ans et plus au cours de la semaine (du dimanche au samedi) ayant précédé le jour du recensement (le 15 mai 2001). Les recensés sont classés dans les catégories « Personnes occupées », « Chômeurs » ou « Inactifs ». La population active comprend les personnes occupées et les chômeurs.

Personnes occupées (pendant la semaine de référence)
Personnes âgées de 15 ans et plus, à l'exclusion des pensionnaires d'un établissement institutionnel, qui, au cours de la semaine (du dimanche au samedi) ayant précédé le jour du recensement (le 15 mai 2001) :

a) avaient fait un travail quelconque à un emploi salarié ou à leur compte ou sans rémunération dans une ferme ou une entreprise familiale ou dans l'exercice d'une profession;

b) étaient temporairement absentes de leur travail ou de l'entreprise, avec ou sans rémunération, toute la semaine à cause de vacances, d'une maladie, d'un conflit de travail à leur lieu de travail, ou encore pour d'autres raisons.

Chômeurs (pendant la semaine de référence)
Personnes âgées de 15 ans et plus, à l'exclusion des pensionnaires d'un établissement institutionnel, qui, pendant la semaine (du dimanche au samedi) ayant précédé le jour du recensement (le 15 mai 2001), étaient sans emploi salarié et sans travail à leur compte, étaient prêtes à travailler et :

a) avaient activement cherché un emploi salarié au cours des quatre semaines précédentes; ou

b) avaient été mises à pied mais prévoyaient reprendre leur emploi; ou

c) avaient pris des arrangements définis en vue de se présenter à un nouvel emploi dans les quatre semaines suivantes.

Inactifs (pendant la semaine de référence)
Personnes âgées de 15 ans et plus, à l'exclusion des pensionnaires d'un établissement institutionnel, qui, pendant la semaine (du dimanche au samedi) ayant précédé le jour du recensement (le 15 mai 2001), n'étaient ni occupées ni en chômage. Les inactifs comprennent les étudiants, les personnes au foyer, les retraités, les travailleurs saisonniers en période de relâche qui ne cherchaient pas un travail et les personnes qui ne pouvaient travailler en raison d'une maladie chronique ou d'une incapacité à long terme.

Population active (pendant la semaine de référence)
Personnes qui étaient soit occupées, soit en chômage pendant la semaine (du dimanche au samedi) ayant précédé le jour du recensement (le 15 mai 2001).

Au cours des recensements précédents, cette variable était appelée « Population active totale ».

Taux d'activité (pendant la semaine de référence)
Pourcentage de la population active pendant la semaine (du dimanche au samedi) ayant précédé le jour du recensement (le 15 mai 2001) par rapport aux personnes âgées de 15 ans et plus à l'exclusion des pensionnaires d'un établissement institutionnel.

Le taux d'activité d'un groupe donné (âge, sexe, état matrimonial, région géographique, etc.) correspond au nombre total d'actifs dans ce groupe, exprimé en pourcentage des personnes âgées de 15 ans et plus, de ce groupe.

Taux d'emploi (pendant la semaine de référence)
Pourcentage de la population occupée au cours de la semaine (du dimanche au samedi) ayant précédé le jour du recensement (le 15 mai 2001), par rapport au pourcentage de la population de 15 ans et plus à l'exclusion des pensionnaires d'un établissement institutionnel.

Le taux d'emploi pour un groupe donné (âge, sexe, état matrimonial, région géographique, etc.) correspond au nombre de personnes occupées dans ce groupe, exprimé en pourcentage des personnes âgées de 15 ans et plus, de ce groupe.

Au cours des recensements antérieurs, cette variable était appelée « Rapport emploi-population ».

Taux de chômage (pendant la semaine de référence)
Pourcentage de la population en chômage par rapport à la population active pendant la semaine (du dimanche au samedi) ayant précédé le jour du recensement (le 15 mai 2001).

Le taux de chômage d'un groupe donné (âge, sexe, état matrimonial, région géographique, etc.) correspond au nombre de chômeurs dans ce groupe exprimé en pourcentage de la population active dans ce groupe pendant la semaine ayant précédé le recensement.

Âge

Âge au dernier anniversaire de naissance (à la date de référence du recensement, soit le 15 mai 2001). Cette variable est établie d'après la réponse à la question sur la date de naissance.

Âge à l'immigration

Âge du recensé lorsqu'il a obtenu pour la première fois le statut d'immigrant reçu. Un immigrant reçu est une personne à qui les autorités de l'immigration ont accordé le droit de résider au Canada en permanence.

Agglomération de recensement (AR)

Se reporter à la définition de Région métropolitaine de recensement (RMR) et agglomération de recensement (AR).

Catégorie de lieu de travail

Lieu de travail des personnes âgées de 15 ans et plus, à l'exclusion des pensionnaires d'un établissement institutionnel, qui ont travaillé depuis le 1er janvier 2000. La variable se rapporte habituellement à l'emploi occupé par les recensés au cours de la semaine ayant précédé le recensement. Toutefois, dans le cas des personnes qui n'ont pas travaillé cette semaine-là, mais qui avaient travaillé à un moment quelconque depuis le 1er janvier 2000, les données portent sur l'emploi occupé le plus longtemps au cours de cette période.

À domicile – Les personnes dont le lieu de travail et la résidence se trouvaient dans le même immeuble, celles qui habitaient la ferme où elles travaillaient, les concierges d'immeuble et les télétravailleurs qui travaillaient à domicile pendant la plus grande partie de leur semaine de travail.

En dehors du Canada – Personnes dont le lieu de travail est à l'extérieur du Canada. Les diplomates, les membres des Forces armées et les autres personnes dénombrées à l'étranger, de même que les nouveaux immigrants ne travaillant pas en ce moment, mais dont l'emploi de plus longue durée depuis le 1er janvier 2000 avait été exercé à l'extérieur du Canada.

Sans adresse de travail fixe – Les personnes qui ne se rendaient pas au même lieu de travail au début de chaque quart, notamment les entrepreneurs en bâtiments, les entrepreneurs paysagistes, les représentants de commerce, les chauffeurs de camion indépendants, etc.

À l'adresse précisée ci-dessous – Les personnes qui ne sont pas incluses dans les catégories ci-dessus et qui se rendent au même lieu de travail (habituel) au début de chaque quart sont incluses ici. Les recensés devaient inscrire le numéro de voirie, la ville, le village, le canton, la municipalité ou la réserve indienne, la province ou le territoire et le code postal de leur lieu de travail. Ceux qui ne connaissaient pas l'adresse complète pouvaient donner uniquement le nom de l'immeuble ou de l'intersection la plus proche.

Les télétravailleurs qui passaient moins que la moitié de la semaine de travail à leur bureau à domicile devaient donner l'adresse complète de leur employeur. Les personnes qui travaillaient à des endroits différents, mais se présentaient à un siège social au début de chaque quart devaient donner l'adresse complète du siège social.

Catégorie de revenu

Situation de la famille économique ou de la personne hors famille économique de 15 ans et plus par rapport aux seuils de faible revenu (SFR) de Statistique Canada.

Catégorie de travailleurs

Variable permettant de classer les personnes qui ont déclaré un emploi selon les catégories suivantes :

a) personnes qui ont travaillé principalement pour un salaire, pour un traitement, à commission, pour des pourboires, à la pièce ou contre rémunération « en nature » (paiements sous forme de biens ou de services, plutôt qu'en espèces);

b) personnes qui ont travaillé surtout à leur compte, avec ou sans aide rémunérée dans une entreprise, une ferme ou à exercer une profession, seules ou avec des associés;

c) personnes qui ont travaillé sans rémunération à exercer une profession ou dans une entreprise ou une ferme familiale appartenant à un parent du même ménage ou exploitée par celui-ci; le travail familial non rémunéré ne comprend pas les travaux ménagers non rémunérés, les soins aux enfants non rémunérés, les soins ou l'aide aux personnes âgées non rémunérés, ni le travail bénévole.

L'emploi déclaré désigne l'emploi que la personne occupait au cours de la semaine (du dimanche au samedi) ayant précédé le recensement (le 15 mai 2001) si elle avait travaillé, l'emploi qu'elle a occupé le plus longtemps depuis le 1er janvier 2000, si la personne n'avait pas travaillé au cours de la semaine de référence. Les personnes ayant occupé deux emplois ou plus cette semaine-là devaient donner des renseignements sur celui auquel elles avaient consacré le plus grand nombre d'heures.

Forme juridique

Forme juridique des entreprises commerciales ou agricoles ou dans l'exercice d'une profession. Cette variable s'applique aux personnes qui travaillaient surtout à leur compte, avec ou sans aide rémunérée, dans l'emploi déclaré, c'est-à-dire l'emploi qu'elles avaient pendant la semaine (du dimanche au samedi) ayant précédé le recensement (le 15 mai 2001) ou l'emploi qu'elles ont occupé le plus longtemps depuis le 1er janvier 2000. Une **entreprise constituée en société** est une entreprise ou une ferme ou l'exercice d'une profession ayant une entité juridique constituée sous le régime de lois provinciales ou fédérales. Une **entreprise** ou une ferme ou l'exercice d'une profession **non constituée en société** ne représente pas une entité juridique distincte; il peut toutefois s'agir d'une société en nom collectif, d'une entreprise familiale ou d'une entreprise exploitée par le propriétaire.

Chambres à coucher

Pièces conçues et meublées pour servir de chambres à coucher et utilisées principalement pour y dormir, même si ce n'est qu'à l'occasion (une chambre d'ami par exemple).

Citoyenneté

Statut légal de citoyenneté du recensé. Les personnes ayant plus d'une citoyenneté devaient indiquer le nom du ou des autres pays dont ils étaient citoyens.

Connaissance des langues non officielles

Indique les langues autres que le français ou l'anglais dans lesquelles le recensé peut soutenir une conversation.

Connaissance des langues officielles

Indique si le recensé peut soutenir une conversation en français seulement, en anglais seulement, en français et en anglais, ou dans aucune des deux langues officielles du Canada.

Division de recensement (DR)

Division de recensement (DR) est le terme général de régions créées en vertu des lois provinciales (comme les comtés, les municipalités régionales de comté et les regional districts) ou d'autres genres de régions. Les divisions de recensement sont des régions géographiques intermédiaires entre la municipalité (subdivision de recensement) et la province.

État du logement

Variable indiquant si, selon le répondant, le logement nécessite des réparations (à l'exception des rénovations ou ajouts souhaités).

État matrimonial légal

Situation conjugale légale d'une personne.

Voici la définition des diverses catégories de réponse :

Jamais légalement marié (célibataire) – Personne qui n'a jamais été mariée (y compris toute personne de moins de 15 ans) ou personne dont le mariage a été annulé et qui ne s'est pas remariée.

Légalement marié (et non séparé) – Personne mariée dont le conjoint est vivant, à moins que le couple ne soit séparé ou divorcé.

Séparé, mais toujours légalement marié – Personne actuellement mariée, mais qui ne vit plus avec son conjoint (pour quelque raison que ce soit autre que la maladie ou le travail) et qui n'a pas obtenu de divorce.

Divorcé – Personne qui a obtenu un divorce et qui ne s'est pas remariée.

Veuf ou veuve – Personne dont le conjoint est décédé et qui ne s'est pas remariée.

Famille de recensement

Couple marié (avec ou sans enfants des deux conjoints ou de l'un d'eux), couple vivant en union libre (avec ou sans enfants des deux partenaires ou de l'un d'eux) ou parent seul (peu importe son état matrimonial) demeurant avec au moins un enfant dans le même logement. Un couple vivant en union libre peut être de sexe opposé ou de même sexe. Les « enfants » dans une famille de recensement incluent les petits-enfants vivant dans le même ménage que leurs grands-parents, en l'absence des parents.

Famille économique

Groupe de deux personnes ou plus qui vivent dans le même logement et qui sont apparentées par le sang, par alliance, par union libre ou par adoption.

Fréquence des unités à faible revenu

Proportion ou pourcentage de familles économiques ou de personnes hors famille économique dans une catégorie donnée dont le revenu est inférieur aux seuils de faible revenu. Ces taux de fréquence sont calculés d'après des estimations non arrondies des familles économiques et des personnes hors famille économique âgées de 15 ans et plus.

Fréquentation scolaire

Fréquentation à plein temps ou à temps partiel (le jour ou le soir) d'une école, d'un collège ou d'une université au cours de la période de neuf mois allant de septembre 2000 au 15 mai 2001. La fréquentation est comptée seulement pour les cours permettant d'accumuler des crédits en vue de l'obtention d'un certificat, d'un diplôme ou d'un grade.

Genre de ménage

Répartition fondamentale des ménages privés en ménages familiaux et en ménages non familiaux. Un ménage familial est un ménage qui comprend au moins une famille de recensement, c'est-à-dire un couple marié avec ou sans enfants, ou un couple vivant en union libre avec ou sans enfants, ou un parent seul avec un ou plusieurs enfants (famille monoparentale). Un ménage unifamilial se compose d'une seule famille de recensement (avec ou sans autres personnes hors famille) qui occupe un logement privé. Un ménage multifamilial se compose de deux familles de recensement ou plus (avec ou sans autres personnes hors famille de recensement) qui occupent le même logement privé.

Un ménage non familial est constitué soit d'une personne vivant seule dans un logement privé, soit d'un groupe de deux personnes ou plus qui partagent un logement privé, mais qui ne forment pas une famille de recensement.

Genre de subdivision de recensement

Les subdivisions de recensement (SDR) sont classées en 46 genres, selon les appellations officielles adoptées par les autorités provinciales ou fédérales. Il y a toutefois deux exceptions, soit la *Subdivision of Unorganized* à Terre-Neuve-et-Labrador et la *Subdivision of County Municipality* en Nouvelle-Écosse, qui constituent des régions géographiques équivalant aux municipalités et qui ont été créées par Statistique Canada et ces provinces pour la diffusion de données statistiques.

Afin de mieux distinguer les SDR les unes des autres, le nom de chaque subdivision de recensement est généralement accompagné d'une indication du **genre de subdivision de recensement**, par exemple, Granby, V (pour la « ville » de Granby) et Granby, CT (pour la « municipalité de canton » de Granby).

Heures consacrées à offrir des soins ou de l'aide aux personnes âgées, sans paye ou sans salaire

Nombre d'heures que la personne a consacrées à offrir des soins ou de l'aide aux personnes âgées, sans salaire, pour des membres du ménage du recensé, pour d'autres membres âgés de la famille ne faisant pas partie du ménage, pour des amis ou des voisins pendant la semaine (du dimanche au samedi) ayant précédé le jour du recensement (le 15 mai 2001).

Les soins ou l'aide aux personnes âgées sans paye ou sans salaire ne comprennent pas le travail bénévole pour un organisme à but non lucratif, un organisme religieux, une oeuvre de charité ou un groupe communautaire ni le travail sans paye dans une ferme ou une entreprise familiale ou dans l'exercice d'une profession.

Heures consacrées aux soins des enfants, sans paye ou sans salaire

Nombre d'heures que la personne a consacrées à donner des soins aux enfants, sans paye ou sans salaire. Sont incluses les heures consacrées à donner des soins aux enfants, sans paye ou sans salaire, pour des membres du ménage du recensé, pour d'autres membres de la famille ne faisant pas partie du ménage, pour des amis ou des voisins ou d'autres membres de la famille à l'extérieur du ménage pendant la semaine (du dimanche au samedi) ayant précédé le jour du recensement (le 15 mai 2001).

Les soins aux enfants sans paye ou sans salaire ne comprennent pas le travail bénévole pour un organisme à but non lucratif, un organisme religieux, une oeuvre de charité ou un groupe communautaire ni le travail sans paye dans une ferme ou une entreprise familiale ou dans l'exercice d'une profession.

Heures consacrées aux travaux ménagers, sans paye ou sans salaire

Nombre d'heures que la personne a consacrées aux travaux ménagers, à l'entretien de la maison ou du jardin, sans paye ou sans salaire, pendant la semaine (du dimanche au samedi) ayant précédé le jour du recensement (le 15 mai 2001). Sont incluses les heures consacrées aux travaux ménagers, sans paye ou sans salaire, pour des membres du ménage du recensé, pour d'autres membres de la famille ne faisant pas partie du ménage, pour des amis ou des voisins.

Les travaux ménagers sans paye ou sans salaire ne comprennent pas le travail bénévole pour un organisme à but non lucratif, un organisme religieux, une oeuvre de charité ou un groupe communautaire ni le travail sans paye dans une ferme ou une entreprise familiale ou dans l'exercice d'une profession.

Identité autochtone

Personne ayant déclaré appartenir à au moins un groupe autochtone, c'est-à-dire Indien de l'Amérique du Nord, Métis ou Inuit (Esquimau) et/ou personne ayant déclaré être un Indien des traités ou un Indien inscrit tel que défini par la *Loi sur les Indiens* du Canada et/ou personne ayant déclaré appartenir à une bande indienne ou à une première nation. Lors du recensement de 1991 et des recensements antérieurs, la population autochtone était déterminée au moyen de la question sur l'origine ethnique (ancêtres). Au recensement de 1996, on a ajouté une question sur la propre perception du recensé face à son identité autochtone. La question du recensement de 2001 est la même que celle de 1996.

Indien inscrit ou Indien des traités

Personnes ayant déclaré être inscrites en vertu de la *Loi sur les Indiens* du Canada. Les Indiens des traités sont des personnes qui sont inscrites en vertu de la *Loi sur les Indiens* et qui peuvent démontrer qu'elles descendent d'une bande qui a signé un traité. La question sur le statut d'Indien inscrit a été posée en 1991; toutefois, la présentation de la question posée au recensement de 1996 était quelque peu différente. En 1991, l'appartenance à une bande indienne était un sous élément de la question 16 portant sur les Indiens inscrits. Le recensé devait indiquer s'il était un Indien inscrit dans la première partie de la question, puis préciser la bande indienne ou la première nation à laquelle il appartenait dans la deuxième partie de la question. En 1996, une question directe a été élaborée en vue de recueillir des données sur le statut d'Indien inscrit ou d'Indien des traités.

Le libellé de la question de 1996 différait légèrement de celui des questions posées aux recensements précédents. Avant 1996, le terme « Indien des traités » n'était pas utilisé dans la question. Il a été ajouté en 1996 à la demande des personnes des provinces de l'Ouest où ce terme est davantage utilisé.

Industrie (basée sur le Système de classification des industries de l'Amérique du Nord de 1997 [SCIAN])

Nature générale de l'activité de l'établissement où travaille la personne. Si la personne n'avait pas d'emploi au cours de la semaine (du dimanche au samedi) ayant précédé le recensement (le 15 mai 2001), elle devait donner des renseignements sur l'emploi qu'elle avait occupé le plus longtemps depuis le 1er janvier 2000. Les personnes qui avaient deux emplois ou plus devaient fournir des renseignements sur celui auquel elles avaient consacré le plus grand nombre d'heures de travail.

Les données sur l'industrie du recensement de 2001 sont produites en fonction du Système de classification des industries de l'Amérique du Nord (SCIAN) de 1997. Ce dernier, qui assure une meilleure comparabilité entre les données sur l'industrie des trois partenaires de l'Accord de libre-échange nord-américain (ALENA) (Canada, États-Unis et Mexique), consiste en un répertoire systématique et détaillé des industries regroupées en 20 secteurs, 99 sous-secteurs et 300 groupes. Les critères utilisés pour créer ces catégories sont la similitude des structures d'intrants, des qualifications de la main-d'oeuvre ou des processus de production utilisés par l'établissement. Pour obtenir plus de renseignements au sujet de cette classification, reportez-vous au *Système de classification des industries de l'Amérique du Nord, Canada, 1997*, n° 12-501-XPF au catalogue.

La variable Industrie (selon le SCIAN de 1997) ne permet pas d'établir de comparaisons directes avec les données sur l'industrie des recensements antérieurs. Il faut utiliser la Classification type des industries de 1980 pour effectuer des comparaisons entre les données des recensements de 1986, 1991, 1996 et 2001.

Langue maternelle

Première langue apprise à la maison dans l'enfance et encore comprise par le recensé au moment du recensement.

Langue parlée à la maison

Langue que le recensé parlait le plus souvent à la maison ou de façon régulière au moment du recensement.

Langue utilisée au travail

Cette question portait sur la langue le plus souvent utilisée au travail par le recensé au moment du recensement. Des données sur les autres langues utilisées au travail de façon régulière ont aussi été recueillies.

Lieu de naissance du répondant

Provinces ou territoires de naissance pour les répondants nés au Canada ou pays de naissance pour les répondants nés à l'extérieur du Canada.

Lieu de résidence 1 an auparavant (mobilité)

La mobilité est déterminée d'après le lien entre le domicile habituel d'une personne le jour du recensement et son domicile habituel un an plus tôt. Il s'agit d'une personne n'ayant pas déménagé si son domicile n'a pas changé dans l'intervalle; sinon, il s'agit d'une personne ayant déménagé. Cette catégorisation correspond à la mobilité (1 an auparavant). Dans la catégorie des personnes ayant déménagé, on peut également distinguer les non-migrants et les migrants; cette distinction correspond au statut migratoire.

Les **personnes n'ayant pas déménagé** sont celles qui, le jour du recensement, demeuraient à la même adresse que celle où elles résidaient un an plus tôt.

Les **personnes ayant déménagé** sont celles qui, le jour du recensement, demeuraient à une autre adresse que celle où elles résidaient un an plus tôt.

Les **non-migrants** sont des personnes ayant déménagé qui, le jour du recensement, demeuraient à une autre adresse mais dans la même subdivision de recensement (SDR) que celle où elles résidaient un an plus tôt.

Les **migrants** sont des personnes ayant déménagé qui, le jour du recensement, demeuraient dans une SDR autre que celle où elles résidaient un an plus tôt (migrants internes) ou qui résidaient à l'extérieur du Canada un an plus tôt (migrants externes).

Les **migrants infraprovinciaux** sont des personnes ayant déménagé qui, le jour du recensement, demeuraient dans une subdivision de recensement autre que celle où elles résidaient un an plus tôt, dans la même province.

Les **migrants interprovinciaux** sont des personnes ayant déménagé qui, le jour du recensement, demeuraient dans une subdivision de recensement autre que celle où elles résidaient un an plus tôt, dans une province différente.

Lieu de résidence 5 ans auparavant (mobilité)

La mobilité est déterminée d'après le lien entre le domicile habituel d'une personne le jour du recensement et son domicile habituel cinq ans plus tôt. Il s'agit d'une personne n'ayant pas déménagé si son domicile n'a pas changé dans l'intervalle; sinon, il s'agit d'une personne ayant déménagé. Cette catégorisation correspond à la mobilité (5 ans auparavant). Dans la catégorie des personnes ayant déménagé, on peut également distinguer les non-migrants et les migrants; cette distinction correspond au statut migratoire.

Les **personnes n'ayant pas déménagé** sont celles qui, le jour du recensement, demeuraient à la même adresse que celle où elles résidaient cinq ans plus tôt.

Les **personnes ayant déménagé** sont celles qui, le jour du recensement, demeuraient à une autre adresse que celle où elles résidaient cinq ans plus tôt.

Les **non-migrants** sont des personnes ayant déménagé qui, le jour du recensement, demeuraient à une autre adresse mais dans la même subdivision de recensement (SDR) que celle où elles résidaient cinq ans plus tôt.

Les **migrants** sont des personnes ayant déménagé qui, le jour du recensement, demeuraient dans une SDR autre que celle où elles résidaient cinq ans plus tôt (migrants internes) ou qui résidaient à l'extérieur du Canada cinq ans plus tôt (migrants externes).

Les **migrants infraprovinciaux** sont des personnes ayant déménagé qui, le jour du recensement, demeuraient dans une subdivision de recensement autre que celle où elles résidaient cinq ans plus tôt, dans la même province.

Les **migrants interprovinciaux** sont des personnes ayant déménagé qui, le jour du recensement, demeuraient dans une subdivision de recensement autre que celle où elles résidaient cinq ans plus tôt, dans une province différente.

Logement privé

Ensemble distinct de pièces d'habitation ayant une entrée privée donnant sur l'extérieur ou sur un corridor, un hall, un vestibule ou un escalier commun à l'intérieur. L'entrée doit donner accès au logement sans que l'on ait à passer par les pièces d'habitation de quelqu'un d'autre. Le logement doit répondre aux deux conditions qui le rendent propre à l'habitation durant toute l'année :

a) avoir une source de chauffage ou d'énergie (comme en atteste la présence d'une cheminée, de fils électriques, de tuyaux ou compteurs pour l'huile [mazout] ou le gaz, d'une génératrice, de bois de chauffage, d'ampoules électriques, d'une thermopompe, de panneaux solaires, etc.);

b) fournir un espace clos permettant de s'abriter des intempéries (comme en atteste la présence de murs d'enceinte et d'un toit ainsi que de portes et fenêtres offrant une protection contre le vent, la pluie et la neige).

Pour les besoins du recensement, on classe les logements privés comme **logements privés ordinaires** et **logements marginaux occupés**. Les logements privés ordinaires se subdivisent en trois grandes catégories : les **logements occupés** (par des résidents habituels), les **logements occupés par des résidents étrangers et/ou temporaires** et les **logements inoccupés**. Les logements marginaux sont classés comme logements occupés par des résidents habituels ou comme logements occupés par des résidents étrangers et/ou temporaires. Les logements marginaux inoccupés le jour du recensement ne font pas partie du parc immobilier.

Logement privé occupé

Logement privé occupé de façon permanente par une personne ou un groupe de personnes. Sont également inclus dans cette catégorie les logements privés dont les résidents habituels sont temporairement absents le jour du recensement. Sauf indication contraire, toutes les données présentées dans les produits sur le logement ont trait aux logements privés occupés et non aux logements privés inoccupés ou aux logements occupés par des résidents étrangers et/ou temporaires uniquement.

Loyer brut

Total des montants mensuels moyens versés par les ménages locataires au titre de l'habitation.

Ménage privé

Personne ou groupe de personnes (autres que des résidents étrangers) occupant un logement privé et n'ayant pas de domicile habituel ailleurs au Canada.

Minorités visibles

Groupe de minorités visibles auquel le recensé appartient. Selon la *Loi sur l'équité en matière d'emploi*, font partie des minorités visibles « les personnes, autres que les Autochtones, qui ne sont pas de race blanche ou qui n'ont pas la peau blanche ».

La population des minorités visibles comprend les groupes suivants : Chinois, Sud-Asiatique, Noir, Philippin, Latino-Américain, Asiatique du Sud-Est, Arabe, Asiatique occidental, Coréen, Japonais, Minorité visible, n.i.a. et Minorités visibles multiples.

Mode d'occupation

Indique si le logement est possédé ou loué par un membre du ménage, ou s'il s'agit d'un logement de bande (dans une réserve ou un établissement indien).

Mode de transport

Mode de transport utilisé pour se rendre au travail par les personnes âgées de 15 ans et plus, à l'exclusion des pensionnaires d'un établissement institutionnel, qui ont travaillé depuis le 1er janvier 2000. Les personnes qui ont indiqué qu'elles n'avaient pas d'adresse de travail fixe, ou ont précisé l'adresse d'un lieu habituel de travail, devaient inscrire le moyen de transport utilisé le plus souvent pour faire la navette entre le domicile et le travail. La variable se rapporte habituellement à l'emploi occupé par les recensés au cours de la semaine ayant précédé le recensement. Toutefois, dans le cas des personnes qui n'ont pas travaillé cette semaine-là, mais qui avaient travaillé à un moment quelconque depuis le 1er janvier 2000, les données portent sur l'emploi occupé le plus longtemps au cours de cette période.

Les personnes qui utilisaient plus d'un moyen de transport devaient indiquer seulement celui qu'elles utilisaient pour faire la plus grande partie du trajet. En conséquence, la question a permis de recueillir des données sur le principal mode de transport utilisé pour se rendre au travail. Elle ne permet toutefois pas d'obtenir des données sur l'utilisation de plusieurs modes de transport, la variation saisonnière dans le choix du mode de transport, ni sur les déplacements faits à d'autres fins que pour faire la navette entre le domicile et le travail.

Origine autochtone

Personne ayant indiqué appartenir à au moins un groupe autochtone à la question sur l'origine ethnique, c'est-à-dire Indien de l'Amérique du Nord, Métis ou Inuit (Esquimau). L'origine ethnique se rapporte au(x) groupe(s) ethnique(s) ou culturel(s) auquel (auxquels) appartenaient les ancêtres du recensé. (Voir Origine ethnique.)

Origine ethnique

Groupe(s) ethnique(s) ou culturel(s) auquel (auxquels) appartenaient les ancêtres du recensé.

Période d'immigration

Tranches d'années établies d'après les réponses à la question sur l'année d'immigration. Par année d'immigration, on entend l'année au cours de laquelle la personne a obtenu le statut d'immigrant reçu pour la première fois.

Période de construction

Période au cours de laquelle l'immeuble ou le logement a été construit.

Personnes hors famille économique

Membres d'un ménage qui ne sont pas membres d'une famille économique. Les personnes qui vivent seules sont toujours comprises dans cette catégorie.

Pièces

Nombre de pièces dans un logement. Une pièce est un espace fermé à l'intérieur d'un logement, fini et habitable toute l'année.

Plus haut niveau de scolarité atteint

Dernière année d'études primaires ou secondaires, terminée ou non, ou dernière année universitaire ou collégiale terminée. Dans la hiérarchie de la scolarité, les études universitaires sont classées au-dessus des études collégiales. En outre, la personne qui a obtenu un grade, certificat ou diplôme se trouve classée à un échelon au-dessus de celle qui a un nombre d'années de scolarité plus élevé, terminées ou non, mais qui n'a pas de titre scolaire.

Population des immigrants

Personnes ayant le statut d'immigrant reçu au Canada, ou l'ayant déjà eu. Un immigrant reçu est une personne à qui les autorités de l'immigration ont accordé le droit de résider au Canada en permanence. Certains immigrants résident au Canada depuis un certain nombre d'années, alors que d'autres sont arrivés récemment. La plupart des immigrants sont nés à l'extérieur du Canada, mais un petit nombre d'entre eux sont nés au Canada.

Population des non-immigrants

Personnes qui sont des citoyens canadiens de naissance. Bien que la plupart de ces personnes soient nées au Canada, un petit nombre d'entre elles sont nées à l'étranger de parents canadiens.

Première langue officielle parlée

Variable élaborée pour l'application de la *Loi sur les langues officielles*.

Présence d'enfants

Nombre d'enfants dans les ménages privés selon le groupe d'âge.

Principales dépenses de propriété ou loyer brut, sous forme de pourcentage du revenu du ménage

Proportion du revenu mensuel total moyen du ménage en 2000 consacrée aux principales dépenses de propriété (dans le cas des logements occupés par leur propriétaire) ou au loyer brut (dans le cas des logements occupés par un locataire). Voici comment ces résultats sont obtenus :

a) **Logements non agricoles occupés par leur propriétaire :**

$$\frac{\text{Principales dépenses de propriété}}{\text{(Revenu annuel total du ménage en 2000) /12}} \times 100 = \_\_\_\_ \%$$

b) **Logements non agricoles occupés par un locataire :**

$$\frac{\text{Loyer brut}}{\text{(Revenu annuel total du ménage en 2000) /12}} \times 100 = \_\_\_\_ \%$$

Profession (basée sur la Classification nationale des professions pour statistiques de 2001 [CNP–S de 2001])

Genre de travail que faisaient les personnes pendant la semaine de référence, défini d'après le type d'emploi occupé par le recensé et la description des tâches les plus importantes qui s'y rattachent. Si le recensé n'avait pas d'emploi au cours de la semaine (du dimanche au samedi) ayant précédé le recensement (le 15 mai 2001), les données portent sur l'emploi qu'il avait occupé le plus longtemps depuis le 1er janvier 2000. Les personnes qui avaient deux emplois ou plus devaient donner des renseignements sur l'emploi auquel elles avaient consacré le plus d'heures de travail.

Les données sur la profession du recensement de 2001 sont produites selon la Classification nationale des professions pour statistiques de 2001 (CNP–S de 2001). Cette classification comprend quatre niveaux d'agrégation. Elle comprend 10 grandes catégories professionnelles englobant 47 grands groupes, lesquels comprennent à leur tour 140 sous-groupes. Ces sous-groupes renferment 520 groupes de base. Les titres de profession sont classés selon le niveau de scolarité, de formation ou de compétence nécessaire pour exercer cette profession, ainsi que le genre de travail exécuté, déterminé d'après les tâches, les fonctions et les responsabilités reliées au poste.

Pour plus de renseignements sur la CNP–S de 2001, se reporter à la *Classification nationale des professions pour statistiques 2001*, n° 12-583-XPF au catalogue.

Province ou territoire

Les termes « province » et « territoire » désignent les principales unités politiques du Canada. Du point de vue statistique, les provinces et les territoires sont des régions de base selon lesquelles les données du recensement sont totalisées et recoupées. Le Canada est divisé en dix provinces et trois territoires.

Région métropolitaine de recensement (RMR) et agglomération de recensement (AR)

Une région métropolitaine de recensement (RMR) ou une agglomération de recensement (AR) est formée d'une ou de plusieurs municipalités adjacentes situées autour d'une grande région urbaine (appelée noyau urbain). Un noyau urbain doit compter au moins 10 000 habitants pour former une agglomération de recensement et au moins 100 000 habitants pour former une région métropolitaine de recensement. Pour être incluses dans une RMR ou une AR, les autres municipalités adjacentes doivent avoir un degré d'intégration élevé avec la région urbaine centrale, lequel est déterminé par le pourcentage de navetteurs établi d'après les données du recensement sur le lieu de travail.

Si la population du noyau urbain d'une AR devient inférieure à 10 000 habitants, l'AR est retirée du programme. Cependant, une RMR restera une RMR même si la population de son noyau urbain devient inférieure à 100 000 habitants. Les régions urbaines comprises dans une RMR ou une AR qui ne sont pas contiguës à un noyau urbain sont appelées banlieues urbaines, tandis que les régions rurales sont appelées banlieues rurales.

Lorsque le noyau urbain d'une AR compte au moins 50 000 habitants d'après les chiffres du recensement, il est subdivisé en secteurs de recensement. Les secteurs de recensement de l'AR sont maintenus même si, ultérieurement, la population de son noyau urbain devient inférieure à 50 000 habitants. Toutes les RMR sont subdivisées en secteurs de recensement.

Religion

Confession religieuse précise ou appartenance à un groupe ou à un organisme religieux, à une secte, à un culte ou à toute autre collectivité ayant adopté une religion ou un système de croyances quelconque.

Revenu total

Revenu total en espèces, reçu par les personnes âgées de 15 ans et plus durant l'année civile 2000, provenant des sources suivantes :

- salaires et traitements (total);
- revenu agricole net;
- revenu non agricole net de l'exploitation d'une entreprise non constituée en société et/ou de l'exercice d'une profession;
- prestations fiscales canadiennes pour enfants;
- pension de sécurité de la vieillesse et supplément de revenu garanti;
- prestations du Régime de rentes du Québec ou du Régime de pensions du Canada;
- prestations d'assurance-emploi;
- autre revenu provenant de sources publiques;
- dividendes, intérêts d'obligations, de dépôts et de certificats d'épargne, et autre revenu de placements;
- pensions de retraite et rentes, y compris les rentes de REÉR et de FERR;
- autre revenu en espèces.

Recettes non comptées comme revenu – Le concept du revenu excluait les gains et les pertes au jeu, les prix gagnés à la loterie, les sommes forfaitaires reçues en héritage au cours de l'année, les gains et les pertes en capital, le produit de la vente d'une propriété, les remboursements d'impôt sur le revenu, les remboursements de prêts reçus, les règlements monétaires forfaitaires d'assurance, les remboursements d'impôt foncier, les remboursements de cotisations à un régime de pensions ainsi que les revenus en nature tels que les repas et l'hébergement gratuits ou les produits agricoles cultivés et consommés à la ferme.

Revenu moyen des particuliers – Revenu total moyen pondéré des personnes âgées de 15 ans et plus qui ont déclaré un revenu en 2000. Pour établir le revenu moyen à partir des données non arrondies, il faut diviser le revenu agrégé d'un groupe de particuliers (par exemple, les hommes de 45 à 54 ans) par le nombre de personnes qui ont déclaré un revenu dans ce groupe.

Les revenus moyen et médian des particuliers, ainsi que les erreurs types de revenu moyen correspondantes, sont calculés pour les personnes qui sont âgées d'au moins 15 ans et qui ont un revenu (positif ou négatif). En ce qui concerne tous les autres univers (p. ex. les familles de recensement ou les ménages privés), ces statistiques sont calculées pour toutes les unités, qu'un revenu ait été déclaré ou non.

Revenu médian des particuliers – Valeur centrale séparant en deux parties égales la répartition par tranches de revenu d'un groupe donné de personnes ayant un revenu; la première partie regroupe les personnes ayant un revenu inférieur à la médiane, et la seconde, les personnes ayant un revenu supérieur à la médiane. Le revenu médian pour un groupe de personnes est calculé à partir des données non arrondies pour les membres de ce groupe (par exemple, les hommes de 45 à 54 ans) qui ont déclaré un revenu.

Les revenus moyen et médian des particuliers, ainsi que les erreurs types de revenu moyen correspondantes, sont calculés pour les personnes qui sont âgées d'au moins 15 ans et qui ont un revenu (positif ou négatif). En ce qui concerne tous les autres univers (p. ex. familles de recensement ou ménages privés), ces statistiques sont calculées pour toutes les unités, qu'un revenu ait été déclaré ou non.

Erreur type de revenu moyen – Estimation de l'erreur type de revenu moyen pour une répartition par tranches de revenu. Si elle est interprétée de la façon décrite ci-après, elle sert d'indicateur brut de la précision avec laquelle le revenu moyen a été estimé. Pour environ 68 % des échantillons qui peuvent être tirés de la base de sondage, la différence entre l'estimation du revenu moyen calculée pour un échantillon et le chiffre correspondant obtenu par un dénombrement exhaustif est inférieure à une erreur type. Pour près de 95 % des échantillons possibles, la différence est de moins de deux erreurs types et, dans environ 99 % des échantillons, elle est inférieure à environ deux erreurs types et demie.

Salarié ou bénéficiaire d'un revenu d'emploi

Revenu total des personnes âgées de 15 ans et plus ayant reçu un revenu au cours de l'année civile 2000 sous forme de salaires et traitements, de revenu net de l'exploitation d'une entreprise non agricole non constituée en société et/ ou dans l'exercice d'une profession et de revenu net provenant d'un travail autonome agricole.

Secteur de recensement (SR)

Les secteurs de recensement (SR) sont de petites régions géographiques relativement stables qui comptent habituellement entre 2 500 et 8 000 habitants. Ils sont créés au sein de régions métropolitaines de recensement et d'agglomérations de recensement dont le noyau urbain compte 50 000 habitants ou plus d'après le recensement précédent.

Un comité de spécialistes locaux (par exemple, des planificateurs, des travailleurs sociaux, des travailleurs du secteur de la santé et des éducateurs) délimitent initialement les SR de concert avec Statistique Canada. Une fois qu'une région métropolitaine de recensement (RMR) ou qu'une agglomération de recensement (AR) a été divisée en secteurs de recensement, les secteurs de recensement sont maintenus même si, ultérieurement, la population du noyau urbain de la RMR ou de l'AR devient inférieure à 50 000 habitants.

Seuils de faible revenu (SFR)

Les mesures du faible revenu appelées seuils de faible revenu (SFR) ont été établies pour la première fois au Canada en 1968, d'après les données sur le revenu du recensement de 1961 et les régimes de dépenses des familles en 1959. À cette époque, les régimes de dépenses indiquaient que les familles canadiennes consacraient environ 50 % de leur revenu total à la nourriture, au logement et à l'habillement. On a arbitrairement estimé que les familles consacrant 70 % ou plus de leur revenu (soit 20 points de pourcentage de plus que la moyenne) à ces biens de première nécessité sont « dans le besoin ». À partir de cette hypothèse, des seuils de faible revenu ont été établis pour cinq différentes tailles de famille.

Par la suite, les seuils de faible revenu ont été révisés d'après les données nationales sur les dépenses des familles pour 1969, 1978, 1986 et 1992. Selon ces données, les familles canadiennes consacraient en moyenne 42 % de leur revenu total aux biens de première nécessité en 1969, contre 38,5 % en 1978, 36,2 % en 1986 et 34,7 % en 1992. Depuis 1992, les données de l'enquête sur les dépenses des familles indiquent que cette proportion est demeurée relativement stable. En ajoutant la différence initiale de 20 points au niveau de base des dépenses au titre des biens de première nécessité, de nouveaux seuils de faible revenu ont été fixés selon la taille de la famille et le degré d'urbanisation. Depuis 1992, ces seuils de faible revenu ont été mis à jour chaque année d'après les changements subis par l'indice des prix à la consommation.

Sexe

Qualité d'homme ou de femme.

Situation des particuliers dans la famille de recensement

Classement des personnes selon qu'elles appartiennent ou non à une famille de recensement.

Membres d'une famille de recensement – Membres d'un ménage qui appartiennent à une famille de recensement. Ces personnes se répartissent dans les catégories suivantes :

Époux et épouses – Personnes de sexe opposé qui sont légalement mariées l'une à l'autre et qui habitent le même logement.

Partenaires en union libre – Personnes de sexe opposé ou de même sexe qui ne sont pas légalement mariées l'une à l'autre, mais qui vivent comme couple dans le même logement.

Parent seul – Mère ou père, sans époux(se) ni partenaire en union libre, qui habite un logement avec au moins un de ses enfants.

Enfants – Fils ou filles apparentés par le sang, par alliance ou par adoption, peu importe leur âge ou leur état matrimonial, qui vivent dans le même logement que leur(s) parent(s), ainsi que les petits-enfants des ménages où les parents sont absents. Les fils et les filles qui vivent avec leur conjoint(e), ou avec un(e) partenaire en union libre ou avec un ou plusieurs de leurs propres enfants, ne sont pas considérés comme des membres de la famille de recensement de leur(s) parent(s), même s'ils vivent dans le même logement. En outre, les fils et les filles qui n'habitent pas dans le même logement que leur(s) parent(s) ne sont pas considérés comme des membres de la famille de ce(s) dernier(s). Les personnes suivantes font donc partie de la catégorie « enfants » :

Fils et/ou filles jamais mariés faisant partie d'une famille de recensement, comme dans le cas des recensements précédant celui de 2001.

Autres fils et/ou filles faisant partie d'une famille de recensement qui n'auraient pas été inclus dans la famille de recensement de leurs parents selon le concept précédent.

Petits-enfants vivant dans le même ménage que leurs grands-parents, en l'absence des parents.

Personnes hors famille de recensement – Membres d'un ménage qui ne font pas partie d'une famille de recensement. Ils peuvent être apparentés à la Personne 1 (p. ex. soeur, beau-frère, cousine ou grand-père de la Personne 1), ou non apparentés (p. ex. chambreur, colocataire ou employé). Les personnes qui vivent seules sont toujours considérées comme des personnes hors famille de recensement.

Situation des particuliers dans le ménage

Classement des personnes selon qu'elles sont des membres d'un ménage familial ou non familial et selon qu'elles sont des membres d'une famille de recensement ou des personnes hors famille de recensement.

Statut d'immigrant reçu

Personne à qui les autorités de l'immigration ont accordé le droit de résider au Canada en permanence.

Statut des générations

Le « statut des générations » du répondant (c.-à-d. « 1re », « 2e » ou « 3e ou plus » des générations) indique si le répondant ou ses parents sont nés au Canada ou à l'extérieur du Canada.

Structure de la famille de recensement

Classement des familles de recensement en couples mariés (avec ou sans enfants des deux conjoints ou de l'un d'eux), en couples en union libre (avec ou sans enfants des deux partenaires ou de l'un deux) et en familles monoparentales selon le sexe du parent. Un couple vivant en union libre peut être de sexe opposé ou de même sexe. Les « enfants » dans une famille de recensement incluent les petits-enfants vivant dans le même ménage que leurs grands-parents, en l'absence des parents.

Subdivision de recensement (SDR)

Subdivision de recensement (SDR) est un terme générique qui désigne les municipalités (telles que définies par les lois provinciales) ou les territoires considérés comme étant des équivalents municipaux à des fins statistiques (par exemple, les réserves indiennes, les établissements indiens et les territoires non organisés).

Superficie des terres

La superficie des terres correspond à la surface en kilomètres carrés des parties des terres des régions géographiques normalisées.

Les données sur les superficies des terres ne sont pas officielles et servent uniquement à calculer la densité de la population.

Taille du ménage

Nombre de personnes dans un ménage privé.

Type de construction résidentielle

Type de construction et/ou caractéristiques du logement (maison individuelle non attenante, appartement dans une tour d'habitation, maison en rangée, habitation mobile, etc.).

Union libre

Par union libre, on entend deux personnes de sexe opposé ou de même sexe qui vivent ensemble en tant que couple sans être légalement mariées l'une à l'autre.

Univers de la population

L'univers de la population du recensement de 2001 comprend les groupes suivants :

- les citoyens canadiens (par naissance ou par naturalisation) et les immigrants reçus ayant un lieu habituel de résidence au Canada;
- les citoyens canadiens (par naissance ou par naturalisation) et les immigrants reçus qui sont à l'étranger, dans une base militaire ou en mission diplomatique;
- les citoyens canadiens (par naissance ou par naturalisation) et les immigrants reçus qui sont en mer ou dans des ports à bord de navires marchands battant pavillon canadien;
- les personnes ayant un lieu habituel de résidence au Canada qui demandent le statut de réfugié et les membres de leur famille vivant avec elles;
- les personnes ayant un lieu habituel de résidence au Canada, qui sont titulaires d'un permis de séjour pour étudiants (visas pour étudiants, permis pour étudiants) et les membres de leur famille vivant avec elles;

- les personnes ayant un lieu habituel de résidence au Canada, qui sont titulaires d'un permis de travail et les membres de leur famille vivant avec elles;

- les personnes ayant un lieu habituel de résidence au Canada, qui sont titulaires d'un permis ministériel (y compris les prolongements) et les membres de leur famille vivant avec elles.

Aux fins du recensement, les personnes des quatre derniers groupes de la liste sont des « résidents non permanents ».

Valeur du logement

Montant en dollars que s'attendrait à recevoir le propriétaire s'il vendait son logement.

Qualité des données

Généralités

Le recensement de 2001 a été une entreprise complexe et de grande envergure. Bien que l'on ait déployé des efforts considérables pour assurer le respect de normes élevées au cours des opérations de la collecte et du traitement, il est inévitable que les estimations résultantes soient entachées d'erreurs. Les utilisateurs des données du recensement doivent savoir que ces erreurs existent et doivent avoir une idée générale de leurs principales composantes afin d'être en mesure de déterminer l'utilité des données produites et d'évaluer les risques qu'ils courent en tirant des conclusions ou en prenant des décisions à partir de ces données.

Des erreurs peuvent se produire pratiquement à toutes les étapes du recensement, depuis la préparation des documents jusqu'au traitement des données, en passant par l'établissement des listes de logements et la collecte des données. Certaines erreurs, qui surviennent par hasard, ont tendance à s'annuler lorsque les réponses fournies par les divers répondants sont agrégées pour un groupe assez important. Dans le cas d'erreurs de cette nature, l'estimation correspondante sera d'autant plus précise que le groupe visé sera grand. C'est pourquoi on conseille aux utilisateurs de faire preuve de prudence lorsqu'ils utilisent des estimations relatives à de petits groupes. Toutefois, certaines erreurs peuvent survenir de façon plus systématique et introduire un « biais » dans les estimations. Comme ce biais persiste quelle que soit la taille du groupe pour lequel les réponses sont agrégées et comme il est particulièrement difficile d'en mesurer l'importance, les erreurs systématiques posent pour la plupart des utilisateurs de données des problèmes plus graves que les erreurs aléatoires mentionnées plus haut.

En ce qui concerne les données du recensement en général, les principaux types d'erreurs sont les suivants :

- les **erreurs de couverture** qui se produisent lorsqu'on oublie des logements ou des personnes, qu'on les dénombre à tort ou qu'on les compte plus d'une fois;

- les **erreurs dues à la non-réponse** qui surviennent lorsqu'on n'a pu obtenir de réponses d'un certain nombre de ménages ou de personnes en raison d'une absence prolongée ou pour toute autre raison;

- les **erreurs de réponse** qui surviennent lorsque le répondant, ou parfois le recenseur, a mal interprété une question du recensement et a inscrit une mauvaise réponse ou s'est tout simplement trompé de case de réponse;

- les **erreurs de traitement** qui peuvent se produire à diverses étapes, notamment lors du **codage**, lorsque les réponses en lettres sont converties en codes numériques; lors de la **saisie des données**, lorsque les préposés à l'entrée des données transfèrent dans un format électronique les réponses figurant au questionnaire du recensement; lors de l'**imputation**, lorsqu'une réponse « valide », mais pas nécessairement exacte, est insérée dans un enregistrement par l'ordinateur pour remplacer une réponse manquante ou « invalide » (« valide » et « invalide » renvoient à la cohérence de la réponse, compte tenu des autres renseignements compris dans l'enregistrement);

- les **erreurs d'échantillonnage** qui s'appliquent uniquement aux questions supplémentaires figurant dans le questionnaire complet distribué à un échantillon de un cinquième des ménages. Ces erreurs résultent du fait que les réponses à ces questions supplémentaires, une fois pondérées pour représenter l'ensemble de la population, diffèrent inévitablement des réponses qu'on aurait obtenues si l'on avait posé ces questions à tous les ménages.

Les types d'erreur mentionnés plus haut ont tous une composante aléatoire et une composante systématique. Toutefois, la composante systématique de l'erreur d'échantillonnage est d'ordinaire très petite comparativement à sa composante aléatoire. Dans le cas des autres erreurs non dues à l'échantillonnage, tant la composante aléatoire que la composante systématique peuvent être importantes.

Erreurs de couverture

Les erreurs de couverture ont une incidence directe sur la précision des chiffres du recensement, c'est-à-dire sur la taille des divers univers du recensement : la population, les familles, les ménages et les logements. Bien que des mesures aient été prises pour corriger certaines erreurs identifiables, les chiffres définitifs sont toujours entachés d'une certaine erreur parce que des personnes ou des logements ont été oubliés, dénombrés à tort ou comptés plus d'une fois.

L'oubli de logements ou de personnes se traduit par un **sous-dénombrement**. Des logements peuvent être oubliés en raison soit d'une mauvaise interprétation des limites du secteur de dénombrement (SD), soit qu'ils n'ont pas l'apparence de logements ou soit qu'ils semblent inhabitables. Des personnes peuvent être oubliées parce que leur logement est oublié ou classé comme inoccupé, ou parce que le répondant a mal interprété les instructions concernant les personnes à inclure sur le questionnaire. Enfin, certaines personnes peuvent être oubliées parce qu'elles n'ont pas de domicile habituel et qu'elles n'ont pas passé la nuit du recensement dans un logement.

Le dénombrement à tort ou le double compte de logements ou de personnes se traduit par un **surdénombrement**. Il peut y avoir surdénombrement de logements lorsque des constructions impropres à l'habitation sont classées comme logements (dénombrement à tort), lorsqu'il existe une certaine ambiguïté au sujet des limites des SD ou lorsque des unités d'habitation (par exemple, des chambres) sont comptées séparément plutôt que d'être considérées comme faisant partie d'un seul logement (double compte). Les personnes peuvent être comptées plus d'une fois parce que leur logement a été compté deux fois ou parce que les lignes directrices concernant les personnes à inscrire dans le questionnaire ont été mal interprétées. À l'occasion, il arrive qu'une personne ne faisant pas partie de l'univers de la population du recensement, comme un résident étranger ou une personne fictive, soit dénombrée à tort. En moyenne, le surdénombrement est moins susceptible de se produire que le sous-dénombrement; les chiffres des logements et des personnes sont donc probablement légèrement sous-estimés.

Pour le recensement de 2001, trois études permettent de mesurer l'erreur de couverture. Dans le contexte de l'Étude sur la classification des logements, on a de nouveau visité des logements classés comme inoccupés afin de vérifier s'ils étaient réellement inoccupés le jour du recensement, et des logements dont le ménage a été classé comme non répondant afin de déterminer le nombre de résidents habituels et leurs caractéristiques. Les chiffres définitifs du recensement ont ensuite été corrigés pour tenir compte des personnes ou des ménages oubliés parce que leur logement avait été classé par erreur comme inoccupé. Il est aussi possible que les chiffres du recensement aient été corrigés pour tenir compte des logements dont le ménage a été classé comme non répondant. En dépit de ces ajustements, les chiffres définitifs peuvent tout de même être entachés d'un certain sous-dénombrement. Le sous-dénombrement tend à être plus élevé pour certains segments de la population comme les jeunes adultes (plus particulièrement ceux de sexe masculin) et les personnes récemment immigrées. L'Étude de la contre-vérification des dossiers permet de mesurer le sous-dénombrement résiduel pour le Canada, de même que pour chaque province et chaque territoire. L'Étude sur le surdénombrement a pour objet d'étudier les erreurs de surdénombrement. Ensemble, les résultats de l'Étude de la contre-vérification des dossiers et de l'Étude sur le surdénombrement fournissent une estimation du sous-dénombrement net.

Autres erreurs non dues à l'échantillonnage

Alors que les erreurs de couverture ont une incidence sur le nombre d'unités comprises dans les divers univers du recensement, d'autres erreurs influent sur les caractéristiques de ces unités.

Il est parfois impossible d'obtenir une réponse complète d'un ménage, même si le logement a été classé comme étant occupé et un questionnaire y a été livré. Il se peut que les membres du ménage aient été absents pendant toute la période du recensement ou, en de rares occasions, que le membre responsable du ménage ait refusé de remplir le questionnaire. Il arrive plus souvent que le questionnaire soit retourné, mais qu'il y ait des questions laissées sans réponse. Des efforts sont déployés afin d'obtenir un questionnaire le plus complet possible. Les recenseurs contrôlent les questionnaires et assurent un suivi à l'égard de l'information manquante. Le travail du recenseur est ensuite vérifié par un surveillant et par un technicien du contrôle qualitatif. Malgré tout, il existe toujours un petit nombre de réponses manquantes à la fin de l'étape de la collecte, c'est-à-dire d'**erreurs dues à la non-réponse**. Bien que les réponses manquantes soient éliminées en cours de traitement en remplaçant chacune d'elles par la réponse correspondante figurant dans un enregistrement « similaire », il est possible que certaines erreurs d'imputation s'y glissent. Cela est particulièrement grave lorsque les personnes non répondantes diffèrent des répondants sous certains aspects; en effet, cette procédure introduit un **biais dû à la non-réponse**.

Même lorsqu'une réponse est obtenue, il se peut qu'elle ne soit pas tout à fait exacte. Il est possible que le répondant ait mal interprété la question ou ait donné une réponse au jugé, surtout lorsqu'il répondait pour le compte d'un autre membre du ménage, qui était peut-être absent. Il est aussi possible que le répondant ait inscrit sa réponse au mauvais endroit sur le questionnaire. Ces erreurs sont désignées sous le nom d'**erreurs de réponse**. Bien que ces erreurs surviennent d'ordinaire parce que les répondants ont fourni des renseignements inexacts, elles peuvent aussi résulter d'erreurs commises par les recenseurs qui ont rempli certaines parties du questionnaire, comme le type de construction résidentielle, ou qui ont effectué le suivi pour obtenir une réponse manquante.

Certaines questions du recensement nécessitent une réponse en lettres. Pendant le traitement, on attribue un code numérique à ces réponses. Il est possible que des **erreurs de codage** se produisent lorsque la réponse écrite est ambiguë, incomplète ou difficile à lire, ou lorsque la liste des codes est longue (p. ex. principal domaine d'études, lieu de travail). L'étape formelle du contrôle qualitatif (CQ) permet de cerner et de rectifier les erreurs de codage et d'en réduire le nombre. À l'intérieur de chaque unité de travail, un échantillon des réponses est codé indépendamment une deuxième fois. La résolution des incohérences entre les premier et deuxième codages détermine la nécessité, s'il y a lieu, de coder à nouveau l'unité de travail. Exception faite pour le codage des variables de l'industrie et de la profession, la plupart des tâches de codage du recensement sont maintenant automatisées, ce qui a pour conséquence de réduire le nombre d'erreurs de codage.

Les renseignements figurant dans les questionnaires sont tapés dans un fichier informatique. Deux méthodes de résolution ordonnée sont utilisées pour limiter le nombre d'**erreurs à la saisie des données**. Dans un premier temps, certains contrôles (comme des vérifications d'étendue) sont effectués à mesure que les données sont entrées. Dans un second temps, on tape de nouveau à l'ordinateur un échantillon tiré de chaque lot de documents, puis on compare les entrées résultantes aux entrées initiales. Le travail non satisfaisant est ainsi circonscrit et corrigé et, si cela est nécessaire, le reste du lot est de nouveau saisi.

Une fois saisies, les données font l'objet de vérifications qui consistent à les soumettre à une série de contrôles informatiques visant à relever les réponses manquantes ou incohérentes. À l'étape de l'imputation, on substitue à ces dernières des réponses déduites à partir des autres données de l'enregistrement ou des réponses tirées d'un enregistrement donneur similaire. L'imputation permet d'obtenir une base de données complète dont les données correspondent aux chiffres du recensement et facilitent les analyses multidimensionnelles. Même si des erreurs peuvent être introduites à l'**étape de l'imputation**, les méthodes utilisées ont fait l'objet de tests rigoureux visant à réduire au minimum les erreurs systématiques.

Diverses études sont réalisées afin d'évaluer la qualité des réponses obtenues dans le cadre du recensement de 2001. Ainsi, on a calculé les taux de non-réponse et les taux de rejet au contrôle pour chaque question. Ces taux peuvent permettre de déterminer le potentiel d'erreurs dues à la non-réponse et d'autres types d'erreurs. De même, les totalisations établies à partir des données du recensement de 2001 ont été ou seront comparées avec les estimations correspondantes obtenues à partir des données des recensements précédents, des enquêtes-échantillon (comme l'Enquête sur la population active) et de divers dossiers administratifs (comme les registres des naissances et le cadastre municipal). Ces comparaisons peuvent permettre de cerner les problèmes de qualité éventuels ou, à tout le moins, de relever les divergences entre les sources.

Outre ces comparaisons entre données agrégées, certaines études de couplage de microdonnées sont actuellement menées afin de comparer les réponses de certains particuliers obtenues au recensement à celles d'une autre source de renseignements. Pour un certain nombre de caractéristiques « stables » (comme l'âge, le sexe, la langue maternelle et le lieu de naissance), on compare les réponses obtenues auprès d'un échantillon de personnes à l'occasion du recensement de 2001 aux réponses obtenues des mêmes personnes à l'occasion du recensement de 1996.

Erreurs d'échantillonnage

Les estimations obtenues en pondérant les réponses recueillies auprès d'un échantillon sont susceptibles d'être entachées d'erreurs en raison de la répartition des caractéristiques au sein de l'échantillon, qui n'est généralement pas identique à la répartition correspondante au sein de la population dans laquelle l'échantillon a été prélevé.

L'erreur susceptible d'être introduite par l'échantillonnage variera en fonction de la rareté relative de la caractéristique étudiée au sein de la population. Lorsque la valeur contenue dans la case est élevée, cette erreur sera relativement faible proportionnellement à cette valeur. Lorsque la valeur contenue dans la case est faible, cette erreur sera relativement importante proportionnellement à cette valeur.

L'erreur susceptible d'être introduite par l'échantillonnage est d'ordinaire exprimée sous forme d'« erreur type ». Il s'agit de la racine carrée de la moyenne, calculée pour l'ensemble des échantillons de même taille prélevés selon le même plan d'échantillonnage, des carrés de l'écart de l'estimation obtenue à partir de l'échantillon par rapport à la valeur pour l'ensemble de la population.

Le tableau ci-dessous fournit des mesures approximatives de l'erreur type due à l'échantillonnage. Ces mesures sont données uniquement à titre indicatif.

Erreur type approximative due à l'échantillonnage pour les données-échantillon du recensement de 2001

Valeur contenue dans la case	Erreur type approximative
50 ou moins	15
100	20
200	30
500	45
1 000	65
2 000	90
5 000	140
10 000	200
20 000	280
50 000	450
100 000	630
500 000	1 400

Les utilisateurs souhaitant déterminer l'erreur d'échantillonnage approximative pour une case de données dont la valeur a été obtenue à partir de l'échantillon de 20 % doivent choisir l'erreur type correspondant à l'entrée dans la colonne « Valeur contenue dans la case » ci dessus qui se rapproche le plus de celle qui figure dans la case de données de la totalisation en cause. En utilisant la valeur ainsi obtenue pour l'erreur type, l'utilisateur peut, en général et à juste titre, être certain que la valeur réelle pour la population dénombrée (ne tenant pas compte des formes d'erreurs autres que l'erreur d'échantillonnage) ne s'écarte pas de la valeur contenue dans la case dans une proportion supérieure ou inférieure à trois fois l'erreur type (p. ex. si la valeur contenue dans la case est 1 000, la fourchette à l'intérieur de laquelle se situe la valeur réelle serait de 1 000 ± [3 x 65] ou de 1 000 ± 195).

Les erreurs types données dans le tableau ci-dessus ne s'appliquent pas aux chiffres de population, de logements, de ménages ou de familles pour la région géographique étudiée (voir Échantillonnage et pondération ci-dessous). On peut déterminer l'effet de l'échantillonnage pour ces valeurs en les comparant à celles des produits correspondants contenant des données intégrales.

Il est à noter que l'effet du plan d'échantillonnage et de la méthode de pondération utilisés dans le cadre du recensement de 2001 variera d'une caractéristique à l'autre et d'une région géographique à l'autre. Il est donc possible que les valeurs de l'erreur type données dans le tableau ci-dessus sous-estiment ou surestiment l'erreur attribuable à l'échantillonnage.

Échantillonnage et pondération

Les données du recensement de 2001 sont soit des données intégrales (c'est-à-dire recueillies auprès de l'ensemble des ménages), soit des données-échantillon (c'est-à-dire recueillies auprès d'un échantillon aléatoire comprenant un ménage sur cinq) que l'on a pondérées pour obtenir des estimations pour l'ensemble de la population. Les données ont été recueillies auprès d'un échantillon de 20 % et pondérées pour compenser pour l'échantillonnage. Tous les en-têtes de tableaux sont annotés en conséquence. On notera que, dans les réserves indiennes et les régions éloignées, toutes les données ont été recueillies auprès de l'ensemble de la population.

Il est possible que, pour une région géographique donnée, le total ou le total partiel pondéré de la population, des ménages, des logements ou des familles diffère du chiffre correspondant figurant dans les publications contenant des données intégrales. Ces variations sont attribuables à l'échantillonnage et au fait que les données intégrales n'excluent pas les pensionnaires d'établissements institutionnels, contrairement aux données-échantillon.

Confidentialité et arrondissement aléatoire

Afin de protéger le caractère confidentiel des renseignements fournis, les chiffres indiqués aux tableaux ont fait l'objet d'un **arrondissement aléatoire** qui supprime toute possibilité d'associer des données statistiques à une personne facilement reconnaissable. Selon cette méthode, tous les chiffres, y compris les totaux et les marges, sont arrondis de façon aléatoire (vers le haut ou vers le bas) jusqu'à un multiple de « 5 » et, dans certains cas, de « 10 ». Cette technique assure une protection efficace contre la divulgation sans ajouter d'erreur significative dans les données du recensement. Les utilisateurs doivent savoir que les totaux et les marges sont arrondis séparément et qu'ils ne correspondent pas nécessairement à la somme des chiffres arrondis séparément dans les répartitions. De plus, il faut s'attendre à ce que les totaux et les autres chiffres correspondants dans diverses totalisations du recensement présentent quelques légères différences. De même, la somme des pourcentages, qui sont calculés à partir de chiffres arrondis, ne correspond pas forcément à 100 %. Les statistiques d'ordre (médiane, quartiles, percentiles, etc.) ainsi que les mesures de dispersion comme l'erreur type sont calculées de la façon habituelle. Lorsqu'une statistique est définie comme le quotient de deux nombres (c'est le cas pour des moyennes, des pourcentages et des proportions), les deux nombres sont arrondis avant d'effectuer la division. S'il s'agit de revenu, de dépenses de propriété, de valeur du logement, d'heures travaillées, de semaines travaillées ou d'âge, la somme est définie comme le produit de la moyenne par la fréquence pondérée arrondie. Sinon, c'est la somme pondérée qui est arrondie. La distorsion importante pouvant résulter de l'arrondissement aléatoire dans le cas des cases de faible valeur mérite aussi d'être signalée. Cette distorsion peut entraîner une perte de précision pour les cases de données renfermant des chiffres peu élevés. De plus, une statistique est supprimée si le nombre actuel d'enregistrements ayant servi au calcul est inférieur à 4 ou si la somme du poids de ces enregistrements est inférieure à 10. En outre, dans le cas de valeurs exprimées en dollars, d'autres règles s'ajoutent. Ainsi, pour les produits normalisés, si toutes les valeurs sont égales, la statistique est supprimée. Pour tous les autres produits, la statistique est supprimée si l'étendue des valeurs est trop petite ou si toutes les valeurs sont inférieures, en valeur absolue, à un certain seuil.

Les utilisateurs devraient, lors de l'agrégation des données arrondies, être conscients de cette distorsion. Les erreurs dues à l'arrondissement ont tendance à s'annuler lorsque les chiffres contenus dans les cases sont agrégés de nouveau. Cependant, il est possible de réduire les distorsions en intégrant dans la mesure du possible les totaux partiels appropriés dans les totalisations.

Les utilisateurs désirant obtenir un maximum de précision peuvent aussi choisir de demander des totalisations personnalisées. Dans le cas de produits personnalisés, l'agrégation se fait à partir des enregistrements dans la base de données du recensement se rapportant aux particuliers. L'arrondissement aléatoire a lieu uniquement après que les cases de données ont été agrégées, ce qui réduit la distorsion au minimum.

Outre l'arrondissement aléatoire, on a adopté la technique de la **suppression des régions**, afin d'assurer encore mieux la confidentialité des réponses des particuliers.

Dans le cadre de la **suppression des régions**, toutes les données caractéristiques se rapportant aux régions géographiques dont la population est inférieure à une taille donnée sont supprimées. L'importance de la suppression est fonction des facteurs suivants :

- Si les données sont totalisées à partir de la base de données intégrales, elles sont supprimées si la population totale de la région est inférieure à 40 personnes.
- Si les données sont totalisées à partir de la base de données-échantillon, elles sont supprimées si la population totale de la région, à l'exclusion des pensionnaires d'un établissement institutionnel, est inférieure à 40 personnes, selon la base de données intégrales ou la base de données-échantillon.

Il y a quelques exceptions à ces règles :

- Les données renfermant une répartition du revenu et les statistiques connexes sont supprimées si la population de la région, à l'exclusion des pensionnaires d'un établissement institutionnel, est inférieure à 250 personnes selon la base de données intégrales ou la base de données-échantillon, ou encore si le nombre de ménages privés est inférieur à 40, selon la base de données-échantillon.
- Les données renfermant une répartition du lieu du travail et les statistiques connexes sont supprimées si le nombre de personnes occupées dans la région est inférieur à 40, selon la base de données-échantillon. Si ces données incluent, en plus, une répartition du revenu, le seuil est changé à 250 personnes, toujours selon la base de données-échantillon.

- Les totalisations traitant à la fois du lieu de travail et du lieu de résidence ainsi que les statistiques connexes sont supprimées si le nombre de personnes occupées dans la région est inférieur à 40 selon la base de données-échantillon ou si la population totale de la région, à l'exclusion des pensionnaires d'un établissement institutionnel, selon la base de données intégrales ou la base de données-échantillon est inférieure à 40 personnes. Si ces totalisations incluent, en plus, une répartition du revenu, le seuil est changé à 250 personnes dans tous les cas et les totalisations sont supprimées si le nombre de ménages privés dans la région du lieu de résidence est inférieur à 40.

- Les données renfermant une répartition sur les couples de même sexe et les statistiques connexes sont supprimées si la population de la région dans les ménages privés est inférieure à 5 000 personnes, selon la base de données-échantillon.

- Si les données sont totalisées à partir de la base de données intégrales et se réfèrent aux codes postaux de six caractères ou encore à des regroupements d'îlots ou de côtés d'îlots, elles sont supprimées si la population totale de la région est inférieure à 100 personnes.

- Si les données sont totalisées à partir de la base de données-échantillon et se réfèrent aux codes postaux de six caractères ou encore à des regroupements d'îlots ou de côtés d'îlots, elles sont supprimées si la population totale de la région, à l'exclusion des pensionnaires d'un établissement institutionnel, et selon la base de données intégrales ou la base de données-échantillon, est inférieure à 100 personnes.

- Si les données se réfèrent à des regroupements d'îlots ou de côtés d'îlots, et renferment une répartition du lieu de travail, elles sont supprimées si le nombre de personnes occupées dans la région est inférieur à 100 selon la base de données-échantillon.

- Si les données se réfèrent à des regroupements d'îlots ou de côtés d'îlots, et renferment, à la fois, une répartition du lieu de travail et du lieu de résidence, elles sont supprimées si le nombre total de personnes occupées dans la région est inférieur à 100 selon la base de données-échantillon ou si la population totale de la région, à l'exclusion des pensionnaires d'un établissement institutionnel, selon la base de données intégrales ou la base de données-échantillon, est inférieure à 100 personnes.

Dans tous les cas, les données supprimées sont incluses dans les totaux ou totaux partiels du niveau d'agrégation supérieur approprié.

La technique de suppression est appliquée à tous les produits renfermant des données infraprovinciales (c'est-à-dire la série des Profils, les tableaux croisés de base, les produits personnalisés et semi personnalisés), qu'il s'agisse de données intégrales ou de données-échantillon.

Pour obtenir de plus amples renseignements sur la qualité des données du recensement, veuillez communiquer avec la Division des méthodes d'enquêtes sociales, Statistique Canada, Ottawa (Ontario), Canada K1A 0T6, ou en composant le (613) 951-4783.

Notes spéciales

Chiffres de population

Les chiffres de population du recensement de 2001 pour une région particulière représentent le nombre de Canadiens dont le domicile habituel est dans cette région, quel que soit l'endroit où ils se trouvent le jour du recensement. Sont également compris dans ces chiffres tous les Canadiens qui demeurent dans un logement de cette région le jour du recensement qui n'ont pas de domicile habituel ailleurs au Canada, de même que ceux qui sont considérés comme des « résidents non permanents » (voir les Notes spéciales). Dans la plupart des régions, la différence entre le nombre de résidents habituels et le nombre de résidents qui demeurent dans cette région le jour du recensement est minime. Toutefois, à certains endroits, notamment dans des régions touristiques ou de villégiature, ou dans celles où l'on trouve d'importants camps de travail, le nombre de personnes qui demeurent dans la région à n'importe quel moment pourrait être bien supérieur au nombre de résidents habituels dont il est ici fait mention. Les chiffres de population tiennent compte des Canadiens qui habitent dans d'autres pays, mais non pas des résidents étrangers qui habitent au Canada (la catégorie des « résidents étrangers » ne comprend pas les « résidents non permanents » [voir les Notes spéciales]). Compte tenu de ces divergences, les utilisateurs ne doivent pas déduire que les chiffres de population correspondent au nombre de personnes qui habitent dans les logements déclarés.

Comparabilité des données de 2001 sur le lieu de travail

Le travail à domicile peut être mesuré de différentes façons. Dans le cadre du recensement, la catégorie des personnes travaillant à domicile comprend les personnes qui résident et travaillent au même endroit, comme les agriculteurs, les télétravailleurs et les travailleurs d'un camp de chantier. Par ailleurs, selon les instructions données dans le Guide du recensement de 2001, les personnes ayant travaillé à domicile une partie du temps et à l'adresse d'un employeur le reste du temps devaient indiquer qu'elles avaient travaillé à domicile si elles avaient travaillé la majeure partie du temps chez elles (par exemple trois jours sur cinq).

D'autres enquêtes de Statistique Canada, telles que l'Enquête sociale générale, l'Enquête sur la dynamique du travail et du revenu et l'Enquête sur le milieu de travail et les employés, recueillent également des données sur les personnes travaillant à domicile. Toutefois, les données de ces enquêtes ne sont pas directement comparables à celles du recensement, étant donné que dans le cadre des enquêtes, les répondants doivent indiquer s'ils font une partie ou la totalité de leur travail rémunéré à domicile, alors qu'au recensement, ils doivent indiquer où ils travaillent habituellement la plupart du temps. Par conséquent, les estimations du travail à domicile tirées du recensement sont inférieures à celles tirées des enquêtes.

La présentation de la question sur le lieu de travail est demeurée à peu près la même pour chaque recensement depuis 1971. Cependant, en 1996, la catégorie « Sans adresse de travail fixe » a remplacé la catégorie « Sans lieu habituel de travail ». Sur le questionnaire du recensement de 1996, une case à cocher a été ajoutée pour la catégorie de réponse « Sans adresse de travail fixe ». Lors des recensements antérieurs, les répondants devaient inscrire « Sans lieu habituel de travail » dans les zones réservées à l'adresse. Il semble y avoir eu un sous-dénombrement des personnes sans lieu de travail fixe lors des recensements antérieurs.

Les annexions, les incorporations et les fusions de municipalités pourraient rendre difficile l'établissement de comparaisons entre des unités et des structures spatiales qui changent dans le temps.

Données sur l'immigration et la citoyenneté

Les questions sur la citoyenneté et l'immigration n'ont pas été posées aux personnes qui vivent sur des réserves indiennes et dans des établissements indiens et qui ont été dénombrées à l'aide du questionnaire 2D du recensement de 2001. Par conséquent, les données ne sont pas affichées pour les réserves indiennes et les établissements indiens aux niveaux géographiques inférieurs. Toutefois, ces données sont comprises dans les totaux pour les plus grandes régions géographiques, telles que les divisions de recensement et les provinces.

Données sur la migration pour les petites régions géographiques

Les chiffres estimatifs sur la migration interne peuvent manquer d'exactitude pour les petites régions géographiques, pour les localités ayant le même nom que d'autres localités situées ailleurs et pour certaines subdivisions de recensement (SDR) dans les cas où des résidents, au lieu d'indiquer le nom de la composante SDR dans laquelle ils résidaient auparavant, ont fourni le nom de la région métropolitaine de recensement ou de l'agglomération de recensement.

Identité autochtone

Les utilisateurs doivent prendre note du fait que le dénombrement partiel de certaines réserves indiennes ou de certains établissements indiens a une plus grande incidence sur les chiffres de population associés à la présente variable que sur la plupart des autres chiffres. L'ampleur de cette incidence sera fonction de la région géographique à l'étude. En 2001, un total de 30 réserves indiennes et établissements indiens ont été partiellement dénombrés dans le contexte du recensement. Les chiffres du recensement ne tiennent pas compte des populations de ces 30 collectivités.

Incidence de la restructuration municipale

Il est possible que les limites et les noms des municipalités (subdivisions de recensement) soient modifiés d'un recensement à un autre par suite d'annexions, de dissolutions et d'incorporations. Le nombre et l'importance de ces modifications ont toutefois augmenté depuis le recensement de 1996, surtout au Québec, en Ontario et en Colombie-Britannique. En général, les données du recensement de 2001 sont diffusées pour un plus petit nombre de subdivisions de recensement de plus grande taille, ce qui a pour effet de compliquer les analyses historiques. Afin d'atténuer l'impact de ces modifications sur la diffusion des données, l'équipe du recensement de 2001 entend produire un profil pour les subdivisions de recensement dissoutes.

Modifications apportées aux concepts relatifs à la famille pour le recensement de 2001

Au recensement de 1996, la définition du concept de famille de recensement était la suivante :

Couple actuellement marié (avec ou sans fils et/ou filles jamais mariés des deux conjoints ou de l'un d'eux), couple vivant en union libre (avec ou sans fils et/ou filles jamais mariés des deux partenaires ou de l'un d'eux) ou parent seul (peu importe son état matrimonial) demeurant avec au moins un fils ou une fille jamais marié(e).

La définition de ce concept n'avait pas été modifiée depuis 1976. Toutefois, au cours de la planification du recensement de 2001, il a été décidé qu'il était nécessaire de le modifier compte tenu des facteurs suivants : 1) les changements apportés aux lois fédérales et provinciales afin que les couples formés de partenaires de même sexe soient considérés sur un pied d'égalité avec les couples formés de partenaires de sexe opposé vivant en union libre, plus particulièrement le Projet de loi C-23, *Loi sur la modernisation de certains régimes d'avantages et d'obligations*, qui a été adopté par le gouvernement du Canada en 2000; 2) les recommandations des Nations Unies dans le cadre d'un processus de normalisation des concepts pour les recensements qui devaient être réalisés en 2000 et en 2001 dans les pays membres; 3) le fait qu'aux recensements précédents un nombre important de personnes âgées de moins de 15 ans aient été classées comme personnes hors famille.

Par conséquent, les changements suivants ont été apportés au concept de famille de recensement pour le recensement de 2001 :

- Deux personnes constituant un couple en union libre formé de partenaires de même sexe et tous les enfants faisant partie de leur ménage sont considérés comme une famille de recensement.

- Les enfants compris dans une famille de recensement peuvent avoir déjà été mariés (pourvu qu'ils n'habitent actuellement pas avec leur époux(se) ou partenaire en union libre). Auparavant, il fallait qu'ils n'aient jamais été mariés.

- Un petit-fils ou une petite-fille vivant dans un ménage à trois générations où le parent (deuxième génération) n'a jamais été marié est, contrairement aux recensements précédents, maintenant considéré(e) comme faisant partie de la famille de recensement du parent, à condition de ne pas habiter avec son époux(se), son/sa partenaire en union libre ou son enfant. Auparavant, la famille de recensement était ordinairement constituée des deux générations les plus anciennes.

- Un petit-fils ou une petite-fille d'un autre membre du ménage où le parent (deuxième génération) n'est pas présent est maintenant considéré(e) comme faisant partie de la famille de recensement du grand-père ou de la grand-mère, à condition que le petit-fils ou la petite-fille n'habite pas avec son époux(se), son/sa partenaire en union libre ou son enfant. Auparavant, un tel petit-fils ou une telle petite-fille n'aurait pas été considéré(e) comme faisant partie de la famille de recensement.

Les trois dernières modifications apportées (définition du terme « enfant ») se traduisent par une augmentation de 1,5 % du nombre total de familles de recensement, et une augmentation de 10,1 % du nombre de familles monoparentales. L'inclusion de couples formés de partenaires de même sexe se traduit par une augmentation de 0,4 % du nombre de familles de recensement à l'échelle nationale.

Le terme famille économique désigne un groupe de deux personnes ou plus qui vivent dans le même logement et qui sont apparentées par le sang, par alliance, par union libre ou par adoption. Cette définition n'a pas été modifiée pour le recensement de 2001. La seule incidence des changements sur le concept de famille économique est que les couples formés de partenaires de même sexe sont maintenant considérés comme étant des partenaires en union libre et donc considérés comme étant apparentés et membres de la même famille économique.

Deux concepts connexes ne faisant pas partie de l'univers des familles sont touchés par la modification apportée à la définition du concept de famille de recensement : union libre et genre de ménage. Avant 2001, deux personnes vivant ensemble comme mari et femme sans être mariées étaient considérées comme formant un couple en union libre. Pour 2001, l'expression « comme mari et femme » a été remplacée par « comme couple » de sorte que les partenaires de même sexe sont maintenant inclus. Le concept de genre de ménage renvoie à la répartition fondamentale des ménages privés en ménages familiaux et en ménages non familiaux. Comme il est fondé sur le concept de famille de recensement, la modification apportée à ce dernier concept a une incidence sur le classement des ménages en ménages familiaux ou non familiaux. La classification détaillée de cette variable est également touchée puisque les couples mariés et les couples en union libre étaient répartis auparavant entre les catégories « sans fils ou filles jamais mariés » et « avec fils ou filles jamais mariés ». En 2001, ces expressions sont remplacées par les termes « sans enfant » et « avec enfants » conformément à la nouvelle définition.

Modifications aux chiffres de population et des logements

Suite à la diffusion des chiffres de population et des logements, des erreurs sont occasionnellement relevées dans les données. Il est impossible d'apporter des changements aux données du recensement de 2001 qui sont présentées dans ces tableaux. Toutefois, les utilisateurs peuvent obtenir les modifications aux chiffres de population et des logements touchant les subdivisions de recensement et d'autres niveaux géographiques en visitant la section consacrée au recensement de 2001 dans le site Web de Statistique Canada à l'adresse suivante : www.statcan.ca. Ils peuvent également communiquer avec le centre régional de consultation de Statistique Canada le plus près au numéro 1 800 263-1136 ou par courriel à infostats@statcan.ca.

Nunavut

Des données du recensement de 2001 sont disponibles pour le Nunavut, nouveau territoire reconnu officiellement le 1er avril 1999.

Les produits de données normalisés diffusés seulement pour le Canada, les provinces et les territoires n'afficheront pas de données pour le Nunavut pour les années de recensement antérieures à 2001.

Les produits de données normalisés diffusés pour les régions métropolitaines de recensement (RMR) et les agglomérations de recensement (AR) afficheront des données pour le Nunavut pour les recensements de 2001, 1996 ou 1991.

Les données de 1996 et de 1991 pour les RMR/AR ont été ajustées le plus possible selon les limites des RMR et des AR de 2001 afin de faciliter les comparaisons de données selon les limites géographiques de 2001.

Période de référence du revenu

Des recensements canadiens ont eu lieu en 1996 et en 2001. Les données de ces recensements portant sur le revenu correspondent à l'année civile précédant l'année du recensement, c.-à-d. 1995 et 2000 respectivement.

Population de 15 ans et plus ayant travaillé depuis 2000

Ce sont les personnes ayant travaillé depuis le 1er janvier 2000, qu'elles aient fait partie ou non de la population active pendant la semaine de référence.

Qualité des données – Comparaison des estimations du revenu tirées du recensement avec des estimations établies à partir des comptes nationaux et de l'Enquête sur la dynamique du travail et du revenu

Les estimations du revenu agrégé en 2000 qui ont été tirées du recensement ont été comparées à des estimations semblables du revenu des particuliers établies à partir des comptes nationaux. Une fois que les estimations du revenu des particuliers ont été ajustées pour tenir compte des différences touchant les concepts et la couverture, on a observé que les estimations du revenu agrégé en 2000 qui sont tirées du recensement sont inférieures de 4,1 % à celles qui sont établies à partir des comptes nationaux. Comme par le passé, les estimations tirées du recensement soutiennent davantage la comparaison pour certaines composantes du revenu et pour certaines provinces que pour d'autres.

Dans le cas des salaires et traitements agrégés, qui constituent la plus grande composante du revenu, les estimations tirées du recensement et celles établies à partir des comptes nationaux sont presque identiques. Bien qu'il y ait une grande différence entre les deux estimations du revenu net provenant d'un travail autonome agricole (la plus petite composante du revenu des particuliers), dans le cas du revenu agrégé provenant d'un travail autonome agricole et d'un travail non agricole, les estimations du recensement ne sont inférieures que de 1 %. Dans l'ensemble, les estimations du revenu d'emploi total tirées du recensement et celles établies à partir des comptes nationaux sont quasi identiques.

Les estimations des prestations de la sécurité de la vieillesse et du supplément de revenu garanti qui sont tirées du recensement sont supérieures d'environ 5 % aux estimations ajustées établies à partir des comptes nationaux. En revanche, les estimations tirées du recensement leur sont inférieures d'environ 9 % dans le cas des prestations du Régime de rentes du Québec ou du Régime de pensions du Canada, et d'environ 6 % dans le cas des prestations d'assurance-emploi. Pour ce qui est des prestations fiscales canadiennes pour enfants, les deux estimations sont quasi identiques. Les estimations des autres transferts gouvernementaux tirées du recensement, qui incluent notamment les allocations sociales, les prestations provinciales de supplément du revenu aux personnes âgées, les pensions d'ancien combattant et les remboursements de la TPS/TVH/TVQ, sont plus faibles que les estimations tirées des comptes nationaux. Dans l'ensemble, les estimations du revenu agrégé tirées du recensement, qui proviennent de tous les transferts gouvernementaux, sont inférieures d'environ 13 %. Comme aux recensements antérieurs, l'estimation du revenu de placement tirée du recensement est de beaucoup inférieure, soit de 32 % en 2000, à l'estimation tirée des comptes nationaux.

Les statistiques du recensement sur le revenu ont également été comparées à des statistiques similaires tirées de l'Enquête sur la dynamique du travail et du revenu (EDTR), qui est tenue chaque année. Les estimations tirées de l'EDTR ont été ajustées pour tenir compte du sous-dénombrement de la population, alors que ce n'est pas le cas pour les estimations du recensement. Cette correction contribue à faire en sorte que les estimations tirées du recensement affichent, par rapport à celles de l'EDTR, un nombre moins élevé de bénéficiaires d'un revenu et de soutiens économiques, qui présente un écart de 3,4 % et de 7,2 % respectivement. Par conséquent, les estimations tirées du recensement sont inférieures à celles de l'EDTR, de 4 % dans le cas des gains agrégés et de 3 % dans le cas du revenu total agrégé des particuliers. À la lumière des erreurs d'échantillonnage dans l'EDTR, la plupart des différences observées entre les provinces ont été jugées acceptables.

Qualité des données concernant la fréquentation scolaire

La qualité générale des variables de l'éducation du recensement de 2001 est acceptable. Toutefois, il importe aux usagers des données du recensement de 2001 sur la fréquentation scolaire de savoir que les chiffres pour la catégorie des 15 à 19 ans qui ne fréquentent pas l'école sont peut-être trop élevés. La proportion de personnes âgées entre 15 et 19 ans qui ont répondu qu'elles n'avaient pas fréquenté l'école au cours de l'année scolaire avant le recensement est passée de 18 % en 1996 à 23 % en 2001. Il est nécessaire d'effectuer de plus amples recherches à cet effet.

Résidents non permanents

En 1991, 1996 et 2001, le Recensement de la population a dénombré à la fois les résidents permanents et non permanents au Canada. Les résidents non permanents sont les personnes qui, au moment du recensement, étaient titulaires d'un permis de séjour pour étudiants, d'un permis de travail ou d'un permis ministériel, ou qui revendiquaient le statut de réfugié. Les membres de leur famille vivant avec elles sont aussi considérés comme des résidents non permanents.

Avant 1991, seuls les résidents permanents du Canada étaient inclus dans le recensement (exception faite pour 1941). Les résidents non permanents étaient considérés comme des résidents étrangers et n'étaient pas dénombrés.

Présentement au Canada, les résidents non permanents forment un segment important de la population, en particulier dans plusieurs régions métropolitaines de recensement. Leur présence peut influer sur la demande de services gouvernementaux tels que les soins de santé, l'éducation, les programmes d'emploi et la formation linguistique. L'inclusion des résidents non permanents au recensement facilite la comparaison avec les statistiques provinciales et territoriales (mariages, divorces, naissances et décès) qui incluent cette population. En outre, l'inclusion des résidents non permanents permet au Canada de mieux refléter la recommandation de l'ONU, à savoir que les résidents à long terme (personnes demeurant dans un pays pour un an ou plus) soient dénombrés au recensement.

Le recensement de 1996 a dénombré 166 715 résidents non permanents au Canada, soit 0,6 % de la population totale. Le nombre avait augmenté quelque peu au recensement de 2001 : 198 645 résidents non permanents, soit 0,7 % de la population totale.

Le total des chiffres de population, de même que ceux de toutes les variables, sont touchés par ce changement apporté à l'univers du recensement. Les utilisateurs doivent faire preuve d'une très grande prudence lorsqu'ils comparent des données de 1991, de 1996 ou de 2001 avec celles de recensements antérieurs pour des régions géographiques où la concentration de résidents non permanents est importante. Celles-ci comprennent les principales régions métropolitaines de recensement de l'Ontario, du Québec et de la Colombie-Britannique.

Même si tous les efforts possibles ont été déployés pour dénombrer les résidents non permanents, des facteurs tels que les problèmes linguistiques, la réticence à remplir un formulaire du gouvernement ou à comprendre l'importance de participer peuvent avoir influé sur le dénombrement de cette population.

Secteurs de recensement en Ontario

On a décelé, dans la base de données, une erreur qui touche la présentation des chiffres de population de 1996 pour deux secteurs de recensement (SR), c'est-à-dire les SR 0520.05 et 0520.06, dans la région métropolitaine de recensement (RMR) de Toronto. Les données pour ces SR sont correctes, mais elles ont été inversées : 0520.05 contient les données de 0520.06 et 0520.06 contient les données de 0520.05. En raison de contraintes opérationnelles, il n'a pas été possible d'effectuer des ajustements à la base de données de 1996 (chiffres ajustés) pour ces deux SR. Il importe de faire preuve de prudence dans l'utilisation de ces données.

Suppression des données sur le revenu

Dans le cadre de la suppression des régions, toutes les données caractéristiques se rapportant aux régions géographiques dont la population est inférieure à une taille donnée sont supprimées. Les données renfermant une répartition du revenu et les statistiques connexes sont supprimées si la population de la région, à l'exclusion des pensionnaires d'un établissement institutionnel, est inférieure à 250 personnes selon la base de données intégrales ou la base de données-échantillon, ou encore si le nombre de ménages privés est inférieur à 40, selon la base de données-échantillon.

Type de construction résidentielle

Au recensement de 2001, on a recueilli des données sur deux nouvelles catégories de la variable Type de construction résidentielle :

Appartement avec accès direct au niveau du sol dans un immeuble de moins de cinq étages et appartement sans accès direct au niveau du sol dans un immeuble de moins de cinq étages.

L'évaluation postcensitaire des données a révélé un problème grave d'erreur de classement pour ces types de logements. Par conséquent, les données ne seront pas diffusées.

Les données sur le type « Appartement dans un immeuble de moins de cinq étages » sont diffusées dans les produits du recensement de 2001. Cette catégorie constitue un regroupement des deux nouvelles catégories susmentionnées, et les données correspondantes sont directement comparables avec celles de la même catégorie utilisée aux recensements précédents et ne posent en outre aucun problème.

Annexe 1. Réserves indiennes et établissements indiens partiellement dénombrés, chiffres de population de 1996 et de 1991

Province	Réserves indiennes et établissements indiens partiellement dénombrés, 2001	Population	
		1996	1991
Québec	Akwesasne (Partie)	¶	¶
	Doncaster 17	0	4
	Kahnawake 14	¶	¶
	Kanesatake	¶	¶
	Lac-Rapide	228	¶
Ontario	Akwesasne (Part) 59 (formerly Akwesasne [Part])	¶	¶
	Bear Island 1	153	¶
	Chippewas of the Thames First Nation 42 (formerly Chippewa of the Thames First Nation)	¶	¶
	Goulais Bay 15A	¶	¶
	Marten Falls 65	204	187
	Moose Factory 68	0	0
	Munsee-Delaware Nation 1	¶	¶
	Ojibway Nation of Saugeen (Savant Lake) (formerly Savant Lake)	¶	171
	Oneida 41	¶	¶
	Pikangikum 14	1 170	1 303
	Rankin Location 15D	¶	¶
	Six Nations (Part) 40 (Brant County)	¶	¶
	Six Nations (Part) 40 (Haldimand-Norfolk Regional Municipality)	¶	¶
	Tyendinaga Mohawk Territory (formerly Tyendinaga 38)	¶	¶
	Wahta Mohawk Territory (formerly Gibson 31)	¶	130
	Whitefish Bay 32A	¶	¶
	Whitesand	115	0
Manitoba	Dakota Tipi 1	¶	72
Saskatchewan	Big Head 124	¶	¶
Alberta	Ermineskin 138	¶	¶
	Little Buffalo	¶	186
	Saddle Lake 125	¶	1 893
Colombie-Britannique	Esquimalt	¶	¶
	Marble Canyon 3	67	¶
	Pavilion 1	76	73

Annexe 2. Secteurs de recensement supprimés par chiffres de population selon la région métropolitaine de recensement et l'agglomération de recensement, recensement de 2001

Secteurs de recensement supprimés	Chiffres de population (données intégrales)	Chiffres de population (données-échantillon (20 %))
Belleville AR		
0010	35	34
0013 **A**	10	4
0014 **A**	33	33
0405	-	-
0407	-	-
Edmonton RMR		
0015.01	5	4
0016.01	-	-
0019.01	-	-
0052.01	-	-
0064.02	-	-
0065.03	-	-
0090.07	-	-
Granby AR		
0003 **A**	38	38
Greater Sudbury RMR		
0013	-	-
Halifax RMR		
0155 ◆◆◆◇◇◇ **A**	15	14
Kitchener RMR		
0106.03 ◆◆◆◇◇◇	5	2
Lethbridge AR		
0010	25	15
London RMR		
0035	-	-
Montréal RMR		
0014.02	23	23
0040	-	-
0071	-	-
0091	-	-
0094.02	-	-
0127.02	17	17
0145	-	-
0189	-	-
0229	-	-
0268.03	-	-
0440	-	-
0832 ¶		-
Ottawa - Hull RMR		
0140.01	20	16
Saint John RMR		
0005	15	6
Saint-Jean-sur-Richelieu AR		
0006	5	-
0010	-	-
0303	-	-
Toronto RMR		
0003	-	-
0376.06 ◇	35	20
0401.05	5	5
Trois-Rivières RMR		
0301	39	38
Vancouver RMR		
0270	-	-
Winnipeg RMR		
0052	-	-

Nota :

Pour obtenir de plus amples renseignements sur les règles de suppression du recensement de 2001, se reporter à « Qualité des données » de la section « Documents de référence » de cette publication.

Centres régionaux de consultation

La Division des services consultatifs de Statistique Canada vous offre un réseau de diffusion de l'information qui couvre tout le Canada au moyen de huit centres régionaux de consultation. Chaque centre de consultation possède une série de publications courantes et des documents de référence qui peuvent être consultés ou achetés, de même que des disquettes, des CD-ROM, des cartes et d'autres produits. On peut photocopier sur place les documents imprimés.

Chaque centre de consultation vous offre un vaste éventail de services additionnels. Les services consultatifs peuvent vous aider à identifier vos besoins en information, établir des sources de données disponibles, consolider et intégrer des données de différentes sources, élaborer des profils, analyser les faits saillants et les tendances, et finalement, offrir de la formation sur les produits, les services, les concepts de Statistique Canada et l'utilisation de données statistiques.

Pour de plus amples renseignements, veuillez composer le numéro sans frais ci-dessous ou envoyer un courriel à infostats@statcan.ca.

Contactez-nous

Numéro sans frais pour les **demandes de renseignements** (Canada et les États-Unis) : 1 800 263-1136

ATS : 1 800 363-7629

Numéro sans frais **pour commander seulement** (Canada et les États-Unis) : 1 800 267-6677

Numéro sans frais **pour commander par télécopieur** (Canada et les États-Unis) : 1 877 287-4369

Courriel : infostats@statcan.ca

Région de l'atlantique

Couvre les provinces suivantes : Terre-Neuve-et-Labrador, la Nouvelle-Écosse, l'Île-du-Prince-Édouard et le Nouveau-Brunswick.

Services consultatifs
Statistique Canada
2e étage, boîte 11
1741, rue Brunswick
Halifax (Nouvelle-Écosse)
B3J 3X8

Téléphone : (902) 426-5331 ou,
sans frais, 1 800 263-1136
Télécopieur : (902) 426-9538
Courriel : infostats@statcan.ca

Région du Québec

Couvre tout le Québec et le Nunavut sauf la région de la Capitale nationale.

Services consultatifs
Statistique Canada
Complexe Guy-Favreau, tour Est,
4e étage
200, boulevard René-Lévesque Ouest
Montréal (Québec)
H2Z 1X4

Téléphone : (514) 283-5725 ou,
sans frais, 1 800 263-1136
Télécopieur : (514) 283-9350
Courriel : infostats@statcan.ca

Région de la Capitale nationale

Couvre la région de la Capitale nationale.

Centre de consultation statistique
(région de la Capitale nationale)
Statistique Canada
Immeuble Principal, pièce 1500
120, avenue Parkdale
Ottawa (Ontario)
K1A 0T6

Téléphone : (613) 951-8116 ou,
sans frais, 1 800 263-1136
Télécopieur : (613) 951-0581
Courriel : infostats@statcan.ca

Région de l'Ontario

Couvre tout l'Ontario sauf la région de la Capitale nationale.

Services consultatifs
Statistique Canada
Immeuble Arthur-Meighen, 10e étage
25, avenue St. Clair Est
Toronto (Ontario)
M4T 1M4

Téléphone : (416) 973-6586 ou,
sans frais, 1 800 263-1136
Télécopieur : (416) 973-7475
Courriel : infostats@statcan.ca

Région des prairies

Il y a trois centres de consultation dans cette région qui couvre le Manitoba, la Saskatchewan, l'Alberta et les Territoires du Nord-Ouest.

Pour le Manitoba :

Services consultatifs
Statistique Canada
Immeuble Via Rail, bureau 200
123, rue Main
Winnipeg (Manitoba)
R3C 4V9

Téléphone : (204) 983-4020 ou,
sans frais, 1 800 263-1136
Télécopieur : (204) 983-7543
Courriel : infostats@statcan.ca

Région des prairies – fin

Pour la Saskatchewan :

Services consultatifs
Statistique Canada
Immeuble Park Plaza, bureau 440
2365, rue Albert
Regina (Saskatchewan)
S4P 4K1

Téléphone : (306) 780-5405 ou,
sans frais, 1 800 263-1136
Télécopieur : (306) 780-5403
Courriel : infostats@statcan.ca

Pour l'Alberta et les Territoires du Nord-Ouest :

Services consultatifs
Statistique Canada
Immeuble Pacific Plaza, bureau 900
10909, avenue Jasper Nord-Ouest
Edmonton (Alberta)
T5J 4J3

Téléphone : (780) 495-3027 ou,
sans frais, 1 800 263-1136
Télécopieur : (780) 495-5318
Courriel : infostats@statcan.ca

Région du pacifique

Couvre la Colombie-Britannique et le territoire du Yukon.

Services consultatifs
Statistique Canada
Library Square Tower, bureau 600
300, rue West Georgia
Vancouver (Colombie-Britannique)
V6B 6C7

Téléphone : (604) 666-3691 ou,
sans frais, 1 800 263-1136
Télécopieur : (604) 666-4863
Courriel : infostats@statcan.ca